Professional XM

Bill Evjen,
Kent Sharkey,
Thiru Thangarathinam,
Michael Kay,
Alessandro Vernet,
Sam Ferguson

Wiley Publishing, Inc.

Professional XML

Published by
Wiley Publishing, Inc.
10475 Crosspoint Boulevard
Indianapolis, IN 46256
www.wiley.com

Published simultaneously in Canada

ISBN: 978-0-471-77777-9

Manufactured in the United States of America

10 9 8 7 6 5 4 3 2 1

Library of Congress Cataloging-in-Publication Data:

Professional XML / Bill Evjen . . . [et al.].
p. cm.
Includes index.
ISBN-13: 978-0-471-77777-9 (paper/website)
ISBN-10: 0-471-77777-3 (paper/website)
1. XML (Document markup language) I. Evjen, Bill.
QA76.76.H94P7638 2007
006.7'4—dc22

2007006214

Credits

Senior Acquisitions Editor
Jim Minatel

Development Editor
Sydney Jones

Technical Editors
Alexei Gorkov
Steve Danielson
Cody Reichenau

Production Editor
William A. Barton

Copy Editors
Mary Lagu
Kathryn Duggan

Editorial Manager
Mary Beth Wakefield

Vice President & Executive Group Publisher
Richard Swadley

Vice President and Publisher
Joseph B. Wikert

Project Coordinator
Erin Smith

Graphics and Production Specialists
Jonelle Burns
Carrie A. Foster
Brooke Graczyk
Denny Hager
Jennifer Mayberry
Barbara Moore
Rashell Smith
Alicia B. South

Quality Control Technicians
Laura Albert
Christy Pingleton

Proofreading and Indexing
Aptara

Anniversary Logo Design
Richard J. Pacifico

To my three little ones—Sofia, Henri, and Kalle.—Bill Evjen

To Babi, for keeping me alive, and putting up with me. Hopefully for a long time to come.—Kent Sharkey

Thanks to my beautiful wife Jacquie for her patience, my cat Peggy for her company (and technical input), and to all my colleagues at API who continue to inspire and challenge me.—Sam Ferguson

About the Authors

Lead Authors

Bill Evjen is an active proponent of .NET technologies and community-based learning initiatives for .NET. He has been actively involved with .NET since the first bits were released in 2000. In the same year, Bill founded the St. Louis .NET User Group (`www.stlnet.org`), one of the world's first such groups. Bill is also the founder and former executive director of the International .NET Association (`www.ineta.org`), which represents more than 450,000 members worldwide.

Based in St. Louis, Missouri, USA, Bill is an acclaimed author (more than 13 books to date) and speaker on ASP.NET and XML Web services. He has written or co-written *Professional C# 2005; Professional VB 2005;* and the best-selling *Professional ASP.NET 2.0,* as well as *ASP.NET Professional Secrets, XML Web Services for ASP.NET, Web Services Enhancements: Understanding the WSE for Enterprise Applications, Visual Basic .NET Bible*, and more. In addition to writing, Bill is a speaker at numerous conferences, including DevConnections, VSLive, and TechEd. Along with these items, Bill works closely with Microsoft as a Microsoft Regional Director and he has received the Microsoft MVP designation for many years.

Bill is the Technical Architect for Lipper (`www.lipperweb.com`), a wholly-owned subsidiary of Reuters, the international news and financial services company. He graduated from Western Washington University in Bellingham, Washington, with a Russian language degree. When he isn't tinkering on the computer, he can usually be found at his summer house in Toivakka, Finland. You can reach Bill at `evjen@yahoo.com`. He presently keeps his weblog at `www.geekswithblogs.net/evjen`.

Kent Sharkey is an independent consultant who lives and codes in the midst of the wilds of Vancouver Island. Before going solo, Kent worked at Microsoft as a Technical Evangelist and Content Strategist, promoting the use of .NET technologies. When not coding or writing, he's off hiking, biking, or canoeing (or exploring the wilds of Azeroth). He shares his house with his wife, Margaret, and two "children," Squirrel and Cica.

Contributing Authors

Thiru Thangarathinam is a Microsoft MVP who specializes in architecting, designing, and developing distributed enterprise class applications using .NET-related technologies. He is the author of the books *Professional ASP.NET 2.0 XML* and *Professional ASP.NET 2.0 Databases* from Wrox press and has coauthored a number of books on .NET-related technologies. He is a frequent contributor to leading technology-related online publications.

Michael Kay is widely known in the XML world as the developer of the Saxon XSLT and XQuery processor, and as the editor of the XSLT 2.0 specification. His Wrox books *XSLT 2.0 Programmer's Reference* and *XPath 2.0 Programmer's Reference* are regarded as the definitive guides to these languages. Michael runs his own company, Saxonica, which develops the Saxon technology and provides support and consultancy for XSLT and XQuery users. His background is as a software designer creating database products for a mainframe manufacturer. He is a Fellow of the British Computer Society and a Visiting Fellow at the University of Reading (UK). In his spare time he sings and plays croquet.

About the Authors

Alessandro Vernet co-founded Orbeon in 1999, which makes Orbeon Forms, an open source product to build and deploy sophisticated forms on the Web. He is one of the authors of *Professional Web 2.0 Programming* and is a member of two W3C Working Groups: the XForms and XML Processing Model Working Groups. Before co-founding Orbeon, Alessandro was at Symantec as part of the VisualCafé team, working on their next-generation RAD for web applications. He holds an MS/CS from the Swiss Institute of Technology (EPFL) in Lausanne, Switzerland, and since 1998 lives in the incredibly energetic Silicon Valley.

Sam Ferguson is a Project Manager with API Software, a Microsoft Gold Certified Partner, based in Glasgow, Scotland. Sam, who lives in Ayrshire, specializes in SQL Server, Microsoft Office Server System 2007, .NET, and all XML-related technologies. In what little spare time he has, Sam enjoys playing golf and is an avid fan of the Glasgow Rangers.

Acknowledgments

This book, like most, took an entire team to get out the door. First and foremost, I would like to thank Jim Minatel for providing me the opportunity to write this book. Big thanks go to Sydney Jones, the book's development editor who kept this book together despite numerous delays.

Thanks to my family for putting up with this second job. I love you all greatly.—Bill Evjen

Contents

Introduction

As many people predicted, XML has changed the world! When XML was introduced, many considered it a revolutionary leap forward in how we look at data representation. Since then, XML has grown considerably and many new technologies have been introduced. The number of new technologies based upon XML is staggering. From Web services, to blogging, to alerts and notifications—there is so much coming out today completely based upon this technology.

This book covers not just the basics of XML and the XML specification, but it also takes a look at the technologies based on XML that are driving the tech industry forward. This book not only introduces these technologies to you, but it also shows you examples of these new technologies in action. So sit back, pull up that keyboard, and let's have some fun!

What You Need for This Book

This book is vendor agnostic as XML can be utilized on any major operating system out there. But this book is also about various technologies that are based upon XML, and for this reason, you will sometimes need specific vendor tools to complete the examples provided in the chapters. In these cases, the locations of the tools or technologies and where you can acquire them are called out in the chapter.

You will find that this book focuses on both Microsoft- and Java-based technologies, and therefore, you are sometimes asked to work with that vendor's specific development tools and environments to complete the examples.

Who Should Read This Book?

This book was written to provide you with the latest and greatest information on XML, and to look at the new technologies and capabilities being built on XML today. We assume you have a general understanding of programming technologies, such as C# or Java. If you understand the basics of these programming languages, then you shouldn't have much trouble following along with this book's content.

If you are brand new to XML, be sure to check out *Beginning XML* by David Hunter and others (published by Wrox; ISBN: 978-0-7645-7077-3) to help you understand the basics.

You may also be wondering whether this book is focused on the Microsoft developer or the Java developer. We're happy to say that it's for both! You will find that there are chapters focused on each of these programming technologies.

What This Book Covers

This book spends its time reviewing the big changes that have occurred in the 2.0 release of ASP.NET. Each major new feature included in ASP.NET 2.0 is covered in detail. The following list tells you something about the content of each chapter.

- **Chapter 1, "XML Syntax."** This first chapter gives a good grounding in the XML specification. This chapter looks at the reasoning to include XML and its related technologies within an application's architecture. In addition to this introduction, this chapter will also look at the syntactical rules of the XML markup language.
- **Chapter 2, "XML Editors."** This chapter takes a look at the XML tools that can be used for working with XML and its related technologies. These are also tools used in the chapters throughout the book. This chapter introduces you to the various tools out there, where they can be found, as well as some basics for working with them.
- **Chapter 3, "XHTML and CSS."** The next set of chapters looks at presenting XML and XML-based presentation technologies. This first chapter focuses on the popular XHTML specification and how it can be used to present content within a browser. In continuing on with the presentation theme, this chapter looks at how to present XML documents visually in a browser using Cascading Style Sheets.
- **Chapter 4, "XSL-FO."** This chapter takes a look at presenting XML using an XML-based presentation markup language—Extensible Stylesheet Language Formatting Objects (XSL-FO), also known as simply XSL.
- **Chapter 5, "Document Type Definitions (DTDs)."** This chapter takes a look at defining an XML structure using DTDs which have been around for quite awhile. Though it is preferred to use XML Schema today, DTDs should still be understood as developers may encounter legacy XML documents.
- **Chapter 6, "XML Schemas."** XML Schemas are the latest and most preferred way to define the structure and data types of an XML document. This is an important topic to understand as it is referenced throughout the book. This chapter takes a deep look into XML Schemas and how to build them.
- **Chapter 7, "RELAX NG."** RELAX NG is a new XML specification that allows you to validate an XML structure as well as make a link to datatype libraries. This standard was born to simplify what was perceived as difficult and complicated about XML Schema. This chapter looks at how to work with RELAX NG.
- **Chapter 8, "XSLT."** This chapter looks at transforming XML documents in a multitude of ways using XSLT. Starting with the basics of XSLT, this chapter gives you an understanding of how and when to use this technology.
- **Chapter 9, "XPath."** XPath allows for the searching and manipulation of particular subsets of an XML document. This chapter takes a look at this popular technology and will focus on the latest release of XPath—version 2.0.
- **Chapter 10, "XQuery."** XQuery is another search and manipulation technology that often competes with XPath. This chapter takes a look at XQuery and what makes it different than XPath. By the end of chapters 9 and 10, you should have a good understanding of both XPath and XQuery and when to use which technology.

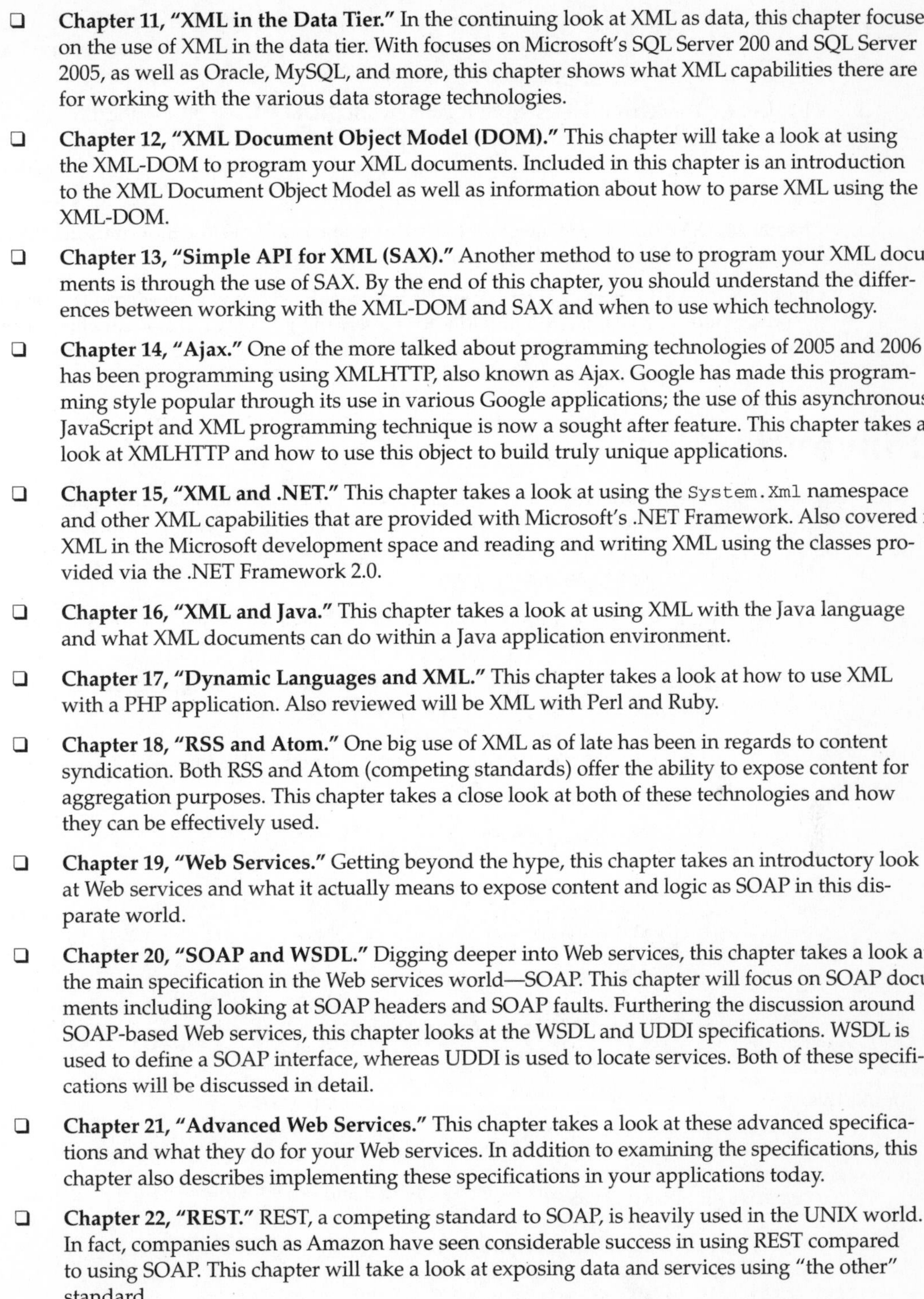

- **Chapter 11, "XML in the Data Tier."** In the continuing look at XML as data, this chapter focuses on the use of XML in the data tier. With focuses on Microsoft's SQL Server 200 and SQL Server 2005, as well as Oracle, MySQL, and more, this chapter shows what XML capabilities there are for working with the various data storage technologies.
- **Chapter 12, "XML Document Object Model (DOM)."** This chapter will take a look at using the XML-DOM to program your XML documents. Included in this chapter is an introduction to the XML Document Object Model as well as information about how to parse XML using the XML-DOM.
- **Chapter 13, "Simple API for XML (SAX)."** Another method to use to program your XML documents is through the use of SAX. By the end of this chapter, you should understand the differences between working with the XML-DOM and SAX and when to use which technology.
- **Chapter 14, "Ajax."** One of the more talked about programming technologies of 2005 and 2006 has been programming using XMLHTTP, also known as Ajax. Google has made this programming style popular through its use in various Google applications; the use of this asynchronous JavaScript and XML programming technique is now a sought after feature. This chapter takes a look at XMLHTTP and how to use this object to build truly unique applications.
- **Chapter 15, "XML and .NET."** This chapter takes a look at using the `System.Xml` namespace and other XML capabilities that are provided with Microsoft's .NET Framework. Also covered is XML in the Microsoft development space and reading and writing XML using the classes provided via the .NET Framework 2.0.
- **Chapter 16, "XML and Java."** This chapter takes a look at using XML with the Java language and what XML documents can do within a Java application environment.
- **Chapter 17, "Dynamic Languages and XML."** This chapter takes a look at how to use XML with a PHP application. Also reviewed will be XML with Perl and Ruby.
- **Chapter 18, "RSS and Atom."** One big use of XML as of late has been in regards to content syndication. Both RSS and Atom (competing standards) offer the ability to expose content for aggregation purposes. This chapter takes a close look at both of these technologies and how they can be effectively used.
- **Chapter 19, "Web Services."** Getting beyond the hype, this chapter takes an introductory look at Web services and what it actually means to expose content and logic as SOAP in this disparate world.
- **Chapter 20, "SOAP and WSDL."** Digging deeper into Web services, this chapter takes a look at the main specification in the Web services world—SOAP. This chapter will focus on SOAP documents including looking at SOAP headers and SOAP faults. Furthering the discussion around SOAP-based Web services, this chapter looks at the WSDL and UDDI specifications. WSDL is used to define a SOAP interface, whereas UDDI is used to locate services. Both of these specifications will be discussed in detail.
- **Chapter 21, "Advanced Web Services."** This chapter takes a look at these advanced specifications and what they do for your Web services. In addition to examining the specifications, this chapter also describes implementing these specifications in your applications today.
- **Chapter 22, "REST."** REST, a competing standard to SOAP, is heavily used in the UNIX world. In fact, companies such as Amazon have seen considerable success in using REST compared to using SOAP. This chapter will take a look at exposing data and services using "the other" standard.

- **Chapter 23, "XML Form Development."** Forms, as popular as they are on the Web, can now be defined using XForms. This chapter takes a close look at XForms and how it can be used, along with other XML-based technologies, to produce various types of forms.
- **Chapter 24, "The Resource Description Framework (RDF)."** The RDF specification allows for the relation of metadata to presentation content. RDF is a framework for describing and interchanging metadata and is introduced in this chapter as well as demonstrated through some examples.
- **Chapter 25, "XML in Office Development."** This chapter takes a close look at using XML in Office development with a particular focus on Microsoft Office.
- **Chapter 26, "XAML."** This chapter takes a look at XAML—the new way Microsoft is promoting the presentation of a GUI. XAML provides for presentation that is fluid and enriching. This chapter takes a look at the basics of XAML and how to build some basic XAML applications.

Conventions

This book uses a number of different styles of text and layout to help differentiate among various types of information. Here are examples of the styles used and an explanation of what they mean:

- New words being defined are shown in *italics*.
- Keys that you press on the keyboard, such as Ctrl and Enter, are shown in initial caps and spelled as they appear on the keyboard.
- File and folder names, file extensions, URLs, and code that appear in regular paragraph text are shown in a `monospaced` typeface.

When we show a block of code that you can type as a program and run, it's shown on separate lines, like this:

```
<?xml version="1.0" encoding="UTF-8" ?>
<Employee>
   <FirstName>Bill</FirstName>
   <LastName>Evjen</LastName>
   <JobTitle>Technical Architect</JobTitle>
   <Company>Lipper</Company>
   <StartDate>10/04/2001</StartDate>
   <WorkLocation>St. Louis, Missouri</WorkLocation>
   <NumberOfDependents>3</NumberOfDependents>
</Employee>
```

or like this:

```
<?xml version="1.0" encoding="UTF-8" ?>
<Employee>
   <FirstName>Bill</FirstName>
   <LastName>Evjen</LastName>
   <JobTitle>Technical Architect</JobTitle>
   <Company>Lipper</Company>
   <StartDate>10/04/2001</StartDate>
```

```
    <WorkLocation>St. Louis, Missouri</WorkLocation>
    <NumberOfDependents>3</NumberOfDependents>
</Employee>
```

Sometimes you see code in a mixture of styles, like this:

```
<?xml version="1.0" encoding="UTF-8" ?>
<Employee>
    <FirstName>Bill</FirstName>
    <LastName>Evjen</LastName>
    <JobTitle>Technical Architect</JobTitle>
    <Company>Lipper</Company>
    <StartDate>10/04/2001</StartDate>
    <WorkLocation>St. Louis, Missouri</WorkLocation>
    <NumberOfDependents>3</NumberOfDependents>
</Employee>
```

When mixed code is shown like this, the code with no background represents code that has been shown previously and that you don't need to examine further. Code with the gray background is what you should focus on in the current example.

We demonstrate the syntactical usage of methods, properties, and so on using the following format:

```
<?[target] [data]?>
```

Here, the italicized parts indicate *placeholder text:* object references, variables, or parameter values that you need to insert.

Most of the code examples throughout the book are presented as numbered listings that have descriptive titles, like this:

Listing 1-8: Creating an XML file

Each listing is numbered (for example: *1-8*) where the first number represents the chapter number and the number following the hyphen represents a sequential number that indicates where that listing falls within the chapter. Downloadable code from the Wrox Web site (`www.wrox.com`) also uses this numbering system so that you can easily locate the examples you are looking for.

Source Code

As you work through the examples in this book, you may choose either to type all the code manually or to use the source code files that accompany the book. All the source code used in this book is available for download at `www.wrox.com`. When you get to the site, simply locate the book's title (either by using the Search box or one of the topic lists) and click the Download Code link. You can then choose to download all the code from the book in one large zip file or download just the code you need for a particular chapter.

Because many books have similar titles, you may find it easiest to search by ISBN; this book's ISBN is 978-0-471-77777-9.

After you download the code, just decompress it with your favorite compression tool. Alternatively, you can go to the main Wrox code download page at `www.wrox.com/dynamic/books/download.aspx` to see the code available for this book and all other Wrox books. Remember, you can easily find the code you are looking for by referencing the listing number of the code example from the book, such as "Listing 1-8." We used these listing numbers when naming the downloadable code files.

Errata

We make every effort to ensure that there are no errors in the text or in the code. However, no one is perfect, and mistakes do occur. If you find an error in one of our books, such as a spelling mistake or faulty piece of code, we would be very grateful if you'd tell us about it. By sending in errata, you may spare another reader hours of frustration; at the same time, you are helping us provide even higher-quality information.

To find the errata page for this book, go to `www.wrox.com` and locate the title using the Search box or one of the title lists. Then, on the book details page, click the Book Errata link. On this page, you can view all errata that have been submitted for this book and posted by Wrox editors. A complete book list including links to each book's errata is also available at `www.wrox.com/misc-pages/booklist.shtml`.

If you don't spot "your" error already on the Book Errata page, go to `www.wrox.com/contact/techsupport.shtml` and complete the form there to send us the error you have found. We'll check the information and, if appropriate, post a message to the book's errata page and fix the problem in subsequent editions of the book.

p2p.wrox.com

For author and peer discussion, join the P2P forums at `p2p.wrox.com`. The forums are a Web-based system for you to post messages relating to Wrox books and technologies and to interact with other readers and technology users. The forums offer a subscription feature that enables you to receive e-mail on topics of interest when new posts are made to the forums. Wrox authors, editors, other industry experts, and your fellow readers are represented in these forums.

At `http://p2p.wrox.com` you will find a number of different forums that will help you not only as you read this book but also as you develop your own applications. To join the forums, just follow these steps:

1. Go to `p2p.wrox.com` and click the Register link.
2. Read the terms of use and click Agree.
3. Supply the information required to join, as well as any optional information you want to provide, and click Submit.

You will receive an e-mail with information describing how to verify your account and complete the joining process.

You can read messages in the forums without joining P2P, but you must join in order to post messages.

After you join, you can post new messages and respond to other users' posts. You can read messages at any time on the Web. If you would like to have new messages from a particular forum e-mailed to you, click the Subscribe to this Forum icon by the forum name in the forum listing.

For more information about how the forum software works, as well as answers to many common questions specific to P2P and Wrox books, be sure to read the P2P FAQs. Simply click the FAQ link on any P2P page.

Part I
XML Basics

1

XML Syntax

Extensible Markup Language (XML) is now in widespread use. Many applications on the Internet or residing on individual computers use some form of XML to run or manage the processes of an application. Earlier books about XML commented that XML was to be the "next big thing." Now, it *is* "the big thing." In fact, there really isn't anything bigger.

For this reason, you want to understand XML and its various applications. This book focuses on some of the more common ways to apply XML to the work you are doing today. Whether you need Web services, searching, or application configuration, you can find immediate uses for XML. This book shows you how to apply this markup language to your work.

This first chapter looks at the basics of XML, why it exists, and what makes it so powerful. Finally, this chapter deals with XML namespaces and how to properly apply them to XML instance documents. If you are already pretty familiar with the basics of XML, feel free to skim this chapter before proceeding.

The Purpose of XML

Before you actually get into the basics of XML, you should understand why this markup language is one of the most talked about things in computing today. To do this, look back in time a bit.

During the days of mainframes, information technology might have seemed complicated, but it actually got a heck of a lot more complicated when we moved from the mainframes and started working in a client-server model. Now the users were accessing information remotely instead of sitting at the same machine where the data and logic were actually stored. This caused all sorts of problems — mainly involving how to visually represent data that was stored on larger mainframes to remote clients. Another problem was application-to-application communication. How was one application sitting on one computer going to access data or logic residing on an entirely different computer?

Two problems had to be resolved. One dealt with computer-to-human communications of data and logic; another dealt with application-to-application communications. This is illustrated in Figure 1-1.

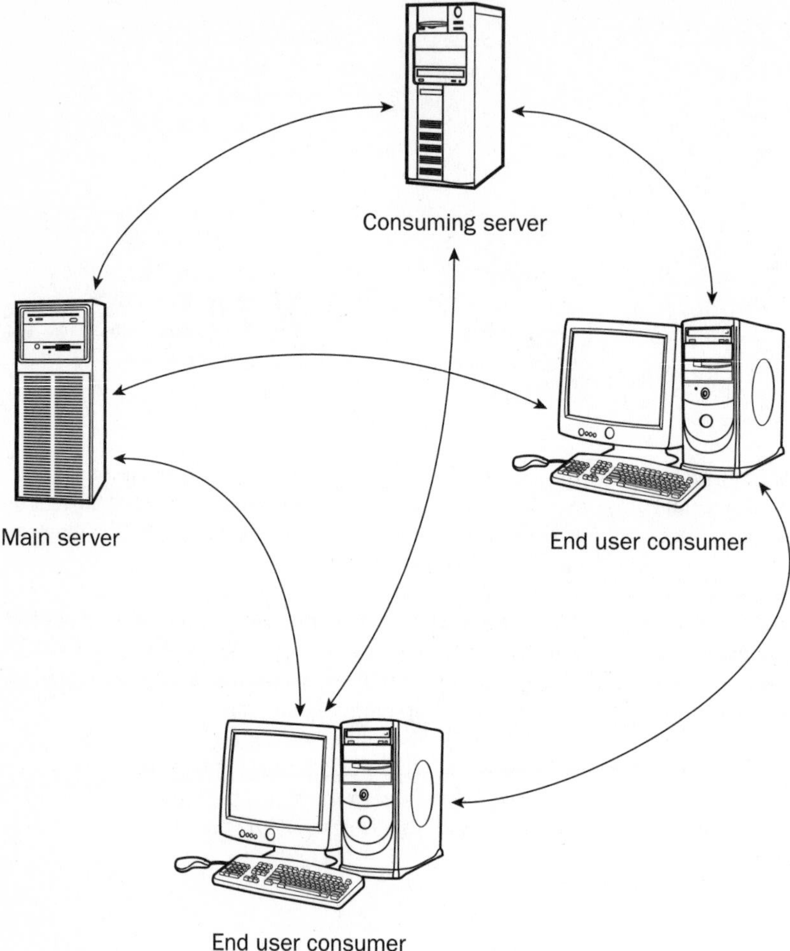

Figure 1-1

The first problem of computer-to-human communication of data and logic was really solved in a large way with the advent of HTML (also known as *HyperText Markup Language*). This markup language packaged data and logic in a way that allowed users to view it via applications specifically designed to present it (the birth of the browser as we know it). Now with HTML and browser applications in place, end users could work through data and logic remotely without too much of a problem.

With that said, it really isn't all about humans is it? There was also a need for other servers, processes, applications, and whatnot to access and act upon data and logic stored elsewhere on a network or across the planet. This created a pursuit to find the best way of moving this data and logic from point A to point B.

It was a tough task. The varying sources of data were often not compatible with the platform where the data was to be served up. A common way to structure and represent the data was needed. Of course, many solutions were proposed — some of which were pretty exciting.

The idea was to *mark up* a document in a manner that enabled the document to be understood across working boundaries. Many systems existed to mark up documents so that other applications could easily understand them. Applying markup to a document means adding descriptive text around items contained in the document so that another application or another instance of an application can decipher the contents of the document.

For instance, Microsoft Word provides markup around the contents of document. What markup is really needed? Well, as you type words into Microsoft Word, you are also providing data to be housed in the document. The reason you don't simply use Microsoft Notepad is that Word gives you the extra capability to change the way in which the data is represented. What this really means is that you can apply *metadata* around the data points contained in the document. For instance, you can specify whether a word, paragraph, or page is bolded, italicized, or underlined. You can specify the size of the text and the color. You can actually alter the data quite a bit. Word takes your instructions and applies a markup language around the data.

Like Word, XML uses markup to provide metadata around data points contained within the document to further define the data element. XML provides such an easy means of creating and presenting markup that it has become the most popular way to apply metadata to data.

In its short lifetime, XML has become the standard for data representation. XML came into its own when the W3C (*The World Wide Web Consortium*) realized that it needed a markup language to represent data that could be used and consumed regardless of the platform. When XML was created in 1998, it was quickly hailed as the solution for data transfer and data representation across varying systems.

In the past, one way to represent data was to place the data within a comma-, tab-, or pipe-delimited text file. Listing 1-1 shows an example of this:

Listing 1-1: An example of a pipe-delimited data representation

```
Bill|Evjen|Technical Architect|Lipper|10/04/2001|St. Louis, Missouri|3
```

These kinds of data representations are in use today. The individual pieces of data are separated by pipes, commas, tabs, or any other characters. Looking at this collection of items, it is hard to tell what the data represents. You might be able to get a better idea based on the file name, but the meaning of the date and the number 3 is not that evident.

On the other hand, XML relates data in a self-describing manner so that any user, technical or otherwise, can decipher the data. Listing 1-2 shows how the same piece of data is represented using XML.

Listing 1-2: Representing the data in an XML document

```
<?xml version="1.0" encoding="UTF-8" ?>
<Employee>
   <FirstName>Bill</FirstName>
   <LastName>Evjen</LastName>
```

(continued)

Listing 1-2 *(continued)*

```
        <JobTitle>Technical Architect</JobTitle>
        <Company>Lipper</Company>
        <StartDate>10/04/2001</StartDate>
        <WorkLocation>St. Louis, Missouri</WorkLocation>
        <NumberOfDependents>3</NumberOfDependents>
    </Employee>
```

You can now tell, by just looking at the data in the file, what the data items mean and how they relate to one another. The data is laid out in such a simple format that is quite possible for even a non-technical person to understand the data. You can also have a computer process work with the data in an automatic fashion.

When you look at this XML file, you may notice how similar XML is to HTML. Both markup languages are related, but HTML is used to mark up text for presentation purposes whereas XML is used to mark up text for data representation purposes.

Both XML and HTML have their roots in the Standard Generalized Markup Language (SGML), which was created in 1986. SGML is a complex markup language that was also used for data representation. With the explosion of the Internet, however, the W3C realized that it needed a universal way to represent data that would be easier to use than SGML. That realization brought forth XML.

XML has a distinct advantage over other forms of data representation. The following list represents some of the reasons XML has become as popular as it is today:

- XML is easy to understand and read.
- A large number of platforms support XML and are able to manage it through an even larger set of tools available for XML data reading, writing, and manipulation.
- XML can be used across open standards that are available today
- XML allows developers to create their own data definitions and models of representation.
- Because a large number of XML tools are available, XML is simpler to use than binary formats when you want to represent complex data structures.

XML Syntax and Rules

Building an XML document properly means that you have to follow specific rules that have been established for the structure of the document. These rules of XML are defined by the XML specification found at `w3.org/TR/REC-xml`. If you have an XML document that follows the rules diligently, it is a *well-formed* XML document.

You want to make sure that the rules are followed closely because if the rules defined in the XML specification are observed, you can use various XML processors (or *parsers*) to work with your documents in an automatic fashion.

XML Parsers

You might not realize it, but you probably already have an XML parser on your computer. A number of computer vendors have provided XML parsers and have even gone as far as to include these parsers in applications that you use each and everyday. The following is a list of some of the main parsers.

- **Microsoft's Internet Explorer XML Parser**—The most popular XML parser on the market is actually embedded in the number-one browser on the market. Microsoft's Internet Explorer comes with a built-in XML parser—Microsoft's XML Parser. Internet Explorer 5.5 comes with Microsoft's XML Parser 2.5 whereas Internet Explorer 6.0 comes with the XML Parser 3.0. This parser includes a complete implementation of XSL Transformations (XSLT) and XML Path Language (XPath) and incorporates some changes to work with Simple API for XML (SAX2). You can get the XML Parser 3.0 via an Internet Explorer download, or you can download the parser directly from `microsoft.com/downloads/details.aspx?familyid=4A3AD088-A893-4F0B-A932-5E024E74519F&displaylang=en`
- **Mozilla's XML Parser (also the Firefox XML Parser)**—Like Internet Explorer, Mozilla includes support for XML parsing. Mozilla has the built-in capability to display XML with CSS.*
- **Apache Xerces**—This open source XML parser can be found online at `http://xerces.apache.org/` and comes under the Apache Software License. This parser is available for Java, C++, and a Perl implementation that makes use of the C++ version. Apache Xerces was originally donated to Apache by IBM in 1999. Until 2004, Apache Xerces was a subproject of the Apache XML Project found at `http://xml.apache.org/`.
- **IBM's XML Parser for Java**—Also known as Xml4j, this parser has become the Apache Xerces2 Java Parser found at `http://xerces.apache.org/xerces2-j/`.
- **Oracle XML Parser**—Oracle provides XML parsers for Java, C, C++, and PL/SQL through its Oracle XML Developer's Kit 10g found at `oracle.com/technology/tech/xml/xdkhome.html`.
- **Expat XML Parser**—Written by James Clark, the tech-lead of the W3C's XML activity that created the XML 1.0 Specification, you can find the Expat parser as a SourceForge project found at `http://expat.sourceforge.net/`. Expat is currently in version 2.0.

XML Elements and Tags

When reading and conversing about XML, you come across the terms *element* and *tag* quite often. What's the difference between the two? Many individuals and organizations incorrectly use these terms interchangeably. Each term has a distinct meaning.

An XML element is the means to provide metadata around text to give it further meaning. For instance, you might be presented with the following bit of XML:

```
<City>Saint Charles</City>
```

In this case, the element is the entire item displayed. XML uses *tags* to surround text in order to provide the appropriate metadata. Figure 1-2 shows the pieces of this bit of code.

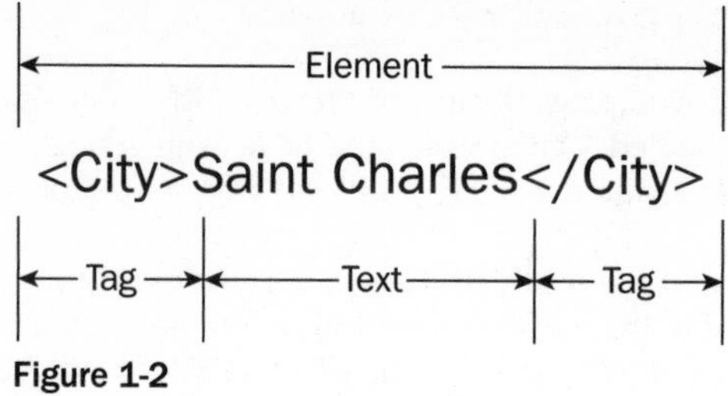

Figure 1-2

From this, you can see that everything from the starting `<City>` to the ending `</City>` is the XML element. An XML element is made up a *start tag*, which precedes the text to be defined, as well as an *end tag*, which comes at the end of the text to be defined. In this case, the start tag is `<City>` and the end tag is `</City>`.

Element Syntax

If there is text to be marked up with XML, then an XML element must contain start and end tags. XML is very strict about its rules, and you must follow them just as strictly if you want to ensure that your XML document is well-formed.

XML Elements Must Have a Start and End Tag

Unlike HTML, where you can bend the rules of the syntax utilized, XML requires a start and end tag if an element contains any text. The following shows two XML elements together.

```
<City>Saint Charles</City>
<State>Missouri</State>
```

Naming Conventions for Elements

You can choose any name that suits your fancy for the elements of your XML document. With that said however, certain rules do restrict the names that you can use for elements.

Element names must start with a letter from an alphabet of one of the languages of the world or an underscore. You cannot start an element name with a number or a special character (such as !, @, #, $, %, and so on).

Examples of improper naming of XML elements include the following:

- `<123Industries></123Industries>`
- `<#Alpha></#Alpha>`
- `<!Yellow></!Yellow>`

Examples of well-formed XML elements include these:

```
<StLouisCardinals></StLouisCardinals>

<Item123></Item123>

<_Wowzer></_Wowzer>

<__></__>
```

Element names cannot contain spaces. This means that the following XML element name is improper and not well-formed:

```
<Bill Evjen></Bill Evjen>
```

Element names cannot start with the word `XML` in any case. For example, the following element names are improper and not well-formed:

```
<xml></xml>

<XML></XML>

<XmlLover></XmlLover>

<XML_Element1></XML_Element1>
```

After you have defined the first character of your XML element, you can subsequently use numbers, periods, underscores, or hyphens. The following are examples of well-formed XML:

```
<St.Louis_Cardinals></St.Louis_Cardinals>

<Item1></Item1>

<Address-Present></Address-Present>
```

Immediately after the opening < and </ of the XML tags, you must start the element name. You cannot have a space first. This means that the following XML element is improper:

```
< Item1></ Item>
```

Although a space is not allowed preceding the element name, you can have a space trailing the element name before the closing of the tag. This use is illustrated in the following example:

```
<Item1 ></Item1 >
```

XML Elements Must Be Properly Nested

When XML documents contain more than one XML element (which they invariably do), you must properly nest the XML elements. You are required to open and close these elements in a logical order. When looking at the preceding XML fragment, you can see that the <City> tag is closed with a </City> tag before the <State> opening tag is utilized. The following fragment is *not* well-formed.

```
<City>Saint Charles
<State></City>Missouri</State>
```

However, you are not required to always close an element before starting another one. In fact, the opposite is true. XML allows for a hierarchical view of the data that it represents. This means that you can define child data of parent data directly in your XML documents; this enables you to show a relationship between the data points.

```
<Location>
   <City>Saint Charles</City>
   <State>Missouri</State>
   <Country>USA</Country>
</Location>
```

The indenting of the XML file is done for readability and is not required for a well-formed document.

This XML fragment starts with the opening XML element <Location>. Before the <Location> element is closed however, three other XML elements are defined — thereby further defining the item. The <Location> element here contains three *subelements* — <City>, <State>, and <Country>. Being subelements, these items must also be closed properly before the <Location> element is closed with a </Location> tag.

You can also continue the nesting of these elements so that they are aligned hierarchically as deep as you wish. For instance, you can use the following structure for your nested XML fragment.

```
<Person>
   <Name>Bill Evjen</Name>
   <Location>
      <City>Saint Charles</City>
      <State>
         <Name>Missouri</Name>
         <StateCode>MO</StateCode>
      </State>
      <Country>USA</Country>
   </Location>
</Person>
```

In this case, the <Person> element contains two child elements or subelements — <Name> and <Location>. The <Name> element is a simple element, whereas the <Location> element is further nested two more times with additional subelements.

Empty Elements

If the text or item you want to define in your XML document is null or not present for some reason, you can represent this item through the use of an empty XML element. An empty XML element takes the following format:

```
<Age/>
```

In this case, the XML element is still present, but is represented as an empty value through a single XML tag. When representing an empty element, you do not need an opening and closing tag, but instead just a single tag which ends with `/>`.

In addition to the empty element representation shown here, you can also have a space between the word used to define the tag and the closing of the tag.

```
<Age />
```

In addition to using a single tag to represent an empty element, you can also use the standard start and end tags with no text to represent an empty element. This is illustrated here:

```
<Person>
   <Name>Bill Evjen</Name>
   <Age></Age>
   <Location>
      <City>Saint Charles</City>
      <State>
         <Name>Missouri</Name>
         <StateCode>MO</StateCode>
      </State>
      <Country>USA</Country>
   </Location>
</Person>
```

Tag Syntax

Tags are defined using greater-than/less-than signs (`<Tag>`). A start tag has a textual name preceded with a `<` and ending with a `>`. An end tag must have the same textual name as its start tag, but it is preceded by a `</` as opposed to a `<`. The end tag is finalized with a `>` just as the start tag is.

The words you use for tag names are entirely up to you, but some basic rules govern how you build tags. The first rule is that the case used for the start tag and the end tag must be the same. Therefore, the `<Location>` tag is not the same as `<location>`. For instance, this is considered improper or malformed XML:

```
<Country>USA</country>
```

Because XML is case-sensitive, the tags shown here are actually completely different tags and, therefore, don't match. For your XML to be well-formed, the XML tags must be of the same case.

```
<Country>USA</Country>
```

Because XML does understand case, you could, theoretically, have the following XML snippet in your XML document:

```
<Name>Bill Evjen</Name>
<name>Bill</name>
```

Although completely legal, you shouldn't actually implement this idea because it causes confusion and can lead to some improper handling of your XML documents. Remember that you want to build XML documents that are easily understandable by the programmers who will build programs that process these documents.

XML Text

The text held within an XML element can be whatever you wish. The entire point of the XML document is to hold information using XML elements as markup. Remember a few rules, however, when you are representing content within your XML elements.

Text Length

You have no rules on the length of the text contained within your XML documents. This means that the content can be of any length you deem necessary.

```
<Message>
   This can go on and on and on and on and on and on and on and on and on
   and on and on ...
</Message>
```

Content

You might think that the content of an XML element is just text for humans to read, but an XML element really can contain just about anything. For instance, you can use binary code to represent an image or other document and then stick this item in your XML document. This is illustrated here with a partial element:

```
<base64Binary>/9j/4AAQSkZJRgABAAgEASABIAAD/7RNoGUGhvdG9ZaG9wIDMuMAA4Qk1NAAQBIAAAAAQ
 ABOEJJTQQNAAAAAAEAAAAAeDhCSu0D8 ...
</base64Binary>
```

Spoken Languages

Of course, XML is for the world, and this means that you can write content in any language you want. Here are some examples of proper XML:

```
<Message> 私は別の言語を話している。</Message>

<Message>_ ______ __ ______ _____.</Message>

<Message>Estoy hablando otra lengua.</Message>

<Message> 我講其它語言。</Message>
```

When working with an XML file that contains a fragment such as this, notice that the XML parser has no problem working with the content. See Figure 1-3.

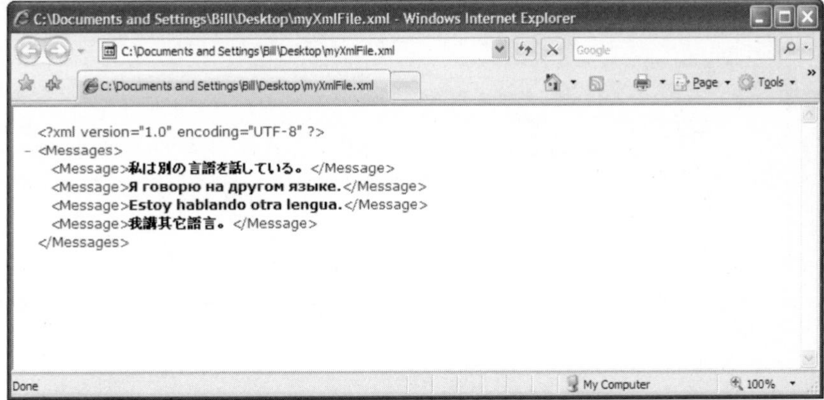

Figure 1-3

Whitespace

Whitespace is a special character in its own right. Whitespace is the space, line feeds, tabs, and carriage returns within your XML document. An example XML document containing various whitespace elements is presented here:

```
<Movies>
   <Favorites>
      <Title>Happy  Gilmore</Title>
      <Title>Grease</Title>
      <Title>Lawrence
             of
             Arabia</Title>
      <Title>Star Wars -         The Empire Strikes Back</Title>
   </Favorites>
</Movies>
```

HTML parsers do a good job of ignoring the whitespace contained within a document. In fact, in HTML, if you want to force the HTML parsers to interpret the whitespace contained within an HTML document, you have to put `<pre>` tags around the text.

XML works in the opposite manner. All whitespace is preserved in XML documents. This means that if there are two spaces between two words, these spaces are maintained by any XML parser and, consequently, they pass to the consuming application. The consuming application can choose whether to process the whitespace. Certain applications or processes strip the whitespace from the document, and others do not.

For example, Microsoft's Internet Explorer receives whitespace from the XML document and then strips it out in the consumption process. The previous XML document produces the results shown in Figure 1-4 when it is viewed in Internet Explorer.

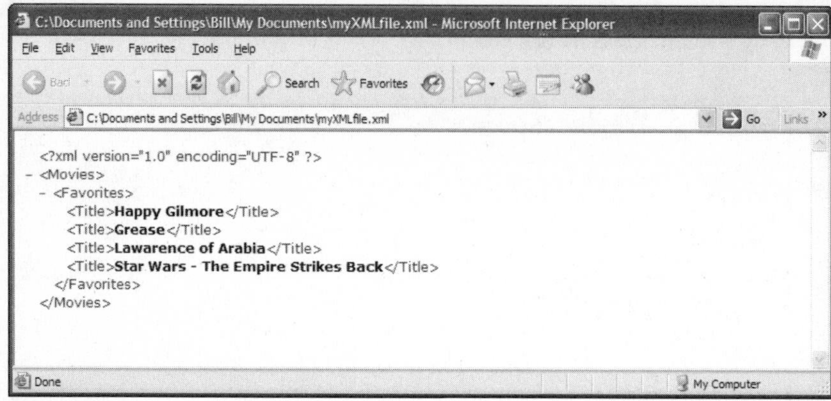

Figure 1-4

Entity References

Although you can put about just anything in the text part of an XML element, some characters cannot be contained as a value within an XML element. Take a look at the following code to see if you can tell where a problem might occur.

Incorrect usage of text within an XML element

```
<Value>Do if 5 < 3</Value>
```

You should be able to tell right away that a processing error will occur because of the character directly after the 5. The *greater than* sign is used to close an XML tag; but here it is used as a textual value within an XML element, and so it will confuse the XML parser. In fact, if you run this in Internet Explorer, you are presented with the error directly. See Figure 1-5.

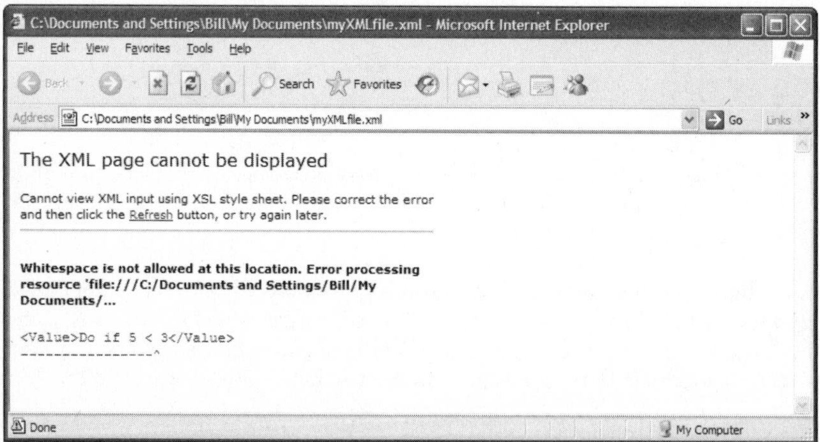

Figure 1-5

You can see that a parsing error is automatically thrown because the XML parser thinks that the less than sign is actually the start of the closing tag of the element. The space behind the character causes the parser to throw an error because it sees a whitespace problem.

The trick is to encode this character so that the XML parser can treat it in the appropriate manner. Five characters that cause an error and, therefore, must be encoded are shown in the following table with their encoded values.

Character	Entity
<	`<`
>	`>`
"	`"`
'	`'`
&	`&`

With this knowledge, you can now write the XML element as follows:

```
<Value>Do if 5 &lt; 3</Value>
```

If you run this element in Internet Explorer, you get the correct output as presented in Figure 1-6.

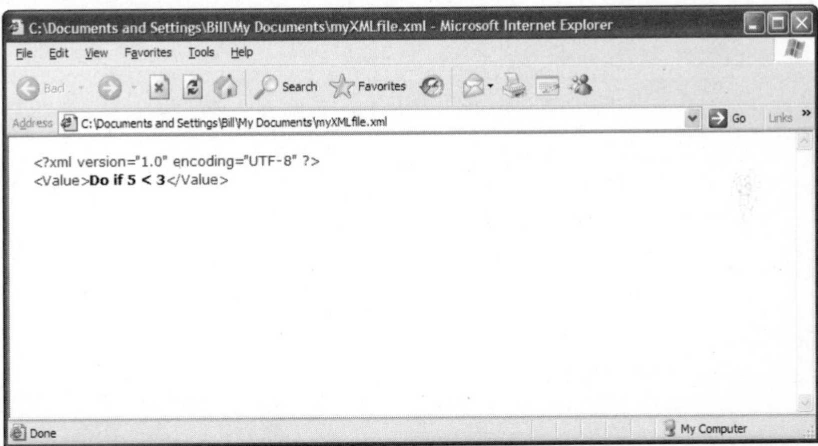

Figure 1-6

The XML with the encoded character was passed to the XML parser used by Internet Explorer, and the XSL stylesheet then converts the encoded character to the format in which it should be represented visually.

CDATA Sections

One way to work with some of the character entities that XML parsers can't easily interpret is to encode the character.

```
<Value>Do if 5 &lt; 3</Value>
```

When you have a lot of items that need this type of encoding (especially if you are representing computer code within your XML document), you should check out the CDATA section capability found in XML.

Creating a CDATA section within the text value of your XML element allows you, with little work on your part, to use as many difficult characters as you wish. Representing the previous code within a CDATA section is accomplished in the following manner:

```
<Value><![CDATA[Do if 5 < 3]]></Value>
```

You can use this method to represent large content sets that might require a lot of escape sequences. This method is shown in Listing 1-3.

Listing 1-3: Representing text using the CDATA section

```
<?xml version="1.0" encoding="UTF-8" ?>
<Value>
   <![CDATA[
   <script runat="server">
    protected void DropDownList1_SelectedIndexChanged(object sender, EventArgs e)
    {
        string[] CarArray = new string[4] {"Ford", "Honda", "BMW", "Dodge"};
        string[] AirplaneArray = new string[3] {"Boeing 777", "Boeing 747",
           "Boeing 737"};
        string[] TrainArray = new string[3] {"Bullet Train", "Amtrack", "Tram"};

        if (DropDownList1.SelectedValue == "Car") {
            DropDownList2.DataSource = CarArray; }
        else if (DropDownList1.SelectedValue == "Airplane") {
            DropDownList2.DataSource = AirplaneArray; }
        else {
            DropDownList2.DataSource = TrainArray;
        }

        DropDownList2.DataBind();
        DropDownList2.Visible = true;
    }

    protected void Button1_Click(object sender, EventArgs e)
    {
        Response.Write("You selected <b>" +
           DropDownList1.SelectedValue.ToString() + ": " +
           DropDownList2.SelectedValue.ToString() + "</b>");
    }
   </script>
   ]]>
</Value>
```

The start of the CDATA section is defined with <![CDATA[. After this entry, you can place as much text as you wish. The XML parser looks for a closing]]> before ending the CDATA section. To make this work, be careful that you don't have this sequence of characters in your text. The previous XML document displayed in IE is shown in Figure 1-7.

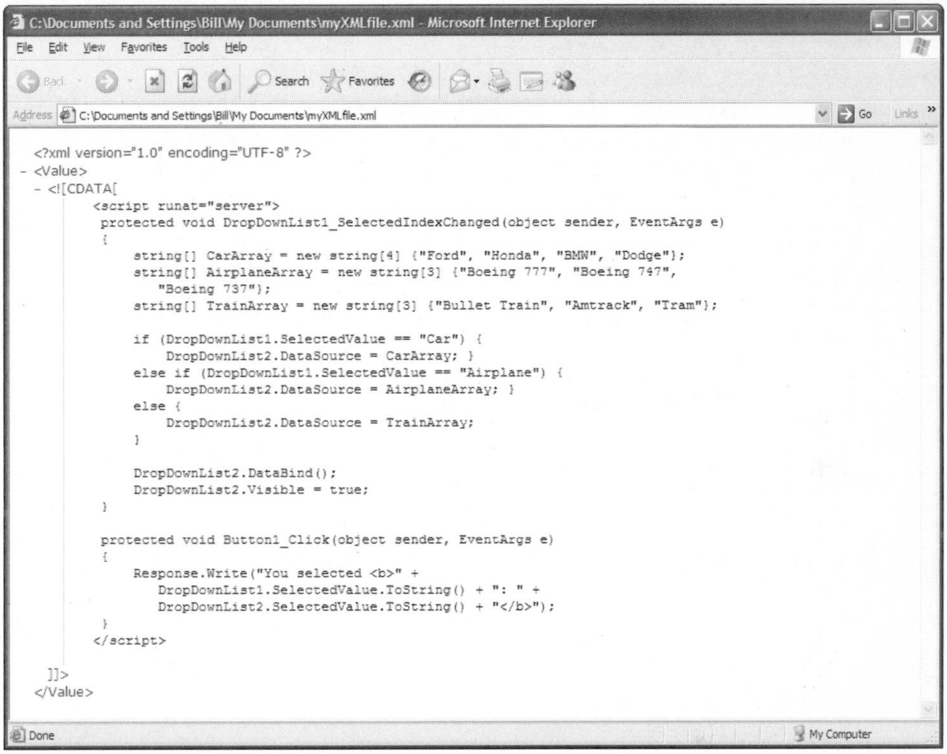

```
<?xml version="1.0" encoding="UTF-8" ?>
- <Value>
  - <![CDATA[
        <script runat="server">
        protected void DropDownList1_SelectedIndexChanged(object sender, EventArgs e)
        {
            string[] CarArray = new string[4] {"Ford", "Honda", "BMW", "Dodge"};
            string[] AirplaneArray = new string[3] {"Boeing 777", "Boeing 747",
               "Boeing 737"};
            string[] TrainArray = new string[3] {"Bullet Train", "Amtrack", "Tram"};

            if (DropDownList1.SelectedValue == "Car") {
                DropDownList2.DataSource = CarArray; }
            else if (DropDownList1.SelectedValue == "Airplane") {
                DropDownList2.DataSource = AirplaneArray; }
            else {
                DropDownList2.DataSource = TrainArray;
            }

            DropDownList2.DataBind();
            DropDownList2.Visible = true;
        }

        protected void Button1_Click(object sender, EventArgs e)
        {
            Response.Write("You selected <b>" +
               DropDownList1.SelectedValue.ToString() + ": " +
               DropDownList2.SelectedValue.ToString() + "</b>");
        }
        </script>
    ]]>
  </Value>
```

Figure 1-7

The XML Document

Now that you have studied the pieces that make up an XML document, you can turn your attention to the entire XML document.

Creating an .xml File

Like all files, XML files have a file extension. In many cases, XML files have an `.xml` file extension, but this is not the only one used. Certain XML files have their own file extensions. For instance, if you have the .NET Framework installed on your computer, it includes many configuration files with a `.config` file extension. If you look at one of these `.config` files within Microsoft's Notepad, you see that they are indeed XML files. (See Figure 1-8.)

XML file are created in a number of ways. Many outstanding tools are out there to help you with the construction and creation of XML files. Tools such as Altova's XMLSpy or Microsoft's Visual Studio 2005 give you what you need to get the job done. Because this is the first XML file you are working with, this example concentrates on building the XML file using Microsoft's Notepad.

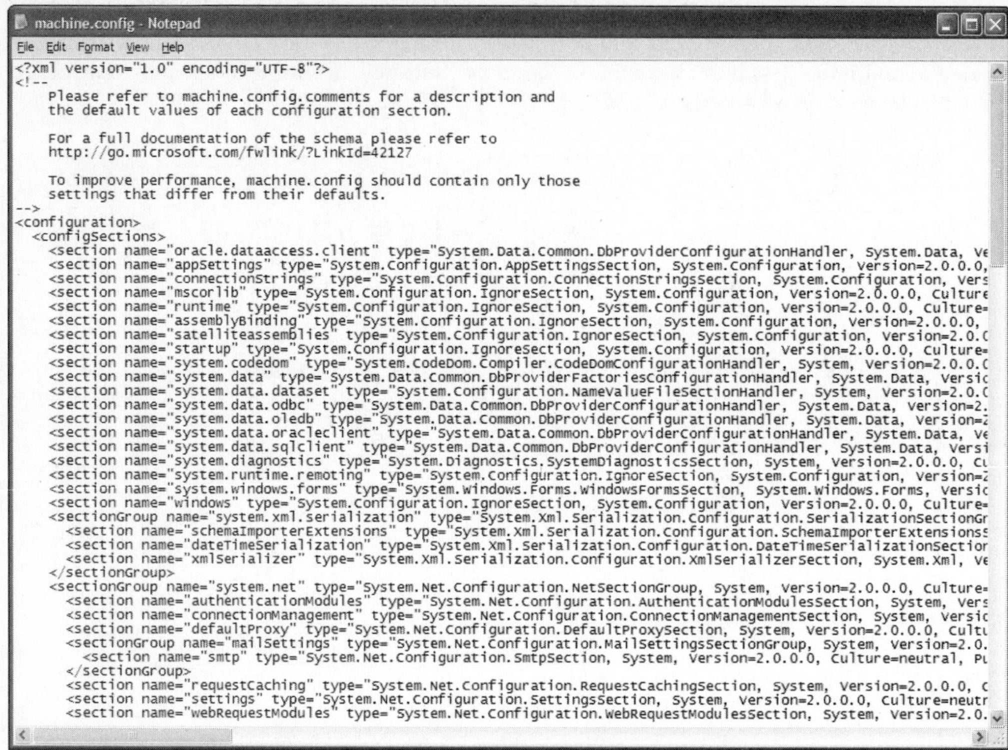

Figure 1-8

XML tools are covered in Chapter 2.

Now, open Notepad and type the XML shown in Listing 1-4.

Listing 1-4: Creating an XML file

```
<?xml version="1.0" encoding="UTF-8" ?>
<Process>
   <Name>Bill Evjen</Name>
   <Address>123 Main Street</Address>
   <City>Saint Charles</City>
   <State>Missouri</State>
   <Country>USA</Country>
   <Order>
      <Item>52-inch Plasma</Item>
      <Quantity>1</Quantity>
   </Order>
</Process>
```

After your have typed this small XML document into Notepad, save it as `myXMLfile.xml`. Make sure you save it as presented in Figure 1-9.

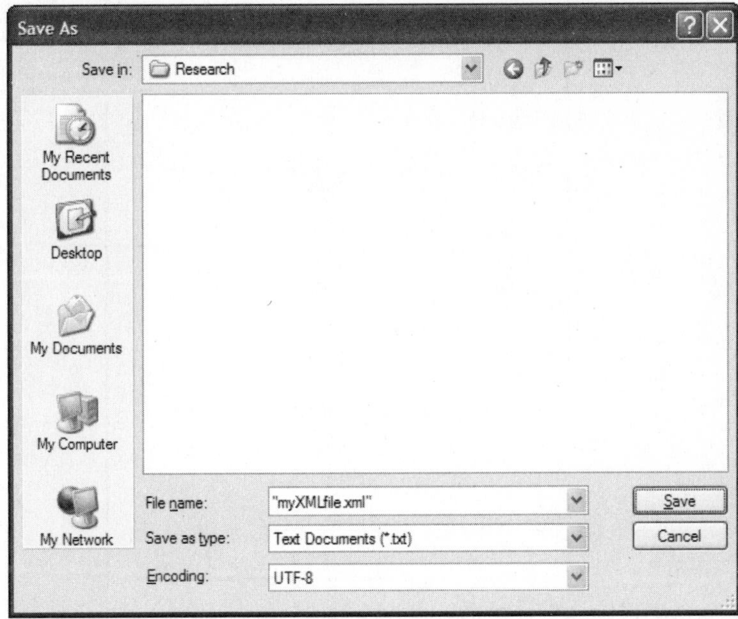

Figure 1-9

Put the name of the file along with the file extension `.xml` in quotes within the Filename text box of the Save As dialog. This ensures that the file won't be saved with a `.txt` file extension. You also want to change the encoding of the file from ANSI to UTF-8 because this is the format used for many XML files. This enables any XML parsers to interpret a larger character base than otherwise.

After you do this, click the Save button and you can then double-click on the new `.xml` file. This opens up in Internet Explorer if you are using a Windows operating system. You might be wondering why Internet Explorer is the default container for XML files. You can actually manually change this yourself by going into the Properties dialog of one of your XML files. Figure 1-10 shows the Properties dialog of the newly created `myXMLfile.xml`.

From the Properties dialog, you can see in the first section that the `Opens with` property is set to Internet Explorer. You can easily change the application used to open the file by clicking the Change button.

Internet Explorer produces the results presented in Figure 1-11.

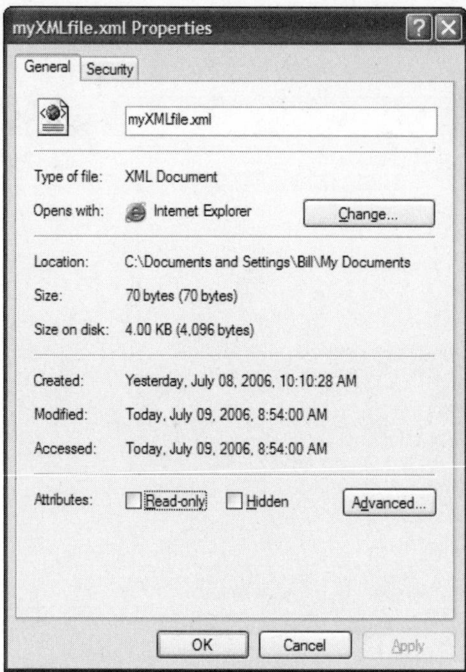

Figure 1-10

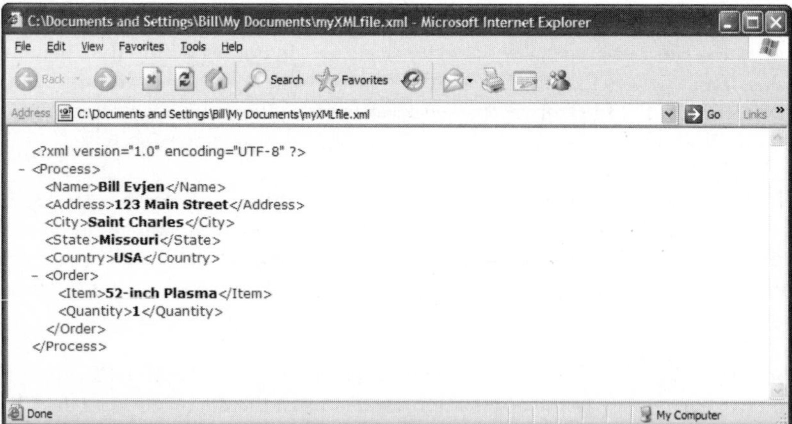

Figure 1-11

You can see that XML files are color-coded for easy viewing. IE is using the Microsoft XML parser and then applies an XSL stylesheet to beautify the results. The interesting part of the XML document as it is presented in IE is that you can expand and collapse the child nodes for easy readability. By default, the XML document is presented with the entire document expanded, but you can start collapsing nodes by clicking the minus button next to nodes that have children associated with them. Figure 1-12 shows various nodes collapsed in IE.

Using Mozilla's Firefox for the same XML file produces the results presented in Figure 1-13.

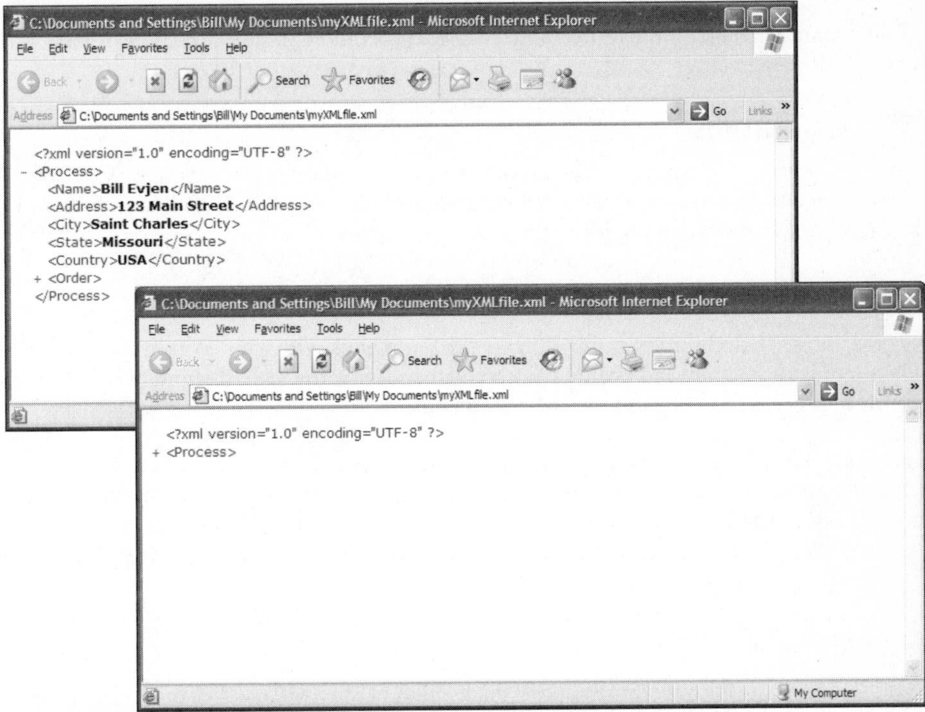

Figure 1-12

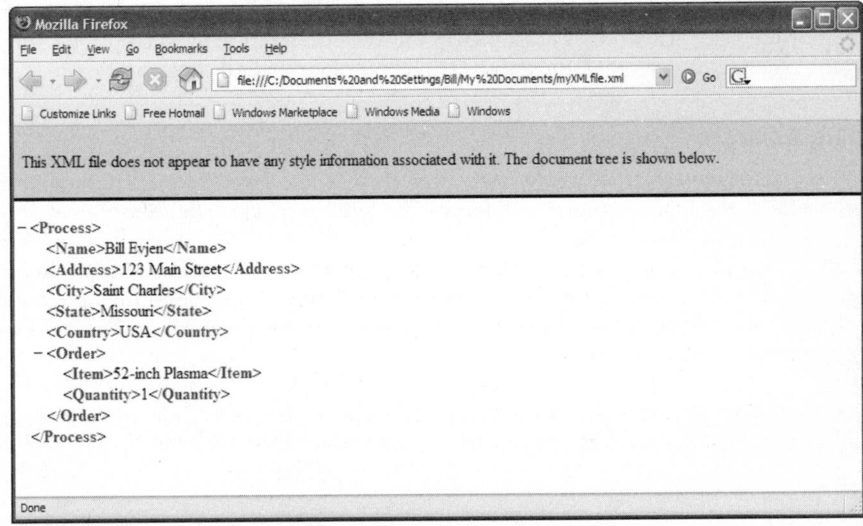

Figure 1-13

As you can see from Figure 1-13, Firefox also allows you to expand and collapse the nodes of the XML document.

Now that you understand a little more about the XML document, the next sections review the construction of the XML document.

The XML Declaration

Typically, you place a declaration at the top of your XML file stating that this is an XML file. It is called the *XML declaration*. It is recommended, but not required, that you use an XML declaration. The XML should be written in the following format:

```
<?xml version="1.0" ?>
```

In this case, the XML declaration starts with a `<?xml` and ends with a `?>`. Within the declaration, you can include a couple of different key/value pairs to further define the XML document to help parsers understand how to process the forthcoming XML document.

If you include the XML declaration, the only required attribute is the `version` attribute. The other possible attributes are `encoding` and `standalone`. One difference between this set of attributes in the XML declaration and normal attributes that you would find in any other XML element is that `version`, `encoding`, and `standalone` are required in this particular order when other attributes have no such requirements.

The version Attribute

The `version` attribute allows you to specify the version of the XML used in the XML document.

```
<?xml version="1.0" ?>
```

This preceding XML declaration signifies that version 1.0 of XML is used in the XML document. All values defined by the version and other attributes in the XML declaration must be placed within quotes. It is important to note that at present, the only version you can use is 1.0.

The encoding Attribute

`encoding` explains how a computer interprets 1's and 0's. These 1's and 0's are put together to represent various characters, and the computer can interpret these digits in a number of different ways.

The United States and its computer encoding formats evolved around an encoding technology called ANCII. ANCII, *American Standard Code for Information Interchange*, is very limiting in that it only allows 256 possible values. It works with the English language, but it is less effective when working with multiple languages with their many characters.

Because XML was developed by an international organization, it is uses Unicode for encoding an XML document. So far, you have seen the use of UTF-8 used for encoding some of the XML documents in this chapter.

```
<?xml version="1.0" encoding="UTF-8" ?>
```

The more common encoding formats used for XML documents are UTF-8 and UTF-16. The difference between the two is that UTF-8 can result in smaller file size because it can use either a single byte (mostly for English characters) or a double byte for other characters. UTF-16 uses a double-byte for all characters.

XML parsers must understand at least UTF-8 and UTF-16. If no encoding directive is provided, then UTF-8 is assumed. Some common character sets are presented in the following table.

Character Set Code Name	Coverage
US-ASCII	English
UTF-8	Compressed Unicode
UTF-16	Compressed UCS
windows-1252	Microsoft Windows Western European
windows-1250	Microsoft Windows Central European
windows-1251	Microsoft Windows Cyrillic
windows-1253	Microsoft Windows Greek
ISO-8859-1	Latin 1, Western European
ISO-8859-2	Latin 2, Eastern European
ISO-8859-3	Latin 3, Southern European
ISO-8859-4	Latin 4, Northern European
ISO-2022-JP	Japanese

The standalone Attribute

Another optional attribute that can be contained within the XML declaration is the `standalone` attribute. The `standalone` attribute signifies whether the XML document requires any other files in order to be understood or whether the file can be completely understood as a *standalone* file. By default, the value of this attribute is set to `no`.

```
<?xml version="1.0" standalone="no" ?>
```

If the document does not depend upon other documents in order to be complete, set the `standalone` attribute to reflect this.

```
<?xml version="1.0" standalone="yes" ?>
```

XML Comments

As in HTML, you can easily place XML comments inside your XML documents. Comments placed inside the XML document are ignored by any XML parser. Listing 1-5 shows how you can add comments to the XML document displayed in Listing 1-4.

Listing 1-5: Adding comments to the previous XML document

```
<?xml version="1.0" encoding="UTF-8" ?>
<Process>
   <!-- Be sure to check name against customer database later -->
   <Name>Bill Evjen</Name>
   <Address>123 Main Street</Address>
   <City>Saint Charles</City>
   <State>Missouri</State>
   <Country>USA</Country>
   <Order>
      <Item>52-inch Plasma</Item>
      <Quantity>1</Quantity>
   </Order>
</Process>
```

An XML comment starts with a `<!--` and ends with a `-->`. Anything found in between these two items is considered the comment and is ignored by the XML parser. You are not required to put XML comments on a single line. You can break them up in multiple lines if you wish. This is illustrated in Listing 1-6.

Listing 1-6: Adding comments on multiple lines

```
<?xml version="1.0" encoding="UTF-8" ?>
<Process>
   <!--
        Be sure to
        check name against
        customer database later
    -->
   <Name>Bill Evjen</Name>
   <Address>123 Main Street</Address>
   <City>Saint Charles</City>
   <State>Missouri</State>
   <Country>USA</Country>
   <Order>
      <Item>52-inch Plasma</Item>
      <Quantity>1</Quantity>
   </Order>
</Process>
```

If you open the XML document in IE, you see that the Microsoft XML parser did indeed interpret the XML comment as a comment because it is shown in gray, unlike the other XML elements. This is illustrated in Figure 1-14.

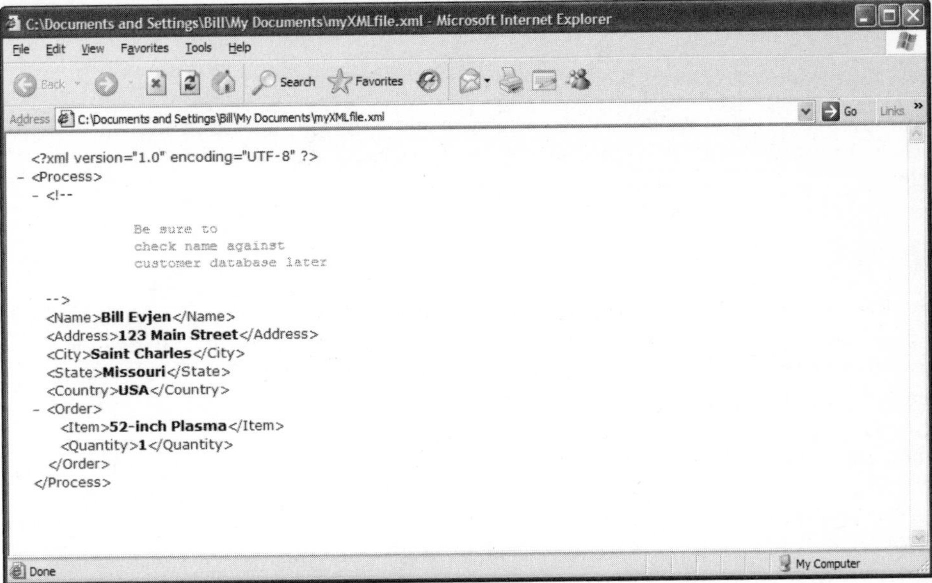

Figure 1-14

XML Processing Instructions

An XML processing instruction lets you direct computer process reactions. You won't see XML processing instructions used in the XML documents you interact with mainly because they are not accepted by all parsers and are often difficult to deal with. An example of an XML processing instruction is illustrated in Listing 1-7.

Listing 1-7: Using XML processing instructions

```
<?xml version="1.0" encoding="UTF-8" ?>
<Process>
   <?CustomerInput INPUT:Evjen?>
   <Name>Bill Evjen</Name>
   <Address>123 Main Street</Address>
   <City>Saint Charles</City>
   <State>Missouri</State>
   <Country>USA</Country>
   <Order>
      <Item>52-inch Plasma</Item>
      <Quantity>1</Quantity>
   </Order>
</Process>
```

In this case, the CustomerInput application that interprets this XML document can use the INPUT instruction and accomplish something with the `Evjen` value as provided by the XML processing instruction.

You would use the following syntax for processing instructions:

```
<?[target] [data]?>
```

The `target` part of the statement is a required item and it must be named in an XML-compliant way. The `data` item itself can contain any character sequence except for the `?>` set of characters, which signify the closing of a processing instruction.

Attributes

So far, you have seen the use of XML elements and tags and how they work within an XML document. One item hasn't yet been discussed — XML attributes. XML elements provide values via an attribute that is basically a key/value pair contained within the start tag of an XML element. The use of an XML attribute is presented in Listing 1-8.

Listing 1-8: Creating an XML file

```
<?xml version="1.0" encoding="UTF-8" ?>
<Process>
   <Name>Bill Evjen</Name>
   <Address type="Home">123 Main Street</Address>
   <City>Saint Charles</City>
   <State>Missouri</State>
   <Country>USA</Country>
   <Order count="1">
      <Item>52-inch Plasma</Item>
      <Quantity>1</Quantity>
   </Order>
</Process>
```

In this case, this XML document has two attributes — `type` and `count`. All attributes must include the name of the attribute followed by an equal sign and the value of the attribute contained within quotes (single or double). It is illegal not to include the quotes.

Illegal XML Element

```
<Address type=Home>123 Main Street</Address>
```

Naming Attributes

The names you give your attributes must follow the same rules that you follow when naming XML elements. This means that the following attributes are illegal.

Illegal Attribute Names

```
<myElement 123type="Value"></myElement>

<myElement #type="Value"></myElement>

<myElement .type="Value"></myElement>
```

Empty Attributes

If an attribute doesn't have a value, you can represent this empty or null value as two quotes next to each other as illustrated here:

```
<Address type="">123 Main Street</Address>
```

Attribute Names Must Be Unique

All attribute names must be unique within an XML element. You cannot have two attributes with the same name in the same element (as presented here):

```
<Address type="Home" type="Mail">123 Main Street</Address>
```

If you use this XML element, you would get an error when parsing the XML document—as illustrated in Figure 1-15.

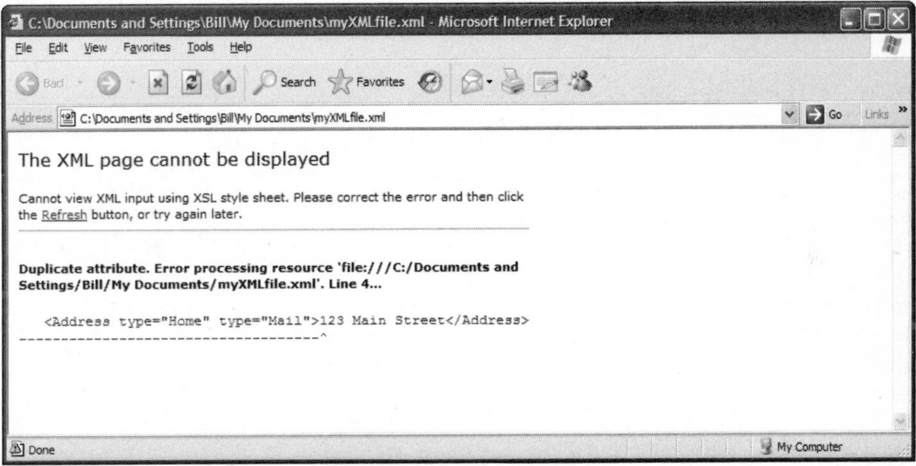

Figure 1-15

This only applies to attributes that are contained within the same XML element. You can have similar attribute names if they are contained within different XML elements. This scenario is shown in Listing 1-9.

Listing 1-9: Creating an XML file

```
<?xml version="1.0" encoding="UTF-8" ?>
<Process>
   <Name>Bill Evjen</Name>
   <Address type="Home">123 Main Street</Address>
   <City>Saint Charles</City>
   <State>Missouri</State>
   <Country>USA</Country>
   <Order type="Express">
      <Item>52-inch Plasma</Item>
      <Quantity>1</Quantity>
   </Order>
</Process>
```

In this case, you can see that there are two attributes that use the name `type`, but because they are contained within different XML elements, you won't encounter any errors in their use.

The xml:lang Attribute

Two built-in XML element attributes can be used in XML documents — `xml:lang` and `xml:space`. The first of these, `xml:lang`, allows you to specify the language of the item represented as the value in the XML element.

You can use as a value either the ISO 639 standard (found at `http://ftp.ics.uci.edu/pub/ietf/http/related/iso639.txt`), the ISO 3166 standard (found at `http://ftp.ics.uci.edu/pub/ietf/http/related/iso3166.txt`), or the IANA language codes (found at `iana.org/assignments/lang-tags/`).

Listing 1-10 shows how you might represent the earlier XML fragment when using the `xml:lang` attribute with the ISO 639 standard.

Listing 1-10: Using ISO 639 with the xml:lang attribute

```
<?xml version="1.0" encoding="UTF-8" ?>
<TranslatedMessages>
   <Message xml:lang="jp"> 私は別の言語を話している。</Message>
   <Message xml:lang="ru">_ ______ __ ______ _____.</Message>
   <Message xml:lang="es">Estoy hablando otra lengua.</Message>
   <Message xml:lang="zh"> 我講其它語言。</Message>
</TranslatedMessages>
```

You can see that the ISO 639 standard is simply a two-letter code that signifies the language to use. The problem with this standard is that it really only allows for 676 languages to be represented and a significant number more than that are used in the world. The ISO 3166 standard has a similar problem, but represents a country as well as a language (as presented in Listing 1-11).

Listing 1-11: Using ISO 3166 with the xml:lang attribute

```
<?xml version="1.0" encoding="UTF-8" ?>
<TranslatedMessages>
   <Message xml:lang="jp-JP"> 私は別の言語を話している。</Message>
   <Message xml:lang="ru-RU">_ ______ __ ______ _____.</Message>
   <Message xml:lang="es-ES">Estoy hablando otra lengua.</Message>
   <Message xml:lang="zh-CN"> 我講其它語言。</Message>
</TranslatedMessages>
```

The xml:space Attribute

When you really want to preserve your whitespace, one option is to also include the attribute `xml:space` within your XML elements where whitespace needs to be maintained. For instance, Listing 1-12 shows using the `xml:space` attribute for maintaining whitespace.

Listing 1-12: Using the xml:space attribute

```
<?xml version="1.0" encoding="UTF-8" ?>
<Movies>
   <Favorites>
      <Title xml:space="default">Happy  Gilmore</Title>
      <Title>Grease</Title>
      <Title xml:space="preserve">Lawrence
```

```
                of
                Arabia</Title>
        <Title xml:space="preserve">Star Wars -       The Empire Strikes Back</Title>
    </Favorites>
</Movies>
```

Two possible values exist for the `xml:space` attribute — `default` and `preserve`. A value of `default` means that the whitespace should not be preserved, and a value of `preserve` means that the whitespace should remain intact.

Notice that the XML parsers do not strip whitespace or act upon the whitespace in any manner because of these attribute settings. Instead, the `xml:space` attribute is simply an instruction to the consuming application that is can choose to act upon if desired.

XML Namespaces

Because developers create their own tag names in XML, you must use *namespaces* to define particular elements. If you are using two XML files within your application and the two files use some of the same tags, namespaces become very important. Even though the tags have the same name, they might have different meanings. For instance, compare the two XML files in Listings 1-13 and 1-14.

Listing 1-13: Book.xml

```
<?xml version="1.0" encoding="UTF-8" ?>
<Book>
    <Title>Professional ASP.NET 2.0</Title>
    <Price>49.99</Price>
    <Year>2005</Year>
</Book>
```

Now take a look at the second XML file. You should be able to see where the problem lies.

Listing 1-14: Author.xml

```
<?xml version="1.0" encoding="UTF-8" ?>
<Author>
    <Title>Mr.</Title>
    <FirstName>Bill</FirstName>
    <LastName>Evjen</LastName>
</Author>
```

A conflict exists with the `<Title>` tag. If you are using both these XML files, you might be able to tell the difference between the tags by just glancing at them; but computers are unable to decipher the difference between two tags with the same name.

The solution to this problem is to give the tag an identifier that enables the computer to tell the difference between the two tags. Do this is by using the XML namespace attribute, `xmlns`. Listing 1-15 shows how you would differentiate between these two XML files by using XML namespaces.

Listing 1-15: Revised Book.xml using an XML namespace

```
<?xml version="1.0" encoding="UTF-8" ?>
<Book xmlns="http://www.xmlws101.com/xmlns/book">
   <Title>Professional ASP.NET 2.0</Title>
   <Price>49.99</Price>
   <Year>2005</Year>
</Book>
```

Notice that you now have added the XML namespace attribute to your root element `<Book>`. Now look at the second file (Listing 1-16).

Listing 1-16: Revised Author.xml using an XML namespace

```
<?xml version="1.0" encoding="UTF-8" ?>
<Author xmlns="http://www.xmlws101.com/xmlns/author">
   <Title>Mr.</Title>
   <FirstName>Bill</FirstName>
   <LastName>Evjen</LastName>
</Author>
```

In this example, the `<Author>` element contains an XML namespace that uniquely identifies this XML tag and all the other tags that are contained within it. Note that you could have put an XML namespace directly in the `<Title>` tag if you wished. By putting the `xmlns` attribute in the root element, not only do you uniquely identify the root element, but you also identify all the child elements contained within the root element.

The value of the `xmlns` attribute is the Universal Resource Identifier (URI). It is not required that the URI be a Web site URL as shown in the example, but this is usually a good idea. The URI can be anything that you wish it to be. For example, it could just as easily be written as `xmlns="myData"` or `xmlns="12345"`. But with this kind of URI, you are not guaranteed any uniqueness because another URI in another file may use the same value. Therefore, it is common practice to use a URL, and this practice serves two purposes. First, it is guaranteed to be unique. A URL is unique, and using it as your URI ensures that your URI won't conflict with any other. The other advantage to using a URL as the URI is that it also identifies where the data originates.

You don't have to point to an actual file. In fact, it is usually better not to do that, but instead to use something like the following:

```
xmlns="http://www.xmlws101.com/[Namespace Name]"
```

If the XML file has an associated XSD file, another option is to point to this file. The XSD file defines the schema of the XML file.

The style of XML namespaces used thus far is referred to as a default namespace. The other type of XML namespaces that is available for your use is a qualified namespace. To understand why you need another type of XML namespace, take a look at the example in Listing 1-17.

Listing 1-17: Author.xml using multiple XML namespaces

```
<?xml version="1.0" encoding="UTF-8" ?>
<Author xmlns="http://www.firstserver.com/xmlns/author">
   <Title xmlns="http://www.secondserver.com/title">Mr.</Title>
   <FirstName xmlns="http://www.thirdserver.com/fn">Bill</FirstName>
   <LastName xmlns="http://www.thirdserver.com/ln">Evjen</LastName>
</Author>
```

As you can see in this example, you use a number of different XML namespaces to identify your tags. First, your `<Author>` tag is associated with the XML namespace from the first server. The `<Title>` tag is associated with the second server, and the `<FirstName>` and `<LastName>` tags are associated with the third server. XML allows you to associate your tags with more than one namespace throughout your document.

The problem is that you might have hundreds or thousands of nodes within your XML document. If one of the namespaces that is repeated throughout the document changes, you have a lot of changes to make throughout the document.

Using qualified namespaces enables you to construct the XML document so that if you need to make a change to a namespace that is used throughout the document, you only have to do it in one spot. The change is reflected throughout the document. Look at Listing 1-18 to see an XML document that uses qualified namespaces.

Listing 1-18: Author.xml using qualified XML namespaces

```
<?xml version="1.0" encoding="UTF-8" ?>
<AuthorNames:Author
 xmlns:AuthorNames="http://www.firstserver.com/xmlns/author"
 xmlns:AuthorDetails="http://www.secondserver.com/xmlns/details">
   <AuthorNames:Title>Mr.</AuthorNames:Title>
   <AuthorNames:FirstName>Bill</AuthorNames:FirstName>
   <AuthorNames:LastName>Evjen</AuthorNames:LastName>
   <AuthorDetails:Book>Professional ASP.NET 2.0</AuthorDetails:Book>
</AuthorNames:Author>
```

In this document, you use an explicit declaration of the namespace. Explicit declarations of namespace prefixes use attribute names beginning with `xmlns:` followed by the prefix. So in the first node, you have explicitly declared two namespaces that you use later in the document.

```
xmlns:AuthorNames="http://www.firstserver.com/xmlns/author"
xmlns:AuthorDetails="http://www.secondserver.com/xmlns/details"
```

Notice that the declaration name follows a colon after `xmlns`. In this example, you declare two qualified namespaces: `AuthorNames` and `AuthorDetails`. Later, when you want to associate an element with one of these explicit declarations, you can use the shorthand (or prefix) to substitute for the full namespace. In your document, you do this by using `<AuthorNames:LastName>` and `<AuthorDetails:Book>`.

Summary

This chapter is a simple review of XML. It is meant to serve as a primer for you to get up to speed in dealing with the technologies that use XML. These technologies are covered throughout the rest of this book.

This chapter looked at the basics of XML, its syntax, and the rules that go into building XML documents. In addition, this chapter reviewed how to build an XML document and to view it in the IE or Firefox.

Finally, this chapter explained how to use namespaces with XML documents. The next chapter covers building and working with XML documents using a number of different developer tools.

2

XML Editors

Although it is certainly possible to work with XML using only a text editor (such as emacs, vi, or even Windows Notepad), having a tool specifically designed or expanded for working with XML can make your life much easier. Beyond creating XML files, these tools add validation, schema creation, mapping, and even advanced features such as XSLT debugging to the mix; making you more productive and more successful when working with XML. In short, you want a dedicated XML editor to make working with XML easier.

This chapter will survey some of the more popular tools available for working with XML, along with the advantages and disadvantages of each.

The XML editors described in this chapter include:

- Microsoft Visual Studio .NET 2003
- Microsoft Visual Studio 2005
- Altova XMLSpy
- Oxygen
- Stylus

Visual Studio .NET 2003

Many developers spend a lot of their time in Microsoft Visual Studio .NET 2003, so it makes sense that it should also provide XML functionality. The XML features of Visual Studio .NET 2003 are somewhat basic, but utilizing them may reduce your need to purchase and learn additional tools.

Basic Editing in Visual Studio .NET 2003

By *basic editing*, I do mean basic. Editing XML with Visual Studio .NET 2003 is pretty much the same experience as editing XML with a text editor, with a few notable exceptions. The first is the addition of IntelliSense when working with XML files using a known schema. (See Figure 2-1) IntelliSense is the term for the drop down list that appears as you type. This list provides a list of the valid text at any point. The benefit here is that you get feedback as to what is valid, and in many cases, the IntelliSense features also save you many keystrokes. For example, in Figure 2-1, you can see the dropdown includes the valid children of the channel element.

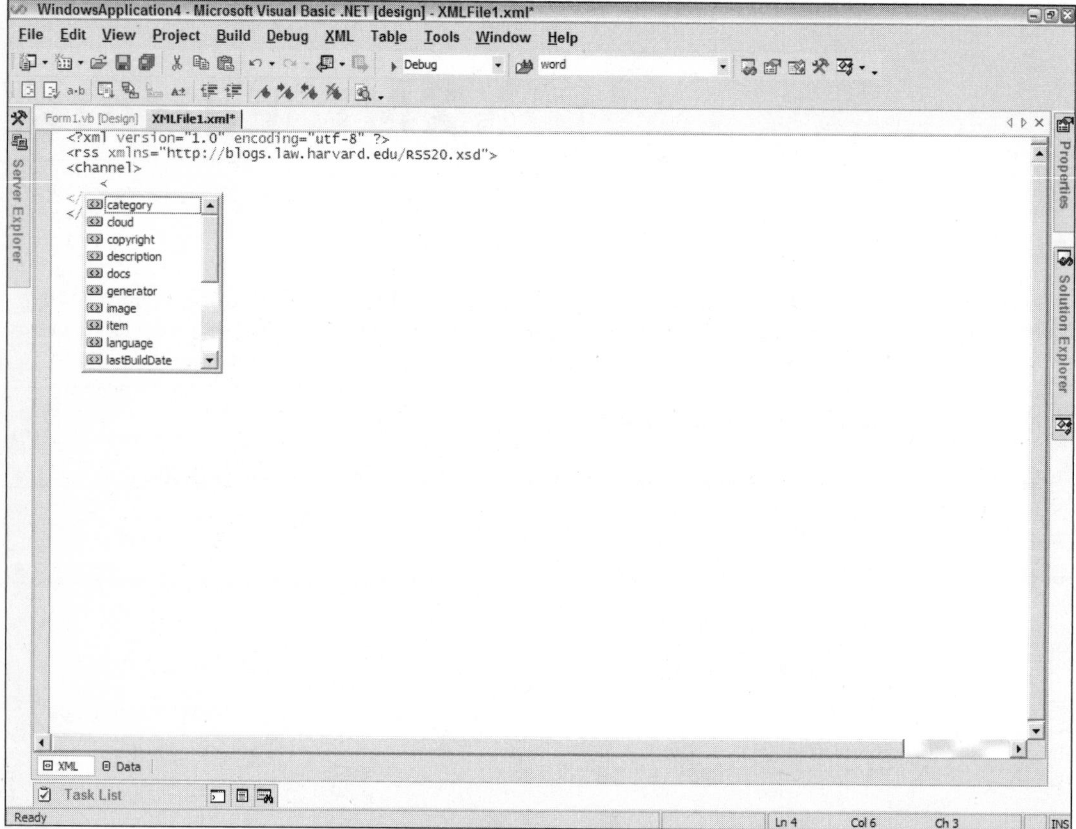

Figure 2-1

IntelliSense helps guarantee a more accurate document in two ways:

- The drop-down list displays only elements that are available while you are typing. This reduces the chance of adding elements at an incorrect location, based on the schema.
- The validation marks (the infamous *squiggles*) show any items in the XML file that would not validate based on the current schema. They provide a means of detecting these errors without requiring additional external tools or a validation step.

Although Visual Studio .NET 2003 is a capable editor, if you need a lot of advanced functionality for editing or creating XML documents, especially for formats that do not have an XML schema, you might want to look elsewhere.

Schema Development in Visual Studio .NET 2003

In addition to creating simple XML files, Visual Studio .NET 2003 supports the creation of W3C XML schemas using either a standard text editor or a graphical designer (see Figure 2-2). Visual Studio .NET 2003 does not support the creation of DTDs, Relax NG, or Schematron schemas.

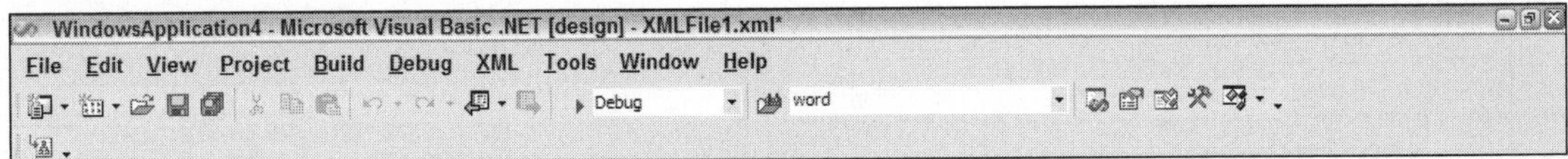

Figure 2-2

Other Features

Visual Studio .NET 2003, however, provides great XML support in the creation and accessing of SOAP-based Web Services. See Chapters 20-22 for more details on these features.

The following table provides a summary of Visual Studio .NET 2003's capabilities as an XML editor.

Benefit	Disadvantage
If you develop for Windows, odds are you have it installed already.	Fairly basic XML editing support
Excellent support for creating and accessing Web Services	Schema support limited to W3C XML schema.
	No support for XSLT debugging.
	Limited support for many XML grammars, such as DocBook, SVG or XQuery.

Visual Studio 2005

Although the XML features of Visual Studio .NET 2003 are a step in the right direction, the features of Visual Studio 2005 clearly show that some people at Microsoft know how to spell XML.

Basic Editing in Visual Studio 2005

Although the core editing experience for Visual Studio 2005 hasn't been improved much from Visual Studio .NET 2003, there are some welcome additions — notably, improved validation aids and the XML visualizers feature.

The squiggles of Visual Studio .NET 2003 told you if a non-validating item was present in your XML file. Visual Studio 2005 adds extra information by providing a ToolTip for the invalid item. Rather than simply identifying the invalid item, Visual Studio 2005 adds suggested changes (see Figure 2-3). This can speed development by reducing the number of trips you need to re-read the schema.

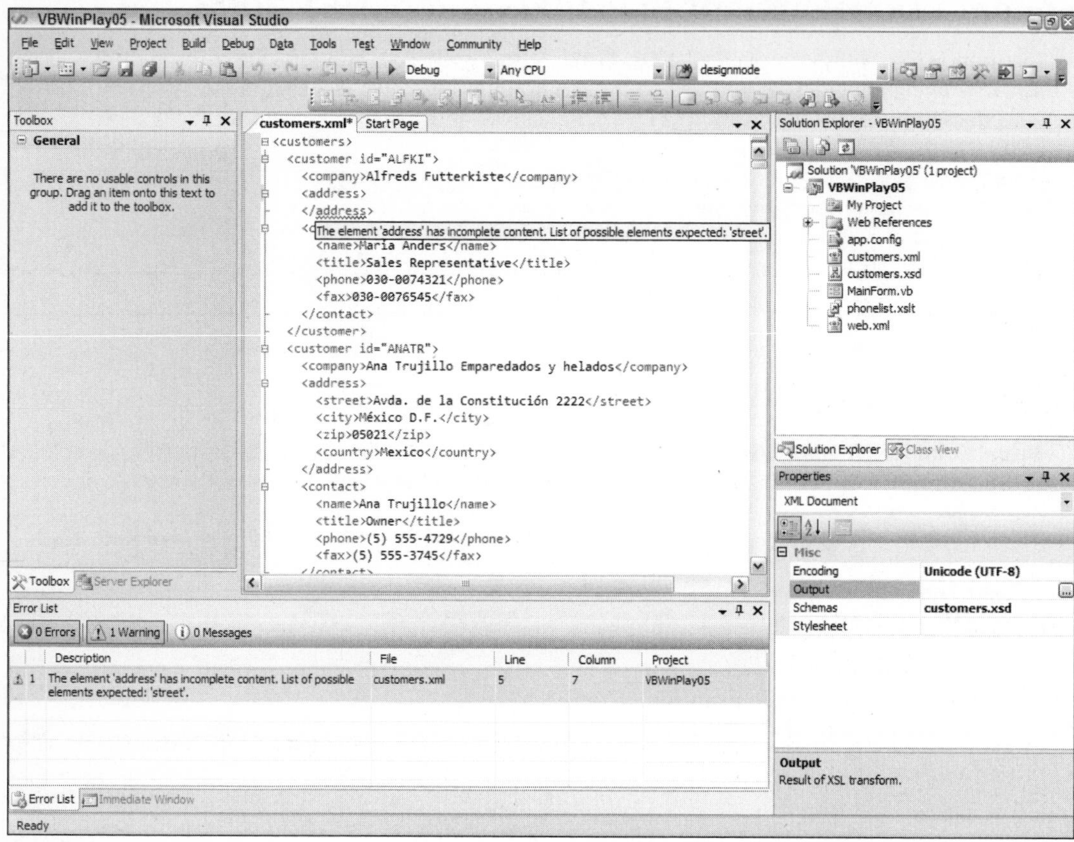

Figure 2-3

In addition to the improved IntelliSense in the main XML editors, Visual Studio 2005 makes working with XML in the core part of your application easier as well. Visualizers are tools that are displayed when debugging code to reveal the current value of variables. If the variable is storing XML, the XML visualizer (see Figure 2-4) enables you to explore the variable and the structure of the XML.

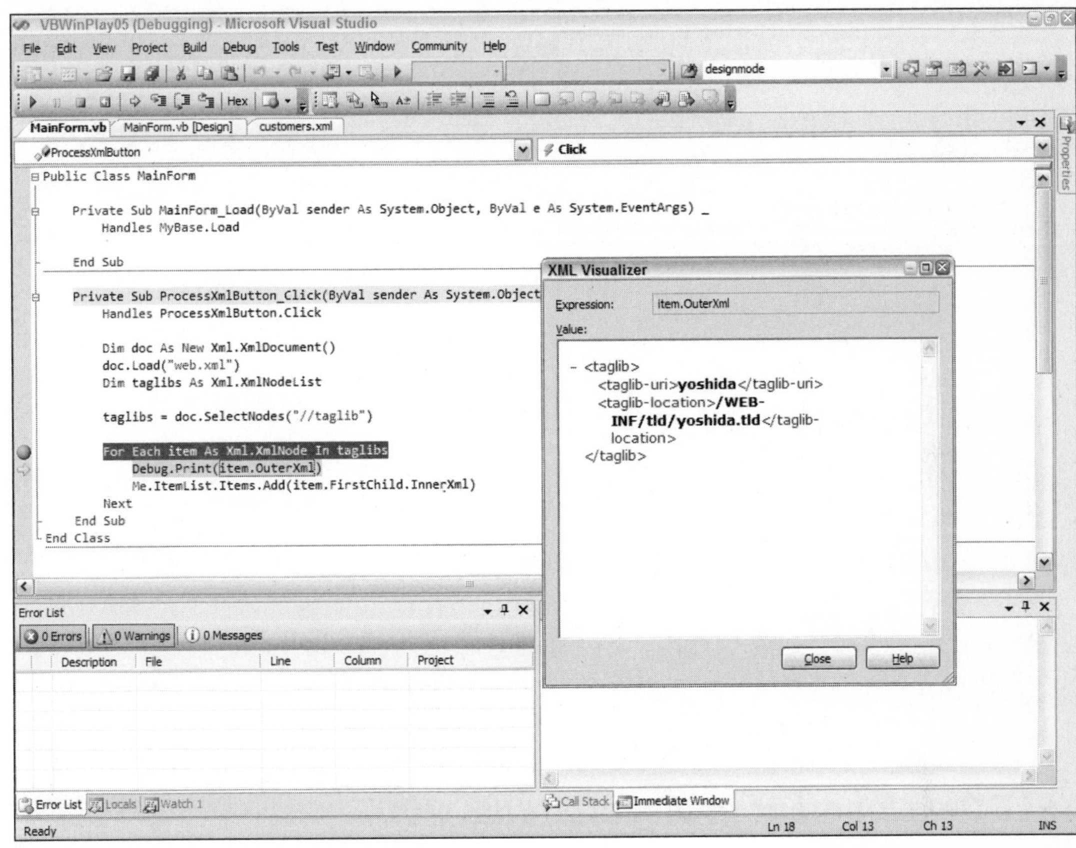

Figure 2-4

Schema Development in Visual Studio 2005

The schema design features of Visual Studio 2005 are similar to those in Visual Studio .NET 2003. They enable developers to create W3C XML schemas using either a text editor or a graphical tool (see Figure 2-5).

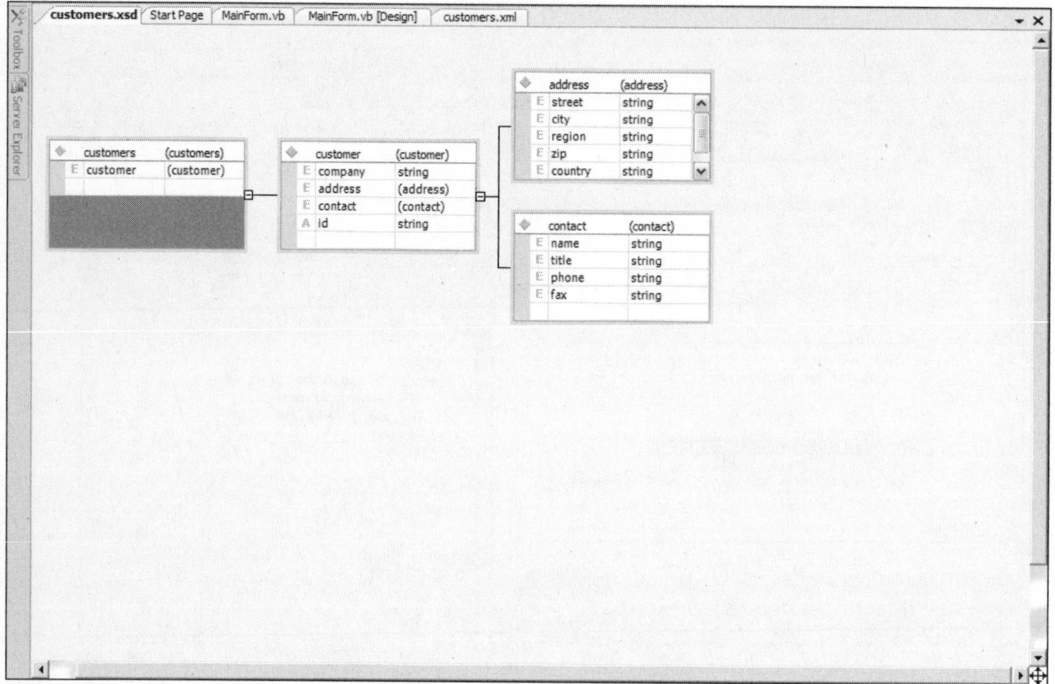

Figure 2-5

XSLT Development in Visual Studio 2005

Although Visual Studio .NET 2003 enabled the creation of XSLT files, Visual Studio 2005 allows you to debug them, too. This debugging (see Figure 2-6) enables you to create breakpoints, step through the templates in the XSLT, and query variables. These features are identical to the features available in normal code debugging using Visual Studio 2005. When you are working with complex templates, this can be an invaluable aid to understanding the flow of the templates.

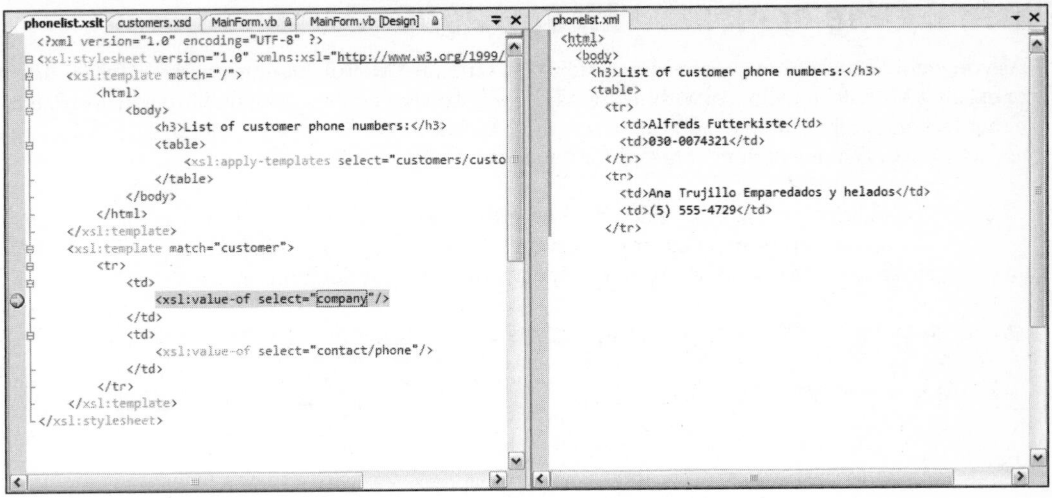

phonelist.xslt | customers.xsd | MainForm.vb | MainForm.vb [Design]

```
<?xml version="1.0" encoding="UTF-8" ?>
<xsl:stylesheet version="1.0" xmlns:xsl="http://www.w3.org/1999/
    <xsl:template match="/">
        <html>
            <body>
                <h3>List of customer phone numbers:</h3>
                <table>
                    <xsl:apply-templates select="customers/custo
                </table>
            </body>
        </html>
    </xsl:template>
    <xsl:template match="customer">
        <tr>
            <td>
                <xsl:value-of select="company"/>
            </td>
            <td>
                <xsl:value-of select="contact/phone"/>
            </td>
        </tr>
    </xsl:template>
</xsl:stylesheet>
```

phonelist.xml

```
<html>
  <body>
    <h3>List of customer phone numbers:</h3>
    <table>
      <tr>
        <td>Alfreds Futterkiste</td>
        <td>030-0074321</td>
      </tr>
      <tr>
        <td>Ana Trujillo Emparedados y helados</td>
        <td>(5) 555-4729</td>
      </tr>
```

Figure 2-6

The following table summarizes Visual Studio 2005's XML editing capabilities.

Benefit	Disadvantage
Improved support for creating valid documents through improvements in IntelliSense.	Schema creation support limited to W3C XML schema
XSLT debugging supported, including breakpoints and inspecting values.	No support for XQuery
Great support for creating, accessing, and debugging Web Services.	No support for XSL:FO
XML visualizers help you view XML structure when working with XML throughout the application.	

Altova XMLSpy 2006

XMLSpy from Altova GmbH is not just one tool, but an entire suite of products for working with XML in many of its forms. In addition, you can extend the capabilities of XMLSpy by adding on one or more of Altova's other products, such as Authentic (graphical XML editor for non-technical people), SchemaAgent (XML Schema repository), MapForce (data and Web services integration), and StyleVision (graphical form/report designer). These tools integrate into XMLSpy, providing additional capabilities beyond its already long list of features.

Basic Editing in Altova XMLSpy 2006

As you would expect from a tool designed for XML editing, XMLSpy has great support for editing new or existing XML documents. As with many other tools described here, you can edit XML documents in either text or a graphical view. You can access these views either via the View menu, or by selecting the appropriate item at the bottom of the editor window.

- **Text:** A basic editing experience. However, the XMLSpy editing window also includes such niceties as auto-completion (if you have an assigned schema), code folding (see Figure 2-7). This can be useful to hide sections of the document you're working on.

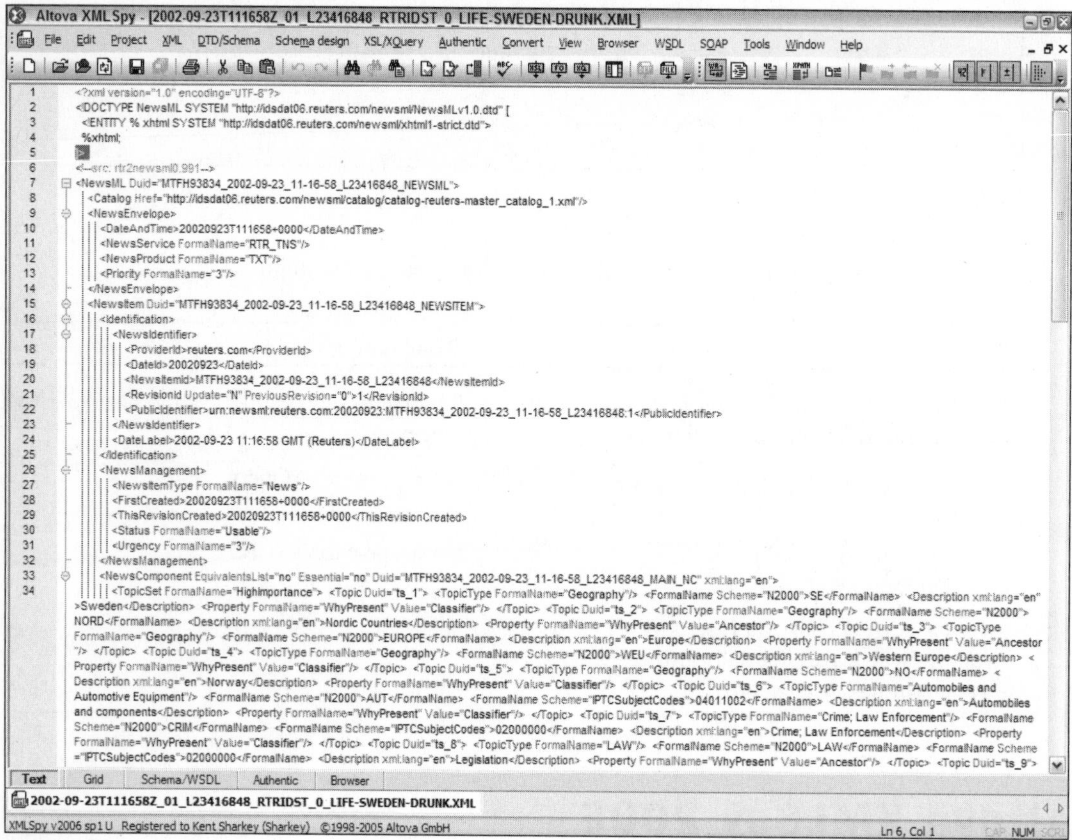

Figure 2-7

- **Grid:** A hierarchical editing surface that shows the logical structure of the XML file in a series of nested grids. This can be a useful editing surface either when you are first working with an XML document, when you want to learn the structure of the document, or when you are working on one area of a document and want to hide the remaining parts of the document. (See Figure 2-8.)

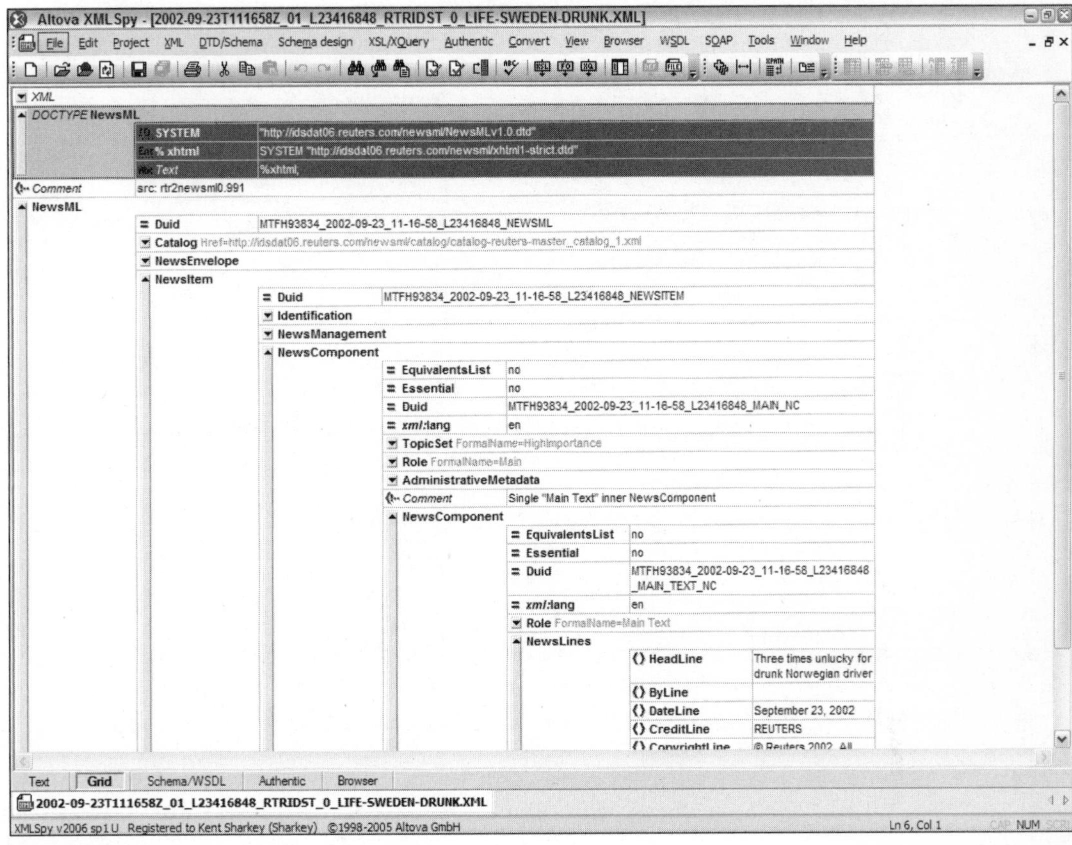

Figure 2-8

- **Schema/WSDL:** This view is only available when working with XML schemas or WSDL documents. It shows one of two views. For the document itself, it shows a list of all the global structures (element definitions, complex and simple types, and so on) in the document. (See Figure 2-9.) The second view, shown when an element or complex type is selected, shows a graphical node-based view of that section of the schema. (See Figure 2-10.) Both of these views provide a graphical view of the structure of the schema, but also allow you to graphically design the schema or WSDL. For more details on this view, see the Schema Development section later in this chapter.

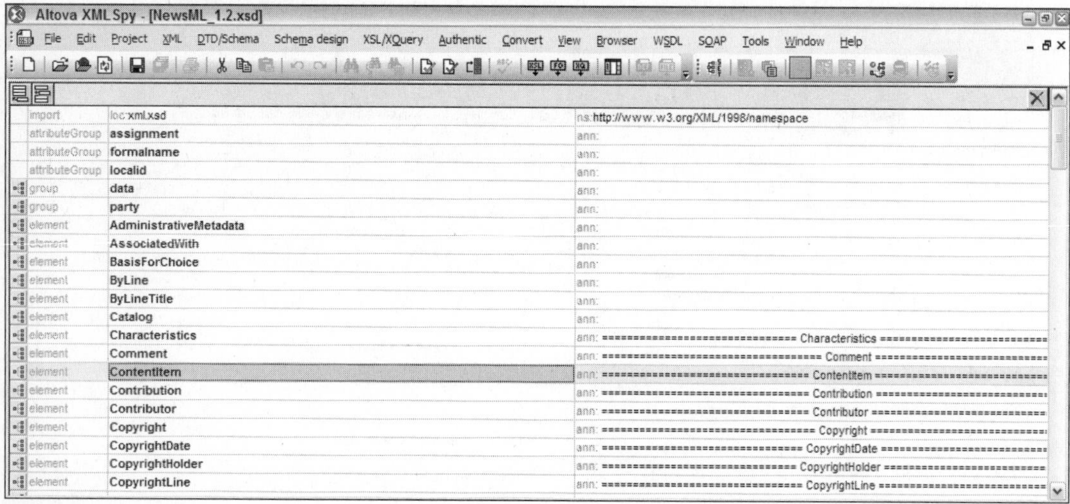

Figure 2-9

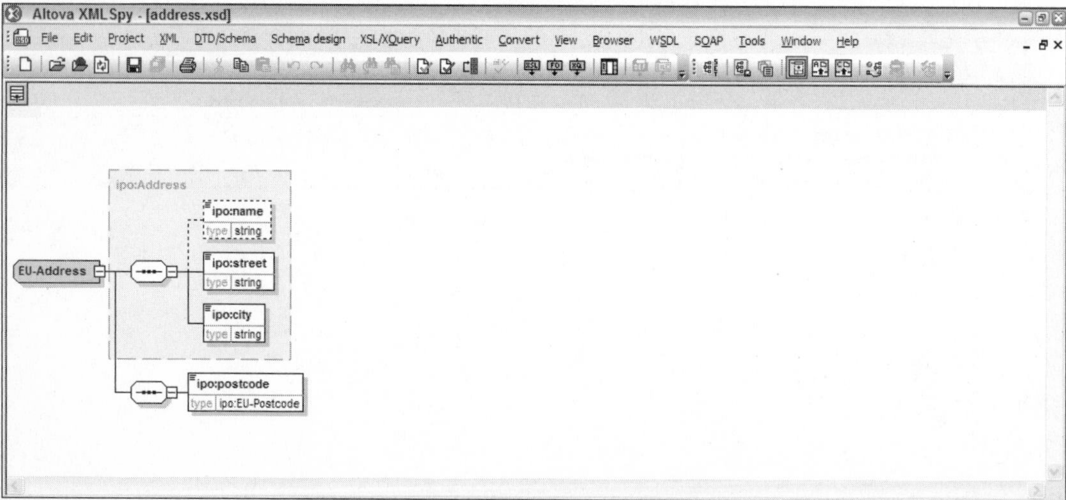

Figure 2-10

- **Authentic:** A view specific to XMLSpy, this displays the XML using a StyleVision stylesheet. A StyleVision stylesheet is a graphical overlay on an XML file. It can include controls, validation, and graphics to make working with XML easier for those not used to dealing with angle brackets. See Figure 2-11.
- **Browser:** Displays the XML document using Internet Explorer (requires IE 5 or above). This can be useful when you are creating XHTML files or XML files with an embedded stylesheet. It can confirm what the files might look like in a browser window. (See Figure 2-12.)

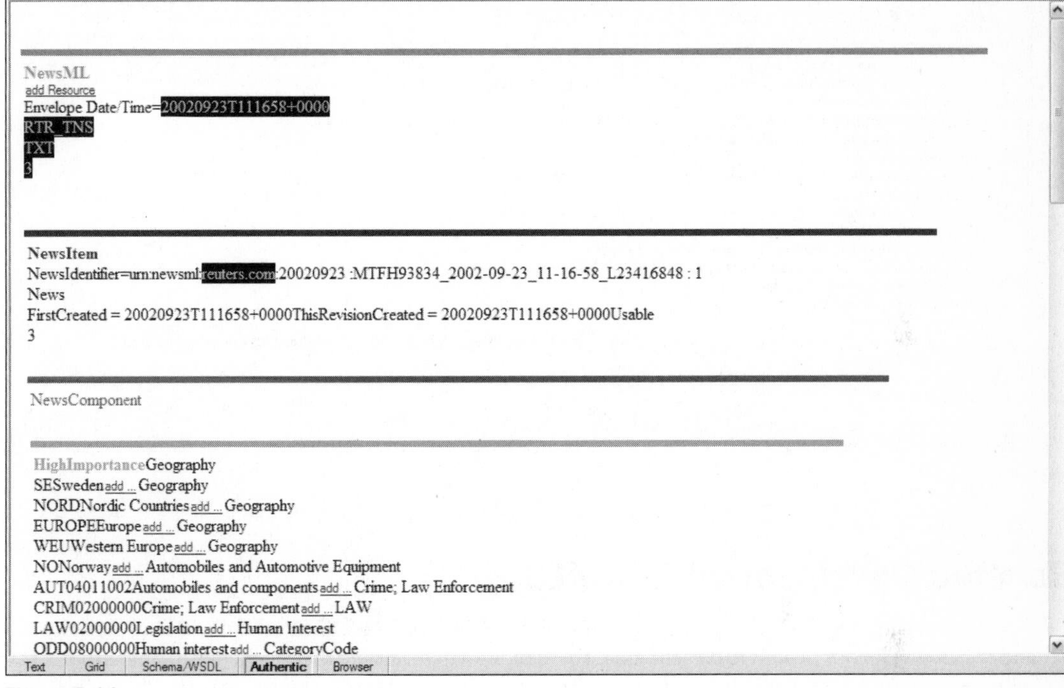

Figure 2-11

```
<?xml version="1.0" encoding="UTF-8" ?>
<!DOCTYPE NewsML (View Source for full doctype...)>
<!-- src: rtr2newsml0.991 -->
<?altova_sps C:\Program Files\Altova\XMLSpy2006\sps\Template\News\NewsML.sps?>
- <NewsML Duid="MTFH93834_2002-09-23_11-16-58_L23416848_NEWSML">
    <Catalog Href="http://idsdat06.reuters.com/newsml/catalog/catalog-reuters-master_catalog_1.xml" />
  - <NewsEnvelope>
      <DateAndTime>20020923T111658+0000</DateAndTime>
      <NewsService FormalName="RTR_TNS" />
      <NewsProduct FormalName="TXT" />
      <Priority FormalName="3" />
    </NewsEnvelope>
  - <NewsItem Duid="MTFH93834_2002-09-23_11-16-58_L23416848_NEWSITEM">
    - <Identification>
      - <NewsIdentifier>
          <ProviderId>reuters.com</ProviderId>
          <DateId>20020923</DateId>
          <NewsItemId>MTFH93834_2002-09-23_11-16-58_L23416848</NewsItemId>
          <RevisionId Update="N" PreviousRevision="0">1</RevisionId>
          <PublicIdentifier>urn:newsml:reuters.com:20020923:MTFH93834_2002-09-23_11-16-
            58_L23416848:1</PublicIdentifier>
        </NewsIdentifier>
        <DateLabel>2002-09-23 11:16:58 GMT (Reuters)</DateLabel>
      </Identification>
    - <NewsManagement>
        <NewsItemType FormalName="News" />
        <FirstCreated>20020923T111658+0000</FirstCreated>
        <ThisRevisionCreated>20020923T111658+0000</ThisRevisionCreated>
        <Status FormalName="Usable" />
        <Urgency FormalName="3" />
      </NewsManagement>
    - <NewsComponent EquivalentsList="no" Essential="no" Duid="MTFH93834_2002-09-23_11-16-58_L23416848_MAIN_NC"
        xml:lang="en">
      - <TopicSet FormalName="HighImportance">
        - <Topic Duid="ts_1">
            <TopicType FormalName="Geography" />
```

Text | Grid | Schema/WSDL | Authentic | Browser

Figure 2-12

Schema Development in XMLSpy

Schema development in XMLSpy is done with either DTDs or W3C XML schema. It does not directly support Relax NG or Schematron schemas. You can, however, create these schemas using either a text editor (see Figure 2-13) or their graphical editor (see Figure 2-14). You can navigate between the two editors by selecting either the Text or Schema/WSD buttons at the bottom of the editor window, or via the View menu. A number of entry helpers are available when you are working with either mode to ensure that you generate a valid schema, including statement completion. These entry helpers change to show the valid options at each point in the document.

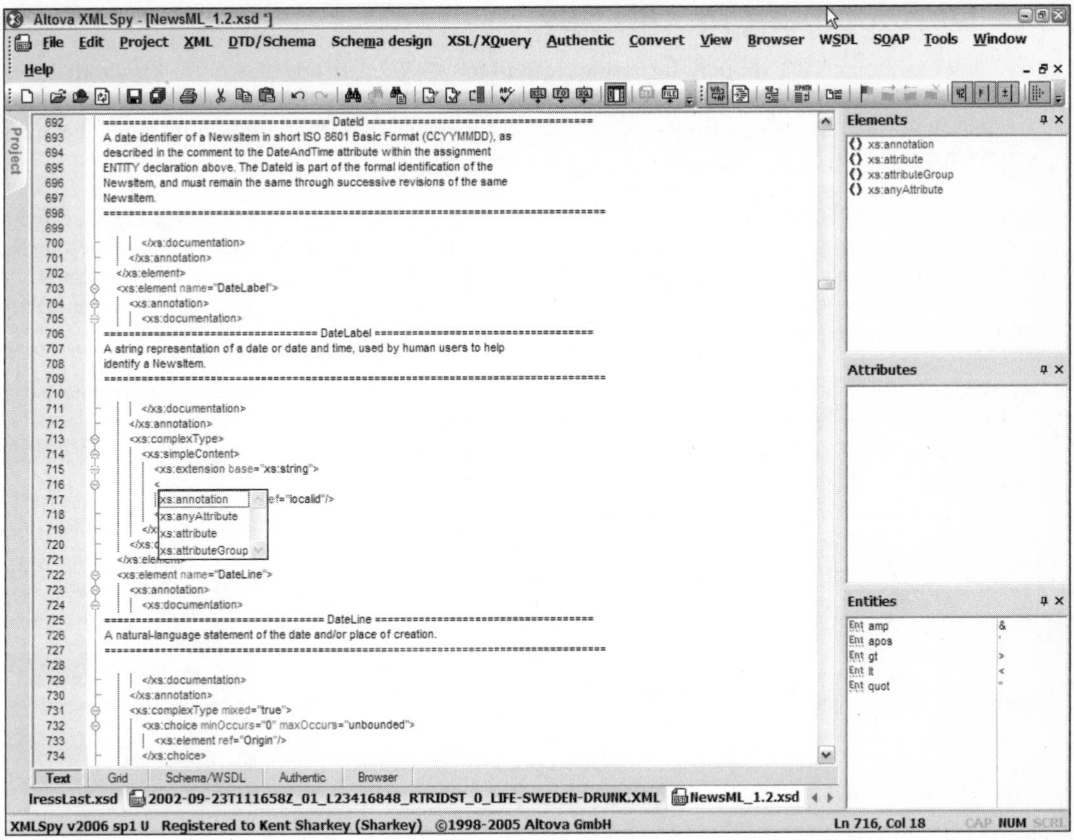

Figure 2-13

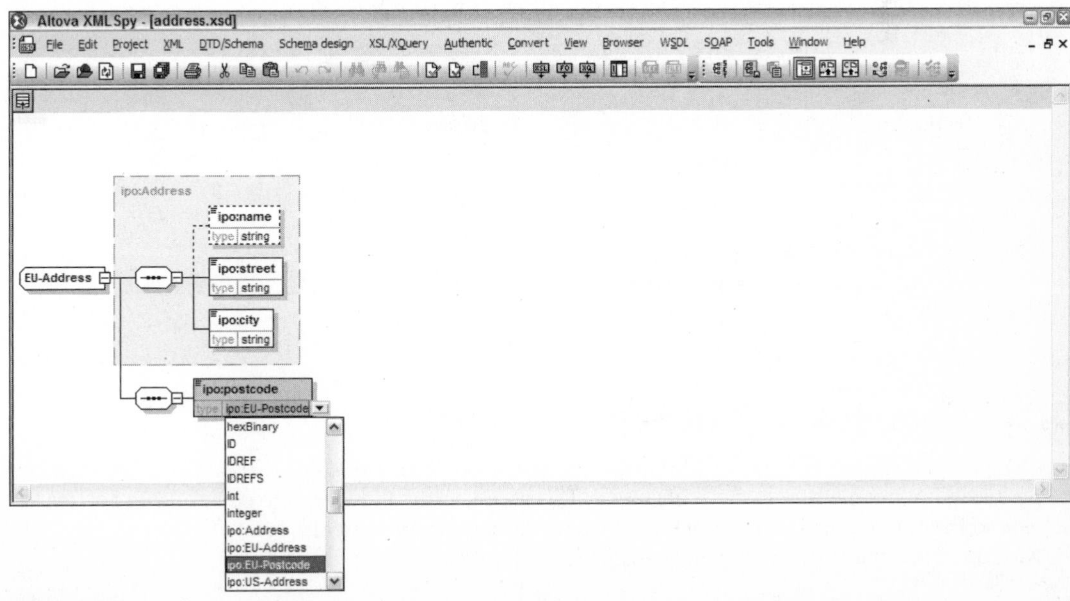

Figure 2-14

XSLT Development in XMLSpy

XMLSpy has strong XSLT support, including support for XSLT 2.0. In addition to the capability to create basic XSLT files, XMLSpy also has support for mapping between two XML schemas using MapForce or generating documents via XSL:FO using StyleVision. However, these features require you to have those products installed.

When generating XSLT documents, XMLSpy has an integrated debugger (see Figure 2-15), accessed by selecting Start Debugger ➪ Go from the XSL/XQuery menu. This debugger enables you to step through your XSLT file, watch for specific variables or XPath statements, and set breakpoints. These can be invaluable assists when you are trying to interpret the sometimes-Byzantine interplay between XPath, individual XSLT templates, and XML.

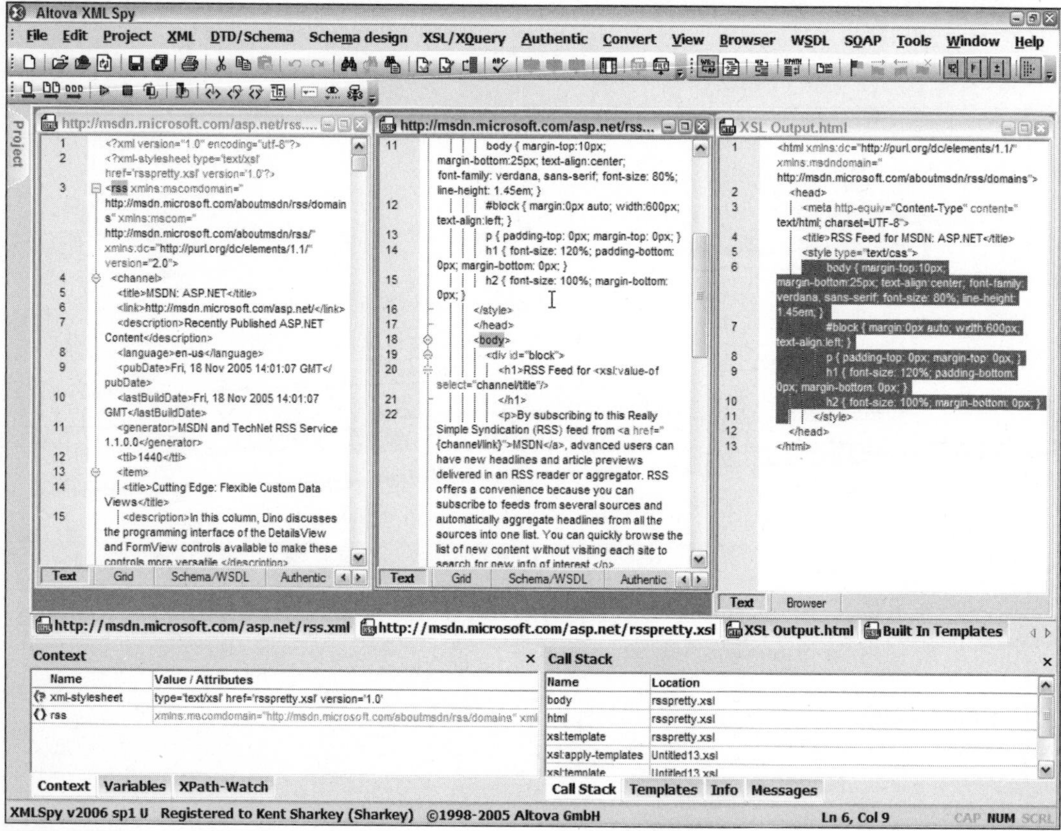

Figure 2-15

Other Features in XMLSpy

One potentially useful feature of XMLSpy is the inclusion of a script editor, accessed via the Switch to Scripting Environment from the Tools menu. This script editor allows you to edit and run macros to extend the environment using either VB Script or JavaScript. You can also create forms that run within XMLSpy, enabling you to add new dialogs. (See Figure 2-16.)

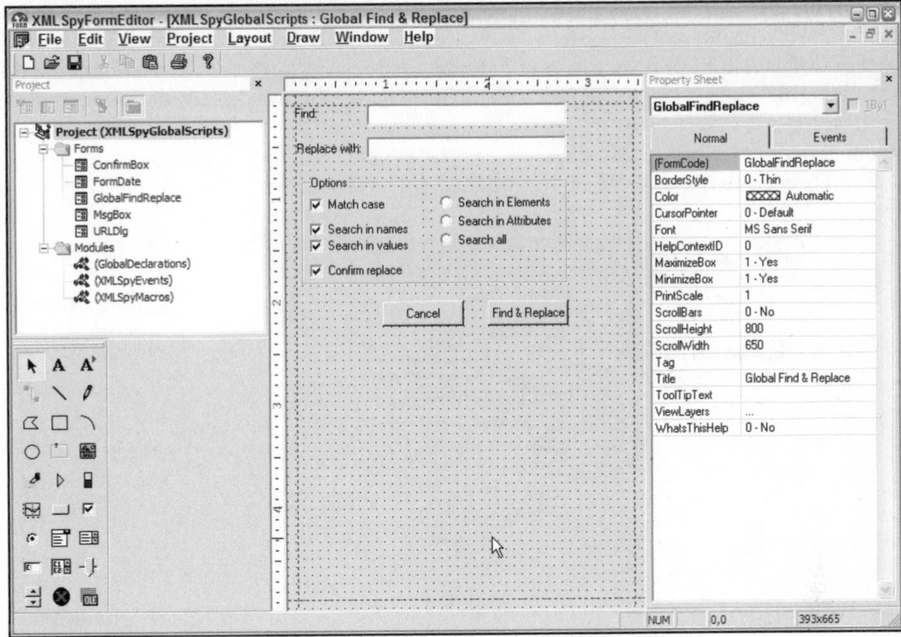

Figure 2-16

The following table summarizes the XML editing features in XMLSpy.

Benefit	Disadvantage
Incredibly full-featured toolset for working with XML, schemas, XSLT and more.	Because of the scope, can be difficult to learn all the features.
Includes macro engine for extending the environment.	Some features require purchasing additional software.
Can be used as a code generator (C#, Java, or C++)	Does not directly support Relax NG or Schematron schemas.
Includes XSLT, XQuery and SOAP debugging.	

Stylus Studio 2006

Stylus Studio is a product of the DataDirect Technologies division of Progress Software is a flexible, extensible tool for working with XML. It is strongest at opening XML from a variety of sources and enabling conversion of many formats into XML.

Basic Editing in Stylus Studio 2006

Stylus Studio supports basic XML editing, but also provides a number of advanced and unique features for working with XML documents. The first feature you notice when you attempt to open an XML file is the incredible number of sources available for opening XML (see Figure 2-17). Stylus Studio can open XML files directly from a number of file systems, as well as relational or object databases. In addition, you can convert nonXML files into XML as you load them by adding a converter or adapter between the source and Stylus Studio. This enables you to convert CSV, delimited, or EDI files directly as you load them.

In addition to opening existing XML files, you can create new XML files using a basic template or an existing data source. Figure 2-18 shows some of the available document wizards that can convert or create XML files.

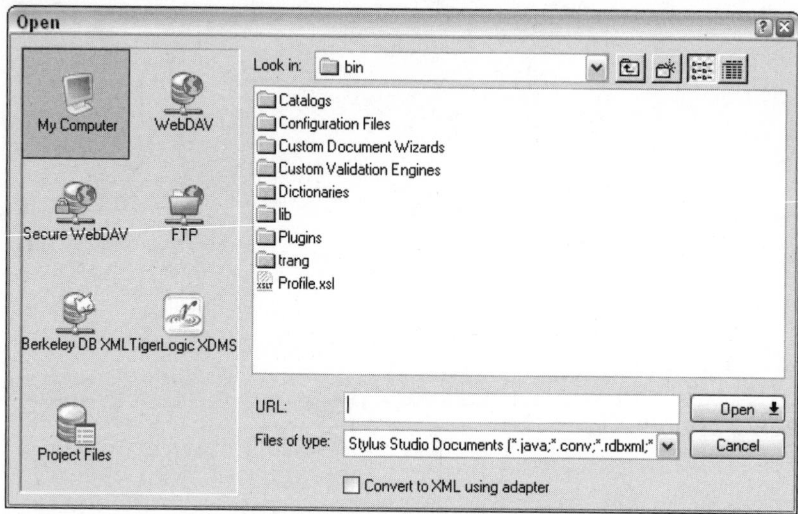

Figure 2-17

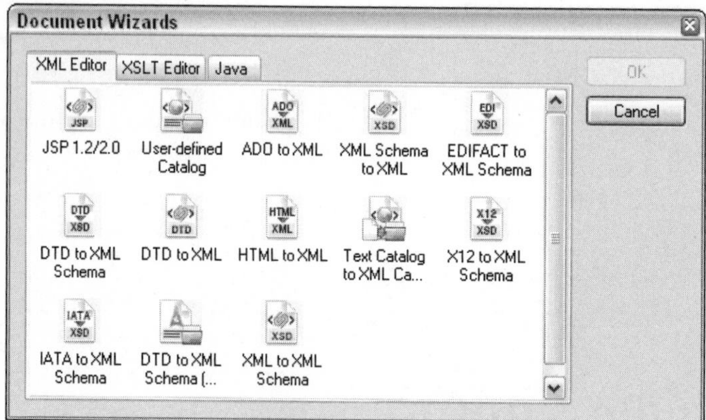

Figure 2-18

Stylus Studio has different views for working with your XML files. In addition to the normal text-based view of your XML, Stylus Studio also includes two graphical views. You can switch between these views via the tabs at the bottom of the editor window. Figure 2-19 shows the tree view. Using this view, you can quickly view and navigate the structure of a document.

In addition, a grid view (as seen in Figure 2-20) adds to the capabilities of the tree view by providing a surface where you can navigate and edit an XML document using a grid at each level in the document. This is very useful when working with documents that contain repeating structures, such as those extracted from databases.

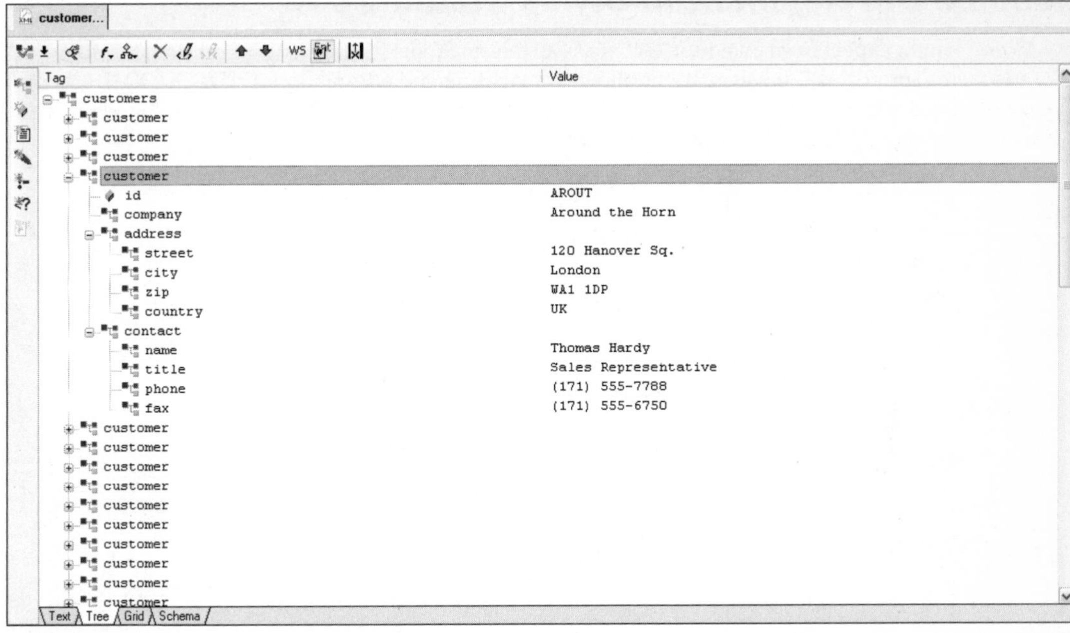

Figure 2-19

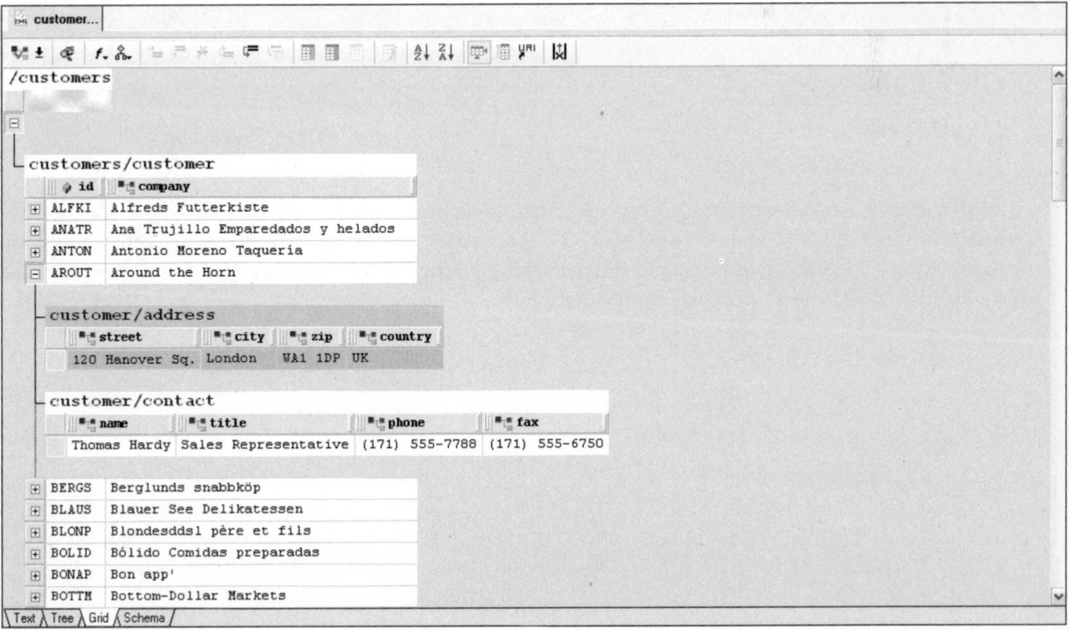

Figure 2-20

Stylus Studio certainly has all the core XML features you need for typical XML work. The grid and tree views make exploring and editing XML files easier. Where Stylus really shines is in its import and conversion capabilities.

Schema Development in Stylus Studio 2006

As you would expect from an editor that is as capable as Stylus is for opening and transforming XML, the schema support is extensive. Stylus allows for creating and editing both DTDs and XML schemas. In addition, it has support for converting between these two formats. Figure 2-21 shows the schema editor window, with both the graphical and text views of the schema.

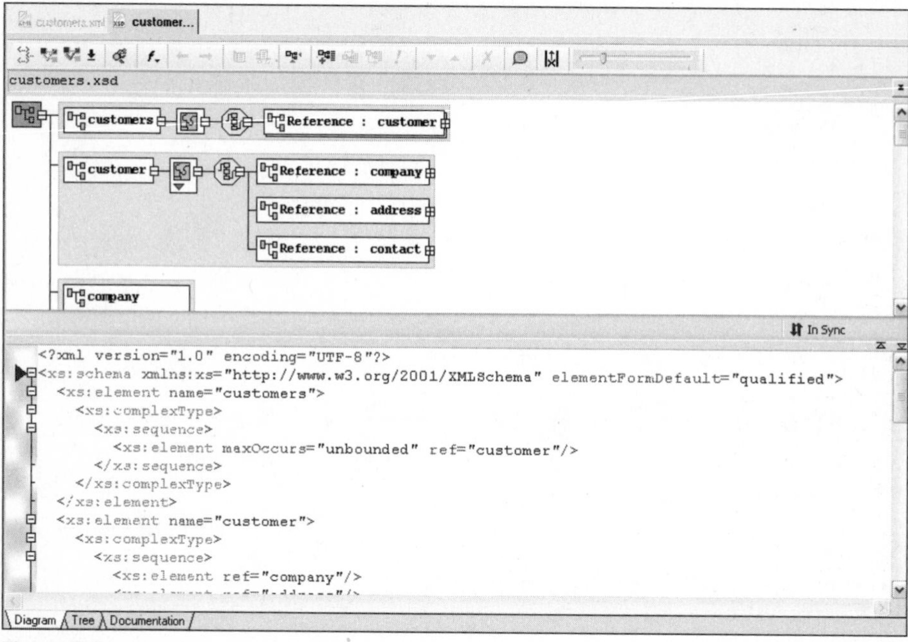

Figure 2-21

After the schema has been created, Stylus can create a set of documentation pages for the schema. This creates a number of HTML pages (see Figure 2-22) based on the schema structure, as well as any annotations available. This can be quite useful when sharing a schema between developers because users can more rapidly learn how to structure their documents.

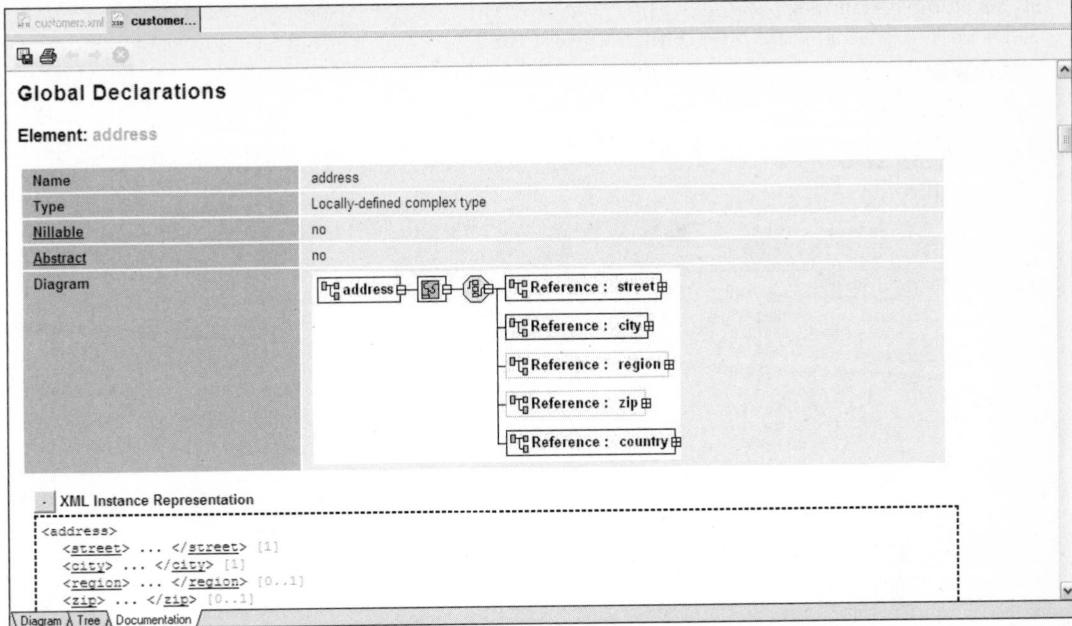

Figure 2-22

XSLT Development in Stylus Studio

Like many of the other editors in this chapter, Stylus Studio supports debugging XSLT (see Figure 2-23). You can set breakpoints in the templates, step through the code, and query values while the transformation is in process. You start the debugger using the commands in the Debug menu.

This debugger can also be used when working with XQuery documents. In addition to debugging XSLT or XQuery statements, you can also generate a profile report of the transformation. This can highlight slow points in the query or transformation by showing the relative timings at each step (see Figure 2-24).

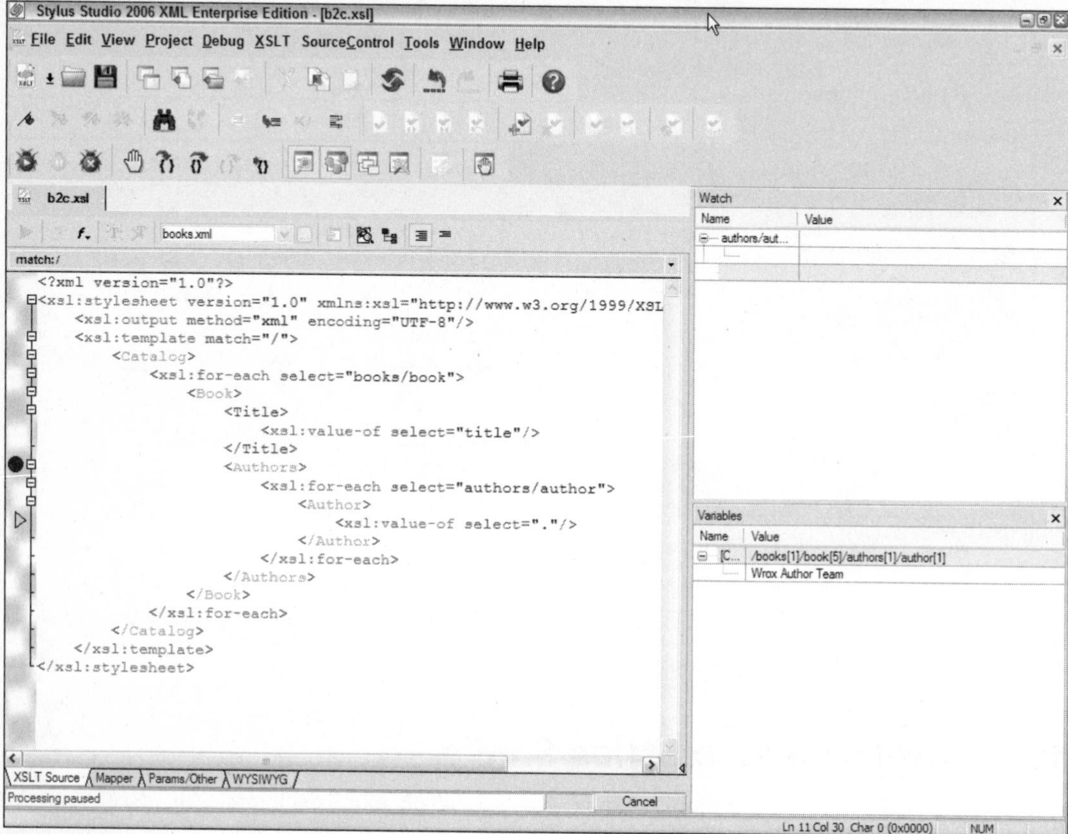

Figure 2-23

One unique capability among these editors is the capability of Stylus to create an XSLT template with a graphical mapper. This enables you to align two similar XML documents or visually define how the XML can be used when generating HTML output. Figure 2-25 shows this mapper in action. Notice how the XSLT is built in the lower window as the tags are mapped between the source and destination files. The transformation can even include additional processing on the elements using Java extensions.

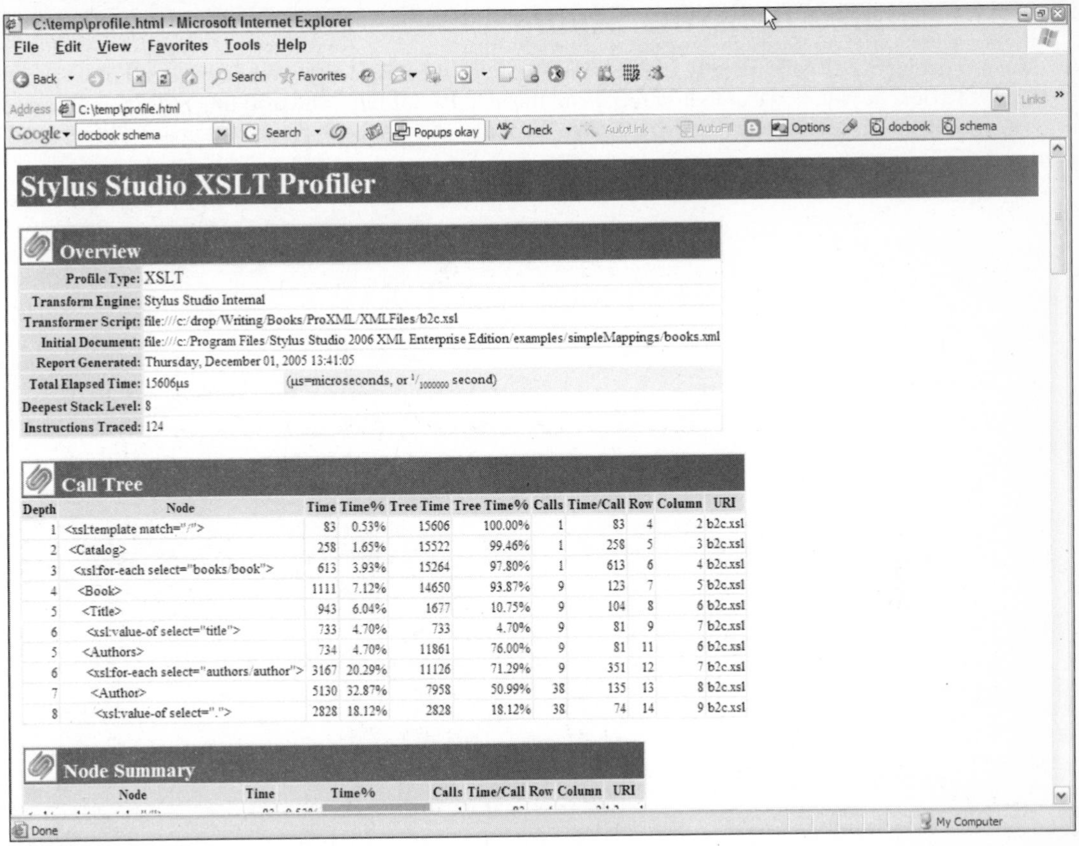

C:\temp\profile.html - Microsoft Internet Explorer

Stylus Studio XSLT Profiler

Overview

Profile Type:	XSLT
Transform Engine:	Stylus Studio Internal
Transformer Script:	file:///c:/drop/Writing/Books/ProXML/XMLFiles/b2c.xsl
Initial Document:	file:///c:/Program Files/Stylus Studio 2006 XML Enterprise Edition/examples/simpleMappings/books.xml
Report Generated:	Thursday, December 01, 2005 13:41:05
Total Elapsed Time:	15606µs (µs=microseconds, or 1/1000000 second)
Deepest Stack Level:	8
Instructions Traced:	124

Call Tree

Depth	Node	Time	Time%	Tree Time	Tree Time%	Calls	Time/Call	Row	Column	URI
1	<xsl:template match="/">	83	0.53%	15606	100.00%	1	83	4	2	b2c.xsl
2	<Catalog>	258	1.65%	15522	99.46%	1	258	5	3	b2c.xsl
3	<xsl:for-each select="books/book">	613	3.93%	15264	97.80%	1	613	6	4	b2c.xsl
4	<Book>	1111	7.12%	14650	93.87%	9	123	7	5	b2c.xsl
5	<Title>	943	6.04%	1677	10.75%	9	104	8	6	b2c.xsl
6	<xsl:value-of select="title">	733	4.70%	733	4.70%	9	81	9	7	b2c.xsl
5	<Authors>	734	4.70%	11861	76.00%	9	81	11	6	b2c.xsl
6	<xsl:for-each select="authors/author">	3167	20.29%	11126	71.29%	9	351	12	7	b2c.xsl
7	<Author>	5130	32.87%	7958	50.99%	38	135	13	8	b2c.xsl
8	<xsl:value-of select=".">	2828	18.12%	2828	18.12%	38	74	14	9	b2c.xsl

Node Summary

Node	Time	Time%	Calls	Time/Call	Row	Column	URI

Figure 2-24

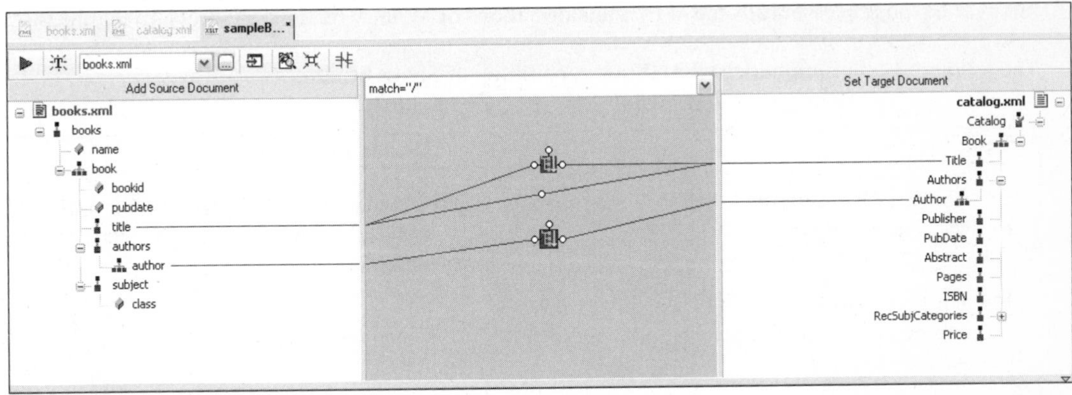

Figure 2-25

Other Features in Stylus Studio

You can debug SOAP calls directly from Stylus Studio by creating a new Web Service call file. You assign the WSDL for the call. You can then directly call the SOAP endpoint. The resulting SOAP request and response files are created, enabling you to save them for later use or documentation (see Figure 2-26).

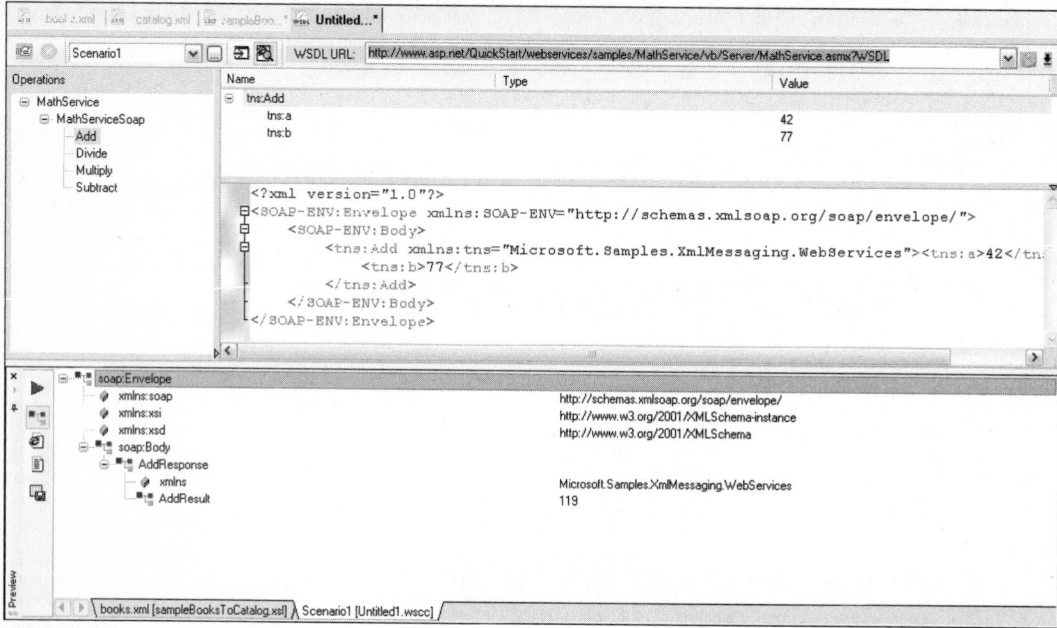

Figure 2-26

Stylus Studio also supports code generation. If you work in Java, Stylus can generate classes that wrap Xalan or Saxon processor calls for XSLT transformations or XQuery queries, as shown in Figure 2-27.

The following table summarizes the editing capabilities of Stylus Studio.

Benefit	Disadvantage
Can convert CSV, delimited, EDI, or other formats to XML when loading.	Schema support limited to DTD and W3C XML schema. No support for Relax NG or Schematron.
Has support for opening and closing files from a number of sources, including relational and object databases.	
Document Wizards enable conversion of files from CSV, tab-delimited, or databases into XML.	
Integrated XSLT mapper allows for visually designing XSLT transformation.	

Benefit	Disadvantage
Support for XQuery, including debugging.	
Can generate Java source code for XSLT or XQuery.	No support for .NET or C++ code generation.

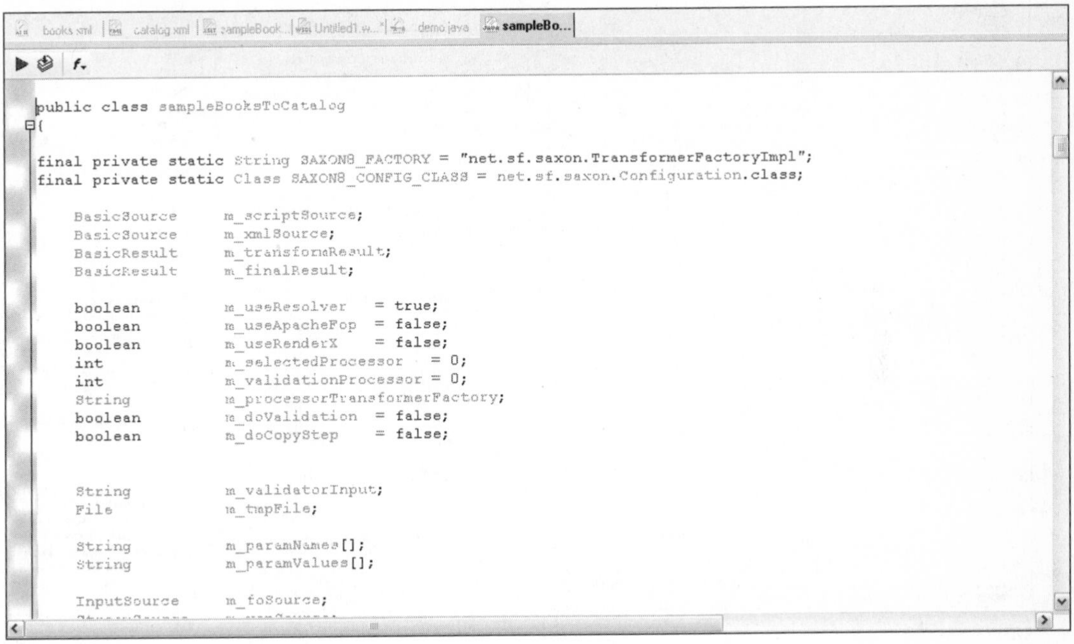
books.xml
catalog.xml
sampleBook...
Untitled1.w...*
demo.java
sampleBo...
public class sampleBooksToCatalog
{
final private static String SAXON8_FACTORY = "net.sf.saxon.TransformerFactoryImpl";
final private static Class SAXON8_CONFIG_CLASS = net.sf.saxon.Configuration.class;
BasicSource m_scriptSource;
BasicSource m_xmlSource;
BasicResult m_transformResult;
BasicResult m_finalResult;
boolean m_useResolver = true;
boolean m_useApacheFop = false;
boolean m_useRenderX = false;
int m_selectedProcessor = 0;
int m_validationProcessor = 0;
String m_processorTransformerFactory;
boolean m_doValidation = false;
boolean m_doCopyStep = false;
String m_validatorInput;
File m_tmpFile;
String m_paramNames[];
String m_paramValues[];
InputSource m_foSource;

Figure 2-27

Oxygen XML Editor 6.2

Oxygen from SyncRO Soft Ltd. is a Java-based XML editor that works on a variety of platforms, including Windows, Mac OS X, and Linux. In addition, it can work in concert with Eclipse, providing all its functionality as a plug-in to Eclipse. One other unique feature of this editor is that it can be deployed and started using Java WebStart technology. This enables you to have a single deploy point for all users, presented as a Web link. Clicking the link downloads the latest version of the application, reducing the need to deploy updates to all users.

Basic Editing in Oxygen XML Editor 6.2

XML editing in Oxygen is capable. It includes both statement completion (Figure 2-28) and Tag insight. Tag insight displays a ToolTip containing any annotations in the schema. This can be a handy reminder of the purpose of each element and is a nice addition.

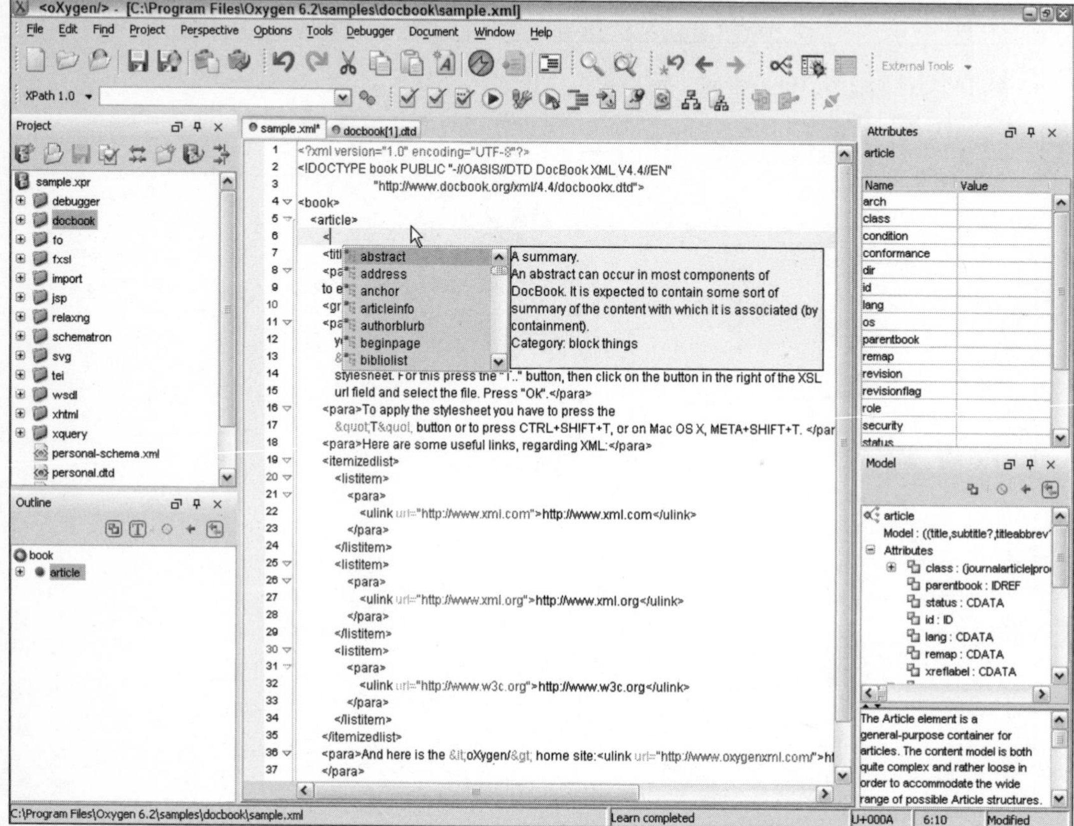

Figure 2-28

Rather than providing multiple views of the XML document in the main window, Oxygen provides the bulk of the graphical views of the document in side windows (see the outline and model windows in Figure 2-29). However, these are not editable views, and they display only a reflection of the existing text view. The graphical Tree editor is opened in a separate window if you'd rather edit the XML document using a graphical model (see Figure 2-29). However, this editor is not as capable as the graphical editor in other products such as XMLSpy or Stylus Studio.

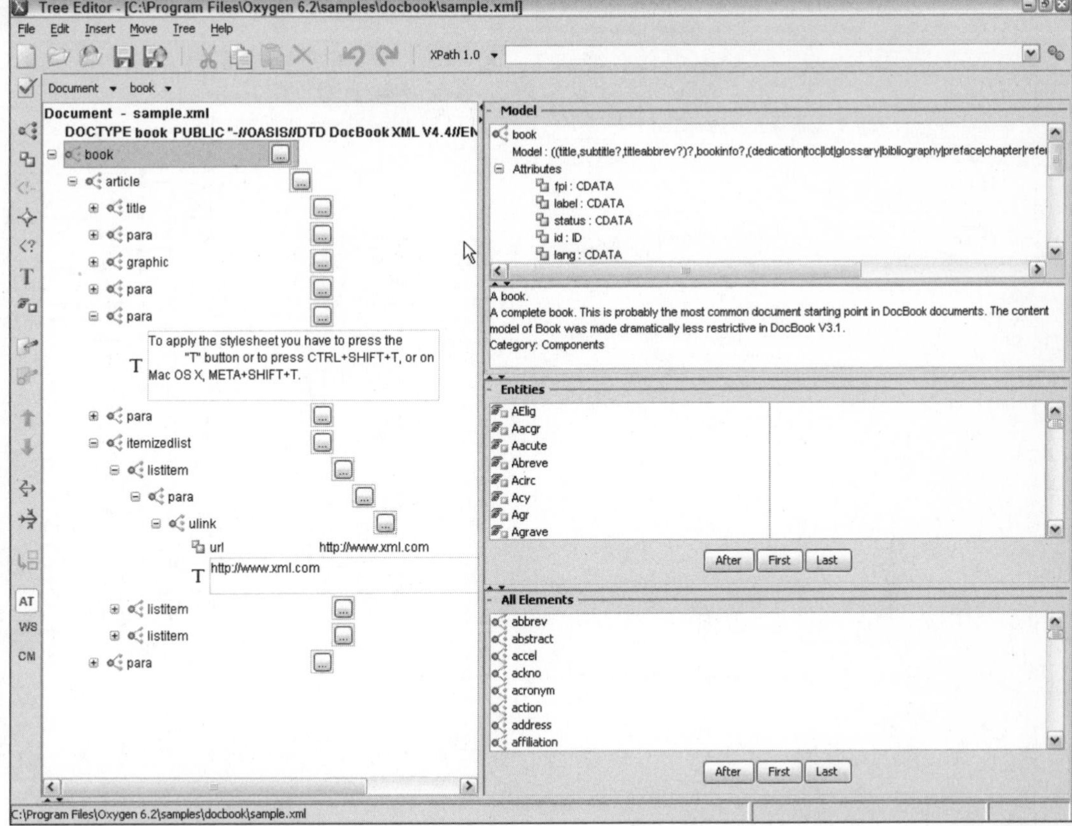

Figure 2-29

Schema Development in Oxygen XML Editor 6.2

Oxygen supports creation of schemas based on DTD, W3C XML Schema, Relax NG (full and compact), or Schematron. In addition, it supports converting between these schema formats using the integrated Trang converter.

Oxygen has the broadest set of available schema formats, including DTD, W3C XML schemas, Relax NG, and Schematron. However, only Relax NG and W3C XML schemas support graphical schema editors (see Figure 2-30). In addition, the graphical view is a static view. Changes can be made only in the text editor window.

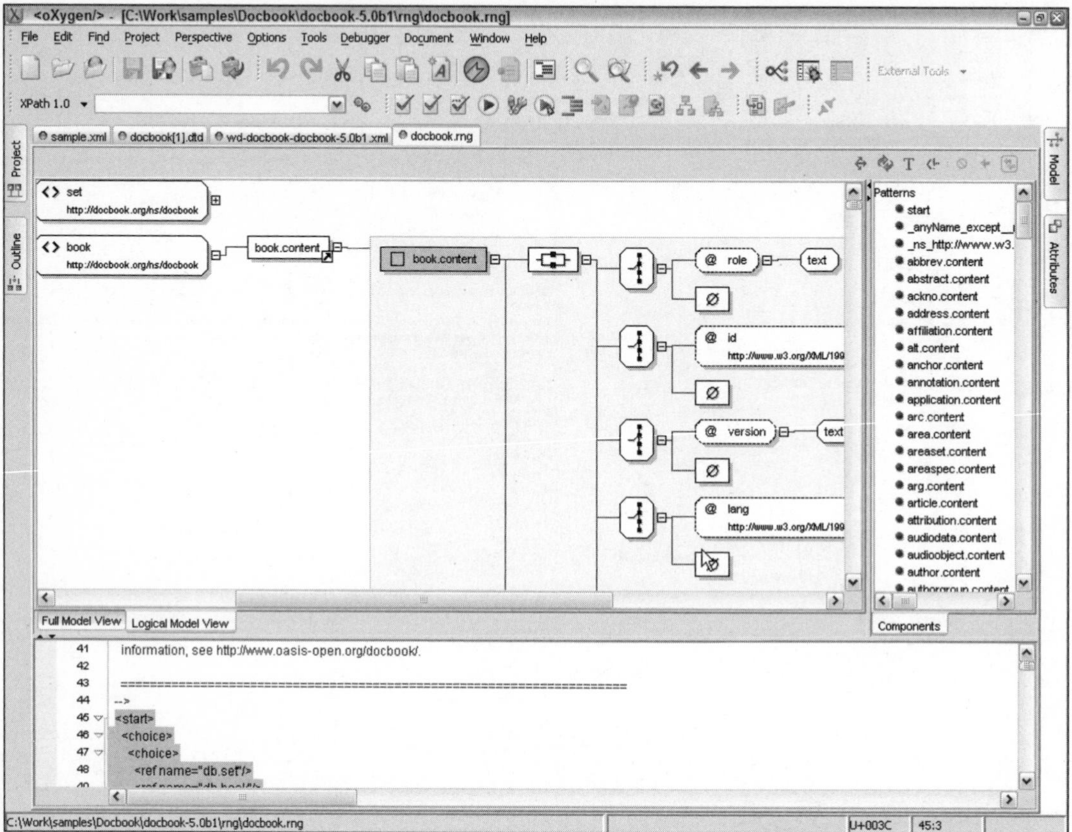

Figure 2-30

Converting between Schema Types in Oxygen XML Editor 6.2

Oxygen is fairly unique in that it gives you a selection of editors to provide support for converting between many of the standard schema formats (see Figure 2-31). This support is added by the integration of the Trang schema converter, which is capable of converting between DTD, XML schema, and Relax NG schema formats.

After your schema is complete, you can generate documentation for the schema. This documentation includes diagrams of each global element and type (see Figure 2-32).

Trang Converter

Input

RELAX NG Schema - XML

RELAX NG Schema - Compact

XML 1.0 DTD

XML Documents

file:/C:/Program%20Files/Oxygen%20XML%20Edit

Choose

Output

RELAX NG Schema - XML

RELAX NG Schema - Compact

XML 1.0 DTD

W3C XML Schema

Options

Encoding UTF-8

Line width - Format and Indent 72

Indent size 2

Choose

Open in editor

Advanced options

Convert

Close

Figure 2-31

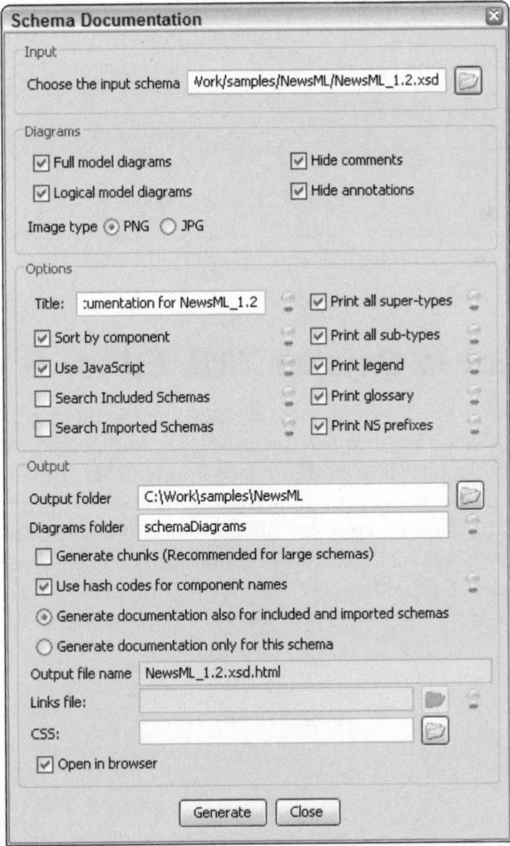

Figure 2-32

The output from this generation can now be viewed by all team members in any browser (see Figure 2-33).

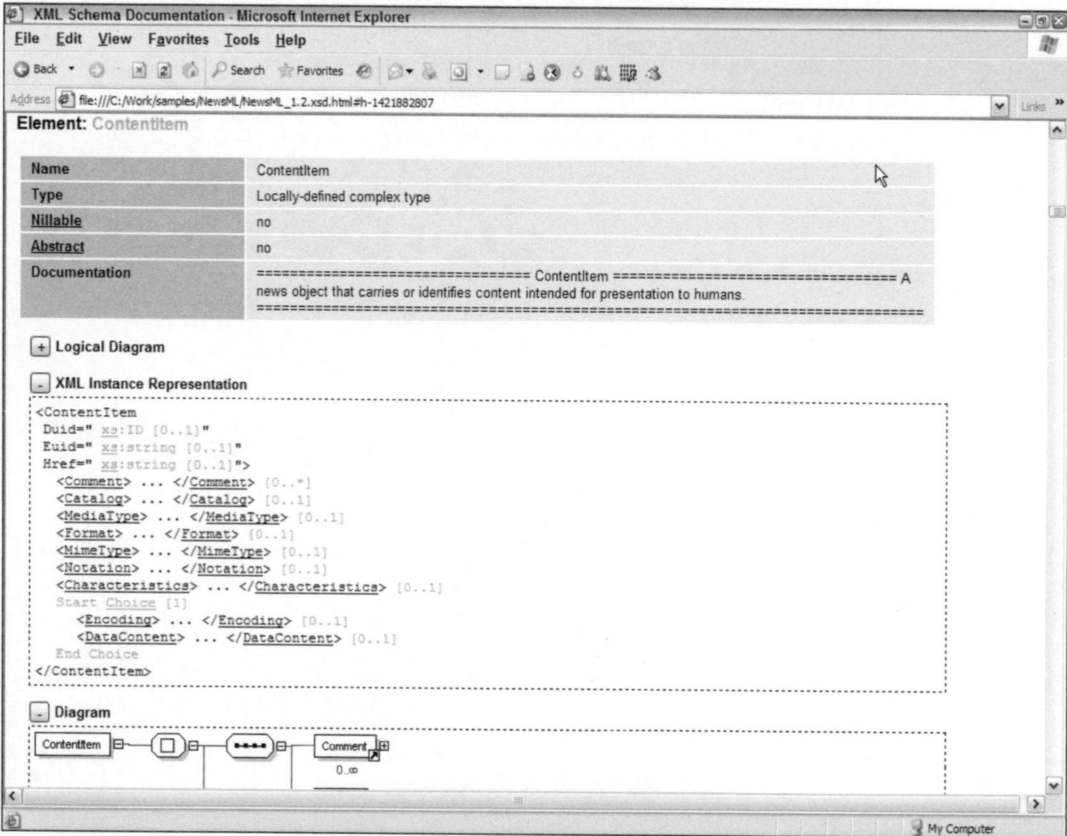

Figure 2-33

XSLT Development in Oxygen XML Editor 6.2

Oxygen supports debugging XSLT templates as do many of the other editors described in this chapter. This includes breakpoints, stepping through the templates, and probing values at runtime. However, Oxygen goes one step further, enabling profiling (see Figure 2-34) of the transformation. This can be a great resource for tuning a slow transformation, highlighting just which templates or section of code is causing the processing to be slow. Oxygen can also use multiple XSLT processors, notably Xalan and versions of Saxon, including XSLT 2.0 processors. These can be used to select the particular XSLT engine you want to use in your development.

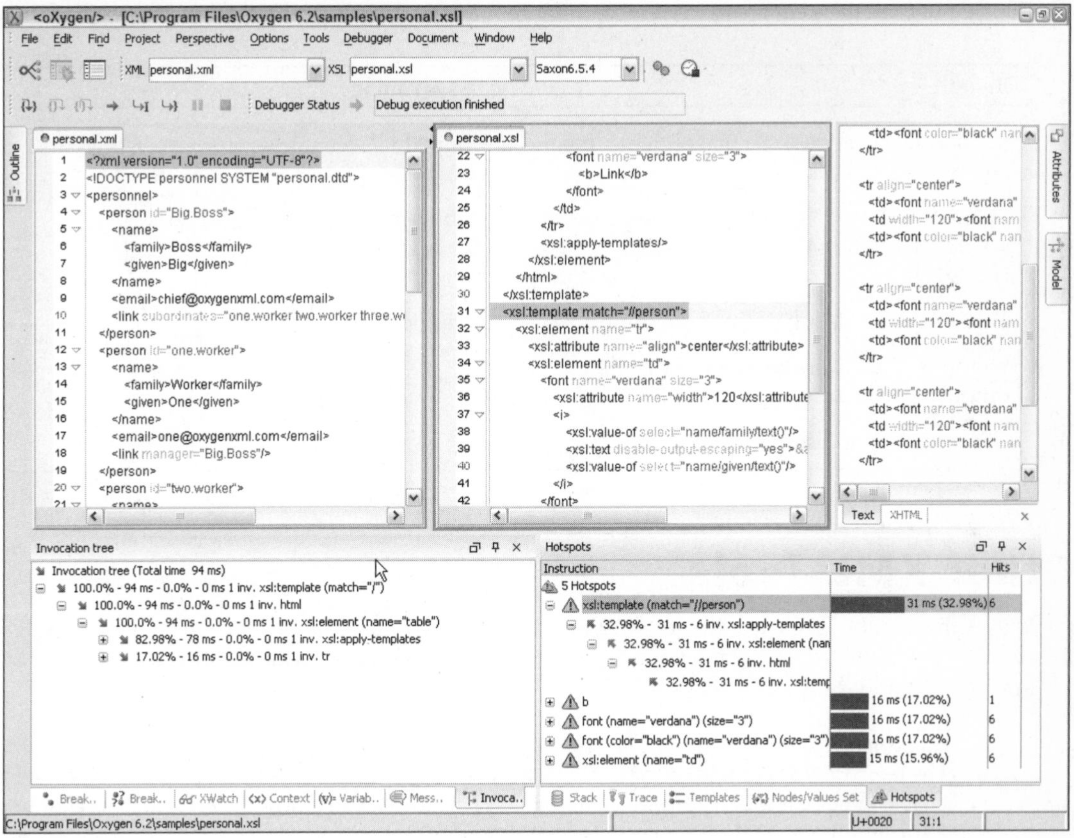

Figure 2-34

Other Features in Oxygen XML Editor 6.2

When you are working with SVG (see Chapter 5), it can sometimes be difficult to visualize the resulting graphic. Oxygen includes an SVG viewer, allowing you to see SVG graphics from within the editor (see Figure 2-35).

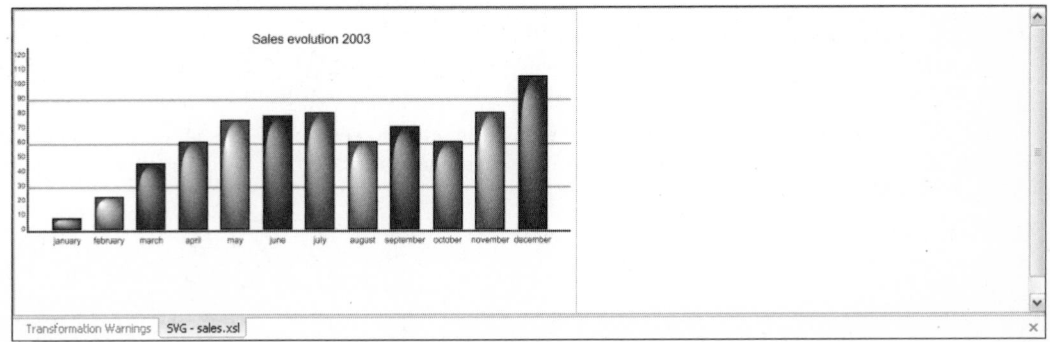

Figure 2-35

The following table summarizes the XML editing capabilities of Oxygen XML Editor 6.2.

Benefit	Disadvantage
Support for Java WebStart makes deployment and upgrading easier.	Limited viewer support for visualizing XML structure.
Support for Relax NG and Schematron schemas as well as W3C XML Schema and DTDs.	Debugging only with XSLT, no XQuery debugging.
Supports XSLT debugging and profiling.	Graphical views are read-only.
Supports XSL:FO, including many common output formats, such as PDF and HTML.	
Can work within Eclipse as a plug-in.	

Other XML Tools

Many other tools exist for working with XML. These include other editors not covered here, as well as special-purpose tools for working with various XML dialects. The following list discusses some of the available editors.

- **Cooktop** — Available at `http://www.xmlcooktop.com/`, this is a free Windows XML editor. The main benefits of this editor (beyond the cost) are the size (full install is about 3MB) and the inclusion of *Code Bits*. These are common snippets for various XML dialects, such as common XSLT templates, XML programming instructions, or namespace declarations. In addition, you can add your own Code Bits to the list.

- **Eclipse** — Although not a dedicated XML editor, Eclipse has a strong plug-in model, enabling third parties to add XML support to the main editor. Oxygen, for example, can work as an Eclipse plug-in as well as a standalone.

- **XMetaL** — The latest iteration of the tool that used to be known as HoTMetaL, now owned by BlastRadius (`xmetal.com`). Probably due to its roots in SGML editing, XMetal is strongest at creating valid XML documents based on XML schemas.

- **Emacs** — Emacs is one of the more popular text editors and is available for almost every platform. It has a strong programmatic platform and has many add-on modes available for editing XML documents such as nXML. nXML adds statement completion, validation, and schema editing (for Relax NG).

- **Vi** — The other popular text editor, vi, has been around seemingly forever and is available for almost every platform. A recent version, Vim, supports add-ins, including many for XML, such as XmlEdit.

Summary

XML is not difficult to create; it is only text after all. Still, creating XML and schemas can be made easier through the use of one of these tools. They reduce the overall amount of typing, make visualizing the XML or schema easier, and reduce the chance for errors or invalid files. Each have their own strengths and target scenarios.

Visual Studio supports the creation of XML and schema files, but it is at its heart a programming environment. Therefore, it is not as strong a tool as some of the dedicated XML tools. However, if you are already using Visual Studio, its XML features may be enough for your needs.

Altova XMLSpy is only one of a family of tools from Altova. It provides solid XML editing features, XSLT/XQuery debugging and more in a single package. In addition, XMLSpy can integrate into common programmer environments such as Visual Studio or Eclipse. This means that you gain the benefit of XMLSpy's functionality within the environment you are familiar with. XMLSpy can support any XML developer, but is best suited for environments that do not need Schematron or Relax NG support.

While Stylus Studio is a powerful Swiss army knife of XML editors, it shines when it comes to its import functionality. Many common data formats, such as CSV, EDI or databases can easily be imported into Stylus Studio and converted into XML. Once in, Stylus Studio continues to provide support in terms of XSLT/XQuery debugging, schema mapping and even code generation. Stylus Studio can support any XML developer, but is best suited for organizations that must deal with a lot of EDI or other file processing.

Oxygen XML editor's main strength is breadth. While most of the other editors described here support DTDs or W3C Schemas, Oxygen includes support for Schematron and Relax NG. While the other editors run on Windows, Oxygen provides OS X and Linux versions. Performance and memory usage may be an issue, however. Oxygen is best suited for organizations that need to support multiple platforms.

Part II
Presentation

3

XHTML and CSS

Although many people think of XML as a data format, many of the important uses for XML are in layout. Of these, one of the most significant is XHTML, or the Extensible HyperText Markup Language. XHTML is the "XML-ized" version of HTML, cleaning up many of the sloppier features of HTML and creating a more standardized, more easily validated document format. The Cascading Stylesheets (CSS) feature, although not an XML format, is widely viewed as important for XHTML development. CSS is a formatting language that can be used with either HTML or XHTML. It is generally viewed as a cleaner replacement for the Font tag and other similar devices that force a particular view. When used in combination with XHTML, the model is that the XHTML document carries all the content of the page, whereas CSS is used to format it. This chapter looks at these two sets of specifications, as well as some validation tools that help ensure your code is valid. In addition, this chapter looks at microformats, a relatively recent set of uses for both XHTML and CSS.

Understanding XHTML

When people hear that XHTML is the XML version of HTML, the first question is usually, "Isn't HTML already XML?" or "What's wrong with HTML that it has to be XML-ized?" I hope that I'll be able to answer both these questions and more in this chapter. For those who are planning on skipping this chapter or who want the answers now, the answers are, "sort of, but not exactly" and "a few fairly major things."

The Evolution of Markup

Markup is information added to text to describe the text. In HTML and XHTML, these are the tags (for example, `<b></b>`) that are added around the text. However, markup isn't just HTML and its family. Rich Text Format (RTF) is another example of a markup language. The text, "**This is bold**, and this isn't" could be marked up in RTF as `{\b\insrsid801189\charrsid801189 This is bold}{\insrsid13238650\charrsid13238650 , and this isn't}`. Other markup languages include TeX and ASN.1. Markup, therefore, is just a way of adding formatting and semantic information. Formatting information includes identifiers such as *bold, italic, first level of heading*, or *beginning of a table*. Semantic information includes identifiers such as *beginning of a section*, a *list item* or similar notations.

The idea of markup is quite old — separate the content from the description of that content. A number of implementations using this concept arose back in the stone ages of computing (the 1960s), including Standard Generalized Markup Language (SGML). SGML was strategy for defining markup. That is, you used SGML to define the tags and attributes that someone else could use to markup a document. This notion was powerful, enabling the production of documents that could be rendered easily in a number of formats.

SGML begat HTML, and it was good. HTML was a markup language loosely defined on the concepts of SGML. It lifted the tagging concept, but simplified it greatly because HTML was intended solely as a means of displaying text on computer screens. Later versions attempted to increase the rigor of the standard, for example, creating a Document Type Description (DTD — the format SGML used as the means of defining a markup language). HTML slowly evolved in a fairly organic fashion: first adding tags and then becoming a standard (4.01). Meanwhile, on an almost parallel track, SGML begat XML, and it was good. XML was an attempt to simplify SGML, creating a technology that provided many of the same capabilities of language definition. Although it wasn't necessarily inevitable, these two cousins decided to get together and produce an offspring, XHTML. XHTML has XML's eye for rigor: XHTML documents must be well-formed XML documents first, and rules around formatting are specific. However, XHTML still has HTML's looks and broad appeal.

The Basics of XHTML

Unfortunately, no one XHTML standard exists. In fact, there are currently six flavors or versions of XHTML:

- **XHTML 1.0 Transitional:** Intended to be a transitional move from HTML 4.01 to XHTML. This flavor included support for some of the newer features of XHTML, while retaining some of the older HTML features (such as `<u>`, `<strike>` or `<applet>`).
- **XHTML 1.0 Frameset:** Another transitional flavor that included support for HTML frameset tags.
- **XHTML 1.0 Strict:** The "real" XHTML. This version included strict rules (see the following section) for formatting the markup in a document.
- **XHTML Basic:** An attempt at creating the smallest possible implementation of XTHML. XHTML Basic is intended for mobile applications that are not capable of rendering complex documents or supporting the full extensibility of XHTML 1.1.
- **XHTML 1.1:** The current version of XHTML. This is an attempt at defining XHTML in a modular fashion, enabling the addition of new features through extension modules (for example, adding MathML or frameset support).
- **XHTML 2.0:** As of this writing, this is still a gleam in the eyes of the committee. It will likely end up being a major new version; it will also break compatibility with a number of XHTML documents. Because of this, I expect that it will be some time before it is in broad usage.

This chapter focuses mostly on XHTML 1.0 Strict and XHTML 1.1 — primarily 1.1. The remaining current versions are primarily compatibility versions, meant to assist developers in migrating older code. XHTML 2.0 is still in the future, and even the planned broken compatibility may change before it becomes a standard.

Validating XHTML

The one main improvement of XHTML over HTML is in enforcement of what constitutes a valid document. XHTML requires that a document follow these rules:

- **No overlapping elements:** Although it was a horrid practice, some people wrote their HTML so that one element started before another was finished, or so that a tag closed before its child tag did. Even worse, some HTML editors created this kind of markup. The result was something that looked like the following:

  ```
  <b>Bold<i>and italic</b></i>
  ```

  As you can see, the bold tag (<b>) is closed before the child italics tag (<i>). Although most browsers were capable of interpreting this code, it did not lend itself to building a parse tree correctly. XHTML does not consider this valid.

- **No unclosed elements:** Some of the HTML elements, such as `<br>`, `<hr>`, and `<img>`, were generally used without closing tags. In XHTML, you must either add a close tag (such as `</br>`) or use the empty element form (`<hr />`) of the element. Note the space before the slash character. Although not absolutely necessary, it is highly recommended. For certain tags (such as a paragraph element or table cell) that are empty but that should contain information, do not use this form; instead include the close element, such as `<p> </p>`.

- **All elements and attributes are written in lowercase:** HTML is not case-sensitive regarding elements and attributes, therefore `<table>`, `<TABLE>` and `<Table>` are all equivalent. However, XML is case-sensitive, meaning that these three elements are different, and only one can be the real table element. Fortunately for my own personal style, all lowercase was defined as the standard, so the real element is `<table>`.

- **All attributes are quoted:** Another code formatting practice used by some authors and HTML editors is quotes around attributes. One argument is that including quotes around attributes, as in `<img src="http://some.url.com/image.png" />` adds two additional characters, bloating the document. Some users prefer the slightly less bandwidth intensive, `<img src=http://some.url.com/image.png>`. However, this practice (especially when included without a closing element, as shown here) makes it more difficult to parse the attribute correctly.

- **All attributes require values:** A few attributes are typically used standalone in HTML, such as the checked attribute for the Checkbox control or selected for options in a list.

```
<input type="checkbox" checked />
<select>
        <option selected>One</option>
  <option>Two</option>
</select>
```

In XHTML, attributes must have a value. Therefore, the correct way of writing these elements should be:

```
<input type="checkbox" checked="checked" />
<select>
       <option selected="selected">One</option>
       <option>Two</option>
</select>
```

- **IDs are id:** In later versions of HTML, two ways of naming elements co-existed; both id and name were used, and often both in the same document. This lead to a great deal of confusion, because users thought each had a unique purpose or meaning. With XHTML, name is now considered invalid, and id should be used when naming elements (all lowercase).
- **Script blocks should be wrapped:** Because XHTML documents are primarily XML documents, normal XML rules apply to the content. Blocks such as CSS or JavaScript may include XML markers (such as <), possibly breaking the document. Because of this, these blocks should be wrapped in CDATA blocks (see Listing 3-1) to ensure they do not affect the validity of the XHTML. Better yet, use an external document and one of the tags that imports that file (see Listing 3-9 later in this chapter).

Listing 3-1: Using CDATA with embedded script

```
<script type="text/JavaScript">
  <![CDATA[
    //JavaScript content here
  ]]>
</script>
```

The next major set of changes you need to make to convert your HTML pages to XHTML is to remove some of the deprecated HTML tags. XHTML 1.0 (especially the Transitional and Frameset varieties) still permits these elements, but they are invalid in future versions, including XHTML 1.1. (See the following table for more discussion of the deprecated elements.) Most of these elements were removed because they caused an intermixing of content and specific layout. The recommended method of adding layout is now with CSS, as you learn later in this chapter. See Listing 3-2 for a simple XHTML 1.1 file.

Deprecated Element	Replacement	Discussion
applet embed	object	Applet, object, and embed were all methods for including content such as Java Applets and ActiveX objects. Rather than maintain these three elements, the object element is used for embedding any external objects.
dir menu	ul	Dir and Menu were little-used elements that provided much of the same functionality as unordered lists (ul).
font basefont blockquote i strike center	CSS	These elements enforced a particular view on the content of a page and merged the content with layout. This functionality is now superseded by CSS, and you should use that technology instead. Browsers (such as screen readers for u the sight impaired) are free to ignore the CSS, if necessary, leaving the content usable.
layer	CSS	A Netscape/Mozilla-specific tag that was used to create dynamic HTML pages. The functionality is roughly replaceable with `div` and `span` tags.
isindex	input type=""	This ancient tag (that I haven't seen for a while) was used to create a search field on a page. This should be replaced with a form containing search fields and "real" server-side search functionality.

Deprecated Element	Replacement	Discussion
style (attribute)	CSS	With XHTML 1.1, the style attribute is also considered deprecated. Although it is not yet removed from the standard, it should be avoided. Instead, use id or class attributes and CSS to apply style to individual elements.

Finally, to ensure your document is processed in the format you intend, you should include a reference to the DTD of the desired level of XHTML. This provides information to the browser or parser, which should then treat your document appropriately. The following table shows the expected DTD.

XHTML Level	DocType Declaration
XHTML 1.0 Transitional	<!DOCTYPE html PUBLIC "-//W3C//DTD XHTML 1.0 Transitional//EN" "http://www.w3.org/TR/xhtml1/DTD/xhtml1-transitional.dtd">
XHTML 1.0 Frameset	<!DOCTYPE html PUBLIC "-//W3C//DTD XHTML 1.0 Frameset//EN" "http://www.w3.org/TR/xhtml1/DTD/xhtml1-frameset.dtd">
XHTML 1.0 Strict	<!DOCTYPE html PUBLIC "-//W3C//DTD XHTML 1.0 Strict//EN" "http://www.w3.org/TR/xhtml1/DTD/xhtml1-strict.dtd">
XHTML Basic	<!DOCTYPE html PUBLIC "-//W3C//DTD XHTML Basic 1.0//EN" "http://www.w3.org/TR/xhtml-basic/xhtml-basic10.dtd">
XHTML 1.1	<!DOCTYPE html PUBLIC "-//W3C//DTD XHTML 1.1//EN" "http://www.w3.org/TR/xhtml11/DTD/xhtml11.dtd">

Listing 3-2: A simple XHTML 1.1 file

```
<?xml version="1.0" encoding="UTF-8"?>
<!DOCTYPE html PUBLIC "-//W3C//DTD XHTML 1.1//EN"
    "http://www.w3.org/TR/xhtml11/DTD/xhtml11.dtd">
<html xmlns="http://www.w3.org/1999/xhtml" xml:lang="en" >
  <head>
    <title>Some Title</title>
  </head>
  <body>
    <p>Page Content</p>
  </body>
</html>
```

How can you ensure your documents are valid? By validating them, of course. That seems to be a circular argument, doesn't it? A number of XHTML validation services and applications are available to ensure the documents you create are both well-formed and valid, most notably the W3C Validation service and Tidy.

W3C Validation Service

As the standards body responsible for HTML and XHTML, it seems appropriate that the W3C has a service available for validating XHTML documents. This service (see Figure 3-1) is available at `http://validator.w3.org`, and enables checking a document by URL, file upload, or text input.

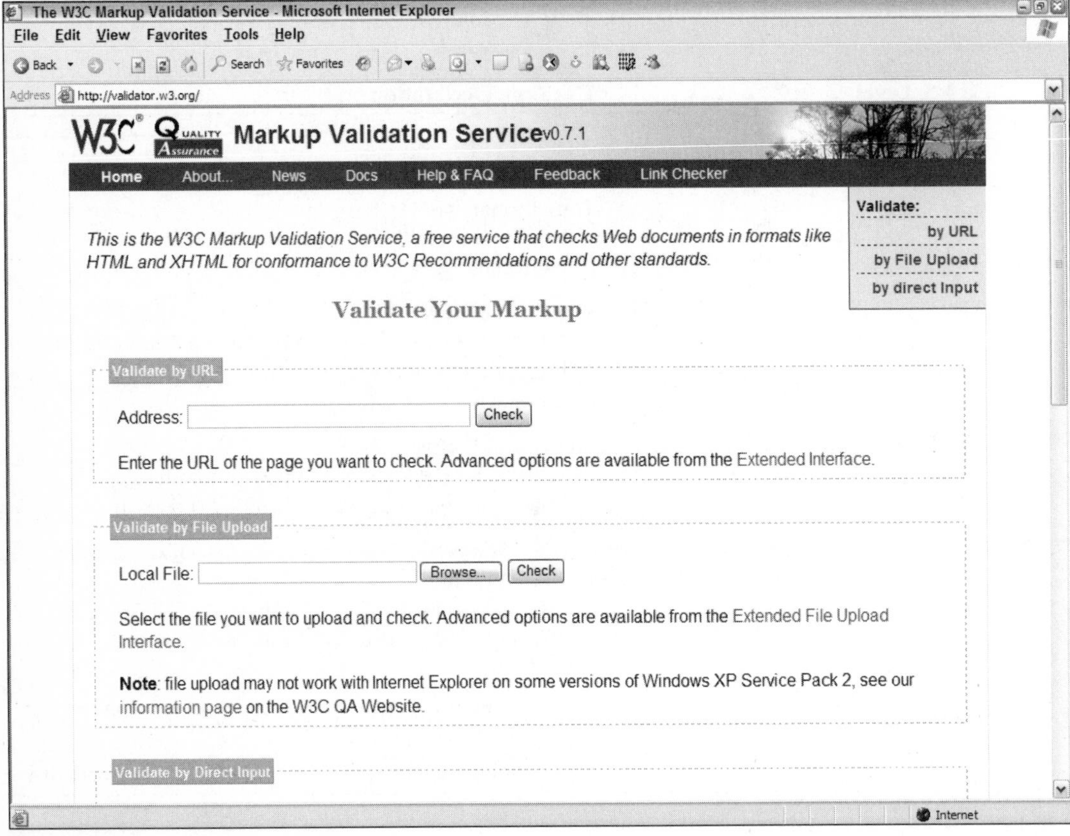

Figure 3-1

Tidy

Tidy is an application that was initially developed at the W3C, but later was taken over by the broader development community. It is a command-line application (see Figure 3-2 for some of the command-line arguments) that can validate a document, return a list of errors, or correct the errors. In addition, a number of wrappers are available that provide direct access to the functionality from the programming language of your choice.

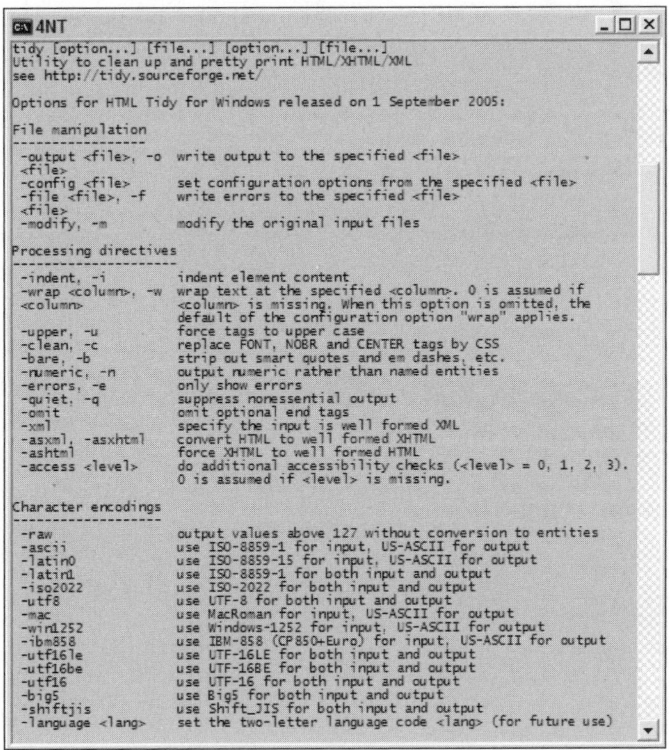

Figure 3-2

The two most common uses for Tidy are to create new, compliant versions of your Web pages, and to clean up errors and formatting. Listing 3-3 shows an HTML file that contains a number of issues. Although this file would still be valid in a browser (see Figure 3-3), you can use Tidy to clean up its problems and convert the document to XHMTL.

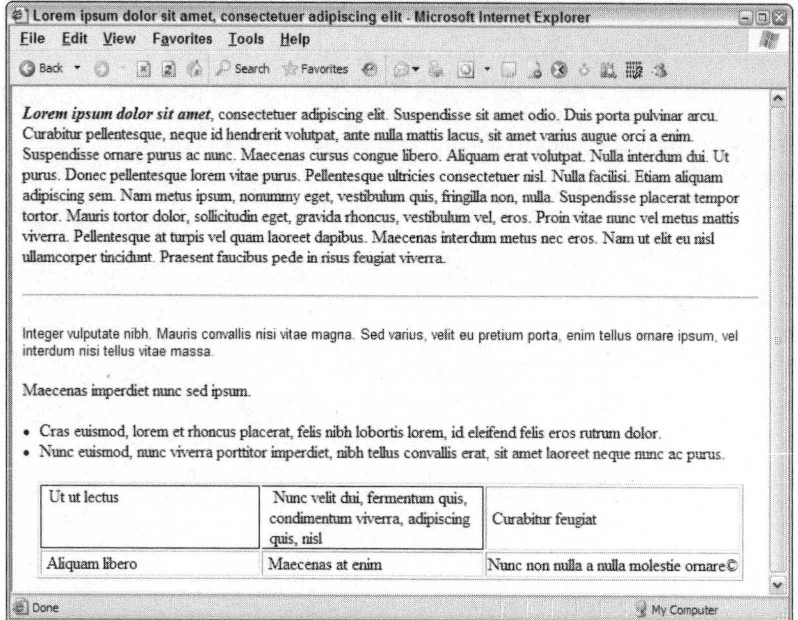

Figure 3-3

Listing 3-3: Not very valid HTML

```
<head>
<title>Lorem ipsum dolor sit amet, consectetuer adipiscing elit</title></head>
<body lang=EN-US BGCOLOR=white text=black link=blue vlink=purple>
<p><b><i>Lorem ipsum dolor sit amet</b></i>, consectetuer adipiscing elit.
Suspendisse sit amet odio. Duis porta pulvinar arcu. Curabitur pellentesque,
neque id hendrerit volutpat, ante nulla mattis lacus, sit amet varius augue
orci a enim. Suspendisse ornare purus ac nunc. Maecenas cursus congue libero.
Aliquam erat volutpat. Nulla interdum dui. Ut purus. Donec pellentesque lorem
vitae purus. Pellentesque ultricies consectetuer nisl. Nulla facilisi. Etiam
aliquam adipiscing sem. Nam metus ipsum, nonummy eget, vestibulum quis,
fringilla non, nulla. Suspendisse placerat tempor tortor. Mauris tortor dolor,
sollicitudin eget, gravida rhoncus, vestibulum vel, eros. Proin vitae nunc vel
metus mattis viverra. Pellentesque at turpis vel quam laoreet dapibus. Maecenas
interdum metus nec eros. Nam ut elit eu nisl ullamcorper tincidunt. Praesent
faucibus pede in risus feugiat viverra.</p>
<hr>
<p><font face="arial" size=2>Integer vulputate nibh. Mauris convallis
nisi vitae magna. Sed varius, velit eu pretium porta, enim tellus ornare ipsum,
vel interdum nisi tellus vitae massa.</font></p>
<p>Maecenas imperdiet nunc sed ipsum.</p>
 <li>Cras euismod, lorem et rhoncus placerat, felis nibh
     lobortis lorem, id eleifend felis eros rutrum dolor.
 <li>Nunc euismod, nunc viverra porttitor imperdiet, nibh
     tellus convallis erat, sit amet laoreet neque nunc ac purus.</li>
</ul>
```

```
<Center>
<table border=1>
 <tr>
  <td width=197 valign=top style='width:2.05in;border:solid windowtext 1.0pt;
  padding:0in 5.4pt 0in 5.4pt'>
  <p>Ut ut lectus</p>
  <td width=197 valign=top style='width:2.05in;border:solid windowtext 1.0pt;
  border-left:none;padding:0in 5.4pt 0in 5.4pt'>
  <p> Nunc velit dui, fermentum quis, condimentum viverra, adipiscing
  quis, nisl</p>
  <td><p> Curabitur feugiat</p></tr><tr><td><p> Aliquam libero</p>
  <td>
  <p> Maecenas at enim</p>
  <td><p>Nunc non nulla a nulla molestie ornare&copy;</p>
</table>
</CENTER>
</body>
```

In the preceding code, a number of errors are present in the HTML (such as a missing root html tag, missing close tags for the last tr, and so on). Also, a number of items that are valid HTML items are not valid in XHTML. For example, the `hr` tag is an empty tag; therefore, it should be written `<hr />`. In addition, many unquoted attributes are present, and the center tag is written in mixed case in one place and in all uppercase elsewhere.

Converting a document as shown in Listing 3-3 is not an uncommon task, but it can be quite difficult to do manually. HTML editing software and users have found just too many ways to hide bad code in Web pages. Running Tidy with the following command-line generates the list of warnings in Listing 3-4. As you can see, it detected many of the expected errors, as well as a few others.

```
tidy -o c:\temp\fixed.htm -f errors.txt -i -w 79 -c -b -asxhtml -utf8 Invalid.htm
```

Note: The options set are:

- Output file is `c:\temp\fixed.htm`
- Send errors to `errors.txt`
- Indent output
- Wrap output to 79 characters or less per line
- Replace deprecated font, center, and `nobr` tags with CSS
- Strip out smart quotes, em dashes, and other formatting characters
- Output should be XHTML
- Output should be encoded as UTF-8

Many other command-line options exist. In addition, many other configuration settings alter the output of Tidy. See the documentation for more details. If you want a common set of parameters, it would be easier to create a configuration file for running Tidy. This is a text file, with the configuration elements listed one per line. With this in place, the previous command-line could be simplified to:

```
tidy -config myconfig.txt Invalid.htm
```

Listing 3-4 shows the result of running Tidy on the sample file.

Listing 3-4: Warnings generated

```
line 1 column 1 - Warning: missing <!DOCTYPE> declaration
line 4 column 7 - Warning: replacing unexpected b by </b>
line 4 column 4 - Warning: replacing unexpected i by </i>
line 3 column 1 - Warning: <li> isn't allowed in <body> elements
line 21 column 2 - Warning: inserting implicit <ul>
line 25 column 1 - Warning: discarding unexpected </ul>
line 21 column 2 - Warning: missing </ul> before <center>
line 27 column 1 - Warning: <table> lacks "summary" attribute
Info: Document content looks like HTML 4.01 Transitional
8 warnings, 0 errors were found!
```

Although the cleaned document may not reflect all the intent of the original (an inappropriate change sometimes occurs), it should be much easier to clean up. Listing 3-5 shows the output of the previous code.

Listing 3-5: Cleaned XHTML output

```
<!DOCTYPE html PUBLIC "-//W3C//DTD XHTML 1.0 Transitional//EN"
    "http://www.w3.org/TR/xhtml1/DTD/xhtml1-transitional.dtd">

<html xmlns="http://www.w3.org/1999/xhtml">
<head>
  <meta name="generator" content=
  "HTML Tidy for Windows (vers 1 September 2005), see www.w3.org" />

  <title>Lorem ipsum dolor sit amet, consectetuer adipiscing elit</title>
<style type="text/css">
/*<![CDATA[*/
 body {
  background-color: white;
  color: black;
 }
 :link { color: blue }
 :visited { color: purple }
 div.c4 {text-align: center}
 td.c3 {width:2.05in;border:solid windowtext 1.0pt; border-left:none;padding:0in
5.4pt 0in 5.4pt}
 td.c2 {width:2.05in;border:solid windowtext 1.0pt; padding:0in 5.4pt 0in 5.4pt}
 p.c1 {font-family: arial; font-size: 80%}
/*]]>*/
</style>
</head>

<body lang="EN-US" xml:lang="EN-US">
  <p><b><i>Lorem ipsum dolor sit amet</i></b>, consectetuer adipiscing elit.
  Suspendisse sit amet odio. Duis porta pulvinar arcu. Curabitur pellentesque,
  neque id hendrerit volutpat, ante nulla mattis lacus, sit amet varius augue
  orci a enim. Suspendisse ornare purus ac nunc. Maecenas cursus congue
  libero. Aliquam erat volutpat. Nulla interdum dui. Ut purus. Donec
  pellentesque lorem vitae purus. Pellentesque ultricies consectetuer nisl.
  Nulla facilisi. Etiam aliquam adipiscing sem. Nam metus ipsum, nonummy eget,
```

```
  vestibulum quis, fringilla non, nulla. Suspendisse placerat tempor tortor.
  Mauris tortor dolor, sollicitudin eget, gravida rhoncus, vestibulum vel,
  eros. Proin vitae nunc vel metus mattis viverra. Pellentesque at turpis vel
  quam laoreet dapibus. Maecenas interdum metus nec eros. Nam ut elit eu nisl
  ullamcorper tincidunt. Praesent faucibus pede in risus feugiat viverra.</p>
  <hr />

  <p class="c1">Integer vulputate nibh. Mauris convallis nisi vitae magna. Sed
  varius, velit eu pretium porta, enim tellus ornare ipsum, vel interdum nisi
  tellus vitae massa.</p>

  <p>Maecenas imperdiet nunc sed ipsum.</p>

  <ul>
    <li>Cras euismod, lorem et rhoncus placerat, felis nibh lobortis lorem, id
    eleifend felis eros rutrum dolor.</li>

    <li>Nunc euismod, nunc viverra porttitor imperdiet, nibh tellus convallis
    erat, sit amet laoreet neque nunc ac purus.</li>
  </ul>

  <div class="c4">
    <table border="1">
      <tr>
        <td width="197" valign="top" class='c2'>
          <p>Ut ut lectus</p>
        </td>

        <td width="197" valign="top" class='c3'>
          <p> Nunc velit dui, fermentum quis, condimentum viverra, adipiscing
          quis, nisl</p>
        </td>

        <td>
          <p> Curabitur feugiat</p>
        </td>
      </tr>

      <tr>
        <td>
          <p> Aliquam libero</p>
        </td>

        <td>
          <p> Maecenas at enim</p>
        </td>

        <td>
          <p>Nunc non nulla a nulla molestie ornare(c)</p>
        </td>
      </tr>
    </table>
  </div>
</body>
</html>
```

Tidy UI

For those less than comfortable with the command-line, Charles Reitzel created a Windows application to enable working visually with Tidy (see Figure 3-4). This is a handy utility if you have only a small amount of HTML to convert. For larger quantities, the command-line (or one of the code wrappers) is a better solution.

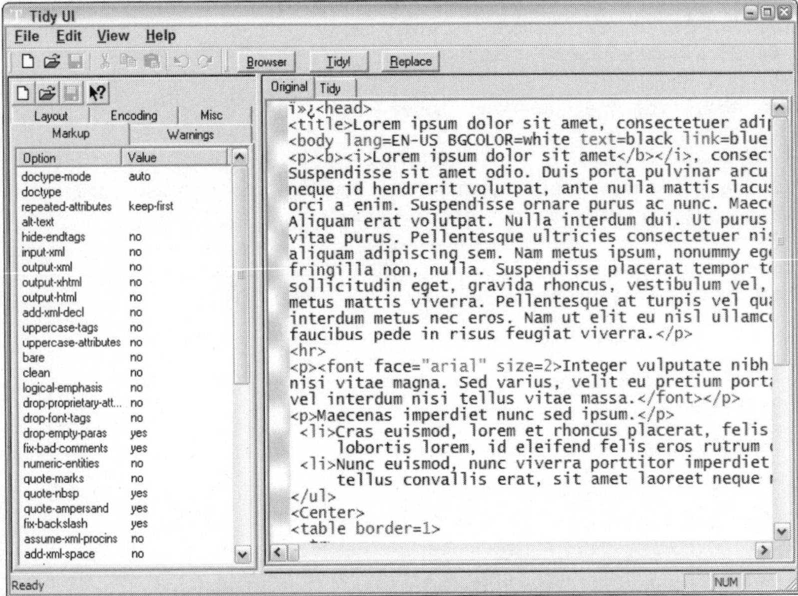

Figure 3-4

Just as with the command-line version, you can easily see the errors and warnings your document generates (see Figure 3-5). Double-clicking the warning or error selects the appropriate line in the edit window.

Level	Line	Col	Message
Warning	1	1	plain text isn't allowed in <head> elements
Warning	1	1	inserting missing 'title' element
Warning	1	1	<head> isn't allowed in <body> elements
Warning	1	1	<title> isn't allowed in <body> elements
Warning	1	1	</head> isn't allowed in <body> elements
Warning	1	1	<body> isn't allowed in <body> elements
Warning	4	7	replacing unexpected b by </b>
Warning	4	4	replacing unexpected i by </i>
Warning	1	1	<li> isn't allowed in <body> elements
Warning	21	2	inserting implicit <ul>
Warning	27	1	<table> lacks "summary" attribute
Warning	1	1	Attribute "lang" not supported in HTML 3.2
Warning	1	1	Text node in <body> in HTML 3.2
Warning	1	1	Text node in <body> in HTML 3.2
Warning	21	2	Attribute "class" not supported in HTML 3.2
Warning	29	3	Attribute "style" not supported in HTML 3.2
Warning	32	3	Attribute "style" not supported in HTML 3.2
Information			Document content looks like HTML 4.01 Transitional

Figure 3-5

The functionality of Tidy has also been exposed through a number of language wrappers. This allows you to integrate the functionality into your own applications. Wrappers are available for COM, .NET, Java, Perl, Python, and many other languages. See the Tidy home page (`http://tidy.sourceforge.net/`) for the full list.

The included project is a simple text editor that includes the capability to run Tidy (using the .NET wrapper) on the content. It is intentionally simple, but shows how you can integrate the Tidy functionality directly in an application.

First, create a new Windows Forms project. The sample project contains three tabs. The first is an edit window, the second a read-only text box containing the tidied XHTML, and the last is a Web browser window for viewing the resulting content. Next, add a reference to the .NET wrapper (see Figure 3-6). If you receive an error while adding the reference, it may be because the TidyATL.dll is not registered (the .NET wrapper is actually a .NET wrapper of the COM wrapper). Register the TidyATL.dll file using the command-line `regsvr32 tidyatl.dll` and try adding the reference again.

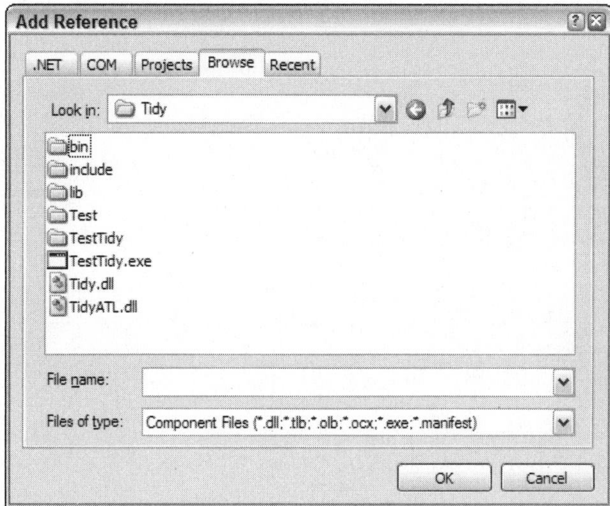

Figure 3-6

Most of the code in the included project is involved in the menus and file handling. The only code that actually calls the Tidy wrapper is in the `TidyText` function (see Listing 3-6). This takes a block of HTML, processes it with Tidy, and returns the result (see Figure 3-7). Each of the command-line properties of Tidy is exposed in an enumeration (`TidyOptionId`). You use the `SetOptBool`, `SetOptInt` and `SetOptValue` methods to set the desired settings. Alternatively, you can load the settings from a configuration file. This file is simply a list containing one parameter per line, along with the value, in the format:

```
property: value
```

For Boolean values, yes/no, true/false or 1/0 can be used for the value. `ParseString` loads the HTML, and `SaveString` returns the cleaned XHTML. You could alternatively use `ParseFile` and `SaveFile` to process files on disc or `CleanAndRepair` to clean a file in place.

Listing 3-6: Using the .NET Tidy wrapper

```
Private Function TidyText(ByVal text As String) As String
    Dim result As String = String.Empty
    Dim t As New Tidy.Document
    With t
        'set options
        .SetOptBool(TidyOptionId.TidyIndentContent, 1)
        .SetOptBool(TidyOptionId.TidyXhtmlOut, 1)
        .SetOptBool(TidyOptionId.TidyMakeClean, 1)
        .SetOptBool(TidyOptionId.TidyIndentContent, 1)
        .SetOptInt(TidyOptionId.TidyIndentSpaces, 2)
        .SetOptValue(TidyOptionId.TidyCharEncoding, "utf8")
         'or .LoadConfig("tidyconfig.txt")

        'parse and return tidy'd html
        .ParseString(text)
        result = .SaveString()
    End With

    Return result
End Function
```

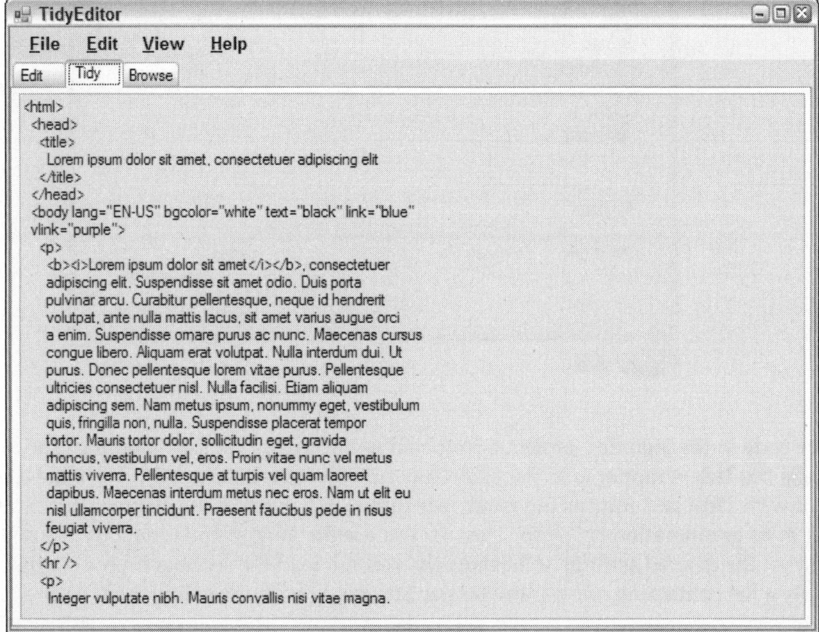

Figure 3-7

The functionality of Tidy and its availability for multiple languages and platforms means you never have an excuse for invalid XHTML pages. Try to develop the habit of running it regularly on your XHTML to ensure it conforms.

The Evil Font Tag

When I first learned HTML, it was a fairly primitive formatting tool. You had your choice of bold, italics, or one of six headline levels. ("And we liked it!") Going further than this meant using the <font> element. Using this element, you could change the look of your Web sites, getting them to look closer to a corporate or other brand, or to make them look more like offline documentation.

However, like a lot of other gifts of technology, things were waiting to bite in this Pandora's Box. Using the <font> element meant that you were hard-coding huge amounts of information directly in the page. Maintaining <font> information as it changed was a chore. In addition, this information was repeated frequently through the document, causing page bloat and slow response times. Fortunately, around the time of HTML 4, CSS came along. As you will soon see, CSS is a way of applying the same type of information as you could using the <font> element (and more), but in a better way. Therefore, the <font> tag has been deprecated, and support for it in browsers will eventually go the way of the <blink> and other extinct HTML elements.

Understanding CSS

Cascading Style Sheets (CSS) is a technology for defining layout or formatting for documents. Although not an XML technology, it is most useful when used in combination with XHTML, and, therefore, it is included here. CSS separates the style information from the actual content. In addition, CSS can save you time when generating pages. Rather than add font, color, or other styling information on every tag of a particular group (for example, making each `h1` tag red and Arial), you apply the CSS style information to a selector and then add that selector to the elements you want formatted that way. That is, rather than sprinkling `<font face="Arial, Helvetica, sans serif" size="3" color="red">Some text</font>` throughout your Web pages, you add something like `<span class="emphasis">Some text</span>`. The emphasis style is defined elsewhere in one spot. Should the appearance of your emphasis text need changing, you no longer need to search through all your documents looking for items to change. Finally, CSS can save bandwidth. By having all your documents refer to the same file(s) containing style information, you save the bandwidth that would be used if this information were scattered throughout your documents. One upcoming benefit of CSS is that you will be able to apply different CSS files based on the desired output (for example, screen vs. printer) for your page.

Basics of CSS

CSS could easily fill a book, such as *Wrox Professional CSS: Cascading Style Sheets for Web Design*, ISBN: 0-7645-8833-8 (`wrox.com/WileyCDA/WroxTitle/productCd-0764588338.html`). Now, however, I'll cover only the basics and let you refer to other material as needed.

Two active levels of CSS exist: CSS 1 (originally ratified in 1996) and CSS 2.1 (as of this writing still a Working Draft that expands on CSS 2.0, originally ratified in 1998). CSS 3.0 is currently a standard in progress; it adds a number of properties that will be useful, such as column layout. However, because it will likely be some time before these properties will be supported by most browsers, I won't cover them here. If you want your CSS to work in the broadest range of browsers, you should stick with CSS 1.0. Some of the CSS 2.0 and 2.1 features are either unsupported or supported using nonstandard extensions in the various browsers.

CSS consists of a number of properties that can be applied to areas on a page. These properties have values that affect how they are rendered, and include such items as color, margins, padding, and text formatting. The following table lists some of the more commonly used properties. Note: This is hardly a comprehensive list; see *Professional CSS* (ISBN: 0-7645-8833-8) for more details.

Property	Description
border	Sets a border around an item. Also border-left, border-top, border-right, and border-bottom set each border individually. Value is a three-part string of style line-width color. Style determines how the line is drawn (for example, solid, dashed, dotted). Line-width can be an actual length (with units) or one designated thin, medium, or thick. Color can be a named color or the RGB value (with a # preceding it). Each of these properties can also be individually enhanced with its own properties, such as border-right-style, border-top-color, and border-left-width.
margin	Sets the margin around the item. This differs from padding in that padding sets the margin between the edge of the item and the content itself. Margins sets the margin between the edge of the item and its container. You can also use margin-left, margin-top, margin-right, and margin-bottom to set each margin individually. Value is an actual length (with units) or a percentage of available space (ending with %)
padding	Sets the spacing around the content of the item. This differs from margin in that margin sets the spacing around the entire item, whereas padding adds spacing between the item's edge, and the content. You can also use padding-top, padding-right, padding-bottom, and padding-left to set each side individually. Value is an actual length (with units) or a percentage of the available space (ending with %).
color background-color	Sets the foreground or background color of an item. Value is either a named color or the RGB value (with a # preceding it). Although not absolutely necessary, if you set one of these, you should set the other as well.
background	Sets a number of the properties of the background, including color, image, and how the image interacts with the page. The value is a five-part string containing the color, image url, the repeat settings for the image, whether the image is fixed or whether it scrolls as the user scrolls the page, and the position of the image. Each of these properties can be set individually as well with the background-color, background-image, background-repeat, background-attachment, and background-position properties.
display	Sets how the item is displayed. The most common example of this is display:none, which hides the content (that is, nothing is created on the page for it). However, a number of options exist for this property, including block, inline-block, inline, and list-item.
text-align	Sets how the text is aligned within the borders of the item.
text-decoration	Adds decoration to the item. The decoration consists of underlining, overlining, blinking and striking through the item.

Property	Description
font-style	Sets the text as italic or oblique (angled like italics, but the other way).
font	Sets all the font properties for an item. Value is a five-part string containing the setting for the style (currently normal, italic, or oblique), variant (currently the only option is small-caps), weight (boldness), size (either a specific size, or a name that describes the size, for example: xx-small, larger), and font family (for example, Arial). Alternatively, but more rarely, the value can be the name of a system font (for example, caption, message-box, menu). Each of the properties can be set individually as well, such as font-family, font-style, font-weight, and font-size.
list-style	Sets how each list item is displayed. Value is a three-part string containing the symbol type to use as a bullet (for example, disc, square, or none), an optional URL to an image to use for the bullets, and the position of the bullet relative to the item. Each of these properties can be set individually as well, with the list-style-image, list-style-position, and list-style-type properties.
height width min-height min-width max-height max-width	Sets the size of items. Value is either an actual size (with units) or a percentage of the available space (ending with '%'). The min- and max- versions control the minimum and maximum dimensions of an item if the browser window is resized. They are not supported by Internet Explorer (up to version 6.0).
float	Removes an item from the normal flow of items on a page and moves it to either the left or right of the screen. Other content flows around this item. See an explanation of multicolumn layout with CSS (in the following section) for one common use of this property.
position	Changes how the item is positioned on the page. Values include static (normal behavior), relative, fixed, and absolute. With relative or absolute, you should also include left and top properties in the selector. When using relative, these values are used to adjust the position of the item relative to where it should appear in the flow of the page. When you use absolute, these values enable you to place the item exactly.
cursor	Sets the mouse pointer when the cursor is placed over it. Value is one of the standard shapes for a mouse pointer (crosshair, wait, move, default, help) or an URL pointing to a custom cursor.
overflow	Sets the behavior used if the content is larger than the assigned size. Values include visible (meaning the content continues beyond the assigned size), hidden (meaning the content is cut off at the margin), scroll (meaning the content is cut off at the margin but a scroll bar is added to view the remaining content) and auto (implementation-dependant behavior). This property can be a useful property when adding a large block of content to a page, such as when adding code samples. You can fix the size of the content and add a scroll bar if the size is larger than the requested space.

You group these properties in selectors. Each selector is applied to one of the following types of items:

- All elements of a named type, for example: `h1 { color: red; }`
- All elements with a particular id or all elements of one type with a particular id, for example: `#doc-body { font-size:0.78em; }` or `h1#headline { color: red; }`
- All elements with a particular class attribute or all elements of one type with a particular class attribute, for example: `.emphasis {font-weight: bold;color:navy; }` or `div.fineprint { font-size: xx-small; }`
- All elements that are contained by another element (descendant selectors), for example `div a { text-decoration: none; }`. This would be when one tag is contained within another tag, such as `<div><a></a></div>`. The a element descends from the div element. A elements not within div elements would not be affected.
- All elements adjacent to one another (adjacent sibling selectors), for example `h1+div { margin-top: 1.5em; }`. This would be when one tag immediately follows another; in this case a `div` immediately follows an `h1` tag. Adjacent sibling selectors are not frequently encountered, but can provide a powerful formatting tool for some documents.
- All elements with a particular attribute or all elements of one type with a particular attribute, for example: `h1[title] {font-size:2.2em; color:navy; }`.
- Specific "pseudo" classes and elements. Certain tags, most notably the a tag, support pseudo-classes to identify specific states for the anchor. These include hover, active, link, visited. Each of these classes can have CSS applied to them for styling. In addition, elements support the lang class to style different languages. Some clients also support pseudo-elements such as before, first-line, first-letter and more. Consult a CSS reference for the complete list of pseudo-elements and selectors, but be aware that many of these have poor support by some browsers.

Listing 3-7 shows examples of these three types of selectors. Selectors are made up of one or more named items and the properties associated with those items surrounded by braces ({}).

Listing 3-7: CSS selectors

```
body {
  margin: 0;
 padding: 0;
 border: 0;
 text-align: center;
 color: #554;
 background: #692 url(images/background.gif) top center repeat-y;
 font: small tahoma, "Bitstream Vera Sans", "Trebuchet MS",
  "Lucida Grande", lucida, helvetica, sans-serif;
 }

#main {
 width: 400px;
 float: left;
 }

#sidebar ul li {
```

```
 list-style: disc url(images/bullet.gif) inside;
 vertical-align: top;
 padding: 0;
 margin: 0;
 }

.content-body {
  line-height: 140%;
  }

h3.content-title {
 margin-top: 5px;
 font-size: medium;
 }
```

The sample CSS in Listing 03-7 includes five selectors. The first is associated with the body tag of the page, but you create element-associated selectors using this format. The selector sets the margins, padding, and border to 0, meaning the content will appear flush with the edges of the browser window. The background property sets the color and assigns an image for the background. The image is set to the top of the page, and it repeats down the page. If the browser window is too wide, the graphic is not repeated.

The second and third selectors show the id form of naming a selector. The first creates a named selector called main. Any tag that includes the attribute `id="main"` has this selector associated with it, setting the width and floating it to the left margin. The second form of the id selector is applied to all `li` tags that are within a `ul` element that is within an area marked with the `id="sidebar"` attribute. This form of the selector is very useful in blocking off sections of your page. For example, you might break down your page into navigation, main, sidebar, and footer sections to define areas of the page, and then create selectors that include that information. This causes tags to appear differently depending on their location on the page.

```
<div id="sidebar">
  <h2>List Title</h2>
  <ul>
    <li><a href='http://www.example.com/someLink'>Item 1</a></li>
    <li><a href='http://www.example.com/someOtherLink'>Item 2</a></li>
  </ul>
</div>
```

The fourth and fifth selectors show the class form of naming a selector. The first creates a selector called `content-body`. Any tag that has the attribute `class="content-body"` has this selector applied to it, setting the line height to 140% of normal. The second form applies only to `h3` tags with a class of content-title. This form of the tag is useful as a means of precisely formatting a block of content. In addition, if you had multiple `h3` tags, you could format some of them by including the `class` attribute.

You can include selectors either directly within the file or as an external file. When adding style information directly to the page, you should identify the style block as CSS and provide an id for reference (see Listing 3-8). In addition, if your styles include any characters significant to XML, such as < and `&`, you should wrap them in a CDATA block.

Listing 3-8: Style information in an XHTML document

```
<?xml-stylesheet href="#internalStyle" type="text/css"?>
<!DOCTYPE html PUBLIC "-//W3C//DTD XHTML 1.0 Strict//EN"
  "http://www.w3.org/TR/xhtml1/DTD/xhtml1-strict.dtd">
<html xmlns="http://www.w3.org/1999/xhtml" lang="en" xml:lang="en">
  <head>
    <title>Title</title>
    <style type="text/css" id="internalStyle">
      <![CDATA[
        body {
          margin: 0;
          padding: 0;
          border: 0;
          text-align: center;
          color: #554;
          background: #692 url(images/background.gif)
            top center repeat-y;
          font: small tahoma, "Bitstream Vera Sans", "Trebuchet MS",
            "Lucida Grande", lucida, helvetica, sans-serif;
        }

        #main {
          width: 400px;
          float: left;
        }

        #sidebar ul li {
          list-style: disc url(images/bullet.gif) inside;
          vertical-align: top;
          padding: 0;
          margin: 0;
        }

        .content-body {
          line-height: 140%;
        }

        h3.content-title {
          margin-top: 5px;
          font-size: medium;
        }

      ]]>
    </style>
  </head>

  <body>
    <div id="main">
      <h3 class="content-title">Some Title</h3>
      <div class="content-body">Lorem ipsum dolor sit amet,
        consectetuer adipiscing elit.</div>
    </div>

    <div id="sidebar">
```

```
        <h2>List Title</h2>
        <ul>
          <li><a href='http://www.example.com/someLink'>Item 1</a></li>
          <li><a href='http://www.example.com/someOtherLink'>Item 2</a></li>
        </ul>
      </div>
    </body>
  </html>
```

Because of the issues around the & and < characters, it is generally best to include CSS information in external files and reference them in your pages. In addition, including the CSS information in a separate file means that the file needs to be downloaded only once, reducing bandwidth requirements. The two ways of including an external style sheet with a document are the XML way and the HTML way. You can use either method, although the XML way is preferred.

The XML way of including an external CSS reference is to use a processing instruction (see Listing 3-9). The xml-stylesheet processing instruction takes the URL of the CSS file and identifies it as the MIME type text/css.

Listing 3-9: An external CSS reference using processing instructions

```
<?xml version="1.0" encoding="utf-8" ?>
<?xml-stylesheet href="sample.css" type="text/css"?>
<!DOCTYPE html PUBLIC "-//W3C//DTD XHTML 1.0 Strict//EN"
  "http://www.w3.org/TR/xhtml1/DTD/xhtml1-strict.dtd">
<html xmlns="http://www.w3.org/1999/xhtml" lang="en" xml:lang="en">
  <head>
    <title>External CSS Reference using PI</title>
  </head>

  <body>
    ...
  </body>
</html>
```

The HTML way of including an external CSS reference, shown in Listing 3-10, still works with XHTML. This method uses a link element. The link includes the URL of the CSS, the MIME type, and an identification of it as the stylesheet using the `rel` attribute.

Listing 3-10: An external CSS reference using the link element

```
<?xml version="1.0" encoding="utf-8" ?>
<!DOCTYPE html PUBLIC "-//W3C//DTD XHTML 1.0 Strict//EN"
  "http://www.w3.org/TR/xhtml1/DTD/xhtml1-strict.dtd">
<html xmlns="http://www.w3.org/1999/xhtml" lang="en" xml:lang="en">
  <head>
    <title>External CSS Reference using PI</title>
    <link href="sample.css" type="text/css" rel="stylesheet" />
  </head>

  <body>
    ...
  </body>
</html>
```

By this point, I would expect you are more than a little curious about where the *Cascading* part of the name comes from. The name comes from the way CSS is applied to an item when multiple selectors apply and when multiple sources of CSS are included in a document. CSS selectors cascade or flow from more local to more general. That is, selectors deemed more important take precedence. The rules governing the application of CSS in these situations are basically as follows:

1. If only a single selector applies to the item, that selector is applied.
2. If two or more selectors apply to an item and they do not conflict, both are applied. That is, they "cascade" together.
3. If two or more selectors apply to an item, and one or more properties conflict, the more specific property is applied. Therefore, if you had a generic h2 selector, and `h2 class="foo"` to apply to an item, the properties of `h2 class="foo"` would override the conflicting value in the generic h2 selector.
4. If a property is assigned to an item in both an external and internal stylesheet, the properties of the internal (more local) stylesheet are applied.

CSS Examples

In addition to simply applying a few styles to a document, CSS is frequently used to perform certain tasks. For example, although many people create their overall page layout with a mixture of tables, they could create a multicolumn layout very simply using CSS. In addition, because you can easily change the CSS for your pages, why not allow your users to select their personal favorites?

Box Layout and Cross-Browser Compatibility

Although Internet Explorer was the first browser to support CSS, even before it was a standard, Explorer has fallen a little behind the standard. Some aspects of CSS 2 are currently unsupported, and even some areas of CSS 1.x are implemented differently in Internet Explorer than in other browsers (or the standards). The most significant of these is the Box model (see Figure 3-8). The *Box Model* is the way that the margins, padding, and borders are constructed around a piece of content.

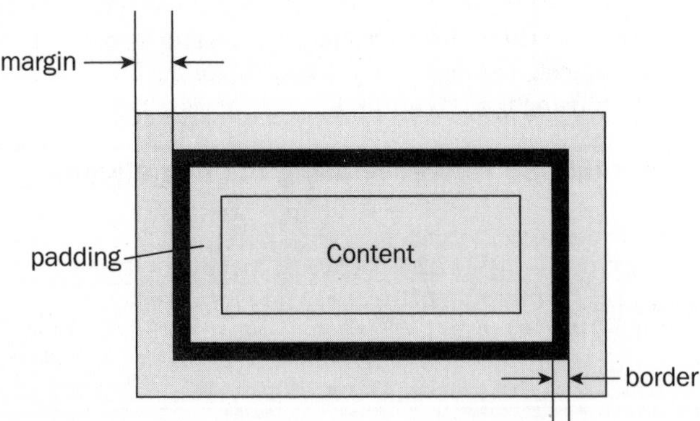

Figure 3-8

Older versions (4.0-5.5) of Internet Explorer are notorious for interpreting the Box Model incorrectly. Figure 3-9 shows this in action, with Internet Explorer 5.0 depicted in the top version, and Firefox 1.5 in the lower. The red line beneath the two grey boxes represents 300 pixels, whereas the green shows 344 pixels. The content box width is set by the combination of the width, margin, border, and padding. In versions of Internet Explorer before 6.0, *width* meant the total width of all these values. Therefore, adding margin, padding, and border made the text area narrower. Internet Explorer 6.0, Firefox, and Opera interpret the width correctly, adding margin, padding, and border to the outside of the width value. This leads to the total width of 344 pixels. The page with its CSS is shown in Listing 3-11.

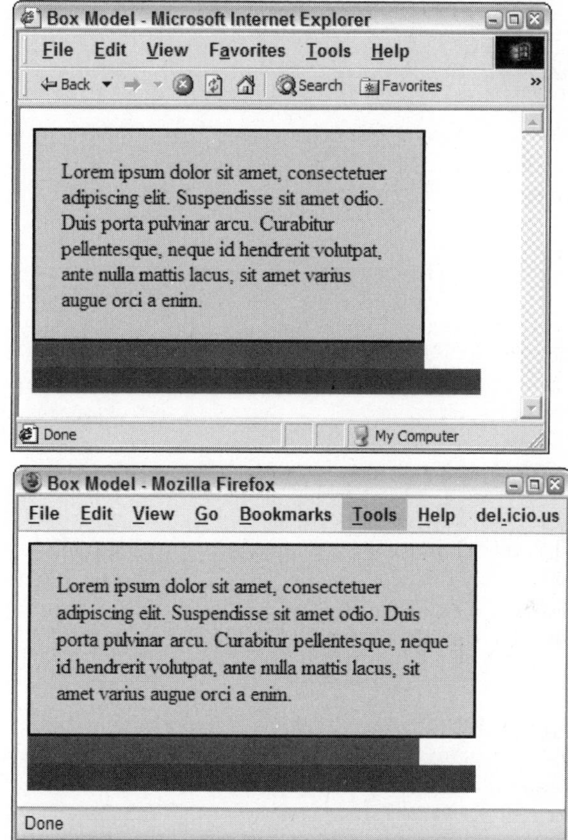

Figure 3-9

Listing 3-11: Box Model differences between browsers

Page:

```
<!DOCTYPE html PUBLIC "-//W3C//DTD XHTML 1.0 Transitional//EN"
    "http://www.w3.org/TR/xhtml1/DTD/xhtml1-transitional.dtd">
<html xmlns="http://www.w3.org/1999/xhtml" >
<head>
    <title>Box Model</title>
```

(continued)

Listing 3-11 *(continued)*

```
    <link href="BoxModel.css" rel="stylesheet" type="text/css" />
</head>
<body>

<div class="border">Lorem ipsum dolor sit amet,
consectetuer adipiscing elit. Suspendisse sit amet odio.
Duis porta pulvinar arcu. Curabitur pellentesque,
neque id hendrerit volutpat,
ante nulla mattis lacus, sit amet varius augue orci a enim. </div>
<div class="rulerIE"> </div>
<div class="rulerCSS"> </div>
</body>
</html>
```

CSS:

```
div.border
{
    border: solid 2px black;
    padding:20px;
    width: 300px;
    background-color: #ccc;
}

div.rulerIE
{
    width:300px;
    background-color: Red;
}
div.rulerCSS
{
    width: 344px;
    background-color: Green;
}
```

Solving the Box Model problem with older versions of IE is a bit of a cottage industry: a number of solutions have been proposed. Most involve adding extra information to the CSS file. This information is ignored by most browsers but interpreted by earlier versions of IE. Some of the more popular ones include:

- **The Box Model Hack:** First proposed by Tantek Çelik of Technorati, this method involves adding a second selector with a false ending. In the following code, the second `div.border` selector overrides the width set in the first. The odd looking line "`voice-family: "\"}\"";`" uses the rarely set `voice-family` property. Most browsers ignore this line because it is not valid. However, versions of Internet Explorer (5.5 and earlier) interpret it as, "`voice-family: }`". That is, IE 5.5 and earlier see this line as the end of the selector and ignore the next two lines. Other browsers ignore this line, and interpret the following two lines, setting the width as appropriate and resetting the voice-family to the default.

```
div.border
{
    border: solid 2px black;
```

```
    padding:20px;
    background-color: #ccc;
    width: 300px;
}
div.border {
  width:344px;
  voice-family: "\"}\"";
  voice-family:inherit;
  width:300px;
}
```

- **The Simplified Box Model Hack:** First proposed by Andrew Clover, this method leverages the string escape method of CSS to include multiple copies of the width. CSS-aware browsers read the correct value, whereas browsers that improperly handle the escapes have the value overridden later in the file.

```
div.border
{
    border: solid 2px black;
    padding:20px;
    background-color: #ccc;
    width: 300px;
}
div.border
{
    \width: 344px;
    w\idth: 300px;
}
```

- **The Modified Simple Box Model Hack:** This method, also known as the Star HTML Hack, was proposed by Edwardson Tan and includes a selector for the invalid `* html` before the desired tag. This, like the other hacks, is ignored as invalid by browsers such as Firefox or Opera and processed by older versions of Internet Explorer (5.5 or earlier).

```
div.border
{
    border: solid 2px black;
    padding:20px;
    width: 300px;
    background-color: #ccc;
}

* html div.border
{
    width: 344px;
}
```

One or all these hacks will likely work for you. Personally, I've found the Simplified Box Model Hack works quite well, and it is simple enough to implement. In general, you should include these hacks in separate CSS files, and use import statements to include them in your normal CSS. That way, you need to change only one line to remove them when you no longer need the hack.

Multicolumn Layout with CSS

Most, if not all, Web sites involve multiple column layouts. The content itself may be in multiple columns, or columns may be used for navigation or other page elements. The classic method of laying out a page like this is to use a combination of tables and 1-pixel transparent graphics to position items on the page. As you can imagine, this technique has a number of problems — it can be difficult to manage, particularly if you've got nested tables. All those tags bulk up the document, increasing download times; and this technique is definitely not accessible to those who read the page using screen readers or similar technologies. Because of this, it's a good idea to replace these pages with CSS to create the multiple column layout. However, doing so has its own problems, most notably browser compatibility with some of the CCS techniques. Even if you ignore older browsers (pre-Internet Explorer 4 or Netscape Navigator 3) that do not support CSS, a few compatibility issues still exist because each browser tends to interpret the CSS standards differently. Some comply only with CSS 1.x, whereas others are compatible CSS 2.x. As with any CSS technique, it is a good idea to validate your pages and to view them in a variety of browsers and platforms to ensure your pages work properly.

Figure 3-10 shows a simple two-column layout using CSS. As you can see, the left Menu Area does not change in size as the browser window is increased. Instead, the main content area expands and contracts to fit the available space. This is the simplest way of creating a page layout with a banner, left navigation area, and main area.

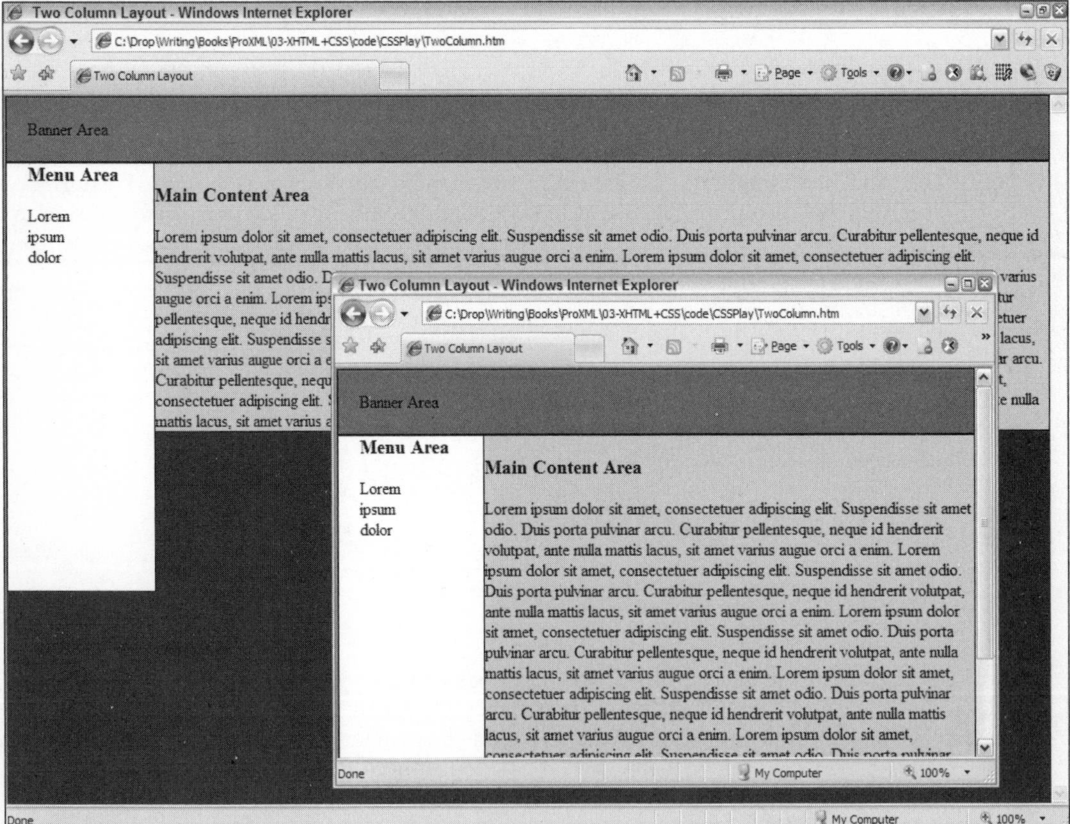

Figure 3-10

Creating this two column layout is a simple matter. The CSS and HTML used are shown in Listing 3-12. The only important selectors are the two highlighted ones setting the width of the menu area, and `float:left`. The float selector causes the area to be removed from the normal processing of the page and positioned at the left margin. Remaining content wraps around this area, so if the main content area's content is longer than the menu area (which it likely will be); you should adjust the padding-bottom to prevent this.

Listing 3-12: Two column layout with CSS

CSS:

```
body
{
    background-color: #0000cc;
    color:#000;
}
#banner
{
    background-color:#00cc00;
    color:#000;
    padding:20px;
    border: solid 1px #000;
}
#leftColumn
{
    float:left;
    width:300px;
    background-color:#fff;
    color:#000;
    border: solid 1px #000;
    padding-left: 20px;
    padding-right:20px;
    padding-bottom:200px;
}

#mainContent
{
    background-color: #ccc;
    color:#000;
    border: solid 1px #000;
}
```

XHTML:

```
<!DOCTYPE html PUBLIC "-//W3C//DTD XHTML 1.0 Transitional//EN"
"http://www.w3.org/TR/xhtml1/DTD/xhtml1-transitional.dtd">
<html xmlns="http://www.w3.org/1999/xhtml">
<head>
    <title>Two Column Layout</title>
    <link href="TwoColumn.css" rel="stylesheet" type="text/css" />
</head>
<body>
    <div id="banner">Banner Area</div>
    <div id="leftColumn">
        <h3>Menu area</h3>
```

(continued)

Listing 3-12 *(continued)*

```
        <div>
            Lorem</div>
        <div>
            ipsum</div>
        <div>
            dolor</div>
    </div>
    <div id="mainContent">
        <h3>Main Content Area</h3>
        <div>
            Lorem ipsum dolor sit amet, consectetuer adipiscing elit.
            Suspendisse sit amet odio.
            Duis porta pulvinar arcu. Curabitur pellentesque, neque id
            hendrerit volutpat, ante
            nulla mattis lacus, sit amet varius augue orci a enim.</div>
    </div>
</body>
</html>
```

Validating CSS

Just as with XHTML, it is best if you validate your CSS before releasing it into the wild. You have at least two main means of validating your CSS. First, you should run your style sheets through a mechanical validator, such as the online one at `http://jigsaw.w3.org/css-validator`. This identifies any major errors you may have, as well as shows you any items that aren't covered in the version of the standard you are targeting.

The second and much more important means of validating your CSS is to look at the resulting page in as many browsers as you think may be used to view your site. Generally, this means Internet Explorer, Netscape Navigator, Firefox, Opera, and any others that appear regularly in your Web server logs. In addition, you probably want to use multiple versions of those programs, and probably also some versions running on multiple platforms. Using virtualization software, such as Microsoft Virtual PC or VMWare, makes it easy to keep all these versions available when you need to test a page.

Using Microformats

Microformats are an interesting new development in the use of XHTML. Rather than propose new XML grammars for items such as contacts, lists, or calendar elements, microformat users recommend using standard XHTML tags, with CSS for formatting for those elements. Among many benefits of this technique are the following:

- You don't need to learn a new XML grammar or to get a standards body to approve it.
- No additional code is required to display microformats in existing browsers and applications.
- Existing XHTML validators can validate the pages produced using microformats by using existing XHTML tags.
- The microformat is human-readable, and at the same time it provides information to software, such as search engines.

There are three basic sets of microformats — simple, elemental microformats, and compound microformats.

Elemental Microformats

Elemental microformats are minimal solutions to a specific XHTML problem (often a single element or an attribute). They provide additional semantic information to the content of the XHTML page. Some of the more notable elemental microformats include:

- `RelNoFollow`: An attribute used to change the way search engines treatlinking tags.
- `Rel-Tag`: An attribute used to identify the topic of a link, page, or other item.

RelNoFollow

The most-used elemental microformat is the `RelNoFollow` microformat. This microformat recommends the addition of the attribute `rel="nofollow"` to some hyperlinks, typically in the comment section of a weblog or forum. The end user does not see the effect of this change in the hyperlink, but it becomes an informational marker for search engines. Typically, search engines follow hyperlinks and apply weighting to the association between the destination page and the linking page. Therefore, if the link is coming from a popular site about some technology, the target page may likely be about that technology as well. However, this relationship has been used by a number of spam groups to increase their status in popular search engines, typically by commenting on popular blogs or news sites. The `RelNoFollow` microformat is a marker for search engines to ignore the target page, reducing the value of such comment spam. You can get more information on the `RelNoFollow` microformat at `http://microformats.org/wiki/relnofollow`.

Rel-Tag

`Rel-Tag` is intended to be metadata added to an article, blog post, or other block of information, that provides the topic of the item. The intent is that the tag points to an aggregation of similar items, a definition of the item, or similar collection. For example, `Rel-Tag` could be used in a weblog post or article to identify that the content involves XHTML by adding the following tag to the content.

```
<a rel="xhtml" href="http://www.technorati.com/tag/xhtml">XHTML</a>
```

An application reading this would realize (because of the rel="xhtml" attribute) that the post was about XHTML. Users then click on the link to discover more links about XHTML. Note that the link doesn't have to point to Technorati, but it could instead point at some other tag aggregation site, such as Delicious (e.g. `http://del.icio.us/tag/xhtml`), Wikipedia (for example, `http://en.wikipedia.org/wiki/Xhtml`), or even the specification itself (for example, `http://www.w3.org/TR/xhtml11/`). `Rel-Tag` suggests the presence of the `rel="xhtml"` attribute, and requires `href` to point to something useful and appropriate for that attribute.

In one sense, Rel-Tags are similar to the META tags that some people add to the head section of XHTML pages. However, they are slightly different in that they are visible. Their visibility makes them a more honest attempt at identifying the content. In the past, many sites have abused META tags by adding them excessively or falsely, in the hope that search engines would misidentify the site as highly relevant to a search subject. For this reason, many of the major search engines have stopped using META tags completely. By adding Rel-Tags to appropriate links on your XHTML pages, you provide this metadata, but in a way that is less prone to abuse. You can get more information on `Rel-Tag` at `http://microformats.org/wiki/reltag`.

Compound Microformats

Compound microformats are XHTML versions of other formats, built using XHTML elements and elemental microformats. The intent is to embed them in XHTML pages. They provide information to both users and applications viewing the page. Three of the most significant compound microformats include:

- **hCard:** An XHTML representation of the vCard standard for contact information.
- **hCalendar:** An XHTML representation of the iCalendar standard for calendaring and events information.
- **hReview:** An XHTML representation for review (as in movie, book, or music reviews) information.

hCard

hCard is a proposed structure for contact information in XHTML, based on the vCard format. Although vCard is text-based, it is not XML. hCard is a combination of recommended structure and class names. The class names provide hooks to provide for additional styling, as well as metadata about the content. Listing 3-13 shows a sample hCard block.

Listing 3-13: hCard

```
<div class="vcard">
 <a class="url fn n" href="http://www.example.com">
 <span class="given-name">John</span>
 <span class="middle-initial">J.</span> <span class="family-name">Bull</span></a>

 <div class="org">Example Corp.</div>
 <div class="adr">
  <div class="street-address">123 Any Drive</div>
  <span class="locality">Springfield</span>,
  <span class="region">KY</span>
  <span class="postal-code">40069</span>
 </div>

 <div class="tel">+1(859) 555-1212</div>
 <a class="url" href="http://blog.johnjbull.com">Home Page</a>
 <a class="email" href="mailto:jbull@example.com">Contact</a>
</div>
```

The hCard information is wrapped in a `div` with an attribute of `vcard`. Within the hCard, the individual elements of the contact item are created in a mixture of `div`, `span`, and `a` tags. The class of these tags clarifies the information's true meaning. The applications processing this block of XHTML can process the data. Humans looking at this block without any style information can still read it (see Figure 3-11). Addition of a simple style sheet can greatly alter the view for humans (see Figure 3-12), without changing the data available for applications processing the hCard.

John J. Bull
Example Corp.
123 Any Drive
Springfield, KY 40069
+1(859) 555-1212
Home Page Contact

Figure 3-11

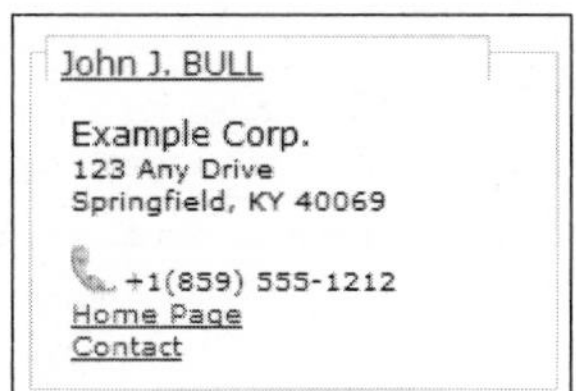

Figure 3-12

hCalendar

hCalendar is a proposed structure for date and event information using XHTML. It is based on the iCalendar standard of the IETF made popular by Apple with their iCal product. It is an excellent way of including event information within XML that is not directly associated with a specific calendaring application. Listing 3-14 shows an example of hCalendar.

Listing 3-14: hCalendar

```
<div class="vevent">
  <abbr class="dtstart" title="20060104T0900-0800">
    January 4, 2006 - 09:00
  </abbr> -
  <abbr class="dtend" title="20060104T1500-0800">
    15:00
    </abbr>
 -   <span class="summary">
     Meeting Planning Meeting
   </span> - at
  <span class="location">
     Room 13
   </span>
   <div class="description">
      We need to use this time to plan an upcoming meeting.
 Lunch will not be provided.
    </div>
</div>
```

The entire calendar item is wrapped in a `div` tag, with a class of `vevent`. Within the `div`, `spans`, and additional `divs` provide the information. The most notable aspect of the hCalendar format is how dates are written. The `abbr` tag is used to identify the start and end dates (and times) of the event. The `title` attribute of the element contains the ISO 8601 version of the date and time (in the previous example, January 4, 2006, 9:00 am in the US Pacific time zone), whereas the content is a more user-friendly rendering of the date and time. This provides useful information to any application processing the hCalendar data, without forcing users to employ that format.

Internet Explorer (version 6.0 and below) does not have support for the `abbr` *element. Or rather, it supports it, but does nothing with it. Other browsers, such as Netscape, Firefox, and Opera render the tag with a dotted underline (as seen in Figure 3-13). Safari behaves intermediately — the tooltip works, but the text is not rendered with the dotted underline.*

January 4, 2006 - 09:00 - 15:00 - Meeting Planning Meeting - at Room 13
We need to use this time to plan an upcoming meeting. Lunch will not be provided.
20060104T0900-0800

Figure 3-13

hReview

hReview is a proposed structure for product reviews on Web pages. It is a combination of a recommended structure, along with recommended class names. A simple hReview block looks like the code in Listing 3-15 (from the specification).

Listing 3-15: hReview

```
<div class="hreview">
 <span><span class="rating">5</span> out of 5 stars</span>
 <h4 class="summary"><span class="item fn">Crepes on Cole</span> is awesome</h4>
 <span>Reviewer: <span class="reviewer fn">Tantek</span> -
 <abbr class="dtreviewed" title="20050418T2300-0700">April 18, 2005</abbr></span>
 <blockquote class="description"><p>
  Crepes on Cole is one of the best little creperies in San Francisco.
  Excellent food and service. Plenty of tables in a variety of sizes
  for parties large and small.  Window seating makes for excellent
  people watching to/from the N-Judah which stops right outside.
  I've had many fun social gatherings here, as well as gotten
  plenty of work done thanks to neighborhood WiFi.
 </p></blockquote>
 <p>Visit date: <span>April 2005</span></p>
 <p>Food eaten: <span>Florentine crepe</span></p>
</div>
```

The entire hReview is enclosed in a `div` tag, with a class of `hreview`. In addition, appropriate `span` tags are identified in the block with the addition of class attributes. The review itself is enclosed in a `blockquote` tag with a class of `description`. Finally, the date and time of the review are included using an abbreviation (`abbr`) tag that includes the date and time in ISO 8601 format (year month day T time timezone). For example, May 4, 2006 at 3:02 AM in the Pacific Time Zone would be written as 20060504T0302-700. Even without an added stylesheet, this is perfectly readable (see Figure 3-14). In addition, applications can extract useful information from the page, including the reviewer, the item reviewed, the rating, and the text of the review. You can get more information about hReview at `microformats.org/wiki/hreview`.

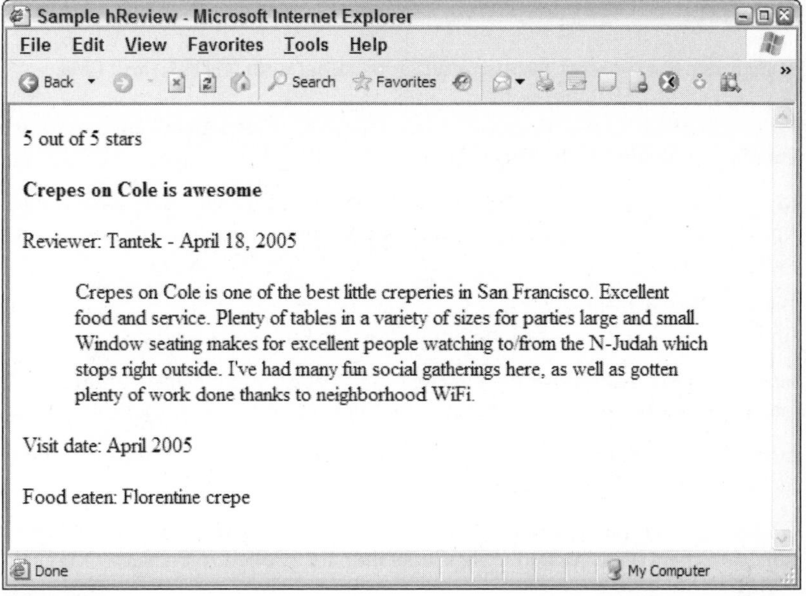

Figure 3-14

Summary

By migrating your HTML development to make it fully XHTML, you gain a number of benefits. It becomes easier for you and your applications to validate and parse XHTML. You can also use all the XML tools and technologies for processing your pages. For example, if your content is valid XML, you can more easily perform XSLT or XQuery with the content. Processing becomes simpler as well because you no longer have to worry about empty tags, case insensitivity, or unquoted attributes.

By changing your formatting to use CSS throughout, you are reducing the bandwidth needs of your XHTML (or HTML) pages and making your site easier to maintain. Rather than scanning through all your pages, you now change selectors in one place and have that change applied to all pages. CSS also provides more flexibility in formatting than other technologies.

Microformats are an intriguing development for embedding semantic information directly in XHTML pages (or other XML files). Although not a standard or even proposed to any standards body, many microformats are based on standards, and a number of people are working to maintain consistency in their use. Future developments may make them easier to include in your pages, and future search engines may extract the information they provide, making searches more valid and accurate.

Resources

This section includes some useful resources when working with XHTML and CSS.

- **World Wide Web Consortium (**`w3.org`**):** The W3C is responsible for standardizing many XML-related technologies, including XHTML and CSS.
- **Tidy (**`http://tidy.sourceforge.net`**):** Download the current source or binaries for Tidy for a variety of platforms. In addition, this contains links to documentation and many language wrappers.
- **Charlie's Tidy Add-ons (**`http://users.rcn.com/creitzel/tidy.html`**):** Tidy UI for Windows and language wrappers for COM, .NET, C++ and Perl.
- **Online XHTML Validator (**`http://validator.w3.org`**):** Handy online way to quickly check a page or block of text to determine if it is XHTML and to identify problems with the code.
- **Online CSS Validator (**`http://jigsaw.w3.org/css-validator/`**):** Online validator to quickly check a CSS file for conformance with the standards.
- **CSS Zen Garden (**`csszengarden.com`**):** An amazing example of what can be done with CSS. Many designers have created style sheets that are applied to the same XHTML, radically altering the resulting view.

4

XSL-FO

This chapter presents a reference and detailed examples of using the features of XSL-FO (e**X**tensible **S**tylesheet **L**anguage - **F**ormatting **O**bjects). It is used to specify the formatting semantics of documents using an XML format.

XSL-FO is used to produce formatted output from an XML data source. One problem of Web based applications has been the difficulty of producing quality printable output to create presentation quality documents available from the browser. XSL-FO, in conjunction with Scalable Vector Graphics (Chapter 5), gives you the tools to provide this service to users in common Web formats.

XSL-FO builds on the other Web based styling technologies like Cascading Style Sheets (CSS(2)), Document Style Semantics and Specification Language (DSSSL). The W3C used these technologies, which were aimed primarily for browser rendering to produce a specification for paginated output not solely targeted to the Web browser. This led to the W3C specification for XSL, which includes XSL-FO and for e**X**tensible **S**tylesheet **L**anguage **T**ransformation (XSLT).

Although this chapter concentrates on producing output documents for printing, the XSL-FO specification provides for other mediums of electronic communication such as text to speech. XSL-FO also includes multilingual support including options for right-to-left, bottom-to-top languages.

At the moment, Web browsers cannot directly display pages marked up with XML-FO objects. To produce output from XSL-FO documents, you use an XSL-FO processor. Examples of the common output supported by free-to-download processors include PDF, Text, PCL and PS.

If you wish to work through the examples presented in this chapter, you need several prerequisites. The applications required for the examples plus alternative applications are listed and examined later in the chapter.

Initially, I present a detailed overview of XSL, where XSL-FO fits in to the XML family, examples of where XSL-FO can be used and a detailed overview of the syntax and properties of the key areas of the XSL-FO implementation.

The Composition of XSL

XSL is a W3C standard developed to allow for the application of stylesheets to XML data. There are three parts to XSL as shown in Figure 4-1.

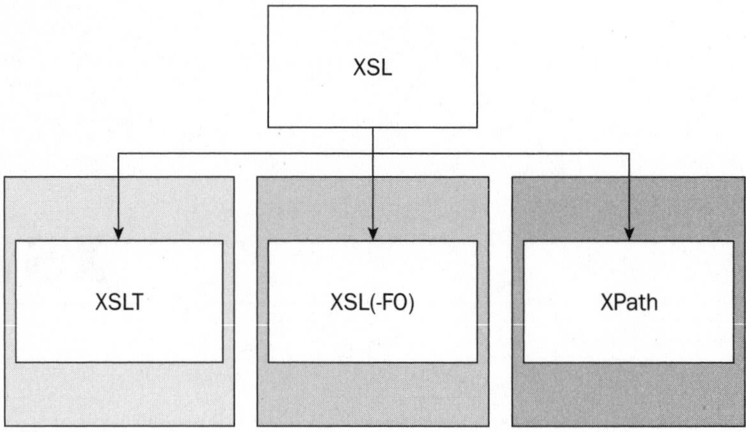

Figure 4-1

Some consider XSL to be composed of only XSLT and XSL-FO but XPath was also required to satisfy the requirements of a transformation and formatting standard. The list that follows gives a short explanation of each of the components.

- **Transformation (XSLT)** — Applying transformations to XML data. This can be used to create other data formats, sort existing data, or query the XML data by selection.
- **Formatting (XSL(-FO))** — The main subject of this chapter, it allows, the formatting of XML data using defined structures.
- **Selection (XPath)** — XPath provides the capability to address sections of the XML document tree.

Transformation is by far the most well-known of the XSL components and inherently utilizes XPath to select the XML data to transform. Both these topics are covered in detail in chapters 9 & 10 but I also use them in an example later in the chapter. Also, XSLT is commonly the first step in producing an XML structure capable of being used with XSL-FO to produce formatted output.

The full specification for XSL can be found on the W3C site w3.org/TR/xsl/. This is a full technical specification that is targeted at developers of processing engines and can be used as a developer's reference. It is most certainly not a tutorial! The site is however very useful as a reference and does explain some of the aims and benefits of the specification.

Some of the potential uses for XSL are shown in Figure 4-2.

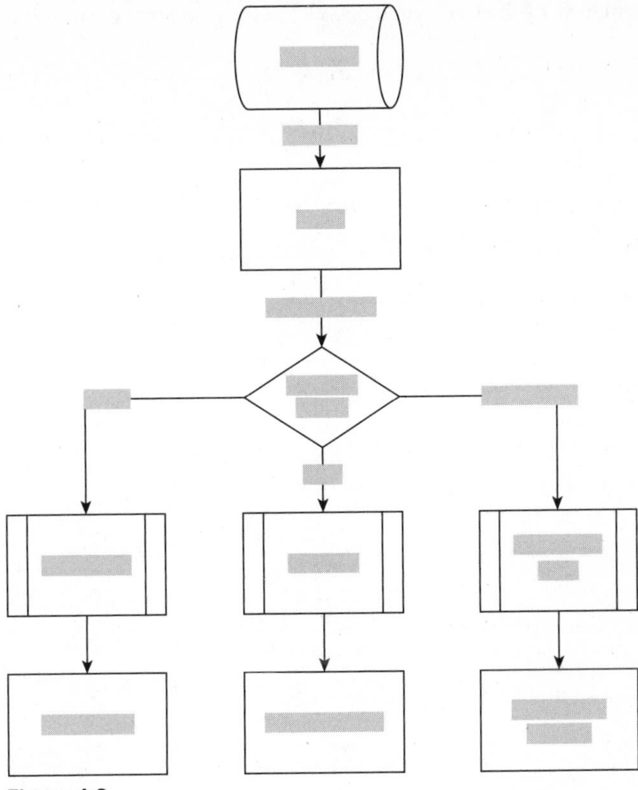

Figure 4-2

In the preceding example, the application extracts data from a data source such as a database, text file or another XML data source. The XSLT transforms the source to a defined XML tree structure in preparation for applying further transformations to the data. Depending on the desired destination, you can apply a stylesheet to the data to produce the appropriate output.

In the previous example, the application applies XSLT to the source, selecting appropriate data to be output within HTML tags. An XSL-FO stylesheet is applied to the source defining the pagination and format of the data to be output in Adobe PDF format. The final transformation performs an XML-to-XML transform to produce a SOAP packet.

You work through an example like this later in the chapter. First, however, you go through the basics of XSL-FO.

XSL-FO Overview

The namespace for XSL-FO is `http://www.w3.org/1999/XSL/Format`. The example that follows shows how the `xsl-fo` namespace is generally introduced using the alias `"fo"`.

```
<?xml version="1.0"?>
<fo:root xmlns:fo="http://www.w3.org/1999/XSL/Format">
```

This and subsequent examples in this book use `fo` as the alias for the namespace.

Each page is split into the following types of areas:

- **Region** — The main area of the page. This is split into further sub-regions as show later in this section.
- **Block Area** — Areas of content such as tables, lists and paragraphs.
- **Line Area** — Areas inside a block that contains one line of text.
- **Inline Area** — Lowest level of an area. An inline area can be a single character. Generally, this is used to display graphics or to insert auto-text or serve as a placeholder for calculations.

Figure 4-3 shows the hierarchical nature of these areas.

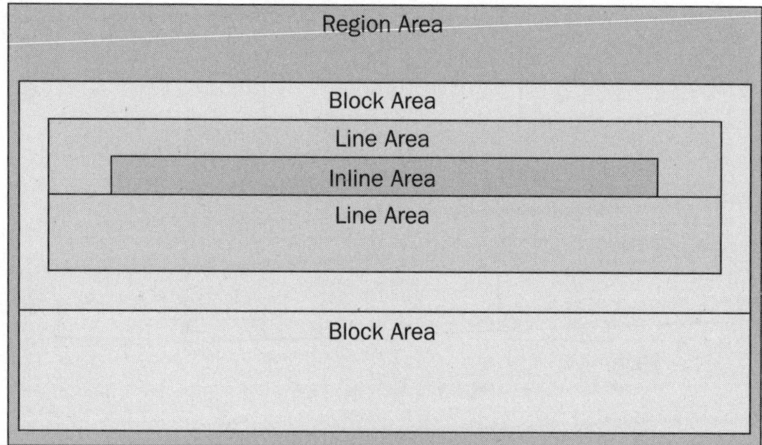

Figure 4-3

You can see how the region area is split on a per page basis by the XSL-FO area tags. Figure 4-4 shows the different areas available within a page followed by a short description of each. Note that a page is contextual in that the size and length of a page is dependent on the output type. For example, a Web page is considered one long page, whereas a PDF document the size of the page is restricted by the selected paper size.

The header and footer regions are self-evident terms. The width of these regions is set to the width of the page; only the height of this region can be set. The header region is defined by the element `fo:region-before` and the footer is defined in by the `fo:region-end` element. One of the previously mentioned features of XSL-FO is support for multiple languages. When the chosen language is a dialect that is read or written from bottom to top, `fo:region:start` is at the foot of the page and `fo:region-end` is at the head.

The start and end regions are the left and right regions of the page. Notice I didn't specify which was which! Again, for multilingual support, the start and end regions can be either on the left or right side of the page. For this example, the start region is the left region of the page and the end region is the right. The height of the start and end regions, is the height of the body region. The width can be set through an attribute for each of the elements.

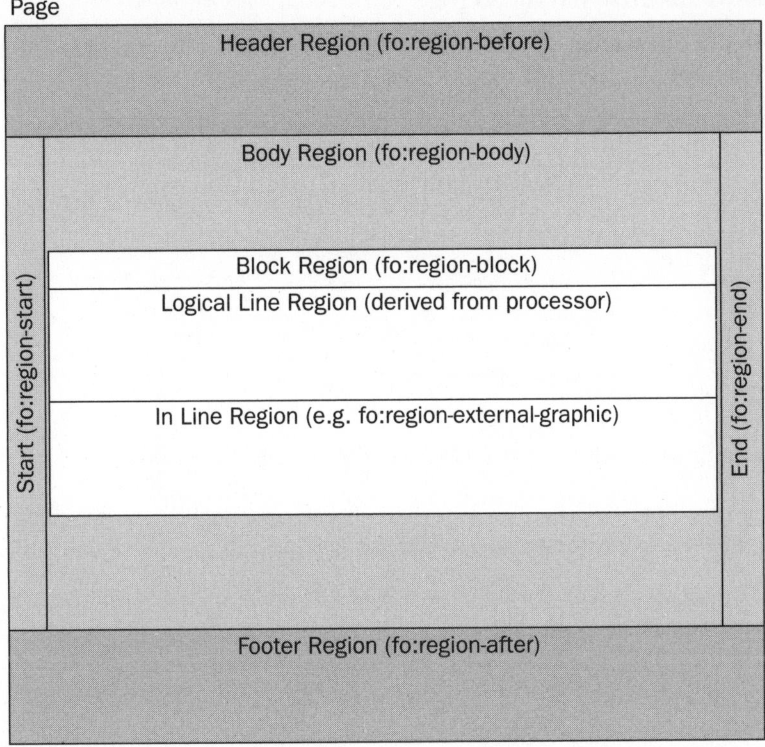

Figure 4-4

No width or height attributes are available for the body region these attributes are defined by the page settings. The body region is the size of the page less any margins set on the page level attributes. The page is discussed in the next section and an example clarifies how the dimensions are determined. The body can actually overlap the header and footer regions if the attributes of the regions are not correctly set.

Page Templates

Now that you understand the structure and breakdown of a page and regions, look at some of the XSL-FO elements that define the settings for each. The first element is the simple page master.

fo:simple-page-master

This element is used to specify the settings for a page. More than one `fo:simple-page-master` can exists in an XSL-FO document, but each page references only one page master template. Each page master is hosted within the `fo:layout-master-set` element. The following settings for a master page template are available:

- **Margin properties** -- margin-top, margin-bottom, margin-left, margin-right
- **master-name** — The name by which any subsequent elements refer to the template
- **page-height** — The height of the page

- **page-width** — The width of the page
- **reference-orientation** — Specifies the rotation (0, 90, 180, 270, -90, -180, -270) in degrees of the area content
- **writing-mode** — Specifies the direction of text. The available values are:
    - lr-tb - l(eft)r(ight)-t(op)b(ottom)
    - rl-tb
    - tb-rl
    - lr
    - rl
    - tb

Each of these setting is specified as an attribute of the `fo:simple-page-master`.

Now look at an example template. The code that follows sets a page master template with a one centimeter margin on each side on a standard A4 size page.

```
<fo:layout-master-set>
  <fo:simple-page-master
      master-name="A4"
      page-height="29.7cm"
      page-width="21cm"
      margin-top="1.0cm"
      margin-bottom="1.0cm"
      margin-left="1.0cm"
      margin-right="1.0cm">
      <fo:region-body/>
   </fo:simple-page-master>
</fo:layout-master-set>
```

The preceding code sets up the page, but you now want to specify the dimensions of the region areas such as the header, footer and body. You can achieve this by adding the appropriate elements into the page master definition. The code that follows shows how to setup the header, footer and body regions by setting the `margin` and `extent` attributes. The `extent` attribute is the height for header and footer regions, and width for the start and end regions. Only one dimension can be set for each of these areas.

```
<fo:layout-master-set>
  <fo:simple-page-master
    master-name="A4"
    page-height="29.7cm"
    page-width="21cm"
    margin-top="1.0cm"
    margin-bottom="1.0cm"
    margin-left="1.0cm"
    margin-right="1.0cm">
    <fo:region-before extent="1.0cm"/>
    <fo:region-body   margin="1.0cm"/>
    <fo:region-after  extent="1.0cm"/>
  </fo:simple-page-master>
</fo:layout-master-set>
```

Figure 4-5 shows how the settings in the preceding code render the page.

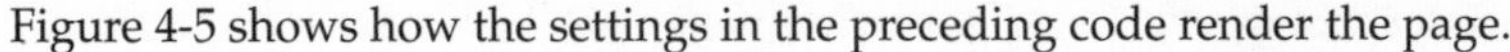

Figure 4-5

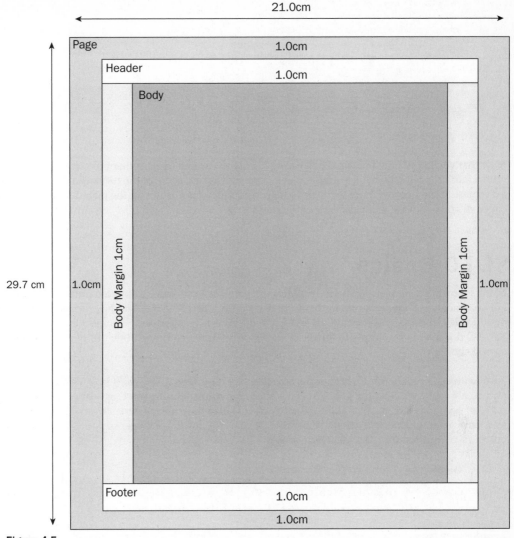

To define a page, the `fo:page-sequence` element is used. One of the attributes of this element is named `master-reference` and is a reference to the page master to be used as the layout template for the page. All the code for the page is stored within the `fo:page-sequence` element. The following code shows an example of this.

```
<fo:layout-master-set>
  <fo:simple-page-master
    master-name="A4"
    page-height="29.7cm"
    page-width="21cm"
```

```
      margin-top="1.0cm"
      margin-bottom="1.0cm"
      margin-left="1.0cm"
      margin-right="1.0cm">
      <fo:region-before extent="1.0cm"/>
      <fo:region-body   margin="1.0cm"/>
      <fo:region-after  extent="1.0cm"/>
    </fo:simple-page-master>
  </fo:layout-master-set>

  <fo:page-sequence master-reference="A4">

  </fo:page-sequence>
```

Now that you know how the regions hang together, you can put some content into them. Here, you start with a fairly simple *hello world* example, but as you go through some of the formatting features, the examples should become more valuable to help you understand. After all the main features have been covered, you begin the main example of the chapter.

XSL-FO Basics

In the following examples you need an XML-FO processor to produce formatted output from your XML-FO documents. All the examples in this section are presented using the Apache processor that can be downloaded from `http://xml.apache.org/fop/`. This is an open-source project that processes the XSL-FO document you supply to the designated output. It is a command line utility and its syntax is discussed shortly.

Also, with a Microsoft Windows operating system you may need a Microsoft Java Virtual Machine. If you do not know whether the Java VM is installed, run or install software diagnostics such as Belarc Advisor (`www.belarc.com`) to audit the software installed on your machine. If you do not have the Java VM, you can download and install the service. Because Microsoft no longer supports the Java VM, various third party sites now provide the download:

- `techtips4u.com/downloads/#MSJavx86`
- `download.windowsupdate.com/msdownload/update/v3-19990518/cabpool/MSJavWU_8073687b82d41db93f4c2a04af2b34d.exe`

In order to make the examples a little easier, you can download the XMLSpy suite of applications on a free 30 day trial from `altova.com`. This provides an XML, XSL, XSLT editor and also a convenient download as a plug in which will install the Apache FOP and configure XMLSpy to use it. This enables you to create a project with an XML document source, XSLT to transform the data into an XSL-FO document and instruct XMLSpy to process the resulting XSL-FO document into PDF. All the subsequent examples in this chapter will use this method and therefore is the recommended method (You still need the Java VM for Microsoft platforms). In scenarios when you wish to see the results of your XSL-FO document in another format, you can use the Apache FOP directly through the command line.

In order to view the examples later in the chapter, you need Adobe Acrobat Reader as this will be the chosen output for the examples.

Hello World for XSL-FO

The following code shows a sample XSL-FO doc for the Hello World example.

```
<?xml version="1.0" encoding="ISO-8859-1"?>
<fo:root xmlns:fo="http://www.w3.org/1999/XSL/Format">

   <fo:layout-master-set>
    <fo:simple-page-master
      master-name="A4"
      page-height="29.7cm"
      page-width="21cm"
      margin-top="1.0cm"
      margin-bottom="1.0cm"
      margin-left="1.0cm"
      margin-right="1.0cm">
      <fo:region-body   margin="1.0cm"/>
      <fo:region-before extent="1.0cm"/>
      <fo:region-after  extent="1.0cm"/>
      </fo:simple-page-master>
      </fo:layout-master-set>

      <fo:page-sequence master-reference="A4">
            <fo:flow flow-name="xsl-region-body">
                  <fo:block>Hello World</fo:block>
            </fo:flow>
      </fo:page-sequence>

</fo:root>
```

Using the command prompt, run the XSL-FO code through the Apache Formatting Objects Processor (FOP). Your command line resembles the following:

```
fop hello.xml -txt hello.txt
```

Run through the Apache Formatting Objects Processor (FOP), the output for a text file looks like the screen in Figure 4-6.

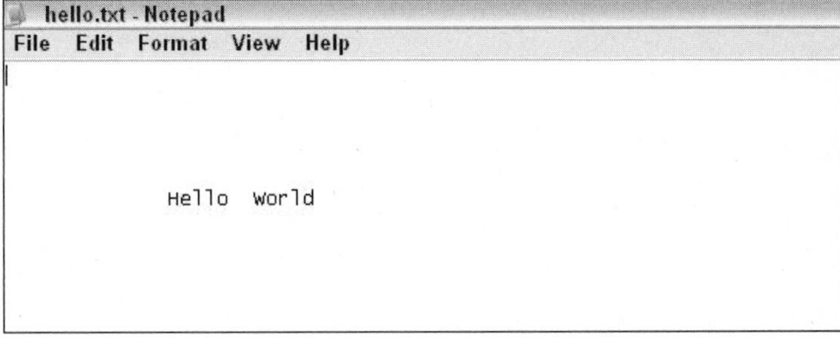

Figure 4-6

If you change the output to a PDF file, as follows:

```
fop hello.xml -pdf hello.pdf
```

The output looks like what you see in Figure 4-7.

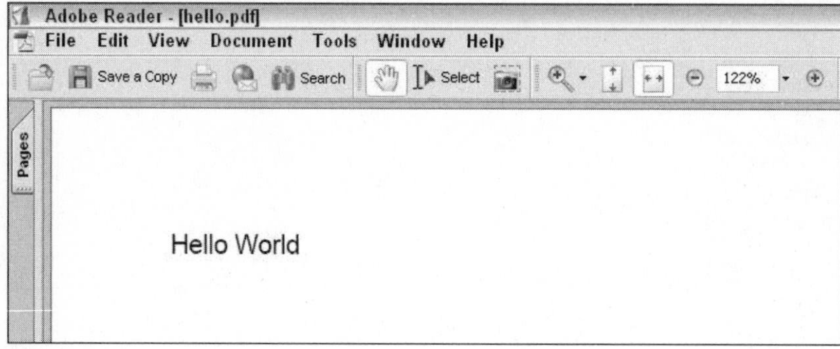

Figure 4-7

Not exactly earth-shattering, but this example enables you to try out using the Apache FOP and is a starting point for looking at some of the other features available within XSL-FO.

Note that the `fo:flow` element in the source XML-FO. The `fo:flow` element is the root level element for all subsequent content. The `fo:flow` does not create an area, areas are created for all the child elements contained within the open and closing tags in the order in which they appear. In our example, the child element is an `fo:block` containing the Hello World text.

Within the fo:flow the attribute flow-name specifies where in the page the flow will be rendered. The allowed values correspond to the regions discussed earlier in the list of possible values:

- `xsl-region-body` — Body
- `xsl-region-before` — Header
- `xsl-region-after` — Footer
- `xsl-region-start` — Left
- `xsl-region-end` — Right

The `fo:block` element usually host paragraphs, tables captions and so on. Formatting is applied to all elements within the block unless the child elements override the formatting. This is a form of inheritance within the XSL-FO model whereby the child elements inherit the formatting properties of their parents or they can override the settings by specifying their own property values.

To apply a font to the text you add the following:

```
<fo:flow flow-name="xsl-region-body">
       <fo:block font-size="20pt" font-weight="bold"
           font-family="verdana">Hello World
</fo:block>
</fo:flow>
```

Basic Formatting

Begin by putting together a slightly better example than our Hello World application. Consider the following XML listing. This is a set of postal codes and that demonstrate some of the basic formatting.

```
<?xml version="1.0" encoding="UTF-8"?>
<ROOT>
  <PostCode>
      <PostCode>G1</PostCode>
      <City>Glasgow</City>
   </PostCode>
   <PostCode>
      <PostCode>EH1</PostCode>
      <City>Edinburgh</City>
   </PostCode>
   <PostCode>
      <PostCode>PA1</PostCode>
      <City>Paisley</City>
   </PostCode>
   <PostCode>
      <PostCode>NE5</PostCode>
      <City>Newcastle</City>
   </PostCode>
</ROOT>
```

You can generate a basic list of all the postcodes and cities they relate to. The following XSLT produces an XML-FO to list each of the postcode elements.

```
<?xml version="1.0"?>
<xsl:stylesheet version="1.0"
  xmlns:xsl="http://www.w3.org/1999/XSL/Transform"
  xmlns:fo="http://www.w3.org/1999/XSL/Format">

  <xsl:template match="/">
   <fo:root xmlns:fo="http://www.w3.org/1999/XSL/Format">

    <fo:layout-master-set>

      <fo:simple-page-master
         master-name="A4"
         page-width="29.7cm"
         page-height="21cm"
         margin-top="1cm"
         margin-bottom="1cm"
         margin-left="1cm"
         margin-right="1cm">
      <fo:region-body/>
      </fo:simple-page-master>

      </fo:layout-master-set>

      <fo:page-sequence master-reference="A4">

      <fo:flow flow-name="xsl-region-body">
          <xsl:apply-templates select="//ROOT/PostCode"/>
```

```
        </fo:flow>

      </fo:page-sequence>

    </fo:root>
  </xsl:template>

  <xsl:template match="//ROOT/PostCode">
    <fo:block><xsl:value-of select="PostCode"/>-<xsl:value-of
select="City"/></fo:block>
  </xsl:template>

</xsl:stylesheet>
```

Using XMLSpy, you can apply the transformation to the XML and view the results in any of the following formats:

- **PDF** — Default
- **Text** — Standard textual representation of results
- **XML** — An XML area tree
- **MIF** — Maker Interchange Format
- **PCL** — Printer Control Language
- **Postscript** — Adobe postscript format

When you take the default PDF, the results look like the screen in Figure 4-8.

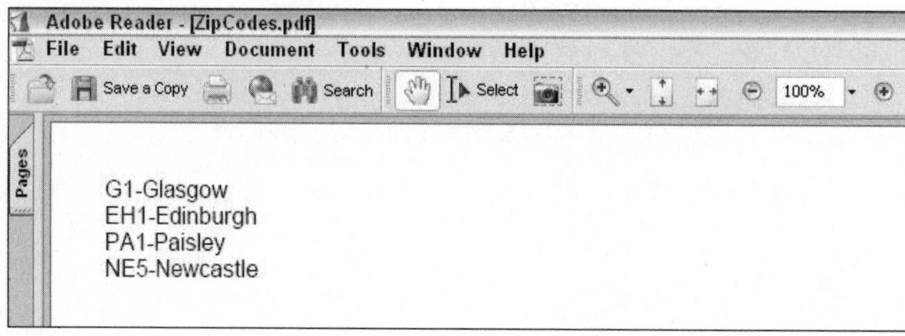

Figure 4-8

Lists

You can now change the transformation to produce XSL-FO that renders the XML using a bulleted list. The `fo:list-block` element contains `fo:list-item` elements which in turn must contain a `fo:list-item:label` and one or more `fo:list-item-body` elements. The `fo-list-item` is optional because it is implicit within the `fo:list-block`. The `fo:list-item-label` allows us to insert a bullet character or as we shall see shortly, a bullet image. The `fo:list-body`, contains the list items themselves.

Within either the `fo:list-block` or `fo:list-body`, you can specify any indents we wish to apply. The attributes `start-indent` and `end-indent` allow us to specify the indent in millimeters, centimeters, etc. There is also a special indent function `body-start()` that sets the start-indent to value calculated from `provisional-distance-between-starts`. The `provisional-distance-between-starts` can be set to a value at the `fo-list-block` element.

```
        <fo:page-sequence master-reference="A4">
          <fo:flow flow-name="xsl-region-body">
                    <fo:list-block provisional-distance-between-starts="2.0cm">
                         <xsl:apply-templates select="//ROOT/PostCode"/>
                        </fo:list-block>
          </fo:flow>

        </fo:page-sequence>

        </fo:root>
    </xsl:template>

    <xsl:template match="//ROOT/PostCode">
        <fo:list-item>
              <fo:list-item-label start-indent="1.0cm" end-indent="1.0cm">
                    <fo:block >
                          <fo:external-graphic src="C:\Wrox\Professional
  XML\Chp4\Code\POSTITL.jpg" content-height="0.5cm"/>
                    </fo:block>
              </fo:list-item-label>
              <fo:list-item-body start-indent="body-start()" >
              <fo:block >
                    <xsl:value-of select="PostCode"/>-<xsl:value-of select="City"/>
              </fo:block>
             </fo:list-item-body>
        </fo:list-item>
    </xsl:template>
```

This code produces the following output shown in Figure 4-9.

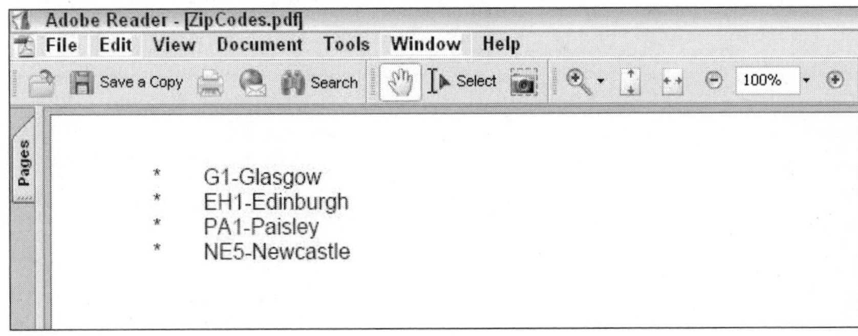

Figure 4-9

You can also use images as the bullet points or include them in the list (for example, a traffic light indicator or progress bar for a task list).

```
<xsl:template match="//ROOT/PostCode">
  <fo:list-item>
      <fo:list-item-label start-indent="1.0cm" end-indent="1.0cm">
          <fo:block >
              <fo:external-graphic src="C:\Wrox\Professional
XML\Chp4\Code\POSTITL.jpg" content-height="0.5cm"/>
              </fo:block>
      </fo:list-item-label>
      <fo:list-item-body start-indent="body-start()" >
          <fo:block >
              <xsl:value-of select="PostCode"/>-<xsl:value-of select="City"/>
          </fo:block>
      </fo:list-item-body>
  </fo:list-item>
</xsl:template>
```

The output is shown in Figure 4-10.

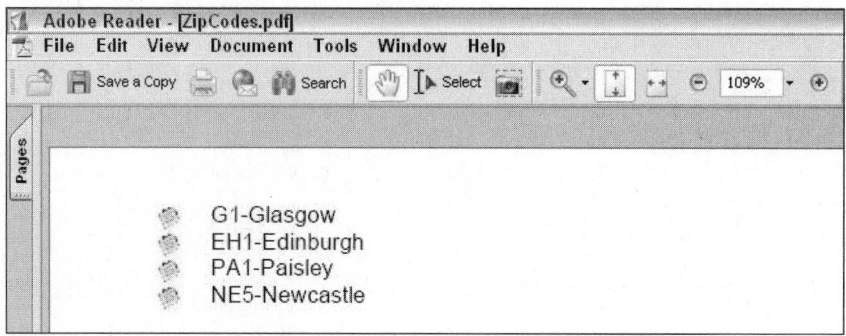

Figure 4-10

Tables

You can put this detail into a neatly formatted table. First, look at the HTML table with XSL-FO elements and attribute equivalents:

HTML	XSL-FO Element	Description/Values
`<TABLE>`	`fo:table-and-caption`	Table and optional caption
`<TH>`	`fo:table-header`	Table header
`<TR>`	`fo:table-row`	Table row
`<TD>`	`fo:table-cell`	Table cell
`<COLUMN>`	`fo-table-column`	Table column
`<TBODY>`	`fo:table-body`	Table body
`<TFOOT>`	`fo-table-footer`	Table footer

HTML	XSL-FO Attribute	Description/Values
<COLSPAN>	number-columns-spanned	number of columns to span on table-cell element
<ROWSPAN>	number of rows to span	number of rows to span in table-row element
NA	empty-cells	show or hide empty cells in table – default is show
NA	table-omit-header-at-break	if table spans multiple pages false (default) displays the header on each page; true does not.
NA	table-omit-footer-at-break	If table spans multiple pages false (default) displays the header on each page; true does not.
<TBODY>	fo:table-body	Table body
<TFOOT>	fo-table-footer	Table footer
<CELLPADDING>	padding-left, padding-right, padding-top, padding-bottom.	Specifies the padding width for cells.
<CELLSPACING>	NA	
Width	column-width	Specifies the width of the table column.

This code shows an example of the table structure within an XSLT that produces the XSL-FO document for sample postal codes.

```
<xsl:template match="/">
  <fo:root xmlns:fo="http://www.w3.org/1999/XSL/Format">

    <fo:layout-master-set>

      <fo:simple-page-master
              master-name="A4"
              page-width="29.7cm"
              page-height="21cm"
              margin-top="1cm"
              margin-bottom="1cm"
          margin-left="1cm"
          margin-right="1cm">
        <fo:region-body/>
      </fo:simple-page-master>

    </fo:layout-master-set>

    <fo:page-sequence master-reference="A4">

      <fo:flow flow-name="xsl-region-body">
```

```
                <fo:table>
                        <fo:table-column column-width="3cm"/>
                        <fo:table-column column-width="3cm"/>
                        <fo:table-body>
                             <fo:table-row background-color="silver">
                                <fo:table-cell border-style="solid" padding-
top="2px" padding-bottom="2px" padding-left="2px" padding-right="2px">
                                       fo:block>Postcode</fo:block>
                                        </fo:table-cell>
                                        <fo:table-cell border-style="solid" padding-
top="2px" padding-bottom="2px" padding-left="2px" padding-right="2px">
                                                 <fo:block>City</fo:block>
                                        </fo:table-cell>
                                </fo:table-row>
                                <xsl:apply-templates select="//ROOT/PostCode">
                                        <xsl:sort data-type="text" select="City"/>
                                </xsl:apply-templates>
                        </fo:table-body>
              </fo:table>
        </fo:flow>

      </fo:page-sequence>

    </fo:root>
  </xsl:template>

  <xsl:template match="//ROOT/PostCode">
 <fo:table-row>
       <fo:table-cell border-style="solid" padding-top="2px" padding-bottom="2px"
padding-left="2px" padding-right="2px">
                <fo:block><xsl:value-of select="PostCode"/></fo:block>
       </fo:table-cell>
         <fo:table-cell border-style="solid" padding-top="2px" padding-bottom="2px"
padding-left="2px" padding-right="2px">
               <fo:block><xsl:value-of select="City"/></fo:block>
        </fo:table-cell>
 </fo:table-row>
  </xsl:template>
```

The results of this transformation in PDF format are shown in Figure 4-11.

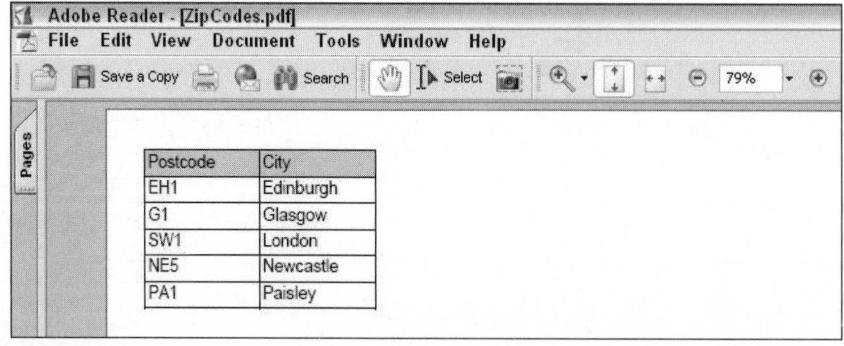

Figure 4-11

A Working Example

You now work through a real-world example to gain a more thorough understanding of the mechanics of the XSL-FO process. The example produces a printable invoice from a given XML set that is formatted and paginated appropriately and available to a consumer (a customer-facing Web site, for example) in PDF format.

A subset of the source XML for the example is shown in the following code (the full file can be downloaded from the companion Web site for this book at wrox.com):

> **It should be noted that depending on the software currently running on your computer, you may receive some warnings while processing and may receive slightly different output. This may also be the case if you are targeting a different browser (when rendering HTML).**
>
> **If you have to ensure the content is presented identically for every target browser, you should test on each target, make changes to the XSL-FO for that target, then your page should use client-side script to check which target you are running on and produce the content accordingly.**

```
<?xml version="1.0" encoding="UTF-8"?>
<ROOT DATE="19/06/2006" Time="10:41:09">
 <Invoice InvoiceID="4561598">
        <InvoiceID>4561598</InvoiceID>
        <ContractID>CH20721    </ContractID>
        <AccountNumber>002585</AccountNumber>
        <CustomerName>Smiths Construction</CustomerName>
        <CustomerAddress1>123 Glassford St</CustomerAddress1>
        <CustomerAddress2>Glasgow</CustomerAddress2>
        <CustomerAddress3>Lanarkshire</CustomerAddress3>
        <CustomerAddress4>Scotland</CustomerAddress4>
        <CustomerPostCode>G2 4YR</CustomerPostCode>
        <DeliveryAddress1>Carlisle Railway Station</DeliveryAddress1>
        <DeliveryAddress2>HARKER</DeliveryAddress2>
        <DeliveryAddress3>CARLISLE</DeliveryAddress3>
        <OrderNumber>TC258567</OrderNumber>
        <OrderName>MICK</OrderName>
        <InvoiceDate>30/06/06</InvoiceDate>
        <HireStatus>HIRE COMPLETE</HireStatus>
        <PreVATTotal>166.28</PreVATTotal>
        <VAT1>29.10</VAT1>
        <InvoiceTotal>195.38</InvoiceTotal>
        <CreditTerms>30</CreditTerms>
        <HireItem>
               <ProductCode>CHAA</ProductCode>
               <Description>JUNCTION BOX </Description>
               <FromDate>01/06/06</FromDate>
               <ToDate>21/06/06</ToDate>
               <Weeks>3.00</Weeks>
               <Rate>10.75</Rate>
               <Quantity>1</Quantity>
               <Discount>50.00</Discount>
               <VATCode>1</VATCode>
               <Value>16.14</Value>
```

```
        </HireItem>
        <HireItem>
                <ProductCode>CHXL 03206</ProductCode>
                <Description>EXT LEAD     </Description>
                <FromDate>01/06/06</FromDate>
                <ToDate>30/06/06</ToDate>
                <Weeks>4.40</Weeks>
                <Rate>1.25</Rate>
                <Quantity>1</Quantity>
                <VATCode>1</VATCode>
                <Value>5.50</Value>
        </HireItem>
        <HireItem>
                <ProductCode>CHXL 01917</ProductCode>
                <Description>EXT LEAD     </Description>
                <FromDate>01/06/06</FromDate>
                <ToDate>30/06/06</ToDate>
                <Weeks>4.40</Weeks>
                <Rate>1.25</Rate>
                <Quantity>1</Quantity>
                <VATCode>1</VATCode>
                <Value>5.50</Value>
        </HireItem>
        <SaleItem>
                <Description>STARTER KEY</Description>
                <Date>01/06/06</Date>
                <Quantity>1</Quantity>
                <Price>2.10</Price>
                <VATCode>1</VATCode>
                <Value>-2.10</Value>
        </SaleItem>
        <SaleItem>
                <Description>DRILL CHUCK KEY</Description>
                <Date>01/06/06</Date>
                <Quantity>1</Quantity>
                <Price>1.75</Price>
                <VATCode>1</VATCode>
                <Value>-1.75</Value>
        </SaleItem>
        <SaleItem>
                <Description>ALLEN KEY</Description>
                <Date>01/06/06</Date>
                <Quantity>1</Quantity>
                <Price>3.10</Price>
                <VATCode>1</VATCode>
                <Value>-3.10</Value>
       </SaleItem>
       <SaleItem>
                <Description>MISC</Description>
                <Date>01/06/06</Date>
                <Quantity>1</Quantity>
                <Price>3.10</Price>
                <VATCode>1</VATCode>
                <Value>-3.10</Value>
        </SaleItem>
  </Invoice>
 </ROOT>
```

The preceding XML represents an invoice produced for a customer who is being charged for hiring equipment from the providing company. The invoice is encapsulated within the <Invoice> tag and has child elements `<HireItem>` showing the specific invoicing details for every individual piece of equipment that has been hired by the customer.

The `<invoice>` section contains all the top level detail for the invoice, such as invoice number, customer details and summary values. The `<HireItem>` section contains the specifics about the equipment such as descriptions and rates charged. The `<SaleItem>` section contains a record of sales purchased by the customer.

The invoice you want to produce shows the invoice header information at the top of the invoice and provides a detailed breakdown of the equipment hired in a list following the header data.

Figure 4-12 shows a high-level layout for the invoice.

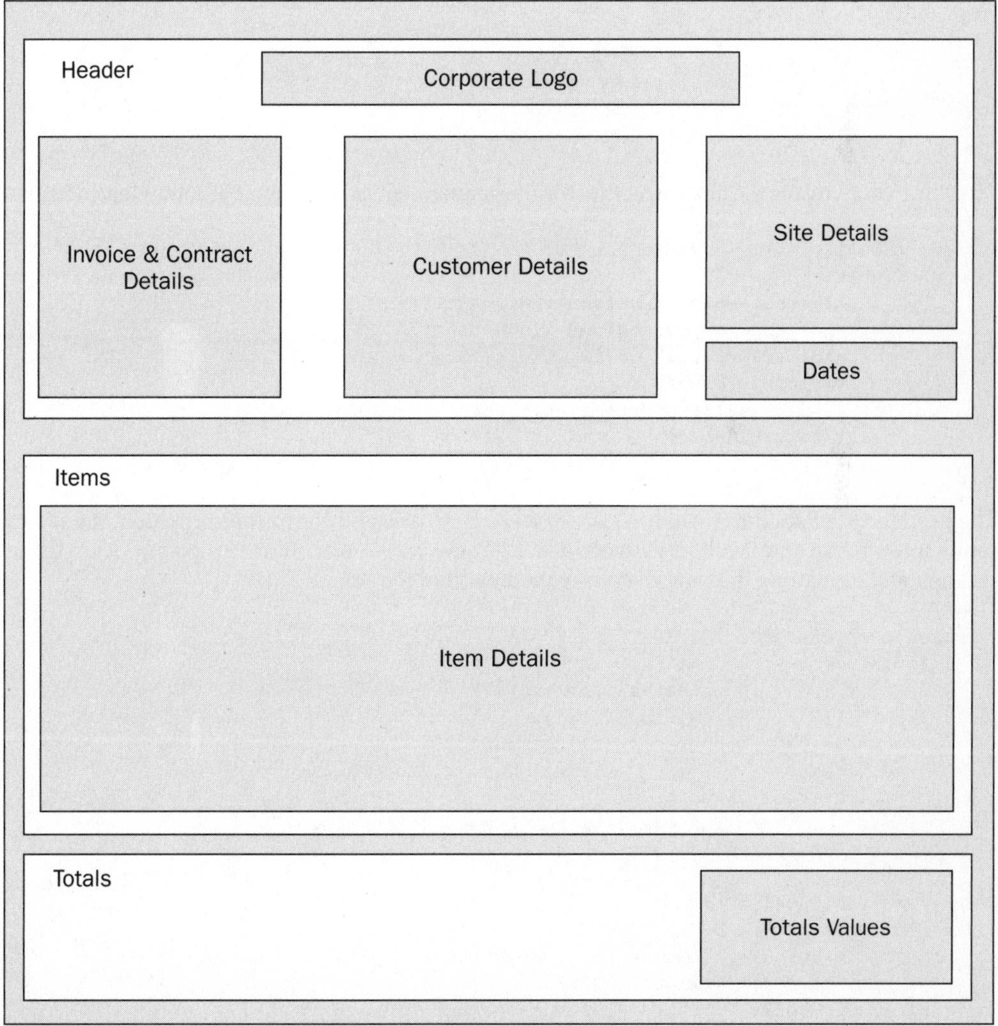

Figure 4-12

The header section has one table that holds the company logo and all the top level invoice details. You create a table and populate it using an apply-templates section for the ROOT/Invoice element.

The initial setup of the invoice, an A4 – landscape oriented format is shown in the following code:

```
<?xml version="1.0"?>
<xsl:stylesheet version="1.0" xmlns:xsl="http://www.w3.org/1999/XSL/Transform"
xmlns:fo="http://www.w3.org/1999/XSL/Format">
<xsl:template match="/">
 <fo:root xmlns:fo="http://www.w3.org/1999/XSL/Format">
       <fo:layout-master-set>
               <fo:simple-page-master master-name="A4"
                                      page-width="29.7cm"
                                      page-height="21cm"
                                      margin-top="1cm"
                                      margin-bottom="1cm"
                                      margin-left="1cm"
                                      margin-right="1cm">
                       <fo:region-body/>
                </fo:simple-page-master>
               </fo:layout-master-set>
               <fo:page-sequence master-reference="A4">
```

The XSLT code creates the table structure for the header data as shown in the following code:

```
<fo:flow flow-name="xsl-region-body">
 <fo:table>
         <fo:table-column column-width="9cm"/>
         <fo:table-column column-width="9cm"/>
         <fo:table-column column-width="9cm"/>
         <fo:table-body>
                <xsl:apply-templates select="//ROOT/Invoice"/>
         </fo:table-body>
         </fo:table>
```

The header comprises three columns. The first holds invoice and contract information, the second customer information and the third delivery details. The `apply-templates` section builds up the table by creating and formatting the cells with relevant data from the source XML.

```
<xsl:template match="//ROOT/Invoice">
 <fo:table-row       background-color="silver"
                     text-align="center"
                     width="27cm">
  <fo:table-cell number-columns-spanned="3">
   <fo:block>
    <fo:external-graphic
      src="C:\Wrox\Professional XML\Chp4\Code\AcmeLogo.JPG"
      content-height="0.5cm"/>
   </fo:block>
  </fo:table-cell>
 </fo:table-row>
 <fo:table-row       background-color="white"
                     width="27cm">
  <fo:table-cell     number-columns-spanned="3"
                     border-style="none">
```

```
    <fo:block font-family="serif" font-weight="bold" font-size="28pt">
      Hire Invoice
    </fo:block>
   </fo:table-cell>
  </fo:table-row>
  <fo:table-row       background-color="white"
                      width="100%">
   <fo:table-cell     padding="2px"
                      border-top-style="solid"
                      border-left-style="solid"
                      border-right-style="solid"
                      width="33%">
    <fo:block>
        Invoice:      <xsl:value-of select="InvoiceID"/>
    </fo:block>
   </fo:table-cell>
   <fo:table-cell     padding="2px"
                      border-top-style="solid"
                      border-left-style="solid"
                      border-right-style="solid"
                      width="33%">
    <fo:block  font-family="serif"
               font-weight="bold"
               font-size="14pt">
       Customer Details
    </fo:block>
   </fo:table-cell>
   <fo:table-cell       padding="2px"
                    border-top-style="solid"
                    border-left-style="solid"
                    border-right-style="solid"
                    width="33%"
                    text-align="right">
    <fo:block    font-family="serif"
          font-weight="bold"
          font-size="14pt">
  Site Address
    </fo:block>
   </fo:table-cell>
  </fo:table-row>
  <fo:table-row   background-color="white"
                  width="100%">
   <fo:table-cell        padding="2px"
                  border-left-style="solid"
                  border-right-style="solid"
                  width="33%">
    <fo:block>
  Contract:      <xsl:value-of select="ContractID"/>
    </fo:block>
   </fo:table-cell>
   <fo:table-cell       padding="2px"
                  border-left-style="solid"
                  border-right-style="solid"
                  width="33%">
    <fo:block>
```

```
        <xsl:value-of select="AccountNumber"/>
          </fo:block>
         </fo:table-cell>
         <fo:table-cell      padding="2px"
                        border-left-style="solid"
                        border-right-style="solid"
                        width="33%"
                        text-align="right">
          <fo:block>
        <xsl:value-of select="DeliveryAddress1"/>
          </fo:block>
         </fo:table-cell>
        </fo:table-row>
      </xsl:template>
```

The preceding code shows the first three rows of the header table. The subsequent header rows are identical to the last two rows with the exception of content.

Some new attributes are shown in the example that must be explained (these are bolded in the code). The first is the attribute `number-columns-spanned`. This enables you to create the HTML equivalent of COLSPAN on the table. For the logo and the header label you want the logo to span the three columns and be centered. You want the header to span the three columns and be left-aligned.

The second attribute is text-align. This attribute simply allows you to specify the alignment of the child content as `left`, `right`, or `center`.

The padding attribute sets the cell padding area that outlines the content. This can be broken down specifically using padding-top, padding-bottom, padding-left and padding-right. You can control cell padding for each dimension of the cell.

You can also applied various font attributes to some of the fo:block elements in the code. Some of the commonly used font attributes are shown in the following list:

- Font-family — Serif, sans-serif, fantasy etc
- Font-size — Can be specified in points, relatively (larger, smaller) or using constants (small, medium, large, x-large etc)
- Font-style — Normal, italic, oblique, backslant or inherit
- Font-weight — Constants (normal, bold, bolder or lighter) or an integer value representing the weighting.

Several attributes enable you to format the border of table cells. The border style is broken down into `border-top-style`, `border-bottom-style`, `border-left-style` and `border-right-style`; these can have the following values:

- **None** — No border
- **Solid** — Single pixel border
- **Dotted** — Single full stop broken border
- **Dashed** — Short line broken border

- **Hidden** — Same as none except when conflict occurs with borders for table elements
- **Double** — Double lined solid border. 1 pixel line, 1 pixel space, 1 pixel line
- **Inset** — Embedded cell style
- **Outset** — Raised cell style
- **Groove** — Embedded border style
- **Ridge** — Raised border style

If you create the subsequent rows for the header table and apply the transformation you achieve the results shown in Figure 4-13.

Figure 4-13

It should be noted that the presentation of the results on screen (in, for example, Adobe Acrobat) are not always exactly what will be printed. It is wise to periodically print to your target printer in order to check the results.

You now wish to show the payment terms on the invoice for the customer. This is just an `fo:block` element neatly formatted and presented under the header table.

```
<fo:block      padding="2px">
 Payment Terms: This invoice must be paid no later than
 <xsl:value-of select="//ROOT/Invoice/CreditTerms"/>
 from the invoice date.
</fo:block>
```

Next you want to render the series of hire item records in a table. First, you build up the table structure and the header record. The XSLT code that follows shows how to achieve this based on the XML data shown previously.

```
<fo:table padding="2px">
<fo:table-column column-width="4cm"/>
<fo:table-column column-width="5cm"/>
<fo:table-column column-width="3cm"/>
<fo:table-column column-width="3cm"/>
```

```
<fo:table-column column-width="2cm"/>
<fo:table-column column-width="2cm"/>
<fo:table-column column-width="2cm"/>
<fo:table-column column-width="2cm"/>
<fo:table-column column-width="2cm"/>
<fo:table-column column-width="2cm"/>
<fo:table-header border-style="solid">
<fo:table-row background-color="white">
<fo:table-cell number-columns-spanned="10">
 <fo:block font-family="serif" font-weight="bold" font-size="20pt">Hire
Items</fo:block>
</fo:table-cell>
</fo:table-row>
<fo:table-row background-color="silver">
<fo:table-cell padding="2px">
 <fo:block>Code</fo:block>
</fo:table-cell>
<fo:table-cell padding="2px">
 <fo:block>Description</fo:block>
</fo:table-cell>
<fo:table-cell padding="2px">
 <fo:block>From Date</fo:block>
</fo:table-cell>
<fo:table-cell padding="2px">
 <fo:block>To Date</fo:block>
</fo:table-cell>
<fo:table-cell padding="2px" text-align="right">
 <fo:block>Weeks</fo:block>
</fo:table-cell>
<fo:table-cell padding="2px" text-align="right">
 <fo:block>Rate</fo:block>
</fo:table-cell>
<fo:table-cell padding="2px" text-align="right">
 <fo:block>Quantity</fo:block>
</fo:table-cell>
<fo:table-cell padding="2px" text-align="right">
 <fo:block>VATCode</fo:block>
</fo:table-cell>
<fo:table-cell padding="2px" text-align="right">
 <fo:block>Discount</fo:block>
</fo:table-cell>
<fo:table-cell padding="2px" text-align="right">
 <fo:block>Value</fo:block>
</fo:table-cell>
</fo:table-row>
</fo:table-header>
<fo:table-body>
<xsl:apply-templates select="//ROOT/Invoice/HireItem"/>
</fo:table-body>
</fo:table>
```

This creates the header record for the list of items that have been hired by the customer on this particular contract. The `apply-templates` section creates and formats each of the records as cells of table shown in the previous code.

The XSLT code is shown here:

```
<xsl:template match="//ROOT/Invoice/HireItem">
 <fo:table-row background-color="white" width="100%">
  <fo:table-cell       border-left-style="solid"
              padding="2px"
              border-right-style="solid">
   <fo:block>
    <xsl:value-of select="ProductCode"/>
   </fo:block>
  </fo:table-cell>
  <fo:table-cell       border-left-style="solid"
              padding="2px"
              border-right-style="solid">
   <fo:block>
    <xsl:value-of select="Description"/>
   </fo:block>
  </fo:table-cell>
  <fo:table-cell       border-left-style="solid"
              padding="2px"
              border-right-style="solid">
   <fo:block>
    <xsl:value-of select="FromDate"/>
   </fo:block>
  </fo:table-cell>
  <fo:table-cell      border-left-style="solid"
              padding="2px"
              border-right-style="solid">
   <fo:block>
    <xsl:value-of select="ToDate"/>
   </fo:block>
  </fo:table-cell>
  <fo:table-cell      border-left-style="solid"
              padding="2px"
              border-right-style="solid">
   <fo:block>
    <xsl:value-of select="Weeks"/>
   </fo:block>
  </fo:table-cell>
  <fo:table-cell      border-left-style="solid"
              padding="2px"
              border-right-style="solid"
              text-align="right">
   <fo:block>
    <xsl:value-of select="Rate"/>
   </fo:block>
  </fo:table-cell>
  <fo:table-cell      border-left-style="solid"
              padding="2px"
              border-right-style="solid"
              text-align="right">
   <fo:block>
    <xsl:value-of select="Quantity"/>
   </fo:block>
```

```
    </fo:table-cell>
    <fo:table-cell        border-left-style="solid"
                 padding="2px"
                 border-right-style="solid"
                 text-align="right">
     <fo:block>
      <xsl:value-of select="VATCode"/>
     </fo:block>
    </fo:table-cell>
    <fo:table-cell        border-left-style="solid"
                 padding="2px"
                 border-right-style="solid"
                 text-align="right">
     <fo:block>
      <xsl:value-of select="Discount"/>
     </fo:block>
    </fo:table-cell>
    <fo:table-cell        border-left-style="solid"
                 padding="2px"
                 border-right-style="solid"
                 text-align="right">
     <fo:block>
      <xsl:value-of select="Value"/>
     </fo:block>
    </fo:table-cell>
    </fo:table-row>
  </xsl:template>
```

If this code is included with the previous XSLT code, the PDF in Figure 4-14 is produced.

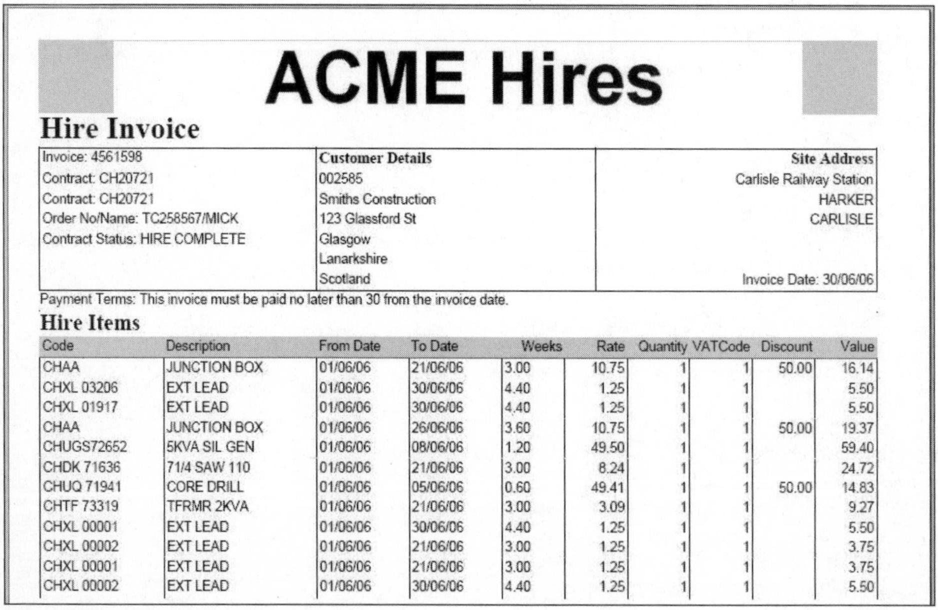

ACME Hires

Hire Invoice

Invoice: 4561598 Contract: CH20721 Contract: CH20721 Order No/Name: TC258567/MICK Contract Status: HIRE COMPLETE	**Customer Details** 002585 Smiths Construction 123 Glassford St Glasgow Lanarkshire Scotland	**Site Address** Carlisle Railway Station HARKER CARLISLE Invoice Date: 30/06/06

Payment Terms: This invoice must be paid no later than 30 from the invoice date.

Hire Items

Code	Description	From Date	To Date	Weeks	Rate	Quantity	VATCode	Discount	Value
CHAA	JUNCTION BOX	01/06/06	21/06/06	3.00	10.75	1	1	50.00	16.14
CHXL 03206	EXT LEAD	01/06/06	30/06/06	4.40	1.25	1	1		5.50
CHXL 01917	EXT LEAD	01/06/06	30/06/06	4.40	1.25	1	1		5.50
CHAA	JUNCTION BOX	01/06/06	26/06/06	3.60	10.75	1	1	50.00	19.37
CHUGS72652	5KVA SIL GEN	01/06/06	08/06/06	1.20	49.50	1	1		59.40
CHDK 71636	71/4 SAW 110	01/06/06	21/06/06	3.00	8.24	1	1		24.72
CHUQ 71941	CORE DRILL	01/06/06	05/06/06	0.60	49.41	1	1	50.00	14.83
CHTF 73319	TFRMR 2KVA	01/06/06	21/06/06	3.00	3.09	1	1		9.27
CHXL 00001	EXT LEAD	01/06/06	30/06/06	4.40	1.25	1	1		5.50
CHXL 00002	EXT LEAD	01/06/06	21/06/06	3.00	1.25	1	1		3.75
CHXL 00001	EXT LEAD	01/06/06	21/06/06	3.00	1.25	1	1		3.75
CHXL 00002	EXT LEAD	01/06/06	30/06/06	4.40	1.25	1	1		5.50

Figure 4-14

You created the header row of the hire items table as a `fo:table-header` because the number of records may cause the table to be rendered on several pages. If the number of hire items requires a new page, the header row is rendered on the second page.

If you add a sufficient number of hire items to the source XML, the rendering of the second page is shown in Figure 4-15.

Hire Items

Code	Description	From Date	To Date	Weeks	Rate	Quantity	VATCode	Discount	Value
CHXL 00002	EXT LEAD	01/06/06	21/06/06	3.00	1.25	1	1		3.75
CHXL 00001	EXT LEAD	01/06/06	21/06/06	3.00	1.25	1	1		3.75
CHXL 00002	EXT LEAD	01/06/06	30/06/06	4.40	1.25	1	1		5.50

Figure 4-15

Any rows included under the `fo:table-header` element are rendered by default on each page of the table. The same concept applies to any records contained in a `fo:table-footer` element. This can be overridden by using the `table-omit-header-at-break` and the `table-omit-footer-at-break` attributes of a `fo:table` element. If you set the values of these attributes to `true`, you stop the rendering of the header record and any footer records on any page other than the start page (in the case of the header) or last page (in the case of the footer) of the table.

The same XML source rendered with the table-omit-header-at-break attribute set to true results in the second page being rendered as shown in Figure 4-16.

CHXL 00002	EXT LEAD	01/06/06	21/06/06	3.00	1.25	1	1		3.75
CHXL 00001	EXT LEAD	01/06/06	21/06/06	3.00	1.25	1	1		3.75
CHXL 00002	EXT LEAD	01/06/06	30/06/06	4.40	1.25	1	1		5.50

Figure 4-16

Next, you want to render the sale items in a table similar to the hire items. The columns are slightly different but the mechanism to render them is mainly the same.

The XSLT code to create and setup the columns for the sale item table is shown here:

```
<fo:table>
 <fo:table-column padding="2px" padding-top="5px" column-width="10cm"/>
 <fo:table-column padding="2px" column-width="5cm"/>
 <fo:table-column padding="2px" column-width="3cm"/>
 <fo:table-column padding="2px" column-width="3cm"/>
 <fo:table-column padding="2px" column-width="3cm"/>
 <fo:table-column padding="2px" column-width="3cm"/>
 <fo:table-header border-style="solid">
  <fo:table-row      background-color="white"
                     border-style="none">
   <fo:table-cell number-columns-spanned="6">
    <fo:block font-family="serif" font-weight="bold" font-size="20pt">
```

```
    Sale Items
        </fo:block>
      </fo:table-cell>
     </fo:table-row>
     <fo:table-row background-color="silver">
      <fo:table-cell>
        <fo:block>Description</fo:block>
      </fo:table-cell>
      <fo:table-cell>
       <fo:block>Date</fo:block>
      </fo:table-cell>
      <fo:table-cell>
       <fo:block>Quantity</fo:block>
      </fo:table-cell>
      <fo:table-cell>
       <fo:block>Price</fo:block>
      </fo:table-cell>
      <fo:table-cell>
       <fo:block>VATCode</fo:block>
      </fo:table-cell>
      <fo:table-cell>
       <fo:block>Value</fo:block>
      </fo:table-cell>
     </fo:table-row>
    </fo:table-header>
    <fo:table-body>
     <xsl:apply-templates select="//ROOT/Invoice/SaleItem"/>
    </fo:table-body>
   </fo:table>
```

The `apply-templates` section for the sale item rows is again very much like the hire items table and is shown here.

```
   <xsl:template match="//ROOT/Invoice/SaleItem">
    <fo:table-row  keep-with-next="always"
            background-color="white"
            width="100%">
     <fo:table-cell          border-left-style="solid"
                  padding="2px"
                  border-right-style="solid">
      <fo:block>
       <xsl:value-of select="Description"/>
      </fo:block>
     </fo:table-cell>
     <fo:table-cell        border-left-style="solid"
                  padding="2px"
                  border-right-style="solid">
      <fo:block>
       <xsl:value-of select="Date"/>
      </fo:block>
     </fo:table-cell>
     <fo:table-cell        border-left-style="solid"
                  padding="2px"
                  border-right-style="solid">
      <fo:block>
```

```
      <xsl:value-of select="Quantity"/>
     </fo:block>
    </fo:table-cell>
    <fo:table-cell          border-left-style="solid"
                  padding="2px"
                  border-right-style="solid">
     <fo:block>
      <xsl:value-of select="Price"/>
     </fo:block>
    </fo:table-cell>
    <fo:table-cell         border-left-style="solid"
                  padding="2px"
                  border-right-style="solid">
     <fo:block>
      <xsl:value-of select="VATCode"/>
     </fo:block>
    </fo:table-cell>
    <fo:table-cell           border-left-style="solid"
                  padding="2px"
                  border-right-style="solid">
     <fo:block>
      <xsl:value-of select="Value"/>
     </fo:block>
    </fo:table-cell>
   </fo:table-row>
  </xsl:template>
```

We have introduced one major difference in the rendering of the table. The row attribute `keep-with-next` has been used and set to the value always. This means that where possible, the rows of the table are rendered in the same area (in most cases, in the same page). If this attribute is omitted, the sale items table is rendered directly after the hire items table regardless of whether all the records in the sales item data set can be displayed on the same page. Figure 4-17 shows this scenario.

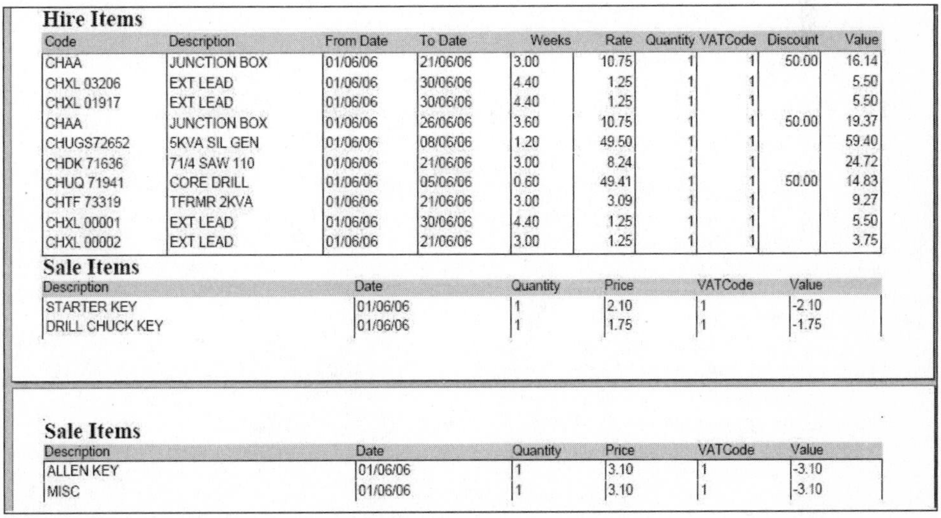

Hire Items

Code	Description	From Date	To Date	Weeks	Rate	Quantity	VATCode	Discount	Value
CHAA	JUNCTION BOX	01/06/06	21/06/06	3.00	10.75	1	1	50.00	16.14
CHXL 03206	EXT LEAD	01/06/06	30/06/06	4.40	1.25	1	1		5.50
CHXL 01917	EXT LEAD	01/06/06	30/06/06	4.40	1.25	1	1		5.50
CHAA	JUNCTION BOX	01/06/06	26/06/06	3.60	10.75	1	1	50.00	19.37
CHUGS72652	5KVA SIL GEN	01/06/06	08/06/06	1.20	49.50	1	1		59.40
CHDK 71636	71/4 SAW 110	01/06/06	21/06/06	3.00	8.24	1	1		24.72
CHUQ 71941	CORE DRILL	01/06/06	05/06/06	0.60	49.41	1	1	50.00	14.83
CHTF 73319	TFRMR 2KVA	01/06/06	21/06/06	3.00	3.09	1	1		9.27
CHXL 00001	EXT LEAD	01/06/06	30/06/06	4.40	1.25	1	1		5.50
CHXL 00002	EXT LEAD	01/06/06	21/06/06	3.00	1.25	1	1		3.75

Sale Items

Description	Date	Quantity	Price	VATCode	Value
STARTER KEY	01/06/06	1	2.10	1	-2.10
DRILL CHUCK KEY	01/06/06	1	1.75	1	-1.75

Sale Items

Description	Date	Quantity	Price	VATCode	Value
ALLEN KEY	01/06/06	1	3.10	1	-3.10
MISC	01/06/06	1	3.10	1	-3.10

Figure 4-17

Setting `keep-with-next` to `true` means that the sales item table split in Figure 4-17 is (where possible) rendered in a contiguous area.

Finally, you want to create a summary table giving the total values for the invoice. The table does not introduce any new features, but the code is presented to complete the example.

```
<fo:table       display-align="after"
         text-align="right"
         font-family="serif"
         font-weight="bold"
         font-size="18pt">
 <fo:table-header border-style="none">
  <fo:table-row  background-color="white"
                border-style="none">
   <fo:table-cell       number-columns-spanned="2"
                text-align="left"
                padding-top="10px">
    <fo:block   font-family="serif"
         font-weight="bold"
         font-size="20pt">
 Invoice Totals
    </fo:block>
   </fo:table-cell>
  </fo:table-row>
 </fo:table-header>
 <fo:table-column padding="2px" column-width="23cm"/>
 <fo:table-column padding="2px" column-width="4cm"/>
 <fo:table-body>
  <fo:table-row border-style="none">
   <fo:table-cell padding-top="5px" padding-right="10px">
    <fo:block>Net</fo:block>
   </fo:table-cell>
   <fo:table-cell padding-top="5px" background-color="silver">
    <fo:block>£<xsl:value-of select="//ROOT/Invoice/PreVATTotal"/></fo:block>
   </fo:table-cell>
  </fo:table-row>
  <fo:table-row>
   <fo:table-cell padding-right="10px">
    <fo:block>VAT</fo:block>
   </fo:table-cell>
   <fo:table-cell background-color="silver">
    <fo:block>£<xsl:value-of select="//ROOT/Invoice/VAT1"/>
    </fo:block>
   </fo:table-cell>
  </fo:table-row>
  <fo:table-row>
   <fo:table-cell padding-right="10px">
    <fo:block>Total</fo:block>
   </fo:table-cell>
   <fo:table-cell background-color="silver">
    <fo:block>£<xsl:value-of select="//ROOT/Invoice/InvoiceTotal"/></fo:block>
   </fo:table-cell>
  </fo:table-row>
 </fo:table-body>
</fo:table>
```

The example in full is available for download from this books companion Web site. It renders as shown in Figure 4-18

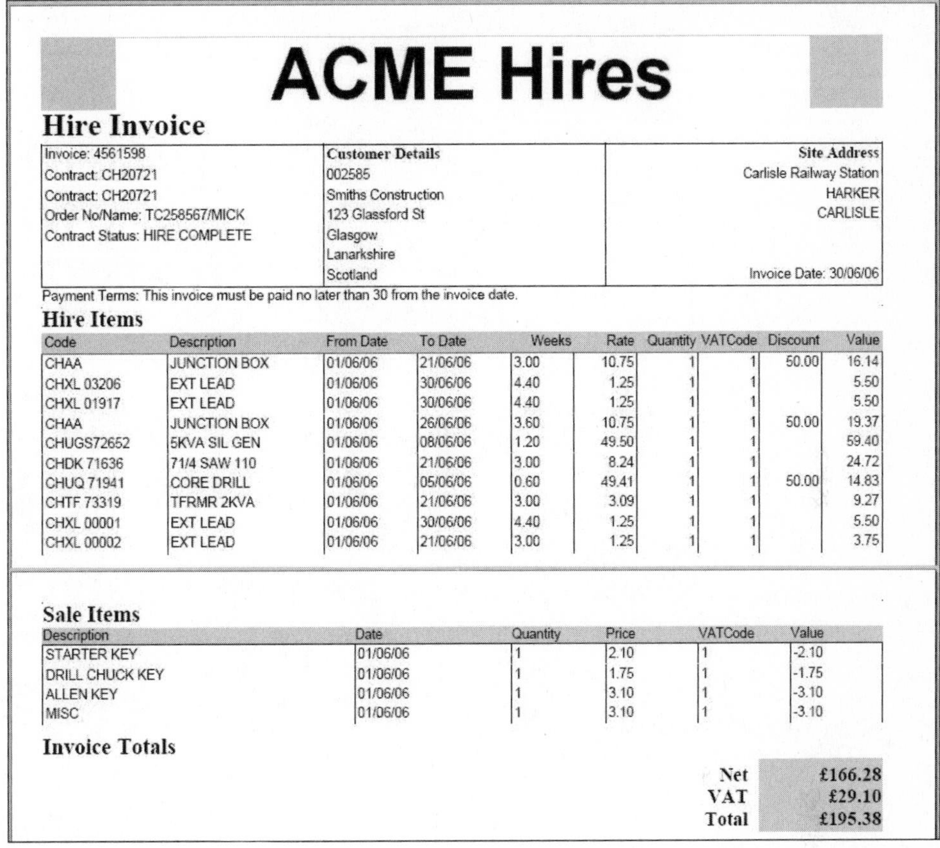

ACME Hires

Hire Invoice

Invoice: 4561598	Customer Details	Site Address
Contract: CH20721	002585	Carlisle Railway Station
Contract: CH20721	Smiths Construction	HARKER
Order No/Name: TC258567/MICK	123 Glassford St	CARLISLE
Contract Status: HIRE COMPLETE	Glasgow	
	Lanarkshire	
	Scotland	Invoice Date: 30/06/06

Payment Terms: This invoice must be paid no later than 30 from the invoice date.

Hire Items

Code	Description	From Date	To Date	Weeks	Rate	Quantity	VATCode	Discount	Value
CHAA	JUNCTION BOX	01/06/06	21/06/06	3.00	10.75	1	1	50.00	16.14
CHXL 03206	EXT LEAD	01/06/06	30/06/06	4.40	1.25	1	1		5.50
CHXL 01917	EXT LEAD	01/06/06	30/06/06	4.40	1.25	1	1		5.50
CHAA	JUNCTION BOX	01/06/06	26/06/06	3.60	10.75	1	1	50.00	19.37
CHUGS72652	5KVA SIL GEN	01/06/06	08/06/06	1.20	49.50	1	1		59.40
CHDK 71636	71/4 SAW 110	01/06/06	21/06/06	3.00	8.24	1	1		24.72
CHUQ 71941	CORE DRILL	01/06/06	05/06/06	0.60	49.41	1	1	50.00	14.83
CHTF 73319	TFRMR 2KVA	01/06/06	21/06/06	3.00	3.09	1	1		9.27
CHXL 00001	EXT LEAD	01/06/06	30/06/06	4.40	1.25	1	1		5.50
CHXL 00002	EXT LEAD	01/06/06	21/06/06	3.00	1.25	1	1		3.75

Sale Items

Description	Date	Quantity	Price	VATCode	Value
STARTER KEY	01/06/06	1	2.10	1	-2.10
DRILL CHUCK KEY	01/06/06	1	1.75	1	-1.75
ALLEN KEY	01/06/06	1	3.10	1	-3.10
MISC	01/06/06	1	3.10	1	-3.10

Invoice Totals

Net	£166.28
VAT	£29.10
Total	£195.38

Figure 4-18

Summary

In this chapter you have seen some powerful uses of XSL-FO. The capability to quickly produce printer friendly documents from an XML source is extremely attractive. Although this chapter has provided a full working example, many other applications of this technology exist and you are encouraged to explore these.

One of the main benefits of XSL-FO that I have moved to the top of my list is the low cost of deployment. For example, a Web server requires only an XML-FO processor, to produce high-quality documents. No need for licensing or for other production and delivery applications such as Microsoft Reporting Services, Crystal Reports or Cognos.

Part III
Defining Structure

5

Document Type Definitions (DTDs)

You know that, as an XML document author, you can create the XML document in whatever structure you decide on. You are able to decide on your own element names, you can determine how the data within these elements is represented, and you can even dictate the complete hierarchy of the data represented in the document. The structure you decide on is referred to as a *vocabulary*. This open set of rules may seem like anarchy, but this is what gives XML its power. It is a creative environment that allows you to build a true representation of your data.

This openness of XML vocabulary does, however, require a set of rules defined on the structure of XML documents. This set of rules, once in place, can then be used to *validate* XML documents that are created or being read. If you want to consume an XML document, you must have a means to run the document through a validation process to make sure it abides by the established rules to ensure easy processing. Otherwise, you must ensure this by laboriously parsing the XML document line by line.

The XML validation process is an important one. This book covers the three main ways to validate an XML document. *Document Type Definitions*, also known as *DTDs*, are ways you can apply this validation process. Other means include XML Schemas and RELAX NG. This chapter takes a look at DTDs and how you can create and work them.

Why Document Type Definitions?

Validation is important. If you plan to share information or services using an XML document between two working processes, applications, or other entities, you must put in place a set of rules that defines the structure of the XML document that is to be passed. You should be able to use the rule definition to perform validation against any XML document.

For instance, suppose you have created an XML document like the one presented in Listing 5-1.

Listing 5-1: A simple XML document

```
<?xml version="1.0" encoding="UTF-8" ?>
<Process>
   <Name>Bill Evjen</Name>
   <Address>123 Main Street</Address>
   <City>Saint Charles</City>
   <State>Missouri</State>
   <Country>USA</Country>
   <Order>
      <Item>52-inch Plasma</Item>
      <Quantity>1</Quantity>
   </Order>
</Process>
```

If your application depends upon a structure like the preceding one, you don't want to receive an XML document that doesn't conform to that structure (for example, Listing 5-2).

Listing 5-2: An XML document that does not follow the prescribed structure

```
<?xml version="1.0" encoding="UTF-8" ?>
<Process>
   <Name>Bill Evjen</Name>
   <Address>123 Main Street</Address>
   <City>Saint Charles</City>
   <State>Missouri</State>
   <Country>USA</Country>
   <Order>
      <Item>52-inch Plasma</Item>
      <Quantity>1</Quantity>
      <Type>New</Type>
   </Order>
</Process>
```

As you look at the XML document presented in Listing 5-2, you can see that it doesn't follow the structure prescribed immediately prior in Listing 5-1. This XML document Listing 5-has an extra element (`<Type>`) that wasn't part of the original requirement. A departure like adding an extra element makes the XML document invalid and can break your consuming process. For this reason, you need a validation process.

The most common form of XML validation is done using XML Schemas. Why, then, would you ever want to learn about any other validation process? You should learn about the DTD format because it was the first method (used for quite some time) to validate the structure of XML documents. Although it has limitations, you may still encounter XML applications that depend on this type of validation. If you do encounter a DTD, you want to understand how to deal with it.

DTDs came from the SGML world. It was a good choice for defining XML documents because many SGML users had already used it to define their documents. Using DTDs in the new world of XML made the migration from SGML to XML that much easier.

DTDs, however, wasn't the best option for defining document structure. One problem was that the method was difficult to learn. DTDs are not written using XML. Instead, the syntax is quite different, and this means that an XML developer has to learn two types of syntaxes when working with XML documents. One other major difficulty is that this form of XML validation doesn't support the use of namespaces — something that is extremely important in XML.

Even though the DTD format is not ideal, you will often see it used. In fact, many of the HTML documents that you deal with today use some form of DTD to define the permissible structure of the HTML document.

For instance, if you create a new HTML document in Microsoft's Visual Studio, you get the results presented in Listing 5-3.

Listing 5-3: A basic HTML file using a DTD to define its structure

```
<!DOCTYPE html PUBLIC "-//W3C//DTD XHTML 1.0 Transitional//EN"
 "http://www.w3.org/TR/xhtml1/DTD/xhtml1-transitional.dtd">
<html xmlns="http://www.w3.org/1999/xhtml" >
<head>
    <title>Untitled Page</title>
</head>
<body>

</body>
</html>
```

At the top of the HTML document, you can see that a `<!DOCTYPE>` element is defined in the first line and that the URL of `http://www.w3.org/TR/xhtml1/DTD/xhtml1-transitional.dtd` is used to show where the DTD document for this HTML document is located.

If you pull up this particular DTD document, `xhtml1-transitional.dtd`, you find a large DTD document. Listing 5-4 shows a partial results from this file, which focuses on the definition of the Headings part of the HTML document.

Listing 5-4: The Headings defined within the xhtml1-transitional.dtd document

```
<!--=================== Headings ==========================================-->

<!--
  There are six levels of headings from h1 (the most important)
  to h6 (the least important).
-->

<!ELEMENT h1  %Inline;>
<!ATTLIST h1
  %attrs;
  %TextAlign;
  >

<!ELEMENT h2 %Inline;>
<!ATTLIST h2
  %attrs;
```

(continued)

Listing 5-4 *(continued)*

```
    %TextAlign;
    >

  <!ELEMENT h3 %Inline;>
  <!ATTLIST h3
    %attrs;
    %TextAlign;
    >

  <!ELEMENT h4 %Inline;>
  <!ATTLIST h4
    %attrs;
    %TextAlign;
    >

  <!ELEMENT h5 %Inline;>
  <!ATTLIST h5
    %attrs;
    %TextAlign;
    >

  <!ELEMENT h6 %Inline;>
  <!ATTLIST h6
    %attrs;
    %TextAlign;
    >
```

This is just a partial result from the `xhtml1-transitional.dtd` file. In the HTML world (also the XHTML world), you can use a number of different DTDs to define the structure used in your HTML document. The following list includes some of the available DTDs that are provided for HTML.

- **HTML 4.01 Strict**—`http://www.w3.org/TR/html401/strict.dtd`
- **HTML 4.01 Transitional**—`http://www.w3.org/TR/html401/loose.dtd`
- **HTML 4.01 Frameset**—`http://www.w3.org/TR/html401/frameset.dtd`
- **XHTML 1.0 Strict**—`http://www.w3.org/TR/xhtml1/DTD/xhtml1-strict.dtd`
- **XHTML 1.0 Transitional**—`http://www.w3.org/TR/xhtml1/DTD/xhtml1-transitional.dtd`
- **XHTML 1.0 Frameset**—`http://www.w3.org/TR/xhtml1/DTD/xhtml1-frameset.dtd`

Internal DTDs

Before you begin building DTD documents, you should understand that a DTD can be defined in several places. A DTD is a set of text elements that follows a specific syntax. This text can be stored in the XML file that it defines, or it can be held in a separate file. If it is held within the same file as the XML it defines, then it is considered an inline DTD. If it is kept in a separate file, it is considered an external DTD and has a `.dtd` file extension.

To show an example of utilizing an internal DTD, suppose you are working with the XML document presented in Listing 5-5.

Listing 5-5: An XML document that needs a DTD

```
<?xml version="1.0" encoding="UTF-8" ?>
<Process>
   <Name>Bill Evjen</Name>
   <Address>123 Main Street</Address>
   <City>Saint Charles</City>
   <State>Missouri</State>
   <Country>USA</Country>
   <Order>
      <Item>52-inch Plasma</Item>
      <Quantity>1</Quantity>
   </Order>
</Process>
```

To place a DTD document within this XML document, you place the DTD definition directly after the `<?xml>` declaration as illustrated in Listing 5-6.

Listing 5-6: Providing the XML document an internal DTD

```
<?xml version="1.0" encoding="UTF-8"?>
<!DOCTYPE Process [
<!ELEMENT Address (#PCDATA)>
<!ELEMENT City (#PCDATA)>
<!ELEMENT Country (#PCDATA)>
<!ELEMENT Item (#PCDATA)>
<!ELEMENT Name (#PCDATA)>
<!ELEMENT Order (Item, Quantity)>
<!ELEMENT Process (Name, Address, City, State, Country, Order)>
<!ELEMENT Quantity (#PCDATA)>
<!ELEMENT State (#PCDATA)>
]>
<Process>
 <Name>Bill Evjen</Name>
 <Address>123 Main Street</Address>
 <City>Saint Charles</City>
 <State>Missouri</State>
 <Country>USA</Country>
 <Order>
         <Item>52-inch Plasma</Item>
         <Quantity>1</Quantity>
 </Order>
</Process>
```

At this point, I won't review the meaning of the DTD declaration. Note that it is possible to declare DTDs internally within the XML document. Many in the industry, however, would say this is an improper way to declare your DTDs. They would tell you it is better to provide some level of abstraction and declare your DTDs externally. Others prefer that the DTD that validates the XML document is encased within the document itself — eliminating the need to deal with two files.

Listing 5-6 shows that when the DTD is declared internally, it is presented immediately following the `<?xml>` declaration and right before the XML document's root element `<Process>`.

If you take the XML file from Listing 5-6 and view the file in Microsoft's Internet Explorer, you see the results illustrated in Figure 5-1.

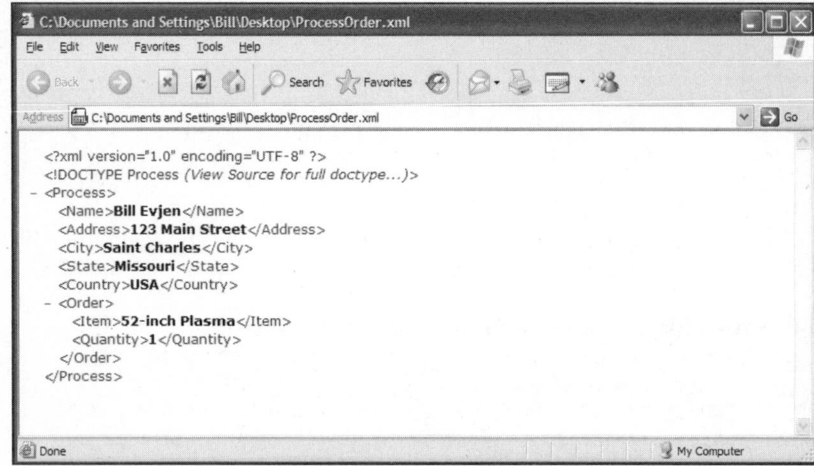

Figure 5-1

From this image, you can see that the DTD is not fully presented, but instead IE instructs you to go to the source file to see the complete DTD. If you look at the same file through Mozilla's Firefox, you see that Firefox doesn't do anything to present the associated DTD document.

Next, this chapter explains how to create the same document as an external DTD.

External DTDs

It is not considered best practice to build DTDs within your XML documents. Instead, it is best to reference an external DTD from the XML file. You want this level of abstraction between the data and the data definition. Tying them together makes future changes more difficult.

An internal DTD is really effective only if you have a single instance of this XML file and you don't plan on having any additional copies of the file. If you create more than a single instance of the XML structure, you must to go into each and every instance to make any change. If a DTD is referenced from your XML file, you can make any change to the document in a single place to have it instantly reflected across all the XML files that use that particular DTD. This level of abstraction is simply more powerful.

Creating an external DTD is simple. In the XML file from Listing 5-5, you simply make a single line reference to the DTD you want to use as your document definition. This is presented in Listing 5-7.

Listing 5-7: Building an XML document with an external DTD

```
<?xml version="1.0" encoding="UTF-8" ?>
<!DOCTYPE Process SYSTEM "ProcessOrder.dtd">
<Process>
   <Name>Bill Evjen</Name>
   <Address>123 Main Street</Address>
   <City>Saint Charles</City>
   <State>Missouri</State>
   <Country>USA</Country>
   <Order>
      <Item>52-inch Plasma</Item>
      <Quantity>1</Quantity>
   </Order>
</Process>
```

In this case, Listing 5-7 shows a reference to the `ProcessOrder.dtd` document by using the `<!DOCTYPE>` declaration within the XML file.

```
<!DOCTYPE Process SYSTEM "ProcessOrder.dtd">
```

This declaration comes after the `<?xml>` declaration and directly prior to the opening of the root element `<Process>`. By using `"ProcessOrder.dtd"` within this `<!DOCTYPE>` declaration, you are stating that the DTD file can be found in the same spot as the XML file itself. If this is not the case, you can assign a different path for the DTD file.

One option is to locate the DTD on the Internet by using a complete URL, as presented here:

```
<!DOCTYPE Process SYSTEM "http://www.wrox.com/files/dtd/ProcessOrder.dtd">
```

This code is directing the parser to look for the DTD using the absolute path to a remote location on the Internet. You can also direct the parser to look for the DTD using an absolute path located within a network as follows:

```
<!DOCTYPE Process SYSTEM "C:\Wrox\Files\DTD\ProcessOrder.dtd">
```

Because the location utilized is a relative URL, you can also provide a relative path as follows:

```
<!DOCTYPE Process SYSTEM "../ProcessOrder.dtd">
```

Or

```
<!DOCTYPE Process SYSTEM "Files/ProcessOrder.dtd">
```

After you have defined where to find the DTD file in your XML file, the next step is to actually create the DTD file. Listing 5-8 shows the `ProcessOrder.dtd` file.

Listing 5-8: The ProcessOrder.dtd

```
<?xml version="1.0" encoding="UTF-8"?>
<!ELEMENT Address (#PCDATA)>
<!ELEMENT City (#PCDATA)>
<!ELEMENT Country (#PCDATA)>
<!ELEMENT Item (#PCDATA)>
<!ELEMENT Name (#PCDATA)>
<!ELEMENT Order (Item, Quantity)>
<!ELEMENT Process (Name, Address, City, State, Country, Order)>
<!ELEMENT Quantity (#PCDATA)>
<!ELEMENT State (#PCDATA)>
```

Save this text file with a `.dtd` file extension, and your DTD file is ready for action.

Building Your Own DTD

Now that you know how to reference your DTD definitions with your XML documents, the next step is to look at how you can build your own DTDs. A number of tools enable you to build DTDs easily, but the first step is to learn how to build them from scratch in Notepad. This can help you understand all the steps that go into making DTDs.

First locate the XML file you want to work with. For this example, you can use the Shakespeare play *Hamlet* as it is represented in XML.

You can find the play Hamlet as XML online at `andrew.cmu.edu/user/akj/shakespeare/`. *On this page, you will find all of Shakespeare's plays, including Hamlet. To get the XML file, simply right-click the file and select Save Target As from the provided menu (in Microsoft's Internet Explorer). If this page is not present at the time of this reading, then simply do a search in an Internet search engine for "*`XML Shakespeare`*" to find a large number of results.*

The `Hamlet.xml` file is a large file that includes all of the parts of the play itself. It is presented partially in Listing 5-9.

Listing 5-9: Part of the Hamlet.xml file

```
<?xml version="1.0"?>
<?xml-stylesheet type="text/css" href="shakes.css"?>

<PLAY>
   <TITLE>The Tragedy of Hamlet, Prince of Denmark</TITLE>

   <PERSONAE>
      <TITLE>Dramatis Personae</TITLE>

      <PERSONA>CLAUDIUS, king of Denmark. </PERSONA>
      <PERSONA>HAMLET, son to the late, and nephew to the present king.</PERSONA>
      <PERSONA>POLONIUS, lord chamberlain. </PERSONA>
      <PERSONA>HORATIO, friend to Hamlet.</PERSONA>
      <PERSONA>LAERTES, son to Polonius.</PERSONA>
```

```
      <PERSONA>LUCIANUS, nephew to the king.</PERSONA>

      <PGROUP>
         <PERSONA>VOLTIMAND</PERSONA>
         <PERSONA>CORNELIUS</PERSONA>
         <PERSONA>ROSENCRANTZ</PERSONA>
         <PERSONA>GUILDENSTERN</PERSONA>
         <PERSONA>OSRIC</PERSONA>
         <GRPDESCR>courtiers.</GRPDESCR>
      </PGROUP>

      <PERSONA>A Gentleman</PERSONA>
      <PERSONA>A Priest. </PERSONA>

      <PGROUP>
         <PERSONA>MARCELLUS</PERSONA>
         <PERSONA>BERNARDO</PERSONA>
         <GRPDESCR>officers.</GRPDESCR>
      </PGROUP>

      <PERSONA>FRANCISCO, a soldier.</PERSONA>
      <PERSONA>REYNALDO, servant to Polonius.</PERSONA>
      <PERSONA>Players.</PERSONA>
      <PERSONA>Two Clowns, grave-diggers.</PERSONA>
      <PERSONA>FORTINBRAS, prince of Norway. </PERSONA>
      <PERSONA>A Captain.</PERSONA>
      <PERSONA>English Ambassadors. </PERSONA>
      <PERSONA>GERTRUDE, queen of Denmark, and mother to Hamlet. </PERSONA>
      <PERSONA>OPHELIA, daughter to Polonius.</PERSONA>
      <PERSONA>Lords, Ladies, Officers, Soldiers, Sailors, Messengers,
       and other Attendants.</PERSONA>
      <PERSONA>Ghost of Hamlet's Father. </PERSONA>
   </PERSONAE>

   <SCNDESCR>SCENE  Denmark.</SCNDESCR>

   <PLAYSUBT>HAMLET</PLAYSUBT>

   <ACT>
      <TITLE>ACT I</TITLE>

      <SCENE>
         <TITLE>SCENE I.  Elsinore. A platform before the castle.</TITLE>
         <STAGEDIR>FRANCISCO at his post. Enter to him BERNARDO</STAGEDIR>

         <SPEECH>
            <SPEAKER>BERNARDO</SPEAKER>
            <LINE>Who's there?</LINE>
         </SPEECH>

         <SPEECH>
            <SPEAKER>FRANCISCO</SPEAKER>
            <LINE>Nay, answer me: stand, and unfold yourself.</LINE>
         </SPEECH>
```

Although this is just a partial view of the XML file, you can see that it is a large file. Even though it is large, very few elements are involved. This means it isn't going to take much effort to create the DTD that you can use to validate the `Hamlet.xml` file.

After you have the `Hamlet.xml` file on your computer, the next step is to start building the DTD for this file. The DTD is a representation of the structure allowed for this large XML document. The first step is to incorporate the *document type declaration* within your `Hamlet.xml` file.

Document Type Declaration

The DTD acronym discussed so far in this chapter refers to *Document Type Definition* — a file that defines the XML structure of particular XML files. Don't get the term *DTD file* confused with the DTD we are talking about now — the *document type declaration* element.

The *document type declaration* is the element that you place within an XML file to declare the DTD (Document Type Definition) to use to validate the XML contained within the document. An example document type declaration is presented here:

```
<!DOCTYPE PLAY SYSTEM "http://www.wrox.com/files/dtd/Hamlet.dtd">
```

A document type declaration starts with a `<!DOCTYPE` and ends with a closing >. The different parts of this particular DTD are presented in Figure 5-2.

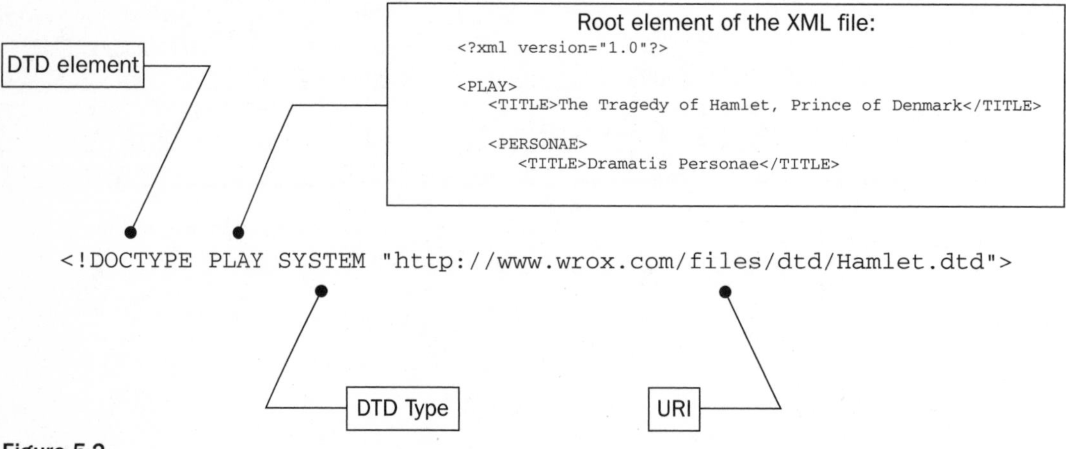

Figure 5-2

This generic construction of the DOCTYPE element is presented here:

```
<!DOCTYPE [root element name] SYSTEM [URI]>
```

Other possible constructions include:

```
<!DOCTYPE [root element name] [inline DTD]>

<!DOCTYPE [root element name] SYSTEM [URI] [inline DTD]>

<!DOCTYPE [root element name] PUBLIC [identifier] [URI]>

<!DOCTYPE [root element name] PUBLIC [identifier] [URI] [inline DTD]>
```

After the initial `<!DOCTYPE>` element declaration, the first item (or attribute) provided is the root element of the XML being defined. In the example from the XML file shown in Listing 5-9, the root element is `<PLAY>`. Therefore, this is the value that must be used in the `<!DOCTYPE>` element.

The SYSTEM and PUBLIC Keywords

You can declare the DTD within the XML document as shown earlier in Listing 5-6. If you are not taking that particular approach, then you are going to want to use the either the SYSTEM or PUBLIC keyword to specify whether your DTD is a private or public DTD.

By far, the most common method is to use the `SYSTEM` keyword, thereby making all your DTDs private. This doesn't inhibit you from sharing your DTDs with other groups, entities, or organizations. When using the `SYSTEM` keyword, you must specify the URI (*unique resource identifier*) of the DTD. In the previous examples, you saw that the URI can be a direct physical path to the file as it relates to the XML file using the DTD:

```
<!DOCTYPE Play SYSTEM "C:\Wrox\Files\DTD\Hamlet.dtd">
```

It can also be an HTTP accessible hyperlink to the DTD file:

```
<!DOCTYPE Play SYSTEM "http://www.wrox.com/files/dtd/Hamlet.dtd">
```

Generally, you should stick to the `SYSTEM` keyword and never use the `PUBLIC` keyword. Using the `PUBLIC` keyword in the `<!DOCTYPE>` element means that a standards body (either an official or non-official standards body) has defined a standard that is available to the public. You might not realize it, but you have already seen this used once in this chapter. In Listing 5-3, a `<!DOCTYPE>` defines the vocabulary of an XHTML document. This `<!DOCTYPE>` is presented here:

```
<!DOCTYPE html PUBLIC "-//W3C//DTD XHTML 1.0 Transitional//EN"
 "http://www.w3.org/TR/xhtml1/DTD/xhtml1-transitional.dtd">
```

In this case, the `<!DOCTYPE>` element contains the root element of the XML document that it defines, html, the `PUBLIC` keyword, its identifier — `"-//W3C//DTD XHTML 1.0 Transitional//EN"`, and finally ending with a URI of `"http://www.w3.org/TR/xhtml1/DTD/xhtml1-transitional.dtd"`.

The first character of the identifier (a dash) means that a non-official standards body developed the DTD. A plus sign instead of a dash (or minus sign) means that an official standards body developed the DTD. The second attribute within the identifier (all the attributes are separated by `//`) specifies the governing body that defined the DTD. In this case, the World Wide Web Consortium, also known as the

W3C, developed this DTD. The third attribute specifies the name of the DTD defined and its version. Then finally, the fourth attribute defines the language used in the definition because this DTD might be available in multiple languages.

Following the identifier is the URI defining the location of the DTD. If you are developing your own public DTD, you follow the same rules as shown here. Remember that you really could achieve the same thing if you just declared your XML vocabulary using the `SYSTEM` keyword and its related structure.

Using the URI and Inline DTD Together

As you examine the possible structures of the `<!DOCTYPE>` element, note that it is possible to combine both the external and internal DTDs.

```
<!DOCTYPE [root element name] SYSTEM [URI] [inline DTD]>

<!DOCTYPE [root element name] PUBLIC [identifier] [URI] [inline DTD]>
```

This means that in addition to invoking a DTD by making an external reference (as shown in Listing 5-10), you can also extend the DTD by using it in combination with some inline DTD markup (as shown in Listing 5-11).

Listing 5-10: Using an external DTD

```
<?xml version="1.0" encoding="UTF-8" ?>
<!DOCTYPE PLAY SYSTEM "http://www.wrox.com/files/dtd/Hamlet.dtd">
<PLAY>
   <TITLE>The Tragedy of Hamlet, Prince of Denmark</TITLE>
   <PERSONAE>
      <TITLE>Dramatis Personae</TITLE>
      <PERSONA>CLAUDIUS, king of Denmark. </PERSONA>
      <PERSONA>HAMLET, son to the late, and nephew to the present king.</PERSONA>
      <PERSONA>POLONIUS, lord chamberlain. </PERSONA>
      <PERSONA>HORATIO, friend to Hamlet.</PERSONA>
      <PERSONA>LAERTES, son to Polonius.</PERSONA>
      <PERSONA>LUCIANUS, nephew to the king.</PERSONA>
      <PGROUP>
         <PERSONA>VOLTIMAND</PERSONA>
         <PERSONA>CORNELIUS</PERSONA>
         <PERSONA>ROSENCRANTZ</PERSONA>
         <PERSONA>GUILDENSTERN</PERSONA>
         <PERSONA>OSRIC</PERSONA>
         <GRPDESCR>courtiers.</GRPDESCR>
      </PGROUP>

<!-- XML cut short for space reasons -->
```

Listing 5-11: Using an external DTD with some inline DTD markup

```
<?xml version="1.0" encoding="UTF-8" ?>
<!DOCTYPE PLAY SYSTEM "http://www.wrox.com/files/dtd/Hamlet.dtd" [
   <!ELEMENT TITLE (#PCDATA)>
]>
```

```
<PLAY>
   <TITLE>The Tragedy of Hamlet, Prince of Denmark</TITLE>
   <PERSONAE>
      <TITLE>Dramatis Personae</TITLE>
      <PERSONA>CLAUDIUS, king of Denmark. </PERSONA>
      <PERSONA>HAMLET, son to the late, and nephew to the present king.</PERSONA>
      <PERSONA>POLONIUS, lord chamberlain. </PERSONA>
      <PERSONA>HORATIO, friend to Hamlet.</PERSONA>
      <PERSONA>LAERTES, son to Polonius.</PERSONA>
      <PERSONA>LUCIANUS, nephew to the king.</PERSONA>
      <PGROUP>
         <PERSONA>VOLTIMAND</PERSONA>
         <PERSONA>CORNELIUS</PERSONA>
         <PERSONA>ROSENCRANTZ</PERSONA>
         <PERSONA>GUILDENSTERN</PERSONA>
         <PERSONA>OSRIC</PERSONA>
         <GRPDESCR>courtiers.</GRPDESCR>
      </PGROUP>

<!-- XML cut short for space reasons -->
```

In this case, not only is the `Hamlet.dtd` utilized, but this DTD is extended by changing the content specification of the `<TITLE>` element by adding an additional inline DTD. Note that not all XML parsers understand such definitions, and you often get validation errors with this type of structure.

Element Declarations

When building your own DTD, whether it is in a separate file or inline within the XML, you are really defining elements, entities, attributes, and notations. You now look at defining elements. When defining a DTD, you must define every XML element using a DTD element declaration. The generic usage of the element declaration is as follows:

```
<!ELEMENT [element name] [content specification]>
```

In this case, the *element name* is the name used for the element being defined, whereas the *content specification* determines what is allowed as a value within the element. This content definition section can get rather complex because it can contain a number of subelements of different types that are part of a specific sequence.

Therefore, to create a DTD for an order form XML document similar to the one used previously in this chapter, you can start by creating an element declaration for the XML document's root element, `<PLAY>`. This DTD document is presented in Listing 5-12.

Listing 5-12: Hamlet.dtd

```
<?xml version="1.0" encoding="UTF-8"?>

<!ELEMENT PLAY (#PCDATA)>
```

You can also see from the element that it is similar to the `<!DOCTYPE>` element used earlier. To declare an element definition, you use the `<!ELEMENT>` element. Just like `<!DOCTYPE>`, `<!ELEMENT>` is case-sensitive. Therefore, it is illegal to write this as `<!Element>` (just as you can't use `<!Doctype>`).

Listing 5-12 shows a single XML element, `PLAY`, being defined. The content specification allowed for the `<PLAY>` element is defined as `#PCDATA`. This essentially means anything is allowed as long as it is parsed character data.

With this definition in `Hamlet.dtd` in place, you can use the following XML structure in an XML document that makes use of this DTD:

```
<PLAY>Here is some sample text</PLAY>
```

This also means that you can have the following:

```
<PLAY></PLAY>
```

But you are not allowed to place items (such as additional nested XML elements) within the `<PLAY>` element like this:

```
<PLAY>
   <TITLE>The Tragedy of Hamlet, Prince of Denmark</TITLE>
   <PERSONAE></PERSONAE>
   <SCNDESCR>SCENE Denmark.</SCNDESCR>
   <PLAYSUBT>HAMLET</PLAYSUBT>
</PLAY>
```

Using the DTD from Listing 5-12, the previous code would be illegal. Next, this chapter reviews how to further define the XML document so that constructions such as the preceding one can be built.

Content Specification with ANY

One method to provide a content specification for an element is to use the `ANY` value. This is illustrated in Listing 5-13.

Listing 5-13: Hamlet.dtd

```
<?xml version="1.0" encoding="UTF-8"?>

<!ELEMENT ACT ANY>
<!ELEMENT GRPDESCR ANY>
<!ELEMENT LINE ANY>
<!ELEMENT PERSONA ANY>
<!ELEMENT PERSONAE ANY>
<!ELEMENT PGROUP ANY>
<!ELEMENT PLAY ANY>
<!ELEMENT PLAYSUBT ANY>
<!ELEMENT SCENE ANY>
<!ELEMENT SCNDESCR ANY>
<!ELEMENT SPEAKER ANY>
<!ELEMENT SPEECH ANY>
<!ELEMENT STAGEDIR ANY>
<!ELEMENT TITLE ANY>
```

This DTD provides a DTD definition for all XML elements contained within the `Hamlet.xml` file. This means that you can use the following syntax and still have a valid XML document:

```
<PLAY>This is my play!</PLAY>
```

But it also means that you can use any child elements that you want, such as the following:

```
<PLAY>
   <TITLE>The Tragedy of Hamlet, Prince of Denmark</TITLE>
   <PERSONAE></PERSONAE>
   <SCNDESCR>SCENE Denmark.</SCNDESCR>
   <PLAYSUBT>HAMLET</PLAYSUBT>
</PLAY>
```

The ANY keyword really means that you can place any character data or any set of elements within the defined item and that specified item is then considered valid. Although this is an easy way to create a DTD definition, it usually isn't the best approach because it provides only *possible* XML elements that may be contained within a valid XML document. It provides a minimal list of rules. This means someone using a DTD such as the one defined in Listing 5-13 could build an XML document such as the one illustrated in Listing 5-14.

Listing 5-14: Hamlet.xml

```
<PLAY>
   <TITLE>The Tragedy of Hamlet, Prince of Denmark</TITLE>
   <PERSONAE></PERSONAE>
   <SCNDESCR>SCENE Denmark.</SCNDESCR>
   <PLAYSUBT>HAMLET</PLAYSUBT>
   <PLAY>Another Play</PLAY>
   <PLAY>
      <TITLE>The Tragedy of Hamlet, Prince of Denmark</TITLE>
      <PERSONAE></PERSONAE>
      <SCNDESCR>SCENE Denmark.</SCNDESCR>
      <PLAYSUBT>HAMLET</PLAYSUBT>
   </PLAY>
</PLAY>
```

From this, you can see that the `<PLAY>` element is used in a number of different ways. For instance, it is used as the root element with a series of child elements. One of the child elements is another couple of `<PLAY>` elements that are used in a completely different manner.

In the end, certain situations may require use of the ANY value for the content specification of elements that you define in the DTD, but in many cases you may prefer to strictly define the child elements or even limit the element to character data only. This is where the value of `#PCDATA` comes in.

Placing Limits on Elements with #PCDATA

As stated, a `#PCDATA` value means that the XML element being defined is allowed to have only parsed character data and is not allowed anything else — including any child elements. Usage of `#PCDATA` is illustrated in the following example:

```
<!ELEMENT SPEAKER (#PCDATA)>
```

Notice that the #PCDATA is held within parenthesis when being included in the element definition. If you go back to the `Hamlet.dtd` (presented in Listing 5-13), you can change all the definitions for the elements that are not allowed to have any subsequent child elements. This change is presented in Listing 5-15.

Listing 5-15: Hamlet.dtd

```
<?xml version="1.0" encoding="UTF-8"?>
<!ELEMENT ACT ANY>
<!ELEMENT GRPDESCR (#PCDATA)>
<!ELEMENT LINE ANY>
<!ELEMENT PERSONA (#PCDATA)>
<!ELEMENT PERSONAE ANY>
<!ELEMENT PGROUP ANY>
<!ELEMENT PLAY ANY>
<!ELEMENT PLAYSUBT (#PCDATA)>
<!ELEMENT SCENE ANY>
<!ELEMENT SCNDESCR (#PCDATA)>
<!ELEMENT SPEAKER (#PCDATA)>
<!ELEMENT SPEECH ANY>
<!ELEMENT STAGEDIR (#PCDATA)>
<!ELEMENT TITLE (#PCDATA)>
```

Now all the elements that disallow child elements are defined using `#PCDATA` instead of `ANY`. Running the `Hamlet.xml` file with this DTD, the validation process succeeds. The additional rules provide more defined structure for the XML files that use this DTD. The processing of these documents has become easier.

Note that one of the limitations of using DTDs (instead of something like XML Schemas) is that you can define the textual content contained within an element only as parsed character data — nothing more specific. As shown, you do this by using `#PCDATA`. Unlike XML Schemas, DTDs don't let you determine that an element can contain only an integer, double, or a string value.

Empty Values

Having an empty element in your XML document may be important as a signal of a Boolean value and nothing more, or it might show a null value that should be stored in the database. DTDs allow for an empty element declaration.

```
<!ELEMENT Member EMPTY>
```

In this case, to declare an empty element, simply use the `EMPTY` keyword in the `<!ELEMENT>` element declaration. Remember that it is case-sensitive.

Child Elements

One of the first steps in building a DTD is to define your root element. Root elements within XML documents generally contain child elements (or nested elements). DTD does allow you to define root elements through the use of the content specification section of the `<!ELEMENT>` element. The root element of the `Hamlet.xml` file is `<PLAY>`. Listing 5-16 shows a revised version of the `Hamlet.dtd` document to further define the `<PLAY>` element and the other elements that allow for child elements.

Listing 5-16: Hamlet.dtd

```
<?xml version="1.0" encoding="UTF-8"?>

<!ELEMENT ACT (TITLE, SCENE+)>
<!ELEMENT GRPDESCR (#PCDATA)>
<!ELEMENT LINE (#PCDATA | STAGEDIR)*>
<!ELEMENT PERSONA (#PCDATA)>
<!ELEMENT PERSONAE (TITLE | PERSONA | PGROUP)+>
<!ELEMENT PGROUP (PERSONA+, GRPDESCR)>
<!ELEMENT PLAY (TITLE, PERSONAE, SCNDESCR, PLAYSUBT, ACT+)>
<!ELEMENT PLAYSUBT (#PCDATA)>
<!ELEMENT SCENE (TITLE | STAGEDIR | SPEECH)+>
<!ELEMENT SCNDESCR (#PCDATA)>
<!ELEMENT SPEAKER (#PCDATA)>
<!ELEMENT SPEECH (SPEAKER | LINE | STAGEDIR)+>
<!ELEMENT STAGEDIR (#PCDATA)>
<!ELEMENT TITLE (#PCDATA)>
```

When defining the required child elements, you define these elements within parenthesis in the `<!ELEMENT>` element itself. Looking specifically at the `<PLAY>` element, you can see that it can contain five child elements:

```
<!ELEMENT PLAY (TITLE, PERSONAE, SCNDESCR, PLAYSUBT, ACT+)>
```

This definition means that the `<PLAY>` element is required to contain a `<TITLE>`, `<PERSONAE>`, `<SCNDESCR>`, `<PLAYSUBT>`, and `<ACT>` child elements. The defined elements are separated using commas. None of the elements are actually required (except for `<ACT>` because of the plus sign — this will be explained shortly). These elements are required to be set in the `<PLAY>` element is this exact order because of their placement in this definition. This means that if `<PERSONAE>` comes before `<TITLE>`, the XML document won't validate.

Because the `PLAY` definition in the DTD document includes a `TITLE` as a possible child element, you must define the `TITLE` child element in the DTD document.

```
<!ELEMENT TITLE (#PCDATA)>
```

Looking through the `Hamlet.dtd` document shown in Listing 5-16, you can see that each of the five child elements are also defined in the document. Some even nest further as their definition includes yet more child elements that must also be defined. The definition of the `ACT` definition shows even more child elements, thereby allowing further nesting in the XML document.

```
<!ELEMENT ACT (TITLE, SCENE+)>
```

Specifying a Number of Instances Required

Some XML documents require you to specify a set number of instances where the child element may occur in the XML document. For instance, suppose you have the XML document shown in Listing 5-17.

Listing 5-17: An XML document with two <Address> child elements

```
<?xml version="1.0" encoding="UTF-8"?>
<!DOCTYPE Mail SYSTEM "Mail.dtd">

<Mail>
   <Name>Bill Evjen</Name>
   <Address>123 Main Street</Address>
   <Address>St. Charles, MO</Address>
   <ZipCode>63301</ZipCode>
</Mail>
```

If you are building a DTD for this bit of XML, your DTD appears as presented in Listing 5-18.

Listing 5-18: Mail.dtd

```
<?xml version="1.0" encoding="UTF-8"?>

<!ELEMENT Mail (Name, Address, Address, ZipCode)>
<!ELEMENT Name (#PCDATA)>
<!ELEMENT Address (#PCDATA)>
<!ELEMENT ZipCode (#PCDATA)>
```

In this case, you can see that the `<Name>`, `<Address>`, and `<ZipCode>` elements are defined, and the `<Mail>` element specifies that it must include child elements for all of these. Note that the `<Address>` child element is mentioned twice — meaning that it has to appear two times in the document. If you include just a single `<Address>` element, the XML document is considered invalid.

Reusing XML Elements

It is also possible to reuse the elements that are defined within the DTD for any number of elements. For instance Listing 5-19 changes the XML document that is presented in Listing 5-17 so that it now includes two sets of addresses.

Listing 5-19: An XML document with two sets of addresses

```
<?xml version="1.0" encoding="UTF-8"?>
<!DOCTYPE Mail SYSTEM "Mail.dtd">

<Mail>
   <Home>
      <Name>Bill Evjen</Name>
      <Address>123 Main Street</Address>
      <Address>St. Charles, MO</Address>
      <ZipCode>63301</ZipCode>
   </Home>
   <Business>
      <Name>Lipper</Name>
      <Address>123 Main Street</Address>
      <Address>St. Louis, MO</Address>
```

```
        <ZipCode>63141</ZipCode>
    </Business>
</Mail>
```

In this case, <Mail> includes two child elements — <Home> and <Business>; each of which makes use of the same <Name>, <Address>, and <ZipCode> elements. For this reason, you only define each of these elements a single time. This is illustrated in the DTD for this XML file in Listing 5-20.

Listing 5-20: Mail.dtd

```
<?xml version="1.0" encoding="UTF-8"?>

<!ELEMENT Mail (Home, Business)>
<!ELEMENT Home (Name, Address, Address, ZipCode)>
<!ELEMENT Business (Name, Address, Address, ZipCode)>
<!ELEMENT Name (#PCDATA)>
<!ELEMENT Address (#PCDATA)>
<!ELEMENT ZipCode (#PCDATA)>
```

From this you can see that the <Name>, <Address>, and <ZipCode> elements are defined only a single time, but they are used by both the <Home> and <Business> elements.

The + Quantifier

You saw earlier that it was possible to force a repeat of the <Address> element as a child element by repeating the number of times it was defined within the <!ELEMENT> element.

```
<!ELEMENT Mail (Name, Address, Address, ZipCode)>
```

This is an easy way to get a specific number of child element instances in the document, but at the same time, it is very restrictive. If you use it, you are always required to have two instances of the <Address> element — no less and no more. Even if you require only a single instance of the <Address> element, you must still include two instances. Also, if you have a foreign address, which in some cases might require three or four <Address> lines, you would still be unable to place more than two instances in the document.

Instead of placing the Address definition in the <!ELEMENT> element twice, another option is to use a quantifier. A quantifier is a symbol that you place after the defined item to specify more or fewer restrictions on the item. This was used in the `Hamlet.dtd` file.

```
<!ELEMENT PLAY (TITLE, PERSONAE, SCNDESCR, PLAYSUBT, ACT+)>
```

Here, the + quantifier is used with the <ACT> element definition. The + quantifier signifies that the <ACT> element can appear one or more times within the <PLAY> element. You can also change the previous <Mail> element definition so that the <Address> element is allowed one or more times using the + quantifier.

```
<!ELEMENT Mail (Name, Address+, ZipCode)>
```

The `Address+` here signifies that the `<Address>` element can appear one or more times within the `<Mail>` element. This means that the following bit of XML in Listing 5-21 is valid:

Listing 5-21: An XML document using the + quantifier

```
<?xml version="1.0" encoding="UTF-8"?>
<!DOCTYPE Mail SYSTEM "Mail.dtd">

<Mail>
   <Name>Bill Evjen</Name>
   <Address>123 Main Street; St. Charles, MO</Address>
   <ZipCode>63301</ZipCode>
</Mail>
```

Here the `<Address>` element is only used a single time. If the author of this XML document, however, wanted to use the `<Address>` element more often, it would be possible to do so. This is illustrated in Listing 5-22.

Listing 5-22: Another instance in using the + quantifier

```
<?xml version="1.0" encoding="UTF-8"?>
<!DOCTYPE Mail SYSTEM "Mail.dtd">

<Mail>
   <Name>Bill Evjen</Name>
   <Address>123 Main Street</Address>
   <Address>Suite 520</Address>
   <Address>St. Charles, MO</Address>
   <ZipCode>63301</ZipCode>
</Mail>
```

In this case, the `<Address>` element is used three times, and this is considered a valid XML document. The + quantifier does signify, however, that the `<Address>` element must be included at least once. This means that the following XML (Listing 5-23) is considered *invalid.*

Listing 5-23: An invalid XML document

```
<?xml version="1.0" encoding="UTF-8"?>
<!DOCTYPE Mail SYSTEM "Mail.dtd">

<Mail>
   <Name>Bill Evjen</Name>
   <ZipCode>63301</ZipCode>
</Mail>
```

As you saw earlier, the child elements are defined within a set of parenthesis and the Address element was followed with a + quantifier to signify that it can have one or more instances. If you want to apply this setting to all the children of the `<Mail>` element, one method would be to use the + quantifier in each of the elements:

```
<!ELEMENT Mail (Name+, Address+, ZipCode+)>
```

Because a + quantifier follows the Name, Address, and ZipCode definitions, all these elements can appear one or more times (in this sequence only). If you want to make such a declaration, another method is to apply the + quantifier to each of the items contained within the parenthesis as shown here:

```
<!ELEMENT Mail (Name, Address, ZipCode)+>
```

In this case, the + quantifier follows the parenthesis, and this means that this quantifier applies to everything contained within the parenthesis. This appeared earlier in the Hamlet.dtd in the <PERSONAE> element definition.

```
<!ELEMENT PERSONAE (TITLE | PERSONA | PGROUP)+>
```

The ? Quantifier

Another quantifier to work with in building your DTD documents is the ? quantifier. The ? quantifier allows you to specify that zero or only a single instance of the child element can be contained within the element. Suppose you have an XML document like the one presented in Listing 5-24.

Listing 5-24: An XML document using the ? quantifier

```
<?xml version="1.0" encoding="UTF-8"?>
<!DOCTYPE Mail SYSTEM "Mail.dtd">

<Mail>
   <Salutation>Mr.</Salutation>
   <Name>Bill Evjen</Name>
   <Address>123 Main Street; St. Charles, MO</Address>
   <ZipCode>63301</ZipCode>
</Mail>
```

In this case, a new XML element <Salutation> is contained as a child element within the <Mail> element. You could probably structure it so that the <Salutation> element is considered optional. This means that the <Salutation> element can appear either zero times or at least once in the document. Also in this case, it doesn't make much sense for the <Salutation> element to appear more than once, thereby making the ? quantifier an ideal choice in defining the child element.

In defining the child element using the ? quantifier, you take a similar approach to that used with the + quantifier. This approach is illustrated in Listing 5-25.

Listing 5-25: The Mail.dtd using the ? quantifier

```
<?xml version="1.0" encoding="UTF-8"?>

<!ELEMENT Mail (Salutation?, Name, Address+, ZipCode)>
<!ELEMENT Salutation (#PCDATA)>
<!ELEMENT Name (#PCDATA)>
<!ELEMENT Address (#PCDATA)>
<!ELEMENT ZipCode (#PCDATA)>
```

In this case, the <Salutation> child element is defined with a ? quantifier specifying that the element can only appear zero or one time within the <Mail> element. This means that the XML document presented in Listing 5-26 is considered valid.

Listing 5-26: A valid XML document using the Mail.dtd

```
<?xml version="1.0" encoding="UTF-8"?>
<!DOCTYPE Mail SYSTEM "Mail.dtd">

<Mail>
   <Salutation>Mr.</Salutation>
   <Name>Bill Evjen</Name>
   <Address>123 Main Street</Address>
   <Address>St. Charles, MO</Address>
   <ZipCode>63301</ZipCode>
</Mail>
```

This example shows the `<Salutation>` element a single time (the maximum allowed). The XML document presented in Listing 5-27 is also valid.

Listing 5-27: Another valid XML document using the Mail.dtd

```
<?xml version="1.0" encoding="UTF-8"?>
<!DOCTYPE Mail SYSTEM "Mail.dtd">

<Mail>
   <Name>Bill Evjen</Name>
   <Address>123 Main Street</Address>
   <Address>St. Charles, MO</Address>
   <ZipCode>63301</ZipCode>
</Mail>
```

Because you use the `?` quantifier, if you use the `<Salutation>` element more than once, you produce an invalid XML document (see Listing 5-28).

Listing 5-28: An invalid XML document

```
<?xml version="1.0" encoding="UTF-8"?>
<!DOCTYPE Mail SYSTEM "Mail.dtd">

<Mail>
   <Salutation>Mr.</Salutation>
   <Salutation>Mr.</Salutation>
   <Name>Bill Evjen</Name>
   <Address>123 Main Street</Address>
   <Address>St. Charles, MO</Address>
   <ZipCode>63301</ZipCode>
</Mail>
```

You can also apply the `?` quantifier, like the `+` quantifier, to an entire set of child elements as presented here:

```
<!ELEMENT Mail (Salutation, Name, Address+, ZipCode)?>
```

Notice how the `?` quantifier is applied to each of the elements *except* the `<Address>` element. The `+` quantifier applies directly to this sequence of elements.

The * Quantifier

The final quantifier is the * quantifier. The use of this quantifier signifies that the child element can be contained within the designated element zero or more times. An example DTD using the * quantifier is presented in Listing 5-29.

Listing 5-29: Using the * quantifier in the Mail.dtd

```
<?xml version="1.0" encoding="UTF-8"?>

<!ELEMENT Mail (Salutation?, Name*, Address+, ZipCode)>
<!ELEMENT Salutation (#PCDATA)>
<!ELEMENT Name (#PCDATA)>
<!ELEMENT Address (#PCDATA)>
<!ELEMENT ZipCode (#PCDATA)>
```

In this case, the <Name> element can appear zero or more times within the XML document that uses this DTD for validation. This means that the XML document presented in Listing 5-30 is considered valid XML.

Listing 5-30: A valid XML document

```
<?xml version="1.0" encoding="UTF-8"?>
<!DOCTYPE Mail SYSTEM "Mail.dtd">

<Mail>
   <Salutation>Mr.</Salutation>
   <Address>123 Main Street</Address>
   <Address>St. Charles, MO</Address>
   <ZipCode>63301</ZipCode>
</Mail>
```

This also means that Listing 5-31 is considered valid.

Listing 5-31: Another valid XML document

```
<?xml version="1.0" encoding="UTF-8"?>
<!DOCTYPE Mail SYSTEM "Mail.dtd">

<Mail>
   <Salutation>Mr.</Salutation>
   <Name>Bill Evjen</Name>
   <Name>or Resident</Name>
   <Address>123 Main Street</Address>
   <Address>St. Charles, MO</Address>
   <ZipCode>63301</ZipCode>
</Mail>
```

Allowing a *Choice*

A *choice* option allows you to specify a selection of available child elements that can be used. For instance, suppose you wanted to allow a choice between <Item>, <Items>, or <Pallets> in your XML document. To accomplish this, you structure a DTD in the following fashion (Listing 5-32).

Listing 5-32: Providing a choice via your DTD

```
<?xml version="1.0" encoding="UTF-8"?>

<!ELEMENT Quantity (Item | Items | Pallet)>
<!ELEMENT Item (#PCDATA)>
<!ELEMENT Items (#PCDATA)>
<!ELEMENT Pallet (#PCDATA)>
```

As you can see by the `<Quantity>` definition, you are providing a choice of three items to the consumer of this DTD—`<Item>`, `<Items>`, or `<Pallets>`. The options provided via the DTD are separated by a vertical bar (or pipe) instead of by commas as is done normally. This means that the following XML document is considered valid:

```
<Quantity>
   <Item>3Q7854P</Item>
</Quantity>
```

This is also considered valid XML:

```
<Quantity>
   <Items>3Q7854P-6TY458P</Items>
</Quantity>
```

Also valid is:

```
<Quantity>
   <Pallet>5H3899K</Pallet>
</Quantity>
```

Although only three items are provided as choices for the child element of the `<Quantity>` element, you can actually place as many options as you wish as long as they are all separated by a vertical bar.

Just like standard child elements, these choice child elements can take quantifiers.

```
<!ELEMENT Quantity (Item | Items | Pallet)+>
```

The use of the + quantifier means that you can have any of the choices one or more times in your document. The following is, therefore, considered valid XML:

```
<Quantity>
   <Item>3Q7854P</Item>
   <Item>6TY458P</Item>
   <Pallet>5H3899K</Pallet>
</Quantity>
```

Attribute Declarations

Not all XML documents contain only elements and their values and nothing more. Many XML documents use attributes to further define the XML document. Just as you can easily define your elements using a DTD, you can also incorporate the associated attributes into an element. The generic usage of the attribute declaration is shown here:

```
<!ATTLIST [element name] [attribute name] [attribute type] [default value]
          [attribute name] [attribute type] [default value]>
```

In this case, the `element name` is the name of the element to which the attribute is added to. The `attribute name` is the name of the attribute. The `attribute type` is a way to qualify the data type (a rather limited process). Finally, the `default value` is the starting value of the item.

Before you begin to create a set of attributes using the `<!ATTLIST>` element, take a look at the following bit of XML:

```
<Name first="Bill" middle="J." last="Evjen" />
```

Here you can see a single element, `<Name>`, which is really an empty element. Although empty, the `<Name>` element contains three attributes. Listing 5-33 shows how to declare attributes within this element.

Listing 5-33: Declaring attributes for the <Name> element

```
<?xml version="1.0" encoding="UTF-8"?>

<!ELEMENT Name EMPTY>
<!ATTLIST Name first CDATA "">
<!ATTLIST Name middle CDATA "">
<!ATTLIST Name last CDATA "">
```

For this example, just a single element defined — `<Name>`. From the DTD you can see that the `<Name>` element is declared as an empty element with three possible attributes. All the attributes are assigned to the `<Name>` element and given a data type of `CDATA`. This data type specification means that the attribute will contain character data. As a default value, nothing is assigned and an empty string is used instead.

Using this DTD, you can write the following bit of XML:

```
<Name first="Bill" last="Evjen" />
```

In this case the first and last attributes are used, but the middle attribute is not used. This is fine because none of the attributes is required to define the attributes within the DTD. This means that the following XML is also valid:

```
<Name last="Evjen" />
```

The following would also be considered valid XML:

```
<Name />
```

Note that the following bit of XML is also considered valid:

```
<Name last="Evjen" first="Bill" />
```

Here you can see that the order of the attributes has been inverted. XML parsers ignore attribute ordering — allowing the attributes to be used in any order.

Attribute Data Types

One of the requirements when declaring your attributes within a DTD is that the attribute be given a specific data type. In the previous example, you saw what is, probably, one of the more common data types used — CDATA. The list of available data types is presented in the following table.

Data Type	Description
CDATA	Any character data.
IDREF	Forces a unique ID to be provided for the attribute.
IDREFS	Allows for multiple IDs to be provided. IDs must be separated by whitespace.
ENTITY	Allows for an entity to be provided. Entities are discussed shortly.
ENTITIES	Allows for multiple entities to be provided. Entities must be separated by whitespace. Entities are discussed shortly.
NMTOKEN	Allows for an XML name token to be provided.
NMTOKENS	Allows for multiple XML name tokens to be provided. Name tokens must be separated by whitespace.
NOTATION	Allows for one or more notations to be provided.

The #REQUIRED Keyword

If you have an attribute value that is required, you simply use the #REQUIRED keyword when declaring the attributes. Listing 5-34 shows how the three attributes for the <Name> element are turned into required attributes.

Listing 5-34: Declaring required attributes for the <Name> element

```
<?xml version="1.0" encoding="UTF-8"?>

<!ELEMENT Name EMPTY>
<!ATTLIST Name first CDATA #REQUIRED>
<!ATTLIST Name middle CDATA #REQUIRED>
<!ATTLIST Name last CDATA #REQUIRED>
```

You make the attribute a required attribute, by utilizing the #REQUIRED keyword. Note that the keyword is case-sensitive. This forces the attribute to be present, even if it is empty. The following XML is considered invalid:

```
<Name first="Bill" last="Evjen" />
```

However, this bit of XML is considered valid:

```
<Name first="Bill" middle="" last="Evjen" />
```

Even though no value is provided, the middle attribute is present and, therefore, the XML document is now considered valid.

Note that when using the `#REQUIRED` keyword, you are no longer required to provide a default value for the attribute because the user of the DTD will be providing one.

The #IMPLIED Keyword

Earlier I provided three attributes with a default value of `""` instead of something actually meaningful. In the case of these three attributes, it doesn't make much sense to provide a default value because everyone has a different name. One way around this problem is to use the `#REQUIRED` keyword and force everyone to provide a value for all three attributes. This can work; but what if you don't want to require all these values? For instance, suppose you want to make the `first` and `last` attributes required, whereas the `middle` attribute can remain optional? In this kind of scenario, using the `#IMPLIED` keyword in your attribute declaration makes complete sense. Listing 5-35 shows its use in the DTD.

Listing 5-35: Declaring implied attributes for the <Name> element

```
<?xml version="1.0" encoding="UTF-8"?>

<!ELEMENT Name EMPTY>
<!ATTLIST Name first CDATA #REQUIRED>
<!ATTLIST Name middle CDATA #IMPLIED>
<!ATTLIST Name last CDATA #REQUIRED>
```

In this case, the `first` and `last` attributes are required. The `middle` attribute, however, is *not* required and it doesn't include a default value if it isn't included. It is as if a null value is provided instead. With this DTD, the following bit of XML is considered valid:

```
<Name first="Bill" middle="J." last="Evjen" />
```

Also, the following bit of XML is just as valid:

```
<Name first="Bill" last="Evjen" />
```

The #FIXED Keyword

The last keyword to review is the `#FIXED` keyword. It enables you to assign an attribute with a default value that cannot be changed for any reason. Listing 5-36 shows an example of the `#FIXED` keyword.

Listing 5-36: Declaring fixed attributes for the <Name> element

```
<?xml version="1.0" encoding="UTF-8"?>

<!ELEMENT Name EMPTY>
<!ATTLIST Name member CDATA #FIXED "true">
<!ATTLIST Name first CDATA #REQUIRED>
<!ATTLIST Name middle CDATA #IMPLIED>
<!ATTLIST Name last CDATA #REQUIRED>
```

To declare an attribute that makes use of the `#FIXED` keyword, you follow the keyword with the default value in quotes. Listing 5-36 shows that the `member` attribute is set to be a fixed attribute with a default value of `true`. With this declaration in place, the following bit of XML is considered valid:

```
<Name member="true" first="Bill" last="Evjen" />
```

Setting the `member` attribute to `false` causes the XML document to be invalid:

```
<Name member="false" first="Bill" last="Evjen" />
```

One interesting point is that the attribute need not be included at all. If it is included, then the required value must be utilized. However, if the attribute is not included, then the XML parser makes use of the value that is provided via the DTD as if it were present. This means that the following bit of XML is also considered valid:

```
<Name first="Bill" last="Evjen" />
```

Using Enumerations as Values

In some instances, you want an attribute to only contain a set of specific values. In these cases, you provide the user of the DTD with a list of enumerated values that can be used with the attribute. This is rather similar to enumerations, or *choices,* that were used when declaring an element.

Suppose you have a member attribute that you want to take a `true` or `false` value and nothing else. You accomplish by providing the `true` and `false` values as enumerations. This syntax is illustrated in Listing 5-37.

Listing 5-37: Declaring enumerations to use with an attribute

```
<?xml version="1.0" encoding="UTF-8"?>

<!ELEMENT Name EMPTY>
<!ATTLIST Name member (true | false) "true">
<!ATTLIST Name first CDATA #REQUIRED>
<!ATTLIST Name middle CDATA #IMPLIED>
<!ATTLIST Name last CDATA #REQUIRED>
```

In this case, the member attribute allows for an enumeration of values — either `true` or `false`. These enumerations must be contained within parenthesis separated by vertical bars. Following the parenthesis is the default value of the member attribute if it is not included by the user of the DTD.

With this DTD, the following bit of XML is considered valid:

```
<Name member="true" first="Bill" last="Evjen" />
```

This also means that the inverse value for the `member` attribute is also valid:

```
<Name member="false" first="Bill" last="Evjen" />
```

Then, if no `member` attribute is provided a default value of `true` is assumed. Even if the `member` attribute is not included, the XML is still valid:

```
<Name first="Bill" last="Evjen" />
```

When working with enumerations, you can also use the keywords discussed earlier. For instance, if you wish to make the member attribute required, you use the syntax in your DTD illustrated in Listing 5-38.

Listing 5-38: Declaring enumerations to use with a required attribute

```
<?xml version="1.0" encoding="UTF-8"?>

<!ELEMENT Name EMPTY>
<!ATTLIST Name member (true | false) #REQUIRED>
<!ATTLIST Name first CDATA #REQUIRED>
<!ATTLIST Name middle CDATA #IMPLIED>
<!ATTLIST Name last CDATA #REQUIRED>
```

From Listing 5-38, you can see that the default value was replaced with a `#REQUIRED` keyword to make the `member` attribute required. Now the user of this DTD is required to give a `true` or `false` value for the `member` attribute in order to have a valid XML document.

Entity Declarations

In the first chapter of this book, you were introduced to entities. An entity is the capability to map a character string to a specific symbol or character. XML already provides some entities out of the box as is presented in the following table.

Character	Entity
<	`<`
>	`>`
"	`"`
'	`'`
&	`&`

In this table, you can see that the entity for the `&` symbol is `&`. To use the `&` symbol in your document, you type `&` in its place and then, when the XML is parsed, the `&` string is converted to the appropriate referenced character.

Entities can be provided as internal or external entities. This section reviews internal entities.

Internal Entities

To declare an internal entity, you use the following syntax:

```
<!ENTITY [entity key] [entity translated value]>
```

As you can see, it is rather simple to create an internal entity within your DTD. To create an entity you use the `<!ENTITY>` declaration within the DTD and simply provide it with a key and a translated value for the XML parser to use when it encounters the key in an XML document. Listing 5-39 shows a DTD making use of the `<!ENTITY>` declaration.

Listing 5-39: Fund.dtd using an entity

```
<?xml version="1.0" encoding="UTF-8"?>

<!ELEMENT Fund (Name, NumberShares, DataProvider)>
<!ELEMENT Name (#PCDATA)>
<!ELEMENT NumberShares (#PCDATA)>
<!ELEMENT DataProvider (#PCDATA)>
<!ENTITY LIP "Lipper Inc., A Reuters Company">
```

In this DTD, a single element is defined that includes three child elements. At the bottom of the DTD, an entity is declared using the `<!ENTITY>` declaration. A key of `LIP` is provided that should then be translated to `Lipper Inc., A Reuters Company` by an XML parser. Listing 5-40 shows this entity being used within an XML document.

Listing 5-40: Fund.xml using Fund.dtd

```
<?xml version="1.0" encoding="UTF-8"?>
<!DOCTYPE Fund SYSTEM "Fund.dtd">

<Fund>
 <Name>XYZ Fund Global Growth</Name>
 <NumberShares>22</NumberShares>
 <DataProvider>&LIP;</DataProvider>
</Fund>
```

From this code, you can see that the entity key is provided as a value of the `<DataProvider>` element. Note that the key, although declared as `LIP` in the DTD, must be preceded with an ampersand and followed by a semi-colon (`&LIP;`). The `Fund.xml` file in Internet Explorer is shown in Figure 5-3.

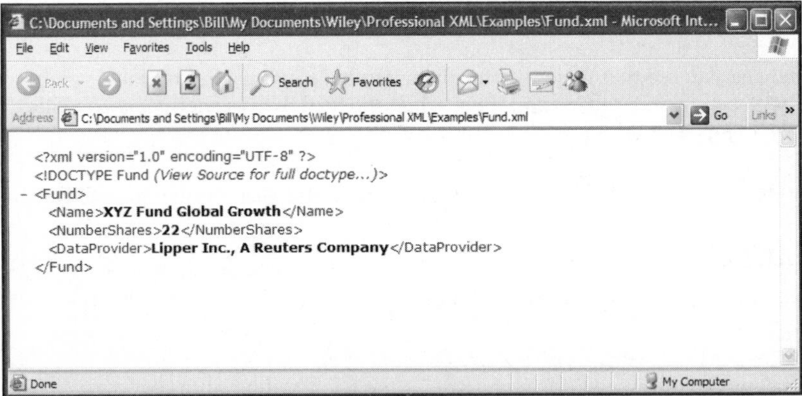

Figure 5-3

From this figure, you can see that the `&LIP;` character sequence was converted by the XML parser to a larger content set because the `<!ENTITY>` declaration was utilized in the DTD.

External Entities

In addition to internal entities, you can also make reference to external entities. This allows you to input XML fragments and other single items into your XML documents. The general usage of an external entity is presented here:

```
<!ENTITY [entity key] SYSTEM [URI]>
```

The difference between this declaration and the internal entity declaration is that this one includes the keyword `SYSTEM` that signifies that this is an external entity. Then, instead of providing the translated value of the entity key, you put a pointer in place to indicate its location.

An example usage is shown here:

```
<!ENTITY LIP SYSTEM "http://www.lipperweb.com/entities/companyname.xml">
```

Notation Declarations

Notation declarations are a rudimentary way of providing some type casting capabilities to the values contained within your XML elements. It is more of a recommendation, and there is no actual enforcement by the XML parsers when you are using a notation declaration. One possible generic usage of the notation declaration is presented here:

```
<!NOTATION [name] SYSTEM [URI or Description]>
```

To create a notation declaration, you use the `<!NOTATION>` declaration. An example of creating an element with a date requirement within your DTD is presented in Listing 5-41.

Listing 5-41: Fund.dtd using a notation

```
<?xml version="1.0" encoding="UTF-8"?>

<!ELEMENT Fund (Name, NumberShares, DataProvider, OrderDate)>
<!ELEMENT Name (#PCDATA)>
<!ELEMENT NumberShares (#PCDATA)>
<!ELEMENT DataProvider (#PCDATA)>
<!ELEMENT OrderDate (#PCDATA)>
<!NOTATION Name SYSTEM "http://www.lipperweb.com/namingstandards.html">
```

Here a notation declaration is utilized to specify that the name needs to follow a specific naming standard and that the standard can be found at a specific URL on the Internet. Using this notation in no way forces XML parsers to make sure that the standard is followed, it is there purely as a reference. You can put anything in place of the hyperlink as well. In fact, the value can be also a MIME type specifying the file type of the value contained within the XML element. For those that move images, documents, or other binary items around via an XML file, this might be a good method to specify to the user of the XML document the MIME type that can be contained within a specified XML element. An example MIME type is `image/png`.

Using XML Tools to Create the DTD

So far in this chapter, you have been creating the DTDs from scratch. The DTD standard has existed for some time now and, for this reason, many XML tools are built-in to make it easy for you to build and consume DTDs.

For instance, using Altova's XMLSpy, you can easily create the DTD for any XML document on the fly. To accomplish this task, select DTD/Schema from the menu and select Generate DTD/Schema from the provided options. This pulls up a dialog box that enables you to name the DTD as you wish. The dialog is presented in Figure 5-4.

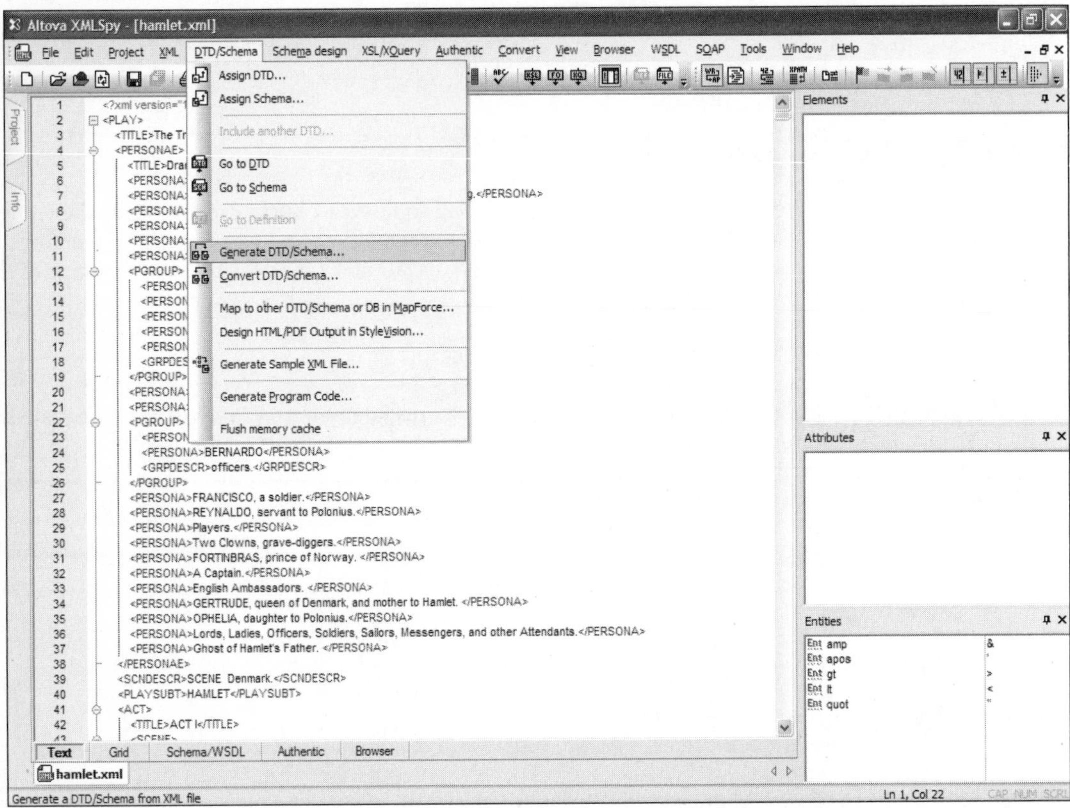

Figure 5-4

DTD Validation

Many tools online and offline enable you to validate your XML documents against a DTD. One such tool online is Validome's DTD and Schema Validator found at `validome.org/grammar/`. This site is shown in Figure 5-5.

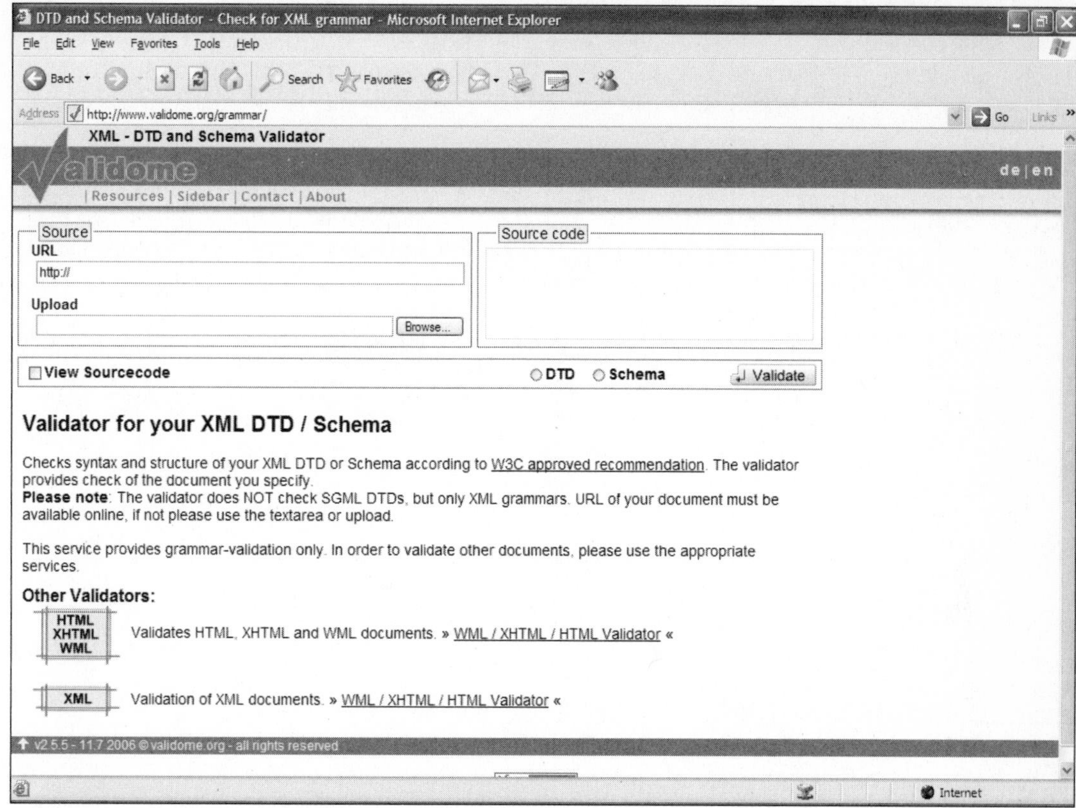

Figure 5-5

This online tool allows you to upload an XML document that contains an inline DTD and also to validate it. The results of the validation are presented in the browser.

Summary

Having an XML document is not always enough. You sometimes need a schema to validate that the XML documents you create or receive are *valid*, meaning that they follow a prescribed structure. This structure enables you to automatically build and consume XML documents.

This chapter looks at one method for defining this structure — DTDs. The next chapter takes a look at one of the more popular methods — XML Schemas.

6

XML Schemas

In the previous chapter, you saw that defining a vocabulary for the XML that you create or work with is an important step in any validation process. If you accept XML documents, you need the means to programmatically validate the structure of those XML documents. *Validating* an XML document means initiating a process to ensure that the XML document follows a set of rules regarding structure. It is quite difficult to process an XML document that is doesn't have the structure you expect.

In the previous chapter, you reviewed using DTDs — or document type definitions in XML validation. *DTDs* are the original way to describe the vocabulary of an XML document. If you look at the XML specification (found at `w3.org/TR/REC-xml/`) you find that DTDs are included in this definition. You don't find the XML Schemas specifications defined in the XML specification. XML Schemas were defined after the creation of the XML specification.

The W3C made the XML Schema a recommendation in October of 2004. You can find the various specifications in the following places on the Internet:

- **XML Schema Part 0: Primer** — `w3.org/TR/xmlschema-0/`
- **XML Schema Part 1: Structures** — `w3.org/TR/xmlschema-1/`
- **XML Schema Part 2: Datatypes** — `w3.org/TR/xmlschema-2/`

XML Schemas are the default way to represent a vocabulary, and they are the best option for new development. This chapter looks at the basics of XML Schemas — including how to build and consume them.

The Issues with DTDs

The previous chapter reviews DTDs and how to use them with your XML documents. It described DTDs as a means to create an XML vocabulary for your XML structures. *Vocabulary* is a valid word to describe how you define the structure of a document. Another word that is used just as often is *schema*, which is a synonym of the word *vocabulary*. They are interchangeable. XML Schemas are another vocabulary for your XML documents.

If DTDs were defined with the XML specification and utilized from the days of SGML, why the need for a new means of creating a vocabulary? The DTD method of defining a vocabulary for XML documents has some issues that require the change.

To understand these issues, look at a sample of a DTD that is embedded within a simple XML document. This document is presented in Listing 6-1.

Listing 6-1: An XML document with an embedded DTD

```
<?xml version="1.0" encoding="UTF-8"?>
<!DOCTYPE Process [
<!ELEMENT Address (#PCDATA)>
<!ELEMENT City (#PCDATA)>
<!ELEMENT Country (#PCDATA)>
<!ELEMENT Item (#PCDATA)>
<!ELEMENT Name (#PCDATA)>
<!ELEMENT Order (Item, Quantity)>
<!ELEMENT Process (Name, Address, City, State, Country, Order)>
<!ELEMENT Quantity (#PCDATA)>
<!ELEMENT State (#PCDATA)>
]>

<Process>
 <Name>Bill Evjen</Name>
 <Address>123 Main Street</Address>
 <City>Saint Charles</City>
 <State>Missouri</State>
 <Country>USA</Country>
 <Order>
        <Item>52-inch Plasma</Item>
        <Quantity>1</Quantity>
 </Order>
</Process>
```

In this listing, you can see some obvious problems. The first is that a DTD definition looks nothing like XML. This makes it the process of learning DTDs more difficult than it should be. After learning the syntax of XML, the XML author also needs to learn another syntax that is quite different from XML. XML Schemas on the other hand make use of the standard XML syntax to create the vocabulary, thereby making the transition to XML Schemas quite simple.

Beyond the overall syntax provided via the DTD document, you can see that an element hierarchy is explicitly defined.

```
<!ELEMENT Process (Name, Address, City, State, Country, Order)>
```

If you have another element besides the element `<Process>` that requires the same set of subelements, DTDs do not let you reuse a set declaration. Instead of providing set declaration that can be reused, DTDs have you declare the construction again. XML Schemas on the other hand allow you to create a group of elements or attributes that can be reused throughout the declaration set.

DTDs also don't give you any extensive datatyping capabilities. Instead, you can perform only simple datatyping. For an example, look at the following DTD statement:

```
<!ELEMENT Quantity (#PCDATA)>
```

In this case, the element <Quantity> is defined with a `#PCDATA` statement, which means that the contents of the `<Quantity>` element can allow only parsed character data. You can't get much more detailed using DTDs. In the XML document that makes use of this element, you see that a number is provided as the content value.

```
<Quantity>1</Quantity>
```

Although this statement is valid for the `#PCDATA` declaration, it would be better if it were more explicit and precise when stating the possible values of the `<Quantity>` element. Using XML Schemas, you can specify that contents of the `<Quantity>` element should be an `int`, `double`, `long`, or any of many other possible datatypes. This capability gives you tremendous power.

Another weakness of DTDs is that they give you a limited model for defining the cardinality of the possible number of times an element can appear in the XML document. You do this using one of a couple of available quantifiers. For instance:

```
<!ELEMENT Mail (Name, Address+, ZipCode)>
```

In this case, the `<Address>` element being utilized as a child element of the `<Mail>` element and the `+` qualifier defines that the `<Address>` element must appear one or more times. Besides the `+` qualifier, you can also use the `?` qualifier.

```
<!ELEMENT Mail (Salutation?, Name, Address+, ZipCode)>
```

The `?` qualifier states that the `<Salutation>` element should appear either zero or only one time within the `<Mail>` element. The last qualifier available in the DTD-world is the `*` qualifier.

```
<!ELEMENT Mail (Salutation?, Name*, Address+, ZipCode)>
```

In this case, the `<Name>` element is defined as something that can appear zero or more times within the `<Mail>` element. You might be looking at these three qualifiers and be wondering where the problem lies, but imagine that you wanted the `<Address>` element to appear three times (no more or less). What if you wanted the `<Address>` element to appear between two and five times in the XML document? This is something that XML Schemas can do. You can get rather specific about how often items appear in the XML document. You definitely want the power to be this specific in your declarations of vocabulary definitions.

After reviewing this chapter, you see that XML Schemas provide you much more control over the vocabulary of your documents. They allow for a more specific validation process. That is why XML Schemas are the most popular methods for validating XML documents.

Building the Root XML Schema Document

Because you already know how to work with XML and understand the XML syntax, you may find that creating the XML Schema document is a simple process. An XML Schema document is an XML file that has an `.xsd` file extension. The next section enables you to create your first XML Schema document and then associate it to any XML documents. These sections look to detail how to create your root element, other elements, simple types, complex types and more.

The XML Declaration

When you create an XML Schema (just as when you create XML documents), you are required to include an XML declaration. This means that your XML Schema starts with the following XML declaration:

```
<?xml version="1.0" ?>
```

This is the minimum requirement for the XML declaration, although you can also specify the encoding and whether the XML document is a standalone document.

```
<?xml version="1.0" encoding="UTF-8" ?>
```

The Root Element

The root element of the XML Schema document is the `<xs:schema>` element. You might also see schema documents written with the `xsd:` namespace prefix as well — `<xsd:schema>`. In addition to the element declaration, you include a namespace declaration.

```
<xs:schema xmlns:xs="http://www.w3.org/2001/XMLSchema">

   <!-- The element and attribute definitions of our document go here -->

</xs:schema>
```

The `xmlns` attribute allows you to specify the prefix and associate it with the W3C's XML Schema namespace `w3.org/2001/XMLSchema`. Because `xs` follows the namespace, this is the item you use preceding all the XML elements of the document. The next sections review some of the other possible attributes of this root element.

attributeFormDefault Attribute

The schema root element can take a series of attributes that enable you to specify some additional behaviors surrounding the use of XML Schema document. The first attribute is the `attributeFormDefault` attribute. From your schema, you can require that XML elements of the instance document prefix their attributes with some characters associated with a particular namespace. Listing 6-2 shows an example of an XML Schema using this attribute.

Listing 6-2: Using the attributeFormDefault attribute in your XML Schema document

```
<?xml version="1.0" encoding="UTF-8" standalone="yes"?>
<xs:schema xmlns:xsi="http://www.w3.org/2001/XMLSchema-instance"
 xmlns:xs="http://www.w3.org/2001/XMLSchema"
 xmlns:be="http://www.lipperweb.com/namespace"
 targetNamespace="http://www.lipperweb.com/namespace"
 attributeFormDefault="qualified">
  <xs:element name="Process">
    <xs:complexType>
```

```
        <xs:sequence>
          <xs:element name="Name">
            <xs:complexType>
              <xs:simpleContent>
                <xs:extension base="xs:string">
                  <xs:attribute name="salutation" type="xs:string" use="required" />
                </xs:extension>
              </xs:simpleContent>
            </xs:complexType>
          </xs:element>
          <xs:element name="Address" type="xs:string" />
          <xs:element name="City" type="xs:string" />
          <xs:element name="State" type="xs:string" />
          <xs:element name="Country" type="xs:string" />
          <xs:element name="Order">
            <xs:complexType>
              <xs:sequence>
                <xs:element name="Item" type="xs:string" />
                <xs:element name="Quantity" type="xs:int" />
              </xs:sequence>
            </xs:complexType>
          </xs:element>
        </xs:sequence>
      </xs:complexType>
    </xs:element>
  </xs:schema>
```

The `attributeFormDefault` can take one of two possible values — `qualified` or `unqualified`. The default value is `unqualified` and means that you don't have to qualify the attribute by adding the prefix. Because the `attributeFormDefault` in this case is set to `qualified`, you must construct the consuming instance document as presented in Listing 6-3.

Listing 6-3: An instance document

```
<?xml version="1.0" encoding="UTF-8"?>
<be:Process xmlns:be="http://www.lipperweb.com/namespace"
 xmlns:xsi="http://www.w3.org/2001/XMLSchema-instance"
 xsi:schemaLocation="http://www.lipperweb.com/namespace C:\mySchema.xsd">
  <Name be:salutation="Mr">Bill Evjen</Name>
  <Address>123 Main Street</Address>
  <City>Saint Charles</City>
  <State>Missouri</State>
  <Country>USA</Country>
  <Order>
     <Item>52-inch Plasma</Item>
     <Quantity>1</Quantity>
  </Order>
</be:Process>
```

In this case, because the `attributeFormDefault` attribute in the XML Schema document, `mySchema.xsd`, is set to `qualified`, the attribute contained within the `<Name>` element makes use of the set prefix.

```
<Name be:salutation="Mr">Bill Evjen</Name>
```

elementFormDefault Attribute

In addition to setting a required prefix for attributes, you can also take the same approach for any elements utilizing the schema. This is presented in Listing 6-4.

Listing 6-4: Using the elementFormDefault attribute in an XML Schema document

```
<?xml version="1.0" encoding="UTF-8" standalone="yes"?>
<xs:schema xmlns:xsi="http://www.w3.org/2001/XMLSchema-instance"
 xmlns:xs="http://www.w3.org/2001/XMLSchema"
 xmlns:be="http://www.lipperweb.com/namespace"
 targetNamespace="http://www.lipperweb.com/namespace"
 attributeFormDefault="unqualified"
 elementFormDefault="qualified">

   <!-- Removed for clarity -->

</xs:schema>
```

Like the `attributeFormDefault` attribute, the `elementFormAttribute` element can take two possible values — `qualified` and `unqualified`. The default value is `unqualified`. Using a value of `qualified` produces instance documents like the one presented in Listing 6-5.

Listing 6-5: An instance document

```
<?xml version="1.0" encoding="UTF-8"?>
<be:Process xmlns:be="http://www.lipperweb.com/namespace"
 xmlns:xsi="http://www.w3.org/2001/XMLSchema-instance"
 xsi:schemaLocation="http://www.lipperweb.com/namespace C:\mySchema.xsd">
  <be:Name salutation="Mr">Bill Evjen</be:Name>
  <be:Address>123 Main Street</be:Address>
  <be:City>Saint Charles</be:City>
  <be:State>Missouri</be:State>
  <be:Country>USA</be:Country>
  <be:Order>
     <be:Item>52-inch Plasma</be:Item>
     <be:Quantity>1</be:Quantity>
  </be:Order>
</be:Process>
```

Using prefixes on elements or even attributes informs the consumer whether these items are in the target namespace or not.

targetNamespace Attribute

As you learn in this book, namespaces are an important part of XML. You can assign your intended namespace to the validation process of the XML document by using the `targetNamespace` attribute within the `<schema>` element. This is presented in Listing 6-6.

Listing 6-6: Using the targetNamespace attribute in your XML Schema document

```
<?xml version="1.0" encoding="UTF-8" standalone="yes"?>
<xs:schema xmlns:xsi="http://www.w3.org/2001/XMLSchema-instance"
 xmlns:xs="http://www.w3.org/2001/XMLSchema"
```

```
    xmlns:be="http://www.lipperweb.com/namespace"
    targetNamespace="http://www.lipperweb.com/namespace"
    attributeFormDefault="unqualified"
    elementFormDefault="qualified">

      <!-- Removed for clarity -->

</xs:schema>
```

The version Attribute

The `version` attribute allows you to easily place a signifier of the version of the XML Schema document directly within the root element. It is important to note that the version attribute has nothing to do with the version of the W3C XML Schema Language which is used, but instead it is the version of the schema document itself. This is shown in Listing 6-7.

Listing 6-7: Using the version attribute in your XML Schema document

```
<?xml version="1.0" encoding="UTF-8" standalone="yes"?>
<xs:schema xmlns:xsi="http://www.w3.org/2001/XMLSchema-instance"
 xmlns:xs="http://www.w3.org/2001/XMLSchema"
 xmlns:be="http://www.lipperweb.com/namespace"
 targetNamespace="http://www.lipperweb.com/namespace"
 attributeFormDefault="unqualified"
 elementFormDefault="qualified"
 version="1.3">

    <!-- Removed for clarity -->

</xs:schema>
```

xml:lang Attribute

The `xml:lang` attribute allows you to signify the language that is utilized for the XML Schema document. This useful if you have versions of the same XML Schema document that are different only because of the element and attribute names that are used. An example of this attribute is presented in Listing 6-8.

Listing 6-8: Using the xml:lang attribute in the XML Schema document

```
<?xml version="1.0" encoding="UTF-8" standalone="yes"?>
<xs:schema xmlns:xsi="http://www.w3.org/2001/XMLSchema-instance"
 xmlns:xs="http://www.w3.org/2001/XMLSchema"
 xmlns:be="http://www.lipperweb.com/namespace"
 targetNamespace="http://www.lipperweb.com/namespace"
 attributeFormDefault="unqualified"
 elementFormDefault="qualified"
 xml:lang="en-US">

    <!-- Removed for clarity -->

</xs:schema>
```

From this example, you can see that the schema is defined as being of language `en-US`, which is a specific culture signifying English as spoken in the United States. Specifying the `xml:lang` attribute with `en-GB` specifies that the document is for English as spoken in the United Kingdom and `fi-FI` signifies that the document is for Finnish as spoken in Finland.

Declaring Elements

Elements, of course, are the main components of any XML document. When you declare the required elements of any instance document that is making use of your XML Schema document, you use several methods.

Elements can be either a *simple type* or a *complex type*. The simple type is the first one reviewed.

Simple Types

Elements are considered simple types if they contain no child elements or attributes. When you declare simple types, three possible simple types are at your disposal—*Atomic types*, *List types*, and *Union types*.

Atomic Types

Atomic types are by far the simplest. For instance, you can have an XML document that is as simple as the one presented in Listing 6-9.

Listing 6-9: An XML document that requires only a single type

```
<?xml version="1.0" encoding="UTF-8"?>
<City xmlns:xsi="http://www.w3.org/2001/XMLSchema-instance"
 xsi:noNamespaceSchemaLocation="AtomicType.xsd">St. Louis</City>
```

In this case, there is only a single element that is quite simple. It doesn't contain any other child elements, and it doesn't contain any attributes or have any rules about its contents. Defining this through an XML Schema document is illustrated in Listing 6-10.

Listing 6-10: Declaring an XML Schema document with a simple type

```
<?xml version="1.0" encoding="UTF-8" standalone="yes"?>
<xs:schema xmlns:xs="http://www.w3.org/2001/XMLSchema">
   <xs:element name="City" type="xs:string" />
</xs:schema>
```

From Listing 6-10, the XML Schema document contains a single element declaration. The `<City>` element declaration—also considered an atomic type—is constructed using the `<xs:element>` element. From here, two attributes are contained within the `<xs:element>` element.

The `name` attribute is used to define the name of the element as it should appear in the XML document. Remember that the value provided here is case-sensitive, meaning that when using this XML Schema document you cannot present the element `<city>` if you want the document to be considered valid.

Besides the `name` attribute, the other attribute presented is the `type` attribute. The `type` attribute allows you to define the datatype of the contents of the `<City>` element. In the XML Schema document that is presented in Listing 6-10, the datatype of the `<City>` element is defined as being of type `string`.

The full list of available datatypes that can be utilized in your element and attribute declarations are presented later in this chapter.

It is rare to declare only a single atomic type and nothing more. In many cases, you use the `<xs:simpleType>` element. This chapter next takes a look at how to construct list types.

List Types

A list type enables you to define a list of values within a single element. Because problems sometimes arise with list types, they are not always considered best practice. It is usually considered better to separate values, with each using its own elements rather than put them all into a single element. Putting multiple values within a single element is illustrated in the XML document presented in Listing 6-11.

Listing 6-11: An XML document that requires only a single type

```
<?xml version="1.0" encoding="UTF-8"?>
<FundIds xmlns:xsi="http://www.w3.org/2001/XMLSchema-instance"
 xsi:noNamespaceSchemaLocation="ListTypes.xsd">
 60003333 600003334 60003335 60003336</FundIds>
```

This XML document contains a single element, `<FundIds>`, which contains what appears as a single value, but really it is four values that are separated with a space. Defining this in an XML Schema document is presented in Listing 6-12.

Listing 6-12: An XML Schema document using a list type

```
<?xml version="1.0" encoding="UTF-8" standalone="yes"?>
<xs:schema xmlns:xs="http://www.w3.org/2001/XMLSchema">
  <xs:element name="FundIds" type="FundIdsType" />
  <xs:simpleType name="FundIdsType">
     <xs:list itemType="xs:int" />
  </xs:simpleType>
</xs:schema>
```

As with previous examples of atomic types, a single declaration begins the document.

```
<xs:element name="FundIds" type="FundIdsType" />
```

In this case, the `<xs:element>` element declares an element with the name of `<FundIds>`, and you can see that it is of type `FundIdsType`. This isn't the type you would normally expect because it is nothing like string, double, or int. Instead it is a type that must be further defined in your XML Schema document.

```
<xs:simpleType name="FundIdsType">
   <xs:list itemType="xs:int" />
</xs:simpleType>
```

The `FundIdsType` is defined using a single `<xs:list>` element. You declare a list type using the `<xs:list>` element. To define the type that is used within the list type itself, you use the `itemType` attribute. In this case, the `itemType` attribute is provided a type of int. No matter which type you define, the items that are contained within the list of items in the single element are separated with a space.

The XML document that was provided as an example shows four fund ids that are separated by a single space.

```
<FundIds>60003333 600003334 60003335 60003336</FundIds>
```

Be aware of a problem when using strings within an element that makes use of the list type. For instance, suppose you have a definition like the one presented in Listing 6-13.

Listing 6-13: An XML Schema document using a list type

```
<?xml version="1.0" encoding="UTF-8" standalone="yes"?>
<xs:schema xmlns:xs="http://www.w3.org/2001/XMLSchema">
  <xs:element name="BaseballTeams" type="BaseballTeamsType" />
  <xs:simpleType name="BaseballTeamsType">
     <xs:list itemType="xs:string" />
  </xs:simpleType>
</xs:schema>
```

This XML Schema defines a list type that is supposed to be a list of string values representing American and Canadian baseball teams. A valid instance document of this type is illustrated in Listing 6-14.

Listing 6-14: An XML document that provides list of baseball teams

```
<?xml version="1.0" encoding="UTF-8"?>
<BaseballTeams xmlns:xsi="http://www.w3.org/2001/XMLSchema-instance"
 xsi:noNamespaceSchemaLocation="ListTypes.xsd">
 Cardinals Yankees Mets Rockies</BaseballTeams>
```

In this case, the XML document is valid and performs as you want. In this case, four items are defined in the list type. This works well because the strings are single words. Imagine instead that the XML document that is making use of this XML Schema document is presented as shown in Listing 6-15.

Listing 6-15: An XML document that provides list of baseball teams

```
<?xml version="1.0" encoding="UTF-8"?>
<BaseballTeams xmlns:xsi="http://www.w3.org/2001/XMLSchema-instance"
 xsi:noNamespaceSchemaLocation="ListTypes.xsd">
 Cardinals Yankees Mets Blue Jays</BaseballTeams>
```

Although four teams are listed in this element, the Blue Jays from Toronto consists of two words that are separated by a single space. The problem is that items are also separated by a space so, when processed, the example from Listing 6-15 appears to consist of five items and not four. This is one of the reasons you should think about separating these types of items into their own elements instead of presenting them within a list type element.

Union types

When working with list types, you might be interested in presenting multiple item types within a single element. For instance, if you are presenting mutual funds, for example, you want a list that consists of the ID of the fund (an `int` value) or the ticker of the fund (a `string` value). If this is the case, you can combine items in a single list, thereby making a union. An example XML Schema document that allows such a construction is presented in Listing 6-16.

Listing 6-16: Allowing a union type from an XML Schema document

```
<?xml version="1.0" encoding="UTF-8" standalone="yes"?>
<xs:schema xmlns:xs="http://www.w3.org/2001/XMLSchema">
   <xs:element name="FundIds" type="FundType" />
   <xs:simpleType name="FundType">
       <xs:union memberTypes="FundIdsType FundTickerType" />
   </xs:simpleType>
   <xs:simpleType name="FundIdsType">
      <xs:list itemType="xs:int" />
   </xs:simpleType>
   <xs:simpleType name="FundTickerType">
      <xs:list itemType="xs:string" />
   </xs:simpleType>
</xs:schema>
```

A few things are going on in this XML Schema document. First, a couple of list types are defined within the document — `FundIdsType` and `FundTickerType`. Each of these list types is using a different datatype — one is using `int` and the other is using `string`.

```
<xs:simpleType name="FundIdsType">
   <xs:list itemType="xs:int" />
</xs:simpleType>
<xs:simpleType name="FundTickerType">
   <xs:list itemType="xs:string" />
</xs:simpleType>
```

To utilize both these list types within a single element, you create a union between the two using the `<xs:union>` element. The `<xs:union>` element from Listing 6-16 utilizes both the list types (in union) through the use of the `memberTypes` attribute. This is where you can place the types that can be part of that union with a space separating the items.

```
<xs:simpleType name="FundType">
   <xs:union memberTypes="FundIdsType FundTickerType" />
</xs:simpleType>
```

Thereafter, the `<xs:element>` element defines a type attribute with a value of the union — `FundType`. This construction makes valid the XML document shown in Listing 6-17.

Listing 6-17: An XML document using the union type

```
<?xml version="1.0" encoding="UTF-8"?>
<FundIds xmlns:xsi="http://www.w3.org/2001/XMLSchema-instance"
 xsi:noNamespaceSchemaLocation="UnionType.xsd">
   60003333 60003334 60003335 60003336 JAXP
</FundIds>
```

Complex Types

In addition to defining simple types by using the <xs:simpleType> element, you can also define elements that contain other child elements or attributes. In these cases, you define a complex type using the <xs:complexType> element. Listing 6-18 defines a simple complex type.

Listing 6-18: Declaring an anonymous complex type

```
<?xml version="1.0" encoding="UTF-8" standalone="yes"?>
<xs:schema xmlns:xs="http://www.w3.org/2001/XMLSchema">
  <xs:element name="Process">
    <xs:complexType>
      <xs:sequence>
        <xs:element name="Name" type="xs:string" />
        <xs:element name="Address" type="xs:string" />
        <xs:element name="City" type="xs:string" />
        <xs:element name="State" type="xs:string" />
        <xs:element name="Country" type="xs:string" />
      </xs:sequence>
    </xs:complexType>
  </xs:element>
</xs:schema>
```

In this case, first a single element is defined — the <Process> element. Before closing the <xs:element> tag to define the <Process> element, you utilize a <xs:complexType> element. The reason that the <xs:complexType> element is used is because numerous subelements are contained within the <Process> element.

Listing 6-18 shows a complex type that is considered an *anonymous complex type*. It is considered anonymous because it is an unnamed type. Instead, the type is really defined by the nested <xs:complexType> element itself.

Within the <xs:complexType> element, an <xs:sequence> element is used to define all the simple types that are contained within the <Process> element. This XML Schema states that the <Process> element must contain a <Name>, <Address>, <City>, <State>, and <Country> element. All the subelements defined are of type string and they all must be contained within the XML document in order for the document to be considered valid. If one of the elements is missing or is repeated more than once, the XML document is considered invalid. Also, if the elements are out of order, the XML document is considered invalid. A sample XML document that makes use of this type is presented in Listing 6-19.

Listing 6-19: Using the complex type

```
<Process xmlns:xsi="http://www.w3.org/2001/XMLSchema-instance"
 xsi:noNamespaceSchemaLocation="ComplexTypes.xsd">
 <Name>Bill Evjen</Name>
 <Address>123 Main Street</Address>
 <City>Saint Charles</City>
 <State>Missouri</State>
 <Country>USA</Country>
</Process>
```

Making the anonymous complex type into a *named complex type* is simple. To create a named complex type, you construct your XML Schema document as shown in Listing 6-20.

Listing 6-20: Declaring a named complex type

```
<?xml version="1.0" encoding="UTF-8" standalone="yes"?>
<xs:schema xmlns:xs="http://www.w3.org/2001/XMLSchema">

  <xs:element name="Process" type="ContactDetails" />

  <xs:complexType name="ContactDetails">
     <xs:sequence>
        <xs:element name="Name" type="xs:string" />
        <xs:element name="Address" type="xs:string" />
        <xs:element name="City" type="xs:string" />
        <xs:element name="State" type="xs:string" />
        <xs:element name="Country" type="xs:string" />
     </xs:sequence>
  </xs:complexType>

</xs:schema>
```

In this case, a single parent element is defined, `<Process>`, of type `ContactDetails`. The `ContactDetails` definition is a named complex type. It is named using the `name` attribute. This works like the anonymous complex type presented earlier.

Looking at Reusability

When you define a named complex type, you get into the area of reusability within your XML Schema document. In Listing 6-20, you can see that the `<Process>` element uses an instance of `ContactDetails` in its definition. Because `ContactDetails` is encapsulated, it can be reused. Listing 6-21 shows an example of how it can be reused in multiple elements.

Listing 6-21: Declaring a named complex type

```
<?xml version="1.0" encoding="UTF-8" standalone="yes"?>
<xs:schema xmlns:xs="http://www.w3.org/2001/XMLSchema">

  <xs:element name="Process">
     <xs:complexType>
        <xs:sequence>
           <xs:element name="BillingAddress" type="ContactDetails" />
           <xs:element name="ShippingAddress" type="ContactDetails" />
        </xs:sequence>
     </xs:complexType>
  </xs:element>

  <xs:complexType name="ContactDetails">
     <xs:sequence>
        <xs:element name="Name" type="xs:string" />
        <xs:element name="Address" type="xs:string" />
        <xs:element name="City" type="xs:string" />
        <xs:element name="State" type="xs:string" />
        <xs:element name="Country" type="xs:string" />
```

(continued)

Listing 6-21 *(continued)*

```
        </xs:sequence>
    </xs:complexType>

  </xs:schema>
```

From this example, you can se that two elements are nested within the `<Process>` element — `<BillingAddress>` and `<ShippingAddress>`. Both these elements are defined as the same type— `ContactDetails`. Figure 6-1 shows how this is represented visually.

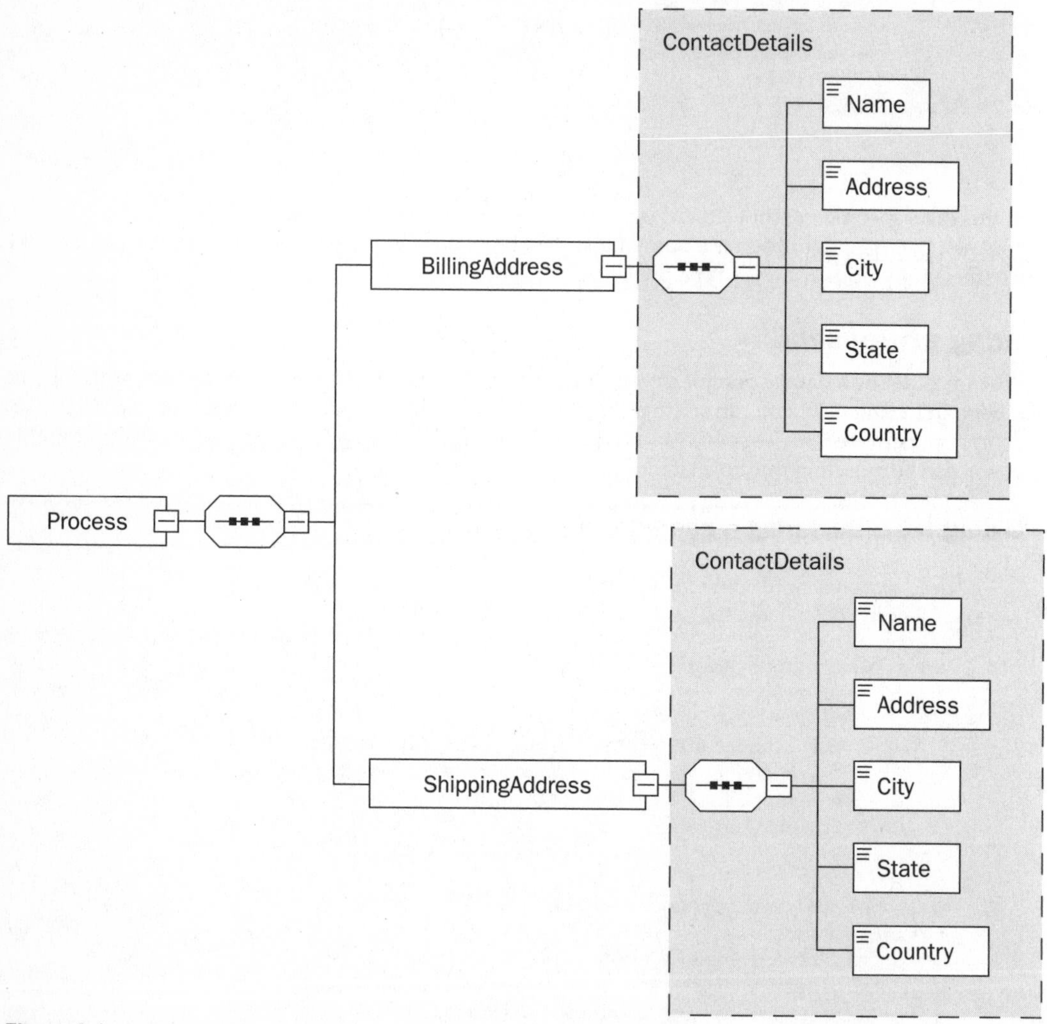

Figure 6-1

Reusing the `ContactDetails` complex type means that you can build a valid XML instance document as presented in Listing 6-22.

Listing 6-22: Process XML document with two ContactDetails instances

```
<?xml version="1.0" encoding="UTF-8"?>
<Process xmlns:xsi="http://www.w3.org/2001/XMLSchema-instance"
 xsi:noNamespaceSchemaLocation="ComplexTypes.xsd">
   <BillingAddress>
      <Name>Bill Evjen</Name>
      <Address>123 Main Street</Address>
      <City>Saint Charles</City>
      <State>Missouri</State>
      <Country>USA</Country>
   </BillingAddress>
   <ShippingAddress>
      <Name>Bill Evjen</Name>
      <Address>123 Main Street</Address>
      <City>Saint Charles</City>
      <State>Missouri</State>
      <Country>USA</Country>
   </ShippingAddress>
</Process>
```

This example shows both instances of the `ContactDetails` type being utilized by different elements.

sequence *and* all

So far, you have been mostly presented with the use of the `<sequence>` element in building complex types. Using `<sequence>` means that all the items in the list are presented in the instance document *in the order in which they are declared within the complex type*. On the other hand, using `<all>` allows the creator of the instance document to place the elements in any order they wish — though it is still a requirement that all the elements appear in the construction. Listing 6-23 details a schema that makes use of the `<all>` element.

Listing 6-23: Using the <all> element

```
<?xml version="1.0" encoding="UTF-8" standalone="yes"?>
<xs:schema xmlns:xs="http://www.w3.org/2001/XMLSchema">
  <xs:element name="Process">
    <xs:complexType>
      <xs:all>
        <xs:element name="Name" type="xs:string" />
        <xs:element name="Address" type="xs:string" />
        <xs:element name="City" type="xs:string" />
        <xs:element name="State" type="xs:string" />
        <xs:element name="Country" type="xs:string" />
      </xs:all>
    </xs:complexType>
  </xs:element>
</xs:schema>
```

Using this construction means that an XML document is considered valid in the following format:

```
<Process xmlns:xsi="http://www.w3.org/2001/XMLSchema-instance"
 xsi:noNamespaceSchemaLocation="ComplexTypes.xsd">
 <Name>Bill Evjen</Name>
 <Address>123 Main Street</Address>
 <City>Saint Charles</City>
 <State>Missouri</State>
 <Country>USA</Country>
</Process>
```

It is also considered valid in this format:

```
<Process xmlns:xsi="http://www.w3.org/2001/XMLSchema-instance"
 xsi:noNamespaceSchemaLocation="ComplexTypes.xsd">
 <Country>USA</Country>
 <Name>Bill Evjen</Name>
 <State>Missouri</State>
 <Address>123 Main Street</Address>
 <City>Saint Charles</City>
</Process>
```

Element Types

As you have noticed, one of the big advantages to XML Schemas is that they are able to datatype their contents in more finely grained manner than a DTD Schema can. A multitude of datatypes are at your disposal when creating elements. You assign a datatype to an element by using the `type` attribute.

```
<xs:element name="Name" type="xs:string" />
```

In this case, an element of `<Name>` is declared, and it is specified to be of type `string`. This means that the contents of the `<Name>` element will always be considered a string value. This means that the following bit of XML is considered valid XML:

```
<Name>Bill Evjen</Name>
```

Although you could also have an element declaration like this one:

```
<xs:element name="Age" type="xs:string" />
```

And this would also be considered valid XML:

```
<Age>23</Age>
```

In this case, however, the `23` value would be considered a string. To give more meaning to any value that you place within the `<Age>` element, it would probably be better to declare the `<Age>` element in the following fashion:

```
<xs:element name="Age" type="xs:int" />
```

Two sets of types at your disposal in the XML Schema world — *primitive datatypes* and *derived datatypes*. The primitive datatypes are the base foundation types, and the derived datatypes build upon the primitive types to create more elaborate types. Figure 6-2 shows a graph of the primitive and derived datatypes available to you when creating XML Schemas.

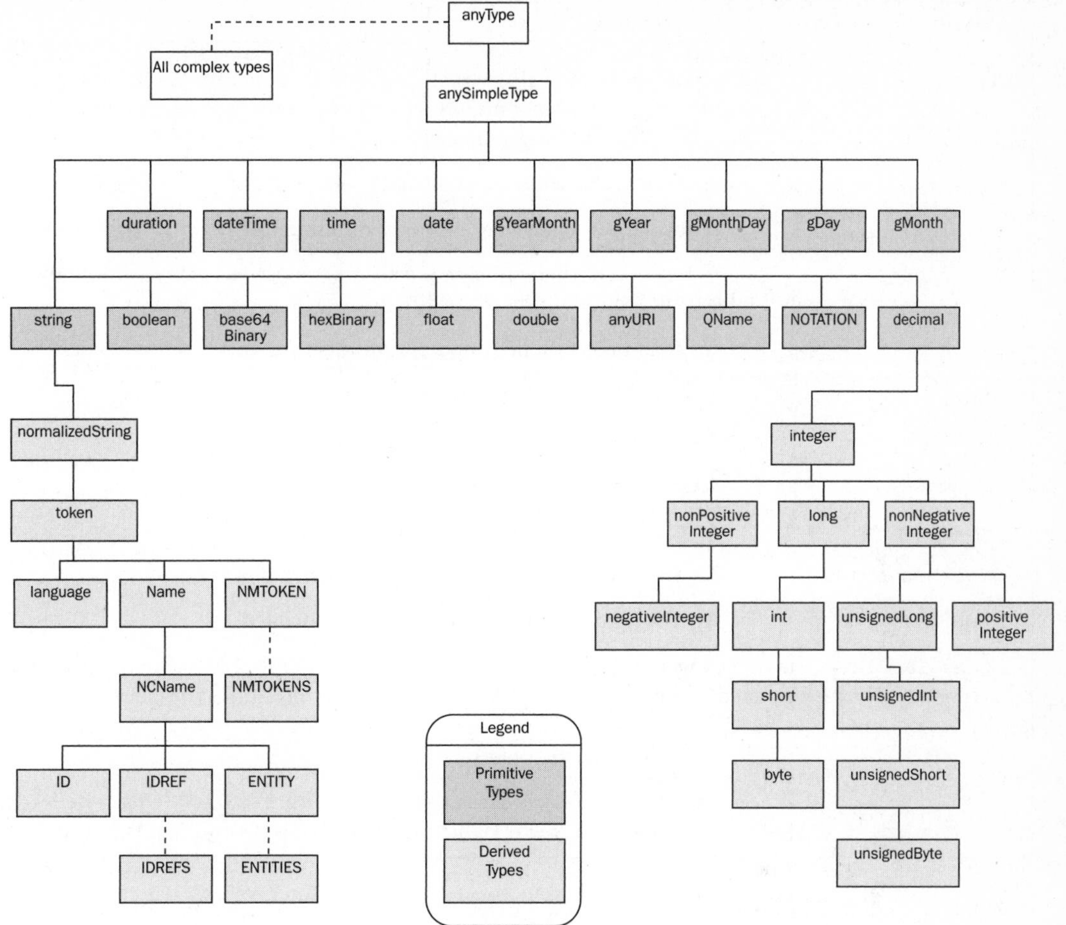

Figure 6-2

In this diagram, you can see a number of primitive datatypes, and only two of them (`string` and `decimal`) have been derived from to create some additional datatypes. The primitive datatypes are detailed in the following table.

Primitive Data Types	Description
`anyURI`	An absolute or relative URI such as `http://www.lipperweb.com/`.
`base64Binary`	A Base64 binary encoded set of data.
`boolean`	A bit-flag option that can be represented as true/false, yes/no, 1/0, on/off or something similar.
`date`	A date consisting of a day/month/year combination according to the Gregorian calendar as it is defined by the ISO 8601 standard.

Table continued on following page

Primitive Data Types	Description
`dateTime`	A date and time value which consists of a date utilizing the day/month/year values and a time set utilizing hour/minute/second as defined by the Gregorian calendar.
`decimal`	A variable precision number that is either positive or negative.
`double`	A double-precision floating point number (64-bit).
`duration`	A duration of time which is a set year/month/day/hour/minute/second length of time according to the Gregorian calendar.
`float`	A single-precision floating point number (32-bit).
`gDay`	A day within the Gregorian calendar.
`gMonth`	A month within the Gregorian calendar.
`gMonthDay`	A month and day within the Gregorian calendar.
`gYear`	A year within the Gregorian calendar.
`gYearMonth`	A year and a month within the Gregorian calendar.
`hexBinary`	A set of binary data that has been hex-encoded.
`NOTATION`	A set of QNames.
`QName`	A qualified name.
`string`	A character string of any length.
`time`	An instance of time. The value range is from 00:00:00 (which represents midnight) to 23:59:59 (which represents one second before midnight).

The datatypes derived from both the string and the decimal primitive datatypes are presented in the following table.

Derived Data Types	Description
`byte`	An integer ranging from -128 to 127. A `byte` type is derived from the `short` type.
`ENTITIES`	A set of `ENTITY` data type values (one or more).
`ENTITY`	An `ENTITY` attribute type as presented in the XML 1.0 specification. An `ENTITY` type is derived from the `NCName` type.
`ID`	An `ID` attribute type as presented in the XML 1.0 specification. The ID type is derived from the `NCName` type.
`IDREF`	A reference to an element with a defined `ID` attribute value. An `IDREF` type is derived from the `NCName` type.
`IDREFS`	A set of `IDREF` attribute types (one or more).

Derived Data Types	Description
int	A numerical value ranging from -2147483648 to 2147483647. The int type is derived from the long type.
integer	A numerical value that consists of a whole number that doesn't contain any decimal places. This number can be negative or positive. The integer type is derived from the decimal type.
language	A representation of a natural language identifier as defined by RFC 3066. The language type is derived from the token type.
long	An integer value ranging from -9223372036854775808 and 9223372036854775807. The long type is derived from the integer type.
Name	A token consisting of characters and represents Names as defined in the XML 1.0 specification. A Name type is derived from the token type.
NCName	A "non-colonized" name as presented in the XML 1.0 specification. An NCName type is derived from the Name type.
negativeInteger	An integer which is made up of a negative value. The negativeInteger type is derived from the nonPositiveInteger type.
NMTOKEN	A set of characters that make up a token value and represents the NMTOKEN attribute as defined in the XML 1.0 specification. The NMTOKEN type is derived from the token type.
NMTOKENS	A set of NMTOKEN attribute types (one or more).
nonNegativeInteger	A positive integer that must be greater than or equal to zero. The nonNegativeInteger type is derived from the integer type.
nonPositiveInteger	A negative integer that must be less than or equal to zero. The nonPositiveInteger type is derived from the integer type.
normalizedString	A whitespace normalized string. The normalizedString type is derived from the string type.
positiveInteger	A positive integer that is greater than zero (but not equal to). A positiveInteger type is derived from the nonNegativeInteger type.
short	An integer value ranging from -32768 to 32767. A short type is derived from the int type.
token	A tokenized string. A token type is derived from the normalizedString type.
unsignedByte	An integer value ranging from 0 to 255. The unsignedByte type is derived from the unsignedShort type.
unsignedInt	An integer value ranging from 0 to 4294967295. The unsignedInt type is derived from the unsignedLong type.
unsignedLong	An integer value ranging from 0 to 18446744073709551615. The unsignedLong type is derived from the nonNegativeInteger type.
unsignedShort	An integer value ranging from 0 to 65535. The unsignedShort type is derived from the unsignedInt type.

Just as these derived datatypes are built upon other types, you can build your own datatypes through the use of the <simpleType> element directly in your XML Schema document.

Listing 6-24 provides an example of creating a custom datatype called MyCountry.

Listing 6-24: Creating a custom datatype called MyCountry

```
<?xml version="1.0" encoding="UTF-8" standalone="yes"?>
<xs:schema xmlns:xs="http://www.w3.org/2001/XMLSchema">

  <xs:element name="Process">
     <xs:complexType>
        <xs:sequence>
           <xs:element name="BillingAddress" type="ContactDetails" />
           <xs:element name="ShippingAddress" type="ContactDetails" />
        </xs:sequence>
     </xs:complexType>
  </xs:element>

  <xs:complexType name="ContactDetails">
     <xs:sequence>
        <xs:element name="Name" type="xs:string" />
        <xs:element name="Address" type="xs:string" />
        <xs:element name="City" type="xs:string" />
        <xs:element name="State" type="xs:string" />
        <xs:element name="Country" type="MyCountry" />
     </xs:sequence>
  </xs:complexType>

  <xs:simpleType name="MyCountry">
     <xs:restriction base="xs:string">
        <xs:enumeration value="USA" />
        <xs:enumeration value="UK" />
        <xs:enumeration value="Canada" />
        <xs:enumeration value="Finland" />
     </xs:restriction>
  </xs:simpleType>

</xs:schema>
```

In the code presented in Listing 6-24, a complex type is used for both the <BillingAddress> and the <ShippingAddress> elements that consists of a series of elements. The element to pay attention to in this example is the <Country> element. The <Country> element is built from a custom derived datatype.

You build a custom datatype using the <simpleType> element and the name attribute (to give a name to your new datatype). In this example, the datatype is named MyCountry. Next, the <restriction> element is used to derive from another datatype using the base attribute — in this case, string. Next, you place a further restriction by making the MyCountry datatype an enumeration of possible string values using the <enumeration> element.

Groups and Choices

You have seen some examples of encapsulation so far in this chapter. Another form of encapsulation places commonly used element groups together in a package that can be used over and over again within your XML Schema document. This can be accomplished using the <group> element.

For instance, suppose you have an XML Schema document as shown in Listing 6-25.

Listing 6-25: Creating a reusable group in your XML Schema document

```
<?xml version="1.0" encoding="UTF-8" standalone="yes"?>
<xs:schema xmlns:xs="http://www.w3.org/2001/XMLSchema">
  <xs:element name="Process">
     <xs:complexType>
        <xs:sequence>
           <xs:element name="OrderNumber" type="xs:positiveInteger" />
           <xs:group ref="ContactDetails" />
        </xs:sequence>
     </xs:complexType>
  </xs:element>
  <xs:group name="ContactDetails">
     <xs:sequence>
        <xs:element name="Name" type="xs:string"/>
        <xs:element name="Address" type="xs:string"/>
        <xs:element name="City" type="xs:string"/>
        <xs:element name="State" type="xs:string"/>
        <xs:element name="Country" type="xs:string"/>
     </xs:sequence>
  </xs:group>
</xs:schema>
```

In this case, you create a group called ContactDetails that encapsulates the <Name>, <Address>, <City>, <State>, and <Country> elements. You define the child elements of the <Process> element; a <group> element is used to incorporate the defined group ContactDetails. To associate the <group> element to the defined group, ContactDetails, you use the ref attribute. Its value is the name of the group.

By specifying the group using a <sequence> element, you are also stating that all the elements of ContactDetails must appear in the order in which they are defined.

Now suppose you want to provide a choice of elements that might appear as a child element of the <Process> element. You can allow choices to single elements or even to entire groups of elements. Suppose you wanted to change the <Process> element construction to allow for either an American or a Canadian address, but you don't want to use the same set of elements to define both of these items. At the same time, you wanted to allow for only a single instance of either of these element groups to appear within the <Process> element. This is the situation where you would use the <choice> element within the XML Schema document. Listing 6-26 provides the XML Schema document that defines this situation.

Listing 6-26: Creating a reusable group in your XML Schema document

```
<?xml version="1.0" encoding="UTF-8" standalone="yes"?>
<xs:schema xmlns:xs="http://www.w3.org/2001/XMLSchema">
  <xs:element name="Process">
    <xs:complexType>
      <xs:sequence>
        <xs:element name="OrderNumber" type="xs:positiveInteger"/>
        <xs:choice>
          <xs:group ref="ContactDetailsUS"/>
          <xs:group ref="ContactDetailsCanada"/>
        </xs:choice>
      </xs:sequence>
    </xs:complexType>
  </xs:element>

  <xs:group name="ContactDetailsUS">
    <xs:sequence>
      <xs:element name="US_Name" type="xs:string"/>
      <xs:element name="Address" type="xs:string"/>
      <xs:element name="City" type="xs:string"/>
      <xs:element name="State" type="xs:string"/>
      <xs:element name="Country" type="xs:string"/>
    </xs:sequence>
  </xs:group>

  <xs:group name="ContactDetailsCanada">
    <xs:sequence>
      <xs:element name="Canada_Name" type="xs:string"/>
      <xs:element name="Address" type="xs:string"/>
      <xs:element name="City" type="xs:string"/>
      <xs:element name="Province" type="xs:string"/>
      <xs:element name="Country" type="xs:string"/>
    </xs:sequence>
  </xs:group>
</xs:schema>
```

In this case, two groups are defined — `ContactDetailsUS` and `ContactDetailsCanada`. The elements between the two groups are similar, but have some differences. For instance, each group uses a unique element name for the name of the contact. The US version uses `<US_Name>` whereas the Canadian version uses `<Canada_Name>`. Also, the US version uses `<State>` whereas the Canadian version uses `<Province>`. The diagram of the schema is presented in Figure 6-3.

Within the `<Process>` element, you are interested in having only one of either of these groups appear. So you use the `<choice>` element.

```
<xs:element name="Process">
  <xs:complexType>
    <xs:choice>
      <xs:group ref="ContactDetailsUS"/>
      <xs:group ref="ContactDetailsCanada"/>
    </xs:choice>
  </xs:complexType>
</xs:element>
```

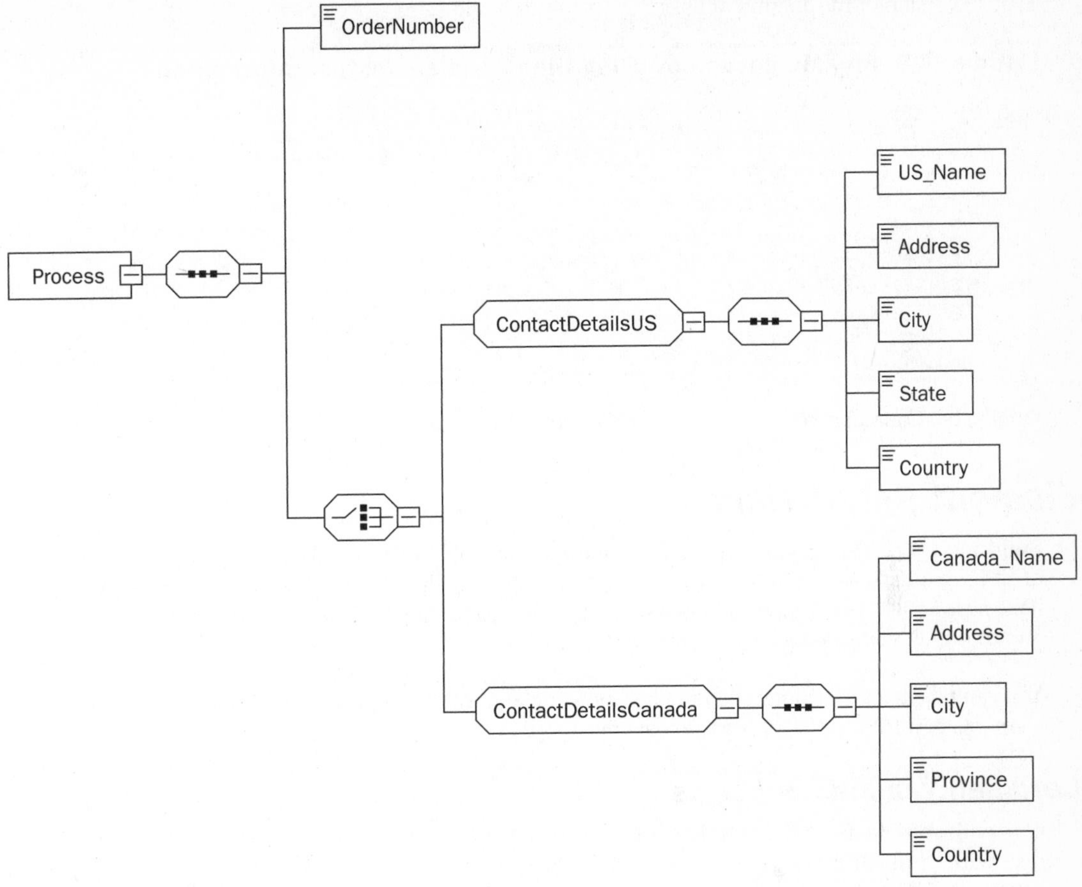

Figure 6-3

Within the <choice> element are all the choices you want to allow. In this case, only two choices are defined — `ContactDetailsUS` and `ContactDetailsCanada`. Allowing only one or the other means that your XML instance document takes the form presented in either Listing 6-27 or 6-28.

Listing 6-27: An XML document using the American contact information

```
<?xml version="1.0" encoding="UTF-8"?>
<Process xmlns:xsi="http://www.w3.org/2001/XMLSchema-instance"
 xsi:noNamespaceSchemaLocation="ComplexTypes.xsd">
   <OrderNumber>1234</OrderNumber>
   <US_Name>Bill Evjen</US_Name>
   <Address>123 Main Street</Address>
   <City>Saint Charles</City>
   <State>Missouri</State>
   <Country>USA</Country>
</Process>
```

The US version of the document uses the <US_Name> and <State> elements.

Listing 6-28: An XML document using the Canadian contact information

```
<?xml version="1.0" encoding="UTF-8"?>
<Process xmlns:xsi="http://www.w3.org/2001/XMLSchema-instance"
 xsi:noNamespaceSchemaLocation="ComplexTypes.xsd">
   <OrderNumber>1234</OrderNumber>
   <Canada_Name>Bill Evjen</Canada_Name>
   <Address>123 Main Street</Address>
   <City>Vancouver</City>
   <Province>British Columbia</Province>
   <Country>Canada</Country>
</Process>
```

Finally, the Canadian version of the document uses the <Canada_Name> and <Province> elements.

Element Restrictions

Building an XML Schema document is all about establishing restrictions. You are defining a set structure of XML that must be in place in order for the XML document to be considered valid. This means, as you have seen so far, that certain elements have to appear, that they have to be spelled in a particular way, and that their values must be of a certain datatype.

You can take the restrictions even further by using a number of available attributes when creating your elements or attributes (attributes are covered shortly).

Cardinality in XML Schemas

One of the problems with DTDs that was mentioned in the beginning part of this chapter was how they deal with cardinality. You want to have a really fine-grained way to define how often (and if) items can appear in a document. Cardinality in XML Schema document is done through the use of the `minOccurs` and `maxOccurs` attributes.

minOccurs

The `minOccurs` attribute specifies the minimum number of times an item may appear. Listing 6-29 shows the `minOccurs` attribute in use.

Listing 6-29: Using the minOccurs attribute with an element

```
<?xml version="1.0" encoding="UTF-8" standalone="yes"?>
<xs:schema xmlns:xs="http://www.w3.org/2001/XMLSchema">
  <xs:element name="Process">
     <xs:complexType>
        <xs:sequence>
           <xs:element name="OrderNumber" type="xs:positiveInteger" />
           <xs:group ref="ContactDetails" />
        </xs:sequence>
     </xs:complexType>
  </xs:element>
```

```
    <xs:group name="ContactDetails">
      <xs:sequence>
        <xs:element name="Salutation" type="xs:string" minOccurs="0" />
        <xs:element name="Name" type="xs:string"/>
        <xs:element name="Address" type="xs:string"/>
        <xs:element name="City" type="xs:string"/>
        <xs:element name="State" type="xs:string"/>
        <xs:element name="Country" type="xs:string"/>
      </xs:sequence>
    </xs:group>
  </xs:schema>
```

In Listing 6-29, a new element is added — `<Salutation>`. This element includes a `minOccurs` attribute with a value set to `0` (zero). This means that the `<Salutation>` element can appear zero or one times in the document. The XML presented in Listing 6-30 is considered valid XML.

Listing 6-30: Using the minOccurs in an instance document

```
<?xml version="1.0" encoding="UTF-8"?>
<Process xmlns:xsi="http://www.w3.org/2001/XMLSchema-instance"
 xsi:noNamespaceSchemaLocation="DefaultValues.xsd">
   <OrderNumber>1234</OrderNumber>
   <Salutation>Mr.</Salutation>
   <Name>Bill Evjen</Name>
   <Address>123 Main Street</Address>
   <City>Saint Charles</City>
   <State>Missouri</State>
   <Country>USA</Country>
</Process>
```

This also means that the code shown in Listing 6-31 is also considered valid XML.

Listing 6-31: Using the minOccurs in an instance document

```
<?xml version="1.0" encoding="UTF-8"?>
<Process xmlns:xsi="http://www.w3.org/2001/XMLSchema-instance"
 xsi:noNamespaceSchemaLocation="DefaultValues.xsd">
   <OrderNumber>1234</OrderNumber>
   <Name>Bill Evjen</Name>
   <Address>123 Main Street</Address>
   <City>Saint Charles</City>
   <State>Missouri</State>
   <Country>USA</Country>
</Process>
```

maxOccurs

The other attribute that helps you to control the number of times an element appears in any of your instance documents is the `maxOccurs` attribute. This attribute controls the maximum number of times an element may appear in your document. Listing 6-32 shows an example of using the `maxOccurs` attribute in your XML Schema document.

Listing 6-32: Using the maxOccurs attribute

```
<?xml version="1.0" encoding="UTF-8" standalone="yes"?>
<xs:schema xmlns:xs="http://www.w3.org/2001/XMLSchema">
  <xs:element name="Process">
     <xs:complexType>
        <xs:sequence>
           <xs:element name="OrderNumber" type="xs:positiveInteger" />
           <xs:group ref="ContactDetails" />
        </xs:sequence>
     </xs:complexType>
  </xs:element>
  <xs:group name="ContactDetails">
     <xs:sequence>
        <xs:element name="Name" type="xs:string"/>
        <xs:element name="Address" type="xs:string"/>
        <xs:element name="City" type="xs:string"/>
        <xs:element name="State" type="xs:string"/>
        <xs:element name="Country" type="xs:string"/>
        <xs:element name="Telephone" type="xs:string" maxOccurs="2" />
     </xs:sequence>
  </xs:group>
</xs:schema>
```

In this case, a `<Telephone>` element is added that can occur once or twice within the XML document. All elements defined here need to occur at least once (unless they have a `minOccurs` attribute set to `0`). This means that you can now have an instance document as presented in Listing 6-33.

Listing 6-33: Using the maxOccurs attribute

```
<?xml version="1.0" encoding="UTF-8"?>
<Process xmlns:xsi="http://www.w3.org/2001/XMLSchema-instance"
 xsi:noNamespaceSchemaLocation="Cardinality.xsd">
   <OrderNumber>1234</OrderNumber>
   <Name>Bill Evjen</Name>
   <Address>123 Main Street</Address>
   <City>Saint Charles</City>
   <State>Missouri</State>
   <Country>USA</Country>
   <Telephone>555-1212</Telephone>
   <Telephone>555-1213</Telephone>
</Process>
```

As you can see from this listing, the `<Telephone>` element has appeared twice in the document. This is allowed to occur because the `maxOccurs` attribute is set to `2`.

A twist on the `maxOccurs` attribute is that you can set it to have an unlimited number of items by setting the value of the attribute to `unbounded`. This is shown in Listing 6-34.

Listing 6-34: Using the maxOccurs attribute

```
<?xml version="1.0" encoding="UTF-8" standalone="yes"?>
<xs:schema xmlns:xs="http://www.w3.org/2001/XMLSchema">
  <xs:element name="Process">
```

```
      <xs:complexType>
         <xs:sequence>
            <xs:element name="OrderNumber" type="xs:positiveInteger" />
            <xs:group ref="ContactDetails" />
         </xs:sequence>
      </xs:complexType>
   </xs:element>
   <xs:group name="ContactDetails">
      <xs:sequence>
         <xs:element name="Name" type="xs:string"/>
         <xs:element name="Address" type="xs:string"/>
         <xs:element name="City" type="xs:string"/>
         <xs:element name="State" type="xs:string"/>
         <xs:element name="Country" type="xs:string"/>
         <xs:element name="Telephone" type="xs:string"
          maxOccurs="unbounded" />
      </xs:sequence>
   </xs:group>
</xs:schema>
```

With this in place, the <Telephone> element can now appear as many times in the document as the instance document author wants (remember that it has to appear at least once in the document).

Default values

You sometimes want to specify whether an element has a default value. You can do this to make XML documents less error-prone and more user-friendly. For instance, suppose you want to provide a new child element called <OrderLocation> to the <Process> element and provide a default value to this element at the same time. You do this by using the default attribute within the element. You accomplish this task as presented in Listing 6-35.

Listing 6-35: Creating an element with a default value attached to it

```
<?xml version="1.0" encoding="UTF-8" standalone="yes"?>
<xs:schema xmlns:xs="http://www.w3.org/2001/XMLSchema">
   <xs:element name="Process">
      <xs:complexType>
         <xs:sequence>
            <xs:element name="OrderNumber" type="xs:positiveInteger" />
            <xs:element name="Location" type="xs:string" default="Seattle" />
            <xs:group ref="ContactDetails" />
         </xs:sequence>
      </xs:complexType>
   </xs:element>
   <xs:group name="ContactDetails">
      <xs:sequence>
         <xs:element name="Name" type="xs:string"/>
         <xs:element name="Address" type="xs:string"/>
         <xs:element name="City" type="xs:string"/>
         <xs:element name="State" type="xs:string"/>
         <xs:element name="Country" type="xs:string"/>
      </xs:sequence>
   </xs:group>
</xs:schema>
```

In this case an XML element called `<Location>` provides the location where the order is to be processed. Using the default attribute within the `<element>` element, you are able to assign a default value of `Seattle`. This means that if no value is present in the instance document, a value of `Seattle` will be assumed. Using an XML Schema document as shown here means you can have an XML document like the one in Listing 6-36.

Listing 6-36: Building the <Location> element

```
<?xml version="1.0" encoding="UTF-8"?>
<Process xmlns:xsi="http://www.w3.org/2001/XMLSchema-instance"
 xsi:noNamespaceSchemaLocation="DefaultValues.xsd">
   <OrderNumber>1234</OrderNumber>
   <Location>San Francisco</Location>
   <Name>Bill Evjen</Name>
   <Address>123 Main Street</Address>
   <City>Saint Charles</City>
   <State>Missouri</State>
   <Country>USA</Country>
</Process>
```

This is a valid instance document. Although a default value is set for the `<Location>` element with the XML Schema document from Listing 6-35, you can easily just override this value by assigning a new value (as shown in Listing 6-36) by setting the value to `San Francisco`. You could have also made use of the default value by building the XML instance document as presented in Listing 6-37.

Listing 6-37: Building the <Location> element using the default value

```
<?xml version="1.0" encoding="UTF-8"?>
<Process xmlns:xsi="http://www.w3.org/2001/XMLSchema-instance"
 xsi:noNamespaceSchemaLocation="DefaultValues.xsd">
   <OrderNumber>1234</OrderNumber>
   <Location />
   <Name>Bill Evjen</Name>
   <Address>123 Main Street</Address>
   <City>Saint Charles</City>
   <State>Missouri</State>
   <Country>USA</Country>
</Process>
```

In this case, the value of `Seattle` is used for the `<Location>` element because nothing is specified. Note that using the `default` attribute means that you can use no value for the `<Location>` element, but at the same time, the `<Location>` element must appear in the document. If the element is not present, the instance document is considered invalid.

Fixed Values

A fixed value is similar to that of a default value with the big difference that the end user cannot change the value. When using a fixed value for an element, you are assigning a value that cannot be changed at all. This is done using the `fixed` attribute rather than the `default` attribute. For instance, if you wanted to set the `<Location>` element to a fixed value of `Seattle`, you would use code like that shown in Listing 6-38.

Listing 6-38: Creating an element with a fixed value attached to it

```
<?xml version="1.0" encoding="UTF-8" standalone="yes"?>
<xs:schema xmlns:xs="http://www.w3.org/2001/XMLSchema">
  <xs:element name="Process">
     <xs:complexType>
        <xs:sequence>
           <xs:element name="OrderNumber" type="xs:positiveInteger" />
           <xs:element name="Location" type="xs:string" fixed="Seattle" />
           <xs:group ref="ContactDetails" />
        </xs:sequence>
     </xs:complexType>
  </xs:element>
  <xs:group name="ContactDetails">
     <xs:sequence>
        <xs:element name="Name" type="xs:string"/>
        <xs:element name="Address" type="xs:string"/>
        <xs:element name="City" type="xs:string"/>
        <xs:element name="State" type="xs:string"/>
        <xs:element name="Country" type="xs:string"/>
     </xs:sequence>
  </xs:group>
</xs:schema>
```

Using this XML Schema means that the following element is valid:

```
<Location>Seattle</Location> <!-- Valid -->
```

Using a value other than Seattle causes your instance document to be considered invalid:

```
<Location>San Francisco</Location> <!-- Invalid -->
```

When using the `fixed` attribute, you may find that it behaves like the `default` attribute. As a consumer of this schema, you are not required to place a value within the `<Location>` element. This means that the following use of the `<Location>` element is also considered valid XML, and a value of `Seattle` is assumed.

```
<Location /> <!-- Valid -->
```

Null Values

In some instances, you want to set items so that a null value is allowed. Sometimes, you also may want to set elements so that they cannot be null as well. In these cases, you use the `nillable` attribute and set this to either `true` or `false`. Its use is presented in Listing 6-39.

Listing 6-39: Creating an element with a value which can be null

```
<?xml version="1.0" encoding="UTF-8" standalone="yes"?>
<xs:schema xmlns:xs="http://www.w3.org/2001/XMLSchema">
  <xs:element name="Process">
     <xs:complexType>
```

(continued)

Listing 6-39 *(continued)*

```
            <xs:sequence>
               <xs:element name="OrderNumber" type="xs:positiveInteger" />
               <xs:element name="Location" type="xs:string" nillable="true" />
               <xs:group ref="ContactDetails" />
            </xs:sequence>
         </xs:complexType>
      </xs:element>
      <xs:group name="ContactDetails">
         <xs:sequence>
            <xs:element name="Name" type="xs:string"/>
            <xs:element name="Address" type="xs:string"/>
            <xs:element name="City" type="xs:string"/>
            <xs:element name="State" type="xs:string"/>
            <xs:element name="Country" type="xs:string"/>
         </xs:sequence>
      </xs:group>
   </xs:schema>
```

Defining Attributes

So far in this chapter, much of the attention has been on XML elements. You saw how easy it is to create element declarations in your XML Schema documents. You can also just as easily create declarations for the attributes.

An attribute is a key/value pair that actually appears inside an element. Attributes are there to further define an element. Any element can contain as many attributes as it needs. Listing 6-40 shows an example of declaring an attribute to be used within the <Name> element.

Listing 6-40: Creating an attribute for the <Name> element

```
<?xml version="1.0" encoding="UTF-8" standalone="yes"?>
<xs:schema xmlns:xs="http://www.w3.org/2001/XMLSchema">
  <xs:element name="Process">
     <xs:complexType>
        <xs:sequence>
           <xs:element name="OrderNumber" type="xs:positiveInteger" />
           <xs:group ref="ContactDetails" />
        </xs:sequence>
     </xs:complexType>
  </xs:element>

  <xs:group name="ContactDetails">
     <xs:sequence>
        <xs:element name="Name">
           <xs:complexType>
              <xs:simpleContent>
                 <xs:extension base="xs:string">
```

```
                    <xs:attribute name="Sex"/>
                </xs:extension>
            </xs:simpleContent>
        </xs:complexType>
    </xs:element>
    <xs:element name="Address" type="xs:string"/>
    <xs:element name="City" type="xs:string"/>
    <xs:element name="State" type="xs:string"/>
    <xs:element name="Country" type="xs:string"/>
  </xs:sequence>
 </xs:group>
</xs:schema>
```

This example shows that the element name can now have an attribute `Sex` contained within. This means that the following construction is possible:

```
<Name Sex="M">Bill Evjen</Name>
```

It is also just as possible to do without the attribute, and the element is still considered valid.

```
<Name>Bill Evjen</Name>
```

With the attribute, the `<Name>` element becomes even more defined. Just as you do when you declare an element declaration, you can declare an attribute by providing the name of the attribute and the datatype of the value it can hold. In this case, the datatype is defined as a `string`, so that it can contain an "`M`" or an "`F`".

An attribute is declared within the `<schema>`, `<complexType>`, or `<attributeGroup>` elements. If there are other declarations within this complex type, such as other elements, the attribute declarations should appear at the bottom of the element declarations. If you are declaring multiple attributes, they do not need to appear in any specific order.

Default Values

The attribute tag within an XML Schema document can contain the attribute `default` as well. This specifies the initial value of the attribute as it is created. If the end user, creating an instance document based upon a schema with this type of attribute declaration, doesn't override the initial value, the default value is used. This is shown in Listing 6-41 within this partial XML Schema document.

Listing 6-41: Creating default values for attributes

```
<xs:element name="Name">
   <xs:complexType>
      <xs:simpleContent>
         <xs:extension base="xs:string">
            <xs:attribute name="Member" default="No" />
         </xs:extension>
      </xs:simpleContent>
   </xs:complexType>
</xs:element>
```

The big difference between defaults for elements and attributes is that when you define a default value for an element, the element must still appear in the XML instance document even if the consumer doesn't specify any value. Attributes, on the other hand, don't need to be present, and the default value is assumed.

use Attribute

The `use` attribute allows you to specify whether the attribute for the element is required. This is an optional attribute itself and can take one of three possible values — `optional`, `prohibited`, or `required`. This is shown in Listing 6-42.

Listing 6-42: Using the use attribute

```
<xs:element name="Name">
   <xs:complexType>
      <xs:simpleContent>
         <xs:extension base="xs:string">
            <xs:attribute name="Member" use="required" />
         </xs:extension>
      </xs:simpleContent>
   </xs:complexType>
</xs:element>
```

The default setting is `optional`.

Putting Restrictions on Attribute Values

At times you don't want to allow the end user to enter any value he wants for an attribute, but instead, you choose to put a limit on the attribute's values. This is done as follows (shown in Listing 6-43):

Listing 6-43: Restrictions being applied to attributes

```
<xs:element name="Name">
   <xs:complexType>
      <xs:simpleContent>
         <xs:extension base="xs:string">
            <xs:attribute name="Age">
               <xs:simpleType>
                  <xs:restriction base="xs:positiveInteger">
                     <xs:minInclusive value="12" />
                     <xs:maxInclusive value="95"" />
                  </xs:restriction>
               </xs:simpleType>
            </xs:attribute>
         </xs:extension>
      </xs:simpleContent>
   </xs:complexType>
</xs:element>
```

This is done by using the <minInclusive> and <maxInclusive> elements. The preceding example specifies an attribute Age where the minimum value that can be utilized is 12 and the maximum value is 95. Therefore, if the end user inputs a value that is not within this range, the XML document is considered invalid.

Earlier in this chapter, you saw how it is possible to use the <xs:restriction> element to put in an enumeration of available options as well:

```
<xs:simpleType name="MyCountry">
   <xs:restriction base="xs:string">
      <xs:enumeration value="USA" />
      <xs:enumeration value="UK" />
      <xs:enumeration value="Canada" />
      <xs:enumeration value="Finland" />
   </xs:restriction>
</xs:simpleType>
```

In this case, the <xs:restriction> element along with the list of <xs:enumeration> elements forces a restriction to only the items in the list.

Other types of restrictions you can utilize include:

```
<xs:restriction base="xs:string">
   <xs:minLength value="1" />
</xs:restriction>
```

Or

```
<xs:restriction base="xs:string">
   <xs:maxLength value="20" />
</xs:restriction>
```

Using <xs:minLength> or <xs:maxLength> allows you to define the length restriction of the element contents. These elements are used to define string restrictions. You could also define numerical restrictions using the <xs:totalDigits> element.

The available constraining facets in the XSD Schema language include:

Primitive Data Types	Description
enumeration	Defines a set of allowed values
fractionDigits	Defines a value with the specific number of decimal digits
length	Sets the units of length that the element can contain
maxExclusive	Defines an upper-level bound value based upon the data type of the element

Table continued on following page

Primitive Data Types	Description
`maxInclusive`	Defines the maximum value
`maxLength`	Defines the maximum number of units of length that is allowed for a value
`minExclusive`	Defines a lower-level bound value based upon the data type of the element
`minInclusive`	Defines the minimum value
`minLength`	Defines the minimum number of units of length that is allowed for a value
`pattern`	Defines an exact structure of a value using regular expressions
`totalDigits`	Defines the total allowed digit (int) values
`whitespace`	Defines how whitespace elements should be treated in the value. Possible values include `Preserve`, `Replace`, or `Collapse`

Attribute Groups

If you have certain attributes that are used across a wide variety of elements, it is easier to create an attribute group in order to manage these attributes. This function allows you to create a group of attributes that you can assign to different elements without having to declare the same attributes over and over again for each element. This is shown in Listing 6-44.

Listing 6-44: Creating an attribute group

```
<xs:attributeGroup name="myAttributes">
   <xs:attribute name="x" type="xs:integer" />
   <xs:attribute name="y" type="xs:integer" />
</xs:attributeGroup>

<xs:complexType name="myElementType">
   <xs:attributeGroup ref="myAttributes" />
</xs:complexType>
```

The idea is to declare a group of attributes within the `<attributeGroup>` element. When you are ready to declare a set of attributes within an element, you simply make a reference to the attribute group using the `<attributeGroup>` element. Within this tag, you simply point to the attribute group reference using the `ref` attribute.

Even when using the attribute groups to define attributes within your elements, you can still provide an element with attributes other than those that the attribute group specifies as is shown in Listing 6-45.

Listing 6-45: Using additional attributes

```
<xs:attributeGroup name="myAttributes">
   <xs:attribute name="x" type="xs:integer" />
   <xs:attribute name="y" type="xs:integer" />
</xs:attributeGroup>

<xs:complexType name="myElementType">
   <xs:attribute name="z" type="xs:integer" />
   <xs:attributeGroup ref="myAttributes" />
</xs:complexType>
```

With this declaration, you assign the attributes that are represented in the attribute group `myAttributes` as well as the new attribute `z`.

In some situations, you don't want to use every attribute that is defined within the attribute group. In these cases, you simply use the `prohibited` keyword with the `use` attribute to turn off the capability for the end user to employ that particular attribute within the element.

Putting XML Schema Document Together

You put XML Schema documents together through the use of either the `<import>` or `<include>` elements. Using these is something I recommend because it allows you to create reusable schema documents that you can use as a foundation whenever you build an XML Schema document.

<import>

Imports allow you to import another entire XML Schema document into the one that you are already working with. This is usually done if the two varying XML Schema documents utilize different namespaces. You use the import statement as shown in the example in Listing 6-46.

Listing 6-46: Importing another XML Schema document

```
<?xml version="1.0" encoding="UTF-8" standalone="yes"?>
<xs:schema xmlns:xs="http://www.w3.org/2001/XMLSchema"
 xmlns:LipperNamespace="http://www.lipperweb.com/OtherNamespace"
 targetNamespace="http://www.lipperweb.com/Namespace"
 elementFormDefault="qualified">

  <xs:import namespace="http://www.lipperweb.com/OtherNamespace"
   schemaLocation="OtherSchema.xsd" />

  <xs:element name="Process">
    <xs:complexType>
      <xs:sequence>
        <xs:element name="Name" type="xs:string" />
        <xs:element name="Address" type="xs:string" />
```

(continued)

Listing 6-46 *(continued)*

```
        <xs:element name="City" type="xs:string" />
        <xs:element name="State" type="xs:string" />
        <xs:element name="Country" type="xs:string" />
      </xs:sequence>
    </xs:complexType>
  </xs:element>
</xs:schema>
```

This import is done using the `<import>` element and two attributes — `namespace` and `schemaLocation`. When doing so, you also want to associate the namespace with a prefix within the `<schema>` element.

```
xmlns:LipperNamespace="http://www.lipperweb.com/OtherNamespace"
```

This allows you to use the items declared in either XML Schema document. If you are referencing an item that is contained in the other schema, you use a construction like the one shown here:

```
<LipperNamespace:OtherElement>value</LipperNamespace:OtherElement>
```

<include>

The `<include>` element is used if the other schema has the same namespace or makes use of no namespace. It is quite similar to the `<import>` element and is a good way to combine two schemas with little work. Listing 6-47 shows an example of using the `<include>` element.

Listing 6-47: Importing another XML Schema document

```
<?xml version="1.0" encoding="UTF-8" standalone="yes"?>
<xs:schema xmlns:xs="http://www.w3.org/2001/XMLSchema"
 targetNamespace="http://www.lipperweb.com/Namespace"
 elementFormDefault="qualified">

  <xs:include schemaLocation="OtherSchema.xsd" />

  <xs:element name="Process">
    <xs:complexType>
      <xs:sequence>
        <xs:element name="Name" type="xs:string" />
        <xs:element name="Address" type="xs:string" />
        <xs:element name="City" type="xs:string" />
        <xs:element name="State" type="xs:string" />
        <xs:element name="Country" type="xs:string" />
      </xs:sequence>
    </xs:complexType>
  </xs:element>
</xs:schema>
```

Commenting XML Schemas

You can apply comments to your XML Schema documents in a couple of ways. The first is fairly simple and straightforward — using standard XML comments.

Standard XML Comments

Because this is an XML document, you can place comments in the XML Schema document just as you can in any other XML or HTML document. Comments are placed between the `<!--` and the `-->` character sets. An example of commenting your schema document using this method is presented in Listing 6-48.

Listing 6-48: Commenting XML Schema documents

```
<?xml version="1.0" encoding="UTF-8" standalone="yes"?>
<xs:schema xmlns:xs="http://www.w3.org/2001/XMLSchema">
  <!-- Schema created by Bill Evjen in the summer of 2006 -->
  <xs:element name="Process">
    <xs:complexType>
      <xs:sequence>
        <xs:element name="Name" type="xs:string" />
        <xs:element name="Address" type="xs:string" />
        <xs:element name="City" type="xs:string" />
        <xs:element name="State" type="xs:string" />
        <xs:element name="Country" type="xs:string" />
      </xs:sequence>
    </xs:complexType>
  </xs:element>
</xs:schema>
```

You can also comment out entire blocks of text or code by putting the comment elements on multiple lines as is presented in Listing 6-49.

Listing 6-49: Commenting XML Schema documents in blocks

```
<?xml version="1.0" encoding="UTF-8" standalone="yes"?>
<xs:schema xmlns:xs="http://www.w3.org/2001/XMLSchema">
  <xs:element name="Process">
    <xs:complexType>
      <xs:sequence>
        <xs:element name="Name" type="xs:string" />
        <xs:element name="Address" type="xs:string" />
        <xs:element name="City" type="xs:string" />
        <!-- Turned off for now
        <xs:element name="State" type="xs:string" />
        <xs:element name="Country" type="xs:string" /> -->
      </xs:sequence>
    </xs:complexType>
  </xs:element>
</xs:schema>
```

From this, you can see that the <State> and <Country> elements have been commented out and will no longer be recognized by any engine.

<annotation>

A child element of the <element> element is the <annotation> element. The <annotation> element allows you to add comments to your schema documents more professionally. The <annotation> element has a couple of child elements at its disposal — <documentation> and <appInfo>.

<documentation>

The <documentation> element allows you to write textual documentation concerning a specific element. An example of its use is presented in Listing 6-50.

Listing 6-50: Using the <documentation> element

```
<?xml version="1.0" encoding="UTF-8" standalone="yes"?>
<xs:schema xmlns:xs="http://www.w3.org/2001/XMLSchema">
  <xs:element name="Process">
    <xs:complexType>
      <xs:sequence>
         <xs:element name="Name" type="xs:string">
            <xs:annotation>
               <xs:documentation>This represents the full name of the
                person making the order (e.g. John Doe).
               </xs:documentation>
            </xs:annotation>
        </xs:element>
        <xs:element name="Address" type="xs:string" />
        <xs:element name="City" type="xs:string" />
        <xs:element name="State" type="xs:string" />
        <xs:element name="Country" type="xs:string" />
      </xs:sequence>
    </xs:complexType>
  </xs:element>
</xs:schema>
```

<appInfo>

The <appInfo> element allows you to stick application-specific documentation in addition to human readable documentation inside the same element.

XML Schema Tools

A number of tools are at your disposal to create and validate XML Schema documents. You can find a large list of such tools at `w3.org/XML/Schema#Tools`. Although a large list is available, I will review only the two that are commonly used by developers — Microsoft's Visual Studio 2005 and Altova's XMLSpy.

Microsoft's Visual Studio 2005

Microsoft made strong efforts to incorporate XML development into its latest development environment. Microsoft's Visual Studio 2005 can do quite a bit more than XML development, but it allows you to create XML-based documents of many kinds easily, including XML Schema documents.

A XSD document type in Visual Studio enables you to visual create schema documents. You can also create hem directly in the code view as well. Figure 6-4 shows Visual Studio 2005 open with the design surface for the schema document.

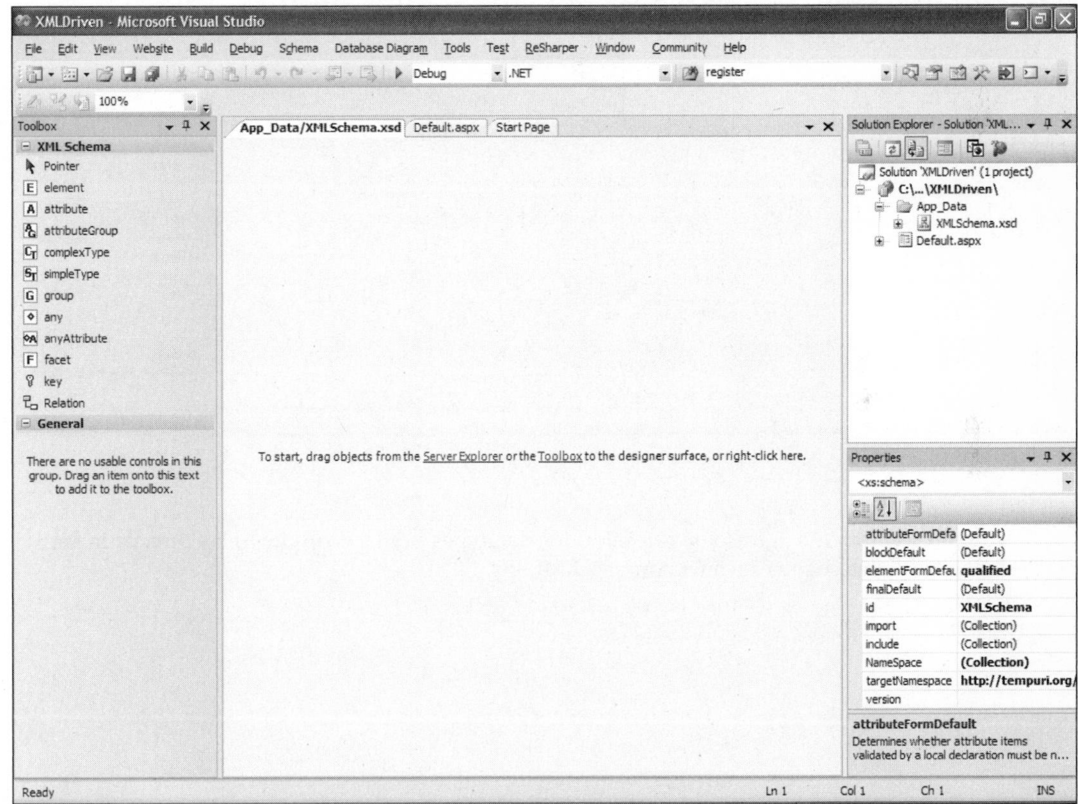

Figure 6-4

From the available Toolbox, you can drag and drop elements directly onto the design surface. The tool creates all the required code on your behalf. Figure 6-5 shows the screen when elements have been created on this design surface.

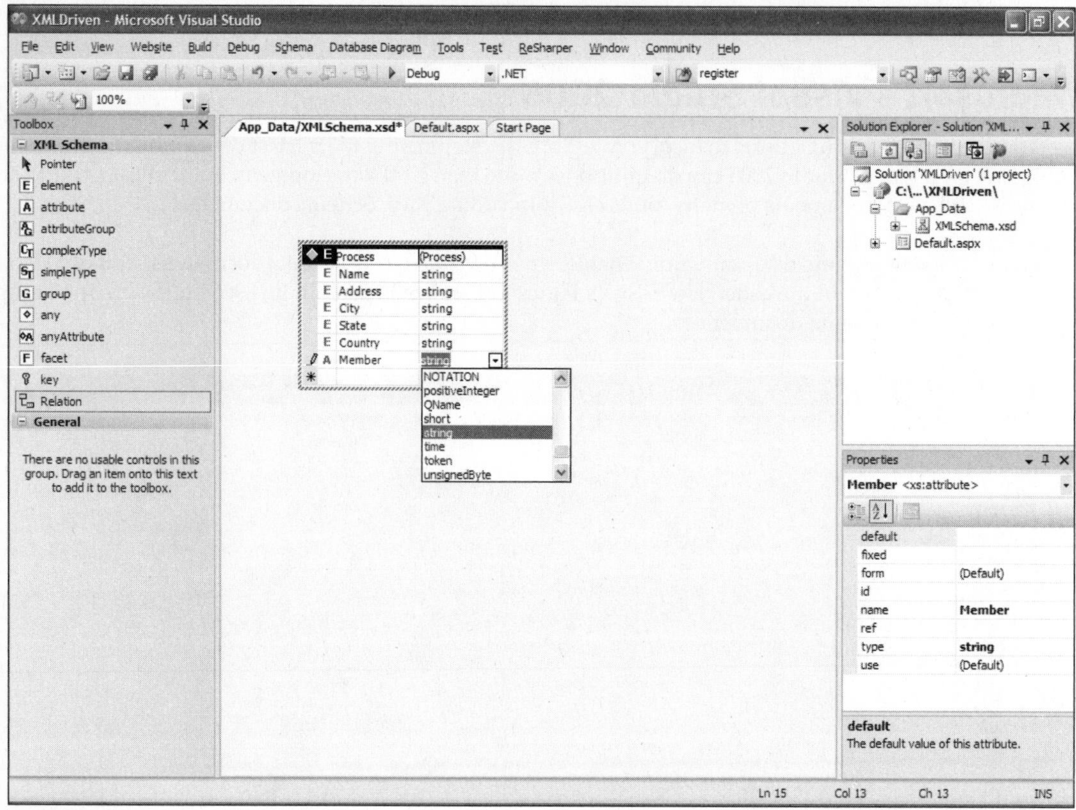

Figure 6-5

As you can see from the figure, you can select the datatypes from a drop-down list directly in the designer. Next, this chapter reviews Altova's XMLSpy.

Altova's XMLSpy

Altova's XMLSpy is a powerful tool recommended for any serious XML programmer. You will find that the XSD capabilities built into the tool allow you to perform pretty much any XSD task including creating schemas from scratch, from other XML documents, and more. Figure 6-6 shows how XMLSpy allows you to code the schema document directly.

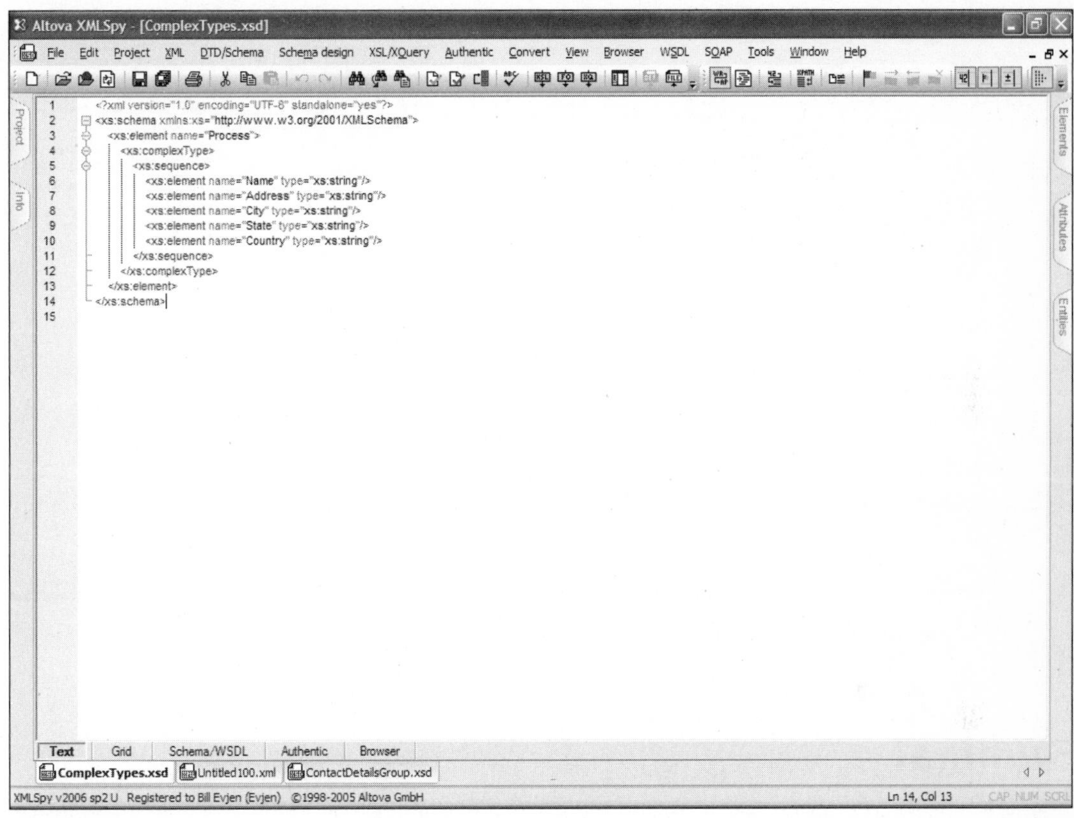

Figure 6-6

You can also design the schema visually and let XMLSpy create the schema code on your behalf. This is presented in Figure 6-7.

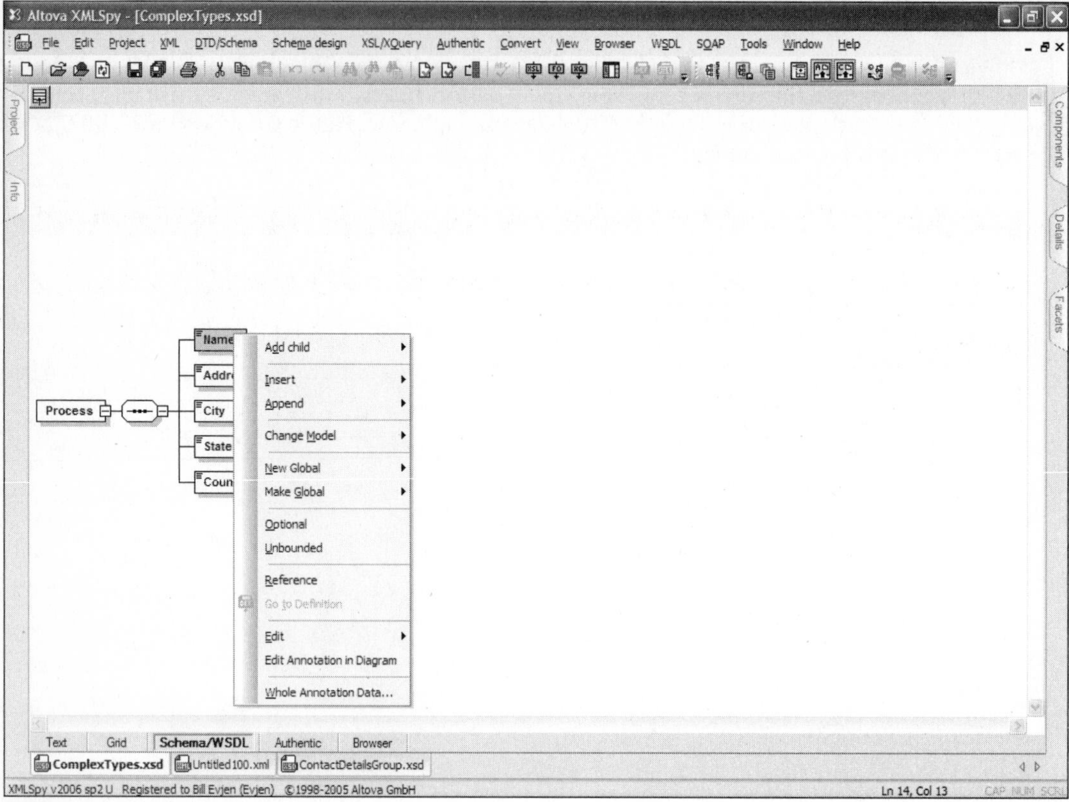

Figure 6-7

Summary

Just as you could probably see the power and reasoning behind DTDs, I hope that you can appreciate that XML Schema documents are that much more powerful. Their power comes in their incredible flexibility. This chapter took a look at the principles you need to build XML Schema documents and focused on building elements, attributes, and more. You will find that schema documents are a big part of most XML technologies — whether you are working with Web services, RSS feeds, or others.

The next chapter looks at another schema technology that is quite flexible as well, but is fairly new on the scene — RELAX-NG.

7

RELAX NG

The previous two chapters looked at two of the more commonly used formats for defining XML vocabularies. This chapter continues this survey of schema languages by looking at RELAX NG. This is a relatively new XML schema definition language from the Organization for the Advancement of Structured Information Standards (OASIS). OASIS is a standards body— similar to the W3C— that was originally created as an improved version of DTDs, and can leverage some of the functionality of XML Schema. To further these goals, RELAX NG was designed to provide a highly readable format that could be used to define complex vocabularies.

This chapter will look at the two forms of the RELAX NG specification: the standard form and the compact form. It will show the way you use these two forms to define XML vocabularies, and compare it with DTDs and XML Schemas. Along the way, you will see how RELAX NG integrates with XML tools and programming languages for validating XML documents and creating objects that map to RELAX NG schemas.

Why Another Schema Language?

At first glance, there seems to be little need for yet another schema language. DTDs have been around since SGML, so most people are aware of them, and most applications can work with them. XML Schema is also commonly available, integrated with many XML tools, and ratified by the W3C. Still, there are great reasons why you should consider using RELAX NG.

The primary reason to use RELAX NG is simplicity. Anyone who has read the W3C XML Schema specification (all three parts) knows that they are not simple. RELAX NG was designed from the outset to be simple to understand and implement. Listing 7-1 shows a RELAX NG schema. Even without knowing the structure of a RELAX NG schema or reading the specification, it is fairly easy to understand the intent of each of the elements.

Listing 7-1: RELAX NG Schema

```
<?xml version="1.0" encoding="UTF-8"?>
<grammar
  xmlns="http://relaxng.org/ns/structure/1.0"
  datatypeLibrary="http://www.w3.org/2001/XMLSchema-datatypes">
    <start>
        <element name="productCatalog">
            <oneOrMore>
                <element name="product">
                    <ref name="productDefinition"></ref>
                </element>
            </oneOrMore>
        </element>
    </start>
    <define name="productDefinition">
        <attribute name="id"><data type="integer"/></attribute>
        <element name="shortName"><text /></element>
        <element name="fullName"><text /></element>
        <element name="description"><text /></element>
        <element name="components">
            <ref name="productDefinition" />
        </element>
    </define>
</grammar>
```

In the preceding schema, you see that it defines a grammar (the root node). Within that grammar, the root element is a `productCatalog`. This `productCatalog` includes one or more products. Each product, in turn, includes a number of sub-elements. The name of each pattern in a RELAX NG schema almost literally guides the reader to describe the structure, and this is one of the main benefits in its use.

In addition to simplicity, RELAX NG was defined to be much more modular and composable than DTDs or XML Schema. Features such as W3C Schema data types can be integrated with RELAX NG schemas. In addition, RELAX NG makes it easy to break your schema into multiple files. This enables you to define standardized schema elements (such as a standard address schema) and combine them into a larger schema.

Finally, RELAX NG provides two forms: a normal syntax that uses XML, and a compact syntax. This enables you to define your XML vocabularies using either the well-formed normal syntax, or the more DTD-like compact syntax.

Defining a RELAX NG Schema

The first step in using RELAX NG, as with other schema languages, is to sketch out your model. Identify the key elements in the XML syntax you are creating, determine the cardinality of each item, and decide if each item should be an element or attribute. When you are moderately comfortable with your decisions, you can begin to document them using RELAX NG syntax.

Defining a RELAX NG syntax is similar to creating one using DTD or W3C XML Schema syntax — the task that the three languages use is the same. Each attempts to describe the rules of a document, so that humans and/or software can know that the document successfully follows the rules. The actual differences between the three can be seen to be minor or major, depending on your perspective.

Listing 7-2 shows a simple DTD, Listing 7-3 shows the equivalent W3C XML Schema version, and 7-4 shows the RELAX NG schema.

Listing 7-2: XML document with an embedded DTD

```
<?xml version="1.0" encoding="UTF-8"?>
<!ELEMENT order (name,address,city,state,country,orderItems)*>
<!ELEMENT name (#PCDATA)>
<!ELEMENT address (#PCDATA)>
<!ELEMENT city (#PCDATA)>
<!ELEMENT state (#PCDATA)>
<!ELEMENT country (#PCDATA)>
<!ELEMENT orderItems (item,quantity)+>
<!ELEMENT item (#PCDATA)>
<!ELEMENT quantity (#PCDATA)>
```

Listing 7-3: W3C XML Schema

```
<?xml version="1.0" encoding="UTF-8"?>
<xs:schema xmlns:xs="http://www.w3.org/2001/XMLSchema"
      elementFormDefault="qualified">
  <xs:element name="order">
    <xs:complexType>
      <xs:sequence minOccurs="0" maxOccurs="unbounded">
        <xs:element name="name"  type="xs:string"/>
        <xs:element name="address"  type="xs:string"/>
        <xs:element name="city"  type="xs:string"/>
        <xs:element name="state" type="xs:string"/>
        <xs:element name="country" type="xs:string"/>
        <xs:element ref="orderItems"/>
      </xs:sequence>
    </xs:complexType>
  </xs:element>
  <xs:element name="orderItems">
    <xs:complexType>
      <xs:sequence maxOccurs="unbounded">
        <xs:element name="item"  type="xs:string"/>
        <xs:element name="quantity" type="xs:int"/>
      </xs:sequence>
    </xs:complexType>
  </xs:element>
</xs:schema>
```

Listing 7-4: Simple RELAX NG Schema

```
<?xml version="1.0" encoding="UTF-8"?>
  <element name="order" xmlns="http://relaxng.org/ns/structure/1.0">
    <zeroOrMore>
      <element name="name"><text /></element>
      <element name="address"><text /></element>
```

(continued)

Listing 7-4 *(continued)*

```
        <element name="city"><text /></element>
        <element name="state"><text /></element>
        <element name="country"><text /></element>
        <element name="orderItems">
          <oneOrMore>
            <element name="item"><text /></element>
            <element name="quantity"><text /></element>
          </oneOrMore>
        </element>
      </zeroOrMore>
    </element>
```

As you can see from these examples, the main differences among the three schema syntaxes are how they use XML and identify cardinality. There are a few other differences, and the rest of this chapter will outline how you can write RELAX NG to define an XML schema.

Declaring Elements

The intent of a schema definition language is to first describe the elements that make up the language you are defining. Therefore, much of RELAX NG is composed of patterns that you will use to define the elements (and attributes) of an XML syntax. Each of the main RELAX NG patterns defines some aspect of the resulting XML.

Simple Elements

The simplest possible definition of an element uses, strangely enough, the `element` pattern:

```
<element name="fullName" xmlns="http://relaxng.org/ns/structure/1.0">
  <text />
</element>
```

This pattern defines a single element, called `fullName`. The declaration includes the current RELAX NG namespace: `http://relaxng.org/ns/structure/1.0`. (Future versions will likely have a different version number.) As with all other XML syntax, you can either use this namespace as the default namespace, or provide a prefix for the RELAX NG elements within your schema. Therefore, both of the RELAX NG schemas in Listing 7-5 are valid.

Listing 7-5: Using namespaces with RELAX NG schemas

```
<element name="contact" xmlns="http://relaxng.org/ns/structure/1.0">
  <choice>
    <element name="fullName">
      <text />
    </element>
    <group>
      <element name="givenName">
```

```
        <text />
      </element>
      <element name="lastName">
        <text />
      </element>
    </group>
  </choice>
</element>

<r:element name="contact" xmlns:r="http://relaxng.org/ns/structure/1.0">
  <r:choice>
    <r:element name="fullName">
      <r:text />
    </r:element>
    <r:group>
      <r:element name="givenName">
        <r:text />
      </r:element>
      <r:element name="lastName">
        <r:text />
      </r:element>
    </r:group>
  </r:choice>
</r:element>
```

The `fullName` element must include some text, as defined by the enclosed `<text />` element. RELAX NG does not allow element patterns to be empty by default; you must include an element within each element definition that describes the expected content for XML files using the schema. If you are defining an XML element that doesn't have content, such as the `<br />` element of XHTML, you should include the `<empty />` element as content in the definition. For example:

```
<element name="isActive">
  <empty />
</element>
```

If the element is only optional, you wrap it in the `<optional>` element as follows.

```
<element name="contact" xmlns="http://relaxng.org/ns/structure/1.0">
  <element name="fullName">
    <text />
  </element>
  <optional>
    <element name="email">
      <text />
    </element>
  </optional>
</element>
```

List Types

You rarely have one of anything with XML. Therefore, you need to be able to define the cardinality of a list of items — that is, how many of the items are valid in a schema.

One common cardinality defines whether an element may occur in any number. This is defined with the `zeroOrMore` element in your schema, as follows:

```
<element name="contacts" xmlns="http://relaxng.org/ns/structure/1.0">
  <zeroOrMore>
    <element name="contact">
      <element name="fullName">
        <text />
      </element>
      <element name="email">
        <text />
      </element>
    </element>
  </zeroOrMore>
</element>
```

Here you can see some of the simplicity of RELAX NG. Rather than describing the cardinality using terms such as `minOccurs/maxOccurs`, you simply wrap the element in a `zeroOrMore` element to define the fact that is optional but may occur in any number.

If the element must occur at least once, you use the `oneOrMore` element instead. For example:

```
<element name="contacts" xmlns="http://relaxng.org/ns/structure/1.0">
  <oneOrMore>
    <element name="contact">
      <element name="fullName">
        <text />
      </element>
      <element name="email">
        <text />
      </element>
    </element>
  </oneOrMore>
</element>
```

RELAX NG includes a third type of element that occurs multiple times: the list. This is for elements that contain multiple items, separated by whitespace. The schema defines the data format and quantity expected. For example, you may have a schema such as the following:

```
<element name="line">
  <element name="startPt">
    <list>
      <data type="float" />
      <data type="float" />
    </list>
  </element>
  <element name="endPt">
    <list>
      <data type="float" />
      <data type="float" />
    </list>
  </element>
</element>
```

The line element contains two child elements, `startPt` and `endPt`, which represent the starting and ending X and Y coordinates for the line. The following XML fragment shows how a valid document might appear using this schema:

```
<line>
  <startPt>1.0 4.5</startPt>
  <endPt>3.2 7.0</endPt>
</line>
```

In this example, the content of each element containing a list is broken using any whitespace character (such as a space or tab), and the data type and quantity are used to determine if the content is valid based on the schema.

Although the previous example uses two explicit `<data>` elements to define the expected quantity of child elements, you can also use the `zeroOrMore` or `oneOrMore` elements to produce more open-ended results. For example:

```
<element name="contacts">
  <zeroOrMore>
    <element name="contact">
      <element name="fullName">
        <text />
      </element>
      <element name="email">
        <text />
      </element>
      <optional>
        <element name="spouseName">
          <text />
        </element>
      </optional>
      <optional>
        <element name="children">
          <list>
            <zeroOrMore>
              <text />
            </zeroOrMore>
          </list>
        </element>
      </optional>
    </element>
  </zeroOrMore>
</element>
```

In this schema, the children node will contain a list of names, separated by whitespace. There may be zero children, or any number. The following XML fragment shows some valid uses for this schema.

```
<contacts>
  <contact>
    <fullName>Foo deBar</fullName>
    <email>foo@debar.com</email>
  </contact>
  <contact>
    <fullName>Bob Sjeruncle</fullName>
```

```
      <email>bob.sjeruncle@example.com</email>
      <spouseName>Mary Sjeruncle</spouseName>
      <children>Rob Tina Anne</children>
    </contact>
    <contact>
      <fullName>Anne Other</fullName>
      <email>anne@example.com</email>
      <children>Thea</children>
    </contact>
</contacts>
```

Each contact may have a child element, and that element will contain some number of names, separated by spaces (or other whitespace).

The only cardinality you cannot explicitly define with RELAX NG is when the minimum or maximum number of entries is something other than 0 or 1. For example, a `manager` element might have between 3 and 10 `reports` elements. However, these types of scenarios are rare, and they can easily be defined through the judicious use of `optional` and other elements.

Union Types

Union types are when two or more nodes may be valid at a given point in a schema. For example, a child node may occur as either an element or an attribute. Or an element might be presented either completely, or broken down into subcomponents. This last scenario is common when adding names to a schema. Do you include the `fullName`, or break it into surname and given names? RELAX NG enables you to handle these scenarios with the `<choice>` element, as shown here:

```
<element name="contacts">
  <zeroOrMore>
    <element name="contact">
      <choice>
        <element name="fullName">
          <text />
        </element>
        <group>
          <element name="surname">
            <text />
          </element>
          <element name="givenName">
            <text />
          </element>
        </group>
      </choice>
      <element name="email">
        <text />
      </element>
    </element>
  </zeroOrMore>
</element>
```

The `choice` element identifies a section of a schema where there may be multiple valid nodes. Each element that occurs within the choice becomes a valid entry at that point in an XML document using the schema. In order to mark a set of child elements as being together, you wrap them in the `<group>`

element, as shown in the previous schema for the surname and givenName elements. Failing to add this would have meant that any one of the fullName, surname or givenName elements could have been used, but that surname and givenName could not be used together. The following XML shows a valid XML fragment using the schema defined previously:

```
<contacts>
  <contact>
    <surname>deBar</surname>
    <givenName>Foo</givenName>
    <email>foo@debar.com</email>
  </contact>
  <contact>
    <fullName>Anne Other</fullName>
    <email>anne@example.com</email>
  </contact>
</contacts>
```

Each contact is identified using either the surname and givenName elements or with the fullName element.

Attributes

A common decision that you must make when you're creating an XML vocabulary is whether a given item should be an element or an attribute. Schemas that use elements for every item are the most extensible, and attribute-based schemas are the most compact. As opposed to DTDs and W3C Schema, in which you define attributes using different syntax than when you're defining elements, RELAX NG attempts to make defining attributes the same as defining elements.

You add attributes to your RELAX NG schemas with the <attribute> element, as shown in Listing 7-6.

Listing 7-6: Defining a schema with attributes

```
<element name="contact" xmlns="http://relaxng.org/ns/structure/1.0">
  <attribute name="fullName" />
  <attribute name="email" />
</element>
```

One change you may notice is that when you're adding attributes with RELAX NG, you don't need to include the <text /> child element like you do with <element>. This is because it is implied for attributes. You can, however, include it without error, as shown here:

```
<element name="contact" xmlns="http://relaxng.org/ns/structure/1.0">
  <attribute name="fullName">
    <text />
  </attribute>
  <attribute name="email">
    <text />
  </attribute>
</element>
```

Just as with elements, attributes added using this syntax are mandatory. To make an attribute optional, you wrap it with the <optional> element, just as you do with elements. For example:

```
<element name="contact" xmlns="http://relaxng.org/ns/structure/1.0">
  <attribute name="fullName" />
  <attribute name="email" />
  <optional>
    <attribute name="notes" />
  </optional>
</element>
```

Order of Elements

Although RELAX NG attempts to use consistent behavior for both attributes and elements, there is one notable difference. The order of attributes is not significant, but the order of elements is. Therefore, using the schema defined in Listing 7-6, either of the two following fragments would be valid:

```
<contact fullName="Foo deBar" email="foo@debar.com" />
<contact email="bob.sjeruncle@example.com" fullName="Bob Sjeruncle" />
```

However, using the equivalent schema with elements, this fragment is valid:

```
<contact>
  <fullName>Foo deBar</fullName>
  <email>foo@debar.com</email>
</contact>
```

The following fragment is not valid, because the two child elements don't appear in the same order as in the schema:

```
<contact>
  <email>foo@debar.com</email>
  <fullName>Foo deBar</fullName>
</contact>
```

If the order of the elements is not significant, you can use the <interleave> pattern to group those elements, like this:

```
<?xml version="1.0" encoding="UTF-8"?>
<element name="order" xmlns="http://relaxng.org/ns/structure/1.0">
    <zeroOrMore>
      <interleave>
        <element name="name">
            <text/>
        </element>
        <element name="email">
            <text/>
        </element>
      </interleave>
    </zeroOrMore>
</element>
```

In this schema, the name and e-mail elements can occur in any order. The `interleave` element is useful when XML documents need extra flexibility. For example, the elements within XHTML documents can occur in any order. Listing 7-7 shows a simplified section of the XHTML schema for the `<head>` element, as it might be defined in RELAX NG.

Listing 7-7: RELAX NG schema for XHTML <head>

```
<?xml version="1.0" encoding="UTF-8"?>
<element name="head" xmlns="http://relaxng.org/ns/structure/1.0">
    <interleave>
        <element name="title">
            <text/>
        </element>
        <zeroOrMore>
            <element name="style">
                <text/>
            </element>
        </zeroOrMore>
        <zeroOrMore>
            <element name="script">
                <text/>
            </element>
        </zeroOrMore>
        <zeroOrMore>
            <element name="meta">
                <text/>
            </element>
        </zeroOrMore>
    </interleave>
</element>
```

When you're writing an XHTML document, you don't normally think of the order you use to add elements, therefore the interleave pattern is ideal.

Another use for the interleave pattern is when an element may have child elements in addition to, or instead of, text. Listing 7-8 shows a schema and Listing 7-9 the XML fragment for this type of scenario.

Listing 7-8: Mixed-content elements — Schema

```
<element name="meetings" xmlns="http://relaxng.org/ns/structure/1.0">
    <oneOrMore>
        <element name="meeting">
            <element name="topic">
                <text/>
            </element>
            <element name="dateTime" datatypeLibrary="">
                <text/>
            </element>
            <optional>
                <element name="notes">
                    <interleave>
                        <zeroOrMore>
                            <element name="keyPoint">
```

(continued)

Listing 7-8 *(continued)*

```
                                        <text/>
                                    </element>
                                </zeroOrMore>
                                <text/>
                            </interleave>
                        </element>
                    </optional>
                </element>
            </oneOrMore>
        </element>
```

Listing 7-9: Mixed-content elements— XML fragment<meetings>

```
  <meeting>
    <topic>Plan new widget</topic>
    <dateTime>2006-04-01T14:30:00Z</dateTime>
    <notes>
Lorem ipsum dolor sit amet, <keyPoint>consectetuer adipiscing elit</keyPoint>.
Fusce id ante et orci facilisis tristique. Suspendisse viverra. <keyPoint>Morbi at
purus</keyPoint> non metus venenatis egestas. Duis nulla ipsum, imperdiet eu,
interdum vitae, mattis ut, diam. <keyPoint>Integer egestas ultricies
lacus</keyPoint>. Suspendisse commodo. Vestibulum diam. Curabitur consectetuer
tempor diam. Aliquam <keyPoint>tincidunt mollis mi</keyPoint>. Suspendisse porta
lorem vitae odio. Mauris accumsan sapien eget ante. Praesent suscipit lobortis
turpis.
    </notes>
  </meeting>
  <meeting>
    <topic>Assign widget tasks</topic>
    <dateTime>2006-04-04T09:00:00Z</dateTime>
    <notes>
Morbi rhoncus, purus ac imperdiet auctor, quam augue euismod diam, ac tempus dolor
metus in odio. Sed ac lacus. Cras pulvinar enim sed justo tempor fermentum. Proin
dictum dapibus urna. Maecenas at velit a <keyPoint>magna congue
pulvinar</keyPoint>. Praesent <keyPoint>consectetuer convallis erat. Cras lobortis
orci eu pede dapibus aliquam. Ut fringilla molestie risus. Nam diam.
<keyPoint>Quisque consequat euismod turpis</keyPoint>.
    </notes>
  </meeting>
</meetings>
```

Because this pattern is fairly common in XML, RELAX NG creates a shortcut method that enables you to describe elements like this: `<mixed>`. Using `<mixed>`, you can simplify the schema in Listing 7-8 to the one shown in Listing 7-10. Notice that the `<mixed>` section does not need to include either the `<interleave>` pattern or `<text />`.

Listing 7-10: Using <mixed>

```
<element name="meetings" xmlns="http://relaxng.org/ns/structure/1.0">
    <oneOrMore>
        <element name="meeting">
            <element name="topic">
```

```
                <text/>
            </element>
            <element name="dateTime" datatypeLibrary="">
                <text/>
            </element>
            <optional>
                <element name="notes">
                    <mixed>
                        <zeroOrMore>
                            <element name="keyPoint">
                                <text/>
                            </element>
                        </zeroOrMore>
                    </mixed>
                </element>
            </optional>
        </element>
    </oneOrMore>
</element>
```

Defining Grammar

Some schemas can have different valid root nodes. For example, the Atom specification allows the root node to either be an `atom:feed` element or `atom:entry`. With W3C schemas, you would have to define this as two schemas. RELAX NG, on the other hand, enables you to create schemas with different root nodes by using two special elements: `grammar` and `start`.

The `grammar` element replaces the normal starting node. The `start` element then contains the various nodes that may be used as the root node in the syntax. Listing 7-11 shows these two elements in action as part of the Atom 1.0 specification.

Listing 7-11: Using grammar and start elements

```
<grammar xmlns:atom="http://www.w3.org/2005/Atom"
  xmlns="http://relaxng.org/ns/structure/1.0"
  datatypeLibrary="http://www.w3.org/2001/XMLSchema-datatypes">
  <start>
    <choice>
      <element name="atom:feed">
        ...
      </element>
      <element name="atom:entry">
        ...
      </element>
    </choice>
  </start>
</grammar>
```

In this schema, the `grammar` element marks the starting point of the schema definition, and includes the namespaces used by the definition. The full Atom specification includes other namespaces, but these have been removed for simplicity. You can define multiple elements within the `grammar` element. Therefore, you need the `start` element to identify the possible root nodes of the document. In this case, the `start` element includes a `choice` element, meaning that multiple elements are possible — either the `atom:feed` or `atom:entry` elements can represent the starting point of an Atom document. Although you can approximate this with W3C XML Schema by identifying each of the root nodes as `minOccurs="0"`, a document with neither may be valid. RELAX NG avoids this outcome.

Reusing Types

There may be times when you want to reuse the structure of a schema. For example, you may use an address structure multiple times within the schema. Alternately, you may want to maintain a library of commonly defined items to be included in your company's schemas. RELAX NG supports both internal and external references to reuse schema patterns.

A common model of writing schemas is to define building block elements, such as `address` or `partClass`, and then include these building blocks at the appropriate location of the schema (that is, to use an internal reference in your schemas). You can do this in RELAX NG with the `ref` and `define` elements.

The `define` element is used to define a type for reference elsewhere in the document. This element has the required attribute name. This name is referenced with the `ref` element to include the defined structure. Listing 7-12 shows these two elements in action.

Listing 7-12: Using define and ref for internal references

```
<?xml version="1.0" encoding="UTF-8"?>
<grammar
  xmlns="http://relaxng.org/ns/structure/1.0"
  xmlns:a="http://relaxng.org/ns/compatibility/annotations/1.0"
  datatypeLibrary="http://www.w3.org/2001/XMLSchema-datatypes">
    <start>
        <element name="orders">
            <oneOrMore>
                <element name="order">
                    <element name="shipToAddress">
                    <ref name="addressType" />
                    </element>
                    <element name="billToAddress">
                        <ref name="addressType" />
                    </element>
                    </element>
            </oneOrMore>
        </element>
    </start>
    <define name="addressType">
        <element name="street">
            <text />
        </element>
        <element name="city">
            <text />
        </element>
        <element name="state">
            <text />
        </element>
        <element name="zip">
            <text />
        </element>
```

```
        <element name="country">
            <text />
        </element>
    </define>
</grammar>
```

The `addressType` definition creates a simple structure that you can use elsewhere in the document. Both the `shipToAddress` and `billToAddress` elements then reference this definition.

External references are basically the same as internal references, with the exception that the defined pattern is located in a separate file. The `externalRef` and `include` elements identify this file with its `href` attribute. This is another useful technique for creating modular RELAX NG schemas. You can create standard definitions of commonly used patterns, and then reference them to complete the schema. Listing 7-13 defines a pattern for a part definition and Listing 7-14 shows how you might reference this file. Although the `include` and `externalRef` patterns are similar in behavior, they serve two logical needs. The `include` pattern acts like an import and must occur as a child node to the `grammar` element. The included document must contain a grammar root node. Conversely, the `externalRef` element may occur at any place in the schema, and the file referenced does not need to be a complete grammar.

Listing 7-13: Using externalRef — External Schema

```
<?xml version="1.0" encoding="UTF-8"?>
<grammar
  xmlns="http://relaxng.org/ns/structure/1.0"
  datatypeLibrary="http://www.w3.org/2001/XMLSchema-datatypes">
    <start><ref name="partDefinition" /></start>
    <define name="partDefinition">
        <attribute name="id"><data type="integer"/></attribute>
        <element name="shortName"><text /></element>
        <element name="fullName"><text /></element>
        <element name="description"><text /></element>
        <element name="components"><ref name="partDefinition" /></element>
    </define>
</grammar>
```

Listing 7-14: Using externalRef — Referencing Schema

```
<?xml version="1.0" encoding="UTF-8"?>
<grammar xmlns="http://relaxng.org/ns/structure/1.0"
    <start>
        <element name="productCatalog">
            <zeroOrMore>
                <element name="part">
                    <externalRef href="externalRefDefinition.rng" />
                </element>
            </zeroOrMore>
        </element>
    </start>
</grammar>
```

Listings 7-13 and 7-14 show two RELAX NG schemas. The first defines a grammar that includes a single element named `partDefinition`. This element defines a single attribute and four child elements. Note that the last child element references itself, meaning that the parts may be defined recursively. This partDefinition file is referenced using the externalRef element in the second schema. The href attribute of the externalRef element points to the URL of the included schema. In this example, the two files are stored in the same directory. Therefore, the URL includes only the filename. You could store all of your external definitions in a single location and reference them with a full URL. The externalRef element acts as though the referenced file replaces the externalRef element. Therefore, the resulting logical schema is as if the contents of the partDefinition file were included within the <element name="part"> pattern.

Merging Schemas

When you begin reusing schema parts with <ref> and <externalRef>, you will eventually need to combine two types that contain multiple definitions for the same name. RELAX NG contains patterns that describe how the schema should combine the multiple definitions.

There are two main ways that RELAX NG can combine schema: the definitions can be combined, or one definition can replace or override the other definitions.

The core pattern used to merge two or more schemas is the <combine> attribute. You include this attribute for elements that have multiple definitions. This attribute must have a value of either choice or interleave, which describes how the schema validates the XML. Listing 7-15 shows the use of the combine attribute.

Listing 7-15: Combine attribute

```
<?xml version="1.0" encoding="UTF-8"?>
<grammar xmlns="http://relaxng.org/ns/structure/1.0">
    <start>
        <element name="orders">
            <zeroOrMore>
                <element name="order">
                    <element name="customer">
                        <ref name="contact"/>
                    </element>
                    <oneOrMore>
                        <element name="orderItem">
                            <element name="item">
                                <ref name="product"/>
                            </element>
                        </element>
                    </oneOrMore>
                </element>
            </zeroOrMore>
        </element>
    </start>
    <!-- These would likely be from separate externalRefs -->
    <define name="contact" combine="choice">
        <attribute name="id"/>
        <element name="fullName">
            <text/>
        </element>
    </define>
    <define name="contact" combine="choice">
        <attribute name="id"/>
```

```
        <element name="given">
            <text/>
        </element>
        <element name="surname">
            <text/>
        </element>
        <element name="price">
            <text/>
        </element>
    </define>
    <define name="product" combine="interleave">
        <attribute name="id"/>
        <attribute name="name"/>
    </define>
    <define name="product" combine="interleave">
        <attribute name="description"/>
    </define>
</grammar>
```

If the `combine` attribute is `choice`, this means that any of the items combined are valid. The following schema fragment is equivalent to the one shown in Listing 7-15:

```
<grammar xmlns="http://relaxng.org/ns/structure/1.0">
    <start>
        <element name="orders">
            <zeroOrMore>
                <element name="order">
                    <element name="customer">
                        <element name="contact">
                            <attribute name="id"/>
                            <choice>
                                <element name="fullName">
                                    <text/>
                                </element>
                                <group>
                                    <element name="given">
                                        <text/>
                                    </element>
                                    <element name="surname">
                                        <text/>
                                    </element>
                                </group>
                            </choice>
                        </element>
                    </element>
                    <oneOrMore>
                        <element name="orderItem">
                            <element name="item">
                                <interleave>
                                    <attribute name="id"/>
                                    <attribute name="name"/>
                                    <attribute name="description"/>
                                </interleave>
                            </element>
                        </element>
```

```
                    </oneOrMore>
                </element>
            </zeroOrMore>
        </element>
    </start>
</grammar>
```

When combining multiple schemas, there may be a case when you need to replace the existing definition with the one from the external definition, such as when the core definition includes a placeholder element that will be provided by the external definition. Alternately, the core definition may include a default implementation (such as an address pattern that defaults to the US formatting), and the external implementations override this behavior for other implementations. The schemas in Listing 7-16 and Listing 7-17 show how you can override a definition in another RELAX NG schema.

Listing 7-16: The replace pattern — Base definition

```
<?xml version="1.0" encoding="UTF-8"?>
<grammar xmlns="http://relaxng.org/ns/structure/1.0">
    <start>
        <element name="orderItems">
            <element name="shipAddress">
                <ref name="address"/>
            </element>
            <oneOrMore>
                <ref name="item"/>
            </oneOrMore>
        </element>
    </start>
    <define name="item">
        <notAllowed/>
    </define>
    <define name="address">
        <element name="street">
            <text/>
        </element>
        <element name="city">
            <text/>
        </element>
        <element name="state">
            <text/>
        </element>
        <element name="zip">
            <text/>
        </element>
    </define>
</grammar>
```

Listing 7-17: The replace pattern — Overriding base

```
<grammar xmlns="http://relaxng.org/ns/structure/1.0">
    <include href="replaceBase.rng">
        <define name="item">
            <attribute name="partNum"/>
            <attribute name="color">
```

```
                <choice>
                    <value>red</value>
                    <value>black</value>
                    <value>blue</value>
                </choice>
            </attribute>
        </define>
        <define name="address">
            <element name="street"><text /></element>
            <element name="city"><text /></element>
            <element name="postalCode"><text /></element>
        </define>
    </include>
</grammar>
```

The `notAllowed` element is a placeholder for an alternate implementation. You can add it at any point in a schema to mark a point where a later element will use `replace` to provide the actual implementation. In the preceding base schema, the `item` element is undefined in the `orderItems` schema. Instead, the `orderItems` includes the `notAllowed` element. The `notAllowed` element will not match any content. The `item` element is defined in the overriding schema. Notice that the replacement definitions for `item` and `address` are written within the `<include>` element. This ensures that it will be included within the original schema. If the `define` elements were not enclosed within the `include` element, they would be considered side-by-side definitions, and you would have to include the `combine` attribute.

Namespaces and Name Classes

RELAX NG also supports the use of namespaces to define elements and attributes that exist within alternate schemas. (See Chapter 1 for more information on namespaces.)

There may be times when you are not absolutely sure what tags may be within a block, such as when you have an element that may contain arbitrary XHTML or another XML dialect. In those cases, you want to describe the possible content, but you don't want to simply leave it as `<text />`. Alternately, you might want to create a pattern where the documents may include any attribute, or any attribute with a given namespace. In these cases, you will make use of the RELAX NG name classes.

The simplest name class is `anyName`. This represents any possible node, regardless of the name or namespace. It is equivalent to the `any` element in W3C XML schema. In the schema shown in Listing 7-18, the `notes` element can include any single element, of any name. That element may include any number of attributes and child elements.

Listing 7-18: Using the anyName element

```
<grammar xmlns="http://relaxng.org/ns/structure/1.0">
  <start>
    <element name="contact">
      <element name="fullName">
        <text />
      </element>
      <element name="email">
        <text />
      </element>
```

(continued)

Listing 7-18 *(continued)*

```
      <element name="notes">
        <ref name="childElement" />
      </element>
    </element>
  </start>
  <define name="childElement">
    <element>
      <anyName />
        <zeroOrMore>
          <attribute>
            <anyName />
          </attribute>
        </zeroOrMore>
        <text />
        <zeroOrMore>
          <ref name="childElement" />
        </zeroOrMore>
    </element>
  </define>
</grammar>
```

In this schema, the `notes` element is defined as a `childElement`. This definition allows any element (the `<element><anyName /></element>` part. Also within the `childElement`, you can have `zeroOrMore` attributes, again with any name. In addition to these elements, the `childElement` pattern may contain `<text />` and `zeroOrMore` child elements using the same definition. This is the definition of well-formed XML. Therefore, the notes element of the contact will be valid as long as it contains any well-formed XML.

In addition to the `anyName` element, REL AX NG includes two other name classes for describing valid content: `nsName` and `except`. You use the `nsName` element to identify the namespace of valid content when you need to include elements or attributes of a specific alternate namespace to your schema. For example, you may need to define a schema in which part of the document should contain a valid SOAP message. The following fragment shows how this would be defined using RELAX NG:

```
<element name="message">
  <element>
    <nsName ns=" http://www.w3.org/2003/05/soap-envelope/" />
  </element>
</element>
```

Both the `anyName` and `nsName` elements may include the `<except>` child. This provides exceptions to the parent. You may have an element that can include any possible child element except specific ones, or more commonly, you may want to exclude specific elements or namespaces as possible children. The following schema fragment shows an element that may have any child element, but only the `xs:type` attribute from the W3C XML schema data types namespace (`http://www.w3.org/2001/XMLSchema`):

```
<element name="item" xmlns:xs="http://www.w3.org/2001/XMLSchema" >
    <zeroOrMore>
        <attribute>
```

```
                <anyName>
                    <except>
                        <nsName ns="http://www.w3.org/2001/XMLSchema"/>
                    </except>
                </anyName>
            </attribute>
        </zeroOrMore>
        <optional>
            <attribute name="xs:type"/>
        </optional>
    </element>
```

This `item` element definition allows for any attribute, except one with the namespace of `http://www.w3.org/2001/XMLSchema`, that includes the data type definitions. This item is added later with the optional attribute that includes both `name` and `ns` attributes.

Annotating Schemas

The RELAX NG specification does not explicitly define an element or pattern for annotating your schema. However, because it supports namespaces and including elements from alternate namespaces in your schemas, you can add annotations using another namespace. The Oxygen XML editor (discussed later in this chapter) adds the `http://relaxng.org/ns/compatibility/annotations/1.0` namespace to documents it creates. You can then use this namespace to add notes to your schema, keeping in mind that they will be ignored by the parser except as needed. The schema in Listing 7-19 includes a couple of annotations that use this namespace.

Listing 7-19: Annotating RELAX NG schemas

```
<grammar xmlns="http://relaxng.org/ns/structure/1.0"
    xmlns:a="http://relaxng.org/ns/compatibility/annotations/1.0">
    <start>
        <a:documentation>Short schema for a personal contact</a:documentation>
        <element name="contact">
            <a:documentation xml:lang="en">
              Full name of the contact ({given Name} {surname}
            </a:documentation>
            <element name="fullName">
                <text/>
            </element>
            <a:documentation>
              E-mail address using RFC 822(http://www.w3.org/Protocols/rfc822/)
            </a:documentation>
            <element name="email">
                <text/>
            </element>
        </element>
    </start>
</grammar>
```

RELAX NG Tools

RELAX NG has not been available as a standard as long as DTDs or W3C XML Schema, so there are fewer tools available for creating or editing RELAX NG files. Many of the most commonly used tools were written by the specification authors themselves. However, because RELAX NG is now an official OASIS standard, more tools are beginning to add support for RELAX NG. Two tools that support the creation of RELAX NG schemas are the Oxygen XML editor and Trang.

Oxygen

As described in Chapter 2, Oxygen is a full-featured XML editor. One of the features that make it unique among similar products is its support for RELAX NG schemas (both the XML form and the compact syntax).

You can create RELAX NG schemas in Oxygen using either a text-based or graphical editor. (RELAX NG compact schemas only allow text-based editing.) Figure 7-1 shows a split screen of the two editors displaying the same schema.

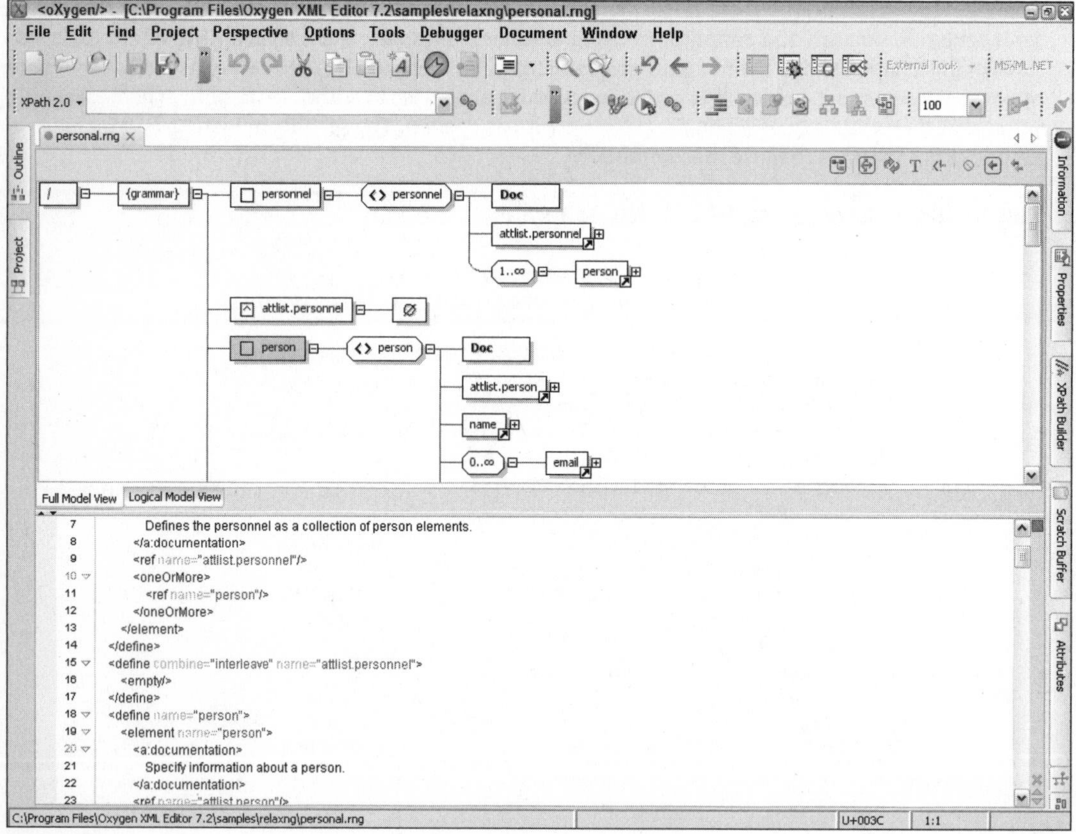

Figure 7-1

In this figure, the central editing area is composed of two parts: the top area is a graphical model of the schema structure, and the lower half is the text of the schema. Oxygen enables you to edit the schema using either section; the other is updated with the changes.

In addition to editing RELAX NG schemas, Oxygen includes a graphical interface to the Trang schema converter. This convertor (see Figure 7-2) enables you to convert between the XML syntax and compact syntax of RELAX NG, as well as convert a DTD into the corresponding RELAX NG schema.

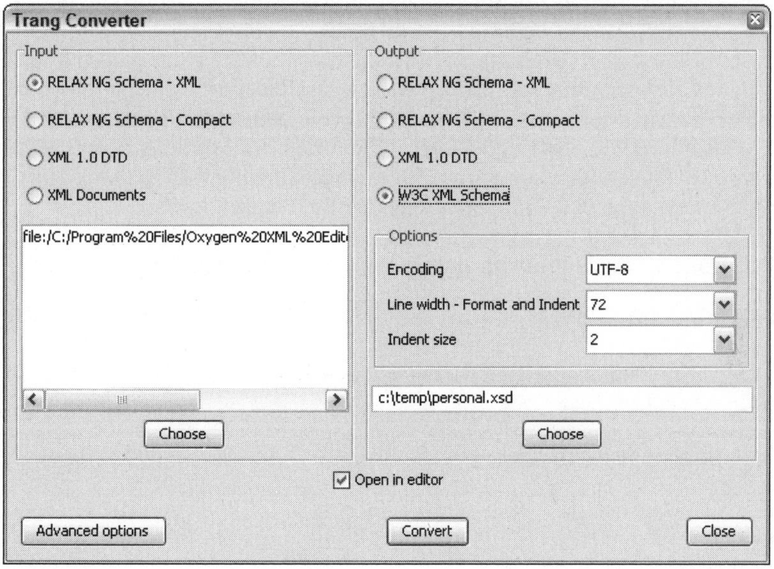

Figure 7-2

Trang

Trang is a multiformat schema converter, originally written by James Clark (one of the authors of the RELAX NG specification). Internally, it uses the RELAX NG syntax, but it is capable of converting RELAX NG (both the XML and compact syntaxes), DTDs, and W3C XML Schemas. It is also capable of inferring a schema based on a number of XML documents. This last capability is useful for generating a schema after the fact based on a set of XML examples, such as when a throwaway format needs to be formalized.

Trang is written in Java and distributed in `jar` format. It is intended for use as a command-line tool, and has no associated GUI (although the Oxygen XML editor provides this support, see the previous section). The basic syntax using Trang is as follows:

```
java -jar trang.jar -I <input format> -O <output format> -i <input options> -o
<output options> <input filename> <output filename>
```

All of the options except the filenames are optional. The input and output formats will be inferred from the extensions of the filenames provided. You can override this behavior by adding the `-I` and `-O` options. There may be multiple input and output option items on the command line. Generally, these options are not needed, and the most common usage is to identify the encoding of the incoming or outgoing document. For example, the following command lines convert the DocBook 4.5 schema from DTD format to RELAX NG syntax, specify UTF-16 for the RELAX NG encoding, and set the indent to 4:

```
java -jar trang.jar -o indent=4 -o encoding=UTF-16
  C:\temp\docbook-xml-4.5\docbookx.dtd c:\temp\docbook\docbook4_5.rng
```

The Trang convertor maintains the structure of the original schema. This means that if the original schema is defined using multiple documents (as with the DocBook DTD), then the resulting RELAX NG schema will use multiple files as well. Comments are also maintained.

Trang can also provide a shortcut approach to writing a schema by inferring the schema from the structure of a number of XML documents. This is useful if you have XML documents that you may have used informally, but for which you now need a format definition (for example, if an internal format will now need to be transmitted to another company). For example, Listing 7-20 shows three XML fragments. Each displays the same type of document, but in slightly different ways.

Listing 7-20: Converting schemas using Trang— Original XML files

contacts1.xml

```
<contacts>
  <contact name="Foo deBar" phone="+1-212-555-1212"
    email="foo@debar.com" />
  <contact name="Bob Sjeruncle" phone="+1-425-555-1212"
    email="bob.sjeruncle@example.com" />
</contacts>
```

contacts2.xml

```
<contacts>
  <contact>
    <fullName>Foo deBar</fullName>
    <email>foo@debar.com</email>
  </contact>
  <contact>
    <fullName>Bob Sjeruncle</fullName>
    <email>bob.sjeruncle@example.com</email>
  </contact>
</contacts>
```

contacts3.xml

```
<contacts>
  <contact id="42">
    <name>
      <first>Foo</first>
      <surname>deBar</surname>
    </name>
  </contact>
  <contact id="13">
    <name>
      <first>Bob</first>
      <surname>Sjeruncle</surname>
    </name>
  </contact>
</contacts>
```

You can generate a schema that applies to all three XML files using the following Trang command.

```
java -jar trang.jar contacts1.xml contacts2.xml contacts3.xml contacts.rng
```

This creates a merged schema that will validate each of the above contact listings (see Listing 7-21).

Listing 7-21: Converting schemas using Trang — RELAX NG Schema

```
<?xml version="1.0" encoding="UTF-8"?>
<grammar ns="" xmlns="http://relaxng.org/ns/structure/1.0"
  datatypeLibrary="http://www.w3.org/2001/XMLSchema-datatypes">
  <start>
    <element name="contacts">
      <oneOrMore>
        <element name="contact">
          <optional>
            <attribute name="email"/>
          </optional>
          <optional>
            <attribute name="id">
              <data type="integer"/>
            </attribute>
          </optional>
          <optional>
            <attribute name="name"/>
          </optional>
          <optional>
            <attribute name="phone"/>
          </optional>
          <optional>
            <choice>
              <element name="name">
                <element name="first">
                  <data type="NCName"/>
                </element>
                <element name="surname">
                  <data type="NCName"/>
                </element>
              </element>
              <group>
                <element name="fullName">
                  <text/>
                </element>
                <element name="email">
                  <text/>
                </element>
              </group>
            </choice>
          </optional>
        </element>
      </oneOrMore>
    </element>
  </start>
</grammar>
```

The resulting RELAX NG schema includes a number of optional items, because the three XML files were structurally distinct. If the structure were more consistent, the resulting schema would be simpler. Notice also that the data type of some of the nodes (such as the id) is identified and added to the schema.

Although you will probably not need to convert schema formats very often, but there may be times when all you have is a schema in one format and you need it in a different format. Trang fills this need admirably — not only for RELAX NG schemas, but for W3C XML Schema and DTDs as well.

RELAX NG Compact

In addition to the regular RELAX NG syntax, there is a compact form of the syntax that does not use XML as a format. Therefore, it can be viewed as a more capable, modernized version of the DTD. The format is similar to the regular form of the syntax. However, the elements are not expressed using XML syntax. Listing 7-22 shows a RELAX NG form of the schema defined in Listing 7-1.

Listing 7-22: RELAX NG compact schema

```
start =
  element productCatalog {
    element product { productDefinition }+
  }
productDefinition =
  attribute id { xsd:integer },
  element shortName { text },
  element fullName { text },
  element description { text },
  element components { productDefinition }*
```

Each of the patterns of the regular RELAX NG syntax has an analog in the compact syntax. The choice of form has more to do with the desire or need to use XML syntax when defining your schema, rather than capabilities of the language. If you need to manipulate the schema using other XML tools, then the regular syntax is most appropriate. If you want to avoid "the angle bracket tax" that XML is sometimes called, look to the compact syntax.

Most of the elements in the XML form of RELAX NG have corresponding items in the compact syntax, but some of the structures do bear describing. Most of these relate to the way you use the compact syntax to define `zeroOrMore`, `oneOrMore`, optional, and similar patterns.

If an element can occur zero or more times in a schema, you use the asterisk (`*`) to mark the pattern as shown previously in Listing 7-22. If the element must occur at least once (`oneOrMore`), you replace the asterisk with a plus sign (+) as shown in the following code:

Optional elements use the question mark (`?`) as shown in the `qty` element.

```
element order {
  element orderDate { text },
  element orderItems {
    element sku { text },
```

```
      element price { text },
      element qty { text }?
    }+
  }
```

In the XML form of RELAX NG, you use the `choice` element to enable one of multiple items. In the compact syntax, you do this with the pipe (|) character. If one or more of the items must occur together (as in the previous group pattern), you wrap them in parentheses like this:

```
element contact {
  (element fullName { text } |
   (element givenName { text }, element surname { text } )),
  element email { text }
}
```

In this schema, either `fullName` or the combination of `givenName` and surname must be used. As the `givenName` and surname must occur together, they are included within a second set of parentheses.

These patterns work the same way for attributes as they do for elements. For example, if an attribute needed a value to be one of a set of options, you use the same notation:

```
element item {
  attribute partNum { text },
  attribute color { "red" | "blue" | "green" | "black" }
}
```

This specifies that the `color` attribute can have a value of `red`, `blue`, `green` or `black`.

Just as with the longer format, you can create named definitions using the compact syntax. For example:

```
element order {
  element shipAddress { address },
  element orderItems { item+ }
}
address =
  element street { text },
  element city { text },
  element state { text },
  element zip { text }
item =
  attribute id { text },
  element name { text }
```

If you combine these definitions, you use |= (for `combine="choice"`) or `&=` (for `combine="interleave"`) to describe how you want the definitions to be included within the main schema.

The compact version of the RELAX NG syntax takes a bit longer to get used to — keeping the various symbols straight can take a while. However, when you are comfortable with these symbols, they can save a great deal of space. For example, the Atom 1.0 specification written using the XML form of RELAX NG is approximately 16KB in size. The equivalent RELAX NG compact syntax form is approximately 7KB. If you must transfer your schema many times, or if the connections are slower, it may make sense to take advantage of this briefer format.

Summary

In a perfect world, there would be only a single schema language that is able to describe any XML document and simple to learn. Sadly, that schema definition language hasn't been written yet, so there are multiple schema definition languages. Each has benefits — and drawbacks — that relate to the choices made by the designers. RELAX NG leans more heavily towards simplicity, although it is a complete language. The syntax is highly approachable and understandable without requiring you to read the entire specification. Because the specification is newer than DTD and W3C XML Schema, there is not much tool support for RELAX NG yet. However, this should improve as more developers see the benefits of this flexible XML schema definition language.

Resources

This section includes links to useful information for working with RELAX NG schemas.

- **RELAX NG home page (**`http://relaxng.org/`**)** — Here you will find information and links to the specifications, tutorials, and tools for RELAX NG and RELAX NG compact.
- **Oxygen (**`oxygenxml.com`**)** — IDE for working with RELAX NG files.
- **Trang (**`http://thaiopensource.com/relaxing/trang.html`**)** — Schema conversion tool that enables migrating schemas between common (and not so common) schema formats, including RELAX NG and RELAX NG compact.

Part IV
XML as Data

8

XSLT

Every tradesman's tool case has one tool that is a little more worn than the others. It is the favorite tool, the "go to" tool that gets used when all other tools have failed, or maybe even the first tool for all problems. For XML developers, that tool is often XSLT (eXtensible Stylesheet Language Transformations). XSLT is a templating language that can be used to convert XML into something else. The result of the transformation can be XML, HTML, XHTML, or even plain text or binary. XSLT is a powerful tool and, like many powerful tools, it has a few sharp edges you should avoid. As XSLT is a functional language, it can seem a little alien at first for developers used to procedural languages such as C# or Java. In addition, XSLT has limited support for variables and conditional logic than either of those languages. This chapter shows you how you can use XSLT in your applications and avoid its potential problems. Examples will show how you can use XSLT standalone, or combined with other programming languages and tools.

What Is XSLT?

XSLT is a transformation language for XML. Its purpose is to take a source tree of XML nodes and convert them into a result by using a series of templates or rules. XSLT is itself an XML syntax (see Listing 8-1). The result of an XSLT transformation does not have to be XML, however. The XSLT specification allows the output to be XML, HTML, or text. In addition, you can target some other form of output, perhaps even binary content.

Listing 8-1: Sample XSLT

```
<?xml version="1.0" encoding="UTF-8"?>
<xsl:stylesheet version="1.0"
xmlns:xsl="http://www.w3.org/1999/XSL/Transform">
  <xsl:output method="xml" version="1.0" encoding="UTF-8" indent="yes"/>
  <xsl:template match="/">
    <contacts>
    <xsl:apply-templates />
    </contacts>
```

(continued)

Listing 8-1 *(continued)*

```
    </xsl:template>
    <xsl:template match="customer">
      <cust>
        <xsl:attribute name="id">
          <xsl:value-of select="generate-id(contact/name)" />
        </xsl:attribute>
        <xsl:attribute name="company">
          <xsl:value-of select="company" />
        </xsl:attribute>
        <xsl:apply-templates select="contact" />
      </cust>
    </xsl:template>
    <xsl:template match="contact" name="contact">
      <xsl:attribute name="name"><xsl:value-of select="name" /></xsl:attribute>
    </xsl:template>
  </xsl:stylesheet>
```

Just as an individual program is composed of a number of classes or modules, an XSLT stylesheet is composed of multiple templates. Each forms a logical subroutine that creates part of the output.

XSLT has less in common with traditional programming languages such as C# or Java and more in common with other declarative languages such as SQL. To program in XSLT, you must create a description of the output based on the source data.

XSLT Syntax

Because XSLT is itself an XML syntax, it defines a number of elements that provide the processing. In addition to these elements, a number of functions are defined for working with the source and result trees. Finally, XSLT makes use of XPath functions (XPath 2.0 in XSLT 2.0) for computation, context, and other work. Therefore, knowledge of XPath (see Chapter 10) helps with XSLT.

Required Items

The root node for an XSLT stylesheet is, appropriately enough, `stylesheet`. It uses the `http://www.w3.org/1999/XSL/Transform` namespace. Alternatively, the specification defines `transform` as a valid synonym for `stylesheet`. Therefore, you may see either term as the root node in an XSLT stylesheet. Either `stylesheet` or `transform` has a single required attribute, `version`. Currently, 1.0 and 2.0 (for XSLT 2.0, obviously) are the only valid values for this attribute. In addition to this attribute, the stylesheet element may also contain references to other namespaces.

Top-level Elements

Typically, after the root node, a number of optional top-level elements provide additional information, either about the document(s) to be processed, or for the output. The valid top-level elements include:

- `import, include`
- `strip-space, preserve-space`

- `decimal-format`
- `output`
- `key`
- `variable`
- `param`
- `template`

Including Additional Stylesheets with include and import

The `import` node imports one stylesheet into another. If this node exists, it must be the first element after the root node. The `import` element enables the modularization of your stylesheets. For example, you could have a stylesheet specific for processing address elements or other common elements. Rather than duplicate this functionality throughout multiple XSLT stylesheets, you could import it when needed. If an element exists in both the parent and the imported stylesheets, the element in the parent stylesheet takes precedence. During processing, lower precedent templates are ignored in favor of higher ones.

The `include` node is similar in functionality to the import node, with one exception. The included stylesheet has the same precedence as the parent. This can lead to errors if both stylesheets include the same definition. Therefore, you should be careful when including other stylesheets to ensure that there are no duplicate templates, parameters, variables, and so on.

The `import` and include elements take a single attribute — `href` — that points at the imported or included stylesheet URL.

Controlling Whitespace and Formatting with strip-space, preserve-space, and decimal-format

The `strip-space` element lists a number of elements that have whitespace removed during processing. Alternatively, the `preserve-space` element defines child elements that maintain their whitespace when processed. Note: This does not affect all nodes, only those text nodes that only contain whitespace. For example, look at the following source fragment and stylesheet:

```
<?xml version="1.0" encoding="UTF-8"?>
<customers>
  <customer id="ALFKI">
    <company>   </company>
    <address>
      <street>Obere Str. 57</street>
      <city>Berlin</city>
      <zip>12209</zip>
      <country>    </country>
    </address>
    <contact>
      <name>Maria Anders</name>
      <title>Sales Representative</title>
      <phone>030-0074321</phone>
      <fax>030-0076545</fax>
    </contact>
  </customer>
```

```
</customers>

<?xml version="1.0" encoding="UTF-8"?>
<xsl:stylesheet version="1.0" xmlns:xsl="http://www.w3.org/1999/XSL/Transform">
  <xsl:output method="xml" version="1.0" encoding="UTF-8" indent="yes"/>
  <xsl:strip-space elements="country"/>
  <xsl:preserve-space elements="company"/>
  <xsl:template match="/">
    <xsl:apply-templates select="customers/customer[@id='ALFKI']"/>
  </xsl:template>
  <xsl:template match="customer">
    <cust>
      <ctry>
        <xsl:attribute name="length">
          <xsl:value-of select="string-length(address/country)"/>
         </xsl:attribute>
        <xsl:value-of select="address/country"/>
      </ctry>
      <name>
        <xsl:attribute name="length">
          <xsl:value-of select="string-length(company)"/>
        </xsl:attribute>
        <xsl:value-of select="company"/>
      </name>
      <contact>
        <xsl:value-of select="contact/name"/>
      </contact>
    </cust>
  </xsl:template>
</xsl:stylesheet>
```

The resulting output is:

```
<cust>
  <ctry length="0"></ctry>
  <name length="3">   </name>
  <contact>Maria Anders</contact>
</cust>
```

Both the `strip-space` and `preserve-space` elements take a single attribute called `elements`. This attribute is either asterisk (*) for all elements or a space-delimited list of the elements to which the rule applies. In the above sample, the whitespace of the country name was stripped, leaving the new element 0 characters long. The `preserve-space` on the company, on the other hand, left the spaces in, and the size was still three.

The `decimal-format` element defines the symbols to be used when formatting numbers in the stylesheet. These rules are then applied using the `format-number` function (covered later in the chapter). A typical use for this element is to create a number of named formats. For example, for US currency you use a comma (,) for grouping thousands and a period (.) as a decimal separator. Meanwhile, European currency would use a period (.) for grouping thousands, and a comma (,) for decimal separator. In addition, you use the `decimal-format` element to change the value displayed when the input value is not a number, infinity, or a negative.

Controlling Output with output and key

The output element defines the format of the result document. This includes defining the output format and any parameters that describe that format.

Attribute	Value	Description
cdata-section-elements	string	This attribute lists the elements that are CDATA wrapped in the output document. Use spaces to delimit multiple elements. This is useful if you are producing HTML output that may include XML content.
doctype-public	string	This attribute defines the public identifier to be used in the document type declaration.
doctype-system	string	This attribute defines the system identifier to be used in the document type declaration.
encoding	string	This attribute is needed only if the output format has an encoding attribute, such as for XML. This inserts the encoding attribute into the output document.
indent	yes/no	If this value is `yes`, the output document is indented to match the hierarchy. This is useful if the XML is intended for human access, although it does increase the size of the document slightly.
media-type	string	This attribute defines the MIME type of the resulting output. For example, if you are outputting `Atom:` and this is XML, the correct MIME type is application/atom+xml.
method	One of: xml, html, text or named type. XSLT 2.0 adds XHTML as a valid value.	Defines the output format, defaults to XML, with one exception. If the root node is <html>, the output format is HTML. To create XHTML output with XSLT 1.0, you can use either the XML output format and include the XHTML namespace and elements, or use the HTML output format and ensure you follow the XHTML rules (always close elements, and so on). This is rarely used, but you can also target any output format by using a qualified name for the method.
omit-xml-declaration	yes/no	If this value is `yes`, the XML declaration is not included in the target document. Typically, you set this to `no` for text or HTML output.
standalone	yes/no	If this value is `yes`, the standalone attribute is added to the XML declaration.
version	string	This character is needed only if the output format has a version, such as for XML. This inserts the version attribute into the output document.

The `key` element creates a named key that is used when searching the source document. Just as each element in an XML document can be identified by a unique identifier, often `id`, the `key` element identifies the attribute or child element that provides the unique identifier for each element. This key pattern can then be used later in the XSLT to retrieve individual items.

For example, look at the following XML source document:

```
<customers>
  <customer id="ALFKI">
    <company>Alfreds Futterkiste</company>
    <address>
      <street>Obere Str. 57</street>
      <city>Berlin</city>
      <zip>12209</zip>
      <country>Germany</country>
    </address>
    <contact>
      <name>Maria Anders</name>
      <title>Sales Representative</title>
      <phone>030-0074321</phone>
      <fax>030-0076545</fax>
    </contact>
  </customer>
  <customer id="ANATR">
    <company>Ana Trujillo Emparedados y helados</company>
    <address>
      <street>Avda. de la Constitución 2222</street>
      <city>México D.F.</city>
      <zip>05021</zip>
      <country>Mexico</country>
    </address>
    <contact>
      <name>Ana Trujillo</name>
      <title>Owner</title>
      <phone>(5) 555-4729</phone>
      <fax>(5) 555-3745</fax>
    </contact>
  </customer>
</customers>
```

You define a key pattern for the customer node using the XSLT in Listing 8-2:

Listing 8-2: Using the Key element and function

```
<?xml version="1.0" encoding="UTF-8"?>
<xsl:stylesheet version="1.0" xmlns:xsl="http://www.w3.org/1999/XSL/Transform">
  <xsl:output method="xml" version="1.0" encoding="UTF-8" indent="yes"/>
  <xsl:key name="cust" match="customer" use="@id"/>
  <xsl:template match="/">
    <result>
      <xsl:for-each select="key('cust','ANATR')">
        <company>
```

```
            <xsl:value-of select="company"/>
          </company>
        </xsl:for-each>
      </result>
    </xsl:template>
  </xsl:stylesheet>
```

The created key, named `cust` searches the `id` attribute of customer nodes to locate the desired elements. This `key` element is different from the `key` function used later in the stylesheet. In the `for-each` element, the `key` function uses the named key to search for a customer with the id `ANATR`. Alternatively, because only a single item can match each key, you use the `select` attribute of `apply-templates` to retrieve the selected company as shown in the following code.

```
<xsl:template match="/">
  <result>
    <xsl:apply-templates select="key('cust', 'TORTU')" />
  </result>
</xsl:template>
<xsl:template match="customer">
  <company><xsl:value-of select="company" /></company>
</xsl:template>
```

Templates

The core of XSLT is in the templates. These provide examples of how the different source elements should be processed when creating the result document. Listing 8-3 shows an XSLT template.

Listing 8-3: XSLT template

```
<xsl:template match="customer">
  <cust>
    <xsl:attribute name="id">
      <xsl:value-of select="generate-id(contact/name)" />
    </xsl:attribute>
    <xsl:attribute name="company">
      <xsl:value-of select="company" />
    </xsl:attribute>
    <xsl:apply-templates select="contact" />
  </cust>
</xsl:template>
```

Each template is composed of the `template` element and either a `match` and/or `name` attribute. The `match` attribute is more common and identifies an XPath pattern in the source document to which the template will apply. The `name` attribute is used only in cases where the `call-template` (covered later in the chapter) is used. In the preceding sample, the template applies to customer elements in the source document. This doesn't mean that it affects all customer elements, however. The caller can select the customer nodes to which the template applies.

The content of the template defines the output of the template. In the preceding template, whenever a customer node is processed, the result document has a `<cust>` node with a number of attributes.

Retrieving Values

The template element does not work alone in producing the result nodes. A number of additional XSLT elements work inside the template to extract values from the source document and produce the result. These include the following:

- value-of — Used to extract a single value based on an XPath statement. This is one of the "work horse" XSLT elements.
- element — Used to create a new element in the result document. Although you can create new elements in the result document simply by including them in the XSLT, element is useful to create a result element based on a value in the source document or a calculation.
- attribute — Used to create a new attribute in the result document. Just like element, this is most useful to create an attribute dynamically.
- text — Used to add text to the result document. Again, this is most useful when creating new text based on the source document, probably with some intermediate processing.
- copy — Used to copy an element from the source document into the result document. This element does not copy any child elements or attributes. This element is commonly used when the result document is similar in structure or naming to the source document.
- copy-of — Used to copy an element and its child elements and attributes from the source document into the result document.

The value-of element extracts a value from the source document, based on an XPath expression and the current context. This element is possibly the most frequently used XSLT element. It has a single required attribute, select, that is the XPath expression, and one optional attribute, disable-output-escaping. The disable-output-escaping attribute is set to either yes or no. If yes, characters that are significant in XML (such as < or >) will be included in the output. If no, these characters are escaped to < and >. If excluded, the default is no. The following element extracts the value of any child element named company, escaping characters as needed.

```
<xsl:value-of select="company" disable-output-escaping="no" />
```

The element and attribute elements create the appropriate nodes in the result tree. Although you can create elements in the result document by including them in the XSLT, these elements make it easier to create these nodes, especially if the desired node is based on the source document. Both of these elements take a single required attribute, name, and an optional namespace attribute. The name is the newly created element or attribute, and namespace defines the namespace URI for the element or attribute.

The following XSLT fragment creates a new element based on the value of the category element in the source document. As the name attribute is generated dynamically, the attribute element is also used to create the name.

```
<xsl:template match="category">
  <xsl:element name="department" >
    <xsl:attribute name="id">
      <xsl:value-of select="text()" />
    </xsl:attribute>
```

```
  </xsl:element>
</xsl:template>

<!-- This would generate: (assuming the current node has
     a child element called category.
  <department id="Beverages"/>
-->
```

The `text` element is used to add text nodes to the result document. Although you can add text by including the new text in the XSLT, the `text` element enables the creation of dynamic content based either on XPath functions or the source document. For example, the following line adds the Unicode character for carriage return (character 13 or hexadecimal 0D) to the result document.

```
<xsl:text>&#x0D;</xsl:text>
```

The `copy` and `copy-of` elements work to copy the current node to the result document. The difference between the two is that `copy-of` includes child elements and attributes, whereas `copy` only reproduces the current node. These two elements are useful when parts of the source and result documents match.

Calling templates

When you have created the templates for your stylesheet, the next step is to call them. With XSLT, two elements are used to call templates: `apply-templates` and `call-template`.

The `apply-templates` element executes templates based on the current context and passes control over to the other template. This is the common method of using templates in your stylesheets. The code that follows shows a parent template using `apply-templates` to execute another template. The line `<xsl:apply-templates select="contact" />` performs an XPath selection based on the current context. The parent template calls the contact template for each instance of a child contact node. That is, the contact template is executed for each node in the node-set defined by `customer[current]/contact`.

```
<xsl:template match="customer">
  <cust>
    <xsl:apply-templates select="contact" />
    <xsl:value-of select="company" />
  </cust>
</xsl:template>
<xsl:template match="contact" name="contact">
  <xsl:attribute name="name"><xsl:value-of select="name" /></xsl:attribute>
</xsl:template>
```

If you exclude the `select` attribute for the `apply-templates`, all child templates are called in the order that they appear in the source document. This is a useful shorthand method when transforming a large block of a source document. The `apply-templates` element also supports sorting the data before the new template is executed (see the following sections).

`Call-template`, on the other hand, executes a single named template based on the current context. It is equivalent to calling a function and passing the current node. After the template completes, "flow" is passed back to the calling template. The parent template in Listing 8-4 uses `call-template` to format the price.

Listing 8-4: Using call-template

```
<?xml version="1.0" encoding="UTF-8"?>
<xsl:stylesheet version="1.0" xmlns:xsl="http://www.w3.org/1999/XSL/Transform">
  <xsl:output method="text" encoding="UTF-16"/>
  <xsl:template match="/">
    <xsl:apply-templates select="//product" />
  </xsl:template>
  <xsl:template match="product">
    <xsl:value-of select="name" />: <xsl:call-template name="price" />
    <xsl:text>&#x0D;</xsl:text>
  </xsl:template>
  <xsl:template name="price">
    <xsl:value-of select="format-number(price, '#.00')" />
  </xsl:template>
</xsl:stylesheet>
```

The `call-template` element is frequently used with conditional logic and/or parameters (see the following sections). For example, you could use it to provide a localized version of a value from the source document.

Multiple Templates for a Single Element

In addition to the `match` and `name` attributes, a template can also include `mode` and `priority` attributes. The `priority` attribute is used in cases where multiple templates apply to a single source element. Templates with a higher priority have precedence and are used; at no time should multiple templates act on the same node-set. The `priority` value must be a number. By default, most templates have a priority of 0.5.

The `mode` attribute is used to override the limitation on a single template acting on an element from the source document. The mode defines a particular action for a template. Other modes may also apply to the same element, but act in a slightly different way. The code in Listing 8-5 shows two templates acting on the same element using the `mode` attribute to identify both the template and the template call.

Listing 8-5: Use of the mode attribute

```
<?xml version="1.0" encoding="UTF-8"?>
<xsl:stylesheet version="1.0" xmlns:xsl="http://www.w3.org/1999/XSL/Transform">
  <xsl:output method="xml" version="1.0" encoding="UTF-8" indent="yes"/>
  <xsl:template match="/">
    <modes>
      <xsl:apply-templates select="//customer[@id='ANATR']" mode="block" />
      <xsl:apply-templates select="//customer[@id='ANATR']" mode="attributes" />
    </modes>
  </xsl:template>
  <xsl:template match="customer" mode="attributes">
    <attributesMode>
      <xsl:attribute name="company">
        <xsl:value-of select="company" /></xsl:attribute>
      <xsl:attribute name="contact">
        <xsl:value-of select="contact/name" /></xsl:attribute>
      <xsl:attribute name="phone">
        <xsl:value-of select="contact/phone" /></xsl:attribute>
    </attributesMode>
```

```
  </xsl:template>
  <xsl:template match="customer" mode="block">
    <blockMode>
      <xsl:value-of select="company"/>:
      <xsl:value-of select="contact/name" />
      (<xsl:value-of select="contact/phone" />)</blockMode>
  </xsl:template>
</xsl:stylesheet>
```

Two templates apply to the `customer` node in the source document. To identify the two, each is given a `mode` attribute. When the template is called using the `apply-templates` element, the desired `mode` is identified. Therefore, despite the attribute's `mode` element being first in the stylesheet, the block `mode` is executed first. The resulting document appears as follows:

```
<?xml version="1.0" encoding="UTF-8"?>
<modes>
  <blockMode>Ana Trujillo Emparedados y helados: Ana Trujillo ((5)
555-4729)</blockMode>
  <attributesMode company="Ana Trujillo Emparedados y helados"
    contact="Ana Trujillo" phone="(5) 555-4729"/>
</modes>
```

Modes provide a handle that can be used by conditional logic to process a given element in different ways. For example, one mode might format dates, currency, and phone numbers for European customers, and another one might do so for U.S. customers.

Conditional Processing

Most programming languages provide some means of conditional logic in the form of `if...else`, `switch` or similar statements. XSLT is no exception: it provides both simple and complex branching using the `if` and `choose/when/otherwise` blocks.

The `if` element is used to provide a single simple test in processing. It takes a single attribute, `test`, that is an expression. If the expression evaluates to `true`, the content of the `if` element is processed. Listing 8-6 shows the use of the `if` element.

Listing 8-6: Using the if element

```
<?xml version="1.0" encoding="UTF-8"?>
<xsl:stylesheet version="1.0" xmlns:xsl="http://www.w3.org/1999/XSL/Transform">
  <xsl:output method="xml" version="1.0" encoding="UTF-8" indent="yes"/>
  <xsl:template match="/">
    <xsl:apply-templates select="customers/customer"/>
  </xsl:template>
  <xsl:template match="customer">
    <company>
      <name><xsl:value-of select="company" /></name>
      <xsl:if test="address/country='USA'">
        <contact><xsl:value-of select="contact/phone" /></contact>
      </xsl:if>
    </company>
  </xsl:template>
</xsl:stylesheet>
```

The test of the if element tests whether the country of the current customer is USA and if so, outputs the phone number. The test attribute can use XPath functions as well as node expressions. If the test requires the use of lesser-than (<) or greater-than (>), you should encode the characters. Therefore, a test to determine if the price of a product is less than $20.00 in the products.xml file looks like this:

```
<xsl:if test="price &lt;= 20">
  <xsl:attribute name="bgcolor">#E0E0E0</xsl:attribute>
</xsl:if>
```

The attribute is created if the price is less-than or equal to 20.

You cannot add an else clause. If you need multiple tests, use the choose element. The choose element is similar to switch statements used by many other languages (or select case in Visual Basic). You define a number of tests, and the first one that evaluates to true is executed. If none of the tests are true, the otherwise element, if present, is used. (See Listing 8-7.)

Listing 8-7: Using the choose, when, and otherwise elements

```
<xsl:choose>
  <xsl:when test="price &lt;= 20">
    <xsl:attribute name="bgcolor">#e0e0e0</xsl:attribute>
  </xsl:when>
  <xsl:when test="price &lt;= 100">
    <xsl:attribute name="bgcolor">#00ff00</xsl:attribute>
  </xsl:when>
  <xsl:otherwise>
    <xsl:attribute name="bgcolor">#FF0000</xsl:attribute>
  </xsl:otherwise>
</xsl:choose>
```

The choose element is a container for when and otherwise elements. Each when element has a test expression. The content of the first valid test is applied to the result document. Therefore, if the price is less than or equal to 20, the background color is set to light gray. If it is greater than 20, but less than 101, the background is set to green. All other items have a background set to red.

Looping

Although templates apply to each node in the selected node-set, on occasion, you need to loop through a set of elements not using a template. This is the purpose of the for-each element. This element takes a single select statement containing an XPath expression. The content of the element is then applied to each node selected by the query. (See Listing 8-8.)

Listing 8-8: Using the for-each element

```
<xsl:for-each select="catalog/row ">
  <xsl:copy-of select="category" />
</xsl:for-each>
```

Given the source XML document in Listing 8-9, it is possible to create a destination document using either for-each (see Listing 8-10) or template (see Listing 8-11).

Should I use for-each or templates?

To developers who come to XSLT from traditional languages, templates are often confusing. XSLT just does not seem "like a real programming language" to people used to writing if statements and loops. So, many stick to creating repeating structures with `for-each`.

For example, given a block of XML similar to the fragment in Listing 8-9 that contains a number of categories and products, you could create a summary report of the products and their prices using `for-each` as shown in Listing 8-10.

```
Chai: 18.00
Chang: 19.00
Chartreuse verte: 18.00
Côte de Blaye: 263.50
Guaraná Fantástica: 4.50
Ipoh Coffee: 46.00
Lakkalikööri: 18.00
...
```

If you do so, however, you miss the true power of XSLT. Templates are just like the subroutines in languages like Java, C#, or C++. Rather than templates being called manually, however, the data itself calls them. Remember that templates represent an example of what the output should look like. They are similar to someone saying, "Put all the yellow triangles in the box and the green squares in the bag." You essentially define an example of the desired result and identify when each result should happen. The data then flows into each appropriate template, creating the result document.

Listing 8-9: A product listing

```
<catalog>
  <row id="1">
    <category>Beverages</category>
    <product>
      <name>Chai</name>
      <price>18.0000</price>
    </product>
  </row>
  <row id="2">
    <category>Beverages</category>
    <product>
      <name>Chang</name>
      <price>19.0000</price>
    </product>
  </row>
...
  <row id="3">
    <category>Condiments</category>
    <product>
      <name>Aniseed Syrup</name>
      <price>10.0000</price>
    </product>
```

(continued)

Listing 8-9 *(continued)*

```
    </row>
    <row id="4">
      <category>Condiments</category>
      <product>
        <name>Chef Anton's Cajun Seasoning</name>
        <price>22.0000</price>
      </product>
    </row>
  ...
  </catalog>
```

Listing 8-10: Using for-each to process XML

```
<?xml version="1.0" encoding="UTF-8"?>
<xsl:stylesheet version="1.0" xmlns:xsl="http://www.w3.org/1999/XSL/Transform">
  <xsl:output method="text" encoding="UTF-16" omit-xml-declaration="yes"/>
  <xsl:template match="/">
  <xsl:for-each select="catalog/row/product">
    <xsl:value-of select="name" />:
    <xsl:value-of select='format-number(price, "#.00")' />
    <xsl:text>&#x0D;</xsl:text>
  </xsl:for-each>
  </xsl:template>
</xsl:stylesheet>
```

The for-each element extracts the matching elements from the XML. The contents of the element are performed for each of these extracted elements; in this case, the name and price are outputted. The internal XSLT function format-number converts the price to a value with two decimal places. Finally, because the output method is text, the `<xsl:text>
</xsl:text>` expression adds a carriage return (hex 13) to force a new line.

Listing 8-11: Using templates to process XML

```
<?xml version="1.0" encoding="UTF-8"?>
<xsl:stylesheet version="1.0" xmlns:xsl="http://www.w3.org/1999/XSL/Transform">
  <xsl:output method="text" encoding="UTF-16" omit-xml-declaration="yes"/>
  <xsl:template match="/">
    <xsl:apply-templates select="catalog/row/product" />
  </xsl:template>
  <xsl:template match="product">
    <xsl:value-of select="name" />: <xsl:value-of select='format-number(price,
"#.00")'/>
    <xsl:text>&#x0D;</xsl:text>
  </xsl:template>
</xsl:stylesheet>
```

The processing for each product occurs in the template identified using the match syntax. Although this is a trivial example, with only a single template, it demonstrates how using templates narrows the scope and makes change easier.

The `for-each` element (as well as the `apply-templates` element) takes an optional child element sort. This enables you to sort the content before the template or loop is applied. This element takes a number of optional attributes as shown in the following table.

Attribute	Description
select	An XPath expression that defines the content to sort on. This is based on the current context. Therefore, it is based on the current selection in a `for-each` or `apply-templates` element.
data-type	The data type of the content — text, numeric, or a qname. The default is text.
lang	The language to be used for the sort, using the language code. It ensures that the correct sorting is applied for the selected language.
order	The sort order, either ascending or descending.
case-order	The sort order when items may begin with either upper- or lowercase characters. Can be either upper-first or lower-first.

Sorting is a resource-intensive process if you have a large document or if you sort within another loop. Therefore, you should apply a sort only if it is needed for your result. The following code applies a sort on a product before the product name and price are written.

```
<xsl:for-each select="catalog/row/product">
  <xsl: sort select="name" data-type="text" />
  <xsl:value-of select="name" />:
  <xsl:value-of select='format-number(price, "#.00")' />
  <xsl:text>&#x0D;</xsl:text>
</xsl:for-each>
```

Variables and Parameters

Stylesheets and templates sometimes require additional data during the transformation of a document, often in the form of calculated values or temporary data. For this reason, XSLT provides both variables and parameters.

Variables provide a name that may hold a value for processing. The value held by the variable may be any valid data type, including the schema types and node-sets. You create a variable using the `variable` element.

```
<xsl:variable name="someName" select="expression">contents</xsl:variable>
```

The `name` attribute is required and identifies the variable. The `select` attribute can be used to assign a value to the variable; alternatively, the content provides the value.

The scope of the variable depends on where it is defined. If defined at the top-level of the stylesheet, it is globally available. If it is defined within another element, then it is only available within that element.

You access the value of a variable (or parameter) elsewhere in the stylesheet using the `$name` syntax.

A `param` element is similar to the `variable` element, but it defines a variable passed to a template. For example, the fragment in Listing 8-12 defines a parameter used to calculate the tax on a product.

Listing 8-12: Using parameters and variables

```
<xsl:template match="/">
  <xsl:apply-templates select="//product">
    <xsl:with-param name="rate" select="0.07" />
  </xsl:apply-templates>
</xsl:template>
<xsl:template match="product">
  <xsl:param name="rate" />
  <xsl:copy>
    <xsl:attribute name="id">
      <xsl:value-of select="generate-id()" />
    </xsl:attribute>
    <xsl:attribute name="name">
      <xsl:value-of select="name" />
    </xsl:attribute>
    <xsl:attribute name="priceWithTax">
      <xsl:value-of select="format-number(price+(price*$rate), '#.00')" />
    </xsl:attribute>
  </xsl:copy>
</xsl:template>
```

The root template calls the product template as you've done elsewhere, but it includes the `with-param` element. This provides the value that is passed to the product template. Therefore, the param named `rate` will hold the value 0.07. This value is used in the final highlighted line to provide the tax rate for the calculation.

Other Functions and Expressions

XSLT leverages the functionality of XPath for most of its functions, providing over 100 different functions for string-handling, date processing, and more. In addition, XSLT supports a number of built-in functions (see the following table).

Function	Description

document	Enables access to XML documents other than the source document. This can be used to merge the nodes of another document with those of the source document.
	`<xsl:for-each select="document(documentURL)/XPath/expression>`
	`..<!-- process content here -->`
	`</xsl:for-each>`

key	Used with the `key` element to generate keys in the result document. See Listing 8-2 for an example of using the `key` function.

Function	Description

generate-id	Used to generate ids for your result document. These ids are guaranteed to be unique based on the current context.
	`<cust>`
	`  <xsl:attribute name="id">`
	`    <xsl:value-of select="generate-id(contact/name)" />`
	`  </xsl:attribute>`
	`</cust>`

format-number	Formats a value based on a supplied mask or pattern. These are characters that will be replaced by the data. For example, the mask ###,###.00 would format numbers to two decimal places, adding a grouping character if they are larger than 1,000.
current	Returns the current node, essentially equivalent to the . `XPath` expression.
system-property	Used to query the implementation for information. Typically, this includes version and vendor information, but the vendor can provide any information using this function.

Extending XSLT

Just like other XML syntaxes, XSLT is not fixed; it can be extended through the use of additional namespaces. This enables implementers to add functionality. One notable and commonly used extension is available with the Microsoft XSLT engine. You can apply script to your templates with the addition of the `msxsl:script` element. This element allows the addition of script code, using JavaScript, VBScript, C#, VB .NET, or another active scripting language. It also permits the addition of procedural functionality to a template.

For example, XSLT 1.0 does not have any means of manipulating text, such as substring extraction or case changing. Script extensions can provide this functionality, as shown in Listing 8-13.

Listing 8-13: Extending XSLT with script

```
<?xml version="1.0" encoding="UTF-8"?>
<xsl:stylesheet version="1.0" xmlns:xsl="http://www.w3.org/1999/XSL/Transform"
   xmlns:msxsl="urn:schemas-microsoft-com:xslt" xmlns:ex="urn:some-URI">
  <xsl:output method="xml" version="1.0" encoding="UTF-8" indent="yes"/>
  <msxsl:script language = "C#"  implements-prefix = "ex">
    <![CDATA[
    string delim = " ";
    public  String upperCase(String value) {
      return value.ToUpper();
    }
    public String firstToken(String value) {
      string[] temp = value.Split(delim.ToCharArray());
      return temp[0];
    }
    public String lastToken(String value) {
      string[] temp = value.Split(delim.ToCharArray());
```

(continued)

Listing 8-13 *(continued)*

```
        return temp[temp.Length-1];
      } ]]>
    </msxsl:script>

    <xsl:template match="/">
    <xsl:apply-templates select="//customer[@id='ANTON']/contact" />
    </xsl:template>
    <xsl:template match="contact">
      <contact>
        <fullName><xsl:value-of select="name" /></fullName>
        <firstName><xsl:value-of select="ex:firstToken(name)" /></firstName>
        <lastName><xsl:value-of select="ex:upperCase(ex:lastToken(name))" />
  </lastName>
      </contact>
    </xsl:template>
  </xsl:stylesheet>
```

When extending XSLT, you must provide additional namespaces for your extensions. The Microsoft-defined namespace for its scripting extensions is `urn:schemas-microsoft-com:xslt`. In addition, a second namespace is added for the script functions themselves. You can include multiple script blocks — even in different languages — as long as each uses a different `implements-prefix`. This prefix is used later when calling the functions. The output of this script is the following:

```
<contact xmlns:msxsl="urn:schemas-microsoft-com:xslt" xmlns:ex="urn:some-URI">
  <fullName>Antonio Moreno</fullName>
  <firstName>Antonio</firstName>
  <lastName>MORENO</lastName>
</contact>
```

Executing XSLT

Obviously, an XSLT stylesheet is only useful if you can apply it to some XML. Apart from executing XML in an XML editor or IDE, you have at least three ways to apply XSLT to XML:

- Using Command-line tools
- Via code
- In a browser

Executing XSLT at the Command-line

If you need to generate a new document based on a source document and standalone XSLT file, a command-line tool may be useful. The two most notable are Open Source Saxon tool and Microsoft's msxsl.exe.

Saxon is an Open Source tool, originally written by Michael Kay. It supports command-line usage and code. It is available for Java and .NET development in two flavors. Saxon-B provides basic conformance support for XSLT 2.0 and XQuery, whereas Saxon-SA provides Schema-aware support and is a commercial package. You execute XSLT using Saxon using the following command-line (Java version shown):

```
java -jar saxon8.jar [options] [Source document] [Stylesheet document] [parameters]
```

The resulting document is displayed in the console. You can send the output to a file either using the `-o` filename option or the output pipe (>). The following line shows using the Saxon processor to execute the sample shown in Listing 8-1 on the `customers.xml` file.

```
java -jar \Tools\saxon\saxon8.jar customers.xml language\sample.xslt
```

The msxsl.exe tool from Microsoft is similar to Saxon. It requires that the MSXML DLLs are also available (at least version 3.0). The command-line parameters and use are also similar:

```
MSXSL source stylesheet [options] [param=value...] [xmlns:prefix=uri...]
```

For example, calling the sample in Listing 8-1 is done with the following:

```
msxsl customers.xml language\sample.xslt -o result.xml
```

Although the MSXSL tool can be used with most XSLT scripts, it cannot process scripts with embedded .NET code, as with Listing 8-13.

Executing XSLT via Code

Both Java and .NET provide built-in functionality for performing XSLT transformations. Other languages also provide this functionality as part of their class libraries. These functions load both source documents and stylesheets and generate the result document. Listing 8-14 shows transforming XML using Java, whereas Listing 8-15 shows using Visual Basic and the .NET Framework to transform XML. Both samples put the resulting XML into a text box for display (see Figure 8-1), but it could also be output to a document or loaded into an XML-handling class.

Listing 8-14: Using XSLT from Java

```
import java.io.*;
import javax.swing.*;
import javax.xml.transform.Transformer;
import javax.xml.transform.TransformerFactory;
import javax.xml.transform.TransformerException;
import javax.xml.transform.stream.StreamSource;
import javax.xml.transform.stream.StreamResult;

private void transformButtonActionPerformed(java.awt.event.ActionEvent evt) {
    if(this.sourceField.getText().length() > 0 &&
            this.stylesheetField.getText().length() >0) {

        try {
            File source = new File(this.sourceField.getText());
            File stylesheet = new File(this.stylesheetField.getText());

            StreamSource sourceSource = new StreamSource(source);
            StreamSource styleSource = new StreamSource(stylesheet);
            Transformer transformer =
                    TransformerFactory.newInstance().newTransformer(styleSource);
            StringWriter w = new StringWriter();
            StreamResult result = new StreamResult(w);
```

(continued)

Listing 8-14 *(continued)*

```
                transformer.transform(sourceSource, result);
                this.resultField.setText(w.getBuffer().toString());

            } catch (TransformerException te) {
                System.out.println ("\n** Transformer error");
                System.out.println("    " + te.getMessage() );
            } catch(Exception e) {
                System.out.println ("\n** General error");
                System.out.println("    " + e.getMessage() );
            }
        }
    }

    private void stylesheetButtonActionPerformed(java.awt.event.ActionEvent evt) {
        int ret = fc.showOpenDialog(this);
        if(JFileChooser.APPROVE_OPTION == ret) {
            this.stylesheetField.setText(fc.getSelectedFile().getPath());
        }
    }

    private void sourceButtonActionPerformed(java.awt.event.ActionEvent evt) {
        int ret = fc.showOpenDialog(this);
        if(JFileChooser.APPROVE_OPTION == ret) {
            this.sourceField.setText(fc.getSelectedFile().getPath());
        }
    }
```

The XSLT functionality is available in the javax.xml.transform package. The main class is the `Transformer`, created by the `TransformerFactory`. This class takes a number of sources, via a DOM, SAX, or a stream. Similarly, it can produce results as a DOM, SAX, or stream.

In this sample, the source and stylesheet files are loaded into `StreamSource` objects. This object can load from a file, stream, or reader to prepare the text for transformation. The source document is transformed, and the result displayed in the resultField JTextArea.

Listing 8-15: Using XSLT from Visual Basic and the .NET Framework

```
Imports System.IO
Imports System.Text
Imports System.Xml
Imports System.Xml.Xsl

Public Class MainForm

    Private Sub SourceXmlButton_Click(ByVal sender As System.Object, _
      ByVal e As System.EventArgs) Handles SourceXmlButton.Click
        With FileOpenDialog
            .Filter = "XML Files|*.xml|All Files|*.*"
            If .ShowDialog = Windows.Forms.DialogResult.OK Then
                Me.SourceXmlField.Text = .FileName
            End If
        End With
```

```
        End Sub

        Private Sub StylesheetButton_Click(ByVal sender As System.Object, _
          ByVal e As System.EventArgs) Handles StylesheetButton.Click
            With FileOpenDialog
                .Filter = "XSLT Files|*.xsl;*.xslt|All Files|*.*"
                If .ShowDialog = Windows.Forms.DialogResult.OK Then
                    Me.StylesheetField.Text = .FileName
                End If
            End With
        End Sub

        Private Sub TransformButton_Click(ByVal sender As System.Object, _
          ByVal e As System.EventArgs) Handles TransformButton.Click
            If File.Exists(Me.SourceXmlField.Text) AndAlso _
              File.Exists(Me.StylesheetField.Text) Then
                Dim trans As New XslCompiledTransform
                Dim out As New StringBuilder
                Using w As XmlWriter = XmlWriter.Create(out)
                    With trans
                        .Load(Me.StylesheetField.Text)
                        .Transform(Me.SourceXmlField.Text, w)
                    End With
                End Using
                Me.ResultField.Text = out.ToString
            End If
        End Sub
    End Class
```

The .NET Framework 2.0 comes with the `XslCompiledTransform` class for performing XSLT transformations. There is also the earlier `XslTransform` class, although this is deprecated. The `XslCompiledTransform` class can load the XSLT stylesheet and source document from a stream, XmlReader, a variable that implements IXPathNavigable, or a file. Similarly, the result of the transformation can be passed to an XmlWriter, file, or Stream. You can also provide arguments to the transformation if necessary.

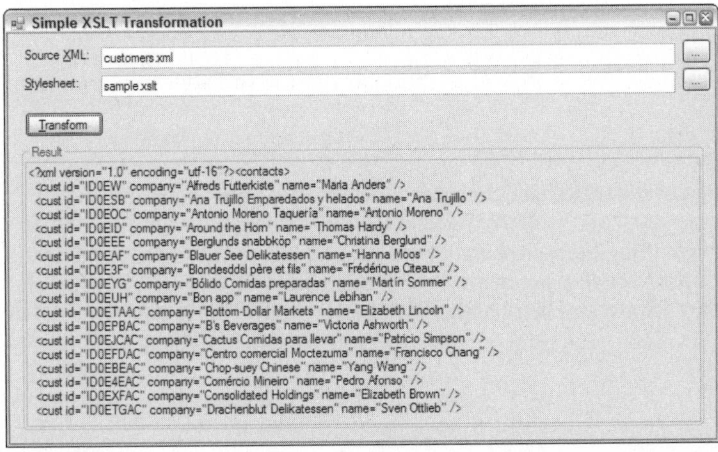

Figure 8-1

Executing XSLT in a Browser

Most modern browsers also support using XSLT when displaying XML documents. This means that you can send XML to the browser and have the client render it into HTML based on your stylesheet. The stylesheet may make the XML more presentable, add more information, or both. For example, Figure 8-2 shows XML being displayed in Internet Explorer. The XML is colorized to identify elements, attributes, and text. Although this is useful when testing XML produced in code, it is less than useful for most viewers.

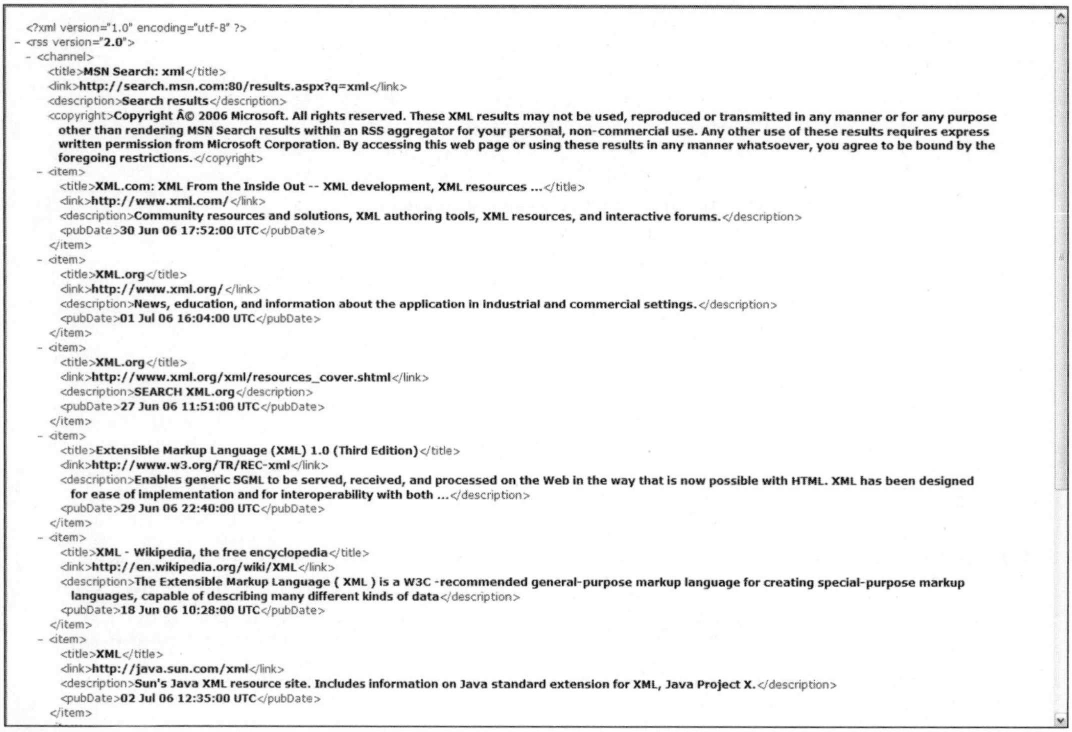

```
  <?xml version="1.0" encoding="utf-8" ?>
- <rss version="2.0">
  - <channel>
      <title>MSN Search: xml</title>
      <link>http://search.msn.com:80/results.aspx?q=xml</link>
      <description>Search results</description>
      <copyright>Copyright Â© 2006 Microsoft. All rights reserved. These XML results may not be used, reproduced or transmitted in any manner or for any purpose
        other than rendering MSN Search results within an RSS aggregator for your personal, non-commercial use. Any other use of these results requires express
        written permission from Microsoft Corporation. By accessing this web page or using these results in any manner whatsoever, you agree to be bound by the
        foregoing restrictions.</copyright>
    - <item>
        <title>XML.com: XML From the Inside Out -- XML development, XML resources ...</title>
        <link>http://www.xml.com/</link>
        <description>Community resources and solutions, XML authoring tools, XML resources, and interactive forums.</description>
        <pubDate>30 Jun 06 17:52:00 UTC</pubDate>
      </item>
    - <item>
        <title>XML.org</title>
        <link>http://www.xml.org/</link>
        <description>News, education, and information about the application in industrial and commercial settings.</description>
        <pubDate>01 Jul 06 16:04:00 UTC</pubDate>
      </item>
    - <item>
        <title>XML.org</title>
        <link>http://www.xml.org/xml/resources_cover.shtml</link>
        <description>SEARCH XML.org</description>
        <pubDate>27 Jun 06 11:51:00 UTC</pubDate>
      </item>
    - <item>
        <title>Extensible Markup Language (XML) 1.0 (Third Edition)</title>
        <link>http://www.w3.org/TR/REC-xml</link>
        <description>Enables generic SGML to be served, received, and processed on the Web in the way that is now possible with HTML. XML has been designed
          for ease of implementation and for interoperability with both ...</description>
        <pubDate>29 Jun 06 22:40:00 UTC</pubDate>
      </item>
    - <item>
        <title>XML - Wikipedia, the free encyclopedia</title>
        <link>http://en.wikipedia.org/wiki/XML</link>
        <description>The Extensible Markup Language ( XML ) is a W3C -recommended general-purpose markup language for creating special-purpose markup
          languages, capable of describing many different kinds of data</description>
        <pubDate>18 Jun 06 10:28:00 UTC</pubDate>
      </item>
    - <item>
        <title>XML</title>
        <link>http://java.sun.com/xml</link>
        <description>Sun's Java XML resource site. Includes information on Java standard extension for XML, Java Project X.</description>
        <pubDate>02 Jul 06 12:35:00 UTC</pubDate>
      </item>
```


Figure 8-2

You add an XSLT stylesheet to an XML document with the xml-stylesheet processing instruction.

```
<?xml-stylesheet type='text/xsl' href='URL to xslt' version='1.0'?>
```

With the addition of the stylesheet, the preceding XML becomes more useful (see Figure 8-3).

The advantage to adding the stylesheet information to the XML is two-fold. First, it means that global changes to multiple XML files are made in only one place — the XSLT file. Second, it pushes the processing required to transform and display the XML to the client. This means that less server-side processing is required.

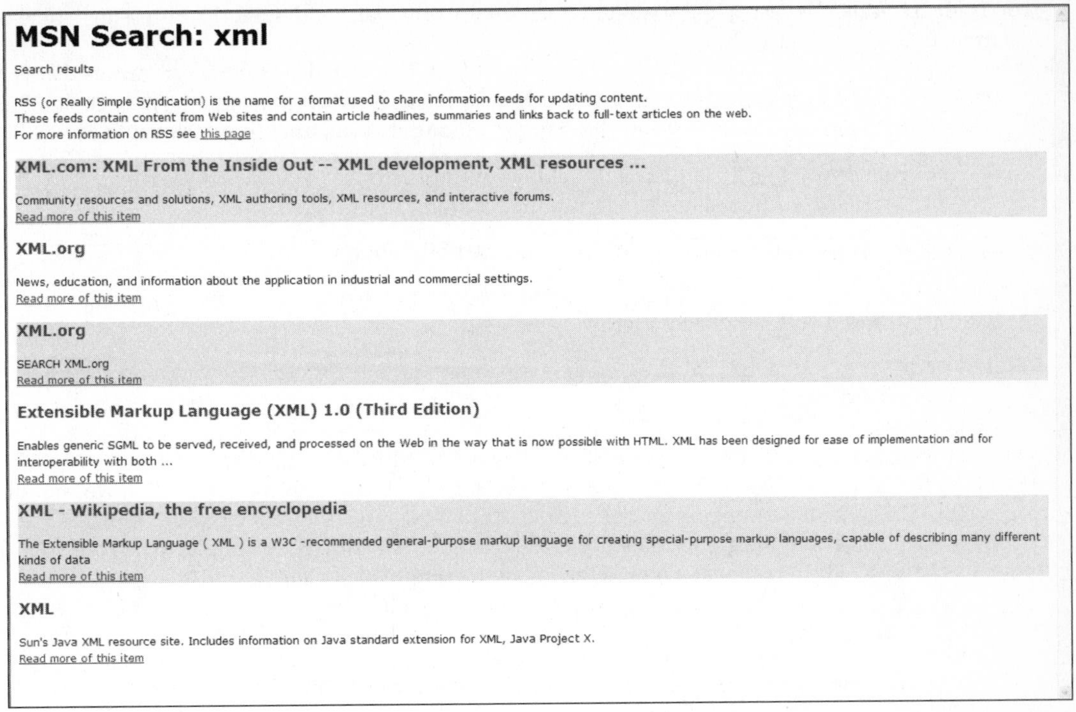

MSN Search: xml

Search results

RSS (or Really Simple Syndication) is the name for a format used to share information feeds for updating content.
These feeds contain content from Web sites and contain article headlines, summaries and links back to full-text articles on the web.
For more information on RSS see this page

XML.com: XML From the Inside Out -- XML development, XML resources ...

Community resources and solutions, XML authoring tools, XML resources, and interactive forums.
Read more of this item

XML.org

News, education, and information about the application in industrial and commercial settings.
Read more of this item

XML.org

SEARCH XML.org
Read more of this item

Extensible Markup Language (XML) 1.0 (Third Edition)

Enables generic SGML to be served, received, and processed on the Web in the way that is now possible with HTML. XML has been designed for ease of implementation and for interoperability with both ...
Read more of this item

XML - Wikipedia, the free encyclopedia

The Extensible Markup Language (XML) is a W3C -recommended general-purpose markup language for creating special-purpose markup languages, capable of describing many different kinds of data
Read more of this item

XML

Sun's Java XML resource site. Includes information on Java standard extension for XML, Java Project X.
Read more of this item

Figure 8-3

Changes with XSLT 2.0

XSLT 2.0 is still a candidate recommendation as I write this, but it should remain constant as it moves to a proposed recommendation and finally to a recommendation. XSLT 2.0 is an evolutionary step from XSLT 1.0. There are no major syntax breaking changes. Instead, it refines the existing model, and improves its clarity and flexibility. The major visible changes within XSLT 2.0 include:

- Support for XPath 2.0 functions
- Addition of XHTML as an output format
- Easier methods for grouping data
- Capability to create multiple output documents
- Capability to create user-defined functions

XSLT 2.0 and XPath 2.0 have been progressing simultaneously through the W3C. The benefit of this is that the functionality of XPath 2.0 is available for use by XSLT 2.0, and the two groups aren't creating similar but incompatible functionality. The greatest benefit is the availability of the XPath functions.

These add a number of necessary capabilities including string, date, and numeric processing. Some of the more useful functions include:

- `round`, `round-half-to-even` — `Round` rounds the number argument to the nearest number; `round-half-to-even` performs the banker's round that rounds 1.5 and 2.5 to 2.
- `concat`, `string-join` — `Concat` combines multiple strings to create a new string; `String-join` takes an additional parameter for the separator to use between each.
- `lower-case`, `upper-case` — Changes the case of the supplied string.
- `substring`, `replace` — `Substring` finds one string within another; `replace` changes one string based on a supplied pattern.
- `year-from-date`, `month-from-date`, `day-from-date` — Extracts the component from the supplied date.

One output format that was missing from XSLT 1.0 was XHTML. Although you could generate XHTML by setting the output format to HTML and ensuring the generated output was XHTML, it was not the same. XSLT 2.0 adds direct support for `output="XHTML"`. You can also use the `doctype-public` and `doctype-system` to add the appropriate declaration in your XHTML. For example, to declare your document as XHTML 1.0 Transitional, you use the following output statement:

```
<xsl:output method="xhtml"
  doctype-system="http://www.w3.org/TR/xhtml1/DTD/xhtml1-transitional.dtd"
  doctype-public="-//W3C//DTD XHTML 1.0 Transitional//EN" version="1.0"
  indent="yes" encoding="UTF-16"/>
```

One common form of report involves data grouped based on some categorization (see Figure 8-4). With XSLT 1.0, creating this type of structure was difficult. XSLT 2.0 adds the `for-each-group` element (see Listing 8-16).

Listing 8-16: Using the for-each-group element

```
<?xml version="1.0" encoding="UTF-8"?>
<xsl:stylesheet version="2.0"
  xmlns:xsl="http://www.w3.org/1999/XSL/Transform"
  xmlns:xs="http://www.w3.org/2001/XMLSchema"
  xmlns:fn="http://www.w3.org/2005/xpath-functions"
  xmlns:xdt="http://www.w3.org/2005/xpath-datatypes"
  exclude-result-prefixes="xs fn xdt">
  <xsl:output method="xhtml"
    doctype-system="http://www.w3.org/TR/xhtml1/DTD/xhtml1-transitional.dtd"
    doctype-public="-//W3C//DTD XHTML 1.0 Transitional//EN" version="1.0"
    indent="yes" encoding="UTF-8"/>
  <xsl:template match="/">
    <html>
      <body>
        <table>
          <tbody>
            <tr>
              <th>Country</th>
              <th>Company</th>
            </tr>
```

```
            <xsl:for-each-group select="customers/customer"
              group-by="address/country">
              <xsl:sort select="address/country" data-type="text"/>
              <tr>
                <td colspan="2" bgcolor="#E0E0E0">
                  <xsl:value-of select="address/country"/>
                </td>
              </tr>
              <xsl:for-each select="current-group()">
                <xsl:sort select="company" data-type="text" />
                <tr>
                  <td> </td>
                  <td>
                    <xsl:value-of select="company"/>
                  </td>
                </tr>
              </xsl:for-each>
            </xsl:for-each-group>
          </tbody>
        </table>
      </body>
    </html>
  </xsl:template>
</xsl:stylesheet>
```

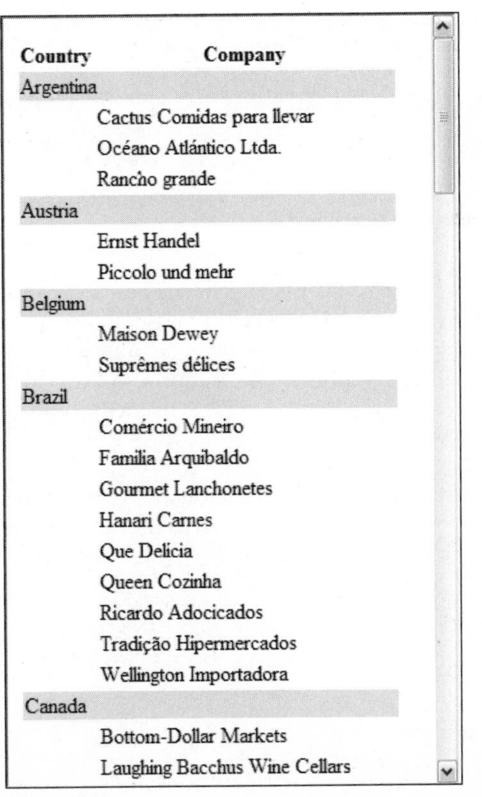

Figure 8-4

The for-each-group element takes a select attribute, as did the for-each element. In addition, it has a group-by attribute. This identifies the expression based on the select attribute that is used to group the output. Within the for-each-group element, the current-group() function returns the items in the current group.

XSLT 1.0 was limited to a single output document for each stylesheet. XSLT 2.0 adds the capability to export multiple documents using the result-document element. It requires you identify the URI for the new document and a format. In essence, it duplicates the output node, but for each output document. Listing 8-17 shows how to use the result-document element.

Listing 8-17: Outputting multiple documents

```
<?xml version="1.0" encoding="UTF-8"?>
<xsl:stylesheet version="2.0"
 xmlns:xsl="http://www.w3.org/1999/XSL/Transform"
  xmlns:xs="http://www.w3.org/2001/XMLSchema"
  xmlns:fn="http://www.w3.org/2005/xpath-functions"
  xmlns:xdt="http://www.w3.org/2005/xpath-datatypes">
  <xsl:output method="text"/>
  <xsl:output method="text" encoding="UTF-16" name="textFormat"/>
  <xsl:template match="/">
    <xsl:for-each-group select="//customer" group-by="address/country">
      <xsl:sort select="address/country" data-type="text"/>
      <xsl:variable name="uri" select="concat(address/country, '.txt')"/>
      <xsl:result-document href="{$uri}" format="textFormat">
        <xsl:for-each select="current-group()">
          <xsl:value-of select="company"/>
          <xsl:text>&#x0D;</xsl:text>
        </xsl:for-each>
      </xsl:result-document>
    </xsl:for-each-group>
  </xsl:template>
</xsl:stylesheet>
```

This stylesheet uses the customers.xml file to generate one text file per country, listing the companies in each country. The primary document is actually empty, although you could also create it as part of the processing. The result-document element takes — at a minimum — the href of the file to create and a named output format. In the preceding example, the href is of the form country.txt. The format attribute points at the named output to create a UTF-16 encoded text file. Within each result-document element, the elements in the current group are written to the file.

Finally, the addition of custom functions takes over many of the abuses of call-template. User-defined functions in XSLT enable encapsulation, just as they do in other programming languages. Each function can have multiple parameters and a return value. Listing 8-18 shows a sample user-defined function.

Listing 8-18: User-defined functions in XSLT 2.0

```
<?xml version="1.0" encoding="UTF-8"?>
<xsl:stylesheet version="2.0"
  xmlns:xsl="http://www.w3.org/1999/XSL/Transform"
  xmlns:xs="http://www.w3.org/2001/XMLSchema"
  xmlns:fn="http://www.w3.org/2005/xpath-functions"
  xmlns:xdt="http://www.w3.org/2005/xpath-datatypes"
  xmlns:ex="some-URI">
  <xsl:output method="xml" version="1.0"
  encoding="UTF-8" indent="yes"
  exclude-result-prefixes="fn xs xdt ex"/>
  <xsl:template match="/">
    <contacts>
      <xsl:apply-templates select="customers/customer/contact"/>
    </contacts>
  </xsl:template>
  <xsl:template match="contact">
    <contact>
      <xsl:value-of select="ex:name-case(name)"/>
    </contact>
  </xsl:template>
  <xsl:function name="ex:name-case" as="xs:string">
    <xsl:param name="value" as="xs:string"/>
    <xsl:sequence select="if(contains($value, ' '))
                          then concat(substring-before($value, ' '),
                                      ' ',
                                      upper-case(substring-after($value, ' ')))
                          else $value"/>
  </xsl:function>
</xsl:stylesheet>
```

To avoid any possible collision with existing functions, you define a new namespace for the user-defined function. This namespace is used in both the call to the function and in the definition. The function element requires a name and, optionally, the data type of the return value. Within the definition of the function, you can include as many parameters as necessary. They must be the first child elements within the function. As with the function, you can also include the type of the parameters. The sequence element generates the return value. The resulting XML displays the last name of each contact in uppercase.

```
<?xml version="1.0" encoding="UTF-8"?>
<contacts>
  <contact>Maria ANDERS</contact>
  <contact>Ana TRUJILLO</contact>
  <contact>Antonio MORENO</contact>
  <contact>Thomas HARDY</contact>
  <contact>Christina BERGLUND</contact>
  <contact>Hanna MOOS</contact>
  <contact>Frédérique CITEAUX</contact>
...
</contacts>
```

Although XSLT 2.0 is not yet a W3C standard, it soon will be. If your XSLT processor supports XSLT 2.0, there really is no excuse not to take advantage of all the new functionality for your stylesheets.

Generating Output with XSLT

XSLT is output-neutral. That is, you can generate just about any type of output from a stylesheet, although XML or HTML are the two most common.

Generating HTML with XSLT

One of the most common uses for XSLT is to create HTML or XHTML from a block of XML. This enables rendering of data for use in browsers without requiring two separate outputs.

RSS is becoming a common XML syntax (see Chapter 19 for more on this), and many sites are using it as a syndication mechanism for news, opinion, or feature releases. Listing 8-19 shows the result of an MSN search for XML displayed as RSS. This search normally provides an XSLT stylesheet but I removed it for this example. Most users do not understand and, therefore, cannot use raw RSS. Therefore, applying an XSLT stylesheet to RSS provides users with a friendlier interface (see Figure 8-5) and more information. Listing 8-20 shows the transformation used to create this.

Listing 8-19: A raw RSS feed

```
<?xml version="1.0" encoding="utf-8"?>
<rss version="2.0">
  <channel>
    <title>MSN Search: xml</title>
    <link>http://search.msn.com:80/results.aspx?q=xml</link>
    <description>Search results</description>
    <copyright>Copyright &#194;&#169; 2006 Microsoft. All rights
    reserved. These XML results may not be used, reproduced or
    transmitted in any manner or for any purpose other than
    rendering MSN Search results within an RSS aggregator for your
    personal, non-commercial use. Any other use of these results
    requires express written permission from Microsoft Corporation.
    By accessing this web page or using these results in any manner
    whatsoever, you agree to be bound by the foregoing
    restrictions.</copyright>
    <item>
      <title>XML.com: XML From the Inside Out -- XML development,
      XML resources ...</title>
      <link>http://www.xml.com/</link>
      <description>Community resources and solutions, XML authoring
      tools, XML resources, and interactive forums.</description>
      <pubDate>30 Jun 06 17:52:00 UTC</pubDate>
    </item>
    <item>
      <title>XML.org</title>
      <link>http://www.xml.org/</link>
      <description>News, education, and information about the
```

```
        application in industrial and commercial
        settings.</description>
        <pubDate>01 Jul 06 16:04:00 UTC</pubDate>
      </item>
...
      <item>
        <title>XML Developer Center</title>
        <link>http://msdn.microsoft.com/xml/</link>
        <description>Microsoft's XML resource site including
        tutorial, XML specification, samples, and XML support in
        Microsoft applications such as Internet
        Explorer.</description>
        <pubDate>02 Jul 06 11:02:00 UTC</pubDate>
      </item>
    </channel>
  </rss>
```

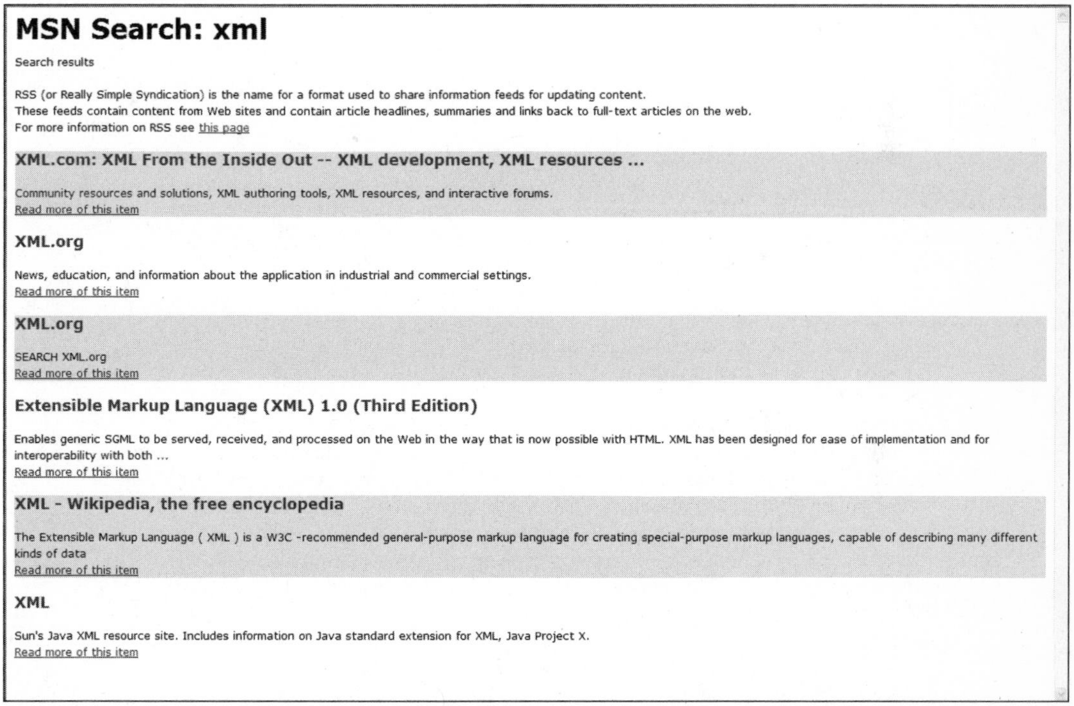

MSN Search: xml

Search results

RSS (or Really Simple Syndication) is the name for a format used to share information feeds for updating content.
These feeds contain content from Web sites and contain article headlines, summaries and links back to full-text articles on the web.
For more information on RSS see this page

XML.com: XML From the Inside Out -- XML development, XML resources ...

Community resources and solutions, XML authoring tools, XML resources, and interactive forums.
Read more of this item

XML.org

News, education, and information about the application in industrial and commercial settings.
Read more of this item

XML.org

SEARCH XML.org
Read more of this item

Extensible Markup Language (XML) 1.0 (Third Edition)

Enables generic SGML to be served, received, and processed on the Web in the way that is now possible with HTML. XML has been designed for ease of implementation and for interoperability with both ...
Read more of this item

XML - Wikipedia, the free encyclopedia

The Extensible Markup Language (XML) is a W3C -recommended general-purpose markup language for creating special-purpose markup languages, capable of describing many different kinds of data
Read more of this item

XML

Sun's Java XML resource site. Includes information on Java standard extension for XML, Java Project X.
Read more of this item

Figure 8-5

Listing 8-20: XSLT Transformation for RSS 2.0

```
<?xml version="1.0" encoding="UTF-8"?>
<xsl:stylesheet version="1.0" xmlns:xsl="http://www.w3.org/1999/XSL/Transform">
  <xsl:output method="html" version="1.0" encoding="UTF-8" indent="yes"/>
  <xsl:template match="/">
    <html>
```

(continued)

Listing 8-20 *(continued)*

```
        <head>
          <title>
            <xsl:value-of select="rss/channel/title"/>
          </title>
          <style type="text/css" media="screen">
          body {
            font-family: verdana, arial, sans-serif;
            font-size: 80%;
            line-height: 1.45em;
          }
          #itemWrapper {}
          #itemWrapperHighlight {
            background-color: #E0E0E0;
          }
          #itemBody{}
          </style>
        </head>
        <body>
          <xsl:apply-templates/>
        </body>
      </html>
    </xsl:template>
    <xsl:template match="channel">
      <h1>
        <xsl:value-of select="title"/>
      </h1>
      <div id="intro">
        <xsl:value-of select="description"/>
        <br/>
        <br/>
        RSS (or Really Simple Syndication) is the name for a format
        used to share information feeds for updating content. <br/>
        These feeds contain content from Web sites and contain article headlines,
        summaries and links back to full-text articles on the web.<br/>
        For more information on RSS see <a
  href="http://en.wikipedia.org/wiki/RSS_(protocol)">this page</a>
      </div>
      <div id="items">
        <xsl:apply-templates select="item">
          <xsl:with-param name="maxItems" select="6"/>
        </xsl:apply-templates>
      </div>
    </xsl:template>
    <xsl:template match="item">
      <xsl:param name="maxItems"/>
      <xsl:if test="count(preceding::item) &lt; $maxItems">
        <div id="itemWrapper">
          <xsl:if test="position() mod 2">
            <xsl:attribute name="id">itemWrapperHighlight</xsl:attribute>
          </xsl:if>
```

```
            <h3 id="itemTitle">
              <xsl:value-of select="title"/>
            </h3>
            <div id="itemBody">
              <xsl:value-of select="description"/>
              <br/>
              <a>
                <xsl:attribute name="href">
                  <xsl:value-of select="url"/>
                </xsl:attribute>
                <xsl:attribute name="alt">
                  <xsl:value-of select="title"/>
                </xsl:attribute>
          Read more of this item
            </a>
            </div>
          </div>
        </xsl:if>
      </xsl:template>
    </xsl:stylesheet>
```

The code consists of three templates, one each for the root (/), channel, and item nodes.

The root node template begins the HTML page and includes information for the head of the document, including the page title and stylesheet information. It then calls `the apply-templates` expression. Remember that excluding the select parameter causes all other templates to be called. In this case, selecting the channel node explicitly produces the same effect.

The channel node template is fairly basic: It extracts a few items from the XML and supplements this with additional text. It is worth noting, however, that `with-param` is used in the call to `apply-templates`. This defines the maximum number of items to display from the feed. You can experiment changing this value to see how it affects the resulting page.

Most of the complexity in the sample is in the item template. The `maxItems` parameter is provided in the call to apply the item template. However, this parameter is not available unless a matching `param` element is included. The test in the conditional `if` statement `<xsl:if test="count(preceding::item) < $maxItems">` translates to, "Count the preceding calls to the item template. If this value is less than the value of the `maxItems` parameter, process the contents of this `if` element." This is a simple means of controlling the number of items displayed from the feed. The third thing to note about the item node template is the `if` element "`<xsl:if test="position() mod 2">`". This test is `true` (that is, non-zero) for odd-numbered items, and `false` for even-numbered items. When `true`, the id of the `itemWrapper` div changes to `itemWrapperHighlight`. This style includes a light grey background in the example. The final noteworthy item in the item template is the technique for adding attributes based on the XML content. The attribute element retrieves the desired item using the `value-of` element, and creates an attribute, in this case the `href` and `alt` attributes for the anchor tag.

You can add an XSLT stylesheet to an XML file using the `xml-stylesheet` processing instruction at the beginning of the XML file (after the XML declaration):

```
<?xml-stylesheet type="text/xsl" href="url to XSLT"?>
```

When building an XSLT to transform XML to HTML, it is best to break the code into separate templates, just as you would break a set of code into separate functions or modules. The template for the channel node can easily be integrated into the root node, or vice versa. However, doing this limits the extensibility of both nodes. Similarly, separating the processing for the item node provides a local template for manipulating just those nodes.

Converting between XML Syntaxes with XSLT

The second major use for XSLT is to convert between XML formats. The purpose might be to align one format with the one used by a business partner, or because of a version change in your own schema. The technique is similar to creating HTML; however, you create a series of templates based on the source schema and define the result document in those templates.

Figure 8-6 shows what the desired output should look like, starting with the `products.xml` document used earlier in this chapter. Notice that the product listing is now grouped by the category, and the product name and price are now attributes of the product element.

```xml
<?xml version="1.0" encoding="UTF-8"?>
<products>
  <beverages>
    <product id="1" name="Chai" priceUSD="$18.00" priceEuro="€18,00"/>
    <product id="2" name="Chang" priceUSD="$19.00" priceEuro="€19,00"/>
    <product id="39" name="Chartreuse verte" priceUSD="$18.00" priceEuro="€18,00"/>
    <product id="38" name="Côte de Blaye" priceUSD="$263.50" priceEuro="€263,50"/>
    <product id="24" name="Guaraná Fantástica" priceUSD="$4.50" priceEuro="€4,50"/>
    <product id="43" name="Ipoh Coffee" priceUSD="$46.00" priceEuro="€46,00"/>
    <product id="76" name="Lakkalikööri" priceUSD="$18.00" priceEuro="€18,00"/>
    <product id="67" name="Laughing Lumberjack Lager" priceUSD="$14.00" priceEuro="€14,00"/>
    <product id="70" name="Outback Lager" priceUSD="$15.00" priceEuro="€15,00"/>
    <product id="75" name="Rhönbräu Klosterbier" priceUSD="$7.75" priceEuro="€7,75"/>
    <product id="34" name="Sasquatch Ale" priceUSD="$14.00" priceEuro="€14,00"/>
    <product id="35" name="Steeleye Stout" priceUSD="$18.00" priceEuro="€18,00"/>
  </beverages>
  <condiments>
    <product id="3" name="Aniseed Syrup" priceUSD="$10.00" priceEuro="€10,00"/>
    <product id="4" name="Chef Anton's Cajun Seasoning" priceUSD="$22.00" priceEuro="€22,00"/>
    <product id="5" name="Chef Anton's Gumbo Mix" priceUSD="$21.35" priceEuro="€21,35"/>
    <product id="15" name="Genen Shouyu" priceUSD="$15.50" priceEuro="€15,50"/>
    <product id="6" name="Grandma's Boysenberry Spread" priceUSD="$25.00" priceEuro="€25,00"/>
    <product id="44" name="Gula Malacca" priceUSD="$19.45" priceEuro="€19,45"/>
    <product id="65" name="Louisiana Fiery Hot Pepper Sauce" priceUSD="$21.05" priceEuro="€21,05"/>
    <product id="66" name="Louisiana Hot Spiced Okra" priceUSD="$17.00" priceEuro="€17,00"/>
    <product id="8" name="Northwoods Cranberry Sauce" priceUSD="$40.00" priceEuro="€40,00"/>
    <product id="77" name="Original Frankfurter grüne Soße" priceUSD="$13.00" priceEuro="€13,00"/>
    <product id="61" name="Sirop d'érable" priceUSD="$28.50" priceEuro="€28,50"/>
    <product id="63" name="Vegie-spread" priceUSD="$43.90" priceEuro="€43,90"/>
  </condiments>
  <confections>
    <product id="48" name="Chocolade" priceUSD="$12.75" priceEuro="€12,75"/>
    <product id="26" name="Gumbär Gummibärchen" priceUSD="$31.23" priceEuro="€31,23"/>
    <product id="49" name="Maxilaku" priceUSD="$20.00" priceEuro="€20,00"/>
    <product id="25" name="NuNuCa Nuß-Nougat-Creme" priceUSD="$14.00" priceEuro="€14,00"/>
    <product id="16" name="Pavlova" priceUSD="$17.45" priceEuro="€17,45"/>
    <product id="27" name="Schoggi Schokolade" priceUSD="$43.90" priceEuro="€43,90"/>
    <product id="68" name="Scottish Longbreads" priceUSD="$12.50" priceEuro="€12,50"/>
    <product id="20" name="Sir Rodney's Marmalade" priceUSD="$81.00" priceEuro="€81,00"/>
    <product id="21" name="Sir Rodney's Scones" priceUSD="$10.00" priceEuro="€10,00"/>
    <product id="62" name="Tarte au sucre" priceUSD="$49.30" priceEuro="€49,30"/>
    <product id="19" name="Teatime Chocolate Biscuits" priceUSD="$9.20" priceEuro="€9,20"/>
    <product id="50" name="Valkoinen suklaa" priceUSD="$16.25" priceEuro="€16,25"/>
    <product id="47" name="Zaanse koeken" priceUSD="$9.50" priceEuro="€9,50"/>
  </confections>
```

Figure 8-6

If you break down the conversion process, you see at least two stages: extracting the category names to ensure they are unique and converting the elements in the product node to attributes. Listing 8-21 shows the XSLT 2.0 stylesheet used to convert the source document. XSLT 2.0 is used to provide access to some of the XPath 2.0 functions, such as `replace` and `lowercase`.

Listing 8-21: Convert.xslt

```
<?xml version="1.0" encoding="UTF-8"?>
<xsl:stylesheet version="2.0"
  xmlns:xsl="http://www.w3.org/1999/XSL/Transform"
  xmlns:xs="http://www.w3.org/2001/XMLSchema"
  xmlns:fn="http://www.w3.org/2005/xpath-functions"
  xmlns:xdt="http://www.w3.org/2005/xpath-datatypes">
  <xsl:import href="formats.xslt"/>
  <xsl:output method="xml" version="1.0" encoding="UTF-8"
    indent="yes" exclude-result-prefixes="fn xs xdt"/>
  <xsl:template match="/">
    <products>
      <xsl:for-each-group select="catalog/row" group-by="category">
        <xsl:sort select="category" data-type="text"/>
        <xsl:variable name="cat" select="category"/>
        <xsl:variable name="catclean"
          select="lower-case(replace(category, '\s+|\\|/', '_'))"/>
        <xsl:element name="{$catclean}">
          <xsl:apply-templates select="//row[category=$cat]">
          </xsl:apply-templates>
        </xsl:element>
      </xsl:for-each-group>    </products>
  </xsl:template>
  <xsl:template match="row">
    <product>
      <xsl:attribute name="id"><xsl:value-of select="@id"/></xsl:attribute>
      <xsl:call-template name="prod"/>
    </product>
  </xsl:template>
  <xsl:template match="product" name="prod">
    <xsl:attribute name="name">
      <xsl:value-of select="product/name"/>
    </xsl:attribute>
    <xsl:attribute name="priceUSD">
      <xsl:value-of
        select="format-number(product/price, '$#.00', 'USD')"/>
      </xsl:attribute>
    <xsl:attribute name="priceEuro">
      <xsl:value-of
        select="format-number(product/price, '¤#,00', 'EURO')"/>
      </xsl:attribute>
  </xsl:template>
</xsl:stylesheet>
```

The first step in this stylesheet is to import the `formats.xslt` file (see Listing 8-22). This file includes a couple of decimal-format declarations used in the stylesheet. Output is defined as XML, and the xpath-functions, xpath-datatypes, and XML Schema namespaces are excluded from the resulting output. This step is not necessary, but reduces the complexity of the output.

Much of the work in the stylesheet is performed in the root template. It uses the XSLT 2.0 element `for-each-group` to loop through the categories in the source document. For XSLT 1.0, you can get a similar result using the `for-each` statement as follows:

```
<xsl:for-each select="catalog/row[not (category = preceding::category)]">
```

The two variables `cat` and `catclean` are needed because some of the categories include ampersands and slashes. These would interfere with the output document and, therefore, they are replaced with underscores. However, they are needed when applying the child template to select the products.

Listing 8-22: Formats.xslt

```
<?xml version="1.0" encoding="UTF-8"?>
<xsl:stylesheet version="1.0" xmlns:xsl="http://www.w3.org/1999/XSL/Transform">
  <xsl:decimal-format name="USD"
    decimal-separator="."
    grouping-separator=","
    NaN="-" />
  <xsl:decimal-format name="EURO"
    decimal-separator=","
    grouping-separator="."
    NaN="-" />
</xsl:stylesheet>
```

As currency formats are commonly used as output in XSLT stylesheets, it makes sense to extract them into a common file that can be imported as needed. The `formats.xslt` file defines two decimal formats using the decimal and grouping separators appropriate for US dollars and Euros.

Debugging XSLT

Just as with any programming effort, it is difficult to get it right the first time. Therefore, many of the XML-processing tools shown in Chapter 2 include XSLT debugging to help you correct any logic errors you may make when writing XSLT stylesheets. Just like code debuggers, these tools enable the developer to step through the templates, examine variables, and set breakpoints to determine how the stylesheet is processing. Figure 8-7 shows a debugging session in Altova XMLSpy. One of the nice features of this debugger is that you can see your script, source document, and result document at the same time as you debug the script.

A number of the product nodes have been processed, as you can see from the output panel. This output is built up as the `value-of` nodes are executed.

Creating breakpoints allows you to ignore the parts of your document that are working as expected. Set a breakpoint at the point in the source document that you want to debug. Then, run the debugger; execution will pause at the breakpoint. The XPath-Watch window (see Figure 8-8) provides insight into the current context and variables. You can then step line by line or template by template through the script as the output document is generated.

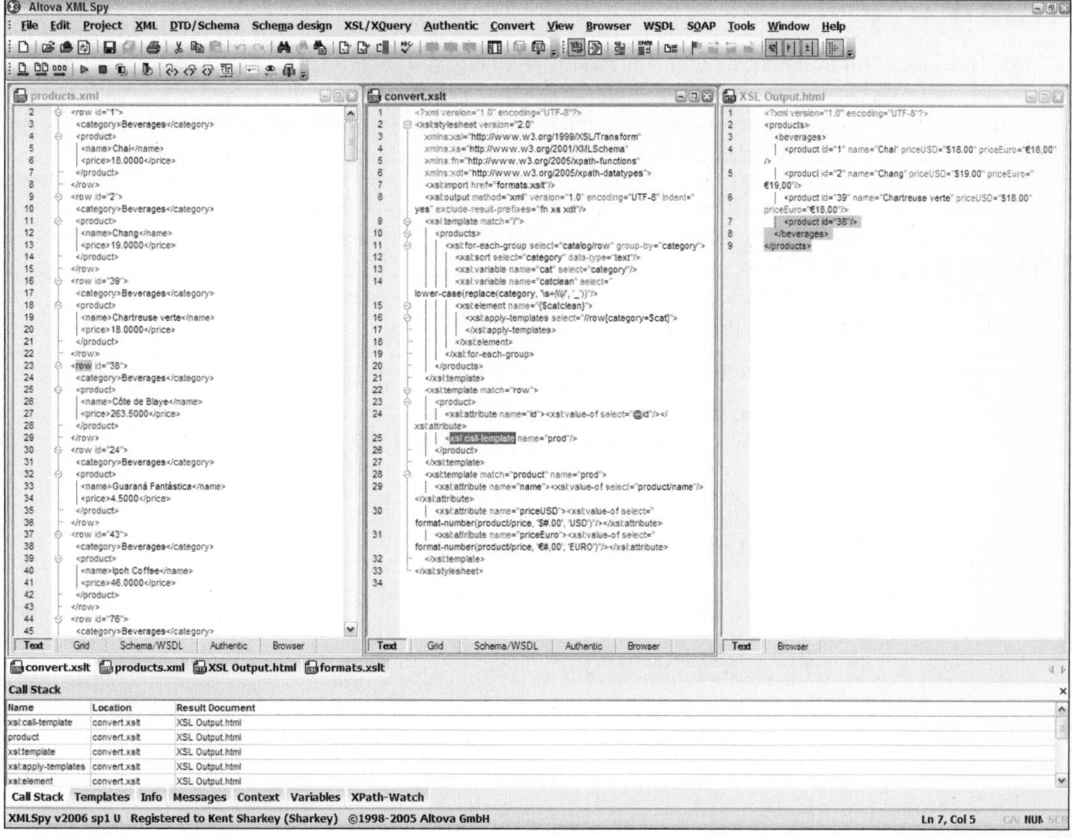

Figure 8-7

XPath-Watch

Name	Value
//row[category=$cat]	
row	id="1"
row	id="2"
row	id="39"
row	id="38"
row	id="24"
row	id="43"
row	id="76"
row	id="67"
row	id="70"
row	id="75"
row	id="34"
row	id="35"
$catclean	beverages

Cont... Varia... XPath-...

Figure 8-8

Summary

XSLT is a powerful tool that many developers turn to when working with XML. Many application frequently need the capability to extract, manipulate, and transform XML into new XML or other formats. Learning the declarative programming model does take a few mindset changes. However, once you've mastered XSLT, you'll find it an invaluable resource when working with any XML syntax.

Resources

- **XSLT 1.0 Specification** — `w3.org/TR/xslt`
- **XSLT 2.0 Specification** — `w3.org/TR/xslt20/`
- **Saxon** — `http://saxon.sourceforge.net/`
  Open Source XSLT and XQuery processor. Distributed as a Java jar file.
- `msxsl.exe` — `microsoft.com/downloads/details.aspx?FamilyID=2fb55371-c94e-4373-b0e9-db4816552e41&DisplayLang=en`
  Command-line XSLT processor from Microsoft.

9

XPath

XPath is a compact expression language to query XML documents. Most of the expressions you will find in XPath are simple to read and understand, even if you are not to use those libraries in your yet an XPath expert. This in part explains the success of the XPath language, which is already in wide use . Among other things, you can use XPath to extract information from an XML document, check the validity of a document, or perform complex queries on a document.

In the first section of this chapter, you learn about some of the major features of the XPath expression language. After reading this section, you will be able to understand most XPath expressions and write your own expressions.

If you are already an XPath expert, you can jump directly to the "Lessons from the Trenches" section. In this section, you will read some lessons that have been learned (often the hard way) over the years by programmers using XPath in real-life situations.

You need a special engine to run XPath expressions. Engines often come in the form of libraries, which you then use from a programming language. This chapter covers XPath libraries available in Java, .NET, and PHP, and shows you how programs.

As always, having the right tool makes a big difference. So the last section of this chapter tells you about some tools that will make your life easier when dealing with XPath expressions.

Major Features of XPath

What follows is a short introduction to some of the most important concepts and features of XPath. Here you will learn how to navigate the tree structure of an XML document with path expressions, about node types, predicates, axes, and sequences.

Nodes

XPath looks at an XML document as a tree of nodes. Let's see what those nodes are through the following example:

```
<catalog>
    <product id="mug">
        <price>5.95</price>
        <description>Custom printed stainless steel coffee mug</description>
    </product>
    <product id="table">
        <price>119.95</price>
        <description>Natural maple bedside table</description>
    </product>
</catalog>
```

From the perspective of XPath, everything in this document is a node. There are seven types of nodes in XPath. The following four are used most frequently:

- Element nodes, such as `catalog` or `product`.
- Attribute nodes, such as `id="mug"`.
- Text nodes, such as `5.95` or `Custom Printed Stainless steel coffee mug`.
- Document node is a somewhat artificial node that stands as the root the tree, with one of its children (and sometimes its only child) being the root element (such as `catalog` in the previous example).

The other three types of nodes that you might encounter occasionally in XPath are as follows:

- Processing instructions
- Namespaces
- Comments

Do not confuse elements with tags. Tags refer to the lexical structure of XML, where `<product>` *and* `</product>` *are opening and closing tags, and elements are what is placed between these tags, such as the* `id`, `price`, *and* `description` *attributes of that product.*

In XPath, you always talk about elements, not tags. If you write an expression that points to the first `product` *element, it returns the whole element, including its attributes and anything else between the opening and closing tags in the textual representation of XML.*

Tree Structure

Nodes are organized in a tree structure as follows:

- Every node has exactly one parent, except the document node, which doesn't have a parent.
- Nodes can have zero or more children nodes.

- Nodes that have same parent are called siblings.
- The ancestors of a node are its parent, the parent of the parent, and so on until you reach the document node.
- The descendants of a node are its children, the children of those children, and so on until you reach and include nodes that don't have any children.

Path Expressions

The tree structure of an XML document is not unlike the structure of a file system. Instead of the elements and attributes used in XML, the file system has directories and files. On UNIX or Windows, you use a particular syntax, called a *path*, to point to a directory or file. The path to a file looks like `C:\windows\system32\drivers\etc\hosts` on Windows or `/etc/hosts` on UNIX. In both cases, you specify directory and file names starting from the root and separating them by a forward or backward slash. For example, `A/B` or `A\B` refers to the child `B` of `A`.

The same is true in XPath. So the `/catalog` specifications in the previous document example signify the following:

- `/catalog` points to the `catalog` element.
- `/catalog/product` points to the two `product` elements, which are children of the catalog element.

Just as with path expressions on UNIX or Windows, you can use `..` (two dots) to refer to parent node. For example:

- `/catalog/product/..` is another (albeit longer) way to point to the `catalog` element.
- `/catalog/..` points to the parent of the `catalog` element, which is the document element.

In the first expression, `/catalog/product` *returns two* `catalog` *elements. So you might wonder if* `/catalog/product/..` *returns the parents of these two elements, and if the parent would be the same if the expression returns the* `catalog` *element twice. This doesn't happen, because a path expression never returns duplicate nodes. So* `/catalog/product/..` *returns just one node: the* `catalog` *element.*

If you prefix a name with `@` (the "at" symbol), it points to an attribute with that name. For instance, the following expression returns the two `id` attributes `"mug"` and `"table"`:

```
/catalog/product/@id
```

Predicates

What if you don't want to get all the products from the catalog, but only those with a price lower than 10 dollars? You can filter the nodes returned by a path expression by adding a condition between square brackets. So to return only the products with a price lower than 10 dollars, you would write this:

```
/catalog/product[price <= 10]
```

There are two types of predicates:

- When the expression in the predicate evaluates to a value of a numeric type, then it is called a *numeric predicate*. A numeric predicate selects the node that has a context position equal to the specified value. Context positions are 1-based (not 0-based). For example:
    - `/catalog/product[1]` returns the first product, the one with `id "mug"`.
    - `/catalog/product[0]` doesn't return any product, because the context position of the first product is 1. Note that this is a valid expression that does not generate an error.
- When the expression does not evaluate to a value of numeric type, it is taken as a Boolean value. If the expression does not evaluate to a Boolean value, it is converted with the `boolean()` function. For example:
    - `/catalog/product[price >=100 and price < 200]` returns products with a price point between 100–200 dollars.
    - `/catalog/product[contains(description, 'table')]` returns products with descriptions that contain the word "table." Note that the predicate expression uses the `contains()` function, and the `'table'` string is within single quotes.

Boolean expressions in predicates

Many developers don't know exactly how the `boolean()` function works, so the best solution is to always write expressions that either return a numeric value or a Boolean value. For example:

- `boolean()` converts an empty string to false and a nonempty string to true, even if the value of the string is the text `"false"`. So to get all the products with nonempty descriptions, you could write this:

```
/catalog/product[string(description)]
```

  However, to ensure that you get numeric or Boolean values, you should write this:

```
/catalog/product[description != '']
```

- `boolean()` converts an empty sequence to false and a node to true. So you could use the following expression to return all the products that have an id attribute:

```
/catalog/product[@id]
```

  However, to state your intention more clearly, you can use the `exists()` function, like this:

```
/catalog/product[exists(@id)]
```

Axes

XPath expressions navigate through a tree. An *axis* is the direction in which this navigation happens. Let's see what this means on the expression `/catalog/product` that you have seen before:

- The first `/` refers to the document node.
- `catalog` selects the `catalog` child element of the document node.
- `/product` selects the `product` elements children of the `catalog` element.

The `/` operator is used here to select child elements. But you can also use it to navigate other *axes*, as they are called in XPath. For example, this expression selects the `product` elements that follow the first product:

```
/catalog/product[1]/following-sibling::product
```

In the case of the document you saw earlier, this returns the second product. You select the `following-sibling` axis by prefixing the last occurrence of `product` with `following-sibling::`. When no axis is specified in front of an element name, the child axis is implied. So you could rewrite the `/catalog/product` expression as follows:

```
/child::catalog/child::product
```

There are 13 axes available in XPath. The eight axes that are most frequently used are these:

- `descendant`
- `descendant-or-self`
- `following-sibling`
- `following`
- `ancestor`
- `preceding-sibling`
- `preceding`
- `ancestor-or-self`

The remaining five axes are these:

- `parent`
- `self`
- `attribute`
- `child`
- `namespace`

In the previous example, the `child` and `attribute` axes were written as `/child::catalog`, which is just a long version of `/catalog`. Similarly, `/catalog/product/attribute::id` is a long version of `/catalog/product/@id`. But it is interesting to note here how these are defined as two distinct axes. One consequence is that an attribute is not a child of the element on which it is defined. The `@id` attribute is not a child of the `product` element, but the `product` element is the parent of the `@id` attribute.

Sequences

You have seen expressions that return more than one element, like `/catalog/product`. They are said to return a sequence. Sequences in XPath are similar to lists in other languages — they can contain items of different types, they can contain duplicates, and items in the sequence are ordered. However, a sequence cannot contain other sequences — they cannot be nested.

Path expressions can return sequences, but you can also build your own sequences using the comma (`,`) operator. For example, the following expression returns a sequence with the two numbers 42 and 43:

```
(42, 43)
```

Lessons from the Trenches

Even starting with little or no knowledge in XPath, you can become productive very quickly. This is because in most cases, simple problems have a simple solution in XPath. But you can also solve complex problems with XPath. While simple in appearance, XPath is in fact a very powerful language. In this section you learn about some more advanced features of the languages. But not those obscure features no one knows about, but those we have found the most useful based on years of practical experience with XPath.

When A != B Is Different from not(A = B)

Are you a genius? Of course you are. Then the same question written in XPath, `you = genius`, returns `true()`. In this case, `you != genius` must return `false()`. No rocket science here: if `A = B` returns `true()`, you expect `A != B` to return `false()`, and the other way around. In other words, you expect `A != B` and `not(A = B)` to be the same.

In most cases they are, but not always. Because of the way XPath compares sequences, the result of the comparison is true if and only if one value in the first sequence and one value in the second, when compared with the specified operator, return `true()`. This causes the following:

- If at least one of the two sequences is empty, the comparison always returns false, so both `() = 42` and `() != 42` return `false()`.
- For some sequences, you can find pairs of values, one in the first sequence and one in the second sequence, that both match the `=` and `!=` operators. For example, `(1, 2) = (1)` returns `true()` because 1 is in both sequences. But `(1, 2) != (1)` also returns `true()`, because 2 from the first sequence is not equal to any value from the second sequence.

Is this all here to confuse you? Certainly not. The way comparison works in XPath has a number of benefits, maybe the most important one in practice being that you can use the = and != operators to check if a value is present in a sequence, like some sort of `contains()` function. For example, `x = (1, 2, 3, 5, 8, 13, 21, 34, 55, 89)`, where x is of type `xs:double`, returns `true()` if x is a Fibonacci number lower than 100.

The Many Faces of a Document

From time to time, you will come across a function in XPath that returns an XML document. If you are using XSLT 1.0 or 2.0, XPath 2.0, XQuery, or XForms, you can use a mix of `instance()`, `doc()`, and `document()`.

XForms is a technology used to create forms. The data you enter in the form is stored in one or more XML documents, which in the XForms jargon are called *XForms instances*. Each document in XForms has an id, as in the following:

```
<xforms:instance id="address">
    <address>
        <street>1 Infinite Loop</street>
        <city>Cupertino</city>
        <state>California</state>
    </address>
</xforms:instance>
```

Assuming that the document in the instance with the address id is also accessible at the URI `http://www.example.org/address.xml`, consider the following XPath expressions:

- `instance('address')`
- `doc('http://www.example.org/address.xml')`
- `document('http://www.example.org/address.xml')`

All three expressions return the same "address" document. You can use the first expression with `instance()` in XForms, the second one with `doc()` wherever you have XPath 2.0 or XQuery expressions, and the third with `document()` within an XPath expression in XSLT 1.0 or 2.0 stylesheets.

Although all three return the same address document, they don't return the same node of the document. `instance()` returns the root element, and `doc()` and `document()` return the root node. This means that to point to the street element, you will need to write the following:

- `instance('address')/street`
- `doc('http://www.example.org/address.xml')/address/street`
- `document('http://www.example.org/address.xml')/address/street`

Note how the name of the root element (`address`) is used with `doc()` and `document()` but not with `instance()`. Granted, the difference between `doc()/document()` on one side and `instance()` on the other side is trivial. But it is surprisingly easy to make a mistake when you're using both functions in the same day. So keep this in mind: the same document can have many faces depending on which function you use.

Tuning Your XPath Expressions

When you write an XPath expression, you describe *what* information you want to extract from an XML document, but you are not saying *how* that information ought to be extracted. Consider, for example, the expression `/phonebook/person[starts-with(phone-number, '323') and last-name = 'Lee']`. Imagine you are running this query on a hypothetical XML document that contains the information found in the phone book. The query retrieves all the persons from Hollywood (area code 323) with the last name Lee. Here are a few ways in which the XPath engine could run this query:

- It can go through the list of persons and start by checking the first condition first. If the first three digits of the phone number are 323, it checks if the last name is Lee.
- A more advanced engine might figure that because the first test on the phone number is more expensive than the straight comparison of the last name with Lee, to run the query more efficiently it will instead do the second comparison first and only perform the comparison on the area code if the last name is Lee.
- An even more advanced engine might maintain an index of the persons based on their last name. With this index, it can quickly locate the persons with the last name Lee. A standalone XPath engine wouldn't typically index XML documents, but this can be expected from an engine running in a database.

The XPath engine has a lot of freedom in the way it runs your XPath queries, and unless you know the engine you are using extremely well, you don't know if a query will run more efficiently because it is written one way instead of another way. So start by writing your queries optimizing for human readability, making your queries explicit and simple to understand. For example:

- Instead of `//person` use `/phonebook/person`, because of the following:
  - Using `/phonebook/person` *might* be more efficient. With `//person`, some engines will traverse every element of the document, but they would only need to go through child elements of the root element with `/phonebook/person`.
  - `/phonebook/person` states your intension more clearly and makes your code more readable.
- In large XPath expressions, avoid duplicating part of the expression. For example, the expression `(count(/company/department[name = 'HR']/employee), avg(/company/department[name = 'HR']/employee/salary))` returns a sequence with two numbers: the number of employees in the HR departments, and their average salary. Instead, write it as `for $hr in /company/department[name = 'HR'] return (count($hr/employee), avg($hr/employee/salary))`. Unlike XQuery, XPath doesn't have a `let` construct for you to declare variables. In some cases however, you can get around this by using the `for` construct.

Don't try to optimize your XPath expression prematurely. Or as 37signals puts it in their book *Getting Real*, "it's a problem when it's a problem." Until then, just write clean and readable expressions.

Function Calls in Path Expressions

You may have seen an expression like `/company/department[@name = 'Engineering']/employee [@firstname = 'Bruce']` used to retrieve the `employee` element that corresponds to that Bruce guy in the engineering department. This is a path expression, and each step of the expression selects some node from the input document relative to the nodes selected by the previous step.

One new feature of XPath 2.0 is that you can have functions calls as a step expression. Consider this document:

```
<company>
    <department id="1" name="HR">
        <employee firstname="John" lastname="Smith" salary="60000"/>
        <employee firstname="Peter" lastname="Strain" salary="70000"/>
        <employee firstname="Carl" lastname="Thompson" salary="80000"/>
    </department>
    <department id="2" name="Engineering">
        <employee firstname="Letticia" lastname="Vallejo" salary="80000"/>
        <employee firstname="Bruce" lastname="Wilson" salary="90000"/>
    </department>
</company>
```

What if you want to return the name of each department and the average salary of the employees working in that department? With imperative languages like Java, C++, or most scripting languages, you would typically use some type of iteration. In XPath, the equivalent would be to use the `for` construct to iterate over the departments and then run the `avg()` function to compute the average salary for each department, like this:

```
for $d in /company/department return avg($d/employee/@salary)
```

When executed on the preceding document, this expression returns `(70000, 85000)`. But instead of having just a list of average salaries, you also want the name of the department, as in: `('HR', 70000, 'Engineering', 85000)`. A simple addition to the previous query will get you the expected result:

```
for $d in /company/department return (string($d/@name), avg($d/employee/@salary))
```

As mentioned earlier, with XPath 2.0 you can use function calls as step expressions. So instead of `string($d/@name)`, you can write `$d/@name/string()`. As long as `$d/@name` returns an attribute node instead of an empty sequence, those two expressions are equivalent. So the one you use is a matter of personal choice. However, keeping simplicity and clarity in mind, it would probably be best to use `$d/name/string()`, which does exactly what you'd think from looking at it: given the element in the variable `$d`, take the attribute `name`, and then take the string value of that attribute.

Note that in cases where `$d/@name` can potentially return an empty sequence, those two expressions are not equivalent anymore, because `string()` applied to an empty sequence returns a zero-length string. So the following occurs:

- `string(())` returns a zero-length string.
- `()/string()` returns an empty sequence.

With XPath 2.0, you can further simplify the expression you saw earlier, getting rid of the <code>for</code> construct altogether to create a much simpler expression such as this:

```
/company/department/(string(@name), avg(employee/@salary))
```

You can push the envelope further. In addition to the average salary for each department, you can get the first name of the person who has the highest salary, like this:

```
/company/department/(string(@name), avg(employee/@salary), employee[@salary =
max(../employee/@salary)]/@firstname/string())
```

This returns `('HR' 70000 'Carl' 'Engineering' 85000 'Bruce')`. Try to imagine how many lines of code you would need with a traditional programming language if you had to extract the same information from a text file with tab separated fields, for example. Indeed, using XML to represent data, and XPath 2.0 to extract information for XML can be quite a time-saver.

Using Comments and Nested Comments

Did you know you could have comments in XPath? You get lured into using XPath because of its simplicity, and as you get more and more familiar with the language, and recognize how powerful it is, your XPath expressions tend to grow in size. Then one day, they get to such a level of heftiness that adding comments within the expression becomes a requirement. And yes, you can do it. For example, the following adds a couple of comments to the expression you saw previously:

```
/company/department/(
    string(@name), (: Department name :)
    avg(employee/@salary), (: Average salary :)
    employee[@salary = max(../employee/@salary)]
        /@firstname/string() (:Employee with highest salary :)
)
```

You start a comment with `(:` and close it with `:)`. One interesting feature of XPath comments is that they can be nested, a feature that is missing from many languages. Here is the use case: you have a complex expression and, maybe the sole purpose of verifying a hypothesis, you would like to run only a subset of that expression. Say that in the preceding expression, you would like to return only the name of each department. For this, you need to comment the rest of the expression — the part that computes the average salary per department and the first name of employee with the highest pay. Because XPath supports nested comments, you don't have to worry about the `:)` after `Average salary` as being interpreted as the end of your comment. You can write this:

```
/company/department/(
    string(@name)
    (:
    , (: Department name :)
    avg(employee/@salary), (: Average salary :)
    employee[@salary = max(../employee/@salary)]
        /@firstname/string() (:Employee with highest salary :)
    :)
)
```

When this expression is executed on the previous document, it returns the sequence `('HR' 'Engineering')`.

Because XPath 2.0 supports nested comments, in most cases you don't need to worry if part of an expression you are commenting out already contains comments. In most cases it does, but not always. Consider the following expression:

```
/company/department[@id = 1 and  @name != ':)']
```

This is a valid XPath expression and when executed on the document shown earlier, it returns the element corresponding to the HR department, because its id is 1 and its name is not equal to the string "(:".

Now look at the second condition in the predicate:

```
/company/department[@id = 1 (: and  @name != ':)' :)]
```

If you run this expression, the XPath engine will throw an error at you that will read something like "Unmatched quote in expression." This is because while the comment is being parsed, the parser only looks for the following two-character sequences:

- `(:`, which signals the beginning of a nested comment
- `:)`, which signals the end of a comment, nested or not

When the parser finds the `:)` that was originally inside a string, it considers it the end of the comment. So essentially the previous expression becomes this:

```
/company/department[@id = 1 ' :)]
```

Notice that the single quote that follows the `:)` is still there, hence the error message "Unmatched quote in expression." Fortunately, this only happens very rarely, and you can usually comment parts of your expressions without any worries, even if the part you are commenting out contains a comment.

Support for nested expressions is one of those features that you could wish every language had, especially XML. Maybe this will be considered for XML 2.0, if there is ever one.

Using Regular Expressions

With XPath 2.0, you get three new functions that let you use regular expressions. But you might be wondering why you need regular expressions in XPath. Regular expressions are useful to extract information from text, and because information is already clearly structured in XML, you should not need regular expressions, right? Although this is certainly true in theory, the documents you have to work with often contain information buried in strings. Consider this document, which represents an order from a customer:

```
<order>
    <number>3837482006122593897</number>
    ...
</order>
```

Here, the order number starts with a six-digit client number, followed by the year, month, and day when the order was processed, and it ends with digits that make the order number unique if the client sent multiple orders in the same day. You can extract the date from the order number with a series of calls to the `substring()` function. However, this `replace()` function in XPath 2.0 makes your job much easier:

```
replace(/order/number,
    '^[0-9]{6}([0-9]{4})([0-9]{2})([0-9]{2})[0-9]{5}$',
    '$1-$2-$3')
```

Execute this XPath expression on the document, and you will get `2006-12-25`, where:

- `[0-9]` matches one digit (i.e. character between 0 and 9).
- Adding `{n}` matches exactly *n* digits. For example `[0-9]{4}` matches 4 digits.
- The `^` at the beginning and the `$` at the end of the expression indicate that the expression matches the whole string, not just a subset of the string.
- Adding parenthesis around parts of the expression enables you to refer to what was matched by this part of the expression with `$x`. You use `$1` to refer to the first parenthesized expression, `$2` to the second, and so on.

Regular expressions that are available in different languages or libraries are similar, but there are quite a few variations. Regular expressions in XPath are a superset of those available in XML Schema, which in turn are based on Perl regular expressions. One difference is that regular expressions in XML Schema do not support the `^` and `$` character, the `{n}` qualifier, or the group semantic using parenthesized expressions. Those features are all used in the previous expression, so it is quite fortunate that XPath offers significant extensions over what is available in XML Schema.

The unordered() Function: Quite an Oddity

There is a function in XPath that takes one parameter and that XPath engines are free to implement by just returning the parameter. It is the `unordered()` function.

The `unordered()` function takes a sequence of items as a parameter and returns a sequence that contains the same items, but not necessarily in the same order. The purpose of this function is not to shuffle items around, but to give an optimization hint to the XPath engine. Consider this expression:

```
/company/department/employee[@salary > 80000]
```

This returns all the employees with a salary higher than 80,000 dollars. In XPath, any expression that uses the / path operator must return nodes in document order. This expression meets that criteria, so if Leticia appears before Bruce in the document, Leticia must be before Bruce in the sequence of nodes returned by the expression.

If the document is stored in an XML database, you might have an index for salaries, and the XPath engine might be able to use that index to quickly retrieve the sequence of employees with a salary higher than 80,000 dollars. But because it is created based on the index, this sequence is ordered by increasing salary. To return nodes in document order, the XPath engine needs to reorder the nodes in the sequence. If you don't care about getting the nodes in document order, you can use the `unordered()` to tell the engine that this last reordering is not necessary, like this:

```
unordered(/company/department/employee[@salary > 80000])
```

If you think that `unordered()` adds clarity to your expressions, then you should use it. But most likely, adding `unordered()` will do more to clutter your XPath expressions. So you should find out if your engine does anything special with `unordered()` before using it. If you are using a standalone engine, most likely `unordered()` won't work. XML databases might handle `unordered()` in a special way, but they are not guaranteed to do so. For example, using `unordered()` in the open source eXist XML database won't have any effect.

Union and Sequence Operators

Consider these two XPath expressions:

- `/r/a | /r/b`
- `/r/a , /r/b`

The first expression uses the union operator (`|`), which already existed in XPath 1.0. The second expression uses the sequence concatenation operator (`,`). When they are executed on the same document, they both return the following sequence, which contains element `a` first and element `b` second:

```
<r>
    <a/>
    <b/>
</r>
```

If you modify the expression to put `/r/b` before `/r/a`, the expression `/r/b | /r/a` still returns the same result, but `/r/b , /r/a` returns a sequence with the `b` element first. This illustrates one difference between the union and concatenation operators: the union operator always returns nodes in document order, and concatenation does not change the order you specified.

Also, the sequence returned by the union operator never contains duplicates, so the following occurs:

- `/r/a | /r/a` returns the `a` element.
- `/r/a , /r/a` returns a sequence that contains the `a` element twice.

You can only use the union operator on nodes, so using the previous example, note the following:

- `/r/a | 1` is not a valid expression.
- `/r/a , 1` returns a sequence with the `a` element first and the atomic value `1` second.

With XPath 2.0, instead of the `|` character, you can use `union`, which is strictly equivalent to `|`.

//h1[1] Different Than (//h1)[1]

Say you want to extract the main title from an XHTML document. Looking for `h1` elements in the document is a good bet, but there might be more than one `h1`, so you decide to take the first one, in document order. At first, you might think that you could use XPath expression `//h1[1]` to do this. Although it will return the first `h1` on some documents, in some cases it will also return other `h1` elements. Consider this document:

```
<body>
    <div>
```

```
            <p/>
            <h1>A</h1>
            <h1>B</h1>
            <p/>
        </div>
        <div>
            <h1>C</h1>
            <p/>
            <h1>D</h1>
            <p/>
        </div>
    </body>
```

Here `//h1[1]` returns the `h1` with A and C, but not B and D. Those are the first `h1` child elements of their parent. The expression `//h1[1]` works this way because the predicate operator (`[]`) has a higher precedence than the `//` operator. So `//h1[1]` is in fact equivalent to `//(h1[1])`, and `not (//h1)[1]`. In this case, it is the later that you want to use to get the first `h1` element in the document.

The precedence of some operators, also sometimes referred to as *operator priority*, is nothing new. In most languages, the multiplication operator has a higher precedence than that additive operator, so 1 + 2 * 3 reads 1 + (2 * 3), not (1 + 2) * 3. Operators can be ranked by their precedence, and for a given language you can assign a number to each operator that represents its precedence. The higher the precedence of an operator is, the higher the number is.

In XPath, the precedence of operators is formally defined by the grammar of the language. It can be quite time-consuming to look at the XPath grammar to figure out what the precedence of an operator is, because the grammar is scattered throughout the XPath specification. Fortunately, the editors have included a table in the appendix with the precedence of each operator. The following table is sorted by ascending precedence, so remember that the lower an operator is in the table, the higher its precedence.

Precedence Number	Operators
1	, (comma)
2	`for, some, even, if`
3	`Or`
4	`And`
5	`eq, ne, lt, le, gt, ge, =, !=, <, <=, >, >=, is, <<, >>`
6	`to`
7	`+, -`
8	`*, div, idiv, mod`
9	`union, |`
10	`intersect, except`
11	`instance of`

Precedence Number	Operators
12	`treat`
13	`castable`
14	`cast`
15	`-(unary),+(unary)`
16	`/,//`
17	`[],()`

Reverse Axis — Evil at Times

An XPath expression can return a sequence. Items in the sequence are in a certain order, and each of them has a context position. For example, consider this document, with three employees—John, Peter, and Carl:

```
<company>
    <employee firstname="John"/>
    <employee firstname="Peter"/>
    <employee firstname="Carl"/>
</company>
```

Now consider these two expressions:

- `/company/employee[1]/following-sibling::employee`
- `/company/employee[3]/preceding-sibling::employee`

The first expression returns the employees that follow the first employee. There is not much to be surprised about here: John is the first employee, so it returns Peter and Carl in that order. The second expression gets the employees before Carl. It returns John and Peter in this order, because all the path expressions in XPath return nodes in document order. This can be summarized as follows:

- The first expression returns Peter, Carl.
- The second expression returns John, Peter.

Now add the predicate [1] to both of those expressions, as follows:

- `/company/employee[1]/following-sibling::employee[1]`
- `/company/employee[3]/preceding-sibling::employee[1]`

When the value of a predicate is of a numeric type, as is the case here, the predicate is called a *numeric predicate*. A numeric predicate is true if the value is equal to the context position and false otherwise. So, the item in each sequence that has a context position equal to 1 is as follows

- The first sequence is composed of Peter and Carl in that order, and Peter is the employee with context position equal to 1.
- The second sequence is composed of John and Peter in that order, and the second employee in the sequence (which in this case is Peter) is the one with a context position equal to 1 (not John, who is the first employee in the sequence).

The reason for this potentially surprising result is that when you use a reverse axis, such as `preceding-sibling`, position is assigned in reverse order. Because a reverse axis is used here, the context position of the last item in the sequence is 1.

You can think of the engine as assigning context position starting from the node where you start your search. If you are going down, as with `following-sibling`, context positions are assigned in document order, but if you are going up, as with `preceding-sibling`, then context positions are assigned in reverse document order. Even if context positions are assigned differently depending on the type of axis you are using, the nodes returned by a path expression are always in document order.

Debugging with trace()

XPath is designed to be used within a host language, such as XSLT. Some host languages provide a tracing facility, such as the `<xsl:message>` construct in XSLT. Other host languages don't, such as XForms. For this reason, the XPath `trace()` function can be quite useful.

> `trace()` *is an XPath 2.0 function. XForms 1.0 uses XPath 1.0, so unfortunately you can't use* `trace()` *in XForms, unless your XForms engine specifically supports XPath 2.0, as does Orbeon Forms.*

`trace()` takes two arguments: a *value*, which is sequence of items, and a *label*, which is a string. It returns the *value* and logs both the *label* and *value* in an implementation-dependent way. Consider what is logged when you execute the following XPath expressions with the open source Saxon engine on the employees document:

- The following expression:
  trace(/company/employee[1]/@firstname, 'Name')

  logs this:

```
Name [1]: attribute(firstname, untypedAtomic): /company/employee[1]/@firstname
```

- The following expression:

```
trace(string(/company/employee[1]/@firstname), 'Name')
```

  logs this:

```
Name: xs:string: John
```

- The following expression:

```
trace(/company/employee, 'Employee')
```

logs this:

```
Employee [1]: element(employee, untyped): /company/employee[1]
Employee [2]: element(employee, untyped): /company/employee[2]
Employee [3]: element(employee, untyped): /company/employee[3]
```

- The following expression:

```
trace(/, 'Document node')
```

logs this:

```
Document node: document-node(): /
```

When you use `trace()` in an expression, there is no guarantee that the function will be executed, because the engine might not need to run that part of the expression, which means that you might not see anything in the trace output. The following expression reads `false() and ...`:

```
false() and trace(true(), 'This doesn't get displayed')
```

This is an `and` expression that starts with `false()`, so whatever comes after that doesn't matter: the result is always `false()`. In cases like this, the XPath engine typically does not run the `trace()` function call.

You can see what an expression returns by putting the whole expression inside a `trace()`, as shown in the previous examples. You can also use it inside a path expression. For example, this returns a sequence of names:

```
/company/employee/string(@firstname)
```

To see what are the employees taken into consideration by this expression, just add a `trace()` step within the path expression, like this:

```
/company/employee/trace(., 'Employee')/string(@firstname)
```

XPath in Java, .NET, and PHP

You can evaluate an XPath expression from a tool, like an XML editor. You will learn about some of the tools that can be used for this purpose in the section "Tools for XPath". But you often need to evaluate an XPath expression from one of your programs, which in most cases means that you will need to use an XPath library. In what follows, you will learn how to use XPath libraries to evaluate XPath expressions in three programming languages: Java, C#, and PHP.

XPath in Java

The Java API for XML Processing (JAXP) is a standard Java API that includes an API for XPath. So using JAXP, you can write code in a way that is mostly independent of a particular XPath implementation. If you write some code using JAXP running a current implementation of XPath, you will be able to easily switch to another XPath implementation in the future. JAXP not only makes your code portable to other XPath implementations, but it also makes your knowledge portable. You will be able to use what you learn here with any implementation of XPath.

JAXP comes out-of-the-box with J2SE 5 and newer. If you are using J2SE 4, you can download the Sun JAXP package from `https://jaxp.dev.java.net/`. Follow this step-by-step procedure to learn how to use JAXP from your Java program:

The code in this procedure uses the Saxon implementation of the JAXP. There are two versions of Saxon: Saxon-SA is the schema aware version, and Saxon-B is the open source version. The only limitation of Saxon-B is that it does not provide any of the schema-aware features, which is not a concern for what you are doing here. You can find more about Saxon and download it from `http://saxon.sourceforge.net/`.

1. All the classes used in the following steps are declared here. Some come from the JAXP library, others come from Saxon, and one comes from SAX (the Simple API for XML).

```
// Classes from JAXP
import javax.xml.xpath.XPathFactory;
import javax.xml.xpath.XPath
import javax.xml.xpath.XpathExpression;
import javax.xml.transform.sax.SAXSource;

// Class from SAX
import org.xml.sax.InputSource

// Classes from Saxon
import net.sf.saxon.xpath.XPathEvaluator;
import net.sf.saxon.om.NamespaceConstant;
```

2. Create an XPath factory. To do this, call the JAXP method `XPathFactory.newInstance()` and pass a URI as parameter. The URI you need to pass to use the Saxon implementation is `http://saxon.sf.net/jaxp/xpath/om`. Instead of using the literal string, you reference the public static final string `NamespaceConstant.OBJECT_MODEL_SAXON` as follows:

```
XPathFactory xpathFactory =
        XPathFactory.newInstance(NamespaceConstant.OBJECT_MODEL_SAXON);
```

3. Use the factory to create XPath object. The object returned by the factory implements the interface `javax.xml.xpath.XPath`, but because this code is using the Saxon implementation, you know that it is an instance of `net.sf.saxon.xpath.XPathEvaluator` so you can just do this:

```
XPath xpath = xpathFactory.newXPath();
```

4. The object that represents the XML document on which the XPath expression is evaluated is XPath implementation dependent. With Saxon, this object implements the `net.sf.saxon.om.NodeInfo` interface, and you create it with the instance of `XPathEvaluator` from step 3. The `XPathEvalutor.setSource()` method used on the third line takes a `SAXSource`, which is created based on the URL of the XML file on which the XPath expression will be evaluated:

```
InputSource inputSource = new InputSource("http://www.example.com/catalog.xml");
SAXSource saxSource = new SAXSource(inputSource);
NodeInfo nodeInfo = ((XPathEvaluator) xpath).setSource(saxSource);
```

5. Now that you have all those objects in place, you can directly evaluate an XPath expression with `xpath.evalute()`. Instead, the following code takes the long route — it first compiles the expression, and then evaluates the expression: You will want to compile your expressions if you are evaluating them multiple times, in which case your program will run more efficiently because the XPath expression will be analyzed and compiled only once.

```
XPathExpression expression = xpath.compile("local-name(/*)");
```

6. Evaluate the expression you just compiled, passing the object that represents the XML document you created in step 4. Specify the type of object you expect in return with the second argument. In this case, you specify the `String` type, so you can safely cast the object returned by `evaluate()` to `String`:

```
expression.evaluate(nodeInfo, XPathConstants.STRING);
```

The full source code for this program is available at `wrox.com`.

XPath on .NET

The XPath implementation that was used in the Java code in the previous section is Saxon. It is also available for the .NET platform. You can download Saxon for .NET from `http://saxon.sourceforge.net/`. To run an XPath expression on a document with Saxon for .NET, follow these steps:

1. You are using `System` and `Saxon.Api` in this program:

```
using System;
using Saxon.Api;
```

2. Create an instance of `Processor`, and then use it to create `XPathCompiler` and `DocumentBuilder`, as follows:

```
Processor processor = new Processor();
XPathCompiler compiler = processor.NewXPathCompiler();
DocumentBuilder builder = processor.NewDocumentBuilder();
```

3. The object `document` that represents the XML document is created by loading the file from a URL. You need to set a base URI on the builder, so it can resolve any URI that could appear in the document, such as a reference to DTDs. Here's how to do this:

```
builder.BaseUri = new Uri("http://www.example.com/");
XdmNode document = builder.Build
    (new Uri("http://www.example.com/catalog.xml"));
```

4. You get to an object that you can use to evaluate the XPath expression by first calling the `Compile()` and then `Load()` methods, which gives you an instance of `XPathSelector`:

```
XPathSelector selector = compiler.Compile("local-name(/*)").Load();
```

5. Use the instance of `XPathSelector` you created in step 4 to set the document that contains the expression to be evaluated , and then call the `Evaluate()` method to evaluate the XPath expression on the document:

```
selector.ContextItem = document;
XdmValue value = selector.Evaluate();
Console.WriteLine(value.ToString());
```

The full source code for this program is available at `wrox.com`.

XPath in PHP

PHP ships with a set of functions that use of the GNOME XML library. Simplicity is one reason why PHP became so popular. Evaluating an XPath expression on a document is just as simple. In just four lines, you can read an XML file, evaluate an XPath expression on that document, and print the result. Consider the following program:

```
$doc = domxml_open_file("catalog.xml");
$xpathContext = $doc->xpath_new_context();
$rootName = $xpathContext->xpath_eval("local-name(/*)");
print($rootName->value);
```

This is what's happening here:

- The first line reads the XML document `catalog.xml` from a file on disk.
- The second line creates an XPath evaluation context for that document.
- With the XPath context, the third line evaluates the expression.
- The fourth line prints the result.

That's it. (You can view this as PHP's contribution to saving trees.)

Tools for XPath

Using the right tool for the job is just as important for programmers as it is for construction workers. The right tool will help you write XPath expressions quickly and avoid errors. A number of tools let you experiment with XPath by writing an expression and quickly seeing what the result will be. This type of tool is particularly appropriate for XPath because it has these characteristics:

- XPath expressions are often short. You can type them quickly. Sometimes a text field is all you need to enter an expression.
- XPath expressions are not destructive. All you can do with XPath is extract information for a document, so your worst expression won't end up reformatting your hard drive.

The tools you learn about in this section let you quickly see what an XPath expression returns when evaluated on a certain document. You can determine which tools suit your environment best.

Online XPath Sandbox

The XPath sandbox is an online tool that doesn't require any installation. All you need is a web browser. You can access it by going to the followingURL: `orbeon.com/ops/goto-example/xpath`

Figure 9-1 shows the relevant part of the page you will see in your browser.

Input:

```
<company>
    <department id="1" name="HR">
        <employee firstname="John" lastname="Smith" salary="60000"/>
        <employee firstname="Peter" lastname="Strain" salary="70000"/>
        <employee firstname="Carl" lastname="Thompson" salary="80000"/>
    </department>
    <department id="2" name="Engineering">
        <employee firstname="Letticia" lastname="Vallejo" salary="80000"/>
        <employee firstname="Bruce" lastname="Wilson" salary="90000"/>
    </department>
</company>
```

XPath:

```
/company/department[@id = '1']
```

Output

```
<department id="1" name="HR">
    <employee firstname="John" lastname="Smith" salary="60000"/>
    <employee firstname="Peter" lastname="Strain" salary="70000"/>
    <employee firstname="Carl" lastname="Thompson" salary="80000"/>
</department>
```

Figure 9-1

You can use this page as follows:

- **Input area** — Use this area to modify the document on which your XPath expression is evaluated.
- **Xpath area** — Type the XPath expression here.
- **Output area** — The result of your expression evaluation on the document is shown here.

The service performs the XPath evaluation as you type, so you don't need to worry about having to click a submit button. If your expression is invalid, an error will be displayed at the top of the page. This service uses the XPath engine in Saxon, which is known as one of the most compliant implementations of XPath.

XPath in Your Browser

XPath is often used to extract information from web pages. More often than not, HTML is not well-formed XML. However, you can transform HTML into XML automatically with tools like HTML Tidy (`http://tidy.sourceforge.net`). This tool has a derived C library called TidyLib; bindings for PHP, Perl, Python, and other languages; and ports, such as JTidy (`http://sourceforge.net/projects/jtidy`), which is written Java.

Writing an XPath expression that extracts the piece of information you are interested in from a web page is often an iterative process. For example, say you want to extract the current value of the Dow from the Google Finance page shown in Figure 9-2.

You can use the XPath Checker add-on for Firefox to extract what you want from this page. Just install Firefox from `https://addons.mozilla.org/firefox/1095/`, restart it, go to the Google Finance page, and choose View XPath from the contextual menu. After looking at the source of the page, you might notice that the values for Dow are located the line of a table with id `mkt0`. Enter the expression **//tr[@id= 'mkt0']** in the XPath Checker window, and make sure that it extracts the expected line, as shown in Figure 9-3.

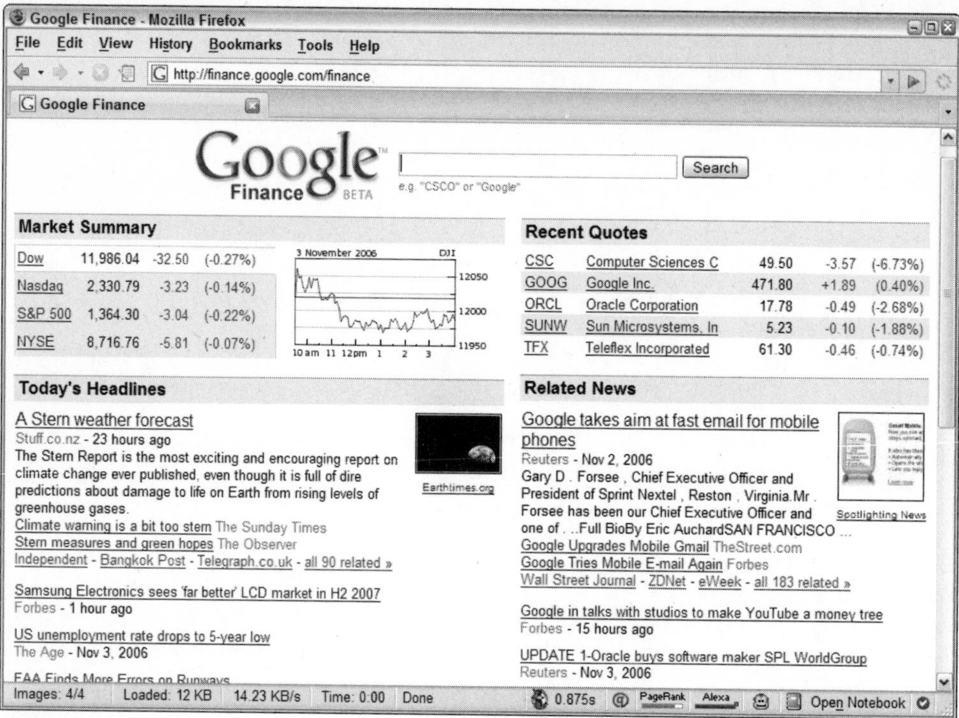

Figure 9-2

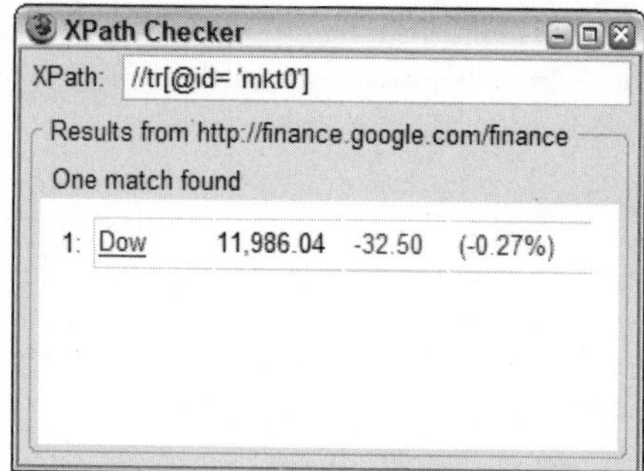

Figure 9-3

The current value for the Dow is in the second column, which you can extract by entering the expression **//tr[@id= 'mkt0']/td[2]**.

XML Editors

Most XML editors like XML Spy (`altova.com/products/xmlspy/xml_editor.html`) and Stylus Studio (`stylusstudio.com/`) provide a way for you to evaluate an XPath expression on a document you have opened in the editor. Figure 9-4 shows the interface provided by XML Spy.

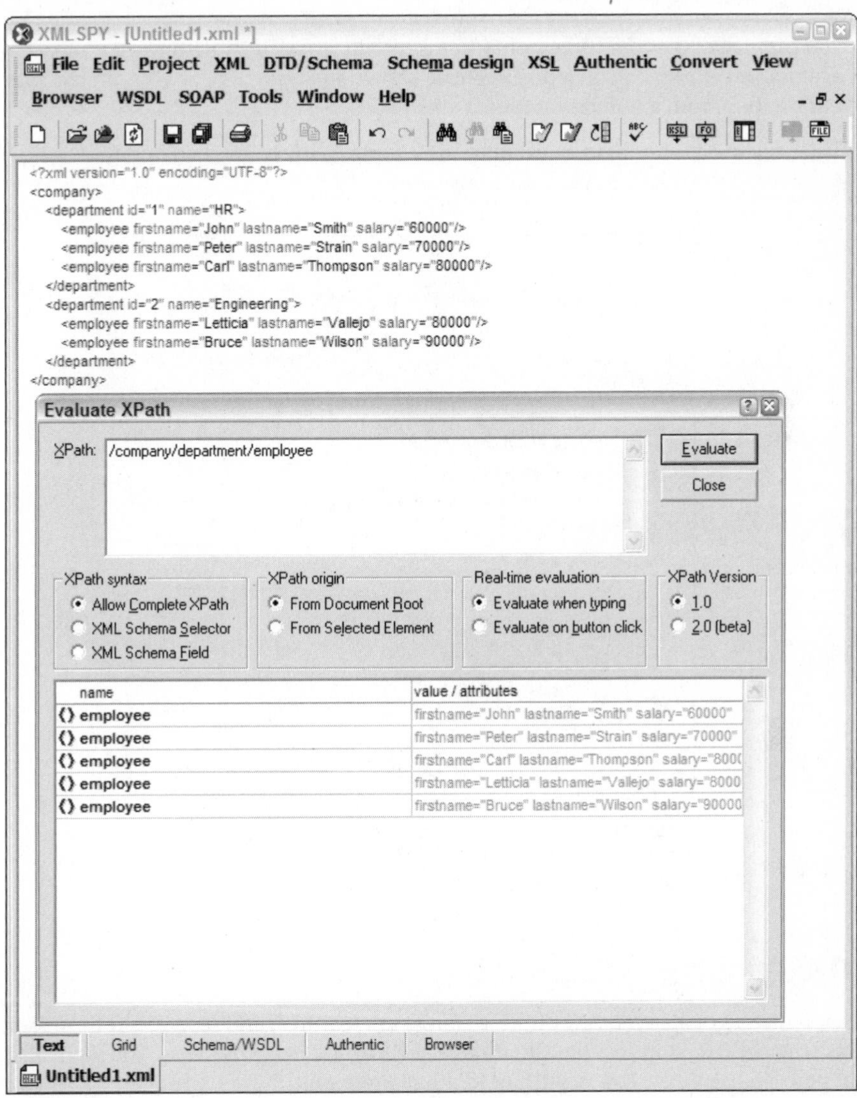

Figure 9-4

Eclipse and IntelliJ

If you already have a Java IDE such as Eclipse (`eclipse.org/`) or IntelliJ (`jetbrains.com/idea/`), you might want to use the XML editor provided by that IDE instead of installing a specialized XML IDE. Eclipse and IntelliJ don't provide a tool to evaluate XPath expressions outside the box, but you can download a third party plug-in as follows:

- You can install the XPathView plug-in for IntelliJ from File ➪ Settings ➪ Plugins. XPathView can evaluate an expression on a document as shown in Figure 9-5, or you can use it to search for information from a number of files.
- The Eclipse-XPath-plugin is a similar plug-in for Eclipse. You can find it at `http://sourceforge.net/projects/eclipse-xpath`.

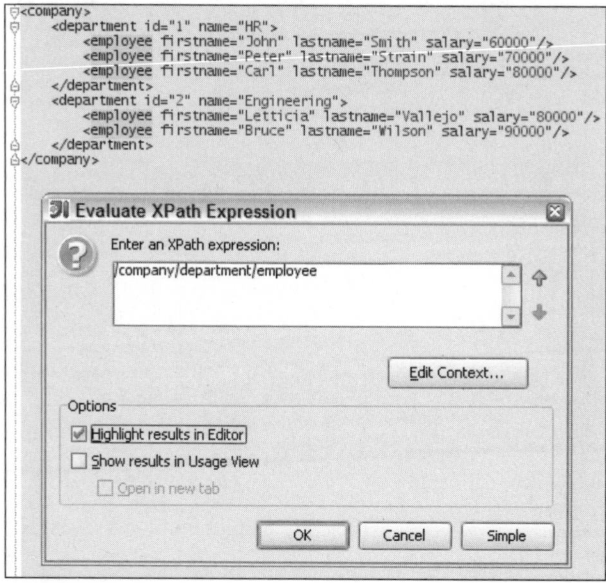

Figure 9-5

Summary

In this chapter, you got an overview of the major XPath features, and read about the lessons that programmers who use XPath in real-life situations have learned over the years. You were also introduced to tools that you can use when you're writing XPath expressions.

There is much more to XPath than what can be covered in just one chapter. If you want to learn more, check out Michael Kay's book *XPath 2.0 Programmer's Reference*. And rest assured, this isn't being recommended just because it is published by the same editor as *Professional XML*: Michael is editor of both the XPath 2.0 and the XSLT 2.0 specification, and he has implemented both in his Saxon product, which is a superior XPath 2.0 and XSLT 2.0 implementation. His book will make also make you an XPath expert.

References

W3C specifications can at times be intimidating, but you might want to check out the following for reference:

- **XPath 2.0 specification** — This contains everything about the syntax and semantic of the language. You can find it at `www.w3.org/TR/xpath20/`.
- **XPath 2.0 and XQuery 1.0 Functions and Operators specification** — One of the great benefits of XPath 2.0 compared to XPath 1.0 is its extensive function library. This library includes everything you need to deal with strings and dates. You can find it at `www.w3.org/TR/xpath-functions/`.
- **XPath 1.0 specification** — Given the choice between using XPath 1.0 and 2.0, you should go with XPath 2.0. But if you have to work with XPath 1.0, then the XPath 1.0 specification is your reference. You can find it at `www.w3.org/TR/xpath`.

10

XQuery

XQuery is a declarative, typed, functional language designed from scratch by the XML Query Working Group specifically for the purpose of querying data stored in XML format. XQuery shares the same data model and the same XML Schema-based type system with other members of the XML standards family such as XPath 2.0 and XSLT 2.0. XQuery is designed to work with XML documents that are untyped (no schema associated with the data), typed with XML Schemas, or a combination of both. XQuery 1.0 is basically a superset of XPath 2.0. In addition to the features of XPath 2.0, it has the following capabilities:

- Adds an `order by` clause to the FLWOR (more on this later) clause to sort in nondocument order
- Adds a `let` clause to the FLWOR clause to name results of expressions for further use
- Provides a way to specify static context items in the query prolog (such as namespace prefix bindings)
- Provides the ability to construct new nodes
- Provides the ability to specify user-defined functions
- Provides the ability to create modules and libraries

In this chapter, you get an in-depth look at the features of XQuery, including its syntax through examples. After that, you will be introduced to the support provided by Java and SQL Server 2005 for XQuery and the steps involved in working with XQuery from within Java and SQL Server 2005.

What Is XQuery?

XQuery is a fairly new language for querying XML data. It was designed from the ground up by the XML Query Working Group of the W3C with the sole purpose of querying data stored in XML format. As mentioned before, it is essentially a superset of XPath 2.0 that gives it all the features of

XPath 2.0 plus a long list of additional features. The great thing about XQuery is that it was built to work with all XML documents, whether they are untyped, typed, or a combination of the two. In all cases, its job is to query data stored in XML format. It does this by using the XPath navigational functionality.

XQuery Use Cases

Application areas for XQuery can be classified broadly as follows:

- **XQuery for query and analysis** — XQuery is excellent for querying huge chunks of data and provides the capability to filter, sort, order, and repurpose the required information. Typical applications include querying XML documents that represent semistructured information, name-value pair property bags, analysis of application logs, transaction logs and audit logs to identify potential application errors and security issues, and so on.
- **XQuery for application integration** — As organizations move away from proprietary application integration approaches and start adopting standards-based application integration approaches, the need for transforming data from internal application-specific formats to standard exchange formats is gaining more focus. Because of its ability to construct and transform XML data, XQuery caters to this need. One typical use of XQuery in the application-integration domain is translating the vocabulary used by one application that uses a native XML database relational data source into a language used by another application that uses an XML relational data format.

Advantages of XQuery

In addition to building on top of XML querying technologies such as XPath, and XSLT, XQuery also provides a number of advantages:

- It is easy to learn if knowledge of SQL and XPath is present.
- When queries are written in XQuery, they require less code than queries written in XSLT do.
- XQuery can be used as a strongly typed language when the XML data is typed, which can improve the performance of the query by avoiding implicit type casts and provide type assurances that can be used when performing query optimization.
- XQuery can be used as a weakly typed language for untyped data to provide high usability.
- Because XQuery requires less code to perform a query than does XSLT, maintenance costs are lower.
- XQuery is supported by major database vendors.

Structure of an XQuery Expression

An XQuery expression consists of two sections — a prolog and a body. A prolog can in turn contain a namespace declaration subsection. Namespace declarations are used to define a mapping between prefix and namespace URI, thereby enabling you to use the prefix instead of the namespace URI in the query body. You can also refer to element names without the prefix by binding a default namespace for element names, using the declare default namespace declaration.

The body of an XQuery expression contains query expressions that define the result of the query. It can, for example, be the signature FLWOR expression (see the "FLWOR Expressions" section in this chapter), an XPath 2.0 expression, or another XQuery expression such as a construction or arithmetic expression.

A Simple XQuery Example

XQuery is used to query an XML document, and for that you need an XML document to talk about while examining the various queries. For the purposes of this chapter, consider the XML document in Listing 10-1, which describes the structure of a set of products.

Listing 10-1: Sample XML file

```
<?xml version="1.0" encoding="utf-8"?>
<Products>
  <Product Category="Helmets">
    <ProductID>707</ProductID>
    <Name>Sport-100 Helmet, Red</Name>
    <ProductNumber>HL-U509-R</ProductNumber>
  </Product>
  <Product Category="Socks">
    <ProductID>709</ProductID>
    <Name>Mountain Bike Socks, M</Name>
    <ProductNumber>SO-B909-M</ProductNumber>
  </Product>
  <Product Category="Socks">
    <ProductID>710</ProductID>
    <Name>Mountain Bike Socks, L</Name>
    <ProductNumber>SO-B909-L</ProductNumber></Product>
  <Product Category="Caps">
    <ProductID>712</ProductID>
    <Name>AWC Logo Cap</Name>
    <ProductNumber>CA-1098</ProductNumber>
  </Product>
</Products>
```

The root element of this XML document is <Products>, which contains an arbitrary number of <Product> elements. Each <Product> element, in turn, contains <ProductID>, <Name>, and <ProductNumber> elements. In addition, the <Product> element also contains a Category attribute.

Just as SQL needs to be able to access any row or column in a relational table, XQuery needs to be able to access any node in an XML document. XML structures have both hierarchy and sequence, and can contain complex structure. Path expressions directly support hierarchy and sequence, and allow you to navigate any XML structure. In its simplest form, an XQuery can simply be an XPath expression. For example, to get a list of all of the product names that are of type `"Socks"`, you could use the following XQuery:

```
doc("Products.xml")/Products/Product[@Category="Socks"]/Name
```

The `doc("Products.xml")` part indicates the XML data store, which is an XML file named `Products.xml` in this case. Given the preceding contents of the `Products.xml` file, the output of this query would be as follows:

```
<Name>Mountain Bike Socks, M</Name>
<Name>Mountain Bike Socks, L</Name>
```

The output of an XQuery statement is a collection of XML elements. In the previous example, it is a collection of <Name> elements.

Enclosed Expressions

In literal XML constructors, you can use curly braces ({ }) to add content that is computed when the query is run. This is called an enclosed expression. For example, in the previous example, if you want all of the <Name> elements to appear within an XML root element named <ProductNames>. This could be accomplished with the following XQuery expression:

```
<ProductNames>
  { doc("Products.xml")/Products/Product[@Category="Socks"]//Name }
</ProductNames>
```

With this addition, the output would be as follows:

```
<ProductNames>

  <Name>Mountain Bike Socks, M</Name>
  <Name>Mountain Bike Socks, L</Name>
</ProductNames>
```

Note that in this query, you used curly braces around the XPath expression within the <ProductNames> element. The braces denote that the content within the braces is an XQuery expression, and not literal content. For example, the following query omits the braces:

```
<ProductNames>
  doc("Products.xml")/Products/Product[@Category="Socks"]//Name
</ProductNames>
```

The output of this query would be as follows:

```
<ProductNames>
  doc("Products.xml")/Products/Product[@Category="Socks"]//Name
</ProductNames>
```

FLWOR Expressions

Similar to the T-SQL `SELECT` statement, XQuery FLWOR statements are the foundation for querying, filtering, and sorting results from an XML document. FLWOR stands for `for`, `let`, `where`, `order by`, and `return` and is pronounced "flower." Although simple XPath expressions are useful, the real power of XQuery shines through with FLWOR expressions.

Take a moment to think about a SQL `SELECT` clause. The main ingredients there are the `SELECT`, `FROM`, and `WHERE` clauses. The `FROM` clause specifies the tables to query. Then the `WHERE` clause is evaluated for each row in the `FROM` clause tables. Those rows that pass the evaluation have those fields that are specified in the `SELECT` clause output.

FLWOR statements are very similar to a SQL `SELECT`. As mentioned previously, it is made up of five parts, or clauses, which do the following:

- `for`—Specifies the XML node list to iterate over, and is akin to the `SELECT` statement's `FROM` clause. The list of XML nodes is specified via an XPath expression. For example, if you wanted to iterate over all of the `<Product>` elements, you would use the XPath expression `doc ("Products.xml")/Products/Product`.
- `let`—Enables you to declare a variable and give it a value.
- `where`—Contains an expression that evaluates to a Boolean, just like the `WHERE` clause in a SQL `SELECT` statement. Each XML node in the XML node list in the `for` clause is evaluated by the `where` clause expression. Those that evaluate to `True` move on; those that don't are passed over.
- `order by`—Allows you to order the results of the query expression in ascending or descending order.
- `return`—Specifies the content that is returned from the FLWOR expression.

In a later section, you get an in-depth look at each of these clauses in the FLWOR expression.

A Simple FLWOR Expression

The simplest XQuery FLWOR expression is something like this:

```
for $p in $doc/Products/Product
return $p
```

This simply returns all the Product elements in the document `$doc`. You can add a bit of substance with an XQuery `where` clause and a slightly more functional XQuery `return` clause, as follows:

```
for $p in $doc/Products/Product
where $p/ProductID = 707
return $p/Name
```

This now returns the product that is identified by product id 707.

If you know SQL, you will probably find this very similar to the corresponding SQL statement:

```
SELECT p.Name FROM Product p WHERE p.ProductID = 707
```

On the other hand, an equivalent query using XPath would be this:

```
$doc/Products/Product[ProductID=707]/Name
```

As you can see, you can produce the same output using XPath as well. So the question is how do you know which style to use and when? It depends on what you're used to. If you've been using XML for years, especially XML with the deep hierarchy found in narrative documents, you'll probably be comfortable with path expressions. But if you're more comfortable with the idea of representing your data as a table, then the FLWOR style might suit you better.

In fact, an XPath path expression is completely equivalent to the previous FLWOR expression, and it's a legal XQuery on its own. In fact, every legal XPath expression is also legal in XQuery. The first query in this section can in fact be written like this:

```
$doc/Products/Product
```

As you'll see, FLWOR expressions are a lot more powerful than path expressions when it comes to doing joins. But for simple queries, the capabilities overlap and you have a choice.

An In-Depth Look at FLWOR Expressions

As mentioned before, the name FLWOR comes from the five clauses that make up a FLWOR expression: `for`, `let`, `where`, `order by`, and `return`. The following sections take a detailed look at each of these clauses.

for Clause

The behavior of the `for` clause is fairly intuitive: it iterates over an input sequence and calculates some value for each item in that sequence, returning a sequence obtained by concatenating the results of these calculations. In simple cases, there's one output item for every input item. For example:

```
for $i in (1 to 10)
return $i * $i
```

This returns the sequence (1, 4, 9, 16, 25, 36, 49, 64, 81, 100).

In this example, the input items are simple numbers, and the output items are also simple numbers. Numbers are an example of what XQuery calls atomic values. Other examples are strings, dates, booleans, and URIs. The XQuery data model allows sequences to contain XML nodes as well as atomic values, and the `for` expression can work on either.

Here's an example that takes nodes as input, and produces numbers as output. It counts the number of product numbers listed for each product:

```
for $p in //Products/Product
return count($p/ProductNumber)
```

This returns the output (1,1,1,1).

A FLWOR expression is just an expression, and you can use it anywhere an expression is allowed — it doesn't have to be at the top level of the query. The `avg()` function computes the average of a sequence of numbers, so you can use that to find the average of a group of elements.

As you can see from the previous example, XQuery is a functional language that you can use to calculate a value by passing the result of one expression or function into another expression or function. Any expression can be nested inside any other, and the FLWOR expression is no exception.

If you're coming from SQL, your instinct was probably to try and do the averaging and rounding in the `return` clause. But the XQuery way is actually much more logical. The `return` clause calculates one value for each item in the input sequence, whereas the `avg()` function applies to the result of the FLWOR expression as a whole.

And you can get from one sequence of nodes to another sequence of nodes. The `for` clause really comes into its own when you have more than one of them in a FLWOR expression. You will be introduced to that when you start looking at joins later in the chapter.

let Clause

The XQuery `let` clause simply declares a variable and gives it a value. For example:

```
let $ProductID := 707
let $productWithProductID707 := //Products/Product[ProductID = $ProductID]
return count($productWithProductID707)
```

Hopefully, the meaning of that is fairly intuitive. In fact, in this example you can simply replace each variable reference by the expression that provides the expression's value. This means that the result is the same as if you used the following:

```
count(//Products/Product[ProductID = 707])
```

In a `for` clause, the variable is bound to each item in the sequence in turn. In a `let` clause, the variable takes only one value. This can be a single item or a sequence, and a sequence can contain nodes, atomic values, or a mixture of the two.

In most cases, variables are used purely for convenience, to simplify the expressions and make the code more readable. If you need to use the same expression more than once, then declaring a variable is also a good hint to the query processor to only do the evaluation once. In a FLWOR expression, you can have any number of `for` clauses, and any number of `let` clauses, and they can be in any order.

There's an important thing to note about variables in XQuery: they can't be updated. This means you can't write something like `let $x := $x+1`. This rule might seem very strange if you're expecting XQuery to behave in the same way as procedural languages like JavaScript. But XQuery isn't that kind of language—it's a declarative language and works at a higher level. There are no rules about the order in which different expressions are executed, and this means that constructs whose result would depend on order of execution (like variable assignment) are banned. This constraint is essential to give optimizers the chance to find execution strategies that can search vast databases in fractions of a second.

where Clause

The XQuery `where` clause in a FLWOR expression performs a very similar function to the `WHERE` clause in a SQL select statement: it specifies a condition to filter the items you are interested in. The `where` clause in a FLWOR expression is optional, but if it appears it must only appear once, after all the `for` and `let` clauses. Here's an example that restates one of the earlier queries, but this time using a `where` clause:

```
for $product in //Products/Product
where $product/ProductID = 707
  and $product/@Category = "Helmets"
return $product/Name
```

This query returns the product with product id `707` with the category of `"Helmets"`.

This style of coding is something that SQL users tend to be very comfortable with: First, define all the tables you're interested in, and then specify a `WHERE` expression to define all the restriction conditions that select subsets of the rows in each table as well as the join conditions that show how the various tables are related.

order by Clause

The `order by` clause enables you to sort the values in the returned result set. The `order by` keyword accepts a sorting expression, which should return an atomic value. Optionally, you can also specify ascending or descending for the sort order. The default sort order is ascending.

To sort the products in ascending order of product id, use the following query:

```
for $product in //Products/Product
order by $product/ProductID ascending
return $product/Name
```

return Clause

Every XQuery FLWOR expression has a `return` clause, and it always comes last. It defines the items that are included in the result. Usually the XQuery return clause generates a single item each time it's evaluated. In general, the `return` clause can also produce a sequence. For example, you can do the following:

```
for $product in //Products/Product[@Category="Socks"]
return $product/Name
```

This selects all the names for products that belong to the category `"Socks"`. However, you can also wrapper the resultant nodes into a root element so that it easily wrappers around the Name elements:

```
<ProductNames>
  {for $product in //Products/Product[@Category="Socks"]
    return $product/Name}
</ProductNames>
```

Generally a FLWOR expression without element constructors can only produce flat lists of values or nodes, and that's not usually enough. You usually want to produce an XML document as the output of the query, and XML documents aren't flat.

As a result, instead of doing purely relational joins that generate a flat output, you want to construct hierarchic output using a number of nested FLWOR expressions. The `return` clause might seem like the least significant part of the FLWOR, but a misplaced `return` can make a big difference. It is recommended that you always align the F (`for`), L (`let`), W (`where`), O (`order by`), and R (`return`) clauses of a single FLWOR expression underneath each other, indenting any nested expressions, so that you can see what's going on.

FLWOR Expressions Versus XPath Expressions

Using a FLWOR expression to define the result sequence when you could express the same sequence using an XPath expression can be overkill in some cases because of the complexity of FLWOR expressions. As a general rule of thumb, you must establish the use cases where the use of a FLWOR expression is justified. The following list provides basic scenarios where the use of FLWOR expressions makes sense:

- If you want to iterate over a sequence of values that are returned as a result of an expression: Use the `for` clause, which binds a variable to successive values of the result set. Examples are the construction of new elements within the scope of the `for` clause and the retention of duplicates.

- If you want to filter the result sequence of the `for` clause based on a predicate that cannot be defined using simple XPath expressions: Use the `where` clause to eliminate unwanted values in the result set. For example:

```
for $i in (1, 2, 3), $j in (3, 4, 5)
where $i < $j
return sum($i + $j)
```

- If you want to sort the result set based on a sorting expression: Use the `order by` clause to define the sort on the result set.
- If you want to define the shape of the returned result set using the results obtained from the `for` clause: Use the `return` statement to perform the shaping of the result set.

If your requirement does not fall in any of these scenarios, you must carefully evaluate the use of FLWOR expressions.

XQuery Functions

XQuery includes an array of built-in functions. These functions are used for all the way from working with string values to numeric values, date and time comparison, node and QName manipulation, sequence manipulation, Boolean values, and more. In addition to the built-in functions, you can also define your own custom functions in XQuery. The following sections explore the XQuery built-in functions.

XQuery Built-In Functions

The XQuery namespace that contains all the XPath functions is identified by `w3.org/2005/02/xpath-functions`. When you use these built-in functions, you can use the prefix `fn:`. For example, you can invoke the `string()` function using the default prefix `fn:string()`. However you can invoke the same function just as `string()` leaving out the `fn:` prefix since `fn:` is the default prefix of the namespace. For example, here are some examples of functions usage inside an XQuery.

- You can use functions to format the contents of an XML element Inside an XML element:

```
<name>{upper-case($Name)}</name>
```

- You can also use functions inside the predicate of a XPath query for performing operations such as string comparisons, and so on to introduce new conditions:

```
doc("Products.xml")/Products/Product[substring(Name,1,5)='Sport']
```

- You can also use functions in a `let` clause before assigning the values to a XQuery variable as follows:

```
let $name := (substring($Name,1,5))
```

As you can see from the previous examples, XQuery built-in functions are very handy and go a long way in effectively applying the power of XQuery to solve real world problems. Now that you have had an idea of the role of the functions supplied with XQuery, let us explore some of the useful built-in functions.

doc() Function

The doc (uri) function returns the root node of the referenced document. The URI reference format is implementation dependent. For example, doc("Products.xml") returns the root node of the Products.xml document.

Aggregate Functions

XQuery provides count, avg, max, min and sum aggregate functions, which do the following:

- count returns the number of items in the sequence.
- avg returns the average (mean) of a sequence of numbers.
- sum returns the sum of a sequence of numbers.
- max returns the number with maximum value from a sequence.
- min returns the number with minimum value from a sequence.

For example, the following query calculates the number of products contained in the Products.xml file:

```
let $products := doc("Products.xml")/Products//Product
return
  <itemCount> {count($products) } </itemCount>
```

In the preceding XQuery, the $products variable represents all the product elements in the Products.xml file. The count($products) function returns the count of products in that sequence. The return clause constructs an element that looks like this:

```
<itemCount> 4 </itemCount>
```

String Functions

XQuery provides the following string functions: concat, starts-with, ends-with, contains, substring, string-length, normalize, upper-case, and lower-case.

The function starts-with (str1, str2) returns true if the beginning of str1 matches the characters in str2. The function ends-with (str1, str2) returns true if the ending characters in str1 match the characters in str2. The function contains(str1, str2) returns true if str1 contains str2.

The following query uses the contains() function to find products in the Products.xml whose category is of type "Socks":

```
for  $product in doc("Products.xml")/Products/Product
where contains($product/@Category, "Socks")
  return $product/Name
```

This results in the following output:

```
<Name>Mountain Bike Socks, M</Name>
<Name>Mountain Bike Socks, L</Name>
```

XQuery User-Defined Functions

The nice thing about XQuery is that if you can't find the right XQuery function out of the box, you are free to write your own. These user-defined functions can be defined in the query or in a separate library. The syntax for user-defined functions is as follows:

```
declare function prefix:function_name($parameter AS datatype)
  AS returnDatatype
{
  (: ...function code here... :)
};
```

The following are the key characteristics of a user-defined function that you need to be aware of while writing user-defined functions:

- The functions use the "`declare function`" keyword.
- The name of the function must be prefixed.
- The data types of the parameters are mostly the same as the data types defined in XML schema.
- The body of the function must be surrounded by curly braces.

Here is an example of a user-defined function:

```
declare function local:minPrice(
  $price as xs:decimal,
  $discount as xs:decimal)
  as xs:decimal
{
  let $disc := ($price * $discount) div 100
  return ($price - $disc)
};
```

And here is an example of how to call the `minPrice` function:

```
<minPrice>
  {local:minPrice($book/price, $book/discount)}
</minPrice>
```

The following is another example that illustrates the declaration and use of a local function. In this case, the function accepts a sequence of employee elements, summarizes them by department, and returns a sequence of dept elements:

```
declare function local:summary($emps as element(employee)*)
  as element(dept)*
{
  for $d in fn:distinct-values($emps/deptno)
  let $e := $emps[deptno = $d]
  return
    <dept>
      <deptno>{$d}</deptno>
      <headcount> {fn:count($e)} </headcount>
      <payroll> {fn:sum($e/salary)} </payroll>
    </dept>
};
```

To prepare a summary of the employees located in Phoenix, invoke the above function as follows:

```
local:summary(fn:doc("Employees.xml")//employee[location = "Phoenix"])
```

XQuery in Java

There are a number of toolkits available to work with XQuery from within Java. This chapter uses the XMLBeans open source implementation from Apache for working with XQuery. XMLBeans is a technology for accessing XML by binding it to Java types. XMLBeans provides several ways to get at the XML, including the following:

- Through XML Schema, which has been compiled to generate Java types that represent schema types. In this way, you can access instances of the schema through JavaBeans-style accessors such as `getXXX` and `setXXX`.
- Reflect into the XML schema itself through an XML Schema Object model as provided by the XMLBeans API.
- With a cursor model through which you can traverse the full XML InfoSet.
- With XML DOM, which is completely supported.

Pre-requisites

Here are the prerequisites to working with XMLBeans:

- **JDK 1.4 and Ant**—Install these if you don't have them already.
- **XMLBeans binaries**—You can download them from`http://xmlbeans.apache.org/sourceAndBinaries/index.html#XMLBeans+Binary+and+Development+Kit`.
- **Saxon XQuery processor for full XQuery support**—For XMLBeans 2.2.0, you need Saxon 8.6.1,which you can download from `http://prdownloads.sourceforge.net/saxon/saxonb8-6-1.zip?download`.
- **An editor for writing Java code**—This could be a text editor or your favorite Java IDE.

With these items installed and configured, you are ready to work with XQuery from Java.

Selecting XML with XQuery

You can use XQuery to retrieve specific pieces of XML as you might retrieve data from a database. XQuery provides syntax for specifying the elements and attributes you're interested in. The XMLBeans API provides a method named `execQuery()` for executing XQuery expressions.

You can call them from and `XmlObject` instance (or a generated type inheriting from it) or an `XmlCursor` instance. First take a look at an example that invokes the `execQuery()` method from an `XmlObject` instance.

Invoking execQuery() from an XmlObject

Note that the XQuery expressions require additional classes on the class path, as noted in the XMLBeans installation instructions. You use the `execQuery` method to execute XQuery expressions. With XQuery expressions, the output XML returned is a copy of XML in the document queried against and this output is an array of type `XmlObject`.

The example in Listing 10-2 retrieves `<Name>` elements from the incoming XML, displaying them directly on the console.

Listing 10-2: Executing an XQuery expression from a Java application

```
package com.wrox.xquery;
import org.apache.xmlbeans.XmlCursor;
import org.apache.xmlbeans.XmlObject;

public class XmlObjectSample
{
  final static String m_namespaceDeclaration =
    "declare namespace xq='http://www.wrox.com/xquery/samples/departments';";

  public static void main(String[] args) throws Exception
  {
    String fileName = args[0];
    XmlObject departmentDoc = XmlObject.Factory.parse(new URL(fileName));
    //Get all the <Name> elements
    String queryExpression =
       "let $d := $this/xq:Departments " +
       "return " +
         "for $n in $d/xq:Department/ xq:Name " +
         "return $n " ;

    XmlObject[] results =
      departmentDoc.execQuery(m_namespaceDeclaration + queryExpression);
    //Print the results.
    if (results.length > 0)
    {
      System.out.println("The query results: \n");
      for (int i=0; i<results.length; i++)
      {           System.out.println(results[i].toString() + "\n");
      }
    }
    else
    {
      System.out.println("No results returned: \n");
    }
  }
}
```

You start by creating an instance of `XmlObject` object passing in the XML filename as an argument:

```
String fileName = args[0];
XmlObject departmentDoc = XmlObject.Factory.parse(new
  URL(filename));
```

After that, you specify the query expression in a string variable:

```
String queryExpression =
  "let $d := $this/xq:Departments " +
  "return " +
      "for $n in $d/xq:Department/xq:Name " +
        "return $n " ;
```

This query expression first gets references to all the <Name> elements in the XML file and returns them as the output. The `$this` variable in the query expression refers to the current position.

You then actually execute the XQuery using the `execQuery()` method, passing in the value that is derived by combining the namespace declaration with the actual query expression:

```
XmlObject[] results =
  departmentDoc.execQuery(m_namespaceDeclaration + queryExpression);
```

You then display the resultant output on the console through the `System.out.println()` method.

To test this Java program, create an XML file named `Departments.xml` with the contents shown in Listing 10-3.

Listing 10-3: Departments.xml file

```
<?xml version="1.0" encoding="utf-8"?>
<Departments xmlns="http://www.wrox.com/xquery/samples/departments">
  <Department>
    <DepartmentID>1</DepartmentID>
    <Name>Engineering</Name>
    <GroupName>Research and Development</GroupName>
  </Department>
  <Department>
    <DepartmentID>2</DepartmentID>
    <Name>Tool Design</Name>
    <GroupName>Research and Development</GroupName>
  </Department>
  <Department>
    <DepartmentID>3</DepartmentID>
    <Name>Sales</Name>
    <GroupName>Sales and Marketing</GroupName>
  </Department>
  <Department>
    <DepartmentID>4</DepartmentID>
    <Name>Marketing</Name>
    <GroupName>Sales and Marketing</GroupName>
  </Department>
  <Department>
    <DepartmentID>5</DepartmentID>
    <Name>Purchasing</Name>
    <GroupName>Inventory Management</GroupName>
  </Department>
</Departments>
```

If you pass the URL of the `Departments.xml` file as a command-line argument at the time of executing the `XmlObjectSample` class, you will get the following output:

```
<Name xmlns="http://www.wrox.com/xquery/samples/departments">Engineering</Name>
<Name xmlns="http://www.wrox.com/xquery/samples/departments">Tool Design</Name>
<Name xmlns="http://www.wrox.com/xquery/samples/departments">Sales</Name>
<Name xmlns="http://www.wrox.com/xquery/samples/departments">Marketing</Name>
<Name xmlns="http://www.wrox.com/xquery/samples/departments">Purchasing</Name>
```

Invoking execQuery() from an XmlCursor

The XML cursor offers a fine-grained model for manipulating data in addition to providing you with a method to execute query expressions. The XML cursor API, analogous to the DOM's object API, is simply a way to point at a particular piece of data. So, just like a cursor helps navigate through a word processing document, the XML cursor defines a location in XML where you can perform actions on the selected XML.

Cursors are ideal for moving through an XML document when there's no schema available. After you've got the cursor at the location you're interested in, you can perform a variety of operations with it. For example, you can execute queries, set and get values, insert and remove fragments of XML, copy fragments of XML to other parts of the document, and make other fine-grained changes to the XML document. Listing 10-4 uses an XML cursor to execute an XQuery query.

Listing 10-4: Using XmlCursor to execute an XQuery expression

```
package com.wrox.xquery;
import org.apache.xmlbeans.XmlCursor;
import org.apache.xmlbeans.XmlObject;
public class XmlCursorSample
{
  final static String m_namespaceDeclaration =
    "declare namespace xq='http://www.wrox.com/xquery/samples/departments';";

  public static void main(String[] args) throws Exception
  {
    String fileName = args[0];
    XmlObject departmentDoc = XmlObject.Factory.parse(new URL(fileName));
    //Get the <Name> elements and return them
    String queryExpression =
      "let $d := $this/xq:Departments " +
      "return " +
        "for $n in $d/xq:Department/xq:Name " +
        "return $n" ;
    XmlCursor resultsCursor = departmentDoc.newCursor().execQuery
      (m_namespaceDeclaration + queryExpression);
    //Print the results
    System.out.println(resultsCursor.xmlText());
  }
}
```

This code creates a new cursor at the start of the document. From there, it uses the `XmlCursor` interface's `execQuery()` method to execute the query expression:

```
XmlCursor resultsCursor = departmentDoc.newCursor().execQuery
  (m_namespaceDeclaration + queryExpression);
```

After executing the query, the results are displayed through the call to the `xmlText()` method of the resultant `XmlCursor`:

```
System.out.println(resultsCursor.xmlText());
```

Here is the output produced by the code.

```
<xml-fragment>
  <Name xmlns="http://www.wrox.com/xquery/samples/departments">Engineering</Name>
  <Name xmlns="http://www.wrox.com/xquery/samples/departments">Tool Design</Name>
  <Name xmlns="http://www.wrox.com/xquery/samples/departments">Sales</Name>
  <Name xmlns="http://www.wrox.com/xquery/samples/departments">Marketing</Name>
  <Name xmlns="http://www.wrox.com/xquery/samples/departments">Purchasing</Name>
</xml-fragment>
```

XQuery in Relational Databases

One of the primary tasks developers are faced with is querying data from some data store and allowing users to view and/or manipulate the information via a Web interface. Typically, the data stores that you query from are traditional relational databases, such as Microsoft SQL Server or Oracle. With relational databases, the de facto means for querying data is SQL. However, with the ever-continuing rise in the popularity of Web services, and the need for a platform-independent, Internet-transferable, data representation format, XML data stores are becoming more and more popular. SQL was never designed for querying semi-structured data stores, and therefore is not suitable for querying XML data stores. So, how do you query an XML data store and retrieve results from such a query? Most developers currently use XSLT and XPath to accomplish this task. However, XPath and XSLT alone are not sufficient for querying the XML data stores, and you need the power of XQuery to be able to maximize the benefits of using XML data stores. Now all the major relational database vendors (including Oracle and Microsoft) support XQuery as part of their database implementations. The following section gives you a quick tour of the XQuery support provided by SQL Server 2005.

XQuery in SQL Server 2005

One of the newly introduced features in SQL Server 2005 is the native XML data type. Using the XML data type, you can create a table that has one or more columns of type XML in addition to relational columns. XML variables and parameters are also allowed. XML values are stored in an internal format as large binary objects (BLOBs) in order to support the XML model characteristics, such as document order and recursive structures, more faithfully.

SQL Server 2005 provides XML schema collections as a way to manage W3C XML Schemas as metadata. An XML data type can be associated with an XML Schema collection to enforce schema constraints on XML instances. When the XML data is associated with an XML Schema collection, it is called *typed XML;* otherwise it is called *untyped XML*. Both typed and untyped XML are accommodated within a single framework, the XML data model is preserved, and query processing enforces XML semantics. The underlying relational infrastructure is used extensively for this purpose. It supports interoperability between relational and XML data, thereby making way for more widespread adoption of the XML features.

XML Data Type Query and Data Modification

You can use a T-SQL SELECT statement to retrieve XML instances. Five built-in methods on the XML data type are provided to query and modify XML instances. These methods accept XQuery. The XQuery type system is aligned with that of W3C XML schema types. Most of the SQL types are compatible with the XQuery type system (for example, decimal). A handful of types (for example, `xs:duration`) are stored in an internal format and suitably interpreted to be compatible with the XQuery type system.

The compilation phase checks static type correctness of XQuery expressions and data modification statements, and uses XML schemas for type inferences in the case of typed XML. Static type errors are raised if an expression could fail at run time due to a type safety violation. Through the XQuery support, you can retrieve entire XML values or you can retrieve parts of XML instances. This is possible by using four XML data type methods that take an XQuery expression as argument: `query()`, `value()`, `exist()` and `nodes()`. A fifth method, `modify()`, allows modification of XML data and accepts an XML data modification statement as input. Here is a brief introduction to each of these methods:

- `query()` — Extracts parts of an XML instance. The XQuery expression evaluates to a list of XML nodes. The subtree rooted at each of these nodes is returned in document order. The result type is untyped XML.
- `value()` — Extracts a scalar value from an XML instance and returns the value of the node the XQuery expression evaluates to. This value is converted to a T-SQL type specified as the second argument of the `value()` method.
- `exist()` — Performs existential checks on an XML instance. It returns 1 if the XQuery expression evaluates to non-null node list; otherwise it returns 0.
- `nodes()` — Yields instances of a special XML data type, each of which has its context set to a different node that the XQuery expression evaluates to.
- `modify()` — Enables you to modify parts of an XML instance, such as adding or deleting subtrees, or replacing scalar values such as the price of a book from 9.99 to 39.99.

Take a brief look at each of these methods. Before that, create a table named `Department` with two columns: an id column and xml_data column that uses the xml data type.

```
CREATE TABLE Department( id int primary key, xml_data xml)
```

Now that the table is created, insert a couple of rows to the table as follows:

```
INSERT INTO Department values(1, '<department id="1">
<name>Engineering</name><groupname>Research and
Development</groupname></department>')
GO
INSERT INTO Department values(2, '<department id="2">
<name>Sales</name><groupname>Sales and Marketing</groupname></department>')
```

Working with the query Method

With the introduction of the XML data type in SQL Server 2005, the `FOR` XML clause now provides the ability to generate an instance of XML directly using the new `TYPE` directive. For example:

```
SELECT * FROM HumanResources.Employee as Employee FOR XML AUTO, TYPE
```

This returns the `Employee` elements as an XML data type instance, instead of the `nvarchar(max)` instance that would have been the case without the `TYPE` directive. This result is guaranteed to conform to the well-formedness constraints provided by the XML data type. Because the result is an XML data type instance, you can also use XQuery expressions to query and reshape the result. For XQuery expressions, you use the `query()` method supported by the XML data type. For example, the following XQuery expression retrieves all the department names from the Department table.

```
SELECT xml_data.query('/department/name') from Department
```

The previous query results in the following output:

```
<name>Engineering</name>
<name>Sales</name>
```

You can also use the `query` method to execute a FLWOR XQuery. For example, you can build an XML document that contains all the department names from the Department table using this query:

```
SELECT xml_data.query('
  <department>
  {
    for $d in //department
    order by $d/name[1]
    return $d/name[1]
  }
  </department>')
FROM Department
```

Here is the output produced by the previous query.

```
<department><name>Engineering</name></department>
<department><name>Sales</name></department>
```

Note that you must declare the namespace of the document if the source column is a typed xml column. Since the xml_data column is not a typed column, there is no need to use the namespace.

Working with the value Method

To the `value` method, you pass an XQuery statement and the return type. As a result, the `value()` method returns a single value that is produced as a result of query execution.

As an example, the following query,

```
SELECT xml_data.value('
/department[1]/name[1]', 'VARCHAR(100)')
from Department Where ID = 1
```

produces the following result.

```
Engineering
```

As you can see from the query, you pass in the data type as a second parameter to the `value()` method. This tells the method to return the value as that type. The `value()` method is very useful when you want to fetch a value from an XML column and insert the value into another table column of a different type.

Working with the exist Method

The `exist()` method allows you to determine whether a node value you are searching for exists. It returns a `1` if the node value is found and a `0` if not.

```
Select xml_data.query('/department//name')
from Department where
xml_data.exist('/department[@id = "1"]') = 1
```

In the previous example, the `exist()` method is used in the `where` clause and acts as the filtering mechanism to retrieve only the name for the department with the id value of `1`. The query also produces `"Engineering"` as the output.

Working with the nodes Method

This method accepts an XQuery statement as a parameter and returns a rowset that contains logical scalar data from the XML variable. It is very similar to the `selectNodes()` function in XML DOM. This method is very useful when you need to shred the data from an XML data type variable into one or many relational table columns.

Working with the modify Method

Through the `modify` method, you can insert, update, or delete values from an XML typed column. To modify the contents of an element, you first need to reference that element using the XPath expression. Once you get to the actual element, you then reference the textual contents using the `text()` method as follows:

```
Update Department
SET xml_data.modify
  ('replace value of
    (/department/name/text())[1]
  with "Engineering and Design"
  ')
Where ID = 1
```

In the previous code, you use `replace value of` to identify the element you want to modify and then you use the `with` to specify the new value.

Now that you have had a look at the update, look at an example for deleting an element. For example, here is how you delete the `<groupname>` (child element of `<department>`) element from the xml_data column.

```
UPDATE Department
SET xml_data.modify
  ('delete /department/groupname[1]')
Where ID = 1
```

Summary

This chapter started with a brief introduction to XQuery by discussing the role of XQuery, its advantages and the structure of an XQuery expression. After that, you looked at one of the key aspects of XQuery-FLWOR expressions that provide you with a consistent way to write and execute query expressions. FLWOR expressions are the central feature of the XQuery language, in the same way as path expressions are at the heart of XPath. Specifically:

- FLWOR expressions have five clauses: `for`, `let`, `where`, `order by`, and `return`. The first two can appear any number of times in any order. The `where` and `order by` clauses are optional, but if used, they must appear in the order given. There is always a `return` clause.
- The semantics are similar to those of a `SELECT` statement in SQL. In most cases, you can think of a FLWOR expression with multiple for clauses as a set of nested loops, but a sorting using order using a rather more complex execution model is needed.
- You can use FLWOR expressions anywhere that you can use any other kind of expression. This means the expressions can be nested within each other, and they can appear in contexts such as an argument to a function like `count()` or `max()`. The only constraint is that the type of value returned by the FLWOR expression (a sequence of items) must be appropriate to the context where the expression is used.

After that, you learned the various functions supported by XQuery including the use of built-in and user-defined functions. You also explored the steps involved in using XQuery from within a Java program through an XMLBeans open-source implementation. As part of this, you learned the two ways of executing XQuery expressions from within a Java application: through XmlObject and XmlCursor. Examples showed you the XQuery implementation in SQL Server 2005.

Now is as good a time as any to start learning XQuery, because it's bound to become more prominent as XML data stores continue their meteoric rise. Furthermore, with the deep XQuery support provided by SQL Server 2005, it is only a matter of time before XQuery becomes pervasive.

11

XML in the Data Tier

Although XML is frequently a part of the data tier — because it stores data — this chapter concentrates on XML and databases. Databases, both relational and native XML, are part of many applications. You must, therefore, often store XML in those databases or retrieve some of the data in XML format. While the conversion of data to XML could be done in an intermediate layer of your application, it is sometimes more efficient to do this work within the database itself. This chapter will look at how you can store and retrieve XML from such common databases as Microsoft SQL Server and Oracle 10g. In addition, this chapter will cover XML databases, and their possible role in your applications.

XML and Databases

Although XML is an excellent format for moving data between platforms, applications, or application tiers, it may not be the best format to use for storing data for your application. As the volume of data increases, so too does the time it takes to search for and manipulate that data. Databases, on the other hand, minimize the query times, even for large data sets. Because of this, you might often combine XML and databases in some applications. This can create mismatches: Data types stored in the database may not be in the same format as XML, and the structure of the two are different. XML tends to be more loosely structured or hierarchical, and relational databases (the most common forms today) are designed around tabular data. Moving data in and out of relational databases can be a code-intensive operation. However, some databases are embracing XML, either as a first-class data type or, at least, for enabling querying and indexing semistructured data.

Retrieving Data as XML

Databases are convenient stores for data in many applications, but you also frequently share the data with clients from other platforms or move the data between tiers of your application and computers. Most native database formats are not optimal for this type of data exchange; however,

XML is ideally suited for these scenarios. You can convert data stored in a database into XML, providing an excellent cross platform format for data exchange. You can also easily write components to convert the rows and columns of relational data into XML. However, many databases are beginning to provide support for retrieving your queries as XML. This may be provided by proprietary extensions to SQL or via the upcoming SQL/XML standard. SQL/XML (or SQL-X) is a proposed extension to the SQL programming language (see Chapter 14 of that specification if you like reading specification documents). Note that this SQL/XML should not be confused with Microsoft's SQLXML. SQL/XML is a proposed extension to the standard SQL language for working with databases. SQLXML is a Microsoft-specific API for integrating SQL Server and XML. The SQL/XML standard defines a number of new SQL keywords:

- **XML** — a data type to hold XML data
- **XMLAgg** — used to group XML data in GROUP BY queries
- **XMLAttributes** — used to add attributes in XML elements
- **XMLConcat** — used to concatenate two or more XML values
- **XMLElement** — used to transform a relational value into an XML element
- **XMLForest** — used to generate a list of XML elements
- **XMLNamespaces** — used to declare namespaces in an XML element
- **XMLSerialize** — used to serialize an XML value as a character string

These extensions are used in two ways. First, the XML data type becomes a native data type for columns. This provides you with a method for storing XML as XML, rather than as text. In addition, when you work with XML in stored procedures, having an XML type ensures that validity and other rules apply to the data. The second use of the new SQL/XML extensions is to create a standard mechanism for querying data and returning it as XML. The `XMLAttributes`, `XMLElement`, `XMLForest`, and `XMLNamespaces` operators create the appropriate structures within a `SELECT` statement. See the Oracle section later in this chapter for samples of using these publishing functions.

In addition to allowing you to directly query using a SQL dialect, many databases are adding support for the relatively new standard XQuery for querying data (see Chapter 11 for more details on XQuery).

Storing XML

When storing XML in a relational database, you usually have three choices:

- *Shred* the XML to fit into the rows and columns of one or more relational tables.
- Store the XML in a Binary Large Object (BLOB) or Character Large Object (CLOB) field.
- Store the XML in a field specialized for storing and/or indexing XML.

Shredding the XML, or converting into rows and columns, is simple, but requires the most processing. In addition, it also means you must make more decisions: Do you process the XML within the database itself — using stored procedures — or in another component of your application? Using stored procedures might provide better performance, but only if the variant of SQL supported by your database provides XML-handling functions. This adds complexity, however, if the elements and attributes of the XML do not align directly with rows and columns. You may need to perform additional processing or conversion of the data when saving and loading. For example, the XML may hold the full name of a client, when you need to save the first and last names separately in the database. Therefore, you would need to separate the name before storing.

Storing XML in BLOB or CLOB fields (for example, text fields) or even a large character field is a simple solution that works with every database. However, the data is essentially meaningless at this point. It is difficult to query text fields in any meaningful way. You can use whatever full-text search is available from the database, but this is certainly less useful than a search that includes the tags. For example, if you had a BLOB field full of resumés in XML format, searching for candidates with experience in .NET using a full-text search would likely give results cluttered with URL values and possibly become a fishing experience. If the search were aware of the structure of the XML, you would have more luck narrowing the scope of the search.

Finally, you can use a dedicated XML field. Not all databases have a native way of storing XML, and the techniques used to store and index the XML vary. The sections that follow describe the features available for some databases.

XML databases add a fourth choice to storing XML: Store it *as is*. The XML is stored natively, and queries are usually carried out using XQuery or XPath. Although XML databases are not as prevalent as relational databases, this feature makes them quite attractive in some scenarios.

Relational Databases

The most common databases in use today fit into the *relational* model. Data is stored as logical rows in one or more tables. Manipulation is typically accomplished with a dialect of Structured Query Language (SQL). Two of the most common relational databases in use today that provide XML features are Microsoft SQL Server and Oracle.

Microsoft SQL Server 2005

Microsoft SQL Server, currently version 2005, is a popular and powerful database server. XML support, including XQuery support and the addition of an XML column type, is one of the primary areas of improvement in this version

Retrieving XML

SQL Server's T-SQL dialect includes the `FOR XML` clause for `SELECT` queries. This clause, which must be the last clause in the `SELECT` statement, causes the data returned from the query to be formatted as XML. This feature was first added with SQL Server 2000, but it has been improved in SQL Server 2005. The actual format of the XML is configurable using one of the optional keywords listed in the following table.

FOR XML Formatting	Notes
RAW	Each row in the query is returned as an XML element. Individual columns are returned as attributes of that element. There is no root node by default, although this can be added. By default, the element name is row. This can be changed by including the name as a parameter to RAW (FOR XML RAW('myrowname')).
AUTO	Each row is returned as an XML element named for the table providing the data. Individual columns returned are attributes of that element. There is no root node by default. If related columns are included, the resulting XML is nested.
EXPLICIT	The structure of the resulting XML must be defined. This provides the most flexibility in creating XML, but also requires the most work by the developer.
PATH	The structure of the resulting XML can be defined. This method, added with SQL Server 2005, is much easier to use than the EXPLICIT model. By default, it creates a structure similar to the AUTO output, but columns are output as elements, not attributes.

RAW format is, as the name implies, the rawest output of SQL data to XML. It generates a document fragment (that is, the result is not a well-formed document because no a single root node exists). Listing 11-1 shows part of the output from the following simple raw query on the Northwind sample database.

The Northwind sample database is available for download from Microsoft at http://www.microsoft.com/downloads/details.aspx?FamilyID=06616211-0356-46A0-8DA2-EEBC53A68034&displaylang=en.

```
SELECT CategoryName, ProductName, UnitPrice
FROM Categories INNER JOIN Products
ON Categories.CategoryID = Products.CategoryID
WHERE CategoryName='Beverages'
ORDER BY ProductName
FOR XML RAW
```

Listing 11-1: Output of FOR XML RAW query

```
<row CategoryName="Beverages" ProductName="Chai" UnitPrice="18.0000" />
<row CategoryName="Beverages" ProductName="Chang" UnitPrice="19.0000" />
<row CategoryName="Beverages" ProductName="Chartreuse verte" UnitPrice="18.0000" />
<row CategoryName="Beverages" ProductName="Côte de Blaye" UnitPrice="263.5000" />
<row CategoryName="Beverages" ProductName="Guaraná Fantástica" UnitPrice="4.5000" />
<row CategoryName="Beverages" ProductName="Ipoh Coffee" UnitPrice="46.0000" />
<row CategoryName="Beverages" ProductName="Lakkalikööri" UnitPrice="18.0000" />
<row CategoryName="Beverages" ProductName="Laughing Lumberjack Lager"
UnitPrice="14.0000" />
<row CategoryName="Beverages" ProductName="Outback Lager" UnitPrice="15.0000" />
<row CategoryName="Beverages" ProductName="Rhönbräu Klosterbier" UnitPrice="7.7500" />
<row CategoryName="Beverages" ProductName="Sasquatch Ale" UnitPrice="14.0000" />
<row CategoryName="Beverages" ProductName="Steeleye Stout" UnitPrice="18.0000" />
```

The AUTO format takes a few guesses about the structure of the resulting XML. It then structures the XML to nest child data appropriately. The output from an AUTO query can be either a complete document or a document fragment, depending on the query. Listing 11-2 shows the output for the following query:

```
SELECT CategoryName, ProductName, UnitPrice
FROM Categories INNER JOIN Products
ON Categories.CategoryID = Products.CategoryID
WHERE CategoryName='Beverages'
ORDER BY ProductName
FOR XML AUTO
```

Listing 11-2: Output for FOR XML AUTO query

```
<Categories CategoryName="Beverages">
  <Products ProductName="Chai" UnitPrice="18.0000" />
  <Products ProductName="Chang" UnitPrice="19.0000" />
  <Products ProductName="Chartreuse verte" UnitPrice="18.0000" />
  <Products ProductName="Côte de Blaye" UnitPrice="263.5000" />
  <Products ProductName="Guaraná Fantástica" UnitPrice="4.5000" />
  <Products ProductName="Ipoh Coffee" UnitPrice="46.0000" />
  <Products ProductName="Lakkalikööri" UnitPrice="18.0000" />
  <Products ProductName="Laughing Lumberjack Lager" UnitPrice="14.0000" />
  <Products ProductName="Outback Lager" UnitPrice="15.0000" />
  <Products ProductName="Rhönbräu Klosterbier" UnitPrice="7.7500" />
  <Products ProductName="Sasquatch Ale" UnitPrice="14.0000" />
  <Products ProductName="Steeleye Stout" UnitPrice="18.0000" />
</Categories>
```

As you can see from the output, the products are nested within the categories node because this is the relationship between the two tables. In this case, the output is well-formed; however, if the WHERE clause hadn't been included, the result would have been a document fragment with multiple Categories nodes and no single root node.

EXPLICIT format is more complex than the preceding two formats because it has no default output. The developer is responsible for defining the structure of the resulting XML. When defining an EXPLICIT query, you must add two columns to the query. These two provide the relationship between each row and its parent. Figure 11-1 shows the desired structure of the output, if it is returned normally.

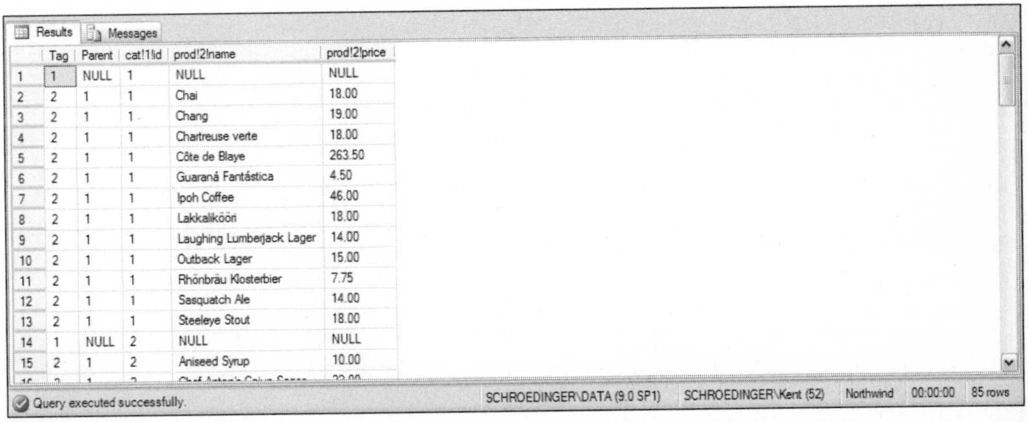

Results | Messages

	Tag	Parent	cat!1!id	prod!2!name	prod!2!price
1	1	NULL	1	NULL	NULL
2	2	1	1	Chai	18.00
3	2	1	1	Chang	19.00
4	2	1	1	Chartreuse verte	18.00
5	2	1	1	Côte de Blaye	263.50
6	2	1	1	Guaraná Fantástica	4.50
7	2	1	1	Ipoh Coffee	46.00
8	2	1	1	Lakkalikööri	18.00
9	2	1	1	Laughing Lumberjack Lager	14.00
10	2	1	1	Outback Lager	15.00
11	2	1	1	Rhönbräu Klosterbier	7.75
12	2	1	1	Sasquatch Ale	14.00
13	2	1	1	Steeleye Stout	18.00
14	1	NULL	2	NULL	NULL
15	2	1	2	Aniseed Syrup	10.00

Query executed successfully. | SCHROEDINGER\DATA (9.0 SP1) | SCHROEDINGER\Kent (52) | Northwind | 00:00:00 | 85 rows

Figure 11-1

```
SELECT 1     as Tag,
       NULL as Parent,
       C.CategoryID as [cat!1!id],
       NULL       as [prod!2!name],
       NULL       as [prod!2!price]
FROM   Categories C, Products P
WHERE  C.CategoryID = P.CategoryID
UNION
SELECT 2 as Tag,
       1 as Parent,
       P.CategoryID,
       ProductName,
       UnitPrice
FROM   Categories C, Products P
WHERE  C.CategoryID = P.CategoryID
ORDER BY [cat!1!id],[prod!2!name]
FOR XML EXPLICIT
```

The Tag column identifies each level in the generated XML, whereas the Parent column identifies the Tag representing the parent of each item. For the top level elements, the Parent column should be `NULL`. In addition, placeholder fields must be added to the root element. This is the purpose of the two `NULL` entries in the first half of the `UNION` query. Finally, the `ElementName!TagNumber!AttributeName!Directive` syntax is used to shape the resulting XML. The term `[cat!1!id]` causes the element name to be `cat` with an attribute id, and this element is placed at the root. `[prod!2!name]` is placed as a child element because of the `position=2`. It assigns the element and attribute names to `prod` and `name` respectively.

Running the preceding query returns the XML shown in Listing 11-3 (not all the XML is shown).

Listing 11-3: Output for FOR XML EXPLICIT query

```
<cat id="1">
  <prod name="Chai" price="18.0000" />
  <prod name="Chang" price="19.0000" />
  <prod name="Chartreuse verte" price="18.0000" />
  <prod name="Côte de Blaye" price="263.5000" />
  <prod name="Guaraná Fantástica" price="4.5000" />
  <prod name="Ipoh Coffee" price="46.0000" />
  <prod name="Lakkalikööri" price="18.0000" />
  <prod name="Laughing Lumberjack Lager" price="14.0000" />
  <prod name="Outback Lager" price="15.0000" />
  <prod name="Rhönbräu Klosterbier" price="7.7500" />
  <prod name="Sasquatch Ale" price="14.0000" />
  <prod name="Steeleye Stout" price="18.0000" />
</cat>
```

The `PATH` format is new with SQL Server 2005. It provides an easier model for manipulating the output than using `EXPLICIT` queries. Creating `PATH` queries is based on the aliases assigned to the result columns. If the alias starts with a `@` character, the data is placed in an attribute. If the alias contains one or more / characters, these create child elements. You could view this as XPath in reverse. For example, in the following query, the field aliased as `product/name` creates a new child element named `product`. That element then has a `name` child. Listing 11-4 shows the output from this query.

```
SELECT ProductID "@id",
 CategoryName "category",
 ProductName "product/name",
 UnitPrice "product/price"
FROM Categories INNER JOIN Products
ON Categories.CategoryID = Products.CategoryID
WHERE CategoryName='Beverages'
ORDER BY ProductName
FOR XML PATH
```

Listing 11-4: Partial output for FOR XML PATH query

```
<row id="1">
  <category>Beverages</category>
  <product>
    <name>Chai</name>
    <price>18.0000</price>
  </product>
</row>
<row id="2">
  <category>Beverages</category>
  <product>
    <name>Chang</name>
    <price>19.0000</price>
  </product>
</row>
<row id="39">
  <category>Beverages</category>
  <product>
    <name>Chartreuse verte</name>
    <price>18.0000</price>
  </product>
</row>
<row id="38">
  <category>Beverages</category>
  <product>
    <name>Côte de Blaye</name>
    <price>263.5000</price>
  </product>
</row>
<row id="24">
  <category>Beverages</category>
  <product>
    <name>Guaraná Fantástica</name>
    <price>4.5000</price>
  </product>
</row>
```

In addition to the parameters outlined here, you can also manipulate the resulting XML to change the resulting structure. The following table shows additional keywords and the formats they can be used with.

Directive	Can be used with	Notes
ELEMENTS	AUTO, RAW, PATH	Causes the column values to be output as elements, not attributes.
ROOT	any	Adds a root node to the resulting XML. The name defaults to root, but you can change this by adding the name as a parameter to the ROOT keyword (FOR XML AUTO, ROOT('rootElement')) (see Listing 11-5).
TYPE	any	Ensures that the output is treated as XML. This becomes important when you are assigning the output of the query to the XML data type in T-SQL. Alternatively, if you are building the XML using nested queries, failing to include the type may cause the inner blocks of XML to be encoded.
XMLSCHEMA	AUTO, RAW	Causes the XML Schema to be added to the resulting XML (see Listing 11-6).
XMLDATA	AUTO, RAW, EXPLICIT	Causes the XML Data Reduced schema to be included in the resulting XML.
BINARY BASE64	any	Outputs binary data Base 64 encoded. This enables output of binary data using simple ASCII.

Listing 11-5 shows an FOR XML PATH query with an additional root node added. This ensures that the resulting XML is a well-formed document.

Listing 11-5: Adding a root node to a FOR XML PATH query

```
SELECT TOP 3 Products.ProductID "@id",
 CategoryName "category",
 ProductName "product/name",
 UnitPrice "product/price"
FROM Categories INNER JOIN Products
ON Categories.CategoryID = Products.CategoryID
WHERE CategoryName='Beverages'
ORDER BY ProductName
FOR XML PATH, ROOT('catalog')
================================
<catalog>
  <row id="1">
    <category>Beverages</category>
    <product>
      <name>Chai</name>
      <price>18.0000</price>
    </product>
  </row>
  <row id="2">
    <category>Beverages</category>
    <product>
      <name>Chang</name>
      <price>19.0000</price>
    </product>
```

```
  </row>
  <row id="39">
    <category>Beverages</category>
    <product>
      <name>Chartreuse verte</name>
      <price>18.0000</price>
    </product>
  </row>
</catalog>
```

Queries can use as many of these additional commands as necessary. Listing 11-6 shows adding both a root node and an XML schema to an AUTO query. This would be useful when transmitting this data to another system because the schema could be then used to validate the document or to create a serializer to convert the XML into an object for further processing.

Listing 11-6: Adding an XML Schema to a FOR XML AUTO query

```
SELECT CategoryName, ProductName, UnitPrice
FROM Categories INNER JOIN Products
ON Categories.CategoryID = Products.CategoryID
WHERE CategoryName='Beverages'
ORDER BY ProductName
FOR XML AUTO, ROOT('catalog'), XMLSCHEMA
==========================================
<catalog>
  <xsd:schema targetNamespace="urn:schemas-microsoft-com:sql:SqlRowSet1"
    xmlns:schema="urn:schemas-microsoft-com:sql:SqlRowSet1"
    xmlns:xsd="http://www.w3.org/2001/XMLSchema"
    xmlns:sqltypes="http://schemas.microsoft.com/sqlserver/2004/sqltypes"
    elementFormDefault="qualified">
    <xsd:import namespace="http://schemas.microsoft.com/sqlserver/2004/sqltypes"
 schemaLocation="http://schemas.microsoft.com/sqlserver/2004/sqltypes/sqltypes.xsd"
    />
    <xsd:element name="Categories">
      <xsd:complexType>
        <xsd:sequence>
          <xsd:element ref="schema:Products" minOccurs="0" maxOccurs="unbounded" />
        </xsd:sequence>
        <xsd:attribute name="CategoryName" use="required">
          <xsd:simpleType>
            <xsd:restriction base="sqltypes:nvarchar" sqltypes:localeId="1033"
               sqltypes:sqlCompareOptions="IgnoreCase IgnoreKanaType IgnoreWidth"
               sqltypes:sqlSortId="52">
              <xsd:maxLength value="15" />
            </xsd:restriction>
          </xsd:simpleType>
        </xsd:attribute>
      </xsd:complexType>
    </xsd:element>
    <xsd:element name="Products">
      <xsd:complexType>
        <xsd:attribute name="ProductName" use="required">
          <xsd:simpleType>
            <xsd:restriction base="sqltypes:nvarchar" sqltypes:localeId="1033"
               sqltypes:sqlCompareOptions="IgnoreCase IgnoreKanaType IgnoreWidth"
```

(continued)

Listing 11-6 *(continued)*

```
                sqltypes:sqlSortId="52">
              <xsd:maxLength value="40" />
            </xsd:restriction>
          </xsd:simpleType>
        </xsd:attribute>
        <xsd:attribute name="UnitPrice" type="sqltypes:money" />
      </xsd:complexType>
    </xsd:element>
  </xsd:schema>
  <Categories xmlns="urn:schemas-microsoft-com:sql:SqlRowSet1"
      CategoryName="Beverages">
    <Products ProductName="Chai" UnitPrice="18.0000" />
    <Products ProductName="Chang" UnitPrice="19.0000" />
    <Products ProductName="Chartreuse verte" UnitPrice="18.0000" />
    <Products ProductName="Côte de Blaye" UnitPrice="263.5000" />
    <Products ProductName="Guaraná Fantástica" UnitPrice="4.5000" />
    <Products ProductName="Ipoh Coffee" UnitPrice="46.0000" />
    <Products ProductName="Lakkalikööri" UnitPrice="18.0000" />
    <Products ProductName="Laughing Lumberjack Lager" UnitPrice="14.0000" />
    <Products ProductName="Outback Lager" UnitPrice="15.0000" />
    <Products ProductName="Rhönbräu Klosterbier" UnitPrice="7.7500" />
    <Products ProductName="Sasquatch Ale" UnitPrice="14.0000" />
    <Products ProductName="Steeleye Stout" UnitPrice="18.0000" />
  </Categories>
</catalog>
```

Although SQL Server does not have support for the SQL/XML extensions, Microsoft is a member of the group working on the standard. As such, future versions of SQL Server may provide access to that functionality as well.

Storing XML

SQL Server 2005 adds support for the XML column type. You can create a table containing one of these columns just as you can for any other data type (see Listing 11-7).

Listing 11-7: Creating a table containing XML data in Microsoft SQL Server

```
CREATE TABLE dbo.Articles(
 id int IDENTITY(1,1) NOT NULL PRIMARY KEY,
 Title nvarchar(255) NOT NULL,
 CreatedOn datetime NOT NULL DEFAULT (getdate()),
 Body xml NULL
)
```

After the table is created, you can populate and query it just as you do any other table:

```
INSERT INTO dbo.Articles(Title, Body)
VALUES('Welcome',
 '<div class="wrapper">Welcome to the system</div>')

SELECT Body FROM dbo.Articles
```

Simply dumping XML into an XML column, although it is useful, has few benefits over using a text column. To improve the process, you can add an XML Schema to the column. Then, adding data to the table triggers validation, ensuring the column contains data of the appropriate type. To do this with SQL Server, you create a schema collection in the database. The `CREATE XML SCHEMA COLLECTION` command creates the schema collection (see Listing 11-8). In addition to adding an entry in the database for the schema, adding a schema collection to a database creates a number of new system tables and views to track the schemas, as well as support validation.

Listing 11-8: Creating an article schema collection

```
CREATE XML SCHEMA COLLECTION ArticleSchemaCollection AS
'<xs:schema xmlns:xs="http://www.w3.org/2001/XMLSchema"
  elementFormDefault="qualified" attributeFormDefault="unqualified"
  targetNamespace="http://example.com/articleSchema.xsd">
  <xs:element name="article">
    <xs:complexType>
      <xs:sequence>
        <xs:element name="encoding">
          <xs:complexType>
            <xs:attribute name="type" />
          </xs:complexType>
        </xs:element>
        <xs:element name="author" type="xs:string"/>
        <xs:element name="body" type="xs:string"/>
        <xs:element name="published" type="xs:dateTime"/>
      </xs:sequence>
    </xs:complexType>
  </xs:element>
</xs:schema>'
```

You can view the new schema collection by querying the sys.xml_schema_collections system view (see Figure 11-2).

After you have created the schema collection, you can apply it to the table. Drop the previous articles table and recreate it using the schema collection (Listing 11-9).

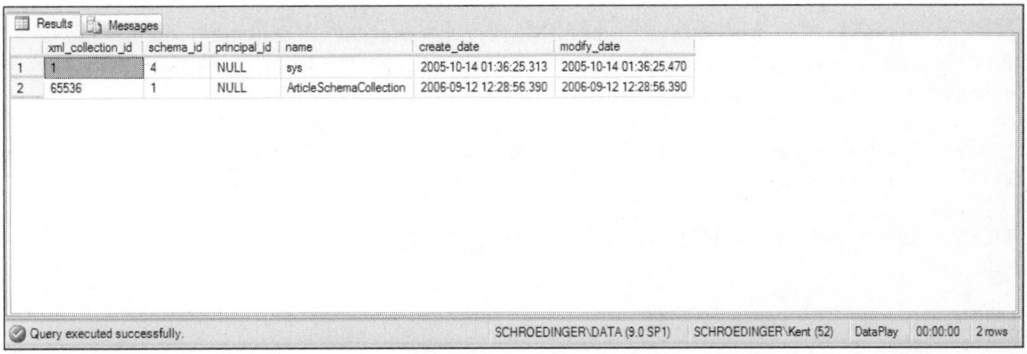

Results | Messages

	xml_collection_id	schema_id	principal_id	name	create_date	modify_date
1	1	4	NULL	sys	2005-10-14 01:36:25.313	2005-10-14 01:36:25.470
2	65536	1	NULL	ArticleSchemaCollection	2006-09-12 12:28:56.390	2006-09-12 12:28:56.390

Query executed successfully. SCHROEDINGER\DATA (9.0 SP1) SCHROEDINGER\Kent (52) DataPlay 00:00:00 2 rows

Figure 11-2

Listing 11-9: Applying a schema collection to a table

```
CREATE TABLE dbo.Articles(
 id int IDENTITY(1,1) NOT NULL PRIMARY KEY,
 Title nvarchar(255) NOT NULL,
 CreatedOn datetime NOT NULL DEFAULT (getdate()),
 Body xml(ArticleSchemaCollection) NULL
)
```

By applying the schema collection to the XML column, SQL Server validates the data on insert/update (Listing 11-10).

Listing 11-10: Inserting into a validating column

```
INSERT INTO dbo.Articles (Title, Body)
     VALUES ('Validated item',
            '<article xmlns="http://example.com/articleSchema.xsd ">
               <encoding type="text/plain" />
               <author>Foo deBar (foo@debar.com)</author>
               <body>This item will be validated upon insert.</body>
               <published>2001-11-17T09:30:47.0Z</published>
             </article>')
```

This item should be saved because it matches the schema. However, if you try the insert with invalid XML (for example, XML missing the body element), it fails. Adding a schema to validate your XML is a good idea unless you need the capability to store less-structured documents.

A second means of storing XML is via the `OPENXML` function, first added with SQL Server 2000. This function enables you to open a block of XML in a stored procedure. After it is open, you can perform other processing on the XML. Essentially, it converts a block of XML into rows and columns.

The format of the `OPENXML` function is:

```
OPENXML( @doc, @xpath, @flags)
WITH row definitions
```

Here, `@doc` points at an in-memory block of XML; `@xpath` is an XPath statement identifying the XML to process, and `@flags` provides additional hints to the processor. The `WITH` clause provides one or more columns into which you convert the XML.

For example, you can use the `OPENXML` function to extract the attributes from the XML shown in Listing 11-2 back into columns with the query shown in Listing 11-11.

Listing 11-11: Using OPENXML to extract attributes

```
DECLARE @idoc int
DECLARE @doc nvarchar(1000)
SET @doc ='<Categories CategoryName="Beverages">
  <Products ProductName="Chai" UnitPrice="18.0000" />
  <Products ProductName="Chang" UnitPrice="19.0000" />
  <Products ProductName="Chartreuse verte" UnitPrice="18.0000" />
  <Products ProductName="Côte de Blaye" UnitPrice="263.5000" />
  <Products ProductName="Guaraná Fantástica" UnitPrice="4.5000" />
```

```
    <Products ProductName="Ipoh Coffee" UnitPrice="46.0000" />
    <Products ProductName="Lakkalikööri" UnitPrice="18.0000" />
    <Products ProductName="Laughing Lumberjack Lager" UnitPrice="14.0000" />
    <Products ProductName="Outback Lager" UnitPrice="15.0000" />
    <Products ProductName="Rhönbräu Klosterbier" UnitPrice="7.7500" />
    <Products ProductName="Sasquatch Ale" UnitPrice="14.0000" />
    <Products ProductName="Steeleye Stout" UnitPrice="18.0000" />
  </Categories>'
  -- Create an internal representation of the XML document.
  EXEC sp_xml_preparedocument @idoc OUTPUT, @doc
  -- Execute a SELECT statement using OPENXML rowset provider.
  SELECT *
  FROM OPENXML (@idoc, '/Categories/Products',1)
        WITH (ProductName  nvarchar(50),
              UnitPrice decimal)
  EXEC sp_xml_removedocument @idoc
```

The `sp_xml_preparedocument` stored procedure loads the block of XML into the `@idoc` variable, and `sp_xml_removedocument` frees the memory and handles used by the variable. The `OPENXML` function first applies the XPath `/Categories/Products` to extract the individual rows. The `ProductName` and `UnitPrice` attributes are mapped to the columns identified in the `WITH` clause. At this point, you can walk the RowSet, perhaps saving the individual items. The preceding code simply returns the resulting RowSet, as shown in Figure 11-3.

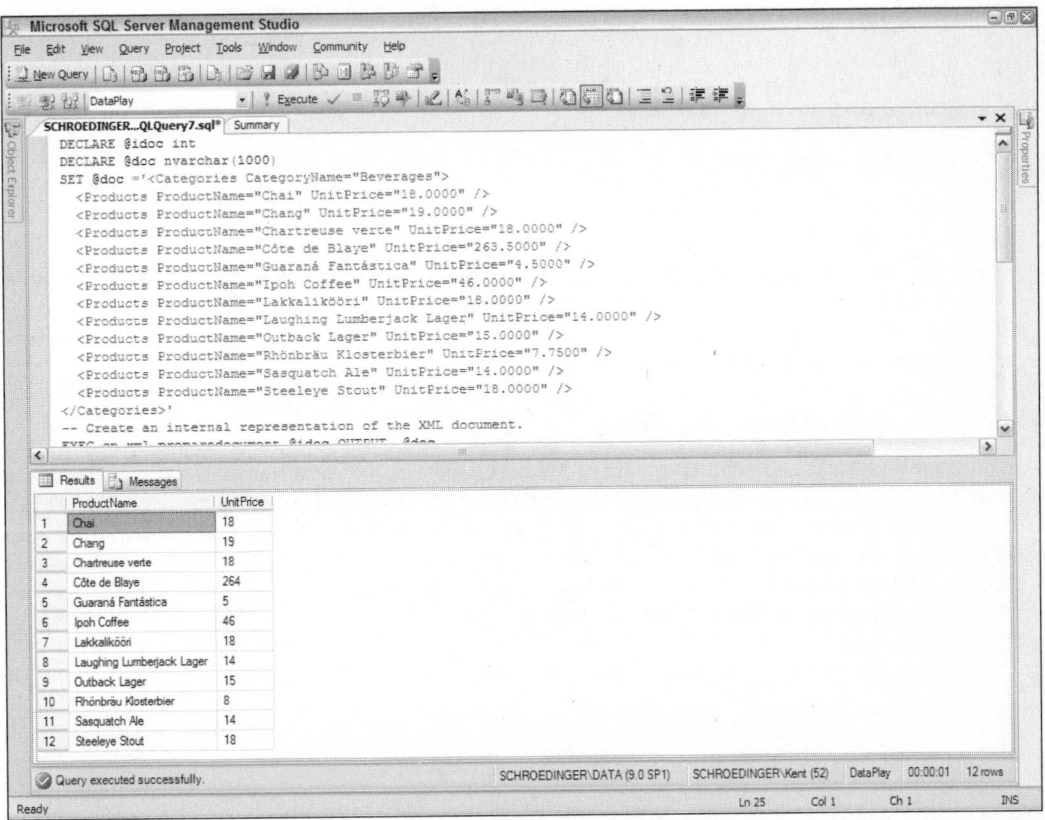

Figure 11-3

Rather than simply returning the resulting rows and columns, you can use the `OPENXML` function to perform a bulk insert, as Listing 11-12 shows.

Listing 11-12: A bulk insert using OPENXML

```
CREATE TABLE NewProducts(
 id int identity(1,1) NOT NULL,
 productName nvarchar(50) NOT NULL,
 unitPrice decimal)
GO

DECLARE @idoc int
DECLARE @doc nvarchar(1000)
SET @doc ='<Categories CategoryName="Beverages">
  <Products ProductName="Chai" UnitPrice="18.0000" />
  <Products ProductName="Chang" UnitPrice="19.0000" />
  <Products ProductName="Chartreuse verte" UnitPrice="18.0000" />
  <Products ProductName="Côte de Blaye" UnitPrice="263.5000" />
  <Products ProductName="Guaraná Fantástica" UnitPrice="4.5000" />
  <Products ProductName="Ipoh Coffee" UnitPrice="46.0000" />
  <Products ProductName="Lakkalikööri" UnitPrice="18.0000" />
  <Products ProductName="Laughing Lumberjack Lager" UnitPrice="14.0000" />
  <Products ProductName="Outback Lager" UnitPrice="15.0000" />
  <Products ProductName="Rhönbräu Klosterbier" UnitPrice="7.7500" />
  <Products ProductName="Sasquatch Ale" UnitPrice="14.0000" />
  <Products ProductName="Steeleye Stout" UnitPrice="18.0000" />
</Categories>'
EXEC sp_xml_preparedocument @idoc OUTPUT, @doc
INSERT INTO NewProducts SELECT *
FROM OPENXML (@idoc, '/Categories/Products',1)
      WITH (ProductName  nvarchar(50),
            UnitPrice decimal)
EXEC sp_xml_removedocument @idoc
```

First, a new table is created. You wrap the `CREATE TABLE` command in an `if exists` statement to avoid any errors caused by the effort to create a table that already exists. The `INSERT INTO` clause then retrieves the list of products and creates new rows for each entry. This technique can be used to load a number of tables quickly from a block of XML.

Additional XML-related features

In addition to storing and retrieving data as XML, SQL Server 2005 adds support for exposing stored procedures or functions as Web services. These Web services are then available to clients via HTTP or TCP. This can provide a method of sharing the functionality of a SQL Server without requiring a dedicated Web service layer or a Web server. You must be running Windows Server 2003 or Windows XP Professional Service Pack 2 or later to get this functionality because it depends on the HTTP.SYS driver, which is present only on those operating systems.

To expose or not to expose?

Exposing Web Services directly from the database is a bit of a controversial exercise.

Those in favor of it believe that providing functionality like this directly from the source allows for more optimization. The database is more aware of the structure of the data and, therefore, can optimize better. For example, indexes can make data retrieval faster than is possible in the business tier code. In addition, joins and views can mean that the data required by the Web service is more readily available in the database itself. Therefore, it makes sense to provide the Web service from the database.

Developers opposed to providing Web service access to the database point out that doing so allows a dangerous direct connection to the database—possibly from the Internet. They argue that the database should be behind a firewall (if not multiple firewalls), and adding another port that can access the data means that the system is that much more vulnerable to attack.

However, keep in mind that just because you have Web services does not mean that the clients are coming from the Internet. They could be coming from within the firewall. In this case, Web services provide platform independence and reduce the need to install database client functionality on client machines. For example, using these SQL endpoints could provide access to data to Unix or other non-Windows workstations that lack SQL connectivity. Finally, Ajax clients could access the Web services without requiring database connectivity. In short, SQL endpoints become another tool in your developer's toolbox: not perfect for all scenarios, but useful when employed correctly.

The basic syntax of the `CREATE ENDPOINT` command is shown in Listing 11-13. Although both `AS HTTP` and `AS TCP` are shown, only one can occur per `create endpoint` command.

Listing 11-13: The CREATE ENDPOINT command

```
CREATE ENDPOINT endPointName [ AUTHORIZATION login ]
STATE = { STARTED | STOPPED | DISABLED }
AS HTTP (
  PATH = 'url',
  AUTHENTICATION =( { BASIC | DIGEST | INTEGRATED | NTLM | KERBEROS } [ ,...n ] ),
  PORTS = ( { CLEAR | SSL} [ ,... n ] )
  [ SITE = {'*' | '+' | 'webSite' },]
  [, CLEAR_PORT = clearPort ]
  [, SSL_PORT = SSLPort ]
  [, AUTH_REALM = { 'realm' | NONE } ]
  [, DEFAULT_LOGON_DOMAIN = { 'domain' | NONE } ]
  [, COMPRESSION = { ENABLED | DISABLED } ]
  )
AS TCP (
  LISTENER_PORT = listenerPort
  [ , LISTENER_IP = ALL | (<4-part-ip> | <ip_address_v6> ) ]
  )
```

(continued)

Listing 11-13 *(continued)*

```
FOR SOAP(
  [ { WEBMETHOD [ 'namespace' .] 'method_alias'
    (   NAME = 'database.owner.name'
      [ , SCHEMA = { NONE | STANDARD | DEFAULT } ]
      [ , FORMAT = { ALL_RESULTS | ROWSETS_ONLY } ]
    )
  } [ ,...n ] ]
  [   BATCHES = { ENABLED | DISABLED } ]
  [ , WSDL = { NONE | DEFAULT | 'sp_name' } ]
  [ , SESSIONS = { ENABLED | DISABLED } ]
  [ , LOGIN_TYPE = { MIXED | WINDOWS } ]
  [ , SESSION_TIMEOUT = timeoutInterval | NEVER ]
  [ , DATABASE = { 'database_name' | DEFAULT }
  [ , NAMESPACE = { 'namespace' | DEFAULT } ]
  [ , SCHEMA = { NONE | STANDARD } ]
  [ , CHARACTER_SET = { SQL | XML }]
  [ , HEADER_LIMIT = int ]
  )
```

The main points to consider when creating an endpoint are:

- **What stored procedure or function (or UDF) will you be exposing?** This is identified in the `WebMethod` clause.
- **What authentication will clients need to use?** Typically, if your clients are part of the same network, you use integrated or NTLM authentication. If clients are coming across the Internet or from non-Windows, you may want to use Kerberos, digest, or basic authentication.
- **What network port will the service use?** The basic choices when creating an HTTP endpoint are CLEAR (port 80) or SSL (port 443). Generally, you should use SSL if the data transmitted requires security and you are using public networks. Note that Internet Information Services (IIS) and other Web servers also use these ports. If you have both IIS and SQL Server on the same machine, you should alternate ports (using CLEAR_PORT or SSL_PORT) for your HTTP endpoints. When creating TCP endpoints, you should select a LISTENER_PORT that is unused on your server.

Listing 11-14 shows the creation of an HTTP endpoint exposing the system stored procedure `sp_monitor`.

Listing 11-14: Creating an HTTP endpoint

```
CREATE ENDPOINT SampleEndpoint
STATE = STARTED
AS HTTP(
   PATH = '/sql',
   AUTHENTICATION = (INTEGRATED ),
   PORTS = (CLEAR),
   CLEAR_PORT = 8888,
   SITE = 'localhost'
   )
FOR SOAP (
```

```
    WEBMETHOD 'GetServerStats'
              (name='master.sys.sp_monitor'),
    WSDL = DEFAULT,
    SCHEMA = STANDARD,
    DATABASE = 'master',
    NAMESPACE = 'http://tempUri.org/'
    );
GO
```

The `CREATE ENDPOINT` command creates an endpoint that responds to SOAP requests via HTTP. In this case, the endpoint is created on the local instance of SQL Server. One Web method is created in the preceding sample. However, you can add multiple `WEBMETHOD` clauses to create multiple methods in a single call. Figure 11-4 shows a portion of the WSDL dynamically created by querying the new endpoint (`http://localhost:8888/sql?WSDL`).

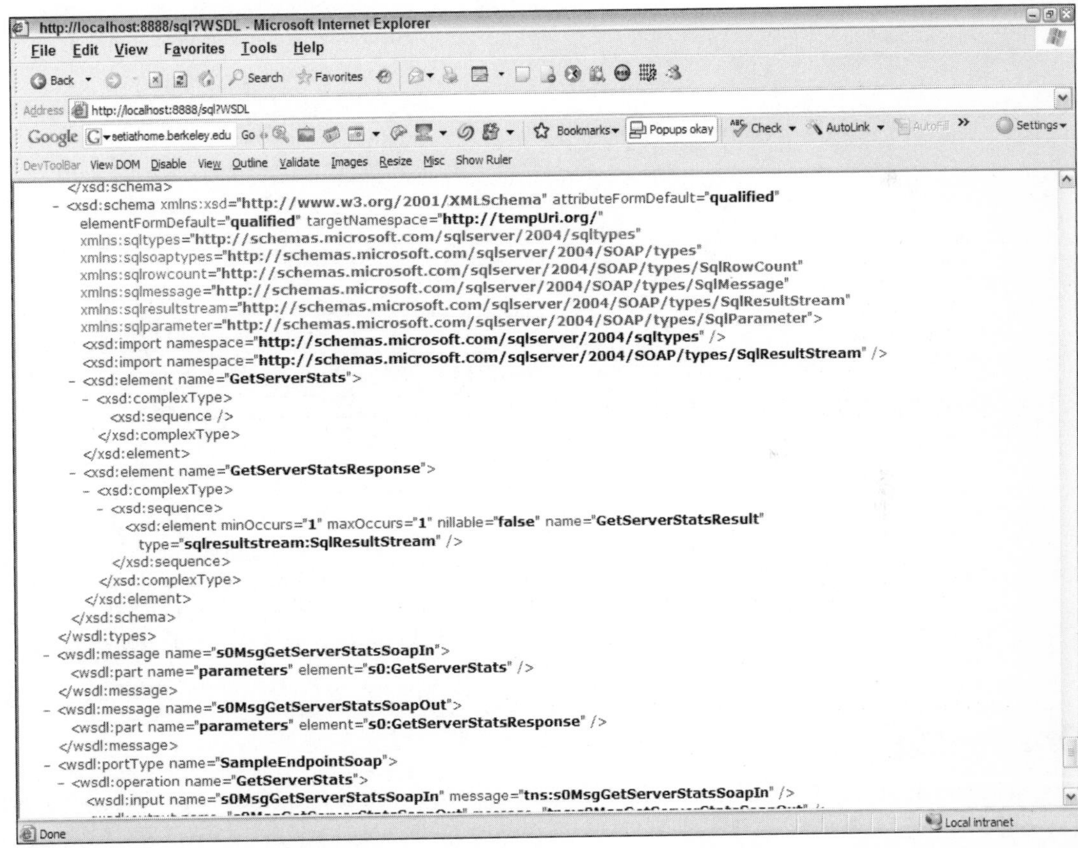

Figure 11-4

After a method is created, you can use any SOAP client to bind to the WSDL and call the HTTP endpoint on the SQL Server. Figure 11-5 shows a portion of the result when you call this Web service using XML Spy.

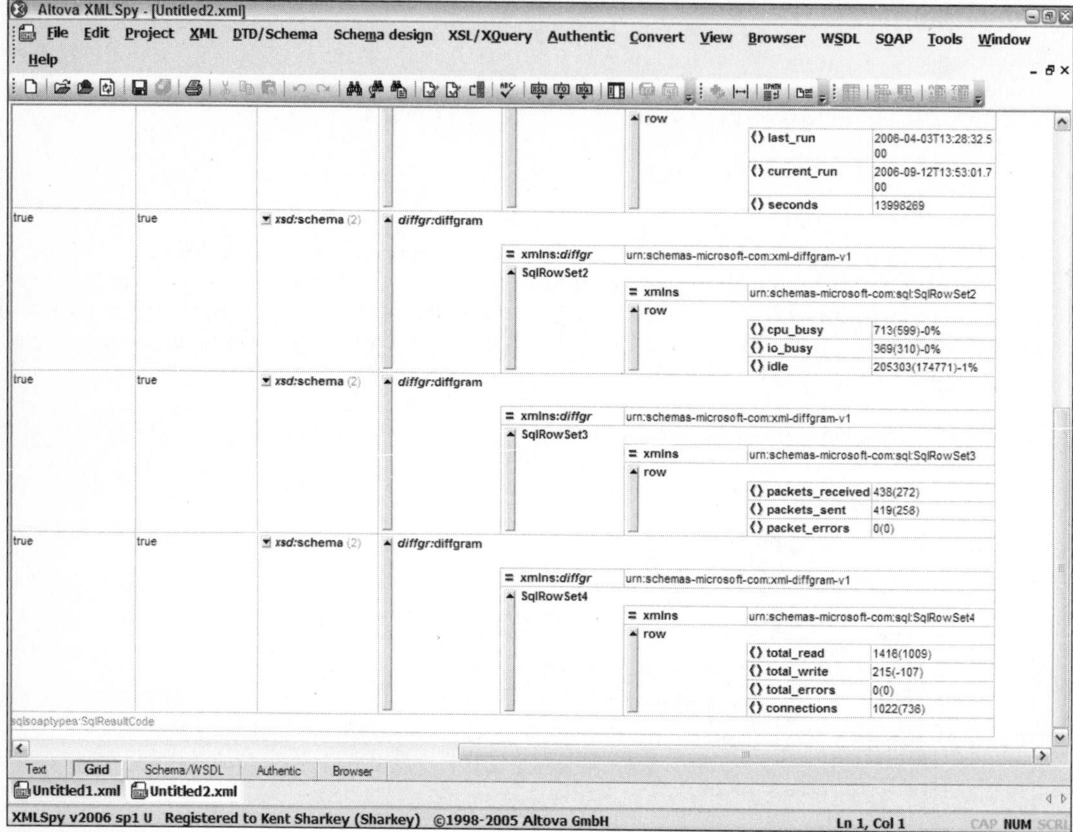

Figure 11-5

One last feature of SQL Server 2005 is not directly related to XML, but can provide a great deal of assistance when working with XML: the capability to use C# or Visual Basic to create stored procedures. This provides a number of benefits in some scenarios, most notably the availability of .NET classes (including the `System.Xml` namespace) for processing data. This means you can perform XPath or XSLT processing within the stored procedure, giving you additional flexibility in processing XML, either for storage or retrieval.

Oracle 10g

Oracle and databases are synonymous for many developers. Oracle is frequently at the forefront in providing database functionality, and its support for XML is yet another example of this. Oracle 10g includes support for SQL/XML and XQuery via the XML DB subsystem. In addition to SQL/XML and XQuery, Oracle adds hierarchical indices, a number of PL/SQL extensions for working with XML.

Retrieving XML

Retrieving XML from Oracle is based on the emerging SQL/XML standard. You can use the operators defined in the standard to construct queries that output XML. Oracle supports most of the proposed operators. However, the XML type in the standard is implemented using the `XMLType` keyword.

To query the table shown in Figure 11-6 and return XML, you construct the following query:

```
SELECT XMLElement("emp", XMLAttributes(employee_id AS id),
         XMLElement("fname",first_name),
         XMLElement("lname",last_name),
         XMLElement("email", email))
FROM employees
WHERE last_name LIKE 'L%';
```

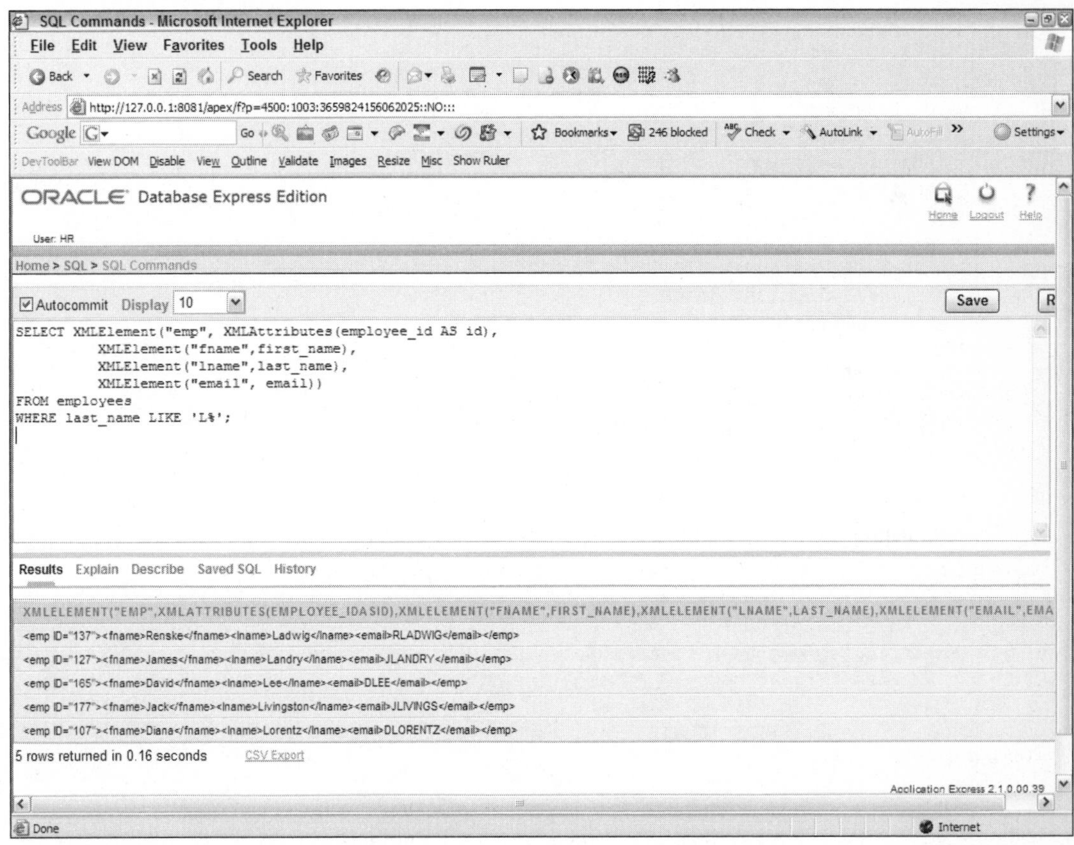

Figure 11-6

The SQL/XML operators convert the data returned into XML elements and attributes. As you can see in the preceding query, the employee_id field is converted into an attribute and applied to a newly created `emp` element, showing that you can easily create elements as needed. As the first and last names are enclosed within the `emp` element, the resulting elements are created as child elements. Listing 11-15 shows the output of the query.

Listing 11-15: Output from SQL/XML query

```
<emp ID="137">
  <fname>Renske</fname>
  <lname>Ladwig</lname>
  <email>RLADWIG</email>
</emp>
<emp ID="127">
  <fname>James</fname>
  <lname>Landry</lname>
  <email>JLANDRY</email>
</emp>
<emp ID="165">
  <fname>David</fname>
  <lname>Lee</lname>
  <email>DLEE</email>
</emp>
<emp ID="177">
  <fname>Jack</fname>
  <lname>Livingston</lname>
  <email>JLIVINGS</email>
</emp>
<emp ID="107">
  <fname>Diana</fname>
  <lname>Lorentz</lname>
  <email>DLORENTZ</email>
</emp>
```

Rather than listing each of the child elements separately, you can use the `XMLForest` command to simplify the query (the following query generates the same output as Listing 11-15):

```
SELECT XMLElement("emp",
  XMLAttributes(employee_id AS id),
     XMLForest(first_name AS "fname",
               last_name AS "lname",
               email AS "email"))
FROM employees
WHERE last_name LIKE 'L%';
```

The `XMLForest` command provides an easy means of adding multiple elements using the one command. Each of the elements listed in the `XMLForest` command is a child element of the preceding `XMLElement`.

The SQL/XML extensions enable you to define complex queries and provide a syntax similar to the normal `SELECT`. For example, the query in Listing 11-16 retrieves the employees and groups them by their departments.

Listing 11-16: Retrieving employees and departments

```
SELECT XMLElement("dept",
       XMLAttributes(d.department_name AS "Name"),
          XMLAgg(
             XMLElement("emp",
                        XMLAttributes(employee_id AS id),
                XMLForest(e.first_name AS "fname",
                          e.last_name AS "lname",
                          e.email AS "email")))) AS out
FROM departments d INNER JOIN employees e
     ON d.department_id = e.department_id
GROUP BY d.department_name;
```

As before, the `XMLElement` and `XMLAttributes` commands are used to identify the tags to use. The `XMLAgg` command is used to group the employees based on the `GROUP BY` clause. Listing 11-17 shows part of the output of this query.

Listing 11-17: Employees and departments

```
<dept Name="Accounting">
  <emp ID="205"><fname>Shelley</fname><lname>Higgins</lname></emp>
  <emp ID="206"><fname>William</fname><lname>Gietz</lname></emp>
</dept>
<dept Name="Administration">
  <emp ID="200"><fname>Jennifer</fname><lname>Whalen</lname></emp>
</dept>
<dept Name="Executive">
  <emp ID="100"><fname>Steven</fname><lname>King</lname></emp>
  <emp ID="101"><fname>Neena</fname><lname>Kochhar</lname></emp>
  <emp ID="102"><fname>Lex</fname><lname>De Haan</lname></emp>
</dept>
```

Storing XML

Oracle supports storing XML in database tables using the `XMLType` column type. This type is similar to the CLOB type in that it stores large amounts of text. In addition to standard CLOB behavior, it ensures that the resulting data is well-formed XML and provides a number of helper methods for working with the resulting document. Listing 11-18 creates a table that stores XML in one column.

Listing 11-18: Creating a table containing XML data in Oracle 10g

```
CREATE TABLE  "ARTICLES"
(
  "ID" NUMBER NOT NULL ENABLE,
  "TITLE" VARCHAR2(255) NOT NULL ENABLE,
  "BODY"  "XMLTYPE",
  CONSTRAINT "ARTICLES_CON" PRIMARY KEY ("ID") ENABLE
)

INSERT INTO Articles(id, Title, Body) VALUES (24, 'An article title',
  XMLType('<article>
```

(continued)

Listing 11-18 *(continued)*

```
        <author>Foo deBar (foo@debar.com)</author>
              <body>This is the article body.</body>
            </article>'));
```

The `XMLType` operator converts the enclosed XML block into the SQL/XML XML type for storage in the Body column.

The table created in Listing 11-18 does not ensure the XML validates against a schema, however. To do that, the schema must be registered with the database. Another benefit in addition to validation is that you can index the schema, allowing queries of the XML data to be almost as fast as queries against indexed tables. Listing 11-19 shows how you would associate a schema with this table.

Listing 11-19: Creating a table containing XML data with a schema

```
DBMS_XMLSCHEMA.registerSchema(
    SCHEMAURL => 'http://example.com/schemas/articles.xsd',
    SCHEMADOC => bfilename('SchemaDir','article.xsd'),
    CSID => nls_charset_id('AL32UTF8'));
/
CREATE INDEX iArticleAuthor ON Articles
(extractValue(Body, '/article/author'));
/
```

The `SchemaUrl` points to the target namespace URL of the schema and may not actually point to a physical file. The `SchemaDoc` value is used to load the actual schema to store in the database. The `CSID` parameter identifies the character encoding used by the document.

SQL/XML also defines a number of operators for extracting data from the supplied XML. This is useful when you want to extract only a few values from a block of XML. The following table shows some of these operators.

Operator	Notes
`existsnode()`	Queries the XML using an XPath statement to determine if the node exists.
`extract()`	Retrieves the document or document fragment described by the XPath query. If the query identifies a single node, the resulting XML is well-formed. If it identifies a number of nodes, the resulting XML is a fragment.
`extractvalue()`	Retrieves the text value for the node identified with the XPath query. The resulting data is converted to the appropriate SQL data type.
`updatexml()`	Changes the XML based on an XPath statement and the new desired value.
`xmlsequence()`	Converts a document fragment into a well-formed document.

For example, the following query returns the value of the author element from the article with an ID of 24:

```
SELECT extractvalue(Body, '/article/author') AS author FROM articles where id=24

// returns: Foo deBar (foo@debar.com)
```

XML Databases

The databases described previously all work with XML from a relational model; they may store XML, but they are designed with rows and columns in mind. Storing XML data is either a matter of dumping the content into a BLOB (Binary Large OBject) field or extracting the information and mapping it to columns. XML databases, on the other hand, store and manipulate XML in a more native form. Three examples of XML databases are the open source Xindice (pronounced Zeen-dee-chay), the eponymous Mark Logic Server, and Berkeley DB XML from Sleepycat Software. These databases store XML natively, without requiring conversion to and from relational tables. Rather than attempt to shoehorn SQL as a query language, they use XQuery or XPath as a query mechanism.

Xindice

Xindice is an open source native XML database. It is part of the tools developed and managed by the Apache Foundation. Although not as full-featured as some commercial databases (it has no support for XQuery for example), binaries and source code are available for a number of Operating Systems. You can download it from the Apache Foundation Web site at `http://xml.apache.org/xindice/`. The samples in this section use Xindice 1.1 syntax, which is slightly different from that used by 1.0. It directly supports access via Java, but other languages are supported via WebDAV queries.

Setting up Xindice requires that you first install an application server. This can be either the freely available Tomcat (also from the Apache Foundation), or a commercial application server, such as BEA Weblogic or IBM Websphere. Xindice is distributed as a WAR (Web ARchive) file for installation into the application server. After it is set up and configured, you can begin to communicate with the database via the included command-line tool or Java.

Retrieving XML

As XML is stored in Xindice as the native format, retrieving XML is simpler than retrieving it from relational databases. You don't need to map columns to XML or to use extensions to SQL to work with the collection. Instead, you process Xindice collections using a provided command-line tool or via Java. Other languages may also be used via an XML-RPC interface.

Xindice stores XML documents in collections; these structures serve as the databases, and they may be nested. Before performing any other processing with Xindice, you must first create a collection in which to store your documents. When querying or adding XML, you reference the collection for the documents. You create a collection either with the command-line interface or via code. Via the command-line, you use the `add_collection` (or `ac`) command:

```
xindice ac -c xmldb:xindice://db -n {collection}
```

Listing 11-20 shows the code used to create a new collection.

Listing 11-20: Creating a Xindice collection

```
private void collectionButtonActionPerformed(java.awt.event.ActionEvent evt) {
    try {
        getDatabase();
        Collection col = DatabaseManager.getCollection(SERVICE_URL);
        CollectionManager service =
            (CollectionManager) col.getService("CollectionManager", "1.0");
        String collectionName = this.collectionField.getText();

        String collectionConfig =
                "<collection compressed=\"true\" " +
                "              name=\"" + collectionName + "\">" +
                "   <filer class=\"org.apache.xindice.core.filer.BTreeFiler\"/>" +
                "</collection>";
        service.createCollection(collectionName,
                DOMParser.toDocument(collectionConfig));
        this.collectionMessage.setText("Collection created");

    } catch (Exception e) {
        System.err.println("Error creating collection " + e.getMessage());
    }

}
```

The first step when working with a Xindice collection is to register the database (see Listing 11-21). Next, the Collection Manager service is loaded and the new collection created. Notice that the parameters of the new collection are passed to the `createCollection` method. In this case the resulting collection is compressed and uses the BTreeFiler.

Listing 11-21: The getDatabase method

```
private static void getDatabase() {
    try {
        Class c = Class.forName(driver);
        Database database = (Database) c.newInstance();
        DatabaseManager.registerDatabase(database);
    } catch (Exception e) {
        System.err.println("Error registering database " + e.getMessage());
    }
}
```

The `getDatabase` routine loads the class for the Xindice implementation (`org.apache.xindice.client.xmldb.DatabaseImpl`), and then it creates a new instance of that class and registers the database. This is required whenever you work with the database, either storing or retrieving information.

Xindice collections are queried using XPath statements. This means that it is relatively simple to retrieve individual items or lists from the collection. However, complex queries or calculations that would be possible in XQuery are not possible currently.

Using the command-line, you perform queries with the `xpath` command:

```
xindice xpath -c xmldb:xindice://{server}:{port}/db/{collection} -q {query}
```

For example, to retrieve the information in a collection named `employees` about `Foo deBar`, you use the following command:

```
xindice xpath -c xmldb:xindice://{server}:{port}/db/employees
    -q emps[lname="deBar"]
```

Figure 11-7 shows a simple application for working with a Xindice collection (see Listing 11-22).

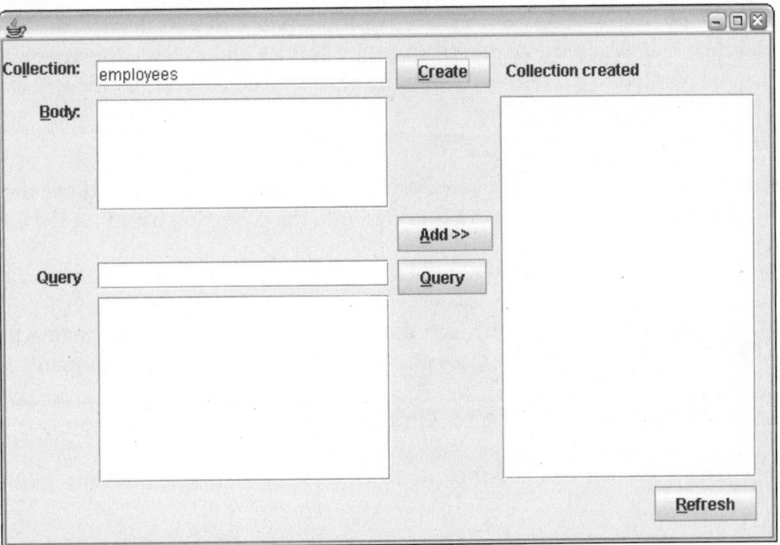

Figure 11-7

Listing 11-22: Using XPath to query a Xindice collection with Java

```
private void queryButtonActionPerformed(java.awt.event.ActionEvent evt) {
    try {
        getDatabase();
        this.queryResults.setText("");
        String url = SERVICE_URL + "/" + this.collectionField.getText();
        Collection col = DatabaseManager.getCollection(url);
        XPathQueryService service =
            (XPathQueryService) col.getService("XPathQueryService", "1.0");
        String xpath = this.queryField.getText();
        ResourceSet resultSet = service.query(xpath);
        ResourceIterator results = resultSet.getIterator();
        StringBuffer buff = new StringBuffer();
        while (results.hasMoreResources()) {
            Resource res = results.nextResource();
            buff.append(res.getContent());
            System.out.println((String) res.getContent());
        }
        this.queryResults.setText(buff.toString());

    } catch(Exception e) {
```

(continued)

Listing 11-22 *(continued)*

```
            System.err.println("Error querying collection " + e.getMessage());
        }
    }
```

The query functionality first connects to the database as before. After you have registered the database, the next step is to load the collection. This is performed by referencing the URL (`xmldb:xindice://localhost:90/db/employees` on my machine; the server and port depend on the URL of your application server). You then retrieve the XPath query service and execute the query. This returns a collection that can be iterated to process each item in the result set. Notice that the key is part of the result.

Storing XML

Storing XML in Xindice is similar to the retrieval: You access the collection and use the `xindice ad` (or `add_document`) command. The document is added into the collection based on the URL used.

```
xindice ad -c xmldb:xindice://{server}:{port}/db/{collection} -f {file}
```

You can also add a number of documents simultaneously with the `-e` switch, listing the extension of all the documents to be added. Listing 11-23 shows the code required to add documents to the collection.

Listing 11-23: Adding documents to Xindice collection

```
private void addButtonActionPerformed(java.awt.event.ActionEvent evt) {

    try {
        getDatabase();
        String url = SERVICE_URL + "/" + this.collectionField.getText();
        Collection col = DatabaseManager.getCollection(url);
        XMLResource document =
                (XMLResource) col.createResource(null, "XMLResource");
        document.setContent(this.bodyField.getText());
        col.storeResource(document);

        this.itemMessage.setText("Item added");
    } catch(Exception e) {
        System.err.println("Error adding item " + e.getMessage());
    }
}
```

The `XMLResource` class provides a number of methods for working with XML. This includes adding the content as I have done here or via a DOM or SAX handle. To confirm the item is listed, you can either query for the new information or retrieve the full list of resources in the collection as shown in Listing 11-24.

Listing 11-24: Retrieving all resources in the Xindice collection

```
private void refreshButtonActionPerformed(java.awt.event.ActionEvent evt) {
    DefaultListModel theList = new DefaultListModel();
    this.itemList.setModel(theList);
```

```
        try {
            //get all items from collection
            getDatabase();
            String url = SERVICE_URL + "/" + this.collectionField.getText();
            Collection col = DatabaseManager.getCollection(url);
            String[] items = col.listResources();

            //add each to list
            for(int i=0;i<items.length;i++) {
                theList.addElement(items[i]);
            }
        } catch (Exception e) {
            System.err.println("Error retrieving items " + e.getMessage());
        }
    }
```

Xindice provides an easy (and inexpensive) way to add a native XML database to your solution. If you are dealing with many small XML documents and don't want to add a relational database to your application, it can provide a useful data storage and query mechanism.

Other Databases

Obviously, not every developer in the world uses one of the databases discussed in this chapter. Many more databases are in use, and many of them also support some interaction with XML. Some of the more notable databases providing support for XML include:

- **Sybase Adaptive Server Enterprise 15**—includes support for SQL/XML and XQuery.
- **Berkeley DB XML**— formerly from Sleepycat Software, now owned by Oracle. Berkeley DB XML is a native XML database with full XQuery support and is capable of being embedded in other applications. Support for Java and C/C++ clients.
- **Mark Logic Server**—native XML database (or Content Server, as the site calls it). It provides support for XQuery and XPath 2.0. In addition, it provides support for partitioning a database across multiple servers for better performance. Support for Java and .NET clients, as well as direct connection from Stylus Studio.

Summary

Databases are rapidly becoming excellent stores for XML data—either natively or using extensions to SQL. Similarly, XQuery support is expanding, providing a common query mechanism for XML and relational data. For those scenarios where the structure of the XML does not allow for the use of relational databases, native XML databases are available to provide data storage. The integration of databases and XML will continue, and tool support should improve—helping developers access the best features of XML and databases in their applications.

Resources

- **MSDN SQL Server Developer Center** — `http://msdn.microsoft.com/sql`
- **Oracle OTN** — `oracle.com/technology/index.html`
- **IBM DB2 Developer Center** — `ibm.com/developerworks/db2/`
- **Mark Logic xq:zone** — `http://xqzone.marklogic.com/`
- **SQL/XML specification** — `sqlx.org/SQL-XML-documents/5FCD-14-XML-2004-07.pdf`

Part V
Programming XML

12

XML Document Object Model (DOM)

XML was introduced to alleviate interoperability problems across platforms and networks. A standard language, combined with a DTD (or another schema construct), provides a way of exchanging data. Not only does data need to be in a standard format, but the way data is accessed should also be standardized. XML provides the constructs for putting data into a standard format, and as you will soon see, the Document Object Model provides a standard way of accessing data. A Web developer, who provides some script inside a Web page that makes use of an XML document, shouldn't have to recode the script to work in every browser. This chapter takes you through a tour of the XML DOM features, including its object model, various classes, and their usage. Specifically you will see:

- The need for XML DOM processing on the client side
- The different classes contained in the XML DOM
- How to work with the various classes of XML DOM
- How to create, read, and modify nodes in an XML document
- How to validate an XML document against an XSD schema using XML DOM
- How to transform an XML document into HTML using XML DOM

What Is DOM?

Some overhead is involved when using XML documents, because extracting data from the tags in an XML document can be arduous. A parser is used to take care of checking a document's validity and extracting the data from the XML syntax. A layer of abstraction between the application and the XML document is made possible by the XML Document Object Model (DOM) specification, which has been standardized by the W3C. This layer of abstraction comes in the form of interfaces that have methods and properties to manipulate an XML document. In other words, when using the DOM, you don't need to worry about the XML syntax directly. For example, the methods, `getAttribute(...)` and `setAttribute(...)`, enable you to manipulate the attributes on an element in an elegant fashion. Legacy systems can use these interfaces to provide access to legacy data as if the data was natively stored in XML. In other words, your legacy data can be made to look like an XML document by implementing the DOM interfaces on top of the legacy database.

Why Client-Side XML Processing?

At first glance, it seems pretty silly to process XML data on the client side when powerful languages such as ASP.NET, Java, and Perl exist to handle processing on the back end. But, if you have been around the world of Web development for any length of time, will know that in some circumstances it makes sense to handle things on the server side, and other conditions that suit processing on the client side.

Processing data on the client side can help relieve server load and give the visitor a better, more responsive experience on your site. For example, the use of server-side programming to perform a task as simple as sorting a column in a table, or formatting some data, is unnecessary; it also forces the users to wait longer than they should have to for such trivial operations. Client-side processing of XML data can be a big help in situations like this.

XML DOM Object Model

Document Object Model is a W3C standard that allows you to put together a document dynamically, and to navigate and manipulate its structure and content. To work with DOM, you use an XML parser to load XML documents into memory. After the documents are loaded, you can then easily manipulate the information in the documents through the Document Object Model (DOM).

You can visualize the DOM's structure as a tree of nodes. The root of the tree is a Document node, which has one or more child nodes that branch off from this trunk. Each of these child nodes may in turn contain child nodes of its own, and so on. For example, consider the XML file shown in Listing 12-1.

Listing 12-1: A sample XML file

```
<?xml version="1.0" encoding="utf-8"?>
<Products>
  <Product Category="Helmets">
    <ProductID>707</ProductID>
    <Name>Sport-100 Helmet, Red</Name>
    <ProductNumber>HL-U509-R</ProductNumber>
  </Product>
  <Product Category="Socks">
    <ProductID>709</ProductID>
    <Name>Mountain Bike Socks, M</Name>
    <ProductNumber>SO-B909-M</ProductNumber>
  </Product>
  <Product Category="Socks">
    <ProductID>710</ProductID>
    <Name>Mountain Bike Socks, L</Name>
    <ProductNumber>SO-B909-L</ProductNumber></Product>
```

```
    <Product Category="Caps">
      <ProductID>712</ProductID>
      <Name>AWC Logo Cap</Name>
      <ProductNumber>CA-1098</ProductNumber>
    </Product>
  </Products>
```

The root element of this XML document is `<Products>`, which contains an arbitrary number of `<Product>` elements. Each `<Product>` element, in turn, contains `<ProductID>`, `<Name>`, and `<ProductNumber>` elements. In addition, the `<Product >` element also contains a category attribute.

If you load this XML file into DOM, DOM loads the XML file into a tree-like structure with the elements, attributes, and text defined as nodes. Some of these node objects have child objects or child nodes. Nodes with no child object are called leaf nodes. Figure 12-1 provides a visual representation of the `Products.xml` file.

According to W3C recommendations, the DOM Level 1 allows navigation within an HTML or XML document and the manipulation of its content. DOM Level 2 extends Level 1 with a number of features such as XML Namespace support, filtered views, ranges, and events. DOM Level 3 builds on Level 2 that allows programs to dynamically access and update the content, structure, and style of documents. The following table describes the main interfaces that form the DOM Level 3 Core module.

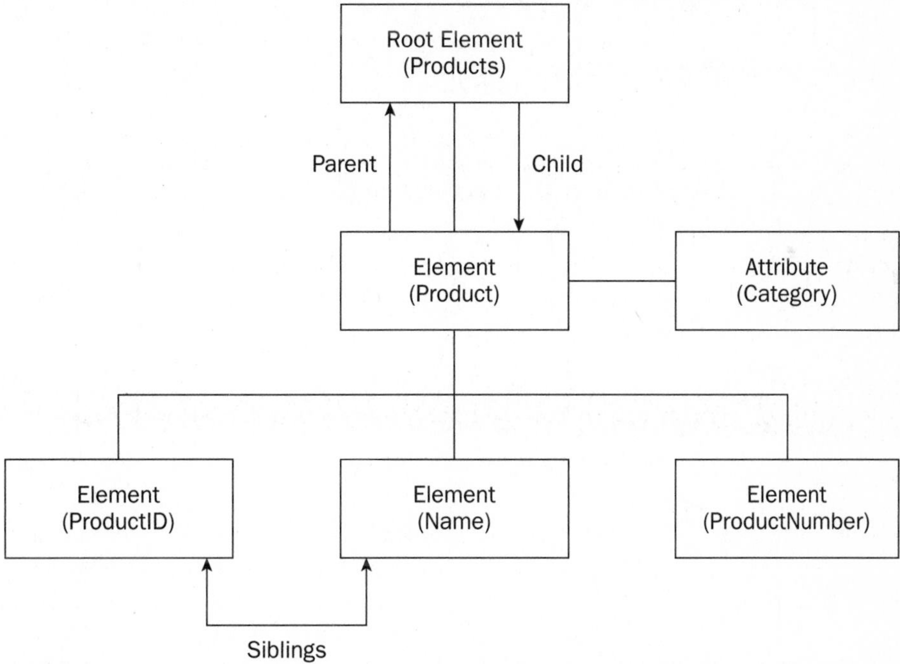

Figure 12-1

Interface	Description
Attr	The Attr interface represents an attribute in an `Element` object
CDataSection	CDATA sections escape blocks of text containing characters that would otherwise be regarded as markup
CharacterData	The CharacterData interface extends Node with a set of attributes and methods for accessing character data in the DOM
Comment	This interface inherits from CharacterData and represents the content of a comment (in other words, all the characters between the starting `<!--` and ending `-->`)
Document	The Document interface represents the entire Hypertext Markup Language (HTML) or XML document
DocumentFragment	DocumentFragment is a light-weight or minimal Document object
DocumentType	Each Document has a `doctype` attribute whose value is either null or a DocumentType object
DOMImplementation	The DOMImplementation interface provides a number of methods for performing operations that are independent of any particular instance of the DOM
Element	The Element interface represents an element in an HTML or XML document
Entity	This interface represents an entity, either parsed or unparsed, in an XML document
EntityReference	EntityReference objects may be inserted into the structure model when an entity reference is in the source document or when the user wants to insert an entity reference
NamedNodeMap	Objects implementing the NamedNodeMap interface represent collections of nodes that can be accessed by name
Node	The Node interface is the primary data type for the entire DOM
NodeList	The NodeList interface provides the abstraction of an ordered collection of nodes, without defining or constraining how this collection is implemented
Notation	This interface represents a notation declared in the document type definition (DTD)
ProcessingInstruction	The ProcessingInstruction interface represents a PI, which is used in XML as a way to keep processor-specific information in the text of the document
Text	The Text interface inherits from CharacterData and represents the textual content (termed character data in XML) of an Element or Attr

Note that every interface that represents a node in the DOM tree extends the Node interface. The next few sections explore some of the important interfaces and the steps involved in using its methods and properties.

Using the Document Interface

The Document interface is the uppermost object in the XML DOM hierarchy. It implements all the basic DOM methods required to work with an XML document. It also provides methods that help you navigate, query, and modify the content and the structure of an XML document. Some of the important methods of the Microsoft's implementation of Document object are described in the following table:

Method	Description
`createElement`	Takes an element name as a parameter and creates an element node by using the name. You cannot create namespace-qualified elements using the `createElement()` method. To create namespace-qualified elements, you need to use the `createElementNS()` method
`createAttribute`	Takes an attribute name as a parameter and creates an attribute node with that name
`createTextNode`	Takes a string as a parameter and creates a text node containing the specified string
`createNode`	Takes three parameters. The `type` parameter is a variant that can be either a string or an integer. The second parameter is a string that represents the name of the node to be created. The third parameter is a string that represents the namespace-URI
`createComment`	Takes a string as a parameter and creates a comment node containing this string
`getElementsByTagName`	Takes a string as a parameter. The string represents the element to be searched. This method returns an instance of the `IXMLDOMNodeList` object, which contains the collection of nodes with the specified element name. You can use the node list to navigate and manipulate the values stored in the named elements
`load`	Takes a string as a parameter that represents the URL or the path of an XML document as its argument and loads the specified document in the DOMDocument object
`loadXML`	Takes a string as a parameter, which contains well-formed XML code or an entire XML document, to load it in the DOMDocument object
`transformNode`	Takes a style sheet object as a parameter, processes the node by applying the corresponding style sheet template on the XML document, and returns the result of transformation
`save`	Takes an object as a parameter. This object can be either DOMDocument or a filename. The `save()` method saves the DOMDocument object at the specified destination

In addition to the preceding methods, the Microsoft implementation of the Document interface also exposes the following properties that can be used to manipulate the information contained in the Document object.

Property	Description
`async`	Specifies whether an asynchronous download is permitted. If you set this property to `true`, the script executes while the XML document is still being loaded. If this property is set to `false`, the script waits until the XML document is loaded before it starts processing the content.
`childNodes`	Returns a list of child nodes that belong to a parent node. The value of this property is of the type `IXMLDOMNodeList`.
`documentElement`	Contains the root element of the XML document represented by the DOM-Document object.
`firstChild`	Returns the first child node of a parent element. This is a read-only property.
`lastChild`	Returns the last child of a parent node.
`parseError`	Returns an `IXMLDOMParseError` object that contains information about the most recently generated error.
`readyState`	Returns the state of the XML document. It indicates whether the document has been loaded completely.
`xml`	Returns an XML representation of a node and its child nodes.
`validateOnParse`	Specifies whether the parser should validate the XML document when parsing.

Now that you have had a brief look at the properties and methods of the Document interface, take a look at an example that shows how to load an XML document through the Document interface.

Loading an XML Document

To traverse an XML document in Internet Explorer, you first have to instantiate the Microsoft XMLDOM parser. In Internet Explorer 5.0 and above, you can instantiate the parser using JavaScript:

```
<script type="text/javascript">
  function loadDocument()
  {
    var doc = new ActiveXObject("Microsoft.XMLDOM");
    ...
  }
</script>
```

Note that the previous XML parser is implemented as an ActiveX object and works only in Internet Explorer.

After the parser is instantiated, you can load a file into it using a series of commands. For example, to load the `Products.xml` file in the parser:

```
<script type="text/javascript">
  function loadDocument()
  {
    var doc = new ActiveXObject("Microsoft.XMLDOM");
    doc.async = false;
    doc.load("Products.xml");
    ...
  }
</script>
```

Note that you set the async property of the XMLDOM object to `false` to ensure that the parser will wait until the document is fully loaded before it does anything else. Next, you invoke the `load()` method to load the contents of the `Products.xml` file into the parser.

At times you might want to load the XML from a string variable and then feed it directly to the parser. To do this, you must use the `loadXML()` method instead of the `load()` method, as in the following example:

```
<script type="text/javascript">
  function loadDocument()
  {
    var xmlContents = '<?xml version="1.0" encoding="iso-8859-1"?>';
    xmlContents += '<Products><Product>';
    xmlContents += '<ProductID>707</ProductID>';
    xmlContents += '<Name>Sport-100 Helmet, Red</Name>';
    xmlContents += '<ProductNumber>HL-U509-R</ProductNumber>';
    xmlContents += '</Product></Products>';
    var doc = new ActiveXObject("Microsoft.XMLDOM");
    doc.async = false;
    doc.loadXML(xmlContents);
    ...
  }
</script>
```

The `loadXML()` method can be extremely useful in scenarios where you are retrieving XML data from the server side dynamically as a string variable. You can take that XML and load it onto an XML DOM object using the `loadXML()` method for subsequent processing.

Using the readyState Property

To check whether a document has been loaded completely, use the `readyState` property. This property stores a numeric value, which represents one of the following states:

- `LOADING (1)` — The loading process is in progress, and data is not yet parsed.
- `LOADED (2)` — The data has been read and parsed, but the object model is not ready.
- `INTERACTIVE (3)` — The object model is available with partially retrieved data set and is in read-only mode.
- `COMPLETED (4)` — The loading process is complete.

To determine whether the XML document is completely loaded and display a message using JavaScript, use the code:

```
if (doc.readyState==4)
{
  alert ("Document is completely loaded");
}
```

Using the Element Interface

The Element interface represents each element in the XML document. It supports the manipulation of elements and the attributes associated with the elements. If the element node contains text, this text is represented in a text node. The Element interface helps manage attributes because this is the only node type that has attributes. This interface has only one read-only property, `tagName`, which retrieves the tag name of the element as a string.

An element is also a `Node` object and inherits different properties of the `Node` object. The methods of the Element interface are shown in the following table:

Method	Description
`getAttribute`	Returns the string containing the value of the specified attribute
`getAttributeNode`	Returns the specified attribute node as an `Attr` object
`getElementsByTagName`	Returns the NodeList of all descendant elements with a given tag name
`removeAttribute`	Removes the specified attribute's value
`removeAttributeNode`	Removes the specified attribute node
`setAttribute`	Creates a new attribute and sets the value for the attribute. If an attribute is present, changes the value for it
`setAttributeNode`	Inserts a new specified attribute to the element, replacing any existing attribute

As mentioned previously, the `getElementsByTagName()` method retrieves all elements of the specified name that occur under the node on which the method is called. For example, to print the value contained in the `Name` element of the first product, you could write the following code:

```
document.write(doc.getElementsByTagName("Name").item(0).text);
```

To display all the values of the `Name` elements, you could loop through the collection of `NodeList` object returned by the `getElementsByTagName()` method:

```
var names = doc.getElementsByTagName("Name");
for (var i = 0; i < names.length; i++)
{
  document.write(names.item(i).text + "  ");
}
```

Creating a New Element

You can create a new element for an XML document using the `createElement()` method of the DOM object. The `createElement()` method takes one parameter — the name of the element that is to be created, as shown:

```
var prodElement = doc.createElement("Product");
```

In the previous code, a variable named `prodElement` is declared and a new element node, `Product`, is created. The reference of the new node is stored in the `prodElement` variable.

Using the Node Interface

The Node interface represents a single node in the document tree structure. All the objects inherit the properties from the Node interface. In addition to the properties and functions, which are associated with them, the Node interface provides basic information like the name of the Node, its text, and its content. The following table lists the different properties of the Node interface:

Property	Description
`attributes`	This returns a `NamedNodeMap` for nodes that have attributes
`baseName`	A read-only property that returns the base name for a node
`childNodes`	A read-only property containing a node list of all children for all the elements that can have them
`dataType`	A read-only property that specifies the data type for the node
`definition`	This property returns the definition of the node in the DTD
`firstChild`	A read-only property that returns the first child node of a node
`lastChild`	A read-only property that returns the last child node of a node
`namespaceURI`	A read-only property. This property returns the Universal Resource Identifier (URI) of the namespace
`nextSibling`	This property returns the next node in the parent's child list
`nodeName`	A read-only property and contains the name of the node, depending on node type
`nodeType`	A read-only property specifying the type of the node
`nodeTypedValue`	This property contains the value of this node as expressed in its data type
`nodeTypeString`	A read-only property and returns the node type in string form
`nodeValue`	This property contains the value of the node, depending on its type
`ownerDocument`	This property returns the Document interface to which the node belongs
`parentNode`	A read-only property and returns the parent node of all nodes except `Document`, `DocumentFragment` and `Attr`, which cannot have parent nodes

Table continued on following page

Property	Description
`parsed`	This property returns a value of `True` if this node and all of its child nodes have been parsed. Otherwise, it returns `False`
`prefix`	This property is read-only property and returns the namespace prefix
`previousSibling`	This property returns the previous node in the parent's child list
`specified`	This property returns a value indicating whether this node is specified or derived from a default value in the DTD or schema
`text`	This property returns the text content of this node and its sub trees
`xml`	This property contains the XML representation of this node and its child nodes

Note that the properties `baseName`, `dataType`, `definition`, `nodeTypedValue`, `nodeTypeString`, `parsed`, `text`, *and* `xml` *are available only in the Microsoft implementation of DOM.*

The following table lists the different methods of the Node interface:

Method	Description
`appendChild`	Adds a new child node to the list of children for this node
`cloneNode`	Creates a clone node that is an exact duplicate of this node
`hasChildNodes`	Determines whether a node has child nodes
`insertBefore`	Inserts a new child node before an existing one. If no child node exists, the new child node becomes the first
`removeChild`	Removes the specified node from the list of child nodes
`replaceChild`	Replaces one child of a node with another and returns the old child
`selectNodes`	Creates a NodeList of all the matching child nodes returned after matching the specified pattern
`selectSingleNode`	Returns a Node interface for the first child node to match the specified pattern
`transformNode`	Processes this node and its child nodes using the specified XSL style sheet and returns the resulting transformation
`transformNodeToObject`	Processes this node and its descendants using the specified XSL style sheet and returns the resulting transformation in the specified object

Note that the methods `selectNodes`, `selectSingleNode`, `transformNode`, *and* `transform NodeToObject` *are available only in the Microsoft implementation of DOM.*

Now that you have had an understanding of the properties and methods of the Node object, look at an example.

When the parser loads an XML document, it gives you a reference to the document itself. From this, you can get a reference to the root element in the document (in this example, the `Products` element) with the property name `documentElement`. The children of that element are, in turn, accessible through the `childNodes` property.

```
var nodes = doc.documentElement.childNodes;
```

The `childNodes` property, and thus the `nodes` variable in this example, contains a node list that is represented by NodeList interface. In accordance with the DOM standard, you can access the elements of a node list by passing a numerical index to the `item()` method, with `0` corresponding to the first node in the list. In this example, therefore, `nodes.item(0)` returns a reference to the first child element of the `Products` element — the `Product` element.

```
document.write(nodes.item(0).text);
```

The result should look something like this:

```
707 Sport-100 Helmet, Red HL-U509-R
```

As you can see, the output shows the concatenated the values of the `ProductID`, `Name` and `ProductNumber` elements. If you just want to print the `ProductID` element value of the first `Product` element, you need to modify the code to look as follows:

```
var nodes = doc.documentElement.childNodes.item(0).childNodes;
document.write(nodes.item(0).text);
```

When you run the code now, the text `707` is displayed in the browser dialog box.

Note that Internet Explorer (and indeed many other DOM implementations) allows you to treat `NodeList` objects as arrays to simplify the code you need to work with them. For example, you could use array syntax to access nodes instead of the item method:

```
var nodes = doc.documentElement.childNodes[0].childNodes;
alert(nodes[0].text);
```

This method of accessing text values within an XML file by numerical index is useful, but it can get a little cumbersome and it can be sometimes error prone as well. Fortunately, there is another way to approach the problem.

Creating a New Node

You create a new node using the `createNode()` method. To create a root element using the `createNode()` method in JavaScript, use the following code:

```
var doc = new ActiveXObject("Microsoft.XMLDOM");
doc.async = false;
doc.load("Products.xml");
```

```
if (doc.childNodes.length == 0)
{
   rootNode = doc.createNode(1,"Products"," ");
   doc.appendChild(rootNode);
   doc.save("Products.xml");
}
```

In the previous code, the DOM object serves as the root node for the tree structure. The length property of the `NodeList` object is used to check the number of child nodes that the root node contains. If this number is equal to `0`, a new node is created using the `createNode()` method. This new node is then added as the root document element using the `appendChild()` method.

Appending a New Child Node

You append a new child node to a DOM tree using the `appendChild()` method of the `Node` object, as shown:

```
var rootElement = doc.documentElement;
var prodElement=doc.createElement("Product");
rootElement.appendChild(prodElement);
```

In the previous code, you first create a reference to the root element of the DOM object. You then create a new element using the `createElement()` method of the `DOMDocument` object in JavaScript. Finally, you append the created element to the last child of the root element using the `appendChild()` method of the `Node` object.

Inserting a Node Before an Existing Node

You insert a node before an existing node in a DOM tree using the `insertBefore()` method of the `Node` object, as shown:

```
var newElement= doc.createElement("ProductIdentifier");
var oldElement = doc.documentElement.childNodes.item(0).childNodes.item(0);
doc.documentElement.childNodes.item(0).insertBefore(newElement, oldElement);
```

In the previous code, you first create a new element called `ProductIdentifier`. You then obtain the reference of the first child of the first node-set within the root element and store a reference to this child node in a variable, `oldElement`. Finally, you insert the newly created node before the first child node using the `insertBefore()` method of the `Node` object.

Removing a Child Node

You can remove a child node from a DOM tree using the `removeChild()` method of the `Node` object, as shown:

```
var elementToBeRemoved = doc.documentElement.childNodes.item(0).firstChild;
doc.documentElement.childNodes.item(0).removeChild(elementToBeRemoved);
```

In the previous code, you first obtain a reference to the first child node of the first node-set of the root element and store this reference in the variable, `elementToBeRemoved`. You use the `removeChild()` method of the `Node` object to remove the node contained in `elementToBeRemoved`.

Replacing a Node

You replace an existing node with a new node using the `replaceChild()` method of the `Node` object. The `replaceChild()` method takes two parameters, the first parameter is the new element and the second parameter is the existing element that needs to be replaced. In the following code, the first `ProductID` element in the document is replaced with the new element named `ProductIdentifier`.

```
var newElement= doc.createElement("ProductIdentifier");
var oldElement=doc.documentElement.childNodes.item(0).childNodes.item(0);
doc.documentElement.childNodes.item(0).replaceChild(newElement, oldElement);
doc.documentElement.childNodes.item(1).childNodes.item(0).
  replaceChild(newElement, oldElement);
```

Accessing Text Values of Elements

In the Microsoft implementation of DOM, the text enclosed within the tags in an XML document is used as a node value, which can be the value of an attribute or the text within an element.

You can display the text within an element using the text property of the `Node` object, as shown:

```
alert(productIDElement.text);
```

You can also set the value of an element or an attribute using this property, as shown:

```
productIDElement.text="100";
```

Using the NodeList Interface

The NodeList interface is a collection of Node and its childNode interfaces. It allows access to all the child nodes. The length property of the NodeList interface is a very important property that returns the number of items in the NodeList collection. The following table describes the different methods of the NodeList interface.

Method	Description
`item`	Returns the item at the index of the Node collection
`nextNode`	Returns null if an invalid index is entered
`reset`	Resets the sequence of the collection

The following code creates a NodeList interface of the `Product` elements using the XML document's `getElementByTagName()` method. With the `Length` property, you can determine the number of nodes in the list and display the node values by accessing each node through the index.

```
var productNodes = doc.getElementsByTagName("Product");
var length = productNodes.length;
for (i = 0; i < length; i++)
  document.write(productNodes.item(i).text + "<br>");
```

When you open the HTML file in the browser, the browser displays the output shown in Figure 12-2.

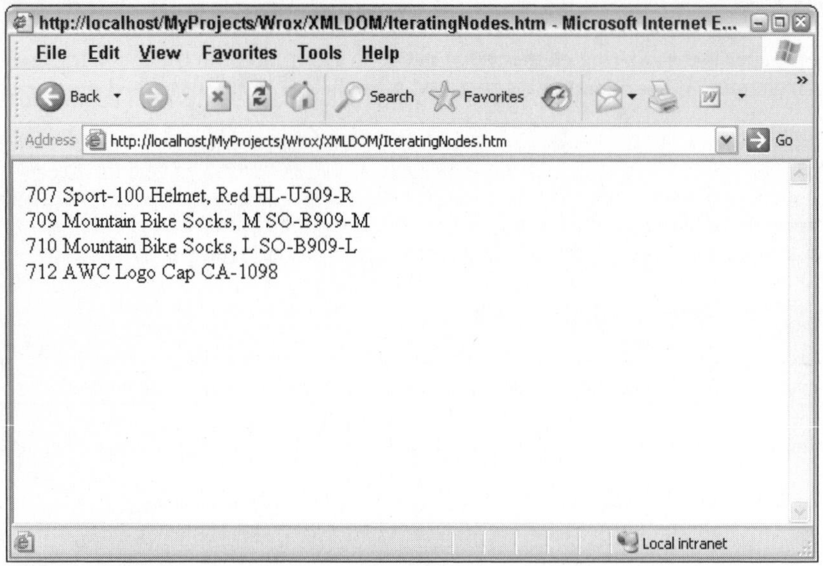

Figure 12-2

Using the NamedNodeMap Interface

The NamedNodeMap interface represents a collection of nodes that can be accessed by name. The following code shows how to create a NamedNodeMap interface of all the attribute nodes of the class element. Then iterate through the collection using the item method to display the attribute name and associated text.

```
var firstChildElement = doc.documentElement.firstChild;
var attributes = firstChildElement.attributes;
for (i = 0; i < attributes.length; i++)
  document.write(attributes.item(i).name + "="
  + attributes.item(i).text + "<br>");
```

When you open the HTML file in the browser, the browser displays the attribute name and associated text. If you use the `Products.xml` file as an example, you will get `"Category=Helmets"` as the output because the `Product` element has only one attribute.

Using the Attr Interface

The Attr interface represents an attribute of an `Element` object. The DOM considers Attr to be a property of an element. The values that are allowed for an Attr interface are defined in DTD. An Attr interface is similar to a Node interface and has the properties and methods of a Node interface. The following table discusses the important properties of the Attr interface.

Property	Description
`Name`	Sets the name of the attribute. It is same as the nodeName property for this Node interface
`specified`	Indicates if the value of the attribute is set in the document
`Value`	Returns or sets the value of the attribute

In addition to the previous methods, all the methods of the Node interface also apply to Attr because Attr is also a Node interface. The following code shows a simple example of using the Attr interface to retrieve the name and value of attributes in an XML document.

```
var firstChildElement = doc.documentElement.firstChild;
var attributes = firstChildElement.attributes;
for (i = 0; i < attributes.length; i++)
  document.write(attributes.item(i).name + "=" +
  attributes.item(i).value + "<br>");
```

When you open the HTML file in the browser, the browser displays the name and the value of the attribute of the first node. In the case of `Products.xml` file, it just displays `Category=Helmets` as the output.

Creating Attributes

Most of the functionality that is included with the Element node is the management of attributes. This example shows how to add new attributes to an existing Element node and how to view attribute contents. Creating attributes can be accomplished with the Document method `createAttribute(...)`. It can then be inserted into the tree with `setAttributeNode(...)`. An even simpler method exists by using the `setAttribute(...)` method on the Element node. This method allows you to work with attribute names that are strings instead of attribute nodes. Listing 12-2 shows an example of how to create an attribute and retrieve its value for display purposes.

Listing 12-2: Using XML DOM to manipulate attributes

```
<html xmlns="http://www.w3.org/1999/xhtml">
<head>
  <title>Working with Attributes</title>
  <script type="text/javascript" language="javascript">
    var doc;

    function btnCreateAndDisplayAttribute_Click()
    {
      loadDocument();
      createAndDisplayAttribute();
    }

    function loadDocument()
    {
      doc = new ActiveXObject("Microsoft.XMLDOM");
      doc.async = false;
```

(continued)

Listing 12-2 *(continued)*

```
        doc.load("Products.xml");
      }

      function createAndDisplayAttribute()
      {
        var docElement = doc.documentElement;
        //Put the attribute myAtt='hello' on rootElement
        docElement.setAttribute('CategoryID', '1');
        //Display the value of the added attribute
        result.innerText = docElement.getAttribute('CategoryID');
      }
    </script>
  </head>
  <body>
    <input type="button" id="btnCreateAndDisplayAttribute"
      value="Create and display attribute"
      onclick="btnCreateAndDisplayAttribute_Click()" />
    <br/><br/><br/>
    <div id="result"></div>
  </body>
  </html>
```

When you click the button control, the page displays the value of the CategoryID attribute, which is `1` in this case.

Using the CharacterData Interface

The CharacterData interface provides the Node object with various properties and methods to manipulate text. These interfaces can handle very large amounts of text and can be implemented by the CDATASection, Comment, and Text Nodes. The CharacterData interface has the following properties:

Property	Description
`data`	This property contains the data for this node, depending on node type
`length`	This property is read-only and contains the length of the data string in characters

The following table lists the methods for CharacterData Interface.

Property	Description
`appendData`	Adds the specified string to existing string data
`deleteData`	Deletes the specified range of characters from string data
`insertData`	Inserts a string of data at the specified position in the string

Property	Description
`replaceData`	Replaces the characters from the specified position in the string with the supplied string data
`substringData`	Returns a substring consisting of the specified range of characters

Look at the following simple example to understand the use of one of the methods of the CharacterData interface.

```
var prodElement = doc.documentElement.firstChild;
var text = prodElement.firstChild.firstChild;
document.write(text.data + "<br>");
var lastTwoCharacters = text.substringData(1, 2)
document.write(lastTwoCharacters  + "<br>");
```

The previous code displays the character data of the first `ProductID` element using the data. `The substringData()` method gets the specified range of characters from the substring of the text (`char-offset = 1` and `num-count= 2`) and displays that specific data. The output produced by the page looks as follows in the browser:

```
707
07
```

Using the Comment Interface

The Comment represents the content which appear between '<!–' and '-->' as a comment entry. The Comment object does not have any properties of its own. It inherits the properties of Node objects as well as CharacterData objects. It inherits the properties as well as the methods of Node and CharacterData objects.

Using the Text Interface

The Text object represents the text of an Element or an Attr object. There is only one node of Text for each block of text. The Text object has properties of Node and CharacterData objects. The Text is also a Node object and therefore inherits the methods of Node objects. The Text interface has one method of its own named `splitText(number)`. This method splits the text in two parts, at the specified character, and returns the rest of the text, till the end of the string into a new text node.

Using the CDATASection Interface

The CDATASection interface represents the content within the CDATA section brackets `![... ]]`. The CDATASection provides characters that should not be parsed by the XML parser. The content of CDATASection is stored as a childNode of a Text node. The CDATASection interface has no methods or properties of its own but inherits those of the Text and Node objects.

If the CDATASection contains text, which includes HTML tags, the CDATASection object allows it to escape from the XML parser. The content of the CDATASection is displayed without the brackets `![...]]`. You can use CDATASection interface to exclude HTML tags while parsing as shown here:

```
<?xml version="1.0"?>
<Products>
  <Product>
    <ProductID></ProductID>
    <Name><![CDATA[<span style="color:red"> Cotton Shirt </span>]]> </Name>
    ----
    ----
</Products>
```

The code required to handle a CDATASection is exactly the same as processing any other node since the CDATASection is also a node.

Handling Errors in XML DOM

At times the XML parsing might generate errors due to reasons such as invalid XML, schema compliant reasons, and so on. To process these errors, the Document object exposes a property called `parseError` through which you can get more details about the exception. This object, derived from the interface `IXMLDOMParseError` provides a set of properties to retrieve the error information. The following table describes the commonly used properties of the `IXMLDOMParseError` object:

Property	Description
`reason`	Stores a string explaining the reason for the error
`line`	Stores a long integer representing the line number for the error
`errorCode`	Contains long integer error code. This property contains the value `0` if there are no errors in the XML document
`linepos`	Stores a long integer representing the line position for the error
`srcText`	Stores a string containing the line that caused the error

You use the `IXMLDOMParseError` object to display the information about the errors encountered while parsing an XML document, as shown here:

```
var doc = new ActiveXObject("Microsoft.XMLDOM");
doc.async = false;
doc.load("Products.xml");
if (doc.parseError.errorCode != 0)
{
  alert("Error Code: " + doc.parseError.errorCode);
  alert("Error Reason: " + doc.parseError.reason);
  alert("Error Line: " + doc.parseError.line);
}
else
{
  alert(doc.documentElement.xml);
}
```

In the previous code, you first create a new DOM object and then use the `if` construct to determine whether the `parseError` property of this object returns any error code. If the error code is greater than `1`, you display the details of the error indicating the error code, reason, and the line number where the error occurred. Otherwise, you display a message box showing the XML of the document.

XML Transformation Using XSL

In this section, you see the steps involved in transforming the contents of an XML file into HTML using the built-in support provided by XML DOM. You can accomplish this in the client side by invoking the methods of XML DOM through JavaScript. First, let's create the XSL file that will be used to transform the `Products.xml` file as shown in Listing 12-3.

Listing 12-3: Products.xsl file used for transforming the Products.xml file

```
<?xml version="1.0" ?>
<xsl:stylesheet version="1.0" xmlns:xsl="http://www.w3.org/1999/XSL/Transform">
  <xsl:output method="html" />
  <xsl:template match="/">
    <table border="1" cellSpacing="1" cellPadding="1">
      <center>
        <xsl:element name="tr">
          <xsl:element name="td">Product ID</xsl:element>
          <xsl:element name="td">
            <xsl:attribute name="align">center</xsl:attribute>
            Name
         </xsl:element>
          <xsl:element name="td">Product Number</xsl:element>
        </xsl:element>
        <xsl:for-each select="//Product">
          <!-- Each product on a separate row -->
          <xsl:element name="tr">
            <xsl:element name="td">
              <xsl:value-of select="ProductID" />
            </xsl:element>
            <xsl:element name="td">
              <xsl:value-of select="Name" />
            </xsl:element>
            <xsl:element name="td">
              <xsl:value-of select="ProductNumber" />
            </xsl:element>
          </xsl:element>
        </xsl:for-each>
      </center>
    </table>
  </xsl:template>
</xsl:stylesheet>
```

The XSL logic shown in Listing 12-3 simply loops through all the `<Product>` elements and for each element it retrieves the values of the `ProductID`, `Name`, and `ProductNumber` elements and displays them in the browser. Now that you have created the XSL file, look at the code of the Web page in Listing 12-4 to perform the transformation.

Listing 12-4: Transforming XML to HTML using XML DOM

```
<html xmlns="http://www.w3.org/1999/xhtml">
<head>
  <title>Transforming XML to HTML</title>
  <script type="text/javascript" language="javascript">
    var xmlDoc;
    var xslDoc;

    function btnTransformXmlToHtml_Click()
    {
      loadDocuments();
      tranformXmlToHtml();
    }

    function loadDocuments()
    {
      //Load the XML Document
      xmlDoc = new ActiveXObject("Microsoft.XMLDOM");
      xmlDoc.async = false;
      xmlDoc.load("Products.xml");
      //Load the XSL Document
      xslDoc = new ActiveXObject("Microsoft.XMLDOM");
      xslDoc.async = false;
      xslDoc.load("Products.xsl");
    }

    function tranformXmlToHtml()
    {
      var output = xmlDoc.transformNode(xslDoc);
      result.innerHTML = output;
    }
  </script>
</head>
<body>
  <input type="button" id="btnTransformXmlToHtml" value="Transform XML"
    onclick="btnTransformXmlToHtml_Click()" />
  <br/><br/><br/>
  <div id="result"></div>
</body>
</html>
```

The preceding Web page contains mostly JavaScript code that loads the XML and XSLT files into memory, processes them, and displays the results. First, you create an instance of the XML DOM and load the `Products.xml` file into memory. Next, you create another instance of XML DOM and load the `Products.xsl` file into memory. Since XSLT files are formatted as XML, you can load them just as you would any other XML file:

You then transform the XML document using the XSL style sheet, and assign the HTML output of the transformation to the innerHTML property of the div control.

```
function tranformXmlToHtml()
{
  var output = xmlDoc.transformNode(xslDoc);
  result.innerHTML = output;
}
```

The `transformNode()` method takes the object that holds the XSL file as an argument. Figure 12-3 shows how the output looks when you click the Transform XML button in the browser.

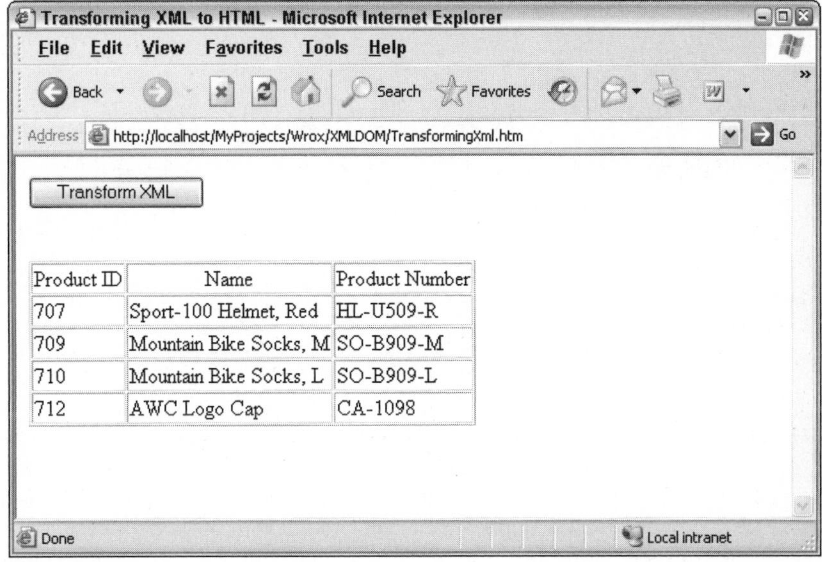

Figure 12-3

XML Validation Using XML DOM

As XML documents become more and more pervasive as a standardized way to exchange data, there is an increasing need for the XML documents to be acceptable to different developers/users. To meet this need, the XML document should conform to a standard structure. One of the ways you can represent this standard structure is through XML Schema Definition (XSD) language. XML Schema is an XML-based representation of the structure of an XML document. Through its support for data types and namespaces, XML Schema has the potential to provide the standard structure for XML elements and attributes.

To determine whether an XML document conforms to an XML Schema, the document must be validated against that XML Schema. Through its support for XML validation, XML DOM allows you to validate XML through its properties.

Before looking at the code required to validate the XML document, create the `Products.xsd` file that will be used to validate the `Products.xml` file. (See Listing 12-5.)

Listing 12-5: Products.xsd schema

```
<?xml version="1.0" encoding="utf-8"?>
<xs:schema xmlns="http://www.wrox.com/samples"
  targetNamespace="http://www.wrox.com/samples" attributeFormDefault="unqualified"
  elementFormDefault="qualified" xmlns:xs="http://www.w3.org/2001/XMLSchema">
  <xs:element name="Products">
    <xs:complexType>
      <xs:sequence>
        <xs:element maxOccurs="unbounded" name="Product">
          <xs:complexType>
            <xs:sequence>
              <xs:element name="ProductID" type="xs:unsignedShort" />
              <xs:element name="Name" type="xs:string" />
              <xs:element name="ProductNumber" type="xs:string" />
            </xs:sequence>
            <xs:attribute name="Category" type="xs:string" use="required" />
          </xs:complexType>
        </xs:element>
      </xs:sequence>
    </xs:complexType>
  </xs:element>
</xs:schema>
```

To connect an XML schema to an XML document, you use an attribute named `xsi:schemaLocation` in the document element to specify the URI of the document's XML schema. To use this attribute so that Internet Explorer will understand it, you assign it a text string, giving the namespace you are using in your XML document, which is `http://www.wrox.com/samples` here, and the URI of the XML schema, which is `Products.xsd` in this case. If the `Products.xsd` file is in the same directory as that of the `Products.xml` file, you can set the `xsi:schemaLocation` attribute to `http://www.wrox.com/samples Products.xsd`. Here is the modified `Products.xml` file using the namespace `http://www.wrox.com/samples`.

```
<?xml version="1.0" encoding="utf-8"?>
<Products xmlns="http://www.wrox.com/samples"
  xmlns:xsi="http://www.w3.org/2001/XMLSchema-instance"
  xsi:schemaLocation="http://www.wrox.com/samples Products.xsd">
  <Product Category="Helmets">
    <ProductID>707</ProductID>
    ----
    ----
</Products>
```

Note that if you are not using a namespace in your XML document, you can use the `xsi:noNamespaceSchemaLocation` attribute and simply specify the location of the XSD.

Now that you have seen the XML and the corresponding XSD schema, Listing 12-6 shows the complete HTML page required for validating the `Products.xml` file with the `Products.xsd` file.

Listing 12-6: Validating an XML file with the XSD file

```
<html xmlns="http://www.w3.org/1999/xhtml">
<head>
  <title>Validating an XML Document</title>
  <script type="text/javascript" language="javascript">
    var doc;
    function btnValidate_Click()
    {
      loadDocument();
    }

    function loadDocument()
    {
      doc = new ActiveXObject("MSXML2.DOMDocument.6.0");
      doc.resolveExternals = true;
      doc.validateOnParse = true;
      doc.async = false;
      if (doc.load("Products.xml"))
        document.write("Document is valid");
      else
        displayErrorInfo();
    }

    function displayErrorInfo()
    {
      document.write("Error code: " + doc.parseError.errorCode + "<br />");
      document.write("Error reason: " + doc.parseError.reason + "<br />");
      document.write("Error line: " + doc.parseError.line);
    }
  </script>
</head>
<body>
  <input type="button" id="btnValidate" value="Validate XML Document"
    onclick="btnValidate_Click()" />
</body>
</html>
```

Note the use of the `validateOnParse` property that is set to `true` to indicate the parser that the XML document needs to be validated at the time of parsing. In addition, you also set the `resolveExternals` property of DOMDocument to `true` in order to use external XSD document for validation. If the XML document is compliant with the XSD schema, you get a message indicating that the `Document is valid`. If the document is not compliant, you get an error message indicating the details of the error code, reason, and line.

Summary

This chapter started with a brief introduction to XML DOM by discussing the role of XML DOM, its advantages and the object model of XML DOM. After that, you looked at how to use the various objects contained in the XML DOM. You also saw the steps involved in creating, reading, and modifying nodes in an XML document using the various classes of XML DOM. In addition, you also understood the steps involved in manipulating attributes stored in an XML document. Finally, you understood the various functions supported by XML DOM including the use of transforming an XML document into HTML using XSL, and the steps involved in validating an XML document.

13

Simple API for XML (SAX)

The Simple API for XML (SAX) is an event-driven programming interface for XML parsing. It was developed by the members of the xml-dev mailing list currently hosted by the Organization for the Advancement of Structured Information Standards (OASIS) (`oasis-open.org`). SAX is not an XML parser, but instead it is a set of interfaces implemented by many XML parsers. SAX was developed as a standardized way to parse an XML, to enable more efficient analysis of large XML documents. SAX is specified as a set of Java interfaces. Initially, if you were going to do any serious work with it, you had to be doing some Java programming, using JDK 1.1 or later. Now, however, a wide variety of languages have their own version of SAX.

In this chapter, you get an in-depth look at the features of SAX including its architecture, and processing flow through examples. Specifically you learn how to,

- Configure a SAX parser and parse an XML document
- Handle elements, attribute lists, character data, and processing instructions
- Handle errors and warnings using SAX
- Search for specific elements in an XML document using SAX
- Write XML elements using SAX
- Validate an XML document with an XSD schema
- Understand the advantages and disadvantages of SAX

Introducing XML Parsing

There are two widely used approaches to parsing XML data:

- Tree-based APIs
- Simple API for XML (SAX)

The following sections discuss each of these approaches.

Tree-Based APIs

One of the most popular XML APIs at the moment is the Document Object Model, which is a standard that was developed by the World Wide Web Consortium (`w3.org`). DOM is what is known as a tree-based API, which means that all of the information and content from the original document must be read into memory and stored in a tree structure before it can be accessed by a client program. After the document has been parsed and stored as an in-memory tree structure, the client application has full access to its contents. It is simple to follow references from one part of the document to another. It is also easy to modify the document by adding and removing nodes from the tree.

Although this approach has some obvious advantages, it has some equally obvious disadvantages. The size of the document affects the performance (and memory consumption) of the program. If the document is very large, it may not be possible to store the entire thing in memory at one time. Also, the whole document must be successfully parsed before any information is available to the client program.

A Simple API for XML (SAX)

It was to solve these and other problems that the members of the XML-DEV mailing list (`www.xml.org`) developed the SAX. Unlike DOM, SAX is an event-driven API. Rather than building an in-memory copy of the document and passing it to the client program, This API requires the client program to register itself to receive notifications when the parser recognizes various parts of an XML document.

In the event-driven scenario, the API itself doesn't allocate storage for the contents of the document. The required content is passed to the event notification method, and then forgotten. Whether the document is 10 kilobytes or 10 megabytes, the application's memory usage and relative performance remain constant. Unlike in the tree-based approach, the client application notifications are received as the document is parsed. This means it can begin processing before the entire document has been read. For many Internet-based applications, where bandwidth may be an issue, this can be extremely useful.

There are, of course, drawbacks to this approach. Application developers are responsible for creating their own data structures to store any document information they must reference later. Because no comprehensive model of the document is available in memory, SAX is unsuitable for sophisticated editing applications. Also, for applications where random access to arbitrary points of the document is required (such as an XSLT implementation), a tree-based API would be more appropriate.

Installing SAX

In reality, SAX is nothing more than a set of Java class and interface descriptions that document a system for writing event-driven XML applications. The SAX specification (along with the source code for a set of Java interfaces and classes) lives on its own Web site (`www.saxproject.org`) and is still maintained and extended by the members of the XML-DEV mailing list. To download SAX, you can go to the home page and then browse for the latest version, or you can go directly to the SourceForge project page at `http://sourceforge.net/project/showfiles.php?group_id=29449`.

The distribution contains all the Java interfaces, the extension interfaces, some helper files, and the documentation, but doesn't include a SAX parser. To actually use SAX, you need to download one of the many XML parsers that have been developed to work with SAX. The parser is the one that has a concrete implementation of the various interfaces and classes that make up the `org.xml.sax` and `org.xml.sax.helpers` Java packages. Some popular Java SAX parsers are shown in the following table:

Parser	Driver identifier	Description
Xerces-J	org.apache.xerces.parsers .SAXParser	The Xerces parser, which is used throughout this chapter, is maintained by the Apache group. It is available at `http://xml.apache.org/xerces2-j`.
AElfred2	gnu.xml.aelfred2.XmlReader	AElfred2 parser is highly conformant as it was written and modified by the creators of SAX. It is available as part of the GNUJAXP project at `gnu.org/software/classpathx/jaxp/`.
Crimson	org.apache.crimson.parser .XMLReaderImpl	The Crimson parser was originally part of the Crimson project at `http://xml.apache.org/crimson/`. It is now included as part of Sun's Java API for XML Parsing available at `http://java.sun.com/xml`.
Oracle	oracle.xml.parser.v2.SAXParser	Oracle maintains a SAX parser as part of its XML toolkit. It can be downloaded from the Oracle Technology Network at `http://otn.oracle.com/tech/xml/index.html`.
XP	com.jclark.xml.sax.SAX2Driver	XP is an XML 1.0 parser written by James Clark. A SAX2 driver was created for use with the latest versions of SAX. More information can be found at `xmlmind.com/_xpforjaxp/docs/`.

In this chapter, I use the Apache XML parsing library developed as part of the Apache Xerces project. You can download Apache Xerces project code from `http://xml.apache.org/xerces2-j/ or http://archive.apache.org/dist/xml/xerces-j/`. After downloading the archive file, unzip it to the desired folder and follow the instructions to set up your environment.

After that, set the CLASSPATH environment variable to the following:

- `<SAX-Installation-Drive>\sax2r3\sax2.jar`
- `<Xerces-Installation-Drive>\Xerces-J\xerces-2_9_0\xercesImpl.jar`

These options allow `java.exe` (the JDK Java runtime) to locate the SAX classes at runtime so you aren't required to supply their location on the command line.

You also need a copy of the Java 2 SDK to compile and execute your SAX application. The examples in this book were compiled using the JDK version 1.5.10. As part of the Java set up, you must also set your PATH variable to Java execution path.

SAX Architecture

In SAX, you can configure the parser with a variety of callback handlers, as shown in Figure 13-1.

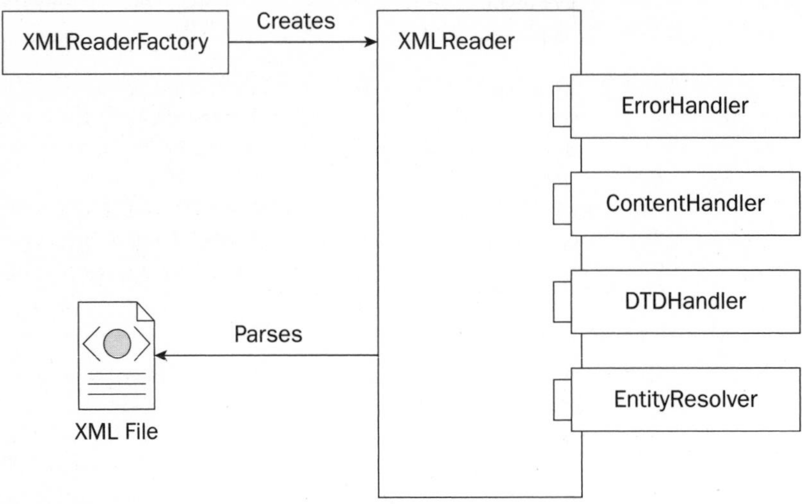

Figure 13-1

When the parser scans an external stream that contains XML markup, it reports the various events involved to those callback handlers. These events include but are not limited to the following:

- Beginning of the document
- End of the document
- Namespace mapping
- Errors in well-formedness
- Validation errors
- Text data
- Start of an element
- End of an element

The SAX API provides interfaces that define the contract for these callback handlers. When you write XML applications that use SAX, you can write implementations for these interfaces and register them with a SAX parser.

Basic SAX Application Flow

Every SAX application goes through the same basic steps to process an XML document.

1. It obtains a reference to an object that implements the XMLReader interface.
2. It creates an instance of an application-specific object that implements one or more of the various SAX *Handler (DTDHandler, ContentHandler, ErrorHandler, and EntityResolver) interfaces.

3. IT registers the object instance with the XMLReader object so that it will receive notifications as XML parsing events occur.

4. It calls the `XMLReader.parse()` method for each XML document that needs to be processed by the application. The object instance that was registered in Step 3 receives notifications progressively as the document is parsed.

It is up to the application-specific object (or objects) to track and process the information that is delivered via the various event notification methods that it implements. For example, an application that wants to strip markup out of an XML document and leave only the text content must implement the `ContentHandler` interface and its specific processing in the `characters()` event callback method. Even though the setup for every SAX application is almost identical, the data structures and algorithms that process the event notifications vary widely depending on what the application is designed to do.

SAX Packages and Classes

SAX contains the packages described in the following table:

Package	Description
org.xml.sax	Defines handler interfaces. Handler implementations of these interfaces are registered with parsers, which call the handler methods in order to report parsing events and errors.
org.xml.sax.ext	Contains two additional, non-mandatory handlers for dealing with DTD declarations and lexical information.
org.xml.sax.helpers	Provides default implementations for some of the core interfaces defined in `org.xml.sax`.

Each of these packages has several classes. For reasons of brevity, I discuss only the important classes in this chapter.

The SAXParser Class

is the `SAXParser` class is an abstract class that wraps an XMLReader implementation class. You obtain a reference to this class by calling the `newSAXParser()` method on the factory class.

```
SAXParserFactory factory=SAXParserFactory.newInstance();
SAXParser parser=factory.newSAXParser();
```

After you have a `SAXParser` object, you can then specify the input for the parsing process using the `parser()` method. The input to the parser can come from a variety of sources, such as InputStreams, files, URLs, and SAX InputSources. You can open an InputStream on the document to be parsed and send the reference to it as an argument to the parse method of the parser. Instead of using an InputStream, you can pass an instance of the `File` class or a URL reference or a SAX `InputSource` as an argument to the parse method. The `InputSource` class defined in the `org.xml.sax` package provides a single input source for an XML entity. A single input source may be a byte stream and/or a character stream. It may also be a public or system identifier.

As this parser object parses the document, the handler methods are called. Some of the important methods of the SAXParser class are as follows:

- `parse`—This is the most important method of this class. Several overloaded parse methods take different parameters, such as `File`, `InputSource`, `InputStream`, and URI. For each of the different input types, you also specify the handler to be used during parsing.
- `getXMLReader`—This method returns the XMLReader that is encapsulated by the implementation of this class.
- `get/setProperty`—These methods allow you to get and set the parser properties, such as the validating parser.

The XMLReader Interface

The `XMLReader` interface is implemented by the parser's driver and is mainly used for reading an XML document. The interface allows you to register an event handler for document processing. Some of the important methods of this interface are:

- `parse`—Two overloaded `parse` methods take input from either an `InputSource` object or a String URI. The method parses the input source document and generates events in your handler. The method call is synchronous and does not return until the entire document is parsed or an exception occurs during parsing.
- `setContentHandler`—This method registers a content event handler. If the content event handler is not registered, all the content events during parsing are ignored. It is possible to change the content handler in the middle of parsing. If a new content handler is registered during parsing, the parser immediately uses the new handler while processing the rest of the document.
- `setDTDHandler`—Like a content handler in the previous paragraph, this method registers a DTD handler. You use DTDHandler to report notation and unparsed entity declarations to the application. If the DTD handler is not registered, all DTD events are ignored. As with the content handler, the DTD handler can be changed during parsing. Because DTDs are supported only for maintaining backward compatibility, you may not be using this handler frequently in your applications.
- `setEntityResolver`—Like the previous two methods, `setEntityResolver` allows you to define an `EntityResolver` that can be changed during processing.
- `setErrorHandler`—Allows you to handle errors generated during parsing.

Receiving SAX Events

To receive SAX events, you write a Java class that implements one of the SAX interfaces, which means your class has all the same functions as the interface does. You specify that a class implements an interface by declaring it like this:

```
public class ProductsReader implements ContentHandler
```

`ProductsReader` is the name of my new class, and `ContentHandler` is the name of the interface. Actually, this is the most important interface in SAX, as it is the one that defines the callback methods for content related events (that is, events about elements, attributes, and their contents). So what you are doing here is creating a class that contains methods that a SAX-aware parser knows about.

The ContentHandler interface contains a whole series of methods, most of which you can ignore in the normal course of events. Unfortunately, when you implement an interface, you have to provide implementations of all the methods defined in that interface. However, SAX provides you with a default, empty implementation, called DefaultHandler. So rather than implement ContentHandler, you can instead extend DefaultHandler, like this:

```
public class ProductsReader extends DefaultHandler
```

By extending the DefaultHandler class, you can trap specific events by picking and choosing which methods to provide to your own implementations. If you leave things as they are, the base class (DefaultHandler in this case) provides its own implementation of them for use by ProductsReader. However, if you provide your own implementations of the methods, they are used instead. In the preceding example, the method invoked would now be ProductsReader.startDocument(). This might do something totally different from DefaultHandler's implementation.

Actually, DefaultHandler is a very important class because it also provides default implementations of the three other core SAX interfaces: ErrorHandler, DTDHandler, and EntityResolver. Throughout this chapter, I extend the DefaultHandler class to leverage the functionalities from any of the existing SAX interfaces.

The DefaultHandler Class

The DefaultHandler class provides a default implementation for all the callback methods defined in the following interfaces:

- ContentHandler — The class implementing this interface receives notifications on basic document-related events such as the start and end of elements and character data.
- ErrorHandler — This interface provides the basic interface for SAX error handlers. The SAX application implements this interface to provide customized error handling.
- DTDHandler — The class implementing this interface receives notification of basic DTD-related events.
- EntityResolver — This interface provides a basic interface for resolving entities. The SAX application implements this interface to provide customized handling for external entities.

You can use only the DefaultHandler in your application and override the desired methods from the four handler interfaces. Some of the important methods of the DefaultHandler class are as follows:

- startDocument/endDocument — These are callback methods called by the parser whenever it encounters a start and end of a parsed document.
- startElement/endElement — These are callback methods called by the parser whenever it encounters a start and end of an element during parsing. The method receives the parameters that indicate the local and qualified name of the element.
- characters — This method receives notification of character data inside an element during parsing.
- processingInstruction — This method receives notification of a processing instruction during parsing.

Using the XMLReader Interface

The primary entry point to any SAX implementation is the XMLReader interface. This interface contains methods for the following:

- Controlling how the underlying XML parser operates (for example, validating versus non-validating)
- Enabling and disabling specific SAX features, such as namespace processing
- Registering object instances to receive XML parsing notifications (via the xxxHandler interfaces)
- Initiating the parsing process on a specific document URI or input source (via the `parse()` methods)

Before an application can use the `XMLReader` interface, it must first obtain a reference to an object that implements it. The decision about how to support the `XMLReader` interface is left up to the implementers of the particular SAX distribution. For instance, the Xerces package supplies a class called `org.apache.xerces.parsers.SAXParser` that implements the `XMLReader` interface. Any application that uses Xerces to provide SAX support can simply create a new instance of the `SAXParser` class and use it immediately.

The SAX specification does define a special helper class (from the org.xml.sax.helpers package) called `XMLReaderFactory` that is intended to act as a class factory for `XMLReader` instances. It has two static methods for creating a new `XMLReader` object instance:

- `createXMLReader()` — Allows you to create an `XMLReader` using the system defaults
- `createXMLReader(String className)` — Allows you to create an XMLReader from the supplied class name

Of course, both of these methods require that the class name of the class that supports the `XMLReader` interface be known in advance. Here is the code required to create the `XMLReader` using the second overload.

```
XMLReader reader =
  XMLReaderFactory.createXMLReader("org.apache.xerces.parsers.SAXParser");
```

In addition, you can obtain a reference to an `XMLReader` class instance by directly instantiating the `SAXParser` class from the Xerces package inside its constructor:

```
   XMLReader reader = (XMLReader)new org.apache.xerces.parsers.SAXParser();
```

Now that you have an `XMLReader` object instance to work with, you can register your class to receive XML parse callback notifications. The following code shows the skeleton implementation required for parsing an XML file.

```
import javax.xml.parsers.SAXParserFactory;
import javax.xml.parsers.SAXParser;
import org.xml.sax.*;
import org.xml.sax.helpers.*;
public class ProductsReader extends DefaultHandler
{
  public static void main(String[] args) throws Exception
```

```
    {
      System.out.println("Start of Products...");
      ProductsReader readerObj = new ProductsReader();
      readerObj.read(args[0]);
      //add processing here
    }

    public void read(String fileName) throws Exception
    {
      XMLReader reader = XMLReaderFactory.createXMLReader
        ("org.apache.xerces.parsers.SAXParser");
      reader.setContentHandler(this);
      reader.parse(fileName);
    }

    public void startDocument()
    {
      //add processing here
    }

    //add other event handlers
    //add other event handlers
  }
```

The previous code uses the `XMLReaderFactory.createXMLReader()` method to get a reference to the `XMLReader` object. After that, you invoke the `setContentHandler()` to register a content event handler. If the application does not register a content handler, all events raised by the SAX parser are ignored. In this case, you pass in the reference to the current context object that has the event handlers for processing the events raised by the SAX parser.

```
reader.setContentHandler(this);
```

When you invoke the `parse()` method, you pass in the name of the XML file to be parsed.

```
reader.parse(fileName);
```

As the XML file is parsed, the SAX parser raises events, such as `startDocument`, `endDocument`, and so on that will be discussed in the next section.

DefaultHandler Class

The `DefaultHandler` class, contained in the `org.xml.sax`.helpers package, is a helper class that is primarily used as the base class for SAX2 applications. It provides default implementations for all of the callbacks present in the SAX handler classes such as `EntityResolver`, `DTDHandler`, `ContentHandler`, and `ErrorHandler`. You can extend this class when you need to implement only part of an interface. The `DefaultHandler` class has a number of predefined methods, called callback methods that the SAX parser calls:

- `characters` — Called by the SAX parser for text nodes
- `endDocument` — Called by the SAX parser when it sees the end of the document
- `endElement` — Called by the SAX parser when it sees the closing tag of an element

- `startDocument`—Called by the SAX parser when it sees the start of the document
- `startElement`—Called by the SAX parser when it sees the opening tag of an element

All the required callback methods are already implemented in the `DefaultHandler` class, but they don't do anything. That means you have to implement only the methods you want to use, such as `startDocument()` to catch the beginning of the document or `endDocument()` to catch the end of the document, as described later in this chapter. The following table lists the significant methods of the `DefaultHandler` class.

Method	Description
`characters`	Handles text nodes
`endDocument`	Handles the end of the document
`endElement`	Handles the end of an element
`error`	Handles a recoverable parser error
`fatalError`	Reports a fatal parsing error
`ignorableWhitespace`	Handles ignorable whitespace (such as that used to indent a document) in element content
`notationDecl`	Handles a notation declaration
`processingInstruction`	Handles an XML processing instruction (such as a JSP directive)
`resolveEntity`	Resolves an external entity
`setDocumentLocator`	Sets a Locator object for document events
`skippedEntity`	Handles a skipped XML entity
`startDocument`	Handles the beginning of the document
`startElement`	Handles the start of an element
`startPrefixMapping`	Handles the start of a namespace mapping
`unparsedEntityDecl`	Handles an unparsed entity declaration
`warning`	Handles a parser warning

Before looking at an example of this, consider the XML document in Listing 13-1, which describes the attributes of a set of products.

Listing 13-1: A sample XML file

```
<?xml version="1.0" encoding="ISO-8859-1"?>
<Products>
  <Product>
    <ProductID>1</ProductID>
    <Name>Adjustable Race</Name>
```

```
      <ProductNumber>AR-5381</ProductNumber>
    </Product>
    <Product>
      <ProductID>2</ProductID>
      <Name>Bearing Ball</Name>
      <ProductNumber>BA-8327</ProductNumber>
    </Product>
    <Product>
      <ProductID>3</ProductID>
      <Name>BB Ball Bearing</Name>
      <ProductNumber>BE-2349</ProductNumber>
    </Product>
    <Product>
      <ProductID>4</ProductID>
      <Name>Headset Ball Bearings</Name>
      <ProductNumber>BE-2908</ProductNumber>
    </Product>
  </Products>
```

The root element of this XML document is `<Products>`, which contains an arbitrary number of `<Product>` elements. Each `<Product>` element, in turn, contains `<ProductID>`, `<Name>`, and `<ProductNumber>` elements.

Now that you took a brief look at the methods, I go into details on how to use them starting with handling the start and end of the document.

The startDocument() and endDocument() Methods

To handle the start and end of a document, you use the `startDocument()` and `endDocument()` methods. These signify the beginning and end of events. Here is an example of using of these methods:

```
public void startDocument() throws SAXException
{
  try{
    System.out.println("Start Document");
  }
  catch(Exception e){
    throw new SAXException(e.toString());
  }
}


public void endDocument() throws SAXException
{
  try{
    System.out.println("End Document");
  }
  catch(Exception e){
    throw new SAXException(e.toString());
  }
}
```

The processingInstruction() Method

You can handle processing instructions by using the `processingInstruction()` method, which is called automatically when the SAX parser finds a processing instruction. The target of the processing instruction is passed to this method, as is the data for the processing instruction, which means you can handle processing instructions as follows:

```
public void processingInstruction(String target, String data) throws SAXException
{
  try{
    System.out.println("PI(Target= " + target + " Data= " + data + ")");
  }
  catch(Exception e){
    throw new SAXException(e.toString());
  }
}
```

Namespace Callbacks

This distinguishes between the namespace of an element, signified by an element prefix and an associated namespace URI, and the local name of an element. Two methods include a namespace, `startPrefixMapping()` and `endPrefixMapping()`. These are invoked when a parser reaches the beginning and end of a prefix mapping, respectively. A prefix mapping is declared using the `xmlns` attribute for a namespace and the namespace declaration typically occurs as part of the root element.

The namespace URI is supplied as an argument to the `startPrefixMapping()` method. This URI is added to `namespaceMappings` object within the body of the `startPrefixMapping()` method. The following code shows an example of the `startPrefixMapping()` method:

```
public void startPrefixMapping (String prefix, String uri) throws SAXException
{
  try{
    namespaceMappings.put(uri,prefix);
  }
  catch(Exception e){
    throw new SAXException(e.toString());
  }
}
```

The mapping ends when the element that declared the mapping is closed, which triggers the `end PrefixMapping()` method.

The `endPrefixMapping()` method, in the following code, removes the mappings when they are no longer available:

```
public void endPrefixMapping(String prefix) throws SAXException
{
  try{
    for (Iterator i=namespaceMappings.keySet().iterator();i.hasNext();)
    {
      String uri=(String) i.next();
      String thisPrefix=(String)namespaceMappings.get(uri);
      if(prefix.equals(thisPrefix)){
        namespaceMappings.remove(uri);
```

```
            break;
          }
        }
      }
      catch(Exception e){
        throw new SAXException(e.toString());
      }
    }
```

The startElement() and endElement() Methods

To handle the start of an element, use the `startElement()` method. This method is passed the namespace URI of the element, the local (unqualified) name of the element, the qualified name of the element, and the element's attributes (as an `Attributes` object).

```
public void startElement(String uri,String localName,String qName,Attributes atts)
  throws SAXException
{
  try
  {
    //Display Start Element name
    System.out.println("Start Element : " + qName);
    //Determine prefix of a namespace
    String prefix=(String)namespaceMappings.get(uri);
    if(prefix.equals(""))
    {
      prefix="[None]";
    }
    System.out.println("  Element(Namespace:Prefix = '" + prefix +
      "' URI = '" + uri + "')");
    //Process Attribute of each element
    for(int i=0;i<atts.getLength();i++)
    {
      System.out.println("    Attribute(name: '" + atts.getLocalName(i) + "',
        value = '" + atts.getValue(i) + "')");
      String attURI=atts.getURI(i);
      String attPrefix="";
      if(attURI.length() >0 )
      {
        attPrefix=(String)namespaceMappings.get(uri);
      }
      if(attPrefix.equals(""))
      {
        attPrefix="[None]";
      }
      if(attURI.equals(""))
      {
        attURI="[None]";
      }
      System.out.println("     Attribute(Namespace:Prefix = '" + attPrefix +
        "' URI = '" + attURI + "')");
    }
  }
  catch(Exception e)
  {
```

```
      throw new SAXException(e.toString());
    }
  }
```

In the `startElement()` callback method, the parameters are the names of the elements and an `org.xml.sax.Attributes` instance. This helper class contains references to the attributes within an element and allows easy iteration through the attributes of the element. To refer to an attribute, use its index or name. Helper methods, such as `getURI(int index)` and `getLocalName(int index)`, provide additional namespace information about an attribute.

In addition to the `startElement()` method, which is called when the SAX parser sees the beginning of an element, you can also implement the `endElement()` method to handle an element's closing tag. The end of the element displays the complete name of the closed element.

```
public void endElement(String uri,String localName,String elemName)
  throws SAXException
{
  try
  {
    System.out.println("End Element : \"" + elemName + "\"");
  }
  catch(Exception e){
    throw new SAXException(e.toString());
  }
}
```

Element Data Callback

This contains additional elements, textual data, or a combination of the two. In XML, the textual data within elements is sent to an application through the `characters()` callback. This method is passed an array of characters, the location in that array where the text for the current text node starts, and the length of the text in the text node.

```
public void characters(char[] ch,int start,int length) throws SAXException
{
  try
  {
    String s=new String(ch,start,length);
    if((s.trim()).equals("")){}
    else{
      System.out.println("Character Encountered :\"" + s.trim() + "\"");
    }
  }
  catch(Exception e){
    throw new SAXException(e.toString());
  }
}
```

The ignorableWhitespace() Method

The `ignorableWhitespace()` method reports white space, often by using the `characters()` method. This occurs when no DTD or XML schema is referenced. The constraints in a DTD or a schema specify that no character data is allowed between the start of one element and the subsequent start of another element. If a reference to a DTD is removed, the white spaces will trigger the `characters()` callback instead of the `ignorableWhitespace()` callback.

```
public void ignorableWhitespace(char[] ch, int start, int length)
  throws SAXException
{
  try
  {
    //Ignores whitespaces or call the characters method
    //characters(ch, start, length);
  }
  catch(Exception e){
    throw new SAXException(e.toString());
  }
}
```

By default, the SAX parser also calls `ignorableWhitespace` when it finds whitespace text nodes, such as whitespace used for indentation. If you want to handle that text like any other text, you can simply pass it on to the characters method you just implemented.

The skippedEntity() Method

The `skippedEntity()` method is issued when an entity is skipped by a nonvalidating parser. The callback gives the name of the entity that can be displayed as the output. The following code shows the empty body of the `skippedEntity()` method:

```
public void skippedEntity(java.lang.String name) throws SAXException
{
  try{
    System.out.println("Entity : " + name);
  }
  catch(Exception e){
    throw new SAXException(e.toString());
  }
}
```

The setDocumentLocator() Method

The `setDocumentLocator()` method sets an `org.xml.sax.Locator` for use in any other SAX event associated with the application. The `Locator` class has several methods, such as `getLineNumber()` and `getColumnNumber()`, which return the current location of the parsing process within an XML file. The following code gives the definition of the `setDocumentLocator()` method:

```
public void setDocumentLocator(Locator locator)
{
  //Locator object can be saved for later use in application
  this.locator=locator;
}
```

Handling Errors and Warnings

The ErrorHandler interface is another callback interface provided by SAX that can be implemented by an application to receive information about parsing problems as they occur. The ErrorHandler interface specifies three notification functions to be implemented by a client application:

Method	Description
warning	Called for abnormal events that are not errors or fatal errors
error	Called when the XML parser detects a recoverable error. For instance, a validating parser would throw this error when a well-formed XML document violates the structural rules provided in its DTD
fatalError	Called when a non-recoverable error is recognized. Non-recoverable errors are generally violations of XML well-formedness rules (for instance, forgetting to terminate an element open tag)

The process for registering to receive notifications on the ErrorHandler interface is similar to that for registering the DefaultHandler interface. First, an object that implements the ErrorHandler interface must be instantiated. The new instance is then passed to the XMLReader.setErrorHandler() method so that the SAX parser is aware of its existence.

As you can see, SAX makes it easy to handle warnings and errors. You can implement the warning() method to handle warnings, the error() method to handle errors, and the fatalError() method to handle errors that the SAX parser considers fatal enough to make it stop processing. Before you handle the errors, you must invoke the setErrorHandler() method as follows:

```
public void read(String fileName) throws Exception
{
  XMLReader reader = XMLReaderFactory.createXMLReader
    ("org.apache.xerces.parsers.SAXParser");
  reader.setContentHandler(this);
  reader.setErrorHandler(this);
  reader.parse(fileName);
}
```

Once you have invoked the setErrorHandler() method, you must implement one of the notification methods as follows:

```
public void warning(SAXParseException e) throws SAXException
{
  System.out.println("Warning: ");
  displayErrorInfo(e);
}

public void error(SAXParseException e) throws SAXException
{
  System.out.println("Error: ");
  displayErrorInfo(e);
}

public void fatalError(SAXParseException e) throws SAXException
```

```
{
  System.out.println("Fatal error: ");
  displayErrorInfo(e);
}

private void displayErrorInfo(SAXParseException e)
{
  System.out.println("   Public ID: " + e.getPublicId());
  System.out.println("   System ID: " + e.getSystemId());
  System.out.println("   Line number: " + e.getLineNumber());
  System.out.println("   Column number: " + e.getColumnNumber());
  System.out.println("   Message: " + e.getMessage());
}
```

The `displayErrorInfo()` helper method displays the details of the exception through the various methods of the `SAXParseException` object.

Searching in an XML File

You can search for a value in an XML file using the methods that the `DefaultHandler` and `XMLReader` interfaces provide. Listing 13-2 shows the `ProductsSearch.java` application that searches for a specific value in the specified XML file. First, you extend the `DefaultHandler` class through the ProductsSearch class. The `startDocument()` method contains statements that prompt the end user to enter the product number. The `characters()` method contains statements that display information such as the product id, name, and product number for the matching product in the console.

Listing 13-2: Searching in an XML file

```
import java.io.*;
import javax.xml.parsers.SAXParserFactory;
import javax.xml.parsers.SAXParser;
import org.xml.sax.*;
import org.xml.sax.helpers.*;

public class ProductsSearch extends DefaultHandler
{
  String key = null;
  String currentTagName = null;
  String productNumber = null;
  String productID = null;
  String name= null;
  int flag = 0;

  public static void main(String[] args) throws Exception
  {
    System.out.println("Start of Products...");
    ProductsSearch readerObj = new ProductsSearch();
    readerObj.read(args[0]);
  }

  public void read(String fileName) throws Exception
  {
```

(continued)

Listing 13-2 *(continued)*

```
      XMLReader reader =
        XMLReaderFactory.createXMLReader("org.apache.xerces.parsers.SAXParser");
      reader.setContentHandler(this);
      reader.parse(fileName);
    }

    public void startDocument() throws SAXException
    {
      System.out.println("Start document");
      InputStreamReader istream = new InputStreamReader(System.in);
      BufferedReader bufRead = new BufferedReader(istream);
      System.out.print("Enter the Product Number:");
      try
      {
        key = bufRead.readLine();
      }
      catch (IOException e){ }
      if (key.length() == 0)
      {
        System.out.println("No Product Number is entered");
        System.exit(0);
      }
  }

    public void endDocument() throws SAXException
    {
      if (flag == 0)
        System.out.println("No matching entry found...");
      System.out.println("End document");
    }

    public void startElement(String uri, String name, String qName, Attributes atts)
    {
      currentTagName = qName;
    }

    public void endElement(String uri, String name, String qName)
    {}

    public void characters(char ch[], int start, int length)
    {
      String value = new String(ch, start, length);
      if (productID  == null && currentTagName.equals("ProductID"))
      {
        productID = value;
      }
      if (name == null && currentTagName.equals("Name"))
      {
        name = value;
      }
      if (currentTagName.equals("ProductNumber"))
```

```
        {
          if (key.equals(value))
          {
            System.out.println("*******");
            System.out.println("Product ID:" + productID);
            System.out.println("Product Name:" + name);
            System.out.println("Product Number:" + key);
            System.out.println("*******");
            flag = 1;
          }
        }
        if (currentTagName.equals("Product"))
        {
          productID = null;
          name = null;
          productNumber = null;
        }
      }
    }
```

In the previous code, you set the name of the current element in a private variable named `currentTagName`, which is used later inside the `characters()` method.

You actually compare the entered product number with the `<ProductNumber>` elements in the `Products.xml` file in the `characters()` method. Note that the sequence of the elements contained in the `<Product>` element is very important to enable the matching code to generate the desired results. To get the desired search output based on the product number, you need to ensure that the `<ProductNumber>` element is the last element inside each of the `<Product>` elements in the `Products.xml` file.

Figure 13-2 shows the console window that prompts the user to enter the product number to be searched.

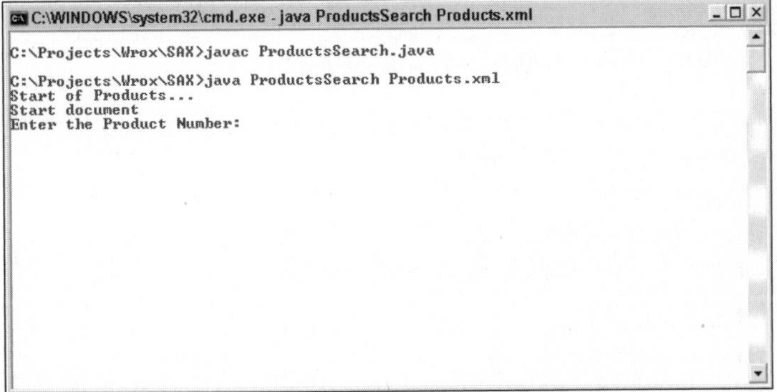

Figure 13-2

In this case, I entered the product number `BE-2908`. The output is shown in Figure 13-3.

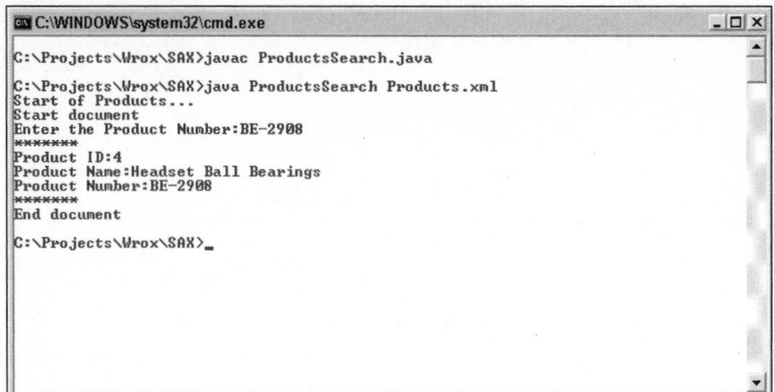

Figure 13-3

The previous figure shows the details of the product that has the product number `BE-2908`.

Writing XML Contents Using SAX

When compared to DOM, writing an XML document using SAX isn't straightforward because of its sequential processing nature. To accomplish this, you need to manually insert the right XML element at the right location. To insert an element, you use the following:

- Use the `startElement()` method to insert the element's start tag
- Use the `characters()` method to insert the text content of the element
- Use the `endElement()` to insert the element's end tag

Listing 13-3 shows the code required to add a new element named `<Discount>` as a child element to each of the `<Product>` elements.

Listing 13-3: Writing XML contents using SAX

```
import java.io.*;
import javax.xml.parsers.SAXParserFactory;
import javax.xml.parsers.SAXParser;
import org.xml.sax.*;
import org.xml.sax.helpers.*;
public class ProductsWriting extends DefaultHandler
{
  static int numberOfLines = 0;
  static String indentation = "";
  static String text[] = new String[1000];

  public static void main(String[] args) throws Exception
  {
    System.out.println("Start of Products...");
    ProductsWriting readerObj = new ProductsWriting();
    readerObj.read(args[0]);
    try
```

```
    {
      FileWriter writer = new FileWriter("Products_New.xml");
      for (int index = 0; index < numberOfLines; index++)
      {
        writer.write(text[index].toCharArray());
        writer.write('\n');
      }
      writer.close();
    }
    catch (Exception e)
    {
      e.printStackTrace(System.err);
    }
  }

  public void read(String fileName) throws Exception
  {
    XMLReader reader = XMLReaderFactory.createXMLReader
      ("org.apache.xerces.parsers.SAXParser");
    reader.setContentHandler(this);
    reader.setErrorHandler(this);
    reader.parse(fileName);
  }

  public void startDocument()
  {
    text[numberOfLines] = indentation;
    text[numberOfLines] += "<?xml version=\"1.0\" encoding=\""+
      "UTF-8" + "\"?>";
    numberOfLines++;
  }

  public void processingInstruction(String target, String data)
  {
    text[numberOfLines] = indentation;
    text[numberOfLines] += "<?";
    text[numberOfLines] += target;
    if (data != null && data.length() > 0)
    {
      text[numberOfLines] += ' ';
      text[numberOfLines] += data;
    }
    text[numberOfLines] += "?>";
    numberOfLines++;
  }

  public void startElement(String uri, String localName,
    String qualifiedName, Attributes attributes)
  {
    text[numberOfLines] = indentation;
    indentation += "    ";
    text[numberOfLines] += '<';
    text[numberOfLines] += qualifiedName;
    if (attributes != null)
    {
```

(continued)

Listing 13-3 *(continued)*

```
        int numberAttributes = attributes.getLength();
        for (int loopIndex = 0; loopIndex < numberAttributes; loopIndex++)
        {
          text[numberOfLines] += ' ';
          text[numberOfLines] += attributes.getQName(loopIndex);
          text[numberOfLines] += "=\"";
          text[numberOfLines] += attributes.getValue(loopIndex);
          text[numberOfLines] += '"';
        }
      }
      text[numberOfLines] += '>';
      numberOfLines++;
    }

    public void characters(char characters[], int start, int length)
    {
      String characterData = (new String(characters, start, length)).trim();
      if(characterData.indexOf("\n") < 0 && characterData.length() > 0)
      {
        text[numberOfLines] = indentation;
        text[numberOfLines] += characterData;
        numberOfLines++;
      }
    }

    public void endElement(String uri, String localName, String qualifiedName)
    {
      indentation = indentation.substring(0, indentation.length() - 4);
      text[numberOfLines] = indentation;
      text[numberOfLines] += "</";
      text[numberOfLines] += qualifiedName;
      text[numberOfLines] += '>';
      numberOfLines++;
      if (qualifiedName.equals("ProductNumber"))
      {
        startElement("", "Discount", "Discount", null);
        characters("10%".toCharArray(), 0, "10%".length());
        endElement("", "Discount", "Discount");
      }
    }

    public void warning(SAXParseException exception)
    {
      System.err.println("Warning: " + exception.getMessage());
    }

    public void error(SAXParseException exception)
    {
      System.err.println("Error: " + exception.getMessage());
    }

    public void fatalError(SAXParseException exception)
```

```
    {
      System.err.println("Fatal error: " + exception.getMessage());
    }
  }
```

In the preceding lines of code, the `endElement()` method is where the majority of the work occurs including identifying the location where the `<Discount>` element needs to be inserted. Since you want to insert the `<Discount>` element right next to `<ProductNumber>`, you check for the presence of `ProductNumber` as the name of the element. After you figure out the exact location, you insert the new element through the combination of `startElement()`, `characters()`, and `endElement()`, methods.

Figure 13-4 shows the contents of the `Products_New.xml` file when viewed in the browser.

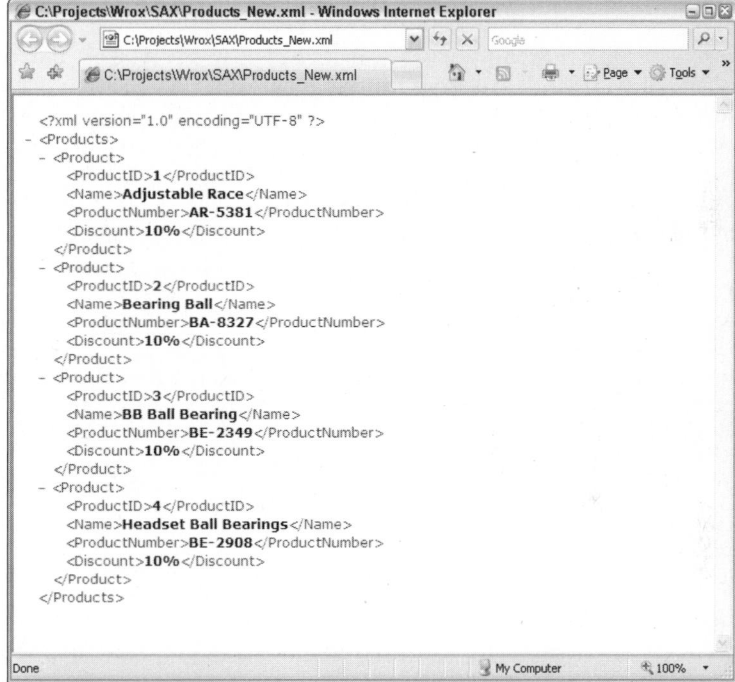

Figure 13-4

XML Validation Using SAX

By default, the Xerces SAX parser is non-validating. This means that even if a document contains a DTD, the parser doesn't check the document contents to make sure that they conform to its rules. Enabling validation requires the use of the `XMLReader.setFeature()` method. SAX offers this method to provide different sets of features in an extensible way. You invoke the `XMLReader.setFeature()` method to enable the schema validation behavior.

```
public void read(String xmlFileName, String xsdSchemaName) throws Exception
{
  String validationFeature = "http://xml.org/sax/features/validation";
  String schemaFeature = "http://apache.org/xml/features/validation/schema";
  XMLReader reader =
    XMLReaderFactory.createXMLReader("org.apache.xerces.parsers.SAXParser");
  reader.setProperty
    ("http://apache.org/xml/properties/schema/external-noNamespaceSchemaLocation",
    xsdSchemaName);
  reader.setFeature(validationFeature, true);
  reader.setFeature(schemaFeature, true);
  reader.setContentHandler(this);
  reader.setErrorHandler(this);
  reader.parse(xmlFileName);
}
```

To set a feature on either `org.apache.xerces.parsers.SAXParser`, you use the method `setFeature(String, boolean)`. To query a feature, you use the SAX `getFeature(String)` method. You can see the complete listing of features that you can set at `http://xerces.apache.org/xerces-j/features.html`.

Before looking at the complete code, consider the XSD file in Listing 13-4, which is named `Products.xsd` and is used for validating the `Products.xml` file.

Listing 13-4: Products.xsd file

```
<?xml version="1.0" encoding="utf-8"?>
<xs:schema attributeFormDefault="unqualified" elementFormDefault="qualified"
  xmlns:xs="http://www.w3.org/2001/XMLSchema">
  <xs:element name="Products">
    <xs:complexType>
      <xs:sequence>
        <xs:element maxOccurs="unbounded" name="Product">
          <xs:complexType>
            <xs:sequence>
              <xs:element name="ProductID" type="xs:unsignedByte" />
              <xs:element name="Name" type="xs:string" />
              <xs:element name="ProductNumber" type="xs:string" />
            </xs:sequence>
          </xs:complexType>
        </xs:element>
      </xs:sequence>
    </xs:complexType>
  </xs:element>
</xs:schema>
```

Listing 13-5 shows the complete code required to validate the Products.xml file with the Products.xsd file. To catch the events raised by the parser, you override the methods of the ErrorHandler interface such as `warning()`, `error()`, `fatalError()`.

Listing 13-5: Validating an XML file with XSD Schema

```
import javax.xml.parsers.SAXParserFactory;
import javax.xml.parsers.SAXParser;
```

```
import org.xml.sax.*;
import org.xml.sax.helpers.*;
public class ProductsSchemaValidation extends DefaultHandler
{
  public static void main(String[] args) throws Exception
  {
    System.out.println("Start of Products...");
    ProductsSchemaValidation readerObj = new ProductsSchemaValidation();
    readerObj.read(args[0], args[1]);
  }

  public void read(String xmlFileName, String xsdSchemaName) throws Exception
  {
    String validationFeature = "http://xml.org/sax/features/validation";
    String schemaFeature = "http://apache.org/xml/features/validation/schema";
    XMLReader reader =
      XMLReaderFactory.createXMLReader("org.apache.xerces.parsers.SAXParser");
    reader.setProperty
     ("http://apache.org/xml/properties/schema/external-noNamespaceSchemaLocation",
      xsdSchemaName);
    reader.setFeature(validationFeature, true);
    reader.setFeature(schemaFeature, true);
    reader.setContentHandler(this);
    reader.setErrorHandler(this);
    reader.parse(xmlFileName);
  }

  public void startDocument() throws SAXException
  {
    System.out.println("Start of the document");
  }

  public void endDocument() throws SAXException
  {
    System.out.println("End of the document");
  }

  public void startElement(String uri, String name, String qName, Attributes atts)
  {
    if ("".equals(uri))
      System.out.println("Start element: " + qName);
    else
      System.out.println("Start element: {" + uri + "}" + name);
  }

  public void endElement(String uri, String name, String qName)
  {
    if ("".equals(uri))
      System.out.println("End element: " + qName);
    else
      System.out.println("End element:   {" + uri + "}" + name);
  }

  public void warning(SAXParseException e) throws SAXException
```

(continued)

Listing 13-5 *(continued)*

```
    {
      System.out.println("Warning: ");
      displayErrorInfo(e);
    }

    public void error(SAXParseException e) throws SAXException
    {
      System.out.println("Error: ");
      displayErrorInfo(e);
    }

    public void fatalError(SAXParseException e) throws SAXException
    {
      System.out.println("Fatal error: ");
      displayErrorInfo(e);
    }

    private void displayErrorInfo(SAXParseException e)
    {
      System.out.println("   Public ID: " + e.getPublicId());
      System.out.println("   System ID: " + e.getSystemId());
      System.out.println("   Line number: " + e.getLineNumber());
      System.out.println("   Column number: " + e.getColumnNumber());
      System.out.println("   Message: " + e.getMessage());
    }
  }
```

If you run the program passing in the Products.xml and Products.xsd as command line arguments, it will work fine, since the XML file is compliant with the XSD file. However, if you change the root element of the `Products.xsd file` from `Products` to `Products1` and rerun the program, you will see the output shown in Figure 13-5.

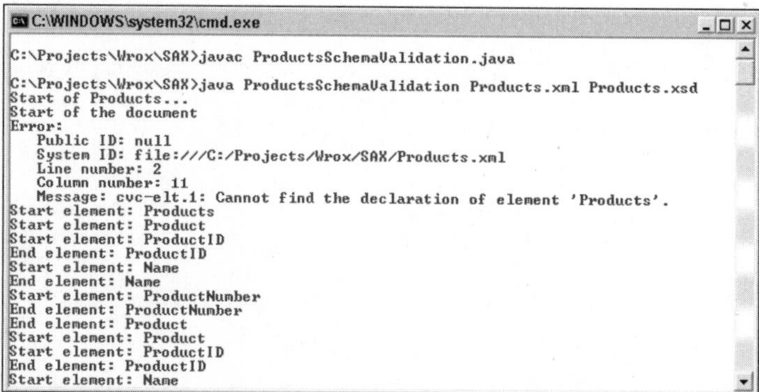

Figure 13-5

The output shown in Figure 13-5 clearly proves that validation works fine and because of that the validation violation is reported by the parser.

Advantages and Disadvantages of SAX

Being event based, SAX offers several benefits to its user. At the same time, it also comes with certain disadvantages. Both sides of this coin are presented in this section.

SAX presents four particularly compelling advantages, each of which is presented here:

- SAX generates the events continually while processing a document. The document analysis can begin immediately, and you need not wait to do the analysis until the entire document is processed. This is equivalent to streaming media, where the media contents are rendered immediately and you need not wait until the entire media is read.
- SAX examines the document contents as it reads the document and immediately generates events on the processing application. Thus, it need not store the data that it has already processed. This puts fewer constraints on the application memory requirements.
- Because the document's contents are not stored in memory, it is easier to process very large documents as compared to other processing techniques such as DOM. Other techniques that require the entire document to be read into memory before processing can sometimes place severe constraints on system resources.
- The application need not process the entire document if it is interested in a certain criterion. After that criterion is met, further processing can be abandoned. Other techniques require the document to be parsed fully before any processing can be done.

SAX does come with certain disadvantages:

- SAX is similar to a one-pass compiler. After it reads part of the document, it cannot navigate backward to reread the data it has processed, unless you start all over again.
- Because SAX does not store the data that it has processed, you cannot modify this data and store it back in the original document.
- Because SAX does not create an in-memory document structure, you cannot build an XML document by using a SAX parser.

Summary

SAX is an excellent API for analyzing and extracting information from large XML documents without incurring the time and space overheads associated with the DOM. In this chapter, you learned how to use SAX to catch events passed to you by a parser, by implementing a known SAX interface, DefaultHandler. You used this to extract some simple information from an XML document. You also looked at error handling, and found out how to implement sophisticated intelligent parsing, and reporting errors. In addition you looked at how to search, update and validate an XML document using SAX.

14

Ajax

Ajax is a new term for a relatively old technique. Ajax is an acronym coined by Jesse James Garrett of Adaptive Path, standing for *A*synchronous *J*avaScript *A*nd XML. Although it is an acronym, people tend to use it without capitalizing each letter.

The core idea behind Ajax is the use of JavaScript within the browser to transfer and process XML from the server. The *asynchronous* refers to the fact that this transfer occurs on a background thread, allowing the client to continue to interact with the Web page. Asynchronous download, combined with the fact that only relatively small amounts of XML are transferred, reduces the need for round tripping the entire browser page. This creates a Web application that seems more performant.

This chapter will look at Ajax, and how to add it to your applications. It looks at the main components of any Ajax solution — JavaScript and the `XMLHttpRequest` object. While not a complete reference on either, the chapter provides basic information on these two topics. In addition, several popular Ajax libraries are highlighted.

The history of Ajax begins around the time of Internet Explorer 5.0, when the `XMLHttpRequest` object (Microsoft.XMLHTTP) was added to the objects accessible from client-side script.

JavaScript is a scripting language created by Netscape to provide dynamic functionality in Navigator. Originally, it was called LiveScript, but it was later renamed to associate it with Java, which was becoming popular at the time. JavaScript is a loosely-typed, *scripting* language. That is, it is not compiled. The code is executed through an interpreter (built into most modern browsers). In addition, data types are limited, and variables can change type based on the data stored. For syntax, it takes many cues from the C/C++ family of programming languages. Therefore, you should expect to end each line with a semicolon and use braces ({}) to identify code blocks. JavaScript is a standard (ECMA), so you may hear it referred to as ECMAScript.

Adding JavaScript to a Web Page

You add JavaScript to a Web page in one of two ways: using a script tag, or by adding short blocks of JavaScript directly to events associated with tags on a Web page.

The script tag is the more common form of adding JavaScript to a Web page. The JavaScript can be included within the tag, or the code may be contained within a separate file referenced by the tag.

```
//script block
<script language="javascript" type="text/javascript">
    alert("Hello world");
</script>

//script in external file
<script type="text/javascript" src="/script/somefile.js"></script>
```

Note that the code identifies the type as `text/javascript`, which is the official MIME type for JavaScript content. You could also use this form when including the JavaScript as a script block, but this is less common.

One problem with adding JavaScript is dealing with browsers that do not accept JavaScript. This is much less of a problem now that most modern browsers can process JavaScript, but a few clients out there are still using Mosaic or Lynx, so it's good technique to comment out (using the HTML comment markers `<!--` and `-->`) the JavaScript to prevent it from appearing in the text of the page on these browsers. Note that this is not necessary if you are including the JavaScript via an external file.

```
// Commenting out JavaScript for older browsers
<script language="javascript">
<!--
    //your JavaScript here
//-->
</script>
```

Notice that the last line in the JavaScript block actually has both the JavaScript (`//`) and HTML (`-->`) comments. This is to prevent the JavaScript interpreter from processing the HTML comment.

Functions in JavaScript

You can write your JavaScript in one of two ways: Either use simple statements, or write one or more functions. Loose statements are executed when the script is loaded, whereas functions are called, typically in response to button clicks or other events. Writing functions reveals one of the first major differences between JavaScript and other C-derived languages.

```
function sayHello() {
    alert("Hello World");
}
```

Notice that the function does not require the addition of the return type. The `alert()` method is a standard JavaScript method that produces a message box containing the text passed in (see Figure 14-1).

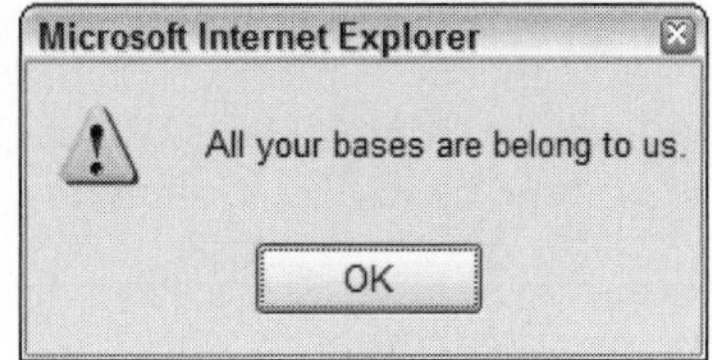

Figure 14-1

In addition to allowing you to create your own functions, JavaScript includes some standard methods you can use in your scripts. Three of these are useful when interacting with users: alert, confirm, and prompt. Alert displays a message box (see Figure 14-1) containing text you specify.

Confirm is similar, but provides OK/Cancel buttons (see Figure 14-2). This enables you to ask simple questions from your scripts.

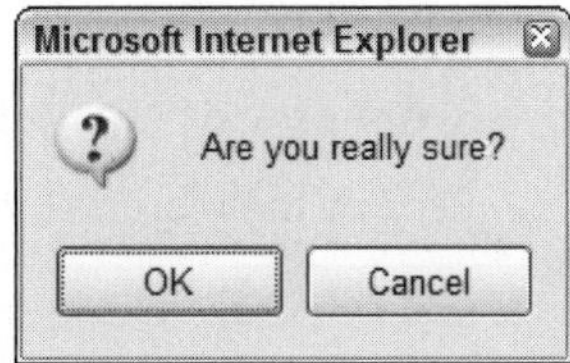

Figure 14-2

Finally, prompt provides a text field, enabling user input (see Figure 14-3).

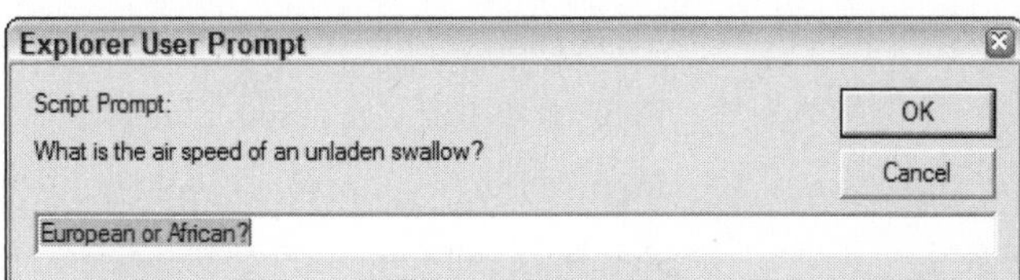

Figure 14-3

Because JavaScript is text that is interpreted at runtime, it enables different methods of processing than do C# or Java. This is evident in the `eval` method: This method takes a block of JavaScript and executes it. It is possible to build up a string containing code based on user input and to execute it on demand. This is a powerful (albeit ripe for misuse) feature that you might want to use in the right circumstances.

Data Types in JavaScript

You are not required to identify the types you use when creating variables. However, it is still a good idea to declare the variables before use. This is done with the `var` keyword.

```
var someVariable, someOtherVariable, aThirdVariable;
```

The previous statement declares three variables that can hold any data type.

Although JavaScript is a loosely-typed language, it is also object-oriented. You can create your own objects (see Listing 14-1) or make use of the built-in objects. Four of the most common built-in objects in JavaScript are the String, Date, Boolean, and Math objects. These objects provide a number of useful static and instance methods. Some of these methods are shown in the following table.

Object	Method/Property	Description
String	`length`	Returns the length of the string
String	`indexOf`	Returns the position of the desired substring (0 based)
String	`lastIndexOf`	Returns the last position of the desired substring (0 based)
String	`substring`	Extracts a substring from a string and returns it
String	`toLowerCase`	Converts the string to lowercase and returns it
String	`toUpperCase`	Converts the string to all uppercase and returns it
Date	`getDate`	Returns the day of the month (1-31)
Date	`getDay`	Returns the day of the week (0-6)
Date	`getMonth`	Returns the month of the year (0-11)
Date	`getYear`	Returns the year
Date	`getFullYear`	Returns the four-digit year
Date	`getTime`	Returns the number of milliseconds since 0:00 GMT January 1, 1970
Date	`parse`	Converts a string that looks like a date to a date object
Date	`set*`	Set versions of the above get* methods for Date
Math	`min`	Returns the smaller of two numbers
Math	`max`	Returns the larger of two numbers
Math	`random`	Returns a random number between 0 and 1
Math	`PI`	Returns the value of pi

Listing 14-1: Creating objects in JavaScript

```
function Person(first, last) {
  this.first=first;
  this.last = last;
}
Person.prototype.toString = function() {
  return this.first + " " + this.last;
}

var p = new Person("John", "Doe");
alert(p.toString());
```

Language Features of JavaScript

The commonly used looping and conditional blocks of C/C++ are also available in JavaScript (see Listing 14-2). These include `if..else`, `switch`, `for` loops, `while` loops, and `do..while` loops.

Listing 14-2: Conditional and loop blocks in JavaScript

```
function isPrime(value) {
    var result = true;

    for(i=2; i<=Math.sqrt(value);i++) {
        if(Math.round(value/i) == value/i) {
            result = false;
            break;
        }
    }
    return result;
}

function getGreeting() {
    var currentTime = new Date();
    var result;
    switch(currentTime.getDay()) {
        case 5:
            result = "TGIF";
            break;
        case 6:
            result = "Saturday";
            break;
        case 0:
            result = "Sunday";
            break;
        default:
            result = "Just another work day";
            break;
    }

    return result;
}
```

In addition to the expected `for` loops, JavaScript also supports `for..in` loops. These enable you to iterate over an array or other object that contains a collection of items (see Listing 14-3). The iterator value is set to the index of the item during each loop through the `for..in` loop.

As you can see from the highlighted code in Listing 5-3, objects are stored as arrays using the property names as keys. You can also iterate over all the properties of an object using the `for..in` syntax.

Listing 14-3: Using the for..in loop

```
var people = new Array();
people[0] = new Person("John", "Bull");
people[1] = new Person("Jane", "Doe");

for(var person in people) {
```

(continued)

Listing 14-3 *(continued)*

```
    alert(people[person].toString());

    for(var prop in people[1]) {
      alert(prop + ": " + people[person][prop]);
    }
  }
```

One area of code that always needs attention is error handling. JavaScript supports the `try..catch` form of exception handling. You wrap the section that might cause an exception in a `try` block. If an exception occurs, the flow of the code moves to the `catch` block (see Listing 14-4). There you can handle the error or provide more information to the user as appropriate.

Listing 14-4: Try..catch blocks in JavaScript

```
try {
  var answer=prompt('Enter an equation', '6*8');
  alert(eval(answer));
} catch(e) {
  alert('Could not evaluate that equation');
}
```

In Listing 14-4, the `eval` method is used to execute the equation entered. If you use the default equation, this should result in a message box showing `48`. However, if you enter an equation with an error or with code that cannot be evaluated, the message box shows the error message.

XMLHttpRequest

`XMLHttpRequest` is an object first added to Internet Explorer 5.0 (as the Microsoft.XMLHTTP ActiveX object), and it is core to Ajax. `XMLHttpRequest` is used to make HTTP queries from a Web page, generally retrieving XML. You can tell that a lot of thought went into the name of the object. The developers of Mozilla (Netscape Navigator and Firefox) obviously recognized the value of this object, and so they added it to those browsers as well. Recently, the World Wide Web Consortium (W3C) started an effort to standardize the functionality of this object as well. In addition, Microsoft has announced that this object would also be available in Internet Explorer 7.

The `XMLHttpRequest` object can make either synchronous or asynchronous requests. Synchronous requests are like any other normal application call: You make the request, and when the data is returned, your code moves on to the next line. This is simple, but remember that a Web request is being made here—a request that may take some time to complete. If the request is made over a slow link, it could take a lot of time, and your Web page will be not responsive during this time. That is, the user will be staring at a page that doesn't allow him to enter any more data or click buttons until the code has run. Therefore, you should always make asynchronous requests when working with the `XMLHttpRequest` object. With an asynchronous request, when you make the call to download the data, it happens on a background thread, allowing the code to continue and the main Web page to keep dealing with the user. Obviously, if your code is happening on another thread, some code must process the result when the `XMLHttpRequest` call is completed. You identify this function when you make the call to download data.

Creating an `XMLHttpRequest` object is slightly more complex than it should be. It is implemented as one of two ActiveX objects in Internet Explorer (depending on the version), but it is a natively available object in Firefox, Opera, and Safari. You must create a method to create this object. Many people write a routine that uses the User Agent to decide how to create it (see Listing 14-5). However, methods similar to this are inherently fragile. New browser versions come out, browser agent strings change, or browsers can be set to impersonate other browsers. Instead, you should use code similar to Listing 14-6 to create the `XMLHttpRequest` object.

Listing 14-5: Creating an XMLHttpRequest object the wrong way

```
var browser=navigator.userAgent.toLowerCase();
var majorVersion = parseInt(navigator.appVersion);
var minorVersion = parseFloat(navigator.appVersion);
var isIE = ((browser.indexOf("msie") != -1) && (browser.indexOf("opera") == -1));
var isMozilla == (browser.indexOf('mozilla')!=-1);
var req;

if(isIE) {
  if(majorVersion = 7) {
    req = new XMLHttpRequest();
  } else if (majorVersion > 6) {
    req = new ActiveXObject("Microsoft.XMLHTTP");
  } else if (majorVersion > 4) {
    req = new ActiveXObject("Msxml2.XMLHTTP");
  }
} else {
  req = new XMLHttpRequest();
}
```

Listing 14-6: Creating an XMLHttpRequest object the correct cross browser way

```
function getReqObj(){
    var result=null;

    if( window.XMLHttpRequest ) {
        result = new XMLHttpRequest();
    } else {
        try {
            result=new ActiveXObject("Msxml2.XMLHTTP");
        } catch(e){
            result=null;
        }
    }

    return result;
}
```

Because exceptions require some time to process, it is best to attempt to avoid them if possible. Therefore, you make a check to `window.XMLHttpRequest`. If the object is available (the code is running within Firefox, Opera, Safari, or Internet Explorer 7), the remainder of the code and any possible exceptions are avoided. Next, the code attempts to create the `Msxml2.XMLHTTP` ActiveX object. This is the current version of the object, and the name is the version agnostic request.

The good news is that with Internet Explorer 7.0, the `XMLHttpRequest` object will become a native object. This means that, at some point (when you want to forget about supporting Internet Explorer 5-6), the preceding code can be simplified to:

```
var req = new XMLHttpRequest();
```

After you have created an instance of the `XMLHttpRequest` object, review the methods and properties it makes available. (See the following table.)

Method	Description
`abort`	Cancels the current request. Because most of your requests should be asynchronous, this method is a useful method for canceling long-running requests.
`getAllResponseHeaders`	Returns a string containing all response headers for the request. Each name:value pair is separated by CR/LF. Note that this value can only be retrieved if the `readyState` (see the following) is 3 or 4. With other states, it should always be null.
`getResponseHeader`	Returns a string containing the value for a requested response header. Note that this value can only be retrieved if the `readyState` (see the following) is 3 or 4. With other states it should always be null.
`open`	Opens a new request, preparing for a call. If an existing request is in progress, this is reset. A number of overridden versions of this method are available (see text).
`send`	Sends the request to the URI assigned in the call to open and prepares the object to receive the returned data. The `send` method takes a single parameter, which can be either a block of text or XML document.
`setRequestHeader`	Adds a custom header to the request. This can be useful for authentication (providing a magic token in the headers of the request), or to modify the behavior of the called service (the header could provide additional parameters for the call or change the identification of the User Agent).
`addEventListener`	Available only with the Mozilla version of the object. Associates an event listener to the object. This can be used to override the behavior of the object or to limit other code from accessing the results of the call.
`dispatchEvent`	Available only with the Mozilla version of the object. Triggers an event that other code may respond to. This can be useful to bubble the events normally if the `addEventListener` captures all returned events.
`openRequest`	Available only with the Mozilla version of the object.

Method	Description
`overrideMimeType`	Available only with the Mozilla version of the object.
`removeEventListener`	Available only with the Mozilla version of the object. Disconnects an event listener connected via `addEventListener`.

In addition to the methods listed in the preceding table, some of the implementation provides a number of properties that can assist you when you are working with the `XMLHttpRequest` object. The following table shows those properties:

Property	Type	Description
`onreadystatechange`	function/ event listener	`OnReadyStateChange` provides a hook for you to add a routine to provide handling for asynchronous requests. The method associated with the event is called when the asynchronous method completes.
`readyState`	enumeration	A read-only value describing the current status of the request. This must be one of the following values: ❑ 0 (Uninitialized): The object has been created, but no `open` method has been called yet. ❑ 1 (Open): `Open` has been called, but not send. ❑ 2 (Sent): `Send` has been called, but no data has been received yet. ❑ 3 (Receiving): Data is partially available. ❑ 4 (Loaded): All data and headers have been received. This is the state most code needs before processing the result.
`responseBody`	byte[]	Only available when using the Internet Explorer version of the object. This property contains the raw content of the response as an array of bytes. It can be helpful when you are using the `XMLHttpRequest` object to return non-text data such as a media file.
`responseText`	string	Returns the body of the response as a string. If the `readyState` is 3, this may not be the complete returned content.

Table continued on following page

Property	Type	Description
responseXML	XML Document	Returns the body of the response as an XML document. Note that this property is really only useful if you are returning XML from the server. If the readyState is 3, the entire document is not yet available, and the document may not be well formed.
status	int (short)	The returned HTTP status code for the request. For example, 200 means a successful request. Note that this is only available if the readyState is 3 or 4.
statusText	string	The returned HTTP status code text for the request. For example, if the status is 500, the statusText property can provide more information on the reason for the error. Note that this is only available if the readyState is 3 or 4.

As you can see from the preceding table, the actual target of the request is set using the open method. The simplest version of this method takes two parameters: method and URI. Method is the HTTP method (typically GET or POST) that the request will use. URI represents the target of the call.

```
var req = GetReqObj();
req.open("GET", "someendpoint.php");
```

In addition to these two parameters, three other parameters are optional:

- **async** — A Boolean value that determines whether the request should be made asynchronously or synchronously. Generally, you want to make your XMLHttpRequest calls asynchronously. Synchronous calls prevent the user from interacting with the rest of your Web page, thereby reducing the overall value of using Ajax. Listing 14-7 shows the basic process when making asynchronous requests.
- **user** — A string identifying the credentials that should be used when processing the request.
- **password** — A string identifying the password for the user passed in the previous parameter.

Listing 14-7: Pseudocode for XMLHttpRequest calls

```
//Create the XMLHttpRequest object
var req = getReqObj();
//set the URL and method and configure call as asynchronous
req.open("GET", "http://someendpoint", true);
//set the function that will respond when the call is complete
req.onreadystatechange = MyFunc;
req.send(data);
```

The `onreadystatechange` property identifies a function that is called whenever the status of the call changes. Therefore, you must determine the overall status of the request in this function. That is, you should determine if the status is 3 (loading) or 4 (complete) before processing any data. Statuses 1 and 2 may be useful to report to your users, however.

The DOM

The last of the major components that make Ajax work is the DOM or Document Object Model. The DOM is the weak link in the process — not because it fails, but because each browser uses slightly different objects to make up the DOM. This means the methods and properties exposed by those objects are different as well. Adding Ajax functionality that works cross browser usually means making one of four choices:

- Ignore the browsers you're not interested in. Many developers target a particular browser and version, usually based on their Web traffic. This solution makes most sense for internal applications that allow you to control the client software. However, for public-facing applications, this choice can have a nasty side effect of alienating potential or current customers. Although supporting only one (or a few) browsers reduces your test needs and increases the chances of success, it also sends the message to users of other browsers, "We don't care about you."
  You should at least strive to provide for users of other browsers. People using your selected browser(s) can have the Ajax experience, whereas other users receive a Web page that requires round-tripping (but is still functional).
- Use only a common subset of functionality that is exposed by all target browsers. By limiting your use of browser-specific features, you increase your chances of success at the expense of adding functionality that may be easier or richer in some browsers. This is the safe option. It does require a fair bit of discipline, however, because you must remember what features work across all browsers and limit yourself to use only those features. Usually the restrictions make this option quite difficult.
- Degrade appropriately. This is one of the more common solutions. It can also be described as, "Keep trying until something works." Using this technique, you first try the most common solution, perhaps attempting to retrieve a particular object. If that fails, you then try the next most common solution. This continues until you either run out of possibilities or you run out of options. For example, a common need is to locate a field in a form based on its ID. Internet Explorer exposes a document.all collection, which is non-standard. Other browsers may or may not support this collection, although current versions of Opera and Firefox (but not Safari) do. If you use a feature such as this, you should check the returned object. If it is null, you should use another method to retrieve the object.
- Have your framework treat all browsers the same. This is a curious option, but it can be quite appealing. The code wrapping the DOM can expose methods making all selected browsers look the same. That is, you create DOM methods where the underlying browser doesn't support them. Microsoft's AJAX Extensions uses this technique to provide all browsers with a DOM similar to Internet Explorer.

The end result, however, is that unless you choose to ignore certain browsers, you should test in a variety of browsers and, preferably, in multiple versions of those browsers before releasing any Ajax application. If you have an existing Web application, you can use your Web server log files to identify which browsers are commonly used for your site to determine which ones you should support.

Objects in the DOM

The following table shows some of the major objects provided by the DOM. As the name DOM implies, the document is the only object described by the W3C standard on the DOM; however, the other objects are provided by most modern browsers.

Object	Description
`document`	Contains methods and properties related to the document (or page) currently open in the browser. You use this object to retrieve the elements of the page.
`location`	Contains methods and properties related to the current URL. The main use here is to send the user to another page, but you can also extract portions of the URL as needed.
`navigator`	Contains methods and properties related to the browser. This information can be useful in querying the capabilities of the browser.
`window`	Contains methods and properties related to the browser window. This is typically used to resize the browser or change the visibility of elements such as status bars.

Of the objects in the previous table, the most important or, at least, the most frequently used is the document object. This object enables you to retrieve, process, or change the contents of the current document. The total number of collections and child objects of this object are staggering: You could literally write a book about them (there so are many). A certain subset of these child objects and methods are used most frequently by developers. These objects and methods enable navigation through the items on the page, allow changes to their properties, and permit the addition of new items. Just a few of the child objects of document are listed in the following table.

Object	Discussion
`all[]`	This child collection is only available with Internet Explorer and is not part of the W3C standard. Still, if all your clients are using Internet Explorer, it can be a handy shortcut. This collection contains all the important items for a Web page: images, links, stylesheets, and forms. The `all[]` collection can be used to retrieve individual items or iterate over the collection, looking for items to process.
`forms[]`	A collection of all the forms on the Web page. This is typically used to locate form elements, such as text fields, for processing.
`documentElement`	The root node of the document. This node is used to further drill down into the document structure.
`body`	Represents the content of the body of the document.

The following table discusses some of the important methods of document.

Method	Discussion
`createElement(tagName)`	Creates a new element and adds it to the current document.
`getElementById`	This is the main method you work with when using Ajax. This method returns the selected element.
`getElementsByTagName`	This common method returns all elements of a given type. Typically, this is used as the input into a loop for further processing.
`write`	Writes content to the current document. Note that this content does not appear if the user looks at the source of the page. Therefore, many sites use this method to write information that should remain somewhat protected. This is not a foolproof method, however, because any use of a HTTP monitoring application or JavaScript debugger shows the content.

In addition to the objects listed in the preceding table and the document object, a number of other objects exist in the DOM. They relate to the objects that normally occur in HTML forms and on pages. For example, a button object relates to the buttons you can add to HTML forms.

Events in the DOM

In addition to supporting methods and properties, many objects in the DOM also support events. You can connect your code to react to these events using the syntax:

```
object.eventHandlerName = JavaScript_function;
```

Event handlers in the DOM can be identified by names that start with `on`. Using them is similar to the `onrequestchange` you saw earlier with the `XMLHttpRequest` object. You assign a JavaScript function to the event handler. When the event occurs, the code in your method is executed. For example, use the following code to trap the `button.onClick` event that occurs when the button is clicked:

```
button.onclick=someJSFunction;
```

A possible problem with the preceding syntax is that it removes any previous handler that may have been set on the `onclick` event handler. Because of this, you should use the syntax:

```
// Internet Explorer
button.attachEvent('click', someJSFunction);

// DOM compliant browsers
Button.addEventListener('click', someJSFunction, false);
```

The previous form adds the function as a handler for the `onclick` method, but does this in addition to any existing handlers. This means that your trapping the event does not break any other code that may already be listening to the event.

Putting It All Together

Now that you've seen the three constituent parts of Ajax, it's time to connect them to add some simple Ajax functionality to a Web page. To explore how JavaScript, `XMLHttpRequest` and the DOM interact, I'll create an application to look up contact phone numbers (see Figure 14-4). The solution uses a simple HTML page as a client (with JavaScript) and an ASP.NET HTTP handler as the server. It should be possible to convert this server-side component to any other server-side Web technology.

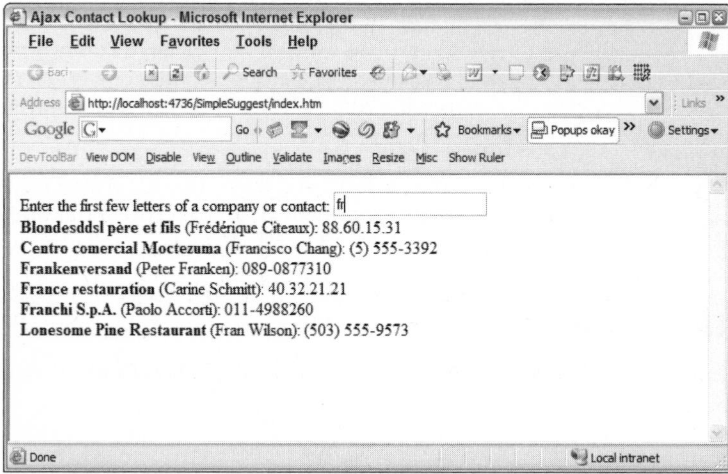

Figure 14-4

The server-side of the solution queries an XML file to retrieve any company or contact that matches the currently entered data, returning up to 10 items that match. Part of the XML file queried is shown in Listing 14-8.

Listing 14-8: Contact information file

```
<customers>
  <customer id="ALFKI">
    <company>Alfreds Futterkiste</company>
    <contact>Maria Anders</contact>
    <phone>030-0074321</phone>
  </customer>
  <customer id="ANATR">
    <company>Ana Trujillo Emparedados y helados</company>
    <contact>Ana Trujillo</contact>
```

```
    <phone>(5) 555-4729</phone>
  </customer>
  <customer id="ANTON">
    <company>Antonio Moreno Taquería</company>
    <contact>Antonio Moreno</contact>
    <phone>(5) 555-3932</phone>
  </customer>
  <customer id="AROUT">
    <company>Around the Horn</company>
    <contact>Thomas Hardy</contact>
    <phone>(171) 555-7788</phone>
  </customer>
  <customer id="BERGS">
    <company>Berglunds snabbköp</company>
    <contact>Christina Berglund</contact>
    <phone>0921-12 34 65</phone>
  </customer>
  <customer id="BLAUS">
    <company>Blauer See Delikatessen</company>
    <contact>Hanna Moos</contact>
    <phone>0621-08460</phone>
  </customer>
...
</customers>
```

In order to retrieve both companies and contacts that match the query, the XPath combines the two queries, using the XPath function `starts-with` to identify desired nodes. As `starts-with` is case-sensitive, it is also necessary to use the `translate` function to perform the search in a case-insensitive way. The full XPath query for any company or customer that starts with `fr` is:

```
customers/customer[starts-with(translate(company,
        'ABCDEFGHIJKLMNOPQRSTUVWXYZ', 'abcdefghijklmnopqrstuvwxyz'), 'fr')
        or starts-with(translate(contact, 'ABCDEFGHIJKLMNOPQRSTUVWXYZ',
        'abcdefghijklmnopqrstuvwxyz'), 'fr')]
```

The `translate` function converts a string to another string based on a mapping. The syntax looks like the following:

```
translate(string-to-convert, mapping-string, result-string)
```

Whenever the code encounters one of the characters in the mapping-string in the string-to-convert, it is replaced with the character at the same position in the result-string. Therefore, using the code shown previously, any alphabetic character is replaced with the lowercase equivalent. Note that this only includes basic letters. Any accented characters should be added to both the second and third parameters in the call to translate. When you do this, make certain that the lowercase character in the third parameter is in the same position as the character in the second parameter. Two `starts-with` clauses are needed because one searches for items matching the company name, whereas the second includes items matching on the contact name. Listing 14-9 shows the output of the preceding query when applied to the contact list. Notice how the query (`fr`) matches the start of both companies and contacts.

Listing 14-9: Selected contacts

```
<customers>
  <customer id="BLONP">
    <company>Blondesddsl père et fils</company>
    <contact>Frédérique Citeaux</contact>
    <phone>88.60.15.31</phone>
  </customer>
  <customer id="CENTC">
    <company>Centro comercial Moctezuma</company>
    <contact>Francisco Chang</contact>
    <phone>(5) 555-3392</phone>
  </customer>
  <customer id="FRANK">
    <company>Frankenversand</company>
    <contact>Peter Franken</contact>
    <phone>089-0877310</phone>
  </customer>
  <customer id="FRANR">
    <company>France restauration</company>
    <contact>Carine Schmitt</contact>
    <phone>40.32.21.21</phone>
  </customer>
  <customer id="FRANS">
    <company>Franchi S.p.A.</company>
    <contact>Paolo Accorti</contact>
    <phone>011-4988260</phone>
  </customer>
  <customer id="LONEP">
    <company>Lonesome Pine Restaurant</company>
    <contact>Fran Wilson</contact>
    <phone>(503) 555-9573</phone>
  </customer>
</customers>
```

Listing 14-10 shows the server-side code that performs the query on the XML and returns the resulting XML. Although it is written for ASP.NET, it could be written in PHP, JSP, ColdFusion, or other server-side code.

Listing 14-10: A server-side query

```
<%@ WebHandler Language="C#" Class="CustomerLookup" %>

using System;
using System.Web;
using System.Web.Caching;
using System.Globalization;
using System.Xml;
using System.Xml.XPath;
using System.Text;
```

```
using System.IO;

public class CustomerLookup : IHttpHandler {

    private const String dataFile = "app_data/contactList.xml";
    private const String cacheKey = "contactList";
    private const Int32 maxResults = 10;

    private HttpContext myContext = null;
    private String xQuery = @"customers/customer[starts-with(translate(company,
        'ABCDEFGHIJKLMNOPQRSTUVWXYZ', 'abcdefghijklmnopqrstuvwxyz'), '{0}')
        or starts-with(translate(contact, 'ABCDEFGHIJKLMNOPQRSTUVWXYZ',
        'abcdefghijklmnopqrstuvwxyz'), '{0}')]";

    public void ProcessRequest (HttpContext context) {
        myContext = context;
        String result = String.Empty;
        String query = context.Request["q"];
        if (!String.IsNullOrEmpty(query)) {
            result = GetContactList(query, maxResults);
        }

        context.Response.ContentType = "text/xml";
        context.Response.Write(result);
    }

    public bool IsReusable {
        get {
            return false;
        }
    }

    private String GetContactList(String root, Int32 count) {
        StringBuilder result = new StringBuilder();
        String filename = myContext.Server.MapPath(dataFile);
        String data = LoadAndCache(filename);
        String query = String.Empty;
        XmlDocument doc = new XmlDocument();
        XPathNavigator nav = null;
        int i = 0;

        doc.LoadXml(data);
        query = String.Format(xQuery, root);
        nav = doc.CreateNavigator();

        XPathNodeIterator iter = nav.Select(query);
        XmlWriterSettings settings = new XmlWriterSettings();
        settings.Encoding = Encoding.UTF8;
        settings.OmitXmlDeclaration = true;

        using (XmlWriter w = XmlWriter.Create(result, settings)) {
```

(continued)

Listing 14-10 *(continued)*

```
            w.WriteStartDocument();
            w.WriteStartElement("result");
            while (iter.MoveNext()) {
                w.WriteNode(iter.Current,false);
                i++;
                if (i == count) {
                    break;
                }
            }
            w.WriteEndElement();
            w.WriteEndDocument();
        }

        return result.ToString();
    }

    private String LoadAndCache(String filename) {
        String result = String.Empty;

        result = myContext.Cache[cacheKey] as String;
        if (String.IsNullOrEmpty(result)) {
            using (StreamReader reader = File.OpenText(filename)) {
                result = reader.ReadToEnd();
            }
            myContext.Cache.Add(cacheKey, result,
                new CacheDependency(filename),
                Cache.NoAbsoluteExpiration, Cache.NoSlidingExpiration,
                CacheItemPriority.Normal, null);
        }

        return result;
    }
}
```

The bulk of the code for an ASP.NET HTTP handler is in the `ProcessRequest` method. This is called for each request, and the developer is responsible for writing the output. This output is generated by the `GetContactList` method. The `GetContactList` method first loads the XML file (and caches the data for performance); then it executes the query using the current data typed by the user. The resulting data is wrapped in a `<result>` element (see Figure 14-5).

The interface for the client application is intentionally simple and would likely be part of a more complex page. The idea is that the user can type in the search field, and the server-side code is called by JavaScript on that page. Listing 14-11 shows the code for the client page and JavaScript.

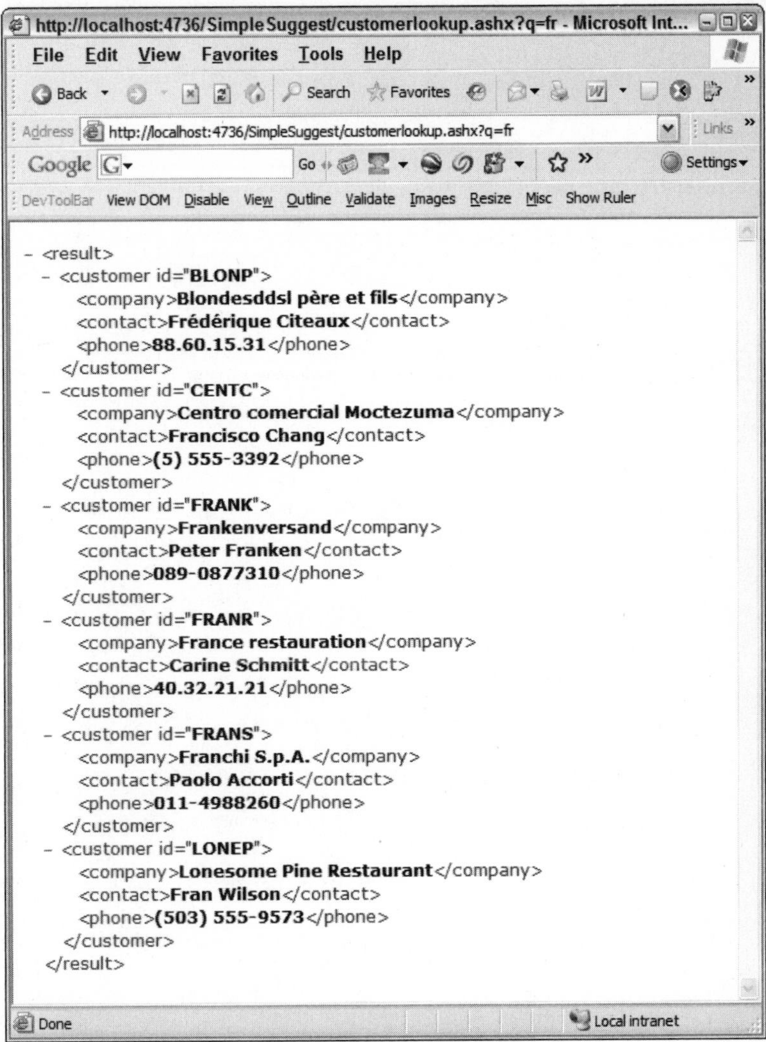

Figure 14-5

Listing 14-11: Client-side code

```
<!DOCTYPE html PUBLIC "-//W3C//DTD XHTML 1.0 Transitional//EN"
    "http://www.w3.org/TR/xhtml1/DTD/xhtml1-transitional.dtd">
<html xmlns="http://www.w3.org/1999/xhtml" >
<head>
    <title>Ajax Contact Lookup</title>
    <script type="text/javascript" src="script/getReqObj.js"></script>
<script language="javascript" type="text/javascript">
```

(continued)

Listing 14-11 *(continued)*

```
<!--

    var req;

    function getContacts() {
        var q = document.getElementById("q").value;
        if("" != q) {
            req = getReqObj();

            if(null != req) {
                req.open("GET", "customerlookup.ashx?q=" + q, true);
                req.onreadystatechange = Process;
                document.getElementById("contactList").innerHTML = "Working";
                req.send(null);
            }
        } else {
            document.getElementById("contactList").innerHTML = "";
        }
    }

    function Process() {
        if(4 == req.readyState) {
            if(200 == req.status) {
                //success
                var data = req.responseXML;
                var result = "";
                var node = data.documentElement.firstChild;

                while(null != node) {
                    var child = node.firstChild;
                    result += "<b>" + child.firstChild.nodeValue + "</b> ";
                    child = child.nextSibling;
                    result += "(" + child.firstChild.nodeValue + "): ";
                    child = child.nextSibling;
                    result += child.firstChild.nodeValue;
                    result += "<br />";
                    node = node.nextSibling;
                }

                document.getElementById("contactList").innerHTML = result;
            } else {
                document.getElementById("contactList").innerHTML = req.statusText;
            }
        }
    }
// -->
</script>
```

```
</head>
<body>
<form>
    Enter the first few letters of a company or contact:
    <input id="q" type="text" onkeyup="getContacts();"/><br />
    <div id="contactList"></div>

</form>
</body>
</html>
```

The other data format: JSON

When processing the returned XML from an `XMLHttpRequest` call, you are essentially left to your own devices and the DOMDocument. Although this is not really a handicap (only a bit of extra friction and a few lines of code), you should know that many developers avoid XML entirely. Instead, these developers use JSON (JavaScript Object Notation, pronounced *Jason*) as a data-exchange format. JSON is a serialized form of JavaScript objects. For example, the data returned from a server-side component similar to the `CustomerLookup` component, but returned using JSON instead of XML looks like the following:

```
{ "customers": { "customer": [
    {"id": "DRACD",
      "company": "Drachenblut Delikatessen",
      "contact": "Sven Ottlieb",
      "phone": "0241-039123"},
    {"id": "DUMON",
      "company": "Du monde entier",
      "contact": "Janine Labrune",
      "phone": "40.67.88.88"},
    {"id": "FISSA",
      "company": "FISSA Fabrica Inter. Salchichas S.A.",
      "contact": "Diego Roel",
      "phone": "(91) 555 94 44"},
    {"id": "LACOR",
      "company": "La corne d'abondance",
      "contact": "Daniel Tonini",
      "phone": "30.59.84.10"},
    {"id": "SPECD",
      "company": "Spécialités du monde",
      "contact": "Dominique Perrier",
      "phone": "(1) 47.55.60.10"},
    {"id": "WANDK",
      "company": "Die Wandernde Kuh",
      "contact": "Rita Müller",
      "phone": "0711-020361"}
  ]
}};
```

The JavaScript file containing the cross-browser code for retrieving the `XMLHttpRequest` object is included, and this method is used to create the object. The first step is to identify the URL and HTTP method that will be used for the page. Notice that the `true` parameter is included to ensure the request is made asynchronously. If this parameter is not included, the request could cause the page to stop responding to the user while the query is being completed. Next, because this call is done asynchronously, you must set the `onreadystatechange` to point to the method that responds when the state of the request changes. Finally, the `send` method sends the request to the desired URL.

Each time the state of the request changes, the method pointed to by the `onreadystatechange` property is called. Therefore, you must determine if you are currently at a state where data has been retrieved (`reqObj.readyState == 4`) before you continue. Similarly, you should examine the `status` property to ensure that the request succeeded (`reqObj.status == 200`). At this point, you can use the various response properties (`responseXML`, `responseText`, and `responseBody` in Internet Explorer) to retrieve the data for further processing. Using the `responseXML` provides you with a `DOMDocument` object that can be used to process the data, using the familiar `firstChild`, `nextSibling`, and `nodeValue` properties. In addition, if cross-browser support is not required, you use the methods of the DOMDocument specific to your implementation (for example, the `childNodes` collection). The resulting data is pushed into the `contactList div` element (see Figure 14-6). Notice that the list of items changes as you type in the text box — without the flicker that might occur if a page round-trip were required to update the list.

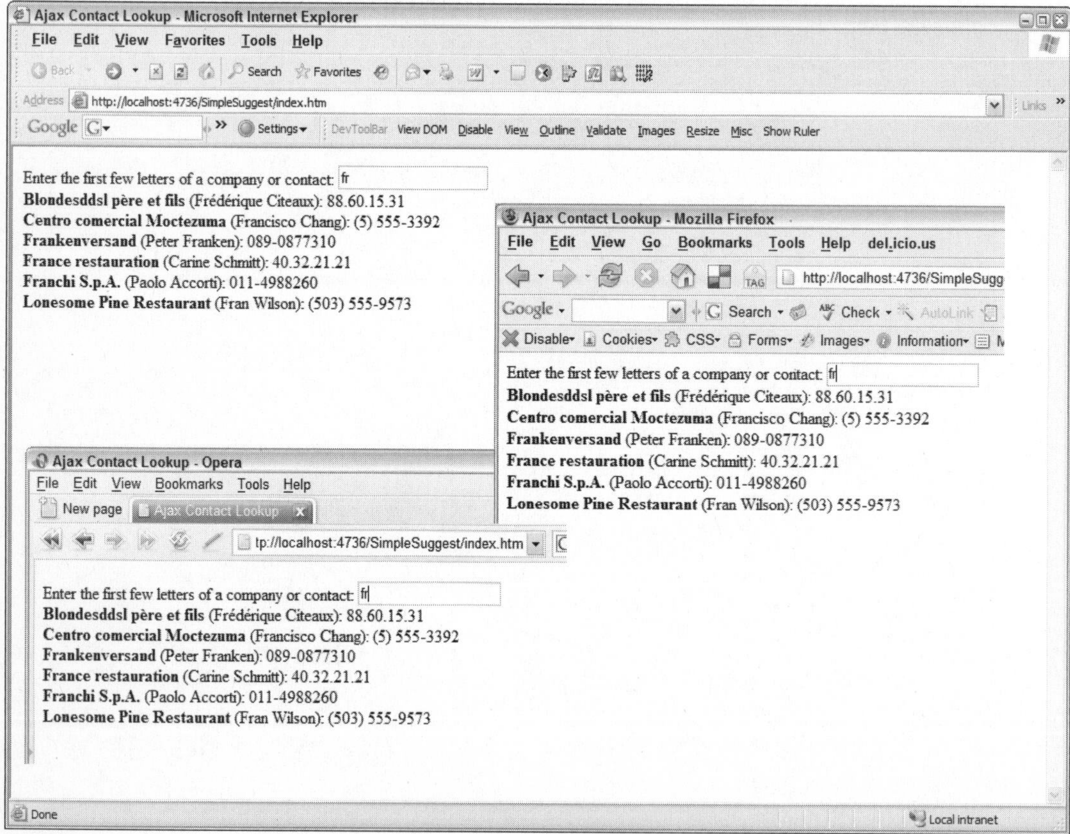

Figure 14-6

As you can see, the syntax is basically name:value pairs. However, the braces ({}) create an object or hash, whereas the brackets ([]) create an array. In the preceding example, an object is created that consists of an array of customer hashtables. Each hashtable is populated with the properties of each customer.

The benefit of JSON data is that you can use the JavaScript `eval` method to convert it back into JavaScript hashtables and arrays. This converts the code required for dumping the returned data into the target div to the following:

```
function getContacts() {
    var result = "";
    for(var i = 0; i < jsonObj.customer.length; i++) {
        result += "<b>" + jsonObj.customer[i].company + "</b> ";
        result += "(" + jsonObj.customer[i].contact + "): ";
        result += jsonObj.customer[i].phone + "<br />";
    }
    document.getElementById("contactList").innerHTML = result;
}
```

Now that you know that JSON exists and what it looks like, we can go back to ignoring it. This is a book on XML, after all.

Ajax Libraries

New Ajax libraries have been appearing almost daily since the term was coined. Most are targeted at one of the main Web development frameworks (JSP, ASP.NET, or PHP), but many others work well with any platform or even simple HTML pages. The libraries themselves range from simple libraries that make communication between client and server easier to libraries of widgets that use JavaScript to support editing. The benefit of using one of these libraries is that it can reduce the amount of code you must write to add Ajax support to your applications.

Mashups

With the number of services growing by the week, many developers are finding that communicating with one service just isn't enough. They are beginning to combine the data and features of multiple services, creating new services: for example, looking up store locations via a geocoding service and then plotting them on a map. These combination services have become known as *mashups*. Notice that I use mashup (without a hyphen), whereas a similar trend of combining music from multiple artists to create a new song is usually termed *mash-up*. Many authors use a single term for both or interchange the two words, however. Still, try to use the correct word the next time you're discussing your latest efforts at a cocktail party. With so many services providing online data or APIs, the number of potential mashups is rapidly becoming unlimited. The Web site Programmable Web (`programmableweb.com`) is a great resource to find useful services, as well as to locate known and potential combinations.

Some of the more notable Ajax libraries include the following: (Note, this list is hardly comprehensive. Dozens of other Ajax libraries are out there for all platforms, with more appearing every week)

- **Microsoft AJAX Library, ASP.NET 2.0 AJAX Extensions, and the ASP.NET AJAX Control Toolkit** — A collection of ASP.NET Ajax tools from Microsoft, formerly known as the "Atlas" project. This library works well with Internet Explorer, Firefox, and Safari. Although the extensions and control library are intended for use with Microsoft's ASP.NET, the core AJAX library can be used with other frameworks as well. Microsoft has demonstrated how it works with PHP pages.
- **Prototype** — Not an Ajax library per se, but a very useful tool for any JavaScript work. Prototype makes creating cross-browser JavaScript easier, and it adds a number of methods for doing common code procedures. Many other libraries, such as Script.aculo.us and moo, are written on top of the functionality provided by Prototype.
- **Script.aculo.us** — Not a standalone library, Script.aculo.us works with Prototype to create a number of common user interface Ajax functions. It is built into Ruby on Rails, and provides much of the Ajax functionality of that framework. Although it is part of Ruby on Rails, it works well with any Web application framework or even with simple HTML pages. In addition, the functionality it provides works cross-browser.
- **AjaxPro** — This is an Ajax library that targets Microsoft's ASP.NET framework, written by Michael Schwarz, and available in open source or commercial versions. It provides a quick method of adding Ajax support to Web applications. It works with ASP.NET 1.1 as well as 2.0.
- **Echo2** — A library of Ajax-enabled controls to add to Java-based Web applications. Works well across all common browsers.
- **Symfony** — A PHP5-based Ajax framework. Works well cross-browser. In addition to Ajax, it also includes support for templating and other Web application functionality.

Although a direct comparison of Ajax libraries is impractical and unfair because each developer's needs for platform and functionality vary, it is worth looking at how these libraries can be used to add common Ajax methods to your Web pages.

Using the Microsoft AJAX Library to Add Ajax Functionality

Microsoft AJAX is a set of technologies that extend ASP.NET 2.0 to add Ajax functionality. In addition to the library, Microsoft provides the AJAX Extensions that extends the HTML elements emitted by ASP.NET and the AJAX Control Toolkit that adds Ajax support to specific controls.

At the core of the Microsoft ASP.NET AJAX Extensions is the ScriptManager control. This outputs the appropriate JavaScript to the client, and provides cross-browser support. In addition, a number of additional controls, such as the UpdatePanel, are available.

Figure 14-7 shows an example of using Microsoft AJAX to create a simple RSS reader. When the drop-down list is changed, the list box is populated with the items from the selected RSS feed. Selecting items from the list causes the contents of the RSS item to be displayed on the right-hand side of the form. Because of the use of Ajax, the updates do not require any postbacks.

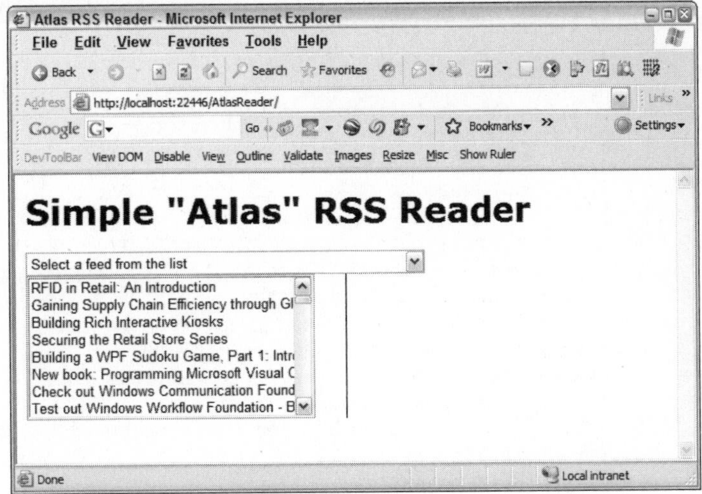

Figure 14-7

Listing 14-12 shows the source code for the RSS reader application. It uses the AJAX Extensions, and the RSSToolkit library written by Dmitry Robson of the ASP.NET team (see Resources).

Listing 14-12: The RSS Reader with the Microsoft AJAX Extensions

```
<%@ Page Language="C#" %>

<%@ Register Assembly="RssToolkit" Namespace="RssToolkit" TagPrefix="rss" %>
<!DOCTYPE html PUBLIC "-//W3C//DTD XHTML 1.0 Transitional//EN"
  "http://www.w3.org/TR/xhtml1/DTD/xhtml1-transitional.dtd">

<script runat="server">

    protected void FeedList_SelectedIndexChanged(object sender, EventArgs e) {
        this.RssData.Url = this.FeedList.SelectedValue;
        this.PostList.DataBind();
    }

    protected void PostList_SelectedIndexChanged(object sender, EventArgs e) {
        this.RssData.Url = this.FeedList.SelectedValue;
        this.ItemBody.Text =
this.RssData.Channel.Items[this.PostList.SelectedIndex].Attributes["description"];
    }

</script>

<html xmlns="http://www.w3.org/1999/xhtml">
<head runat="server">
    <title>Simple RSS Reader using Microsoft ASP.NET 2.0 AJAX Extensions</title>
    <link href="styles.css" rel="stylesheet" type="text/css" />

</head>
```

(continued)

Listing 14-12 *(continued)*

```
<body>
    <h1>Simple RSS Reader using Microsoft ASP.NET 2.0 AJAX Extensions</h1>
    <form id="form1" runat="server">
    <asp:ScriptManager ID="sm" runat="server" EnablePartialRendering="true" />

        <div>
            <asp:DropDownList runat="server" ID="FeedList"
                OnSelectedIndexChanged="FeedList_SelectedIndexChanged"
                Width="380px" AutoPostBack="true" EnableViewState="false">
                <asp:ListItem Text="Select a feed from the list" Value="" />
                <asp:ListItem Text="MSDN: XML"
                  Value="http://msdn.microsoft.com/xml/rss.xml" />
                <asp:ListItem Text="'Atlas' Forum"
                  Value="http://forums.asp.net/rss.aspx?ForumID=1007&amp;Mode=0" />
            </asp:DropDownList><br />
            <div class="leftContent">
                <asp:UpdatePanel runat="server" ID="ListPanel">
                    <ContentTemplate>
                        <asp:ListBox runat="server" ID="PostList"
                            DataSourceID="RssData" DataTextField="title"
                            AutoPostBack="true"
                            OnSelectedIndexChanged="PostList_SelectedIndexChanged"
                            Rows="8"
                            CssClass="leftContent" Width="274px"
                            EnableViewState="false">
                        </asp:ListBox>
                    </ContentTemplate>
                    <Triggers>
                    <asp:AsyncPostBackTrigger ControlID="FeedList"
                       EventName="SelectedIndexChanged" />
                    </Triggers>
                </asp:UpdatePanel>

            </div>
            <div class="rightContent">
                <asp:UpdatePanel runat="server"
                                 UpdateMode="Conditional"
                                 ID="ItemPanel">
                    <ContentTemplate>
                        <asp:Label ID="ItemBody" runat="server" />
                    </ContentTemplate>
                    <Triggers>
                        <asp:AsyncPostBackTrigger ControlID="PostList"
                           EventName="SelectedIndexChanged" />
                    </Triggers>
                </asp:UpdatePanel>
                <br />
                <br />
                <rss:RssDataSource ID="RssData" runat="server"
                  Url="http://msdn.microsoft.com/rss.xml" />
            </div>
        </div>
```

```
    </form>
</body>
</html>
```

The first step in using the AJAX Extensions is to load the ScriptManager control. This must be included within a control that includes the `runat="server"` attribute. At runtime, this renders the appropriate JavaScript block to the client. With Internet Explorer, the code generated becomes:

```
<script src="/AtlasReader/WebResource.axd?d=AUY39WO
iwTRIogu9AIMyv6Z5UsRE7EaRGPSTsch0K6Lyz2EON7S15vqL-
bgMC0KchPDT06BtbeFjyRdgUFdpkB6kgBIS3V36a7l7XfDiYLz-
EYY1MiTpqdR4XfUdtZYO0L6toHqkLPPJbUJy038yHwt9ninEaeJ4
FkHeGh3sdKA1&amp;t=632980743289843750" type="text/javascript">
</script>
```

The Web resource actually points to about 11K lines of JavaScript code used by the rest of the framework. The `EnablePartialRendering` property means that only those sections of the page that have changed will be updated. This ensures that flickering is kept to a minimum.

Listing 14-13 contains the stylesheet used for the sample. The two selectors `.leftContent` and `.rightContent` cause the two sections to appear side by side.

Listing 14-13: Styles.css

```
body {
    font-family:Verdana,Arial, Sans-Serif;
    font-size:0.8em;
}

.leftContent
{
    float:left;
    width: 250px;
    padding-right: 30px;
    border-right: solid 1px black;
}

.rightContent
{
    padding-left: 30px;
    margin: 5px 5px 5px 5px;
}
```

The black box of the AJAX Extensions is the UpdatePanel. This control is used as a marker by the attached JavaScript code (that is, it does not produce any HTML output in itself). It identifies the controls that will be updated dynamically and the events that trigger the updates. In the preceding code, there are two UpdatePanels. One updates the Listbox that is populated with the post titles, and the other updates the content of each post item. The Triggers section of the control identifies the events that cause the contained controls to be updated. The code listed is actually executed on the server-side via Ajax, and the results are rendered to the page. The end result is a better experience for your clients, with less flicker and more feedback.

Using Prototype to Add Ajax Functionality

Prototype is a popular library, created by Sam Stephenson, which contains not only Ajax functionality but also a number of shortcuts for general JavaScript programming. Although it is not as large or full-featured as some of the other libraries, it has so many helpful shortcuts that many other libraries (such as Script.aculo.us that follows) are built on top of Prototype.

Listing 14-14 shows the client-side code for the contact lookup application created earlier. It has been modified to use Prototype and shows some of the added functionality of this library.

Listing 14-14: Client-side code using Prototype

```
<!DOCTYPE html PUBLIC "-//W3C//DTD XHTML 1.0 Transitional//EN"
"http://www.w3.org/TR/xhtml1/DTD/xhtml1-transitional.dtd">
<html xmlns="http://www.w3.org/1999/xhtml" >
<head>
    <title>Ajax Contact Lookup</title>
    <script type="text/javascript" src="scripts/prototype.js"></script>
<script language="javascript" type="text/javascript">
<!--
    function getContacts() {
        if("" != $F("q")) {
            var url="customerlookup.ashx";
            var parms = "q=" + $F("q");
            var target="contactList";
            var ajax = new Ajax.Updater(target,
                                        url,
                                        {method: "get",
                                         parameters: parms,
                                         onComplete: updateContent,
                                         onFailure: reportError
                                        });
        } else {
            $("contactList").innerText = "";
        }
    }
    function reportError(request) {
        $F("contactList") = request.statusText;
    }

    function updateContent(req) {
        var resp = req.responseXML;
        var result = "";

        var node = resp.documentElement.firstChild;
        var nodes = resp.getElementsByTagName('customer');
        for(i=0;i<nodes.length;i++) {
            result += dumpRow(nodes[i]);
        }

        $("contactList").innerHTML = result;
    }

    function dumpRow(row) {
```

```
        var child = row.firstChild;
        var result = "";
        result += "<b>" + getValue(child) + "</b> ";
        child = child.nextSibling;
        result += "(" + getValue(child) + "): ";
        child = child.nextSibling;
        result += getValue(child);
        result += "<br />";
        return result;
    }

    function getValue(node) {
        return Try.these(
            function() {return node.firstChild.nodeValue;},
              function() {return node.text;}
            );
    }

// -->
</script>
</head>
<body>
<form>
    Enter the first few letters of a company or contact:
    <input id="q" type="text" onkeyup="getContacts();"/><br />
    <div id="contactList"></div>

</form>
</body>
</html>
```

The first step in using Prototype is to include the library on the page. You can download Prototype from `http://prototype.conio.net`. The current version (as of this writing) is 1.4.0.

One of the most common tasks developers face when building JavaScript applications is accessing the elements on a page, particularly form fields. Prototype includes two handy shorthand functions for returning this data: `$(name)` returns the element on the page, whereas `$F(name)` returns the value of the item. Although not earth-shattering in complexity, these two functions can save a lot of typing. In addition to these two functions, two others not shown include `$H(object)` for creating hashtables, and `$A(object)` for creating arrays.

In addition to the JavaScript shortcuts, Prototype also includes Ajax functionality in the form of three main classes:

- **Ajax.Request** — used to make individual requests to server-side code. This object wraps the `XMLHttpRequest` object, and makes it easier to add simple requests that work cross-browser.
- **Ajax.Updater** — used to update a region of the Web page based on server-side code. This object extends the `Ajax.Request` object to automatically change the contents of a named region of the page based on the returned data.
- **Ajax.PeriodicalUpdater** — used to update a region of the Web page based on server-side code at regular intervals. This object extends the `Ajax.Updater`, adding timer functionality so that the update happens as the timer fires.

Prototype alone may be enough to help you with your Ajax applications. Alternatively, one of the libraries that use Prototype as a starting point could be just what you need to make your Web applications more dynamic.

Ajax Resources

A huge number of resources are available for learning more about Ajax. The concept has blossomed, creating cottage industries of Ajax libraries, conferences, and even online magazines offering information.

- `http://adaptivepath.com/publications/essays/archives/000385.php` — The essay that coined the term Ajax and repopularized the use of JavaScript.
- `wrox.com/WileyCDA/WroxTitle/productCd-0471777781.html` — Professional Ajax book from Wrox (ISBN: 0-471-77778-1).
- `http://prototype.conio.net/` — Home to the Prototype JavaScript framework.
- `http://script.aculo.us/` — Home to the Scriptaculous JavaScript framework.
- `http://atlas.asp.net/` — Home of Microsoft's AJAX Extensions for adding Ajax support to ASP.NET 2.0 applications.
- `http://www.ajaxpro.info` — Home of the Ajax.NET framework for adding Ajax support for ASP.NET applications.
- `nextapp.com/platform/echo2/echo/` — Home of the Echo2 framework for adding Ajax support for Java Web applications.
- `symfony-project.com/` — Home of the Symfony framework for adding Ajax support for PHP5 Web applications.
- `http://blogs.msdn.com/dmitryr/archive/2006/03/26/561200.aspx` — Dmitry Robson's blog post announcing his RSS Toolkit for ASP.NET.

Summary

Ajax can help make your browser-based applications appear faster and more like desktop applications. It requires a working knowledge of JavaScript and may cause a few more debugging headaches, but it can create a dynamic view of your application that results in more productive, happier clients. The benefits for clients who access your Web application over slower connections are even greater, because these clients can appreciate the reduced round-tripping. For larger Ajax implementations, you can look at a pre-existing Ajax library, or you can roll your own (everyone else has, it seems).

15

XML and .NET

Microsoft has been working for years to make using XML in the .NET world as easy as possible. You can't help but notice the additional capability and the enhancements to overall XML usage introduced in new each version of the .NET Framework. In fact, Bill Gates highlighted Microsoft's faith in XML in his keynote address at the Microsoft Professional Developers Conference 2005 in Los Angeles. He stated that XML is being pushed deeper and deeper into the Windows core each year. If you look around the .NET Framework, you will probably agree.

In addition to a series of namespaces in the .NET Framework that deal with XML and other XML-related technologies, you also find support for XML in Microsoft's products such as Visual Studio 2005, ASP.NET, ADO.NET, SQL Server, BizTalk, and a plethora of others.

This and the following two chapters step away from focusing on a specific XML technology. Instead, they focus on how specific vendors' technologies use XML. This chapter takes a look at XML in the .NET world, while the next few chapters look at XML in the worlds of Java, PHP, and more. You start by looking specifically at the Microsoft's embrace of XML.

The Serialization of XML

The .NET Framework makes it rather simple to serialize an object, such as a class, to XML. This has a lot of value in that you can take any objects you create in the .NET world, serialize them to XML, and then transport this XML over the wire or save it to disk for later retrieval. The serialization of an object means that it is written out to a stream, such as a file or a socket (this is also known as *dehydrating* an object). The reverse process can also be performed: An object can be deserialized (or rehydrated) by reading it from a stream.

For this entire process, the .NET Framework provides you with the `System.Xml.Serialization` namespace. This namespace contains all the classes and interfaces you need to support the serialization and deserialization of objects to and from XML.

Serializing Using the XmlSerializer Class

For an example of the serialization capabilities supported by the .NET Framework, you can create a C# console application. In this console application, you first create a class to be serialized to XML using the `XmlSerializer` class found in the `System.Xml.Serialization` namespace. Listing 15-1 provides you with the class you will use first. Place this class inside the project of the console application.

Listing 15-1: A simple class that will later be used in the serialization process

```
using System;
using System.Collections.Generic;
using System.Text;

namespace XmlSerializationProject
{
    public class StockOrder
    {
        private string _symbol;
        private int _quantity;
        private DateTime _OrderTime = DateTime.Now;

        public string Symbol
        {
            get { return _symbol; }
            set { _symbol = value; }
        }

        public int Quantity
        {
            get { return _quantity; }
            set { _quantity = value; }
        }

        public DateTime OrderTime
        {
            get { return _OrderTime; }
            set { _OrderTime = value; }
        }
    }
}
```

After the `StockOrder` class is in place in your console application project, the next step is to populate some of the properties this class exposes and use the `XmlSerializer` to convert the object to XML. The code for the console application is shown in Listing 15-2.

Listing 15-2: Serializing the StockOrder class to XML

```
using System;
using System.Collections.Generic;
using System.Text;
using System.Xml.Serialization;

namespace XmlSerializationProject
```

```
{
    class Program
    {
        static void Main(string[] args)
        {
            try
            {
                XmlSerializer classSerialization =
                    new XmlSerializer(typeof(StockOrder));

                StockOrder so = new StockOrder();
                so.Symbol = "MSFT";
                so.Quantity = 100;

                classSerialization.Serialize(Console.Out, so);
                Console.ReadLine();
            }
            catch (System.Exception ex)
            {
                Console.Error.WriteLine(ex.ToString());
                Console.ReadLine();
            }
        }
    }
}
```

In the previous listing, the `Serialize` method of the `XmlSerializer` instance is what you use to serialize the object to a specified stream. In the case of Listing 15-2, the `Serialize` instance is using two parameters — the first specifying the stream (in this case, `Console.Out`) and the second specifying the object to be serialized (in this case, `so`). The output generated from this simple application is illustrated in Figure 15-1.

file:///C:/Documents and Settings/Billy/My Documents/Visual Studio 2005/Projects/XmlSeria...
<?xml version="1.0" encoding="IBM437"?>
<StockOrder xmlns:xsi="http://www.w3.org/2001/XMLSchema-instance" xmlns:xsd="htt
p://www.w3.org/2001/XMLSchema">
<Symbol>MSFT</Symbol>
<Quantity>100</Quantity>
<OrderTime>2005-10-02T10:51:10.1141536-05:00</OrderTime>
</StockOrder>

Figure 15-1

The output shows that each public property is represented as an XML element which has the same name as the exposed property from the `StockOrder` class. Along that vein, the root element of the XML document has the same name as the class — `StockOrder`.

As with a typical XML document, the output includes a version specification of the XML as well as the `encoding` attribute with the value of `IBM437`. This encoding value is used because the console application really ends up using the `TextWriter` object to output the XML. Using some other type of object, the `XmlTextWriter` object, for instance, enables you more direct control over the encoding type used in the XML creation.

Besides the `encoding` attribute, a couple of namespaces are added to the XML document on your behalf:

```
xmlns:xsi="http://www.w3.org/2001/XMLSchema-instance"

xmlns:xsd="http://www.w3.org/2001/XMLSchema"
```

The end result shows that the simple object that was created has been output with a single set of results to the console application through the use of the `XmlSerializer` object. Next, you examine how you go about changing some of the output that is generated for you by the .NET Framework.

Changing the Output of the Serialized Object

The XML serialization that was generated and displayed in Figure 15-1 may be acceptable for your object serialization, but then again, you might want to modify the output so that it is more to your liking. For instance, if you want to change the name used for the root node, you can easily accomplish this task through the use of `XmlRootAttribute` class as shown in Listing 15-3.

Listing 15-3: Using the XmlRootAttribute class to change the root element's name

```
using System;
using System.Collections.Generic;
using System.Text;
using System.Xml.Serialization;

namespace XmlSerializationProject
{
    class Program
    {
        static void Main(string[] args)
        {
            try
            {
                XmlRootAttribute ra = new XmlRootAttribute();
                ra.ElementName = "ReutersStockOrder";

                XmlSerializer classSerialization =
                    new XmlSerializer(typeof(StockOrder), ra);

                StockOrder so = new StockOrder();
                so.Symbol = "MSFT";
                so.Quantity = 100;

                classSerialization.Serialize(Console.Out, so);
                Console.ReadLine();
            }
            catch (System.Exception ex)
            {
                Console.Error.WriteLine(ex.ToString());
                Console.ReadLine();
            }
        }
    }
}
```

Using the `XmlRootAttribute` class, you can programmatically alter how the `XmlSerializer` object serializes the respective class to XML. In this case, Listing 15-3 simply changes the name of the root element by first creating an instance of the `XmlRootAttribute` class and then using the `ElementName` property to make an assignment.

After you have instantiated the `XmlRootAttribute` class and set it up as desired, you assign the instance to the serialization process by adding it as a parameter in the instantiation of the `XmlSerializer` object.

```
XmlSerializer classSerialization = new XmlSerializer(typeof(StockOrder), ra);
```

Employing the code from Listing 15-3, you get the results illustrated in Figure 15-2.

```
file:///C:/Documents and Settings/Billy/My Documents/Visual Studio 2005/Projects/XmlSeria...
<?xml version="1.0" encoding="IBM437"?>
<ReutersStockOrder xmlns:xsi="http://www.w3.org/2001/XMLSchema-instance" xmlns:x
sd="http://www.w3.org/2001/XMLSchema">
  <Symbol>MSFT</Symbol>
  <Quantity>100</Quantity>
  <OrderTime>2005-10-04T10:53:49.635576-05:00</OrderTime>
</ReutersStockOrder>
```

Figure 15-2

In addition to changing the name used in the root element programmatically, you can also accomplish the same task declaratively directly in the `StockOrder.cs` file. This is illustrated in Listing 15-4.

Listing 15-4: Changing the name used in the root element declaratively

```
using System;
using System.Collections.Generic;
using System.Text;

namespace XmlSerializationProject
{
    [XmlRoot(ElementName = "ReutersStockOrder")]
    public class StockOrder
    {
       // Code removed for clarity
    }
}
```

Using the `XmlRoot` attribute prior to the class declaration is another way to accomplish this task. Within the attribute declaration, you can use the `ElementName` named property to provide an overriding name for the root element — in this case, `ReutersStockOrder`. This could also have been accomplished using the following syntax:

```
[XmlRoot("ReutersStockOrder")]
public class StockOrder
{
   // Code removed for clarity
}
```

In addition to the `ElementName` property, other properties include: `DateType`, `IsNullable`, and `Namespace`. Listing 15-5 shows an example of adding a new property, a namespace, to the generated output.

Listing 15-5: Adding a namespace to the serialized output

```
using System;
using System.Collections.Generic;
using System.Text;
using System.Xml.Serialization;

namespace XmlSerializationProject
{
    [XmlRoot(ElementName = "ReutersStockOrder",
        Namespace = "http://www.reuters.com/namespaces/")]
    public class StockOrder
    {
       // Code removed for clarity
    }
}
```

Listing 15-5 not only changes the name used in the root element, but it also adds another namespace to this root element. The results are shown in Figure 15-3.

```
file:///C:/Documents and Settings/Billy/My Documents/Visual Studio 2005/Projects/XmlSeria...
<?xml version="1.0" encoding="IBM437"?>
<ReutersStockOrder xmlns:xsi="http://www.w3.org/2001/XMLSchema-instance" xmlns:x
sd="http://www.w3.org/2001/XMLSchema" xmlns="http://www.reuters.com/namespaces/"
>
  <Symbol>MSFT</Symbol>
  <Quantity>100</Quantity>
  <OrderTime>2005-10-04T11:09:32.1608608-05:00</OrderTime>
</ReutersStockOrder>
```

Figure 15-3

You can also programmatically add namespaces and prefixes to the serialization process through the use of the `XmlSerializerNamespaces` class. This is illustrated in Listing 15-6:

Listing 15-6: Adding namespaces and prefixes to the serialization process

```
using System;
using System.Collections.Generic;
using System.Text;
using System.Xml.Serialization;

namespace XmlSerializationProject
{
    class Program
    {
        static void Main(string[] args)
        {
            try
            {
                XmlSerializer classSerialization =
```

```
                    new XmlSerializer(typeof(StockOrder));

                XmlSerializerNamespaces serName =
                    new XmlSerializerNamespaces();

                serName.Add("reu", "http://www.reuters.com/ns/");
                serName.Add("lip", "http://www.lipperweb.com/ns/");

                StockOrder so = new StockOrder();
                so.Symbol = "MSFT";
                so.Quantity = 100;

                classSerialization.Serialize(Console.Out, so, serName);
                Console.ReadLine();
            }
            catch (System.Exception ex)
            {
                Console.Error.WriteLine(ex.ToString());
                Console.ReadLine();
            }
        }
    }
}
```

The changes made to the console application include the addition of the `XmlSerializerNamespaces` class. In the application, an instance of this class is created (`serName`), and using the `Add` method allows you to define a prefix (`reu` or `lip`) as well as the namespace — both `string` values. The other and final change to the application is the parameter `XmlSerializerNamespaces`, which is added to the `Serialize` method of the `XmlSerializer` object instance (`classSerialization`).

After the prefixes and namespaces are in place in the application and ready to use, the next step is to change the `StockOrder.cs` file so that these namespaces are utilized by either the entire class or by particular properties declared in the class. This is illustrated in Listing 15-7.

Listing 15-7: Utilizing namespaces in the StockOrder.cs file

```
using System;
using System.Collections.Generic;
using System.Text;
using System.Xml.Serialization;

namespace XmlSerializationProject
{
    [XmlRoot(Namespace="http://www.lipperweb.com/ns/")]
    public class StockOrder
    {
        private string _symbol;
        private int _quantity;
        private DateTime _OrderTime = DateTime.Now;

        [XmlElement(Namespace="http://www.reuters.com/ns/")]
        public string Symbol
        {
```

(continued)

Listing 15-7 *(continued)*

```
            get { return _symbol; }
            set { _symbol = value; }
        }

        public int Quantity
        {
            get { return _quantity; }
            set { _quantity = value; }
        }

        public DateTime OrderTime
        {
            get { return _OrderTime; }
            set { _OrderTime = value; }
        }
    }
}
```

From Listing 15-7, you can see that by simply using the `XmlRoot` and `XmlElement` attributes, the same programmatically declared namespaces can be used in the serialization process. The nice thing is that the prefixes will be properly placed in the appropriate elements contained in the XML document as well. This is illustrated in Figure 15-4.

```
file:///C:/Documents and Settings/Billy/My Documents/Visual Studio 2005/Projects/XmlSeria...
<?xml version="1.0" encoding="IBM437"?>
<lip:StockOrder xmlns:reu="http://www.reuters.com/ns/" xmlns:lip="http://www.lip
perweb.com/ns/">
  <reu:Symbol>MSFT</reu:Symbol>
  <lip:Quantity>100</lip:Quantity>
  <lip:OrderTime>2005-10-05T09:30:39.7770864-05:00</lip:OrderTime>
</lip:StockOrder>
```

Figure 15-4

The results show that through the use the `XmlRoot` attribute, the root element and all the elements but one (`<Symbol>`) are provided with the appropriate namespace prefixes. `<Symbol>` was written as `<reu:Symbol>` because the declarations done by the `XmlRoot` attribute are overridden through the use of the `XmlElement` attribute.

Not only can you declaratively alter the serialized output by adding an attribute before the class declaration in the `StockOrder.cs` file (as shown previously), but you can also perform a similar operation by adding an `XmlElement` attribute before any property declarations contained in the same class.

For instance, if you look at the `<OrderTime>` element in Figure 15-4, note that you are getting back a very detailed version (universal time) of `DateTime`.

```
2005-10-04T11:09:32.1608608-5:00
```

What if you wanted this to be a different type of date, one that is easily passed to other bits of code? Using the `XmlElement` attribute, you can assign data types to use for your properties. This is illustrated in Listing 15-8.

Listing 15-8: Assigning a specific data type to an element

```
using System;
using System.Collections.Generic;
using System.Text;
using System.Xml.Serialization;

namespace XmlSerializationProject
{
    public class StockOrder
    {
        private string _symbol;
        private int _quantity;
        private DateTime _OrderTime = DateTime.Now;

        public string Symbol
        {
            get { return _symbol; }
            set { _symbol = value; }
        }

        public int Quantity
        {
            get { return _quantity; }
            set { _quantity = value; }
        }

        [XmlElement(DataType = "date")]
        public DateTime OrderTime
        {
            get { return _OrderTime; }
            set { _OrderTime = value; }
        }
    }
}
```

Just as you used the `XmlRoot` attribute before the class declaration, you can easily add `XmlElement` attributes to any of your properties to further refine how the XML will be serialized. In this case, the `DataType` value is given a value of `date`, which is an XML-Schema-defined data type. The new output of serialized XML is shown in Figure 15-5.

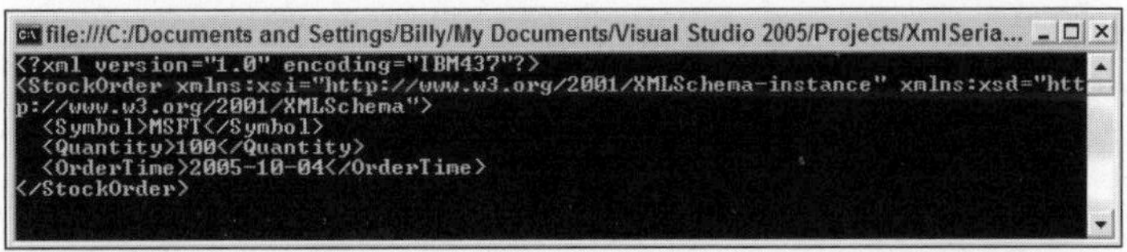

Figure 15-5

In addition to the `DataType` property for the `XmlElementAttribute` class, you can also use the attributes detailed in the following table.

Public Property	Description
`DataType`	Allows you to get or set the XML Schema defined data type of the XML element (for example, `date`).
`ElementName`	Allows you to get or set the name of the element that will be generated.
`Form`	Allows you to get or set a value that specifies whether the element is qualified.
`IsNullable`	Allows you to determine whether the `XmlSerializer` object should serialize elements where a null value is held. This property takes a `Boolean` value.
`Namespace`	Allows you to get or set a namespace for a particular XML element.
`Order`	Allows you to get or set the order in which elements are serialized or deserialized.
`Type`	Allows you to get or set the object type that is used to represent the XML element.
`TypeId`	Provides a unique identifier.

Deserializing XML

After an extensive look at the serialization process, next take a look at how you can reverse this process and deserialize an XML document back into a usable object in your code. For this, you use the same `XmlSerializer` object, but instead of using the `Serialize` method, you make use of the object's `Deserialize` method.

For an example of using the `Deserialize` method, you first establish a serialized object in a flat file. Listing 15-9 shows the `MyXML.xml` file that you need for this example.

Listing 15-9: The MyXML.xml file

```
<?xml version="1.0" encoding="utf-8"?>
<MultiStockOrder>
  <StockOrderMultiple>
    <StockOrder>
      <Symbol>MSFT</Symbol>
      <Quantity>100</Quantity>
      <OrderTime>2005-10-04</OrderTime>
    </StockOrder>
    <StockOrder>
      <Symbol>INTC</Symbol>
      <Quantity>110</Quantity>
      <OrderTime>2005-10-04</OrderTime>
    </StockOrder>
```

```
    <StockOrder>
      <Symbol>RTRSY</Symbol>
      <Quantity>200</Quantity>
      <OrderTime>2005-10-04</OrderTime>
    </StockOrder>
  </StockOrderMultiple>
</MultiStockOrder>
```

Instead of an XML file with just a single stock order in an XML file, this XML file has an array of orders (3), which will all be deserialized and placed into an array of your customized type, `StockOrder`. Next, you create a new class that contains an array of `StockOrder` objects in your console application. This class, `MultiStockOrder.cs`, is displayed in Listing 15-10.

Listing 15-10: A class representing an array of StockOrder objects

```
using System;
using System.Collections.Generic;
using System.Text;

namespace XmlSerializationProject
{
    public class MultiStockOrder
    {
        public StockOrder[] StockOrderMultiple;
    }
}
```

This class and the previous `StockOrder.cs` class define the syntax that your XML document from Listing 15-9 takes. Figure 15-6 illustrates just this.

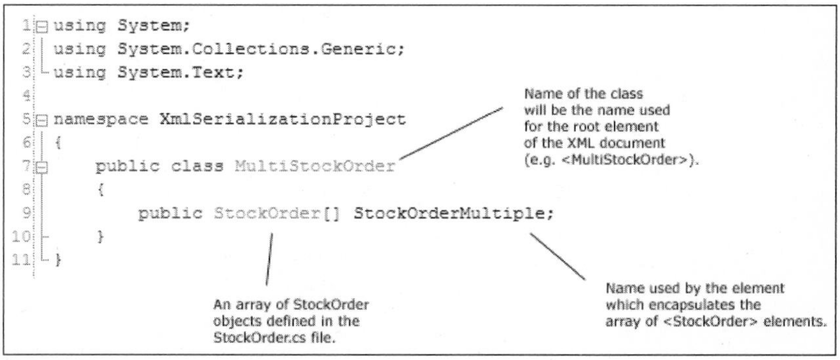

```
using System;
using System.Collections.Generic;
using System.Text;

namespace XmlSerializationProject
{
    public class MultiStockOrder
    {
        public StockOrder[] StockOrderMultiple;
    }
}
```

Name of the class will be the name used for the root element of the XML document (e.g. <MultiStockOrder>).

An array of StockOrder objects defined in the StockOrder.cs file.

Name used by the element which encapsulates the array of <StockOrder> elements.

Figure 15-6

Next, deserializing this into a usable object is rather simple in .NET. Listing 15-11 shows how the `MultiStockOrder` object is deserialized from a file on disk, `MyXML.xml` and how the file's contents are used.

Listing 15-11: The deserialization of XML to the MultiStockOrder object

```
using System;
using System.Collections.Generic;
using System.Text;
using System.Xml;
using System.Xml.Serialization;
using System.IO;

namespace XmlSerializationProject
{
    class Program
    {
        static void Main(string[] args)
        {
            try
            {
                FileStream dehydrated = new
                   FileStream("C:/MyXML.xml", FileMode.Open);

                XmlSerializer serialize = new
                   XmlSerializer(typeof(MultiStockOrder));

                MultiStockOrder myOrder = new MultiStockOrder();
                myOrder = (MultiStockOrder) serialize.Deserialize(dehydrated);

                foreach(StockOrder singleOrder in myOrder.StockOrderMultiple)
                {
                   Console.WriteLine("{0}, {1}, {2}",
                      singleOrder.Symbol,
                      singleOrder.Quantity,
                      singleOrder.OrderTime.ToShortDateString());
                }

                dehydrated.Close();
                Console.ReadLine();

            }
            catch (System.Exception ex)
            {
                Console.Error.WriteLine(ex.ToString());
                Console.ReadLine();
            }
        }
    }
}
```

The `Deserialize` method takes a few constructions. Some of them include the following:

```
Deserialize(Stream)
Deserialize(TextReader)
Deserialize(XmlReader)
```

From this list, you can see that the `Deserialize` method takes a couple of possible inputs. The first, is a stream, and from the code Listing 15-11, you can determine this is what is being used (a `FileStream` object). Other possibilities include a `TextReader` object, or even an `XmlReader` object, which you look at shortly.

In Listing 15-11, first the `FileStream` object is used to pull the data from the `MyXML.xml` file. Then, as before, the `XmlSerializer` object is instantiated, but this time it is cast as a new object type—`MultiStockOrder`. From there, an instance of the `MultiStockOrder` is created and populated through the deserialization of the `XmlSerializer`.

```
myOrder = (MultiStockOrder) serialize.Deserialize(dehydrated);
```

At this point, the `MultiStockOrder` instance (`myOrder`) contains everything that was stored in the `MyXML.xml` file. Now the job is to iterate through each of the single orders contained in the class instance. This is done by using a `foreach` statement where each of the values for each order is output to the console. In the end, the console application produces the results illustrated in Figure 15-7.

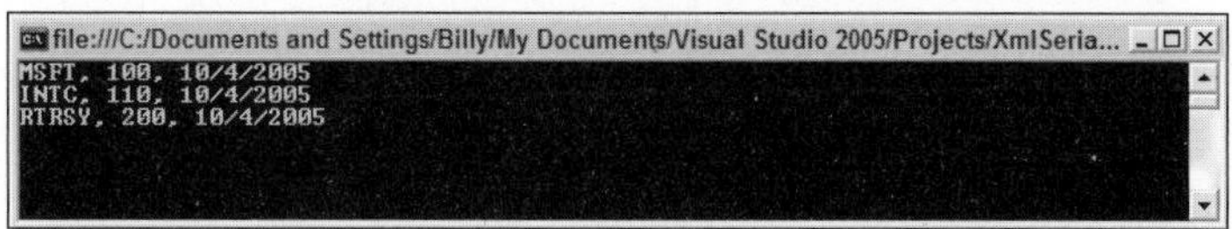

Figure 15-7

From this example, you can see that it is quite easy to serialize objects to XML and then deserialize that XML back into a usable object.

XmlWriter

Don't think of an XML document as just a string of characters and angle brackets that form a larger document; instead, it is an *InfoSet* or a representation of data as an object. When writing XML to a stream or a file, you might think it's easiest to simply use string concatenation to build a large string that you then write to a stream or file. I strongly warn against taking this approach. A far better approach is to use the .NET Framework, which provides you with an XML writer through the `XmlWriter` class.

`XmlWriter` is an abstract class that allows you to specify an uncached, forward-only stream that writes an XML document. The style in which the XML document is created is controlled by the `XmlWriterSettings` class. The `XmlWriterSettings` class, which is new to .NET 2.0, enables you to configure the behavior of the `XmlWriter` object even before you instantiate it.

Writing XML Using XmlTextWriter

Before venturing into the `XmlWriterSettings` class, take a look at a simple example of using the `XmlTextWriter` to construct an XML document to be written to disk. `XmlTextWriter` is a class that implements `XmlWriter` and enables you to output XML to files or an open stream. An example of this is illustrated in Listing 15-12.

Listing 15-12: Using the XmlTextWriter class to construct XML to be written to disk

```
using System;
using System.Collections.Generic;
using System.Text;
using System.Xml;
using System.Xml.Serialization;
using System.IO;

namespace XmlSerializationProject
{
    class Program
    {
        static void Main(string[] args)

        {
            try
            {
                XmlSerializer classSerialization =
                    new XmlSerializer(typeof(StockOrder));

                StockOrder so = new StockOrder();
                so.Symbol = "MSFT";
                so.Quantity = 100;

                XmlTextWriter tw = new
                   XmlTextWriter("C:/MyXml.xml", Encoding.UTF8);
                classSerialization.Serialize(tw, so);
                tw.Close();

                Console.Write("Written to disk");
                Console.ReadLine();
            }
            catch (System.Exception ex)
            {
                Console.Error.WriteLine(ex.ToString());
                Console.ReadLine();
            }
        }
    }
}
```

The code in Listing 15-12 continues some of the previous examples illustrated using the `StockOrder` class. This example again uses the `XmlSerializer` class to serialize an object to XML using the `Serialize` method. However, this time instead of outputting the results to a console application, an instance of the `XmlTextWriter` class is used as the output destination.

The `XmlTextWriter` class is being instantiated as follows:

```
XmlTextWriter tw = new XmlTextWriter("C:/MyXml.xml", Encoding.UTF8);
```

In this case, the first parameter points to the file to be created and the second parameter specifies the encoding to use for the XML document. Other possible encodings include:

- `ASCII`
- `BigEndianUnicode`
- `Default`
- `Unicode`
- `UTF32`
- `UTF7`
- `UTF8`

In this example, UTF8 is used as the encoding, and the results are specified to be written to the file `MyXml.xml` located in the root directory. After the `XmlTextWriter` object is in place, the next step is to use the `XmlSerializer` object, which takes an instance of `XmlWriter` in one of its constructions.

```
classSerialization.Serialize(tw, so);
```

In this case, being passed to the `Serialize` method includes the instance of the `XmlTextWriter` object (`tw`) and an instance of the `StockOrder` object (`so`). After running the application, you get a message that the XML has been written to disk. Looking into the root directory, you find the `MyXml.xml` file with the results illustrated in Figure 15-8.

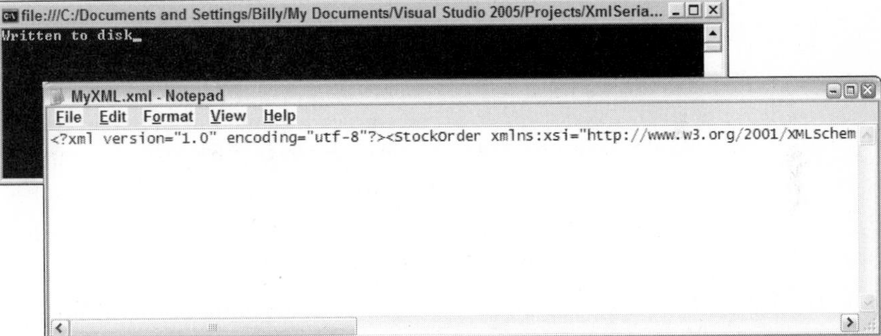

Figure 15-8

You can notice a few things from the output displayed in Figure 15-8. First, the encoding has indeed been specified as you want it—to UTF8. You can find this in the XML document's `<?xml>` declaration. The other item to pay attention to (because it isn't as apparent from looking at the figure) is that I have the `MyXml.xml` document open in Notepad with word-wrapping turned off. The XML document is written out in a single, long string. Although this is fine for computers and programs, it isn't always that helpful to any humans who might have to open and alter the XML contents from time to time.

Writing XML Using XmlWriter

Next, instead of using the `XmlTextWriter` object to write your serialized XML to disk, take a look at performing the same operation with the `XmlWriter` object. This enables you to use the `XmlWriterSettings` object later to play around with the XML output. The following table details the properties of the `XmlWriterSettings` class.

Property	Initial Value	Description
`CheckCharacters`	`True`	This property, if set to `True`, performs a character check on the contents of the `XmlWriter` object. Legal characters can be found at `www.w3.org/TR/REC-xml#charsets`.
`CloseOutput`	`False`	Allows you to close the XmlWriter instance and if set to `true`, allows to also close the underlying stream.
`ConformanceLevel`	`ConformanceLevel.Document`	Allows the XML to be checked to make sure that it follows certain specified rules. Possible conformance-level settings include `Document`, `Fragment` and `Auto`.
`Encoding`	`Encoding.UTF8`	Defines the encoding of the XML generated.
`Indent`	`False`	Defines whether the XML generated should be indented. Setting this value to `true` properly indents child nodes from parent nodes.
`IndentChars`	`Two spaces`	Specifies the number of spaces by which child nodes are indented from parent nodes. This setting only works when the `Indent` property is set to `true`.
`NewLineChars`	`\r\n`	Assigns the characters that are used to define line breaks.
`NewLineHandling`	`NewLineHandling.Replace`	Deals with the normalization of line breaks in the output. Possible settings include `Replace`, `Entitize`, and `None`.
`NewLineOnAttributes`	`False`	Defines whether a node's attributes should be written to a new line in the construction. This occurs only if the property is set to `true`.
`OmitXmlDeclaration`	`False`	Defines whether an XML declaration should be generated in the output. This omission only occurs if this property is set to `true`.
`OutputMethod`	`Xml`	Defines the output to use. Possible settings include `Xml`, `Html`, `Text`, and `AutoDetect`.

Using the `XmlWriterSettings` object, you can alter how the XML is written to disk. Instead of just a straight line of XML, use this new object to change this and some other settings. This is illustrated in Listing 15-13.

Listing 15-13: Using the XmlWriterSettings object to alter the XML output

```
using System;
using System.Collections.Generic;
using System.Text;
using System.Xml;
using System.Xml.Serialization;
using System.IO;

namespace XmlSerializationProject
{
    class Program
    {
        static void Main(string[] args)

        {
            try
            {
                XmlSerializer classSerialization =
                    new XmlSerializer(typeof(StockOrder));

                StockOrder so = new StockOrder();
                so.Symbol = "MSFT";
                so.Quantity = 100;

                XmlWriterSettings settings = new XmlWriterSettings();
                settings.CheckCharacters = true;
                settings.Encoding = Encoding.Unicode;
                settings.Indent = true;

                XmlWriter xw = XmlWriter.Create("C:/MyXml.xml", settings);

                classSerialization.Serialize(xw, so);
                xw.Close();

                Console.Write("Written to disk");
                Console.ReadLine();
            }
            catch (System.Exception ex)
            {
                Console.Error.WriteLine(ex.ToString());
                Console.ReadLine();
            }
        }
    }
}
```

In this bit of code, before the `XmlSettings` object is created, an instance of the `XmlWriterSettings` is created and certain properties are assigned values to change elements like the encoding and to break up the lines and indent the XML generated. After the `XmlWriterSettings` object is established, you assign this instance of the `XmlWriterSettings` object to the `XmlWriter` object. This is done through the `XmlWriter` object's `Create` method.

Looking at the new `MyXml.xml` file in the root directory, you see the following results after running this console application. (See Figure 15-9.)

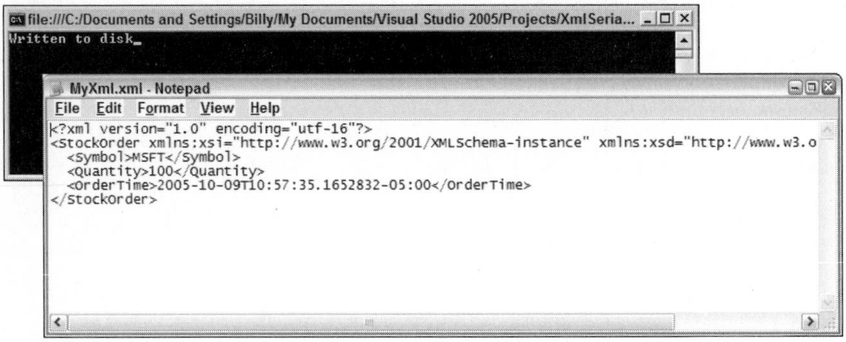

Figure 15-9

In this instance of opening the XML document in Notepad, I still have the Word Wrap feature turned off, but (as you can) see the XML contains the proper line breaks and indents. This makes the XML more readable and manageable. Also, because the encoding was set in through the `XmlWriterSettings` object to `Encoding.Unicode`, the encoding specified in the XML document is now set to `utf-16`.

Writing XML Programmatically Using XmlWriter

You can also use the `XmlWriter` object to create XML programmatically. This is illustrated in Listing 15-14.

Listing 15-14: Building XML programmatically with the XmlWriter object

```
using System;
using System.Collections.Generic;
using System.Text;
using System.Xml;
using System.IO;

namespace XmlProject
{
    class Program
    {
        static void Main(string[] args)

        {
            try
            {
                XmlWriterSettings settings = new XmlWriterSettings();
                settings.CheckCharacters = true;
```

```
                settings.Encoding = Encoding.Unicode;
                settings.Indent = true;

                XmlWriter xw = XmlWriter.Create("C:/MyXml.xml", settings);
                xw.WriteStartDocument();
                xw.WriteStartElement("StockOrder");
                xw.WriteStartElement("Symbol");
                xw.WriteValue("MSFT");
                xw.WriteEndElement(); // Symbol
                xw.WriteStartElement("Quantity");
                xw.WriteValue(100);
                xw.WriteEndElement(); // Quantity
                xw.WriteStartElement("OrderTime");
                xw.WriteValue(DateTime.Now.ToUniversalTime());
                xw.WriteEndElement(); // OrderTime
                xw.WriteEndElement(); // StockOrder
                xw.WriteEndDocument();

                xw.Close();

                Console.Write("Written to disk");
                Console.ReadLine();
            }
            catch (System.Exception ex)
            {
                Console.Error.WriteLine(ex.ToString());
                Console.ReadLine();
            }
        }
    }
}
```

First, establish any settings via the `XmlWriterSettings` class. In this case, you use the same settings form as before — setting the encoding and providing line breaks and indentation as appropriate. From there, the `XmlWriter` is established through the `Create` method passing in the string of the file to write to and the instance of the `XmlWriterSettings` class.

From there, the XML Infoset is created using some of the many methods that are available to the `XmlWriter` class. The idea here is to open an element, add any required attributes, add any values, and then close the element. You need to perform this write in a procedural manner. Before any elements can be added, however, you must open the document itself. This is done through the `WriteStartDocument` method.

```
xw.WriteStartDocument();
```

After the document has been started, or opened, the next step is to create the first element in the document. Of course, the first element created is the root element — `StockOrder`. This is done by using the `WriteStartElement` method.

```
xw.WriteStartElement("StockOrder");
```

Whenever you start (or open) an element, you must also end (or close) the element. As you can see from the previous example, however, the `StockOrder` element is not closed until the end of the document. You have to shut the elements in the appropriate order to achieve a properly structured XML document. The root element's closing node doesn't appear till the very end of the document, and this is where you use the `WriteEndElement` method for the `StockOrder` element.

```
xw.WriteEndElement();
```

After you start an element using the `WriteStartElement` method, your next step is to either start creating some attributes for that particular element, give the element a value, or close the element (if the element will be empty). An example of writing a value to an element is shown here:

```
xw.WriteValue(DateTime.Now.ToUniversalTime());
```

After you have completed creating the document and closed all the elements contained in the document, the last step is to end the document using the `WriteEndDocument` method.

```
xw.WriteEndDocument();
```

Finally, you can't write the document to disk (as is specified in the `Create` method of the `XmlWriter` instance) until you instantiate the `Close` method of the instance.

```
xw.Close();
```

Running this console application produces an XML file, `MyXml.xml` (as specified programmatically in this example).

XmlReader

The `XmlReader` class is an abstract class that allows you to specify an uncached, forward-only access to XML data. Similar to the way the `XmlWriter` class utilizes the `XmlWriterSettings` class, the style in which the XML document is read is controlled by the `XmlReaderSettings` class. The `XmlReaderSettings` class, which is new to .NET 2.0, allows you to configure the behavior of the `XmlReader` object before you even instantiate it.

For an example of this, try reading some XML from a file on disk. Use one of the previously presented XML files, as shown in Listing 15-15.

Listing 15-15: The MyXml.xml file that the XmlReader will utilize

```
<?xml version="1.0" encoding="utf-8"?>
<MultiStockOrder>
  <StockOrderMultiple>
    <StockOrder>
      <Symbol>MSFT</Symbol>
      <Quantity>100</Quantity>
      <OrderTime>2005-10-04</OrderTime>
    </StockOrder>
    <StockOrder>
```

```
        <Symbol>INTC</Symbol>
        <Quantity>110</Quantity>
        <OrderTime>2005-10-04</OrderTime>
      </StockOrder>
      <StockOrder>
        <Symbol>RTRSY</Symbol>
        <Quantity>200</Quantity>
        <OrderTime>2005-10-04</OrderTime>
      </StockOrder>
    </StockOrderMultiple>
  </MultiStockOrder>
```

With the XML file in place, the next step is to build a console application that can read through this XML document and work with some of the elements and their values. This is illustrated in Listing 15-16.

Listing 15-16: Using the XmlReader object to read the MyXml.xml file

```
using System;
using System.Collections.Generic;
using System.Text;
using System.Xml;
using System.IO;

namespace XmlProject
{
    class Program
    {
        static void Main(string[] args)

        {
            try
            {
                XmlReaderSettings settings = new XmlReaderSettings();
                settings.IgnoreWhitespace = true;
                settings.IgnoreComments = true;
                settings.CheckCharacters = true;

                FileStream myStockOrders = new
                   FileStream("C:/MyXml.xml", FileMode.Open);

                XmlReader xr = XmlReader.Create(myStockOrders, settings);

                while (xr.Read())
                {
                    if (xr.NodeType == XmlNodeType.Element &&
                        "Symbol" == xr.LocalName)
                    {
                        Console.WriteLine(xr.Name + " " +
                           xr.ReadElementContentAsString());
                    }
```

(continued)

Listing 15-16 *(continued)*

```
                }

                xr.Close();

                Console.WriteLine("Done");
                Console.ReadLine();
            }
            catch (System.Exception ex)
            {
                Console.Error.WriteLine(ex.ToString());
                Console.ReadLine();
            }
        }
    }
}
```

As you review this bit of code, note that the first step is to instantiate the `XmlReaderSettings` class and assign it some values. In this case, the `IgnoreWhitespace`, `IgnoreComment`, and the `CheckCharacters` properties are set. After the `XmlReaderSettings` instance is ready to go, the next step is to retrieve the XML file through the use of the `FileStream` object and assign both the XML document and the settings applied through the `XmlReaderSettings` object to the `XmlReader` object (`xr`).

The `Read()` method of the `XmlReader` reads `true` if there is anything to be read in the document, including whitespace, comments, and similar items. This is why these items are set to be ignored through the `XmlReaderSettings` instance in the program. Because of this, a check is done on the element being read to determine if it is an XML element using the `NodeType` property, and then a second check is done to see if the element has the name `Symbol` by comparing it to the `LocalName` property.

```
if (xr.NodeType == XmlNodeType.Element && "Symbol" == xr.LocalName)
{
   // Code removed for clarity
}
```

After the element is found, its name (it will be `Symbol` if it passed the check) and the value of the element are then written to the console.

```
Console.WriteLine(xr.Name + " " + xr.ReadElementContentAsString());
```

In this case, the name of the element is retrieved through the `Name` property, and the value of the element is retrieved through the `ReadElementContentAsString` method. In addition to the `ReadElementContentAsString` method, you can use many other data types as well (this is also explained in more detail shortly).

Once run, the console application produces the results illustrated in Figure 15-10.

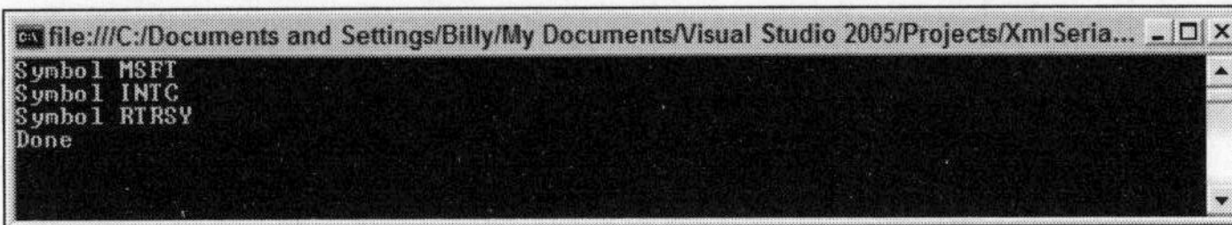

Figure 15-10

Reading XML with a Schema Validation

One problem with the XML reading example from the previous section is that the code can process *any* XML document, and if that document contains a `<Symbol>` element somewhere in its contents, then the node's name and value are used by the console application. This is a problem because you are really interested in processing only XML documents for stock orders that follow the `MyXml.xml` document pattern. This is why working with XML schemas is such a powerful tool.

The nice thing with the `XmlReader` object is that you can provide an XSD schema to be applied to an inputted document through the `XmlReaderSettings` class. Listing 15-17 shows an example of this validation check on the retrieved XML document.

Listing 15-17: Performing schema validations with the XmlReader instance

```
using System;
using System.Collections.Generic;
using System.Text;
using System.Xml;
using System.Xml.Schema;
using System.IO;

namespace XmlProject
{
    class Program
    {
        static void Main(string[] args)
        {
            try
            {
                XmlSchemaSet mySchema = new XmlSchemaSet();
                mySchema.Add(null, "C:/MyXml.xsd");

                XmlReaderSettings settings = new XmlReaderSettings();
                settings.IgnoreWhitespace = true;
                settings.IgnoreComments = true;
                settings.CheckCharacters = true;
                settings.Schemas.Add(mySchema);
                settings.ValidationType = ValidationType.Schema;
                settings.ValidationFlags =
                   XmlSchemaValidationFlags.ReportValidationWarnings;
                settings.ValidationEventHandler += new
                   ValidationEventHandler(settings_ValidationEventHandler);

                FileStream myStockOrders = new
```

(continued)

Listing 15-17 *(continued)*

```
                    FileStream("C:/MyXml.xml", FileMode.Open);

                XmlReader xr = XmlReader.Create(myStockOrders, settings);

                while (xr.Read())
                {
                    if (xr.NodeType == XmlNodeType.Element &&
                        "Symbol" == xr.LocalName)
                    {
                        Console.WriteLine(xr.Name + " " +
                           xr.ReadElementContentAsString());
                    }
                }

                xr.Close();

                Console.WriteLine("Done");
                Console.ReadLine();
            }
            catch (System.Exception ex)
            {
                Console.Error.WriteLine(ex.ToString());
                Console.ReadLine();
            }
        }

        static void settings_ValidationEventHandler(object sender,
           ValidationEventArgs e)
        {
            throw new Exception("Your XML is invalid.");
        }
    }
}
```

As you look over the code, note that the first step is to import in the `System.Xml.Schema` namespace because you want to use the `XmlSchemaSet` class in your code. The `XmlSchemaSet`, which is a new class as of the .NET Framework 2.0, is an object to represent the XSD document that you want to validate the XML data to. The creation of the `XmlSchemaSet` instance is done using the `Add` method.

```
XmlSchemaSet mySchema = new XmlSchemaSet();
mySchema.Add(null, "C:/MyXml.xsd");
```

Now that the schema you want to use is ready and in place, the next step is to add this instance to the `XmlReaderSettings` object that is created.

```
settings.Schemas.Add(mySchema);
settings.ValidationType = ValidationType.Schema;
settings.ValidationFlags = XmlSchemaValidationFlags.ReportValidationWarnings;
settings.ValidationEventHandler += new
   ValidationEventHandler(settings_ValidationEventHandler);
```

First off, the schema stored in the `XmlSchemaSet` is associated with the `XmlReaderSettings` instance by using the `Schemas.Add` method and passing in the `XmlSchemaSet` instance, `mySchema`. Next, you declare through the `ValidationType` property that you are specifying a schema. Other options include: `Auto`, `DTD`, `None`, and `XDR`. From there, you then specify through the `ValidationFlags` property that you are interested in reporting validation warnings, and then you simply make an association to a validation event handler to handle any validation errors that might occur. It is important to note that the Auto and XDR options of the ValidationType property are obsolete in the .NET Framework 2.0.

When you are running the console application against an XML document that doesn't follow the rules defined in the `MyXml.xsd` schema, you see something similar to what is illustrated in Figure 15-11.

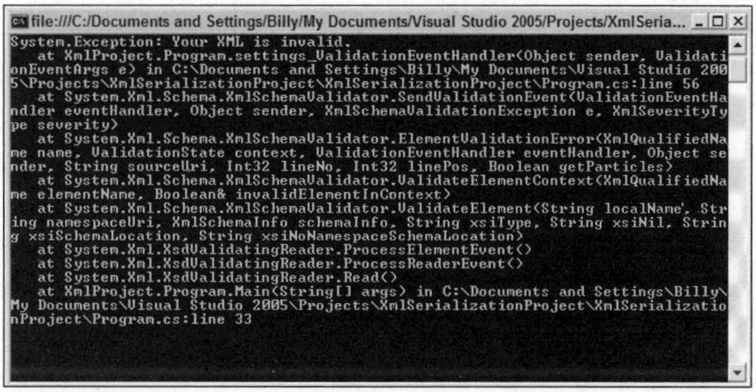

Figure 15-11

Casting XML Types to .NET-Compliant Types

.NET CLR-compliant types are not 100% inline with XML types. For this reason, the .NET Framework 2.0 has introduced some new methods in the `XmlReader` that simplify the process of casting from one of these XML types to .NET types.

You saw an earlier example of this being done with one of the new classes. Using the `ReadElementContentAs` method, you can easily perform the required casting.

```
string userName =
   (string) myXmlReader.ReadElementContentAs(typeof(System.String), null);

DateTime myDate =
   (DateTime) myXmlReader.ReadElementContentAs(typeof(System.DateTime), null);
```

A whole series of direct casts through new classes are available:

- `ReadElementContentAsBase64`
- `ReadElementContentAsBinHex`
- `ReadElementContentAsBoolean`
- `ReadElementContentAsDateTime`

- ReadElementContentAsDecimal
- ReadElementContentAsDouble
- ReadElementContentAsFloat
- ReadElementContentAsInt
- ReadElementContentAsLong
- ReadElementContentAsObject
- ReadElementContentAsString

This makes it easy to perform operations like those shown in Listing 15-17:

```
Console.WriteLine(xr.Name + " " + xr.ReadElementContentAsString());
```

Reading XML Using XPathDocument

`XmlReader` is great, don't get me wrong; but it is a forward-only, non-cached way of reading XML data. Sometimes, instead of reading XML in this way, you want to hold the XML Infoset in memory while you jump from one point in the document to another to query the information you are interested in using.

XPath (discussed heavily in Chapter 10) is a great way to query XML for what you want. For this reason, the class, `XPathDocument`, in the .NET Framework. `XPathDocument` stores the XML data in memory and allows you to jump to any point of the document using XPath queries.

Note that if you are interested in altering or writing to the XML document in any manner, then you want to use the .NET Framework class, `XmlDocument` to accomplish this task. `XmlDocument` allows for reading and writing of an XML document, while `XPathDocument` allows only reading. With that said , if you are interested in *just* reading from the XML document, then you want to use `XPathDocument` because it is easier to use and performs better than `XmlDocument` does.

For an example of reading an XML document using the `XPathDocument` object, again turn to the stock order XML file, `MyXml.xml`, and use XPath to query a list of stock symbols from the document. This is illustrated in Listing 15-18.

Listing 15-18: Querying XML using XPath and the XPathDocument object

```
using System;
using System.Collections.Generic;
using System.Text;
using System.Xml;
using System.Xml.XPath;
using System.IO;

namespace XmlProject
{
    class Program
    {
```

```
            static void Main(string[] args)
            {
                try
                {
                    FileStream myStockOrders = new
                       FileStream("C:/MyXml.xml", FileMode.Open);

                    XPathDocument myDocument = new XPathDocument(myStockOrders);
                    XPathNavigator docNavigation = myDocument.CreateNavigator();

                    foreach(XPathNavigator node in
                        docNavigation.Select
                        ("//MultiStockOrder/StockOrderMultiple/StockOrder/Symbol"))
                    {
                        Console.WriteLine(node.Value.ToString());
                    }

                    Console.WriteLine("Done");
                    Console.ReadLine();
                }
                catch (System.Exception ex)
                {
                    Console.Error.WriteLine(ex.ToString());
                    Console.ReadLine();
                }
            }
        }
    }
```

To use the `XPathDocument` class, you should first import the `System.Xml.XPath` namespace into the application. From the example in Listing 15-18, you can see that the instantiation of the `XPathDocument` object is passed the `FileStream` object which holds the `MyXml.xml` file contents.

Then, using a `foreach` command, you are able to iterate through everything retrieved from the XPath query — `//MultiStockOrder/StockOrderMultiple/StockOrder/Symbol`. For each item found with this XPath query, the value of the element is printed to the screen of the console application giving you the results shown in Figure 15-12.

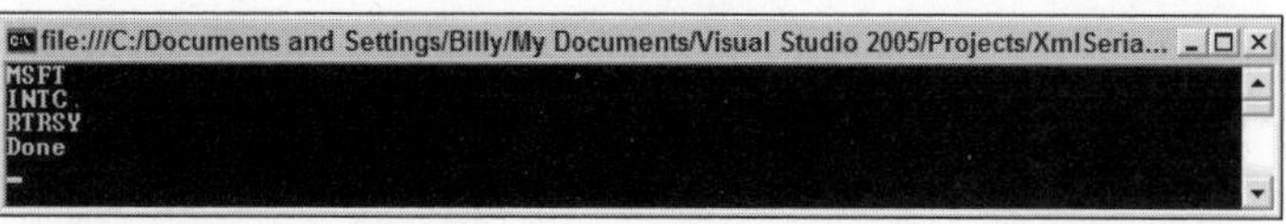

Figure 15-12

XML in ASP.NET 2.0

Most Microsoft-focused Web developers have usually relied on either Microsoft SQL Server or Microsoft Access for their data storage needs. Today, however, a considerable amount of data is stored in XML format, so considerable inroads have been made toward improving Microsoft's core Web technology to work easily with this format.

The XmlDataSource Server Control

ASP.NET 2.0 introduced a series of data source controls to bridge the gap between your data stores (such as XML) and the data-bound controls at your disposal. These new data controls not only enable you to retrieve data from various data stores, but they also let you easily manipulate the data (using paging, sorting, editing, and filtering) before the data is bound to an ASP.NET server control.

With XML being as important as it is, a specific data source control has been added to ASP.NET 2.0 just for retrieving and working with XML data. The XmlDataSource control enables you to connect to your XML data and to use this data with any of the ASP.NET data-bound controls. Just like the SqlDataSource and the ObjectDataSource controls (which are some of the other data source controls), the XmlDataSource control also enables you not only to retrieve data, but also to insert, delete, and update data items. With the world turning more and more to XML data formats, such as Web services, RSS feeds, and more, this control is a valuable resource for your Web applications.

To show the XmlDataSource control in action, first create a simple XML file and include this file in your application. Listing 15-19 shows a simple XML file of Russian painters that you can use.

Listing 15-19: Painters.xml

```
<?xml version="1.0" encoding="utf-8" ?>
<Artists>
   <Painter name="Vasily Kandinsky">
      <Painting>
         <Title>Composition No. 218</Title>
         <Year>1919</Year>
      </Painting>
   </Painter>
   <Painter name="Pavel Filonov">
      <Painting>
         <Title>Formula of Spring</Title>
         <Year>1929</Year>
      </Painting>
   </Painter>
   <Painter name="Pyotr Konchalovsky">
      <Painting>
         <Title>Sorrento Garden</Title>
         <Year>1924</Year>
      </Painting>
   </Painter>
</Artists>
```

Now that the `Painters.xml` file is in place, the next step is to use an ASP.NET DataList control and to connect this DataList control to an `<asp:XmlDataSource>` control. This is illustrated in Listing 15-20.

Listing 15-20: Using a DataList control to display XML content

```
<%@ Page Language="C#"%>

<html xmlns="http://www.w3.org/1999/xhtml" >
<head runat="server">
    <title>XmlDataSource</title>
```

```
</head>
<body>
    <form id="form1" runat="server">
        <asp:DataList ID="DataList1" Runat="server" DataSourceID="XmlDataSource1">
            <ItemTemplate>
                <p><b><%# XPath("@name") %></b><br />
                <i><%# XPath("Painting/Title") %></i><br />
                <%# XPath("Painting/Year") %></p>
            </ItemTemplate>
        </asp:DataList>

        <asp:XmlDataSource ID="XmlDataSource1" Runat="server"
         DataFile="~/Painters.xml" XPath="Artists/Painter">
        </asp:XmlDataSource>
    </form>
</body>
</html>
```

This is a simple example, but it shows you the power and ease of using the XmlDataSource control. You should pay attention to only two attributes in this example. The first is the `DataFile` attribute. This attribute points to the location of the XML file. Because the file resides in the root directory of the application, it is simply `~/Painters.xml`. The next attribute included in the XmlDataSource control is the `XPath` attribute. The XmlDataSource control uses XPath for the filtering of XML data. In this case, the XmlDataSource control is taking everything within the `<Painter>` set of elements. The value `Artists/Painter` means that the XmlDataSource control navigates to the `<Artists>` element and then to the `<Painter>` element within the specified XML file.

The DataList control next must specify the `DataSourceID` as the XmlDataSource control. In the `<ItemTemplate>` section of the DataList control, you can retrieve specific values from the XML file by using XPath commands. The XPath commands filter the data from the XML file. The first value retrieved is an element attribute (`name`) that is contained in the `<Painter>` element. If you are retrieving an attribute of an element, you preface the name of the attribute with an `@` symbol. In this case then, you simply specify `@name` to get at the painter's name. The next two XPath commands go deeper into the XML file and get the specific painting and the year of the painting. Remember to separate nodes with a `/`. When run in the browser, this code produces the results illustrated in Figure 15-13.

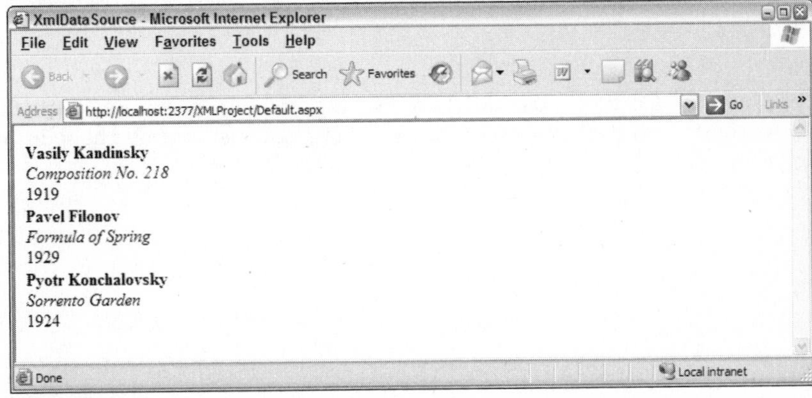

Figure 15-13

Besides working from static XML files like the `Painters.xml` file shown earlier, the XmlDataSource file has the capability to work from dynamic, URL-accessible XML files. One popular XML format that is pervasive on the Internet today is the blog or weblog. Blogs, or personal diaries, can be viewed in the browser, through an RSS-aggregator, or just as pure XML.

As you look at my blog in Figure 15-14, you can see the XML it produces directly in the browser. (You can find a lot of blogs to play with for this example at `weblogs.asp.net`.)

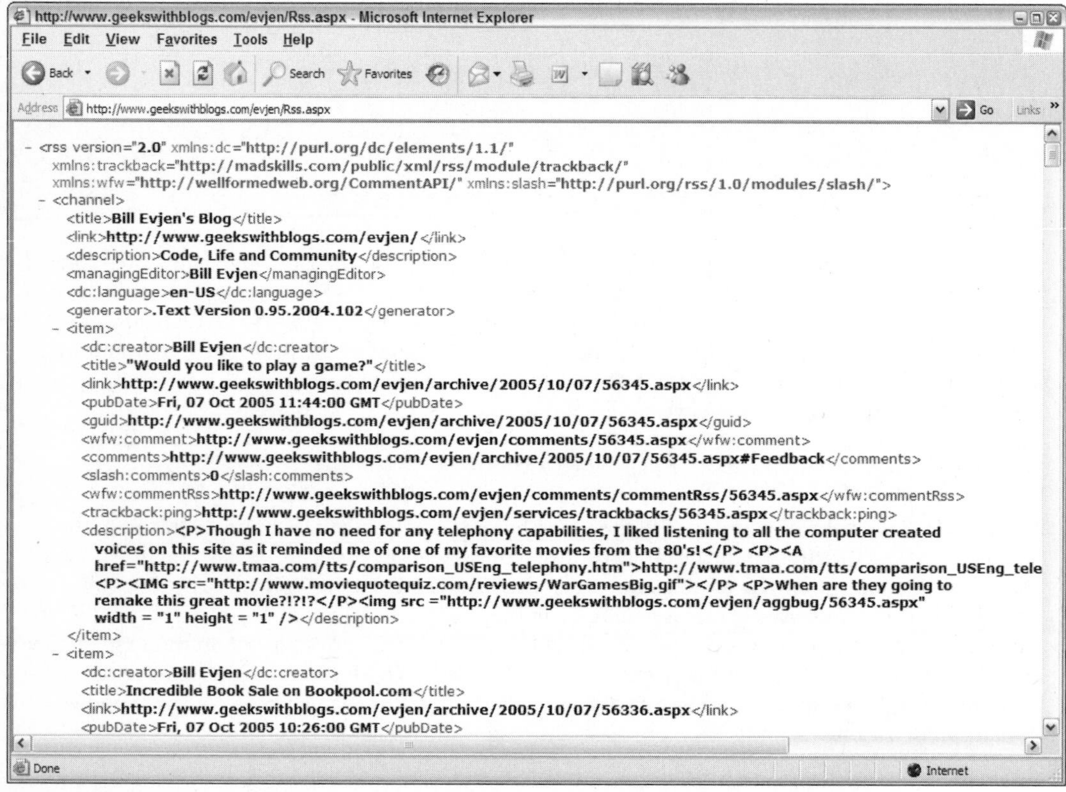

Figure 15-14

Now that you know the location of the XML from the blog, you can use this XML with the XmlDataSource control and display some of the results in a DataList control. The code for this example is shown in Listing 15-21.

Listing 15-21: Working with an RSS feed

```
<%@ Page Language="C#"%>

<html xmlns="http://www.w3.org/1999/xhtml" >
<head runat="server">
    <title>XmlDataSource</title>
</head>
<body>
    <form id="form1" runat="server">
        <asp:DataList ID="DataList1" Runat="server" DataSourceID="XmlDataSource1">
            <HeaderTemplate>
                <table border="1" cellpadding="3">
            </HeaderTemplate>
            <ItemTemplate>
                <tr><td><b><%# XPath("title") %></b><br />
                <i><%# XPath("pubDate") %></i><br />
                <%# XPath("description") %></td></tr>
            </ItemTemplate>
            <AlternatingItemTemplate>
                <tr bgcolor="LightGrey"><td><b><%# XPath("title") %></b><br />
                <i><%# XPath("pubDate") %></i><br />
                <%# XPath("description") %></td></tr>
            </AlternatingItemTemplate>
            <FooterTemplate>
                </table>
            </FooterTemplate>
        </asp:DataList>

        <asp:XmlDataSource ID="XmlDataSource1" Runat="server"
         DataFile="http://geekswithblogs.net/evjen/Rss.aspx"
         XPath="rss/channel/item">
        </asp:XmlDataSource>
    </form>
</body>
</html>
```

Looking at the code in Listing 15-21, you can see that the `DataFile` points to a URL where the XML is retrieved. The `XPath` property filters out all the `<item>` elements from the RSS feed. The DataList control creates an HTML table and pulls out specific data elements from the RSS feed, such as the `<title>`, `<pubDate>`, and `<description>` elements.

Running this page in the browser, you get something similar to the results shown in Figure 15-15.

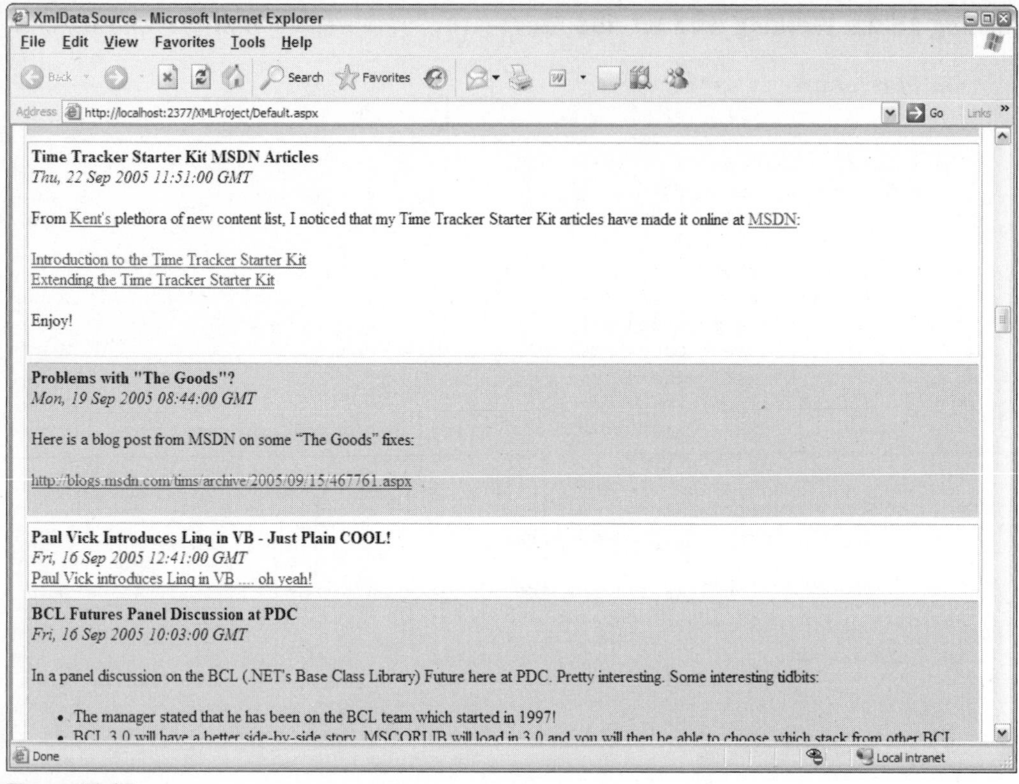

Figure 15-15

This approach also works with XML Web services, even ones for which you can pass in parameters using HTTP-GET. You just set up the `DataFile` value in the following manner:

```
DataFile="http://www.someserver.com/GetWeather.asmx/ZipWeather?zipcode=63301"
```

The XmlDataSource Control's Namespace Problem

One big issue with the XmlDataSource control is that when you are using the XPath capabilities of the control, it is unable to understand namespace qualified XML. The XmlDataSource control chokes on any XML data that contain namespaces and, for this reason, it is important to yank out any prefixes and namespaces that are contained in the XML.

To make this a bit easier, the XmlDataSource control includes the attribute `TransformFile`. This attribute applies your XSLT transform file to the XML pulled from the XmlDataSource control. That means you can use an XSLT transform file to transform your XML so that the prefixes and namespaces are completely removed from the overall XML document. An example of this XSLT document is illustrated in Listing 15-22.

Listing 15-22: Building an XSLT document which removes all prefixes and namespaces

```
<?xml version="1.0" encoding="UTF-8"?>
<xsl:stylesheet version="1.0"
 xmlns:xsl="http://www.w3.org/1999/XSL/Transform">
   <xsl:output method="xml" version="1.0" encoding="UTF-8" indent="yes"/>
   <xsl:template match="*">
      <!-- Remove any prefixes -->
      <xsl:element name="{local-name()}">
          <!-- Work through attributes -->
          <xsl:for-each select="@*">
             <!-- Remove any attribute prefixes -->
             <xsl:attribute name="{local-name()}">
                <xsl:value-of select="."/>
             </xsl:attribute>
          </xsl:for-each>
      <xsl:apply-templates/>
      </xsl:element>
   </xsl:template>
</xsl:stylesheet>
```

Now with this XSLT document in place within your application, you can use the XmlDataSource control to pull XML data and to strip that data of any prefixes and namespaces.

```
<asp:XmlDataSource ID="XmlDataSource1" runat="server"
 DataFile="NamespaceFilled.xml" TransformFile="~/RemoveNamespace.xsl"
 XPath="ItemLookupResponse/Items/Item"></asp:XmlDataSource>
```

The Xml Server Control

Since the very beginning of ASP.NET, there has always been a server control called the Xml server control. This control performs the simple operation of XSLT transformation upon an XML document. This control is rather easy to use. All you do is point to the XML file you wish to transform using the `DocumentSource` attribute and indicate the XSLT transform file using the `TransformSource` attribute.

To see this in action, use the `Painters.xml` file that was shown in Listing 15-19. The next step is to create your XSLT transform file. The process is shown in Listing 15-23.

Listing 15-23: The XSLT transformation file

```
<?xml version="1.0" encoding="utf-8"?>

<xsl:stylesheet version="1.0"
    xmlns:xsl="http://www.w3.org/1999/XSL/Transform">

  <xsl:template match="/">
      <html>
      <body>
        <h3>List of Painters &amp; Paintings</h3>
        <table border="1">
```

(continued)

Listing 15-23 *(continued)*

```
            <tr bgcolor="LightGrey">
              <th>Name</th>
              <th>Painting</th>
              <th>Year</th>
            </tr>
            <xsl:apply-templates select="//Painter"/>
          </table>
        </body>
      </html>
    </xsl:template>

    <xsl:template match="Painter">
      <tr>
        <td>
          <xsl:value-of select="@name"/>
        </td>
        <td>
          <xsl:value-of select="Painting/Title"/>
        </td>
        <td>
          <xsl:value-of select="Painting/Year"/>
        </td>
      </tr>
    </xsl:template>

  </xsl:stylesheet>
```

With the XML document and the XSLT document in place, the final step is to combine the two using the Xml server control provided by ASP.NET. This is illustrated in Listing 15-24.

Listing 15-24: Combining the XML and XSLT documents using the Xml server control

```
<%@ Page Language="C#" %>

<html xmlns="http://www.w3.org/1999/xhtml" >
<head id="Head1" runat="server">
    <title>XmlDataSource</title>
</head>
<body>
    <form id="form1" runat="server">
        <asp:Xml ID="Xml1" runat="server" DocumentSource="~/Painters.xml"
          TransformSource="~/PaintersTransform.xsl"></asp:Xml>
    </form>
</body>
</html>
```

The end result is shown in Figure 15-16.

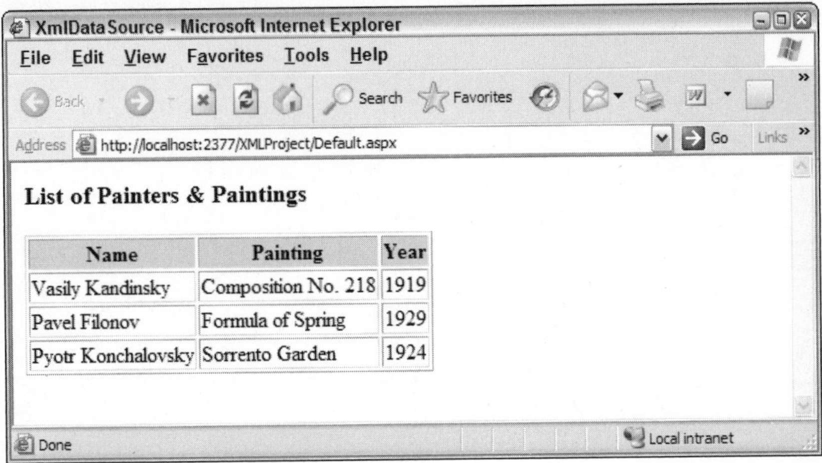

Figure 15-16

Summary

From this chapter, I hope you learned how committed Microsoft is to putting XML capabilities into its overall framework. XML use in the world will only continue to grow, and for this reason, Microsoft is working to make it easier and easier with each release to use XML data from end-to-end in your applications, workflow-processes, and more.

This chapter takes a good look at some of the more important XML capabilities provided in the .NET Framework 2.0, but this is just a scratch on the surface. This topic is really deserving of an entire book of its own.

16

XML and Java

In this chapter, you examine how XML and Java work together. In some ways XML and Java are excellent bedfellows; they're both children of the 1990s and fit in well with modern concepts of Internet and Web-based application architectures, and they both have a solid foundation in Unicode. When it comes to the details, however, there's sometimes a mismatch: For example, the mapping from XML Schema data types to classes in the Java class library is less than perfect.

Java and XML can interact in many different ways. This chapter takes a bottom-up approach, starting with the lowest-level interfaces and working steadily upward. The most important interfaces are covered in detail elsewhere in this book, so this chapter gives more of an overview: a comparative study of the different interfaces, explaining their capabilities and their strengths and weaknesses. Its goal is to enable you to choose the right interface for the job at hand without necessarily providing a detailed reference for each class and method.

At the lowest level, Java applications can read and write *lexical XML*, that is, XML represented in character form with angle-bracket markup. Reading lexical XML is called parsing; writing lexical XML is called serialization (although that term is overloaded, unfortunately). The first section of the chapter discusses how a Java application can interact with a parser and a serializer.

The next level up is the construction of tree-based representations of XML documents in memory. The best-known tree model is the DOM, which is described in more detail in Chapter 13. However, DOM has come under some criticism in the Java world, and a number of attempts have been made to create better models. At least three such programs have a significant user base, namely JDOM, DOM4J, and XOM. I give a brief overview of these models to help you make an informed choice.

What DOM and these other tree models have in common is that they are generic object models: They use Java objects to represent elements, attributes, and text nodes. Wouldn't it be better to translate these generic objects into objects that reflect the semantics of the information you want to manipulate, such as customers, orders, and products? This brings us to the next level up, which is data binding: the capability to define the mapping between the XML representation of data and a Java object model.

But there's a higher level still. Rather than writing your business logic in Java, which involves moving the data between a Java representation and an XML representation, you can write the business logic in declarative languages such as XPath, XSLT, and XQuery, where the data is manipulated entirely in its native XML form. Java, however, still has a role in controlling the overall structure of the application and linking together modules written in these special-purpose languages. So in the final part of the chapter, you examine how Java relates to these declarative XML-processing languages.

Reading and Writing XML

This first section of the chapter looks at how you can manipulate lexical XML (XML as a character or byte stream) from a Java application. You look first at the input side (parsing), then at output (serialization).

Because this is a bottom-up approach to the chapter, it risks giving too much prominence to these interfaces. Remember that these are low-level interfaces. They represent the foundation on which other things are built. You may find that you never have to use these interfaces directly because you can take advantage of the superstructure built on top of them. But it's worth knowing that they are there and that they offer things you can't achieve at a higher level of the stack.

Parsing from Java

Until recently, the only standard low-level interface for parsing from Java was the SAX interface. SAX is sufficiently important that the whole of Chapter 13 is devoted to it. This section starts with a quick overview of SAX and then moves on to a new contender in this area, the StAX interface.

SAX: Push Parsing

SAX is a *push* interface. The parser is in control: It reads the XML input stream, and when it finds something of interest like a start tag, an end tag, or a processing instruction, it notifies the application by calling an appropriate method. The application registers a `ContentHandler` with the parser; the `ContentHandler` implements methods such as `startElement()`, `endElement()`, `characters()`, `comment()`, and `processingInstruction()`. The parser calls these methods when the relevant events occur.

That's a very cursory overview, of course, but you can afford to take a bird's eye view because all the detail is covered in Chapter 13.

Writing Java applications to use the SAX interface is traditionally considered to be rather difficult. The reasons for this include the following:

- Programmers like to be in control. It's difficult to write an application as a set of methods without knowing which method is going to be called next. Of course, that's exactly what you have to do when you write a GUI application that responds to events such as button clicks; but knowing that doesn't make it any easier.
- Closely related to this, it can be hard to keep track of the context. If an element representing, say, an invoice has a flexible structure, it can be hard to know what processing to perform as each event occurs, and where to put the logic, for example, that assigns a value to fields that were absent from the input.

SAX is, however, extremely efficient. The interface is designed to avoid unnecessary creation of objects, which is always an expensive operation in Java. If you're not careful you can throw away all these performance benefits at the application level, but that's a general characteristic of low-level interfaces.

One of the nice features of SAX is that it lends itself very well to the construction of pipelines. A pipeline consists of a sequence of processing stages, each of which takes XML as its input and produces XML as its output. In principle, the XML that passes from one stage to another could be represented any way you like: It could be as a file of lexical XML or as a DOM tree in memory, for example. It might seem like an abstract notion to represent an XML document as a sequence of events pushed from one stage of the pipeline to the next, and it certainly isn't one that comes naturally to many people. But it's actually a very effective way of doing it. Unlike lexical XML, you avoid the overhead of having one stage in the pipeline serialize the XML, while the next stage parses it again. And unlike when you use a DOM or other tree representations, you don't need to tie down memory — this, of course, becomes increasingly important as the size of your documents increases. (It's also important if you are processing many concurrent transactions.)

Figure 16-1 shows a typical push pipeline implemented using SAX. At the source of the pipeline is a SAX parser followed by a schema validation stage, followed by two application-level processing stages that manipulate the content before passing it to a SAX-based serializer that acts as the final destination. One of the advantages of such a pipeline is that the different stages don't all have to use the same technology: You can write SAX-based pipeline filters in XSLT or XQuery as well as in Java.

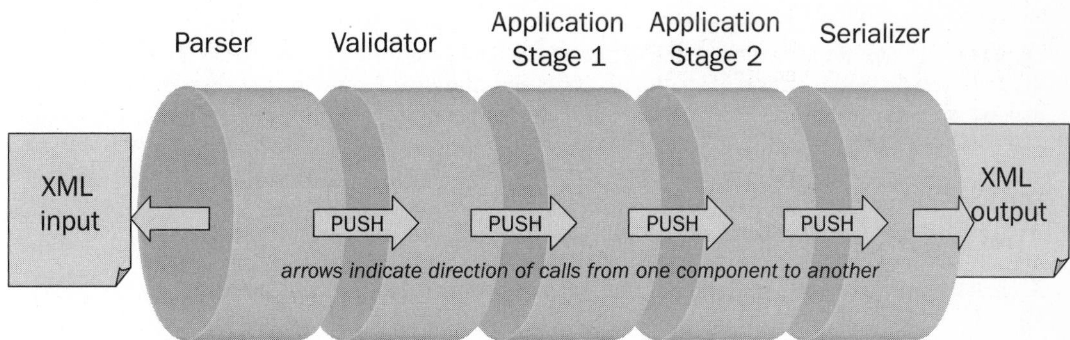

Figure 16-1

SAX parsers are widely available. The field has consolidated so that most people nowadays use Xerces, a product that originated in IBM and was donated to the Apache project. It is probably installed on your machine as a built-in component of the Sun JDK — that's if you're using J2SE 5.0. In JDK 1.3 and 1.4, a different parser, called Crimson, was bundled in. Of course, one of the reasons for having standard interfaces is that it's possible to swap one implementation with another without applications noticing. Other SAX parsers you might come across include one from Oracle (part of the Oracle XDK toolkit), and if you use the GNU Classpath library, its default SAX parser is Ælfred2.

You come back to pipelines in a moment, after looking at the new alternative for low-level parsing, namely StAX.

StAX: Pull Parsing

When Microsoft came out with its XML tools for the .NET platform (see Chapter 15), it decided to include a parser with a very different API, referred to as a pull API. Instead of having the parser in control, calling the application when it comes across something of interest, the application is now in control, executing a series of `getNext()` calls to ask the parser for more data. It's not clear to what extent StAX was actually based on the .NET ideas, but it's certainly true to say that .NET popularized this alternative approach to low-level parsing, and the Java community responded to the interest that Microsoft created.

For many programmers, this style of interface comes naturally. It's easier to call on a service than to be called by it; it makes it easier to understand the flow of control and the sequence of events, and easier to see where to put the conditional logic that says, "If the next thing is an X, do this; if it's a Y, then do that."

When it was first proposed, many advocates of pull parsing claimed that it was potentially faster. I think the case for that is unproven. In the quest for ultimate parsing speed, many apparently small things can make a big difference. For example, it's important to minimize the number of times characters are moved from one buffer to another. This is affected by the fine detail of the API design, but it's unclear that either pull or push interfaces are superior in this regard. The best parsers in both categories seem to be within 20 percent of each other in processing speed (I won't say which way, because they are playing leapfrog with each other), and in my view this is unlikely to be significant in terms of overall application performance.

The StaX interface, also known as JSR (for Java Specification Request) 173, has been in gestation for a long time. The initiative came from BEA Systems back in 2002, bringing together previous projects that had previously lacked critical mass. But StAX doesn't find its way into the Java mainstream until J2SE 6.0, which many users won't be adopting until 2008 or beyond. The years in between have been rather frustrating for users keen to try the technology, with long intervals between parser releases that turned out to be rather buggy and with poor interoperability between the different products. One of the best implementations at the time of writing is probably Woodstox, written by Tatu Saloranta (`woodstox.codehaus.org`).

One of the attractions of a pull interface for parser vendors is that you can layer a push interface on top of a pull interface, but not the other way around. This is illustrated in Figure 16-2.

Here a control program pulls data from the parser (by calling its `getNext()` method) and pushes it to the application (by calling the SAX `ContentHandler` methods such as `startElement()`, `endElement()`, and so on).

Note how this is another example of a pipeline. In a pipeline, the components can either pull data from the previous stage in the pipeline, or they can push data to the next stage. The problem is that only one component can be in charge. Upstream from that component, everyone has to pull; downstream, everyone has to push. The Figure 16-3 illustrates this.

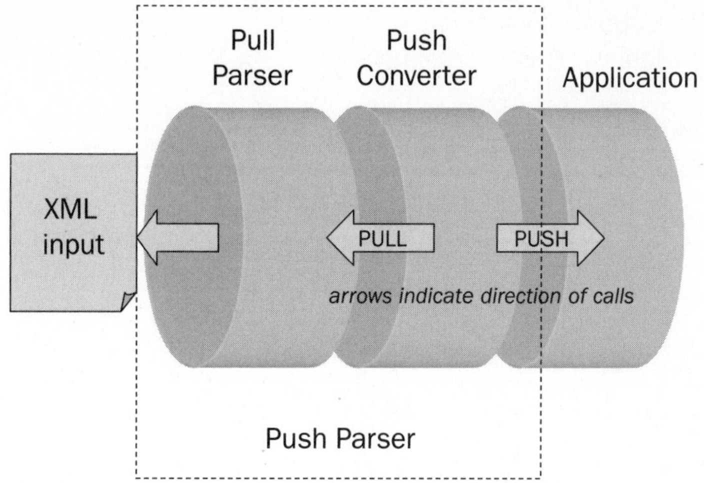

Figure 16-2

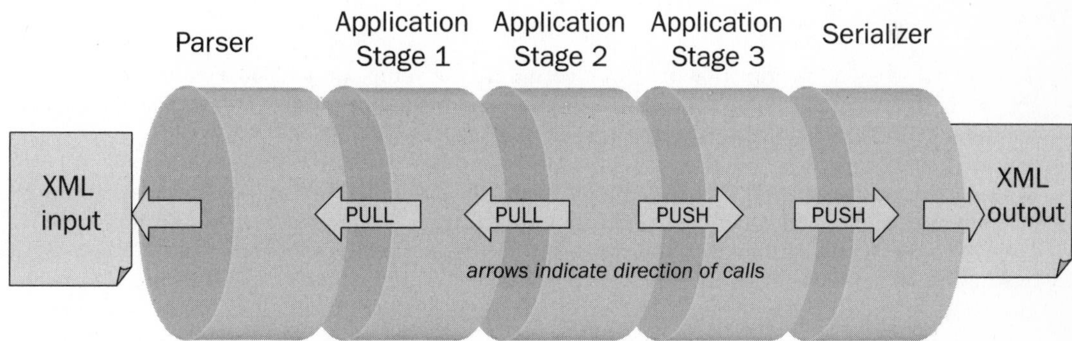

Figure 16-3

If you want to connect a pipeline that pushes data to one that pulls it, you can do this in two ways.

- The first pipeline can build a tree in memory (for example, a DOM), and the second pipeline can read from the tree, as shown in Figure 16-4.
- The two pipelines can operate in different threads or processes, which allows more than one control loop. This requires some fairly difficult concurrent programming and is not to be attempted lightly; the overhead of coordinating multiple threads can quickly eliminate any performance gains. Typically, the two threads communicate via a cyclic buffer holding a queue of events, as shown in the diagram that follows.

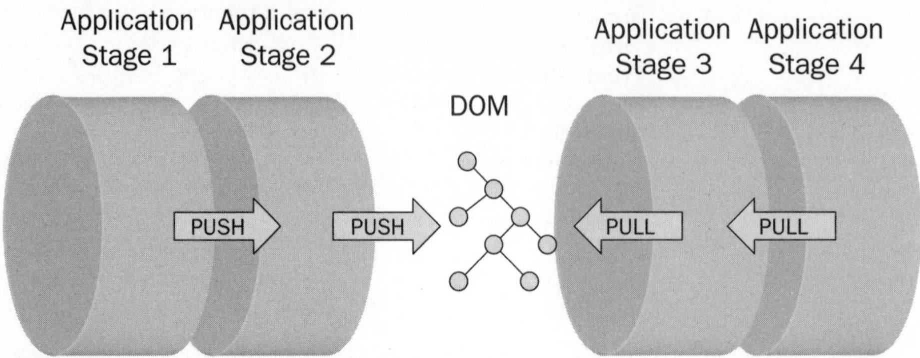

Figure 16-4

One of the potential attractions of the StAX pull interface is that in time, you can pull data not only from a parser analyzing lexical XML, but from other sources of XML. For example, an XSLT or XQuery engine enables you to read the results of a transformation or query into your application using this style of API. Of course, this is equally true of SAX, but it might well be an area where the added programming convenience proves decisive.

So far I've discussed the principles of StAX. Because it's not yet well-established enough to justify a chapter of its own in this book, the following sections go into a little more detail to make the ideas more concrete.

StAX, in fact, offers two pull APIs, the cursor API and the iterator API. Why two? Because one optimizes performance, whereas the other optimizes usability. The team that defined the specification wasn't prepared to trade one for the other. You can regard the iterator API as a layer on top of the cursor API, making it a bit more user-friendly. The implementation, however, doesn't necessarily work that way internally.

In the lower-level cursor API, the interface offered by the parser is called `XMLStreamReader`. Its main methods are `hasNext()`, which tests whether there are more parsing events to come, and `next()`, which gets the next such event. The `next()` method returns an integer identifying the event, for example `START_ELEMENT`, `END_ELEMENT`, `CHARACTERS`, or `COMMENT`. You can request further details of the current event from the `XMLStreamReader`. For example, if you are positioned on a `START_ELEMENT` event, you can call `getName()` to determine the name of the element. One reason this API is efficient is that it doesn't give you any information unless you actually ask for it. (However, the efficiency is limited by the fact that a conformant XML parser is obliged to check that the XML is well-formed. For example it must detect when an element name contains invalid characters even if the application doesn't ask to see the element name).

Attributes and namespaces can also be read directly from the `XMLStreamReader`. After a `START_ELEMENT` event, a call on `getAttributeCount()` tells you how many attributes the element has, and you can then call methods such as `getAttributeName(N)` and `getAttributeValue(N)` to find details of the Nth attribute. Similar methods are available for namespace declarations (which in StAX are not treated as attributes).

The higher-level API in StAX is the iterator API, presented by the interface `XMLEventReader`. This has two similar methods `hasNext()` and `nextEvent()` that you can use to read though the input document.

Unlike the next() method of the cursor API, however, nextEvent returns an Event object, which provides properties directly to the current event. When it encounters an element start tag, the relevant event can be cast to a StartElement event, which offers a method getAttributeByName() to find the attribute with a given qualified name. The iterator API also maintains the full namespace context on your behalf. So if the document contains attributes such as xsi:type, whose value contains a QName, you can use this namespace context to see what namespace the prefix xsi refers to, without having to track all the namespace declarations in your application. Clearly, this interface is likely to be a bit less efficient because it is collecting information just in case you happen to need it.

Both the iterator and the cursor API allow you to do something that's not possible in SAX, namely to skip forward. For example, if you hit the start tag of an element that you're not interested in, you can fast-forward to the corresponding end tag. This gives a potential performance boost by reducing unnecessary chit-chat and also simplifies your application code, which no longer has to deal with the events for the unwanted subtree.

Another thing that's much easier to do cleanly in a pull API rather than a push API is to abandon processing. If you have read as much of the document as you need to see, in StAX you just stop reading. (It's a good idea to issue a close() to give the parser a chance to tidy up, but if you don't, the garbage collector will take care of it eventually.) In SAX, the only way an application can ask the parser to stop is to throw an exception. That's much messier: For a start, exceptions are expensive, and also, it can be difficult to distinguish it from a real application error, especially when the application is part of a complex pipeline.

I hope you've learned enough about pull parsing to give you a feel for whether this is an interface you should look at more closely. If it is, then you can find plenty of reference information on the Web. The best place to look is probably the J2SE 6.0 JavaDoc specification in package javax.xml.stream and its subpackages. You don't actually need J2SE 6.0 to use StAX, however. Parsers such as Woodstox come with a copy of the interface definitions that you need.

Writing XML (Serialization)

Having looked at the interfaces available to a Java program for reading XML, you can now turn to the other side of the coin: How do you write a file containing lexical XML?

One option is simply to create a PrintWriter and write to it:

```
PrintWriter w = new PrintWriter(new File("output.xml"));
w.write("<a>here is some XML</a>");
w.close();
```

This isn't something I would recommend, although I have to admit I've done it often enough myself when I was in a hurry. The main traps to avoid are the following:

- Make sure that special characters in text and attribute nodes are properly escaped, for example that & is written as & and < as <
- You need to make sure that the character encoding of the file as written to disk matches the character encoding specified in the XML declaration.
- It's entirely your responsibility to make sure that the document is well-formed, for example that all namespaces are properly declared.

There's also a more subtle reason why this is not the preferred interface. After you've committed your code to writing lexical XML (angle brackets, escaped ampersands and all), you won't be able to deploy your application so readily in a pipeline. Pipelines are the key to writing reusable software components in an XML-based application (which is why I keep coming back to the subject), and you should always bear in mind that someone else might one day want to modify the output of your program by adding a postprocessing stage to the pipeline. Unless you write your XML using a higher-level interface than basic print statements, this won't be possible without expensive reparsing.

Furthermore, if you use an XML serialization library, you can probably tweak the output in many ways without changing your application. An obvious example is switching indentation on or off: Indented output makes life much easier if the XML must be read by human beings, but it can add significant overhead when transmitted over a network.

So now, look at the alternatives. In this section, you see approaches that enable your Java application to write directly to a serializer. If you've got the data in a tree representation such as DOM or one of the other tree models discussed later in the chapter, you can also serialize directly from the tree. But you don't want to build a tree in memory just so that you can serialize it.

Using a JAXP Serializer

In its very first incarnations, the JAXP (Java API for XML Processing) suite of interfaces provided control over two aspects of XML processing: XML parsing, and XSLT transformation. You look at the transformation API more closely later in this chapter. It so happens that the XSLT specification includes the definition of a serializer that converts XSLT's internal tree representation of XML into lexical XML output. It uses an `<xsl:output>` declaration in the stylesheet to control the details of how this is done. The designers of the JAXP interface decided to structure the interface so that you can invoke the serialization component whether or not you have done a transformation.

In fact, no class or interface in JAXP explicitly calls itself a serializer. Instead, something called an identity transformer can convert one representation of XML (provided as a `Source`) into a different representation (the `Result`), without modifying the XML en route. Three kinds of `Source` objects are defined: a `DOMSource`, a `SAXSource`, and a `StreamSource`, as well as three kinds of `Result` objects: `DOMResult`, `SAXResult`, and `StreamResult`. An `IdentityTransformer` can convert any kind of `Source` into any kind of `Result`. Moreover, implementers can provide additional kinds of `Source` or `Result`, further adding to the possibilities.

Because a `StreamResult` represents XML lexically, any identity transformer that produces a `StreamResult` as its output is acting as an XML serializer.

To serialize XML from a Java application, you want the identity transformer in the form of a `TranformerHandler`. The way you achieve this is:

```
TransformerFactory factory = TransformerFactory.newInstance();
TransformerHandler serializer =
                ((SAXTransformerFactory)factory).newTransformerHandler();
serializer.setResult(new StreamResult(new File("output.xml")));
```

Technically, before doing this, you should check that the `TransformerFactory` is one that offers this optional feature, but as far as I know all the implementations in common use do.

The interface TransformerHandler extends the SAX ContentHandler interface, so you can now write your output by calling the ContentHandler methods:

```
serializer.startDocument();
serializer.startElement("", "a", "a", new AttributesImpl());
String s = "some XML content";
serializer.characters(s.toCharArray(), 0, s.length());
serializer.endElement("", "a", "a");
serializer.endDocument();
```

This approach has a number of advantages. The serialization library takes care of all the details of escaping and character encoding, reducing the risk of bugs in your application. And because you are writing to the standard ContentHandler interface, it's easy to change your application so it pipes the output into a different ContentHandler, one which performs further application processing rather than doing immediate serialization.

You can also set serialization properties using this interface. Here's an example that illustrates how to do this. The output is serialized as HTML (which will only be useful, of course, if the elements you are writing are valid HTML elements — but that applies equally to any vocabulary).

```
Transformer trans = serializer.getTransformer();
trans.setOutputProperty(OutputKeys.METHOD, "html");
trans.setOutputProperty(OutputKeys.INDENT, "yes");
trans.setOutputProperty(OutputKeys,ENCODING, "iso-8859-1");
```

Serializing Using StAX

I've already discussed StAX as a pull parser API, which is how most people think of it. But in fact, StAX has a push API as well. The SAX ContentHandler interface, used in the previous section, was primarily designed as an interface allowing an XML parser to push events to a Java application. This explains why it's a little bit clumsy when you use it, as you just did, to push events from a Java application to a serializer. By contrast, the StAX push API is designed primarily to allow applications to push events to other components, such as serializers, so it is more user-friendly from the point of view of the component doing the pushing.

As with the pull API, the StAX push API comes in two flavors. The cursor-level interface is called XMLStreamWriter (mirroring XMLStreamReader), whereas the iterator-level interface is XMLEventWriter (mirroring XMLEventReader).

Here's how you might serialize a simple document using the XMLStreamWriter interface:

```
XMLOutputFactory factory = XMLOutputFactory.newInstance();
XMLStreamWriter serializer = factory.createXMLStreamWriter(
        new FileOutputStream(new File("output.xml")));
serializer.writeStartDocument("iso-8859-1", "1.0");
serializer.writeStartElement("", "a");
serializer.writeCharacters("some XML content");
serializer.writeEndElement();
serializer.writeEndDocument();
```

You can also call `setProperty()` on the `XMLStreamWriter` object to set serialization properties, but unlike the JAXP interface, it has no standard property names. You have to look in the documentation to see what properties are available for your chosen implementation. Woodstox, for example, has a property that allows you to control whether empty elements should be written in minimized form (such as `<empty/>`).

The StAX serialization interface is slightly more convenient to use than the JAXP `ContentHandler` interface, but I will probably continue to use the SAX interface until StAX implementations are more widely available and offer serialization properties similar to those available in JAXP. Some features, such as HTML serialization, are available only through the JAXP interface.

This completes a tour of the lowest level of XML interfaces for Java, the interfaces for reading and writing lexical XML. In the next section, you explore the next level: generic tree models for XML.

XML Tree Models

Chapter 12 is devoted to a detailed exposition of the DOM, the most commonly used tree model for XML. Once again, in this section, you step back from the details to look at the role of the DOM as part of the wider picture of Java interfaces to XML. It also discusses some of the alternative tree models that have appeared in the Java world, specifically JDOM, DOM4J, and XOM.

It's easy to see why tree models are popular. It's much easier to manipulate the content of an XML document at the level of a tree of nodes than it is to deal with events in the order they are reported by a parser. This method puts the application back in control. Rather than dealing with the data in the order it appears in the document (which is the case when you use either a push or a pull parser interface), a tree representation of the document in memory enables you direct access, navigating around the structure to locate the information that your application needs. It's rather like the difference between processing a sequential file (who does that nowadays?) and using a database.

One of the two problems with tree models is performance. Tree models tend to take up a lot of memory (ten times the original source document size is not untypical), and they also take time to build because of the number of objects that need to be allocated. The other disadvantage is that navigation around the structure can be extremely tedious. Most tree models allow you to mix low-level procedural navigation (`getFirstChild()`, `getNextSibling()` and so on) with the use of XPath expressions for a more declarative approach, but using XPath brings its own performance penalty because it usually involves parsing and optimizing XPath expressions on the fly.

The DOM interface, although it remains the most popular tree model used in the Java world, has problems of its own. Most of these stem from its age: It was designed originally to handle HTML rather than XML, and it was first adapted to handle XML before namespaces were invented. The result is that namespaces still feel very much like a bolt-on extra. Another significant problem is that DOM was devised (by W3C) as a programming-language-independent interface, with Java being just one of the language bindings. This means that many of its idioms are very un-Java-like. This includes its exception handling, the way that collections (lists and maps) are handled, the use of shorts to represent enumerated constants, and many other details. This problem is partly cosmetic, but there is a deeper impact because it diminishes the extent to which DOM code fits well architecturally into the Java world view.

Because DOM was developed by a standards committee, it has grown rather large. In fact, the W3C working group no longer exists, having been replaced by an interest group. The specifications are no longer being developed, and some of the work that was done by the working group is now in a somewhat undefined state of limbo. But the material that was published as formal Recommendations is quite large enough. Not all of this has yet made it into Java, which confuses the issue further. Some parts that have made it into Java, notably the Event model, go well beyond what one expects to find in a tree representation of XML documents and are far more concerned with user-interface programming in the browser (or elsewhere). This reflects the historical origins of the DOM as the underpinning object model for Dynamic HTML.

The DOM, remember, is a set of interfaces — not an implementation. Several implementations of these interfaces exist: in fact, there can be any number. You can write your own implementation if you want, and this is not just a fanciful notion. By writing a DOM interface to some underlying Java data source, you can make the data appear to the world as XML, and thus make it directly accessible to any XML process that accepts DOM input, for example XSLT transformations and XQuery queries.

The fact that DOM is a set of interfaces with multiple implementations, combined with the fact that it is a large and complex specification, leads inevitably to the result that different implementations are not always as compatible as one would like. It can be difficult to write application code to DOM interfaces that actually works correctly with all implementations. It's very easy to make assumptions that turn out to be faulty: I once wrote the test

```
if (x instanceof Element) ...
```

in a DOM application. It failed when it ran on the Oracle DOM implementation because in that implementation some objects that are not element nodes nevertheless implement the DOM `Element` interface. This is perfectly legal according to the specification, but not what one might expect.

A further criticism of the DOM is that it doesn't reflect modern thinking as to the true information model underlying XML. It retains information that most applications don't care about, such as CDATA sections and entity references. It throws away some information that applications do care about, such as DTD-defined attribute types, and it models namespaces in a way that makes them very difficult to process.

For some users, the final straw is that DOM isn't even stable. Unlike its policy with every other interface in the JDK class library, Sun's policy for DOM allowed incompatible changes to be made to the interfaces in J2SE 5.0, with the result that it can be quite difficult to write applications that work on multiple versions of the JDK. This affects providers of DOM interfaces more than users, but since the interface is only as good as the products that implement it, the effect is a general decline in support for DOM as a preferred interface.

Alternatives to DOM

A number of alternatives to DOM have been proposed to address the shortcomings outlined in the previous section. You look at three of them: JDOM, DOM4J, and XOM. Each of these has an open source implementation and an active user community. None of them is actually part of the JDK, which creates the serious disadvantage that the interfaces are not recognized by other APIs in the Java family such as JAXP and XQJ (discussed later in this chapter). However, as you see in this chapter, this has not meant that they are islands of technology with no interoperability.

JDOM

JDOM, produced by a team led by Jason Hunter, was the first attempt to create an alternative tree model.

JDOM's main design aim was to be significantly easier to use than DOM for the Java programmer. The most striking difference in its design is that it uses concrete classes rather than interfaces. All the complexities and abstractions of factory classes and methods are avoided, which is a great simplification. The decision has another significant effect, which has both advantages and disadvantages: There is only one JDOM. If you write an application that works on a JDOM tree, it will never work on anything else. You can't make a different tree look like a JDOM tree by implementing the JDOM interfaces; the best you can do is to bulk copy your data into a JDOM tree. This might seem like a significant disadvantage, but most people won't need to do this. The big advantage, however, is that because there is only one JDOM, it has no compatibility problems with different implementations.

Another striking feature of the JDOM model is that no abstract class represents a node. Each of the various kinds of node has its own concrete class, such as `Element`, `Comment`, and `ProcessingInstruction`, but there is no generic class that all nodes belong to. This means that you end up using the class `Object` a lot. A generic interface called `Parent` exists for nodes that can have children (element and document nodes), and there is also a generic class for nodes that can be children (text nodes, comments, elements, and so on), but nothing for the top level. When programming using JDOM, I have found this is a bewildering omission.

This small example gives a little feel of the navigation interfaces in JDOM. Suppose you have an XML document like the one that follows, and you have this data in a JDOM tree that you want to copy to a Java HashMap:

```
<currencies>
  <currency code="USD">1.00</currency>
  <currency code ="EUR">0.79</currency>
  <currency code ="GBP">0.53</currency>
  <currency code ="JPY">118.29</currency>
  <currency code ="CAD">1.13</currency>
</currency>
```

Here's the Java code to do it:

```
HashMap map = new HashMap();
Document doc = new SaxBuilder().build(new File('input.xml'));
for (Iterator d = doc.getDescendants(); d.hasNext();) {
    Object node = d.next():
    if (node instanceof Element and
                   ((Element)node).getName().equals("currency")) {
        map.put(node.getAttributeValue("code"), node.getValue());
    }
}
```

All the tree models struggle with the problem of how to represent namespaces. JDOM, true to its philosophy, concentrates on making the easy cases easy. Elements and attributes have a three-part name (prefix, local name, and namespace URI). Most of the time, that's all you need to know. Occasionally, in some documents, you may need to know about namespaces that have been declared even if they aren't used in any element or attribute names (they might be used in a QName-valued attribute such as `xsi:type`).

To cover such cases, an element also has a property `getAdditionalNamespaces()`, which returns namespaces declared on the element, excluding its own namespace. If you want to find all the namespaces that are in scope for an element, you have to read this property on the element itself, on its parent, and so on — all the way up the tree.

An effect of this design decision is that when you make modifications to a tree, such as moving an element or renaming it, the namespaces usually take care of themselves, except in the case where your document contains QName-valued attributes. In that case, you must take great care to ensure that the namespace declarations remain in scope.

JDOM comes with a raft of "adapters" that allow data to be imported and exported from/to a variety of other formats including, of course, DOM and SAX. To create a tree by parsing XML, you simply write

```
Document doc = new SaxBuilder().build(new File('input.xml'));
```

Serialization is equally easy: you can serialize the whole document by writing

```
new XMLOutputter().output(doc, System.out);
```

If you want to customize the way that serialization is done, you can supply the `XMLOutputter` with a `Format` object on which you set preferences. For example, you can set the option `setExpandEmptyElements()` to control whether empty element tags are used.

JDOM also provides interfaces to allow XPath or XSLT access to the document. This exploits the JAXP interfaces to allow different XSLT and XPath processors to be selected. Of course, you can only choose one that understands the JDOM model. (In fact, Saxon has support for JDOM and doesn't use this mechanism: You can wrap a JDOM document in a wrapper that allows Saxon to recognize it directly as a Source object.)

Overall, the keynote of JDOM is simplicity. Simplicity is its strength, but also its weakness. It makes easy things easy, but it can also make difficult things rather hard or impossible.

For more information about JDOM and to download the software, visit`jdom.org/`.

DOM4J

DOM4J started as an attempt to build a better JDOM. It is sometimes said that it is a *fork* of JDOM, but I don't think this is strictly accurate in terms of the actual code. Rather, it is an attempt to redo JDOM the way some people think it should have been done.

Unlike JDOM, DOM4J uses Java interfaces very extensively. All nodes implement the `Node` interface, and this has sub-interfaces for `Element`, `Attribute`, `Document`, `CharacterData`, and so on. These interfaces, in turn, have abstract implementation classes, with names such as `AbstractElement`, and `AbstractDocument`. `AbstractElement` has two concrete subclasses: `DefaultElement`, which is the default DOM4J class representing an element node, and `BaseElement`, which is a helper class designed to allow you to construct your own implementation. (Why would you want your own implementation? Essentially, you use it to add your own data to a node or use methods that allow you to navigate more easily around the tree.)

So you can see immediately that in contrast to JDOM, this is heavy engineering. The designers have taken the theory of object-oriented programming and applied it rigorously. The result is that you can do far more with DOM4J than you can with JDOM, but you must be a rather serious developer to want all this capability.

Here's the same code that you used earlier for JDOM reworked for DOM4J.

```
HashMap map = new HashMap();
Document doc = ...;
Element root = doc.getRootElement();
for (Iterator d = root.elementIterator("currency"); d.hasNext();) {
    Element node = (Element)d.next():
    map.put(node.attributeValue("code"), node.getStringValue());
}
```

It's not a great deal different. DOM4J methods are a bit more strongly typed than their JDOM equivalents, but any benefit you get from this is eliminated by the fact that both interfaces were designed before Java generics hit the scene in J2SE 5.0. That means the objects returned by iterators have to be cast to the expected type. The DOM4J code is a bit shorter because you have a wider range of methods to choose from, but the downside of that is that you have a longer spec to wade through before you find them!

In addition to the simple navigational methods that allow you to get from a node to its children, parent, or siblings, DOM4J offers some other alternatives. For example you can define a `Visitor` object which visits nodes in the tree, having its `visit()` method called to process each node as it is traversed: This feels strangely similar to writing a SAX ContentHandler, except that the `visit()` method is free to navigate from the node being visited to its neighbors.

An interesting feature of DOM4J is that it's possible to choose implementation classes for the DOM4J nodes that implement DOM interfaces as well as DOM4J interfaces. In principle, this means you can have your cake and eat it, too. However, I'm not sure how useful this really is in practice. Potentially, it creates a lot of extra complexity.

Like JDOM, the DOM4J package includes facilities allowing you to build a DOM4J tree from various sources, including lexical XML, SAX, StAX, and DOM, and to export to various destinations, again including lexical XML, SAX, StAX, and DOM. The serialization facilities work in a very similar way to JDOM. DOM4J also has a built-in XPath 1.0 engine, and you can use it with JAXP XSLT engines.

So if you can sum up JDOM by saying it is about simplicity, you can say the DOM4J is about solid support for advanced object-oriented development approaches and design patterns.

DOM4J is found at `dom4j.org/`.

XOM

The most recent attempt to create the perfect tree model for XML in the Java world is XOM. The focus of the XOM project is 100% fidelity and conformance to the XML specifications and standards. In particular, it attempts to do a much better job than previous models of handling namespaces. XOM is developed by Elliotte Rusty Harold, and although it's open source, he maintains strong control to ensure that the design principles are adhered to.

It's worth asking why namespaces are such a problem. In lexical XML, a namespace declaration on a particular element binds a prefix to a namespace URI. This prefix can be used anywhere within the content of this element as a shorthand for the namespace URI. When you come to apply this to a tree model, this creates a number of problems:

- Are the prefixes significant, or can a processor substitute one prefix for another at whim? After much debate, the consensus now is that you have to try to preserve the original prefixes for two reasons: First, because users have become familiar with them, and second, they can be used in places (such as XPath expressions within attribute content) where the system has no chance of recognizing them and, therefore, changing them.
- If prefixes are significant, what happens when an element becomes detached from the tree where the prefix is defined? Tree models support *in-situ* updates, and they have all struggled with defining mechanisms that allow update of namespace declarations without the risk of introducing inconsistencies.

As well as concentrating on strict XML correctness, XOM also has some interesting internal engineering, designed to reduce the problems that occur when you use tree models to represent very large documents. XOM allows you to build the tree incrementally, to discard the parts of the document you don't need while the tree is being built, to process nodes before tree construction has finished, and to discard parts of the tree you have finished with. This makes it a very strong contender for dealing with documents whose size is 100Mb or larger.

Like JDOM, XOM uses classes rather than interfaces. Harold justifies this choice vigorously and eloquently: He claims that interfaces are more difficult for programmers to use, and more important, interfaces do not enforce integrity. You can write a class that ensures that the String passed to a particular method will always be a valid XML name, but you cannot write an interface that imposes this constraint. In addition, an interface can't impose a rule that one method must be called before another method is called. When you work with interfaces, you recognize the possibility of multiple implementations, and you have no control over the quality or interoperability of the various implementations. This is all good reasoning, but it does mean that, just as there is only one JDOM, there is only one XOM. You can't write a XOM wrapper around your data so that XOM applications can access it as if it were a "real" XOM tree.

XOM does allow and even positively encourages the base classes (such as `Element`, `Attribute`, and so on) to be subclassed. The design has been done very carefully to ensure that subclasses can't violate the integrity of the system. Many methods are defined as `final` to ensure this. Users sometimes find this frustrating, but it's done with good reason. The capability to subclass means that you can add your own application-dependent information to the nodes, and you can add your own navigation methods. So you might have a method `getDollarValue()` on an `Invoice` element that returns the total amount invoiced without exposing to the caller the complex navigation needed to find this data.

At the level of navigational methods, XOM is not so very different from JDOM and DOM4J. Here's that familiar fragment of code rewritten for XOM, to prove it:

```
HashMap map = new HashMap();
Document doc = ...;
Element root = doc.getRootElement();
Elements currencies = root.getChildElements("currency");
for (int i=0; i<currencies.size(); i++) {
    Element node = currencies.get(i):
    map.put(node.getAttributeValue("code"), node.getValue());
}
```

One interesting observation is that this is the first version of this code that doesn't involve any Java casting. In the absence of Java generics, XOM has defined its own collection class `Elements` (rather like DOM's `NodeList`) to achieve type safety.

It won't come as a surprise to learn that XOM also comes with converters to and from DOM and SAX; you can build a document by creating a `Builder` using any SAX parser (represented by an `XMLReader` object). It also has interfaces to XSLT and XPath processors; and, of course, XOM also has its own serializer.

Closely related to XOM, but a quite separate package from a different developer (Wolfgang Hoschek) is a toolkit called NUX. This integrates XOM tightly with the Saxon XPath and XQuery engine and with StAX parsers such as Woodstox. It offers binary XML serialization options and a number of features geared towards processing large XML documents at high speed in streaming mode. For users with large documents and a need for high performance, the combination of XOM, Saxon, and NUX is almost certainly the most effective solution available unless the user wants to pay large amounts of money.

So the keywords for XOM are strict conformance to XML standards and high performance engineering, especially for large documents.

You can find out more about XOM at `.xom.nu/`, and about NUX at `http://dsd.lbl.gov/nux/`. Saxon (which has both open source and commercial versions) is at `saxonica.com/`.

This concludes our tour of the Java tree models. You don't have any reference information to help you actually program against these models, but there's enough here to help you decide which is right for you and to find the detail you need online.

In the next section of the chapter, you move up a level in the tier of Java XML interfaces, to discuss data binding.

Java/XML Data Binding

So far, the interfaces you've been looking at don't try to hide the fact that the data you are working with is XML. Documents consist of elements, attributes, text nodes, and the like. When you manipulate them at the level of a sequential parser API like SAX or StAX, or at the level of a document object model like DOM, JDOM, DOM4J, or XOM, you must understand what elements, attributes, and text nodes are, and how they relate to each other.

The idea of data binding is to move up a level. To find out the zip code of an address, you no longer need to call `element("address").getAttributeValue("zipcode")`; instead you call `address.getZipCode()`.

In other words, data binding maps (or *binds*) the elements and attributes of the XML document representation to objects and methods in your Java program whose structure and representation reflect the semantics of the data you are modeling, rather than reflecting the XML data model.

It's probably true to say that data binding works better for data-oriented XML than for document-oriented XML. In fact, some data binding products have difficulty coping with some of the constructs frequently found in document-oriented XML, such as comments and mixed content. These products aren't actually aiming to achieve fidelity to the XML representation. A number of products and interfaces implement this general idea. The accepted standard, however, is the JAXB interface, also referred to on occasion as JSR (Java Specification Request) 31. JAXB brings together the best ideas from a number of previous technologies, but it hasn't completely displaced them: You may find yourself working with the open-source Castor product, for example, which has similar concepts but is not JAXB-compliant. Other products you might come across include JBind, Quick, and Zeus. Some more specialized products use similar concepts: The C24 Integration Objects package, for example, focuses on conversions between different XML-based and non-XML formats for financial messages. It achieves the interoperability by means of a data binding framework.

JAXB is technically a specification rather than a product, but for many users the term is synonymous with the reference implementation, which comes as part of the Java Web Services Developers Pack (JWSDP). The JAXB 2.0 specification was finalized during 2006, but because this is only a broad overview, you don't need to be too concerned with the differences.

Data binding generally starts with an XML Schema description of the XML data. Among the considerable advantages to using an XML Schema, rather than (for example) a DTD, the most obvious one is that XML Schema defines a rich set of data types for the content of elements and attributes (dates, numbers, strings, Booleans, URIs, durations, and so on). Less obviously, XML Schema has also gone to great lengths to ensure that when you validate a document against a schema you don't get just a yes/no answer and perhaps some error messages. You get a copy of the document (the so-called PSVI, or post-schema-validation-infoset) in which every element and attribute has been annotated with type information derived from the schema. In fact, some of the restrictions in XML Schema (that are so painful when you use it for validation) are there explicitly to support data binding. The notorious UPA (Unique Particle Attribution) rule says that a model is ambiguous (and, therefore, invalid) if more than one way of matching the same data exists. Data binding requires conversion of an XML element to a Java object, and the schema determines which class of object you end up with. It's not enough, for example, to say that a book can consist of a sequence of chapters followed by a sequence of appendices; you must be able to decide without any ambiguity (and also without backtracking) whether the element you're now looking at is a chapter or an appendix. For Relax NG, it would be good enough to say, "If it could be either, that's fine; the document is valid." But for XML Schema, that's not good enough because the XML Schema is about more than validation.

I can explain it with an example. Here's an XML structure containing a name and address:

```
<customer>
  <name>
    <first>Jean</first>
    <last>Dupont</last>
  </name>
  <address>
    <line>18bis rue d'Anjou</line>
    <line/>
    <postal-code>75008</postal-code>
    <city>Paris</city>
    <country>France</country>
  </address>
</customer>
```

Mapped to Java, you might want to see:

```
Class Customer {
  PersonalName getName();
  Address getAddress();
}

Class PersonalName {
  String getFirstName();
  String getLastName();
}

Class Address {
  List<String> getAddressLines();
  String getPostalCode();
  String getCity();
  String getCountry();
}
```

It can get more complicated than this, of course. For example, one might want ID/IDREF links in the XML to be represented as methods that traverse the relationships between Java objects.

Rather than starting with an XML document instance and converting it to a set of Java objects, a data binding tool starts with an XML schema and converts it to a set of Java classes. These classes can then be compiled into executable code. Typically, the executable code contains methods that construct the Java objects from the XML document instance (a process called *marshalling*) or that create the XML document instance from the Java objects (called *unmarshalling*).

The process of creating class definitions from a schema can be fully automated. You then end up with a default representation of each construct in the schema. However, you can often get a much more effective representation of the schema if you take the trouble to supply extra configuration information to influence the way the class definitions are generated. JAXB provides two ways of doing this: You can add the information as annotations to the source schema itself, or you can provide it externally. Using external configuration information is more appropriate if you don't control the schema (for example, if you are defining a Java binding for an industry schema such as FpML).

Although it's usual to start with an XML Schema, JAXB also allows you to work in the opposite direction. Instead of generating a set of Java classes from a schema, you can generate a schema from a set of Java classes. The model is pleasingly symmetric, as you can see from Figure 16-5.

In JAXP, a Java class is generally derived from an element definition in the schema. Most of the customization options are concerned with how the Java class name relates to the name of the XML element declaration. This is used to get a name that fits in with Java naming conventions, and also to resolve conflicts when the same name is used for more than one purpose.

Java package names are derived by default from the XML namespace URI. For example, the namespace URI `http://www.example.com/ipo` converts to the java package name `com.example.ipo`. This works well if you stick to the recommended naming conventions — but very badly if you don't!

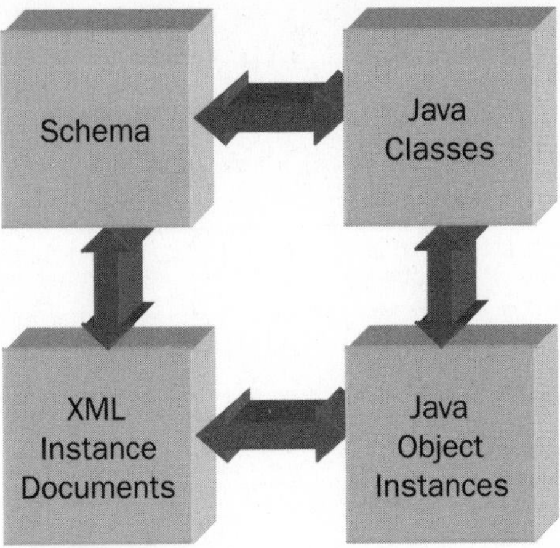

Figure 16-5

Within the package, a number of interfaces represent the complex types defined in the schema, and a number of interfaces represent the element declarations. A class, `ObjectFactory`, allows instances of the elements to be created. Further classes are generated to represent enumeration data types in the schema by using the Java *type-safe enumeration* pattern.

Within an element, attributes and simple-valued child elements are represented as properties (with getter and setter methods). Complex-valued child elements map to further Java classes (this includes any element that is allowed to have attributes, as well as elements that can have child elements).

The following table shows a default mapping of the built-in types defined in XML Schema to data types in Java. Some of these are straightforward; others require more discussion.

XML Schema Type	Java Data Type
`xs:string`	`java.lang.String`
`xs:integer`	`java.math.BigInteger`
`xs:int`	`int`
`xs.long`	`long`
`xs:short`	`short`
`xs:decimal`	`java.math.BigDecimal`
`xs:float`	`float`
`xs:double`	`double`
`xs:boolean`	`boolean`
`xs:byte`	`byte`

Table continued on following page

XML Schema Type	Java Data Type
`xs:QName`	`javax.xml.namespace.QName`
`xs:dateTime`	`javax.xml.datatype.XMLGregorianCalendar`
`xs:base64Binary`	`byte[]`
`xs:hexBinary`	`byte[]`
`xs:unsignedInt`	`long`
`xs:unsignedShort`	`int`
`xs:unsignedByte`	`short`
`xs:time`	`javax.xml.datatype.XMLGregorianCalendar`
`xs:date`	`javax.xml.datatype.XMLGregorianCalendar`
`xs:gYear, gYearMonth, gMonth, gMonthDay, gDay`	`javax.xml.datatype.XMLGregorianCalendar`
`xs:anySimpleType`	`java.lang.Object` (for elements), `java.lang.String` (for attributes)
`xs:duration`	`javax.xml.datatype.Duration`
`xs:NOTATION`	`javax.xml.namespace.QName`
`xs:anyURI`	`java.lang.String`

Notice how, in some cases, no suitable class is available in the core Java class library, so new classes had to be invented. This is particularly true for the date and time types because although a lot of commonality exists between the XML Schema dates and times and classes such as `java.util.Date`, many differences exist in the details of how things such as `timezones` are handled.

One might have expected `xs:anyURI` to correspond to `java.net.URI`. It doesn't because the detailed rules for the two are different — `xs:anyURI` accepts URIs whether or not they have been `%HH` encoded, whereas `java.net.URI` corresponds more strictly to the RFC definitions.

For derived types, the rules are quite complex. For example, a user-defined type in the schema derived from `xs:integer` whose value range is within the range of a java `int` is mapped to a java `int`.

List-valued elements and attributes (that is, a value containing a space-separated sequence of simple items) are represented by a Java List. Union types in the schema are represented using a flag property in the Java object to indicate which branch of the union is chosen.

When you do the mapping in the opposite direction, from Java to XML Schema, you aren't restricted to the types in the right-hand column of the preceding table. For example, if your data uses the `java.util.Date` type, this is mapped to an `xs:dateTime` in the schema.

After you have established the Java class definitions, customized as far as you consider necessary, you can unmarshall an XML document to populate the classes with instances. Suppose that you started with the sample purchase order schema published in the W3C primer (`http://www.w3.org/TR/xmlschema-0/`), and that the relevant classes are generated into package `accounts.ipo`.

Start by creating a `JAXBContext` object, naming this package, and then adding an `Unmarshaller`:

```
JAXBContext jaxb = JAXBContext.newInstance("accounts.ipo");
Unmarshaller u = jaxb.createUnmarshaller();
```

Now you can unmarshall a purchase order from its XML representation:

```
PurchaseOrder ipo =
           (PurchaseOrder)u.unmarshall(new FileInputStream("order.xml"));
```

And now you can manipulate this as you would any other Java object:

```
Items items = ipo.getItems();
for (Iterator iter = items.getItemList().iterator(); iter.hasNext()) {
    ItemType item = (ItemType)iter.next();
    System.out.println(item.getQuantity());
    System.out.println(item.getPrice());
}
```

Marshalling (converting a Java object to the XML representation) works in a very similar way using the method

```
Marshaller.marshal(Object jaxbElement, ...);
```

Marshalling involves converting values to a lexical representation, and this can be customized with the help of a `DatatypeConverter` object supplied by the caller.

I hope this overview of JAXB gives you the flavor of the technology and helps you to decide whether it's appropriate for your needs. If you're handling data rather than documents, and if you have a lot of business logic processing the data in Java form, then JAXB or other data binding technologies can certainly save you a lot of effort. This suggests that they are ideal in a world where applications are Java-centric, with XML being used around the edges to interface the applications to the outside world. It's probably less appropriate in an application architecture where XML is central. In that case, you are probably writing the business logic in XSLT or XQuery, and that brings us to the subject of the next and final section of this chapter.

Controlling XSLT, XQuery, and XPath Processing from Java

XSLT, XQuery, and XPath are well-covered in other chapters of this book, and none of that information is repeated here. Rather, the aim here is to show how these languages work together with Java.

In many cases, Java is used simply as a controlling framework to collect the appropriate parameters, fire off an XSLT transformation, and dispose of the results. For example, you may have a Java servlet whose only real role in life is to deal with an incoming HTTP request by running the appropriate transformation. Today, that is probably an XSLT transformation. In the future, XQuery may play an increasing role, especially if you use an XML database.

The key here is to decide which language the business logic is to be written in. You can write it in Java, and then use XSLT simply to format the results. My own inclination, however, is to use XSLT and XQuery as fourth-generation application development languages, containing the bulk of the real business logic. This relegates Java to the role of integration glue, used to bind all the different technology components together.

It is possible to mix applications written in different languages, however. The best approach to doing this in the XML world is the pipeline pattern: Write a series of components, each of which transforms one XML document into another; and then string them together, one after another, in a pipeline. The different components don't have to use the same technology: Some can be XSLT, some XQuery, and some Java.

The components in a pipeline must be managed using some kind of control structure. You can write this yourself in Java; or you can use a high-level pipeline language. The pipeline might well start with an XForms processor that accepts user input from a browser window and feeds it into the pipeline for processing. Different stages in the pipeline might handle input validation (perhaps using a schema processor), database access, and output formatting. No standards exist for high-level pipeline languages yet, but the W3C has started work in this area, and in the meantime, a number of products are available (take a look at Orbeon for an example: `www.orbeon.com`). You can also implement the design pattern using frameworks such as Cocoon.

Why are pipelines so effective? First, they provide a very effective mechanism for component reuse. By splitting your work into a series of independent stages, the code for each stage becomes highly modular and can be deployed in other pipelines. The second reason is that pipelines can be dynamically reconfigured to meet different processing scenarios. For example, if management asks for a report about particular activity, it's easy to add a step at the appropriate place in the pipeline that monitors the relevant data flow and "siphons off" a summarized data feed without changing the existing application except to reconfigure the pipeline.

The reason for discussing pipelines here (yet again) is that this kind of thinking has influenced the design of the APIs you are about to look at—in particular, the JAXP API for controlling XSLT transformations.

XPath APIs fit less well into the structure of this section. If you're using XPath from Java on its own, you're probably using it in conjunction with one of the object models discussed in the second section of this chapter (DOM, JDOM, DOM4J or XOM). That's likely to be a Java-centric architecture, using XPath essentially as a way of navigating around the tree-structured XML representation without all the tedious navigation code that's needed otherwise. For that reason, this section does not cover XPath in any detail. Instead, it focuses on the JAXP interface for XSLT, and the XQJ interface for XQuery.

These APIs all have very different origins. The JAXP transformation API was created (originally under the name TrAX) primarily by the developers of the first four XSLT 1.0 engines to appear on the Java scene around 1999–2000: James Clark's original xt processor, Xalan, Saxon, and Oracle. All these had fairly similar APIs, and TrAX was developed very informally to bring them together. It only became a reality, however, when Sun decided to adopt it and formalize the specification as part of the JDK, developing the XML parser part of the JAXP API at the same time. This history shows why one of the important features of JAXP is that it enables users to select from multiple implementations (that is to choose an XML parser and an XSLT processor) without having compile-time dependencies on any implementation in their code.

XQJ, the XQuery API for Java, was a much later development than JAXP, just as XQuery standardization itself lags behind XSLT by about seven years (and counting). By this stage, the Java Community Process was much more formalized (and politicized), so development was slower and less open. Like JAXP, however, development was driven by vendors. The key participants in the XQJ process were database vendors, and as a result, the specification has a strong JDBC-like feel to it. It supports the notion that there is a client and a server who communicate through a Connection. Some XQJ implementations might not actually work that way internally, but that's the programming style.

Let's now look at these two families of interfaces in turn.

JAXP: The Java API for XML Processing

In its original form, JAXP contained two packages: the `javax.xml.parsers` package to control XML parsing, and `javax.xml.transform` to control XSLT transformation and serialization. More recently, other packages have been added, notably `javax.xml.validation` to control schema validation (not only XML Schema, but other schema languages such as Relax NG), and `javax.xml.xpath` for standalone XPath processing. In addition, the `javax.xml.datatype` package contains classes defining Java-to-XML data type mappings (you saw these briefly in the previous section on JAXB data binding), and the `javax.xml.namespace` package contains a couple of simple utility classes for handling namespaces and QNames.

Be a bit careful about which versions of these interfaces you are using. Java JDK 1.3 was the first version to include XML processing in the JDK, which was achieved by including JAXP 1.1. (Previously, JAXP had been a component that you had to install separately.) JDK 1.4 moved forwards and incorporated JAXP 1.2, whereas JDK 1.5 (or J2SE 5.0 as the Sun marketing people would like us to call it) rolled on to JAXP 1.3. If you want the schema validation and XPath support, or support for DOM level3, you need JAXP 1.3. This comes as standard with JDK 1.5, as already mentioned, but you can also download it to run on JDK 1.4. Unfortunately, it's a messy download and installation because it only comes as part of the very large Java Web Services Developer Pack product. To make matters worse, if you develop an application that uses JAXP 1.3, you're not allowed to distribute JAXP 1.3 with the application. Your end users have to download it and install it individually. Perhaps Sun is just trying to encourage you to move forward to J2SE 5.0.

The same story occurs again with JAXP 1.4, which contains the StAX Streaming API and pull parser discussed at the beginning of this chapter. JAXP 1.4 is bundled with J2SE 6.0. You can get a freestanding download for J2SE 5.0, but it changes every week, so I'm not sure I'd recommend it for serious work.

Also note that when you download or install JAXP, you get both the interface and a reference implementation (usually the Apache implementation). This generates some confusion about whether JAXP is merely an API or a specific product. In fact, it's the API — that's what the "A" stands for — and the product serves as a reference implementation because an API with nothing behind it is very little use.

You'll look at these packages individually in due course. But first, look at the factory mechanism which is shared (more-or-less) by all these packages, for choosing an implementation.

The JAXP Factory Mechanism

The assumption behind the JAXP factory mechanism is that you, as the application developer, want to choose the particular processor to use (whether it's an XML parser, an XSLT processor, or a schema validator). But you also want the capability to write portable code that works with any implementation, which means your code must have no compile-time dependencies on a particular product's implementation classes: It should be possible to switch from one implementation to another simply by changing a configuration file.

The same mechanism is used for all these processors, but the XSLT engine is the example here. JAXP comes bundled with the Apache Xalan engine, but many people use it with other processors, notably Saxon because that supports the more advanced XSLT 2.0 language specification.

You start off by instantiating a Factory class:

```
TransformerFactory factory = TransformerFactory.newInstance();
```

This looks simple, but it's actually quite complex. `TransformerFactory` is a concrete class, delivered as part of the JAXP package. It's actually a factory in more than one sense. The real `TransformerFactory` class is a factory for its subclasses — its main role is to instantiate one of its subclasses, and there is one in every JAXP-compliant XSLT processor. Its subclasses, as you see later, act as factories for the other classes in the particular implementation. The Saxon implementation, for example, is class `net.sf.saxon.TransformerFactoryImpl`.

So if you organize things so that Saxon is loaded, then you find that the result of this call is actually an instance of `net.sf.saxon.TransformerFactoryImpl`. It's often a good idea to put a message into your code at this point to print out the name of the actual class that was loaded, because many problems can occur if you think you're running one processor and you're actually running another. Another tip is to set the Java system property `jaxp.debug` to the value `true` (you can do this with the switch `-Djaxp.debug=true` on the command line). This gives you a wealth of diagnostic information that shows which classes are being loaded and why.

How does the master `TransformerFactory` decide which implementation-specific `TransformerFactory` to load? This is where things can get tricky. The procedure works like this:

1. Look to see if there is a Java system property named `javax.xml.transform.TransformerFactory`. If there is, its value should be the name of a subclass of `TransformerFactory`. For example, if the value of the system property is `net.sf.saxon.TransformerFactoryImpl`, Saxon should be loaded.
2. Look for the properties file `lib/jaxp.properties` in the directory where the JRE (Java runtime) resides. This can contain a value for the property `javax.xml.transform.TransformerFactory`, which again should be the required implementation class.
3. Search the classpath for a JAR file with appropriate magic in its JAR file manifest. You don't need to worry here what the magic is: The idea is simply that if Saxon is on your classpath, Saxon gets loaded.
4. If all else fails, the default `TransformerFactory` is loaded. In practice, at least for the Sun JDK, this means Xalan.

A couple of problems can arise in practice, usually when you have multiple XSLT processors around. If you've got more than one XSLT processor on the classpath, searching the classpath isn't very reliable. It can also be difficult to pick up your chosen version of Xalan, rather than the version that shipped with the JDK (which isn't always the most reliable).

As far as choosing the right processor is concerned, my advice is to set the system property. Searching the classpath is simply too unpredictable, especially in a complex Web services environment, where several applications may actually want to make different choices. In fact, if the environment gets really tough, it can be worth ignoring the factory mechanism entirely and just instantiating the chosen factory directly:

```
TransformerFactory factory = new net.sf.saxon.TransformerFactoryImpl();
```

But if you don't want that compile time dependency, setting the system property within your code seems to work just as well:

```
System.setProperty("javax.xml.transform.TransformerFactory",
                   "net.sf.saxon.TransformerFactoryImpl");
TransformerFactory factory = TransformerFactory.newInstance();
```

Another problem with the JAR file search is that it can be very expensive. With a lot of JAR files on the classpath, it sometimes takes longer to find an XML transformation engine than to do the transformation. Of course, you can and should reduce the impact of this by reusing the factory. You should never have to instantiate it more than once during the whole time the application remains running.

You've seen the mechanism with regard to the `TransformerFactory` for XSLT processors, and the same approach applies (with minor changes) to factories for SAX and DOM parsers, schema validators, XPath engines, and StAX parsers.

One difference is that some of these factories are parameterized. For the schema validator, you can ask for a `SchemaFactory` that handles a particular schema language (for example XML Schema or Relax NG), and for XPath you can request an XPath engine that works with a particular document object model (DOM, JDOM, and so on). These choices are expressed through URIs passed as string-valued parameters to the `newInstance()` method on the factory class. Although they appear to add flexibility, a lot more can also go wrong. One of the things that can go wrong is that some processors have been issued with manifests that the JDK doesn't recognize, because of errors in the documentation. Again, the answer is to keep things as simple as you can by setting system properties explicitly.

The JAXP Parser API

The SAX and DOM specifications already existed before JAXP came along, so the only contribution made by the JAXP APIs is to provide a factory mechanism for choosing your SAX or DOM implementation. Don't feel obliged to use it unless you really need the flexibility it offers to deploy your application with different parsers. Even then, you might find better approaches: For example SAX2 introduced its own factory mechanism shortly after JAXP first came out, and many people suggest using the SAX2 mechanism instead (the `XMLReaderFactory` class in package `org.xml.sax.helpers`).

For SAX, the factory class is called `javax.xml.parsers.SAXParserFactory`. Its `newInstance()` method returns an implementation-specific `SAXParserFactory`; you can then call the method `newSAXParser()` on that to return a `SAXParser` object, which is in fact just a thin wrapper around the `org.xml.sax.XMLReader` object that does the real parsing.

The DOM mechanism is similar. The factory class is named `javax.xml.parsers.DocumentBuilderFactory`; after you have an implementation-specific `DocumentBuilderFactory`, you can call `newDocumentBuilder()` to get a `DocumentBuilder` object, which has a `parse()` method that takes lexical XML as input and produces a DOM tree as output.

After you've instantiated your parser you're in well-charted waters that are discussed elsewhere in this book.

If you're adventurous, you can write your own parser. Your creation doesn't have to do the hard work of parsing XML; it can delegate that task to a real parser written by experts. It can just pretend to be a parser by implementing the relevant interfaces and making itself accessible to the factory classes. You can exploit this idea in a number of ways. Your parser, when it is loaded, can initialize configuration settings on the real parser underneath, so your parser is, in effect, just a preconfigured version of the standard system parser. Also, your parser can filter the communication between the application and the real parser underneath. For example, you could change all the attribute names to uppercase or you could remove all the whitespace between elements. This is just another way of exploiting the pipeline idea, another way of configuring the components in a pipeline so that each component does just one job. SAX provides a special class `XMLFilterImpl` to help you write a pseudo-parser in this way.

The JAXP Transformation API

The interface for XSLT transformation differs from the parser interface in that it isn't just a layer of factory methods; it actually controls the whole process.

It's, therefore, quite a complex API, but (as is often the way) 90% of the time you only need a small subset.

As discussed earlier, you start by calling `TransformerFactory.newInstance()` to get yourself an implementation-specific `TransformerFactory`.

You can then use this to compile a stylesheet, which you do using the rather poorly named `newTemplates()` method. This takes as its argument a `Source` object, which defines where the stylesheet comes from. (A stylesheet is simply an XML document, but it can be represented in many different ways.) `Source` is a rather unusual interface, in that it's really just a marker for the collection of different kinds of sources that the particular XSLT engine happens to understand. Most accept the three kinds of `Source` defined in JAXP, namely a `StreamSource` (lexical XML in a file), a `SAXSource` (a stream of SAX events, perhaps but not necessarily from an XML parser), and a `DOMSource` (a DOM tree in memory). Some processor may accept other kinds of `Source`; for example, Saxon accepts source objects that wrap a JDOM, DOM4J, or XOM document node.

The next stage is to create a `Transformer`, which is the object that actually runs the transformation. You do this using the `newTransformer()` method on the `Templates` object. The `Templates` object (essentially, the compiled stylesheet in memory) can be used to run the same transformation many times, typically on different source documents or with different parameters—perhaps in different threads. Creating the compiled stylesheet is expensive, and it's a good idea to keep it around in memory if you're going to use it more than once. By contrast, the `Transformer` is cheap to create, and its main role is just to collect the parameters for an individual run of the stylesheet; so my usual advice is to use it once only. Certainly, you must never try to use it to run more than one transformation at the same time.

Here's a simple example that shows how to put this together. It transforms `source.xml` using stylesheet `style.xsl` to create an output file `result.html`, setting the stylesheet parameter `debug` to the value `no`.

```
TransformerFactory factory = TransformerFactory.newFactory();
Source styleSrc = new StreamSource(new File("style.xsl"));
Templates stylesheet = factory.newTemplates(styleSrc);
```

```
Transformer trans = stylesheet.newTransformer();
trans.setParameter("debug", "no");
Source docSrc = new StreamSource(new File("source.xml"));
Result output = new StreamResult(new File("result.html"));
trans.transform(docSrc, output);
```

One little subtlety in this example is worth mentioning. The class `StreamSource` has various constructors, including one that takes an `InputStream`. Instead of giving it a new `File` as the input, you can give it a new `FileInputStream`. But there's a big difference: With a `File` as input, the XSLT processor knows the base URI of the source document or stylesheet. With a `FileInputStream` as input, all the XSLT processor sees is a stream of bytes, and it has no idea where they came from. This means that it can't resolve relative URIs, for example those appearing in `xsl:include` and `xsl:import`. You do have the option to supply a base URI separately using the `getSystemId()` method on the Source object, but it's easy to forget to do it.

You can call various methods to configure the `Transformer`, for example to supply values for the `<xsl:param>` parameters defined in the stylesheet, but its main method is the `transform()` method which actually runs the transformation. This takes two arguments: a `Source` object, which this time represents the source document to be transformed, and a `Result` object, which describes the output of the transformation. Like `Source`, this is an interface rather than a concrete class. An implementation can decide how many different kinds of `Result` it will support. Most implementations support the three concrete `Result` classes defined in JAXP itself, which mirror the `Source` classes: `StreamResult` for writing (serialized) lexical XML, `SAXResult` for sending a stream of events to a SAX `ContentHandler`, and `DOMResult` for writing a DOM tree.

That's the essence of the transformation API. It's worth it to be familiar with a few variations, if only to learn which methods you don't need for a particular application:

- As well as running an XSLT transformation you can run a so-called identity transformation, which simply copies the input to the output unchanged. To do this, you call the factory's `newTemplates()` method without supplying a source stylesheet. Although an identity transformation doesn't change the document at the XML level, it can be very useful because it can convert the document from any kind of `Source` to any kind of `Result`, for example from a `SAXSource` to a `DOMResult` or from a `DOMSource` to a `StreamResult`. If your XSLT processor supports additional kinds of source and result, this becomes even more powerful.
- Rather than running the transformation using the `transform()` method, you can run it as a filter in a SAX pipeline. In fact, you can do this in two separate ways. One way is to create a `SAXTransformerFactory` and call its `newTransfomerHandler()` method. The resulting `SAXTransformerHandler` is, in fact, a SAX `ContentHandler` that can be used to receive (and, of course, transform) the events passed by a SAX parser to its `ContentHandler` directly. The other way, also starting with a `SAXTransformerHandler`, is to call the `newXMLFilter()` method to get an `XMLFilter`, which as you saw earlier is a pretend-XML-parser. This pretend parser can be used to feed its output document in the form of SAX events to an application that is written in the form of a SAX `ContentHandler` to process SAX output.

The `SAXTransformerFactory` also allows the stylesheet to be processed in a pipeline in a similar way, but this feature is rarely needed.

- The JAXP interface allows you to supply two important plug-in objects: an `ErrorListener`, which receives notification of errors and decides how to report them, and a `URIResolver`, which decides how URIs used in the stylesheet should be interpreted (a common use is to get a cached copy of documents from local filestore, identified by a catalog file). Be aware that the `ErrorListener` and `URIResolver` supplied to the `TransformerFactory` itself are used at compile time, whereas those supplied to the `Transformer` are used at runtime.

The JAXP Validation API

New in JAXP 1.3, the validation API allows you to control validation of a document against a schema. This is a schema with a small *s*. The API is designed to be independent of the particular schema technology you use. The idea is that it works equally well with DTDs, XML Schema, or Relax NG, and perhaps even other technologies such as Schematron.

Validation is often done immediately after parsing, and, of course, it can be done inline with parsing—that is, as the next step in the processing pipeline. But it can make sense to do validation at other stages in the pipeline as well. For example it is useful to validate that the output of a transformation is correct XHTML. The validation API is, therefore, quite separate from the parsing API (and some validators—Saxon is an example—are distributed independently of any XML parser).

The API itself is modelled very closely on the transformation API. The factory class is called `SchemaFactory`, and its `newInstance()` method takes as a parameter a constant identifying the schema language you want to use. With the resulting implementation-specific `SchemaFactory` object, you can call a `newSchema()` method to parse a source schema to create a compiled schema, in much the same way as `newTemplates()` gives you a compiled stylesheet. The resulting `Schema` object has a method `newValidator()` that, as you would expect, returns a `Validator` object. This is the analog of the `Transformer` in the transformation API, and sure enough, it has a `validate()` method with two arguments: a `Source` to identify the document being validated, and a `Result` to indicate the destination of the post-validation output document. (You can omit this argument if you only want a success/failure result.)

If you want to do validation in a SAX pipeline, the `Schema` object offers another method `newValidatorHandler()`. This returns a `ValidatorHandler` that, like a `TransformerHandler`, accepts SAX events from an XML parser and validates the document that they represent.

Here's an example that validates a document supplied in the form of a DOM, creating a new DOM representing the post-validation document. As well as having attribute values normalized and defaults expanded, it differs from the original by having type annotations, which can be interrogated using methods available in DOM level 3 such as `Node.getTypeInfo()`.

```
SchemaFactory schemaFactory =
        SchemaFactory.newInstance("http://www.w3.org/2001/XMLSchema");
// create a grammar object.
Schema schemaGrammar = schemaFactory.newSchema(new File("schema.xsd"));
Validator schemaValidator = schemaGrammar.newValidator();
//validate xml instance against the grammar.
schemaValidator.validate(new StreamSource("instance.xml"));
System.err.println("Validation successful");
```

After the discussion of the main components of the JAXP API, move on now to XQJ, the Java API for XQuery, or rather, as the order of the initials implies, the XQuery API for Java. (If you think that's an arbitrary distinction, you need to study the byzantine politics involved in defining the name.)

XQJ: The XQuery API for Java

Unlike the other APIs discussed in this chapter, XQJ is not a completely stable specification at the time of writing. You can get early access copies of the specifications, but there is no reference implementation you can download and play with. Nevertheless, it's implemented in a couple of products already (for example, Saxon and the DataDirect XQuery engine), and it seems very likely that many more will follow. A great many XQuery implementations are trying to catch a share of what promises to be a big market. They won't all be successful, so using a standard API is a good way to hedge your bets when it comes to choosing a product.

Because the detail might well change, in this chapter, you get an overview of the main concepts.

XQJ does reuse a few of the JAXP classes, but it's obvious to the most casual observer that it comes from a different stable. In fact, it owes far more to the design of data-handling APIs like JDBC.

The first object you encounter is an `XQDataSource`. Each implementation has to provide its own `XQDataSource` object. Unlike JAXP, there's no factory that enables you to choose the right one; that's left to you (or to a framework such as J2EE) to sort out. You can think of an `XQDataSource` as an object that represents a database.

From this object you call `getConnection()` to get a connection to the database. The resulting `XQConnection` object has methods like `getLoginTimeout()`, so it's clear that the designers are thinking very much in client-server terms with the connection representing a communication channel between the client and the server. Nevertheless, it's sufficiently abstract that it's quite possible for an implementation to run the server in the same thread as the client (which is what Saxon does).

After you've got a connection, you can compile a query. This is done using the `prepareExpression()` method on the `Connection` object. This architecture means that a compiled query is closely tied not only to a specific database but to a specific database connection. The result of the method is an `XQPreparedExpression` object. Rather surprisingly, this fulfills the roles of both the `Templates` and the `Transformer` objects in the JAXP transformation API. You can set query parameters on the `XQPreparedExpression` object, which means that it's not safe to use it in multiple threads at the same time. (This feels like a design mistake that might well be corrected before the final spec is frozen.)

You can then evaluate the query by calling the `executeQuery()` method on the `XQPreparedExpression`. This returns an `XQResultSequence`, which is a representation of the query results that has characteristics of both a List and an Iterator. In fact, two varieties of `XQResultSequence exist`, one of which allows only forward scrolling through the results, whereas the other allows navigation in any direction.

The items in the query result are represented using an object model that's fairly close to the abstract XDM data model defined in the XQuery specification itself. The items in the sequence are `XQItem` objects. These can be either nodes or atomic values. If they are nodes, you can access them using the `getNode()` method which returns a DOM representation of the node; if they are atomic values you can access the value using a method such as `getBoolean()` or `getInt()` according to the actual type of the value. (The mapping between XML Schema data types and Java types seems to be slightly different from the one that JAXB uses.)

Some interesting methods allow the results of a query to be presented using other APIs discussed in this chapter. For example, `getItemAsStream()` returns a StAX stream representation of a node in the query results, whereas `writeItemToSAX()` allows it to be represented as a stream of SAX events.

For more details of the XQJ interface, you can download the early access specifications from `http://jcp.org/en/jsr/detail?id=225`. But this is not yet a mature specification, so you must carefully investigate how the interface is implemented in different products.

Summary

In this chapter, you have taken a lightning tour through the main places where Java and XML meet. You started with the lowest level interfaces — the streaming pull and push parser APIs, SAX and StAX. Then you moved up a level to the various tree-structured document object models: DOM, JDOM, DOM4J, and XOM.

For data centric applications where the business logic resides in Java, you looked at Java XML data binding interfaces, typified by the JAXP specification. Then you examined the interfaces used to control high-level, XML-based languages such as XSLT and XQuery from a Java application framework.

Some of these APIs are covered in much more detail elsewhere in this book. For others, you have to go to the reference materials for the APIs, which can, in every case, be found online. Although there isn't enough detail in this chapter to enable you to write code using any of these interfaces, you should now have enough background to enable you to study the reference manuals. You have already acquired a broad understanding of the key concepts and, in particular, an understanding of the range of different interfaces available and their relationship to each other.

17

Dynamic Languages and XML

Although much attention is currently directed to Java and .NET, many developers work with dynamic programming languages such as Perl, Python, and Ruby. Dynamic languages differ from languages such as Java or C# in that the variables are usually not fixed to a particular type. For example, the following code fragment is perfectly valid in a dynamic language:

```
var x;
x = 5;
x = "testing";
```

Notice that the variable declaration does not identify the type of the variable, and that it may be used to store numeric, string or even object values. In most dynamic languages, the variable declaration is not even needed: You can simply begin to use a variable. Some languages, such as Python and Ruby, go even further, supporting what has become known as duck typing. With duck typing, a variable is treated as a particular type as long as it supports the same method and property calls as the desired type does. That is, if a block of code is expecting a method called `toString`, then any object may be used as long as it supports a `toString` method. This demonstrates a powerful feature in dynamic languages, the ability to rapidly prototype and test a block of code. (The term duck typing derives from the old expression, "If it walks like a duck, and quacks like a duck, it must be a duck.")

Dynamic languages are frequently also known as scripting languages, as many of them are interpreted languages that may be used directly from the command-line, without requiring a separate compilation step. These two features — dynamic variables and flexibility in release — outline the benefits many developers see in dynamic languages: It is very easy to rapidly develop and iterate applications written in dynamic languages. In addition, some programming concepts are much more difficult to implement in statically typed languages when compared with dynamic languages.

Dynamic languages are also ideal for manipulating XML. Most have strong text-manipulation capabilities, and libraries for processing XML in a variety of ways. This chapter looks at three of the most commonly used dynamic languages (Perl, Python, and Ruby). For each of these languages, it will show some of the common methods of using these languages to read and write XML and related technologies.

Perl

Perl is one of the oldest, and most powerful of the scripting languages. Originally created by Larry Wall in 1987, he wanted to name it Pearl, after the Parable of the Pearl. However, that name was already taken by another programming language, so he shortened it to Perl. Later, the name has been said to be an acronym (Practical Extraction and Report Language), however this name is a fairly contrived example of creating the acronym after the fact.

Perl is available for most, if not all, platforms and is currently at version 5.8. Its forte is text-processing, and it is typically used in scenarios where you need to search through large amounts of text to find the information you need, such as processing log files. This section focuses on the most basic XML parsers available in Perl, showing you techniques for reading and writing XML using the commonly available libraries for Perl. Note, however, that Perl supports a great many more libraries and methods of working with XML: see *Programming Perl* ISBN 0-596-00027-8 (aka "The Camel Book") for more details on Perl. The samples in this section were created using ActivePerl 5.8.8 (Build 819), but they should work with any Perl installation with few or no changes.

Reading and Writing XML

Perl supports three main types of parsers for working with XML: tree-based, object-based, and stream-based. Each is useful in different situations. Object-based parsers convert the XML into Perl objects, enabling you to work with XML without keeping track of angle brackets. Tree-based parsers enable you to work with the XML in memory, moving forward and backward as needed to process the XML. Finally, stream-based parsers move rapidly through the XML document, raising events that you can use in your code to process the XML. Generally, object-based parsers "feel" the most natural for those used to dealing with a programming language. Rather than deal with XML as a separate format, object-based parsers enable the developer to use the techniques they already know to work with the format. Tree-based parsers are generally based on the XML DOM, and thus are the easiest to port between languages. They create a common model in memory, of the XML as a tree with a single root, and branches reaching out to terminal leaf nodes. Finally, stream-based parsers are generally the fastest if you need forward-only access to the XML. In addition, they usually have the lowest memory requirements because they only store a portion of the document in memory at any time. These parsers are best if you need only a small part of the XML file, or if you will only need to process the file once, and in order.

Reading XML

The simplest library for processing XML with Perl is named, strangely enough, XML::Simple. This library was originally created for processing configuration files, but it can be used with many XML files. It is an object-based parser, converting the XML into Perl data structures, such as hashrefs and arrays. XML::Simple has two main methods: `XMLin` loads a block of XML and converts it into a mixture of arrays and associative arrays, whereas `XMLout` does the opposite. In Perl, arrays are zero-based lists of items, and associative arrays are collections of name-value pairs. Listing 17-1 shows how this library can be used to process the XML that is shown in Listing 17-2.

Listing 17-1: Using XML::Simple to read XML with Perl

```
use XML::Simple;

my $file = 'customers.xml';
```

```
# default behaviour
print "Default behaviour\n";
my $doc = XMLin($file);
print XMLout($doc->{customer}->{ALFKI});
print "\n============================\n";

# Coerces structure into arrays (outputs as elements)
print "Output as elements\n";
my $doc = XMLin($file, ForceArray=>1);
print XMLout($doc->{customer}->{ALFKI});
print "\n============================\n";

# Does not use id as key, creates array of customers
print "Display 0th customer\n";
my $doc = XMLin($file, KeyAttr=>[]);
print XMLout($doc->{customer}->[0]);
print "\n============================\n";

# Return selected elements
print "Return selected elements\n";
my $doc = XMLin($file);
print $doc->{customer}->{AROUT}->{contact}->{phone}, "\n";
```

Listing 17-2: Sample XML used in reading samples

```
<customers>
  <customer id="ALFKI">
    <company>Alfreds Futterkiste</company>
    <address>
      <street>Obere Str. 57</street>
      <city>Berlin</city>
      <zip>12209</zip>
      <country>Germany</country>
    </address>
    <contact>
      <name>Maria Anders</name>
      <title>Sales Representative</title>
      <phone>030-0074321</phone>
      <fax>030-0076545</fax>
    </contact>
  </customer>
  <customer id="ANATR">
    <company>Ana Trujillo Emparedados y helados</company>
    <address>
      <street>Avda. de la Constitución 2222</street>
      <city>Mexico D.F.</city>
      <zip>05021</zip>
      <country>Mexico</country>
    </address>
    <contact>
      <name>Ana Trujillo</name>
      <title>Owner</title>
```

(continued)

Listing 17-2 *(continued)*

```
      <phone>(5) 555-4729</phone>
      <fax>(5) 555-3745</fax>
    </contact>
  </customer>
  <customer id="ANTON">
    <company>Antonio Moreno Taqueria</company>
    <address>
      <street>Mataderos  2312</street>
      <city>Mexico D.F.</city>
      <zip>05023</zip>
      <country>Mexico</country>
    </address>
    <contact>
      <name>Antonio Moreno</name>
      <title>Owner</title>
      <phone>(5) 555-3932</phone>
    </contact>
  </customer>
  .
  .
  .
</customers>
```

In the previous code, the directive `use XML::Simple;` loads it into your script. It uses the `XMLIn` command to import the XML, and `XMLout` to print it to the system console. Each of the runs loads the same file, but using the various parameters to force the in-memory representation to change. Listing 17-3 shows the output of the code in Listing 17-1.

Installing Perl modules

To use `XML::Simple` in your Perl scripts, first ensure that you have it as part of your distribution. It is included with the ActivePerl distribution by default. If you do not have this library installed, you can install it from Comprehensive Perl Archive Network (CPAN). CPAN is a Web site (`cpan.org`) that provides a common location for finding and downloading Perl libraries. As of this writing, there are almost 11,000 modules available. These range from modules for specific operating systems, image and text processing, and, of course, XML handling. The `XML::Simple` page on CPAN is at `http://search.cpan.org/~grantm/XML-Simple-2.16/lib/XML/Simple.pm.`

Perl interpreters generally have the capability of automatically downloading and compiling modules from CPAN. This means that you generally do not need to navigate manually through the CPAN site, find the module you need, download it, and compile. If you do not have the module installed, or if there is a more recent version of the module available, the code will be downloaded and Perl will attempt to compile the module. This compilation generally means you need a make program (such as `nmake.exe` or `dmake.exe`) available on your computer, and on the system path. Once downloaded and compiled, the module will be available to your applications.

Listing 17-3: Reading XML with XML::Simple

```
Default behaviour
<opt company="Alfreds Futterkiste">
  <address city="Berlin" country="Germany" street="Obere Str. 57" zip="12209" />

  <contact name="Maria Anders" fax="030-0076545" phone="030-0074321"
    title="Sales Representative" />
</opt>

============================
Output as elements
<opt>
  <address>
    <city>Berlin</city>
    <country>Germany</country>
    <street>Obere Str. 57</street>
    <zip>12209</zip>
  </address>
  <company>Alfreds Futterkiste</company>
  <contact>
    <name>Maria Anders</name>
    <fax>030-0076545</fax>
    <phone>030-0074321</phone>
    <title>Sales Representative</title>
  </contact>
</opt>

============================
Display 0th customer
<opt id="ALFKI" company="Alfreds Futterkiste">
  <address city="Berlin" country="Germany" street="Obere Str. 57" zip="12209" />

  <contact name="Maria Anders" fax="030-0076545" phone="030-0074321"
     title="Sales Representative" />
</opt>

============================
Return selected elements
(171) 555-7788
```

By default, `XML::Simple` converts the document into a hashref (associative array). Therefore, the first customer appears in memory as shown in Listing 17-4. Each of the elements in the original XML file is now represented as a name-value pair.

Listing 17-4: Structure of the customer in memory

```
$VAR1 = {
          'address' => {
                        'country' => 'Germany',
                        'zip' => '12209',
                        'city' => 'Berlin',
```

(continued)

Listing 17-4 *(continued)*

```
                         'street' => 'Obere Str. 57'
                     },
          'contact' => {
                         'fax' => '030-0076545',
                         'name' => 'Maria Anders',
                         'title' => 'Sales Representative',
                         'phone' => '030-0074321'
                     },
          'company' => 'Alfreds Futterkiste'
        };
```

You have a number of options for adjusting the resulting structure. For example, the `ForceArray` parameter of `XMLin` converts each element into an array. Listing 17-5 shows the resulting in-memory structure.

Listing 17-5: Structure of the customer in memory with ForceArray

```
$VAR1 = {
          'address' => [
                         {
                           'country' => ['Germany'],
                           'zip' => ['12209'],
                           'city' => ['Berlin'],
                           'street' => ['Obere Str. 57']
                         }
                       ],
          'contact' => [
                         {
                           'fax' => ['030-0076545'],
                           'name' => ['Maria Anders'],
                           'title' => ['Sales Representative'],
                           'phone' => ['030-0074321']
                         }
                       ],
          'company' => ['Alfreds Futterkiste']
        };
```

In addition to the `XML::Simple` module, Perl supports a number of other XML processing modules. Stream-based parsing is available from the `XML::Parser` module. In fact, this module forms the basis of many of the other XML parsers for Perl, including `XML::Simple`. When using `XML::Parser` in streaming mode, you supply up to three handlers; these are called for the start, end, and contents of each tag. Listing 17-6 shows a script to count the occurrences of cities in the customer file.

Listing 17-6: Counting cities with stream-based parsing

```
use XML::Parser;

my $file = 'customers.xml';

my $parser = new XML::Parser();
```

```
my %cities;
my $flag = 0;

sub start_handler {

  my $p = shift;
  my $elem = shift;

  if ($elem =~ /city/) {
    $flag = 1;
  }
}

sub end_handler {
  my $p = shift;
  my $elem = shift;
  if ($elem =~ /customers/) {
    foreach $city (keys %{$cities}) {
      print $city, ": ", %{$cities}->{$city}, "\n";
    }
  }
}
sub char_handler {
  if($flag) {
    my ($p, $data) = @_;
    $cities->{$data}++;
    $flag = 0;
  }
}

$parser->setHandlers(Start => \&start_handler,
                     End   => \&end_handler,
                     Char  => \&char_handler);

$parser->parsefile($file);
```

Three handlers are defined and assigned to the parser. Of the three, only `char_handler` may need some explanation; it is called for each text element in the XML.

The code creates a hash table. The key for each of the elements in the hash table will be the city names, while the value will be the count of that city. As the XML needs to be read only once, using a streaming parser such as `XML::Parser` means that the code should run faster than it might with another form of parser, as the parser itself does not need to create any additional memory structures. In `start_handler`, which is called at the beginning of each element, the code determines if it is in the `city` element, setting a flag if so. If not, it continues. Similar code could handle multiple elements. If the flag is set, the `char_handler` routine increments the count for that city in the hash and turns off the flag. Finally, when the end of document is reached in `end_handler`, the count of each city is dumped to the output. Listing 17-7 shows a portion of the output of this script.

Listing 17-7: Output of the Perl stream-based parsing

```
Reims: 1
Barquisimeto: 1
Mexico D.F.: 5
Strasbourg: 1
Graz: 1
Lille: 1
Leipzig: 1
Charleroi: 1
Bruxelles: 1
Resende: 1
San Francisco: 1
Eugene: 1
Warszawa: 1
Elgin: 1
```

Writing XML

Writing XML with Perl and `XML::Simple` is a matter of building up the correct structure in memory and using `XMLout` to write the resulting XML structure. The items in an array are converted into elements, whereas the items in a hashref are converted into attributes. The code in Listing 17-8 shows how to create a simple in-memory structure. Note that the formatting is for clarity; the definition of the structure could fit on one line.

Listing 17-8: Writing XML with XML::Simple

```
use XML::Simple;

my $cfg = {'version' => '1.0',
           'section' => {
           'name' => 'Section 1',
           'setting' => [
                          {
                            'name' => 'Setting#1',
                            'value' => 'Value#1'
                          },
                          {
                            'name' => 'Setting#2',
                            'value' => 'Value#2'
                          },
                          {
                            'name' => 'Setting#3',
                            'value' => 'Value#3'
                          }
                        ]
            }
            };


# write out Perl variable
print XMLout($cfg, RootName=>'configuration', XMLDecl=>1);
```

The `XMLout` command takes the memory structure created and writes the XML version to the console. As there was no root node defined in the `$cfg` variable, only the value for the version, this is added during the call to `XMLout`. In addition, the standard XML declaration is included by including the `XMLDecl` parameter. If you were creating this XML to be part of a larger structure, you would likely avoid this step. Listing 17-9 shows the output of this script.

Listing 17-9: Output of writing XML with XML::Simple

```
<?xml version='1.0' standalone='yes'?>
<configuration version="1.0">
  <section name="Section 1">
    <setting name="Setting#1" value="Value#1" />
    <setting name="Setting#2" value="Value#2" />
    <setting name="Setting#3" value="Value#3" />
  </section>
</configuration>
```

Support for Other XML Formats

Beyond `XML::Simple` and `XML::Parser`, many other modules exist for working with XML and Perl. CPAN (see the Resources section later in this chapter) lists over 3700 current modules; they include everything from simple processing, through specific XML formats such as Atom or DocBook, to XSLT and XSL:FO processors. Some of the most notable modules include:

- `XML::Parser::PerlSAX` — A stream-based parser with full SAX support.
- `XML::Twig` — A tree-based parser, optimized for working with extremely large documents. Documents can be loaded entirely in memory or chunked to conserve memory.
- `XML::DOM` — A tree-based parser with W3C DOM support. Good for porting DOM code, but rather non-Perl.

Python

Python is an interpreted scripting language that has been around for quite some time. It was created by Guido van Rossum in 1990. The name is not derived from the snake, but is in fact a reference to the television show, "Monty Python's Flying Circus." This reference tends to be repeated throughout Python code, resulting in many samples making reference to spam and parrots.

Python has many of the text-processing features of Perl, but with a more readable syntax and more object-orientation. One of the core tenets of Python coding is that readability is more important than brevity. While it may take more code in Python to perform a given task compared to some languages (most notably Perl), you are much more likely to understand just what the code is intended to do, even months later. In addition to text-processing, the breadth of libraries means that Python can write just about any type of application. It has been embraced fairly strongly by Web developers. The first version of Microsoft's Site Server was written in Python. In addition, the popular video-sharing site YouTube is reported to be written, "almost entirely in Python."

Python is available for almost every platform imaginable, including the new IronPython implementation for Microsoft's .NET platform. The current version as of this writing is 2.5. This section focuses on some of the more commonly used XML parsers. As with Perl, there are many more modules available. The Python Cheese Shop Web site (`python.org/pypi`) is the official central repository of Python modules. As of this writing, it lists over 1850 packages, of which there are approximately 50 for working with XML. While this seems lower than other languages, this is likely due to the strength of the core XML modules. For more details on Python, see *Beginning Python* (ISBN 978-0-7645-9654-4) or the Python Web site (`python.org`). The samples in this section were created using the Windows version of Python version 2.5.

Reading and Writing XML

Since Python 2, the standard library includes support for processing XML, including modules that include DOM, SAX, pull, and object-based syntaxes.

The DOM implementation is a tree-based model, and is modeled on the W3C DOM implementation. As with other DOM implementations, the result is an in-memory structure that contains the whole document. You can then move forward and backward through the document as necessary. SAX and pull provide lighter-weight models for reading XML. The SAX parsing is similar to the other implementations: You provide a number of event handlers that are called while the document is being read. Pull parsers, on the other hand, are generally called in a loop. Each time through the loop, the current position is advanced. Both SAX and pull parsers are best when you need to read through a document in a forward-only fashion, or when the document is quite large. Finally, object-based parsers convert the XML into Python data structures. While this provides the most natural, or Pythonic, means of working with XML, it is also typically the least portable code.

Reading XML

The DOM support in Python is included in the `xml.dom` and `xml.dom.minidom` libraries. The `xml.dom` library is a full implementation of the W3C DOM, while the `xml.dom.minidom` was designed as a lightweight version of the DOM, removing support for some of the less used features. Although reading XML with the DOM may not be the most "Pythonesque" means of processing XML, it is the most portable technique. For more details on the DOM, see Chapter 12. Listing 17-10 shows loading the `customers.xml` file using Python with the `minidom` library.

Listing 17-10: Loading XML using DOM in Python

```
from xml.dom.minidom import parse

doc = parse("customers.xml")
print doc.documentElement.childNodes.length

print "========="
print "\tusing toxml"
print "Print first customer"
print doc.documentElement.childNodes[1].toxml()
print "========="
print "\tusing toprettyxml"
print doc.documentElement.childNodes[1].toprettyxml()

print "========="
print "getElementsByTagName returns array of customers"
```

```
customers = doc.getElementsByTagName("customer")
print customers[15].toprettyxml('..', '\n')

print "========="
print "Return Attribute"
print customers[34].attributes.item(0).value
```

In order to use the DOM objects, you import them into the Python script. The first line in the preceding code imports the `parse` object, which is used to load the local file. There is also a `parseString` object that is used to load string data containing XML. At this step, the memory structure of the XML document is generated. After it is loaded, you can use the DOM methods described in Chapter 12 to extract the nodes in the document. Each of the nodes in the minidom have the methods `toxml()` and `toprettyxml()` included. These methods are non-standard, and are used to export the node in XML. The difference between the two is that the `toprettyxml` supports the addition of parameters for altering the format. In the code in Listing 17-10, the code retrieves the first child of the root element, and prints it to the console. The first call, using `toxml` looks like the code in Listing 17-11 (extra lines have been removed).

Listing 17-11: Output using toxml

```
  using toxml
Print first customer
<customer id="ALFKI">
  <company>
    Alfreds Futterkiste
  </company>
  <address>
    <street>
      Obere Str. 57
    </street>
    <city>
      Berlin
    </city>
    <zip>
      12209
    </zip>
    <country>
      Germany
    </country>
  </address>
  <contact>
    <name>
      Maria Anders
    </name>
    <title>
      Sales Representative
    </title>
    <phone>
      030-0074321
    </phone>
    <fax>
      030-0076545
    </fax>
  </contact>
</customer>
```

In contrast, the default printout using `toprettyxml` creates a more compact document, as seen in Listing 17-12.

Listing 17-12: Output using toprettyxml

```
  using toprettyxml
<customer id="ALFKI">
    <company>Alfreds Futterkiste</company>
    <address>
      <street>Obere Str. 57</street>
      <city>Berlin</city>
      <zip>12209</zip>
      <country>Germany</country>
    </address>
    <contact>
      <name>Maria Anders</name>
      <title>Sales Representative</title>
      <phone>030-0074321</phone>
      <fax>030-0076545</fax>
    </contact>
  </customer>
```

Alternately, you can use the properties of the `toprettyxml` to alter the characters used to indent the lines and the character to use at the end of lines.

Rather than use the DOM, you may want to use stream-based parsing. Tree-based parsers that provide a DOM interface have a bit of a bad reputation for memory use. This is because they must load the entire XML document into memory and create the in-memory representation of the DOM. Stream-based parsers, such as those based on SAX, do not have this limitation, because they hold only a small fraction of the document in memory at any one time. They are also incredibly fast at processing files. The major problem with stream-based processors, however, is that they are forward-only. If you want to move backwards through the document, stream-based parsers do not give you this capability. For more details on SAX, see Chapter 13. The Python SAX parser is defined in the `xml.sax` library. Within that library, there are three main functions that are used.

Class	Description
`make_parser`	Creates a SAX parser. Before using this parser, you must set the class that will perform the processing. This class must inherit from `xml.sax.handler.ContentHandler`.
`parse`	Calls the `ContentHandler` to process the document. The class needs to be created first using `make_parser`. Takes a file as a parameter.
`parseString`	Calls the `ContentHandler` to process the document. The class needs to be created first using `make_parser`. Takes a string as a parameter.

Listing 17-13 shows using the SAX parser with Python.

Listing 17-13: Parsing XML with SAX using Python

```
from xml.sax import make_parser
from xml.sax.handler import ContentHandler

file = "customers.xml"

class CityCounter(ContentHandler):
  def __init__(self):
    self.in_city = 0
    self.cities = {}

  def startElement(self, name, attrs):
    if name == 'city':
      self.in_city = 1

  def endElement(self, name):
    if name == 'customers':
      for city, count in self.cities.items():
        print city, ": ", count

  def characters(self, text):
    if self.in_city:
      self.in_city = 0
      if self.cities.has_key(text):
        self.cities[text] = self.cities[text] + 1
      else:
        self.cities[text] = 1

#main routine
p = make_parser()
cc = CityCounter()
p.setContentHandler(cc)
p.parse(file)
```

As with other SAX-based parsers, you create one or more methods that are called by the parser when specific XML nodes are processed. In this case, the three methods are created in a class that inherits from the default SAX content handler (`xml.sax.handler.ContentHandler`). This enables chaining, in case you wanted to have multiple SAX processors working on the same XML file. This class is assigned to the parser using the `setContentHandler` method. In addition, you could use the `setErrorHandler` method to identify a handler that will be called if an error occurs during the processing of the XML. When the parse method of the SAX parser begins the processing, your methods are called as needed. Just as with other SAX implementations, the `startElement` method is called at the beginning of each element, `endElement` for the close of the element, and `characters` is called for the content of the element. You can test this script on the command line using the command (assuming that `Python.exe` is on your system path):

```
python streamcustomers.py
```

Listing 17-14 shows a portion of the output of this script.

Listing 17-14: Output of the Python SAX processor

```
Boise :  1
Leipzig :  1
Caracas :  1
Strasbourg :  1
Lille :  1
Barcelona :  1
Oulu :  1
Aachen :  1
Warszawa :  1
Marseille :  1
Montreal :  1
Mannheim :  1
Elgin :  1
Reggio Emilia :  1
Toulouse :  1
Walla Walla :  1
Madrid :  3
San Cristobal :  1
Sevilla :  1
Kobenhavn :  1
Munchen :  1
Bruxelles :  1
London :  6
Helsinki :  1
Lisboa :  2
Portland :  2
Seattle :  1
Bräcke :  1
```

Writing XML

Just as Python has methods for reading, it also has a number of ways to write XML.

XML Bookmark Exchange Language (XBEL) is an XML format defined by the Python XML Special Interest Group as a format for applications to share Web browser bookmarks. It has many of the features of OPML, but has the advantage that it is not tied as closely to the implementation of one program as OPML is. In addition, it has a DTD, enabling validation. You can read more about the XBEL format at the XBEL Resources page (`http://pyxml.sourceforge.net/topics/xbel/`). Listing 17-15 shows the creation of a small XBEL file using Python.

Listing 17-15: Writing XML with Python

```
from xml.dom.minidom import getDOMImplementation
from xml.dom import EMPTY_NAMESPACE

class simpleXBELWriter:

  def __init__(self, name):
```

```
    impl = getDOMImplementation()
    doctype = impl.createDocumentType("xbel",
      "+//IDN python.org//DTD XML Bookmark Exchange Language 1.0//EN//XML",
      "http://www.python.org/topics/xml/dtds/xbel-1.0.dtd")

    self.doc = impl.createDocument(EMPTY_NAMESPACE,
      "xbel", doctype)
    self.doc.documentElement.setAttribute("version", "1.0")

    root = self.doc.createElement("folder")
    self.doc.documentElement.appendChild(root)

  def addBookmark(self, uri, title, desc=None):
    book = self.doc.createElement("bookmark")
    book.setAttribute("href", uri)

    t = self.doc.createElement("title")
    t.appendChild(self.doc.createTextNode(title))
    book.appendChild(t)

    if(desc):
      d = self.doc.createElement("desc")
      d.appendChild(self.doc.createTextNode(desc))
      book.appendChild(d)
    self.doc.getElementsByTagName("folder")[0].appendChild(book)

  def Print(self):
    print self.doc.toprettyxml()

w = simpleXBELWriter("Some useful bookmarks")
w.addBookmark("http://www.geekswithblogs.net/evjen",
  "Bill Evjen's Weblog")
w.addBookmark("http://www.acmebinary.com/blogs/kent",
  "Kent Sharkey's Weblog")
w.addBookmark("http://www.wrox.com",
  "Wrox Home Page",
  "Home of great, red books")
w.Print()
```

Just as with other DOM implementations, you create each node at the document level and append it where necessary. In the code in Listing 17-15, a doctype is first created, to enable validating parsers to check the resulting document. This uses the doctype defined for XBEL documents.

The basic structure of an XBEL document is a root node (xbel) containing multiple folder elements. The sample shown in Listing 17-15 creates only a single folder and inserts all bookmarks into it. In a more robust implementation of an XBEL generator, you would want to enable multiple nested folders. Title and, optionally, description elements are added to each bookmark. Listing 17-16 shows the resulting XML.

Listing 17-16: A created XBEL document

```
<?xml version="1.0" encoding="UTF-8"?>
<!DOCTYPE xbel PUBLIC
  "+//IDN python.org//DTD XML Bookmark Exchange Language 1.0//EN//XML"
  "http://www.python.org/topics/xml/dtds/xbel-1.0.dtd">
<xbel version="1.0">
  <folder>
    <bookmark href="http://www.geekswithblogs.net/evjen">
      <title>Bill Evjen's Weblog</title>
    </bookmark>
    <bookmark href="http://www.acmebinary.com/blogs/kent">
      <title>Kent Sharkey's Weblog</title>
    </bookmark>
    <bookmark href="http://www.wrox.com">
      <title>Wrox Home Page</title>
      <desc>Home of great, red books</desc>
    </bookmark>
  </folder>
</xbel>
```

Support for Other XML Formats

As you might expect, what you have seen is only the tip of a huge iceberg. Python has a number of additional libraries for working with XML. Some of the most notable ones are:

- **xml.marshal** — Part of the PyXML distribution. This library enables a simple means of converting between Python objects and XML.
- **XSLT** — A number of XSLT processors are available for Python, including 4XSLT, Pyana, and libxslt.
- **Web services** — A number of Python Web service clients exist, including XML-RPC (xmlrpclib) and SOAP (SOAPpy).

Ruby

Ruby is an interpreted scripting language, designed with object-orientation and simplicity in mind. It was written by Yukihiro "Matz" Matsumoto in 1995. He wanted to create a language that used the best parts of his favorite languages (Perl, Smalltalk, Eiffel, Ada, and Lisp). At the same time, he wanted to create a language that was expressive. That is, one that was simple to use and understand, but with a great deal of power. The name is a slight tribute to Perl, as Matz decided that keeping with the name of a precious gem would be appropriate.

Ruby has many of the features of Perl and Python, as well as features of more academic languages. It shares the text-processing capabilities of Perl and Python, as well as the dynamic nature of these languages. From the more academic languages, Ruby obtained lambda expressions — powerful inline functions — as well as strict object-orientation. It is this last feature that truly distinguishes Ruby from the previous two languages. While both Perl and Python have some aspects of object-orientation, they are more or less recent additions to the language. Ruby, on the other hand, was designed around the concepts of object-oriented programming. Recently, Ruby has grown in popularity, partly because of its completeness, but also due to the increasing popularity of a Web interface written to use it: Ruby on Rails.

Reading and Writing XML

Ruby has support for both reading and writing XML via the REXML library. This library is part of the base Ruby class library. This library was originally modeled off of the Electric XML library. This library was written in Java by The Mind Electric. However, the API is designed to fit into the Ruby way of doing things. This means, "Keep the common case simple, and the uncommon, possible." As such, the API does not completely follow standards, such as the W3C DOM. Instead, it forms a close, but more easily developed model.

Reading XML

Ruby has two main methods for reading XML content:

- A tree-based method that is similar, but not identical, to working with the DOM. While it maintains the XML file in a tree-based memory structure, it does not provide all the methods required by the W3C DOM implementation. Although this makes porting code that uses the W3C model more difficult to port to Ruby, it means that the resulting API is closer to the natural way of working with Ruby.
- A stream-based method based on SAX2. This method more closely follows the SAX model, as described in Chapter 13. The core parser handles three events: one that occurs at the beginning of each element, one at the end, and one for text nodes. You provide the parser with a file or block of XML to process, and it begins executing the methods in order. Although SAX processing is much faster than DOM processing, it is inherently a forward-only pass through the XML. In Ruby, you create a SAX parser by inheriting from a class, and overriding the appropriate methods (see below).

While some differences between the Ruby tree-based model and the W3C DOM are minor, they can trip you up. See the following table for some of the mostly commonly encountered differences between the two.

W3C DOM method	Ruby equivalent	Description
`documentElement`	`root` or `root_node`	Returns the root element of the XML file
`addChild`	`<<` or `add`	Adds a new node to the document tree.
`childNodes`	`get_elements`	Returns the collection of elements below the current element.
`attributes`	`attribute`	Returns the collection of attributes for the selected element. Attributes can be identified by numerical index (starting with 1) or the name of the attribute.

Table continued on following page

W3C DOM method	Ruby equivalent	Description
`firstChild`	`elements[1]`	The elements method returns the collection of child elements of the selected element. Children can be identified by numerical index (starting with 1), string name, or via an XPath statement.
`nextSibling`	`next_element`	Returns the next sibling when iterating through a set of elements.
`getElementsByTagName`	`get_elements`	Both methods take an XPath statement, and return the collection of elements that match that statement.

Listing 17-17 shows some of the methods of REXML in use on the customer.xml file shown earlier (Listing 17-2).

Listing 17-17: Reading XML with Ruby

```
require "rexml/document"
include REXML

doc = Document.new(File.new('customers.xml'), 'r')

puts ">>Print the full first element"
puts doc.root.elements[1]

puts
puts ">>Print the id of the first customer"
puts doc.root.elements['customer'].attributes['id']

puts
puts ">>Select an element via an XPath and display it"
puts doc.elements["//customer[@id='HUNGC']"]

puts
puts ">>Iterate over child elements"
el = doc.elements["//customer[@id='ANTON']"]
puts el.elements["company"].text
el.elements["contact"].each_element{|e| puts e.name+ ": " +e.text }

puts
puts ">>Select elements via XPath and display child elements"
el2 = doc.each_element("//customer/address[country='Canada']/city"){|e| puts
e.text}
```

Listing 17-16 begins with a required statement to load in the REXML library's document handling. Next, REXML is included, so that all references to objects in that namespace don't need the REXML prefix (that is, `Document.new`, not `REXML::Document.new`). The file is loaded into a Document object. It is at this point that the tree structures are built up in memory. The first highlighted line in the listing shows one difference between the REXML structure and the W3C DOM. The root element in Ruby is `root`, rather than the `documentElement` in the DOM.

Elements can be extracted from the document via the `elements` method. Notice that the first element is numbered 1, rather than 0. Alternatively, the name of the element or attribute can be used to identify the item in the collection. The third highlighted line in the preceding code shows a third method: Each of the collection methods (`elements` and `attributes`), as well as the `each_???` methods accept an XPath statement to restrict the selection.

The last two samples in the previous listing show the `each_element` method that iterates over child elements. This is a shorthand method for `doc.elements.each`. As described earlier, the `each_element` also accepts an XPath statement to restrict the returned children. The output of the code in Listing 17-17 should look similar to Listing 17-18.

Listing 17-18: Output of Ruby tree-based processing

```
>>Print the full first element
<customer id='ALFKI'>
    <company>Alfreds Futterkiste</company>
    <address>
      <street>Obere Str. 57</street>
      <city>Berlin</city>
      <zip>12209</zip>
      <country>Germany</country>
    </address>
    <contact>
      <name>Maria Anders</name>
      <title>Sales Representative</title>
      <phone>030-0074321</phone>
      <fax>030-0076545</fax>
    </contact>
  </customer>

>>Print the id of the first customer
ALFKI

>>Select an element via an XPath and display it
<customer id='HUNGC'>
    <company>Hungry Coyote Import Store</company>
    <address>
      <street>City Center Plaza 516 Main St.</street>
      <city>Elgin</city>
      <region>OR</region>
      <zip>97827</zip>
      <country>USA</country>
    </address>
    <contact>
      <name>Yoshi Latimer</name>
      <title>Sales Representative</title>
      <phone>(503) 555-6874</phone>
      <fax>(503) 555-2376</fax>
    </contact>
```

(continued)

Listing 17-18 *(continued)*

```
  </customer>

>>Iterate over child elements
Antonio Moreno Taquería
name: Antonio Moreno
title: Owner
phone: (5) 555-3932

>>Select elements via XPath and display child elements
Montreal
Tsawassen
Vancouver
```

In addition to the methods listed previously, the Ruby XML implementation includes a number of methods that are designed to get information on the structure of the document. These methods use common Ruby idioms, making the code feel more Ruby-like. The following table outlines some of these methods.

Method	Description
`each_element`	Iterates over the child elements of the selected element. Can be passed an XPath statement to restrict the elements iterated over.
`has_elements?`	Returns `true` if the current node has child elements.
`has_attributes?`	Returns `true` if the current node has attributes.
`has_text?`	Returns `true` if the current node has a child text node.
`text=`	Assigns a value as the inner text for an element.

Listing 17-19 shows some of these methods being used to query the structure of the XML.

Listing 17-19: Getting structure information with Ruby

```
require "rexml/document"
include REXML

doc = Document.new(File.new('customers.xml'), 'r')

#get information about element
el = doc.elements["//customer[@id='RICAR']"]
if el.has_attributes?
  puts  el.name+ " has attributes"
  el.attributes.each {|name, value| puts name+ ": " +value}
end

def dump_element(e)
  if e.has_elements?
    puts
    puts e.name+ " has children"
```

```
      e.each_element{|el| dump_element(el)}
    else
      if e.has_text?
        puts e.name+ ": " +e.text
      end
    end
  end

  if el.has_elements?
      dump_element(el)
  end
```

Listing 17-20 shows the output of the preceding code.

Listing 17-20: XML Structure Information

```
customer has attributes
id: RICAR

customer has children
company: Ricardo Adocicados

address has children
street: Av. Copacabana, 267
city: Rio de Janeiro
region: RJ
zip: 02389-890
country: Brazil

contact has children
name: Janete Limeira
title: Assistant Sales Agent
phone: (21) 555-3412
```

In addition to the tree-based document parsing, REXML supports a stream-based parser. With this technique, you create one or more listener classes with methods that are called as the document is processed. You create a listener class by inheriting from the `StreamListener` class. You must then override the methods of the `StreamListener` class to provide the implementation you desire. The following table describes the most common methods you should override.

Method	Description
`tag_start`	Called when the parser first encounters a new tag. The name of the new element will be passed to the method, as well as the attributes for the element. The attributes are provided in an array of name-value pairs. This method is usually used to prepare for the processing by identifying the elements you are interested in.
`tag_end`	Called when the parser encounters the end of an element. This is usually used to undo whatever settings where enabled when the corresponding `tag_start` method was called, such as turning off flags or decrementing counters.
`text`	Called when the parser encounters a text node. This is often where the bulk of the processing occurs when using stream-based parsers.

Listing 17-21 shows some of these methods processing the customers XML file.

Listing 17-21: Reading XML using streams with Ruby

```
require 'rexml/document'
require 'rexml/streamlistener'
include REXML
include Parsers

class Listener
  include StreamListener
  def initialize
    @cities = Hash.new(0)
    @flag = false
   end

  def tag_start(name, attributes)
    if name == 'city'
      @flag = true
    end
  end

  def tag_end(name)
    if name == 'customers'  #end of document
      puts
      dump_list
    end
  end

  def text(text)
    if @flag
      puts "Adding " +text
      @cities[text] = @cities[text] + 1
      @flag = false
    end
  end

  def dump_list()
    puts ">> Count of each city"
    @cities.each {|key, value| puts key+ ": " +value.to_s }
    puts "==="
  end
end

listener = Listener.new
parser = StreamParser.new(File.new("customers.xml"), listener)
parser.parse
```

The Listener class includes the `StreamListener` mixin and contains five methods, three of which are used by the streaming parser (`tag_start`, `tag_end` and `text`). The `tag_start` method is called as each new tag is reached by the parser, whereas `tag_end` is called at the end.

The tag_start method receives two parameters: the name of the element and an array containing the keys and values of the attributes for that element. As the code is identifying cities, it simply sets a flag if the parser has reached a city element.

The counting is done within the text method. As this will be called many times throughout the life of the application, however, it uses the @flag variable to determine if it is within a city element. If this is the case, the entry for the city in the hash table @cities is incremented. As Ruby is a dynamic language, if the city did not have an entry in the hash table, one would be created at this point, and the value set to 1. Finally, the flag is turned off. This could also have been done in the tag_end method.

Once the end of the document has been reached (identified by the tag_end method being called on the customers end element), the contents of the hash table are printed to the console. This method uses a Ruby block to print each entry in the @cities hash table.

Listing 17-22 shows a portion of the output from the code in Listing 17-21.

Listing 17-22: Output of the Ruby stream-based processor

```
Adding Lyon
Adding Reims
Adding Stuttgart
Adding Oulu
Adding Resende
Adding Seattle
Adding Helsinki
Adding Warszawa

>> Count of each city
Stuttgart: 1
Butte: 1
Kobenhavn: 1
Tsawassen: 1
London: 6
Brandenburg: 1
Cunewalde: 1
Marseille: 1
Berlin: 1
Sao Paulo: 4
Portland: 2
Lyon: 1
Albuquerque: 1
Warszawa: 1
Lille: 1
Frankfurt a.M.: 1
```

Writing XML

Writing XML with the REXML library is quite simple. The Document class is used to create the new document, whereas Element and Attribute classes add elements and attributes, respectively.

Writing XML using Ruby is significantly different from using the W3C DOM. Instead of sticking with the API used with the DOM, the authors of the Ruby library chose to follow common Ruby idioms. The following table outlines some of these methods.

Method	Description
`Document.new`	`new( source = nil, context = {} )` Constructor for the `Document` class. Creates a new document, using the provided file, string, or IO stream. If no parameter is supplied, it creates the document in memory. The context parameter is deprecated.
`XMLDecl.new`	`XMLDecl.new(version, encoding, standalone)` Returns the XML declaration string. Defaults are: version=1.0, encoding=UTF-8, and standalone=false.
`Element.new`	`new ( arg = UNDEFINED, parent=nil, context=nil )` Creates a new element. The arg parameter can either be a string, providing a name for the newly created element, or another element, meaning that this new element is a shallow copy of the provided element. If parent is provided, the newly created element is a child of the parent. The context parameter provides a number of options for the content of the element.

`Element.add_element`	`add_element(arg=nil, arg2=nil)`
	Adds a new child element. The two arguments are the name of the newly added element and an optional hashtable containing the attributes for the new element. For example, the line in Listing 17-17 below:
	
	`book3 = folder.add_element("bookmark",`
	`{"href"=>"http://www.wrox.com"})`

`Element.add_attribute`	`add_attribute( key, value=nil )` Adds a new child attribute. The first parameter can be either an existing `Attribute` object, which would be copied into the parent element, or a string, in which case that becomes the name of the new attribute. The second parameter provides the value of the attribute.
`Element.<<`	`<< item` An alias for the `add` method. This is handy shorthand for adding new elements to the document.

Listing 17-23 shows the creation of a simple XBEL (XML Bookmarks Exchange Language) document using REXML. Note that this sample uses a number of different techniques on purpose; it shows the choices available for creating new elements and attributes.

Listing 17-23: Writing XML with Ruby

```
require "rexml/document"
include REXML

doc = Document.new
doc << XMLDecl.new
doc << Element.new("xbel")
doc.root.attributes["version"] = "1.0"

folder = Element.new("folder")
folder << Element.new("title").add_text("Some useful bookmarks")

book1 = folder.add_element("bookmark")
book1.add_attribute("href", "http://www.geekswithblogs.net/evjen")
book1.add_element("title").add_text("Bill Evjen's Weblog")

book2 = Element.new("bookmark")
book2.add_attribute("href", "http://www.acmebinary.com/blogs/kent")
book2 << Element.new("title") << Text.new("Kent Sharkey's Weblog")
folder << book2

book3 = folder.add_element("bookmark", {"href"=>"http://www.wrox.com"})
book3 << Element.new("title") << Text.new("Wrox Home Page")
book3 << Element.new("desc") << Text.new("Home of great, red books")

doc.root.add_element(folder)
doc.write(File.new("output.xml", "w"), 2)
```

First, the REXML library is loaded with the `require` statement, and aliased with the `include REXML` statement. This eliminates the inclusion `REXML::` at every use of the library. The XML document is created, and the standard XML declaration added. Next, the root element is added, along with an attribute.

Listing 17-24 shows the resulting XML document.

Listing 17-24: Output from Ruby

```
<?xml version='1.0'?>
<xbel version='1.0'>
  <folder>
    <title>Some useful bookmarks</title>
    <bookmark href='http://www.geekswithblogs.net/evjen'>
      <title>Bill Evjen&apos;s Weblog</title>
    </bookmark>
    <bookmark href='http://www.acmebinary.com/blogs/kent'>
      <title>Kent Sharkey&apos;s Weblog</title>
    </bookmark>
    <bookmark href='http://www.wrox.com'>
      <title>Wrox Home Page</title>
      <desc>Home of great, red books</desc>
    </bookmark>
  </folder>
</xbel>
```

New elements can be created either standalone (with `Element.new`), or as part of the existing structure (with `add_element`). Similarly, attributes can be added via `add_attribute`, or using `Attribute.new`. Finally, the append method (<<) is overridden to permit adding either elements or attributes. The choice in methods allows you to either select the method that works best for you or for the situation at hand.

Notice from the output that the text is automatically encoded in the case of the single quote characters. In addition, other characters not appropriate in XML files (such as `&` or `"`) will be encoded. This behavior can be overridden by adding the `:raw` value to the context (for `Element.new`). You may use this format when you are writing the entries to a CDATA block or other location where the characters may actually be valid.

Support for Other XML Formats

The base libraries for Ruby also include support for creating and accessing Web services using either SOAP or XML-RPC. In addition, they provide support for working with RSS and W3C XML Schemas. External libraries are generally installed as Ruby gems, a packaging format built into Ruby. As of this writing, there are approximately 1200 Ruby gems, many providing support for various XML formats. Some of the more notable Ruby gems include:

- **Amrita2** — An XHTML templating engine that provides for the transformation of XML documents into XHTML. It is similar in concept to XSLT, but does not follow that standard.
- **FeedTools** — A powerful library for working with RSS, Atom and CDF (Channel Definition Format) files.
- **XMPP4R** — A library for communicating with the XML format used by the Jabber instant messenger protocol.

Summary

Dynamic languages provide their own benefits when working with XML. Their ability to rapidly prototype and iteratively develop a solution make writing routines for reading or writing XML faster than their static cousins like Java or C#. When your compilation cycle is reduced to the time it takes to save the file you are working on, you can be more productive with your code. In addition, as each of these languages has been available for quite some time, many libraries have been created for working with common XML formats. Many even provide a variety of techniques for working with XML: from tree-based syntaxes that work like the W3C DOM, through stream-based interfaces like SAX, all the way to object-based syntaxes that make XML work like the native objects of the language.

Perl, through its powerful implementation of regular expressions, is almost synonymous with text processing. As XML is simply text, it should come as no surprise that Perl works quite well with XML. Whether it is through a low level API, such as `XML::Simple`, more capable APIs (such as `XML::Parser`), or through a library for a specific syntax (such as the SOAP or SVG libraries), Perl provides a capable, if slightly opaque, language for processing XML.

The breadth of libraries for Python truly expresses a common motto of Python, "Batteries included." If you need simply to manipulate XML for a configuration file, or other simple format, you can make use of the powerful built-in functionality. If you need to read or write a specific format of XML, it is almost guaranteed that there is a library out there to help you. This, combined with the expressiveness of the Python language makes it an ideal choice for developing with XML.

Although Ruby does not have native support for a wide variety of XML formats, its native XML handling with REXML provides a rapid means of reading and writing just about any format. Support for creating and calling Web services and other common syntaxes, such as RSS, XML-RPC and others is a nice added bonus. While the total number of libraries is generally less than for Perl or Python, those that are integrate so easily into the nature of the language that it sometimes seems like they were always part of the language.

Resources

A number of additional resources are available for working with Perl, Python, and Ruby and XML.

Perl Resources

- **Perl Home Page** — `perl.org`
- **CPAN, the Comprehensive Perl Archive Network (Collection of Perl Libraries)** — `cpan.org/`
- **Perl.com (Great source of Perl information)** — `perl.com/`

Python Resources

- **Python Home Page** — `python.org`
- **Python Package Index (Collection of Python Libraries)** — `http://cheeseshop.python.org`
- **Starship Python (another great collection of libraries)** — `http://starship.python.net/index.html`
- **Iron Python Home Page (.NET implementation of Python)** — `gotdotnet.com/workspaces/workspace.aspx?id=ad7acff7-ab1e-4bcb-99c0-57ac5a3a9742`

Ruby Resources

- **Ruby Home Page** — `ruby-lang.org`
- **Ruby XML** — `rubyxml.com`
- **The Ruby Garden (Collection of Ruby Libraries)** — `rubygarden.org/`
- **Ruby Forge (Central location for Ruby Open Source applications)** — `rubyforge.com`

Part VI
XML Services

18

RSS and Atom

"Content is King!"

"Content is everywhere."

"It's all about the content."

It's obvious from these comments that spring up frequently in newsgroups, forums, technical articles, and elsewhere that many people consider content important. However, just what is *content* and how do you get it in and out of your applications?

Content is the actual information on a Web site — the technical articles, the blog posts, the media files. Content is basically everything on your average Web site except the navigation elements and advertisements.

You share your content with others when they visit your Web site. If the content on your site changes over time, and people want to stay current on that information, they must check your site frequently to see if anything has changed. Different solutions have been proposed to this problem — from *push* technologies such as PointCast to *pull* technologies such as CDF (Channel Definition Format), RSS, and Atom. Although push technologies have fallen by the wayside, RSS and Atom are increasing in importance, especially because they are used in Weblogs (blogs), news sites, and podcasting.

Although RSS and Atom are generally thought of in terms of Web sites, they also have importance for non-Web applications. A database or desktop application can provide a feed of updates via RSS or Atom. Client applications can use this feed to stay in sync.

This chapter looks at means of reading and writing these two families of XML formats.

What Is RSS?

When you discuss RSS, you have to specify which format of RSS you mean. RSS has gone through a number of iterations since it was first published as RSS 0.90 by Netscape back in 1999. The following table discusses the versions of RSS you are likely to encounter.

Version (Year)	Comments
0.90 (1999)	RDF Site Summary was the initial public version of RSS and was intended as a syndication format for their portal (my.netscape.com). As the title indicates, it was based on the Resource Description Framework (RDF). More information on this version is available from the specification page listed in the resource section at the end of this chapter.
0.91 (1999 and 2000)	Netscape's version was a simplification of the 0.90 version. It removed the need for the document to be RDF compatible. A DTD was available for validation as part of the specification.
	Dave Winer's version was (in his own words) a cleanup of Netscape's 0.91. In addition, it was an attempt to maintain forward momentum of RSS. The specification is similar to Netscape's RSS 0.91 with the removal of the DTD requirement. This was the most available version of RSS for a while, although I think it is now surpassed by RSS 2.0.
0.92 (2000)	An updated version of Userland's 0.91 specification. This version was fairly broadly available, and a number of feeds in this format are still available today. The most important additions to 0.91 were the `enclosure` and `category` elements of item.
1.0 (2000)	A new version initially created to be less ambiguous than previous versions. RSS 1.0 has no relation to the previous versions and was based on RDF. This version is described in this specification.
2.0 (2002)	Also known as version 0.94. This is an updated version of 0.92 that includes optional elements. There is no relationship between version 1.0 and 2.0. This is the first version in the 0.9x/2.0 family that included support for extending RSS via namespaces directly in the specification.

With all these versions "in the wild," you may be confused about how to write code to process RSS. However, these versions really fit into two main families: the RSS 0.9 x/2.0 family and the RSS 1.0 family. As each new version of the 2.0 family was designed, developers maintained backward compatibility as much as possible. Therefore, a parser written to work with version 2.0 should work with versions 0.91 and 0.92 as well. Listing 18-1 shows a sample RSS 2.0 document, and Listing 18-2 shows an RSS 1.0 document.

Listing 18-1: A sample RSS 2.0 feed

```
<?xml version="1.0" encoding="utf-8"?>
<rss xmlns:dc="http://purl.org/dc/elements/1.1/" version="2.0">
  <channel>
    <title>MSDN: Microsoft XML Developer Center</title>
```

```
    <link>http://msdn.microsoft.com/xml/</link>
    <description>The latest information from the Microsoft XML Developer
Center.</description>
    <language>en-us</language>
    <pubDate>Sat, 22 Oct 2005 13:01:25 GMT</pubDate>
    <lastBuildDate>Sat, 22 Oct 2005 13:01:25 GMT</lastBuildDate>
    <generator>MSDN RSS Service 1.1.0.0</generator>
    <ttl>1440</ttl>
    <item>
      <title>XML for Fun: Displaying Your iTunes Library</title>
      <description>In this week's article we'll show you how to extract your song
library as XML from iTunes so that you can use the data from within other
applications as well.</description>
<link>http://msdn.microsoft.com/coding4fun/xmlforfun/ITunesLib/default.aspx</link>
      <dc:creator>Peter Bernhardt</dc:creator>
      <guid isPermaLink="false">Titan_1166</guid>
      <pubDate>Fri, 24 Jun 2005 17:13:48 GMT</pubDate>
    </item>
    <item>
      <title>Introduction to XQuery in SQL Server 2005</title>
      <description>Discover how XQuery works in SQL Server 2005: the FLWOR
statement, operators in XQuery, the if-then-else construct, XML constructors,
built-in XQuery functions, type casting operators, and more.</description>
      <link>http://msdn.microsoft.com/sql/default.aspx?pull=/library/en-
us/dnsql90/html/sql2k5_xqueryintro.asp</link>
      <dc:creator>Prasadarao K. Vithanala</dc:creator>
      <guid isPermaLink="false">Titan_851</guid>
      <pubDate>Wed, 15 Jun 2005 18:42:31 GMT</pubDate>
    </item>
  </channel>
</rss>
```

Important points to note in this feed are:

- The root element is rss.
- There is no defined schema for this feed type, nor is there a default namespace.
- It uses namespaces to provide extensions.

Listing 18-2 shows a sample RSS 1.0 feed.

Listing 18-2: A sample RSS 1.0 feed

```
<?xml version='1.0' encoding='utf-8'?>
<rdf:RDF
xmlns:rdf='http://www.w3.org/1999/02/22-rdf-syntax-ns#'
xmlns:dc='http://purl.org/dc/elements/1.1/'
xmlns='http://purl.org/rss/1.0/'>
<channel rdf:about='http://www.xml.com/'>
<title>XML.com</title>
<link>http://www.xml.com/</link>
<description>XML.com Articles and Weblogs</description>
<dc:rights>Copyright 2005, O'Reilly Media, Inc.</dc:rights>
```

(continued)

Listing 18-2 *(continued)*

```
<dc:language>en-us</dc:language>
<items>
<rdf:Seq>
<rdf:li rdf:resource='http://www.xml.com/pub/a/2005/11/09/fixing-ajax-
xmlhttprequest-considered-harmful.html' />
<rdf:li rdf:resource='http://www.xml.com/pub/a/2005/11/09/rexml-processing-xml-in-
ruby.html' />
</rdf:Seq>
</items>
</channel>
<item rdf:about='http://www.xml.com/pub/a/2005/11/09/fixing-ajax-xmlhttprequest-
considered-harmful.html?CMP=OTC-TY3388567169'>
 <title>Fixing AJAX: XmlHttpRequest Considered Harmful</title>
 <link>http://www.xml.com/pub/a/2005/11/09/fixing-ajax-xmlhttprequest-considered-
harmful.html?CMP=OTC-TY3388567169</link>
 <description><![CDATA[<img src='http://www.xml.com/2005/11/09/graphics/111-
bad_httpreq.gif' width='111px' height='91px' alt='tile image' align='left' />Jason
Levitt shows us how to work around XmlHttpRequest restrictions in order to get more
joy from third-party web services.]]></description>
 <dc:creator>Jason Levitt</dc:creator>
 <dc:date>2005-11-09T15:20:36-08:00</dc:date>
</item>
<item rdf:about='http://www.xml.com/pub/a/2005/11/09/rexml-processing-xml-in-
ruby.html?CMP=OTC-TY3388567169'>
 <title>REXML: Processing XML in Ruby</title>
 <link>http://www.xml.com/pub/a/2005/11/09/rexml-processing-xml-in-
ruby.html?CMP=OTC-TY3388567169</link>
 <description><![CDATA[<img src='http://www.xml.com/2005/11/09/graphics/111-
ruby.gif' width='111px' height='91px' alt='tile image' align='left' />Ruby web
apps, including those built with Rails, don't always use XML to represent data. But
sometimes you just don't have a choice. Koen Vervloesem shows us how to process XML
in Ruby using Ruby Electric XML (REXML).]]></description>
 <dc:creator>Koen Vervloesem</dc:creator>
 <dc:date>2005-11-09T15:16:47-08:00</dc:date>
</item>
</rdf:RDF>
```

Major points to note in this example are:

- The root element is `rdf:RDF`. RSS 1.0 depends heavily on the Resource Description Framework (RDF) specification.
- The use of namespaces to provide extension support.
- Heavy reliance on Dublin Core to provide metadata, such as post date/time, creator, and language.
- The use of `rdf:about` to provide an URI for each major element (channel, item).
- The use of the `rdf:Seq` block to identify the order of the items in the feed.
- The use of CDATA blocks to encode HTML content in the description (this is actually common in RSS 2.0 feeds as well).

Specifications

The specifications for RSS 2.0 and 1.0 vary in their stringency and guidance when building feeds. Although much of the information is self-explanatory, it's worth discussing some areas in detail, because they are common sources of error.

RSS 2.0

RSS 2.0 is arguably the most common RSS feed produced today, as well as being the simplest specification (running about 10 pages). However, it is also the most misinterpreted of the three main syndication formats.

The core structure of an RSS 2.0 feed consists of:

- A root node of `rss`, with a version attribute (should be 2.0).
- One (and only one) `channel` node within the `rss` node. This node serves as a container for the remainder of the document and provides information about the feed. The following table discusses the elements of the channel node. Other elements may be added if the namespace is included in the feed.
- One or more item nodes within the channel node. These are the individual items of the feed.

Element	Required / Optional	Notes
title	Required	A name for the feed. This is typically the same as the name for the site or application it comes from.
link	Required	The URL for the Web site producing the feed. In the case of application-specific feeds, this should be to a site providing more information on the content of the feed.
description	Required	A longer description of the source and content of the feed.
language	Optional	The language the channel is written in, using the language-locale format. For example, en-us for the United States English, fr-ca for Canadian French, or fr-be for Belgian French.
copyright	Optional	Any copyright notice for the content in the feed.
managingEditor	Optional	The e-mail address of the person responsible for the content of the feed.
webMaster	Optional	The e-mail address for the person responsible for the technical source of the feed. Typically, this is the same as managingEditor, but it may be different if one person creates the feed and another makes it available for reading.

Table continued on following page

Element	Required / Optional	Notes
pubDate	Optional	The last publication date for the feed. See following sidebar on Dates and RSS because this is one of the primary sources for errors and incompatibilities in RSS 2.0 feeds.
lastBuildDate	Optional	Similar to the pubDate, the lastBuildDate is the date (and time) when the feed was last built. Generally, pubDate and lastBuildDate are the same. However, if the feed needs to be changed without publishing a new item (such as when there is a correction or update), only lastBuildDate changes. This date could be used by a client to determine if an update has occurred, although this is rarely done.
category	Optional	The name of a category describing the content of the feed. Multiple category elements may exist in the channel.
generator	Optional	The application used to create the feed. Basically for information only.
docs	Optional	The URL of the RSS 2.0 specification — `http://blogs.law.harvard.edu/tech/rss`. This serves a similar purpose to a namespace URL by providing a location to get more information about the structure of the feed.
cloud	Optional	A rarely used element identifying the *cloud* Web service that can be used to notify clients of changes to the feed. I have never seen such a service, and most RSS processors actually only make use of the `ttl` element shown next.
ttl	Optional	"Time To Live" is the time (in minutes) that clients should wait before re-querying the feed. This should be set to a value based on the average change frequency of the RSS feed. For example, a news site might update hourly, so the ttl value should be 60. Alternatively, a personal RSS feed might update occasionally, so a value of daily (1440) would be good enough.
image	Optional	Information used to attach a graphic for the feed. This is sometimes used to customize the appearance of the feed icon for aggregators, but is rarely used by aggregators.
rating	Optional	A rarely used element containing the PICS rating — that is, the Platform for Internet Content Selection, a standard way of identifying the type and rating of content. The intent is to enable teachers and parents to manage what children may be exposed to on the Internet. This is only useful if your Web site requires a PICS rating.
textInput	Optional	A rarely used element (I don't think I've ever seen this outside of the specification, and even the specification states: "The purpose of the textInput element is something of a mystery."). Best to just ignore this field and move on.

Element	Required / Optional	Notes
skipHours	Optional	A rarely used element (I don't think I've ever seen this outside of the specification).
skipDays	Optional	A rarely used element (I don't think I've ever seen this outside of the specification). This is a hint to applications reading the feed that no updates are permitted on the days listed (space delimited).

Dates and RSS

RSS 2.0 uses the slightly outdated RFC 822 for its date format. This format has the general structure:

```
Day of Week, Year Month Day Hour:Minute:Second Timezone
```

where Day of Week is an optional value. For example, the following are all valid date formats based on the specification:

- `Tue, 15 Nov 2005 16:00:01 PDT`
- `13 Feb 2006 07:37:00-0800`
- `Wed, 02 Oct 2002 13:00:00 GMT`

This format can get confusing in that the time zone value can be any of the following: UT, GMT, EST, EDT, CST, CDT, MST, MDT, PST, PDT, Z, A, M, N, or a numeric offset (+/-0000 to +/-1200). These refer to Greenwich Mean Time (UT or Universal Time), a US-centric time zone and Military time (the A, M or N values, although these are generally considered deprecated) or an offset. Making it slightly worse, RSS 2.0 also allows two-digit years. All this variability means that parsing these dates can be difficult. For .NET developers, this is a problem because .NET supports a later RFC, 1123. This RFC simplified the date structure to remove the support for US time zones. In addition, it removed the requirement of the day of week value. While the day of the week value may appear, it is not required. Dates compatible with RFC 1123 are also compatible with the older RFC 822, but not vice versa.

However, the default parser in .NET throws an exception when passed any of the US time zones. That is, `DateTime.Parse("Tue, 15 Nov 2005 16:00:01 PDT")` throws an exception as this format is no longer supported with the later RFC.

RSS 1.0 avoids many of these issues (as does Atom, as we shall see soon) by using the ISO 8601 standard for its date format:

```
Year-Month-DayTHour:Minute:SecondTimeZone
```

Where time zone can either be Z for Universal Time or the time zone offset in numeric form (+/-Hours:Minutes e.g. -08:00 or +5:00)

The following table discusses the elements of the item node:

Element	Required / Optional	Notes
title	Optional (see notes)	The title of the item. This is usually the headline. Although optional, it is highly recommended if you want a useful feed. One of title or description must be present in a feed.
link	Optional (see notes)	The URL of the item. This can be omitted for information-only feeds, but this is rare. The content of this element is also interpreted differently by some sites. Most feeds use this element to point to the URL of the main post. However, posts that refer to content that exists elsewhere, such as a blog post about a Web site, actually point to the original Web site, not the blog post. Either use is acceptable, as long as you are consistent.
description	Optional (see notes)	Either the excerpt or the full post. This is one of those "religious arguments" frequent in the computer industry. Many people believe that the feed should only contain a brief excerpt of the actual post, requiring users to go to the Web site to read the full post. This form reduces the overall bandwidth of the feed, particularly when large posts are syndicated. Alternatively, it does reduce the overall value of the feed, especially for aggregating sites.
author	Optional	The e-mail address of the author of the post. This is included here primarily for feeds that may contain posts by multiple authors.
category	Optional	The name of a category describing the content of the feed. Multiple category elements may exist in the item. Client applications can use these categories to organize or filter the content.
comments	Optional	URL of a page for entering comments.

Element	Required / Optional	Notes
enclosure	Optional	For a long time, this was a rarely used element. Then came podcasting, and it became a popular tag. The enclosure element is used to identify an external media item associated with this item. Often, it is a music item or video. Applications processing this element (podcasting software) download this media item automatically. The enclosure element takes the form: <enclosure url="url" length="bytes" type="mime" /> Where url is the URL of the item, bytes is the length of the item (in bytes, as a courtesy to applications downloading it), and mime is the MIME type of the media. For example: <enclosure url="http://www.cbc.ca/quirks/media/2005-2006/mp3/qq-2006-02-11.mp3" length="22280320" type="audio/mpeg"/>
guid	Optional	A string uniquely identifying the item. This is one of the other major inconsistencies in the RSS specification. Many RSS feeds use the URL of the post here, with the optional attribute isPermaLink set to true: <guid isPermaLink="true">http://www.foo.com/23.html</guid> Other sites use it simply as a URI: <guid isPermaLink="false">Titan_5052</guid> The only required consistency is that within the feed, the guid element should be unique. Beyond that, you're on your own.
pubDate	Optional	The date and time of the posting in RFC 822 format
source	Optional	A rarely used element. This is essentially a self reference to the feed URL for the item in case it is viewed separately. It takes the form: <source url="url to feed">Feed title</source>

Categories versus tags

There are two primary ways of identifying the topic of an item in a feed. Although the RSS 2.0 specification includes the `comments` element, some blogging engines do not support creating or adding categories. This limitation has led to the tagging movement, originally proposed by Technorati. The idea of either format is to identify the general scope of the content of the feed item. That is, to mark it as being about photography, music, or the Olympics. Software processing the feed would then associate items with the same category or tag.

The `category` element is an optional element for each item, and an item can include multiple category elements. The format is:

```
<category domain="taxonomy">value</category>
```

The domain value is optional and should point to the URI describing the category's taxonomy. Just as with a namespace URI, this could be a schema or other description of the structure of the categories, or it could be a unique value for each category. For example, MSDN includes categories in the article feeds.

```
<category domain="mscomdomain:Subject">XML</category>
```

The `tag` element is something that can be added to the body of the description of an item and is a simple HTML anchor tag:

```
<a href="taxonomy" rel="tag">value</a>
```

The href for the taxonomy should point to the URL of any site that organizes content by tag. The suggested default is `http://www.technorati.com/tag/[tagname]`, but it could also be Wikipedia, Flickr, Delicious, or other site, as long as the last item on the query string is the tag name. For example:

```
<a href="http://www.technorati.com/tag/XML" rel="tag">XML</a>
```

You can make the choice of category versus tag, if the blogging engine or other RSS generator doesn't support the addition of category tags. However, even if your blogging engine supports adding categories, you may want to also provide tags. They are a low-weight way of adding information to the feed. In addition, using a tag enables your content to be combined with the growing body of other content associated with that tag.

RSS 2.0 is certainly easy to create, and it is broadly accepted. Parsing these feeds from multiple sources can be a bit of a headache, however, because of the variability in the interpretation of the specification and lack of an XML schema for validation. Because of this, I highly recommend use of an online validator, such as `www.feedvalidator.org`.

RSS 1.0

RSS 1.0 is a very extensible syndication format based on the W3C's Resource Description Framework (RDF). Although not as simple as RSS 2.0 (the specification is 18 pages to RSS 2.0's 10 pages, not counting the additional pages of the RDF specification), it certainly has fewer ambiguities. When referring to the acronym for RSS 1.0, it expands to *RDF Site Summary* in a nicely recursive acronym of an acronym. It is the logical child of RSS 0.9 (but not 0.91 or 0.92) and improves on that format. The main goals were to standardize the then orphaned RSS 0.9 and enable additional expansion and evolution by adding modules. In addition, the specification is much more precise, reducing misinterpretation.

The core structure of an RSS 1.0 feed consists of:

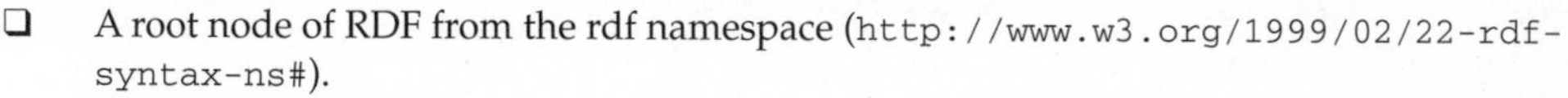

- A root node of RDF from the rdf namespace (`http://www.w3.org/1999/02/22-rdf-syntax-ns#`).
- One (and only one) channel node within the `RDF` element. This contains information about the channel itself. The following table discusses the common elements of this node.
- An `items` element within the `channel` element. This includes pointers to all the item elements of the feed, in order.
- One or more item nodes. Note that (unlike in RSS 2.0) these are not contained within the channel node, but are child elements of the `RDF` element. The following table discusses the elements of the item nodes.
- Optionally, one image node. This node is associated with the feed and is usually an icon (88x31 pixels) for the home site.
- Optionally, one textinput node.
- Liberal use of the `rdf:about` attribute to provide extra information for the elements. This attribute is required for the channel, image, item, and textinput nodes. The following table discusses the standard elements of the RSS 1.0 channel.

Element	Required / Optional	Notes
title	Required	A name for the feed. This is typically the same as the name for the site or application it comes from.
link	Required	URL to the home page for the feed.
description	Required	A description of the channel's content.
image	Required (see notes)	Occasionally used. This element is only required if an image element is also in the feed. It is typically an icon (88x31 pixels) used by the site.

items	Required	A listing of pointers to the item nodes elsewhere in the document. This is used to provide the order of the items using an `rdf:Seq` (sequence) element:
		`<rdf:Seq>`
		`<rdf:li rdf:resource='http://url.to.item1' />`
		`<rdf:li rdf:resource='http://url.to.item2' />`
		`<rdf:li rdf:resource='http://url.to.item3' />`
		`</rdf:Seq>`

Table continued on following page

Element	Required / Optional	Notes
textinput	Required (see notes)	Not frequently used. This element is required only if a `textinput` element is also used in the feed. Contains a pointer to that `textinput` with an `rdf:resource` attribute:
rdf:about	Required	An XML attribute that points to the URI identifying the channel. Generally, this is the URL of the feed, but this is not required.

The following table discusses the standard elements of the RSS 1.0 item.

Element	Required / Optional	Notes
title	Required	The title or headline of the item.
link	Required	The URL of the item.
description	Optional	A brief description or excerpt of the item.

In addition to the `channel` and `item` elements, RSS 1.0 feeds can also include `image` and `textinput` elements. These elements are rarely used. If they do exist, however, you also need matching elements in the channel to point to them. The `image` element is used to provide a graphic for the feed, typically an icon. The `textinput` element is a bit of a throwback to the days when pages contained their own search mechanism (for example, the `isindex` tag) and is intended to provide a mechanism for searching the RSS feed.

In addition to the core RSS elements, RSS 1.0 also includes support for extensibility through modules. These are namespace-identified extensions that add information to the feed. The three most commonly used modules are:

- **Dublin Core** — Standard metadata elements used here, and in RDF generally. These include items such as author, date, language, and so on.
- **Syndication** — Provides hints to readers about how frequently the feed should be updated. This fits the same role as the `skipDays`, `ttl`, and `skipHours` elements of RSS 2.0.
- **Content** — One of the ongoing discussions around RSS is whether the description should hold the entire body of the item. If it is just an excerpt, the `content:encoded` element can be used to hold the entire post.

Although RSS 1.0 is slightly more difficult to read and write than RSS 2.0, it has the benefit of being a more accurate specification. That is, with less ambiguity in the specification, multiple implementations of RSS 1.0 are more likely to match. This is definitely not the same for RSS 2.0, where it sometimes seems that each person creating a feed has interpreted the specification differently.

What Is Atom?

As you saw in the discussion of the various semicompatible variants of RSS, it can be anything but *Really Simple*. Partly because of this complexity and partly because of the management of the RSS 2.0 specification, some developers decided to begin work on Atom. The idea was to take the best features of RSS and fix the parts that caused confusion during implementation.

The core structure of an Atom 1.0 feed consists of:

- The root node is `feed`, with a pointer to the Atom namespace (`http://www.w3.org/2005/Atom`).
- Channel information in the feed itself as child elements.
- One or more entry elements, containing the content.
- One curious feature of Atom is that the root node could also be a single `entry`. Although you probably won't encountered this often when processing an Atom feed, it does mean that entries can be isolated from the overall feed and still remain valid.

Listing 18-3 shows a simple Atom 1.0 feed.

Listing 18-3: A sample Atom 1.0 feed

```
<?xml version="1.0" encoding="UTF-8" standalone="yes"?>

<feed xmlns="http://www.w3.org/2005/Atom" xml:lang="en-US">
<title type="html">AtomEnabled.org</title>
<subtitle type="html">Your one stop shop for all Atom API and syndication
information.</subtitle>

<link href="http://www.atomenabled.org/atom.xml" rel="self"/>
<link href="http://www.atomenabled.org" rel="alternate" title="AtomEnabled.org"
type="text/html"/>
<id>tag:blogger.com,1999:blog-6356614</id>
<updated>2005-09-15T13:33:06Z</updated>
<generator uri="http://www.blogger.com/" version="5.15">Blogger</generator>
<div class="info" xmlns="http://www.w3.org/1999/xhtml">This is an Atom formatted
XML site feed. It is intended to be viewed in a Newsreader or syndicated to another
site. Please visit the <a
href="http://help.blogger.com/bin/answer.py?answer=697">Blogger Help</a> for more
info.</div>
<convertLineBreaks
xmlns="http://www.blogger.com/atom/ns#">false</convertLineBreaks>
<entry xmlns="http://www.w3.org/2005/Atom">
<author>
<name>Sam Ruby</name>
</author>
```

(continued)

Listing 18-3 *(continued)*

```
<published>2005-09-15T06:27:00-07:00</published>
<updated>2005-09-15T13:33:06Z</updated>
<link href="http://www.atomenabled.org/2005/09/atomenableds-atom-feed.php"
rel="alternate" title="AtomEnabled's Atom Feed" type="text/html"/>
<id>tag:blogger.com,1999:blog-6356614.post-112679118686717868</id>
<title type="html">AtomEnabled's Atom Feed</title>
<content type="xhtml" xml:base="http://www.atomenabled.org" xml:space="preserve">
<div xmlns="http://www.w3.org/1999/xhtml">This site's <a
href="http://www.atomenabled.org/atom.xml">Atom feed</a> has been converted to Atom
1.0.  Addionally, the Feed Validator is <a
href="http://feedvalidator.org/news/archives/2005/09/15/atom_03_deprecated.html">no
w issuing deprecation warnings</a> whenever it encounters Atom 0.3 feeds.</div>
</content>
<draft xmlns="http://purl.org/atom-blog/ns#">false</draft>
</entry>
<entry xmlns="http://www.w3.org/2005/Atom">
<author>
<name>Sam Ruby</name>
</author>
<published>2005-07-31T13:08:00-07:00</published>
<updated>2005-08-01T02:37:13Z</updated>
<link href="http://www.atomenabled.org/2005/07/introduction-to-atom.php"
rel="alternate" title="Introduction to Atom" type="text/html"/>
<id>tag:blogger.com,1999:blog-6356614.post-112284122983872666</id>
<title type="html">Introduction to Atom</title>
<content type="xhtml" xml:base="http://www.atomenabled.org" xml:space="preserve">
<div xmlns="http://www.w3.org/1999/xhtml">An <a
href="http://www.atomenabled.org/developers/syndication/">introduction</a> to <a
href="http://www.atomenabled.org/developers/syndication/atom-format-spec.php">The
Atom Syndication Format</a> has been placed into the <a
href="http://www.atomenabled.org/developers/">Developers</a> &gt; <a
href="http://www.atomenabled.org/developers/syndication/">Syndication</a> section
of this website.</div>
</content>
<draft xmlns="http://purl.org/atom-blog/ns#">false</draft>
</entry>
</feed>
```

Important points to note about this feed are:

- The root element of the document is `feed`.
- Use of namespaces to provide extensions.
- Content for each entry marked to identify the encoding type of the element (text, html, or xhtml).

The following table discusses the channel information elements.

Element	Required / Optional	Notes
title	Required	A name for the feed. This is typically the same as the name for the site or application it comes from.

link	Optional (but highly recommended)	The URL of the feed. In addition to the URL itself, the link element should have the `rel="self"` attribute to identify this URL as the one for the feed.
		
		In addition to this URL, the feed may have additional link elements pointing to related links with a `rel="alternate"` attribute and the MIME type. For example, in addition to the link for the Atom feed, you may also include a link to the hosting Web site:
		
		`<link rel="self" href="http://debar.com/foo/feed.atom" />`
		
		`<link rel="alternate" href="http://debar.com/foo" type="text/html" />`
		
		`<link rel="license" href=" http://creativecommons.org/licenses/by/2.5/" type="application/rdf+xml"`

id	Required	A unique identifier (URI) for the feed.
updated	Required	The date and time the feed was last changed. See Dates and Atom for details.

author	Required (see notes)	The creator of the feed. The author field, like most of the people-related elements in Atom, is in the form:
		
		`<author>`
		
		`<name>Foo deBar</name>`
		
		`<uri>http://debar.com/blogs/foo</uri>`
		
		`<email>foo@debar.com</email>`
		
		`</author>`
		
		Only name is required.
		
		The author element must either exist on every entry or in the feed. If you are certain there will be an author for every entry, you can treat it as optional here, and vice versa. It definitely doesn't hurt to have it in both places.

Table continued on following page

Element	Required / Optional	Notes
category	Optional	Multiple category elements can exist in Atom feeds. They are similar to the category elements in RSS. They provide information about the topic of the content. The structure of the category element is different from that in RSS, however. In Atom, a category has `term`, `scheme`, and `label` attributes: `<category term="xml" scheme="scheme" label="XML" />` `Term` is the only required attribute and represents the category or topic of the feed. `Scheme` is the organizing set of categories (or taxonomy). `Label` is a human-readable version of the term, if needed.
generator	Optional	The application generating the Atom feed. A place for generators to either brag about their accomplishments or provide the target for user-anger.
icon	Optional	A URL to a graphic for the feed. Generally, this would be an icon or other small graphic. It should generally be square.
logo	Optional	A URL to a graphic for the feed. This differs from `icon` in that it should be twice as wide as it is high.
rights	Optional	The rights conferred for the item, such as "copyright 2006 Foo deBar."
subtitle	Optional	An extra catchy phrase for the feed.

Dates and Atom

With all the variability possible when you process dates with RSS, it is almost refreshing to deal with dates in Atom. All dates must be in the RFC 3339 format (or the ISO 8601 or W3C date format if you'd rather look at those sites):

`YYYY-MM-DDTHH:MM:SS-hh:mm` (alternately the `Z` character can be used instead of a time zone)

For example, all the following are valid dates for Atom:

```
2006-02-21T16:28:00-08:00

2006-01-01T12:00:00.00Z

2005-04-01T13:29:43.2+01:00
```

The Atom entry element can also be the root node in a document. If it is, the Atom namespace should be attached to the entry node. Most of the other entry features and child elements are similar to those in RSS. The following table covers the entry node elements used by Atom.

Element	Required / Optional	Notes
title	Required	The title for the entry. The title should not contain markup, but should be plain text.
id	Required	A unique identifier for the entry. This may be a URI, but you should not assume that the URI is actually the URL for the item.
updated	Required	The date and time the entry was last updated (or created). See Dates and Atom for more details.
category	Optional	See the category description under the feed element 18-in a previous table. There can be multiple category elements per entry.
content	Optional	The content of the entry. In addition to the content itself, there should be a type attribute. The type attribute identifies the format of the content and should be one of the standard MIME types. Typically, `type="text"`, `type="html"` or `type="xhtml"` are the most common type values. If the content element is empty, there should be a summary element (containing the content).
author	Required (see notes)	The person who created the entry. This element can be optional if the feed itself contains an author. However, in the interest of making parsing easier, it's probably a good idea to include the author element for each entry as well.
contributor	Optional	The person responsible for the entry. This differs from the author element in that there is only one author, but many people may have contributed information leading to the creation of the entry. Multiple contributor elements may exist per entry.

Table continued on following page

Element	Required / Optional	Notes
link	Optional	The URL of the entry, or the content pointed at by the entry. Multiple links per entry may exist, but they should differ by the type and/or hreflang. Each link should have the following attributes: * `href`=The URL of the item (Required). * `rel`=Optional attribute describing the relationship of the link to the content. One of *self* (the content is the entry itself), *related* (the link points to related information, such as company-specific information), *alternate* (the link points at another form of the entry, such as a PDF version), *enclosure* (the link points at a large file, such as audio or video), or *via* (the link points to the original source of the entry). * `type`=Optional MIME type of the content referenced by the link. * `hreflang`=Optional language of the content pointed at by the href. This enables you to have multiple translations pointed at by the same entry. * `title`=Optional text to display for the link * `length`=Optional length (in bytes) of the content referenced by the link.
published	Optional	Date and time the entry was created. See Dates and Atom for more details.
rights	Optional	Any copyright information associated with the entry.
source	Optional	Information about the original source of the Atom entry. Because a feed may actually contain entries created from multiple Atom feeds, this element can be used to provide information about the original feed for the entry.
summary	Optional	A short version of the content. This should have a type attribute (as described under *content* earlier). It should be different from the content (an excerpt or abstract) if present.

Reading RSS and Atom

Reading RSS basically breaks down into two main activities: parsing the channel information and parsing the items. Generally, it is the items that are more important. If you are parsing only one or two feeds or feeds from the same source, it can be a fairly easy process. However, if you are trying to create a generic RSS reader, or even just a reader that works with both RSS 1.0 and 2.0 feeds, it is a different matter. Some feeds ignore date; others may ignore `pubDate` and add a Dublin Core date instead. Similarly, in some feeds the `guid` element points to a URN, whereas in others it is a URL. Some put the entire post into the `description`, whereas others include a `content:body` element. In short, writing a good, general-purpose RSS parser is difficult, and the lack of a DTD or XML Schema doesn't make things easier. It is impossible or even really difficult, but you must be aware of variability when writing the parser and try to test it on multiple feeds.

In addition to the general RSS variability, RSS 1.0 and 2.0 have radically different structures. If you are provided only a URL to an RSS feed, you should try to determine which of these two you have. To determine which you have, you can either use the MIME type or the document itself. The MIME type of an RSS 1.0 document should be `application/rdf+xml`, whereas the MIME type of an RSS 2.0 document should be `application/rss+xml`. (Atom documents should be `application/atom+xml` for those who don't want to extrapolate.) However, many feeds are actually encoded using the MIME type `text/xml`. This means that you can't use MIME type alone to differentiate the feed type. The root node can also be used to identify most documents. RSS 2.0 uses `rss` as a root node, whereas RSS 1.0 uses `RDF` and Atom `feed`. Further differentiating the feed type usually isn't necessary, as RSS 2.0 feeds should also be valid 0.91(Userland) or 0.92 feeds.

Reading Atom is similar to reading RSS, except that it is a much more predictable affair. Because the Atom specification is far more easily interpreted than the RSS 2.0 specification, developers are more likely to get it right. The one major cause of errors is that many feeds are still in Atom 0.3 format—the version that was available before ratification of the standard. This is mostly accurate compared with Atom 1.0, but a few notable differences exist. The following table outlines these differences.

Item	Notes
namespace	In 0.3, the namespace was `http://purl.org/atom/ns#`, whereas for 1.0, it is `http://www.w3.org/2005/Atom`.
version	0.3 required the addition of a version attribute (as in RSS 2.0). This requirement has been removed.
subtitle	This element was named `tagline` in 0.3.
rights	This element was named `copyright` in 0.3.
updated	This element was named `modified` in 0.3.
published	This element was named `issued` in 0.3.
category	This element did not exist in 0.3.
icon	This element did not exist in 0.3.
logo	This element did not exist in 0.3.
source	This element did not exist in 0.3.
id	This element optional for the feed in 0.3; now it is required for both feed and entry elements.

Reading with .NET

Either of the two .NET idioms for dealing with XML (`XmlReader`, and `XmlDocument`) can be used for reading RSS and Atom documents. The benefits and consequences of each of these technologies are discussed in the following sections.

It might be tempting to make assumptions about the structure of the document—such as assuming that the title element is always the first child of an item. However, unless you have created all of the feeds you are processing, this will likely cause a break—quickly and when it puts you in the worst light (like during a demo to your CEO). Either use XPath statements to retrieve the appropriate elements or use conditional logic to retrieve the correct elements.

XmlDocument

`XmlDocument` is probably the one many people start with, loading the document into a DOM for processing. It certainly has the benefit of ease of use and familiarity. After it is loaded, you can use the `SelectNodes` and `SelectSingleNode` to extract the nodes you'd like. Alternately, you can walk the DOM, processing the feed as needed. Listing 18-4 shows a simple Console application that displays information from an Atom 1.0 feed.

Although it is simple, it is overkill to use the `XmlDocument`. It takes time and memory to build up the DOC structure in memory. In addition, the DOM is best when you need bi-directional access to the content. If you intend to go forward only through the feed, you are probably better served by the `XmlReader`. Listing 18-4 shows how to use XmlDocument to read Atom 1.0.

Listing 18-4: Using XmlDocument to read Atom 1.0

```
using System;
using System.Xml;

class Reader {
    [STAThread]
    static void Main(string[] args) {
        if (args.Length < 1) {
            Console.WriteLine("Simple Atom Reader");
            Console.WriteLine("Usage: simplereader <URL to RSS 2.0 feed>");
            Console.WriteLine(@"\tsimplereader
                http://www.oreillynet.com/pub/feed/20");
        } else {

            XmlDocument doc = new XmlDocument();
            doc.Load(args[0]);
            XmlNamespaceManager mgr = new XmlNamespaceManager(doc.NameTable);
            mgr.AddNamespace("atom", "http://www.w3.org/2005/Atom");
            XmlElement root = doc.DocumentElement;

            //display some items from the feed
            Console.WriteLine("Feed Information");
            Console.WriteLine("Title:\t\t{0}",
                root.SelectSingleNode("atom:title", mgr).InnerText);
            Console.WriteLine("Subtitle:\t{0}",
                root.SelectSingleNode("atom:subtitle", mgr).InnerText);
            Console.WriteLine("URL:\t\t{0}",
                root.SelectSingleNode("atom:link[@rel='self']/@href",
```

```
                mgr).InnerText);

            Console.WriteLine("Items");
            foreach (XmlNode item in doc.SelectNodes("//atom:entry", mgr)) {
                Console.WriteLine("\tTitle:\t\t{0}",
                    item.SelectSingleNode("atom:title", mgr).InnerText);
                Console.WriteLine("\tLink:\t\t{0}",
                    item.SelectSingleNode("atom:link/@href", mgr).InnerText);

                XmlNode contentNode = item.SelectSingleNode("atom:summary", mgr);
                //default to showing the summary,
                // but show the content if it is available
                if(null == contentNode) {
                    contentNode = item.SelectSingleNode("atom:content", mgr);
                }

                if (null != contentNode) {
                    Console.WriteLine(contentNode.InnerText);
                }

                Console.WriteLine();
            }

            Console.WriteLine("Press Enter to end program");
            Console.ReadLine();
        }
    }

}
```

Because Atom actually lists a namespace, it's best to use an Xml`NamespaceManager` when working with Atom documents. The DOM. `XmlNamespaceManager` makes it easier to identify elements when you are using the `SelectNodes` and `SelectSingleNode` methods.

Displaying safe RSS

As RSS and Atom become more popular and because it is so easy to simply display the existing feed content on Web pages, it is becoming more and more important to ensure what you display is safe. Many HTML tags can be used to hijack pages, and these should be stripped before displaying the page. Although it is not absolutely necessary when re-displaying feeds you trust (ones you've created and no others), it is incredibly important to remove tags that might allow someone to alter or break your pages. There are three main solutions. I'll call them *Safest*, *Safer*, and *Safish*.

The safest solution is to remove all HTML tags from the content. However, this is hardly a useful suggestion in most cases because the tags (especially links) are the most useful part of the post. The next (*Safer*) solution is to wrap the displayed tag in an IFrame with the `security="restricted"` attribute. This limits the capabilities of the code, preventing script from running and the display of new browser windows. However, this attribute has limited availability (only in Internet Explorer 6.0 SP1); therefore, it is not a valid solution except for intranet scenarios. Therefore, the *Safish* solution is likely the best option in most scenarios. Before displaying HTML from an arbitrary feed, you should strip out the elements and attributes listed in 18-the following table.

Element/Attribute	Reason
script	Running any form of script from unknown sources is a request to have your Web site hacked.
object embed applet	These tags add ActiveX, Java, or other non-HTML elements to the page. ActiveX objects, in particular, are dangerous because they have full access to the client machine; however, any of these items can perform nasty tricks by being embedded in a browser.
frame iframe frameset	These tags allow for the addition of sub pages to a Web page. Apart from likely breaking the layout of your page, they can be used by an unscrupulous feed provider to execute code or otherwise manipulate the client.
on{something}	Similar to script removal, action attributes (such as onclick, onblur, or others) can be used to execute script.
meta link	These tags *should* only appear in the head of HTML pages and not in RSS feeds. In addition, browsers should not interpret them if they are in the body of a page (as they would be if they are from an RSS or Atom feed). However, to be safe, they should be stripped.
style	Both style elements and attributes can be used to import graphics and other items that can have a detrimental effect on your pages. Although most added style information is harmless, it is still better to be safe. Even more or less harmless style information can have a detrimental effect, if it overrides a global style. For example adding, "`a {color: #fff;}`" to styles, can cause all anchor tags to change in appearance.
img a	Although these tags can both be used to execute mischief on your Web pages, their removal is only optional. Likely, these tags are the main reasons you're thinking of displaying the RSS feed(s). Therefore, I'll leave this decision up to you. (Personally, I'd leave them in, but only link to RSS feeds I trusted.)

XmlReader

`XmlReader`, as you saw in Chapter 16, is the low-level, pull parser in .NET. You use the methods of the `XmlReader` to pull elements and attributes from the XML. `XmlReader` is a forward-only parser, meaning that you cannot go backwards through the XML. As only a small fraction of the content is in memory at any time, `XmlReader` excels when working with large documents for speed and memory usage. Listing 18-5 shows using `XmlReader` to serialize RSS 2.0 content into the `RssFeed` class. (To save space, not all properties are shown).

Listing 18-5: Reading RSS 2.0 with XmlReader

```
using System;
using System.Collections.Generic;
using System.Text;
using System.Xml;
using System.IO;
```

```
namespace Wrox.ProXml {
    public class RssFeed {

        #region Private Members
        private Dictionary<String, String> _properties =
            new Dictionary<String, String>();
        private List<RssEntry> _entries = new List<RssEntry>();

        #endregion

        #region C'tors
        public RssFeed() {
            //set up default properties
            this.Title = String.Empty;
            this.Link = String.Empty;
            this.Description = String.Empty;
            this.Language = "en-us";
            this.Copyright = "copyright 2006";
            this.ManagingEditor = string.Empty;
            this.PubDate = DateTime.Now.ToString("R");

        }

        #endregion

        #region Properties
        public Dictionary<String, String> Properties {
            get { return _properties; }
        }
        public List<RssEntry> Entries {
            get { return _entries; }
        }
        public string Title {
            get { return this.Properties["title"]; }
            set { this.Properties["title"] = value; }
        }
        public string Link {
            get { return this.Properties["link"]; }
            set { this.Properties["link"] = value; }
        }
        public string Description {
            get { return this.Properties["description"]; }
            set { this.Properties["description"] = value; }
        }
        public string Language {
            get { return this.Properties["language"]; }
            set { this.Properties["language"] = value; }
        }
        public string Copyright {
            get { return this.Properties["copyright"]; }
            set { this.Properties["copyright"] = value; }
        }
        public string ManagingEditor {
            get { return this.Properties["managingEditor"]; }
```

(continued)

Listing 18-5 *(continued)*

```
            set { this.Properties["managingEditor"] = value; }
        }
        public string PubDate {
            get { return this.Properties["pubDate"]; }
            set { this.Properties["pubDate"] = value; }
        }
        #endregion


        #region Read XML
        public void Load(String filename) {
            XmlReader reader = null;
            XmlReaderSettings settings = new XmlReaderSettings();

            settings.CheckCharacters = true;
            settings.CloseInput = true;
            settings.IgnoreWhitespace = true;

            reader = XmlReader.Create(filename, settings);
            this.Load(reader);
        }
        public void Load(Stream inputStream) {
            XmlReader reader = null;
            XmlReaderSettings settings = new XmlReaderSettings();

            settings.CheckCharacters = true;
            settings.CloseInput = true;
            settings.IgnoreWhitespace = true;

            reader = XmlReader.Create(inputStream, settings);
            this.Load(reader);
        }
        public void Load(XmlReader inputReader) {
            inputReader.MoveToContent();

            //move into the channel

            while (inputReader.Read()) {

                if (inputReader.IsStartElement() && !inputReader.IsEmptyElement) {
                    switch (inputReader.LocalName.ToLower()) {
                        case "channel":
                            //do nothing in this case
                            break;
                        case "item":
                            //delegate parsing to the RssEntry class
                            RssEntry entry = new RssEntry();
                            entry.Load(inputReader);
                            this.Entries.Add(entry);
                            break;
                        default:
```

```
                        string field = inputReader.LocalName;
                        this.Properties[field] = inputReader.ReadString();
                        break;
                    }
                }
            }
        }
        #endregion

    }
}
```

The class uses a `Dictionary` to track the properties and an array for the child items. The `Dictionary` allows for the growth of the class to store necessary properties, including additional namespaces if they are added to the RSS. To make processing the class friendlier, additional named properties are created for title, link, description, and other elements of the RSS.

The `Load` method (highlighted in the listing) processes the RSS to populate the `Dictionary`. The additional two `Load` methods are provided to make it easier for end users to create the `XmlReader` that processes the RSS. The processing is fairly basic: the content of the child elements of the `channel` element are moved over *as is* to the properties `Dictionary`. Parsing of the item elements is delegated to the `RssEntry` class, as shown in Listing 18-6.

Listing 18-6: Reading RSS items with XmlReader

```
using System;
using System.Collections.Generic;
using System.Text;
using System.Xml;
using System.IO;

namespace Wrox.ProXml {
    public class RssEntry {

        private Dictionary<String, String> _properties =
            new Dictionary<String, String>();

        public RssEntry() {
            //set up default properties
            this.Title = String.Empty;
            this.Link = String.Empty;
            this.Description = String.Empty;
        }

        #region Properties
        public Dictionary<String, String> Properties {
            get { return this._properties; }
        }
        public String Title {
            get { return this.Properties["title"]; }
            set { this.Properties["title"] = value; }
        }
```

(continued)

Listing 18-6 *(continued)*

```
        public String Link {
            get { return this.Properties["link"]; }
            set { this.Properties["link"] = value; }
        }
        public String Description {
            get { return this.Properties["description"]; }
            set { this.Properties["description"] = value; }
        }
        #endregion

        public void Load(System.Xml.XmlReader inputReader) {
            while (inputReader.Read()) {
                if (inputReader.Name == "item" &&
                    inputReader.NodeType == XmlNodeType.EndElement) {
                    break;
                }
                if (inputReader.IsStartElement() && !inputReader.IsEmptyElement) {
                    String field = inputReader.LocalName;
                    this.Properties[field] = inputReader.ReadString();
                }
            }
        }
    }
}
```

As with the `RssFeed`, a `Dictionary` is used to store the values of the RSS elements.

After you have the RSS feed serialized into the `RssFeed` and `RssEntry` classes, displaying them becomes easy, as Listing 18-7 shows.

Listing 18-7: Using the RssFeed and RssEntry classes

```
RssFeed feed = new RssFeed();
feed.Load(this.UrlField.Text);
MessageBox.Show(String.Format("Title: {0}\nItems: {1}",
    feed.Title, feed.Entries.Count.ToString()),
    "Feed Information");
foreach (RssEntry entry in feed.Entries) {
    MessageBox.Show(entry.Description, entry.Title);
}
```

Reading RSS with Java

Reading RSS with Java is basically the same as with .NET. One method of reading RSS and Atom popular with Java developers (that is not available as part of the standard .NET class library) is Simple API for XML (SAX). This is an event-based parser for XML. The SAX code reads the XML and calls methods in your code when it encounters new elements, text, or errors in the document. This mechanism makes parsing small documents (like RSS feeds) fast and requires low memory overhead. See Chapter 14 for more details on SAX. Listing 18-8 shows reading RSS 1.0 documents with SAX.

Listing 18-8: Reading RSS 1.0 with SAX

```
package com.wrox.proxml;

import java.io.*;
import java.util.Stack;
import javax.xml.parsers.ParserConfigurationException;
import javax.xml.parsers.SAXParser;
import javax.xml.parsers.SAXParserFactory;
import org.xml.sax.*;
import org.xml.sax.helpers.DefaultHandler;

public class RSSReader extends DefaultHandler {
    static private Writer out;
    static String lineEnd =  System.getProperty("line.separator");

    Stack stack = new Stack();
    StringBuffer value = null;

  public static void main(String args []) {
    // create an instance of RSSReader
    DefaultHandler handler = new RSSReader();

    try {
      // Set up output stream
      out = new OutputStreamWriter(System.out, "UTF8");

      // get a SAX parser from the factory
      SAXParserFactory factory = SAXParserFactory.newInstance();
      SAXParser saxParser = factory.newSAXParser();

      // parse the document from the parameter
      emit("Feed information for " + args[0] + lineEnd);
      saxParser.parse(args[0], handler);

    } catch (Exception t) {
      System.err.println(t.getClass().getName());
      t.printStackTrace(System.err);
    }
  }

  public void startElement(String namespaceURI,String sName,
    String qName,Attributes attrs) throws SAXException {
    String eName = sName; // element name
    if ("".equals(eName)) eName = qName; // namespaceAware = false
    stack.push(eName);
    value = new StringBuffer();
  }

  public void endElement(String namespaceURI,String sName,String qName)
    throws SAXException {
    String element = null;
    String section = null;
```

(continued)

Listing 18-8 *(continued)*

```
        if(!stack.empty()){
            element = (String)stack.pop();
        }
        if(!stack.empty()){
            section = (String)stack.peek();
        }

        if (null != element && null != section ){
            if (section.equalsIgnoreCase("channel")) {
                if(element.equalsIgnoreCase("title")) {
                    emit("Title:\t" + value + lineEnd);
                } else if (element.equalsIgnoreCase("link")){
                    emit("Link:\t" + value + lineEnd);
                }
            } else if (section.equalsIgnoreCase("item")) {
                if(element.equalsIgnoreCase("title")) {
                    emit("\tTitle:\t" + value + lineEnd);
                } else if (element.equalsIgnoreCase("description")) {
                    emit("\t" + value + lineEnd);
                }
            }
        }
      }

      public void characters(char buf [], int offset, int len)
        throws SAXException {
        String s = new String(buf, offset, len);
        value.append(s);
      }

      private static void emit(String s) throws SAXException {
        try {
          out.write(s);
          out.flush();
        } catch (IOException e) {
          throw new SAXException("I/O error", e);
        }
      }
    }
```

The code sets up the handlers for `startElement` and `endElement` and parses the RSS 1.0 document. At the start of each element, the new element is added to a `Stack`, and a new `StringBuffer` is created to hold the contents of the element. Most of the processing takes place in the `endElement` handler. This pops the element name that is ending off of the stack and determines where in the document the current element is located.

Writing RSS and Atom

Writing RSS or Atom is definitely easier than reading it. All you need to do is decide on the flavor you'd like to output and stick with it, validating as you go. The prime reasons feeds fail to validate are that users have neglected to ensure that dates are in correct format and all additional namespaces are included in the feed. Even enclosures or other more advanced features are fairly easy to add to feeds.

Writing with .NET

Writing RSS or Atom with .NET is easiest with the `XmlWriter` class. It provides methods for adding attributes and child elements, and it can write to either files or streams. Listings 18-9 and 18-10 show the extensions to the `RssFeed` and `RssEntry` classes to include saving RSS feeds.

Listing 18-9: Writing RSS 2.0 with XmlWriter

```
public void Save(string filename) {
    XmlWriter writer = null;
    XmlWriterSettings settings = new XmlWriterSettings();
    settings.CheckCharacters = true;
    settings.CloseOutput = true;
    settings.Encoding = Encoding.UTF8;

    writer = XmlWriter.Create(filename, settings);
    this.Save(writer);
}

public void Save(System.IO.Stream outputStream) {
    XmlWriter writer = null;
    XmlWriterSettings settings = new XmlWriterSettings();
    settings.CheckCharacters = true;
    settings.CloseOutput = true;
    settings.Encoding = Encoding.UTF8;

    writer = XmlWriter.Create(outputStream, settings);
    this.Save(writer);
}

public void Save(System.Xml.XmlWriter outputWriter) {
    outputWriter.WriteStartDocument();
    outputWriter.WriteStartElement("rss");
    outputWriter.WriteAttributeString("version", "2.0");
    outputWriter.WriteStartElement("channel");
    outputWriter.WriteElementString("title", this.Title);
    outputWriter.WriteElementString("link", this.Link);
    outputWriter.WriteElementString("description", this.Description);
    outputWriter.WriteElementString("language", this.Language);
    outputWriter.WriteElementString("copyright", this.Copyright);
    outputWriter.WriteElementString("managingEditor", this.ManagingEditor);
    outputWriter.WriteElementString("pubDate", this.PubDate);
```

(continued)

Listing 18-9 *(continued)*

```
        foreach (RssEntry entry in this.Entries) {
            entry.Save(outputWriter);
        }

        outputWriter.WriteEndElement();       //channel

        outputWriter.WriteEndElement();      //rss
        outputWriter.WriteEndDocument();
        outputWriter.Close();
    }
```

The three overloaded methods provide the user of the `RssFeed` class with flexibility when saving the output. However, the first two delegate to the third that creates the RSS using the `XmlWriter` class. Creating XML using the `XmlWriter` can sometimes feel a little repetitive, because you are repeatedly calling the various WriteXXX methods. However, this is preferable (in my opinion) to using the classes of the XML DOM to build up the structure in memory. Remember to close the `XmlWriter` or call `Flush()` to ensure the content is actually written.

Listing 18-10: Writing RSS 2.0 items with XmlWriter

```
    public void Save(System.Xml.XmlWriter outputWriter) {
        outputWriter.WriteStartElement("item");
        outputWriter.WriteElementString("title", this.Title);
        outputWriter.WriteElementString("link", this.Link);
        outputWriter.WriteElementString("description", this.Description);
        outputWriter.WriteEndElement();      //item
    }
```

Writing with Java

Choices for writing RSS or Atom with Java are slightly more limited. Using only the core J2SE class library, your best choice is the DOM. Other libraries exist to make it easier, such as StAX, JDOM, or even serializing to and from Java objects. Listing 18-11 shows creating an RSS 2.0 document using the DOM.

Listing 18-11: Writing RSS 2.0 with DOM

```
    package com.wrox.proxml;

    import java.io.*;
    import javax.xml.*;
    import javax.xml.parsers.*;
    import javax.xml.transform.*;
    import javax.xml.transform.dom.DOMSource;
    import javax.xml.transform.stream.StreamResult;
    import org.w3c.dom.*;

    public class RSSWriter {
```

```
Document doc;
Element  channel;

public RSSWriter() {
    DocumentBuilderFactory factory = DocumentBuilderFactory.newInstance();
    try {
        DocumentBuilder builder = factory.newDocumentBuilder();
        doc = builder.newDocument();
        Element rss = doc.createElement("rss");
        rss.setAttribute("version", "2.0");
        doc.appendChild(rss);
        channel = doc.createElement("channel");
        rss.appendChild(channel);
    } catch (Exception ex){
        ex.printStackTrace();
    }
}

public void setFeedTitle(String title){
    this.addElement(channel, "title", title);
}
public void setFeedLink(String link) {
    this.addElement(channel, "link", link);
}
public void setFeedDescription(String description){
    this.addElement(channel, "description", description);
}

public Element addItem(String title, String link, String desc){
    Element item = doc.createElement("item");
    addElement(item, "title", title);
    addElement(item, "link", link);
    addElement(item, "description", desc);
    addElement(item, "guid", link).setAttribute("isPermaLink", "false");
    channel.appendChild(item);
    return item;
}

public void Save(OutputStream out){
    try {
        Transformer transformer =
        TransformerFactory.newInstance().newTransformer(  );
        Source source = new DOMSource( doc );
        Result output = new StreamResult( out );
        transformer.transform( source, output );
    } catch (TransformerException tex) {
        tex.printStackTrace();
    }
}
```

(continued)

Listing 18-11 *(continued)*

```
    private Element addElement(Element parent, String name, String value){
        Element el = doc.createElement(name);
        el.setTextContent(value);
        parent.appendChild(el);
        return el;
    }


    public static void main(String[] args) {
        RSSWriter writer = new RSSWriter();
        writer.setFeedTitle("Test feed");
        writer.setFeedLink("http://www.example.com");
        writer.setFeedDescription("Sample RSS 2.0 feed");
        writer.addItem("Item 1",
                "http://www.example.com/1",
                "Some more lengthy description of item 1");
        writer.addItem("Item 2",
                "http://www.example.com/2",
                "Description of the second item");
        writer.Save(System.out);
    }

}
```

The DOM makes it easy to create and manipulate XML documents. The only mistake users make when working with the DOM is to forget to `appendChild` when adding elements to the DOM. For this reason, and to reduce repetition in the code, I'll usually create one or more `addElement` methods as shown in the preceding sample. This encapsulates the creation of the element and appends the new element at the appropriate location in the document.

Class Libraries Available for Processing RSS and Atom

Rather than process the RSS with the XML functionality natively, you may want to use an RSS parsing library. Generally, these hide many of the ambiguities in the different feed types and make your life a little easier. Some of the more notable RSS parsing libraries are:

- **RSS.NET (**`http://www.rssdotnet.com/`**)** — Library for RSS 2.0 feeds for .NET.
- **My.Blogs (**`http://msdn.microsoft.com/library/default.asp?url=/library/en-us/dnvs05/html/MyBlogsGetStart.asp`**)** — A library for parsing and creating RSS 1.0, RSS 2.0 and Atom feeds. Written in and designed for Visual Basic 2005 developers.
- **Rome (**`http://wiki.java.net/bin/view/Javawsxml/Rome`**)** — A Java library for processing RSS 1.0, 2.0 and Atom feeds (as well as a few more arcane versions, such as both versions of 0.91). This library also supports extensions to add parsing for additional namespaces.
- **RSSLib4J (**`http://sourceforge.net/projects/rsslib4j/`**)** — Library for processing RSS 1.0 and 2.0 feeds in Java.
- **Atom.NET (**`http://atomnet.sourceforge.net/`**)** — Library for processing Atom feeds with .NET. Sadly, this library is still not 1.0 compliant.

Summary

Atom and RSS provide a means of sharing information and providing a (relatively) standard means of notifying users of change. The rise of blogs, podcasts, and RSS aggregators mean that more and more people are using RSS, even if they are not aware of it. Most common browsers even handle and display RSS and Atom. In addition, future versions of Windows will ship with built-in infrastructure for downloading and displaying these feeds. RSS and Atom are rapidly becoming an important dialect of XML.

Resources

Specifications and tools can help you when processing RSS and Atom. In addition, see the preceding section on class libraries available for processing feeds.

- RSS 2.0 specification. `http://blogs.law.harvard.edu/tech/rss`
- RSS 1.0 specification. `http://web.resource.org/rss/1.0/spec`
- Atom 1.0 specification — IETF RFC 4287 (`.ietf.org/rfc/rfc4287.txt`). Although it reads like any official protocol document (don't read while operating heavy machinery, or when you shouldn't be sleeping), it is precise and informative.
- FeedValidator — Online RSS/Atom validator (`feedvalidator.org`). You should always use this tool to test your feed before releasing it into the wild. It is capable of validating any of the common RSS feed versions, Atom, and many of the common extensions (such as Dublin Core). You can alternatively download and use this locally. It is written in Python.

19

Web Services

If there is one term in this book that you will hear more than any other in the halls of information technology, it is the term *Web services*. Computer magazines, Web sites, and other sources have many reasons to tout the benefits of this XML-based technology. It is simply a powerful and extensible way of moving datasets from one point to another in this cyber world we live in today.

Over the last few years, Web services have grown from being a concept the industry has simply kept its eye on, to a reality that is now planned for in quite a number of recurring IT projects. Web services are filling a need that has existed in the IT industry for some time now, and the major vendors of the world are literally rushing in with solutions that their customers can use to address this need.

This chapter looks at the Web services world (at least to the extent possible in the limited space this chapter offers), including how some of the major vendors of the world make it rather simple for you to build and consume Web services using their tools and technologies. After this chapter, the next few chapters include more discussion on SOAP, WSDL, and the WS-* specifications.

Why Web Services?

One of the first steps in understanding Web services and why so much hype surrounds them is to first understand the problems that they are meant to address. Ever since the industry has moved away from monolithic mainframe computers to the client/server model, users have been wondering how to move data and calculations from one point in the enterprise to another. The Web services model is simply a step toward solving this problem.

Web services are meant to address the problems of connecting disparate systems, creating single repositories, and working towards the holy grail of programming — *code reuse*. Typically in a major enterprise, you rarely find that the computing thought of an entire organization and its data repositories reside on a single vendor's platform. In most instances, organizations are made up of a patchwork of systems — some based on Unix, some on Microsoft, and some on other systems. There probably won't be a day when everything resides on a single vendor's platform, and all the data moves seamlessly from one server to another. For that reason, various systems must be able to talk to one another despite their differences. If disparate systems can communicate easily, moving unique datasets around the enterprise becomes a simple process that eliminates the need for replication of systems and data stores.

Instead of being looked at as only a means to represent data as XML was viewed when first introduced, the markup language has now become a structure that can bring the necessary integration into the enterprise. XML's power comes from the fact that it can be used regardless of the platform, language, or data store of the system using it to expose datasets.

XML is considered ideal for data representation purposes because it enables developers to structure XML documents as they see fit. For this reason, it is also a bit chaotic. Sending self-structured XML documents between dissimilar systems doesn't make a lot of sense — it requires custom building of both the exposure and consumption models for each communication pair.

Vendors and the industry as a whole, however, soon realized that XML needed a specific structure. If rules are in place to clarify communication, the communication between the disparate systems becomes just that much easier. With rules in place, tool vendors can automate the communication process and the creation of all components for applications using the defined communication protocol.

The industry came together with the goal of defining a common ground for communication, and it settled on using SOAP (*Simple Object Access Protocol*) as the standard XML structure. The problem that SOAP solved was not a new one. Previous attempts at a solution included component technologies such as Distributed Component Object Model (DCOM), Remote Method Invocation (RMI), Common Object Request Broker Architecture (CORBA), and Internet Inter-ORB Protocol (IIOP). These first efforts failed because each of these technologies was either driven by a single vendor or (worse yet) was very vendor-specific. It was, therefore, impossible to implement any of these across the entire industry.

SOAP enables you to expose and consume calculations, complex data structures, or just tables of data that have all their relations in place. SOAP is relatively simple and easy to understand. Like various other Web-based technologies such as PHP or ASP.NET, Web services are also primarily engineered to work over HTTP. With that said, though, there are moves in enterprise to also send SOAP structures via other transport protocols such as TCP. Even though those moves are in place, Web services are still being built to flow primarily over HTTP. If you use HTTP, the datasets you send or consume can flow over the same Internet wires that are already established, thereby bypassing many firewalls (as they move through port 80). Implementing Web services over HTTP is rather simple because these networks are already in place and ready to use.

So what's actually going across the wire? As I just stated, Web services generally use SOAP over HTTP using the HTTP Post protocol. An example SOAP request (from the client to the Web service residing on a Web server) takes the structure shown in Listing 19-1.

Listing 19-1: A sample SOAP request

```
POST /MyWebService/Service.asmx HTTP/1.1
Host: www.wrox.com
Content-Type: text/xml; charset=utf-8
Content-Length: 19
SOAPAction: "http://www.wrox.com/HelloWorld"
```

```
<?xml version="1.0" encoding="utf-8"?>
<soap:Envelope xmlns:xsi="http://www.w3.org/2001/XMLSchema-instance"
 xmlns:xsd="http://www.w3.org/2001/XMLSchema"
 xmlns:soap="http://schemas.xmlsoap.org/soap/envelope/">
  <soap:Body>
    <HelloWorld xmlns="http://www.wrox.com/" />
  </soap:Body>
</soap:Envelope>
```

Take note that this is a request which is sent to the Web service from the client (or consumer) to invoke the `HelloWorld` WebMethod (WebMethods are discussed later in this chapter). An example SOAP response from this Web service is shown in Listing 19-2.

Listing 19-2: A sample SOAP response

```
HTTP/1.1 200 OK
Content-Type: text/xml; charset=utf-8
Content-Length: 14

<?xml version="1.0" encoding="utf-8"?>
<soap:Envelope xmlns:xsi="http://www.w3.org/2001/XMLSchema-instance"
 xmlns:xsd="http://www.w3.org/2001/XMLSchema"
 xmlns:soap="http://schemas.xmlsoap.org/soap/envelope/">
  <soap:Body>
    <HelloWorldResponse xmlns="http://www.wrox.com/">
      <HelloWorldResult>Hello World</HelloWorldResult>
    </HelloWorldResponse>
  </soap:Body>
</soap:Envelope>
```

In the examples from Listings 19-1 and 19-2, you can see that what is contained in this message is an actual XML file. Beyond the normal XML declaration of the `<xml>` node, you see a structure of XML that constitutes the SOAP message. A SOAP message uses a root node of `<soap:Envelope>` that contains the `<soap:Body>` or the body of the SOAP message. Other elements that can be contained in the SOAP message (but are not shown in the preceding example) include a SOAP header, `<soap:Header>`, and a SOAP fault`<soap:Fault>`.

For more information about the structure of a SOAP message, be sure to check out the SOAP specifications. You can find them at the W3C Web site, `w3.org/tr/soap`. *SOAP will also be discussed in the next chapter of this book.*

The Composition of Web Services

As you come to understand the Web services model, you are also consistently introduced to a number of its specifications and capabilities. The vendors have done an excellent job by making it relatively easy to build and consume Web services in their development environments. In fact, in this chapter, you learn how to build and consume Web services using both .NET and Java. Whether you are building or consuming Web services, however, guarantee your success by making sure you understand the structure of the Web services model before you begin your first venture.

Understanding a few pillars of Web services development makes your job a lot easier. Not all the specifications or technologies that are used to build and consume Web services are required for every job, but you should review and understand everything before you start using Web services within any of your applications. Building Web services (whether in .NET or Java) gives you the following:

- An industry-standard way to represent data
- A way to transfer data in a common message format
- A way to describe a Web service to potential consumers
- A path to discovery of Web services on remote servers

Representing and Communicating Data in Web Services

As you are probably quite aware, Web services are heavily dependent upon XML. XML markup is used for data representation purposes, and XML Schemas are used to describe data types utilized by the Web services. XML is simply an excellent way to represent data. XML can be packaged and sent across the wire making the Web services model work. If you use XML, you immediately notice that a large number of platforms support XML, and they can manage it through an even larger set of tools available for XML data reading, writing, and manipulation.

Basing the data on XML and then standardizing the XML to the SOAP specification (discussed earlier in this chapter), make it easy to communicate your defined data representations from one point to another. Many Web services use HTTP to transport an XML document between disparate systems. When you transport your SOAP message in this manner, it flows easily through firewalls without any hindrance. Most firewalls are already configured to allow information from the Internet to flow freely through their walls.

You will find that the Web services communication model is not that different from other models you see in the Web world. When you have an application making a request of a Web service, this client triggers an HTTP Web request to the remote Web service. The request, in turn, most likely triggers a response from the server where the Web service resides. In the request from the client, the request message carries information about the function (WebMethod) to be called and any parameters that are required by the function. After the server that hosts the Web service receives the request message from the client, it initiates the function and returns a response message that contains the data returned by the function. The response message can be a simple statement that some particular action was taken, or it can contain a complete table of data from a database. What you want returned is really up to you.

In the past, it was quite possible to work with DCOM to port data from one point to another to solve almost the same problem that Web services are now addressing. However, with DCOM, requests and responses were required to ride on top of a proprietary communication protocol. This kind of architecture is not an effective way to provide data in a universal format such as XML. If your goal is to allow information to be sent and consumed regardless of the platforms used, DCOM does not achieve it.

Describing Web Services

Think of Web services as remote APIs (since they are basically just that). You have a method that you want to implement. Let's suppose the method wasn't built by you and resides somewhere else in the world on equipment that you have no control over — *how can you go about providing that remote method what it needs in order to get instantiated?*

When you find a Web service that you want to include in your application, you must first figure out how to supply the Web service with the parameters it needs in order for it to work. That need also extends a bit further. Even if you know the parameters and types that are required for instantiation, you also need to understand the types that are passed to your application in return. Without these pieces of information, using Web services would prove rather difficult.

Just as there are standard ways to represent data as well as standard ways to move this data over the Internet using Web services, there is a standard way to get a description of the Web service you are interested in consuming. *Web Services Description Language* (WSDL) is a specification of XML that describes the Web services you are interested in consuming. Listing 19-3 shows a sample WSDL file from a simple Calculation Web service that contains a single WebMethod called `Addition` (`a+b`).

Listing 19-3: A sample WSDL file

```
<?xml version="1.0" encoding="utf-8"?>
<wsdl:definitions xmlns:soap="http://schemas.xmlsoap.org/wsdl/soap/"
 xmlns:tm="http://microsoft.com/wsdl/mime/textMatching/"
 xmlns:soapenc="http://schemas.xmlsoap.org/soap/encoding/"
 xmlns:mime="http://schemas.xmlsoap.org/wsdl/mime/"
 xmlns:tns="http://www.wrox.com/" xmlns:s="http://www.w3.org/2001/XMLSchema"
 xmlns:soap12="http://schemas.xmlsoap.org/wsdl/soap12/"
 xmlns:http="http://schemas.xmlsoap.org/wsdl/http/"
 targetNamespace="http://www.wrox.com/"
 xmlns:wsdl="http://schemas.xmlsoap.org/wsdl/">
  <wsdl:types>
    <s:schema elementFormDefault="qualified"
     targetNamespace="http://www.wrox.com/">
      <s:element name="Addition">
        <s:complexType>
          <s:sequence>
            <s:element minOccurs="1" maxOccurs="1" name="a" type="s:int" />
            <s:element minOccurs="1" maxOccurs="1" name="b" type="s:int" />
          </s:sequence>
        </s:complexType>
      </s:element>
      <s:element name="AdditionResponse">
        <s:complexType>
          <s:sequence>
            <s:element minOccurs="1" maxOccurs="1" name="AdditionResult"
             type="s:int" />
          </s:sequence>
        </s:complexType>
      </s:element>
    </s:schema>
  </wsdl:types>
  <wsdl:message name="AdditionSoapIn">
    <wsdl:part name="parameters" element="tns:Addition" />
  </wsdl:message>
  <wsdl:message name="AdditionSoapOut">
    <wsdl:part name="parameters" element="tns:AdditionResponse" />
  </wsdl:message>
  <wsdl:portType name="CalculationSoap">
    <wsdl:operation name="Addition">
```

(continued)

Listing 19-3 *(continued)*

```
      <wsdl:input message="tns:AdditionSoapIn" />
      <wsdl:output message="tns:AdditionSoapOut" />
    </wsdl:operation>
  </wsdl:portType>
  <wsdl:binding name="CalculationSoap" type="tns:CalculationSoap">
    <soap:binding transport="http://schemas.xmlsoap.org/soap/http" />
    <wsdl:operation name="Addition">
      <soap:operation soapAction="http://www.wrox.com/Addition" style="document" />
      <wsdl:input>
        <soap:body use="literal" />
      </wsdl:input>
      <wsdl:output>
        <soap:body use="literal" />
      </wsdl:output>
    </wsdl:operation>
  </wsdl:binding>
  <wsdl:binding name="CalculationSoap12" type="tns:CalculationSoap">
    <soap12:binding transport="http://schemas.xmlsoap.org/soap/http" />
    <wsdl:operation name="Addition">
      <soap12:operation soapAction="http://www.wrox.com/Addition"
       style="document" />
      <wsdl:input>
        <soap12:body use="literal" />
      </wsdl:input>
      <wsdl:output>
        <soap12:body use="literal" />
      </wsdl:output>
    </wsdl:operation>
  </wsdl:binding>
  <wsdl:service name="Calculation">
    <wsdl:port name="CalculationSoap" binding="tns:CalculationSoap">
      <soap:address
       location="http://www.wrox.com/Calculation/Calculation.asmx" />
    </wsdl:port>
    <wsdl:port name="CalculationSoap12" binding="tns:CalculationSoap12">
      <soap12:address
       location="http://www.wrox.com/Calculation/Calculation.asmx" />
    </wsdl:port>
  </wsdl:service>
</wsdl:definitions>
```

From this WSDL document, you can see that the input and output types are defined directly in the document. It also defines the location of the Web services and the different types of SOAP calls you can make to the Web service (using SOAP 1.1 or 1.2). Any client that uses this WSDL document can build the means to communicate with the defined Web service directly.

Discovering Web Services

To use a Web service, you have to be provided with the WSDL document or you have to know the URL endpoint of the WSDL file. How do you find the Web services you are interested in consuming if you don't have access to the location of the WSDL file or if someone or some process hasn't provided it to you?

Note that if you don't want to provide the means for discovering for your Web services, you don't need to build the discovery mechanism around it. If you wish to provide your Web services to the public, however, you must provide a means for users to locate it.

To allow users to discover Web services, various companies, such as Microsoft and IBM, have worked to create the required mechanics of discovery. It is accomplished through another XML specification known as UDDI (known in its full form as *Universal Description, Discovery, and Integration*).

You will find implementations of the UDDI specification on the Microsoft Windows Server 2003 server.

It is interesting to note that UDDI implementations are themselves Web services that employ the UDDI specifications to define a standard way to publish and discover information about Web services. The XML schemas associated with UDDI define four types of information that enable a developer to use a published Web service. The following table lists the types of information that UDDI provides.

Information Provided	Description
Business details	The business contact information for the person or company that is providing the particular Web service.
Service detail	A name and description of the Web service.
Bindings detail	The specific access points for this service instance. It allows for display of additional instance-specific details.
Bindings details	Classifications that specify the field of operation of a business or a service (for example, a geographic location or an industry sector). These enable users of the registry to confirm the importance of a particular Web service.

The UDDI capabilities mentioned here are not the only way to publish and classify your Web services. Other directories that have sprung up on the Internet, and I am sure more will appear as the number of Web services grows. Presently, one of the better Web service directories (besides the one mentioned previously from Microsoft) is XMethods found at `xmethods.com/`.

Building Web Services with C#

Because Web services are so widely accepted across the industry, you can use a large list of programming languages to build them. This chapter focuses on using both C# and Java to build some Web services. Later I will show you how to consume these same services.

Building an XML Web service means that you are interested in exposing some information or logic to another entity either within your organization, to a partner, or to your customers. In a more granular sense, building a Web service means that you, as a developer, simply make one or more methods from a class you create that is enabled for SOAP communication.

When building C# Web services using the .NET Framework, you can use the main IDE for Microsoft development, Visual Studio, or you can even go as far to use Notepad for your Web services development.

Note that the examples in this chapter are using Visual Studio 2005 based upon the .NET Framework 2.0.

The first step is to actually create a new Web site by choosing File ➪ New ➪ Web Site from the Visual Studio menu (depending on your version). This launches the New Web Site dialog. Select ASP.NET Web Service, as shown in Figure 19-1. Building a Web service means that you are interested in exposing some information or logic to another entity either within your organization, to a partner, or to your customers. In a more granular sense, building a Web service means that you, as a developer, simply make one or more methods from a class you create enabled for SOAP communication.

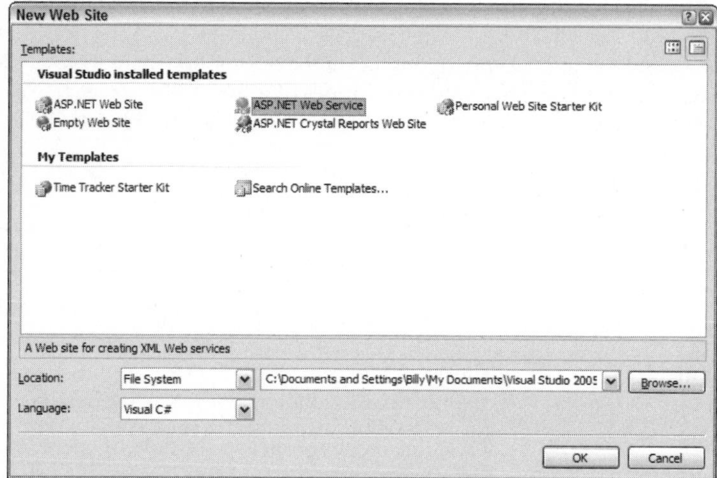

Figure 19-1

Visual Studio creates a few files you can use to get started. In the Solution Explorer of Visual Studio (see Figure 19-2) you find a single Web service file named `Service.asmx`; its code-behind file, `Service.cs`, is located in the `App_Code` folder.

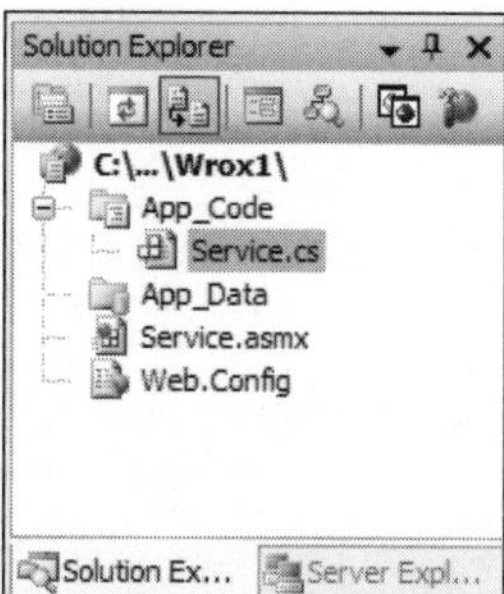

Figure 19-2

For this example, you expose as a Web service the Customers table from the sample Northwind database found in SQL Server 2000. For this example, delete the `Service.asmx` and `Service.cs` files and then right-click the project and select Add New Item from the provided menu. Add a new Web service and give it the name of `Customers.asmx`.

Adding this new Web services to your project actually produces a couple of file. The first is the Web service file — `Customers.asmx`. The second file for this Web service is the code-behind file which you find in the App_Code folder of the solution. The name of this file is `Customers.asmx.cs` (or `Customers.asmx.vb` if you are using Visual Basic).

If you open the `Customers.asmx` file in Visual Studio, you see that the file contains only the `@WebService` page directive, as illustrated in Listing 19-4.

Listing 19-4: Contents of the Customers.asmx file

```
<%@ WebService Language="C#" CodeBehind="~/App_Code/Customers.cs"
    Class="Customers" %>
```

You use the `@WebService` directive instead of the `@Page` directive.

The simple `WebService` directive has only four possible attributes. The following list explains these attributes:

- `Class` — Required. It specifies the class used to define the methods and data types visible to the Web service clients.
- `CodeBehind` — Required only when you are working with a Web service file using the code-behind model. It enables you to work with Web services in two separate and more manageable pieces instead of a single file. The `CodeBehind` attribute takes a string value that represents the physical location of the second piece of the Web service — the class file containing all the Web service logic. In ASP.NET 2.0, it is best to place the code-behind files in the App_Code folder, starting with the default Web service created by Visual Studio when you initially opened the Web service project.
- `Debug` — Optional. It takes a setting of either `True` or `False`. If the `Debug` attribute is set to `True`, the Web service is compiled with debug symbols in place; setting the value to `False` ensures that the Web service is compiled without the debug symbols in place.
- `Language` — Required. It specifies the programming language that is used for the Web service.

Next, for this Web service, you only need to expose a single method — `GetCustomers()`. This is illustrated in Listing 19-5.

Listing 19-5: Exposing the Customers table from the Northwind database in SQL Server

```
using System;
using System.Web;
using System.Web.Services;
using System.Web.Services.Protocols;
using System.Data;
using System.Data.SqlClient;
```

(continued)

Listing 19-5 *(continued)*

```
[WebService(Namespace = "http://www.wrox.com/")]
[WebServiceBinding(ConformsTo = WsiProfiles.BasicProfile1_1)]
public class Customers : System.Web.Services.WebService
{
    public Customers () {

    }

    [WebMethod]
    public DataSet GetCustomers()
    {
        SqlConnection conn;
        SqlDataAdapter myDataAdapter;
        DataSet myDataSet;
        string cmdString = "Select * From Customers";

        conn = new
           SqlConnection("Server=localhost;uid=sa;pwd=;database=Northwind");
        myDataAdapter = new SqlDataAdapter(cmdString, conn);

        myDataSet = new DataSet();
        myDataAdapter.Fill(myDataSet, "Customers");

        return myDataSet;
    }
}
```

For .NET-based Web services, you should pay attention to a couple of things. Note that you are notifying .NET that this is a Web service in a couple of ways. The first is by using the Web service file extension of `.asmx`. The second thing of note is illustrated in Listing 19-5. The `Customers` class is turned into a Web service through the use of the `[WebService]` attribute directly preceding the class.

```
[WebService(Namespace = "http://www.wrox.com/")]
```

In this case, not only is the `WebService` attribute applied to the class, but the `Namespace` property is also assigned a value (always a good idea). Another possible property to assign within the `WebService` attribute is `Description`. Using this property applies a description of the Web service in the WSDL file and might make it easier for developers to understand what the Web service provides.

Something that is new the .NET Framework 2.0 release is the new `[WebServiceBinding]` attribute. It builds the Web service responses so that they conform to the WS-I Basic Profile 1.0 release (found at `http://www.ws-i.org/Profiles/BasicProfile-1.0-2004-04-16.html`).

Besides the attributes that are applied to the `Customers` class, you can also see (from Listing 19-5) that this class inherits from the `System.Web.Services.WebService` class. The only method doing anything in this class is the `GetCustomers()` method, which basically dishes out everything contained in the Customers table from the Northwind database in a single response. Your Web service class (`Customers`) can contain as many methods as you deem necessary, but only the methods that are marked with the `[WebMethod]` attribute are actually exposed out to any consumer. This is only done for the `GetCustomers()` method — also known as a WebMethod.

Using the Microsoft Web Services Test Page

One nice feature provided by the Microsoft Web services development environment is a developer testing page (or a potential consumer testing page as well) for Web services. Pulling up the `.asmx` file in the browser produces the visual test page for the Web service that is being exposed. Remember, usually each Web service is URL-accessible; so to view the visual representation of the Web service, you simply type in the URL of the Web service. An example of this is `http://localhost:1364/Wrox1/Customers.asmx`. The visual test page for the Web services is presented in Figure 19-3.

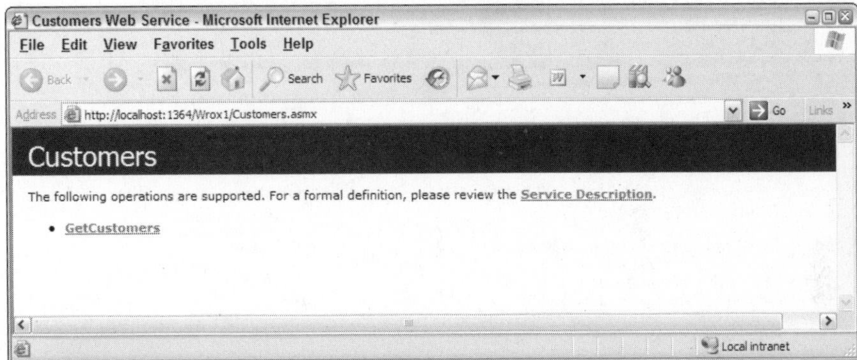

Figure 19-3

This Web interface to your Web service provides the user with the name of your service as well as a list of all the available WebMethods that the consumer can utilize from the Web service. From the preceding figure, you can see that the name of the Web service is provided in the dark blue band at the top of the page (`Customers`) and that the `GetCustomers()` WebMethod is the only method exposed from this Web service.

The other item of importance on the page is a link to the WSDL document for the Web service. This link is provided between the Web service title in the blue band and the list of available WebMethods on the page. Again, the WSDL document is a description of the interface to the Web service. Clicking the link `Service Description` pulls up a new page in the browser that shows you the complete WSDL document (as shown in Figure 19-4).

With this WSDL document, the consumer (or the consumer's IDE) can learn how to consume the Web service. Note that a .NET-based Web service does not have an actual `.wsdl` file in the project that can be referenced directly in the browser. Instead, the WSDL file is invoked by referencing the name of the file which holds the Web service and tacking on a `?WSDL` at the end.

```
http://localhost:1364/Wrox1/Customers.asmx?WSDL
```

Instead of having an actual file in the system, ASP.NET creates one for you dynamically. This doesn't mean that you can't create your own WSDL files. You can do so, but most users stick with the dynamically created WSDL files to represent the interface of their Web services.

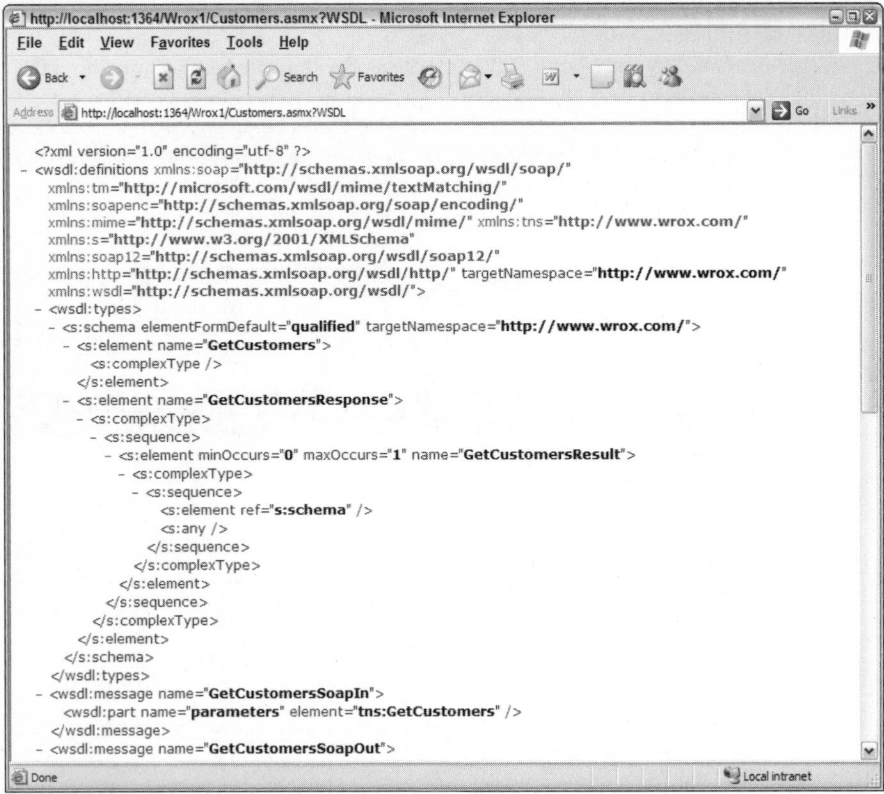

Figure 19-4

Testing the WebMethod

Besides the link to the Web service's WSDL file and a list of methods from the service, the ASP.NET Web service test page also provides consumers with the capability to test actual WebMethods directly in the browser. If a consumer clicks the WebMethod link (`GetCustomers`) in the browser, he is taken to a page where he can test the WebMethod to see how it performs. The `GetCustomers()` WebMethod page is shown in Figure 19-5.

The WebMethod test page enables the consumer to actually test the exposed method. If the method requires parameters, he can find text boxes on the test page in addition to the Invoke button which is shown in Figure 19-5. Because the `GetCustomers()` WebMethod doesn't require any input parameters to invoke the service, you will not find these text boxes in the figure — just the Invoke button.

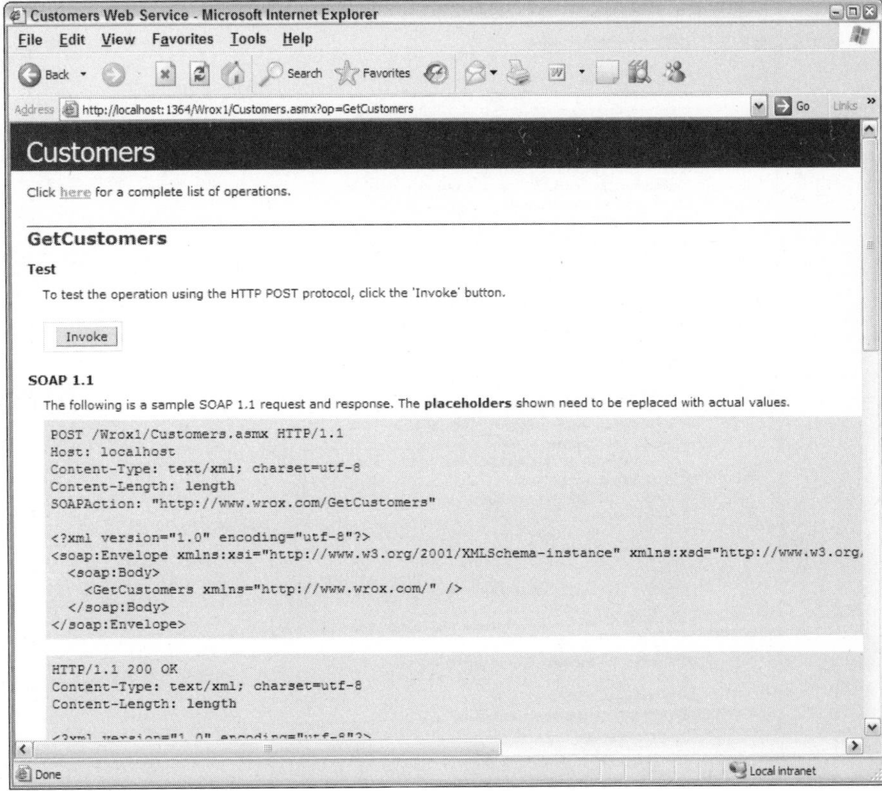

Figure 19-5

In addition to an HTTP-POST form that allows you to invoke WebMethod, you also find some visual documentation that shows the developer what kind of SOAP structure is required to invoke the service as well as the SOAP response the consumer can expect in return. When building Web services in .NET 2.0, you also find documentation for SOAP 1.2 and HTTP-POST requests as well.

Clicking the Invoke button on the page causes the test page to send an HTTP-POST request to the WebMethod. You then see the following response in a new browser instance (shown in Figure 19-6).

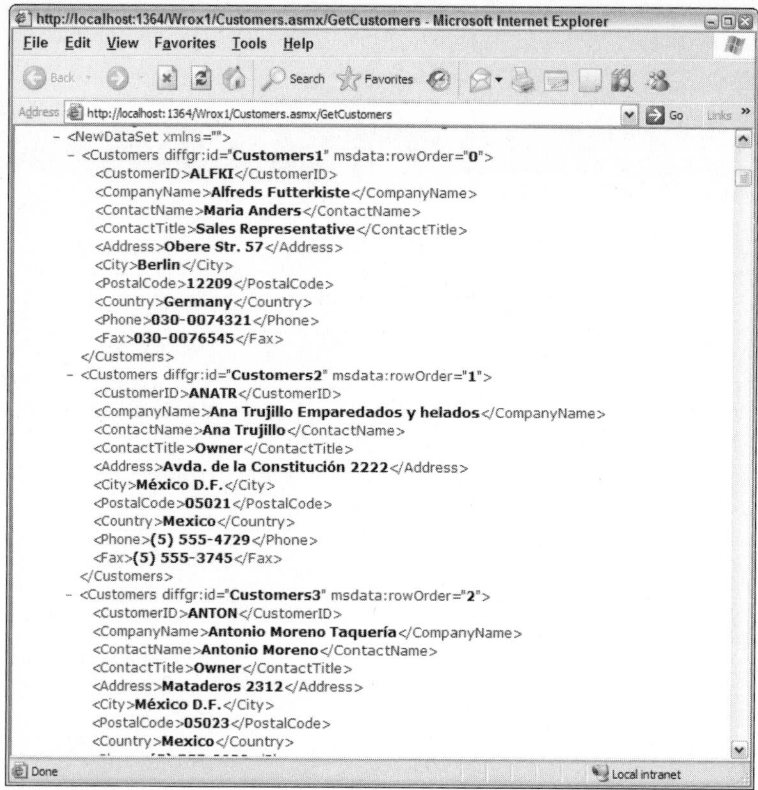

Figure 19-6

Altering the Protocols Used by the Web Service

By default in .NET 2.0, SOAP and HTTP-POST requests are allowed to any Web services on the platform. .NET 1.0 did allow for HTTP-GET requests, but this feature was removed in the default installation starting with .NET 1.1.

To enable HTTP-GET, make changes to your `web.config` file as shown in Listing 19-6.

Listing 19-6: Enabling HTTP-GET in your Web service applications

```
<configuration xmlns="http://schemas.microsoft.com/.NetConfiguration/v2.0">
   <system.web>
      <webServices>
         <protocols>
            <add name="HttpGet"/>
         </protocols>
      </webServices>
   </system.web>
</configuration>
```

Creating a <protocols> section in your web.config file enables you to add or remove protocol communications. For example, you can add missing protocols (such as HTTP-GET) by using the syntax shown previously, or you can remove protocols as the following example shows:

```
<configuration xmlns="http://schemas.microsoft.com/.NetConfiguration/v2.0">
   <system.web>
      <webServices>
         <protocols>
            <remove name="HttpGet"/>
            <remove name="HttpPost"/>
            <remove name="HttpSoap"/>
            <remove name="Documentation"/>
         </protocols>
      </webServices>
   </system.web>
</configuration>
```

You don't want to remove everything shown in this code because that would leave your Web service with basically no capability to communicate; but you can see the construction required for any of the protocols that you do want to remove. The node removing Documentation is interesting because it can eliminate the capability to invoke the Web services interface test page if you don't want to make that page available for any reason.

Building Web Services with Java

XML is a cross platform neutral-data format and Java is a cross-platform programming language. These technologies provide a perfect solution for developing network independent and extensible applications; they enable interoperability, portability, and flexibility. They also provide a standard solution for integrating heterogeneous applications and systems ranging from cell phones to large-scale enterprise applications. An application can be written in Java and ported to various supported platforms (known as "Write Once, Run Anywhere"). In addition, XML also has the capability to talk to Java as well as non-Java applications running on diverse platforms.

With the overwhelming success of XML and Java in enterprise applications, the use of XML has required the development of parsers and other supporting technologies to process the XML data. Many XML-based technologies have been developed over the last few years using vendor-specific APIs that require specific vendor implementation knowledge. The introduction of the Java XML APIs provides standard interfaces that are independent of any vendor-specific implementation. For example, in using a JAXP-compliant parser, this standardization provides better support for maintaining application code and enables the application provider to exchange the underlying implementation of the parser. This change does not require any modification in the application code because the method calls are the same due to compliance of the two parsers.

This chapter presents an introduction to developing Java Web services through the use of Apache Axis and Jakarta Tomcat. Before looking at the Web service implementation, here is a quick introduction to Axis and Tomcat.

Introduction to Axis and Tomcat

Axis is essentially a SOAP engine that provides a framework for constructing SOAP processors such as clients, servers, gateways, etc. In addition to being the third generation of Apache SOAP, the Axis also includes:

- A simple stand-alone server
- A server that plugs into servlet engines such as Tomcat
- Extensive support for the Web Service Description Language (WSDL)
- Emitter tooling that generates Java classes from WSDL

Tomcat is a Java Servlet container and Web server from the Jakarta project of the Apache software foundation. A Web server dishes out Web pages in response to requests from a user sitting at a web browser. But Web servers are not limited to serving up static HTML pages; they can also run programs in response to user requests and return the dynamic results to the user's browser. Tomcat is very good at this because it provides both Java Servlet and Java Server Pages (JSP) technologies (in addition to traditional static pages and external CGI programming). The result is that Tomcat is good choice for use as a Web server for many applications; also if you want a free Servlet and JSP engine. It can be used standalone or used behind traditional Web servers such as Apache http, with the traditional server serving static pages and Tomcat serving dynamic servlet and JSP requests.

For the purposes of this chapter, I will use the combination of Tomcat (as a Web server) and Axis (as the SOAP runtime engine) for the development and deployment of Java Web services.

Setting Up Axis and Tomcat

Before you can begin using Axis, you need to download a copy of Jakarta Tomcat and Apache Axis:

- Jakarta TOMCAT (`http://tomcat.apache.org/download-60.cgi`)
- Apache AXIS (`apache.org/dyn/closer.cgi/ws/axis/1_4`)

For TOMCAT to start properly, set the `JAVA_HOME` system environment variable to `<Drive_Name> Program Files\Java\jdk1.6.0` through Control Panel ➪ System ➪ Advanced ➪ Environment Variables. If you don't have JDK 1.6.0 already installed, download it from the `http://java.sun.com` Web site.

To configure AXIS, set the `CLASSPATH` environment variable to `<axis_home>\axis-1_4\lib\axis.jar; <axis_home>\axis-1_4\lib\commons-discovery-0.2.jar; <axis_home>\axis-1_4\lib\commons-logging-1.0.4.jar; <axis_home>\axis-1_4\lib\jaxrpc.jar; <axis_home>\axis-1_4\lib\saaj.jar; <axis_home>\axis-1_4\lib\wsdl4j-1.5.1.jar; <axis_home>\axis-1_4\;`

After installing Tomcat and decompressing Axis, copy the axis folder from `<axis-home>/webapps` to `<tomcat-home>/webapps`. This gives you the following folder:

```
<tomcat-home>/webapps/axis
```

Start Tomcat by executing the startup script from the <tomcat-home>/bin folder. For example, on Windows:

```
C:\apache-tomcat-5.5.20\bin> startup
```

Now you can test your installation by directing your Web browser to the following URL:

```
http://localhost:8080/axis
```

Click on Validation or go directly to the URL:

```
http://localhost:8080/axis/happyaxis.jsp
```

This page tells you if Axis located the libraries that it needs to run properly. If you have any errors, you are provided with links to the required libraries that you need to install. Follow the links, download the libraries, and copy the JAR files to the <tomcat-home>/webapps/axis/WEB-INF/lib folder.

> *Note you may need to restart Tomcat for the changes to take effect; execute the shutdown script followed by the startup script from the* <tomcat-home>/bin *folder.*

Finally, you might want to test your installation by listing the currently deployed Web services. Bring up the Axis home page by navigating to http://localhost:8080/axis from the browser. If the installation is successful, you should see an output similar to Figure 19-7.

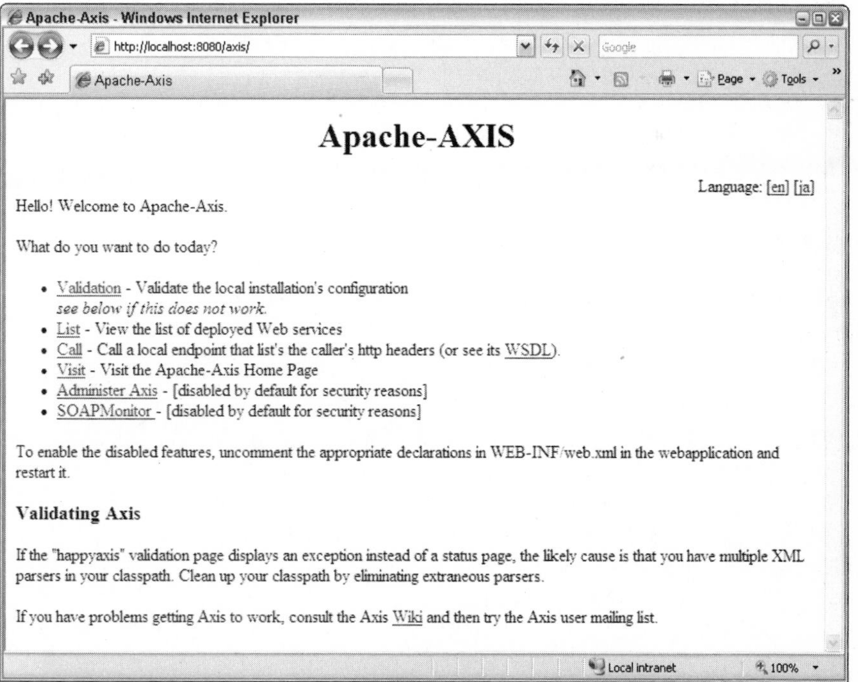

Figure 19-7

If you click List on the Axis homepage, you should initially see two services:

- AdminService
- Version

Click on the wsdl link for the Version service to validate that Axis is properly serving its content.

Publishing Web Services Using Axis

Now that you have set up your Web application to use Axis as the SOAP engine, it's time to publish the Web services. Axis provides two ways to deploy the Web services.

- Instant deployment through renaming `.java` to `.jws`
- Advanced deployment through the `.wsdd` (Web Service Deployment Descriptor) configuration file

The next two sections examine both of these approaches in detail.

Instant Deployment Through Renaming .java to .jws

The simplest and most straightforward way to deploy Web services is to rename the `.java` file to `.jws` and place it in the root of your Web application. JWS stands for Java Web Service. For example, consider the following java class named `HelloWorld.java`.

```
public class HelloWorld {
   public static String HelloWorld(String name){
      return "Hello : " + name;
   }
}
```

To expose this as a Web service, you simply rename it to `HelloWorld.jws` and place it in the root of your Web application. That's all there is to deploying the Web service. With that, you are ready to access the WSDL contents of the Web service by navigating to `http://localhost:8080/axis/HelloWorld.jws` using the browser. Figure 19-8 shows the output generated by the browser.

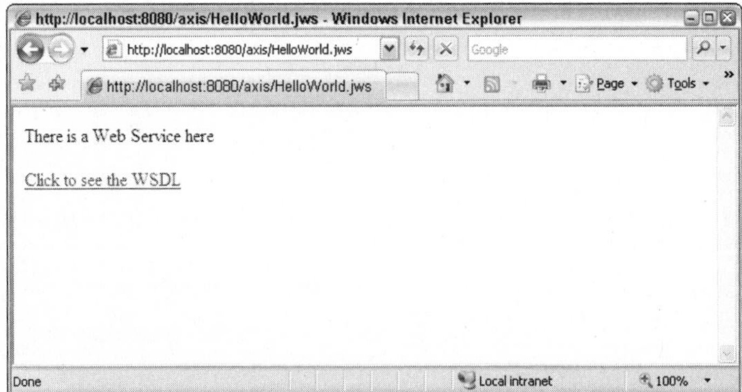

Figure 19-8

In the Consuming Web Services with Java"section, you will see the steps involved in consuming this service from a client application.

As you can see, this approach is very simple. However, one of the major caveats of using this technique is that you are forced to use mainly primitive data types and some very common Java classes such as `java.util.Date` as method arguments and return types. In other words, you cannot use your custom classes (also sometimes referred to as Value Objects or VOs) as method parameters or return types. This is where the advanced deployment comes into your rescue, which is the topic of focus for the next section.

Advanced Deployment

The advanced deployment allows you to use your own classes as parameter values and return type of methods. These parameter values are called Value Objects. Value Objects are typically used to represent the collection of data that needs to be passed on via methods. To illustrate the advanced deployment approach, let us consider a slightly complex service, wherein you retrieve the product data from a SQL Server 2005 database, convert the resultset into a Product object, and return that from the service.

First, to be able to access SQL Server data, you must download the corresponding JDBC driver. You can download the JDBC driver for SQL Server 2005 from the link (`http://www.microsoft.com/downloads/details.aspx?FamilyId=6D483869-816A-44CB-9787-A866235EFC7C&displaylang=en`) in Microsoft Web site. Once you unzip the installation zip file in a local file, ensure that the path to the `sqljdbc.jar` file is also set in the `CLASSPATH` environment variable.

Creating the Service Implementation

Create a new java class file named `ProductService.java` and place it under the `<Drive_Name>\Projects\Wrox\WebServices\com\wrox\webservices` folder. This is shown in Listing 19-7.

Listing 19-7: Exposing the Product data from the AdventureWorks database in SQL Server

```
package com.wrox.webservices;

import java.sql.Connection;
import java.sql.DriverManager;
import java.sql.PreparedStatement;
import java.sql.ResultSet;

public class ProductService
{
   public static Product getProduct(int productID)
   {
      Product obj = new Product();
      try
      {
         Class.forName("com.microsoft.sqlserver.jdbc.SQLServerDriver");
         String connectionUrl =
        "jdbc:sqlserver://localhost;database=AdventureWorks;user=sa;password=thiru";
         Connection con = DriverManager.getConnection(connectionUrl);
         con.setAutoCommit(false);
         PreparedStatement pstmt = con.prepareStatement
```

(continued)

Listing 19-7 *(continued)*

```
                ("SELECT ProductID, Name, ProductNumber, Color FROM " +
                " Production.Product WHERE ProductID = ?");
            pstmt.setInt(1, productID);
            ResultSet rs = pstmt.executeQuery();
            while (rs.next())
            {
                obj.setProductID(rs.getInt("ProductID"));
                obj.setName(rs.getString("Name"));
                obj.setProductNumber(rs.getString("ProductNumber"));
                obj.setColor(rs.getString("Color"));
            }
            rs.close();
            pstmt.close();
            con.close();
        }
        catch (Exception e)
        {
            e.printStackTrace();
        }
        return obj;
    }
}
```

To start with, you load the Microsoft JDBC driver for SQL Server 2005 by calling the `Class.forName()` method passing in the name of the class that represents the SQL Server driver.

```
Class.forName("com.microsoft.sqlserver.jdbc.SQLServerDriver");
```

After that, you specify the connection string to the database using the JDBC connection string syntax. Once the connection string is set, the next step is to get reference to the Connection object, which can be accomplished using the `DriverManager.getConnection()` method.

```
String connectionUrl =
   "jdbc:sqlserver://localhost;database=AdventureWorks;user=sa;password=thiru";
Connection con = DriverManager.getConnection(connectionUrl);
```

Next, you obtain reference to the `PreparedStatement` object through the `prepareStatement()` method of the Connection object. To the `prepareStatement()` method, you pass in the SQL statement to be executed as an argument.

```
PreparedStatement pstmt = con.prepareStatement
   ("SELECT ProductID, Name, ProductNumber, Color FROM " +
   " Production.Product WHERE ProductID = ?");
```

Here you set the value of the `ProductID` parameter by invoking the `setInt()` method of the `Prepared Statement` object. Finally you execute the SQL query through the invocation of `executeQuery()` method, which returns a `ResultSet` object with results from the execution of the query.

```
pstmt.setInt(1, productID);
ResultSet rs = pstmt.executeQuery();
```

Once you have the `ResultSet` object, you can then invoke its `getXXX()` methods to get to the specific column values.

```
while (rs.next())
{
   obj.setProductID(rs.getInt("ProductID"));
   obj.setName(rs.getString("Name"));
   obj.setProductNumber(rs.getString("ProductNumber"));
   obj.setColor(rs.getString("Color"));
}
```

Finally, you return the Product object as a return value to the caller.

```
return obj;
```

The Product class used in Listing 19-8 is declared as follows:

Listing 19-8: Implementation of Product class

```
package com.wrox.webservices;

public class Product
{
   private int productID;
   private String name;
   private String productNumber;
   private String color;

   public int getProductID()
   { return productID; }
   public void setProductID(int productIDVal)
   { productID = productIDVal; }

   public String getName()
   { return name; }
   public void setName(String nameVal)
   { name = nameVal; }

   public String getProductNumber()
   { return productNumber; }
   public void setProductNumber(String productNumberVal)
   { productNumber = productNumberVal; }

   public String getColor()
   { return color; }
   public void setColor(String colorVal)
   { color = colorVal; }
}
```

As you can see from Listing 19-8, the `Product` class just has a set of getter/setter methods that allow you to work with the various attributes of a Product.

The Product class file is also stored in the same location `<Drive_Name>\Projects\Wrox\WebServices\com\wrox\webservices`. Now compile the `ProductService.java` file using the command line compiler javac. For the compiler to identify the Product class, your `CLASSPATH` variable must also include the location `C:\Projects\Wrox\WebServices\`. Instead of setting the `CLASSPATH` environment variable, you can also specify the classpath switch at the time of invoking the compiler.

Creating a Web Service Deployment Descriptor (WSDD) File

Now that you have created the service implementation, the next step is to create a WSDD file that contains the service deployment information. To really use the flexibility available to you in Axis, you should get familiar with the Web Service Deployment Descriptor (WSDD) format. A deployment descriptor contains a bunch of things you want to "deploy" into Axis, meaning make available to the Axis engine. For `ProductService`, create a WSDD file called `Deploy.wsdd` and add the following contents to it.

```
<deployment xmlns="http://xml.apache.org/axis/wsdd/"
   xmlns:java="http://xml.apache.org/axis/wsdd/providers/java">
   <service name="ProductProcessor" provider="java:RPC">
      <parameter name="className" value="com.wrox.webservices.ProductService"/>
      <parameter name="allowedMethods" value="getProduct"/>
      <beanMapping qname="myNS:Product" xmlns:myNS="urn:ProductService"
         languageSpecificType="java:com.wrox.webservices.Product"/>
   </service>
</deployment>
```

The `<service>` element enables you to specify the details of the service including the name of the class as well the methods that are allowed to act as Web methods. The `<beanMapping>` sub-element points to your custom bean. This element allows Axis to handle (most appropriately serialize and de-serialize) the Java classes that are not handled by default by Axis (mostly primitive) and they follow the Java bean style setter and getter methods. You have to define as many bean mappings as the beans used by the Web method and the beans used within those beans.

Now go ahead and deploy the `deploy.wsdd` file using the `AdminClient` utility:

```
java org.apache.axis.client.AdminClient -llocal:///AdminService deploy.wsdd
```

You should see an output similar to Figure 19-9:

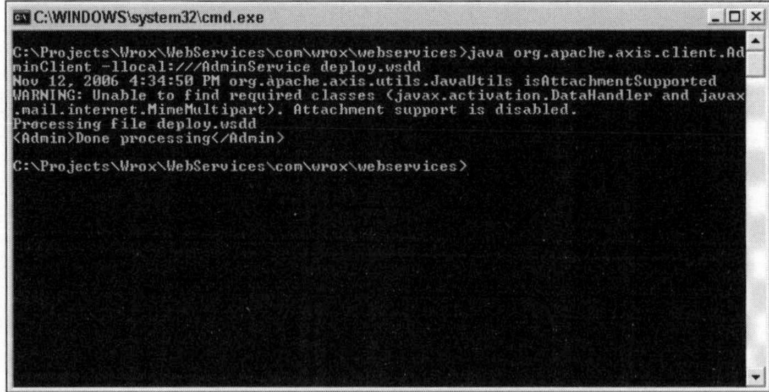

Figure 19-9

Now that you have created the Web service, you are ready to consume it from a client application, which will be covered in the "Consuming Web Services with JAVA" section.

Consuming Web Services with C#

Earlier in this chapter, you got a preview of how to build a simple Web service that exposed the Customers table from the Northwind database of SQL Server. This Web service was written in C# and, once it is in place, any consumer (regardless of the consumer's underlying platform) can consume this Web service.

So where can you consume Web services when using C#? Remember that the Web services you come across can be consumed in Windows Forms applications, mobile applications, databases, and more. You can even consume Web services with other Web services so you can have a single Web service made up of what is basically an aggregate of other Web services. Anything that is connected to HTTP and can understand XML in some fashion can utilize the Customers Web service that was created earlier in this chapter.

Next, you see how to consume the Customers Web service in a C#-based ASP.NET application.

Consuming Web Services Using ASP.NET

The first step in the process of consuming a Web service using ASP.NET is to create an ASP.NET project using Visual Studio 2005. This process creates a single page called `Default.aspx` in the project. The Solution Explorer for this project is shown in Figure 19-10.

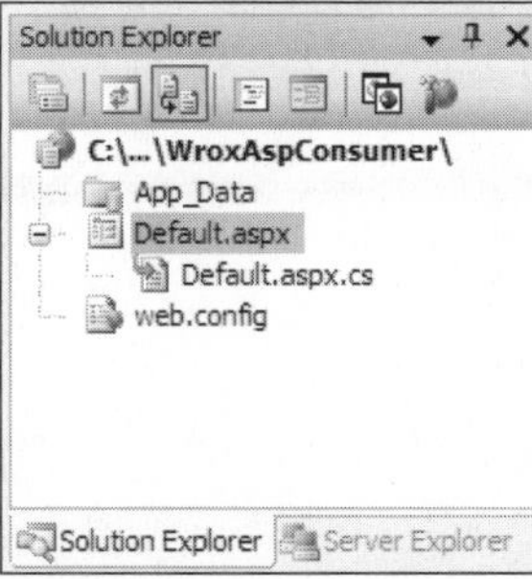

Figure 19-10

Adding a Web Reference to Your ASP.NET Project

Now that the project is in place, right-click the project name and select Add Web Reference from the provided menu. You also see an Add Reference option in the menu, but this is for referencing objects that reside on the same server. Because you are hoping to make a reference to a remote object, you next use the Add Web Reference option. This selection from the menu pulls up the Add Web Reference dialog box.

From the Add Web Reference dialog, you can search for Web services that are located within the same project, the same server, or which are contained within UDDI. For this solution, be sure to select the option that enables you to find Web services that reside on the same server.

You might not find the earlier Customers Web service on the local machine depending on how that service was built. By default, Visual Studio 2005 uses a built-in Web server to launch, run, and test the Web services. If this default Web server is not running, then your new ASP.NET project will not find the Web service anywhere on the server. To get around this, either open another instance of Visual Studio 2005 and run the Customers Web service project or build the Customers Web service within Internet Information Services (IIS).

To find the Customers Web service, you really have to type only the URL endpoint of the service in the address bar of the dialog. Visual Studio figures out where the location of the dynamically created WSDL document on its own when just referencing `Customers.asmx`. However, if you are consuming a Web service from another platform, you must type the location of the WSDL document in the address bar instead.

After the reference has been made, you then should rename the reference. The reference has the default name of `localhost` (if the Web service resides on the same server as the consuming application) or it will have something a bit cryptic such as `com.wrox.www` if located elsewhere on the Internet. For this example, I renamed the reference `Wrox` as shown in Figure 19-11.

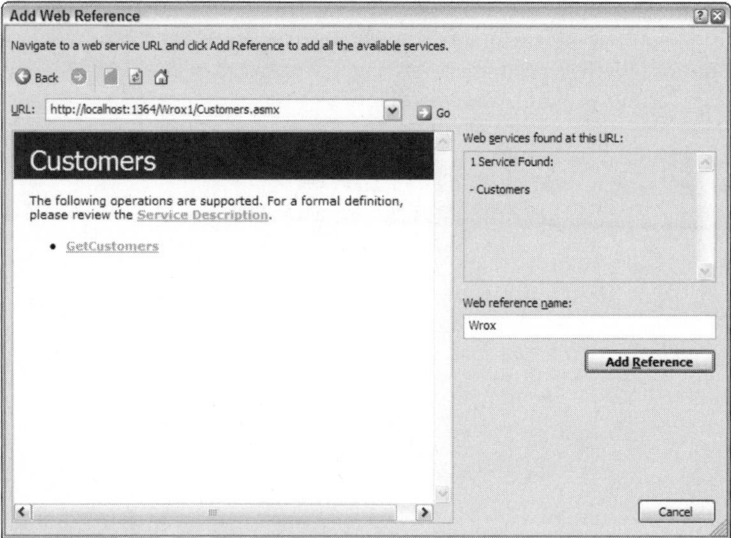

Figure 19-11

After you have the Add Web Reference dialog the way you want it, click the Add Reference button in the dialog to have Visual Studio generate everything you need to consume the Web service.

So, after making this reference, what is created for you? If you look at the Solution Explorer of Visual Studio shown in Figure 19-12, you see the additions.

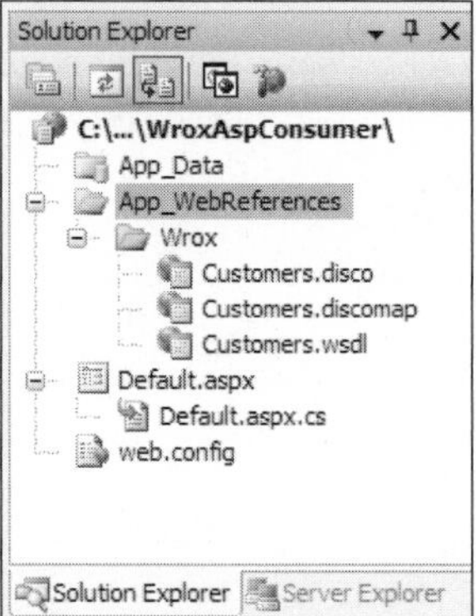

Figure 19-12

From Figure 19-12, you can see that the WSDL document was pulled down to the application as well as some additional DISCO (discovery) documents. In addition to the WSDL document, you also find that a change was made to the ASP.NET application's `web.config` file.

```
<appSettings>
   <add key="Wrox.Customers"
    value="http://localhost:1364/Wrox1/Customers.asmx"/>
</appSettings>
```

This `<appSettings>` value gives you an object reference to the Customers Web service that can now be utilized in your code.

Building the Consuming Web Page

Now turn your attention to the `Default.aspx` page that is in the ASP.NET solution. Now that a reference is in place in the project, the next step is to build the means on the ASP.NET page to utilize this object in some fashion.

On the design part of the `Default.aspx` page, place a Button and a GridView control so that your page looks something like the one shown in Figure 19-13.

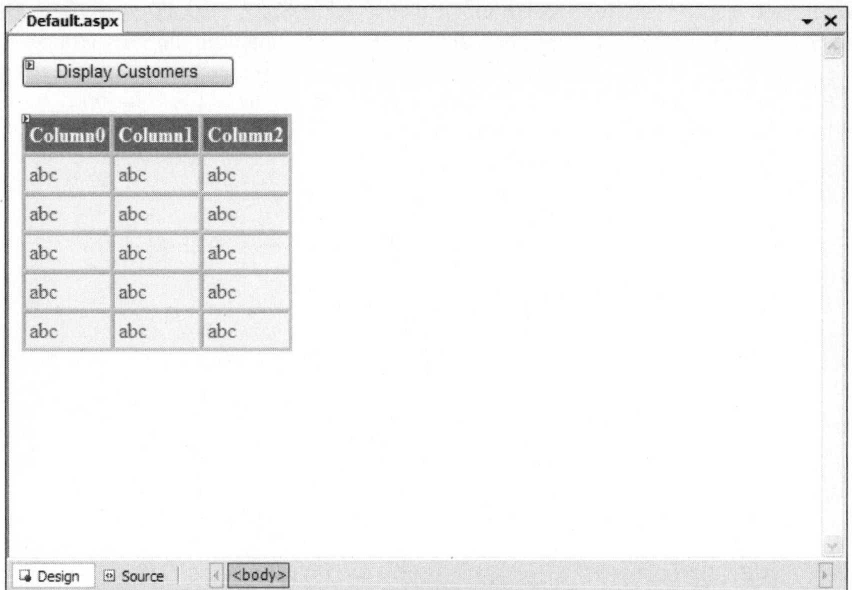

Figure 19-13

The idea is that, when the end user clicks the button contained on the form, the application sends a SOAP request to the Customers Web service and gets back a SOAP response containing the Customers table from the Northwind database, which is then bound to the GridView control on the page. Listing 19-9 shows the code for this simple application.

Listing 19-9: Consuming the Customers Web service in an ASP.NET page

```
using System;
using System.Data;
using System.Configuration;
using System.Collections;
using System.Web;
using System.Web.Security;
using System.Web.UI;
using System.Web.UI.WebControls;
using System.Web.UI.WebControls.WebParts;
using System.Web.UI.HtmlControls;

public partial class _Default : System.Web.UI.Page
{
    protected void Button1_Click(object sender, EventArgs e)
    {
        Wrox.Customers ws = new Wrox.Customers();
        GridView1.DataSource = ws.GetCustomers();
        GridView1.DataBind();
    }
}
```

The code from Listing 19-9 is the code from the code-behind page, `Default.aspx.cs`. This code-behind file contains only a single event — the `Button1_Click` event. This event occurs when the end user clicks the single button on the ASP.NET page. When this happens, first the Web service reference is instantiated as `ws`:

```
Wrox.Customers ws = new Wrox.Customers();
```

Then the result from the `ws` object's `GetCustomers()` method is assigned to the `DataSource` property of the GridView control before being data bound to the control. These three simple lines of code give you the results illustrated in Figure 19-14.

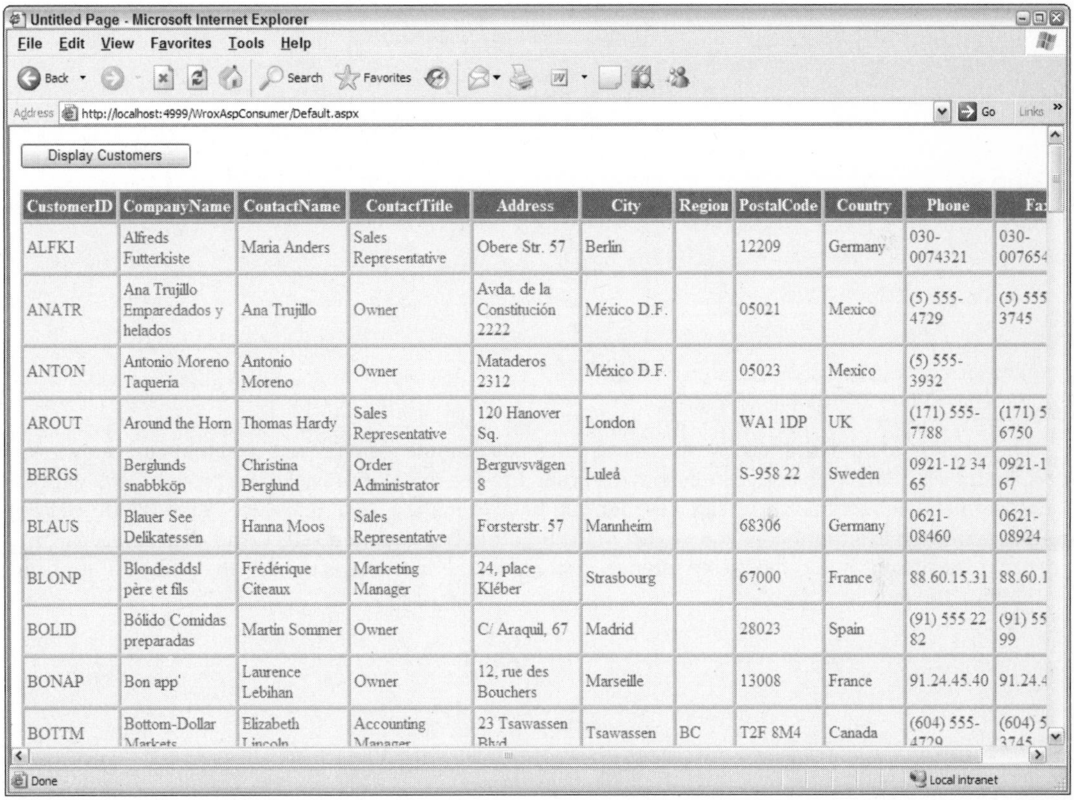

Untitled Page - Microsoft Internet Explorer

File Edit View Favorites Tools Help

Address http://localhost:4999/WroxAspConsumer/Default.aspx

Display Customers

CustomerID	CompanyName	ContactName	ContactTitle	Address	City	Region	PostalCode	Country	Phone	Fa
ALFKI	Alfreds Futterkiste	Maria Anders	Sales Representative	Obere Str. 57	Berlin		12209	Germany	030-0074321	030-007654
ANATR	Ana Trujillo Emparedados y helados	Ana Trujillo	Owner	Avda. de la Constitución 2222	México D.F.		05021	Mexico	(5) 555-4729	(5) 555 3745
ANTON	Antonio Moreno Taquería	Antonio Moreno	Owner	Mataderos 2312	México D.F.		05023	Mexico	(5) 555-3932	
AROUT	Around the Horn	Thomas Hardy	Sales Representative	120 Hanover Sq.	London		WA1 1DP	UK	(171) 555-7788	(171) 5 6750
BERGS	Berglunds snabbköp	Christina Berglund	Order Administrator	Berguvsvägen 8	Luleå		S-958 22	Sweden	0921-12 34 65	0921-1 67
BLAUS	Blauer See Delikatessen	Hanna Moos	Sales Representative	Forsterstr. 57	Mannheim		68306	Germany	0621-08460	0621-08924
BLONP	Blondesddsl père et fils	Frédérique Citeaux	Marketing Manager	24, place Kléber	Strasbourg		67000	France	88.60.15.31	88.60.1
BOLID	Bólido Comidas preparadas	Martín Sommer	Owner	C/ Araquil, 67	Madrid		28023	Spain	(91) 555 22 82	(91) 55 99
BONAP	Bon app'	Laurence Lebihan	Owner	12, rue des Bouchers	Marseille		13008	France	91.24.45.40	91.24.4
BOTTM	Bottom-Dollar Markets	Elizabeth Lincoln	Accounting Manager	23 Tsawassen Blvd.	Tsawassen	BC	T2F 8M4	Canada	(604) 555-4729	(604) 5 3745

Done Local intranet

Figure 19-14

In the end, a dataset is exposed from a remote server and then, using standards such as SOAP, you are able to consume this dataset over HTTP and use it inside your application. It was simple to achieve this remote procedure call because it is based upon standards.

Consuming Web Services Using Windows Forms

To show you the power of consuming Web services, you can look at another example of consumption. Remember, after the data is exposed as a Web service and becomes consumable by someone, you really can't control how that data is utilized. For instance, although you just saw the consumption of the Customers table into an ASP.NET application (which is a browser-based application), the consumer can also take this SOAP response and use it in a thick-client application (Windows Forms, for instance), a console application, a Windows service, and even another Web service.

Next, to show another example of consumption, you can work through an example of consuming the `GetCustomers()` WebMethod in a Windows Forms application. To accomplish this, open up Visual Studio 2005 and create a new Windows Forms project in C#. This gives you a project like the one shown in Figure 19-15.

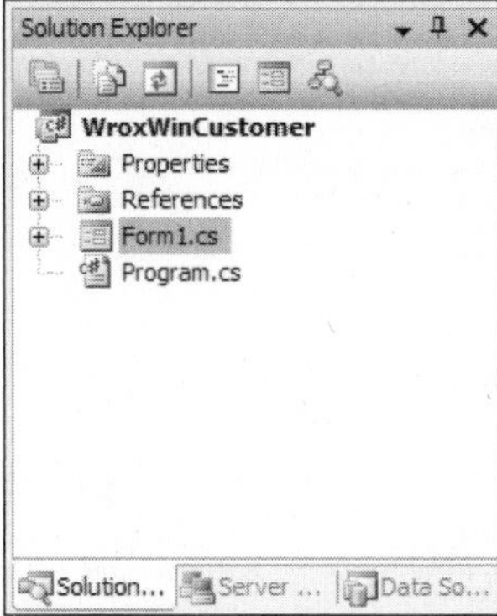

Figure 19-15

The creation of the Windows Forms project gives you a single form (`Form1.cs`) that you can work with. Like the ASP.NET Web application shown earlier, to have this Windows Forms project work with the Customers Web service you created earlier, you have to make a Web Reference in the Windows Forms project. To do this, right-click the project in the Solution Explorer and select Add Web Reference from the provided menu. To add the Web reference, go through the same steps used in the ASP.NET application, naming the reference `Wrox`.

This does a few things to your project as shown in Figure 19-16.

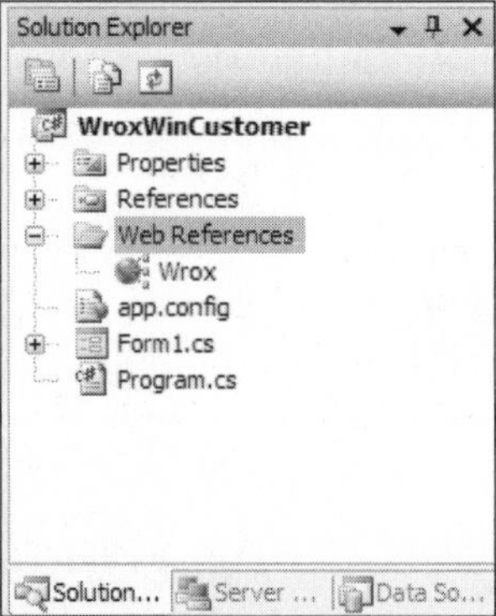

Figure 19-16

Instead of making a reference in this fashion, you can also use the Data Sources tab (shown in the bottom-right-hand corner of Figure 19-16) to add a reference to the Web service. Doing it through the Data Sources dialogs also adds a proxy class to the Visual Studio toolbox that you can then easily use in your project.

For this example, I simply add a DataGridView control to the form and a little bit of style (just for alternating rows). In the code-behind of the form, the only thing to add is an instantiation of the Web service reference and then a process to bind this instantiation to the DataGridView control on the form. The code-behind for the `Form1_Load` event is shown in Listing 19-10.

Listing 19-10: Calling the Web service from a Windows Forms application

```
using System;
using System.Collections.Generic;
using System.ComponentModel;
using System.Data;
using System.Drawing;
using System.Text;
using System.Windows.Forms;

namespace WroxWinCustomer
{
    public partial class Form1 : Form
    {
        public Form1()
        {
            InitializeComponent();
        }

        private void Form1_Load(object sender, EventArgs e)
        {
            Wrox.Customers ws = new Wrox.Customers();
            dataGridView1.DataMember = "Customers";
            dataGridView1.DataSource = ws.GetCustomers();
        }
    }
}
```

In this example, you use the DataGridView control's `DataMember` property and assign the name of the class you are consuming as well as assigning the `DataSource` property to be the dataset which is returned from the `GetCustomers()` method call. The result of this operation is shown in Figure 19-17.

I hope that after you see how this simple Web service was consumed in a Web application as well as in a thick-client application, you recognize how powerful the Web services model is and how usable it is in almost any environment. That's the power of Web services and that is why everyone is so excited about them.

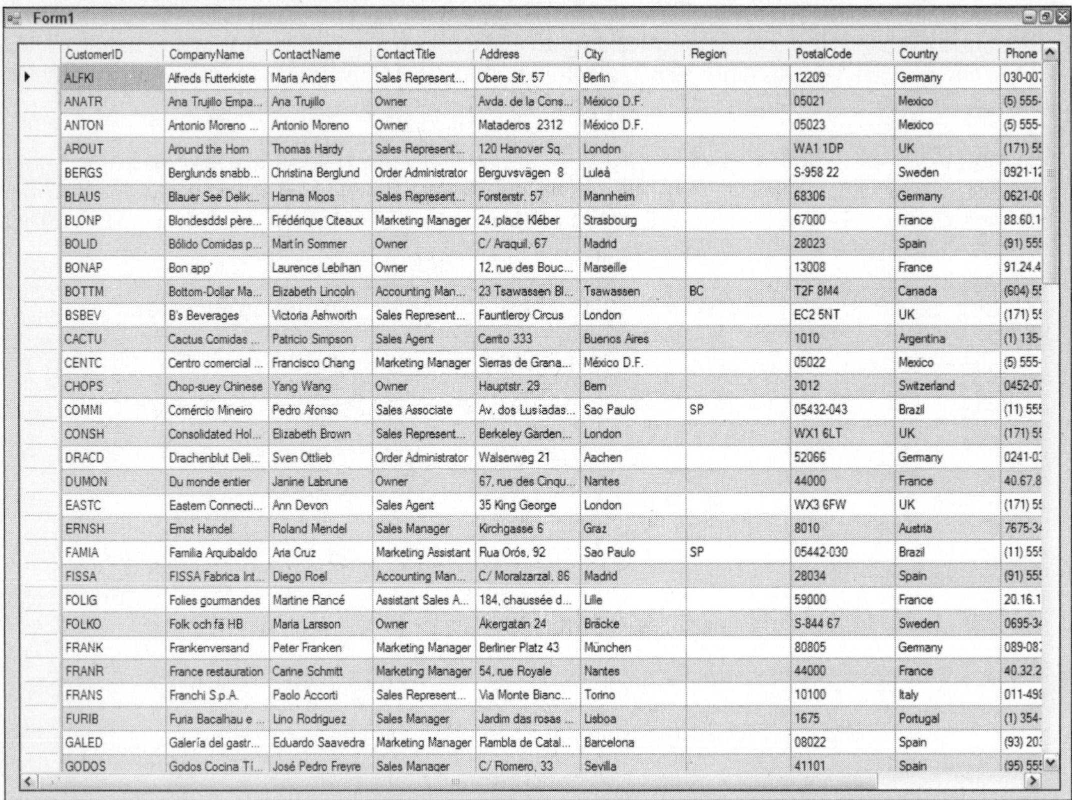

CustomerID	CompanyName	ContactName	ContactTitle	Address	City	Region	PostalCode	Country	Phone
ALFKI	Alfreds Futterkiste	Maria Anders	Sales Represent...	Obere Str. 57	Berlin		12209	Germany	030-007
ANATR	Ana Trujillo Empa...	Ana Trujillo	Owner	Avda. de la Cons...	México D.F.		05021	Mexico	(5) 555-
ANTON	Antonio Moreno ...	Antonio Moreno	Owner	Mataderos 2312	México D.F.		05023	Mexico	(5) 555-
AROUT	Around the Horn	Thomas Hardy	Sales Represent...	120 Hanover Sq.	London		WA1 1DP	UK	(171) 55
BERGS	Berglunds snabb...	Christina Berglund	Order Administrator	Berguvsvägen 8	Luleå		S-958 22	Sweden	0921-12
BLAUS	Blauer See Delik...	Hanna Moos	Sales Represent...	Forsterstr. 57	Mannheim		68306	Germany	0621-08
BLONP	Blondesddsl père...	Frédérique Citeaux	Marketing Manager	24, place Kléber	Strasbourg		67000	France	88.60.1
BOLID	Bólido Comidas p...	Martín Sommer	Owner	C/ Araquil, 67	Madrid		28023	Spain	(91) 555
BONAP	Bon app'	Laurence Lebihan	Owner	12, rue des Bouc...	Marseille		13008	France	91.24.4
BOTTM	Bottom-Dollar Ma...	Elizabeth Lincoln	Accounting Man...	23 Tsawassen Bl...	Tsawassen	BC	T2F 8M4	Canada	(604) 55
BSBEV	B's Beverages	Victoria Ashworth	Sales Represent...	Fauntleroy Circus	London		EC2 5NT	UK	(171) 55
CACTU	Cactus Comidas ...	Patricio Simpson	Sales Agent	Cerrito 333	Buenos Aires		1010	Argentina	(1) 135-
CENTC	Centro comercial ...	Francisco Chang	Marketing Manager	Sierras de Grana...	México D.F.		05022	Mexico	(5) 555-
CHOPS	Chop-suey Chinese	Yang Wang	Owner	Hauptstr. 29	Bern		3012	Switzerland	0452-07
COMMI	Comércio Mineiro	Pedro Afonso	Sales Associate	Av. dos Lusíadas...	Sao Paulo	SP	05432-043	Brazil	(11) 555
CONSH	Consolidated Hol...	Elizabeth Brown	Sales Represent...	Berkeley Garden...	London		WX1 6LT	UK	(171) 55
DRACD	Drachenblut Deli...	Sven Ottlieb	Order Administrator	Walserweg 21	Aachen		52066	Germany	0241-03
DUMON	Du monde entier	Janine Labrune	Owner	67, rue des Cinqu...	Nantes		44000	France	40.67.8
EASTC	Eastern Connecti...	Ann Devon	Sales Agent	35 King George	London		WX3 6FW	UK	(171) 55
ERNSH	Ernst Handel	Roland Mendel	Sales Manager	Kirchgasse 6	Graz		8010	Austria	7675-34
FAMIA	Familia Arquibaldo	Aria Cruz	Marketing Assistant	Rua Orós, 92	Sao Paulo	SP	05442-030	Brazil	(11) 555
FISSA	FISSA Fabrica Int...	Diego Roel	Accounting Man...	C/ Moralzarzal, 86	Madrid		28034	Spain	(91) 555
FOLIG	Folies gourmandes	Martine Rancé	Assistant Sales A...	184, chaussée d...	Lille		59000	France	20.16.1
FOLKO	Folk och fä HB	Maria Larsson	Owner	Åkergatan 24	Bräcke		S-844 67	Sweden	0695-34
FRANK	Frankenversand	Peter Franken	Marketing Manager	Berliner Platz 43	München		80805	Germany	089-087
FRANR	France restauration	Carine Schmitt	Marketing Manager	54, rue Royale	Nantes		44000	France	40.32.2
FRANS	Franchi S.p.A.	Paolo Accorti	Sales Represent...	Via Monte Bianc...	Torino		10100	Italy	011-498
FURIB	Furia Bacalhau e ...	Lino Rodriguez	Sales Manager	Jardim das rosas ...	Lisboa		1675	Portugal	(1) 354-
GALED	Galería del gastr...	Eduardo Saavedra	Marketing Manager	Rambla de Catal...	Barcelona		08022	Spain	(93) 203
GODOS	Godos Cocina Tí...	José Pedro Freyre	Sales Manager	C/ Romero, 33	Sevilla		41101	Spain	(95) 555

Figure 19-17

I hope that after you see how this simple Web service was consumed in a Web application as well as in a thick-client application, you recognize how powerful the Web services model is and how usable it is in almost any environment. That's the power of Web services and that is why everyone is so excited about them.

Consuming Web Services with Java

In the "Building Web Services with Java" section, you created two different Web services. One using the instant deployment (named `HelloWorld.jws`) and another one using the advanced deployment approach (named `ProductService.java`). This section will demonstrate the steps involved in consuming these services from Java client applications. First, let us start with the `HelloWorld.jws` service.

Consuming the HelloWorld Service

For the purposes of this example, create a new Java file named `HelloWorldClient.java` and modify its code to look as shown in Listing 19-11.

Listing 19-11: Implementation of client for the product service

```
package com.wrox.webservices;

import org.apache.axis.client.Call;
import org.apache.axis.client.Service;
import org.apache.axis.encoding.XMLType;
import org.apache.axis.utils.Options;
import javax.xml.rpc.ParameterMode;

public class HelloWorldClient
{
   public static void main(String [] args) throws Exception {
      Options options = new Options(args);
      String endpoint = "http://localhost:" + options.getPort() +
         "/axis/HelloWorld.jws";
      args = options.getRemainingArgs();
      if (args == null || args.length != 2) {
         System.err.println("Usage: HelloWorldClient <HelloWorld> arg1 ");
         return;
      }
      String method = args[0];
      if (!(method.equals("HelloWorld"))){
         System.err.println("Usage: HelloWorld arg1 ");
          return;
      }
      String name = new String(args[1]);
      Service  service = new Service();
      Call call  = (Call) service.createCall();
      call.setTargetEndpointAddress( new java.net.URL(endpoint) );
      call.setOperationName( method );
      call.addParameter( "name", XMLType.XSD_STRING, ParameterMode.IN );
      call.setReturnType( XMLType.XSD_STRING );
      String result = (String)call.invoke(new Object[] { name });
      System.out.println(result);
   }
}
```

To start with, create an instance of the `org.apache.axis.utils.Options` class and pass in the arguments array passed to the main method. Through the `getPort()` method of the `Options` object, you retrieve the port number in which the Web service is hosted. In addition to the port number, the input arguments passed to the main method also include the name of the method as well as the argument to be passed to the method. You retrieve these two values and assign them to local variables for later use.

Then you create a new Service instance and then use the Service object to create a service call through the `createCall()` method. In this case, you create it directly rather than using a `ServiceFactory` because Axis only supports JAX-RPC calls. This approach enables you to keep everything generic because of which the `HelloWorldClient` doesn't need to know anything about the `HelloWorld` service and let the Web service framework handle the underlying complexities.

```
Service  service = new Service();
Call call  = (Call) service.createCall();
```

Next, you specify the location of the Web service using the `setTargetEndpointAddress()` method, to which you pass in the endpoint of the Web service.

```
call.setTargetEndpointAddress( new java.net.URL(endpoint) );
```

Here you define the operation name to execute through the call to the `setOperationName()` method.

```
call.setOperationName( method );
```

Here you tell the service call that you have an input parameter and an output parameter. You set the input parameter name to name and map its String type to the corresponding XSD type. Since the output parameter is of String type, you set the return type to `XSD_STRING`.

```
call.addParameter( "name", XMLType.XSD_STRING, ParameterMode.IN );
call.setReturnType( XMLType.XSD_STRING );
```

Then you invoke the Web service through the `Call.Invoke()` method call passing in the name input parameter.

```
String result = (String)call.invoke(new Object[] { name });
```

Finally, you capture the response returned from the service and typecast that into a String. You then display the value of the result variable by calling the `System.out.println()` method.

```
System.out.println(result);
```

Running the Client Application

Now that you have created the client application, you are ready to run the application. First, compile the `HelloWorldClient.java` using the compiler. After that, enter the following command from the command prompt to initiate the client application.

```
java com.wrox.webservices.HelloWorldClient -p8080 HelloWorld "Thiru"
```

In the previous command:

- The switch `p` specifies the port number
- `HelloWorld` indicates the name of the Web service method to be invoked
- `"Thiru"` is the argument passed to the `HelloWorld` method

The result of the previous command displays output similar to Figure 19-18:

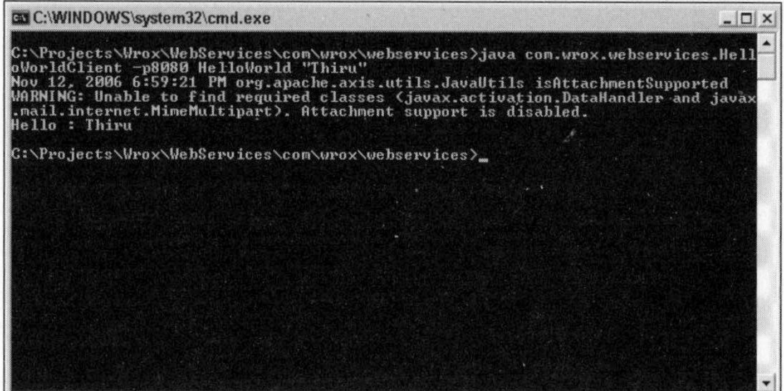

Figure 19-18

Consuming the ProductService

In this section, you will see the steps involved in consuming the `ProductService`. Remember that the `ProductService` has a method named `getProduct` that accepts a `productID` as an argument and returns the details of that product in the form of a Product object. To start with, create a new Java class named `ProductClient` and add the code shown in Listing 19-12 to it.

Listing 19-12: Implementation of Client for the Product Service

```
package com.wrox.webservices;

import org.apache.axis.AxisFault;
import org.apache.axis.client.Call;
import org.apache.axis.client.Service;
import org.apache.axis.utils.Options;
import javax.xml.namespace.QName;
import javax.xml.rpc.ParameterMode;

public class ProductClient
{
   public static void main(String [] args) throws Exception
   {
      Options options = new Options(args);
      Service  service = new Service();
      Call call = (Call) service.createCall();
      QName qn = new QName( "urn:ProductService", "Product" );
      call.registerTypeMapping(Product.class, qn,
         new org.apache.axis.encoding.ser.BeanSerializerFactory(Product.class, qn),
         new org.apache.axis.encoding.ser.BeanDeserializerFactory(Product.class,
         qn));
      Product result = null;
      try {
         call.setTargetEndpointAddress( new java.net.URL(options.getURL()) );
         call.setOperationName( new QName("ProductProcessor", "getProduct") );
```

(continued)

Listing 19-12 *(continued)*

```
            call.addParameter("productID", org.apache.axis.encoding.XMLType.XSD_INT,
               ParameterMode.IN);
            call.setReturnType(org.apache.axis.encoding.XMLType.XSD_ANYTYPE);
            result = (Product) call.invoke( new Object[] { 1 } );
        }
        catch (AxisFault fault) {
            System.out.println("Error : " + fault.toString());
        }
        System.out.println("Name : " + result.getName());
        System.out.println("Product ID : " + result.getProductID());
        System.out.println("Product Number : " + result.getProductNumber());
        System.out.println("Colr : " + result.getColor());
    }
}
```

To start with, create a new Service instance and then as the Service to create a call through the `createCall()` method.

```
Service  service = new Service();
Call call = (Call) service.createCall();
```

To help us manage the command line options, Apache provides the following class: `org.apache.axis.utils.Options`. From this class, you can extract the URL of the destination Web Service through its `getURL()` method. Then you set the `setTargetEndpointAddress()` method of the `Call` object to the target endpoint to connect:

```
call.setTargetEndpointAddress( new java.net.URL(options.getURL()) );
```

Next, you define the operation name to execute; this involves the creation of a `QName`. The `QName` uses the `ProductService` namespace (that was specified in the `deploy.wsdd` file) and the name of the method on the `ProductService` that you want to execute, which is `getProduct` in this case.

```
call.setOperationName( new QName("ProductProcessor", "getProduct") );
```

Here you tell the call that you have an input parameter and an output parameter. You set the input parameter name to `productID` and map its `int` type to the corresponding XSD type. Since the output parameter is an object of type `Product`, you set the return type to `XSD_ANYTYPE`.

```
call.addParameter("productID", org.apache.axis.encoding.XMLType.XSD_INT,
   ParameterMode.IN);
call.setReturnType(org.apache.axis.encoding.XMLType.XSD_ANYTYPE);
```

Finally, you invoke the Web service through the `Call.Invoke()` method call passing in the input parameters as an object array.

```
result = (Product) call.invoke( new Object[] { 1 } );
```

Note that in the previous line of code, you set the product id to a hard-coded value, which is 1 in this case. You capture the response returned from the service and typecast that into a `Product` object. You then display the values contained in the Product object through the `System.out.println()` method.

Running the Client Application

After compiling the `ProductClient.java,` enter the following command from the command prompt.

```
java com.wrox.webservices.ProductClient -llocal://
```

You should see an output similar to Figure 19-19.

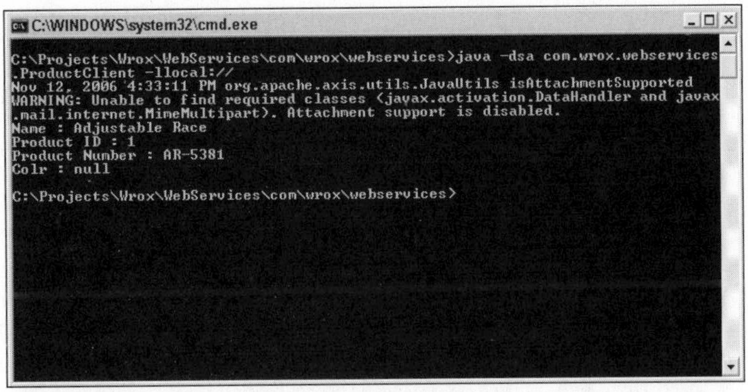

```
C:\WINDOWS\system32\cmd.exe

C:\Projects\Wrox\WebServices\com\wrox\webservices>java -dsa com.wrox.webservices
.ProductClient -llocal://
Nov 12, 2006 4:33:11 PM org.apache.axis.utils.JavaUtils isAttachmentSupported
WARNING: Unable to find required classes (javax.activation.DataHandler and javax
.mail.internet.MimeMultipart). Attachment support is disabled.
Name : Adjustable Race
Product ID : 1
Product Number : AR-5381
Colr : null

C:\Projects\Wrox\WebServices\com\wrox\webservices>
```

Figure 19-19

Caching Web Services

A cache on a system is an in-memory store where data, objects, and various items are stored for reuse. Many applications and Web sites use caching today in order to increase performance. How is this done? Take a look at the browser as a prime example of a device that uses caching to greatly increase performance.

When you pull up a page in your browser for the first time, the browser takes the items from the page (most notably the images) and stores these objects in memory. The next time you return to the same page, the browser uses the in-memory images and data to generate the page (if no changes were made to the original page). Using the in-memory version of the objects to generate the page greatly enhances performance.

Using an in-memory store is also an easy way to greatly increase the performance of your Web services with very little work on your end. Looking at .NET-based Web services, you can use a feature that allows you to use an *output caching* capability. Output caching is a capability to store responses that are generated from your Web service to use for subsequent requests.

Output caching can be controlled in dealing with Web services on the WebMethod level by using the `CacheDuration` property. This is illustrated in Listing 19-13.

Listing 19-13: Caching using the CacheDuration property

```
[WebMethod(CacheDuration=45)]
public DataSet GetCustomers()
{
   SqlConnection conn;
   SqlDataAdapter myDataAdapter;
   DataSet myDataSet;
   string cmdString = "Select * From Customers";

   conn = new SqlConnection("Server=localhost;uid=sa;pwd=;database=Northwind");
   myDataAdapter = new SqlDataAdapter(cmdString, conn);

   myDataSet = new DataSet();
   myDataAdapter.Fill(myDataSet, "Customers");

   return myDataSet;
}
```

The value provided through the `CacheDuration` property is a number that represents the number of seconds that ASP.NET stores the response from the Web service in memory. In this example, the WebMethod `GetCustomers()` returns a large result set of customers that most probably doesn't change very often; therefore, it is a prime candidate for caching. This dataset is cached by ASP.NET for 45 seconds. After 45 seconds, the cache is destroyed and the response is generated again (and stored again).

It is important to understand caching behaviors. If your WebMethod requires input parameters, then the caching occurs for each unique set of data based upon the parameters input into the system. For instance, if a consumer of a WebMethod that requires a single parameter invokes the WebMethod using a single parameter value of `A` to get a response, this response is cached according to the instructions provided through the `CacheDuration` property. Then, if a second consumer of the WebMethod uses a parameter value of `B` to get his response, this response is also cached along with the result that came from using a parameter value of `A`. At this point, two cached results exist in memory: one with the result set from a parameter value of `A` and another with the result set from the parameter value of `B`. If a third consumer uses either `A` or `B` and the cache has not expired for either of these result sets, the cached copy of the response is used.

Understanding this process is important. If your WebMethod can return a wide variety of result sets to the consumer from all the possible parameter values that can be provided by the end user, caching might not be that beneficial. Use caching intelligently.

Asynchronous Consumption of Web Services

When you are building your applications that consume SOAP messages from Web services out there in the world, you may notice that working with these Web services synchronously can be slow and inefficient for applications that depend upon good performance.

In most cases, you are not in control of the actual Web services that you are consuming. Some Web services might return a SOAP response to you quickly, whereas others might return a response very slowly — to the detriment of your consuming application.

Typically, when you have worked with Web services, you have done so in a *synchronous* manner. When you make synchronous invocations of any Web service, your application simply sends a SOAP request and waits for a response before any application processing continues. While the consuming application is waiting for the response from the Web service, the consuming application is locked to the end user. This process is shown in Figure 19-20.

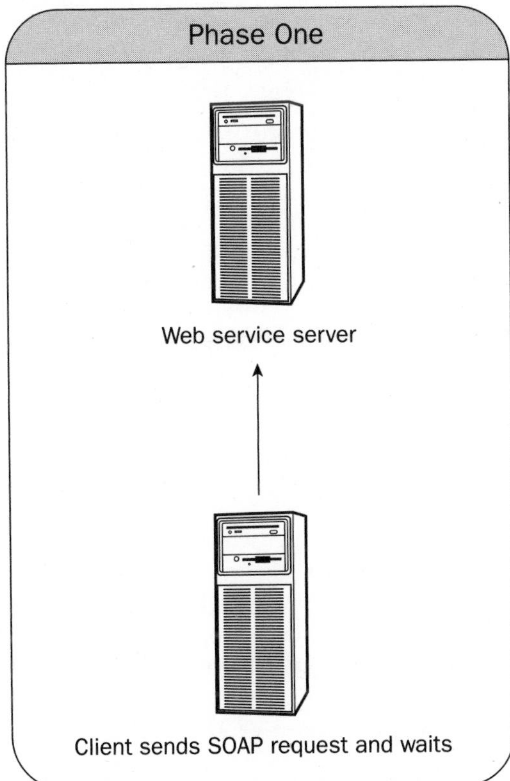

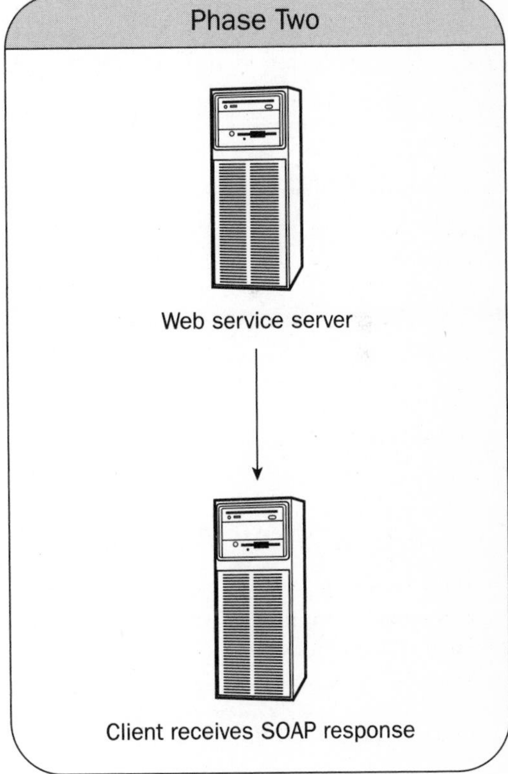

Figure 19-20

To improve efficiency, you can work with slower Web services *asynchronously* rather than synchronously. An asynchronous invocation of a Web service is the opposite of a synchronous invocation. When your consuming application makes an asynchronous invocation of a Web service, it can work on other things while it waits for the response from the Web service. After working on something else, your application can then return to receive the response. Figure 19-21 shows you what an asynchronous invocation of a Web service looks like.

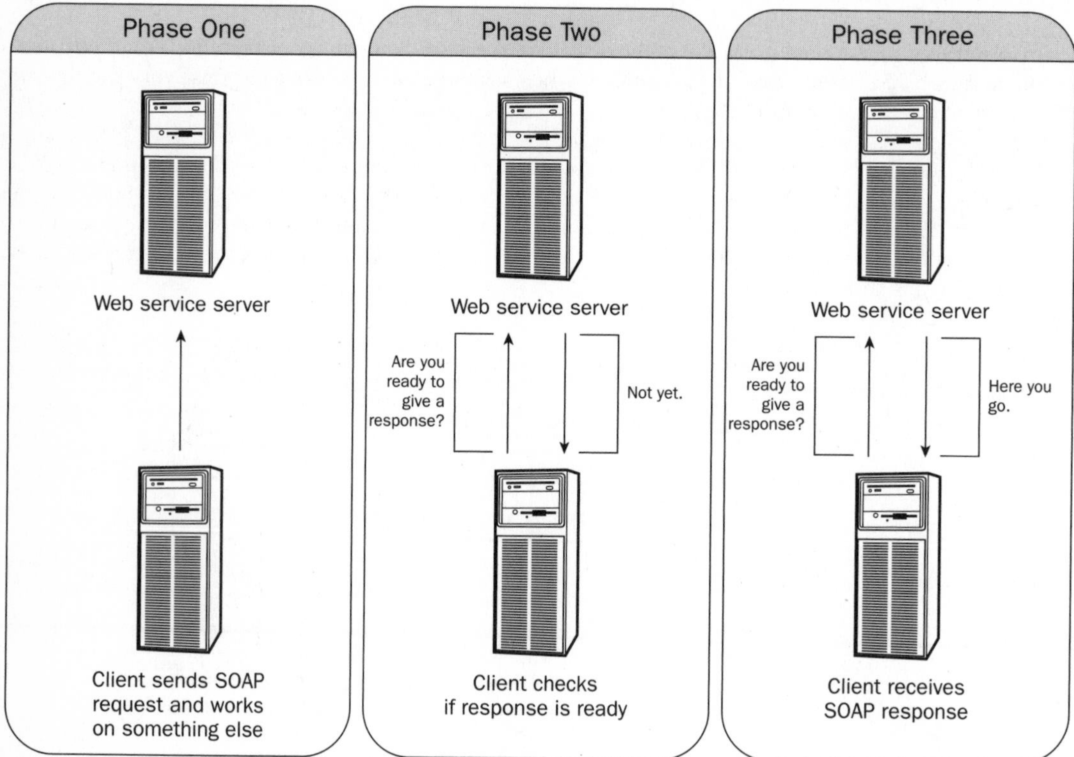

Figure 19-21

Building a Slow Web Service

How can you build your Web services to be consumed asynchronously? Well, nothing really. The asynchronous communication that might be required is provided for on the consuming side of the equation. However, for an example of this, you first have to have a *slow* Web service in place. This slow Web service (shown in Listing 19-14) uses a `for` loop to do a small count before returning a result.

Listing 19-14: Building a slow Web service

```
using System;
using System.Web;
using System.Collections;
using System.Web.Services;
using System.Web.Services.Protocols;
```

```
[WebService(Namespace = "http://www.wrox.com/")]
[WebServiceBinding(ConformsTo = WsiProfiles.BasicProfile1_1)]
public class SlowBoy : System.Web.Services.WebService {

    public SlowBoy () {
    }

    [WebMethod]
    public int TakeLongTime() {
        int x = 0;
        for (int y = 1; y <= 1000; y++)
        {
            y += 1;
            x = y;
        }

        return x;
    }

}
```

You can see that this Web service simply runs through a loop 1000 times before sending back the value of `1000` — all done through the wonderful name of `TakeLongTime()`. Now, the next step is to consume this Web service asynchronously from a consuming application.

Consuming the TakeLongTime() WebMethod Asynchronously

If you look at the WSDL document for the SlowBoy Web service, you see a definition is in place for the `TakeLongTime()` WebMethod. However, when you build a .NET application that consumes this Web service, notice that you have access to two other methods: `BeginTakeLongTime()` and `EndTakeLongTime()`. These Begin and End methods are created for you with no action on your part required. You need these two methods to invoke the Web service in an asynchronous manner.

To see an example of using the `BeginTakeLongTime()` and the `EndTakeLongTime()` methods in your client application, take a look at the code in Listing 19-15. This ASP.NET application sends off a SOAP request to the Web service. Then, while the request is being processed by the Web service, the client application continues its own processing by running a counter until the Web service is ready to return a SOAP response back. When the Web service is ready to provide a response, this response is retrieved and both numbers are displayed to the browser screen. For this example, create a simple ASP.NET page that contains two Label controls that display the output — `Label1` and `Label2`.

Listing 19-15: Asynchronous invocation of a Web service

```
<%@ Page Language="C#" %>

<!DOCTYPE html PUBLIC "-//W3C//DTD XHTML 1.0 Transitional//EN"
 "http://www.w3.org/TR/xhtml1/DTD/xhtml1-transitional.dtd">
```

(continued)

Listing 19-15 *(continued)*

```
<script runat="server">
    protected void Page_Load(object sender, EventArgs e)
    {
        AsyncTest.SlowBoy ws = new AsyncTest.SlowBoy();

        IAsyncResult asyncCheck = ws.BeginTakeLongTime(null, null);
        int x = 0;

        while (asyncCheck.IsCompleted == false)
        {
            x += 1;
        }

        Label1.Text = x.ToString();
        Label2.Text = ws.EndTakeLongTime(asyncCheck).ToString();
    }
</script>

<html xmlns="http://www.w3.org/1999/xhtml" >
<head runat="server">
    <title>Asynchronous invocation</title>
</head>
<body>
    <form id="form1" runat="server">
    <div>
        <asp:Label ID="Label1" runat="server" Text="Label"></asp:Label><br />
        <br />
        <asp:Label ID="Label2" runat="server" Text="Label"></asp:Label>
    </div>
    </form>
</body>
</html>
```

Because the developer of the consuming application anticipates a long wait if it directly invokes the `TakeLongTime()` method, another option is for the application to instead invoke the `BeginTakeLongTime()` method. By using the `BeginTakeLongTime()` method, the client application retains control — instead of being forced to wait around to get a response from the Web service. The client application is then free to do whatever it wants before returning to retrieve the result from the Web service.

After the SOAP request is sent to the Web service, the client application can use the `IAsyncResult` instance to check whether the method call has been completed. In this case, the client application checks whether the method call has been completed by using `asyncCheck.IsCompleted`. If the asynchronous invocation is not complete, the client application increases the x variable by one before making the check again. The client application does this until the Web service is ready to return a response. The example of the result returned to the browser is illustrated in Figure 19-22.

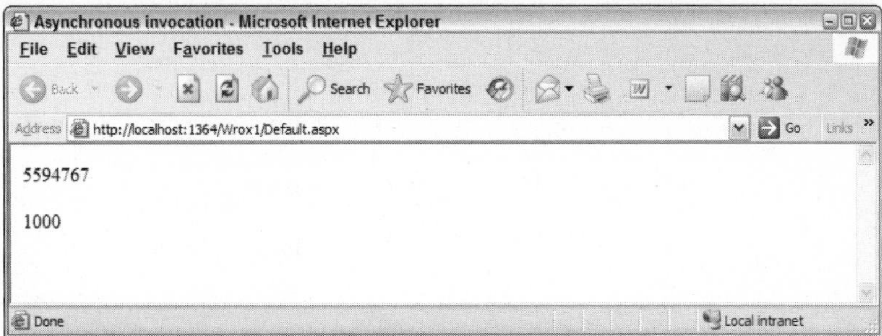

Figure 19-22

As you can tell, this powerful capability can add a lot to the performance of your consuming applications.

Summary

This chapter was a whirlwind tour of Web services in both the .NET world as well as the Java world. It is definitely a topic that merits an entire book of its own. The chapter showed you the power of exposing your data and logic as SOAP and also how to consume these SOAP messages directly in the thin- or thick-client applications you build.

In addition to pointing out the power you have for building and consuming basic Web services, the chapter spent some time helping you understand caching and performance. A lot of power is built into this model; everyday the Web services model is making stronger inroads into various enterprise organizations. It is becoming more likely that in order to get at some data or logic you need for your application, you will employ the tactics presented here.

The next chapter is going to take a look at SOAP and WSDL in greater detail including how to extend SOAP to give your Web services some advanced features.

20

SOAP and WSDL

When you start working with the Web services space, you quickly realize that so much in this space resolves completely around SOAP and WSDL. SOAP, or *Simple Object Access Protocol,* is the language that Web services speak to transmit messages over the wire. WSDL, or *Web Services Description Language,* is the XML structure used to describe the SOAP messages involved in the request/response process.

This chapter investigates both of these technologies and how to use them to your advantage in the applications you are building today. It reviews the basics of SOAP and WSDL, as well as how you can go about extending both these technologies using various tools and technologies that are at your disposal in the industry today.

SOAP Speak

SOAP is an XML-based technology. It is an agreed-upon standard of XML markup used in the transmission of messages across a corporate network or the public Internet. SOAP is the most important pillar in the Web services model.

The proposed Web services model is presented in Figure 20-1 and involves a process of search, discovery, definition, and communication. The first three steps in this process are one-time steps, but these steps are required to get to where you really want to go — the communication step. This step is the step that deals with SOAP. Web service communication is done through the use of SOAP.

As you look over this diagram, notice that not every step mentioned is required to participate in the Web services world. Also, in certain instances, some of these steps can be combined into a single step. For example, the 'Find a Service' section and the 'Discovery' section can be one and same thing. The idea is that when you want to consume a Web service, you first need to find that service. This discovery process can be as simple as having someone e-mail you a link to the Web service's WSDL file, or it can be a more complicated operation that involves searching a directory of some kind (such as UDDI).

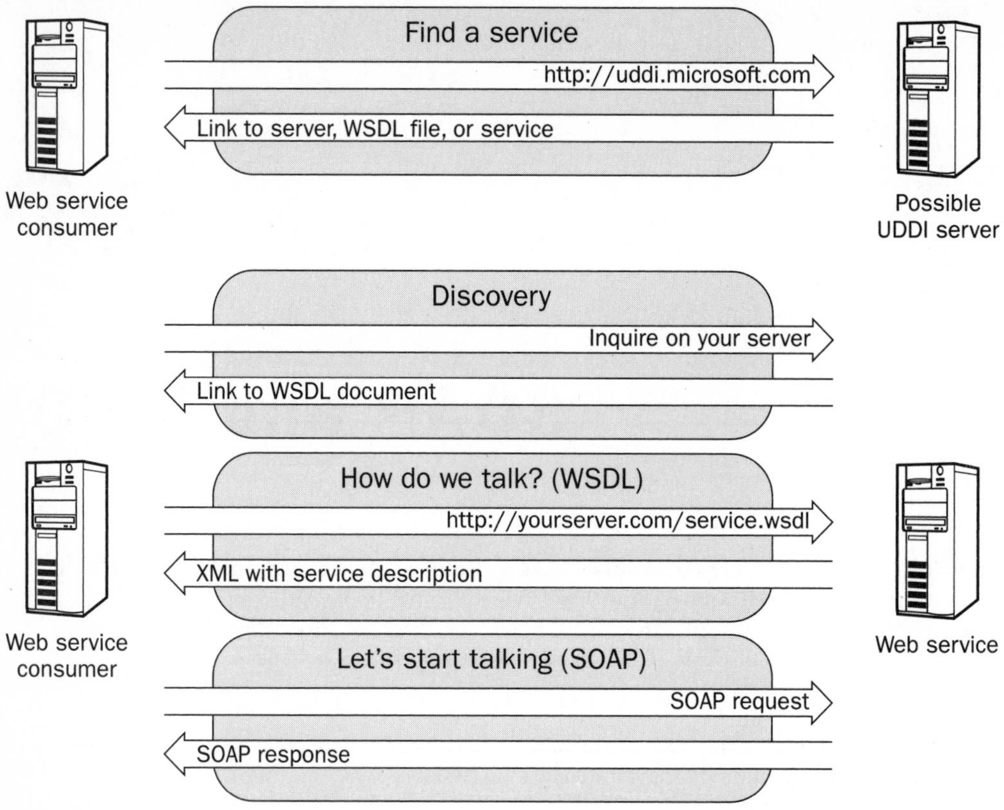

Figure 20-1

After you have found the service you want to consume, the act of discovery should bring you to the location of the Web service's WSDL file. The WSDL file is an XML description of the Web service's interface. After you have found the WSDL file of the Web service, you can create a proxy class (or your environment automatically creates one for you) that enables you to send messages back and forth to the Web service.

Although this chapter focuses on SOAP as the means of communication to be used between disparate objects, you have, of course, other options. For instance, XML-RPC, ebXML, and REST can be used in a similar manner to SOAP. They all provide structure to any remote-procedural call you need. You might not find all the pillars of these other RPC formats defined in Figure 20-1, but the concepts are the same.

The Basics of SOAP

Presently SOAP is in version 1.2. You can find the full specification for SOAP 1.2 on the W3C site located at `w3.org/TR/soap/`.

As of the writing of this book, SOAP 1.2 has existed for only a short time, and much of the use of SOAP in the world still focuses around SOAP 1.1. For instance, in the .NET world, SOAP 1.1 is the basis of Web services for .NET 1.0 and 1.1. Only .NET 2.0 allows you to expose and consume Web services using SOAP 1.2; although SOAP 1.2 is not the default format provided in .NET 2.0.

SOAP 1.1 was developed in March 2000, and it was accepted as a note by the W3C on May 8, 2000. The companies that worked on the development of SOAP include Microsoft, DevelopMentor, IBM, Lotus, and UserLand Software.

SOAP 1.2 was accepted on June 24, 2003 after more than 400 issues from SOAP 1.1 were addressed. SOAP 1.1 required a set of clarifications to clean up ambiguities found in its specification. These ambiguities in SOAP 1.1 had sometimes led to differences in interpretations among the various vendors. When the specification engenders differences in interpretation, interoperability issues invariably arise. To prevent these varied interpretations, SOAP 1.2 is a lot more specific.

SOAP is not a proprietary technology; that is, it is not run or controlled by IBM or Microsoft. It is, instead, an open standard. Therefore, you can use SOAP as you wish for free. The software vendors of the world have come to support SOAP, and you will be hard pressed to find a vendor that isn't making some sort of inroads into getting its platform to understand and work with this XML-based technology.

Remember: SOAP Is XML!

The first thing to either make note of (or remember) is that SOAP is just an agreed-upon structure of XML. SOAP uses XML grammar for a number of reasons as detailed here:

- XML is an open standard.
- XML is consumable upon most platforms.
- A tremendous amount of industry support exists for XML.
- XML is also very human-friendly.
- A number of developer tools, applications, and parsers are available today for XML.

These points make it pretty easy to see why SOAP is constructed to be based upon this technology. Because of its use of XML and the general simplicity of SOAP, you should find that working with its remote procedure call method is a lot easier than working with other methods, such as CORBA or DCOM, which provide similar functionality.

Transport Protocols for SOAP

SOAP-based services exist to meet the business need to share data among departments, with customers, or with partners. In many instances, the data that is to be shared must travel from one database to another between completely incompatible systems. SOAP is the tool that allows companies to share information from one point to another without the need to concern themselves with the platforms of the consumers. Now that you have entered into the Web services world, the first question from your data consumers will not be, "What platform is the data on?" Instead the question will be, "Can you expose that data to me as SOAP?"

In most cases, the Web services that people build make use of HTTP. Most systems, applications, and platforms are connected to the outside world in order to gain access to the Internet. The Internet has become a powerful means of human-to-human communication, even as it becomes an ever stronger force for machine-to-machine communication. These machines communicate with one another through this Internet connection — also known as HTTP.

Putting SOAP on top of HTTP is powerful. SOAP allows you to send data that is a lot more complex and meaningful than the name/value pairs that you can send using HTTP-GET or HTTP-POST. Also, if you send complex data types from one machine to another using something other than HTTP, you have the problem of firewalls to contend with. Almost all machines or servers are behind a firewall of some kind. If you have a server that isn't behind a firewall, you are just asking for some malicious person to come in and mess with your machine and its contents. Firewalls, basically, block all entrances to the server. If the entrances are blocked, however, how can anyone use SOAP to communicate with a machine?

Communication is possible because one of the doors to this server is usually open. Port 80 on almost every server is used for access to the Internet. SOAP rides along (again, using HTTP) right through this open door to the server. Because SOAP is just a set of ASCII characters, it cannot harm the receiving server, so the information is let in without any problems.

More and more Web services are also starting to utilize *Transmission Control Protocol* (TCP) for message transmission as an alternative to HTTP. You should consider using TCP when performance and reliability are important factors to you.

Looking Closely at the SOAP Specification

SOAP was developed to be simple. It is a lightweight protocol that is used in the communication of messages from one point to another. It works in a decentralized and distributed environment, typically using HTTP as its mode of transport (although, as I stated, this is not a requirement). The SOAP specification itself is made up of the following parts, which are covered in this chapter:

- A description of the SOAP envelope and how to package a SOAP message so that it can be sent via a transmission protocol such as HTTP
- The serialization rules for SOAP messages
- A definition of the protocol binding between SOAP and HTTP
- The capability to use SOAP for RPC-like binding

One of the more important aspects of the SOAP specification is the makeup of the SOAP message or SOAP packet. Be sure you understand the structure of this packet in order to extend and mold it within your own Web services.

To understand it better, take a closer look at the SOAP message and all its parts.

The SOAP Message

The SOAP message is simple, and it was meant to be just that. The SOAP message is what is sent over the wire generally using HTTP, with or without the HTTP Extension Framework (HTTP-EF). SOAP messages are meant to be one-way. Nothing is built into these messages that warrants any response. SOAP does not contain any built-in functions or methods that cause specific events to be initiated. As you are probably already aware, the SOAP message is an agreed-upon structure of XML. The XML specification is simply used as the means of marking up the data to send.

The problem is that Web services generally require a request and response action to occur. Web services tend to get around this problem by sending the SOAP message within the HTTP request and response messages.

The typical SOAP message consists of a SOAP envelope, header, and body section. The SOAP envelope is a mandatory element that is the root element of the entire package. Within the SOAP envelope is an optional header element and a mandatory body element. Figure 20-2 shows an example of the structure of a SOAP message.

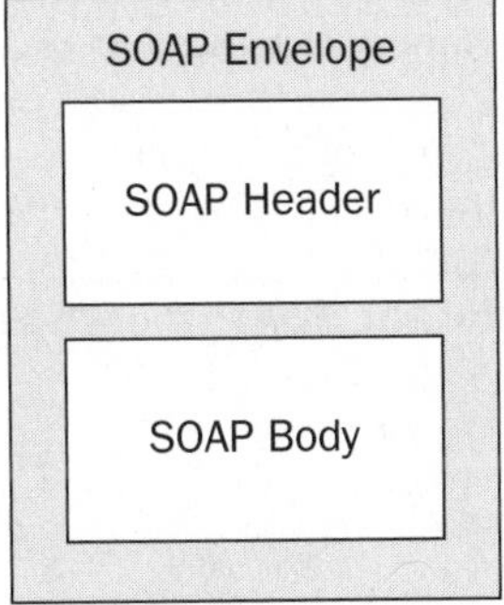

Figure 20-2

Because this entire message is an XML document, it has a single root element (the SOAP envelope element), just like any typical XML document.

The SOAP Envelope

The first step to understanding this structure is to actually review the pieces themselves. Listing 20-1 shows a typical SOAP 1.1 envelope (minus the body information).

Listing 20-1: The SOAP envelope in SOAP 1.1

```
<?xml version="1.0" encoding="utf-8" ?>
<soap:Envelope xmlns:soap="http://schemas.xmlsoap.org/soap/envelope/"
 xmlns:xsi="http://www.w3.org/2001/XMLSchema-instance"
 xmlns:xsd="http://www.w3.org/2001/XMLSchema">
   <soap:Body>
      <!-- The message contents go here -->
   </soap:Body>
</soap:Envelope>
```

SOAP 1.2 is not that much different as you can see in Listing 20-2.

Listing 20-2: The SOAP envelope in SOAP 1.2

```
<?xml version="1.0" encoding="utf-8"?>
<soap:Envelope xmlns:soap="http://www.w3.org/2003/05/soap-envelope"
 xmlns:xsi="http://www.w3.org/2001/XMLSchema-instance"
 xmlns:xsd="http://www.w3.org/2001/XMLSchema">
   <soap:Body>
      <!-- The message contents go here -->
   </soap:Body>
</soap:Envelope>
```

The SOAP envelope is specified as the root element and is qualified by using the SOAP namespace `http://schemas.xmlsoap.org/soap/envelope/` in the SOAP 1.1 message, whereas the namespace is `http://www.w3.org/2003/05/soap-envelope` in SOAP 1.2. This SOAP element, qualified by one of these namespaces in your code, is simply expressed as `<soap:Envelope>`.

The structures defined here, however, are not an absolute requirement; you could also have simply designed the SOAP message as illustrated in Listing 20-3.

Listing 20-3: An example of another SOAP message structure

```
<?xml version="1.0" encoding="utf-8"?>
<env:Envelope xmlns:env="http://www.w3.org/2003/05/soap-envelope">
   <env:Body>
      <!-- The message contents go here -->
   </env:Body>
</env:Envelope>
```

The SOAP Body

Although not every element of a SOAP message is required in the transmission of the message, the SOAP body element is required within your SOAP message. The SOAP body can be considered the main part of the message, where the data part of the message is housed. The SOAP body contains data that is specific to the method call such as the method name and all the input parameters that might be required by the Web service. Your Web service then uses the SOAP body element to return data to the client. The SOAP body can also contain any error information to be sent back to the client.

Looking at the SOAP Body of the Request

Remember that because request and response SOAP messages are going across the wire, both the request and the response SOAP messages must contain a SOAP body section. If you look more specifically at the request payload that is sent in the SOAP body, notice that its contents map directly to a method that has been exposed through the Web service server. Also note that the required arguments (or parameters) for consuming the exposed method are defined in the payload.

For an example of this, examine a simple `Add()` Method as exposed out from a C# 2.0 Web service. This is illustrated in Listing 20-4.

Listing 20-4: A simple Add() Method as exposed from a C# 2.0 Web service

```
[WebMethod]
public int Add(int a, int b) {
   return (a + b);
}
```

With this Web service in place, you can see that the consumer is required to invoke this remote method by passing in two required parameters — variable a (of type int) and variable b (also of type int). Looking at the actual contents of the SOAP body for the request, you can see that the SOAP body maps directly to the Add() method. This is presented in Listing 20-5.

Listing 20-5: The contents of the SOAP body for the SOAP request

```
<soap:Body>
   <Add xmlns="http://www.wrox.com/ws">
      <a>20</a>
      <b>4</b>
   </Add>
</soap:Body>
```

As you can tell from the preceding code example, the method and its parameters are serialized into XML, and the method name is now the first child element of the <soap:Body> element. The parameters of the method are also serialized into XML. The first parameter, variable a, is turned into an <a> element, and the b parameter is converted to a <b> element.

Looking at the SOAP Body of the Response

After a Web service receives this SOAP request, an associated SOAP response from the Web service is sent back to the originating client. Just like the SOAP request that came from the client, the payload of the SOAP body in the response is also serialized into XML.

The response from the request shown in Listing 20-4 is presented in Listing 20-6.

Listing 20-6: The contents of the SOAP body for the SOAP response

```
<soap:Body>
   <AddResponse xmlns="http://www.wrox.com/ws">
      <AddResult>24</AddResult>
   </AddResponse>
</soap:Body>
```

In the case of the response SOAP body message, the method name is turned into an element bearing the same name, but with the word Response tacked onto it. The result that is returned is encased within the <AddResult> element, which is the method name with the word Result appended to it.

The SOAP Header

Unlike the SOAP body element, which is required in each and every SOAP message, the SOAP header portion of the SOAP message is an optional element. This section of the SOAP message is used to provide information that is related to what is contained within the SOAP body element—*the metadata of the actual message*. The convenient thing about the SOAP header is that the recipient of a message that contains contents in a SOAP header is not required to deal with its contents. The consumer of the message may not want to work with some of the information contained in the SOAP header. Therefore, the recipient need not consume all the SOAP header data points.

What should you be transmitting in the SOAP headers of the Web services that you build? This is really an open question. If you look at the SOAP specification, notice it doesn't really state what should be included. This really means that you can include whatever the heck you want. Some common elements that are added to SOAP headers include the following:

- Authentication
- Transaction management
- Timestamps
- Routing information
- Encryption information
- Digital signing management

Of course, you can use SOAP headers for any number of things, but these points give you a general idea of what you can do. Listing 20-7 shows a sample SOAP header.

Listing 20-7: A sample SOAP header

```
<?xml version="1.0" encoding="utf-8"?>
<soap:Envelope xmlns:soap="http://www.w3.org/2003/05/soap-envelope"
 xmlns:xsi="http://www.w3.org/2001/XMLSchema-instance"
 xmlns:xsd="http://www.w3.org/2001/XMLSchema">
   <soap:Header>
      <RequiredServiceHeader xmlns="http://www.wrox.com/ws">
         <Username>Bill Evjen</Username>
         <Password>Bubbles</Password>
      </RequiredServiceHeader>
    </soap:Header>
    <soap:Body>
       <HelloWorld xmlns="http://www.wrox.com/ws" />
    </soap:Body>
</soap:Envelope>
```

In this example, the SOAP request includes credentials that are sent in with the SOAP message in order to authenticate the user before a SOAP response is issued to the requestor. As you can see, this is quite a powerful tool.

Later in this chapter in the section "Working with SOAP Header," I will show you how to build and consume some Web services using SOAP headers in your messages.

The SOAP header element needs to come before the SOAP body declaration in the message. The SOAP header is a child element to the SOAP envelope element. The SOAP header contains a single *SOAP header block*. This SOAP header block is the `<RequiredServiceHeader>` section. It is possible to have multiple header blocks contained with in a single SOAP header instance.

This next section reviews some of the attributes that can be placed within a SOAP header block.

The actor Attribute

One possible attribute available for your SOAP header blocks is the `actor` attribute. Note that this attribute is available only in SOAP 1.1 messages. This attribute is not available in SOAP 1.2. It is replaced with the `role` attribute (discussed shortly).

The actor attribute allows you to easily assign SOAP header blocks for specific SOAP intermediaries. Remember that not all SOAP messages are going to be sent from point A to point B (point-to-point Web services), but instead, your SOAP messages may travel through any number of middle-men (SOAP intermediaries) along the way. A SOAP intermediary is an application that is capable of both receiving and sending SOAP messages as it comes into contact with them. These intermediaries may also be acting upon information that is contained in a SOAP header block that they are designated to work with.

This means that you might have SOAP header blocks contained in your message that, in some cases, could be intended for one of these SOAP intermediaries and not for the final recipient of the SOAP message. If this is the case, it is possible to use the `actor` attribute within the SOAP header block to specify that the enclosed header element is intended only for a particular SOAP intermediary that the SOAP message might come in contact with. After the SOAP message is received by the SOAP intermediary, the SOAP header is not forwarded with the rest of the SOAP message.

To specify that the SOAP header is intended for the first SOAP intermediary that the SOAP message comes in contact with, the value of the `actor` attribute needs to be the URI:

```
http://schemas.xmlsoap.org/soap/actor/next
```

An example of using the actor attribute in a SOAP header is presented in Listing 20-8.

Listing 20-8: Using the SOAP header's actor attribute

```
<?xml version="1.0" encoding="utf-8" ?>
<soap:Envelope xmlns:soap="http://schemas.xmlsoap.org/soap/envelope/"
 xmlns:xsi="http://www.w3.org/2001/XMLSchema-instance"
 xmlns:xsd="http://www.w3.org/2001/XMLSchema">
   <soap:Header>
      <RequiredServiceHeader
       soap:actor="http://schemas.xmlsoap.org/soap/actor/next"
       xmlns="http://www.wrox.com/ws">
         <Username>Bill Evjen</Username>
         <Password>Bubbles</Password>
      </RequiredServiceHeader>
   </soap:Header>
   <soap:Body>
      <HelloWorld xmlns="http://www.wrox.com/ws" />
   </soap:Body>
</soap:Envelope>
```

If you wish to give the SOAP header block to a SOAP intermediary other than the first (one as shown previously), the value of the `actor` attribute needs to be the URI of the intended location.

The role Attribute

The `role` attribute is simply a renamed replacement of the `actor` attribute. Therefore, if you are using SOAP 1.1, use the `actor` attribute. If you are using SOAP 1.2, use the `role` attribute. There is no change in the behavior of this attribute. It is shown in Listing 20-9.

Listing 20-9: Using the SOAP header's role attribute

```
<?xml version="1.0" encoding="utf-8"?>
<soap:Envelope xmlns:soap="http://www.w3.org/2003/05/soap-envelope"
 xmlns:xsi="http://www.w3.org/2001/XMLSchema-instance"
 xmlns:xsd="http://www.w3.org/2001/XMLSchema">
   <soap:Header>
      <RequiredServiceHeader
       soap:role="http://www.w3.org/2003/05/soap-envelope/role/next"
       xmlns="http://www.wrox.com/ws">
         <Username>Bill Evjen</Username>
         <Password>Bubbles</Password>
      </RequiredServiceHeader>
   </soap:Header>
   <soap:Body>
      <HelloWorld xmlns="http://www.wrox.com/ws" />
   </soap:Body>
</soap:Envelope>
```

The `role` attribute value of `http://www.w3.org/2003/05/soap-envelope/role/next` provides the same meaning as the `actor` attribute's URI (`http://schemas.xmlsoap.org/soap/actor/next`) when you want to designate the intermediary for which the SOAP message is intended. Besides this standard URI, other possibilities include `http://www.w3.org/2003/05/soap-envelope/role/none` and `http://www.w3.org/2003/05/soap-envelope/role/ultimateReceiver`. The `...role/none` URI means that the defined SOAP header block is not really meant for any particular intermediary, but instead is there for processing by other SOAP header blocks. The `...role/ultimateReceiver` URI is the default value (even if no `role` attribute value is specified) and means that the SOAP header block is meant for the last receiver in the chain.

The mustUnderstand Attribute

The SOAP header's `mustUnderstand` attribute is an optional attribute that enables you to specify whether the end user can ignore the SOAP header. Again, the intermediary that receives the SOAP header is the one that is specified through the use of the `actor` or `role` attributes.

The value of the `mustUnderstand` attribute for SOAP 1.1 is either `0` or `1`. If the value is set to `1`, the recipient of that SOAP header block must process the SOAP header or fail to receive the entire message. A value of `0` means that the recipient is not required to process the SOAP header. SOAP 1.2 changes the possible values of the `mustUnderstand` attribute from `0` and `1` to `false` and `true` respectively.

SOAP 1.1 Faults

With all the applications that are developed, as you know very well, problems are bound to occur with some of the Web services that people are trying to consume. Simply put, errors happen. When errors occur, due to problems on the server or because of invalid inputs from the client, you want to output an appropriate error message to the client.

This is where the SOAP fault element comes into play. The SOAP fault is contained with the SOAP body and is sent in the payload if an error occurs. Some development platforms output SOAP exceptions automatically on your behalf. After a client receives a SOAP fault message, it can then act upon this message in some logical manner.

For instance, if you send a SOAP message with the `mustUnderstand` attribute set to `true`, but the SOAP packet receiving the request doesn't understand the SOAP header, you get a faultcode specifying that the SOAP header was not understood. The SOAP 1.1 packet that is returned to you looks like the one illustrated in Listing 20-10.

Listing 20-10: A SOAP 1.1 fault message

```
<?xml version="1.0" encoding="utf-8" ?>
<soap:Envelope xmlns:soap="http://schemas.xmlsoap.org/soap/envelope/"
 xmlns:xsi="http://www.w3.org/2001/XMLSchema-instance"
 xmlns:xsd="http://www.w3.org/2001/XMLSchema">
   <soap:Body>
      <soap:Fault>
         <faultcode>soap:MustUnderstand</faultcode>
         <faultstring>System.Web.Services.Protocols.SoapHeaderException:
            SOAP header RequiredServiceHeader was not understood.
            at System.Web.Services.Protocols.SoapHeaderHandling.
              EnsureHeadersUnderstood(SoapHeaderCollection headers)
            at System.Web.Services.Protocols.SoapServerProtocol.
              WriteReturns(Object[] returnValues, Stream outputStream)
            at System.Web.Services.Protocols.WebServiceHandler.
              WriteReturns(Object[] returnValues)
            at System.Web.Services.Protocols.WebServiceHandler.Invoke()
         </faultstring>
      </soap:Fault>
   </soap:Body>
</soap:Envelope>
```

Looking over this SOAP fault, notice that the `<soap:Fault>` element is contained within the `<soap:Body>` element. From this simple fault message, you can see what the error is and the details concerning it. To expand upon this, the next section reviews the possible child elements contained within the `<soap:Fault>` block.

<faultcode>

The `<faultcode>` element is a SOAP 1.1 specific element. As a child of the `<soap:Fault>` element, the `<faultcode>` element is used to give the error code, and thereby inform the consuming application (or developer) about the type of error encountered. The preceding example shows a fault code of MustUnderstand, meaning that a portion of the SOAP message was not understood. The following table defines the possible fault codes at your disposal for a SOAP 1.1 message.

Name	Description
Client	The receiver didn't process the request because the request was improperly constructed or is malformed in some way.
Server	The receiving application faulted when processing the request because of the processing engine and not due to any fault of the sender or the composition of the message sent.
MustUnderstand	The SOAP header element had a mustUnderstand attribute set to true and the processing endpoint did not understand it or didn't obey the processing instructions.
VersionMismatch	The call used an invalid namespace for the SOAP envelope element.

One last note on the <faultcode> element is that it is a required element whenever you provide a SOAP 1.1 fault.

<faultstring>

The <faultstring> element provides a human-readable version of an error report. This element contains a string value that briefly describes the error encountered. This element is also required in any SOAP 1.1 fault message.

<faultactor>

The <faultactor> element describes the point in the process where the fault occurred. This is identified by the URI of the location where the fault was generated. This is meant for situations where the SOAP message is being passed among a number of SOAP intermediaries and, therefore, the location where the fault occurred must be identified. This is a required element within the SOAP fault element *only* if the fault occurred within one of the SOAP intermediaries. If the fault occurred at the endpoint, the endpoint is not required to populate the element, although it can do so.

<detail>

The <detail> element carries the application-specific error information related to the SOAP body element. The fault elements previously described are, in most cases, enough for disclosing the error information. It is always good, however, to have more than enough information when you are trying to debug something. The <detail> element can be used to provide that extra bit of information that can facilitate the debug process. For instance, you can carry the line in the code where the error occurred.

SOAP 1.2 Faults

The purpose of a SOAP fault hasn't changed from SOAP 1.1 to SOAP 1.2, but instead, the structure of the SOAP 1.2 fault message has changed. Listing 20-11 shows a typical SOAP 1.2 fault message where the SOAP header was misunderstood because the `mustUnderstand` attribute was set to `true`.

Listing 20-11: A SOAP 1.2 fault message

```
<?xml version="1.0" encoding="utf-8"?>
<soap:Envelope xmlns:soap="http://www.w3.org/2003/05/soap-envelope"
 xmlns:xsi="http://www.w3.org/2001/XMLSchema-instance"
 xmlns:xsd="http://www.w3.org/2001/XMLSchema">
   <soap:Body>
      <soap:Fault>
         <soap:Code>
            <soap:Value>soap:MustUnderstand</soap:Value>
         </soap:Code>
         <soap:Reason>
            <soap:Text xml:lang="en">
               System.Web.Services.Protocols.SoapHeaderException:
               SOAP header RequiredServiceHeader was not understood.
               at System.Web.Services.Protocols.SoapHeaderHandling.
                 EnsureHeadersUnderstood(SoapHeaderCollection headers)
               at System.Web.Services.Protocols.SoapServerProtocol.
                 WriteReturns(Object[] returnValues, Stream outputStream)
               at System.Web.Services.Protocols.
                 WebServiceHandler.WriteReturns(Object[] returnValues)
               at System.Web.Services.Protocols.
                 WebServiceHandler.Invoke()
            </soap:Text>
         </soap:Reason>
      </soap:Fault>
   </soap:Body>
</soap:Envelope>
```

Looking over this SOAP 1.2 fault message, you can see that the `<soap:Fault>` element is contained within the `<soap:Body>` element just as it is in SOAP 1.1. The difference lies in the child elements that are contained within the `<soap:Fault>` element itself. These child elements are reviewed next.

<Code>

The `<Code>` element is a mandatory element in a SOAP 1.2 fault message. This is a section where you can define the error codes that triggered the error message in the first place. This parent element can contain one or two possible child elements: `<Value>` and `<Subcode>`. Each of these child elements are discussed in the following sections.

<Value>

A `<Value>` element is a mandatory element that is nested within the `<Code>` element. Like the `<fault-code>` element from a SOAP 1.1 fault message, the `<Value>` element is used to specify a high-level SOAP fault code. Possible values for the `<Value>` element are shown in the following table.

Name	Description
Sender	The receiver didn't process the request because the request was improperly constructed or is malformed in some way.
Receiver	The receiving application faulted when processing the request because of the processing engine and not due to any fault of the sender or the composition of the message sent.
DataEncodingUnknown	Either the SOAP header block or SOAP body element used an encoding that the Web service doesn't support.
MustUnderstand	The SOAP header element had a mustUnderstand attribute set to true and the processing endpoint did not understand it or didn't obey the processing instructions.
VersionMismatch	The call used an invalid namespace for the SOAP envelope element.

<Subcode>

The <Subcode> element is an optional element. This element allows you to specify errors that might occur with specific elements. If you use this element, you have to provide a child <Value> element to the <Subcode> element to communicate an error type, as shown in the preceding table.

<Reason>

The <Reason> element has the same purpose as the <faultstring> element from SOAP 1.1. The <Reason> element can contain one or more child <Text> elements that define a human-readable error report.

<Text>

The <Text> element contains the textual string that provides a human-readable error report. This is a child element of the <Reason> element. A <Text> element must contain the lang attribute that defines the language used in the contents of the <Text> element. For instance, in the example from Listing 20-11, you can see that English is used as a value of the <Text> element's lang attribute.

```
<soap:Text xml:lang="en">
   <!-- Contents removed for clarity -->
</soap:Text>
```

<Node>

If you are routing a message through one or more SOAP intermediaries and one of these intermediaries is the cause of the fault, you must include a <Node> element. The <Node> element defines the URI of the SOAP intermediary which caused the fault to occur.

<Role>

The <Role> element defines the role of the node that caused the fault to occur. The possible values are represented in the following table.

Name	Description
`http://www.w3.org/2003/05/soap-envelope/role/next`	A SOAP intermediary acting upon the SOAP message.
`http://www.w3.org/2003/05/soap-envelope/role/ultimateReceiver`	The end and ultimate receiver of the SOAP message.

<Detail>

The `<Detail>` element has the same meaning here as the <detail> element does in SOAP 1.1.

SOAP Encoding of Data Types

Along with the programming language you use to build your Web services, you are passing some specific data types from the methods that the consumers invoke. It doesn't matter if your Web services are written in Java, .NET, or something else. That data is being sent across the wire as a SOAP message. Therefore, the data type that is sitting on the SOAP payload needs to maintain its specified data type so that, on the receiving end, the data can be interpreted correctly. For instance, if your method returns an integer of `22`, the value that is received on the other end must remain an integer of `22` and not become a string value of `"22"`. Changes in the data type value would make dealing with Web services quite difficult.

One of the reasons that Web services are so powerful is that the data types are maintained from point A to point B in the message transmission cycle. The process of converting the data types from the application code to a data type that SOAP recognizes is called *SOAP encoding*.

The types that are serialized into SOAP are the same types that are specified in the XML Schema specification found at `www.w3.org/TR/xmlschema-2`. These data types are pretty standard, and most of the data types that you want to pass into SOAP can be serialized in a manner that works for you. So, for example, you are easily able to serialize primitive types such as String, Char, Byte, `Boolean`, `Int16`, `Int32`, `Int64`, `UInt16`, `UInt32`, `UInt64`, `Single`, `Double`, `Guid`, `Decimal`, `DateTime` (as XML's `timeInstant`), `DataTime` (as XML's `date`), `DateTime` (as XML's `time`), and `XmlQualifiedName` (as XML's `QName`).

Tracing SOAP Messages

So far, you have seen several examples of how the SOAP message is constructed. If you are a developer dealing with SOAP, you invariably need to see the SOAP messages that are being sent back and forth across the wire for debugging purposes. If you want to see the entire SOAP message, how do you go about it? Well, actually, it is fairly simple, but you must take a few steps to set it up.

Web services toolsets that are present on certain platforms have some tracing capabilities built into them. For instance, IBM's WebSphere has a SOAP tracing capability built into it, as does Microsoft's Web Services Enhancements (WSE) toolset. Another possibility includes some open-source tools such as PocketSOAP (found at `pocketsoap.com`).

This chapter discusses two tools for monitoring SOAP messages for the purposes of SOAP debugging — one is the Microsoft Trace Utility, and the other is Altova's SOAP debugging capabilities found in the XMLSpy Enterprise Edition.

The Microsoft Trace Utility

To view SOAP messages as they are sent back and forth across the wire, you must download the Microsoft SOAP Toolkit 3.0 from Microsoft's MSDN site at `msdn.microsoft.com/webservices/Downloads`. The SOAP Toolkit 3.0 includes a number of tools, but you really only need to install the Trace Utility tool that is encased inside this offering.

You can use the Trace Utility within the SOAP Toolkit to trace SOAP messages as they are being sent and received by a Web service client application. One nice feature of this tool is that it is free.

Using the Trace Utility

You must take a few preliminary steps in order to use the Trace Utility. First, you need a Web service that you can consume. Next, you must build an application that consumes this Web service and is able to send a SOAP request to it that causes the Web service to issue a response in return.

The Trace Utility runs the request and response messages through a port that it has opened and is monitoring. After the Trace Utility receives one of these messages, it records the message and then forwards the message to the appropriate port for handling.

To see this in action, open up the Trace Utility. You are then presented with a blank application. To start a new SOAP debugging session, select File ➪ New ➪ Formatted Trace from the menu of the application. What opens next is the Trace Setup window that enables you to specify the local port number that you want the Trace Utility tool to use, as well as the destination host and port number. This dialog is shown in Figure 20-3.

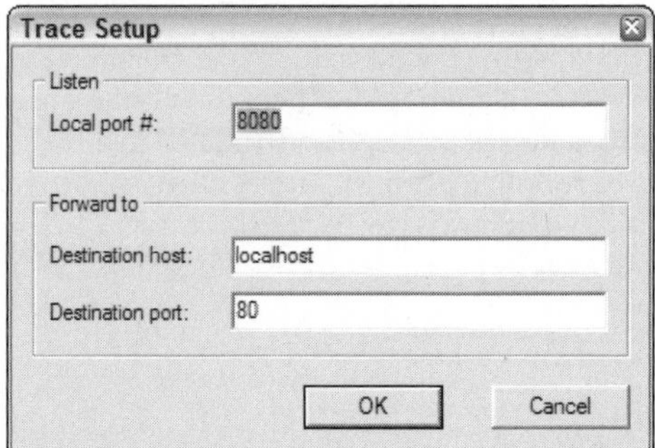

Figure 20-3

After you click the OK button, tracing is enabled, and you are ready to run your consuming application in order to have the SOAP messages that are communicated and recorded by the Trace Utility application. To do this, however, you have to set up your application to run through port 8080 as specified in the Trace Setup dialog from Figure 20-3.

Modifying the Consuming Application

In .NET 1.*x*, you accomplish this by changing the URL attribute in the `Reference.cs` or the `Reference.vb` file contained in your Web Reference to include the new specified port.

```
this.Url = "http://localhost:8080/XMLWS/WebService1.asmx";
```

In .NET 2.0, you accomplish this by changing the URL in the `web.config` or `app.config` file of your application.

```
<appSettings>
   <add key="localhost.Service" value="http://localhost:8080/XMLWS/Service.asmx"/>
</appSettings>
```

Viewing the SOAP Messages

After you have your consuming application set to run through port 8080, then you can run the application as you normally would. The Trace Utility application then traces all the SOAP communications that occur between your application and the Web services it is working with.

Both the Web service client application and the Trace Utility tool from Microsoft should be open when you are doing this. After you have run the application to invoke the remote Web service, you find the results directly in the Trace Utility.

Looking at the Trace Utility, you can see an entry in the left pane of the application. The set of numbers you see, 127.0.0.1, is your local IP address. Expand the plus sign next to this IP address and you see Message #1. Highlight Message #1 to see the SOAP messages show up in the other two panes within the utility. Figure 20-4 shows what the Trace Utility looks like after you have taken these steps.

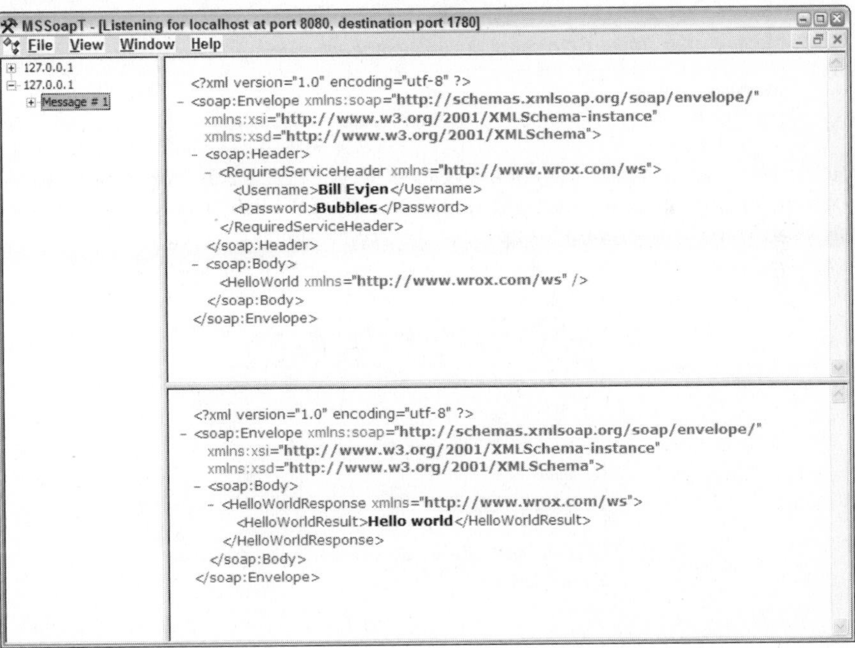

Figure 20-4

After completing these steps, you can watch the SOAP messages that are sent to and from your Web services. This is quite beneficial for debugging and for forming your SOAP messages to the appropriate format. Remember that you shouldn't be doing this tracing operation on production clients or Web services because it greatly hurts the performance of these items. Also, the Trace Utility has some limitations when working with SOAP 1.2. The image shown in Figure 20-4 is a set of SOAP 1.1 messages. When you use this tool with a SOAP 1.2 message, notice that all the beautiful formatting of the SOAP messages is removed and you are left with a single, long, and unformatted string of XML which is the SOAP 1.2 message. It still works, but the result is harder to visualize and decipher.

XMLSpy's SOAP Debugging

When debugging your SOAP messages, the other option you have is Altova's XMLSpy's SOAP debugging capabilities. Note that you have this capability only when using the XMLSpy 2006 Enterprise Edition.

Using the SOAP Debugging Capabilities

To get the SOAP debugging capabilities of XMLSpy up and running, the first step (after you have XMLSpy open, of course) is to select SOAP ➪ SOAP Debugger Session. This launches a dialog that asks for the WSDL file to use for the operation. This dialog is presented in Figure 20-5.

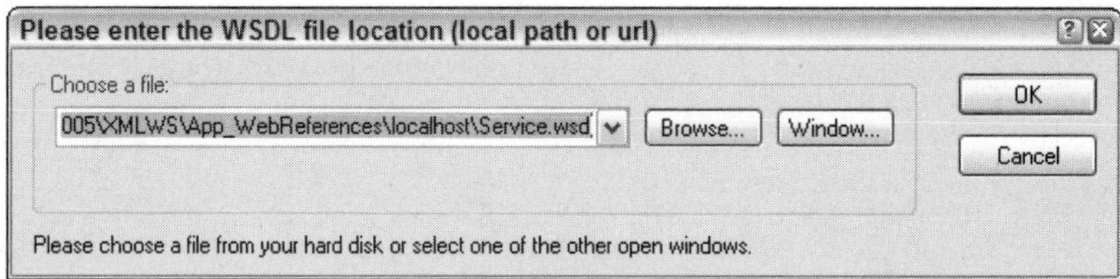

Figure 20-5

After you have pointed to the location of the WSDL file, click the OK button to proceed. After clicking the OK button, you are presented with a dialog to configure the listening and forwarding ports. Similar to the Microsoft Trace Utility tool, XMLSpy monitors communication on a specific port that you must configure your application to work with. This dialog is presented in Figure 20-6.

Figure 20-6

When you have the ports set up as you wish, click the OK button and you are presented with everything wired up for SOAP debugging as presented in Figure 20-7.

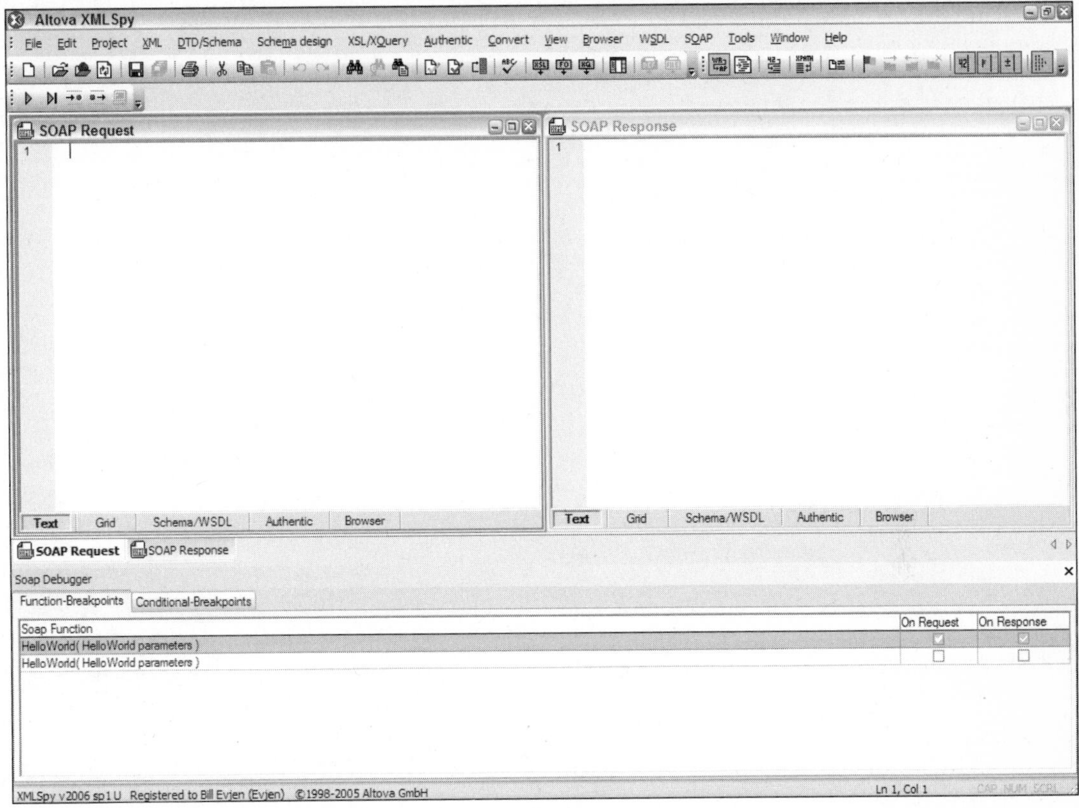

Figure 20-7

From this figure, you can see that (at the bottom of the IDE) two `HelloWorld` methods are presented in the Soap Function list. This is because the WSDL file I am using comes from a C# 2.0 Web service that exposes a Hello World method using SOAP 1.1 and another that uses SOAP 1.2; so it really uses two separate methods.

To take the final steps to use this SOAP debugging tool, check the check boxes for the methods you are interested in monitoring. Looking at Figure 20-7, you can see that I am interested in both the request and the response because I have checked both check boxes. After the appropriate check boxes are checked, click the green arrow found directly above the SOAP Request dialog to start the proxy server. You are now ready to run your application.

Running your application captures only the SOAP request at first, and the application pauses while waiting for a response. The request is presented in the SOAP Request dialog of XMLSpy as shown in Figure 20-8.

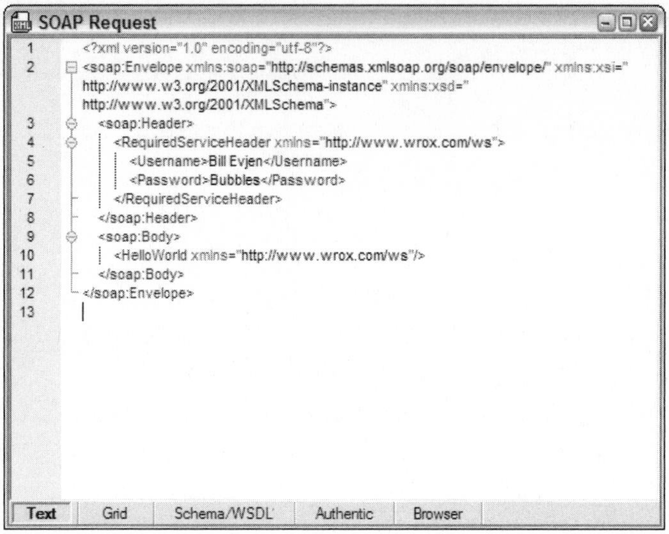

SOAP Request

```
<?xml version="1.0" encoding="utf-8"?>
<soap:Envelope xmlns:soap="http://schemas.xmlsoap.org/soap/envelope/" xmlns:xsi="
http://www.w3.org/2001/XMLSchema-instance" xmlns:xsd="
http://www.w3.org/2001/XMLSchema">
  <soap:Header>
    <RequiredServiceHeader xmlns="http://www.wrox.com/ws">
      <Username>Bill Evjen</Username>
      <Password>Bubbles</Password>
    </RequiredServiceHeader>
  </soap:Header>
  <soap:Body>
    <HelloWorld xmlns="http://www.wrox.com/ws"/>
  </soap:Body>
</soap:Envelope>
```

Text | Grid | Schema/WSDL | Authentic | Browser

Figure 20-8

In this figure, you can see the SOAP request. Now that the SOAP request is shown in this dialog, you can press the green arrow again to actually send the SOAP request to the Web service. You are presented with a SOAP response as shown in Figure 20-9.

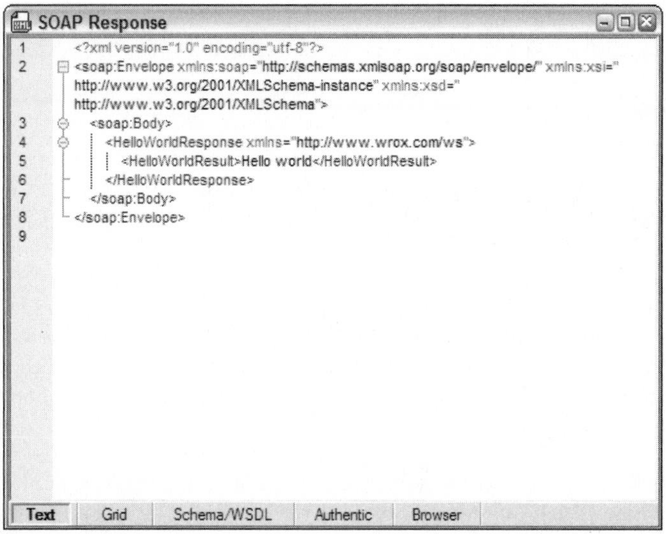

SOAP Response

```
<?xml version="1.0" encoding="utf-8"?>
<soap:Envelope xmlns:soap="http://schemas.xmlsoap.org/soap/envelope/" xmlns:xsi="
http://www.w3.org/2001/XMLSchema-instance" xmlns:xsd="
http://www.w3.org/2001/XMLSchema">
  <soap:Body>
    <HelloWorldResponse xmlns="http://www.wrox.com/ws">
      <HelloWorldResult>Hello world</HelloWorldResult>
    </HelloWorldResponse>
  </soap:Body>
</soap:Envelope>
```

Text | Grid | Schema/WSDL | Authentic | Browser

Figure 20-9

After the response is retrieved, you click the green arrow again to forward the response onto the actual consuming application. The nice thing with XMLSpy is that you can look at the SOAP messages in a couple of different formats. The request and response shown in Figures 21-8 and 21-9 are the text views of the SOAP message. It is also possible, however, to look at the request or response in a Grid view as well as a Browser view, which gives the same view as the Trace Utility tool shown earlier. The Grid view is presented in Figure 20-10.

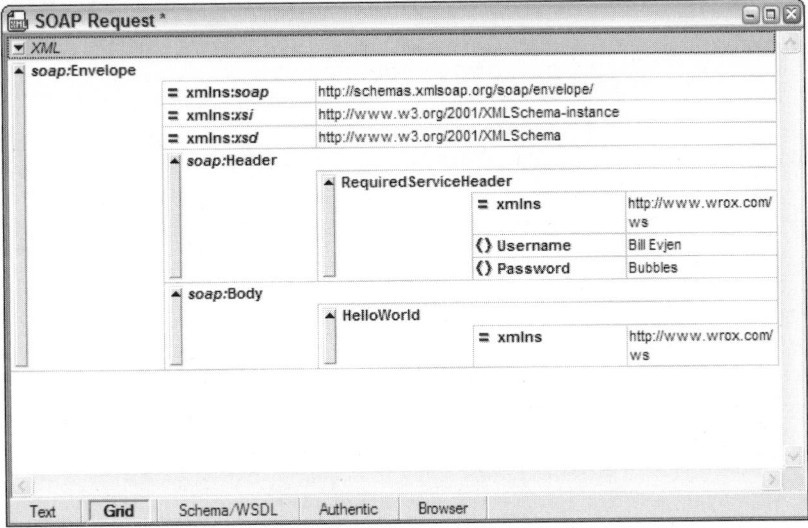

Figure 20-10

Using XMLSpy to Issue SOAP Requests

Probably one of the more exciting SOAP capabilities found in XMLSpy 2006 Enterprise Edition is its capability to issue SOAP requests directly from the tool itself to the Web services you are interested in testing or consuming. If you are a Web services developer, you no longer have to build a consuming application in order to test your Web services; instead, you can use XMLSpy and to test the Web services you are interested in.

To accomplish this, select SOAP ➪ Create New SOAP Request from the XMLSpy menu. This launches a dialog where you specify the location of the WSDL file (this is the same dialog which was presented earlier in Figure 20-5). From this dialog, point to the location of the WSDL file for the Web service you are interested in consuming. After you have specified the location of the WSDL file, click OK and you are presented with a dialog asking you which service you are interested in consuming. This is presented in Figure 20-11.

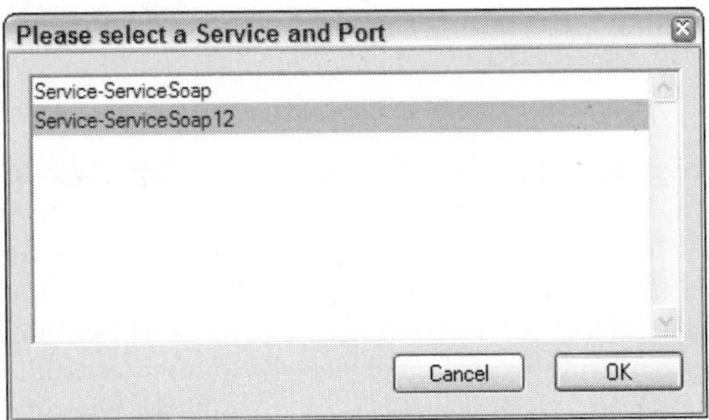

Figure 20-11

In this case, I have selected Service-ServiceSoap12, which is the SOAP 1.2 version of my Web service (the other is the SOAP 1.1 version). After I select OK, I select the Method I am interested in consuming. For this Web service, there is only one — `HelloWorld()` (shown in Figure 20-12).

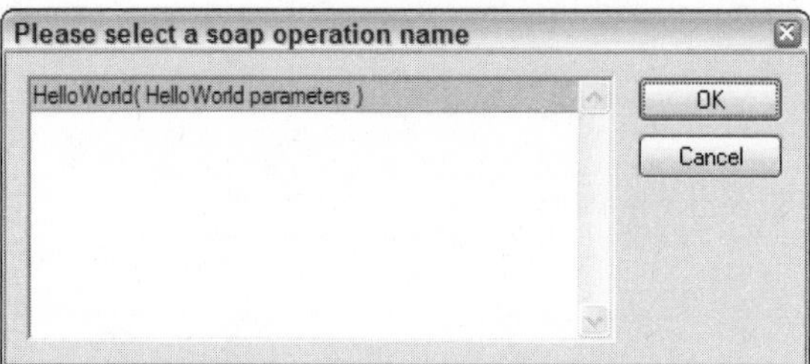

Figure 20-12

After you click OK in this dialog, you are presented with a sample SOAP request to be sent to the `HelloWorld()` Method. This is illustrated in Figure 20-13.

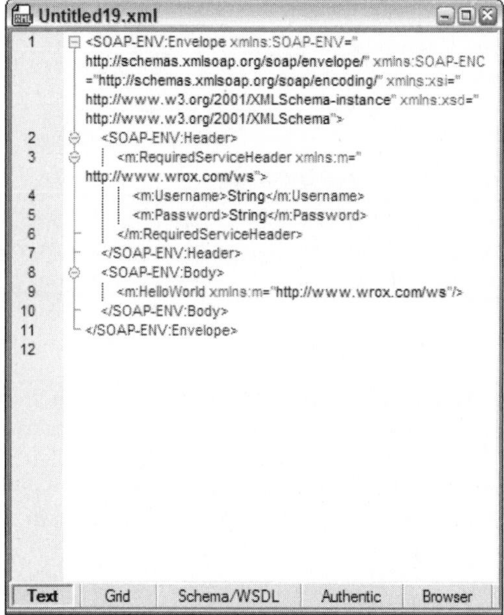

Figure 20-13

Looking over this SOAP request, you can see that it is perfectly structured for sending to the `HelloWorld()` Method. The only problem is that XMLSpy doesn't know which parameters I want to send to the Web service in order to invoke it. (This service doesn't require any parameters for the `HelloWorld()` method.) It also doesn't know what to place inside the SOAP header block that this message contains. In place of the values, it puts the name of the data type as illustrated in the following code:

```
<m:RequiredServiceHeader xmlns:m="http://www.wrox.com/ws">
   <m:Username>String</m:Username>
   <m:Password>String</m:Password>
</m:RequiredServiceHeader>
```

The nice thing about this tool is that you can go into this message and change the values from `String` to whatever you want before sending the message to the Web service. So, change the values and then select SOAP ➪ Send Request To Server from the XMLSpy menu. This sends the structured SOAP message to the Web service you have specified, and it receives and displays the response in the same way as the SOAP request was displayed. This is presented in Figure 20-14.

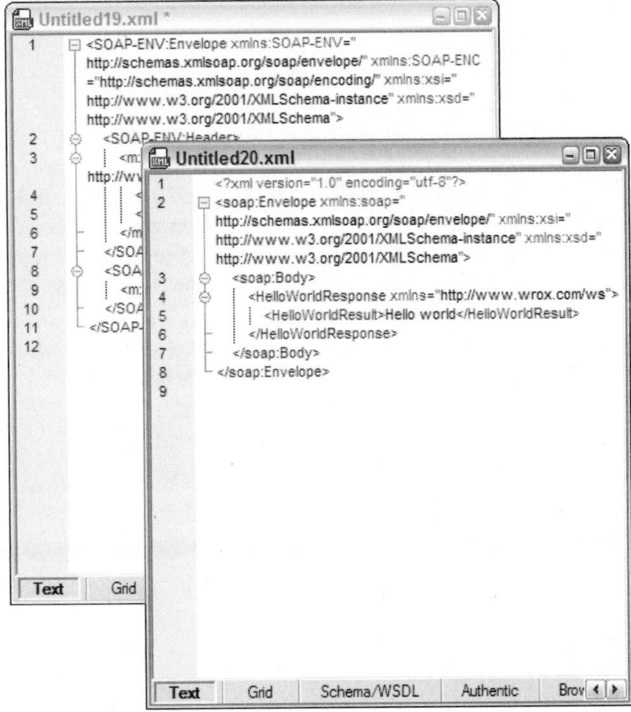

Figure 20-14

As you can see, although the Trace Utility does allow for basic SOAP tracing for debugging purposes, XMLSpy ups it a notch by adding other ways of viewing the data and easier ways to invoke the services.

Working with SOAP Headers

Earlier in this chapter, you learned the purpose of SOAP headers and the value of using them in the Web service you build. SOAP headers provide an excellent means of adding metadata to a SOAP message. Next, you see that it is relatively simple to add and work with SOAP header blocks in your SOAP messages. You look at how to do so using C# 2.0.

Creating SOAP Messages Using SOAP Headers

This example uses Visual Studio 2005 to create a C# 2.0 Web service that exposes a simple `HelloWorld()` method. To start, delete the default `.asmx` file (Web service file) that comes with the default Web service project. Then, create a new Web service file and name the new `.asmx` file `HelloSoapHeader.asmx`. The initial step is to add a class that is an object representing what is to be placed in the SOAP header by the client, as shown in Listing 20-12.

Listing 20-12: A class representing the SOAP header

```
public class HelloHeader : SoapHeader
{
   public string Username;
   public string Password;
}
```

The class, representing a SOAP header object, has to inherit from the .NET Framework `SoapHeader` class from the `System.Web.Services.Protocols` namespace. The `SoapHeader` class serializes the payload of the `<soap:header>` element into XML for you. In the example in Listing 20-12, you can see that this SOAP header requires two elements — simply a username and a password, both of type `String`. The names you create in this class are those used for the subelements of the SOAP header construction, so it is important to name them descriptively. Listing 20-13 shows the Web service class that instantiates an instance of the `HelloHeader` class.

Listing 20-13: A Web service class that utilizes a SOAP header

```
[WebService(Namespace = "http://www.wrox.com/helloworld")]
[WebServiceBinding(ConformsTo = WsiProfiles.BasicProfile1_1)]
public class HelloSoapHeader : System.Web.Services.WebService
{

    public HelloHeader myHeader;

    [WebMethod]
    [SoapHeader("myHeader")]
    public string HelloWorld() {
        if (myHeader == null) {
           return "Hello World";
        }
        else {
           return "Hello " + myHeader.Username + ". " +
              "<br>Your password is: " + myHeader.Password;
        }
    }
}
```

The Web service, `HelloSoapHeader`, has a single method — `HelloWorld()`. Within the Web service class, but outside of the method itself, you create an instance of the `SoapHeader` object. This is done with the following line of code:

```
public HelloHeader myHeader;
```

Now that you have an instance of the `HelloHeader` class that you created earlier called `myHeader`, you can use that instantiation in your method. Because Web services can contain any number of methods, it is not a requirement that all methods use an instantiated SOAP header. You specify whether a method will use a particular instantiation of a SOAP header object by placing the `SoapHeader` attribute before the method declaration.

```
[WebMethod]
[SoapHeader("myHeader")]
public string HelloWorld() {

   // Code here

}
```

In this example, the `SoapHeader` attribute takes a `string` value of the name of the instantiated `SoapHeader` class — in this case, `myHeader`.

From here, the method actually makes use of the `myHeader` object. If the `myHeader` object is not found (meaning that the client did not send in a SOAP header with his constructed SOAP message), a simple `Hello World` is returned. However, if values are provided in the SOAP header of the SOAP request, those values are used within the returned `string` value.

Consuming SOAP Messages Using SOAP Headers

It really isn't difficult to build a consuming application that makes a SOAP request to a Web service using SOAP headers. When using .NET, just as with the Web services that don't include SOAP headers, you need to make a Web Reference to the remote Web service directly in Visual Studio.

For an example of consuming this application using a standard ASP.NET Web page, create a simple `.aspx` page with a single Label control. The output of the Web service is placed in the Label control. The code for the ASP.NET page is shown in Listing 20-14.

Listing 20-14: An ASP.NET page working with an Web service using SOAP headers

```
<%@ Page Language="C#" %>

<script runat="server">
    protected void Page_Load(object sender, System.EventArgs e) {
        localhost.HelloSoapHeader ws = new localhost.HelloSoapHeader();
        localhost.HelloHeader wsHeader = new localhost.HelloHeader();

        wsHeader.Username = "Bill Evjen";
        wsHeader.Password = "Bubbles";
        ws.HelloHeaderValue = wsHeader;

        Label1.Text = ws.HelloWorld();
    }
</script>
```

Two objects are instantiated. The first is the actual method, `HelloWorld()`. The second, which is instantiated as `wsHeader`, is the `HelloHeader` object. After both of these objects are instantiated and before you make the SOAP request in the application, you construct the SOAP header. This is as easy as assigning values to the `Username` and `Password` properties of the `wsHeader` object. After these properties are assigned, you associate the `wsHeader` object to the `ws` object through the use of the `HelloHeaderValue` property. After you have made the association between the constructed SOAP header object and the actual method object (`ws`), you can make a SOAP request just as you would normally do:

```
Label1.Text = ws.HelloWorld();
```

Running the page produces a result in the browser as shown in Figure 20-15.

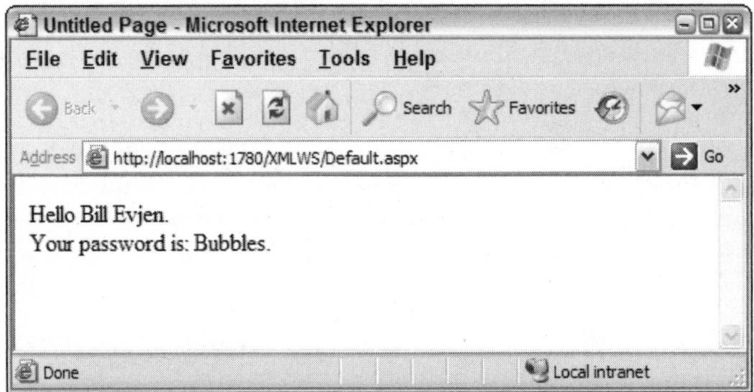

Figure 20-15

What is more interesting, however, is that the SOAP request reveals that the SOAP header was indeed constructed into the overall SOAP message, as shown in Listing 20-15.

Listing 20-15: The SOAP request

```
<?xml version="1.0" encoding="utf-8" ?>
<soap:Envelope xmlns:soap="http://schemas.xmlsoap.org/soap/envelope/"
 xmlns:xsi="http://www.w3.org/2001/XMLSchema-instance"
 xmlns:xsd="http://www.w3.org/2001/XMLSchema">
   <soap:Header>
      <HelloHeader xmlns="http://www.wrox.com/helloworld/">
         <Username>Bill Evjen</Username>
         <Password>Bubbles</Password>
      </HelloHeader>
   </soap:Header>
   <soap:Body>
      <HelloWorld xmlns="http://www.wrox.com/helloworld/" />
   </soap:Body>
</soap:Envelope>
```

This returns the SOAP response shown in Listing 20-16.

Listing 20-16: The SOAP response

```
<?xml version="1.0" encoding="utf-8" ?>
<soap:Envelope xmlns:soap="http://schemas.xmlsoap.org/soap/envelope/"
 xmlns:xsi="http://www.w3.org/2001/XMLSchema-instance"
 xmlns:xsd="http://www.w3.org/2001/XMLSchema">
   <soap:Body>
      <HelloWorldResponse xmlns="http://www.wrox.com/helloworld/">
         <HelloWorldResult>Hello Bill Evjen.&lt;br&gt;Your password is:
          Bubbles</HelloWorldResult>
      </HelloWorldResponse>
   </soap:Body>
</soap:Envelope>
```

Defining Web Services Using WSDL

In order for others to be able to interact with the Web services that you build or simply to enable them to interact with the Web services that any of your client applications might need to consume, you need some sort of description of the Web service. This description is provided through the use of a *Web Services Description Language* (*WSDL*) document. This file is also known as *Wiz-dull*, but you can call it what you want. A WSDL document is an XML document that describes the Web service and can be used by any consuming application.

As you have already seen in this chapter, you are usually required to interact with WSDL files before you start working with the Web services you are interested in consuming. The WSDL document is an important part of any Web service that you want to expose to consumers. This document describes to the end user, the consumer of your Web service, what parameters need to be passed into the Web service. It also tells the users what they should expect to get in return.

Version 1 of the Web Service Description Language specification was finished in the fall of 2000 by a group of companies, including IBM and Microsoft, to help define the Web services that people were building on their systems. The whole concept of Web services demands interoperability; therefore, it made sense for system competitors to sit down together to figure out how their respective Web services can describe themselves to client applications, regardless of their platforms. Luckily these companies realized the best way to achieve the goal of interoperability is to have just one standard in place. Consequently, they have worked together on a standard format to describe the interfaces of Web services that we can all use—WSDL.

In the beginning this wasn't so. At first, both IBM and Microsoft introduced their own Web service description languages. IBM called its standard NASSL, *Network Accessible Service Specification Language*. Microsoft also had a version called SCL, *Service Contract Language*. Both these specifications described the Web services on their respective systems, but these two specifications were not able to understand one another. Therefore, people on a Microsoft system were unable to understand NASSL, and people on any IBM or Java system were unable to understand SCL. The difficulties that ensued caused both companies to see the light and to come together to develop WSDL.

WSDL took hold and has now gone on to version 1.1, which was submitted to the World Wide Web Consortium (`www.w3.org/tr/wsdl`) in March of 2001.

The diagram shown in Figure 20-16 demonstrates how WSDL fits in with the rest of the Web service technology pillars discussed so far.

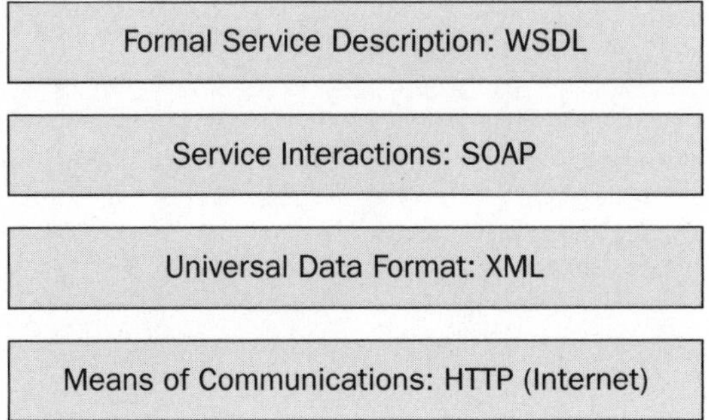

Figure 20-16

You are building client applications that must interact with Web services. You figure out how to perform these interactions by using the formal service description WSDL. Of course, you are never absolutely required to use WSDL files as a means of providing a description of the interface — you have other more informal ways to do this. There are, however, good reasons for you to have a WSDL file in place and to allow consumers to interact with it. First and foremost, it provides a standard way to understand the interface. By having a standard in place, it is possible to build tools that can interact with these WSDL documents on the developer's behalf. Having a standard means that these tools know what to expect from a WSDL document and, therefore, perform all the operations that are required to interact with the defined Web service. For instance, when working with Visual Studio and the .NET Framework, these technologies will build a proxy class on your behalf to take care of marshalling the SOAP messages back and forth to the Web service. If the WSDL document doesn't follow any standard, the tools could have problems interacting with the document. As a result, you might be required to build a proxy class by hand. WSDL documents are created in different ways depending on the platform on which you are building your Web services. If you are using the .NET Framework, the WSDL document is generated for you dynamically. Other platforms, such as J2EE, also provide you with the necessary tools for automatic WSDL generation.

An example of a simple Web service's WSDL file is shown in Listing 20-17. This Web service, called `Calculator`, has only two methods: `Add()` and `Subtract()`. The interfaces of both methods are defined in the WSDL document. You review all the parts of this document in the rest of this chapter.

Listing 20-17: The WSDL document for the Calculator Web service

```
<?xml version="1.0" encoding="utf-8"?>
<wsdl:definitions xmlns:soap="http://schemas.xmlsoap.org/wsdl/soap/"
 xmlns:tm="http://microsoft.com/wsdl/mime/textMatching/"
 xmlns:soapenc="http://schemas.xmlsoap.org/soap/encoding/"
 xmlns:mime="http://schemas.xmlsoap.org/wsdl/mime/"
 xmlns:tns="http://www.wrox.com/ws" xmlns:s="http://www.w3.org/2001/XMLSchema"
 xmlns:soap12="http://schemas.xmlsoap.org/wsdl/soap12/"
 xmlns:http="http://schemas.xmlsoap.org/wsdl/http/"
 targetNamespace="http://www.wrox.com/ws"
```

```
  xmlns:wsdl="http://schemas.xmlsoap.org/wsdl/">
   <wsdl:types>
     <s:schema elementFormDefault="qualified"
      targetNamespace="http://www.wrox.com/ws">
       <s:element name="Add">
         <s:complexType>
           <s:sequence>
             <s:element minOccurs="1" maxOccurs="1" name="a" type="s:int" />
             <s:element minOccurs="1" maxOccurs="1" name="b" type="s:int" />
           </s:sequence>
         </s:complexType>
       </s:element>
       <s:element name="AddResponse">
         <s:complexType>
           <s:sequence>
             <s:element minOccurs="1" maxOccurs="1" name="AddResult" type="s:int" />
           </s:sequence>
         </s:complexType>
       </s:element>
       <s:element name="Subtract">
         <s:complexType>
           <s:sequence>
             <s:element minOccurs="1" maxOccurs="1" name="a" type="s:int" />
             <s:element minOccurs="1" maxOccurs="1" name="b" type="s:int" />
           </s:sequence>
         </s:complexType>
       </s:element>
       <s:element name="SubtractResponse">
         <s:complexType>
           <s:sequence>
             <s:element minOccurs="1" maxOccurs="1" name="SubtractResult"
              type="s:int" />
           </s:sequence>
         </s:complexType>
       </s:element>
     </s:schema>
   </wsdl:types>
   <wsdl:message name="AddSoapIn">
     <wsdl:part name="parameters" element="tns:Add" />
   </wsdl:message>
   <wsdl:message name="AddSoapOut">
     <wsdl:part name="parameters" element="tns:AddResponse" />
   </wsdl:message>
   <wsdl:message name="SubtractSoapIn">
     <wsdl:part name="parameters" element="tns:Subtract" />
   </wsdl:message>
   <wsdl:message name="SubtractSoapOut">
     <wsdl:part name="parameters" element="tns:SubtractResponse" />
   </wsdl:message>
   <wsdl:portType name="CalculatorSoap">
     <wsdl:operation name="Add">
```

(continued)

Listing 20-17 *(continued)*

```
      <wsdl:input message="tns:AddSoapIn" />
      <wsdl:output message="tns:AddSoapOut" />
    </wsdl:operation>
    <wsdl:operation name="Subtract">
      <wsdl:input message="tns:SubtractSoapIn" />
      <wsdl:output message="tns:SubtractSoapOut" />
    </wsdl:operation>
  </wsdl:portType>
  <wsdl:binding name="CalculatorSoap" type="tns:CalculatorSoap">
    <soap:binding transport="http://schemas.xmlsoap.org/soap/http" />
    <wsdl:operation name="Add">
      <soap:operation soapAction="http://www.wrox.com/ws/Add" style="document" />
      <wsdl:input>
        <soap:body use="literal" />
      </wsdl:input>
      <wsdl:output>
        <soap:body use="literal" />
      </wsdl:output>
    </wsdl:operation>
    <wsdl:operation name="Subtract">
      <soap:operation soapAction="http://www.wrox.com/ws/Subtract"
       style="document" />
      <wsdl:input>
        <soap:body use="literal" />
      </wsdl:input>
      <wsdl:output>
        <soap:body use="literal" />
      </wsdl:output>
    </wsdl:operation>
  </wsdl:binding>
  <wsdl:binding name="CalculatorSoap12" type="tns:CalculatorSoap">
    <soap12:binding transport="http://schemas.xmlsoap.org/soap/http" />
    <wsdl:operation name="Add">
      <soap12:operation soapAction="http://www.wrox.com/ws/Add" style="document" />
      <wsdl:input>
        <soap12:body use="literal" />
      </wsdl:input>
      <wsdl:output>
        <soap12:body use="literal" />
      </wsdl:output>
    </wsdl:operation>
    <wsdl:operation name="Subtract">
      <soap12:operation soapAction="http://www.wrox.com/ws/Subtract"
       style="document" />
      <wsdl:input>
        <soap12:body use="literal" />
      </wsdl:input>
      <wsdl:output>
        <soap12:body use="literal" />
      </wsdl:output>
    </wsdl:operation>
```

```
    </wsdl:binding>
    <wsdl:service name="Calculator">
      <wsdl:port name="CalculatorSoap" binding="tns:CalculatorSoap">
        <soap:address location="http://localhost:1780/XMLWS/Calculator.asmx" />
      </wsdl:port>
      <wsdl:port name="CalculatorSoap12" binding="tns:CalculatorSoap12">
        <soap12:address location="http://localhost:1780/XMLWS/Calculator.asmx" />
      </wsdl:port>
    </wsdl:service>
  </wsdl:definitions>
```

Yes, it is a bit lengthy, but it is worth it. You should become familiar with a WSDL document so that you can read it to determine what the Web service needs to run effectively. You might be wondering why you need to do this if the development environments out there can so easily review and interpret these documents for you. Actually, you have a lot of reasons to learn how a WSDL document works.

One reason is that when you are dealing with a Web service, you might not always have access to either the IDEs or development environments you are working with. In such a case, you benefit by being able to open up the WSDL document so you can understand what is going on.

One of the biggest reasons to know how the WSDL file works, however, is that (as all programmers should know by now) developers are not always perfect. Most likely, some WSDL documents out there have errors in them. If this is the case, you want to be able to open up the WSDL document and find the error so that you can modify the document and use it in your applications.

The Structure of WSDL Documents

The WSDL document that was reviewed earlier is a complete WSDL document based on a Calculator Web service with two simple methods. When looking over the code of the WSDL document, you should note that the WSDL document is just a list of definitions using XML grammar.

This grammar is used to describe the protocols that are needed to communicate with the Web service, discover the Web service's interface, and learn the location of the Web service. The grammar of WSDL describes message network endpoints or ports. The diagram in Figure 20-17 shows the message structure of a WSDL document.

Starting from the top of the diagram in Figure 20-17, the first level of the WSDL document contains the *services*. Each service description refers to the Web service that the end user wants to invoke within his client applications. The service includes all the available methods that the creator of the Web service has exposed or the collection of available endpoints.

Beyond this is the *port*. The port is referenced from the service and points to the network address of an endpoint and all the bindings that the endpoint adheres to. For example, a Web service might have a port description of multiple bindings such as SOAP, HTTP-POST, and HTTP-GET.

The *binding* describes the transport and encoding particulars for a *portType*. The portTypes refer to the operations anticipated by a particular endpoint type, without any specifics relating to transport or encoding.

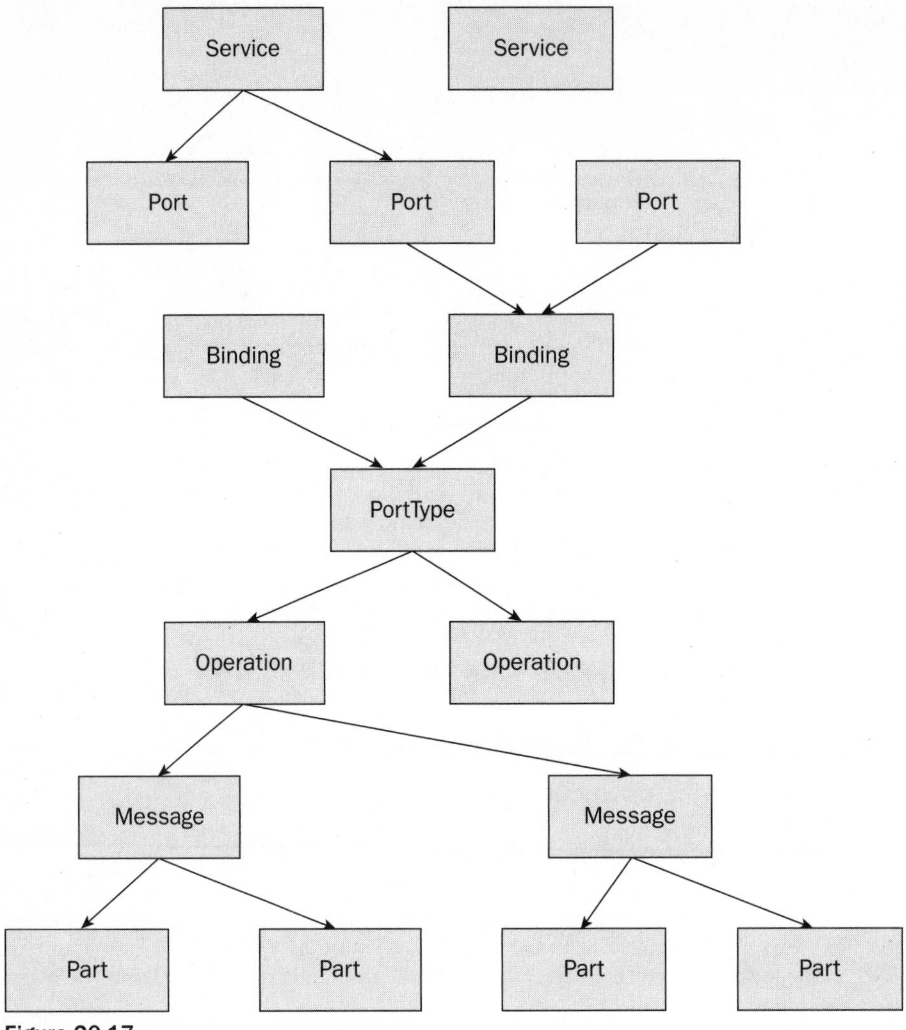

Figure 20-17

The *operation* details all the messages that are involved in dealing with the service at the endpoint. For instance, a Web service that returns a value after a request entails two messages, a request and a response. Each *message* makes a reference to XSD Schemas to detail the different parts of the message. Each piece of data that makes up part of a message is referred to as a *part*.

Next, take a look at each of the parts of the WSDL document so you can better understand what is going on.

<definitions>

The WSDL document contains a root element, just like other XML documents. Directly preceding the start of the `<definitions>` element is the XML declaration.

```
<?xml version="1.0" encoding="utf-8"?>
```

This specifies what the WSDL document truly is — an XML file. The next line in the WSDL document is the root element, `<definitions>`. The code in Listing 20-18 shows the `<definitions>` element for the earlier WSDL file.

Listing 20-18: Breaking down the <definitions> element

```
<wsdl:definitions xmlns:soap="http://schemas.xmlsoap.org/wsdl/soap/"
 xmlns:tm="http://microsoft.com/wsdl/mime/textMatching/"
 xmlns:soapenc="http://schemas.xmlsoap.org/soap/encoding/"
 xmlns:mime="http://schemas.xmlsoap.org/wsdl/mime/"
 xmlns:tns="http://www.wrox.com/ws" xmlns:s="http://www.w3.org/2001/XMLSchema"
 xmlns:soap12="http://schemas.xmlsoap.org/wsdl/soap12/"
 xmlns:http="http://schemas.xmlsoap.org/wsdl/http/"
 targetNamespace="http://www.wrox.com/ws"
 xmlns:wsdl="http://schemas.xmlsoap.org/wsdl/">

</wsdl:definitions>
```

The `<definitions>` element includes a number of namespaces. The following table describes some of the namespaces that you might see in various WSDL documents.

Prefix	Namespace URI	Definition
`wsdl`	`http://schemas.xmlsoap.org/wsdl/`	WSDL namespace for WSDL framework.
`soap`	`http://schemas.xmlsoap.org/wsdl/soap/`	WSDL namespace for WSDL SOAP 1.1 binding.
`soap12`	`http://schemas.xmlsoap.org/wsdl/soap12/`	WSDL namespace for WSDL SOAP 1.2 binding.
`http`	`http://schemas.xmlsoap.org/wsdl/http/`	WSDL namespace for WSDL HTTP GET & POST binding.
`mime`	`http://schemas.xmlsoap.org/wsdl/mime/`	WSDL namespace for WSDL MIME binding.
`soapenc`	`http://schemas.xmlsoap.org/soap/encoding/`	Encoding namespace as defined by SOAP.
`soapenv`	`http://schemas.xmlsoap.org/soap/envelope/`	Envelope namespace as defined by SOAP.
`xsi`	`http://www.w3.org/2000/10/XMLSchema-instance`	Instance namespace as defined by XSD.
`xsd`	`http://www.w3.org/2000/10/XMLSchema`	Schema namespace as defined by XSD.
`tns`	`(various)`	The "this namespace" (`tns`) prefix is used as a convention to refer to the current document.

Along with these namespaces, you also have the option (not shown in this example) of using the attribute name within the `<definitions>` element. If you use this example, the name attribute could take the following form:

```
<definitions name="Calculator" ...
```

This really doesn't have any purpose except to provide some sort of lightweight description for any user who might be looking at the WSDL document and trying to figure out the overall purpose of the Web service that he is trying to consume. Another optional element that is used in the example is `targetNamespace`. This attribute defines the namespace for each of the items in the WSDL document. This means that all the elements contained within this WSDL file belong to this namespace, much the same as a `targetNamespace` declaration in an XSD file. Along with the `targetNamespace` are a number of other namespaces for HTTP-POST, HTTP-GET, and SOAP binding, as well as for MIME.

<types>

In the WSDL example from the Calculator Web service, a couple of types are defined. These are shown in Listing 20-19.

Listing 20-19: Breaking down the <types> element

```
<wsdl:types>
  <s:schema elementFormDefault="qualified"
   targetNamespace="http://www.wrox.com/ws">
    <s:element name="Add">
      <s:complexType>
        <s:sequence>
          <s:element minOccurs="1" maxOccurs="1" name="a" type="s:int" />
          <s:element minOccurs="1" maxOccurs="1" name="b" type="s:int" />
        </s:sequence>
      </s:complexType>
    </s:element>
    <s:element name="AddResponse">
      <s:complexType>
        <s:sequence>
          <s:element minOccurs="1" maxOccurs="1" name="AddResult" type="s:int" />
        </s:sequence>
      </s:complexType>
    </s:element>
    <s:element name="Subtract">
      <s:complexType>
        <s:sequence>
          <s:element minOccurs="1" maxOccurs="1" name="a" type="s:int" />
          <s:element minOccurs="1" maxOccurs="1" name="b" type="s:int" />
        </s:sequence>
      </s:complexType>
    </s:element>
    <s:element name="SubtractResponse">
      <s:complexType>
        <s:sequence>
          <s:element minOccurs="1" maxOccurs="1" name="SubtractResult"
```

```
                  type="s:int" />
              </s:sequence>
            </s:complexType>
          </s:element>
        </s:schema>
      </wsdl:types>
```

The information within the <types> element includes the type definitions that are needed in the message exchange. In order to define these types, you should use the XML Schema Definition Language (XSD). The XSD language is described in detail in Chapter 6.

XSD is used to provide the most interoperability possible to a Web service by using a language that is widely accepted as the standard way of describing types within XML documents.

The code example from Listing 20-19 starts with the definition of the types that are required for the `Add()` and `Subtract()` methods. For both methods, you first find `a` parameter, which is of type `int`. The second parameter is the `b` parameter, which is also of type `int`. It is possible to fully describe various complex types and the sequence of these types using XSD within the <types> element of the WSDL document.

In the end, what's being returned from both methods is a single item of the type `int`. This message is defined by `AddResponse` and `SubtractResponse`. Notice that the inbound message has the same name as the method that it is exposing (in this case, `Add` or `Subtract`), and the outbound message has the same name as the method, but with the word Response appended to it (in this case, `AddResponse` or `SubtractResponse`).

> *A large number of types are at your disposal. Be sure to review the available types by looking back on Chapter 6. If you are going to be passing back an undefined type, be sure to use the type* `anyType` *in the following manner:* `type="s:anyType"`*. This represents a parameter of any type.*

<message>

Messages consist of one or more parts. The sample WSDL document uses a number of different <message> elements which are presented in Listing 20-20.

Listing 20-20: Breaking down the <message> element

```
<wsdl:message name="AddSoapIn">
  <wsdl:part name="parameters" element="tns:Add" />
</wsdl:message>
<wsdl:message name="AddSoapOut">
  <wsdl:part name="parameters" element="tns:AddResponse" />
</wsdl:message>
<wsdl:message name="SubtractSoapIn">
  <wsdl:part name="parameters" element="tns:Subtract" />
</wsdl:message>
<wsdl:message name="SubtractSoapOut">
  <wsdl:part name="parameters" element="tns:SubtractResponse" />
</wsdl:message>
```

You see all the type definitions that play a role in the data that is being transported back and forth across the wire, but the <message> element is the piece of the pie that packages this up. The <message> element is protocol independent and is really only concerned with the message and all the parts of the message that are going to be sent and received.

The <message> element can have a single attribute, the name attribute. The name attribute is just that — a name. It doesn't really have any special meaning except that it provides a unique identifier among all messages defined within the enclosing WSDL document. In this example, all the messages have the name of the method, plus the protocol of the part. You can give the <message> elements any name that you choose, because WSDL makes no distinction about the name that is used, just as long as no naming conflicts exist among the messages.

You can think of the <part> elements as the payload of the messages. In the <message> example that is laid out, you can see a message for each request and response for each of the methods available. It is possible to have multiple <part> elements defining requests that cover both HTTP-GET and HTTP-POST messages, whereas the response information contains a single <part> element.

The SOAP <part> elements used in Listing 20-20 are interesting. If you use SOAP, the <part> elements basically correspond to the SOAP request or response. These <part> elements do not contain the parameter type definitions like the other <part> elements do, but instead they point to the type definitions that were defined in the <types> element earlier. Going back to this definition, you see a type definition for Add and AddResponse as well as for Subtract and SubtractResponse.

<portType>

The job of the <portType> element is to define all the operations that can be used. A port type is a set of certain abstract operations and the abstract messages involved.

The WSDL document example has a couple of different <portType> definitions, although it is possible to have a number more. The code shown in Listing 20-21 reviews these definitions.

Listing 20-21: Breaking down the <portType> element

```
<wsdl:portType name="CalculatorSoap">
  <wsdl:operation name="Add">
    <wsdl:input message="tns:AddSoapIn" />
    <wsdl:output message="tns:AddSoapOut" />
  </wsdl:operation>
  <wsdl:operation name="Subtract">
    <wsdl:input message="tns:SubtractSoapIn" />
    <wsdl:output message="tns:SubtractSoapOut" />
  </wsdl:operation>
</wsdl:portType>
```

The <portType> element can take a single attribute, the name attribute. This attribute provides you with a unique identifier for the <portType> element, so that this <portType> is set out from the other <portType> elements.

A single Web service can support a number of different protocols. The structure of the data depends on the protocol that you use to invoke the Web service. Because of this, you need a way to map from the operations to the endpoints from which they can be accessed. The `<portType>` element takes care of this mapping.

You can place a `portType` definition for each of the protocols available to you for this Web service. For instance, you can have individual `portType` definitions for using SOAP, HTTP-POST, and HTTP-GET. The operation name is the method available from the Web service. If other methods are available to you, additional `<operation>` elements would be defined as well.

For each `<operation>` element, you can also provide an optional `<documentation>` element. This element is discussed later in this chapter. The other elements that you can use within the `<operation>` element include `<input>`, `<output>`, and `<fault>`. Each `<operation>` can contain only one of each of these available elements. There can only be one input into a Web service, just as there can only be one output. Each of these three elements has a `name` and a `message` attribute.

The `<input>` element specifies the request to a Web service. The `<output>` element specifies the response of the Web service. The `<fault>` element details any error messages that may be output by the Web service.

<binding>

Now that you have definitions in place for the different logical ports at your disposal, you can define how the end user binds to a port where the operation is obtainable. You do this by using the `<binding>` element. The following code presented in Listing 20-22 is one of the two `<binding>` elements used in the sample WSDL document.

Listing 20-22: Breaking down the <binding> element

```
<wsdl:binding name="CalculatorSoap" type="tns:CalculatorSoap">
  <soap:binding transport="http://schemas.xmlsoap.org/soap/http" />
  <wsdl:operation name="Add">
    <soap:operation soapAction="http://www.wrox.com/ws/Add" style="document" />
    <wsdl:input>
      <soap:body use="literal" />
    </wsdl:input>
    <wsdl:output>
      <soap:body use="literal" />
    </wsdl:output>
  </wsdl:operation>
  <wsdl:operation name="Subtract">
    <soap:operation soapAction="http://www.wrox.com/ws/Subtract"
     style="document" />
    <wsdl:input>
      <soap:body use="literal" />
    </wsdl:input>
    <wsdl:output>
      <soap:body use="literal" />
    </wsdl:output>
  </wsdl:operation>
</wsdl:binding>
```

The <binding> that is shown in this example is using SOAP. The other binding that is in the main WSDL document includes a <binding> definition for SOAP 1.2.

The <binding> element contains a name attribute. This attribute's value is the name of the Web service class with the word SOAP attached to it. The <binding> element also contains a type attribute. This attribute is a reference to the <portType> name attribute that was used earlier.

<soap:binding>

The example from Listing 20-22 shows that a number of different elements are enclosed within the <binding> element. The first is the <soap:binding> element. By using this <soap:binding> element, you are specifying that this protocol is bound to the SOAP specification that uses a SOAP packet for transport. The SOAP packet is made up of the envelope, header, and body. The <soap:binding> element can contain two attributes. The first is the transport attribute. The transport attribute, a URI, specifies the protocol that is going to be used in transporting the SOAP packet. The value of this attribute in the example is http://schemas.xmlsoap.org/soap/http. This transport value is specifying that the SOAP packet will be transported over HTTP.

The style attribute enables you to specify one of the two available binding styles at your disposal. The optional values are rpc and document. The preceding example is using the style attribute with the value of document. A setting of document means that the SOAP will be transported using a single document message. Using rpc means that the SOAP message will be sent using an RPC-oriented operation. RPC messages are made up of parameters and return values. If a style value isn't specified, assume that document is the style setting.

<soap:operation>

Contained within the <operation> element is a <soap:operation> element. The <operation> element is associated with each of the available methods from the Web service. The <soap:operation> element is used to show how the operation should be bound. In this case, it is to the SOAP protocol. The soapAction attribute specifies the value of the SOAPAction header for this operation.

The style attribute is the same as it is in the <soap:body> element. The possible values of this attribute include both rpc and document.

The <soap:operation> element can take up to one <input> and one <output> element. Each <input> and <output> element can contain either a <soap:body>, <soap:header> or a <soap:headerfault>. The sample WSDL document that is used in this chapter contains only a <soap:body> element for both the <input> and <output> elements.

<soap:body>

The <input> or <output> element can contain a <soap:body> element. This indicates that the message parts are part of the SOAP body element. A number of available attributes can be used within the <soap:body> element.

In the example used in this chapter, the <soap:body> contains a use attribute. The use attribute specifies whether the message parts are being encoded. The possible values of the use attribute include encoded or literal.

The value encoded means that a URI is used to determine how the message is mapped to the SOAP body. If encoded is set as the value, an encodingStyle attribute must be present. The value of the encodingStyle attribute is a list of URIs, each divided by a single space. The URIs signify encoding used within the message, and they are ordered from the most restrictive to the least restrictive.

If literal is used as the value of the use attribute, the message parts represent a concrete schema definition. When this value is set to literal, the message parts are sent literally and not altered in the process.

<service>

The <service> element contains the endpoints for the Web service. The code shown in Listing 20-23 demonstrates this.

Listing 20-23: Breaking down the <service> element

```
<wsdl:service name="Calculator">
  <wsdl:port name="CalculatorSoap" binding="tns:CalculatorSoap">
    <soap:address location="http://localhost:1780/XMLWS/Calculator.asmx" />
  </wsdl:port>
  <wsdl:port name="CalculatorSoap12" binding="tns:CalculatorSoap12">
    <soap12:address location="http://localhost:1780/XMLWS/Calculator.asmx" />
  </wsdl:port>
</wsdl:service>
```

In this example, the Web service has two ports or endpoints. One available port is for SOAP 1.1 and another is for SOAP 1.2. The binding attribute in the <port> element points to the associated <binding> element. Contained within the <port> element is an <soap:address> child element that specifies the URI of the endpoint.

Like the other elements that are part of the WSDL document, the <port> element can also take a name attribute that allows it to have a unique identifier in order to differentiate itself from the other <port> elements.

<import>

Although not shown in any of the examples, you can use the <import> element within a WSDL document. Using the <import> element enables you to associate a namespace with a document location. The following code shows this:

```
<definitions>
     <import namespace="uri" location="uri"/>
</definitions>
```

Basically you can actually import parts of another WSDL document directly into the WSDL document that you are working with. For instance, if you have a type definition in a separate file, your file should look like Listing 20-24:

Listing 20-24: The <types> section in its own WSDL file

```
<wsdl:types>
  <s:schema elementFormDefault="qualified"
   targetNamespace="http://www.wrox.com/ws">
    <s:element name="Add">
      <s:complexType>
        <s:sequence>
          <s:element minOccurs="1" maxOccurs="1" name="a" type="s:int" />
          <s:element minOccurs="1" maxOccurs="1" name="b" type="s:int" />
        </s:sequence>
      </s:complexType>
    </s:element>
    <s:element name="AddResponse">
      <s:complexType>
        <s:sequence>
          <s:element minOccurs="1" maxOccurs="1" name="AddResult" type="s:int" />
        </s:sequence>
      </s:complexType>
    </s:element>
    <s:element name="Subtract">
      <s:complexType>
        <s:sequence>
          <s:element minOccurs="1" maxOccurs="1" name="a" type="s:int" />
          <s:element minOccurs="1" maxOccurs="1" name="b" type="s:int" />
        </s:sequence>
      </s:complexType>
    </s:element>
    <s:element name="SubtractResponse">
      <s:complexType>
        <s:sequence>
          <s:element minOccurs="1" maxOccurs="1" name="SubtractResult"
           type="s:int" />
        </s:sequence>
      </s:complexType>
    </s:element>
  </s:schema>
</wsdl:types>
```

You can now import this `.wsdl` file directly into the WSDL document that you are working on. The partial code example presented in Listing 20-25 shows how this is done.

Listing 20-25: A WSDL document containing an imported type definition

```
<?xml version="1.0" encoding="utf-8"?>
<wsdl:definitions xmlns:soap="http://schemas.xmlsoap.org/wsdl/soap/"
 xmlns:tm="http://microsoft.com/wsdl/mime/textMatching/"
 xmlns:soapenc="http://schemas.xmlsoap.org/soap/encoding/"
 xmlns:mime="http://schemas.xmlsoap.org/wsdl/mime/"
 xmlns:tns="http://www.wrox.com/ws" xmlns:s="http://www.w3.org/2001/XMLSchema"
 xmlns:soap12="http://schemas.xmlsoap.org/wsdl/soap12/"
```

```
    xmlns:http="http://schemas.xmlsoap.org/wsdl/http/"
    targetNamespace="http://www.wrox.com/ws"
    xmlns:wsdl="http://schemas.xmlsoap.org/wsdl/">

     <import namespace="http://www.wrox.com/ws"
      location="http://localhost/SomeLocation/TypeDefinition.wsdl" />

     <wsdl:message name="AddSoapIn">
       <wsdl:part name="parameters" element="tns:Add" />
     </wsdl:message>

     <!-- The rest removed for clarity -->

   </wsdl:definitions>
```

This causes the types that are defined in a separate WSDL document to be planted in the spot where the <import> element is located. You may have pieces of a WSDL document that are easy to carve off and use numerous times in other WSDL documents.

The <import> element takes two attributes. The first is the `namespace` attribute and the second is the `location` attribute. The `location` attribute specifies the location of the actual file that you want to import into the WSDL document.

Using the <import> element properly enables you to separate your WSDL documents into reusable blocks that can be inserted when needed.

<documentation>

It is not always possible for the end user to figure out what is going on in a particular Web service by looking at the WSDL file or any Web services test page. One option to enable the Web service consumer to understand a Web service better is for the Web service developer to use the <documentation> element to further define the methods available. You can use this element to help others understand what is meant by the argument `CityDays2007` in your method. The end user might be able to tell that the `CityDays2007` takes an `int`, but he might not know the actually meaning of the argument. Even after testing it on the test page, he may be no closer to figuring it out.

It is always best to give as much information as possible if you want users to consume your Web services with a smile. Do this by providing documentation notes within your WSDL files, as well by using the <documentation> element.

The <documentation> element is allowed anywhere within the WSDL document. I advise you to use this element to place documentation information in as many places as possible to make it easier for end user to consume your Web services.

For instance, in the example used throughout this chapter, the <documentation> element is placed within the <operation> element in order to give the end user more information about what the operation actually does. The code presented in Listing 20-26 shows an example of this.

Listing 20-26: Using the <documentation> element in a WSDL file

```
<wsdl:operation name="Add">
  <documentation>Adds two numbers together for
   the mathematically impaired.</documentation>
  <wsdl:input message="tns:AddSoapIn" />
  <wsdl:output message="tns:AddSoapOut" />
</wsdl:operation>
```

The preceding code is somewhat self-explanatory. Because you know a little more about this particular operation, you also know how to work more effectively with the Web service you are looking to consume.

Summary

This chapter reviewed some of the core technologies behind Web services. Make sure you understand the details of both SOAP and WSDL if you are planning on either exposing or consuming application data or logic via these means. It will make your life that much easier.

SOAP is a standard way of representing the message structure, and this chapter showed you this basic structure with a review of the SOAP envelope, header, and body. It also demonstrated SOAP faults and how to send effective SOAP error messages back to the consuming client.

The Web Services Description Language is a new XML-based language that is used to describe Web service regardless of the underlying platform on which the Web services reside. Now that you know how a WSDL document is constructed, you will be better able to discern the structure of a Web service from these documents.

21

Advanced Web Services

Web services have already changed the way developers model their applications. Web services allow developers to easily expose application logic and data with relatively little work. Various vendors have now built into their toolsets the means to easily expose and consume Web services.

Although the Web services model is great, it originally generated a little bit of worry in the enterprise. *Where is the security? What about sending binary objects such as images? What about the routing of SOAP messages?* These were good questions because they pointed out what the Web services model was lacking — a common way to provide security, send attachments, establish routing, and more.

Companies such as IBM and Microsoft started working on a number of specifications that addressed these needs. These were

- WS-Security
- WS-Timestamp
- WS-Attachments

Developers watched these new specifications with great excitement, and wanted to begin using them immediately. This desire gave birth to the various WS-* (WS-star) technologies. This chapter takes a look at these advanced specifications and what they do for your Web services. In addition to examining the specifications, this chapter also describes implementing these specifications in your applications today.

Expanding on a Foundation

The XML Web services model is here to stay. In fact, it is so popular and solves so many of the problems developers face that its adoption rate is quite outstanding. After this model was introduced, however, many companies found that it was missing some core pieces that would enable organizations to use the new technology as it was intended.

Most notably, users complained that Web services lacked some enterprise basics such as a standard way to provide different types of credentials, to route SOAP messages, and to perform certain transactions such as encryption, digital signing, and more. Many more issues arose, but these were some of the most vital ones.

Individual vendors might be able to come up with their own solutions for these problems, but doing so violated the basic concept of the Web Services model — Interoperability.

If you want Web Services to work with credentials, encryption, or transactions between disparate systems, you must have common standards agreed upon by the industry at large. This ensures that your XML Web services will work with requests to and from Unix-based systems. So, in a sense, the XML Web services model and this book are based upon the concept of *interoperability*. Everyone wants specifications that provide a common language and enable us to tie our systems together. This has been a goal of the enterprise for quite awhile, and it is slowly starting to be realized.

Web Services Framework — *The Paper*

The vendors developing their own Web Services model, based on the original industry-wide agreements of XML, SOAP and HTTP, foresaw the need for advanced functionality for enterprise-level Web Services. Because of this, both Microsoft and IBM submitted a paper to the W3C in April of 2003 at a Web Services workshop entitled Web Services Framework. The paper contained a laundry list of specifications that the two companies felt would bring about true enterprise-level Web services. These specifications would further the goal of achieving decentralized interoperability.

The paper pinpoints specific functionality that must be developed into specifications for the proposed Web Services Framework. The following section contains the companies' vision of the functionality needed for Web Services.

Message Envelope and Controlled Extensibility

This functionality enables users of SOAP routing to tag parts of the XML message. Tagging reveals what parts of the message can and cannot be ignored by the processors. The SOAP intermediate processors can then work with only those parts of the message meant for them and can ignore the parts meant for the final recipient.

Binary Attachments

This functionality allows for sending of non-textual items along with the SOAP message. It is expensive to serialize and deserialize nontextual items (such as images). If items can be attached to the SOAP message in their binary formats, this serialization process is not needed.

Message Exchange aka Routing

Not all SOAP messages are sent point-to-point. Some messages go through any number of intermediaries. Some of the intermediaries may also send a response back to the original sender. Therefore, the model must allow this type of communication to occur.

Message Correlation

A single message may not always be able to fully encapsulate everything necessary for an application process. Therefore, the model must be able to correlate multiple messages.

Guaranteed Message Exchange

Both parties, the sender and the receiver, want certain message guarantees when a message is sent or received. The sender wants a guarantee or notification that the message was received. The receiver wants to ensure that a message is received only once and that there aren't duplicate messages from the sender.

Digital Signature

Senders must be able to digitally sign the messages that they send so that the recipients have a guarantee that the message is from the anticipated sender and that the message sent has not been altered in transport.

Encryption

The model requires method to encrypt either part of the message or the entire message independent of the protocol. The specification cannot be tied to any particular form of encryption.

Transactions and Activities

SOAP messages require some sort of transactioning capabilities. They must support long-running transactions.

Service Description

A service description specification that fully details the interface of the Web Service can inform the consumer about the consumption including the types of protocols used and the types and parameters required for interaction.

Process Flow Contract Description

A Process Flow Contract Description enhances the service description to show the consumer the sequence that occurs as the messages work through the process. The message that can terminate the entire flow process is also included.

Inspection

Consumers require a way to inspect a known destination for Web service endpoints. They need service descriptions as well as process flow contracts.

Discovery

Discovery means the capability to find specific Web Services and their contracts based upon characteristics of the services themselves.

Since this paper was released, IBM and Microsoft have been working together, releasing a number of different specifications that address these core functions that they discussed in this document. For instance, the functionality of Discovery has been worked out with the UDDI specification created by Microsoft, IBM and others.

In the end, this long list of functionality can be lumped into three distinct categories — those that deal with the wire, those that deal with description, and those that deal with discovery.

The *wire* specifications include the following functionalities named in the paper:

- Message envelope and controlled extensibility
- Message Exchange aka Routing
- Guaranteed Message Exchange
- Transactions and Activities
- Digital Signature
- Encryption

The *description* specifications needed include:

- Service Description
- Process Flow Contract Description

The *discovery* specifications include:

- Inspection
- Discovery

In the end, this paper submitted by these two major vendors was the roadmap they have worked with since then. You, an IT professional who deals with Web Services, can be assured that the functionality described here will be included in the specifications from all major vendors and their partners. It can provide enterprise clients with the advanced functionality they require in their real-world Web Services.

WS-I.org

In order to achieve truly interoperable Web Services from all the IT vendors, a new organization addresses interoperability-related issues in connection with the WS-* specifications. The Web Services Interoperability group, WS-I.org (quite conveniently found at `ws-i.org`), is a group made up of major vendors including Microsoft, IBM, BEA, and a number of global, corporate customers including Rational, NEC, Borland, Hewlett-Packard, and others. (See Figure 21-1.)

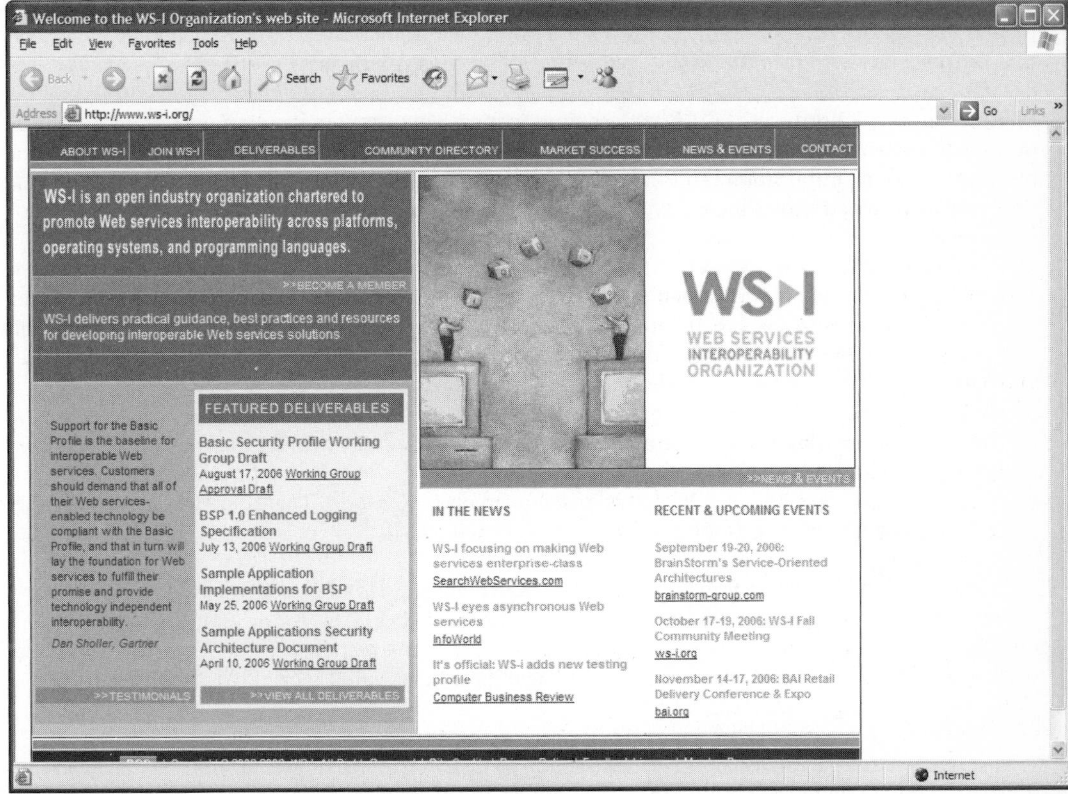

Figure 21-1

This group's mission is to test and address interoperability of the advanced Web service specifications between the different vendors' platforms. They do this by providing the best means of testing this interoperability as well as offering thoughtful leadership and guidance on interoperability.

Extending XML Web Services

If you use these specifications or new ones that may come out in the future, you must apply the structures that are laid out in them. How do you do this? To understand how you can change your SOAP messages so that they start working with these specifications, examine how you can extend SOAP.

SOAP Basics

As stated in the previous two chapters, Simple Object Access Protocol is an XML-based technology. It is used as a common message format in the transmission of messages from a Web service to any end point that is able to consume and understand these SOAP messages. This functionality is an important pillar in the Web services model.

SOAP is not the only means of communication available for a Web service in this multiplatform world. In fact, Web services on non-.NET platforms use other means, including XML-RPC and ebXML, to structure the messages sent from the Web services that sit on those platforms.

Many vendors' platforms use SOAP as the common message format in the exchange of information packets from one point to another. SOAP is a lightweight XML format that is platform-neutral. If your platform or calling application can consume XML over HTTP, you can work with the SOAP packets that are sent and received across the wire. That's the miracle of SOAP.

You can build or consume Web services on the .NET platform without understanding the structure of SOAP or even knowing that it is used as the communication protocol. Still, it is a good idea to understand exactly what SOAP is. It helps to understanding the structure of the SOAP packets that are sent across the wire if you wish to extend them in order to enhance the performance of your Web services.

SOAP 1.1, the main SOAP version used today, was developed in March of 2000 and was accepted as a note by the W3C on May 8, 2000. The companies that worked on the development of SOAP include Microsoft, DevelopMentor, IBM, Lotus, and UserLand Software. SOAP is not a proprietary technology, run or controlled by Microsoft or IBM. It is, instead, an open standard. Therefore, you can use SOAP on almost any platform as long as the platform can work with XML.

The SOAP message was meant to be simple. The SOAP message is what is sent over the wire using HTTP, with or without the HTTP Extension Framework (HTTP-EF). SOAP messages are meant to be one-way. Nothing is built into these messages that warrants any response. SOAP does not contain any built-in functions or methods that cause specific events to be initiated. The SOAP message is XML, and XML is simply a way of marking up data.

Web services require a request and response action to take place. SOAP gets around this problem by sending the SOAP message within the HTTP request and response messages.

The typical SOAP message consists of a SOAP Envelope, Header, and Body section. The SOAP Envelope is a mandatory element that is the root element of the entire package. Within the SOAP Envelope element is an optional Header element and a mandatory Body element. Figure 21-2 shows the structure of a SOAP message.

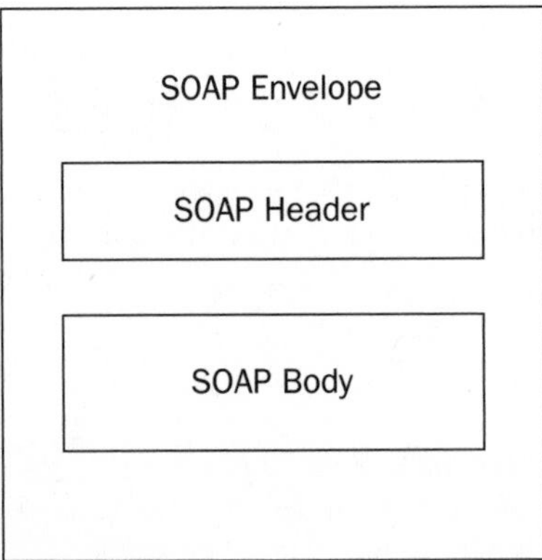

Figure 21-2

Because this entire message is an XML document, it has a single root element (the SOAP Envelope element), just like any typical XML document.

SOAP Headers

The SOAP header element is an optional element used to provide information related to what is contained within the SOAP Body element. The convenient thing about the SOAP header is that you are not required to inform the end user beforehand about the information you place there. Basically, the SOAP header is used to transmit supporting information about the payload that is contained within the SOAP Body.

The SOAP specification doesn't make any rules about what the SOAP header must contain, and this lack of restriction makes the SOAP header a powerful tool. Basically the SOAP header is a container that is sent along with the SOAP body and therefore, you can place any type of information within it.

The SOAP header is where you usually place the WS-* specifications within the SOAP document. How exactly do the various vendors interject these specifications within the SOAP message? The next section takes a look at how Microsoft builds upon a SOAP message to include these advanced specifications.

SOAP Extensions

If you are using a Microsoft-based Web service, SOAP Extensions can intercept and work with a SOAP message before it is sent past certain points.

In .NET, there are specific points in the short life of a SOAP message that is being sent and received when you are able to jump in and interact with it. The following diagram (Figure 21-3) shows you where, in the process of sending a SOAP message, you can work with it.

Serialization is the process whereby an object is converted into a format that enables it to be readily transported. In this case, the format is XML. When you serialize an object within ASP.NET in the context of XML Web services, it is formatted into XML and then sent via a SOAP packet. In the SOAP packet, the XML payload can be *deserialized*. The process of deserialization, as you would expect, is the conversion of an XML payload back into the object that was originally sent.

ASP.NET provides these means of interacting with the SOAP message process before or after serialization and deserialization so that you can inspect or modify the SOAP message. The capability to inspect the SOAP message throughout its journey gives you quite a bit of power. On either the client or server, you can manipulate SOAP messages to perform specific actions based upon items found in the SOAP payload. These points of interaction include `BeforeSerialize`, `AfterSerialize`, `BeforeDeserialize`, and `AfterDeserialize`.

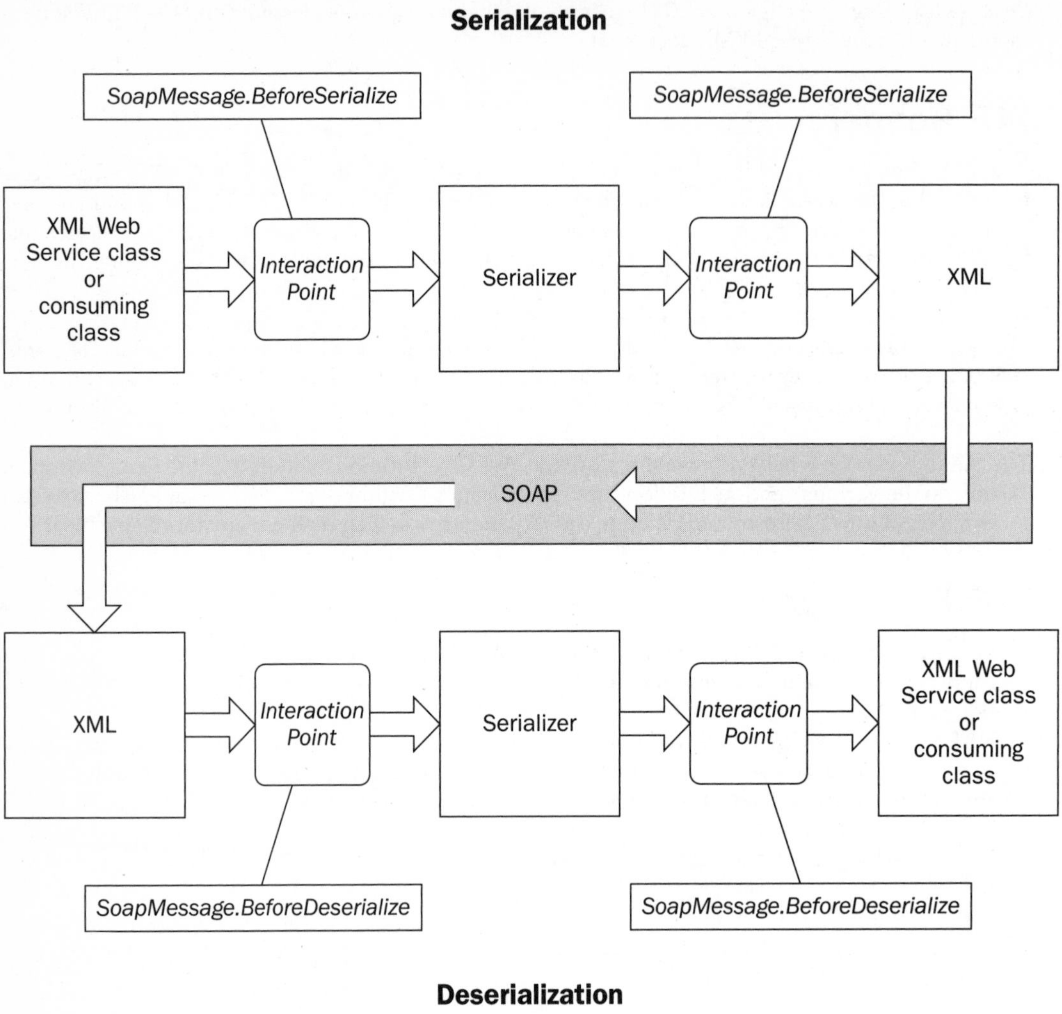

Serialization

SoapMessage.BeforeSerialize | SoapMessage.BeforeSerialize

XML Web Service class or consuming class → Interaction Point → Serializer → Interaction Point → XML

SOAP

XML → Interaction Point → Serializer → Interaction Point → XML Web Service class or consuming class

SoapMessage.BeforeDeserialize | SoapMessage.BeforeDeserialize

Deserialization

Figure 21-3

WS-* Specifications

A tremendous amount of WS-* specifications exist. Really all it takes to create one is for some individuals or organizations to get together and declare one to the world in some fashion. A number of non-profit organizations work on specifications and release them to the public. Some of these organizations include the aforementioned WS-I.org, as well as OASIS (`oasis-open.org`), and the W3C (`w3c.org`).

The following is a review of some of the more notable specifications.

WS-Security

When Web Services were initially introduced, they were not massively adopted. They lacked the security model most companies required before they could begin building technologies within the enterprise.

The specification WS-Security was developed by Microsoft, IBM, and VeriSign. It works on three main areas to make Web Services secure — credential exchange, message integrity, and message confidentiality.

Credential Exchange

WS-Security enables two entities to exchange their security credentials within the message itself. WS-Security doesn't mention the type of credentials needed for an exchange; therefore, it allows any type of credentials to be used.

Message Integrity

Messages can be sent through multiple routers and, in effect, bounce from here to there before they reach their final destination. You must ensure that the messages are not tampered with in transport. As messages move from one SOAP router to another, malicious people can make can make additions or subtractions in the SOAP nodes, thereby destroying the integrity of the message. As SOAP routers become more prevalent, using WS-Security to check for message tampering will increase in popularity.

Message Confidentiality

Encryption is one of the more important functions to apply to your SOAP messages. When your messages are zipping across the virtual world they can be intercepted and opened for viewing by parties who shouldn't be looking at their contents.

For this reason, it is beneficial to somehow scramble the contents of a message. When it reaches the intended receiver, he can use your encryption key and descramble the message to read the contents.

WS-Addressing

The Web Service Addressing protocol is a SOAP-based protocol that is used to route SOAP packets from one point to another over HTTP, TCP, or some other transport protocols. It is especially designed to route the SOAP packet through several points before it reaches its final destination.

To accomplish this, the path for the SOAP message is specified in the SOAP header along with the SOAP message. Therefore, when a SOAP message is sent, the message path is also connected to this message.

For example, you want to get a message from point A to point D, but in order to do this, you must route the SOAP message through points B and C along the way.

Figure 21-4 shows how this might look visually.

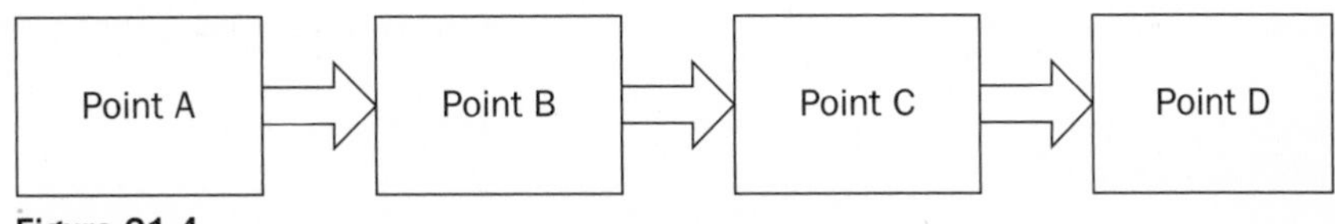

Figure 21-4

In Figure 21-4, point A is the initial SOAP sender. This is where you place the WS-Addressing information into the SOAP header. Points B and C are the routing points, known as either the SOAP nodes or SOAP routers. When they receive a SOAP message with a WS-Addressing specification about the final destination, these two points forward this message onto the next point. Point D is the ultimate receiver of the SOAP message that is specified in the SOAP header.

Contained within the SOAP header itself is a forward message path, an optional reverse path, and the points through which the message must be routed. The entire message path can be described directly in the SOAP header, so there's no need to include it elsewhere. These paths can be created dynamically at runtime as well.

WS-Attachments

WS-Attachments is a specification that was developed by Microsoft and IBM to ease the difficulty of adding attachments to SOAP messages. This specification was published in June of 2002. SOAP is a great way of representing data as XML, but it can be difficult to include images and documents within this structure.

You can do so today with Web services, but you use significant overhead to serialize an image into an acceptable XML form such as `base64` using DIME. The receiver also bears a tremendous cost in processor power when he attempts to deserialize the message on the other end.

In addition to this problem, it is difficult to represent other XML documents in the payload of the SOAP messages, especially if these XML documents or XML fragments don't conform to the encoding type used in the SOAP message itself.

For these problems, WS-Attachments was created and can be used to keep other objects such as images, documents, and XML fragments from being serialized into the body of the SOAP message. This substantially increases performance for these types of payloads.

WS-Coordination

As companies start developing a multitude of Web services within their enterprise, they realized that many Web services have relationships with one another. WS-Coordination has been developed to describe the relationships of Web services with one another.

WS-Coordination is meant to be expanded by other specifications that further define specific coordination types. For instance, WS-AtomicTransaction works with WS-Coordination to create a coordination type that deals with the transactioning of Web services.

WS-MetadataExchange

WS-MetadataExchange enables you to define what services can be found at a particular site by making pointer references to the documents of a Web service that define the Web service's interface.

Core Specifications

The WS-* list goes on and on. The following table looks at some of the present specifications in light detail (shown in alphabetical order).

WS-* Specification	Description
WS-Acknowledgement	Ensures reliable messaging by enabling the receiver to send a "receipt" for the message. Similar to the WS-ReliableMessaging specification.
WS-ActiveProfile	Provides the means to apply a federated identity to the active requestor. This works in conjunction with the WS-Federation specification.
WS-Addressing	Provides the means to apply message-based routing. This specification is considered a replacement to the WS-Routing and WS-Referral specifications. A similar specification to WS-Addressing is the WS-Callback specification.
WS-Attachments	Provides the means of applying one or more binary objects to your message using DIME. Using DIME is now considered obsolete by most vendors because MTOM is the preferred way to move binary objects.
WS-AtomicTransaction	Provides the means to apply atomic transactions to your messaging. Atomic transactions are "all or nothing" transaction types. This specification works with the WS-Coordination specification and is meant to be a replacement to the WS-Transaction specification.
WS-Authorization	Provides the means for a Web service vendor to describe how their Web services manage authorization data and policies.
WS-BaseFaults	Provides a way to define an XML Schema type for base faults. Allows for commonality in how SOAP faults are represented.
WS-BaseNotification	Provides a means to allow for a publish/subscribe mechanism for messaging. WS-BaseNotification works as part of the WS-Notification family which many subspecifications depend upon.
WS-BPEL	Formally known as BPEL4WS (Business Process Execution Language for Web Services), this specification provides the mechanics to apply workflow to messaging. This specification is considered a replacement for XLANG and WSFL.
WS-BrokeredNotification	Provides a publish/subscribe mechanism for messaging. WS-BrokeredNotification works as part of the WS-Notification family.
WS-BusinessActivity	Provides the means (along with WS-AtomicTransaction) to provide transactions to your messaging. WS-BusinessActivity types of transactions are meant to be longer-lived transactions and can perform other actions based upon any possible failure points.

Table continued on following page

WS-* Specification	Description
WS-CAF	Also known as the Web Services Composite Application Framework, this specification is really a collection of three specifications: Web Service Context (WS-CTX), Web Service Coordination Framework (WS-CF), and Web Service Transaction Management (WS-TXM). The purpose of WS-CAF is to help in the sharing of information and the transactioning of messages for composite applications.
WS-Callback	Provides the means to dynamically specify where to send asynchronous responses after receiving a request. A similar specification is the WS-Addressing specification.
WS-CF	Known as the Web Service Coordination Framework, this specification provides the means to specify a software agent to handle context management. This specification is part of the WS-CAF set of specifications.
WS-Coordination	Provides a means to apply transactions to your services. This specification works with WS-AtomicTransaction and WS-BusinessActivity to specify the transactioning functionality.
WS-Choreography	Provides the means to work within a peer-to-peer environment with any number of participants.
WS-CTX	Known as the Web Service Context, this specification provides the means the means of managing, sharing, and accessing context information between Web services. This specification is part of the WS-CAF set of specifications.
DIME	Known as Direct Internet Message Encapsulation, DIME provides the means to encapsulate binary data into a series of records. This allows for these types of objects to be delivered in a more performant manner than otherwise. DIME is now considered obsolete now by many vendors because MTOM is more capable.
WS-Discovery	Provides the means to discover services through a multicast discovery protocol. Any service that wishes to be discovered simply sends an announcement when the service wishes to either join or leave a discovery pool.
WSDM	Known as Web Services Distributed Management, this specification allows for the provision of management information via standards.
WS-EndpointResolution	Enables you to select endpoints from a group of available endpoints. This specification is meant to work with server farms or mobile devices.
WS-Enumeration	Provides the means of enumerating a sequence of XML elements meant for traversing logs, message queues, or other linear information models.

WS-* Specification	Description
WS-Eventing	Provides the capability to subscribe or accept subscriptions from event notification messages. This specification competes with the WS-Events specification.
WS-Events	Provides the means to publish/subscribe to events via services. This specification competes with the WS-Eventing specification.
WS-Federation	Provides a means to manage and broker the trust relationships between entities via messaging.
WSFL	Known as the Web Services Flow Language, this specification provides the means to apply workflow to services through either a usage pattern or interaction pattern. WS-BPEL is the replacement for WSFL.
WS-Inspection	Provides the means to inspect a site for a list of available services. This specification is replaced by the WS-MetadataExchange specification.
WS-Manageability	Provides all the administration tasks available from a service as services themselves. This specification is replaced by WS-Management.
WS-Management	Provides the means to manage services using messaging and events. This specification is a replacement of the WS-Manageability specification.
WS-MessageData	Provides the capability to incorporate a specific message meta-data header.
WS-MessageDelivery	Provides the capability to build transport-agnostic services that provide their endpoints in the messages themselves. This specification is a competing specification to WS-Addressing.
WS-MetadataExchange	Provides the means to retrieve policies and an interface definition document. This specification is replacement to WS-Inspection.
MTOM	Known as Message Transmission Optimization Mechanism, MTOM provides the means to encapsulate binary data using XML-binary Optimized Packaging (XOP). MTOM is considered the recommended way to encapsulate binary objects rather than the MIME or DIME specifications.
WS-Notification	Allows for a publish/subscribe mechanism for messaging. WS-BaseNotification, WS-BrokeredNotification, and WS-Topics are part of the WS-Notification family of specifications.
WS-PassiveProfile	Provides the means for passive requestors (such as Web browsers) to supply identity using WS-Federation. When using this specification, the end-user is limited to the HTTP protocol.
WS-Policy	Provides the means to define a service's requirements, preferences, and capabilities.

Table continued on following page

WS-* Specification	Description
WS-PolicyAssertions	Provides the means to apply a set of common message policy assertions that can be specified within a policy. This specification works in conjunction with the WS-Policy specification.
WS-PolicyAttachment	Provides the means to reference policies from WSDL documents, associate policies with deployed Web services, as well as UDDI entities.
WS-Privacy	Provides the means for organizations to supply their privacy statements.
WS-Provisioning	Provides the means to facilitate interoperability between provisioning systems.
WS-Referral	Provides the means to define routing behaviors of messages received. This specification is generally used in conjunction with WS-Routing and is replaced by the WS-Addressing specification.
WS-Reliability	Provides the means to supply guaranteed message delivery and order. This specification competes with the WS-ReliableMessaging specification.
WS-ReliableMessaging	Provides the means to supply guaranteed message delivery with regard to software components, system, or network failures. This specification completes with the WS-Reliability specification.
WS-ResourceFramework	Also known as WSRF, this is really a definition for a family of specifications such as WS-ResourceProperties, WS-ResourceLifetime, WS-BaseFaults, and WS-ServiceGroup. Each of these specifications is provided to allow for the access of stateful services.
WS-ResourceLifetime	Provides the timeframe in which services can destroy their acquired state. The possible options include immediate or scheduled.
WS-ResourceProperties	Provides the capability to query or change a stateful resource.
WS-Routing	Provides the capability to route messages through any number of intermediaries. This specification is usually used in conjunction with WS-Referral. This specification is considered obsolete by many vendors and has been replaced by WS-Addressing or WS-MessageDelivery.
WS-SecureConversation	Provides the means to manage and authenticate message exchanges between parties using security context exchanges or session keys.
WS-Security	Provides the means to apply credentials to messages in order to make the message transport-agnostic.
WS-SecurityPolicy	Provides the capability for Web service vendors to supply their security policies via the WS-Security specification.
WS-ServiceGroup	Provides the capability to group stateful resources that might be applied to a domain-specific purpose.

WS-* Specification	Description
WS-Topics	Provides the means to allow for the grouping of topics that are used in the publish/subscribe mechanism for messaging. This specification is used in the WS-Notification family of specifications.
WS-Transaction	Provides the means to supply coordination types when used in conjunction with the WS-Coordination specification. This specification is considered obsolete and is replaced by the WS-AtomicTransaction and WS-BusinessActivity specifications.
WS-TransmissionControl	Provides the means to ensure message reliability.
WS-Trust	Provides the means for entities to exchange tokens.
WS-TXM	Known as Web Services Transaction Management, this specification allows for transaction protocols to be applied to a coordination framework. This specification is part of the WS-CAF set of specifications.

In this long table, you see plenty of specifications. Many companies put out specifications to augment their messaging frameworks even though the functionality is already provided via other specifications. Many vendors try to achieve their goals within a specification that is in competition with other specifications.

Vendors spend so much of their time creating specifications because they want interoperability within their product frameworks. A globally accepted specification allows this to happen. Most of the specifications defined in the preceding table are not actually implemented in any of the vendors' technologies. Only a small handful have been actually implemented and made workable across two vendors' platforms.

The rest of this chapter covers some specific technologies that implement these specifications. First, you investigate Microsoft's Web Services Enhancements 3.0.

Looking at Microsoft's Web Services Enhancements 3.0

Microsoft and the other vendors are not in the business of creating specifications; they're in the business of making software. When the specifications for advanced features in Web services were developed, Microsoft had to implement them within its Web services model. It wanted to allow .NET Web service developers to start building Web services immediately using these features. The capabilities of Web services are defined and established within the .NET Framework. The .NET Framework can't keep up with the new specifications that are being pumped out by Microsoft, IBM, and others. The new versions of the .NET Framework are planned to be years apart — not months — and users want these specifications now.

Therefore, Microsoft has decided to release the capabilities to work with Web Services Enhancements for Microsoft .NET (WSE) sooner than the release of the next version of the .NET Framework.

The first version the WSE was released as a beta in the summer of 2002 and, although not a full implementation of all the available WS-* specifications, it included a number of classes that allow you to build advanced Web Services using selected specifications from the various specs out at the time. Since then, two other releases of WSE have come from Microsoft. The following details what is in each of the WSE releases.

The WSE 1.0 Contents

The first release of the WSE was not a full implementation of all the advanced Web service specifications available, but instead represented a smaller subset of specifications from the advanced Web service protocols. This WSE version one includes some of the more important specifications that many customers will consider number-one priorities. This first version of WSE included the capabilities for working with:

- WS-Security
- WS-Routing
- WS-Referral
- WS-Attachments (using DIME)

The WSE 2.0 Contents

WSE 2.0 release in 2003 offered the following WS-* specification implementations as well as the following functionality:

- WS-Security 1.0 full implementation
- WS-Trust
- WS-SecureConversation
- A new adapter for Microsoft's BizTalk

The WSE 3.0 Contents

The WSE 3.0 is the most recent WSE release and further extends the previous two releases. The WSE 3.0 release includes the following specification releases as new functionalities:

- WS-Security 1.1
- Updated WS-Trust and WS-SecureConversation sections
- MTOM support
- 64-bit support
- A new adapter for Microsoft's BizTalk 2006

Functionality Provided by the WSE

As you can see, some important specifications are provided via WSE. The WS-Security implementation is by far the largest and most exciting aspect of the WSE. It is also the most asked-for implementation among all the advanced Web service specifications. WSE allows you to use this implementation to provide credentials with your Web services. You can send in usernames and passwords in the SOAP header of the SOAP messages that are sent onto the Web service provider. The passwords that in the SOAP messages are encrypted, thereby providing a higher level of security. An additional feature, a companion to the capability to provide credentials for verification with your SOAP messages, is the capability to use X.509 certificates in addition to usernames and passwords.

In addition to being able to provide credentials with your SOAP messages, you can digitally sign your SOAP messages. This is done to assure the receiver of a digitally signed SOAP message that the message was not altered in transport by some known or unknown entity.

The last thing provided with the WS-Security implementation is the capability to encrypt and decrypt SOAP messages. This is an important feature when you start dealing with SOAP routing Your SOAP messages go beyond point-to-point services and hop off paths that are protected by SSL.

WS-SecureConversation and WS-Trust provide the means to manage and authenticate message exchanges between parties using security context exchanges or session keys.

The WSE 3.0 implementation works with MTOM and enables you to send items, such as images, that are expensive to serialize into XML for SOAP message transport. The initial WSE 1.0 version provided a WS-Attachments implementation that works with DIME.

These capabilities as a whole have been collected and are available as the final version of WSE. You can use them to build the advanced Web services scenarios required for working with Web services in the enterprise.

How the WSE Works

The WSE is a powerful collection of classes that allow you to work with the advanced Web service specifications. It does this by intercepting all SOAP requests and SOAP responses and running these requests through various WSE filters.

Your XML Web service can receive SOAP messages (incoming requests) through a WSE input filter. Any SOAP messages that are sent from the XML Web service (outgoing requests) are sent through a WSE output filter.

On the client-side of things, the client application that is working with an XML Web service sends out all SOAP messages to the XML Web service through a WSE output filter. Then all SOAP responses that come from the XML Web service are intercepted and run through a WSE input filter. This entire process is shown in Figure 21-5.

The XML Web service automatically uses these input and output filters from the WSE because of certain settings in the `Web.config` file. The client application automatically uses the WSE's filters when you make changes to the proxy class. In the end, it is these filters that give you the powerful capability to build advanced WS-* specifications into your SOAP messages whether you are working on the client-side, the server-side or both.

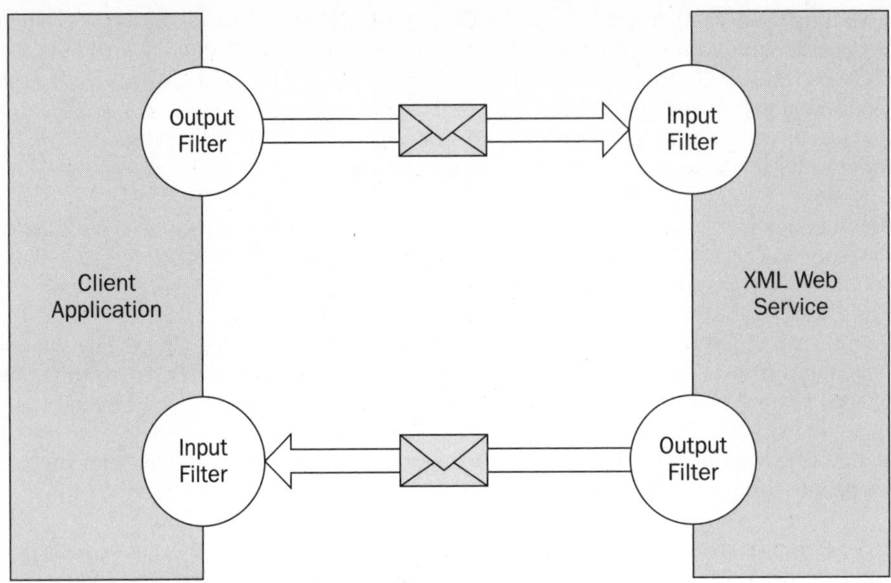

Figure 21-5

So what are these filters doing for you? The output filters take the SOAP messages and, in most cases, apply element constructions to the SOAP header of the SOAP message. In some cases, they also work with the SOAP body of the SOAP message to apply encryption. The input filters are doing the reverse. They take incoming SOAP messages and analyze the SOAP headers and any decode any encrypted SOAP bodies to automatically make sense of their construction.

Building a WSE 3.0 Example — The Server

As an example of using WSE 3.0, you now build a server and a client that utilize some of the features provided via this framework. In this example, you build a Web service (the server-side application) which will provide a simple `Add()` method. This `Add()` method, however, requires a username and password combination that must be packaged in the SOAP header in the WS-Security format.

The WSE provides you with an implementation of WS-Security that you can use in the construction of your Web service for consumers and providers. WS-Security provides you with a number of different security implementations including credential exchange, encryption, and digital signing. This chapter focuses on the first aspect of WS-Security mentioned here — credential exchange.

WSE's WS-Security implementation enables both the consumer and the provider of the Web Service to get credentials verified from a source that is trusted by both parties. The request for the credential verification and the token that is generated from the request are placed directly in the SOAP message itself, in most cases in the SOAP header. Wherever the message is sent, the sender is assured that the security credentials and the related authorization token are always with the message, even if it is transported through any number of intermediaries. You will see this later in the book when working with the routing and referral of SOAP messages.

One of the great things about the WSE implementation of WS-Security is that not only can you work with username and password combinations to provide authentication and authorization to your XML Web services, but you can use with other security credential mechanisms such as using X.509 certificates along with your SOAP messages.

Just as in the previous chapter you created your own class to apply usernames and passwords to the SOAP header of the SOAP message, you now work with the classes of the WSE that apply your usernames and passwords to the SOAP header. The difference is that the WSE classes do this in a manner that conforms to the specifications for credential exchange laid out in WS-Security. The structure that is applied to the SOAP header for credential representation is, therefore, consistent and understandable when passed to other vendor's platforms, such as IBM's WebSphere.

The WSE provides us with a class, the `UsernameTokenManager` class, for working with credential exchanges that involve usernames and passwords. In order to work with the `UsernameTokenManager` class, you use credential verifier source that can inherit from this class. After this class is in place, you configure the `Web.config` file that is contained within the Web service's application root to work with this particular class. You can then program the Web service to work with this new class.

Creating a Class That Verifies Credentials

For authorizing access to the XML Web service, you need a source that can obtain username and password combinations from some type of data store. The class that you create must be able to perform necessary validation on the usernames and passwords coming in with the SOAP messages. In this simple example, our password validation process ensures only that the password is exactly the same as the username in the message.

Your first step is to create a Web service project within Visual Studio 2005 using C#. Within the project, right-click the project's name and choose Add ASP.NET Folder ⇨ App_Code. After you have the App_Code folder in place, right-click the project again and select Add New Item. You are adding a class to the Web Service project. Name the file `myPasswordProvider.cs`.

In order to start applying WSE techniques to this class and to the Web service that you are going to build in a bit, you make a reference to the WSE class within your project. To do this, right-click the project again and this time select Add Reference.

The Add Reference dialog opens on the .NET tab by default. From this section of the dialog, you make reference to the `Microsoft.Web.Services3.dll` (shown here in Figure 21-6). If you don't see this DLL, you haven't installed WSE 3.0. This requires a separate download from the .NET Framework 2.0 download.

To make reference to this assembly, highlight this DLL and click the OK button in the Add Reference dialog. Notice the reference to the assembly in the `Web.config` file.

```
<assemblies>
   <add assembly="Microsoft.Web.Services3, Version=3.0.0.0, Culture=neutral,
    PublicKeyToken=31BF3856AD364E35" />
</assemblies>
```

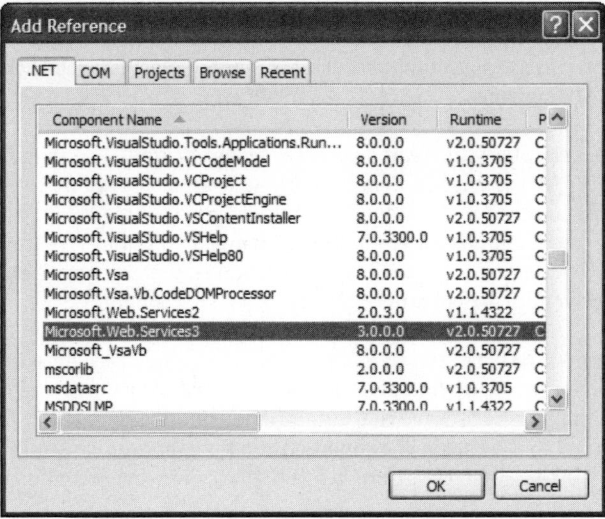

Figure 21-6

Now you can start building the `myPasswordProvider` class. This class inherits from `UsernameToken Manager`. The purpose of this class is to validate the username and password combinations. To accomplish this, you override the `AuthenticateToken()` method provided via `UsernameTokenManager` and obtain the correct password from the username. In this example, the `AuthenticateToken()` method simply returns the `Username` property in string form as the password, meaning that the username and the password are required to be the same for the credential set to be considered valid. Listing 21-1 shows the code required for the `myPasswordProvider.cs` file.

Listing 21-1: The myPasswordProvider.cs file

```
using Microsoft.Web.Services3.Security.Tokens;

namespace WSExample
{
    /// <summary>
    /// Validates the username and password found in a SOAP message
    /// </summary>
    public class myPasswordProvider : UsernameTokenManager
    {
        protected override string AuthenticateToken(UsernameToken token)
        {
            string password = token.Username;

            return password;
        }
    }
}
```

Looking this class over, you can see that the `myPasswordProvider` class inherits from `UsernameToken Manger` and overrides the `AuthenticateToken()` method, which in this case simply returns the `Username` property as the password required from the consumer. Next, you review how to configure the application to use WSE 3.0 and to apply the rest of the required settings.

Configuring the Application To Use the WSE 3.0

Now that you have your `myPasswordProvider` class in place, you have to make reference to the WSE from within the `Web.config` file. To do all the wiring required to get the WSE framework up and running in your application, you apply a lot of different configuration settings in both the `Web.config` and any policy files that you are using. You can easily just go through these XML files yourself and apply all the configurations, but you can also use the WSE Settings 3.0 Tool.

The WSE Settings 3.0 Tool installs itself within Visual Studio along with the rest of the WSE 3.0 framework, so you have to use Visual Studio if you want to utilize the Settings Tool.

The Settings Tool makes it quite easy to configure your Web service to get you up and running rather quickly. To configure your Web service to work with the WSE by using the Settings Tool, right-click the project name within Solution Explorer and select WSE Settings 3.0. Clicking WSE Settings 3.0 pulls up the Settings Tool dialog. This dialog includes a number of tabs including General, Security, Routing, Policy, TokenIssuing, Diagnostics, and Messaging, as shown in Figure 21-7.

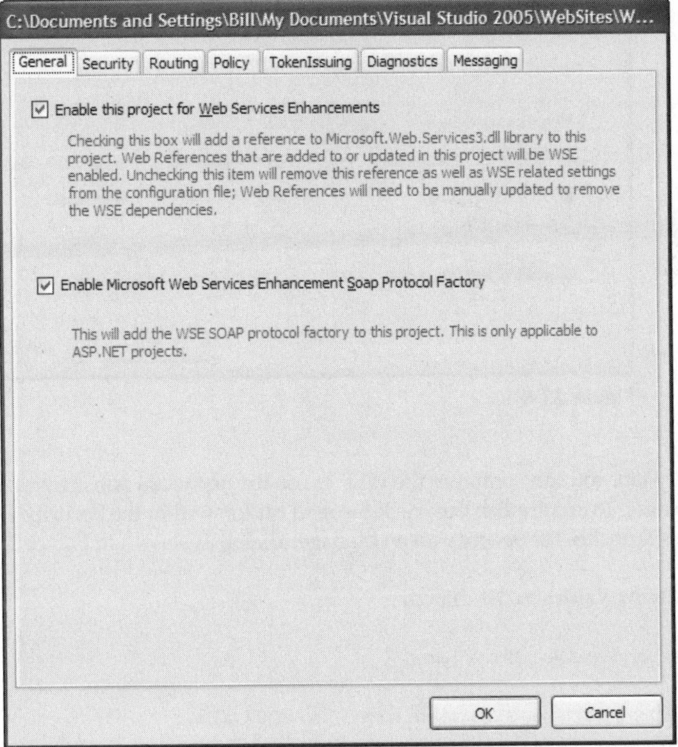

Figure 21-7

To get started building a Web service to work with the WSE, you click the first check box of the General tab. This check box enables the project to work with the WSE. It does this by automatically making a reference to the `Microsoft.Web.Services3` DLL in your project. Because you are working with an ASP.NET Web Service project, also click the second check box.

The Security tab (shown in Figure 21-8) allows you to make changes to the `Web.config` file through the GUI that handles the WSE's security implementation. From this page, you can specify your token managers as well as details on any certificates.

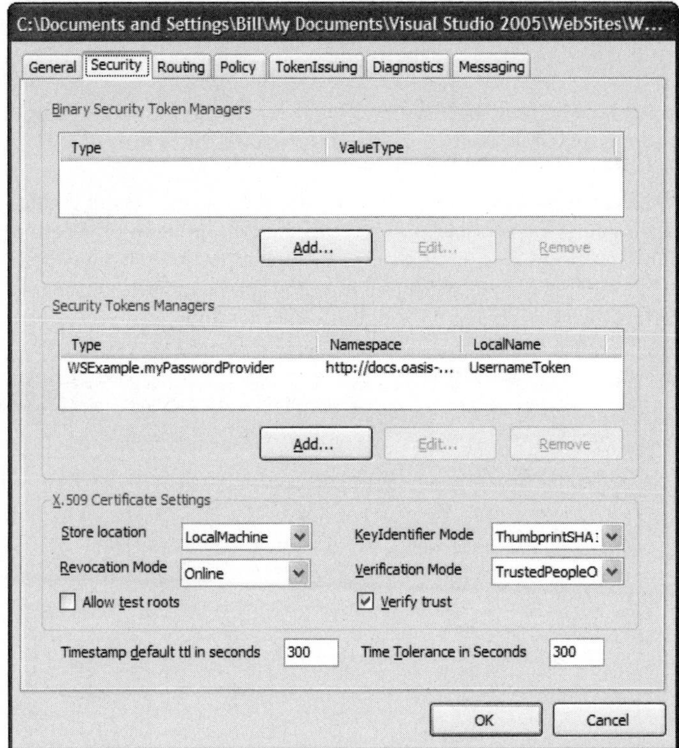

Figure 21-8

Using the Security tab, you can configure the WSE to use the new class you created, `myPasswordProvider`, as the token manager. To accomplish this, click the Add button within the Security Token Managers section of the dialog. This launches the SecurityToken Manager dialog as shown in Figure 21-9.

Provide the following values to the dialog.

Type: `WSExample.myPasswordProvider`

```
Namespace: http://docs.oasis-open.org/wss/2004/01/
   oasis-200401-wss-wssecurity-secext-1.0.xsd
```

LocalName: `UsernameToken`

Click OK in the SecurityToken Manager dialog and open the Policy tab. This tab can establish a policy for using a specific username. It is presented in Figure 21-10.

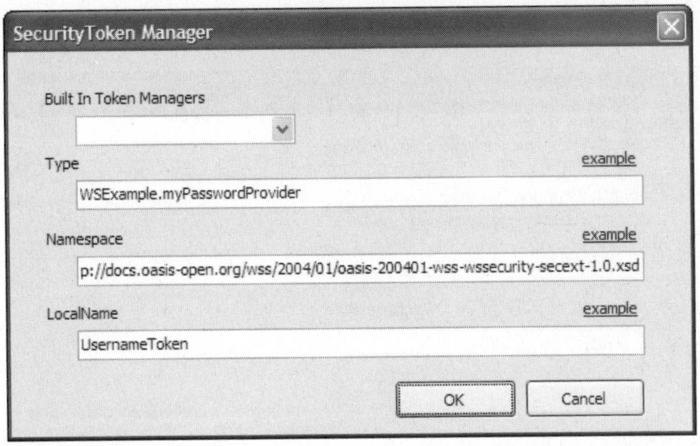

Figure 21-9

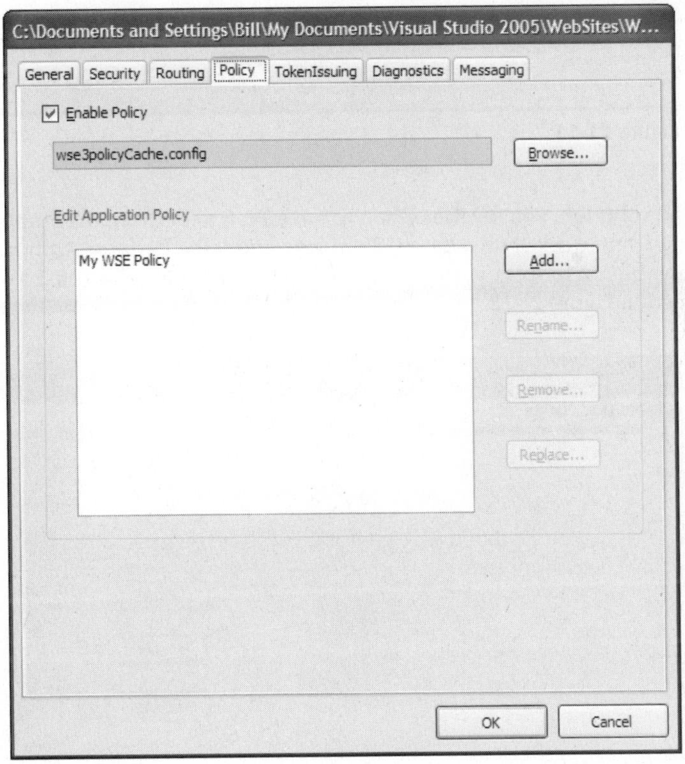

Figure 21-10

To set a policy, check the Enable Policy check box and select the Add button to add a new policy. The first step in the dialog is to establish whether you want to secure a service or a client. In this case, you are interested in securing a service through the use of a username setting. Your dialog should be similar to the one presented in Figure 21-11.

WSE Security Settings Wizard
Authentication Settings
Choose application type and authentication method
Do you want to secure a service or a client?
Secure a service application
Secure a client application
Choose Client Authentication Method
Anonymous
Username
Certificate
Windows
The client provides a username and password as credentials in the request which the service authenticates. The service ensures that the client has secured the request with the server's public certificate. The response message is secured with a symmetric key that was supplied by the client
< Back
Next >
Cancel

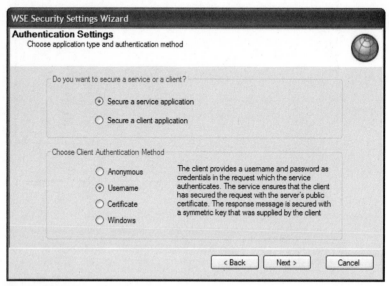

Figure 21-11

If you click the Next button, you see the option to have WSE to perform the authorization process. For this example, you want to select this option. Therefore, check the Perform Authorization check box and click the Add User button to specify a specific user. In this case, I have selected `BEvjen` as the user. This dialog is presented in Figure 21-12.

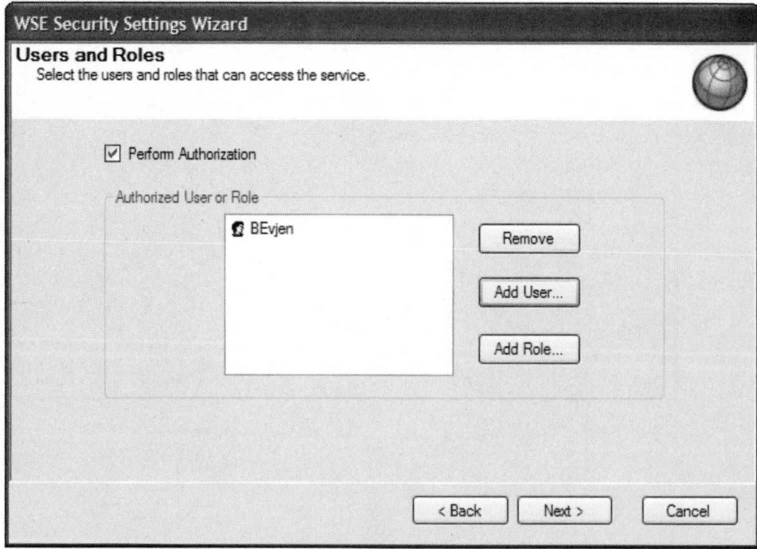

Figure 21-12

The next page in the dialog allows you to set the message-protection level. In this case, you can simply leave the default settings which allow for WS-Security 1.1 Extensions. You could also require the credentials to be signed and encrypted and used with an X.509 certificate, but for this example simply select None (rely on transport protection). This dialog is presented in Figure 21-13.

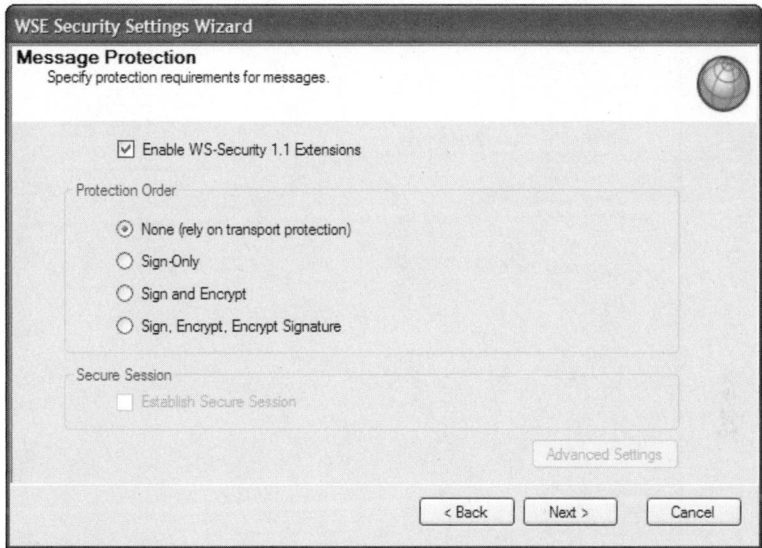

Figure 21-13

If you are working with an X.509 certificate, the last page in the dialog allows you to determine details about the X.509 certificate. You can check the check box that signifies the certificate will be signed within the code.

After these pages in the dialog, you are finally offered a summary page that details everything to be applied. All these setting are actually applied in the set `wse3policyCache.config` file.

Configuring Diagnostics

The service is now configured for the WSE, but as the final step in the configuration process, go to the Diagnostics tab and select the check box to enable this feature. This means that all the SOAP messages that are sent to and from the client are recorded to an XML file. This is quite handy when analyzing your Web services. This page in the dialog is presented in Figure 21-14.

Don't leave the tracing feature on with production Web services. Performance is greatly hindered when this capability is enabled.

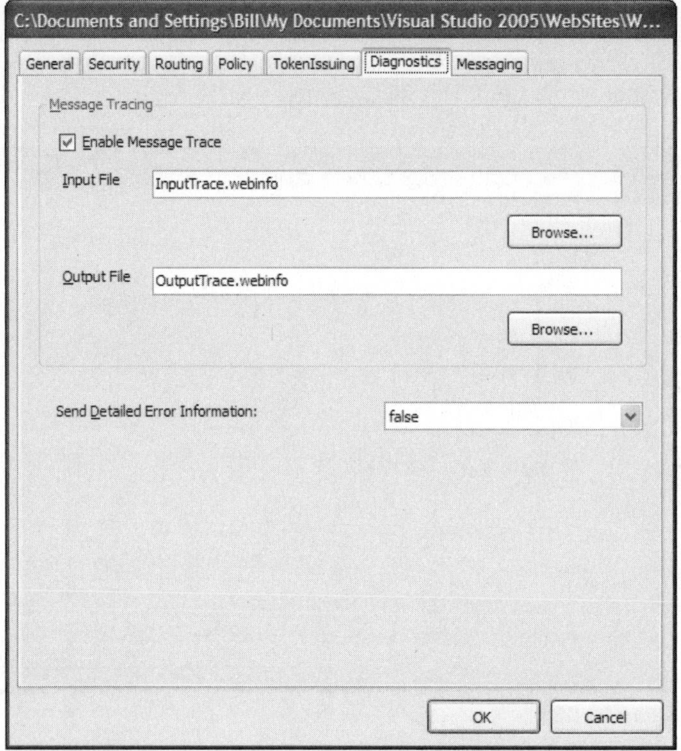

Figure 21-14

The Result of the WSE Settings 3.0 Tool Configuration

After you have set all these values for your service through the settings tool, you may notice that a `wse3policyCache.config` file has been added to your project. In the `Web.config` file, you see that the WSE is engineered to work with this file. The settings applied to the `Web.config` file are presented in Listing 21-2.

Listing 21-2: The Web.config file after using the WSE Settings 3.0 Tool (partial file)

```
<microsoft.web.services3>
   <security>
      <securityTokenManager>
         <add type="WSExample.myPasswordProvider"
          namespace="http://docs.oasis-open.org/wss/2004/01/
             oasis-200401-wss-wssecurity-secext-1.0.xsd"
          localName="UsernameToken" />
      </securityTokenManager>
   </security>
   <policy fileName="wse3policyCache.config" />
   <diagnostics>
      <trace enabled="true" input="InputTrace.webinfo"
```

```
        output="OutputTrace.webinfo" />
    </diagnostics>
</microsoft.web.services3>
```

In this partial bit of configuration code found in the `Web.config` file, you can see that the security token manager is the `myPasswordProvider` class that was built earlier. Also, the policy that is used is assigned through setting the filename of the policy file within the `<policy>` element.

```
<policy fileName="wse3policyCache.config" />
```

Looking at the `wse3policyCache.config` file, you can see all the settings you applied are contained within the file as shown in Listing 21-3.

Listing 21-3: The wse3policyCache.config file

```
<policies xmlns="http://schemas.microsoft.com/wse/2005/06/policy">
  <extensions>
    <extension name="authorization"
     type="Microsoft.Web.Services3.Design.AuthorizationAssertion,
              Microsoft.Web.Services3, Version=3.0.0.0, Culture=neutral,
              PublicKeyToken=31bf3856ad364e35" />
    <extension name="usernameForCertificateSecurity"
     type="Microsoft.Web.Services3.Design.UsernameForCertificateAssertion,
              Microsoft.Web.Services3, Version=3.0.0.0, Culture=neutral,
              PublicKeyToken=31bf3856ad364e35" />
    <extension name="x509"
     type="Microsoft.Web.Services3.Design.X509TokenProvider,
              Microsoft.Web.Services3, Version=3.0.0.0, Culture=neutral,
              PublicKeyToken=31bf3856ad364e35" />
    <extension name="requireActionHeader"
     type="Microsoft.Web.Services3.Design.RequireActionHeaderAssertion,
              Microsoft.Web.Services3, Version=3.0.0.0, Culture=neutral,
              PublicKeyToken=31bf3856ad364e35" />
    <extension name="usernameOverTransportSecurity"
     type="Microsoft.Web.Services3.Design.UsernameOverTransportAssertion,
              Microsoft.Web.Services3, Version=3.0.0.0, Culture=neutral,
              PublicKeyToken=31bf3856ad364e35" />
  </extensions>
  <policy name="My WSE Policy">
    <authorization>
      <allow user="BEvjen" />
      <deny user="*" />
    </authorization>
    <usernameOverTransportSecurity />
    <requireActionHeader />
  </policy>
</policies>
```

In this case, you can see that the named policy, My WSE Policy, has an authorization section that denies all users except user `BEvjen`.

```
<authorization>
  <allow user="BEvjen" />
  <deny user="*" />
</authorization>
```

Now with the wiring to the WSE framework in place, you are now ready to build your Web service.

Building the Web Service

With the wiring for the framework of the WSE in place, you don't have to do much to have your Web services make use of this established framework. For an example of creating a service that requires the client to work with the settings applied to the `Web.config` and policy file, build the sample service shown in Listing 21-4.

Listing 21-4: Building a service that uses the WSE

```
using System.Web.Services;
using Microsoft.Web.Services3;

[WebService(Namespace = "http://tempuri.org/")]
[WebServiceBinding(ConformsTo = WsiProfiles.BasicProfile1_1)]
[Policy("My WSE Policy")]
public class Service : System.Web.Services.WebService
{
    [WebMethod]
    public int Add(int a, int b) {
        return (a + b);
    }

}
```

In this case, you have a Web service that performs a simple `Add()` function. This isn't much different from how you would normally go about building a C# Web service, but there are some minor differences.

From Listing 21-4, a different namespace is imported into the file—`Microsoft.Web.Services3`. This allows you to apply the class attribute `Policy`, which you use to specify the policy file that you wish to use for this service.

```
[Policy("My WSE Policy"]
public class Service : System.Web.Services.WebService
{

}
```

That's it. Now you can review how to create a simple ASP.NET client that works with this new service.

Building a WSE 3.0 Example—The Client Application

A little extra work is involved in creating a Web service that works according to the WS-Security specifications, but it is well worth this extra price. Now that you have a Web Service that accepts SOAP headers that conform to this structure, your consumers can construct their SOAP headers accordingly.

First, to create a client application that can make use of this new service, create a new ASP.NET Web project and within this project, make a reference to the new service that you built in the example earlier in this chapter. To make this reference, right-click on the project where you are creating your ASP.NET page and select Add Web Reference. Then type in the URL path of the WSDL file of the Web Service or of an `.asmx` file in the Add Web Reference dialog's address bar. If the dialog finds the Web service's endpoint, you just click the Add Reference button to create a reference to this remote object.

After you make a reference to the `WSE_Auth` Web Service, Visual Studio 2005 reviews and validates the WSDL document, and then makes the proper references to the service in your project. Notice that the Web Reference folder in your project has expanded and is either showing localhost (meaning that the Web Service is local on your server), or it shows the root URL of the location of the Web Service (but backwards!), for example, `com.wrox.www`.

The name of this reference here is important, and my recommendation is to change it to something meaningful by right-clicking the name and choosing Rename. This helps you understand your code a little better, especially if you are consuming multiple Web Services. This name is how you make reference to the Web Service in your code.

As when you created the WSE 3.0 Web service, you are going to have to enable the project for Web Services Enhancements in the WSE Settings 3.0 dialog. This adds the `Microsoft.Web.Service3.dll` to your project and makes the necessary changes to the `Web.config` file.

By creating an instance of this proxy class in the code of your project, you have programmatic access to the methods provided from the Web Service. To see an example of this, use the `Page_Load` event handler in the `Default.aspx` page and input the following code. (See Listing 21-5.)

Listing 21-5: The Page_Load event in the Default.aspx page

```
using System;
using Microsoft.Web.Services3.Security.Tokens;

public partial class _Default : System.Web.UI.Page
{
    protected void Page_Load(object sender, EventArgs e)
    {
        localhost.ServiceWse ws = new localhost.ServiceWse();

        UsernameToken ut = new UsernameToken("BEvjen", "BEvjen");
        ws.SetClientCredential<UsernameToken>(ut);
        ws.SetPolicy("examplePolicy");

        int result = ws.Add(10, 20);

        Response.Write(result.ToString());
    }
}
```

Try to understand what is going on with the consuming side of the application. First of all, you are working with a Web service in much the same manner as you would have before the WSE came along, although some differences exist.

The first step is to import the `Microsoft.Web.Services3.Security.Tokens` namespace to get access to the `UsernameToken` object. This object is used to provide your username and password to be incorporated in the SOAP message.

The next step is the same as it was before the WSE. You instantiate the proxy class that you have created. In this case, however, you find that new service has the `Wse` extension.

```
localhost.ServiceWse ws = new localhost.ServiceWse();
```

Next, you create an instance of the `UsernameToken` object that populates your username and password into the SOAP header. This `UsernameToken` object reference is called `ut`. In addition to instantiating the object, this bit of code also gives `ut` a value. In this case, you assign it the value of `BEvjen` as the username and the same string, `BEvjen`, as the password.

```
UsernameToken ut = new UsernameToken("BEvjen", "BEvjen");
```

After you have given your application side `UsernameToken` object the appropriate values, you then assign the `UsernameToken` object to the SOAP request that the consuming application sends off to the Web Service.

```
ws.SetClientCredential<UsernameToken>(ut);
ws.SetPolicy("examplePolicy");
```

You assign your `UsernameToken` object using the `SetClientCredential()` method. You must have a policy for security credentials in place. To accomplish this task, you need to create a `wse3policyCache.config` file in your project. This configuration file has the following code:

```
<policies xmlns="http://schemas.microsoft.com/wse/2005/06/policy">
  <extensions>
    <extension name="usernameOverTransportSecurity"
     type="Microsoft.Web.Services3.Design.UsernameOverTransportAssertion,
            Microsoft.Web.Services3, Version=3.0.0.0, Culture=neutral,
            PublicKeyToken=31bf3856ad364e35" />
    <extension name="requireActionHeader"
     type="Microsoft.Web.Services3.Design.RequireActionHeaderAssertion,
            Microsoft.Web.Services3, Version=3.0.0.0, Culture=neutral,
            PublicKeyToken=31bf3856ad364e35" />
  </extensions>
  <policy name="examplePolicy">
    <usernameOverTransportSecurity />
    <requireActionHeader />
  </policy>
</policies>
```

In this case, the policy is called `examplePolicy` and is the value which is used in the `SetPolicy()` method from earlier.

You have finished constructing the SOAP header that is used in the request, and you can then continue to work with the Web service request in the same manner as you did before the WSE. In this case, you simply call the particular Web Method you want and pass it any needed parameters. In this case, two parameters are required and you are assigning the value of the instantiation to a `Response.Write()` statement in order to display the result of the call on the ASP.NET page.

```
int result = ws.Add(10, 20);

Response.Write(result.ToString());
```

The Result of the Exchange

So, in the end, what happened in the request and response to the Web service? This is actually the more important part of the entire discussion and the reason that you want to use the WSE for building the Web service. Take a look at the request from the consumer to the provider first. You do this by reviewing the `.webinfo` files that you had the WSE to create for you. This SOAP message is shown in Listing 21-6.

Listing 21-6: The SOAP request from the consumer to the provider

```
<soap:Envelope xmlns:soap="http://schemas.xmlsoap.org/soap/envelope/"
 xmlns:xsi="http://www.w3.org/2001/XMLSchema-instance"
 xmlns:xsd="http://www.w3.org/2001/XMLSchema"
 xmlns:wsa="http://schemas.xmlsoap.org/ws/2004/08/addressing"
 xmlns:wsse="http://docs.oasis-open.org/wss/2004/01/
               oasis-200401-wss-wssecurity-secext-1.0.xsd"
 xmlns:wsu="http://docs.oasis-open.org/wss/2004/01/
               oasis-200401-wss-wssecurity-utility-1.0.xsd">
   <soap:Header>
      <wsa:Action>http://tempuri.org/Add</wsa:Action>
      <wsa:MessageID>urn:uuid:5405b840-e7cc-4b62-a235-bbd79785bad7</wsa:MessageID>
      <wsa:ReplyTo>
         <wsa:Address>
          http://schemas.xmlsoap.org/ws/2004/08/
             addressing/role/anonymous
         </wsa:Address>
      </wsa:ReplyTo>
      <wsa:To>http://localhost:2263/WSE/Service.asmx</wsa:To>
      <wsse:Security soap:mustUnderstand="1">
         <wsu:Timestamp wsu:Id="Timestamp-4c73c5af-2f3c-4b19-b172-9054289b400f">
            <wsu:Created>2006-09-23T22:43:21Z</wsu:Created>
            <wsu:Expires>2006-09-23T22:48:21Z</wsu:Expires>
         </wsu:Timestamp>
         <wsse:UsernameToken
          xmlns:wsu="http://docs.oasis-open.org/wss/2004/01/
                  oasis-200401-wss-wssecurity-utility-1.0.xsd"
          wsu:Id="SecurityToken-37cd48a5-99de-4fbf-885f-10e5325bb61d">
            <wsse:Username>BEvjen</wsse:Username>
            <wsse:Password
             Type="http://docs.oasis-open.org/wss/2004/01/
                  oasis-200401-wss-username-token-profile-1.0#PasswordDigest">
             Ifj+616Z9JM+eMHcyVj7RFzHiVE=
            </wsse:Password>
```

(continued)

Listing 21-6 *(continued)*

```
            <wsse:Nonce>7nb2/FzjzpYsrnoeJseL1Q==</wsse:Nonce>
            <wsu:Created>2006-09-23T22:43:21Z</wsu:Created>
         </wsse:UsernameToken>
      </wsse:Security>
   </soap:Header>
   <soap:Body>
      <Add xmlns="http://tempuri.org/">
         <a>10</a>
         <b>20</b>
      </Add>
   </soap:Body>
</soap:Envelope>
```

There is a lot to this message it seems, but if you look at the actual SOAP body, only the instantiating of the SOAP WebMethod is taking place.

```
<soap:Body>
   <Add xmlns="http://tempuri.org/">
      <a>10</a>
      <b>20</b>
   </Add>
</soap:Body>
```

All the real action is taking place in the SOAP header. This is where all the WSE action is occurring. Quite a bit of information is concentrated into three areas. The first section is the WS-Addressing part of the message and this section deals with the routing of SOAP messages among other actions. The second section is the `<wsu:Timestamp>` node. This section deals with the time stamping of SOAP messages. The last section in this SOAP header example is the `<wsse:UsernameToken>` node. This is the area of the SOAP header that you concentrate in this chapter. This is where the SOAP request security credentials are represented.

```
<wsse:UsernameToken
 xmlns:wsu="http://docs.oasis-open.org/wss/2004/01/
              oasis-200401-wss-wssecurity-utility-1.0.xsd"
 wsu:Id="SecurityToken-37cd48a5-99de-4fbf-885f-10e5325bb61d">
   <wsse:Username>BEvjen</wsse:Username>
   <wsse:Password
    Type="http://docs.oasis-open.org/wss/2004/01/
            oasis-200401-wss-username-token-profile-1.0#PasswordDigest">
    Ifj+616Z9JM+eMHcyVj7RFzHiVE=
   </wsse:Password>
   <wsse:Nonce>7nb2/FzjzpYsrnoeJseL1Q==</wsse:Nonce>
   <wsu:Created>2006-09-23T22:43:21Z</wsu:Created>
</wsse:UsernameToken>
```

The first thing to note is that this bit of XML in the SOAP header is an XML representation of the `UsernameToken` object that is created on the consuming side and which is passed to the Web service provider. Within the `<wsse:UsernameToken>` node is a unique ID which is given to the `UsernameToken` instance to differentiate it from other requests.

More importantly, a representation of the username and password that the user entered into the application appears in the SOAP header. Notice that it has been hashed and that this is specified by a type definition in the password node of the SOAP header.

The `<wsse:Nonce>` node, which is generated from cryptographic random number generators, uniquely identifies the request. A timestamp is also put on the request with the `<wsu:Created>` node.

After the credentials are verified and accepted by the Web service, the response is sent back to the client as shown in Listing 21-7.

Listing 21-7: The SOAP response from the provider to the consumer

```
<soap:Envelope xmlns:soap="http://schemas.xmlsoap.org/soap/envelope/"
 xmlns:xsi="http://www.w3.org/2001/XMLSchema-instance"
 xmlns:xsd="http://www.w3.org/2001/XMLSchema"
 xmlns:wsa="http://schemas.xmlsoap.org/ws/2004/08/addressing"
 xmlns:wsse="http://docs.oasis-open.org/wss/2004/01/
               oasis-200401-wss-wssecurity-secext-1.0.xsd"
 xmlns:wsu="http://docs.oasis-open.org/wss/2004/01/
               oasis-200401-wss-wssecurity-utility-1.0.xsd">
   <soap:Header>
      <wsa:Action>http://tempuri.org/AddResponse</wsa:Action>
      <wsa:MessageID>urn:uuid:232efd00-6dab-40a1-aed7-487e1abfeb96</wsa:MessageID>
      <wsa:RelatesTo>urn:uuid:673fdd6e-3b2a-474e-ace8-56a8134adc50</wsa:RelatesTo>
      <wsa:To>http://schemas.xmlsoap.org/ws/2004/08/
            addressing/role/anonymous
      </wsa:To>
      <wsse:Security>
         <wsu:Timestamp wsu:Id="Timestamp-8a213916-c2e9-4d7b-a1e5-b13c9cdc1ee4">
         <wsu:Created>2006-09-24T14:47:03Z</wsu:Created>
            <wsu:Expires>2006-09-24T14:52:03Z</wsu:Expires>
         </wsu:Timestamp>
      </wsse:Security>
   </soap:Header>
   <soap:Body>
      <AddResponse xmlns="http://tempuri.org/">
         <AddResult>30</AddResult>
      </AddResponse>
   </soap:Body>
</soap:Envelope>
```

For this return, only a small amount of information in the SOAP header deals with the SOAP message's timestamp and validity. Beyond this bit of information, there isn't anything else needed in the SOAP header. The SOAP body contains a return value.

Summary

The advanced Web service specifications that extend the Web Services model and enable enterprises to build great Web Services are truly outstanding. Many specifications exist already or are in production. The IT community is demanding the chance to use these specifications immediately in creating their enterprise-level Web Services. Many corporations have been unable to implement Web Services to a great extent because the services lacked many essential features such as security and the capability to properly encrypt messages.

Now the implementation of these specifications is appearing in a number of vendors' platforms. This chapter introduced the Microsoft implementation with this third release of the WSE. Using it, businesses can take a new and fresh look at the Web Services model and how it can play in their distributed application environment.

22

REST

In the Web Services family, SOAP is the "cool kid" that gets all the attention, but REST is the child that gets work done quietly in the background. *REpresentational State Transfer* (REST) is the Web Service for the rest of us. Apart from the fact that the acronym needs work (it was coined for a PhD dissertation), REST is really just a description of how the Web works: by moving (transferring) from page to page (the state). Each page you visit is the representation of that state. REST is all about simple links and using simple messages and query strings to get the job done.

Although the process of REST may not be obvious with the general Web pages you visit, think about a shopping site. You browse through a list of products, changing the state of the application and the representation of that state in your browser. Finally, you find the item you've been dreaming of for so long, and you click the link to buy it. State is added to an invisible shopping cart. Viewing the cart's contents is another click away. Increasing the quantity of items purchased is a matter of setting the number, and clicking an Update button. Deleting is just as easy. Everything is managed through simple GET and POST requests. You get many of the benefits of SOAP without having to build SOAP requests, understand WS-something-or-other, or process WSDL. Instead, you define the XML you'd like to pass between client and server.

Introducing the Basics of REST

Some users accept this fairly strict definition of REST, but many others consider any Web service that can be accessed using simple GETs or POSTs as being REST. To differentiate these two camps, I'll refer to these two concepts as *pure* REST and *just-enough* REST.

Pure REST

In a *pure REST* system, resources are the entities exposed by the service: the products you sell, the customer records you view, the pages you interact with. Each resource should have a unique URL that defines it, such as `http://www.mysystem.com/products/5323`. Accessing that URL using an HTTP GET request should return a representation of that resource, in this case a block of XML (or XHTML). In a pure REST system, GET requests cannot change the resource. Changes are performed by other HTTP verbs, as outlined in the following table.

HTTP Verb	Action
GET	Request for a resource. No change is made to the resource. Returns an XML representation of that resource.
POST	Creates a new resource. Returns an XML representation of that resource.
PUT	Updates an existing resource. Returns an XML representation of that resource.
DELETE	Deletes a resource from the system.

Those who do a lot of database programming should see some familiar items. These four actions map closely to the common CRUD (Create, Retrieve, Update, and Delete) that are done in database applications. Although these are not exact matches by any means, it is good to keep this relationship in mind when planning your own REST services. Just as your SELECT statements do not actually change your database, GET posts to a pure REST service should not change any data.

Just-enough REST

In a *just-enough REST* system, only GET and POST (or even just GET) URLs are used. In this model, all the operations of the service can be accessed via a query string in a browser. Part of the rationale for this is that many clients do not support the PUT and DELETE verbs, leaving GET and POST to perform multiple duties.

The Danger of GET

Many people attempt to define *just-enough* REST interfaces that use nothing but GET requests, rationalizing that this makes testing easier, because the user can type all URLs into a browser to make them work. (You'll sometimes see this referred to as the *query-line* or *url-line*.) This method is fine if your service is read-only; however, it can lead to many problems if you provide for other CRUD calls using GET requests. For example, imagine having a URL like: `http://www.example.com/products/delete/42` or `http://www.example.com/products.aspx?delete=42`. Although this would be harmless and possibly useful when used correctly, remember that this URL could be saved as a bookmark — or worse, recorded by a search engine or Web crawling application. After it is saved, this URL could be accessed again in the future, with possibly disastrous results. For example, Google produced a product called the Google Web Accelerator. Its noble aim was to make Web browsing faster by pre-downloading the links from pages you view. It did this by accessing all the links (using GET requests) on the page in the background. Now imagine what would happen if you view a page that contains links to delete URLs? To avoid the embarrassment of losing all your data, remember: GET requests should not change the data and have no side-effects.

Accessing REST Services

Many REST services are available on the Internet. Many of them are read-only services, offering only GET requests and providing some information. Just a few of the most useful are listed in the following table. See the list in the Resources section at the end of this chapter for more.

Service	Description
Yahoo Geocode	Determines the latitude and longitude for a given address (works best with US addresses).
Amazon Product Search	Enables searching Amazon's product catalogues and purchasing products.
Amazon Open Search	Enables searching a number of search engines simultaneously.
eBay Product Search	Enables searching through eBay's product catalog.
Flickr Photo Search	Enables searching through the photographs posted to Flickr by photographer, topic, or other criteria.

Accessing REST Service Examples

One of the easier services to call, but still a very useful one, is Yahoo's Geocoding service. This provides the longitude and latitude for a given address. This data can then be used to map the location with one of the mapping services. The Geocoding service is a just-enough REST API using command-line parameters to identify the location. In addition, the call requires a unique token identifying the application calling the service. The token helps Yahoo identify heavy users of the system. In addition, each IP address calling the service is limited to 50,000 calls per day.

The Geocode service is accessed by sending a GET request to `http://api.local.yahoo.com/MapsService/V1/geocode` with the following parameters.

Parameter	Description
appid	(Required) The unique string used to identify each application using the service. Note that this parameter name is case-sensitive. For testing purposes, you can use either YahooDemo (used by the Yahoo samples themselves) or ProXml (registered for the samples in this book). However, your own applications should have unique application IDs. You can register them at http://api.search.yahoo.com/webservices/register_application.
street	(Optional) The street address you are searching for. Note: this should be URL-encoded. That is, spaces should be replaced with + characters, and high ASCII or characters such as <, /, > etc. should be replaced with their equivalent using '%##' notation.

Table continued on following page

Parameter	Description
city	(Optional) The city for the location you are searching for. Should be URL-encoded, although this is really only necessary if the city name contains spaces or high ASCII characters.
state	(Optional) The US state (if applicable) you are searching for. Either the two letter abbreviation or full name (URL-encoded) will work.
zip	(Optional) The US ZIP code (if applicable) you are searching for. This can be in either 5-digit or 5-digit — 4-digit format.
location	(Optional) A free form field of address information containing the URL-encoded and comma-delimited request. For example: location=1600+Pennsylvania+Avenue+NW,+Washington,+DC

The return from the call is a block of XML corresponding to the XML schema:

```
<?xml version="1.0" encoding="utf-8"?>
<xs:schema xmlns:xs="http://www.w3.org/2001/XMLSchema"
  xmlns="urn:yahoo:maps" targetNamespace="urn:yahoo:maps"
  elementFormDefault="qualified">
  <xs:element name="ResultSet">
    <xs:complexType>
      <xs:sequence>
        <xs:element name="Result" type="ResultType" minOccurs="0" maxOccurs="50"/>
      </xs:sequence>
    </xs:complexType>
  </xs:element>
  <xs:complexType name="ResultType">
    <xs:sequence>
      <xs:element name="Latitude" type="xs:decimal"/>
      <xs:element name="Longitude" type="xs:decimal"/>
      <xs:element name="Address" type="xs:string"/>
      <xs:element name="City" type="xs:string"/>
      <xs:element name="State" type="xs:string"/>
      <xs:element name="Zip" type="xs:string"/>
      <xs:element name="Country" type="xs:string"/>
    </xs:sequence>
    <xs:attribute name="precision" type="xs:string"/>
    <xs:attribute name="warning" type="xs:string" use="optional"/>
  </xs:complexType>
</xs:schema>
```

For example, calling the service for the US Whitehouse:

```
http://api.local.yahoo.com/MapsService/V1/geocode?appid=YahooDemo&street=1600+Penns
ylvania+Avenue+NW&city=Washington&state=DC
```

The previous call returns the following XML:

```
<?xml version="1.0" encoding="UTF-8"?>
<ResultSet xmlns:xsi="http://www.w3.org/2001/XMLSchema-instance"
```

```
xmlns="urn:yahoo:maps" xsi:schemaLocation="urn:yahoo:maps
http://api.local.yahoo.com/MapsService/V1/GeocodeResponse.xsd">
  <Result precision="address">
    <Latitude>38.8987</Latitude>
    <Longitude>-77.037223</Longitude>
    <Address>1600 PENNSYLVANIA AVE NW</Address>
    <City>WASHINGTON</City>
    <State>DC</State>
    <Zip>20502-0001</Zip>
    <Country>US</Country>
  </Result>
</ResultSet>
```

Notice that the full, corrected address is returned along with the latitude and longitude. Therefore, this service can also be used for address correction.

Listing 22-1 shows a class designed to wrap the Geocode service. The class provides two methods for generating the geographic location based on an address. In a real system, this class would likely include either other overrides as well as other geographic or mapping functions. Note that this class uses the `System.Web.HttpUtility` class. Therefore, you will need to add a reference to the `System.Web.dll`.

Listing 22-1: Wrapping the Geocode service

```
using System;
using System.Collections.Generic;
using System.Text;
using System.Net;
using System.Web;
using System.Xml;

namespace ProXml.Samples.Rest {
    public class Mapping {
        private const string BaseUrl =
          "http://api.local.yahoo.com/MapsService/V1/geocode";
        private const string AppId = "ProXML";  //replace with your own code

        public GeographicLocation Geocode(string street,
          string city,
          string state,
          string zip) {
            GeographicLocation result = null;
            UriBuilder uri = new UriBuilder(BaseUrl);
            StringBuilder q = new StringBuilder();

            q.AppendFormat("appid={0}&", AppId);

            if(0!=street.Length) {
                q.AppendFormat("street={0}&", HttpUtility.UrlEncode(street));
            }
            if (0!=city.Length) {
                q.AppendFormat("city={0}&", HttpUtility.UrlEncode(city));
            }
```

(continued)

Listing 22-1 *(continued)*

```
        if (0!=state.Length) {
            q.AppendFormat("state={0}&", HttpUtility.UrlEncode(state));
        }

        if (0!=zip.Length) {
            q.AppendFormat("zip={0}&", HttpUtility.UrlEncode(zip));
        }

        uri.Query = q.ToString(0, q.Length - 1);

        WebRequest req = WebRequest.Create(uri.ToString());
        WebResponse resp = req.GetResponse();

        result = ExtractLocation(resp.GetResponseStream());

        return result;
    }

    public GeographicLocation Geocode(string location) {
        GeographicLocation result = null;
        UriBuilder uri = new UriBuilder(BaseUrl);
        StringBuilder q = new StringBuilder();

        q.AppendFormat("location={0}", HttpUtility.UrlEncode(location));
        uri.Query = q.ToString();

        WebRequest req = WebRequest.Create(uri.ToString());
        WebResponse resp = req.GetResponse();

        result = ExtractLocation(resp.GetResponseStream());

        return result;

    }

    private GeographicLocation ExtractLocation(System.IO.Stream stream) {
        GeographicLocation result = new GeographicLocation();

        using (XmlReader r = XmlReader.Create(stream)) {
            while (r.Read()) {
                if (r.IsStartElement() && !r.IsEmptyElement) {
                    switch (r.Name.ToLower()) {
                        case "latitude":
                            r.Read(); //skip to content
                            result.Latitude = Double.Parse(r.Value);
                            break;
                        case "longitude":
                            r.Read(); //skip to content
                            result.Longitude = Double.Parse(r.Value);
                            break;
                        default:
                            break;
```

```
                    }
                }
            }
        }
        return result;
    }
  }
}
```

The class contains two overloaded methods for retrieving the location of an address. One method takes a single string, location, whereas the other takes street, city, and so forth. Most of the code involved is creating the appropriate URL for the query and does not involve XML processing, with the exception of the `ExtractLocation` method.

The `ExtractLocation` method uses the .NET `XmlReader` class to process the returned XML. Alternatively, you could use SAX or other lightweight XML handling method. As the XML returned is a small amount, you could also use the DOM to extract the appropriate elements. However, because doing so requires extra processing (generating a DOM usually requires the underlying framework to create the document tree), this solution is not used here. In this routine, the `XmlReader` is created and the read loop initialized. Note that the `XmlReader.Create` method is only available with the .NET Framework 2.0. For earlier versions of .NET, you use the line:

```
using(XmlTextReader r = new XmlTextReader(stream)) {
```

The code retrieves only the latitude and longitude from the response XML; however, it should be easy enough to add support for the other elements as well. You should also extend the return type (`GeographicLocation`), as shown in Listing 22-2.

Listing 22-2: GeographicLocation class

```
using System;
using System.Collections.Generic;
using System.Text;

namespace ProXml.Samples.Rest {
    public class GeographicLocation {
        private double _lat = 0.0;
        private double _long = 0.0;

        public double Latitude {
            get { return _lat; }
            set { _lat = value; }
        }
        public double Longitude {
            get { return _long; }
            set { _long = value; }
        }
    }
}
```

After you have the class, you can use it in an application. In this case, I simply create a Windows Forms application to test its functionality (see Figure 22-1).

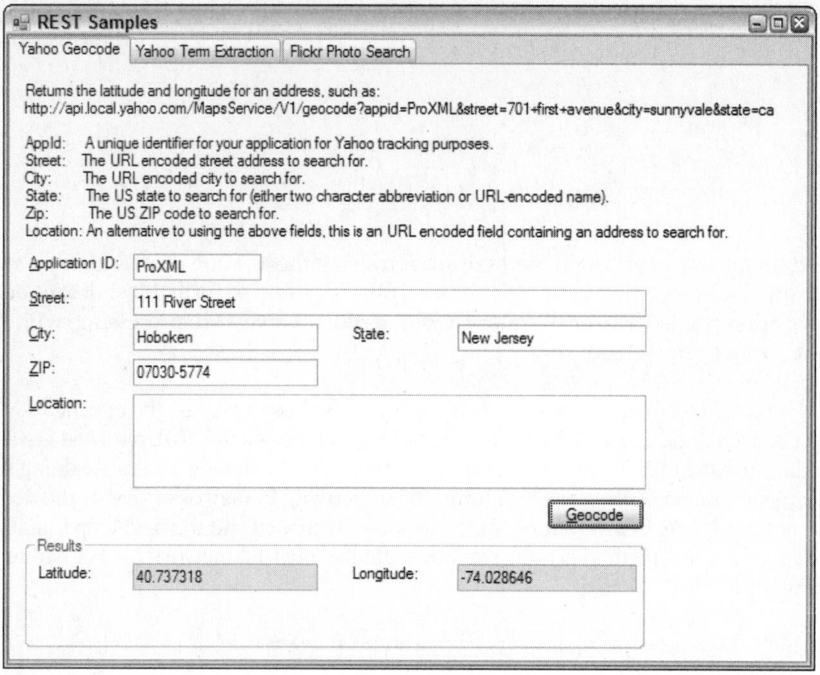

Figure 22-1

Listing 22-3 has the code for the Geocode test application.

Listing 22-3: Testing the Geocode service

```
private void GeoCodeButton_Click(object sender, EventArgs e) {
    ProXml.Samples.Rest.GeographicLocation result = new
        ProXml.Samples.Rest.GeographicLocation();
    ProXml.Samples.Rest.Mapping m =
        new ProXml.Samples.Rest.Mapping();

    //clear the results first
    this.LatitudeField.Text = "";
    this.LongitudeField.Text = "";

    if (0 != this.LocationField.Text.Length) {
        // use the location variant
    } else {
        // use the street/city/state variant
        result = m.Geocode(this.StreetField.Text,
            this.CityField.Text,
            this.StateField.Text,
            this.ZipField.Text);

        if (null != result) {
```

```
                this.LatitudeField.Text = result.Latitude.ToString();
                this.LongitudeField.Text = result.Longitude.ToString();
            }
        }
    }
```

Because all the XML processing is in the `Mapping` class itself, the code to call the function is quite simple.

A second service Yahoo provides requires slightly different handling for both input and output, and so it is worth showing. The Term Extraction service, part of Yahoo search services, returns the important words and phrases in a block of text. This can be useful for categorizing articles or blog posts. As the submitted text can easily be larger than the 2K limit on GET requests, the submission should be made via POST. In addition, the XML returned contains multiple result values, each containing one of the significant terms or phrases.

The Term Extraction service can be accessed via the REST interface at:

```
http://api.search.yahoo.com/ContentAnalysisService/V1/termExtraction
```

The following table shows the parameters available for Yahoo Term Extraction.

Parameter	Description
appid	(Required) The unique string used to identify each application using the service. Note that this parameter name is case-sensitive. For testing purposes, you can use either YahooDemo (used by the Yahoo samples themselves) or ProXml (registered for the samples in this book). However, your own applications should have unique application IDs. You can register them at `http://api.search.yahoo.com/webservices/register_application`.
context	(Required) The block of text that the terms will be extracted from. This should be URL-encoded. If this text is larger than the 2K GET limit, you use a POST request to process it.
query	(Optional) A query to help identify the topic of the context. For example, a block of text may discuss a number of different topics, which would all be included in the extraction. For example, a search for 'java' would likely include topics involving coffee, Indonesia, and programming languages. If you only want one topic extracted, provide a query to limit the extraction to the desired topic.
output	(Optional) Currently one of XML or JSON, defaulting to XML. JSON (Javascript Object Notation) is a non-XML notation for data, consisting of the objects serialized to text that can be converted back to Javascript objects via the eval method. Because this is a non-XML format, that's the last time I'll mention it here.
callback	(Optional) Used only if the output is set to JSON. This is the name of a client-side Javascript method to call to process the returned JSON data.

For example, you could call the service using a short block of text as a GET request:

```
http://api.search.yahoo.com/ContentAnalysisService/V1/termExtraction?appid=ProXML&c
ontext=The+Dunlin,+Calidris+alpina,+is+a+small+wader.+It+is+a+circumpolar+breeder+i
n+Arctic+or+subarctic+regions.&query=bird
```

This returns the following XML containing the key words in the sentence:

```
<ResultSet xmlns:xsi="http://www.w3.org/2001/XMLSchema-instance"
xmlns="urn:yahoo:cate"
  xsi:schemaLocation="urn:yahoo:cate
http://api.search.yahoo.com/ContentAnalysisService/V1/TermExtractionResponse.xsd">
  <Result>subarctic regions</Result>
  <Result>wader</Result>
  <Result>alpina</Result>
  <Result>regions</Result>
</ResultSet>
```

Listing 22-4 shows a class designed to wrap this service.

Listing 22-4: Wrapping the Term Extraction service

```
using System;
using System.Collections.Generic;
using System.Text;
using System.Net;
using System.Web;
using System.Xml;

namespace ProXml.Samples.Rest {
    public class ContentAnalysis {
        private const string BaseUrl =
"http://api.search.yahoo.com/ContentAnalysisService/V1/termExtraction";
        private const string AppId = "ProXML"; //replace with your own AppID

        public List<string> ExtractTerms(string context, string query) {
            List<string> result = null;
            UriBuilder uri = new UriBuilder(BaseUrl);
            StringBuilder q = new StringBuilder();

            q.AppendFormat("appid={0}&", AppId);
            q.AppendFormat("context={0}&", HttpUtility.UrlEncodeUnicode(context));

            if (0 != query.Length) {
                q.AppendFormat("query={0}&", HttpUtility.UrlEncode(query));
            }

            WebRequest req = WebRequest.Create(uri.ToString());
            //using Post as content may be longer than the 2K limit for GET
```

```
            req.Method = "POST";
            req.ContentType = "application/x-www-form-urlencoded";
            System.IO.Stream stream = req.GetRequestStream();
            Byte[] buffer = Encoding.UTF8.GetBytes(q.ToString(0,q.Length-1));
            stream.Write(buffer, 0, buffer.Length);
            stream.Close();
            WebResponse resp = req.GetResponse();

            result = BuildResponse(resp.GetResponseStream());

            return result;
        }

        private List<string> BuildResponse(System.IO.Stream stream) {
            List<string> result = new List<string>();

            using (XmlReader r = XmlReader.Create(stream)) {
                while (r.Read()) {
                    if (r.IsStartElement("Result")) {
                        result.Add(r.ReadElementContentAsString());
                    }
                }
            }
            return result;
        }
    }
}
```

The code is basically the same as that for the Geocode service with two major exceptions marked in the listing. First, because the request requires a POST, the `Method` property of the WebRequest is set to `POST`. In addition, the `ContentType` is set to `application/x-www-form-urlencoded`. This sets the `Content-Type` header on the request to ensure the Web server handles the query correctly. Finally, the query (containing the URL-encoded block of text) is written to the Request stream.

Because all the returned terms are wrapped in a `Result` element, parsing the resulting XML is easier. The `IsStartElement` has a version where you can include the element name you are searching for. After this is found, the resulting content can be retrieved with the `ReadElementContentAsString` method. Note that this method is only available with the .NET Framework 2.0. For version 1.1 and earlier, you should change the code for the `if` statement to:

```
if (r.IsStartElement("Result") && !r.IsEmptyElement) {
    r.Read(); //skips to the content
    result.Add(r.Value);
}
```

Just as with the Geocode service, you can create a simple test application (see Figure 22-2).

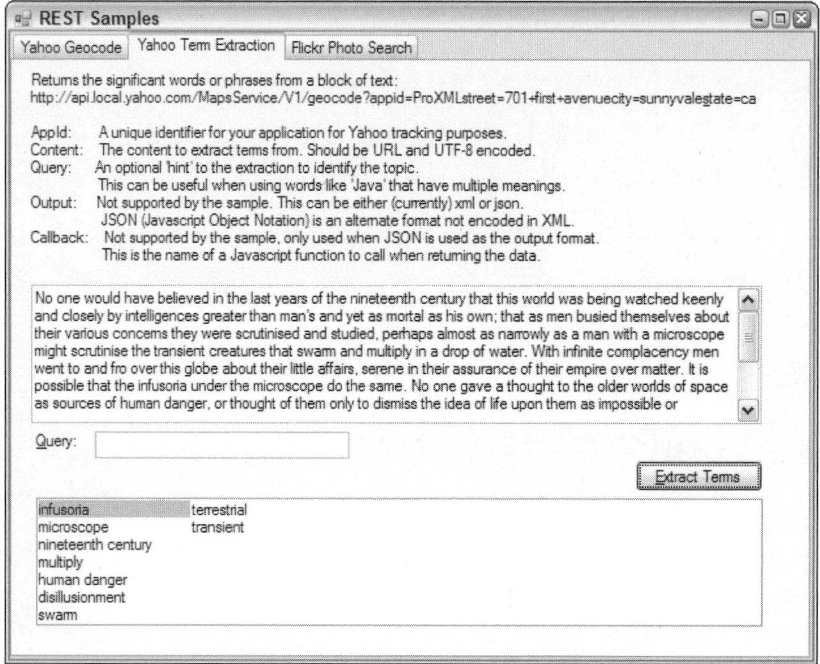

Figure 22-2

Listing 22-5 shows the code required to test the Extraction Wrapper class.

Listing 22-5: Testing the Term Extraction Wrapper class

```
private void ExtractButton_Click(object sender, EventArgs e) {
    ProXml.Samples.Rest.ContentAnalysis con =
      new ProXml.Samples.Rest.ContentAnalysis();
    List<string> result = con.ExtractTerms(this.ContextField.Text,
        this.QueryField.Text);
    this.TermList.DataSource = result;

}
```

As a final example of calling existing REST services, Flickr provides a search service. This enables users to search the thousands of photographs that have been uploaded to Flickr. You can search by photographer, tag (topic), group (a named selection), or other criteria. The following table discusses the available parameters. A typical search takes the form:

```
http://www.flickr.com/services/rest/?api_key={unique
key}&method=flickr.photos.search&tags=okapi
```

Parameter	Description
api_key	(Required) The api_key parameter is similar to the Yahoo appid parameter in that it is a unique key used to identify each application accessing the service. You can apply for your own key at: `http://www.flickr.com/services/api/key.gne`.
method	(Required) This identifies which of Flickr's methods you are calling (they all have the same URL). Flickr provides a number of methods beyond search. For more details, see the API documentation at: `http://www.flickr.com/services/api/`. For an example of what is possible to create using the APIs, see the Organizr application (`http://www.flickr.com/tools/organizr.gne`)
tags	(Optional) Tags are small blocks of text that can be attached to a photograph to identify its content, such as *London*, *summer*, or *wedding*. You can think of it as a category. When searching by tag, this parameter is a comma-delimited list of tags you want to search. By default, a photo containing any of these tags is returned. If you want to perform an AND search, see tag_mode below. (The sample code does not use this parameter).
tag_mode	(Optional) This controls whether the tag search is performed using an OR query (the default) or an AND query. Use the value `any` or omit it to do an OR query, or use `all` to select photos that have all the desired tags.
	Many other parameters are supported, but not used by the sample application. See `http://www.flickr.com/services/api/flickr.photos.search.html` for the full list.

The XML returned from the service contains the ID information that can be used to create URLs to the photographs stored:

```
<rsp stat="ok">
  <photos page="1" pages="2" perpage="100" total="168">
    <photo id="91638599" owner="28255546@N00" secret="40a011bce6" server="16"
title="Okapi" ispublic="1" isfriend="1" isfamily="1"/>
    <photo id="91239219" owner="33394998@N00" secret="56e0d475dc" server="27"
title="Golgota" ispublic="1" isfriend="0" isfamily="0"/>
    <photo id="91207836" owner="33394998@N00" secret="1fc7d87431" server="30"
title="wenteltrap bouwen 2" ispublic="1" isfriend="0" isfamily="0"/>
    <photo id="90845302" owner="18081671@N00" secret="7b7ce51d35" server="42"
title="20060119 009" ispublic="1" isfriend="0" isfamily="0"/>
    <photo id="90845301" owner="18081671@N00" secret="fbad93dd15" server="15"
title="20060119 008" ispublic="1" isfriend="0" isfamily="0"/>
    <photo id="90845303" owner="18081671@N00" secret="dfbe7d90c8" server="39"
title="20060119 010" ispublic="1" isfriend="0" isfamily="0"/>
    <photo id="90795717" owner="18081671@N00" secret="e87de9ad47" server="33"
title="20060119 005" ispublic="1" isfriend="0" isfamily="0"/>
    <photo id="90795718" owner="18081671@N00" secret="dc776cf56c" server="43"
title="20060119 006" ispublic="1" isfriend="0" isfamily="0"/>
    ...
  </photos>
</rsp>
```

To create the URL to the photo, you must first decide on the size of the photo you would like. The basic URL form is:

```
http://static.flickr.com/{server-id}/{id}_{secret}.jpg
```

In addition, you can add a suffix to select a different size, as outlined in the following table:

Suffix	Image Size
none	Returns the image sized to 500 pixels along the longer axis. For example: `http://static.flickr.com/13/90283787_838c56eb46.jpg`
m	Returns the image scaled to 240 pixels along the longer axis. For example: `http://static.flickr.com/29/89924158_adebcfd8b6_m.jpg`
s	Returns the image scaled to a 75 pixel square. Note that this may cause some distortion in the original image because of scaling. For example: `http://static.flickr.com/34/90039890_d1113850b4_s.jpg`
t	Returns a thumbnail version of the image, scaled to 100 pixels on the longest axis. For example: `http://static.flickr.com/29/52619028_e9541b248a_t.jpg`
b	Returns a large version of the image, scaled to 1024 pixels along the longest axis. Note that this will only return an image if the original is larger than1024 pixels wide or high. For example: `http://static.flickr.com/27/67687221_107c1f3c06_b.jpg`
o	Returns the original image. Note that the extension in this case may not actually be jpg, but will be the extension appropriate to whatever format the photograph was posted as. For example: `http://static.flickr.com/23/33000424_82bd503826_o.jpg`

Listing 22-6 shows the code required to wrap the Flickr Photo Search service.

Listing 22-6: Wrapping the Flickr Photo Search service

```
using System;
using System.Collections.Generic;
using System.Text;
using System.Net;
using System.Web;
using System.Xml;
using System.IO;
```

```
namespace ProXml.Samples.Rest {

    public class Photos {
        private const string BaseUrl = "http://www.flickr.com/services/rest/";
        private const string AppId = "c0cbd699d50f296fa5b237eb4bdfbd1d"; //replace
with your own AppID
        private const string FlickrPhotoSearch = "flickr.photos.search";

        public PhotoInformation[] Search(string tags) {
            List<PhotoInformation> result = null;
            UriBuilder uri = new UriBuilder(BaseUrl);
            StringBuilder q = new StringBuilder();

            q.AppendFormat("api_key={0}&", AppId);
            q.AppendFormat("method={0}&", FlickrPhotoSearch);
            q.AppendFormat("tags={0}", HttpUtility.UrlEncodeUnicode(tags));
            uri.Query = q.ToString();

            WebRequest req = WebRequest.Create(uri.Uri);
            WebResponse resp = req.GetResponse();

            result = BuildPhotoList(resp.GetResponseStream());

            return result.ToArray();
        }

        private List<PhotoInformation> BuildPhotoList(System.IO.Stream input) {
            const string BasePhotoUrl = "http://static.flickr.com";
            UriBuilder ub = new UriBuilder(BasePhotoUrl);
            PhotoInformation pi = null;
            List<PhotoInformation> result = new List<PhotoInformation>();

            using (StreamReader read = new StreamReader(input)) {
                XmlReader r = XmlReader.Create(read);
                while (r.Read()) {
                    if (r.IsStartElement("photo")) {
                        pi = new PhotoInformation();
                        pi.Title = r.GetAttribute("title");

                        //build thumbnail URL
                        ub.Path = String.Format("{0}/{1}_{2}_t.jpg",
                            r.GetAttribute("server"),
                            r.GetAttribute("id"),
                            r.GetAttribute("secret"));
                        pi.ThumbnailUrl = ub.ToString();

                        //and photo URL
                        ub.Path = String.Format("{0}/{1}_{2}.jpg",
                            r.GetAttribute("server"),
                            r.GetAttribute("id"),
                            r.GetAttribute("secret"));
                        pi.Url = ub.ToString();

                        result.Add(pi);
                    }
```

(continued)

Listing 22-6 *(continued)*

```
                    }
                }
                return result;
            }
        }
    }
```

Just like the other services, the XML processing is isolated, in this case within the `BuildPhotoList` method. This method processes the returned XML, finding the `photo` elements. These contain the information needed to create the URLs to the graphics. The URLs are reconstructed in the `PhotoInformation` class (see Listing 22-7)

Listing 22-7: PhotoInformation class

```
using System;
using System.Collections.Generic;
using System.Text;

namespace ProXml.Samples.Rest {
    public class PhotoInformation {
        private string _thumb;
        private string _url;
        private string _title;

        public string ThumbnailUrl {
            get { return _thumb; }
            set { _thumb = value; }
        }

        public string Url {
            get { return _url; }
            set { _url = value; }
        }

        public string Title {
            get { return _title; }
            set { _title = value; }
        }

        public override string ToString() {
            if (String.Empty != _title) {
                return _title;
            } else {
                return _thumb;
            }
        }
    }
}
```

After this class is created, searching and retrieving photos is quite easy (see Figure 23.3). Listing 22-8 shows the code that calls this class. Two methods are used: the first performs the initial search based on the keyword(s) provided. The second updates the image whenever a new item is selected in the list.

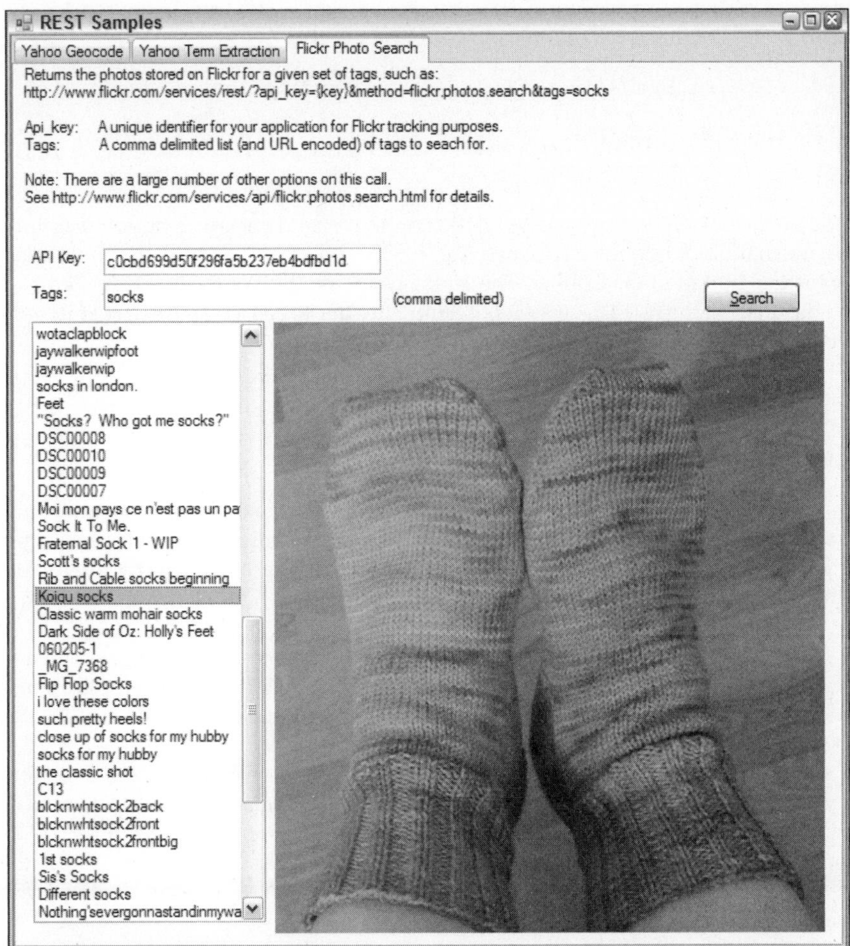

Figure 22-3

Listing 22-8: Using the Flickr Photo Search Wrapper class

```
private void PhotoSearchButton_Click(object sender, EventArgs e) {

    ProXml.Samples.Rest.Photos call =
      new ProXml.Samples.Rest.Photos();
    ProXml.Samples.Rest.PhotoInformation[] result =
      call.Search(this.TagsField.Text);
    PhotoList.DataSource = result;
}
private void PhotoList_SelectedIndexChanged(object sender, EventArgs e) {
    PreviewImage.ImageLocation = "";
    //get the selected item
    ProXml.Samples.Rest.PhotoInformation pi = null;
    ListBox lb = (ListBox)sender;
```

(continued)

Listing 22-8 *(continued)*

```
        pi = (ProXml.Samples.Rest.PhotoInformation)lb.SelectedItem;

        PreviewImage.ImageLocation = pi.Url;
    }
```

The code is for the Search button and the ListBox on the form. The Search button uses the wrapper class to retrieve the first block of photos returned (up to 500) and creates an array of PhotoInformation objects. This array is then bound to the ListBox. The `ToString()` method of the class is called to display the text value for each item in the list. This way it is a simple matter to retrieve the selected item from the ListBox to display the selected image.

Creating REST Services

For those who don't want to be limited to the existing REST services, you can create your own services. Another possible reason for creating your own services is to expose legacy data. Just as you expose this data using Web services, you can expose it via REST services to provide a fairly interoperable means of making the data available to others.

The first step in creating a REST service is to decide what resources you want to provide with this service, that is, the entities maintained by the service. For example, in a Web log application, the resources are the posts and comments in the system. In a shopping application, the resources are the items to buy.

The next step in defining a REST service is to identify the HTTP verbs and URLs that you will use. Here is where you decide whether to create a pure REST service, or a just-enough REST service. By limiting yourself to GET and POST, your service can be called via a browser. Unless your service is read-only, you probably want to add some parameter to differentiate the various requests. Alternately, calling the PUT and DELETE methods of a pure REST service is more difficult for users accessing your service than using a simple browser interface.

Just-enough REST Service Example

To demonstrate how to create a just-enough REST interface, I'll create a simple contact management system. While this is a fairly simple solution, it shows many of the mechanics needed by REST services.

As described previously, the first step in creating a REST service is to identify the resources managed by the system. In this case, the resources will be contacts (in a simple XML layout). With the exception of requesting a list of contacts, all exchanges will consist of individual entries. Listing 22-9 shows an example entry in the system.

Mashups

With the number of REST services growing, it was only a matter of time before people started to combine them, creating what are called mashups. For example, they used the location information from a Flickr user search as input to a Yahoo Geocode, plotting the result on a Google map. Many of these applications are listed at `programmableweb.com`.

Listing 22-9: Sample contact

```
<contact id="12">
  <fName>Charlene</fName>
  <lName>Locksley</lName>
  <email>cl823@public.com</email>
</contact>
```

Now that the resources have been defined, the next step is to define the HTTP verbs and URLs that are used by the system. The service is intended for use from a browser, so both HTTP GET and HTTP POST are supported by the system. As this service is intended to provide read/write access to the contacts, the service needs a way of adding, updating, and deleting entries. The list that follows shows some of the URLs that are supported by the system. For each of the URLs, only the query string is shown. All of the requests are made to a single URL on the system: (`http://localhost/restcontacts/rest.ashx`)

- `?method=getcontact` — Returns a list of all the contacts entered into the system. (See Figure 22-4)

Figure 22-4

- `?method=getcontact&id=3` — Returns an individual contact from the system. based on the id requested. The contact is formatted like the XML shown in Listing 22-9. (See Figure 22-5.)

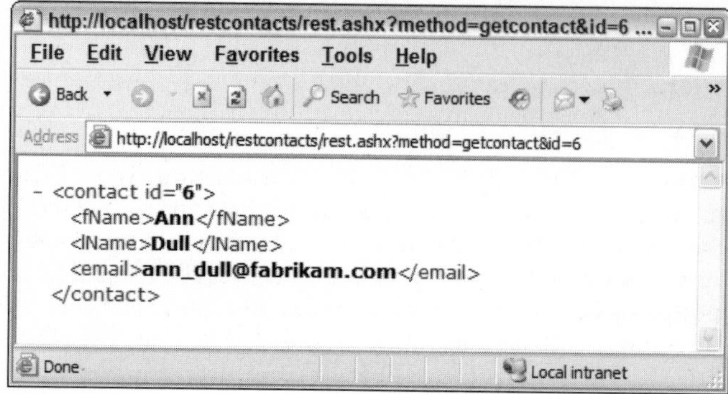

Figure 22-5

- `?method=getcontact&email=user@server.com` — Returns an individual contact from the system. based on a search of the e-mail addresses. The contact is formatted as the XML shown above.
- `?method=insertcontact&fname=name&lname=name&email=address` — Inserts a new entry in the list of contacts. Returns the newly added contact, with the assigned id value. (See Figure 22-6)

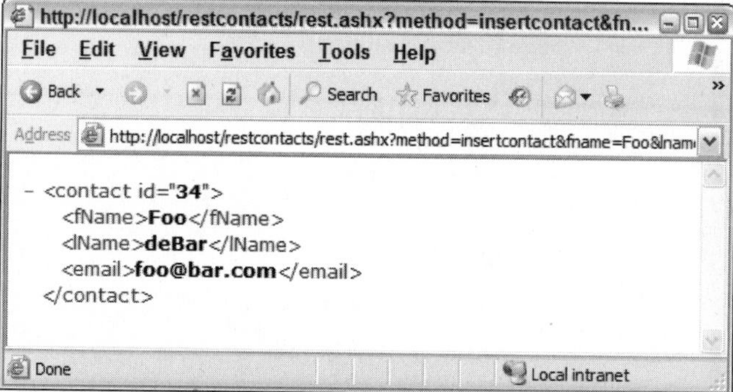

Figure 22-6

- `?method=insertcontact` — Inserts a new entry in the list of contacts. This form is intended for POST calls, and the request body should include the contact information as the XML above, without the id attribute. Returns the newly added contact, with the assigned id value.
- `?method=updatecontact&id=3&fname=new&lname=new&email=new` — Updates one of the existing contacts in the system, returning the updated contact. (See Figure 22-7.)

Figure 22-7

- `?method=updatecontact` — Updates one of the existing contacts in the system. This form is intended for use in POST requests. The request body should contain the updated contact information as the XML above (without the id value). Returns the updated contact.
- `?method=deletecontact&id=3` — Deletes a contact from the system, returning the deleted contact as XML.

Because all the methods for this service are accessible from GET requests, testing the service can be done using a browser. Figures 22-4 through 22-7 show how to access the various methods of the service.

The REST service you'll be creating is based on an ASP.NET HTTP Handler. HTTP Handlers are files in ASP.NET that respond to requests. Although you could create this using an ASP.NET page, doing so doesn't return a complete page, but only a block of XML. Using the handler is a cleaner scenario. The simplest HTTP handler is a file with the extension `ashx` as shown in Listing 22-10.

Listing 22-10: A basic HTTP handler in ASP.NET

```
<%@ WebHandler Language="VB" Class="Handler" %>

Imports System
Imports System.Web

Public Class Handler : Implements IHttpHandler

    Public Sub ProcessRequest(ByVal context As HttpContext) _
        Implements IHttpHandler.ProcessRequest

    End Sub

    Public ReadOnly Property IsReusable() As Boolean _
        Implements IHttpHandler.IsReusable

        Get
            Return False
        End Get
    End Property

End Class
```

The bulk of the work in creating an HTTP handler is in the code in the `ProcessRequest` method. This method is responsible for building the appropriate response content and setting the correct content type for the response. The `IsReusable` method is a marker method to determine if the Web server can use this HTTP handler for multiple requests. Unless you are certain your `ProcessRequest` method is completely safe for multiple threads, it is generally safer to have `IsReusable` return `false`.

Listing 22-11 shows the implementation of the `RestHandler`.

Listing 22-11: The RestHandler

```
<%@ WebHandler Language="VB" Class="RestHandler" %>

Imports System
Imports System.Web
Imports ProXml.Samples.Rest

Public Class RestHandler : Implements IHttpHandler

    Public Sub ProcessRequest(ByVal context As HttpContext) _
        Implements IHttpHandler.ProcessRequest

        Dim req As HttpRequest = context.Request
        Dim resp As HttpResponse = context.Response

        Dim method As String = "unknown"
        resp.ContentType = "application/xml"
        If req("method") IsNot Nothing Then
            method = req("method").ToLower()
        End If

        Select Case method
            Case "getcontact"
                Dim contact As Contact
                If req("id") IsNot Nothing Then
                    'they are looking for a single user
                    Dim id As Integer = Int32.Parse(req("id"))
                    contact = ContactManager.GetContact(id)
                    If contact IsNot Nothing Then
                        resp.Write(contact.ToString())
                    Else
                        Throw New HttpException(404, _
                            "Could not find Contact with that ID")
                    End If
                ElseIf req("email") IsNot Nothing Then
                    'search by email
                    contact = ContactManager.GetContact(req("email"))
                    If contact IsNot Nothing Then
                        resp.Write(contact.ToString())
                    Else
                        Throw New HttpException(404, _
                            "Could not find Contact")
                    End If
                Else
```

```
                    'return all users
                    Dim Contacts() = ContactManager.GetContacts()
                    resp.Write("<contacts>")
                    For Each c As Contact In Contacts
                        resp.Write(c.ToString())
                    Next
                    resp.Write("</contacts>")
                End If
            Case "insertcontact"
                If req("fname") Is Nothing Then
                    'try reading from the body
                    resp.Write(ContactManager.InsertContact(req.InputStream))

                Else
                    resp.Write(ContactManager.InsertContact(req("fname"), _
                        req("lname"), req("email")))
                End If
            Case "updatecontact"
                If req("id") IsNot Nothing Then
                    Dim id As Integer = Int32.Parse(req("id"))
                    If req("fname") Is Nothing Then
                        'contact is in the body
                        resp.Write(ContactManager.UpdateContact(id, _
                            req.InputStream))
                    Else
                        resp.Write(ContactManager.UpdateContact(id, _
                            req("fName"), req("lName"), req("email")))
                    End If
                End If
            Case "deletecontact"
                If req("id") IsNot Nothing Then
                    Dim id As Integer = Int32.Parse(req("id"))
                    resp.Write(ContactManager.DeleteContact(id))
                End If
            Case Else
        End Select
    End Sub

    Public ReadOnly Property IsReusable() As Boolean _
        Implements IHttpHandler.IsReusable

        Get
            Return False
        End Get
    End Property

End Class
```

Although the code is lengthy, it is primarily the code for dispatching requests. The method parameter on the query string identifies which action to perform. However, each method includes multiple possible actions (such as the various `getcontact` methods). The handler delegates the actual changes to the data to the various static methods on the `ContactManager` class (see Listing 22-13). All these methods return one or more `Contact` objects (see Listing 22-12).

Listing 22-12: The Contact class

```
Imports System.Text
Imports System.Xml

Public Class Contact

#Region "Properties"
    Private _id As Integer
    Private _firstName As String
    Private _lastName As String
    Private _email As String

    Public Property ID() As Integer
        Get
            Return _id
        End Get
        Friend Set(ByVal value As Integer)
            _id = value
        End Set
    End Property

    Public Property FirstName() As String
        Get
            Return _firstName
        End Get
        Set(ByVal value As String)
            _firstName = value
        End Set
    End Property

    Public Property Lastname() As String
        Get
            Return _lastName
        End Get
        Set(ByVal value As String)
            _lastName = value
        End Set
    End Property

    Public Property EMail() As String
        Get
            Return _email
        End Get
        Set(ByVal value As String)
            _email = value
        End Set
    End Property
#End Region

#Region "Public Methods"
    Public Overrides Function ToString() As String
        Dim sb As New StringBuilder()
```

```
        Dim ws As New XmlWriterSettings

        With ws
            .CheckCharacters = True
            .CloseOutput = True
            .ConformanceLevel = ConformanceLevel.Fragment
            .Encoding = Encoding.UTF8
            .OmitXmlDeclaration = True
        End With

        Using w As XmlWriter = XmlWriter.Create(sb, ws)
            w.WriteStartElement("contact")
            w.WriteAttributeString("id", Me.ID)
            w.WriteElementString("fName", Me.FirstName)
            w.WriteElementString("lName", Me.Lastname)
            w.WriteElementString("email", Me.EMail)
            w.WriteEndElement() 'contact
        End Using

        Return sb.ToString()
    End Function
#End Region

End Class
```

The `Contact` class is a simple class, with only a few properties. The only notable part of the class is the `ToString` method that returns the XML representation of the class. The handler calls this when the contact is output.

The contacts will be stored in a database. This database includes only a single table. The structure of the contacts table is as follows.

Column	Type	Size	Description
id	int	n/a	Identity column used as the primary key.
fName	nvarchar	50	First name of the contact.
lName	nvarchar	50	Last name of the contact.
email	nvarchar	50	E-mail address of the contact.

The `ContactManager` class (Listing 22-13) performs the bulk of the work of the handler in a set of static methods. Of note are the two methods intended for use by POST requests.

Listing 22-13: The Contact Manager class

```
Imports System.Data.SqlClient
Imports System
Imports System.Collections.Generic

Public Class ContactManager
```

(continued)

Listing 22-13 *(continued)*

```
    Public Shared Function GetContacts() As Contact()
        Dim result As New List(Of Contact)
        Dim c As Contact
        Dim reader As SqlDataReader
        Dim sql As String = "SELECT id, fname, lname, email FROM Contacts"

        reader = DAL.ExecuteSqlText(sql)
        While reader.Read()
            c = New Contact
            c.ID = reader.GetInt32(0)
            c.FirstName = reader.GetString(1)
            c.Lastname = reader.GetString(2)
            c.EMail = reader.GetString(3)
            result.Add(c)
        End While
        reader.Close()

        Return result.ToArray()
    End Function

    Public Shared Function GetContact(ByVal id As Integer) As Contact
        Dim result As Contact = Nothing
        Dim reader As SqlDataReader
        Dim sql As String = _
            "SELECT id, fname, lname, email FROM Contacts WHERE id=" & id

        reader = DAL.ExecuteSqlText(sql)
        While reader.Read()
            result = New Contact
            result.ID = reader.GetInt32(0)
            result.FirstName = reader.GetString(1)
            result.Lastname = reader.GetString(2)
            result.EMail = reader.GetString(3)
        End While
        reader.Close()

        Return result
    End Function

    Public Shared Function GetContact(ByVal email As String) As Contact
        Dim result As Contact = Nothing
        Dim reader As SqlDataReader
        Dim sql As String = _
            String.Format("SELECT id, fname, lname, email " & _
            "FROM Contacts WHERE email='{0}'", _
            email)

        reader = DAL.ExecuteSqlText(sql)
        While reader.Read()
            result = New Contact
            result.ID = reader.GetInt32(0)
            result.FirstName = reader.GetString(1)
            result.Lastname = reader.GetString(2)
            result.EMail = reader.GetString(3)
```

```
        End While
        reader.Close()

        Return result
    End Function

    Public Shared Function InsertContact(ByVal firstName As String, _
        ByVal lastName As String, ByVal email As String) As Contact
        Dim result As Contact = Nothing

        result = GetContact(email)

        If result Is Nothing Then
            'user does not exist, we can create
            Dim sql As String = _
                String.Format("INSERT INTO Contacts(fname, lname, email) " & _
                "VALUES ('{0}', '{1}', '{2}')", _
                firstName, lastName, email)
            If DAL.Execute(sql) Then
                result = GetContact(email)
            End If
        End If

        Return result
    End Function

    Public Shared Function InsertContact(ByVal block As IO.Stream) As Contact
        Dim result As Contact = Nothing
        Dim firstName As String = String.Empty
        Dim lastName As String = String.Empty
        Dim email As String = String.Empty

        Using r As Xml.XmlReader = Xml.XmlReader.Create(block)
            While r.Read()
                If r.IsStartElement() AndAlso Not r.IsEmptyElement Then
                    Select Case r.Name.ToLower
                        Case "fname"
                            r.Read()
                            firstName = r.Value
                        Case "lname"
                            r.Read()
                            lastName = r.Value
                        Case "email"
                            r.Read()
                            email = r.Value
                    End Select
                End If
            End While
        End Using
        result = InsertContact(firstName, lastName, email)

        Return result
    End Function

    Public Shared Function UpdateContact(ByVal id As Integer, _
```

(continued)

Listing 22-13 *(continued)*

```
        ByVal firstName As String, ByVal lastName As String, _
        ByVal email As String) As Contact

        Dim result As Contact = GetContact(id)

        If result IsNot Nothing Then
            Dim sql As String = _
                String.Format("UPDATE Contacts SET fname='{0}', " & _
                "lname='{1}', email='{2}' WHERE id={3}", _
                firstName, lastName, email, id)
            If DAL.Execute(sql) Then
                result = GetContact(id)
            End If
        End If

        Return result
    End Function

    Public Shared Function UpdateContact(ByVal id As Integer, _
        ByVal block As IO.Stream) As Contact

        Dim result As Contact = GetContact(id)

        Dim firstName As String = String.Empty
        Dim lastName As String = String.Empty
        Dim email As String = String.Empty

        Using r As Xml.XmlReader = Xml.XmlReader.Create(block)
            While r.Read()
                If r.IsStartElement() AndAlso Not r.IsEmptyElement Then
                    Select Case r.Name.ToLower
                        Case "fname"
                            r.Read()
                            firstName = r.Value
                        Case "lname"
                            r.Read()
                            lastName = r.Value
                        Case "email"
                            r.Read()
                            email = r.Value
                    End Select
                End If
            End While
        End Using
        result = UpdateContact(id, firstName, lastName, email)

        Return result
    End Function

    Public Shared Function DeleteContact(ByVal id As Integer)
        dim result as Contact = nothing
        Dim c As Contact = GetContact(id)

        If c IsNot Nothing Then
```

```
            Dim sql = String.Format("DELETE FROM Contacts WHERE id={0}", id)
            If DAL.Execute(sql) Then
                result = c
            End If
        End If
        Return result
    End Function
End Class
```

The code is mostly simple SQL processing and, ideally, is used to call stored procedures. The most notable methods are the two intended for use with POST requests (InsertContact and UpdateContact). When posting data using HTTP, the body of the request contains information. This data is encoded via a MIME type. The most common MIME type for POST data is `application/x-www-form-urlencoded` if an HTML form sends the information. This format looks similar to a query string, but is contained in the body of the request to avoid the 2K limit on the length of a query string. Most server-side tools process this form of request to create a hash table, just as they create query string variables. Alternately, the POST body could contain the XML representation submitted (and the MIME type of `application/xml`). In this case, the code extracts the values from the XML for handling.

The actual data access is isolated from the `ContactManager` class in the simple DAL class (see Listing 22-14).

Listing 22-14: The Data Access Layer class

```
Imports System.Data.SqlClient
Imports System.Configuration
Imports System.Data

Public Class DAL
    Private Shared _conn As SqlClient.SqlConnection

    Shared Sub New()
        Dim connectionstring As String
        connectionstring = _
ConfigurationManager.ConnectionStrings("contactsConnection").ConnectionString
        _conn = New SqlClient.SqlConnection(connectionstring)
    End Sub

    Public Shared Function ExecuteQuery(ByVal query As String, _
        ByVal parms As SqlParameter()) As SqlDataReader

        Dim result As SqlDataReader = Nothing
        Dim cmd As New SqlCommand(query, _conn)
        cmd.CommandType = CommandType.StoredProcedure
        cmd.Parameters.AddRange(parms)

        If _conn.State <> ConnectionState.Open Then
            _conn.Open()
        End If

        result = cmd.ExecuteReader(CommandBehavior.CloseConnection)

        Return result
```

(continued)

Listing 22-14 *(continued)*

```
    End Function
    Public Shared Function ExecuteSqlText(ByVal sql As String) _
        As System.Data.SqlClient.SqlDataReader

        Dim result As SqlDataReader = Nothing
        Dim cmd As New SqlCommand(sql, _conn)
        cmd.CommandType = CommandType.Text

        If _conn.State <> ConnectionState.Open Then
            _conn.Open()
        End If
        result = cmd.ExecuteReader(CommandBehavior.CloseConnection)

        Return result
    End Function

    Public Shared Function Execute(ByVal sql As String) As Boolean
        Dim result As Boolean = False
        Dim cmd As New SqlCommand(sql, _conn)

        Try
            If _conn.State <> ConnectionState.Open Then
                _conn.Open()
            End If

            result = CBool(cmd.ExecuteNonQuery())
        Finally
            If _conn.State = ConnectionState.Open Then
                _conn.Close()
            End If
        End Try

        Return result
    End Function

End Class
```

The connection string stored in the web.config file for the RestContacts project is as follows. Note that the connectionString attribute should be all on a single line in the web.config file. The connection string points to a database stored in the app_data directory of the project. Therefore, the AttachDbFilename attribute is used to identify the database file. In addition, the |DataDirectory| marker is used. This string is used to represent the current Web application's app_data directory.

```
<connectionStrings>
  <add name="contactsConnection"
    providerName="System.Data.SqlClient"
    connectionString="Data Source=.\SQLEXPRESS;
    AttachDbFilename=|DataDirectory|contacts.mdf;
    Integrated Security=True;
    User Instance=True"/>
</connectionStrings>
```

The DAL class provides a number of static methods for executing various SQL statements, including stored procedures and simple SQL text.

A Pure REST Service Example

To demonstrate creating a pure REST interface, I'll convert the example used in the just-enough REST interface and make it function as a pure REST interface as well.

The following table describes the URLs that the service exposes. Notice that we are overloading the POST request for those clients that do not support the PUT verb.

URL	Verb	Response
/all	GET	Returns a list of all available contacts entered into the system.
/#	GET	Returns a specific contact from the system by searching on id.
/email	GET	Returns a specific contact from the system by searching on e-mail.
/	POST	Inserts a new contact into the system, returning the contact (with assigned id).
/#	POST	Updates a contact with new information. The contact must exist in the system.
/#	PUT	Updates a contact with new information. Contact must exist in the system.
/#	DELETE	Deletes the contact from the system. The contact must exist in the system.

Core to many pure REST applications is a URL rewriting module. This URL rewriter converts the URLs in the system into the actions that perform the tasks. In the case of the contact manager service, it rewrites a URL such as `http://server/restcontacts/23` as `http://server/restcontacts/rest.ashx?method=getcontact&id=23`. The actual rewriting may be performed by the Web server or by the server-side code. Apache (via the `mod_rewrite` module) has excellent URL rewriting capabilities, and many systems using Apache employ this module to define regular expressions to rewrite URLs. IIS, on the other hand, has relatively weak URL rewriting capabilities, limited to static mappings. To supplement this system of URL rewriting, you can write an ISAPI module, an ASP.NET HTTP Module, or virtual path provider. For the pure REST contact manager, I create a simple HTTP module to rewrite the URLs.

An ASP.NET HTTP Module is a class that implements the `System.Web.IHttpModule` interface. This interface (see Listing 22-15) provides two methods. The `Init` method is called when IIS loads the HTTP Module. In it, you connect event handlers to process the request at the appropriate stage in the page lifetime. The `Dispose` method is called when IIS is unloading the class and is used to perform any cleanup needed by the module, such as closing files or database handles.

Listing 22-15: System.Web.IHttpModule

```
Public Interface IHttpModule
      ' Methods
      Sub Dispose()
      Sub Init(ByVal context As HttpApplication)
End Interface
```

In addition to these two methods, the HTTP Module also needs to have handlers for the stages in the page lifetime that it processes. For the REST module, the `AuthenticateRequest` stage is chosen to process the URL rewriting. This event is fired early enough in the process of a request so that security can be added later without changing the behaviour. The `BeginRequest` event also works in this case, but if authentication is added to the system, the module processes based on the rewritten URL, not the desired one.

The actual implementation of the HTTP module is shown in Listing 22-16. It adds a single handler to process the `AuthenticateRequest` event. This event is used to rewrite the request URL.

Listing 22-16: REST HTTP module

```
Imports Microsoft.VisualBasic
Imports System.Text
Imports System.Xml
Imports System.Net
Imports System.IO

Public Class ContactModule
    Implements IHttpModule

    Public Sub Dispose() Implements System.Web.IHttpModule.Dispose
        'this space left intentionally blank
    End Sub

    Public Sub Init(ByVal context As System.Web.HttpApplication) _
        Implements System.Web.IHttpModule.Init
        'set up connection to Application events
        AddHandler context.AuthenticateRequest, _
            AddressOf Me.AuthenticateRequest

    End Sub

    Private Sub AuthenticateRequest (ByVal sender As Object, ByVal e As EventArgs)
        Dim app As HttpApplication = CType(sender, HttpApplication)
        Rewrite(app.Request.Path, app)
    End Sub

    Protected Sub Rewrite(ByVal requestedPath As String, _
        ByVal app As HttpApplication)

        'You would probably want to make these mappings via
        ' a separate configuration section in web.config
        Dim context As HttpContext = app.Context
```

```
        Dim method As String = app.Request.HttpMethod.ToLower
        Dim tail As String = _
            requestedPath.Substring(app.Request.ApplicationPath.Length)
        If tail.StartsWith("/") Then
            tail = tail.Substring(1)
        End If

        If Not File.Exists(app.Server.MapPath(requestedPath)) Then
            'tail should have the id or name to work with
            'and method the HTTP verb
            Select Case method
                Case "get"
                    If IsNumeric(tail) Then
                        context.RewritePath("~/rest.ashx", False, _
                            "method=getcontact&id=" & tail, False)
                    ElseIf tail = "all" Then
                        'special case to retrieve all contacts
                        context.RewritePath("~/rest.ashx", False, _
                            "method=getcontact", False)
                    Else
                        'assuming an email search
                        context.RewritePath("~/rest.ashx", False, _
                            "method=getcontact&email=" & tail, False)
                    End If
                Case "post"
                    If IsNumeric(tail) Then
                        'overriding POST to also work as a PUT,
                        ' for those clients without PUT support
                        context.RewritePath("~/rest.ashx", False, _
                            "method=updatecontact&id=" & tail, False)
                    Else
                        context.RewritePath("~/rest.ashx", False, _
                            "method=insertcontact", False)
                    End If

                Case "put"
                    context.RewritePath("~/rest.ashx", False, _
                        "method=updatecontact&id=" & tail, False)

                Case "delete"
                    context.RewritePath("~/rest.ashx", False, _
                        "method=deletecontact&id=" & tail, False)
            End Select
        End If

    End Sub
End Class
```

The `Rewrite` method, like the main method in the earlier REST service, is primarily a dispatcher. In this case, if the file cannot be found on disk, the method determines the HTTP verb used and any trailing query parameters. It then uses the `RewritePath` method of the HttpContext to rewrite the URL to the just-enough equivalent.

After the HTTP Module is completed, it must be added to the `web.config` file for the virtual root it will work with. Listing 22-17 shows the code to be added for the `ContactModule`.

Listing 22-17: Adding HTTP module to web.config

```
<configuration>
    <system.web>
        <httpModules>
           <add name="ContactModule" type="ContactModule"/>
        </httpModules>
    </system.web>
</configuration>
```

Because of the format of the URLs, one last step is required before using the HTTP module. Because the requests do not have an extension, IIS would normally attempt to process these requests. You must map these requests to be processed by ASP.NET or you will receive 404 errors. Under IIS 5.1 (Windows XP), this is done by adding a handler for the `.*` extension (see Figure 22-8.)

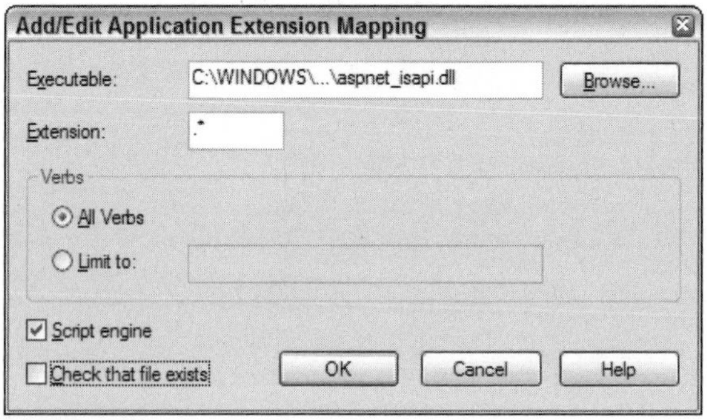

Figure 22-8

The wildcard mapping is used for IIS 6.0 in Windows Server 2003 (see Figure 22-9). Notice that the Check That File Exists is unchecked. This is necessary because the majority of requests that the REST sample supports do not actually exist as files on disk.

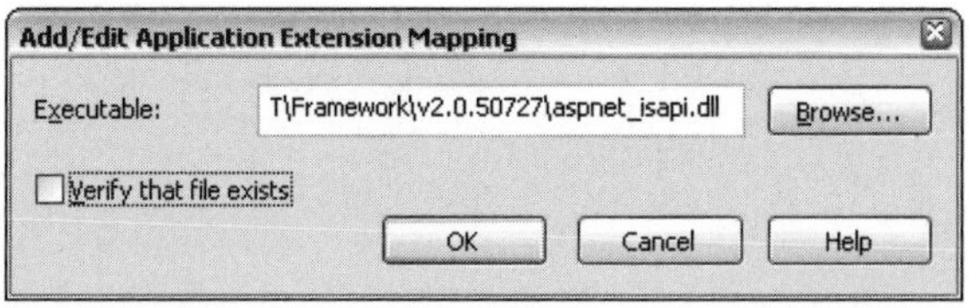

Figure 22-9

Testing the pure REST service is slightly more difficult than testing the just-enough service, because you must create the HTTP PUT and DELETE verbs. In addition, the body of the request must be set for some of the requests. Therefore, it is a good idea to get an HTTP debugging tool, such as Fiddler or curl (see the Resources list at the end of the chapter). These tools let you create requests against your service, set the POST/PUT body, and trace the results, including the HTTP headers. Figure 22-10 shows a test of inserting a new contact into the system using Fiddler.

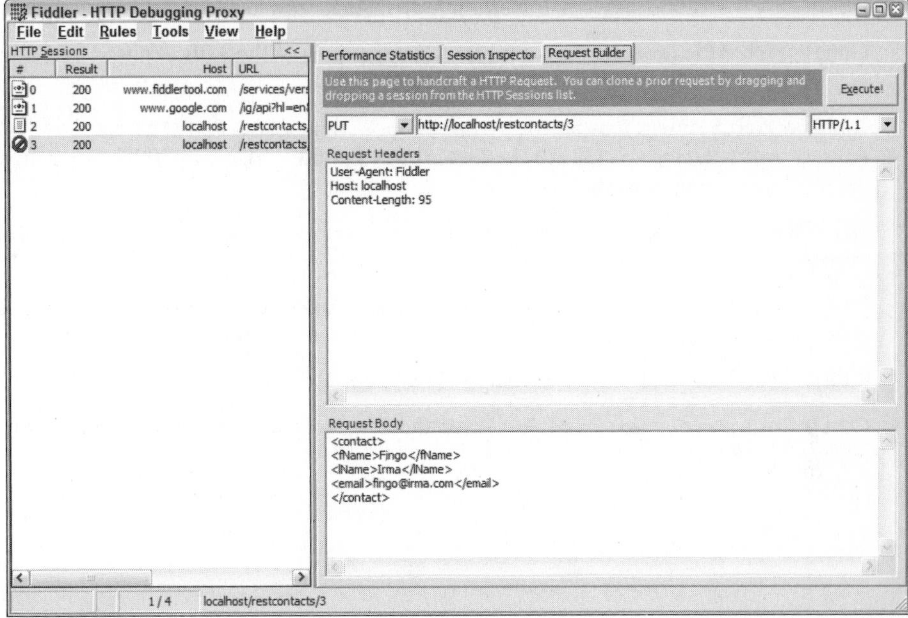

Figure 22-10

Figure 22-11 shows the resulting response.

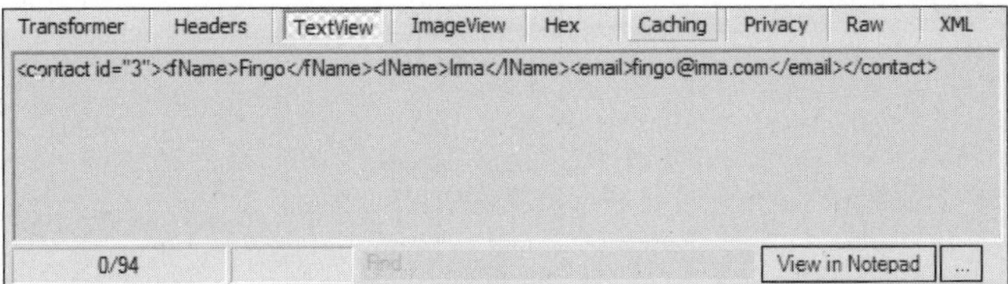

Figure 22-11

Summary

Although SOAP provides many means for creating robust services with routing, transactions, and other powerful features, sometimes all you need is a simple, scalable interface to data. REST services are one means of providing that simple interface. REST relies on simple, stateless HTTP requests and stable but composable URLs to provide a highly scalable interface for Web services. REST is easy to comprehend and work with, using only the GET and POST methods of HTTP; but it provides a clean mechanism for working with data if all the methods are used.

Resources

- **Yahoo Developer Network** (`http://developer.yahoo.net`) — Descriptions of the APIs exposed by the Yahoo services, including Maps, Flickr and Del.icio.us.
- **Google Web APIs** (`google.com/apis`) — Descriptions of the APIs exposed by Google services, including search and maps.
- **Amazon Web Services** (`amazon.com/gp/browse.html/102-0240740-9496941?%5F encoding=UTF8&node=3435361`) — Descriptions of the APIs exposed by Amazon, including the product catalog, search and queue service.
- **eBay Developers Program** (`http://developer.ebay.com/rest/`) — Descriptions of the APIs exposed by eBay.
- **Programmable Web** (`programmableweb.com/`) — Great resource site listing many of the available sites exposing APIs.
- **Fiddler** (`fiddlertoolcom`) — Excellent HTTP debugging tool.
- **Curl** (`http://curl.haxx.se/`) — Command-line tool for testing HTTP (and many, many other protocols).

Part VII
Applying XML

23

XML Form Development

Everyone is familiar with forms, either paper or electronic: a set of fields to be completed. Different types of fields exist, such as fill in the blank text boxes, pick one or pick many items, and so on. Some sort of validation usually ensures that fields are filled out (or filled out correctly). The completed form may need to be transmitted electronically. So, why do we need yet another form syntax? Because this new syntax eliminates some limitations of the previous implementations.

This chapter looks at using defining electronic forms using the W3C XForms standard, and the most commonly used proprietary standard, InfoPath. While neither of these methods is as familiar or offers the ease of development of XHTML forms, both bring benefits to the developer. Both syntaxes enforce best practices in software design, separating the model of the data from the implementation. This makes code and form reuse a much easier process. In addition, by enforcing XML standards, you can use other XML standards, such as XSLT or XPath when working with these XML form implementations. Finally, XForms is intended as the forms model of XHTML 2.0, currently a work in progress. Therefore, its importance will only increase as time goes by.

Creating Forms

The most common form syntax in use for electronic forms is that used in HTML/XHTML. Most developers are familiar with this syntax: an outer `<form>` tag that contains attributes identifying the target of the form and the means to encode the contents. Individual fields are contained within the `<form>` tags. Listing 23-1 shows a typical XHTML form.

Listing 23-1: An XHTML form

```
<form action="http://example.com/search" method="post">
    Text to search for: <input type="text" name="q" />
    <input type="submit" text="Search" />
</form>
```

This seems simple. So, what's the problem? The most notable problems with the XHTML model are:

- In the XHTML model, forms are all single step. The user completes the form and sends it to the target. If more information is needed, the target creates a new form. Creating multistep forms, such as wizards or polls, is a difficult process. Coordination of the steps and supporting the user moving back through the steps is even more difficult.
- XHTML forms are essentially a collection of name/value pairs. The data is flat: No way exists to present or create any structure over the data, such as one that identifies a group of fields as participating in an address.
- Validation and similar form handling requires the addition of script. Although this is not a problem, it does add another moving part to the system, increasing the chance of an error. In addition, because the script is not XML (it's usually JavaScript), you cannot use XML tools or technologies like XSLT.

Obviously, XForms is intended to solve these problems. XForms is currently a W3C Recommendation, now in the second edition of the 1.0 specification (as of March 2006). In addition, XForms is expected to be part of XHTML 2.0, a standard that is currently working its way through the approval process.

When you first begin to look at XForms, it may seem odd compared to other XML syntaxes. XForms does not define a visual UI as do XHTML or SVG. It does not define a new query syntax like XPath or XQuery. It does not define a schema for the form design or structure. No form element serves as a container for controls. These differences are all by design because XForms is intended to leverage existing standards. It uses XPath as the query syntax to identify nodes in XML data, and it uses XML schema to identify the data types of the form. Finally, although XForms does provide a set of UI controls, it uses them within the UI syntax of the containing XML. For example, you can use XForms syntax within XHTML pages, SVG documents, or any other XML syntax. When you use XForms with XHTML, you add the XForms controls within the XHTML page. By not requiring a new syntax for identifying the physical appearance of the forms, XForms makes it easier to use the same technique across multiple user interfaces.

XForms splits the actual form into three logical pieces: the model, the presentation, and the submit protocol (see Figure 23-1). By separating the form into these three components, XForms allows each to be used independently.

XForms Model

The XForms model is the data used by the form, including both the initial data displayed to the user and that submitted to the server. It contains information about the structure of the XML, as well as any constraints or calculations that will be applied to the data. This model is typically added to the `<head>` of an XHTML page, allowing it to be used anywhere on the page.

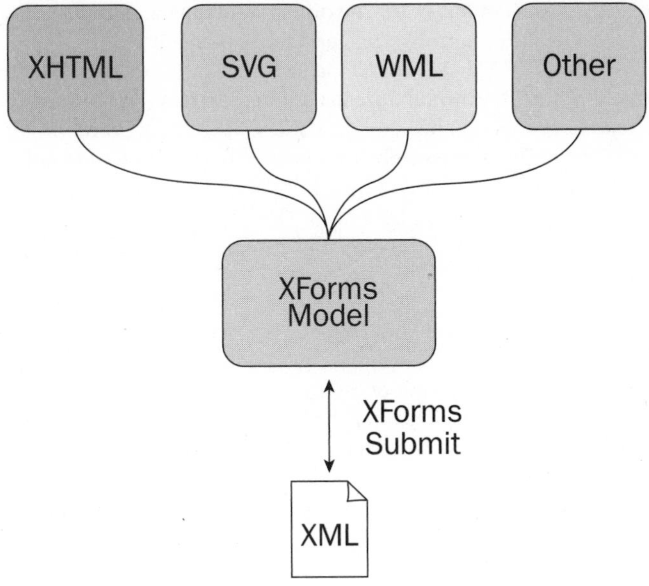

Figure 23-1

Listing 23-2 shows the XForms model for the query form shown in Listing 23-1.

Listing 23-2: The XForms model

```
<model>
   <instance>
     <search>
       <q>Enter search here</q>
     </search>
   </instance>
   <submission action="http://example.com/search"
               method="post"
               id="search"/>
</model>
```

Notice that this `model` does not include controls to identify the fields the form will search. These appear later in the page. Instead, you have the identification of the data used and the action to perform when the `model` is activated. In this case, some input data is sent via HTTP post to some end point (`http://example.com/search`). Although the example shown here is trivial (and it could easily be argued that the original XHTML version is simpler), it still demonstrates a few benefits of the XForms model. In the XHTML version, the query item is identified as a text box (`<input type="text">`), whereas in the XForms version, this binding is not present. Therefore, the XForms model in Listing 23-2 is not limited to being used on an XHTML page. The same model can be associated with an SVG document, WML page, or even a proprietary XML syntax. It provides reuse of a given action.

The `model` element serves as a container for the other elements used to describe the data. These optional child elements are the `instance`, `submission`, and `bind` elements.

The `instance` element defines the initial data used when displaying the form. This may be static data (such as the usual *Type here to enter* data), default values, or dynamic content. The `instance` element represents an *instance* or sample of the model that is used to populate the fields. It should be a valid document based on the schema in use. In the sample in Listing 23-2, the `instance` holds a single node, `search`. This, in turn, has a single child element: `q`. This element holds the default value for the search field. If the instance were to be defined dynamically, it would have been written using linking syntax as shown in the following line.

```
<instance src="http://example.com/sourceUrl" />
```

The submission element defines the target of the model. It is similar to the `action` attribute of XHTML or HTML forms. One major difference between XHTML and XForms forms, however, is that multiple submission elements can appear in each model.

In addition, the submission element has a number of optional attributes that provide further control over the submission process (see the following table).

Attribute	Description
`ref`	An XPath expression that defines the data in the instance to be submitted. This is useful when most of the data in the instance is read-only. Using this attribute, you can define the changing data and submit only that data.
`action`	Like the XHTML form tag, this attribute defines the target URL for the submission.
`method`	Like the XHTML form tag, this attribute defines the HTTP method to use for the submission. Unlike XHTML, however, no default value exists for this attribute.
`replace`	Optional attribute that defines how to replace the instance data after submission. The default is to replace *all* the instance data. However, you can also set it to *instance* to replace the data in a named instance, *none* to replace none of the data, or use a *qname* to identify the data to replace.
`version`	Identifies the version of XML to use when serializing the data for submission, typically *1.0*.
`indent`	Optional attribute that determines if additional whitespace should be added when serializing the data. Typically, you set this to *yes* if the target needs human-readable data, and to *no* if you want to reduce the data volume.
`mediatype`	String identifying the mediatype to use when submitting the data. This should either be `application/xml`, or a subtype that is compatible, such as `application/atom+xml`.
`encoding`	Optional attribute that defines the encoding to use when serializing the data before submission.

Attribute	Description
omit-xml-declaration	Optional attribute that determines whether the serialized data includes the XML declaration.
standalone	Optional attribute that determines whether the serialized data includes the standalone attribute on the XML declaration.
cdata-section-elements	Space-delimited string listing the child elements that are wrapped with CDATA sections before submission.
separator	String value that defines the character that are used to separate name/value pairs during encoding. The default value is `;`.
includenamespace prefixes	Space-delimited list of namespace prefixes that should be included in the serialized data. If this is omitted, the default behavior is to include all namespaces. However, this means that the XForms namespace are included in the serialized data unnecessarily. Typically, if you use this attribute, include only the namespace prefixes used to define the data in your model.

The `bind` element is one of the methods of connecting user interface controls to the instance. The `bind` element serves as a named mapping of data to user interface. Typically, this element is used to create a global mapping, as opposed to the other methods that associate individual controls to their data. You see this and the other methods of connecting the two in the user interface section that follows.

The complete XHTML page containing the query model is shown in Listing 23-3.

Listing 23-3: XHTML page with XForms query

```
<?xml version="1.0" encoding="UTF-8"?>
<html xmlns="http://www.w3.org/1999/xhtml"
  xmlns:xf="http://www.w3.org/2002/xforms"
  xmlns:ex="someURI">
  <head>
    <title>Search</title>
    <xf:model>
      <xf:instance>
        <ex:search>
          <ex:q>default value</ex:q>
        </ex:search>
      </xf:instance>
      <xf:submission action="http://example.com/search" method="post" id="search"/>
    </xf:model>
  </head>
  <body>
    <p>
      <xf:input ref="ex:q">
        <xf:label>Text to search for:</xf:label>
      </xf:input>
      <br/>
      <xf:submit submission="search">
```

(continued)

Listing 23-3 *(continued)*

```
          <xf:label>Search</xf:label>
        </xf:submit>
      </p>
    </body>
  </html>
```

The page includes the XForms and XHTML namespaces. In addition, another namespace is defined for the instance. Although this last step is not completely essential, it is a good practice. Remember that this instance is not required to physically be part of this document and could, instead, be coming from some dynamic source such as a JSP, ASP.NET, or PHP file.

The model serves as the container for the instance, or sample data, and the submission. In this simple case, the instance consists of a root node with a single child. This particular form might have been much simpler in XHTML. However, this simple example shows you some of the benefits of XForms. The default value is set when the form is loaded (see Figure 23-2). In addition, notice the isolation between the model and the user interface. This isolation enables you to more easily use this same model in other XForms applications. As you move on to more complex XForms forms, more benefits become evident.

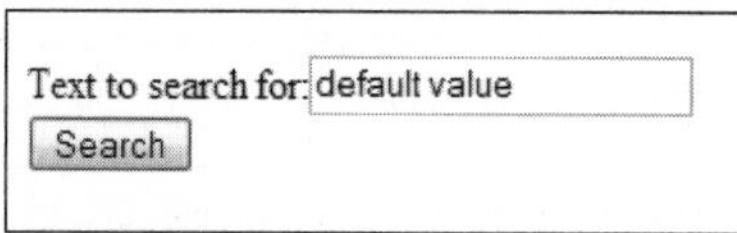

Figure 23-2

You are not limited to a single model in each XForms form. Listing 23-4 shows a form containing two models. The `model` attribute is used to identify the model providing data and structure for each control.

Listing 23-4: Hosting multiple models

```
<?xml version="1.0" encoding="UTF-8"?>
<html xmlns="http://www.w3.org/1999/xhtml" xmlns:xf="http://www.w3.org/2002/xforms"
xmlns:ex="someURI" xmlns:my="someOtherURI">
  <head>
    <title>Hosting multiple models</title>
    <xf:model id="model1">
      <xf:instance>
        <ex:contact>
          <ex:name>Foo deBar</ex:name>
          <ex:title>Consultant</ex:title>
        </ex:contact>
      </xf:instance>
    </xf:model>
    <xf:model id="model2">
      <xf:instance>
        <my:company>
          <my:name>Foobar Ent.</my:name>
        </my:company>
      </xf:instance>
```

```
      </xf:model>
    </head>
    <body>
      <h1>Hosting multiple models</h1>
      <xf:input ref="/ex:contact/ex:name" model="model1">
        <xf:label>Name: </xf:label>
      </xf:input><br /><br />
      <xf:input ref="/my:company/my:name" model="model2">
        <xf:label>Company: </xf:label>
      </xf:input>
    </body>
  </html>
```

Each model in the page is identified using the `id` attribute. Later, the desired model is selected via the model attribute on user interface controls. The resulting document (see Figure 23-3) displays one field from each of the two models. Each block of content could be simultaneously sent to the appropriate submission target.

Hosting multiple models

Name: Foo deBar

Company: Foobar Ent.

Figure 23-3

Just like XHTML (or HTML) and other form creation languages, XForms defines a number of user interface controls for creating items. These include simple text-entry fields, lists, check boxes, and file upload fields. One of the important distinctions between the XForms UI controls and their XHTML equivalents is that the XForms controls do not define their eventual appearance on the page. That is, the XHTML select element is defined as creating a list, and it has attributes that define the appearance of the eventual list (such as the number of elements to display); but the XForms select has no such definition of appearance. XForms clients are free to render the control in whatever form they desire, as long as the *behavior* remains constant. Therefore, a multiselect list can appear as a list box or as a series of check boxes. Either would provide the intent of a multiselect list. The XForms implementation is responsible for selecting the actual user interface.

XForms Controls

The controls defined with XForms are similar to their XHTML counterparts, and include:

- **input** — This is the XForms TextBox control (see Figure 23-4), and is similar to the XHTML input `type="text"` control.

```
<input ref="contact/name">
  <label>Name</label>
</input>
```

Figure 23-4

- **textarea** — Used to enter multiple lines of text (see Figure 23-5). This is equivalent to the XHTML input `type="textarea"` control.

```
<textarea ref="contact/address">
  <label>Address</label>
</textarea>
```

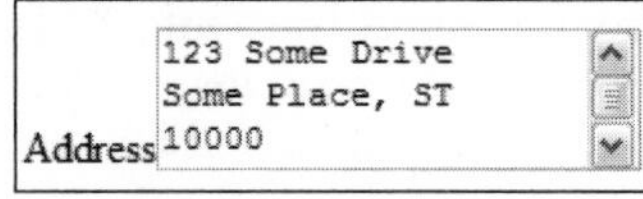

Figure 23-5

- **secret** — An input field that does not display the inputted text (see Figure 23-6), typically used for passwords or other information that should remain hidden. This is equivalent to the XHTML `input type="password"` field.

```
<secret ref="contact/password">
  <label>Password:</label>
</secret>
```

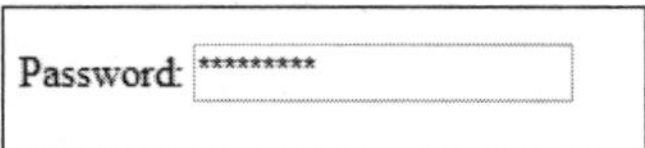

Figure 23-6

- **output** — A field that displays content. This is comparable to a standalone Label control. Typically, the information comes from the model, but this is not essential.

```
<output ref="contact/company" />
```

- **select** — A field that enables selection from a list, as shown in Figure 23-7. This is equivalent to the XHTML select field. However, although the XHTML select field defines the output as a list box, this control does not. Both single and multiple selections are supported by the XForms select control. The options for the list can either be included in the definition of the select field or populated through binding. To include options in the definition, use one or more `<item>` elements, with label and value children. The label becomes the visible entry in the list, whereas the value is what is written to the model.

```
<select ref="/contact/lang">
  <label>Languages spoken: </label>
  <item>
    <label>English</label>
    <value>en</value>
  </item>
  <item>
    <label>French</label>
```

```
        <value>fr</value>
      </item>
      <item>
        <label>Spanish</label>
        <value>es</value>
      </item>
      <item>
        <label>German</label>
        <value>de</value>
      </item>
    </select>
```

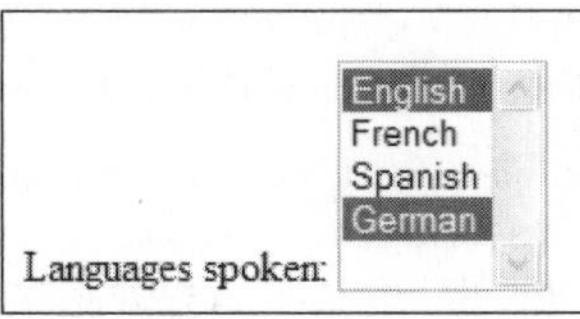

Figure 23-7

- **select1** — A version of the select control that ensures only a single item is selected, as shown in Figure 23-8. The implementation may render this control as a combo box, list box, or as a list of option buttons.

```
<select1 ref="ccard">
  <label>Department</label>
  <item>
    <label>Development</label>
    <value>dev</value>
  </item>
  <item>
    <label>Human Resources</label>
    <value>hr</value>
  </item>
  <item>
    <label>Management/label>
    <value>mgmt</value>
  </item>
</select1>
```

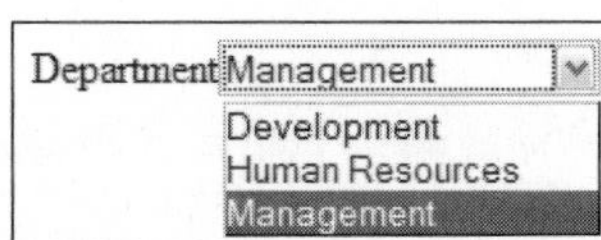

Figure 23-8

- **range** — A control that allows the user to select a value from a range of values, as shown in Figure 23-9. No equivalent to this control exists in XHTML, although some environments (such as Windows Forms) have this type of control. Those environments typically render this control either as a text box with associated up and down values or as a gauge.

```
<range ref="hireDate" start="1996" end="2006" step="1">
  <label>Hire Date:</label>
</range>
```

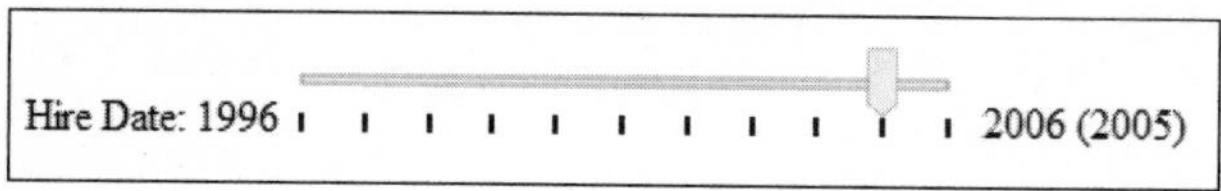

Figure 23-9

As you can see from the preceding sample, the `range` element has three additional attributes. The `start` and `end` attributes define the lower and upper bounds of the range, whereas the step attribute defines the frequency of the available choices.

- **upload** — A control that enables file upload, as shown in Figure 23-10, equivalent to the XHTML input `type="file"` field. This field requires more information than the others because you must define the fields that hold the URI and media type of the selected file.

```
<upload ref="photo" mediatype="image/*">
  <label>Select photo: </label>
  <filename ref=@filename />
  <mediatype ref=@mediatype/>
</upload>
```

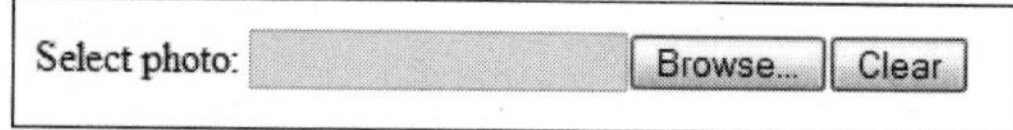

Figure 23-10

Two additional controls initiate an action, such as a calculation or submitting data.

- **submit** — A control that causes the data to be submitted to the server. This is equivalent to the `input type="submit"` of XHTML. Typically, this control renders as a button, but that is not required. This control does not refer to an element in the model. Instead, it refers to a submission element in the model by id. It enables the separation of the user interface from the action performed when the item is clicked.

```
<submit submission="contactForm">
  <label>Save</label>
</submit>
```

- **trigger** — A control that initiates some action, such as a calculation. This is equivalent to the `input type="button"` of XHTML. As you would expect, this is typically rendered using a button.

```
<trigger>
  <label>Add</label>
</trigger>
```

Common Control Children

Keen-eyed developers might note that no static text or label control is listed in the preceding section. XForms defines a common child element (label) that provides this functionality. This and other child elements that may be applied to any of the controls include:

- label — Provides a caption for the control.
- help — Provides assistance to the user during the completion of the form.
- hint — Provides assistance to the user during the completion of the form. This differs from the help element as it is generally less intrusive than help.
- alert — Provides a message used if the data entered is not valid.

Rather than using a standalone label control as in XHTML, XForms requires a label child element for all controls. This provides two benefits. First, the implementation can provide additional support for merging the two items, such as mnemonics or arranging the two controls close to one another. It also ensures that a label defines what each field represents. The label is also provides a handy way of identifying field captions when you need to apply CSS to the page.

The message element provides a means of communicating to the user. The message element defines a string that is displayed, either constantly or in reaction to a particular event. This element has an optional attribute — `level` — that defines how the message should be displayed. This attribute can be *modal*, *modeless* or *ephemeral*. Each implementation is responsible for defining the result of these three levels, but on desktop implementations, they are usually rendered as *modal dialog*, *modeless dialog* and *tooltip*, respectively.

The `setvalue` element assigns a value to the control when an event occurs (see Listing 23-5). This can be an alternative to using the `calculate` attribute when you are interested only in when particular events, such as `xforms-invalid` or `DOMFocusIn`, occur.

Listing 23-5: Adding message and setvalue elements

```
<input ref="ex:startDate">
  <label>Start Date: </label>
  <message level="ephemeral" ev:event="DOMFocusIn">
  Enter the start date for the report
  </message>
  <setvalue ev:event="xforms-ready">2006-04-01</setvalue>
</input>
```

The `hint` element is intended to assist the user while he is completing the form. The content of the `hint` can either be inline, as shown in the code listing, or from the instance or an external source (via the `src` attribute). Implementations typically show the `hint` using a ToolTip if available. Therefore, the `hint` element is equivalent to the following.

```
<message level="ephemeral" ev:event="xforms-hint">Message</message>
```

The `help` element is also intended to assist the user, but this assistance is more visible. For example, the FireFox implementation displays the `help` beside the field (see Figure 23-11). However, X-Smiles does not seem to display the `help` element. The help content can either be inline or from the instance or external source. The `help` element is equivalent to the following message.

```
<message level="modeless" ev:event="xforms-help"
  ev:propagate="stop">Message</message>
```

Listing 23-6 shows adding the help, hint and alert elements to form items.

Listing 23-6: Adding help, hint, and alert elements

```
<input ref="my:name">
  <label>Name: </label>
  <help>Help for the name field</help>
  <hint>Hint for the name field</hint>
  <alert>Alert for the name field</alert>
</input>
<input ref="my:value">
  <label>Integer Value: </label>
  <help>Help for the value field</help>
  <hint>Hint for the value field</hint>
  <alert>Alert for the value field</alert>
</input>
```

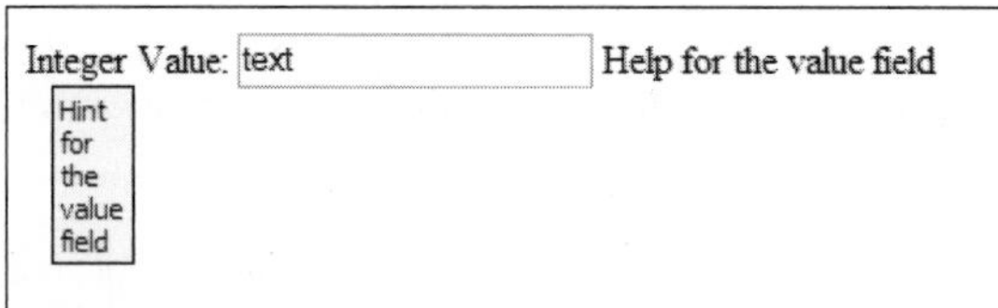

Figure 23-11

The `alert` element is displayed if the field's value is invalid. As shown earlier, the implementation is responsible for the result, but the typical response is to display an error dialog (see Figure 23-12). Some implementations, such as X-Smiles, also highlight the fields containing errors.

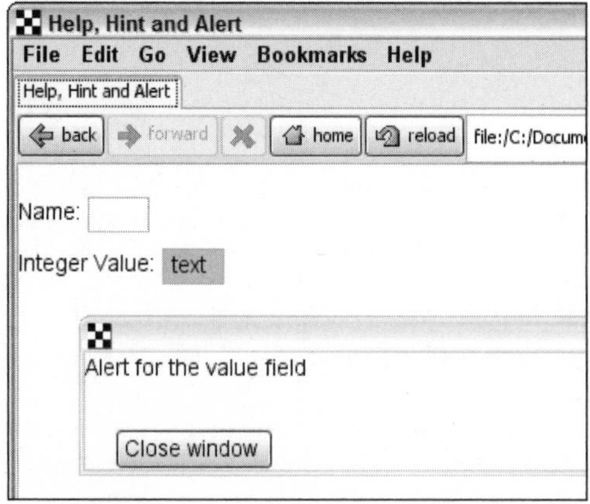

Figure 23-12

Changing Control Appearance

Many of the controls have multiple appearances. For example, the select and select1 controls may be rendered either as a list, or by using check boxes/option buttons (see Figure 23-13). This is not required, however, and each implementation is responsible for the final rendering. As an example, the X-Smiles implementation uses the same rendering for all settings for the select control.

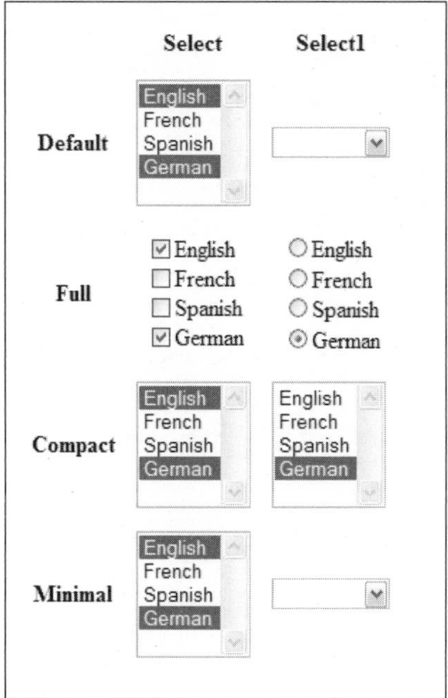

Figure 23-13

In addition, if the XForms content is in an XHTML container, the author can add CSS selectors or other elements, as needed, to style the controls and their labels.

Grouping Controls

When you are developing forms, note that data frequently fits into logical groups. For example, a form may have a number of fields that describe an address; those fields are a logical group. Alternately, when designing your forms, you may want certain fields to appear together, even on an independent page. XForms provides grouping functions to create these logical or visible groupings.

To create a simple association among multiple fields, use the group element. This is a container element that provides a hint to the implementation to associate the controls. Listing 23-7 shows a fragment containing two sets of the same controls; with and without a group element wrapping them. The result is shown in Figure 23-14.

Listing 23-7: Simple control grouping

```
<xf:input ref="ex:firstName">
  <xf:label>First Name: </xf:label>
</xf:input>
<xf:input ref="ex:lastName">
  <xf:label>Last Name: </xf:label>
</xf:input>
<xf:input ref="ex:title">
  <xf:label>Title: </xf:label>
</xf:input>
<br/>
<xf:group>
  <xf:label>Name: </xf:label>
  <xf:input ref="ex:firstName">
    <xf:label>First: </xf:label>
  </xf:input>
  <xf:input ref="ex:lastName">
    <xf:label>Last: </xf:label>
  </xf:input>
</xf:group>
<xf:input ref="ex:title">
  <xf:label>Title: </xf:label>
</xf:input>
```

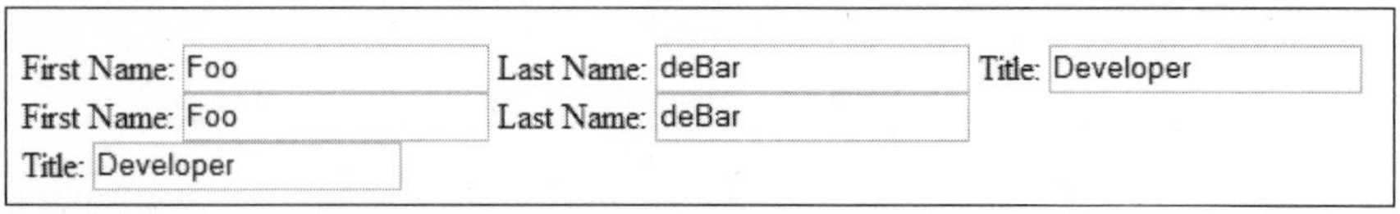

First Name: Foo Last Name: deBar Title: Developer
First Name: Foo Last Name: deBar
Title: Developer

Figure 23-14

Like other user interface controls, the group control accepts common child elements and attributes, such as `label`, `ref`, and so on. Using the `ref` attribute can simplify your forms if you are creating a form for a nested block of XML. The `ref` attribute can identify a common parent for the contained controls. Without the `ref` attribute, you must provide the full XPath expression for a child element. Listing 23-8 shows the `group` element with and without using `ref`.

Listing 23-8: Using ref with group

```
<xf:group>
  <xf:input ref="exp:employee/exp:name">
    <xf:label>Employee:</xf:label>
  </xf:input>
  <xf:input ref="exp:employee/exp:employeeID">
    <xf:label>Employee ID:</xf:label>
  </xf:input>
</xf:group>
<xf:group ref="exp:employee">
  <xf:input ref="exp:name">
    <xf:label>Employee:</xf:label>
  </xf:input>
```

```
    <xf:input ref="exp:employeeID">
      <xf:label>Employee ID:</xf:label>
    </xf:input>
  </xf:group>
```

Without the reference, you must provide the full XPath to retrieve the employee name. With the intermediate `ref`, the context of all fields within the group is set to the employee element.

Although the `group` element does not really provide any feature that is not available in XHTML, the `switch` element does. The `switch` element enables the creation of multipage forms, such as wizards. Using `switch` elements, and the associated `case` elements, you define pages. The logic behind the form can then direct users to pages based on their input. Listing 23-9 shows a simple three-page form that steps the user through a set of questions.

Listing 23-9: Using switch to create multiple pages

```
  <xf:switch>
    <xf:case id="one" selected="true">
      <xf:input ref="ex:name">
        <xf:label>What is your name?</xf:label>
      </xf:input>
      <xf:trigger>
        <xf:label>Next</xf:label>
        <xf:toggle ev:event="DOMActivate" case="two"/>
      </xf:trigger>
    </xf:case>
    <xf:case id="two">
      <xf:textarea ref="ex:quest">
        <xf:label>What is your quest?</xf:label>
      </xf:textarea><br />
      <xf:trigger>
        <xf:label>&lt;</xf:label>
        <xf:toggle ev:event="DOMActivate" case="one"/>
      </xf:trigger>
      <xf:trigger>
        <xf:label>&gt;</xf:label>
        <xf:toggle ev:event="DOMActivate" case="three"/>
      </xf:trigger>
    </xf:case>
    <xf:case id="three">
      <xf:input ref="ex:color">
        <xf:label>What is your favorite color?</xf:label>
      </xf:input><br />
      <xf:trigger>
        <xf:label>&lt;</xf:label>
        <xf:toggle ev:event="DOMActivate" case="two"/>
      </xf:trigger>
      <xf:trigger>
        <xf:label>Finish</xf:label>
        <xf:toggle ev:event="DOMActivate" case="summary"/>
      </xf:trigger>
    </xf:case>
```

(continued)

Listing 23-9 *(continued)*

```
    <xf:case id="summary">
      <xf:output value="ex:name">
        <xf:label>Name:</xf:label>
      </xf:output>
      <br />
      <xf:output value="ex:quest">
        <xf:label>Quest:</xf:label>
      </xf:output>
      <br />
      <xf:output value="ex:color">
        <xf:label>Color:</xf:label>
      </xf:output>
      <br />
      <br />
      <xf:trigger>
        <xf:label>Start again</xf:label>
        <xf:toggle ev:event="DOMActivate" case="one"/>
      </xf:trigger>
    </xf:case>
  </xf:switch>
```

Each page of information is contained within a `case` element. The element should have an id to identify the case. This is used when navigating between pages. Figure 23-15 shows the three pages of this form.

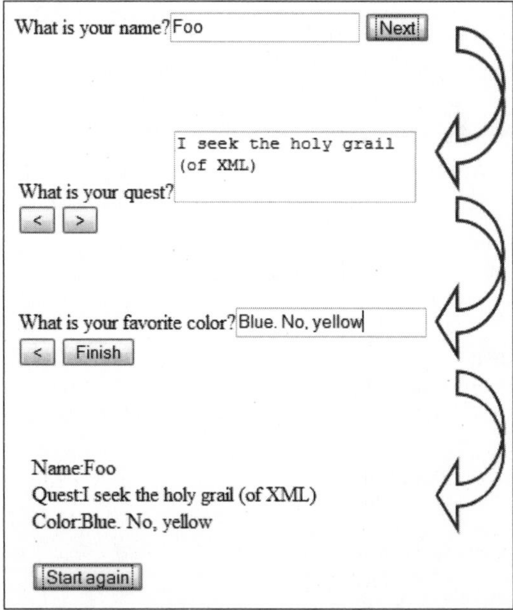

Figure 23-15

The cases do not need to be the entire content on each page, as shown here. You could have one section of the form that changes based on the selection made on another form.

The final form of complex user interfaces uses the `repeat` element. This creates a repeating section of other controls and is the typical way of creating a table-like structure in XForms. The contained controls are repeated for each element in a list of nodes (see Figure 23-16). See the binding section that follows for the syntax for binding to a repeating section.

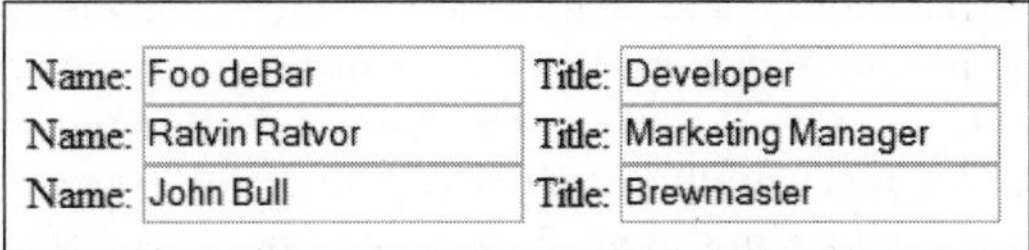

Figure 23-16

Binding Instance Data

After you have the model and the user interface, the next step is to connect the two of them. XForms performs this act using binding via XPath expressions. After a user interface control has been bound to a field in the model, it is automatically updated as the underlying data changes.

Binding is done with the `bind` element, and the `ref` and `nodeset` attributes. The `bind` element is an optional child element of the model. The `ref` and `nodeset` attributes are typically applied directly to controls, although `nodeset` is also used in the `bind` element. Binding can either be simple or complex. *Simple binding* refers to a single node bound to a control, like the input element. The `ref` attribute is used to select a single node via an XPath expression. Complex binding associates multiple nodes with a single control, as is done with select controls. The `nodeset` attribute identifies the desired nodes via an XPath expression.

The `bind` element describes the rules that apply to a later reference to an element. Multiple bind elements can exist in the model element. Each identifies an XPath expression and can represent either a single node or nodeset. The bind rules are applied whenever that node or nodeset is displayed later in the form. When defining a `bind` element, you can apply additional attributes to the element to control how the binding occurs. These additional attributes, referred to as the model item properties, are described in the following table.

Attribute	Description
`type`	This attribute is equivalent to the `xsi:type` attribute and identifies the data type of the binding. Adding the attribute here, as opposed to in the schema or instance, overrides default behavior. It also guarantees the intended type. One additional benefit of using this attribute is that it can be applied to attributes or elements. Therefore, you can use the binding to guarantee that an `id` attribute uses an `xs:integer` value.
`readonly`	Prevents the user of the form from changing the value. This also provides a hint to the user interface that implementations may use to grey out the field or otherwise identify the field as read-only data.

Table continued on following page

Attribute	Description
`required`	Ensures that the data is given a value before the form is submitted. The user interface implementation may use this to provide additional feedback to the user.
`relevant`	Identifies bindings to be included in the serialization and tab order. This is typically used in multipart wizards or forms that have optional sections. If a binding is set to `relevant=false`, it is ignored. Rather than an explicitly entered value, however, it is usually a calculated value. For example, the following fragment identifies three bindings. The discount field is only relevant if the product of the price and quantity bindings is greater than 100 (see Figure 23-17).

```
<xf:model>
  <xf:instance>
    <ex:data>
      <ex:item>
        <ex:price xsi:type="xs:decimal"/>
        <ex:qty xsi:type="xs:integer">1</ex:qty>
        <ex:discount xsi:type="xs:decimal"/>
        <ex:total xsi:type="xs:decimal"/>
      </ex:item>
    </ex:data>
  </xf:instance>
  <xf:bind nodeset="ex:item/ex:price" required="true()" />
  <xf:bind nodeset="ex:item/ex:qty" required="true()" />
  <xf:bind nodeset="ex:item/ex:discount"
    relevant="../ex:price*../ex:qty &gt; 100"
    calculate="../ex:price*../ex:qty*0.1" readonly="true()" />
    <xf:bind nodeset="ex:item/ex:total" readonly="true()"
    calculate="((../ex:price * ../ex:qty)-../ex:discount)" />
</xf:model>
```

Attribute	Description
`calculate`	Provides an expression that is used to calculate the value of a field.
`constraint`	Provides an expression that must be `true` for the model to be considered valid. This is useful to provide validation for your forms. The following fragment tests to ensure that the `to` field is later than the `from` field.

```
<xf:model>
  <xf:instance>
    <ex:dateRange>
      <ex:from xsi:type="xs:date"/>
      <ex:to xsi:type="xs:date" />
      <ex:days xsi:type="xs:integer" />
    </ex:dateRange>
  </xf:instance>
  <xf:bind nodeset="ex:from" required="true()" />
  <xf:bind nodeset="ex:to" required="true()"
    constraint="days-from-date(.) &gt; days-from-date(../ex:from)" />
  <xf:bind nodeset="ex:days"
    calculate="days-from-date(../ex:to) - days-from-date(../ex:from)"
    readonly="true()" />
</xf:model>
```

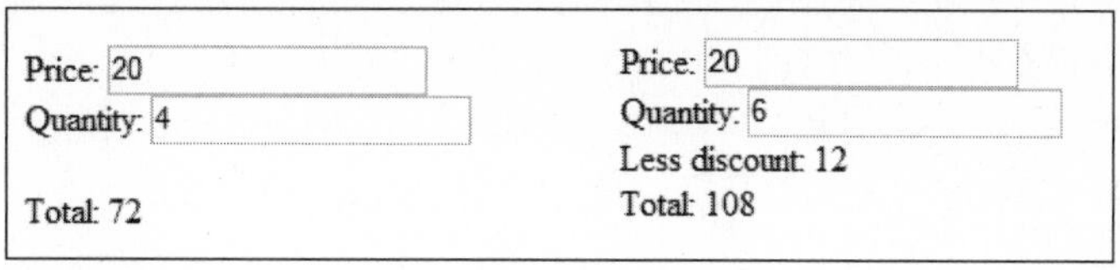

Price: 20
Quantity: 4

Total: 72

Price: 20
Quantity: 6
Less discount: 12
Total: 108

Figure 23-17

The `ref` attribute associates the single node identified by an XPath expression to a control. If an appropriate `bind` element is present, those rules are applied. The XPath expression is applied based on the current context and can include additional XPath or XForms functions (see Listing 23-10).

Listing 23-10: Simple binding

```
<xf:input ref="exp:date">
  <xf:label>Date:</xf:label>
</xf:input>
<xf:input ref="exp:date" />
```

The `nodeset` attribute identifies a set of data for controls that require more information, such as select and select1. Although these controls still have a `ref` attribute that identifies the value of the controls, they also need to be bound to a list of items to display. This list is identified using either the `<choices>` element, or the `<itemset nodeset=" ">` child element (see Listing 23-11). The `choices` element is used to hard-code the list of items to display. The `itemset` extracts a set of nodes from the target instance.

Listing 23-11: Complex binding

```
<?xml version="1.0" encoding="UTF-8"?>
<html xmlns="http://www.w3.org/1999/xhtml"
  xmlns:xf="http://www.w3.org/2002/xforms"
  xmlns:ev="http://www.w3.org/2001/xml-events"
  xmlns:xsi="http://www.w3.org/2001/XMLSchema-instance"
  xmlns:xs="http://www.w3.org/2001/XMLSchema"
  xmlns:ex="someURI">
  <head>
    <title>Data binding</title>
    <xf:model>
      <xf:instance>
        <ex:months selected="apr">
          <ex:month value="jan">January</ex:month>
          <ex:month value="feb">February</ex:month>
          <ex:month value="mar">March</ex:month>
          <ex:month value="apr">April</ex:month>
          <ex:month value="may">May</ex:month>
          <ex:month value="jun">June</ex:month>
          <ex:month value="jul">July</ex:month>
          <ex:month value="aug">August</ex:month>
          <ex:month value="sep">September</ex:month>
          <ex:month value="oct">October</ex:month>
          <ex:month value="nov">November</ex:month>
          <ex:month value="dec">December</ex:month>
```

(continued)

Listing 23-11 *(continued)*

```
        </ex:months>
      </xf:instance>
    </xf:model>
  </head>
  <body>
    <p>
      <xf:input ref="@selected">
        <xf:label>Selected: </xf:label>
      </xf:input><br />
      <xf:select ref="@selected">
        <xf:itemset nodeset="/ex:months/ex:month">
          <xf:label ref="." />
          <xf:value ref="@value" />
        </xf:itemset>
      </xf:select>
    </p>
  </body>
</html>
```

The `ref` attribute points at the selected attribute of the root element, whereas the `nodeset` expression in the `itemset` extracts the list of months to display. Both the `choices` and `itemset` elements require that you identify the text to display and the value for each item. This is done with the `label` and `value` elements respectively. Figure 23-18 shows this form running. The input control is also bound to show how changing either field updates the model and the controls. Try changing the text in the input field to **nov** to see the select field update.

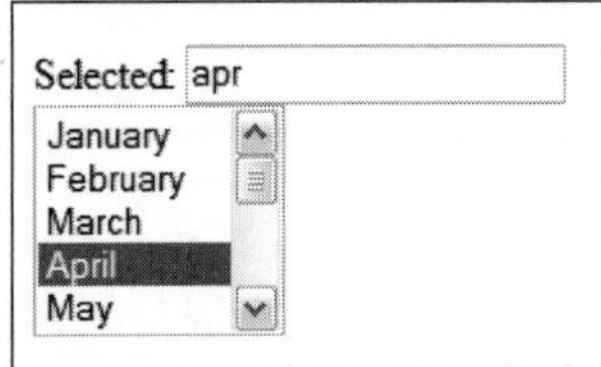

Figure 23-18

The second use of the `nodeset` attribute occurs when you are displaying repeating elements (see Listing 23-12).

Listing 23-12: Using the repeat element

```
<xf:repeat nodeset="ex:employee">
  <xf:input ref="ex:name">
    <xf:label>Name: </xf:label>
  </xf:input>
  <xf:input ref="ex:title">
    <xf:label>Title: </xf:label>
  </xf:input>
</xf:repeat>
```

The entire group of repeating elements is bound to the nodeset identified by the XPath expression, `"ex:employee"`. This also sets the context, so that the contained controls are mapped to the children of that node. Each of the controls within the repeat element repeats for each node in the selected set.

When the type of the data is identified, either by including a schema in the model or by adding the `type` attribute to the `instance` or a `bind` expression, many implementations change the appearance of the controls to data-type-aware versions. The most commonly used version occurs when the data type is `"xs:date"` or one of the related date types. Many implementations provide a date picker control (see Figure 23-19).

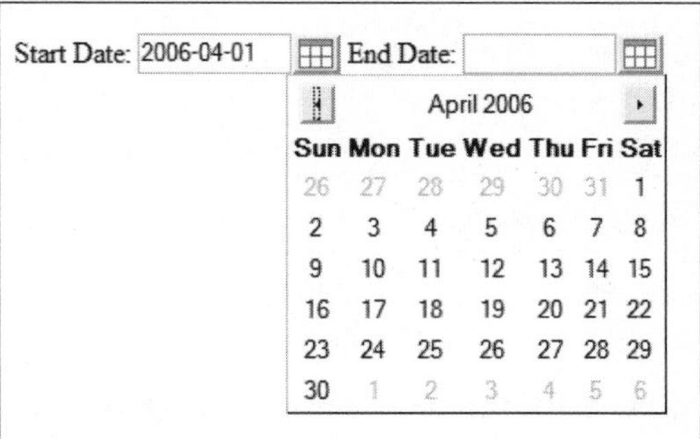

Figure 23-19

XForms Submit Protocol

After the user is finished interacting with the XForm, it is time to submit the form. The behavior during submission is defined by the active submission element. During submission, the data is serialized into a form for transmission. It is then sent to the target URL.

The first step in the submission process is the serialization of the form into the form needed. This is determined by the relationship of the protocol defined in the `action` attribute and the method used. Therefore, a different serialization model is used for sending the data via HTTP GET than for saving the file locally using a PUT. The following table outlines some of the more common combinations.

Protocol	Method	Serialization format
HTTP, HTTPS	GET	application/x-www-form-urlencoded
HTTP, HTTPS, mailto	POST	application/xml
HTTP, HTTPS, file	PUT	application/xml

The fragment in Listing 23-13 defines a form that saves the data locally.

Listing 23-13: Submitting XForms

```
<model>
  <instance>
    <ex:contact>
      <ex:firstName>Foo</ex:firstName>
      <ex:lastName>deBar</ex:lastName>
      <ex:title>Developer</ex:title>
    </ex:contact>
  </instance>
  <submission id="submit1"
    method="put"
    action="file:///C:/temp/output.xml"
    includenamespaceprefixes="ex"/>
  <submission id="submit2"
    method="GET"
    action="http://server/endPoint"
    includenamespaceprefixes="ex"
    separator="&amp;"/>
</model>
```

Listing 23-14 shows the output of each of the submission methods.

Listing 23-14: Data serialization

PUT/file (application/xml):

```
<?xml version="1.0" encoding="utf-8"?>
<ex:contact xmlns="http://www.w3.org/1999/xhtml"
  xmlns:ex="someURI">
  <ex:firstName>Foo</ex:firstName>
  <ex:lastName>deBar</ex:lastName>
  <ex:title>Developer</ex:title>
</ex:contact>
```

GET/HTTP (application/x-www-form-urlencoded):

```
http://localhost:32932/work/Dump.aspx?firstName=Foo&lastName=deBar&title=Developer
```

POST/HTTP (application/xml):

```
<ex:contact xmlns="http://www.w3.org/1999/xhtml" xmlns:ex="someURI">
          <ex:firstName>Foo</ex:firstName>
          <ex:lastName>deBar</ex:lastName>
          <ex:title>Developer</ex:title>
        </ex:contact>
```

Multipart-POST/HTTP (application/multipart):

```
-----------------------------57052814523281
Content-Type: application/xml
```

```
Content-ID: &lt;41bb.26e9@mozilla.org&gt;


<ex:contact xmlns="http://www.w3.org/1999/xhtml" xmlns:ex="someURI">
          <ex:firstname>Foo</ex:firstname>
          <ex:lastname>deBar</ex:lastname>
          <ex:title>Developer</ex:title>

        </ex:contact>
-----------------------------57052814523281-
```

The `includenamespaceprefixes` attribute is applied to restrict the namespaces in the XML to the XHTML and example namepaces.

Note that for the GET request, the separator is set to `"&"`. This ensures that each parameter is sent as a name/value pair. If you fail to do this, the default separator (`;`) is sent.

XForms Logic

A form populated based on some XML and XPath expressions is useful for displaying data, but a form frequently has to perform some processing as well. Therefore, you must add logic or code to react to changes made by the user. XForms provides this capability through events and actions. *Events* are associated with form elements to react to data updates, navigation, errors or other stages in the creation and editing of the form. *Actions* are elements that are invoked based on these events.

Events

Events are at the core of XForms development. They are raised at significant parts of the form's lifetime and cause either the implementation or added code to execute when the event occurs. XForms uses the XML Events module (`w3.org/2001/xml-events`) for defining these events. The event can be caught by any element, although they are frequently associated with trigger controls and actions (see the following). XForms events fall into four broad categories:

- **Initialization** — These events are important in the creation and rendering of the form by the implementation. They include the `xforms-model-construct` event, that is passed to each control, causing them to render themselves onto the form, and the `xforms-ready` that is fired when the form is complete and ready for editing. These events are not usually used by the developer, although `xforms-ready` can be used to notify the user that the form is ready for his input.
- **Interaction** — These events are thrown as the user navigates through the form and changes values. Some examples of these events are the `xforms-submit` (occurs when the form is submitted), `xforms-recalculate` (occurs when any value is changed), and `xforms-focus` (occurs as a control receives focus).
- **Notification** — These events occur when controls are used, such as when a button is clicked or text is entered in a field. They include the most commonly used event, `DOMActivate` (the default event for a control, such as a button click) as well as `xforms-value-changed`, `xforms-insert`, and the `xforms-valid`/`xforms-invalid` events.

- **Error indication** — These events are thrown when major errors occur in the processing of a form. They include `xforms-compute-exception`, which occurs when a major calculation error occurs (such as division by zero). You should handle these events to avoid the default processing, which frequently causes the form to be closed.

You process events by associating them with a control or element such as `action`. When the event occurs, the action is executed.

Actions

Actions are behaviors that you want invoked at points in the lifespan of a form. For example, actions can be used to insert data, change values in fields, or recalculate the form. Typically, actions are performed using trigger elements, but this is not always the case; they can be associated with any form control. The following table discusses the commonly used actions available to XForms developers.

Action	Description
`action`	Enables the developer to combine multiple actions into a set. Each of the child elements of this action are performed in sequence, so you could add a new row to a repeat element and set the value of each of the fields.
`dispatch`	Invokes the desired event. This provides the means of forcing a particular event to occur, such as an error message (using xforms-help). Many of the following actions can also be carried out through dispatch.
`recalculate`	Recalculates the form. Although this is typically done when the fields change, the `recalculate` action can force this behavior.
`revalidate`	Runs all data validation on the form. Although this is typically done as the fields change, the revalidate action can force this behavior.
`Refresh`	Forces the data back to the original instance data, removing changes.
`setfocus`	Sets the focus to a particular control. The control is identified using an `id` attribute. <xf:trigger> <xf:label>Setfocus</xf:label> <xf:action ev:event="DOMActivate"> <xf:setfocus control="B" /> </xf:action> </xf:trigger>
`setvalue`	Assigns a value to a field in the model. The field is identified using an XPath expression. <xf:trigger> <xf:label>Set A to 20</xf:label> <xf:action ev:event="DOMActivate"> <xf:setvalue ref="@a">20</xf:setvalue> </xf:action> </xf:trigger>

<table>
<tr><th>Action</th><th>Description</th></tr>
<tr><td>Send</td><td>Submits the form. This is equivalent to using a submit element, and requires the id of the submit element.</td></tr>
<tr><td>Insert</td><td>Adds a new row to a repeat element. This creates the new fields required for the node. Data from the last member of the existing collection is used to fill these fields. The developer is responsible for identifying the location of the newly added row using the two attributes position (either "before" or "after") and at (the index).
<pre><xf:trigger>
  <xf:label>Add</xf:label>
  <xf:action ev:event="DOMActivate">
    <xf:insert nodeset="ex:employee"
       position="after"
       at="count(//ex:employee)" />
  </xf:action>
</xf:trigger></pre></td></tr>
<tr><td>Delete</td><td>Deletes a row from a repeat element. The index must be provided.
<pre><xf:trigger>
  <xf:label>Delete</xf:label>
  <xf:delete ev:event="DOMActivate"
      nodeset="ex:employee"
      at="index('empitem')" />
</xf:trigger></pre></td></tr>
<tr><td>setindex</td><td>Selects a row in a repeat element. Many implementations highlight the selected row for clarity.</td></tr>
</table>

XForms Sample

Most of the forms in this chapter have been small to highlight one or more XForms features. In order to show a more realistic example, I'll create an expense report form (see Figure 23-20). This demonstrates how many of the features of XForms interact to enable you to create not just simple forms, but full-blown XML applications.

The first step in creating an XForms form is to define the model. In order to benefit from the automatic data validation and improved controls, I decided to base the form on a schema. In addition, the instance is loaded from a separate file. This means you can easily change the default instance by editing this secondary file. So that I don't need to create a server-side component to process the generated XML, the submission is set to use PUT to write a local file. You may need to adjust the paths to these three files for testing.

```
<xf:model schema="http://server/expenseReport.xsd">
  <xf:instance src="http://server/baseReport.xml" />
  <xf:submission id="saveXML" method="put"
      action="file:///C:/temp/output.xml"
      includenamespaceprefixes="exp" />
</xf:model>
```

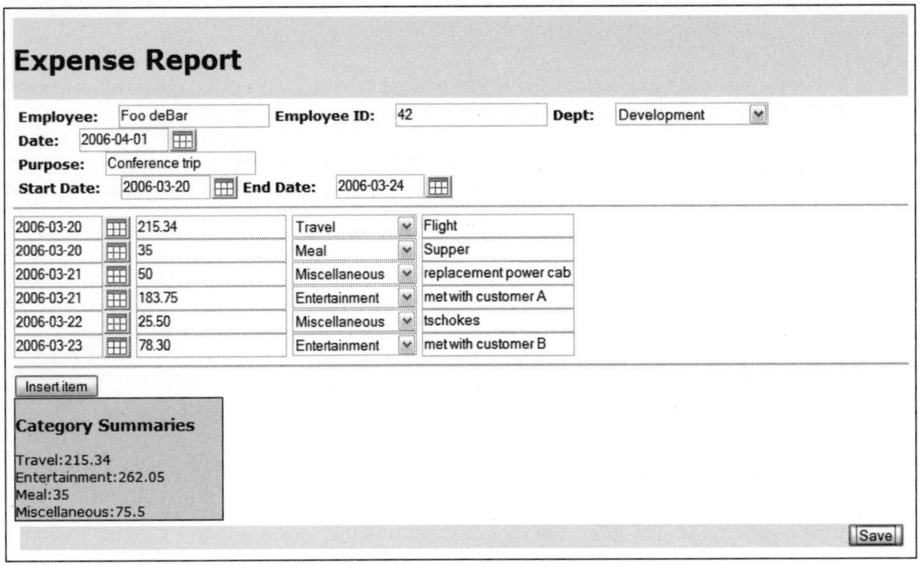

Figure 23-20

The four fields at the bottom of the form that provide the summary data are populated using binding expressions. This ensures that, as the data changes, these fields are updated automatically. The binding expression ensures the data is displayed using the correct data type and provides the calculation that determines the value. Each of the four expressions is identical, with the exception of the target field and the expense type to sum:

```
<xf:bind nodeset="exp:summary/exp:travelSummary"
      type="xs:decimal"
      calculate="sum(//exp:expenseItem/exp:amount[../exp:type='Travel'])" />
```

Lookup fields are frequently used when designing forms. These provide a set of selections for the user, reducing data entry errors and increasing data consistency. The data for the list part of the lookup field may be part of the primary instance, but it is often necessary to provide the data from elsewhere. This is done by adding secondary instances to the model. You refer to these later by referencing the `id` attribute of the instance. The department and expense type drop-down lists are populated using the following instances:

```
<xf:instance id="departments">
  <departments>
    <department id="dev">
      <name>Development</name>
    </department>
    <department id="sal">
      <name>Sales</name>
    </department>
  </departments>
</xf:instance>
<xf:instance id="expenseTypes">
```

```
    <expenseType xmlns="">
      <option value="Travel" />
      <option value="Entertainment" />
      <option value="Meal" />
      <option value="Miscellaneous" />
    </expenseType>
  </xf:instance>
  ...
  <xf:select1 ref="exp:dept">
    <xf:label>Dept:</xf:label>
    <xf:itemset nodeset="instance('departments')/department">
      <xf:label ref="name" />
      <xf:value ref="@id" />
    </xf:itemset>
  </xf:select1>
```

The central section of the form is composed of a repeating section for each expense item. Adding a new item to the list is done through a trigger. This uses the insert element to add a new item to the appropriate nodeset.

```
<xf:repeat id="lineitems" nodeset="exp:expenseItem">
  <xf:input ref="exp:date" />
  <xf:input ref="exp:amount" />
  <xf:select1 ref="exp:type">
    <xf:itemset nodeset="instance('expenseTypes')/option">
      <xf:label ref="@value" />
      <xf:value ref="@value" />
    </xf:itemset>
  </xf:select1>
  <xf:input ref="exp:description" />
</xf:repeat>
<hr />
<xf:trigger>
  <xf:label>Insert item</xf:label>
  <xf:action ev:event="DOMActivate">
    <xf:insert position="after" nodeset="exp:expenseItem"
    at="index('lineitems')" />
  </xf:action>
</xf:trigger>
```

Listing 23-15 shows the complete source for the expense report form.

Listing 23-15: Complete expense report form

```
<?xml version="1.0" encoding="utf-8"?>
<html xmlns="http://www.w3.org/1999/xhtml"
xmlns:xf="http://www.w3.org/2002/xforms"
xmlns:ev="http://www.w3.org/2001/xml-events"
xmlns:xsi="http://www.w3.org/2001/XMLSchema-instance"
xmlns:xs="http://www.w3.org/2001/XMLSchema"
xmlns:exp="http://example.com/expenseReport">
  <head>
```

(continued)

Listing 23-15 *(continued)*

```
    <xf:model schema="http://server/expenseReport.xsd">
      <xf:instance src="http://server/baseReport.xml" />
      <xf:submission id="saveXML" method="put"
      action="file:///C:/temp/output.xml"
      includenamespaceprefixes="exp" />
      <xf:bind nodeset="exp:summary/exp:travelSummary"
      type="xs:decimal"
      calculate="sum(//exp:expenseItem/exp:amount[../exp:type='Travel'])" />
      <xf:bind nodeset="exp:summary/exp:entSummary"
      type="xs:decimal"
      calculate="sum(//exp:expenseItem/exp:amount[../exp:type='Entertainment'])" />
      <xf:bind nodeset="exp:summary/exp:mealSummary"
      type="xs:decimal"
      calculate="sum(//exp:expenseItem/exp:amount[../exp:type='Meal'])" />
      <xf:bind nodeset="exp:summary/exp:miscSummary"
      type="xs:decimal"
      calculate="sum(//exp:expenseItem/exp:amount[../exp:type='Miscellaneous'])" />
      <xf:instance id="departments">
        <departments xmlns=""
        xmlns:xsi="http://www.w3.org/2001/XMLSchema-instance">
          <department id="dev">
            <name>Development</name>
          </department>
          <department id="sal">
            <name>Sales</name>
          </department>
        </departments>
      </xf:instance>
      <xf:instance id="expenseTypes">
        <expenseType xmlns="">
          <option value="Travel" />
          <option value="Entertainment" />
          <option value="Meal" />
          <option value="Miscellaneous" />
        </expenseType>
      </xf:instance>
    </xf:model>
    <link href="sample.css" type="text/css" rel="stylesheet">
    </link>
  </head>
  <body>
    <div id="wrapper">
      <div id="header">Expense Report</div>
      <div id="content">
        <xf:group ref="exp:employee">
          <xf:input ref="exp:name">
            <xf:label>Employee:</xf:label>
          </xf:input>
          <xf:input ref="exp:employeeID">
            <xf:label>Employee ID:</xf:label>
          </xf:input>
          <xf:select1 ref="exp:dept">
```

```
        <xf:label>Dept:</xf:label>
        <xf:itemset nodeset="instance('departments')/department">
          <xf:label ref="name" />
          <xf:value ref="@id" />
        </xf:itemset>
      </xf:select1>
    </xf:group>
    <xf:group>
      <xf:input ref="exp:date">
        <xf:label>Date:</xf:label>
      </xf:input>
      <br />
      <xf:input ref="exp:purpose">
        <xf:label>Purpose:</xf:label>
      </xf:input>
      <br />
      <xf:group>
        <xf:input ref="exp:startDate">
          <xf:label>Start Date:</xf:label>
        </xf:input>
        <xf:input ref="exp:endDate">
          <xf:label>End Date:</xf:label>
        </xf:input>
      </xf:group>
    </xf:group>
  </div>
  <hr />
  <xf:repeat id="lineitems" nodeset="exp:expenseItem">
    <xf:input ref="exp:date" />
    <xf:input ref="exp:amount" />
    <xf:select1 ref="exp:type">
      <xf:itemset nodeset="instance('expenseTypes')/option">
        <xf:label ref="@value" />
        <xf:value ref="@value" />
      </xf:itemset>
    </xf:select1>
    <xf:input ref="exp:description" />
  </xf:repeat>
  <hr />
  <xf:trigger>
    <xf:label>Insert item</xf:label>
    <xf:action ev:event="DOMActivate">
      <xf:insert position="after" nodeset="exp:expenseItem"
      at="index('lineitems')" />
    </xf:action>
  </xf:trigger>
  <div id="summary">
    <xf:group ref="exp:summary">
      <xf:label>
        <h3>Category Summaries</h3>
      </xf:label>
      <xf:output ref="exp:travelSummary">
        <xf:label>Travel:</xf:label>
      </xf:output>
```

(continued)

Listing 23-15 *(continued)*

```
          <br />
          <xf:output ref="exp:entSummary">
            <xf:label>Entertainment:</xf:label>
          </xf:output>
          <br />
          <xf:output ref="exp:mealSummary">
            <xf:label>Meal:</xf:label>
          </xf:output>
          <br />
          <xf:output ref="exp:miscSummary">
            <xf:label>Miscellaneous:</xf:label>
          </xf:output>
          <br />
        </xf:group>
      </div>
      <div id="footer">
        <xf:submit submission="saveXML">
          <xf:label>Save</xf:label>
        </xf:submit>
      </div>
    </div>
  </body>
</html>
```

Alternatives to XForms

Although XForms is a W3C standard, some forms packages have obviously been available for many years. With the advent of XML, many of these packages began to use XML to define the form layout. In addition, while XForms worked its way through the standards bodies, other competing XML formats were defined. The most notable of these is Microsoft InfoPath, but other similar designers include Adobe LifeCycle Designer.

Microsoft InfoPath

InfoPath is the member of the Office family used to create XML forms. It is positioned primarily as a Web Service and SharePoint client, but it can also be used standalone to create XML files. InfoPath uses a similar model to XForms to define its forms (see Figure 23-21). There is a model, a user interface, and a submission mechanism. In the case of InfoPath, the model is the XML Schema or WSDL definition of a block of XML or Web Service. Alternatively, a SQL Server or Microsoft Access database can be used, and the schema is derived from the table structure. The user interface is created using the InfoPath tool (see Figure 23-22). The submission mechanism is typically a Web Service, although you can also use InfoPath to save XML files.

As you can see from the architecture diagram, XSLT is used to create the user interface. The InfoPath file includes this XSLT, as well as any associated XSD or XML files and a manifest file. These are stored in one file using the ZIP file format, although the extension is XSN.

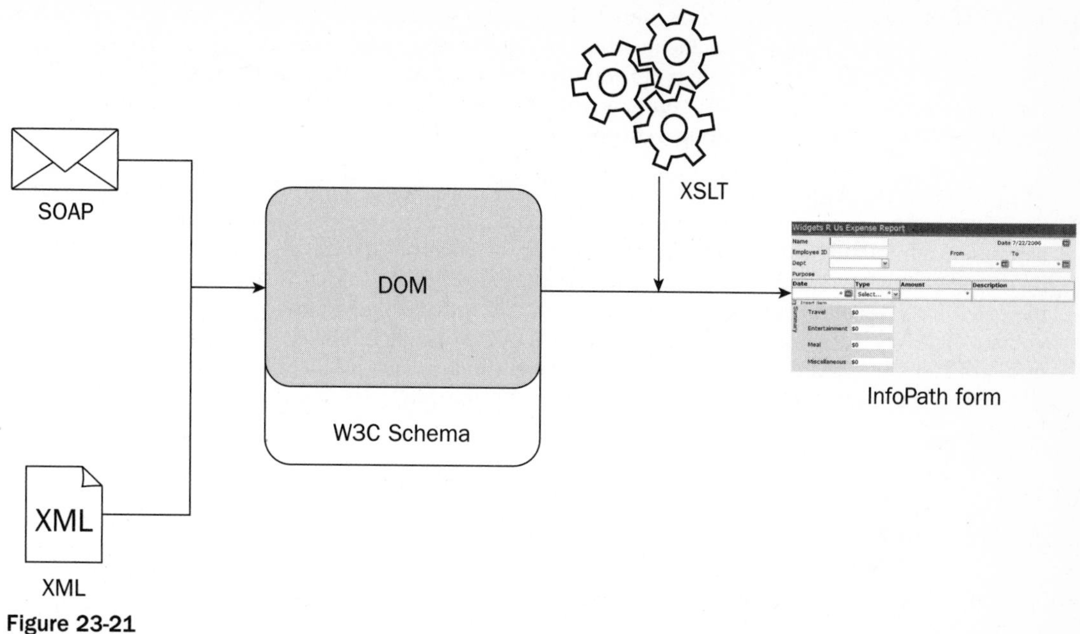

Figure 23-21

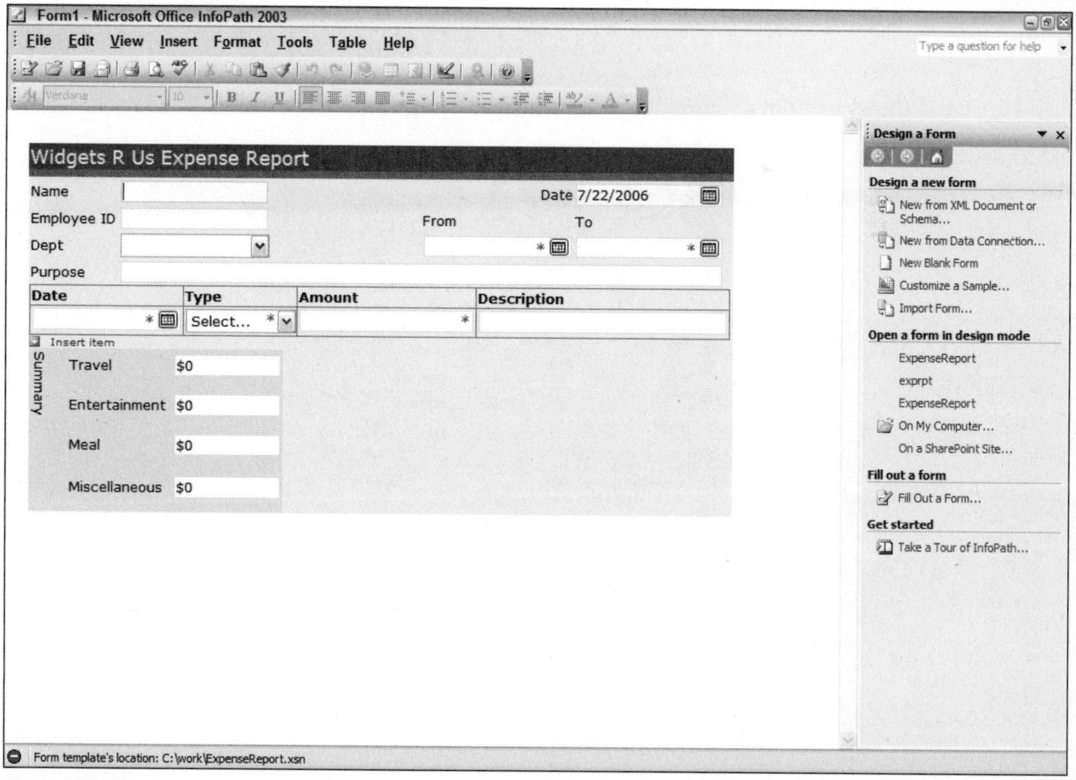

Form1 - Microsoft Office InfoPath 2003

File Edit View Insert Format Tools Table Help

Type a question for help

Widgets R Us Expense Report

Name

Date 7/22/2006

Employee ID

From To

Dept

Purpose

Date	Type	Amount	Description
*	Select... *	*	

Insert item

Summary

Travel $0

Entertainment $0

Meal $0

Miscellaneous $0

Design a Form

Design a new form

New from XML Document or Schema...

New from Data Connection...

New Blank Form

Customize a Sample...

Import Form...

Open a form in design mode

ExpenseReport

exprpt

ExpenseReport

On My Computer...

On a SharePoint Site...

Fill out a form

Fill Out a Form...

Get started

Take a Tour of InfoPath...

Form template's location: C:\work\ExpenseReport.xsn

Figure 23-22

The InfoPath designer enables the creation of form-based solutions using a drag-and-drop model. You can drag elements or groups of elements from the right sidebar over to the design surface. The designer chooses a control based on the data type; however, this can be overridden if necessary. The available controls include a number of layout options, such as table and freeform layouts. You can also add additional secondary data sources to populate portions of the form.

The programming of an InfoPath form can take one of at least three forms. First, it supports a declarative model for applying rules and formatting based on the data. These rules typically take the form of XPath expressions. InfoPath includes designers to assist in the creation of these expressions, so that most users do not need to know XPath to create them (see Figure 23-23). Although this scenario is fine for most simple cases, InfoPath also provides a more programmatic approach using JavaScript. Using this model, you attach JavaScript functions to events or objects in the designer. Finally, through the addition of the InfoPath Toolkit for Visual Studio, you can integrate InfoPath development with Visual Studio .NET 2003, or Visual Studio 2005 to use C#, Visual Basic, and the .NET Framework to extend your InfoPath forms.

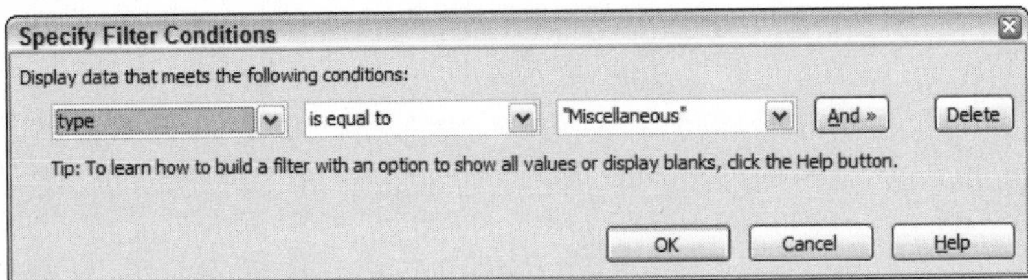

Figure 23-23

Figure 23-24 shows an InfoPath form that uses the same ExpenseReport schema used in the earlier example.

Widgets R Us Expense Report

Name Foo deBar
Date 4/1/2006
Employee ID 42
From 3/26/2006
To 4/1/2006
Dept Development
Purpose Conference trip

Date	Type	Amount	Description
3/27/2006	Travel	$365.34	Airfare
3/27/2006	Meal	$23.40	Meal at destination
3/28/2006	Meal	$5.00	Meal
3/28/2006	Miscellaneou	$50	Replacement power cable
3/28/2006	Entertainmei	$250	Meal with customers from Gizmos R
*	Select... *	*	

Insert item

Select... / Travel / Meal / Entertainment / Miscellaneous

Summary
Travel $
Entertainment $
Meal $28.4
Miscellaneous $50

Figure 23-24

As with the earlier XForms example, the fields are bound to the data in the model. The central table enables the user to add multiple expense items. The drop-down lists for the department and type are populated from the XML as well. The department list comes from the secondary `departments.xml` file, whereas the expense type list is populated from the values of the enumeration in the schema. Some validation is preformed automatically based on the data types in the schema, and required fields are marked in the editor.

As described previously, fields can also be populated dynamically, either through code or XPath expressions. As with XForms, these expressions update as the data changes. The four summary fields are populated based on the expense items entered using an XPath expression like the following.

```
sum(amount[type = "Travel"])
```

As the underlying XML changes, this XPath expression is reapplied. This ensures that the summary totals for each category are updated on any change. You can confirm this by changing the type or amount of each expense item. The resulting XML is shown in Listing 23-16.

Listing 23-16: XML produced by InfoPath

```
<?xml version="1.0" encoding="utf-8"?>
<?mso-infoPathSolution solutionVersion="1.0.0.6"
  productVersion="11.0.6565" PIVersion="1.0.0.0"
  href="http://server/ExpenseReport.xsn"
  name="urn:schemas-microsoft-com:office:infopath:Expense-Report:http---example-
com-expenseReport" language="en-us" ?>
<?mso-application progid="InfoPath.Document"?>
<exp:expenseReport xmlns:exp="http://example.com/expenseReport"
xmlns:xsi="http://www.w3.org/2001/XMLSchema-instance"
xmlns:my="http://schemas.microsoft.com/office/infopath/2003/myXSD/2006-07-19T04:04:
02"
xmlns:ns1="http://example.com/depts">
  <exp:employee>
    <exp:name>Foo deBar</exp:name>
    <exp:employeeID>42</exp:employeeID>
    <exp:dept>dev</exp:dept>
  </exp:employee>
  <exp:date>2006-04-01</exp:date>
  <exp:purpose>Conference trip</exp:purpose>
  <exp:startDate>2006-03-26</exp:startDate>
  <exp:endDate>2006-04-01</exp:endDate>
  <exp:expenseItem>
    <exp:date>2006-03-27</exp:date>
    <exp:type>Travel</exp:type>
    <exp:amount>365.34</exp:amount>
    <exp:description>Airfare</exp:description>
  </exp:expenseItem>
  <exp:expenseItem>
    <exp:date>2006-03-27</exp:date>
    <exp:type>Meal</exp:type>
    <exp:amount>23.40</exp:amount>
    <exp:description>Meal at destination</exp:description>
  </exp:expenseItem>
```

(continued)

Listing 23-16 *(continued)*

```
    <exp:expenseItem>
      <exp:date>2006-03-28</exp:date>
      <exp:type>Meal</exp:type>
      <exp:amount>5.00</exp:amount>
      <exp:description>Meal</exp:description>
    </exp:expenseItem>
    <exp:expenseItem>
      <exp:date>2006-03-28</exp:date>
      <exp:type>Miscellaneous</exp:type>
      <exp:amount>50</exp:amount>
      <exp:description>Replacement power cable</exp:description>
    </exp:expenseItem>
    <exp:expenseItem>
      <exp:date>2006-03-28</exp:date>
      <exp:type>Entertainment</exp:type>
      <exp:amount>250</exp:amount>
      <exp:description>Meal with customers from Gizmos R
      Them</exp:description>
    </exp:expenseItem>
    <exp:summary>
      <exp:travelSummary>365.34</exp:travelSummary>
      <exp:entSummary>250</exp:entSummary>
      <exp:mealSummary>28.4</exp:mealSummary>
      <exp:miscSummary>50</exp:miscSummary>
    </exp:summary>
  </exp:expenseReport>
```

Comparing XForms and InfoPath

Because they are the two leading choices for creating XML-based forms, it's worth comparing XForms with InfoPath. Functionally, they are similar, but they differ in support levels and functionality (see the following table).

Feature	Xforms	InfoPath
Standardization	W3C standard	Proprietary
Programmability	Declarative (XPath)	Declarative (XPath) JavaScript .NET Framework (with the InfoPath Toolkit for Visual Studio .NET 2003)
Browser support	Any (with an appropriate plug-in)	None (although InfoPath 2007 supports running in any browser)
Designer support	Available	Built-in
Event-driven programming model	Yes	Yes

Feature	Xforms	InfoPath
Data Model	Inline model W3C Schema	W3C Schema WSDL SQL Server/Access
Output	XML x-www-urlencoded other based on implementation	XML SOAP
XPath support	1.0	1.0

Like most other decisions concerning software, the decision may already be made for you. Either company standards or policy may point you at either a proprietary solution or to a more standards-based solution.

Summary

Although XForms hasn't exactly taken the world by storm by ripping the forms out of XHTML and custom development, it is poised to become more important in the future. The merger of XForms into XHTML 2.0 and the support now built into many browsers mean that developers will have a native XML solution for creating, editing, and distributing form-based solutions.

If you are already developing a solution that leverages Microsoft Office or Adobe Acrobat, you may want to look at their proprietary solutions for your form-based needs. InfoPath and Lifecycle Designer provide graphical designers to create the forms, simple no-code data binding via XPath statements.

Resources

A number of XForms clients are available from both commercial vendors and open-source development teams.

- **XForms specification** (`.w3.org/tr/xforms`)—Second edition of the XForms specification on the Worldwide Web Consortium's Website.
- **X-Smiles** (`x-smiles.org/`)—Java-based XML viewer that supports XForms, as well as SVG, XHTML, and other standards.
- **FireFox XForms extension** (`mozilla.org/projects/xforms/`)—Extension supports running XForms in Firefox 1.5x. This extension is integrated into Firefox 2.0.
- **formsPlayer** (`formsplayer.com/`)—ActiveX-based XForms implementation enables running XForms in Internet Explorer or other ActiveX containers.
- **XForms implementations** (`w3.org/MarkUp/Forms/#implementations`)—Full list of current XForms implementations.

- **InfoPath Developer Center on MSDN** (`msdn2.microsoft.com/en-us/office/aa905434.aspx`)—Development information for the use of InfoPath to build form-based solutions.
- **Adobe Lifecycle Designer** (`adobe.com/products/server/adobedesigner/`)—Adobe application for designing XML-based forms.

24

The Resource Description Framework (RDF)

As you have seen throughout this book, XML is a great technology to deal with data warehousing, data representation, data presentation, and more. A problem area in XML, however, is how to represent *metadata* in a standard way.

Metadata is quite literally *data about data*. You might find a dataset that makes little sense without the context surrounding it. Perhaps it would make better sense if it had some relations in place that map to additional data points or if it were related to existing data points to show a larger set of relations across boundaries.

An easy-to-understand structure surrounding metadata not only helps you comprehend the data you are presented with, but also gives you a mechanism to discover this data.

For instance, if you are conducting a search for the word *Hemingway*, you find all sorts of information that utilize this keyword. But do you want to know about books on the life of Ernest Hemingway, movies starring Mariel Hemingway, or information on the books written by author Ernest Hemingway?

This is where the relationships between the data make sense. Having data relations in place enables you to more easily pinpoint the data and facilitates research and data discovery that would be difficult otherwise. This chapter takes a look at how to use the Resource Description Framework (RDF) to create the metadata around any data that you represent in your XML documents.

The Core Structure of RDF

RDF does a good job of structuring itself like human thought patterns. The relationship between the data points mirrors the way you would structure these data points yourself. For instance, in the Hemingway example, you might structure a data relationship something like, "The book *The Sun Also Rises* has the author of *Ernest Hemingway*."

In this case, you have three entities—also called a *triples* or a *statement*. These data points include

- **A subject**—The item of focus. In the case of the Hemingway example, the subject is the book *The Sun Also Rises*. Any metadata provided is meant to further define this subject.
- ***A predicate***—a term that provides a property or relation to the subject. This is also considered the verb of the statement.
- ***An object***—A term that works with the predicate to apply a specific relation between the object and subject.

You can break the sentence apart as shown in the diagram in Figure 24-1.

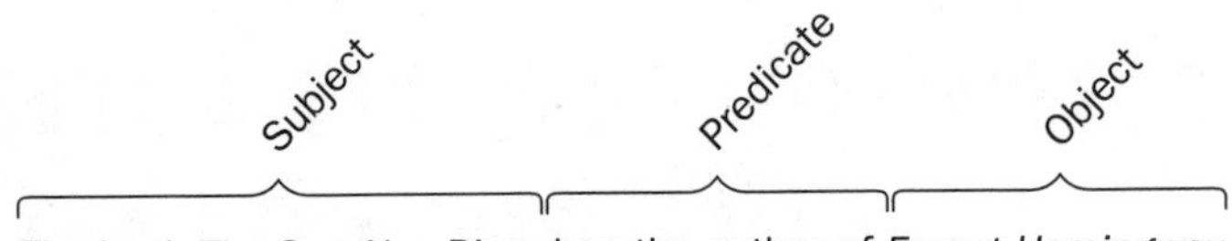
Subject
Predicate
Object
The book *The Sun Also Rises* has the author of *Ernest Hemingway*

Figure 24-1

Instead of having just a subject value within your data store, such as the book *The Sun Also Rises*, using RDF you can also put in place relations such as those presented in Figure 24-1. In fact, you can continue the triples structure and branch out to all kinds of actual relations.

As stated, the three items taken together (the subject, predicate, and object) are referred to as a statement. A series of statements taken together are referred to as a *model*.

A model is basically a hierarchical set of statements that are interrelated in some fashion. For instance, if you add statements around Hemingway, you come up with the logical model presented in Figure 24-2.

As you can see, the relationships between the items are the predicates. Each item is either a subject or an object (in most cases, an item can be both depending on the combinations of subjects and objects you are working with). In this diagram, you see a large list of RDF statements which includes all the triples, as shown in the following table.

Subject	Predicate	Object
Ernest Hemingway	wrote a book called	The Sun Also Rises
Ernest Hemingway	wrote a book called	For Whom the Bell Tolls
Ernest Hemingway	had a granddaughter named	Mariel Hemingway
The Sun Also Rises	was published in	the year 1926
For Whom the Bell Tolls	was published in	the year 1940
The Sun Also Rises	was published by	Charles Scribner's Sons
For Whom the Bell Tolls	was published by	Charles Scribner's Sons
Mariel Hemingway	was in a movie named	Manhattan

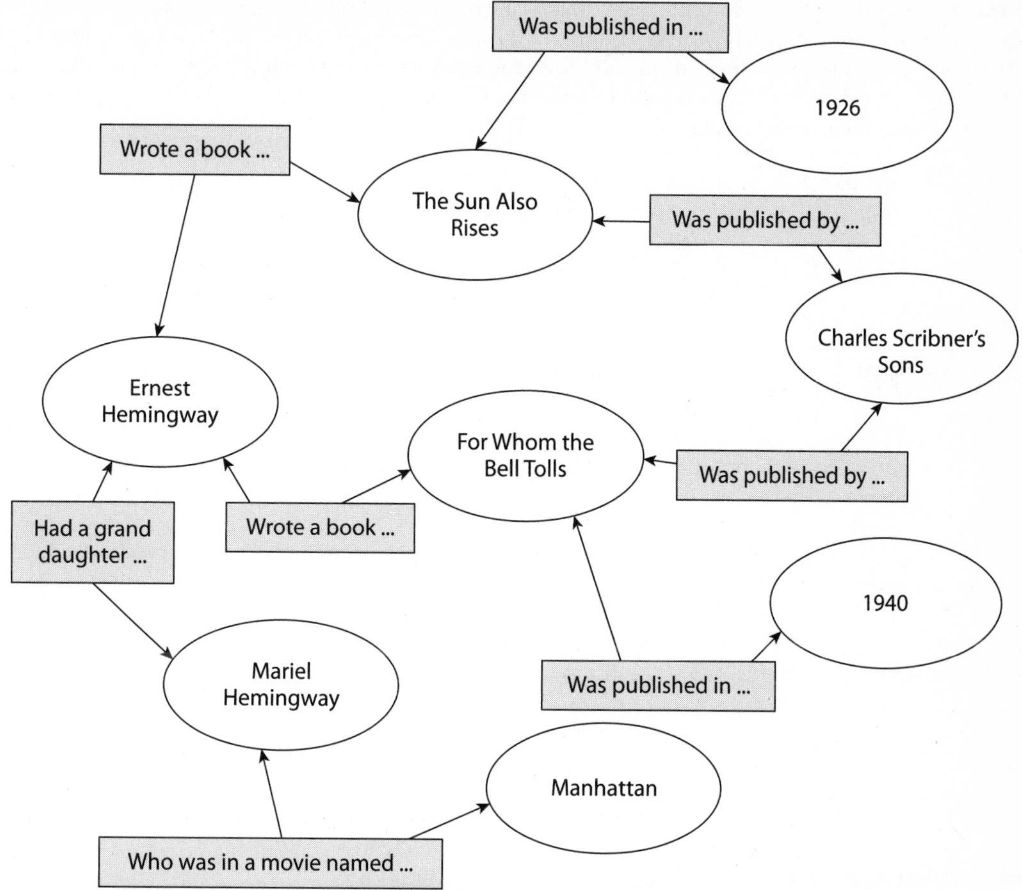

Figure 24-2

You can see that relationships really can go on forever because everything is related to something somewhere. Try to focus your RDF statements on the most meaningful and relevant relationships.

RDF creates these relations by relying upon unique identifiers: the triples that make up the RDF statement. Many folks are aware of the URL, or the *Uniform Resource Locator*, which is used to uniquely identify a Web page or Web resource on the Internet. When you type a URL in the address bar of the browser, you are directed to a specific resource.

In addition to URLs, you find URIs, also known as *Uniform Resource Identifiers*. Not everything can be a URL-accessible resource, so URIs were created to allow for other items to have unique identifiers. An example URI is presented here:

```
http://www.lipperweb.com/myURI
```

Most URIs appear to be URLs (of actual Web resources). Although a URI need not be a Web site URL (like the one in the previous example), this is usually a good idea. The URI can be anything you want it to be. For example, you could write one using terms like `myData` or `12345`. This kind of URI does not guarantee any uniqueness, however. Another URI in another file elsewhere may use the same value. Therefore, it is common practice to use a URL as the value of your URI. In the end, this practice really serves two purposes. First, it guarantees a unique URI that won't conflict with any other. The other advantage of using a URL as the URI is that an URL identifies where the data originated.

When constructing your URIs, you don't have to point to an actual file. In fact, it is usually better not to do just that, but instead to use something like the following:

```
http://www.mydomain.com/myNamespaceName
```

The RDF Graph Model

RDF is mainly represented through a graph model. However, you may find XML representations of the RDF document. The RDF tools present in the industry today visually represent this XML document as an RDF graph.

The simplest form of an RDF graph is a single triplet that is composed of a subject, predicate, and object. An example is presented in Figure 24-3.

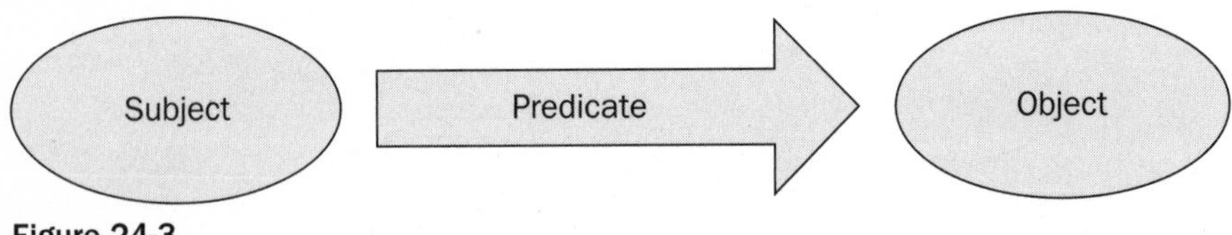

Figure 24-3

When working with a graph, note the two main parts of the graph:

- Nodes
- Arcs

A node is either the subject or the object. The arc on the other hand is the predicate. An arc is the item that connects two nodes, thereby forming a relationship between the nodes. An arc also has a *direction*. In this case, the subject is acting upon the object using the predicate.

Although the nodes in Figure 24-3 might look similar, you can always tell which node is the subject and which node is the object by the direction in which the predicate is applied. For instance, if you go back to the Ernest Hemingway example, you can find the set of nodes presented in Figure 24-4.

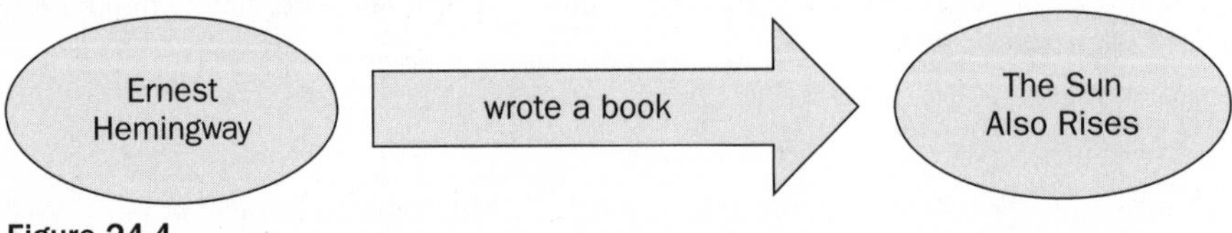

Figure 24-4

From this figure, you can plainly see that the *Ernest Hemingway* node is the subject and that the *The Sun Also Rises* node is the object. You determine this by the direction of the predicate, *wrote a book*, which is pointing to the *The Sun Also Rises* node—implying that the *Ernest Hemingway* node is acting upon it.

Graphs, of course, get more complex as more nodes are added. This is because you add the relationships between the nodes which are present (using predicates). For instance, you can add another node that has a relationship to the object, *The Sun Also Rises*, to the diagram presented in Figure 24-4. This extension is shown in Figure 24-5.

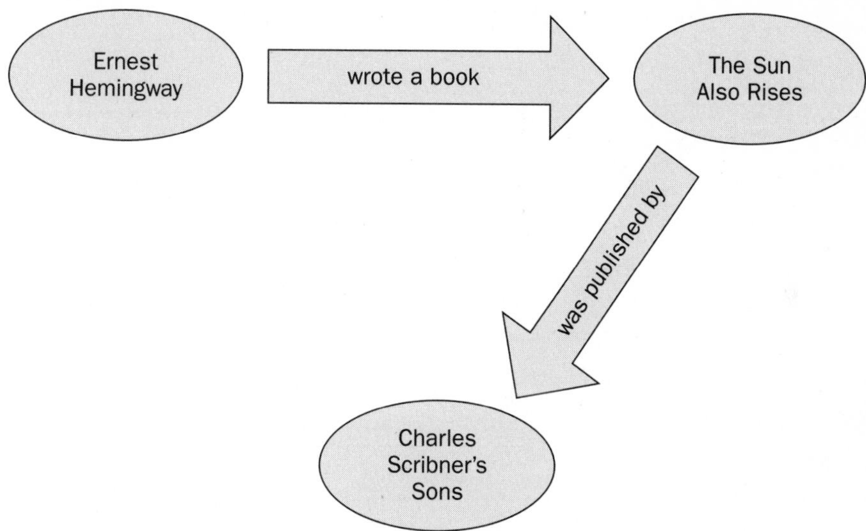

Figure 24-5

In this case, you have three nodes that have some sort of relationship among them, even if it is indirect. In this case, you have *Ernest Hemingway* who wrote a book called *The Sun Also Rises* which was published by a company by the name of *Charles Scribner's Sons*. All the nodes are related in a way, and the two predicates define that relationship between the nodes. You could provide additional metadata to the RDF graph, thereby showing a circular relationship. This is shown in Figure 24-6.

From the diagram in Figure 24-6, you can see that all three nodes now have a direct relationship. *Ernest Hemingway* has a relationship with the book, *The Sun Also Rises*, because he wrote the book. *Ernest Hemingway* also has a relationship to the company, *Charles Scribner's Sons*, because this firm was his publisher.

A triples, which is broken down as the subject, predicate, and object, is called a *statement*. A statement is usually represented in a graph as shown in Figure 24-7.

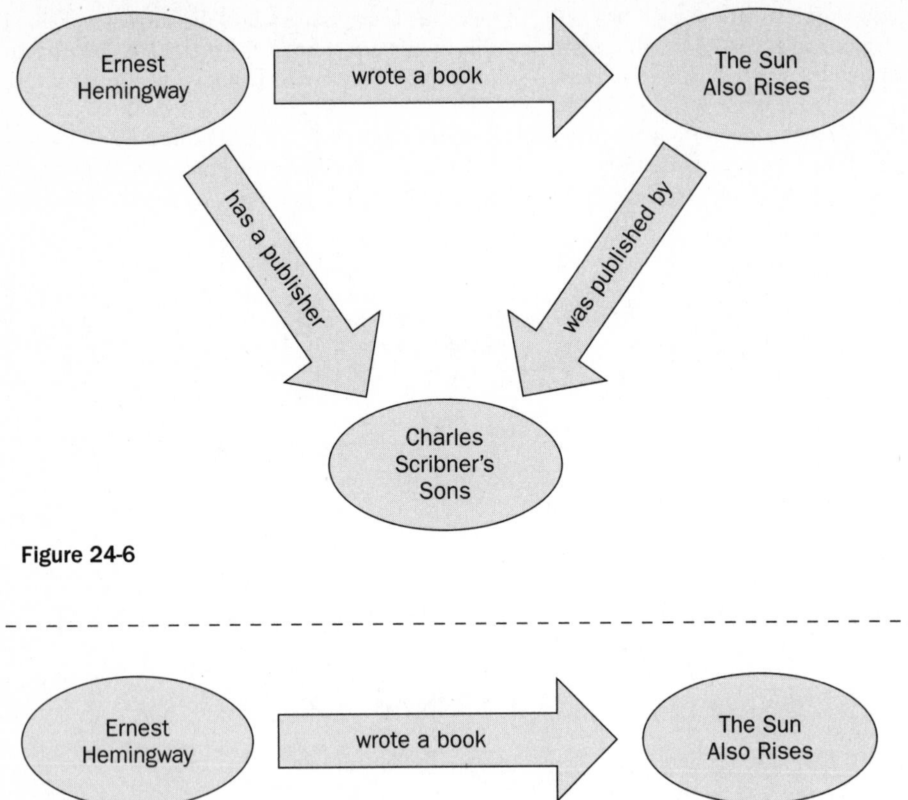

Figure 24-6

Figure 24-7

In this case, the statement definition is presented using a dashed line that forms a box around the entire triples.

Using Altova's SemanticWorks

One RDF tool out there is Altova's SemanticWorks (found at `altova.com`). This tool allows you to work with an RDF document as either a graph or as XML. Altova's SemanticWorks is a good way to visually design your RDF document. Using it, you can later look at the underlying RDF schema that was created by the tool around your graph.

Using this tool with the previous Ernest Hemingway example, you can visually create what is presented in Figure 24-8.

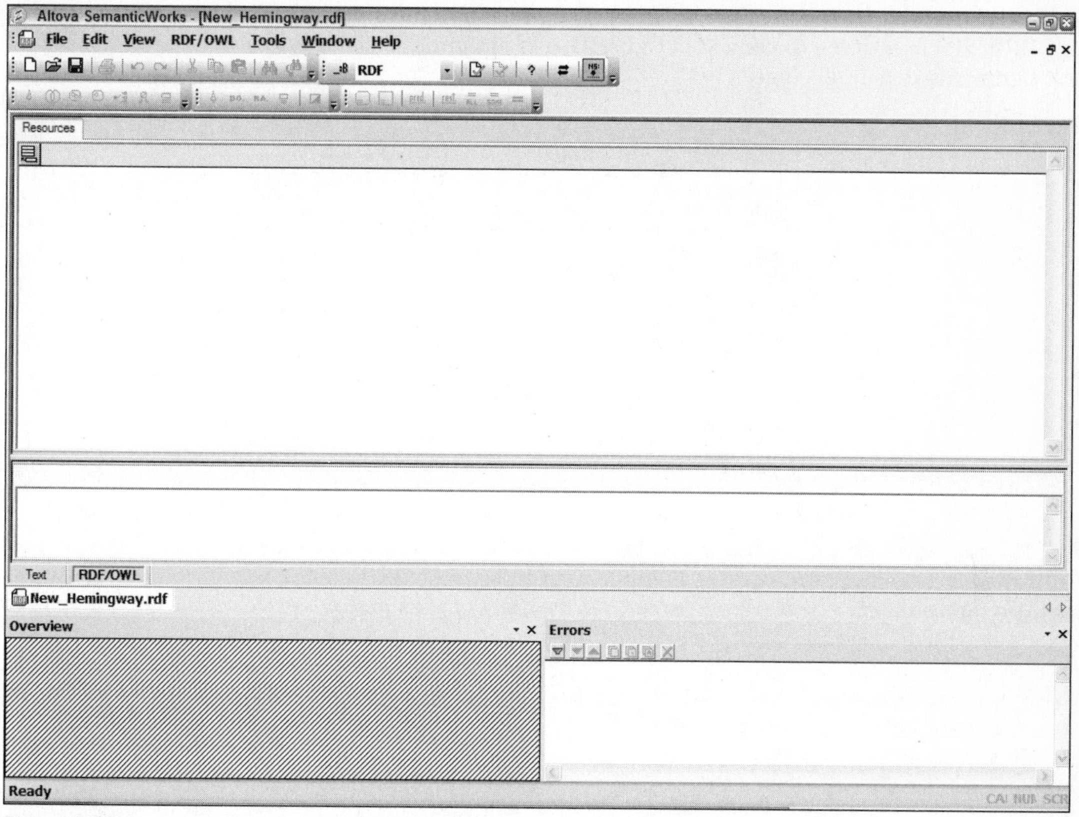

Figure 24-8

In this figure, you can see that the tool provides a good visual representation of the RDF model. You can see a number of statements defined. Note there is even a statement contained within a statement. Again, the statements are defined with the dashed, squared boxes that always surround a triples statement.

This example shows a complete RDF graph. You can use this designer to create a brand new graph from scratch. The first step is to open up Altova's SematicWorks and modify the document to work in RDF mode. You simply set the drop-down box in the menu to RDF as shown in Figure 24-9.

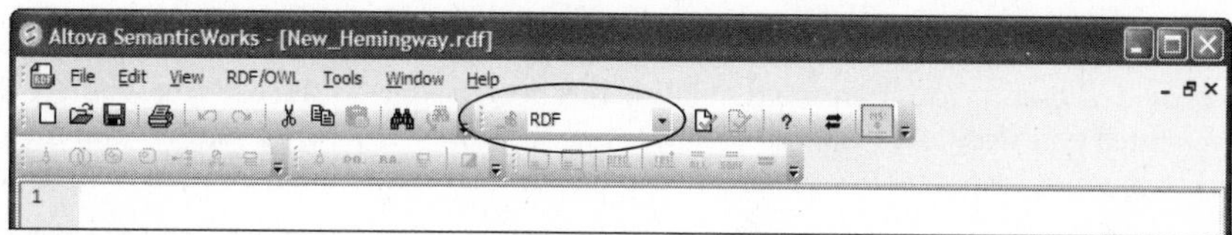

Figure 24-9

Next, you set up a namespace prefix to use in the RDF document. Select Tools ➪ URIref Prefixes. The URIref Prefixes dialog (presented in Figure 24-10) pops up. This dialog enables you to create the prefixes that are used in the document.

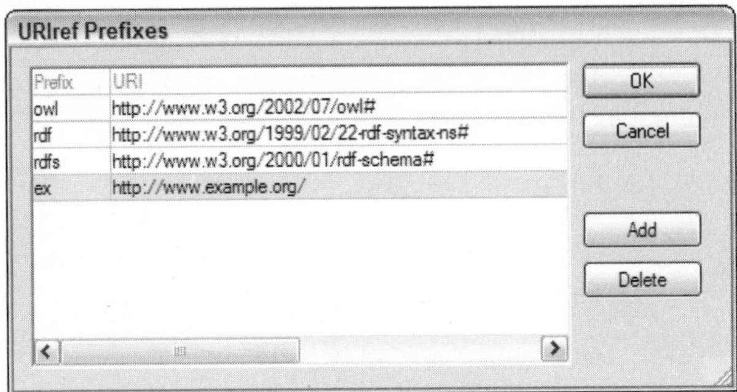

Figure 24-10

To add a new prefix, click the Add button in the dialog and a new prefix line is added to the list. For this example, type the prefix `ex` in the Prefix column and provide a URI in the second column. In this case, you can use `http://www.example.org/` as the URI of the `ex` prefix. Next, click the OK button to continue with the construction of the RDF document.

You see a Resources tab on the RDF document with a single toolbar strip at the top. In the toolbar strip, you find a single button. Clicking this button enables you to add a new resource to the RDF document as illustrated in Figure 24-11.

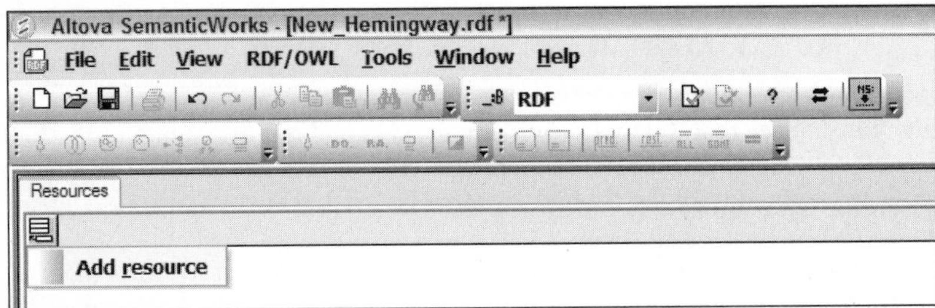

Figure 24-11

To add a new resource to your RDF document, click the button in the toolbar and select Add resource from the provided menu. You then see that a line has been added to the list box where you can type the name of resource you want. At first, the resource has the name `urn:unnamed-1`. You must rename this resource. For the first resource, use the following definition on the resource line:

```
ex:Ernest_Hemingway
```

In this case, `ex:` is the prefix of the resource. This `ex` value maps back to the URI you defined in the URIref Prefixes dialog earlier in the example. After you have associated the resource to the prefix you want (because you can have more than one custom prefix), you then type the name of the resource. In this case, the name of the resource is `Ernest_Hemingway` (with the underscore). The following is an incorrect value:

```
ex:Ernest Hemingway
```

This is incorrect because of the space between the words Ernest and Hemingway. The name that is placed here is actually used in the namespace value within the XML RDF document. For instance, if you use the correct form: `ex:Ernest_Hemingway`, you get the following namespace value:

```
http://www.example.org/Ernest_Hemingway
```

This works, of course, because it is a properly structured value (being a continuous string). If you put a space between `Ernest` and `Hemingway`, the following URI results:

```
http://www.example.org/Ernest Hemingway
```

This, of course, is invalid because it is in two parts.

Now you have a resource in place within your RDF document. The resource list must also include all the pieces of the triples — all the subjects, predicates, and objects. Complete your list using the following resource values:

- `ex:Ernest_Hemingway`
- `ex:The_Sun_Also_Rises`
- `ex:Charles_Scribners_Sons`
- `ex:was_published_by`
- `ex:wrote_a_book`

After these five items in place within Altova's SemanticWorks, you should see something similar to the screen shown in Figure 24-12.

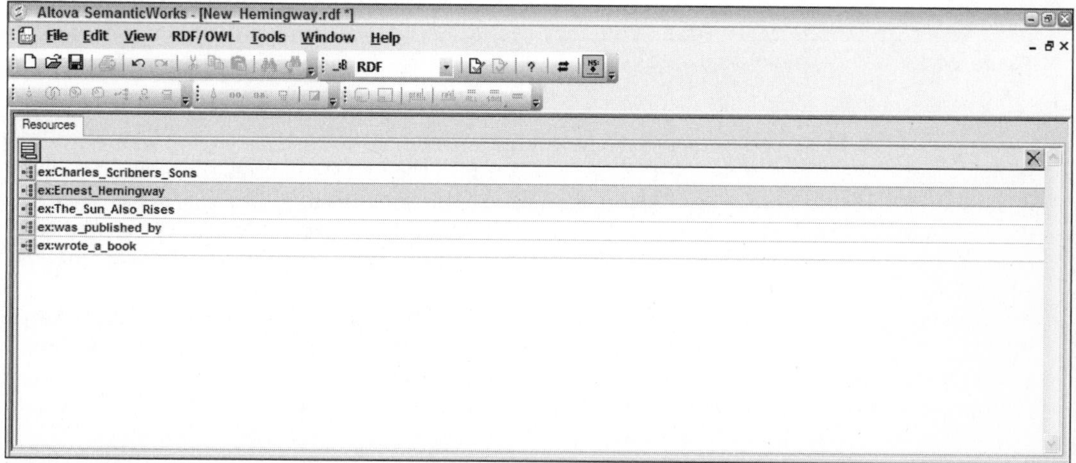

Figure 24-12

In this example, you can see that all five resources are listed in the document. The list is presented alphabetically. Although the resources exist within the document, no relationship exists between the items. In order to create these relationships, which are the core of the RDF document, you use the SemanticWorks tool. To access the tool, press the icon to the left of the `ex:Ernest_Hemingway` resource. This brings up a visual representation of the resource. The resource is presented as a bubble on the design surface and is labeled with its URI. This is shown in Figure 24-13.

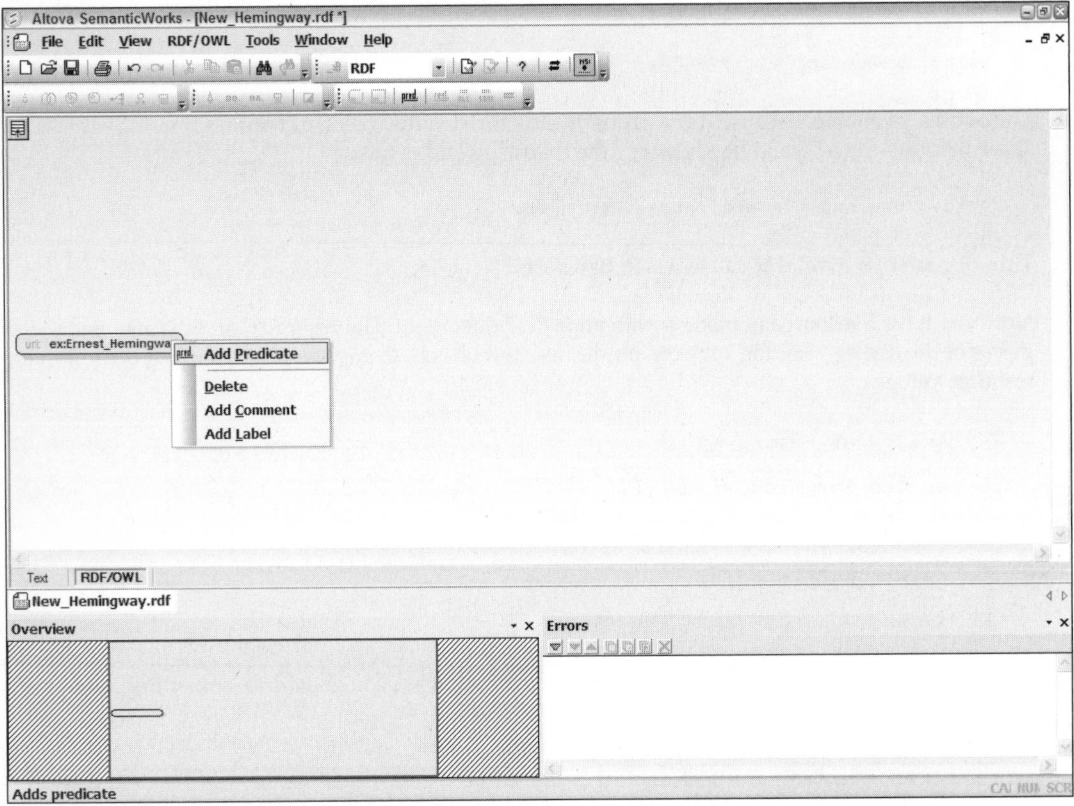

Figure 24-13

Looking at Figure 24-13, you can see that a little more is going on. You see the `ex:Ernest_Hemingway` resource and also the start of the creation of a relationship. The first step in creating a relationship with this resource is adding a predicate. Because the `ex:Ernest_Hemingway` resource is, in fact, a subject, the next step is to add a predicate that can act upon an object (the object is added after the predicate is created).

To associate a predicate to this subject, right-click on the `ex:Ernest_Hemingway` bubble and select Add Predicate from the provided menu. This creates a box next to the `ex:Ernest_Hemingway` resource. After the predicate is added, the predicate box has a drop-down list that can be initiated by clicking the arrow button within the box. This is illustrated in Figure 24-14.

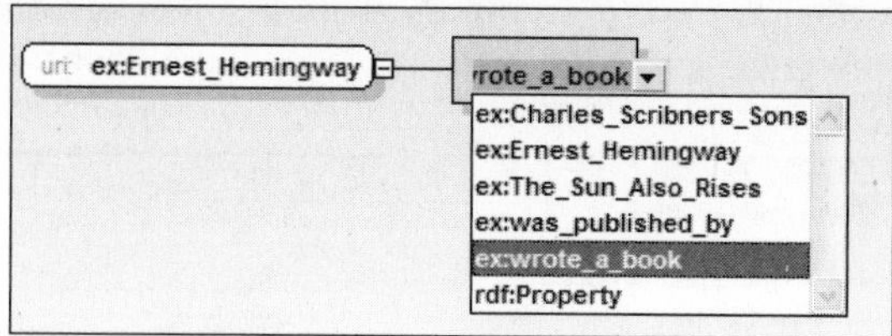

Figure 24-14

You now select the appropriate predicate from the list. In this case, the appropriate choice is the `ex:wrote_a_book` option. Now that the `ex:Ernest_Hemingway` subject has an associated predicate, you associate this predicate with an object. To accomplish this task, right-click the predicate and select Add Resource Object from the provided menu. This is illustrated in Figure 24-15.

Figure 24-15

In the example in Figure 24-15, a new object is added to the predicate. The object behaves just as the predicate behaved when it was added to the diagram. A bubble which represents the object appears on the screen, and you are provided with a drop- down list to choose the object from the list of resources that you defined earlier. In this case, you select the `ex:The_Sun_Also_Rises` option from the list of options presented in the drop-down list.

With these three items in place, you have created your first triples. You have a subject, predicate, and an object all related through a relationship you defined. This is as far as you can go here. You must also define statements in succession and relate the statements through the joint use of subjects and objects. For instance, you cannot define another predicate by clicking the object `ex:The_Sun_Also_Rises` in the design surface. Instead, you go back to your resource list by clicking the small button located at the upper-left corner of the design surface. After you are back to the resource list (shown earlier in Figure 24-12), you can click the icon next to the `ex:The_Sun_Also_Rises` resource to further define it. In the first statement that you created, the `ex:The_Sun_Also_Rises` resource was the object, but in the next case, this resource is the only one found on the design surface and is in the left-most position—signifying that it is now the subject of the statement. From this point in the design surface, you simply right-click the new resource and select Add Predicate from the menu provided—just as you did before with the `ex:Ernest_Hemingway` resource.

In this case, your predicate is `ex:was_published_by`, and the object of this statement is `ex:Charles_Sribners_Sons`. With this relationship in place, you have built two statements which are related through their common use of the `ex:The_Sun_Also_Rises` resource.

If you go back to the ex:Ernest_Hemingway resource in design view, you can expand all the nodes until you get the result presented in Figure 24-16.

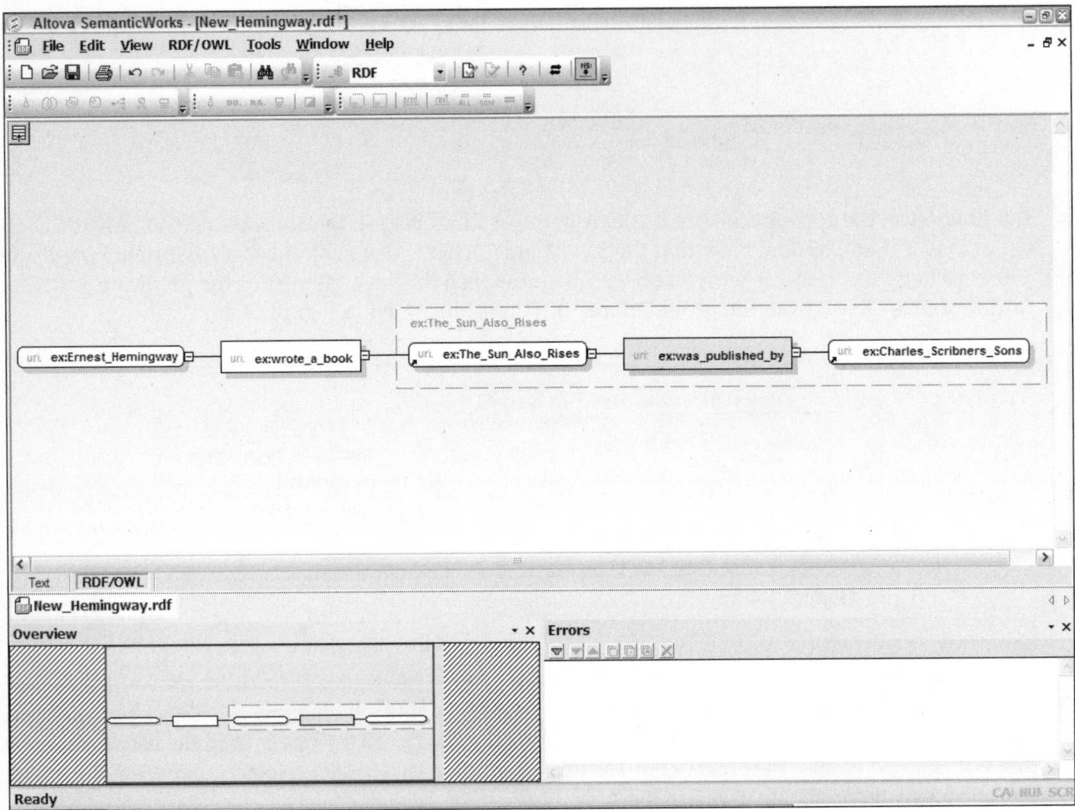

Figure 24-16

In this example, the ex:Ernest_Hemingway statement is connected to the ex:The_Sun_Also_Rises statement though the relations that you defined earlier. You can see that the ex:The_Sun_Also_Rises statement is a full statement with a subject, predicate, and object because it is surrounded with a dashed box.

Now that you have designed this RDF document completely within Altova's SemanticWorks application, you can view the XML behind this RDF graph. To do this, click the Text button within the tool. This switches the view from the RDF graph view to the XML text view. The XML view is illustrated in Figure 24-17.

The next section looks more closely at creating RDF documents using XML rather than graph design.

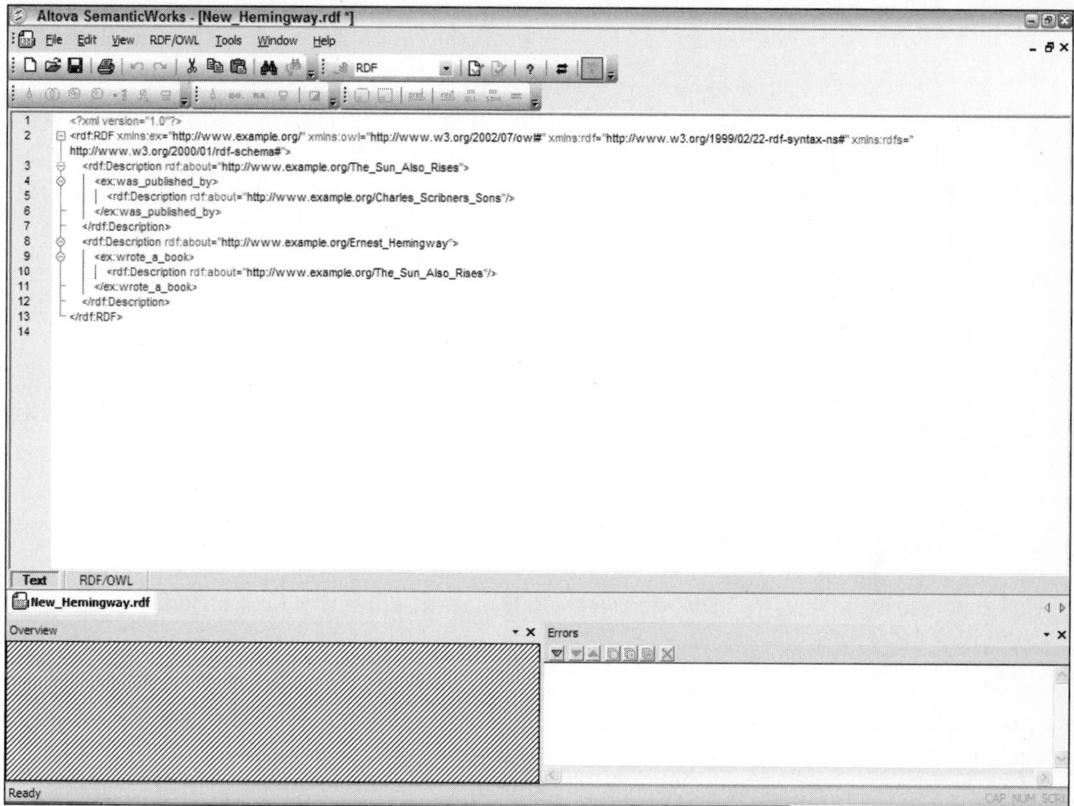

Figure 24-17

The RDF XML Schema

The Ernest Hemingway example that I put together in the visual designer of Altova's SemanticWorks tool generated the bit of XML shown in Listing 24-1.

Listing 24-1: An example RDF document—Hemingway.rdf

```
<?xml version="1.0"?>
<rdf:RDF xmlns:ex="http://www.example.org/"
 xmlns:rdf="http://www.w3.org/1999/02/22-rdf-syntax-ns#">
   <rdf:Description rdf:about="http://www.example.org/Ernest_Hemingway">
      <ex:wrote_a_book>
         <ex:book rdf:about="http://www.example.org/The_Sun_Also_Rises"/>
      </ex:wrote_a_book>
      <ex:wrote_a_book>
         <ex:book rdf:about="http://www.example.org/For_Whom_the_Bell_Tolls"/>
      </ex:wrote_a_book>
```

(continued)

Listing 24-1 *(continued)*

```
        <ex:had_a_grand-daughter>
           <ex:person rdf:about="http://www.example.org/Mariel_Hemingway"/>
        </ex:had_a_grand-daughter>
     </rdf:Description>
     <rdf:Description rdf:about="http://www.example.org/Mariel_Hemingway">
        <ex:starred_in_movie>
           <ex:movie rdf:about="http://www.example.org/Manhattan"/>
        </ex:starred_in_movie>
     </rdf:Description>
  </rdf:RDF>
```

As you can see, the RDF document is a normal XML document. It follows the XML syntax and begins with an `<?xml>` element just as other XML document would. The root element, `<rdf>` starts by defining a couple of namespaces. The two namespaces include

- `http://www.w3.org/1999/02/22-rdf-syntax-ns#`
- `http://www.example.org`

The first item in the list is the namespace of the RDF schema, which should be included by default in all your RDF documents. The second namespace is your own. In this case, it is `xmlns:ex="http://www.example.org/"` so it can be used as a custom prefix throughout the document.

Each subject in the document is then defined using an `<rdf:Description>` element. For instance, the description of `Mariel_Hemingway` in the document includes the following code:

```
<rdf:Description rdf:about="http://www.example.org/Mariel_Hemingway">
   <ex:starred_in_movie>
      <ex:movie rdf:about="http://www.example.org/Manhattan"/>
   </ex:starred_in_movie>
</rdf:Description>
```

If you study this bit of code and how it relates to other elements, you can see that the URI is indeed the identifier of the resource. Using the `<rdf:Description>` element, you select the `rdf:about` attribute to assign the URI to the item. In this case, it is `http://www.example.org/Mariel_Hemingway`.

Now that the subject is in place, the next step is to assign the predicate. You use the custom prefix and assign a defining element, which is the predicate itself.

```
<ex:starred_in_movie>

</ex:starred_in_movie>
```

The predicate is the `<ex:starred_in_movie>` element. This means that the action is applied to anything assigned within this element. This is now the object of the statement.

```
<ex:starred_in_movie>
   <ex:movie rdf:about="http://www.example.org/Manhattan"/>
</ex:starred_in_movie>
```

This predicate is acting upon the `<ex:movie>` element. Again, this element uses the `rdf:about` attribute to assign the URI of the resource. The URI of the movie `Manhattan` is utilized for the `<ex:movie>` element.

After adding this complete `<rdf:Description>` element, you have a full statement. Each of the items of the statement is presented here:

- **Subject** — `http://www.example.org/Mariel_Hemingway`
- **Predicate** — `<ex:starred_in_movie></ex:starred_in_movie>`
- **Object** — `http://www.example.org/Manhattan`

You can have more than one predicate per statement as you see here:

```
<rdf:Description rdf:about="http://www.example.org/Ernest_Hemingway">
   <ex:wrote_a_book>
      <ex:book rdf:about="http://www.example.org/The_Sun_Also_Rises"/>
   </ex:wrote_a_book>
   <ex:wrote_a_book>
      <ex:book rdf:about="http://www.example.org/For_Whom_the_Bell_Tolls"/>
   </ex:wrote_a_book>
   <ex:had_a_grand-daughter>
      <ex:person rdf:about="http://www.example.org/Mariel_Hemingway"/>
   </ex:had_a_grand-daughter>
</rdf:Description>
```

In this case, three predicates are used:

- `<ex:wrote_a_book>` associated to the object `The_Sun_Also_Rises`
- `<ex:wrote_a_book>` associated to the object `For_Whom_the_Bell_Tolls`
- `<ex:had_a_grand-daughter>` associated to the object `Mariel_Hemingway`

One of the objects (`Mariel_Hemingway`) is even further defined with its own statement. This is how two statements are related to each other.

From this XML document, you see that you can extend the metadata definition and incorporate as many additional subjects, predicates, and objects as you wish. The order in which they appear in the document is not important because the document is webbed together through the use of the URIs utilized in the statements.

Summary

This chapter introduced you to RDF. RDF was originally designed to deal with an area of XML that was not yet incorporated into the larger XML architecture. When you are sharing massive amounts of data, it is important to show the relationships between data points. This is where RDF comes into play.

RDF bridges that gap between data points and allows you to put in place the data relations that can make the data more meaningful to the consumer.

This chapter looked at both the XML representation of the RDF document and the RDF graph mode, which is the more common method of representing RDF. Graph models are shown using nodes, arcs, and arc directions.

Finally, this chapter looked at using the Altova's SemanticWorks tool to create RDF graphs and XML.

25

XML in Office Development

Many applications that process XML do it as an intermediate step in creating documents. Many of those documents are created with Microsoft Office by users who are more familiar with the Office tools than with angle brackets. Because Microsoft Office products are some of the most commonly used applications for working with documents, it makes sense that Microsoft added XML processing to these applications. Although it attempts to hide the angle brackets more often than an XML purist may like, Office makes creating and processing XML documents easy for average users. This chapter looks at creating and editing XML with the most commonly used Office tools. In addition, the newer alternatives of Office 2007 and Open Office are shown.

While any editions of Office 2003 (or Office 2007) can be used to save XML, only the Professional and Enterprise editions provide the advanced XML features.

Using XML with Microsoft Excel

Microsoft Excel is one of the most commonly used applications in business. Although it is a spreadsheet application, designed for calculations, Excel files may store more data for business than any other data format.

Saving Excel workbooks as XML

Excel 2003 added the capability to save workbooks as XML, using a format Microsoft calls SpreadsheetML. Spreadsheet can now be transmitted as text, rather than in the default binary format. You can now use tools such as XSLT or XQuery on the resulting XML files. The SpreadsheetML format ensures a high degree of compatibility with the original document. If you open this XML file on a computer that has Excel 2003 (or later) installed, you see the original document. Only a little functionality is lost: Mostly the lost functions are those that are not logically able to move across platforms like embedded controls and subdocuments.

Figure 25-1 shows a simple annuity calculator spreadsheet, and Listing 25-1 gives you a portion of this file saved as SpreadsheetML. Much of the file has been excluded for brevity. The full file is approximately 250KB, compared with 80KB in the binary form.

Microsoft Excel - Annuity investment calculator1

	A	B	C	D	E		F
1	**Annuity investment**						
2	*Present value*	10,000.00		*Value after 7 years*	$	14,430	
3	*Interest rate*	5.25%		*Monthly payment after 7 years*	$	63	
4	*Term (in years)*	20		*Value after 20 years*	$	28,511	
5	*Contribution each month (reinvested interest)*	100.0%		*Monthly payment after 20 years*	$	124	
6							
7	*Month*	*Balance*	*Interest earned*	*Interest + balance*	*Amount paid to investor*		*New balance*
8	1	10,000.00	43.75	10,043.75	0.00		10,043.75
9	2	10,043.75	43.94	10,087.69	0.00		10,087.69
10	3	10,087.69	44.13	10,131.83	0.00		10,131.83
11	4	10,131.83	44.33	10,176.15	0.00		10,176.15
12	5	10,176.15	44.52	10,220.67	0.00		10,220.67
13	6	10,220.67	44.72	10,265.39	0.00		10,265.39
14	7	10,265.39	44.91	10,310.30	0.00		10,310.30
15	8	10,310.30	45.11	10,355.41	0.00		10,355.41
16	9	10,355.41	45.30	10,400.71	0.00		10,400.71
17	10	10,400.71	45.50	10,446.21	0.00		10,446.21
18	11	10,446.21	45.70	10,491.92	0.00		10,491.92
19	12	10,491.92	45.90	10,537.82	0.00		10,537.82
20	13	10,537.82	46.10	10,583.92	0.00		10,583.92
21	14	10,583.92	46.30	10,630.23	0.00		10,630.23
22	15	10,630.23	46.51	10,676.73	0.00		10,676.73
23	16	10,676.73	46.71	10,723.44	0.00		10,723.44
24	17	10,723.44	46.92	10,770.36	0.00		10,770.36
25	18	10,770.36	47.12	10,817.48	0.00		10,817.48
26	19	10,817.48	47.33	10,864.81	0.00		10,864.81
27	20	10,864.81	47.53	10,912.34	0.00		10,912.34
28	21	10,912.34	47.74	10,960.08	0.00		10,960.08
29	22	10,960.08	47.95	11,008.03	0.00		11,008.03
30	23	11,008.03	48.16	11,056.19	0.00		11,056.19
31	24	11,056.19	48.37	11,104.56	0.00		11,104.56

Annuity

Ready NUM

Figure 25-1

Listing 25-1: Annuity spreadsheet as XML

```
<?xml version="1.0"?>
<?mso-application progid="Excel.Sheet"?>
<Workbook xmlns="urn:schemas-microsoft-com:office:spreadsheet"
 xmlns:o="urn:schemas-microsoft-com:office:office"
 xmlns:x="urn:schemas-microsoft-com:office:excel"
 xmlns:dt="uuid:C2F41010-65B3-11d1-A29F-00AA00C14882"
 xmlns:ss="urn:schemas-microsoft-com:office:spreadsheet"
 xmlns:html="http://www.w3.org/TR/REC-html40">
 <DocumentProperties xmlns="urn:schemas-microsoft-com:office:office">
  <LastAuthor>Guy Some</LastAuthor>
  <LastPrinted>2001-04-09T17:58:15Z</LastPrinted>
  <Created>2000-10-19T23:21:30Z</Created>
  <LastSaved>2001-04-20T18:48:39Z</LastSaved>
  <Company>Stuff Is Us</Company>
  <Version>11.6568</Version>
 </DocumentProperties>
 <CustomDocumentProperties xmlns="urn:schemas-microsoft-com:office:office">
```

```
  <_TemplateID dt:dt="string">TC010175321033</_TemplateID>
 </CustomDocumentProperties>
 <ExcelWorkbook xmlns="urn:schemas-microsoft-com:office:excel">
  <WindowHeight>8985</WindowHeight>
  <WindowWidth>11175</WindowWidth>
  <WindowTopX>1365</WindowTopX>
  <WindowTopY>60</WindowTopY>
  <ProtectStructure>False</ProtectStructure>
  <ProtectWindows>False</ProtectWindows>
 </ExcelWorkbook>
 <Styles>
  <Style ss:ID="Default" ss:Name="Normal">
   <Alignment ss:Vertical="Bottom"/>
   <Borders/>
   <Font/>
   <Interior/>
   <NumberFormat/>
   <Protection/>
  </Style>
  <Style ss:ID="s16" ss:Name="Comma">
   <NumberFormat ss:Format="_(* #,##0.00_);_(* \(#,##0.00\);_(* &quot;-
&quot;??_);_(@_)"/>
  </Style>
  <Style ss:ID="s18" ss:Name="Currency">
   <NumberFormat
    ss:Format="_(&quot;$&quot;* #,##0.00_);_(&quot;$&quot;*
\(#,##0.00\);_(&quot;$&quot;* &quot;-&quot;??_);_(@_)"/>
  </Style>
...
<Worksheet ss:Name="Annuity" ss:Protected="1">
  <Table ss:ExpandedColumnCount="9" ss:ExpandedRowCount="665" x:FullColumns="1"
   x:FullRows="1" ss:StyleID="s24" ss:DefaultRowHeight="10.5">
   <Column ss:StyleID="s24" ss:AutoFitWidth="0" ss:Width="117"/>
   <Column ss:StyleID="s24" ss:AutoFitWidth="0" ss:Width="66.75"/>
   <Column ss:StyleID="s24" ss:Width="53.25"/>
   <Column ss:StyleID="s24" ss:AutoFitWidth="0" ss:Width="98.25"/>
   <Column ss:StyleID="s24" ss:AutoFitWidth="0" ss:Width="91.5"/>
   <Column ss:StyleID="s24" ss:Width="90.75"/>
   <Column ss:Index="8" ss:StyleID="s24" ss:Width="72.75"/>
   <Column ss:StyleID="s24" ss:Width="46.5"/>
   <Row ss:AutoFitHeight="0" ss:Height="24">
    <Cell ss:StyleID="s23"><Data ss:Type="String">Annuity investment</Data></Cell>
    <Cell ss:Index="4" ss:StyleID="s25"/>
   </Row>
   <Row ss:AutoFitHeight="0" ss:Height="24">
    <Cell ss:StyleID="s26"><Data ss:Type="String">Present value</Data></Cell>
    <Cell ss:StyleID="s42"><Data ss:Type="Number">10000</Data></Cell>
    <Cell ss:Index="4" ss:StyleID="s26"><Data ss:Type="String">Value after 7
years</Data></Cell>
    <Cell ss:StyleID="s27" ss:Formula="=R[89]C[-1]"><Data
ss:Type="Number">14429.627004010901</Data></Cell>
    <Cell ss:StyleID="s27"/>
   </Row>
   <Row ss:AutoFitHeight="0" ss:Height="24">
```

(continued)

Listing 25-1 *(continued)*

```
    <Cell ss:StyleID="s26"><Data ss:Type="String">Interest rate</Data></Cell>
    <Cell ss:StyleID="s39"><Data ss:Type="Number">5.2499999999999998E-
2</Data></Cell>
    <Cell ss:Index="4" ss:StyleID="s26"><Data ss:Type="String">Monthly payment
after 7 years</Data></Cell>
    <Cell ss:StyleID="s27" ss:Formula="=R[88]C[-2]"><Data
ss:Type="Number">62.854629140059927</Data></Cell>
    <Cell ss:StyleID="s27"/>
   </Row>
...
```

Because SpreadsheetML must maintain this compatibility, it includes sections for the styles, borders, and other formatting of the document, as well as the actual data. The actual data is included in a `<Worksheet>` element that maps to each of the pages in an Excel workbook. Each `<Worksheet>` contains a `<Table>` element, made up of a series of `<Row>` elements that contain multiple `<Cell>` elements. These `<Cell>` elements have attributes that point to the styles stored elsewhere in the document, the formula (if any) in the cell, and the value. Listing 25-2 shows a simple XSLT file that extracts the data and produces a simpler view of it (see Listing 25-3).

Listing 25-2: An XSLT transform of Excel

```
<?xml version="1.0" encoding="UTF-8"?>
<xsl:stylesheet version="2.0"
  xmlns:xsl="http://www.w3.org/1999/XSL/Transform"
  xmlns:xs="http://www.w3.org/2001/XMLSchema"
  xmlns:fn="http://www.w3.org/2005/xpath-functions"
  xmlns:xdt="http://www.w3.org/2005/xpath-datatypes"
  xmlns:ss="urn:schemas-microsoft-com:office:spreadsheet">
  <xsl:output method="xml" version="1.0" encoding="UTF-8" indent="yes"/>
  <xsl:template match="/">
    <data>
      <xsl:attribute name="type">
        <xsl:value-of select="/ss:Workbook/ss:Worksheet/@ss:Name"/>
      </xsl:attribute>
      <xsl:apply-templates select="/ss:Workbook/ss:Worksheet/ss:Table/ss:Row"/>
    </data>
  </xsl:template>
  <xsl:template match="ss:Row">
    <row>
      <xsl:apply-templates select="ss:Cell"/>
    </row>
  </xsl:template>
  <xsl:template match="ss:Cell">
    <col>
      <xsl:value-of select="ss:Data"/>
      </col>
  </xsl:template>
</xsl:stylesheet>
```

The transform is slightly complicated by the need to include the namespaces used by the document. In particular, the `urn:schemas-microsoft-com:office:spreadsheet` URI is used to map the elements in the spreadsheet file.

Listing 25-3: After transform

```
<?xml version="1.0" encoding="UTF-8"?>
<data xmlns:fn="http://www.w3.org/2005/xpath-functions"
  xmlns:ss="urn:schemas-microsoft-com:office:spreadsheet"
  xmlns:xdt="http://www.w3.org/2005/xpath-datatypes"
  xmlns:xs="http://www.w3.org/2001/XMLSchema"
  type="Annuity">
 <row>
        <col>Annuity investment</col>
        <col></col>
 </row>
 <row>
        <col>Present value</col>
        <col>10000</col>
        <col>Value after 7 years</col>
        <col>14429.627004010901</col>
        <col></col>
 </row>
 <row>
        <col>Interest rate</col>
        <col>5.2499999999999998E-2</col>
        <col>Monthly payment after 7 years</col>
        <col>62.854629140059927</col>
        <col></col>
 </row>
        <row>
        <col>Term (in years)</col>
        <col>20</col>
        <col>Value after 20 years</col>
        <col>28511.140205640702</col>
        <col></col>
 </row>
 <row>
        <col>Contribution each month (reinvested interest)</col>
        <col>1</col>
        <col>Monthly payment after 20 years</col>
        <col>124.1928944863005</col>
        <col></col>
        <col></col>
 </row>
...
</data>
```

For more information on the Excel XML format, see the reference schemas page noted in the Resources section that follows.

Editing XML documents

You can also use Excel to edit XML documents, starting with the 2003 edition. This is especially useful when the XML documents require some calculations or intermediate functions. In addition, many office workers are much more comfortable working in Excel than with XML. Providing a familiar interface increases the likelihood of their actually using the application.

To use Excel to edit XML, you must first set up a mapping. This mapping identifies the cells that map to the elements in an XML file or XSD schema. Figure 25-2 shows an Excel file for a purchase order before any mapping has been done.

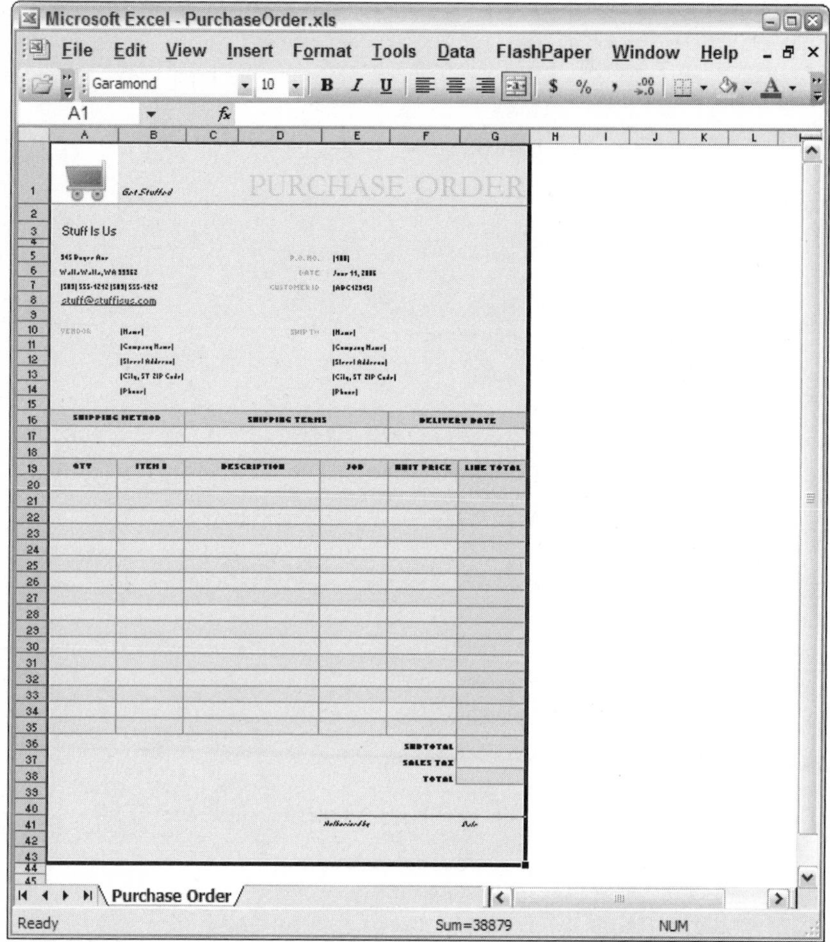

Figure 25-2

Before using this file to edit or create XML files, you must add a mapping. The mapping can be done to a sample XML file or to an XML schema. In this case, it is mapped to a simple purchase order XSD file (see Listing 25-4).

Listing 25-4: A Purchase order schema

```
<xsd:schema xmlns:xsd="http://www.w3.org/2001/XMLSchema">

  <xsd:annotation>
    <xsd:documentation xml:lang="en">
     Purchase order schema for Example.com.
```

```
    Copyright 2000 Example.com. All rights reserved.
   </xsd:documentation>
  </xsd:annotation>

  <xsd:element name="purchaseOrder" type="PurchaseOrderType"/>

  <xsd:element name="comment" type="xsd:string"/>

  <xsd:complexType name="PurchaseOrderType">
    <xsd:sequence>
      <xsd:element name="shipTo" type="USAddress"/>
      <xsd:element name="billTo" type="USAddress"/>
      <xsd:element ref="comment" minOccurs="0"/>
      <xsd:element name="items"  type="Items"/>
    </xsd:sequence>
    <xsd:attribute name="orderDate" type="xsd:date"/>
  </xsd:complexType>

  <xsd:complexType name="USAddress">
    <xsd:sequence>
      <xsd:element name="name"   type="xsd:string"/>
      <xsd:element name="street" type="xsd:string"/>
      <xsd:element name="city"   type="xsd:string"/>
      <xsd:element name="state"  type="xsd:string"/>
      <xsd:element name="zip"    type="xsd:decimal"/>
    </xsd:sequence>
    <xsd:attribute name="country" type="xsd:NMTOKEN"
                   fixed="US"/>
  </xsd:complexType>

  <xsd:complexType name="Items">
    <xsd:sequence>
      <xsd:element name="item" minOccurs="0" maxOccurs="unbounded">
        <xsd:complexType>
          <xsd:sequence>
            <xsd:element name="productName" type="xsd:string"/>
            <xsd:element name="quantity">
              <xsd:simpleType>
                <xsd:restriction base="xsd:positiveInteger">
                  <xsd:maxExclusive value="100"/>
                </xsd:restriction>
              </xsd:simpleType>
            </xsd:element>
            <xsd:element name="USPrice"  type="xsd:decimal"/>
            <xsd:element ref="comment"   minOccurs="0"/>
            <xsd:element name="shipDate" type="xsd:date" minOccurs="0"/>
          </xsd:sequence>
          <xsd:attribute name="partNum" type="SKU" use="required"/>
        </xsd:complexType>
      </xsd:element>
    </xsd:sequence>
  </xsd:complexType>

  <!-- Stock Keeping Unit, a code for identifying products -->
```

(continued)

Listing 25-4 *(continued)*

```
    <xsd:simpleType name="SKU">
      <xsd:restriction base="xsd:string">
        <xsd:pattern value="\d{3}-[A-Z]{2}"/>
      </xsd:restriction>
    </xsd:simpleType>

  </xsd:schema>
```

You create the mapping by first associating the XSD file with the document. Select Data ➪ XML ➪ XML Source to open the XML Source side bar. Because no existing maps are associated with this document, the sidebar is currently empty. Click the XML Maps button, and add the po.xsd file to the mapping. Because two top-level elements are in the schema, you must select purchaseOrder as the root node (see Figure 25-3).

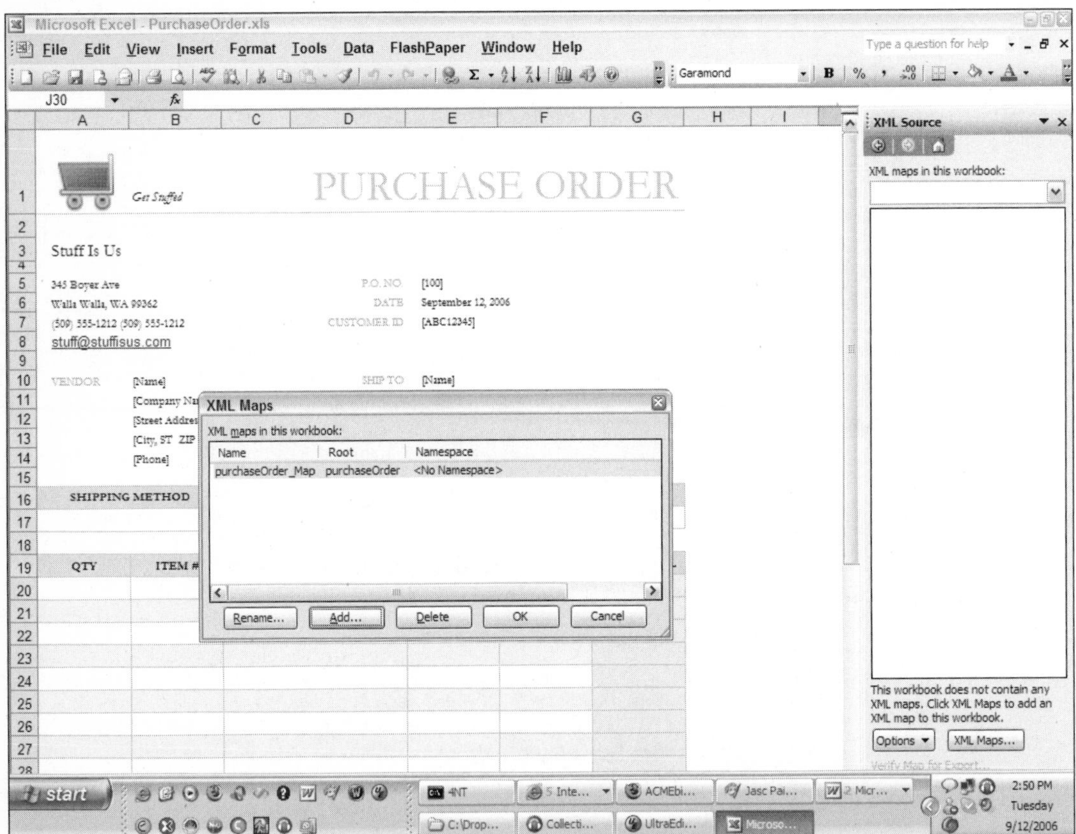

Figure 25-3

After the XML Maps dialog has been closed, the new XML map appears in the sidebar, and you're ready to begin to map the XML data to the cells in the spreadsheet. Drag the fields over to the spreadsheet, dropping them into the appropriate cells. For example, drop the orderDate field onto cell E6, the quantity element onto the first cell in the Qty column, and so on. The cell is highlighted, and selecting highlighted cells also selects the matching element in the XML Source side panel (see Figure 25-4).

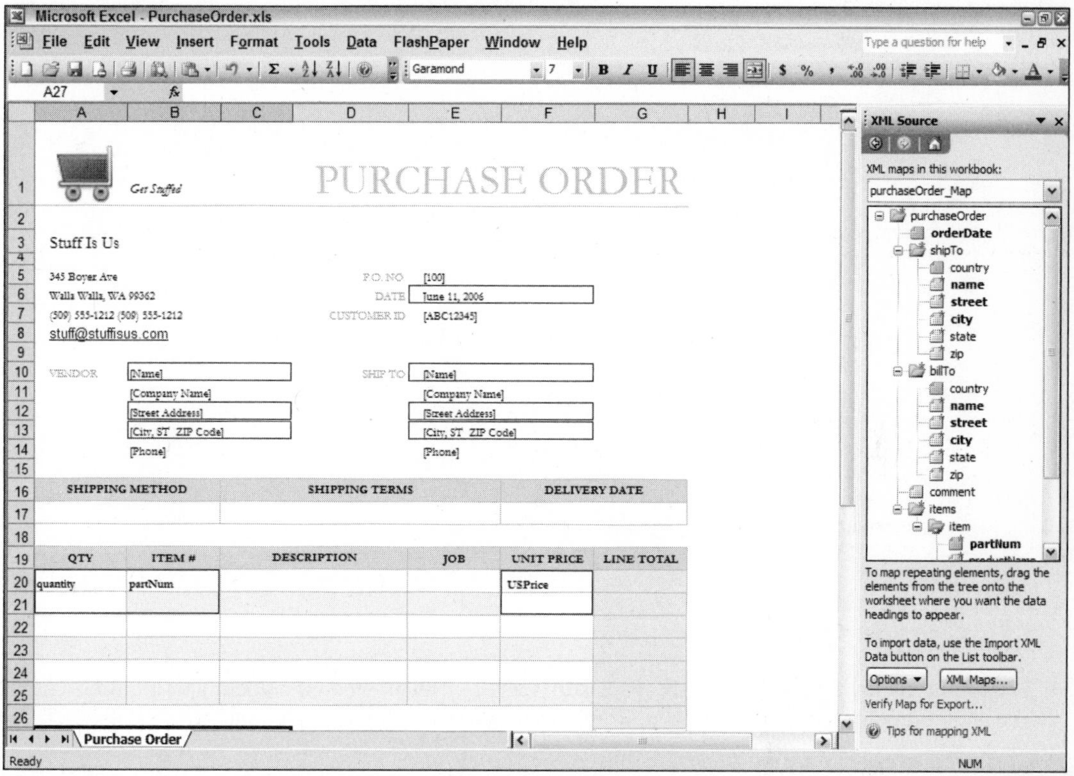

Figure 25-4

With the mapping in place, you can now use the spreadsheet as you normally would, work with formulas, add data, and so on. Table areas, such as the line item area in the purchase order, are treated as lists by Excel. This enables adding multiple rows.

Saving the XML can be done either by selecting Data, XML, Export, or by selecting the XML Data option when using the Save As dialog. This saves the XML (see Listing 25-5), and leaves no association to Excel.

Listing 25-5: An XML file created with Excel

```
<?xml version="1.0" encoding="UTF-8" standalone="yes"?>
<purchaseOrder orderDate="2006-04-01">
  <shipTo country="USA">
    <name>Foo deBar</name>
    <street>123 Any Drive</street>
    <city>New York</city>
    <state>NY</state>
```

(continued)

Listing 25-5 *(continued)*

```
      <zip>10012</zip>
    </shipTo>
    <billTo country="USA">
      <name>Guy Some</name>
      <street>985 Street Avenue</street>
      <city>Redmond</city>
      <state>WA</state>
      <zip>98052</zip>
    </billTo>
    <items>
      <item partNum="1234">
        <productName>Widgets</productName>
        <quantity>3</quantity>
        <USPrice>50</USPrice>
        <comment>The blue ones, if possible</comment>
        <shipDate>2006-04-02</shipDate>
      </item>
      <item partNum="1121">
        <productName>Gizmos</productName>
        <quantity>23</quantity>
        <USPrice>12.41</USPrice>
        <comment>No rush on those</comment>
        <shipDate>2006-04-06</shipDate>
      </item>
    </items>
  </purchaseOrder>
```

You won't frequently use Excel to create or edit XML. However, when the document requires a number of calculations as an intermediate step, Excel can provide a highly capable tool.

Using XML with Microsoft Word

The feature set of Microsoft Word brings it almost within reach of the quality achieved by some desktop publishing applications. Therefore, it should come as no surprise that it has extensive XML support. Word can be used to both create XML documents in WordML format or in a custom schema.

Saving Word documents as XML

The capability to save documents in WordprocessingML (or WordML) was added with Word 2003. This XML dialect attempts to recreate much of the functionality of Word, but renders it in XML. As you might expect, WordML can be rather verbose. As an example, the resume shown in Figure 25-5 is 39KB in `.doc` format, but 44KB in XML format. This may not seem like much, but keep in mind that this is a one-page document. For a more realistic example, Chapter 3 is 666 KB as a `.doc` file and 852 KB as XML — approximately a 27 percent increase in size. Because you are attempting to create as accurate a representation of the `.doc` format as possible, you can expect to find the formatting information within the document, as well as any revisions or other metadata. If you are familiar with Rich Text Format (RTF), the XML structure should look familiar because the XML format is basically an XML version of that format.

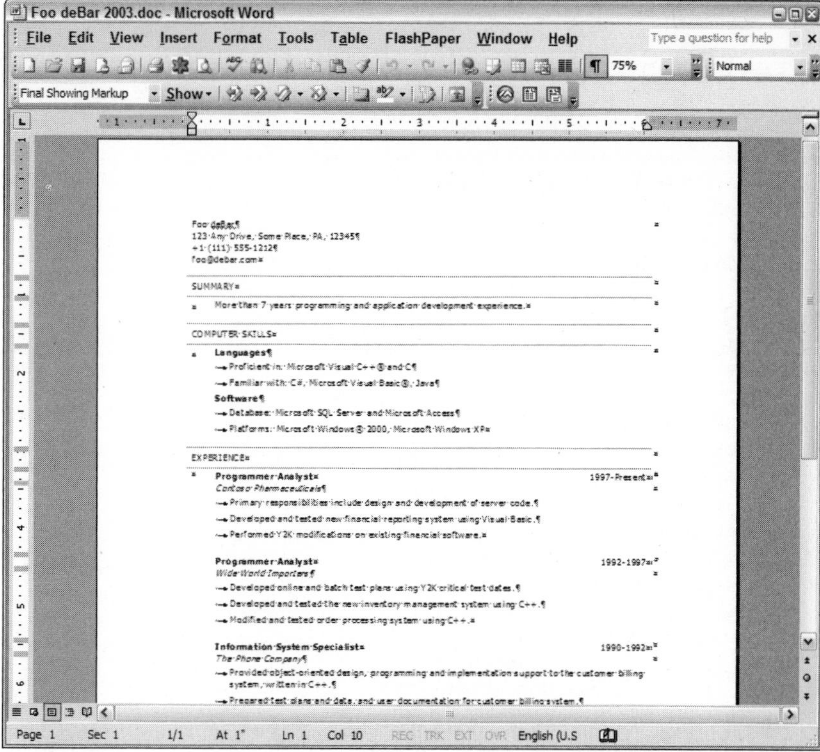

Figure 25-5

Listing 25-6 shows a couple of fragments of this XML.

Listing 25-6: WordML

```
<?xml version="1.0" encoding="UTF-8" standalone="yes"?>
<?mso-application progid="Word.Document"?>
<w:wordDocument xmlns:w="http://schemas.microsoft.com/office/word/2003/wordml"
xmlns:v="urn:schemas-microsoft-com:vml"
xmlns:w10="urn:schemas-microsoft-com:office:word"
xmlns:sl="http://schemas.microsoft.com/schemaLibrary/2003/core"
xmlns:aml="http://schemas.microsoft.com/aml/2001/core"
xmlns:wx="http://schemas.microsoft.com/office/word/2003/auxHint"
xmlns:o="urn:schemas-microsoft-com:office:office"
xmlns:dt="uuid:C2F41010-65B3-11d1-A29F-00AA00C14882"
w:macrosPresent="no"
w:embeddedObjPresent="no"
w:ocxPresent="no"
xml:space="preserve">
  <o:DocumentProperties>
  </o:DocumentProperties>
  <o:CustomDocumentProperties>
  </o:CustomDocumentProperties>
```

(continued)

Listing 25-6 *(continued)*

```
<w:fonts>
 </w:fonts>
 <w:lists>
 </w:lists>
 <w:styles>
 </w:styles>
 <w:shapeDefaults>
 </w:shapeDefaults>
 <w:docPr>
 </w:docPr>
 <w:body>
   <wx:sect>
     <w:tbl>
       <w:tblPr>
         <w:tblW w:w="8924" w:type="dxa"/>
         <w:tblLayout w:type="Fixed"/>
       </w:tblPr>
       <w:tblGrid>
         <w:gridCol w:w="446"/>
         <w:gridCol w:w="22"/>
         <w:gridCol w:w="6120"/>
         <w:gridCol w:w="180"/>
         <w:gridCol w:w="2156"/>
       </w:tblGrid>
       <w:tr>
         <w:tblPrEx>
           <w:tblCellMar>
             <w:top w:w="0" w:type="dxa"/>
             <w:bottom w:w="0" w:type="dxa"/>
           </w:tblCellMar>
         </w:tblPrEx>
         <w:trPr>
           <w:cantSplit/>
         </w:trPr>
         <w:tc>
           <w:tcPr>
             <w:tcW w:w="8924" w:type="dxa"/>
             <w:gridSpan w:val="5"/>
             <w:tcBorders>
               <w:top w:val="nil"/>
               <w:left w:val="nil"/>
               <w:bottom w:val="single" w:sz="4" wx:bdrwidth="10"
                w:space="0" w:color="999999"/>
               <w:right w:val="nil"/>
             </w:tcBorders>
           </w:tcPr>
           <w:p>
             <w:r>
               <w:t>Foo deBar</w:t>
             </w:r>
           </w:p>
           <w:p>
             <w:r>
               <w:t>123 Any Drive, Some Place, PA, 12345</w:t>
```

```
                </w:r>
              </w:p>
              <w:p>
                <w:r>
                  <w:t>+1 (111) 555-1212</w:t>
                </w:r>
              </w:p>
              <w:p>
                <w:pPr>
                  <w:pStyle w:val="E-mailaddress"/>
                </w:pPr>
                <w:r>
                  <w:t>foo@debar.com</w:t>
                </w:r>
              </w:p>
            </w:tc>
          </w:tr>
...
  </w:body>
</w:wordDocument>
```

Notice that this format includes the processing instruction `<?mso-application progid="Word.Document"?>` at the beginning of the document. This identifies the `ProgID` or program identifier of the application that executes if this document is opened from the Desktop or via Internet Explorer. The `ProgID` is a value stored in the Windows Registry that points at the current executable for Word.

Next comes the rather lengthy collection of namespaces, the most important of which is `http://schemas.microsoft.com/office/word/2003/wordml` used by the bulk of the elements. In addition, the namespace for Vector Markup Language (VML) is included. Any drawing elements included in the document are rendered using this namespace. Note that the namespaces are a mix of URL-style and URN-style namespaces. The URL-style namespaces are simply unique identifiers that do not point at schema documents. For this reason, the Office team tends to use URN-style namespaces because they do not imply the existence of a schema document.

The bulk of the document is composed of the `<w:body>` element. This contains the text of the document, as well as pointers to the styles and explicit formatting stored elsewhere in the document. Each paragraph is denoted as a `<w:p>` element, such as the summary heading:

```
<w:p>
  <w:pPr>
    <w:pStyle w:val="Heading1"/>
  </w:pPr>
  <w:r>
    <w:t>Summary</w:t>
  </w:r>
</w:p>
```

The `<w:t>` element contains the actual text, whereas the `<w:pStyle>` is a pointer to an element in the `<w:styles>` section, where the Heading1 style is defined as:

```
<w:style w:type="paragraph" w:styleId="Heading1">
  <w:name w:val="heading 1"/>
  <wx:uiName wx:val="Heading 1"/>
  <w:basedOn w:val="Normal"/>
```

```
    <w:next w:val="Normal"/>
    <w:rsid w:val="00DE7766"/>
    <w:pPr>
      <w:pStyle w:val="Heading1"/>
      <w:spacing w:before="80" w:after="60"/>
      <w:outlineLvl w:val="0"/>
    </w:pPr>
    <w:rPr>
      <wx:font wx:val="Tahoma"/>
      <w:caps/>
    </w:rPr>
  </w:style>
```

In addition to saving in WordML, you can apply an XSLT transformation to the document when it is saved. This enables you to create a simplified or customized version of the document when needed. For example, applying the XSLT listed in Listing 25-7 results in the simple HTML document shown in Listing 25-8.

Listing 25-7: SimpleWord.xsl

```
<?xml version="1.0" encoding="UTF-8"?>
<xsl:stylesheet version="2.0"
 xmlns:xsl="http://www.w3.org/1999/XSL/Transform"
 xmlns:fo="http://www.w3.org/1999/XSL/Format"
 xmlns:xs="http://www.w3.org/2001/XMLSchema"
 xmlns:fn="http://www.w3.org/2005/xpath-functions"
 xmlns:xdt="http://www.w3.org/2005/xpath-datatypes"
 xmlns:w="http://schemas.microsoft.com/office/word/2003/wordml"
 xmlns:o="urn:schemas-microsoft-com:office:office">
<xsl:output encoding="UTF-8" standalone="omit" method="html"  indent="yes" />
  <xsl:template match="/">
    <html>
      <head>
        <title>
          <xsl:value-of select="/w:wordDocument/o:DocumentProperties/o:Title"/>
        </title>
      </head>
      <body>
        <xsl:apply-templates select="/w:wordDocument/w:body"/>
      </body>
    </html>
  </xsl:template>
  <xsl:template match="w:p">
    <div>
      <xsl:if test="exists(w:pPr)">
        <xsl:attribute name="class">
          <xsl:value-of select="w:pPr/w:pStyle/@w:val"/>
        </xsl:attribute>
      </xsl:if>
      <xsl:value-of select="w:r/w:t"/>
    </div>
  </xsl:template>
</xsl:stylesheet>
```

The template selects from all the included <w:p> elements. These are converted to <div> tags in the resulting HTML. If there is a child <w:pPr> element, the style is applied to the <div>. Finally, the text of each paragraph is extracted and added to the <div>. The resulting HTML provides a simpler view of the document (see Listing 25-8).

Listing 25-8: Output of SimpleWord.xsl

```
<?xml version="1.0" encoding="UTF-8"?>
<html xmlns:fn="http://www.w3.org/2005/xpath-functions"
  xmlns:fo="http://www.w3.org/1999/XSL/Format"
  xmlns:o="urn:schemas-microsoft-com:office:office"
  xmlns:w="http://schemas.microsoft.com/office/word/2003/wordml"
  xmlns:xdt="http://www.w3.org/2005/xpath-datatypes"
  xmlns:xs="http://www.w3.org/2001/XMLSchema">
  <head>
    <title>Foo deBar</title>
  </head>
  <body>
    <div>Foo deBar</div>
    <div>123 Any Drive, Some Place, PA, 12345</div>
    <div>+1 (111) 555-1212</div>
    <div class="E-mailaddress">foo@debar.com</div>
    <div class="Heading1">Summary</div>
    <div class="Heading1"></div>
    <div class="Text">More than 7 years programming and application development
experience.</div>
    <div class="Heading1">Computer skills</div>
    <div class="Heading1"></div>
    <div class="Title">Languages</div>
    <div class="bulletedlist">Proficient in: Microsoft Visual C++ (r)  and C</div>
    <div class="bulletedlist">Familiar with: C#, Microsoft Visual Basic (r) ,
Java</div>
    <div class="Title">Software</div>
    <div class="bulletedlist">Database: Microsoft SQL Server and Microsoft
Access</div>
    <div class="bulletedlistlastline">Platforms: Microsoft Windows (r)  2000,
Microsoft Windows XP</div>
    <div class="Heading1">Experience</div>
    <div></div>
    <div class="Title">Programmer Analyst</div>
    <div class="Dates">1997-Present</div>
    <div></div>
    <div>Contoso Pharmaceuticals</div>
    <div class="bulletedlist">Primary responsibilities include design and
development of server code.</div>
    <div class="bulletedlist">Developed and tested new financial reporting system
using Visual Basic.</div>
    <div class="bulletedlistlastline">Performed Y2K modifications on existing
financial software.</div>
    <div></div>
    <div class="Title">Programmer Analyst</div>
    <div class="Dates">1992-1997</div>
    <div></div>
```

(continued)

Listing 25-8 *(continued)*

```
    <div class="Location">Wide World Importers</div>
    <div class="bulletedlist">Developed online and batch test plans using Y2K
critical test dates.</div>
    <div class="bulletedlist">Developed and tested the new inventory management
system using C++.</div>
    <div class="bulletedlistlastline">Modified and tested order processing system
using C++.</div>
    <div></div>
    <div class="Title">Information System Specialist</div>
    <div class="Dates">1990-1992</div>
    <div></div>
    <div>The Phone Company</div>
    <div class="bulletedlist">Provided object-oriented design, programming and
implementation support to the customer billing system, written in C++.</div>
    <div class="bulletedlist">Prepared test plans and data, and user documentation
for customer billing system.</div>
    <div class="bulletedlistlastline">Problem-solved hardware issues with fault-
tolerant hard drives.</div>
    <div class="Heading1">Education</div>
    <div></div>
    <div class="Title">Oak Tree University</div>
    <div class="Dates">1989</div>
    <div></div>
    <div class="Location">Salt Lake City, Utah</div>
    <div class="bulletedlist">B.S., Computer Science</div>
    <div></div>
  </body>
</html>
```

In addition to generating this simple document, you could also extract any tables or graphics used by the document or use the style definitions to create a CSS stylesheet.

Editing XML documents

Just as with Excel, you can use Word to edit XML documents. Also as with Excel, you must first create a mapping between the XML data and the document. With Word, you add one or more XML schemas to the document. Word uses this schema to validate the contents of the document. This can be an invaluable resource when using Word to create highly structured documents.

Listing 25-9 shows an XML schema for a simple resume format (for a more full-featured resume schema, see the HR-XML version listed in the resources). The schema contains sections for contact information, experience, and education.

Listing 25-9: A simple resume schema

```
<?xml version="1.0" encoding="UTF-8"?>
<xs:schema xmlns="http://www.example.com/resume-simple"
  xmlns:xs="http://www.w3.org/2001/XMLSchema"
  targetNamespace="http://www.example.com/resume-simple"
  elementFormDefault="qualified"
  attributeFormDefault="unqualified" version="1.0">
```

```
<xs:element name="resume">
  <xs:annotation>
    <xs:documentation>Simple resume schema</xs:documentation>
  </xs:annotation>
  <xs:complexType mixed="true">
    <xs:sequence>
      <xs:element name="name" type="nameType"/>
      <xs:element name="address" type="addressType"/>
      <xs:element name="objectives" type="xs:string"/>
      <xs:element name="experience" type="experienceType" maxOccurs="unbounded"/>
      <xs:element name="education" type="educationType" maxOccurs="unbounded"/>
      <xs:element name="interests" type="xs:string"/>
    </xs:sequence>
  </xs:complexType>
</xs:element>
<xs:complexType name="nameType">
  <xs:sequence>
    <xs:element name="firstName" type="xs:string"/>
    <xs:element name="lastName" type="xs:string"/>
    <xs:element name="middleInitials" type="xs:string" minOccurs="0"/>
  </xs:sequence>
</xs:complexType>
<xs:complexType name="addressType">
  <xs:sequence>
    <xs:element name="street" type="xs:string"/>
    <xs:element name="city" type="xs:string"/>
    <xs:element name="region" type="regionType"/>
    <xs:element name="postalCode" type="pcodeType"/>
  </xs:sequence>
</xs:complexType>
<xs:simpleType name="regionType">
  <xs:restriction base="xs:string">
    <xs:length value="2"/>
  </xs:restriction>
</xs:simpleType>
<xs:simpleType name="pcodeType">
  <xs:restriction base="xs:string">
    <xs:minLength value="5"/>
  </xs:restriction>
</xs:simpleType>
<xs:complexType name="experienceType">
  <xs:sequence>
    <xs:element name="yearFrom" type="xs:int"/>
    <xs:element name="yearTo" type="xs:int"/>
    <xs:element name="company" type="xs:string"/>
    <xs:element name="position" type="xs:string"/>
    <xs:element name="description" type="xs:string"/>
  </xs:sequence>
</xs:complexType>
<xs:complexType name="educationType">
  <xs:sequence>
    <xs:element name="yearFrom" type="xs:int"/>
    <xs:element name="yearTo" type="xs:int"/>
    <xs:element name="institution" type="xs:string"/>
```

(continued)

Listing 25-9 *(continued)*

```
        <xs:element name="degree" type="xs:string"/>
        <xs:element name="description" type="xs:string"/>
      </xs:sequence>
    </xs:complexType>
  </xs:schema>
```

You add this schema to a Word document or template using the XML Schema tab of the Tools, Templates and Add-ins dialog (see Figure 25-6). If you have a number of related schemas, you can create a Schema Library to work with them together.

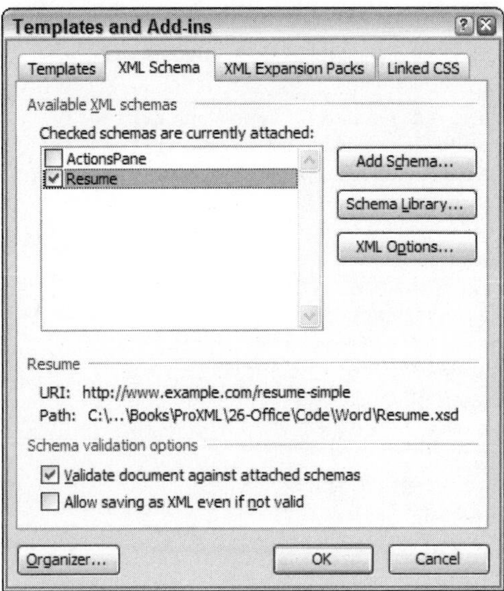

Figure 25-6

As when you use Excel, the next step is to mark up the document to identify the regions that will be populated with the XML data. Figure 25-7 shows a document with the mapping visible. The element markers can be hidden if they are disruptive. However, showing the markers can increase the likelihood that the fields will be filled in correctly. Alternatively, if you were creating a document template for producing XML data, you would probably add fields within the elements, protect the document, and hide the element markers.

When editing the document, Word provides validation. In Figure 25-7, you can see that a validation error is currently active. This is shown by the purple squiggly at the side of the elements that have errors. In addition, these elements are highlighted in the XML Structure sidebar. Hovering over either the item in the side bar or the main document reviews the error.

After the document is completed and it passes validation, you can save it as a complete document in WordProcessingML or save only the data. Listing 25-10 shows the output of the data from the preceding document. Notice no reference back to Word is included. Only the data identified by the schema is present.

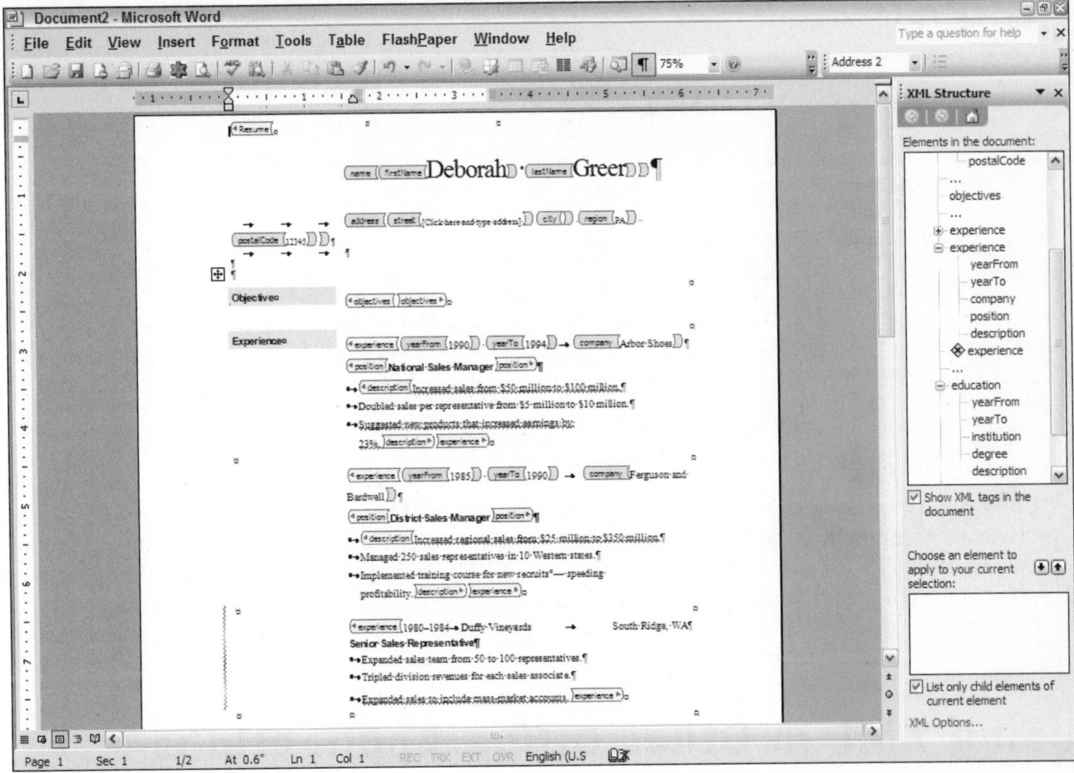

Figure 25-7

Listing 25-10: Resume data as XML

```
<?xml version="1.0" encoding="UTF-8" standalone="no"?>
<resume xmlns="http://www.example.com/resume-simple">
  <name>
    <firstName>Deborah</firstName>
    <lastName>Greer</lastName>
  </name>
  <address>
    <street>1337 42nd Avenue</street>
    <city>Blahford</city>
    <region>MA</region>
    <postalCode>12345</postalCode>
  </address>
  <objectives>Develop with XML, change the world
    one angle bracket at a time.</objectives>
  <experience>
    <yearFrom>1990</yearFrom>
    <yearTo>1994</yearTo>
    <company>Arbor Shoes</company>
    <position>National Sales Manager</position>
```

(continued)

Listing 25-10 *(continued)*

```
      <description>Increased sales from $50 million to $100 million.
        Doubled sales per representative
        from $5 million to $10 million.
        Suggested new products that increased earnings by 23%.</description>
    </experience>
    <education>
      <yearFrom>1971</yearFrom>
      <yearTo>1975</yearTo>
      <institution>South Ridge State University</institution>
      <degree>B.A., Business Administration and Computer Science.</degree>
      <description>Graduated summa cum laude.</description>
    </education>
    <interests>South Ridge Board of Directors, running,
      gardening, carpentry, computers.</interests>
  </resume>
```

Users in most workplaces have at least a passing knowledge of Microsoft Word. Therefore, it makes sense to use it for manipulating XML documents. The capability to save as XML, optionally with a transformation, means that you can use Word to generate simple XML formats. In addition, the XML editing feature extends the powerful forms capabilities of Word to generate valid XML documents. You might use this as the front end to a Web service, for example, using Word to generate the payload for the request.

Using XML in Other Office Applications

In addition to the big two applications of Excel and Word, the various editions of Microsoft Office include other applications that either save or edit XML. Two of the more commonly used are Access and InfoPath.

Microsoft Access

Microsoft Access is the data access component in the Microsoft Office suite. Whereas SQL Server is the tool targeted at DBAs and Microsoft FoxPro the dedicated developer, Access has always been the ease-of-use database. You can use Access either to create applications that store data externally or against its own data format.

Importing XML

Because XML is frequently used as an intermediate data format, it should come as no surprise that Access is capable of importing XML. This import by default attempts to identify each of the tables in the XML and creates new Access tables with a similar structure. However, this is often not the behavior you want. You may want to create the table structure or map one XML format to a target table. Both of these options are available with Access.

In addition to importing both structure and data, you can limit the import to structure only. Access attempts to infer the type of each element in the XML and generates the appropriate column type. If you want better control over this process, you can import an XML schema file instead of an XML file (see Figure 25-8). This uses the type information in the schema file to better define the resulting table (see Figure 25-9). Each global type in the schema becomes a table. Relationships are maintained through the creation of primary/foreign keys. You can then import valid XML into the resulting table without errors.

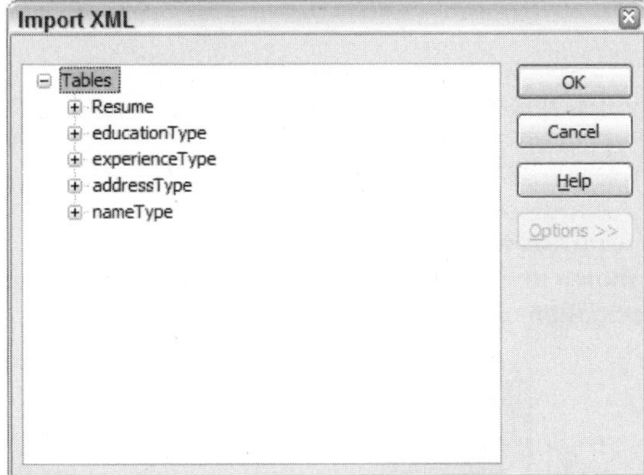

Figure 25-8

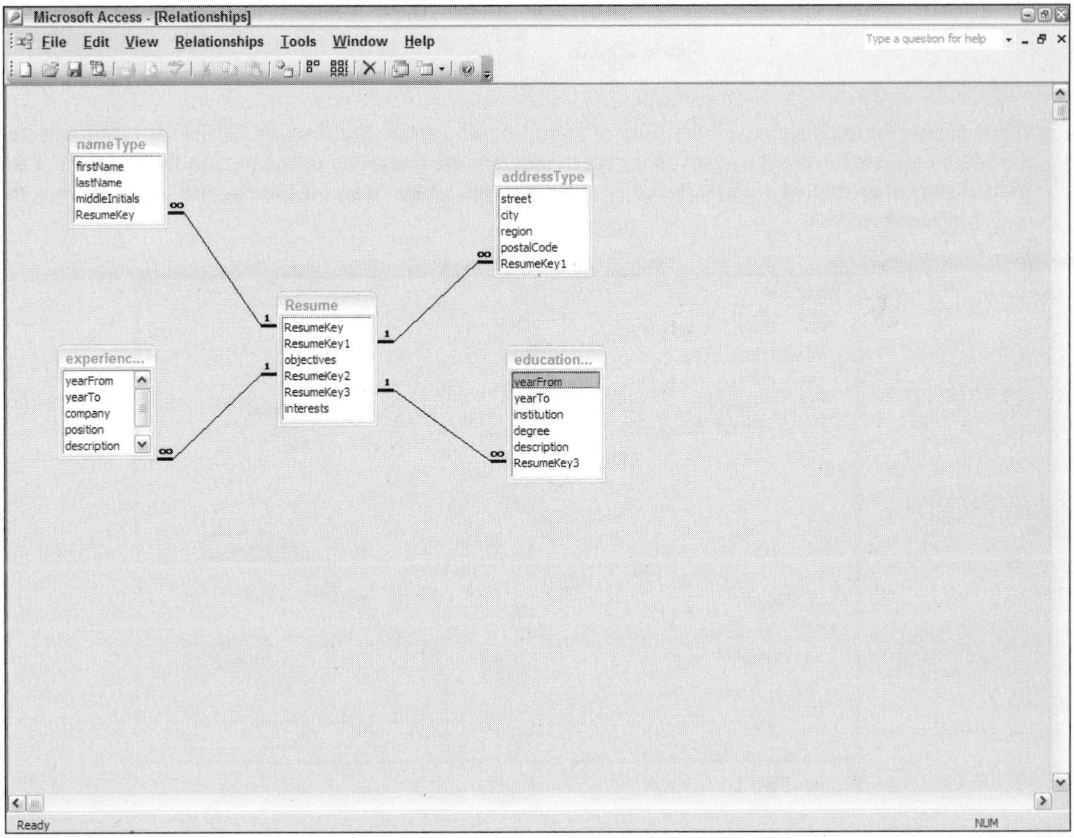

Figure 25-9

If the XML does not completely align with the target table format, you can also apply a transformation during import. This identifies an XSLT stylesheet file that is applied to the XML before import.

Although this import is one-way, it can be a useful means of creating a tool for managing an XML file. As you learn in a moment, it is equally easy to get XML back out of an Access database.

Saving as XML

Tables, queries, views, forms, and reports in Microsoft Access can all be exported as XML. This means that you can dump the data in one or more tables as XML or use the definition of the object to generate an appropriate XML schema or transformation.

The simplest use of this feature is to select an object, then File ➪ Export ➪ Select XML as the output format. You see the dialog shown in Figure 25-10. This gives you the option of exporting the data, the schema, and/or the presentation of the data (for example an XSLT file).

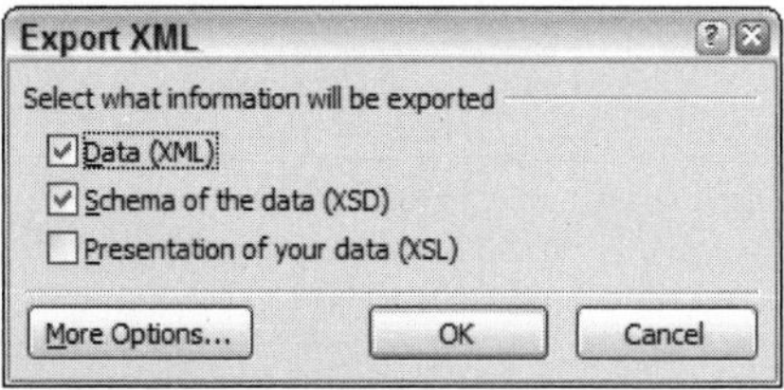

Figure 25-10

When saving tables, you have the option of including any related tables (see Figure 25-11) by selecting the More Options button. This can be useful to recreate the hierarchy of the data in the XML file. Listing 25-11 is part of an export of the Categories and Products tables from the Northwind database that ships with Microsoft Access.

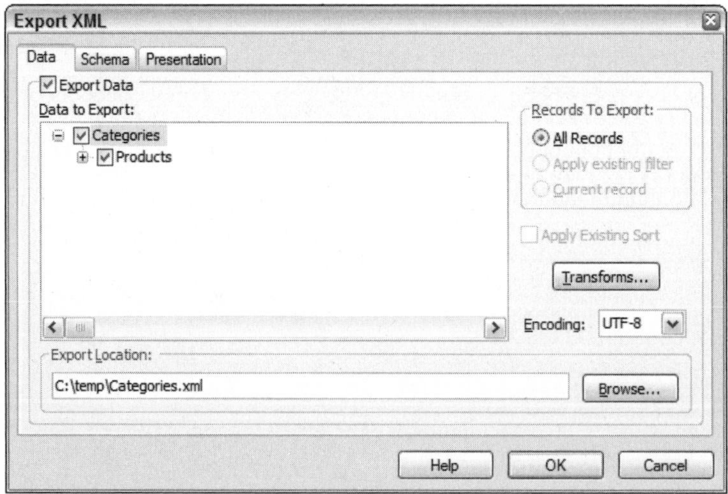

Figure 25-11

Listing 25-11: Exporting related tables

```
<dataroot xmlns:od="urn:schemas-microsoft-com:officedata"
  xmlns:xsi="http://www.w3.org/2001/XMLSchema-instance"
  xsi:noNamespaceSchemaLocation="Categories.xsd"
  generated="2006-06-11T16:53:13">
<Categories>
<CategoryID>1</CategoryID>
<CategoryName>Beverages</CategoryName>
<Description>Soft drinks, coffees, teas, beers, and ales</Description>
<Picture>base64 encoded image</Picture>
<Products>
<ProductID>1</ProductID>
<ProductName>Chai</ProductName>
<SupplierID>1</SupplierID>
<CategoryID>1</CategoryID>
<QuantityPerUnit>10 boxes x 20 bags</QuantityPerUnit>
<UnitPrice>18</UnitPrice>
<UnitsInStock>39</UnitsInStock>
<UnitsOnOrder>0</UnitsOnOrder>
<ReorderLevel>10</ReorderLevel>
<Discontinued>0</Discontinued>
</Products>
<Products>
<ProductID>2</ProductID>
<ProductName>Chang</ProductName>
<SupplierID>1</SupplierID>
<CategoryID>1</CategoryID>
<QuantityPerUnit>24 - 12 oz bottles</QuantityPerUnit>
<UnitPrice>19</UnitPrice>
<UnitsInStock>17</UnitsInStock>
<UnitsOnOrder>40</UnitsOnOrder>
<ReorderLevel>25</ReorderLevel>
<Discontinued>0</Discontinued>
</Products>
...
</dataroot>
```

You can see a reference to a schema file (in the exported XML in Listing 25-11) generated during the export. This schema file (see Listing 25-12 for part of this document) contains the usual XSD definition of the XML, as well as additional information used by Access

Listing 25-12: An exported XML schema

```
<?xml version="1.0" encoding="utf-8"?>
<xsd:schema xmlns:xsd="http://www.w3.org/2001/XMLSchema"
xmlns:od="urn:schemas-microsoft-com:officedata">
  <xsd:element name="dataroot">
    <xsd:complexType>
      <xsd:sequence>
        <xsd:element ref="Categories" minOccurs="0"
        maxOccurs="unbounded" />
```

(continued)

Listing 25-12 *(continued)*

```
      </xsd:sequence>
      <xsd:attribute name="generated" type="xsd:dateTime" />
    </xsd:complexType>
  </xsd:element>
  <xsd:element name="Categories">
    <xsd:annotation>
      <xsd:appinfo>
        <od:index index-name="CategoryName"
        index-key="CategoryName" primary="no" unique="yes"
        clustered="no" />
        <od:index index-name="PrimaryKey" index-key="CategoryID"
        primary="yes" unique="yes" clustered="no" />
      </xsd:appinfo>
    </xsd:annotation>
    <xsd:complexType>
      <xsd:sequence>
        <xsd:element name="CategoryID" minOccurs="1"
        od:jetType="autonumber" od:sqlSType="int"
        od:autoUnique="yes" od:nonNullable="yes" type="xsd:int" />
        <xsd:element name="CategoryName" minOccurs="1"
        od:jetType="text" od:sqlSType="nvarchar"
        od:nonNullable="yes">
          <xsd:simpleType>
            <xsd:restriction base="xsd:string">
              <xsd:maxLength value="15" />
            </xsd:restriction>
          </xsd:simpleType>
        </xsd:element>
        <xsd:element name="Description" minOccurs="0"
        od:jetType="memo" od:sqlSType="ntext">
          <xsd:simpleType>
            <xsd:restriction base="xsd:string">
              <xsd:maxLength value="536870910" />
            </xsd:restriction>
          </xsd:simpleType>
        </xsd:element>
        <xsd:element name="Picture" minOccurs="0"
        od:jetType="oleobject" od:sqlSType="image">
          <xsd:simpleType>
            <xsd:restriction base="xsd:base64Binary">
              <xsd:maxLength value="1476395008" />
            </xsd:restriction>
          </xsd:simpleType>
        </xsd:element>
...
</xsd:schema>
```

The preceding XML schema contains a root element of `dataroot`. This includes the XML schema namespace and an additional URN (`urn:schemas-microsoft-com:officedata`) that is used to identify hints for Microsoft Access should the data be imported back into Access. These hints include any indexes to apply to the resulting table, any keys on the table, and the data type to map to the XSD type.

In addition to using Access to generate XML schemas, you can also use the export function to generate a view of the data using XSLT. This generates two files: an XSLT stylesheet that renders HTML output and either an HTML page or an Active Server Page (ASP) file that uses the XSLT to render the data. The end result is a fairly accurate rendition of the original object. Figure 25-12 shows the output from one of the reports in the Northwind database.

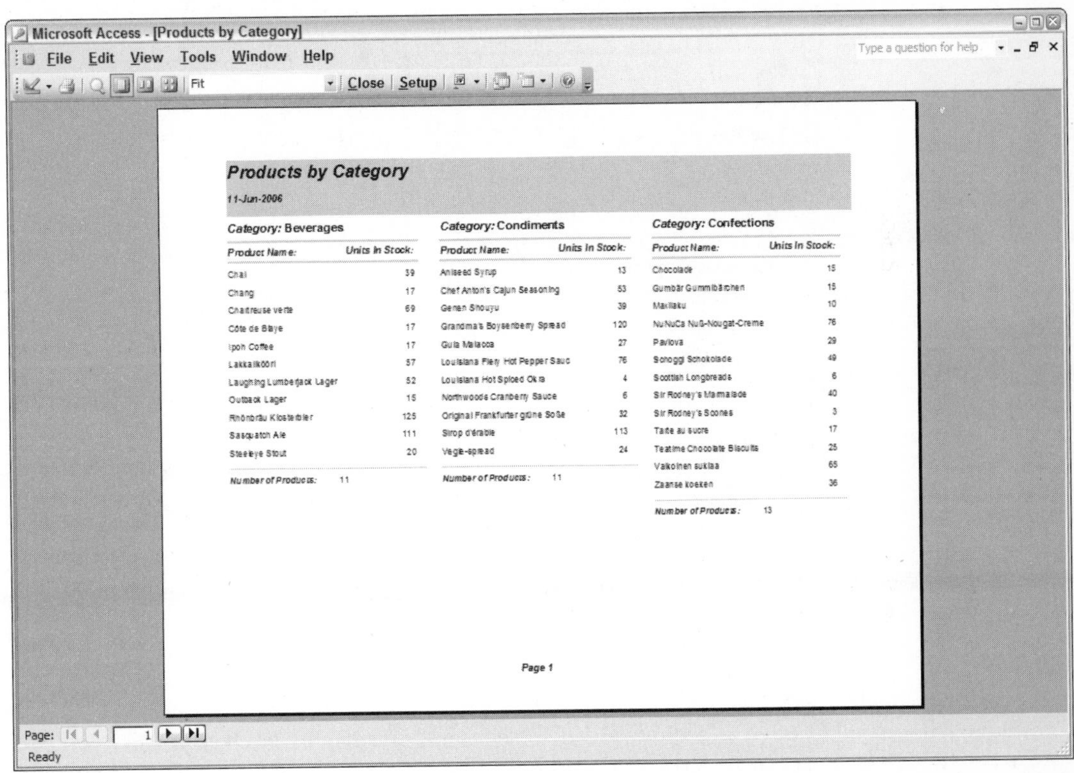

Figure 25-12

Figure 25-13 shows the resulting HTML file that leverages the transformation.

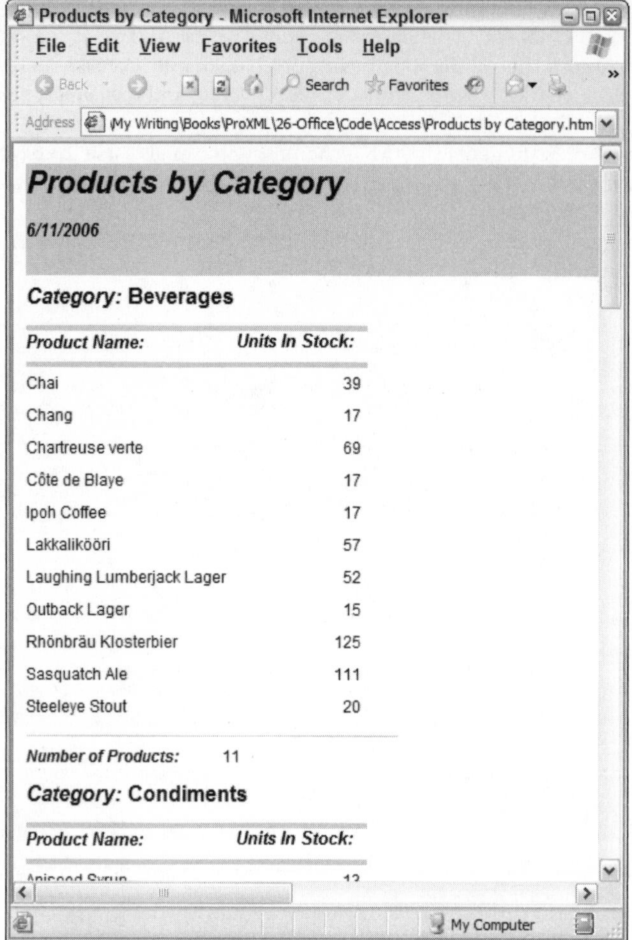

Figure 25-13

Although not as full featured as dedicated XML tools from Altova, Stylus, or Oxygen, Microsoft Access can help the average user create XML, XSD, and XSLT files based on his data. These files can be used as-is or as the starting point for further refinements.

Microsoft InfoPath

Microsoft InfoPath is the first tool from Microsoft designed to support XML from the ground up. It is a form-based tool and, as such, it has properties similar to the Word editing capabilities. However, it does much more than simply enable the creation of XML files. It is a capable Web Service client and schema editor. InfoPath is covered in more detail in Chapter 24.

Office 2007 — Open XML Format

As I write this, Office 2007 has just gone to Beta 2 and should be commercially available by the time the book is on the shelves. Apart from the ribbon and other highly visible changes to the Office user interface, the biggest change relates to XML developers. The native file format for most of the documents is now XML — or rather, a number of XML files bound together in a ZIP format. Figure 25-14 shows the contents of a simple DOCX file.

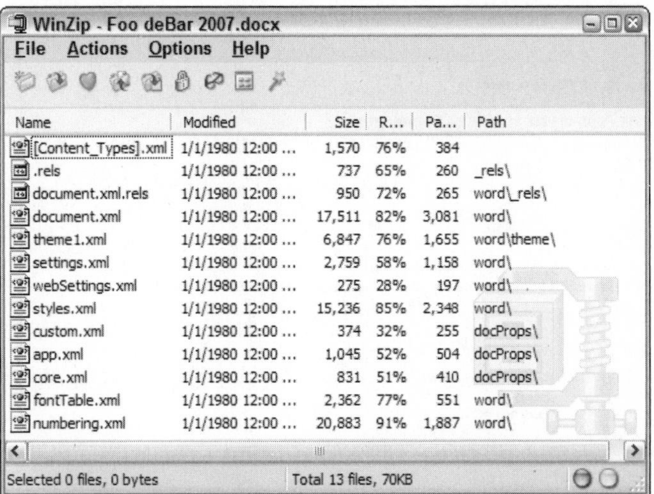

Figure 25-14

The files stored within the document contain the actual text, as well as the formatting and other elements. The most commonly used files are:

- **[Content_Types].xml** — A manifest file containing the list of the XML files that make up the document. This also includes the MIME types of each of the documents. The document.xml MIME type is defined as: `application/vnd.openxmlformats-officedocument.wordprocessingml.document.main+xml`.
- **document.xml** — The actual text of the document, in XML format (WordProcessingML for Word documents, SpreadsheetML for Excel documents). Note that this only includes the content that made up the `<w:body>` element of the Word 2003 WordML document (see Figure 25-15), albeit in a different schema.
- **.rels, document.xml.rels** — Any files that have relationships with other files include an entry like this. Relationships are pointers to other required files. For example, the `document.xml.rels` file contains pointers to the `settings.xml`, `theme1.xml`. `styles.xml`, `fontTable.xml`, and `numbering.xml` files (see Listing 25-13) because these are all needed to correctly render the Word document. Similarly, the root `.rels` file has pointers to the `document.xml` file and the files in the `docProps` folder. If the document contained images or hyperlinks, these items would also be listed in the relationships file, and stored separately. This helps to reduce the overall size of the `document.xml` file.

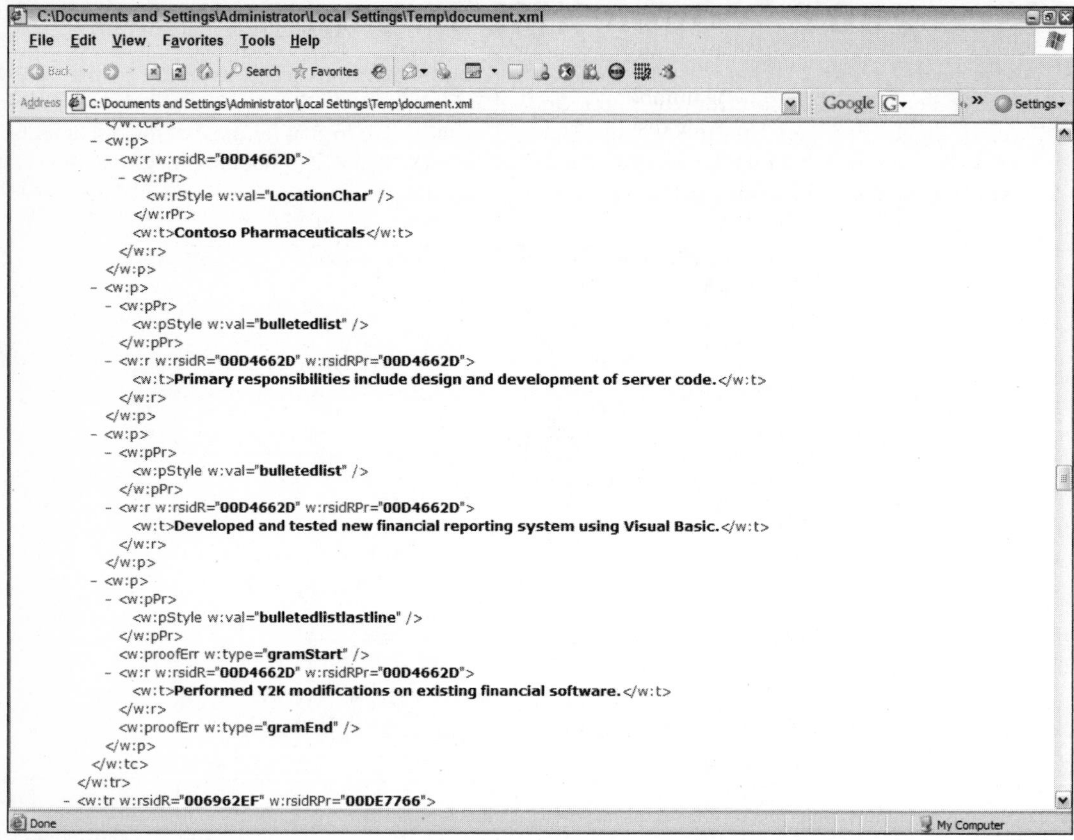

Figure 25-15

The previous documents are the only required elements for a Word 2007 document. In addition, there are a number of optional files that may occur:

- **theme1.xml** — Contains information about the selected font, color, and format schemes applied to the document, if appropriate.
- **settings.xml** — Configuration settings defined for the document. For example, the document template applied to the file, whether revision marks are turned on, and so on.
- **webSettings.xml** — Configuration settings specific to opening the document in Internet Explorer.
- **styles.xml** — The styles available in the document.
- **custom.xml** — Contains any custom user-defined metadata applied to the document.
- **app.xml** — Contains application-specific metadata. For Word, this includes the number of pages, characters, whether document protection is enabled, and so on.
- **core.xml** — Basic metadata about the document, such as the author, last save date, and so on.

- **fontTable.xml** — Listing of the used fonts in the document, as well as their attributes. These attributes can be used to identify a replacement font if the original is not present.
- **numbering.xml** — The numbering definitions part of the document. This defines how numbered and bulleted lists are displayed. The document references these schemes when displaying lists.
- **media** — Subdirectory where all attached media files, such as images, are stored. A reference pointing to this document in located in the `document.xml.rels` file.

Listing 25-13: Document.xml.rels

```
<?xml version="1.0" encoding="utf-8" standalone="yes"?>
<Relationships
  xmlns="http://schemas.openxmlformats.org/package/2006/relationships">

<Relationship Id="rId3"
Type="http://schemas.openxmlformats.org/officeDocument/2006/relationships/settings"
  Target="settings.xml" />
  <Relationship Id="rId2"
  Type="http://schemas.openxmlformats.org/officeDocument/2006/relationships/styles"
  Target="styles.xml" />
<Relationship Id="rId1"
Type="http://schemas.openxmlformats.org/officeDocument/2006/relationships/numbering
"
  Target="numbering.xml" />
  <Relationship Id="rId6"
  Type="http://schemas.openxmlformats.org/officeDocument/2006/relationships/theme"
  Target="theme/theme1.xml" />
<Relationship Id="rId5"
Type="http://schemas.openxmlformats.org/officeDocument/2006/relationships/fontTable
"
  Target="fontTable.xml" />
<Relationship Id="rId4"
Type="http://schemas.openxmlformats.org/officeDocument/2006/relationships/webSettin
gs"
  Target="webSettings.xml" />
</Relationships>
```

The basic flow for processing a document using OpenXML format should be the following:

1. Read the `_rels\.rels` file to determine the file containing the document. Typically, this is the item identified as rId1, but this is not essential. Look for the relationship that contains a pointer to the `http://schemas.openxmlformats.org/officeDocument/2006/relationships/officeDocument` schema:

```
<Relationship Id="rId1"

Type="http://schemas.openxmlformats.org/officeDocument/2006/relationships/officeDoc
ument"
  Target="word/document.xml" />
```

2. Open the document file and process.
3. If you need additional information, refer to the `document.xml.rels` file to locate the files needed. All currently have types defined as a subset of the URN `http://schemas.openxmlformats.org/officeDocument/2006/relationships.`

The OpenXML specification does not only define Word documents; it also defines Excel and PowerPoint documents. It is also an extensible and flexible document format. See the References section that follows for the current specification.

OpenOffice — The Open Document Format

Although Microsoft Office is by far the most popular set of applications for editing common documents, it is not the only set. Recently, a new competitor has increased in popularity: OpenOffice, also known as the Sun Java Desktop. This increasing popularity is partly because it is not Office, but also because of the file format used by these applications. OpenOffice uses a fully documented open XML format for its data. In addition, like Open XML, it uses multiple XML documents, separating the content from the formatting. These multiple documents are stored in a ZIP file, which represents the document created by the tools of OpenOffice.

As the Open Document Format is actually stored in ZIP format, you can open it with WinZip or similar tool and view the created documents. Figure 25-16 shows the files created for a simple OpenOffice Writer file.

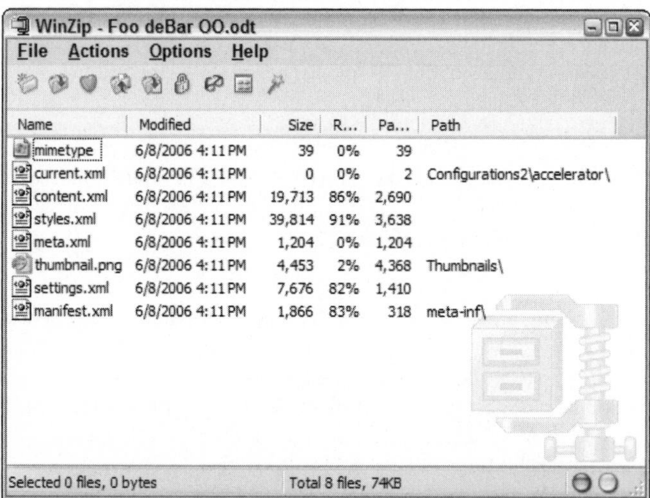

Figure 25-16

The files stored within the ODF file contain not only the content of the document, but also the formatting and application configuration used. The typical files you see are the following:

- **mimetype** — A text file containing the MIME type for the document. For Writer documents, this is `application/vnd.oasis.opendocument.text`.
- **content.xml** — An XML file containing the actual text of the document, as well as the association of the styles used. Listing 25-14 shows a part of this document.
- **styles.xml** — An XML file containing the description of the styles used by the document.
- **meta.xml** — An XML file containing the metadata for the document using Dublin Core syntax. This includes the author, creation date and similar information.
- **thumbnail.png** — A graphics file showing the first page of the document. This is used by the operating system or other preview views of the file.
- **settings.xml** — An XML file that contains application settings for this document. This includes information such as the size and position of the window, printer settings and so on.
- **manifest.xml** — An XML file that lists the files stored in the document (see Figure 25-17). Each file is identified with a file-entry entry, which gives the MIME type of the file as well as the logical path within the XML file used to store the file.

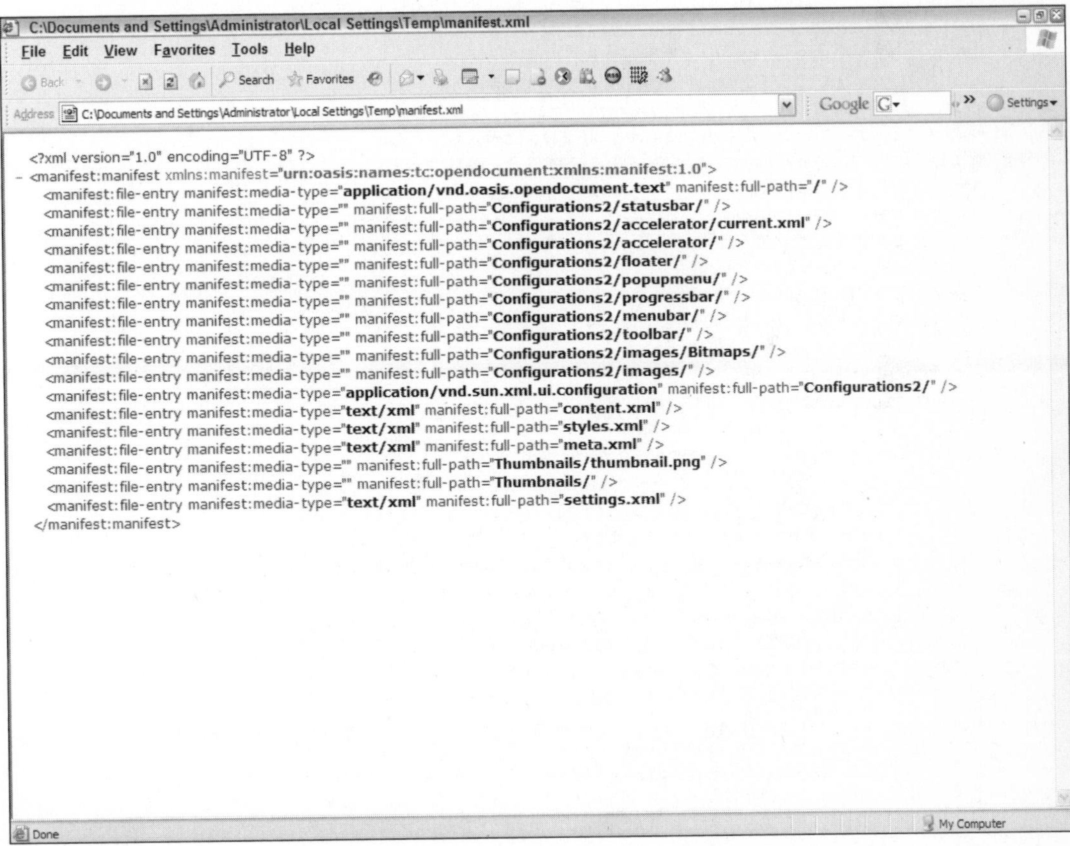

Figure 25-17

Listing 25-14: Content.xml file

```
<?xml version="1.0" encoding="utf-8"?>
<office:document-content
xmlns:office="urn:oasis:names:tc:opendocument:xmlns:office:1.0"
xmlns:style="urn:oasis:names:tc:opendocument:xmlns:style:1.0"
xmlns:text="urn:oasis:names:tc:opendocument:xmlns:text:1.0"
xmlns:table="urn:oasis:names:tc:opendocument:xmlns:table:1.0"
xmlns:draw="urn:oasis:names:tc:opendocument:xmlns:drawing:1.0"
xmlns:fo="urn:oasis:names:tc:opendocument:xmlns:xsl-fo-compatible:1.0"
xmlns:xlink="http://www.w3.org/1999/xlink"
xmlns:dc="http://purl.org/dc/elements/1.1/"
xmlns:meta="urn:oasis:names:tc:opendocument:xmlns:meta:1.0"
xmlns:number="urn:oasis:names:tc:opendocument:xmlns:datastyle:1.0"
xmlns:svg="urn:oasis:names:tc:opendocument:xmlns:svg-compatible:1.0"
xmlns:chart="urn:oasis:names:tc:opendocument:xmlns:chart:1.0"
xmlns:dr3d="urn:oasis:names:tc:opendocument:xmlns:dr3d:1.0"
xmlns:math="http://www.w3.org/1998/Math/MathML"
xmlns:form="urn:oasis:names:tc:opendocument:xmlns:form:1.0"
xmlns:script="urn:oasis:names:tc:opendocument:xmlns:script:1.0"
xmlns:ooo="http://openoffice.org/2004/office"
xmlns:ooow="http://openoffice.org/2004/writer"
xmlns:oooc="http://openoffice.org/2004/calc"
xmlns:dom="http://www.w3.org/2001/xml-events"
xmlns:xforms="http://www.w3.org/2002/xforms"
xmlns:xsd="http://www.w3.org/2001/XMLSchema"
xmlns:xsi="http://www.w3.org/2001/XMLSchema-instance"
office:version="1.0">
  <office:scripts />
  <office:font-face-decls>
  </office:font-face-decls>
  <office:automatic-styles>
  </office:automatic-styles>
  <office:body>
    <office:text>
      <text:sequence-decls>
      </text:sequence-decls>
      <table:table table:name="Table1" table:style-name="Table1">
        <table:table-column table:style-name="Table1.A" />
        <table:table-column table:style-name="Table1.B" />
        <table:table-column table:style-name="Table1.C" />
        <table:table-row table:style-name="Table1.1">
          <table:table-cell table:style-name="Table1.A1"
          table:number-columns-spanned="3"
          office:value-type="string">
            <text:p text:style-name="P1">Foo deBar</text:p>
            <text:p text:style-name="Standard">123 Any Drive, Some
            Place, PA, 12345</text:p>
            <text:p text:style-name="Standard">+1 (111)
            555-1212</text:p>
            <text:p text:style-name="E-mail_20_address">
            foo@debar.com</text:p>
...
```

OpenDocument versus Open XML

The battle over the format of your documents has begun once again because the OpenDocument and Open XML formats are now both offering to help your word processing documents, spreadsheets, presentations, and other documents become cross-platform XML documents. OpenDocument is supported by Sun, IBM, the OASIS consortium, and others, and it is an ISO standard (26300). OpenXML is supported by Microsoft, ECMA, and is targeted (as of this writing) towards also becoming an ISO standard.

Choosing between these two formats on technical merit is difficult: Both use one or more XML files, stored in a ZIP format. Both leverage existing work and standards, such as namespaces, VML, XSD, XLink, SVG, and so on. Both use references heavily to connect parts of the document. OpenXML requires slightly more work to do this because it often requires you to follow two references: the first to the appropriate `.rels` file, and the second to the file containing the data.

Invariably, the choice between these two document formats is likely to be more of a business decision. Do you need to work with Word, Excel, and the rest of Microsoft Office 2007? Then use Microsoft Office. Would you rather align yourself with an Open Source file format or products such as Lotus Notes (that will support ODF in the future)? Use OpenOffice. Alternatively, as both file formats are XML, it is likely that you will be able to use XSLT to transform one document format into the other, allowing you to support both standards.

Just as with the OpenXML format, much of processing ODF involves following references. For example, the style reference `E-mail_20_address` is defined within the `styles.xml` file.

The basic flow for processing an ODF file is to open the `\meta-inf\manifest.xml` file to locate needed files. The bulk of the information is located in the `content.xml` file.

Summary

While the applications of Office are not normally considered XML tools, they continue to add support for creating and editing XML. Most of the Office tools provide the capability of creating both simple XML documents based on a defined schema, as well as saving the full document in XML format. These documents maintain almost complete fidelity with the original.

Going forward, both Office 2007 and Open Office using XML as a native format opens up a number of opportunities for developers. As both use well-defined and open XML specifications, it is possible to create and edit these documents using standard XML tools, such as DOM, XPath, XSLT and XQuery. While the two have separate file formats, it should be possible to create tools that migrate between the two formats.

The next chapter looks at another Microsoft standard — XAML — and how you can use this new XML syntax to create rich, powerful user interfaces for your applications.

Resources

This section contains links to Web sites and documents to help you when working with XML and Office.

- **Office Developer Center on MSDN** (`http://msdn.microsoft.com/office`)—Information on developing for Office, including many XML resources.
- **Office Reference Schemas** (`microsoft.com/office/xml/default.mspx`) —Information on WordProcessingML, SpreadsheetML, and other formats used by the 2003 family of Office documents.
- **OpenXML Specification** (`ecma-international.org/news/TC45_current_work/Ecma%20TC45%20OOXML%20Standard%20-%20Draft%201.3.pdf`) —Specification for the OpenXML formats used by Office 2007 in PDF format. Note: the specification is over 4000 pages.
- **OpenOffice** (`openoffice.org`) —Home to the Open Office suite of products, and the Open Document Format.
- **HR-XML** (`hr-xml.org`) —Group working on creating standardized formats and schemas for common Human Resources documents and processes, such as resumes, employee performance tracking, and more.

26

XAML

One of the newest technologies in the programming world is XAML — an XML language used to write applications on the Windows Presentation Foundation (WPF). *XAML* stands for *Extensible Application Markup Language*. This new way of creating applications within a Microsoft environment was introduced in 2006 and is part of the .NET Framework 3.0. So when you run any WPF application, you must have the .NET Framework 3.0 installed on the client machine. WPF applications are available for Windows Vista, Windows XP, and Windows Server 2003 (the only operating systems that allow for the install of the .NET Framework 3.0).

XAML is the XML declaration used to create a form t represents all the visual aspects and behaviors of the WPF application. Although it's possible to work with a WPF application programmatically, WPF is a step in the same direction the industry is heading — towards *declarative programming*. *Declarative programming* means that instead of creating objects through programming in a compiled language like C#, VB, or Java, you declare everything through XML-type programming. For instance, you can declare a basic WPF form (with only a single button on the form) as shown in Listing 26-1.

Listing 26-1: Window1.xaml

```
<Window x:Class="XAML_Example.Window1"
    xmlns="http://schemas.microsoft.com/winfx/2006/xaml/presentation"
    xmlns:x="http://schemas.microsoft.com/winfx/2006/xaml"
    Title="XAML_Example" Height="300" Width="300">
  <Grid>
      <Button Margin="107,112,110,132" Name="button1">Button</Button>
  </Grid>
</Window>
```

In this case, the form is declared with XAML using the `<Window>` element as the root element of the XML document. The `<Grid>` element defines the entire design surface of the form, and the form contains a single button using the `<Button>` element. Running the application produces the results presented in Figure 26-1.

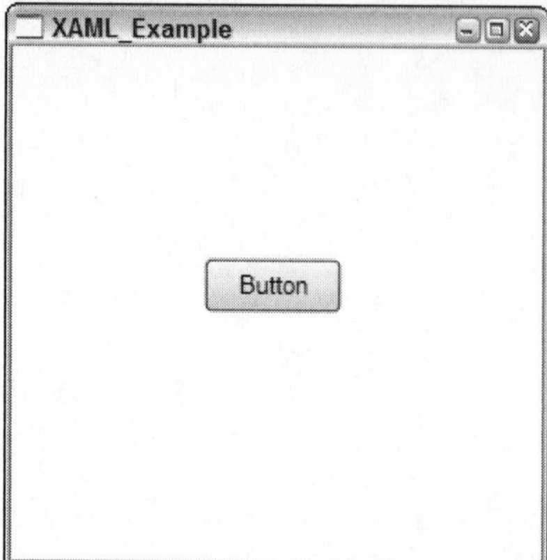

Figure 26-1

With Web technologies and Microsoft's Windows Forms already available, why was another presentation technology needed? The next section answers this question.

Thin or Thick?

When a developer sits down to build an application, one of the first decisions that he makes is whether the application should be a thin- or thick-client. Thin-client applications are browser-based applications, usually `.html`, `.jsp`, `.aspx`, `.asp`, or `.php` pages, whereas thick-client or smart-client applications are usually completely local executables on the client machine.

Over the past few years, thin-client applications have become the preferred application type. Companies such as Google, Microsoft, and others have proven that browser-based applications can add a lot of value to the enterprise. Thin-client applications have made tremendous headway mainly because of just how easily end users can access them, as well as how easy they are to deploy.

To access a thin-client application, you just type a specific URL in a browser of your choice. It really requires only two things — a browser and Internet or intranet access. The deployment and maintenance of thin-client applications also offer powerful advantages. Instead of having an instance of the application reside on each and every end user machine, only a single instance of the thin-client application resides on a server. It is available to anyone who can access the server. This makes for easy upgrade and management of the application. You only have to change the code of this single instance to give every end user automatic access to the latest and greatest version of the application. Another important reason for building a browser-based application is that it can run on any type of vendor operating system. A thick-client application does not guarantee this.

Despite the fact that an instance of the thick-client application must reside on each end user's machine, this technology offers a superior richness that can't be found in a thin-client version of the application. Also, thick-client applications do not require Internet or intranet connections in order to function. A thick-client application can run completely *offline* or in a disconnected mode. Probably one of the biggest reasons for choosing a thick-client application comes down to performance. Thin-client applications are quite synchronous in nature. Most actions you take require a request-response action to occur with the application instance that resides on the remote server. Thick-client applications, on the other hand, don't require this request-response action. In fact, you can create a thick-client application that is asynchronous — allowing it to perform multiple tasks at the same time. Another big advantage to this application style is that it enables you to be fully integrated within the end-user's platform. A thick-client application has access to thread priorities on the client machine, File IO operations, and more. There is definitely a lot of power in this application style.

One More Application Style — Windows Presentation Foundation

Microsoft, considering the issues of both of the application styles, created a new application style that works to combine the best of both these models. WPF applications can run as a thick-client application (directly from an executable) or even within the browser. Microsoft has spent a considerable amount of time building an application model that focuses on the user interface of the application. The graphic capabilities of the WPF application style are completely new and are expected to revolutionize how applications behave. The graphic capabilities are more *Flash-like* and fluid than the traditional thick-client application. It includes a vector-based composition engine that makes full use of the end user's high-powered graphic card. WPF offers many more capabilities in its framework. These capabilities are presented in Figure 26-2.

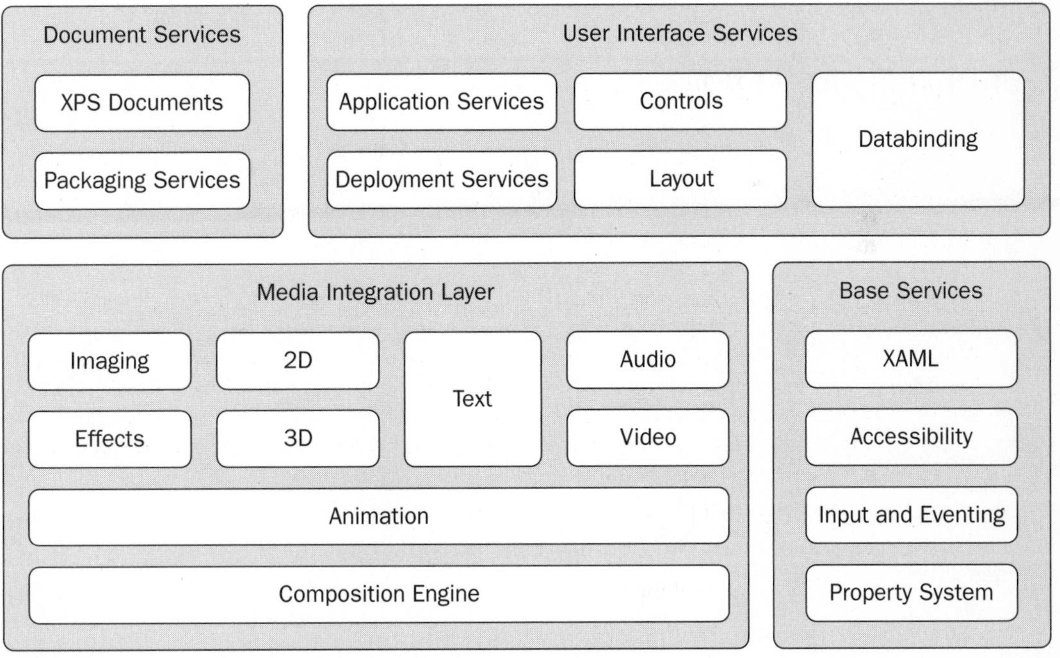

Figure 26-2

As you can see, XAML is one of the base services. As stated earlier, you can use XAML as a means to build an application through the process of declarative programming. For instance, you can create an instance of a button using C# programming as shown in the following code:

```
Button myButton = new Button();
myButton.Content = "This is my button text";
myButton.Background = new SolidColorBrush(Colors.Yellow);
```

Or you can use XAML to accomplish the same thing:

```
<Button Name="button1" >This is my button text
   <Button.Background>
      Yellow
   </Button.Background>
</Button>
```

In the end, either of these methods produces the same results. The C# code found in a class file actually gets compiled and run to produce a large button on the page, whereas the XAML code is interpreted into a class file that is compiled and produces the same large button. Building WPF applications using XAML allows you to separate business logic from presentation. This feature has demonstrated value within the ASP.NET world that uses the same model. Using XAML is easy, and you can work with any type of tool to build your WPF application — including Notepad!

XAML enables you to point to events that happen within a code-behind page just as ASP.NET does in its declarative model. For instance, working with the button example presented in the first part of the chapter, you can add a click event by using the `Click` attribute (as shown in Listing 26-2):

Listing 26-2: Window1.xaml

```
<Window x:Class="XAML_Example.Window1"
    xmlns="http://schemas.microsoft.com/winfx/2006/xaml/presentation"
    xmlns:x="http://schemas.microsoft.com/winfx/2006/xaml"
    Title="XAML_Example" Height="300" Width="300"
    >
  <Grid>
    <Button Margin="10,10,0,0" Name="button1" Click="button1_Click" Height="23"
     HorizontalAlignment="Left" VerticalAlignment="Top" Width="75">
     Button</Button>
    <Label Margin="16.37,44.7233333333334,22,24" Name="label1" FontWeight="Bold"
     FontSize="150" FontFamily="Verdana">1</Label>
  </Grid>
</Window>
```

In this case, you add a reference through the use of the `Click` attribute for a `button1_Click` method. This means that whenever the button is actually clicked on the form, the `button1_Click` event is triggered.

In addition to the new Button control, a Label control has been added. The Label control, `label1`, has a defined margin (which you can get pretty exact about if you look closely at the numbers). If you attempt to design this same thing using Visual Studio 2005, your form in the design surface would resemble the screen shown in Figure 26-3.

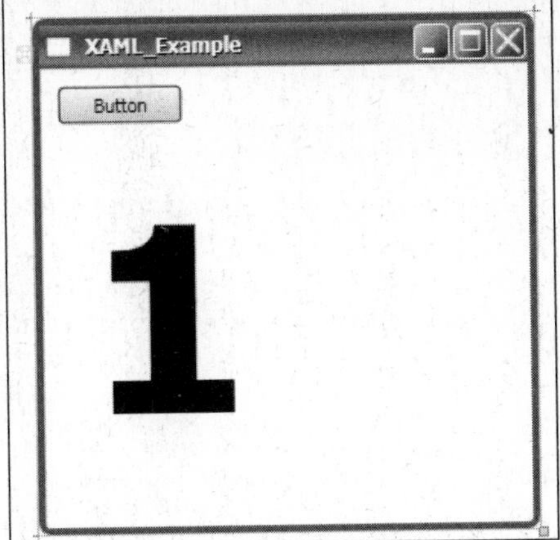

Figure 26-3

The `Click` attribute points to an event that is contained within the code-behind file for this form — `Window1.xaml.cs`. This file is presented in Listing 26-3.

Listing 26-3: Window1.xaml.cs

```
using System.Windows;
using System.Windows.Controls;

namespace XAML_Example
{
    /// <summary>
    /// Interaction logic for Window1.xaml
    /// </summary>

    public partial class Window1 : System.Windows.Window
    {
        int buttonValue = 1;

        public Window1()
        {
            InitializeComponent();
        }

        void button1_Click(object sender, RoutedEventArgs e)
        {
            buttonValue += 1;
            this.label1.Content = buttonValue.ToString();
        }
    }
}
```

In this case, when the button on the form is clicked, the `button1_Click` event is triggered. This increases the `buttonValue` variable by one and assigns its value to the `Content` attribute of the `label1` control (its text value). This means that every time the button on the form is clicked, the number shown on the form is increased by one.

WPF Within Visual Studio 2005

WPF applications can be built directly within Visual Studio 2005. It requires a toolkit called the Visual Studio 2005 Extensions for .NET Framework 3.0. After the toolkit is installed, you should find that you have project types that are relevant to the .NET Framework 3.0. This is illustrated in Figure 26-4, which shows the project dialog box in Visual Studio 2005 after the installation of the toolkit.

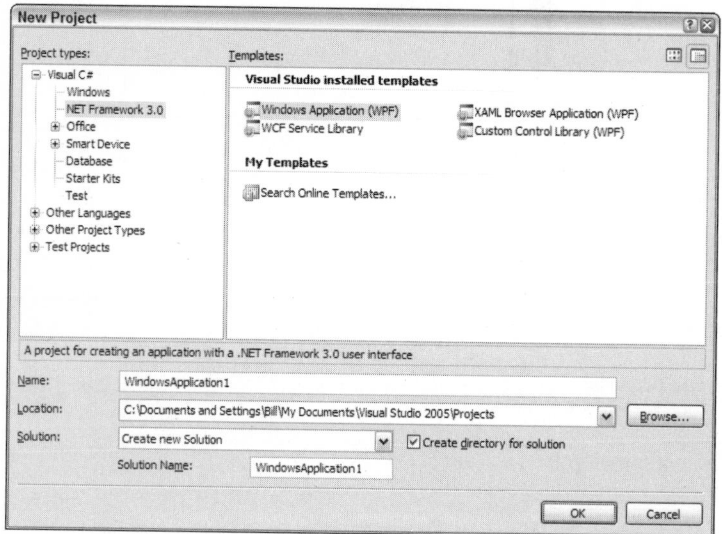

Figure 26-4

A new view of the WPF application has been incorporated into Visual Studio 2005, as shown in Figure 26-5.

This example presents a Design view of the project showing the WPF form as it would appear when compiled and run. You can also see another view of the same form in XAML. Like most .NET applications built from Visual Studio, it enables you to drag and drop controls directly onto the design surface of the WPF form or to type the controls directly into the XAML document using declarative programming.

Nesting Controls

Through XAML, you can add hierarchy to your controls. XML is a hierarchal language, and you can add that same level of hierarchy to deal with controls in your applications. For instance, in the ListBox control, you can normally insert textual items directly in the selectable options for the end user. This is presented in Listing 26-4.

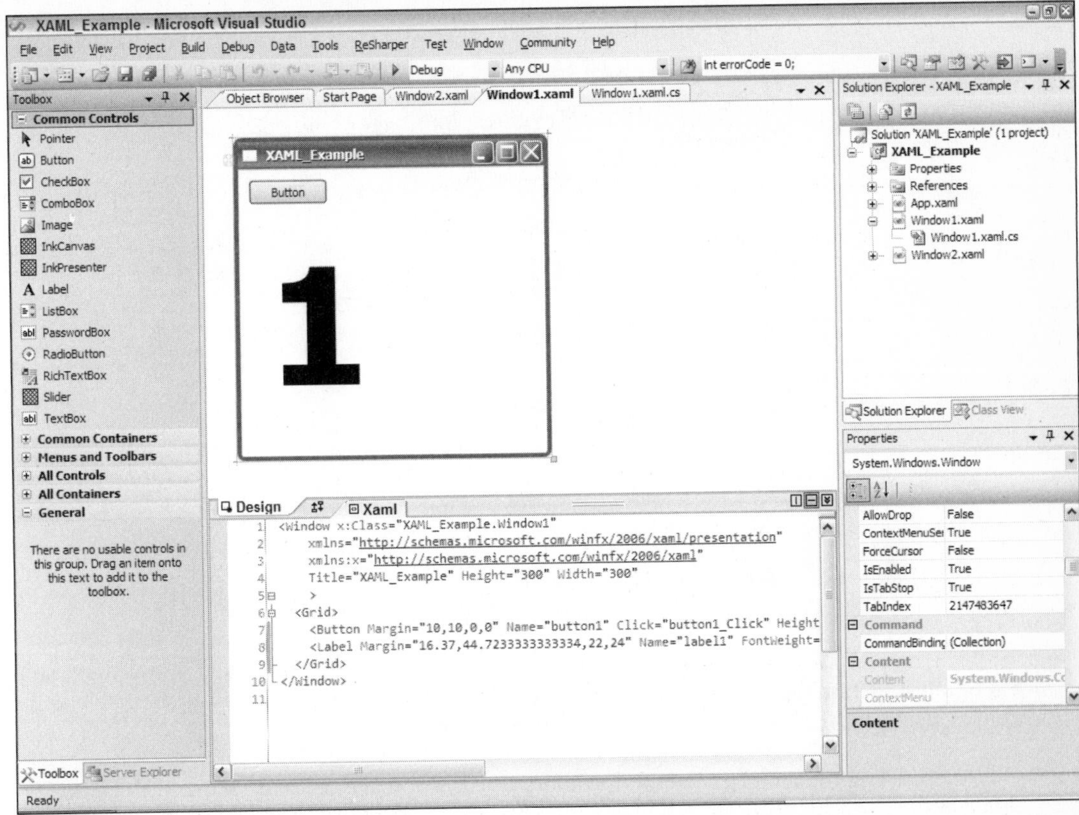

Figure 26-5

Listing 26-4: Showing three elements within the ListBox control

```
<Window x:Class="XAML_Example.Window1"
    xmlns="http://schemas.microsoft.com/winfx/2006/xaml/presentation"
    xmlns:x="http://schemas.microsoft.com/winfx/2006/xaml"
    Title="XAML_Example" Height="300" Width="300"
    >
    <Grid>
      <ListBox Margin="15,15,15,110" Name="listBox1">
        <Label Name="label1" Content="Hello, I'm a Label Control" />
        <Label Name="label2" Content="Hello, I'm a Label Control" />
        <Image Name="image1" Source="whiteLipper.gif" />
      </ListBox>
  </Grid>
</Window>
```

In this case, you have a ListBox control with three child elements. Interestingly, two of the selectable elements are Label controls, whereas the third element is an image. You can nest pretty much anything that you want within something else. WPF takes on the Parent-Child relationship. Please note that images have to be included in the solution for this to work. The preceding bit of XAML code produces the results shown in Figure 26-6.

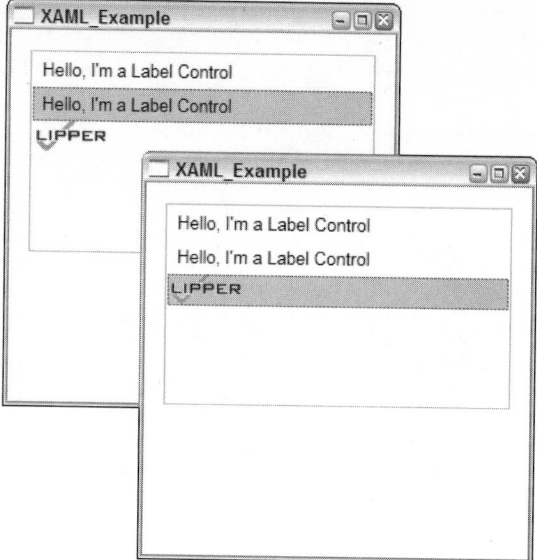

Figure 26-6

From this example, you can see that this ListBox takes traditional text such as the first two items shown in the figure. The third item is the most interesting because it is an image. It is just as selectable as the textual items. They are all simply child elements of the parent ListBox control.

This type of nesting capability can be used in many places. For instance, to use the same logo image within a button, you simply nest the image within the `<Button>` control as shown in Listing 26-5.

Listing 26-5: Nesting an image within a Button control

```
<Window x:Class="XAML_Example.Window1"
    xmlns="http://schemas.microsoft.com/winfx/2006/xaml/presentation"
    xmlns:x="http://schemas.microsoft.com/winfx/2006/xaml"
    Title="XAML_Example" Height="300" Width="300"
    >
    <Grid>
       <Button Height="45" HorizontalAlignment="Left" Margin="25,0,0,55"
        Name="button1" VerticalAlignment="Bottom" Width="87">
          <Image Name="image1" Source="whiteLipper.gif" />
       </Button>
    </Grid>
</Window>
```

This bit of code includes a typical `<Button>` control, but nested within the opening and closing `<Button>` elements is an Image control declaration. This produces the results presented in Figure 26-7.

Figure 26-7

Case Study: Building a Document Viewer Using XAML

Windows Presentation Foundation is very effective in the area of presentation. A tremendous amount of attention has been put onto layout, fonts, and vector graphics. A common practice is to view documents directly within an application — either documents that are created or contained within the application or documents that reside elsewhere. WPF is excellent at document presentation. This section, however, focuses on simply constructing and presenting a document directly from the XAML file.

Create the WPF Application

To accomplish this task, create a new WPF Application (WPF) project. First, you can expand the default form. From the Visual Studio toolbox, drag and drop a FlowDocumentReader control onto the design surface of the form. Initially, this gives you only a small navigation-like control that you can position on the page. You end up with something like the control shown in Figure 26-8.

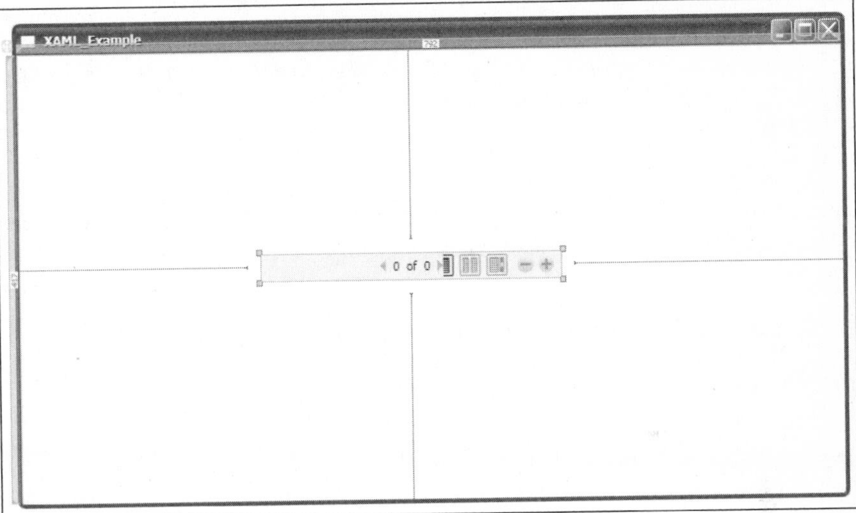

Figure 26-8

In this figure, you see the navigation system for document viewing, which also includes the area in which you will present the document. In order to make room for the document that you create inside this control, expand the FlowDocumentReader control so that it takes up all the space on the form. Now that the control is in place on the form, the next step is to create the document to be presented.

Building the Document

For this part of the application, you build the entire document directly in the XAML file itself. At this stage, you XAML file should appear as illustrated in Listing 26-6.

Listing 26-6: The XAML document at this point

```
<Window x:Class="XAML_Example.MyDocument"
    xmlns="http://schemas.microsoft.com/winfx/2006/xaml/presentation"
    xmlns:x="http://schemas.microsoft.com/winfx/2006/xaml"
    Title="XAML_Example" Height="450" Width="800"
    >
    <Grid>
    <FlowDocumentReader Margin="5,5,5,5" Name="flowDocumentReader1" />
  </Grid>
</Window>
```

Looking this code over, you can see a single `<FlowDocumentReader>` element on the form, positioned with a 5-pixel margin on each of its sides. At this point, the document reader is now in place on the form, but it doesn't contain a document of any kind. The next step is to build the document.

To accomplish this task, you nest some additional XML elements within the `<FlowDocumentReader>` element, such as a `<FlowDocument>`. You use these to define your document. Some of the child elements of the `<FlowDocument>` element include `<BlockUIContainer>`, `<Paragraph>`, `<List>`, `<Section>`, and `<Table>`.

The `<BlockUIContainer>` element allows you to position other WPF controls within the document. For instance, if you want to keep the title and text as presented in Listing 26-6, but you also want to include a RichTextBox control on the document; you simply use the `<BlockUIContainer>` illustrated in Listing 26-7.

Listing 26-7: Using the <BlockUIContainer> element in your document

```
<Window x:Class="XAML_Example.MyDocument"
    xmlns="http://schemas.microsoft.com/winfx/2006/xaml/presentation"
    xmlns:x="http://schemas.microsoft.com/winfx/2006/xaml"
    Title="XAML_Example" Height="450" Width="800"
    >
    <Grid>
      <FlowDocumentReader Margin="5,5,5,5" Name="flowDocumentReader1">
        <FlowDocument>
          <Paragraph>
            <Italic><Bold>This is the title of the document</Bold></Italic>
          </Paragraph>
          <Paragraph>
            This is the start of the document ...
          </Paragraph>
          <BlockUIContainer>
            <RichTextBox Name="richTextBox11" />
          </BlockUIContainer>
        </FlowDocument>
      </FlowDocumentReader>
  </Grid>
</Window>
```

Now the document that you are creating has three parts to it — two paragraph parts and a part that contains a single control (the RichTextBox control). Running this application produces the results presented in Figure 26-9.

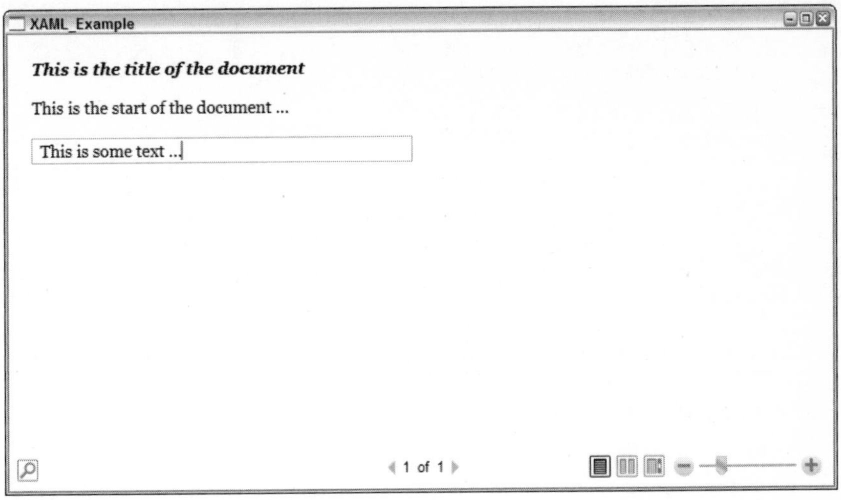

Figure 26-9

You already saw the <Paragraph> section in action with the title and the plain text that was placed at the top of the document. Remember that items can nest inside each other quite easily in XAML, and this means that the <Section>, <List>, and <Table> elements allow for easy nesting of other elements, as does the base <Paragraph> element. For a good example of this, look at Listing 26-8 where you create some list items in the document using the <List> element.

Listing 26-8: Using the <List> element in your document

```
<Window x:Class="XAML_Example.MyDocument"
    xmlns="http://schemas.microsoft.com/winfx/2006/xaml/presentation"
    xmlns:x="http://schemas.microsoft.com/winfx/2006/xaml"
    Title="XAML_Example" Height="450" Width="800"
    >
    <Grid>
      <FlowDocumentReader Margin="5,5,5,5" Name="flowDocumentReader1">
        <FlowDocument>
          <Paragraph>
            <Italic><Bold>This is the title of the document</Bold></Italic>
          </Paragraph>
          <Paragraph>
            This is the start of the document ...
          </Paragraph>
          <List>
            <ListItem>
              <Paragraph>
                Item One
              </Paragraph>
            </ListItem>
            <ListItem>
              <Paragraph>
                Item Two
              </Paragraph>
```

```
            </ListItem>
          </List>
        </FlowDocument>
      </FlowDocumentReader>
  </Grid>
</Window>
```

You can see that a list is created using the <List> element within the <FlowDocument> element. The <List> element can take any number of <ListItem> elements that, in turn, can contain what you deem necessary. In this case, each list item is a <Paragraph> element. These two list items produce the results presented in Figure 26-10.

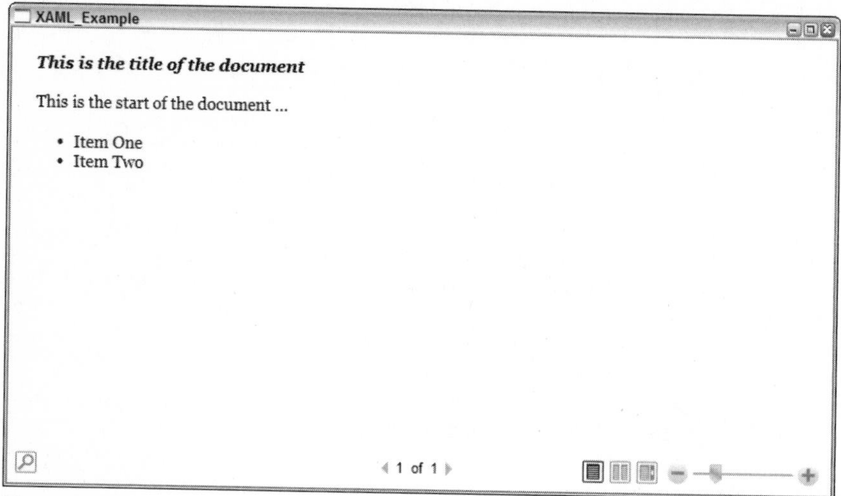

Figure 26-10

The nice thing about this control is that is allows you to easily display a large set of content in columns within the document viewer. To see this in action, go to the Lorem Ipsum Web site found at www.lipsum.com. This site enables you to generate a large amount of gibberish text to use in this example. To build your XAML document with this text, wrap each of the provided paragraphs in a <Paragraph> element. In the end, your XAML document should be similar to the one presented in Listing 26-9.

Listing 26-9: Building the main document using lorem ipsum text

```
<Window x:Class="XAML_Example.MyDocument"
    xmlns="http://schemas.microsoft.com/winfx/2006/xaml/presentation"
    xmlns:x="http://schemas.microsoft.com/winfx/2006/xaml"
    Title="XAML_Example" Height="450" Width="800"
    >
  <Grid>
    <FlowDocumentReader Margin="5,5,5,5" Name="flowDocumentReader1">
      <FlowDocument>
        <Paragraph>
          <Italic>
            <Bold>This is the title of the document</Bold>
```

```
            </Italic>
          </Paragraph>
          <Paragraph>
            Lorem ipsum dolor sit amet, consectetuer adipiscing elit. Praesent mattis
            euismod eros. Aliquam lobortis rhoncus purus ...
          </Paragraph>
          <Paragraph>
            Ut elit lectus, volutpat in, dictum vitae, faucibus vel, nisl. Integer
            dictum pede vel lacus. Vestibulum turpis erat, gravida ...
          </Paragraph>
          <Paragraph>
            Pellentesque habitant morbi tristique senectus et netus et malesuada
            fames ac turpis egestas. Vivamus iaculis ...
          </Paragraph>
        </FlowDocument>
      </FlowDocumentReader>
    </Grid>
</Window>
```

The code shown in this example is slimmed down for presentation purposes. The paragraphs are cut short, and the example you see in the figures for this example actually include 20 paragraphs instead of the three that are shown here.

In this case, you have a document that should include 20 `<Paragraph>` sections from the Lorem Ipsum site. The `<Paragraph>` section at the top represents the title of the document. When you run this application, you get the results presented in Figure 26-11.

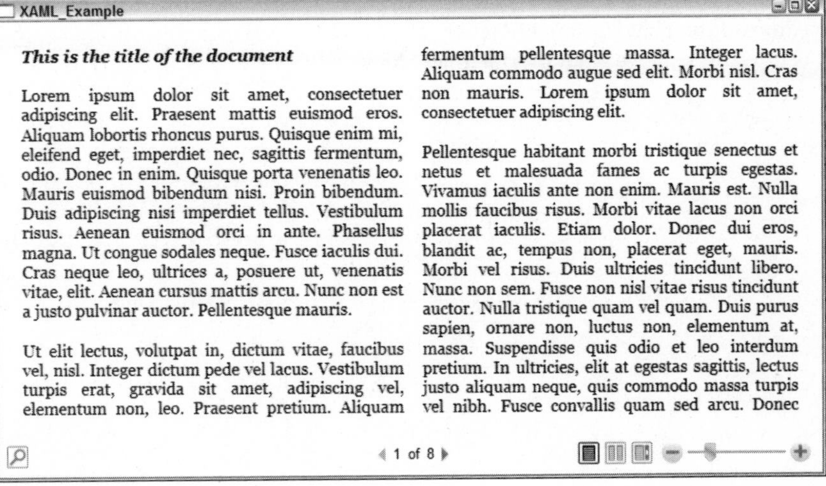

Figure 26-11

Using this little bit of XAML code, you can easily place a document within the application. The FlowDocumentReader control does an excellent job of making your documents easy to read. Notice that the text is divided into two separate columns for easy readability. You can see at the bottom of the application that it contains eight pages. This is controlled by the amount of text contained in the application and the font size of the text. There are a number of features on the control toolbar at the bottom of the application.

Viewing the Document

On the left part of the control panel is a magnifying glass. When you click this icon, a text box appears next to it. This text box enables you to search through the document quite quickly and easily. To the right of the magnifying glass and the search text box, you see a navigation control that allows you to click the arrows that take you to the next page or the previous page. To the right of the navigation controls, are three page view controls. The three available page views include:

- **Page Mode** — This is the mode presented in Figure 27-11. It enables you to see a single page that usually includes multiple columns.
- **Two Page Mode** — This is similar to the Page Mode, but has two distinct pages within the application.
- **Scroll Mode** — Like a Web page, this mode allows you to see the document as a single and continuous page with the appropriate scroll bars for pages that are too long or wide.

You can see a good example of the Scroll Mode and the Two Page Mode in Figure 26-12.

The FlowDocumentReader control allows you to control how you read the document. You can not only change the page format, but you can also click the plus or minus sign in the control panel to manipulate the font size. Clicking the plus sign causes the text to get larger as you can see in Figure 26-13.

Another feature of the FlowDocumentReader control is that it adapts quite nicely to any resolution. For instance, Figure 26-14 shows what the document looks like when it is expanded to a larger resolution.

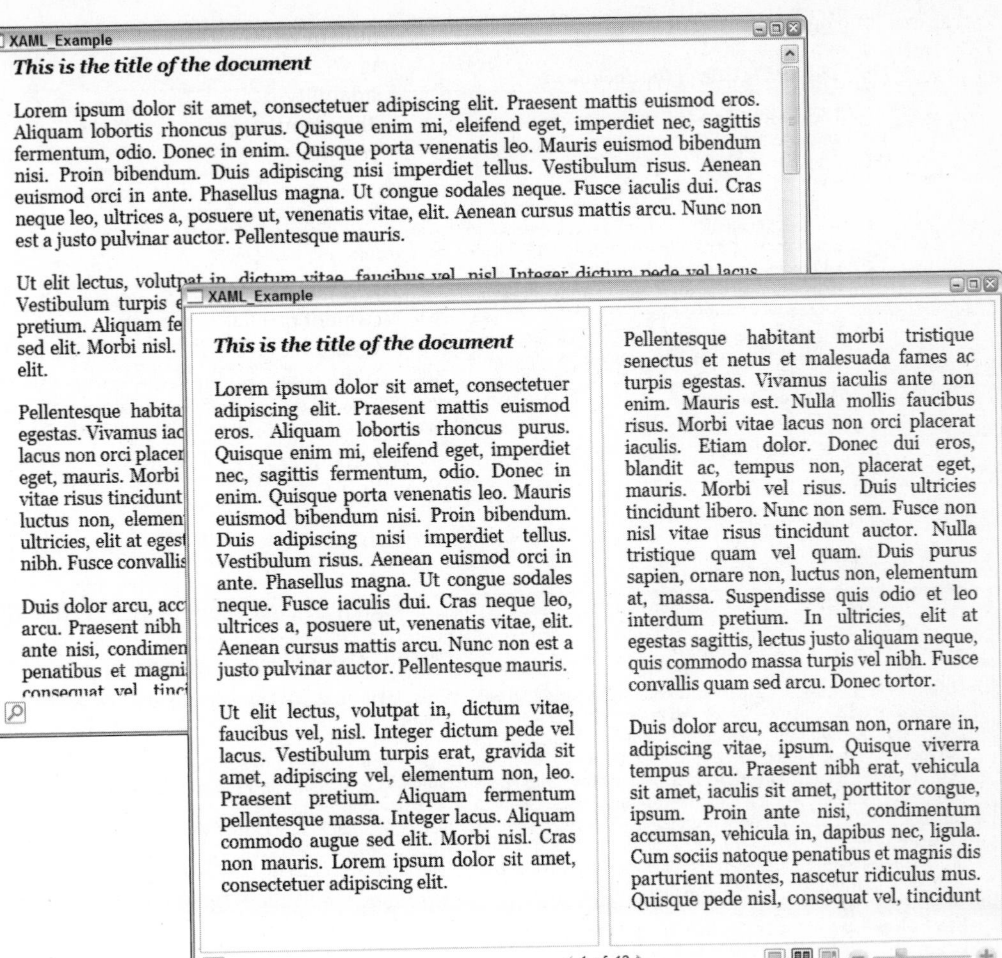

XAML_Example
This is the title of the document
Lorem ipsum dolor sit amet, consectetuer adipiscing elit. Praesent mattis euismod eros. Aliquam lobortis rhoncus purus. Quisque enim mi, eleifend eget, imperdiet nec, sagittis fermentum, odio. Donec in enim. Quisque porta venenatis leo. Mauris euismod bibendum nisi. Proin bibendum. Duis adipiscing nisi imperdiet tellus. Vestibulum risus. Aenean euismod orci in ante. Phasellus magna. Ut congue sodales neque. Fusce iaculis dui. Cras neque leo, ultrices a, posuere ut, venenatis vitae, elit. Aenean cursus mattis arcu. Nunc non est a justo pulvinar auctor. Pellentesque mauris.
XAML_Example
This is the title of the document
Lorem ipsum dolor sit amet, consectetuer adipiscing elit. Praesent mattis euismod eros. Aliquam lobortis rhoncus purus. Quisque enim mi, eleifend eget, imperdiet nec, sagittis fermentum, odio. Donec in enim. Quisque porta venenatis leo. Mauris euismod bibendum nisi. Proin bibendum. Duis adipiscing nisi imperdiet tellus. Vestibulum risus. Aenean euismod orci in ante. Phasellus magna. Ut congue sodales neque. Fusce iaculis dui. Cras neque leo, ultrices a, posuere ut, venenatis vitae, elit. Aenean cursus mattis arcu. Nunc non est a justo pulvinar auctor. Pellentesque mauris.
Ut elit lectus, volutpat in, dictum vitae, faucibus vel, nisl. Integer dictum pede vel lacus. Vestibulum turpis erat, gravida sit amet, adipiscing vel, elementum non, leo. Praesent pretium. Aliquam fermentum pellentesque massa. Integer lacus. Aliquam commodo augue sed elit. Morbi nisl. Cras non mauris. Lorem ipsum dolor sit amet, consectetuer adipiscing elit.
Pellentesque habitant morbi tristique senectus et netus et malesuada fames ac turpis egestas. Vivamus iaculis ante non enim. Mauris est. Nulla mollis faucibus risus. Morbi vitae lacus non orci placerat iaculis. Etiam dolor. Donec dui eros, blandit ac, tempus non, placerat eget, mauris. Morbi vel risus. Duis ultricies tincidunt libero. Nunc non sem. Fusce non nisl vitae risus tincidunt auctor. Nulla tristique quam vel quam. Duis purus sapien, ornare non, luctus non, elementum at, massa. Suspendisse quis odio et leo interdum pretium. In ultricies, elit at egestas sagittis, lectus justo aliquam neque, quis commodo massa turpis vel nibh. Fusce convallis quam sed arcu. Donec tortor.
Duis dolor arcu, accumsan non, ornare in, adipiscing vitae, ipsum. Quisque viverra tempus arcu. Praesent nibh erat, vehicula sit amet, iaculis sit amet, porttitor congue, ipsum. Proin ante nisi, condimentum accumsan, vehicula in, dapibus nec, ligula. Cum sociis natoque penatibus et magnis dis parturient montes, nascetur ridiculus mus. Quisque pede nisl, consequat vel, tincidunt
1 of 12

Figure 26-12

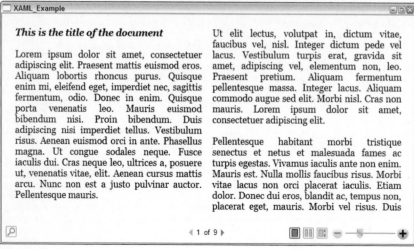

XAML_Example

This is the title of the document

Lorem ipsum dolor sit amet, consectetuer adipiscing elit. Praesent mattis euismod eros. Aliquam lobortis rhoncus purus. Quisque enim mi, eleifend eget, imperdiet nec, sagittis fermentum, odio. Donec in enim. Quisque porta venenatis leo. Mauris euismod bibendum nisi. Proin bibendum. Duis adipiscing nisi imperdiet tellus. Vestibulum risus. Aenean euismod orci in ante. Phasellus magna. Ut congue sodales neque. Fusce iaculis dui. Cras neque leo, ultrices a, posuere ut, venenatis vitae, elit. Aenean cursus mattis arcu. Nunc non est a justo pulvinar auctor. Pellentesque mauris.

Ut elit lectus, volutpat in, dictum vitae, faucibus vel, nisl. Integer dictum pede vel lacus. Vestibulum turpis erat, gravida sit amet, adipiscing vel, elementum non, leo. Praesent pretium. Aliquam fermentum pellentesque massa. Integer lacus. Aliquam commodo augue sed elit. Morbi nisl. Cras non mauris. Lorem ipsum dolor sit amet, consectetuer adipiscing elit.

Pellentesque habitant morbi tristique senectus et netus et malesuada fames ac turpis egestas. Vivamus iaculis ante non enim. Mauris est. Nulla mollis faucibus risus. Morbi vitae lacus non orci placerat iaculis. Etiam dolor. Donec dui eros, blandit ac, tempus non, placerat eget, mauris. Morbi vel risus. Duis

1 of 9

Figure 26-13

XAML_Example

This is the title of the document

Lorem ipsum dolor sit amet, consectetuer adipiscing elit. Praesent mattis euismod eros. Aliquam lobortis rhoncus purus. Quisque enim mi, eleifend eget, imperdiet nec, sagittis fermentum, odio. Donec in enim. Quisque porta venenatis leo. Mauris euismod bibendum nisi. Proin bibendum. Duis adipiscing nisi imperdiet tellus. Vestibulum risus. Aenean euismod orci in ante. Phasellus magna. Ut congue sodales neque. Fusce iaculis dui. Cras neque leo, ultrices a, posuere ut, venenatis vitae, elit. Aenean cursus mattis arcu. Nunc non est a justo pulvinar auctor. Pellentesque mauris.

Ut elit lectus, volutpat in, dictum vitae, faucibus vel, nisl. Integer dictum pede vel lacus. Vestibulum turpis erat, gravida sit amet, adipiscing vel, elementum non, leo. Praesent pretium. Aliquam fermentum pellentesque massa. Integer lacus. Aliquam commodo augue sed elit. Morbi nisl. Cras non mauris. Lorem ipsum dolor sit amet, consectetuer adipiscing elit.

Pellentesque habitant morbi tristique senectus et netus et malesuada fames ac turpis egestas. Vivamus iaculis ante non enim. Mauris est. Nulla mollis faucibus risus. Morbi vitae lacus non orci placerat iaculis. Etiam dolor. Donec dui eros, blandit ac, tempus non, placerat eget, mauris. Morbi vel risus. Duis ultricies tincidunt libero. Nunc non sem. Fusce non nisl vitae risus tincidunt auctor. Nulla tristique quam vel quam. Duis purus sapien, ornare non, luctus non, elementum at, massa. Suspendisse quis odio et leo interdum pretium. In ultricies, elit at egestas sagittis, lectus justo aliquam neque, quis commodo massa turpis vel nibh. Fusce convallis quam sed arcu. Donec tortor.

Duis dolor arcu, accumsan non, ornare in, adipiscing vitae, ipsum. Quisque viverra tempus arcu. Praesent nibh erat, vehicula sit amet, iaculis sit amet, porttitor congue, ipsum. Proin ante nisi, condimentum accumsan, vehicula in, dapibus nec, ligula. Cum sociis natoque penatibus et magnis dis parturient montes, nascetur ridiculus mus. Quisque pede nisl, consequat vel, tincidunt vel, ullamcorper et, nibh. Nulla facilisi. Suspendisse potenti. Praesent ac nisi. Fusce et ipsum. Morbi pretium, arcu ut ultricies tincidunt, urna ligula semper nisl, ut lacinia sem neque sed urna. Morbi tempus hendrerit purus. Praesent mattis elementum velit.

Sed euismod risus quis erat porttitor rutrum. Pellentesque cursus tempor diam. Etiam nulla purus, tristique ut, condimentum sed, volutpat in, ipsum. In hac habitasse platea dictumst. Nulla facilisi. Cras vel tellus a purus laoreet aliquet. Aenean mattis eleifend erat. Cras nisl massa, gravida in, gravida a, imperdiet vestibulum, tortor. Nam interdum, sapien vel suscipit laoreet, arcu erat gravida dolor, faucibus viverra lacus nisl id lacus. Sed vestibulum mauris nec massa. Sed eget mi. Sed nisl lorem, tincidunt nec, ultrices eget, pellentesque at, est. Vestibulum lorem quam, dapibus vel, interdum ac, posuere ac, tellus.

Curabitur metus tellus, posuere in, euismod sit amet, euismod quis, nunc. Nam non metus ut sapien tempus egestas. Nullam egestas metus at quam. Fusce a libero posuere est vulputate mattis. Nullam quis enim. Donec eget felis in arcu sollicitudin auctor. Proin vel tellus. Pellentesque nec urna. Nullam eu libero in urna imperdiet condimentum.

1 of 4

Figure 26-14

As you can see in Figure 26-14, the document has automatically expanded to take advantage of all the available real estate of the screen. You could also shrink the application so that it is quite small. The text adapts quite well to any situation.

Adding an Image to the Document

In some of the earlier XAML examples, you learned you can add anything you want to the document using the XAML declaration. To see this in more detail, you can add an image to the document. It is possible to add an image to the document directly in the XAML code. This is illustrated in Listing 26-10.

Listing 26-10: Adding an image to the document

```
<Window x:Class="XAML_Example.MyDocument"
    xmlns="http://schemas.microsoft.com/winfx/2006/xaml/presentation"
    xmlns:x="http://schemas.microsoft.com/winfx/2006/xaml"
    Title="XAML_Example" Height="450" Width="800"
    >
  <Grid>
    <FlowDocumentReader Margin="5,5,5,5" Name="flowDocumentReader1">
      <FlowDocument>
        <Paragraph>
          <Italic>
            <Bold>This is the title of the document</Bold>
          </Italic>
        </Paragraph>
        <Paragraph>
          Lorem ipsum dolor sit amet, consectetuer adipiscing elit. Praesent mattis
          euismod eros. Aliquam lobortis rhoncus purus ...
        </Paragraph>
        <Paragraph>
          Ut elit lectus, volutpat in, dictum vitae, faucibus vel, nisl. Integer
          dictum pede vel lacus. Vestibulum turpis erat, gravida ...
        </Paragraph>
        <Paragraph>
          Pellentesque habitant morbi tristique senectus et netus et malesuada
          fames ac turpis egestas. Vivamus iaculis ...
        </Paragraph>
        <Paragraph>
          <Image Source="Sunset.jpg" />
          <Italic>This is an image.</Italic>
        </Paragraph>
      </FlowDocument>
    </FlowDocumentReader>
  </Grid>
</Window>
```

In this case, after the third `<Paragraph>` element, another `<Paragraph>` element is added. This `<Paragraph>` element is put in place simply to define a place where you can put the image. In this case, the `<Image>` element is used; it requires only a `Source` attribute to point to the location of the image. To place the image within the document and to give the text below it a style that is different from the text of the main document, use the `<Italic>` element to apply style.

If you run the example, you see that the image is embedded in the overall document. This is illustrated in Figure 26-15.

Figure 26-15

Again, the FlowDocumentReader control makes some smart decisions about the image on your behalf. First off, the image shown in Figure 26-15 is much smaller than the actual image. The FlowDocumentReader control is sizing the image to fit in the column and treats the image much like it treats the rest of the text contained within the document. This is shown in Figure 26-16. When you enlarge the viewing area of the document, you can see that the image also is enlarged to take advantage of the new viewable area of the screen.

If you switch the document viewing mode to scroll mode, you also see that the image now fills the entire width of the screen.

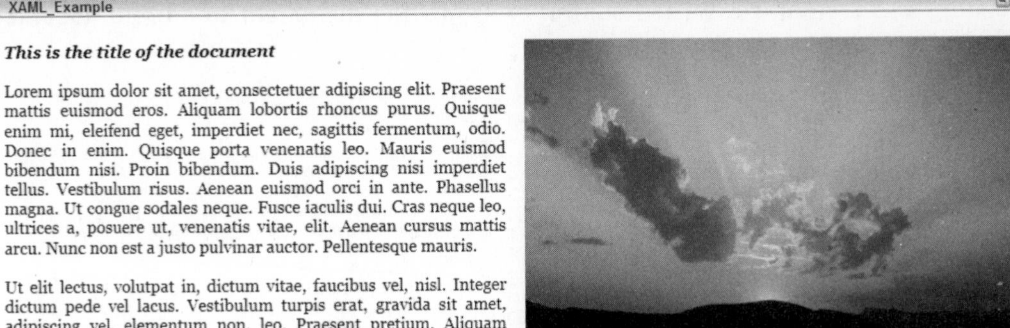

Figure 26-16

Final Step: Saving the Document as an XPS File

The last step in working with the FlowDocumentReader control is to change the WPF application so that the document you created can be saved as an XPS document. *XPS*, or *XML Paper Specification*, is a paginated representation of electronic paper that is described in XML. This specification was developed by Microsoft.

XPS documents must be viewed in an XPS viewer. Microsoft provides a viewer that allows you to see the document directly in Internet Explorer. Other viewers for other platforms are also being developed. To export the new document that you created in the FlowDocumentReader, you add something that initiates the export process. For this example, add a Button control to the WPF document. The code to do this is presented in Listing 26-11.

Listing 26-11: Adding a Button control to export the document to an XPS document

```
<Window x:Class="XAML_Example.MyDocument"
    xmlns="http://schemas.microsoft.com/winfx/2006/xaml/presentation"
    xmlns:x="http://schemas.microsoft.com/winfx/2006/xaml"
    Title="XAML_Example" Height="450" Width="800"
    >
  <Grid>
    <FlowDocumentReader Margin="5,50,5,5" Name="flowDocumentReader1">
      <FlowDocument>
        <Paragraph>
          <Italic>
            <Bold>This is the title of the document</Bold>
          </Italic>
        </Paragraph>
        <Paragraph>
          Lorem ipsum dolor sit amet, consectetuer adipiscing elit. Praesent mattis
          euismod eros. Aliquam lobortis rhoncus purus ...
        </Paragraph>
        <Paragraph>
          Ut elit lectus, volutpat in, dictum vitae, faucibus vel, nisl. Integer
          dictum pede vel lacus. Vestibulum turpis erat, gravida ...
        </Paragraph>
        <Paragraph>
          Pellentesque habitant morbi tristique senectus et netus et malesuada
          fames ac turpis egestas. Vivamus iaculis ...
        </Paragraph>
        <Paragraph>
          <Image Source="Sunset.jpg" />
          <Italic>This is an image.</Italic>
        </Paragraph>
      </FlowDocument>
    </FlowDocumentReader>
    <Button Height="23" HorizontalAlignment="Right" Margin="0,5,5,0" Name="button1"
     VerticalAlignment="Top" Width="100" Click="SaveToXPS">Save to XPS</Button>
  </Grid>
</Window>
```

As you can see, the Button control is added using the `<Button>` element, and its location is defined using the `Margin` attribute. Also notice that the FlowDocumentReader control has changed a bit — its location is altered to make way for the Button control by redefining the `Margin` attribute. The interesting this about XAML is that the order in which the elements appear in the code is not the order in which they appear in the application. Visually, the button control is at the top of the application now, but it is defined below the `<FlowDocumentReader>` element within the XAML. This is because everything is positioned using the `Margin` attributes. This means that these elements can actually appear anywhere you want within the application. The <Button> control on the page should appear as shown in Figure 26-17.

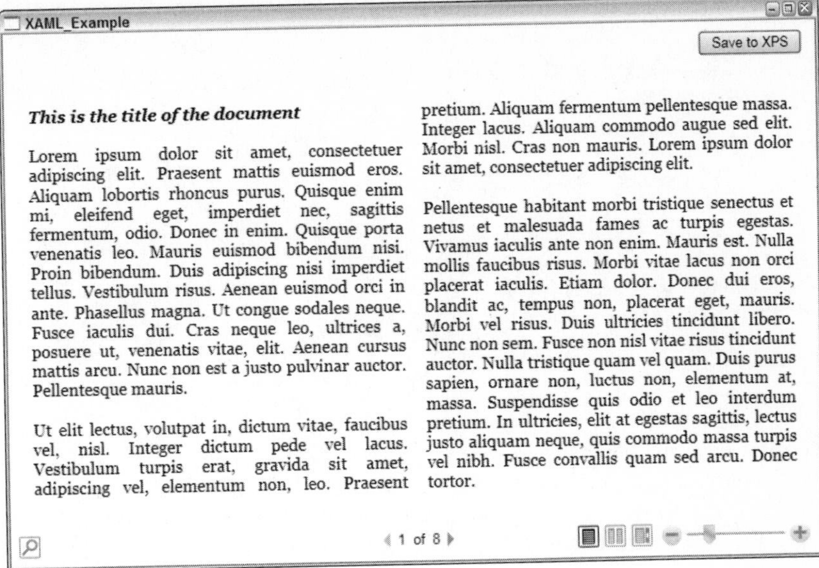

Figure 26-17

Looking at the code of the `<Button>` element, you can see a `Click` attribute as well. This defines the method that should be called in the `MyDocument.xaml.cs` file when the button is clicked. This is the bit of code which converts the document you created and to an XPS document. This code is presented in Listing 26-12.

Listing 26-12: Saving the document to an XPS file

```
using System.IO;
using System.IO.Packaging;
using System.Windows;
using System.Windows.Documents;
using System.Windows.Xps;
using System.Windows.Xps.Packaging;

namespace XAML_Example
{
    public partial class MyDocument : System.Windows.Window
    {
        public MyDocument()
        {
            InitializeComponent();
        }

        void SaveToXPS(object sender, RoutedEventArgs e)
        {
            DocumentPaginator dp =
```

(continued)

Listing 26-12 *(continued)*

```
            ((IDocumentPaginatorSource)flowDocumentReader1.Document).DocumentPaginator;
                Package pkg = Package.Open("myDocument.xps", FileMode.Create);
                XpsDocument xpsdoc = new XpsDocument(pkg);

                XpsDocumentWriter xpsWriter =
                   XpsDocument.CreateXpsDocumentWriter(xpsdoc);
                xpsWriter.Write(dp);

                xpsdoc.Close();
                pkg.Close();
            }
        }
    }
```

You must import some extra namespaces into the file using statements. These enable you to work with some of the classes that output the contents to an XPS file—such as `System.IO.Packaging`, `System.Windows.Documents`, `System.Windows.Xps`, and `System.Windows.Xps,Packaging`. The `SaveToXPS()` method creates a new instance of an XPS document in memory using the `XpsDocument` object:

```
XpsDocument xpsdoc = new XpsDocument(pkg)
```

This instance of the XPS document points to an actual XPS document that is to be created from the `Package` object. This object is passed in as a parameter to the class instantiation. Using the `XpsDocumentWriter` object, you can write the contents of the `flowDocumentReader1` control on your page to the XPS document, which is saved to disk as `myDocument.xps`.

If you have the Microsoft XPS viewer installed on your machine, you can now open the `myDocument.xps` file (by double-clicking the file). It automatically opens in this viewer. An example of the document being open in the XPS viewer is presented in Figure 26-18.

As you can see, the new XPS specification provides an easy way to create electronic versions of your documents that appear just as they would on paper. This is quite similar to the PDF model.

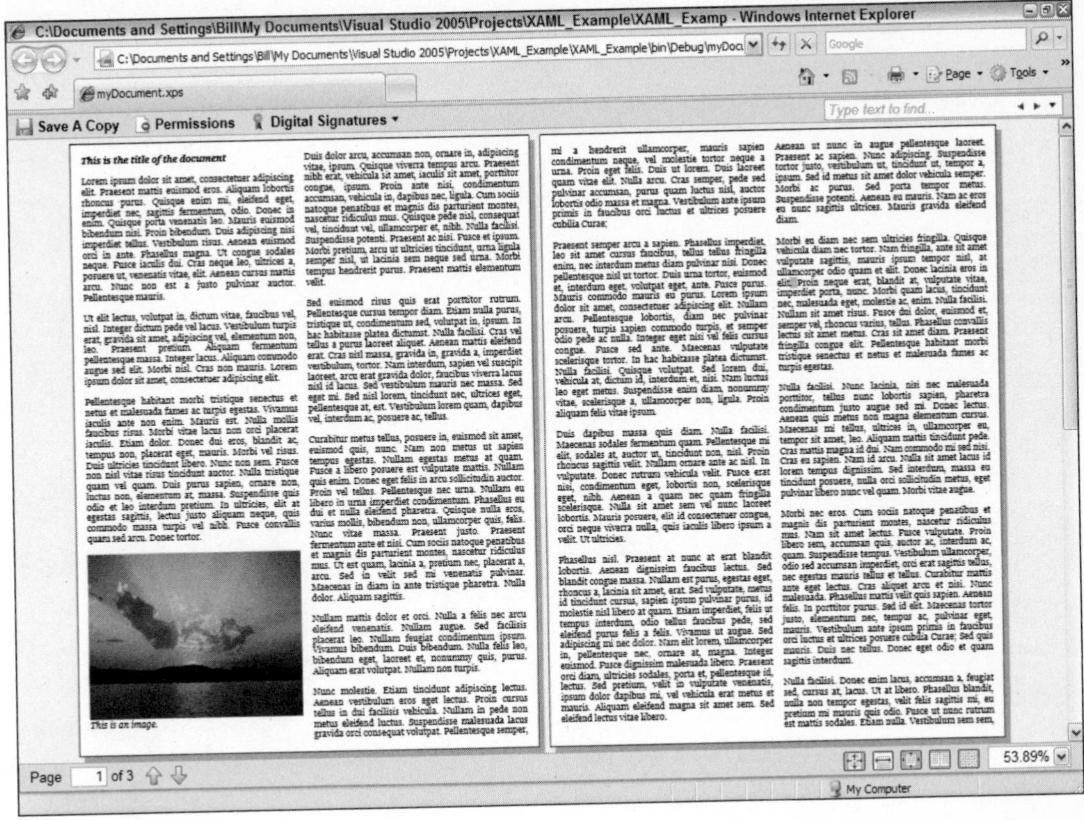

Figure 26-18

Summary

This brief introduction to XAML shows you the direction in which the programming community is heading, not just for Microsoft-based technologies but other technologies as well. Instead of working in traditional code — such as C#, Visual Basic, or Java — new emphasis is being placed on declarative languages that are interpreted to code in the compilation process. XAML is one of these declarative languages. All declarative languages, whether ASP.NET, XAML, or any other, are using XML to represent the language.

As you have seen throughout this book, XML is powerful. It is one thing to learn the basic rules of syntax for XML — it is another to apply it to the technologies which make use of the XML specification. It's these XML-based technologies that are changing the world of IT.

Index

SYMBOLS AND NUMERICS

A

D

F

I

J

P

Q

R

S

T

U